Mobil
Travel Guide

W9-CAG-781

New England

2006

Connecticut

Maine

Massachusetts

New Hampshire

Rhode Island

Vermont

ExxonMobil
Travel Publications

WITHDRAWN

Athens Regional Library
2025 Baxter Street
Athens, GA 30606

Madison County Library
P O Box 38 1315 Hwy 98 West
Danielsville, GA 30633
(706)795-5597
Member: Athens Regional Library System

Acknowledgements

We gratefully acknowledge the help of our representatives for their efficient and perceptive inspections of the lodging and dining establishments listed; the establishments' proprietors for their cooperation in showing their facilities and providing information about them; and the many users of previous editions who have taken the time to share their experiences. Mobil Travel Guide is also grateful to all the talented writers who contributed entries to this book.

Mobil, Exxon, and Mobil Travel Guide are trademarks of Exxon Mobil Corporation or one of its subsidiaries. All rights reserved. Reproduction by any means, including, but not limited to, photography, electrostatic copying devices, or electronic data processing, is prohibited. Use of information contained herein for solicitation of advertising or listing in any other publication is expressly prohibited without written permission from Exxon Mobil Corporation. Violations of reserved rights are subject to prosecution.

Copyright © 2006 EMTG, LLC. All rights reserved. Except for copies made by individuals for personal use, this publication may not be reproduced in whole or in part by any means whatsoever without written permission from Mobil Travel Guide, 7373 N Cicero Ave, Lincolnwood, IL 60712; phone 847/329-5930; info@mobiltravelguide.com.

Maps: © MapQuest.com, Inc. This product contains proprietary property of MapQuest.com, Inc. Unauthorized use, including copying, of this product is expressly prohibited.

www.mobiltravelguide.com

Front cover photo: Portland Head Lighthouse, Maine

The information contained herein is derived from a variety of third-party sources. Although every effort has been made to verify the information obtained from such sources, the publisher assumes no responsibility for inconsistencies or inaccuracies in the data or liability for any damages of any type arising from errors or omissions.

Neither the editors nor the publisher assumes responsibility for the services provided by any business listed in this guide or for any loss, damage, or disruption in your travel for any reason.

ISBN: 0-7627-3926-6

ISSN: 1549-5647

Manufactured in the United States of America.

10 9 8 7 6 5 4 3 2 1

Contents

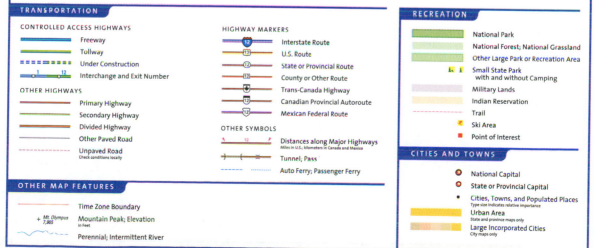

MAP SYMBOLS

TRANSPORTATION

CONTROLLED ACCESS HIGHWAYS
Freeway
Tollway
Under Construction
Interchange and Exit Number

OTHER HIGHWAYS
Primary Highway
Secondary Highway
Divided Highway
Other Paved Road
Unpaved Road
Check conditions locally

HIGHWAY MARKERS
Interstate Route
U.S. Route
State or Provincial Route
County or Other Route
Trans-Canada Highway
Canadian Provincial Autoroute
Mexican Federal Route

OTHER SYMBOLS
Distances along Major Highways
Miles in U.S., kilometers in Canada and Mexico
Tunnel; Pass
Auto Ferry; Passenger Ferry

RECREATION

National Park
National Forest; National Grassland
Other Large Park or Recreation Area
Small State Park
with and without Camping
Military Lands
Indian Reservation
Trail
Ski Area
Point of Interest

CITIES AND TOWNS

National Capital
State or Provincial Capital
Cities, Towns, and Populated Places
Type size indicates relative importance
Urban Area
State and province maps only
Large Incorporated Cities
City maps only

OTHER MAP FEATURES

Time Zone Boundary
Mt. Olympus 7,965 Mountain Peak; Elevation
in Feet
Perennial; Intermittent River

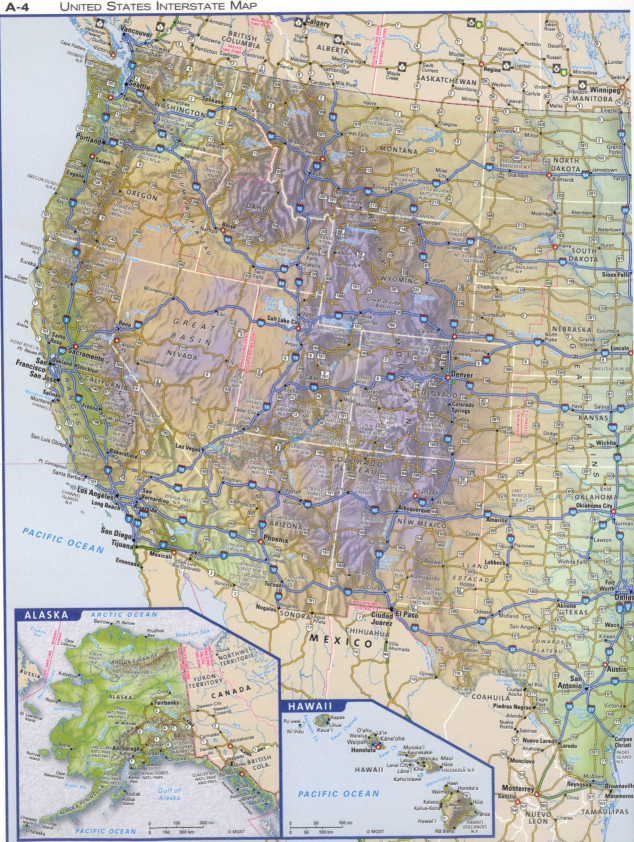

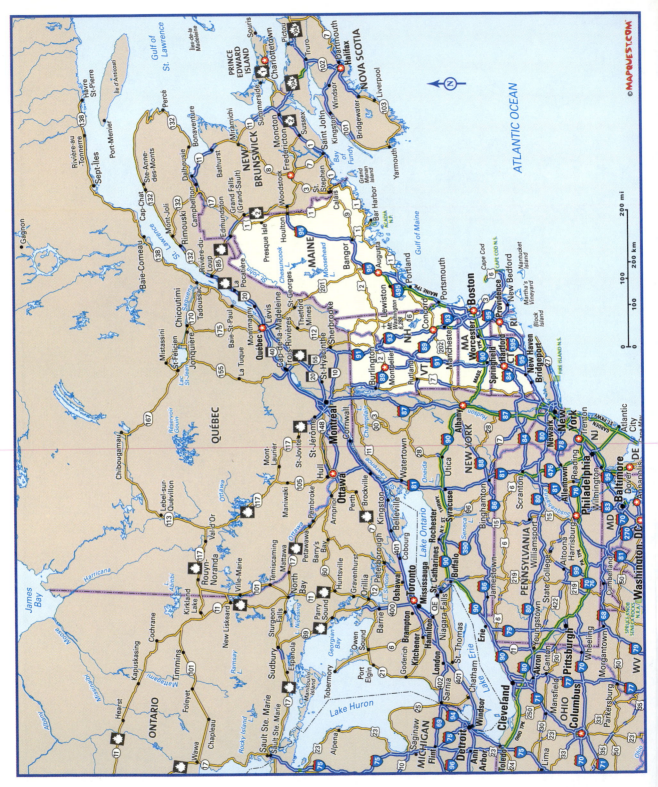

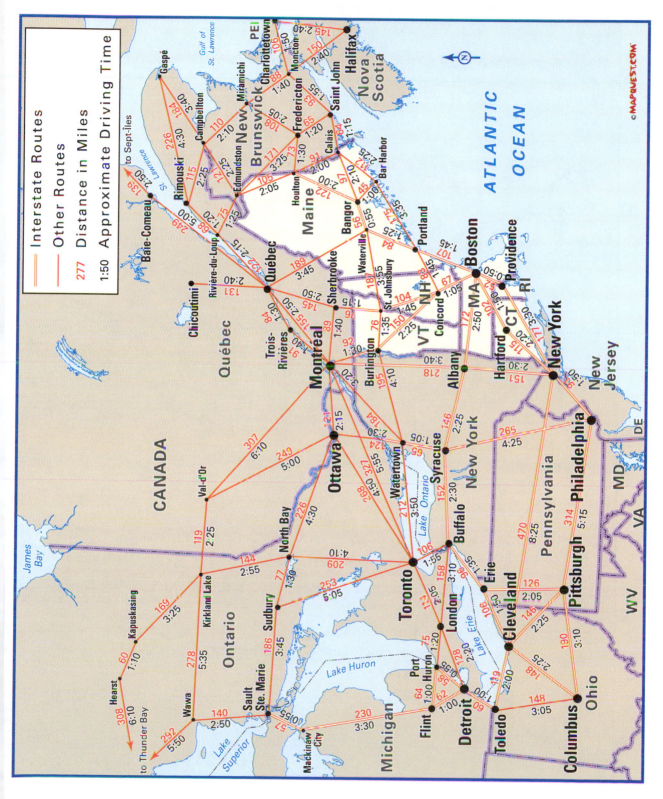

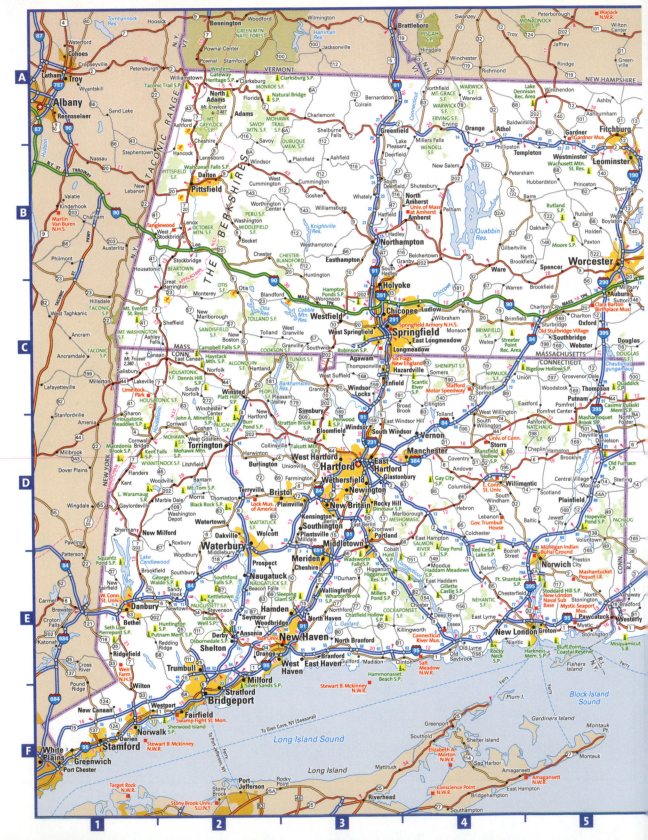

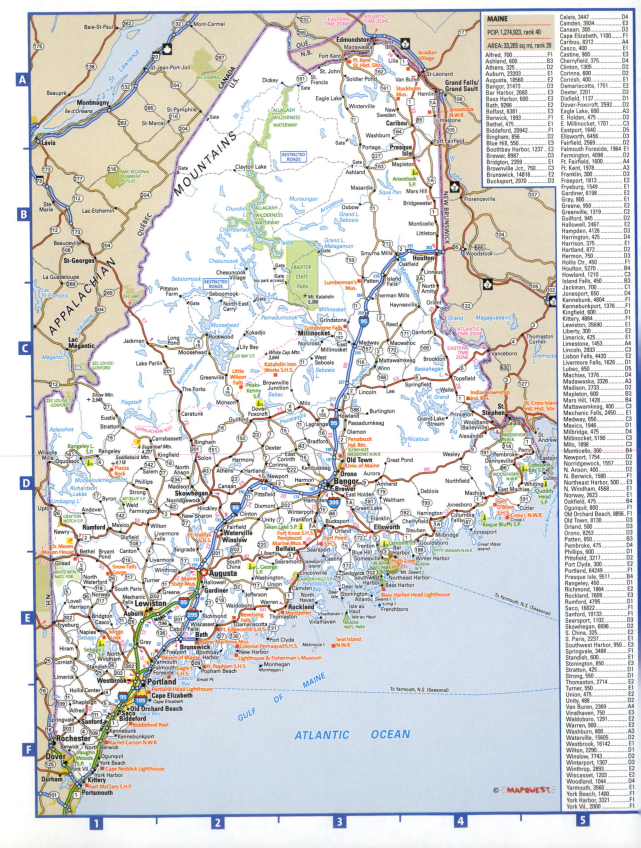

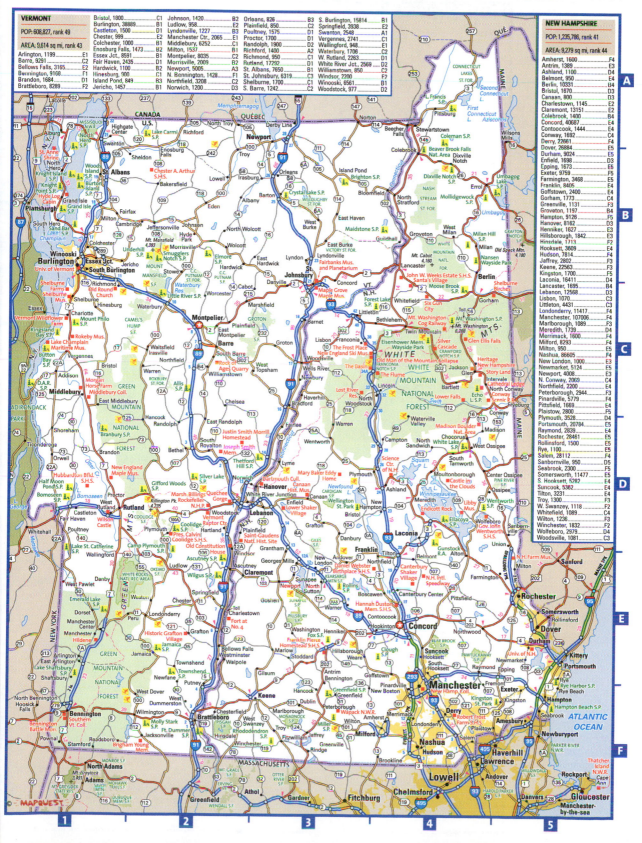

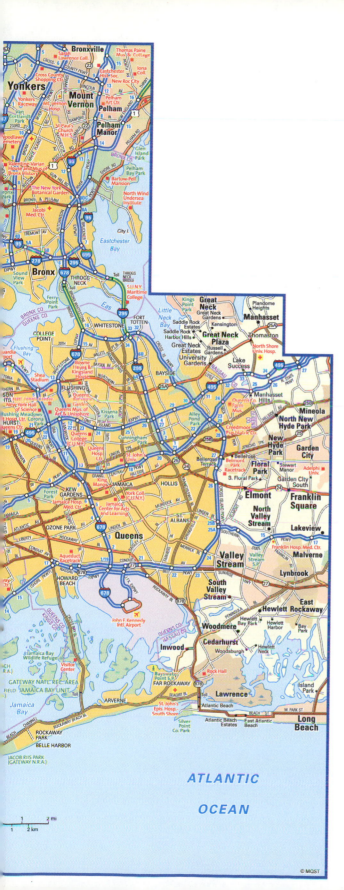

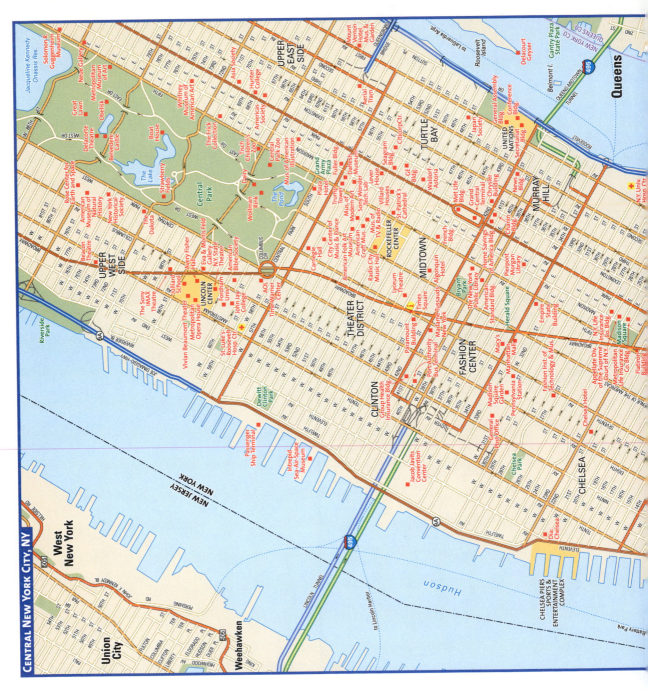

Distances in chart are in miles. To convert miles to kilometers, multiply the distance in miles by 1.609

Example: New York, NY to Boston, MA = 215 miles or 346 kilometers (215 x 1.609)

	ALBUQUERQUE, NM	ATLANTA, GA	BALTIMORE, MD	BILLINGS, MT	BIRMINGHAM, AL	BISMARCK, ND	BOISE, ID	BOSTON, MA	BUFFALO, NY	BURLINGTON, VT	CHARLESTON, SC	CHARLESTON, WV	CHARLOTTE, NC	CHEYENNE, WY	CHICAGO, IL	CINCINNATI, OH	CLEVELAND, OH	DALLAS, TX	DENVER, CO	DES MOINES, IA	DETROIT, MI	EL PASO, TX	HOUSTON, TX	INDIANAPOLIS, IN	JACKSON, MS	KANSAS CITY, MO	LAS VEGAS, NV	LITTLE ROCK, AR	LOS ANGELES, CA	LOUISVILLE, KY	MEMPHIS, TN
ALBUQUERQUE, NM		1490	1902	991	1274	1333	966	2240	1808	2178	1793	1568	1649	538	1352	1409	1619	754	438	1091	1608	263	994	1298	1157	894	578	900	806	1320	1033
ATLANTA, GA	1490		679	1889	150	1559	2218	1100	910	1158	317	503	238	1482	717	476	726	792	1403	967	735	1437	800	531	386	801	2067	528	2237	419	389
BALTIMORE, MD	1902	679		1959	795	1551	2401	422	370	481	583	352	441	1665	708	521	377	1399	1690	1031	532	2045	1470	600	1032	1087	2445	1072	2705	602	933
BILLINGS, MT	991	1889	1959		1839	413	626	2254	1796	2181	2157	1755	2012	455	1246	1552	1597	1433	554	1007	1534	1255	1673	1432	1836	1088	965	1530	1239	1547	1625
BIRMINGHAM, AL	1274	150	795	1839		1509	2170	1215	909	1241	466	578	389	1434	667	475	725	647	1356	919	734	1292	678	481	241	753	1852	381	2092	369	241
BISMARCK, ND	1333	1559	1551	413	1509		1039	1846	1388	1773	1749	1347	1604	594	838	1144	1189	1342	693	675	1126	1597	1582	1024	1548	801	1378	1183	1702	1139	1337
BOISE, ID	966	2218	2401	626	2170	1039		2697	2239	2624	2520	2182	2375	737	1708	1969	2040	1711	833	1369	1977	1206	1952	1852	2115	1376	760	1808	1033	1933	1954
BOSTON, MA	2240	1100	422	2254	1215	1846	2697		462	214	1003	741	861	1961	1003	862	654	1819	2004	1326	741	2465	1890	940	1453	1427	2757	1493	3046	964	1353
BUFFALO, NY	1808	910	370	1796	909	1388	2239	462		375	899	431	695	1502	545	442	197	1393	1546	868	277	2039	1513	508	1134	995	2299	1066	2572	545	927
BURLINGTON, VT	2178	1158	481	2181	1241	1773	2624	214	375		1061	782	919	1887	930	817	567	1763	1931	1253	652	2409	1916	878	1479	1366	2684	1437	2957	915	1297
CHARLESTON, SC	1793	317	583	2157	466	1749	2520	1003	899	1061		468	204	1783	907	622	724	1109	1705	1204	879	1754	1110	721	703	1102	2371	900	2554	610	760
CHARLESTON, WV	1568	503	352	1755	578	1347	2182	741	431	782	468		265	1445	506	209	255	1072	1367	802	410	1718	1192	320	816	764	2122	745	2374	251	606
CHARLOTTE, NC	1649	238	441	2012	389	1604	2375	861	695	919	204	265		1637	761	476	520	1031	1559	1057	675	1677	1041	575	625	956	2225	754	2453	464	614
CHEYENNE, WY	538	1482	1665	455	1434	594	737	1961	1502	1887	1783	1445	1637		972	1233	1304	979	100	633	1241	801	1220	1115	1382	640	843	1076	1116	1197	1217
CHICAGO, IL	1352	717	708	1246	667	838	1708	1003	545	930	907	506	761	972		302	346	936	1015	337	283	1543	1108	184	750	532	1768	662	2042	299	539
CINCINNATI, OH	1409	476	521	1552	475	1144	1969	862	442	817	622	209	476	1233	302		253	958	1200	599	261	1605	1079	116	700	597	1955	632	2215	106	493
CLEVELAND, OH	1619	726	377	1597	725	1189	2040	654	197	567	724	255	520	1304	346	253		1208	1347	669	171	1854	1328	319	950	806	2100	882	2374	356	742
DALLAS, TX	754	792	1399	1433	647	1342	1711	1819	1393	1763	1109	1072	1031	979	936	958	1208		887	752	1218	647	241	913	406	554	1331	327	1446	852	466
DENVER, CO	438	1403	1690	554	1356	693	833	2004	1546	1931	1705	1367	1559	100	1015	1200	1347	887		676	1284	701	1127	1088	1290	603	756	984	1029	1118	1116
DES MOINES, IA	1091	967	1031	1007	919	675	1369	1326	868	1253	1204	802	1057	633	337	599	669	752	676		606	1283	992	481	931	194	1429	567	1703	595	720
DETROIT, MI	1608	735	532	1534	734	1126	1977	741	277	652	879	410	675	1241	283	261	171	1218	1284	606		1799	1338	318	960	795	2037	891	2310	366	752
EL PASO, TX	263	1437	2045	1255	1292	1597	1206	2465	2039	2409	1754	1718	1677	801	1543	1605	1854	647	701	1283	1799		758	1489	1051	1085	717	974	801	1499	1112
HOUSTON, TX	994	800	1470	1673	678	1582	1952	1890	1513	1916	1110	1192	1041	1220	1108	1079	1328	241	1127	992	1338	758		1033	445	795	1474	447	1558	972	586
INDIANAPOLIS, IN	1298	531	600	1432	481	1024	1852	940	508	878	721	320	575	1115	184	116	319	913	1088	481	318	1489	1033		675	485	1843	587	2104	112	464
JACKSON, MS	1157	386	1032	1836	241	1548	2115	1453	1134	1479	703	816	625	1382	750	700	950	406	1290	931	960	1051	445	675		747	1735	269	1851	594	211
KANSAS CITY, MO	894	801	1087	1088	753	801	1376	1427	995	1366	1102	764	956	640	532	597	806	554	603	194	795	1085	795	485	747		1358	382	1632	516	536
LAS VEGAS, NV	578	2067	2445	965	1852	1378	760	2757	2299	2684	2371	2122	2225	843	1768	1955	2100	1331	756	1429	2037	717	1474	1843	1735	1358		1478	274	1874	1611
LITTLE ROCK, AR	900	528	1072	1530	381	1183	1808	1493	1066	1437	900	745	754	1076	662	632	882	327	984	567	891	974	447	587	269	382	1478		1706	526	140
LOS ANGELES, CA	806	2237	2705	1239	2092	1702	1033	3046	2572	2957	2554	2374	2453	1116	2042	2215	2374	1446	1029	1703	2310	801	1558	2104	1851	1632	274	1706		2126	1839
LOUISVILLE, KY	1320	419	602	1547	369	1139	1933	964	545	915	610	251	464	1197	299	106	356	852	1118	595	366	1499	972	112	594	516	1874	526	2126		386
MEMPHIS, TN	1033	389	933	1625	241	1337	1954	1353	927	1297	760	606	614	1217	539	493	742	466	1116	720	752	1112	586	464	211	536	1611	140	1839	386	
MIAMI, FL	2155	661	1109	2554	812	2224	2883	1529	1425	1587	583	994	730	2147	1382	1141	1250	1367	2069	1632	1401	1959	1201	1196	915	1466	2733	1190	2759	1084	1051
MILWAUKEE, WI	1426	813	805	1175	763	767	1748	1100	642	1027	1003	601	857	1012	89	398	443	1010	1055	378	380	1617	1193	279	835	573	1808	747	2082	394	624
MINNEAPOLIS, MN	1339	1129	1121	839	1079	431	1465	1417	958	1343	1319	918	1173	881	409	714	760	999	924	246	697	1530	1240	596	1151	441	1677	814	1951	711	940
MONTRÉAL, QC	2172	1241	564	2093	1289	1685	2535	313	397	92	1145	822	1003	1799	841	815	588	1772	1843	1165	564	2363	1892	872	1514	1359	2596	1446	2869	920	1306
NASHVILLE, TN	1248	242	716	1648	194	1315	1976	1136	716	1086	543	395	397	1240	474	281	531	681	1162	725	541	1328	801	287	423	559	1826	355	2054	175	215
NEW ORLEANS, LA	1276	473	1142	1955	351	1734	2234	1563	1254	1588	783	926	713	1502	935	820	1070	525	1409	1117	1079	1118	360	826	185	932	1854	455	1917	714	396
NEW YORK, NY	2015	869	192	2049	985	1641	2491	215	400	299	773	515	631	1755	797	636	466	1589	1799	1121	622	2235	1660	715	1223	1202	2552	1262	2820	739	1123
OKLAHOMA CITY, OK	546	944	1354	1227	729	1136	1506	1694	1262	1632	1248	1022	1102	773	807	863	1073	209	681	546	1062	737	449	752	612	348	1124	355	1352	774	487
OMAHA, NE	973	989	1168	904	941	616	1234	1463	1005	1390	1290	952	1144	497	474	736	806	669	541	136	743	1236	910	618	935	188	1294	570	1567	704	724
ORLANDO, FL	1934	440	904	2333	591	2003	2662	1324	1221	1383	379	790	525	1926	1161	920	1045	1146	1847	1411	1180	1738	980	975	694	1245	2512	969	2538	863	830
PHILADELPHIA, PA	1954	782	104	2019	897	1611	2462	321	414	371	685	454	543	1725	768	576	437	1501	1744	1091	592	2147	1572	655	1135	1141	2500	1175	2760	678	1035
PHOENIX, AZ	466	1868	2366	1199	1723	1662	993	2706	2274	2644	2184	2035	2107	1004	1819	1876	2085	1077	904	1558	2074	432	1188	1764	1482	1360	285	1367	369	1786	1500
PITTSBURGH, PA	1670	676	246	1719	763	1311	2161	592	217	587	642	217	438	1425	467	292	136	1246	1460	791	292	1893	1366	370	988	857	2215	920	2476	394	780
PORTLAND, ME	2338	1197	520	2352	1313	1944	2795	107	560	233	1101	839	959	2059	1101	960	751	1917	2102	1424	838	2563	1988	1038	1550	1525	2855	1590	3144	1062	1451
PORTLAND, OR	1395	2647	2830	889	2599	1301	432	3126	2667	3052	2948	2610	2802	1166	2137	2398	2469	2140	1261	1798	2405	1767	2381	2280	2544	1805	1188	2237	971	2362	2382
RAPID CITY, SD	841	1511	1626	379	1463	320	930	1921	1463	1848	1824	1422	1678	305	913	1219	1264	1077	404	629	1201	1105	1318	1101	1458	710	1035	1093	1309	1215	1247
RENO, NV	1020	2440	2623	960	2392	1372	430	2919	2460	2845	2741	2403	2595	959	1930	2191	2262	1933	1054	1591	2198	1315	2072	2073	2337	1598	442	2030	519	2155	2175
RICHMOND, VA	1876	527	152	2053	678	1645	2496	572	485	630	428	322	289	1760	802	530	471	1309	1688	1126	627	1955	1330	641	914	1085	2444	983	2682	572	843
ST. LOUIS, MO	1051	549	841	1341	501	1053	1628	1181	749	1119	850	512	704	892	294	350	560	635	855	436	549	1242	863	239	505	252	1610	416	1856	264	294
SALT LAKE CITY, UT	624	1916	2100	548	1868	960	342	2395	1936	2322	2218	1880	2072	436	1406	1667	1738	1410	531	1067	1675	864	1650	1549	1813	1074	417	1507	691	1631	1652
SAN ANTONIO, TX	818	1000	1671	1500	878	1599	1761	2092	1665	2036	1310	1344	1241	1046	1270	1231	1481	271	946	1009	1490	556	200	1186	644	812	1272	600	1356	1125	739
SAN DIEGO, CA	825	2166	2724	1302	2021	1765	1096	3065	2632	3020	2483	2393	2405	1179	2105	2234	2437	1375	1092	1766	2373	730	1487	2122	1780	1695	337	1703	124	2144	1841
SAN FRANCISCO, CA	1111	2618	2840	1176	2472	1749	646	3135	2677	3062	2934	2620	2759	1176	2146	2407	2478	1827	1271	1807	2415	1181	1938	2290	2232	1814	575	2012	385	2372	2144
SEATTLE, WA	1463	2705	2775	816	2657	1229	500	3070	2612	2997	2973	2571	2827	1234	2062	2368	2413	2208	1329	1822	2350	1944	2449	2249	2612	1872	1256	2305	1148	2364	2440
TAMPA, FL	1949	455	960	2348	606	2018	2677	1380	1276	1438	434	845	581	1941	1176	935	1101	1161	1862	1426	1194	1753	995	990	709	1259	2526	984	2553	878	845
TORONTO, ON	1841	958	565	1762	958	1354	2204	570	106	419	1006	537	802	1468	510	484	303	1441	1512	834	233	2032	1561	541	1183	1028	2265	1115	2538	589	975
VANCOUVER, BC	1597	2838	2908	949	2791	1362	633	3204	2745	3130	3106	2705	2960	1368	2196	2501	2547	2342	1463	1956	2483	2087	2583	2383	2746	2007	1390	2439	1291	2497	2574
WASHINGTON, DC	1896	636	38	1953	758	1545	2395	458	384	517	539	346	397	1659	701	517	370	1362	1686	1025	526	2008	1433	596	996	1083	2441	1036	2702	596	896
WICHITA, KS	707	989	1276	1067	838	934	1346	1616	1184	1554	1291	953	1145	613	728	785	995	367	521	390	984	898	608	674	771	192	1276	464	1513	705	597

	MIAMI, FL	MILWAUKEE, WI	MINNEAPOLIS, MN	MONTRÉAL, QC	NASHVILLE, TN	NEW ORLEANS, LA	NEW YORK, NY	OKLAHOMA CITY, OK	OMAHA, NE	ORLANDO, FL	PHILADELPHIA, PA	PHOENIX, AZ	PITTSBURGH, PA	PORTLAND, ME	PORTLAND, OR	RAPID CITY, SD	RENO, NV	RICHMOND, VA	ST. LOUIS, MO	SALT LAKE CITY, UT	SAN ANTONIO, TX	SAN DIEGO, CA	SAN FRANCISCO, CA	SEATTLE, WA	TAMPA, FL	TORONTO, ON	VANCOUVER, BC	WASHINGTON, DC	WICHITA, KS
ALBUQUERQUE, NM	2155	1426	1339	2172	1248	1276	2015	546	973	1934	1954	466	1670	2338	1395	841	1020	1876	1051	624	818	825	1111	1463	1949	1841	1597	1896	707
ATLANTA, GA	661	813	1129	1241	242	473	869	944	989	440	782	1868	676	1197	2647	1511	2440	527	549	1916	1000	2166	2618	2705	455	958	2838	636	989
BALTIMORE, MD	1109	805	1121	564	716	1142	192	1354	1168	904	104	2366	246	520	2830	1626	2623	152	841	2100	1671	2724	2840	2775	960	565	2908	38	1276
BILLINGS, MT	2554	1175	839	2093	1648	1955	2049	1227	904	2333	2019	1199	1719	2352	889	379	960	2053	1341	548	1500	1302	1176	816	2348	1762	949	1953	1067
BIRMINGHAM, AL	812	763	1079	1289	194	351	985	729	941	591	897	1723	763	1313	2599	1463	2392	678	501	1868	878	2021	2472	2657	606	958	2791	758	838
BISMARCK, ND	2224	767	431	1685	1315	1734	1641	1136	616	2003	1611	1662	1311	1944	1301	320	1372	1645	1053	960	1599	1765	1749	1229	2018	1354	1362	1545	934
BOISE, ID	2883	1748	1465	2535	1976	2234	2491	1506	1234	2662	2462	993	2161	2795	432	930	430	2496	1628	342	1761	1096	646	500	2677	2204	633	2395	1346
BOSTON, MA	1529	1100	1417	313	1136	1563	215	1694	1463	1324	321	2706	592	107	3126	1921	2919	572	1181	2395	2092	3065	3135	3070	1380	570	3204	458	1616
BUFFALO, NY	1425	642	958	397	716	1254	400	1262	1005	1221	414	2274	217	560	2667	1463	2460	485	749	1936	1665	2632	2677	2612	1276	106	2745	384	1184
BURLINGTON, VT	1587	1027	1343	92	1086	1588	299	1632	1390	1383	371	2644	587	233	3052	1848	2845	630	1119	2322	2036	3020	3062	2997	1438	419	3130	517	1554
CHARLESTON, SC	583	1003	1319	1145	543	783	773	1248	1290	379	685	2184	642	1101	2948	1824	2741	428	850	2218	1310	2483	2934	2973	434	1006	3106	539	1291
CHARLESTON, WV	994	601	918	822	395	926	515	1022	952	790	454	2035	217	839	2610	1422	2403	322	512	1880	1344	2393	2620	2571	845	537	2705	346	953
CHARLOTTE, NC	730	857	1173	1003	397	713	631	1102	1144	525	543	2107	438	959	2802	1678	2595	289	704	2072	1241	2405	2759	2827	581	802	2960	397	1145
CHEYENNE, WY	2147	1012	881	1799	1240	1502	1755	773	497	1926	1725	1004	1425	2059	1166	305	959	1760	892	436	1046	1179	1176	1234	1941	1468	1368	1659	613
CHICAGO, IL	1382	89	409	841	474	935	797	807	474	1161	768	1819	467	1101	2137	913	1930	802	294	1406	1270	2105	2146	2062	1176	510	2196	701	728
CINCINNATI, OH	1141	398	714	815	281	820	636	863	736	920	576	1876	292	960	2398	1219	2191	530	350	1667	1231	2234	2407	2368	935	484	2501	517	785
CLEVELAND, OH	1250	443	760	588	531	1070	466	1073	806	1045	437	2085	136	751	2469	1264	2262	471	560	1738	1481	2437	2478	2413	1101	303	2547	370	995
DALLAS, TX	1367	1010	999	1772	681	525	1589	209	669	1146	1501	1077	1246	1917	2140	1077	1933	1309	635	1410	271	1375	1827	2208	1161	1441	2342	1362	367
DENVER, CO	2069	1055	924	1843	1162	1409	1799	681	541	1847	1744	904	1460	2102	1261	404	1054	1688	855	531	946	1092	1271	1329	1862	1512	1463	1686	521
DES MOINES, IA	1632	378	246	1165	725	1117	1121	546	136	1411	1091	1558	791	1424	1798	629	1591	1126	436	1067	1009	1766	1807	1822	1426	834	1956	1025	390
DETROIT, MI	1401	380	697	564	541	1079	622	1062	743	1180	592	2074	292	838	2405	1201	2198	627	549	1675	1490	2373	2415	2350	1194	233	2483	526	984
EL PASO, TX	1959	1617	1530	2363	1328	1118	2235	737	1236	1738	2147	432	1893	2563	1767	1105	1315	1955	1242	864	556	730	1181	1944	1753	2032	2087	2008	898
HOUSTON, TX	1201	1193	1240	1892	801	360	1660	449	910	980	1572	1188	1366	1988	2381	1318	2072	1330	863	1650	200	1487	1938	2449	995	1561	2583	1433	608
INDIANAPOLIS, IN	1196	279	596	872	287	826	715	752	618	975	655	1764	370	1038	2280	1101	2073	641	239	1549	1186	2122	2290	2249	990	541	2383	596	674
JACKSON, MS	915	835	1151	1514	423	185	1223	612	935	694	1135	1482	988	1550	2544	1458	2337	914	505	1813	644	1780	2232	2612	709	1183	2746	996	771
KANSAS CITY, MO	1466	573	441	1359	559	932	1202	348	188	1245	1141	1360	857	1525	1805	710	1598	1085	252	1074	812	1695	1814	1872	1259	1028	2007	1083	192
LAS VEGAS, NV	2733	1808	1677	2596	1826	1854	2552	1124	1294	2512	2500	285	2215	2855	1188	1035	442	2444	1610	417	1272	337	575	1256	2526	2265	1390	2441	1276
LITTLE ROCK, AR	1190	747	814	1446	355	455	1262	355	570	969	1175	1367	920	1590	2237	1093	2030	983	416	1507	600	1703	2012	2305	984	1115	2439	1036	464
LOS ANGELES, CA	2759	2082	1951	2869	2054	1917	2820	1352	1567	2538	2760	369	2476	3144	971	1309	519	2682	1856	691	1356	124	385	1148	2553	2538	1291	2702	1513
LOUISVILLE, KY	1084	394	711	920	175	714	739	774	704	863	678	1786	394	1062	2362	1215	2155	572	264	1631	1125	2144	2372	2364	878	589	2497	596	705
MEMPHIS, TN	1051	624	940	1306	215	396	1123	487	724	830	1035	1500	780	1451	2382	1247	2175	843	294	1652	739	1841	2144	2440	845	975	2574	896	597
MIAMI, FL		1478	1794	1671	907	874	1299	1609	1654	232	1211	2390	1167	1627	3312	2176	3105	954	1214	2581	1401	2688	3140	3370	274	1532	3504	1065	1655
MILWAUKEE, WI	1478		337	939	569	1020	894	880	514	1257	865	1892	564	1198	2063	842	1970	899	367	1446	1343	2145	2186	1991	1272	607	2124	799	769
MINNEAPOLIS, MN	1794	337		1255	886	1337	1211	793	383	1573	1181	1805	881	1515	1727	606	1839	1216	621	1315	1257	2014	2055	1654	1588	924	1788	1115	637
MONTRÉAL, QC	1671	939	1255		1094	1632	383	1625	1300	1466	454	2637	607	282	2963	1758	2756	714	1112	2232	2043	2931	2972	2907	1522	330	3041	600	1547
NASHVILLE, TN	907	569	886	1094		539	906	703	747	686	818	1715	569	1234	2405	1269	2198	626	307	1675	954	2056	2360	2463	701	764	2597	679	748
NEW ORLEANS, LA	874	1020	1337	1632	539		1332	731	1121	653	1245	1548	1108	1660	2663	1643	2431	1002	690	1932	560	1846	2298	2731	668	1302	2865	1106	890
NEW YORK, NY	1299	894	1211	383	906	1332		1469	1258	1094	91	2481	367	313	2920	1716	2713	342	956	2189	1861	2839	2929	2864	1150	507	2998	228	1391
OKLAHOMA CITY, OK	1609	880	793	1625	703	731	1469		463	1388	1408	1012	1124	1792	1934	871	1727	1331	505	1204	466	1370	1657	2002	1403	1295	2136	1350	161
OMAHA, NE	1654	514	383	1300	747	1121	1258	463		1433	1228	1440	928	1561	1662	525	1455	1263	440	932	927	1630	1672	1719	1448	971	1853	1162	307
ORLANDO, FL	232	1257	1573	1466	686	653	1094	1388	1433		1006	2169	963	1422	3091	1955	2884	750	993	2360	1180	2467	2918	3149	82	1327	3283	860	1434
PHILADELPHIA, PA	1211	865	1181	454	818	1245	91	1408	1228	1006		2420	306	419	2890	1686	2683	254	895	2160	1774	2779	2900	2835	1062	522	2968	140	1330
PHOENIX, AZ	2390	1892	1805	2637	1715	1548	2481	1012	1440	2169	2420		2136	2804	1335	1308	883	2343	1517	651	987	358	750	1513	2184	2307	1655	2362	1173
PITTSBURGH, PA	1167	564	881	607	569	1108	367	1124	928	963	306	2136		690	2590	1386	2383	341	611	1859	1519	2494	2599	2534	1019	321	2668	240	1046
PORTLAND, ME	1627	1198	1515	282	1234	1660	313	1792	1561	1422	419	2804	690		3223	2019	3016	670	1279	2493	2189	3162	3233	3168	1478	668	3301	556	1714
PORTLAND, OR	3312	2063	1727	2963	2405	2663	2920	1934	1662	3091	2890	1335	2590	3223		1268	578	2925	2057	771	2322	1093	638	170	3106	2633	313	2824	1775
RAPID CITY, SD	2176	842	606	1758	1269	1643	1716	871	525	1955	1686	1308	1386	2019	1268		1151	1720	963	628	1335	1372	1368	1195	1970	1429	1328	1620	712
RENO, NV	3105	1970	1839	2756	2198	2431	2713	1727	1455	2884	2683	883	2383	3016	578	1151		2718	1850	524	1870	642	217	755	2899	2426	898	2617	1568
RICHMOND, VA	954	899	1216	714	626	1002	342	1331	1263	750	254	2343	341	670	2925	1720	2718		834	2194	1530	2684	2934	2869	805	660	3003	108	1274
ST. LOUIS, MO	1214	367	621	1112	307	690	956	505	440	993	895	1517	611	1279	2057	963	1850	834		1326	968	1875	2066	2125	1008	782	2259	837	441
SALT LAKE CITY, UT	2581	1446	1315	2232	1675	1932	2189	1204	932	2360	2160	651	1859	2493	771	628	524	2194	1326		1419	754	740	839	2375	1902	973	2094	1044
SAN ANTONIO, TX	1401	1343	1257	2043	954	560	1861	466	927	1180	1774	987	1519	2189	2322	1335	1870	1530	968	1419		1285	1737	2275	1195	1714	2410	1635	624
SAN DIEGO, CA	2688	2145	2014	2931	2056	1846	2839	1370	1630	2467	2779	358	2494	3162	1093	1372	642	2684	1875	754	1285		508	1271	2481	2601	1414	2720	1531
SAN FRANCISCO, CA	3140	2186	2055	2972	2360	2298	2929	1657	1672	2918	2900	750	2599	3233	638	1368	217	2934	2066	740	1737	508		816	2933	2643	958	2834	1784
SEATTLE, WA	3370	1991	1654	2907	2463	2731	2864	2002	1719	3149	2835	1513	2534	3168	170	1195	755	2869	2125	839	2275	1271	816		3164	2577	140	2769	1843
TAMPA, FL	274	1272	1588	1522	701	668	1150	1403	1448	82	1062	2184	1019	1478	3106	1970	2899	805	1008	2375	1195	2481	2933	3164		1383	3297	916	1448
TORONTO, ON	1532	607	924	330	764	1302	507	1295	971	1327	522	2307	321	668	2633	1429	2426	660	782	1902	1714	2601	2643	2577	1383		2711	563	1217
VANCOUVER, BC	3504	2124	1788	3041	2597	2865	2998	2136	1853	3283	2968	1655	2668	3301	313	1328	898	3003	2259	973	2410	1414	958	140	3297	2711		2902	1977
WASHINGTON, DC	1065	799	1115	600	679	1106	228	1350	1162	860	140	2362	240	556	2824	1620	2617	108	837	2094	1635	2720	2834	2769	916	563	2902		1272
WICHITA, KS	1655	769	637	1547	748	890	1391	161	307	1434	1330	1173	1046	1714	1775	712	1568	1274	441	1044	624	1531	1784	1843	1448	1217	1977	1272	

© MapQuest.com, Inc.

Welcome

Dear Traveler,

Since its inception in 1958, Mobil Travel Guide has served as a trusted advisor to auto travelers in search of value in lodging, dining, and destinations. Now in its 48th year, the Mobil Travel Guide is the hallmark of our ExxonMobil family of travel publications, and we're proud to offer an array of products and services from our Mobil, Exxon, and Esso brands in North America to facilitate life on the road.

Whether you're looking for business or pleasure venues, our nationwide network of independent, professional evaluators offers their expertise on thousands of travel options, allowing you to plan a quick family getaway, a full-service business meeting, or an unforgettable Mobil Five-Star celebration.

Your feedback is important to us as we strive to improve our product offerings and better meet today's travel needs. Whether you travel once a week or once a year, please take the time to contact us at www.mobiltravelguide.com. We hope to hear from you soon.

Best wishes for safe and enjoyable travels.

Lee R Raymond

Lee R. Raymond
Chairman and CEO
Exxon Mobil Corporation

A Word to Our Readers

Travelers are on the roads in great numbers these days. They're exploring the country on day trips, weekend getaways, business trips, and extended family vacations, visiting major cities and small towns along the way. Because time is precious and the travel industry is ever-changing, having accurate, reliable travel information at your fingertips is critical. Mobil Travel Guide has been providing invaluable insight to travelers for more than 45 years, and we are committed to continuing this service well into the future.

The Mobil Corporation (known as Exxon Mobil Corporation since a 1999 merger) began producing the Mobil Travel Guide books in 1958, following the introduction of the US interstate highway system in 1956. The first edition covered only five Southwestern states. Since then, our books have become the premier travel guides in North America, covering all 50 states and Canada.

Since its founding, Mobil Travel Guide has served as an advocate for travelers seeking knowledge about hotels, restaurants, and places to visit. Based on an objective process, we make recommendations to our customers that we believe will enhance the quality and value of their travel experiences. Our trusted Mobil One- to Five-Star rating system is the oldest and most respected lodging and restaurant inspection and rating program in North America. Most hoteliers, restaurateurs, and industry observers favorably regard the rigor of our inspection program and understand the prestige and benefits that come with receiving a Mobil Star rating.

The Mobil Travel Guide process of rating each establishment includes:

- Unannounced facility inspections

- Incognito service evaluations for Mobil Four-Star and Mobil Five-Star properties

- A review of unsolicited comments from the general public

- Senior management oversight

For each property, more than 450 attributes, including cleanliness, physical facilities, and employee attitude and courtesy, are measured and evaluated to produce a mathematically derived score, which is then blended with the other elements to form an overall score. These quantifiable scores allow comparative analysis among properties and form the basis that we use to assign our Mobil One- to Five-Star ratings.

This process focuses largely on guest expectations, guest experience, and consistency of service, not just physical facilities and amenities. It is fundamentally a relative rating system that rewards those properties that continually strive for and achieve excellence each year. Indeed, the very best properties are consistently raising the bar for those that wish to compete with them. These properties proactively respond to consumers' needs even in today's uncertain times.

Only facilities that meet Mobil Travel Guide's standards earn the privilege of being listed in the guide. Deteriorating, poorly managed establishments are deleted. A Mobil Travel Guide listing constitutes a positive quality recommendation; every listing is an accolade, a recognition of achievement. Our Mobil One- to Five-Star rating system highlights its level of service. Extensive in-house research is constantly underway to determine new additions to our lists.

- The Mobil Five-Star Award indicates that a property is one of the very best in the country and consistently provides gracious and courteous service, superlative quality in its facility, and a unique ambience. The lodgings and restaurants at the Mobil Five-Star level consistently and proactively respond to consumers' needs and continue their commitment to excellence, doing so with grace and perseverance.

- Also highly regarded is the Mobil Four-Star Award, which honors properties for outstanding achievement in overall facility and for providing very strong service levels in all areas. These award winners provide a distinctive experience for the ever-demanding and sophisticated consumer.

○ The Mobil Three-Star Award recognizes an excellent property that provides full services and amenities. This category ranges from exceptional hotels with limited services to elegant restaurants with a less-formal atmosphere.

○ A Mobil Two-Star property is a clean and comfortable establishment that has expanded amenities or a distinctive environment. A Mobil Two-Star property is an excellent place to stay or dine.

○ A Mobil One-Star property is limited in its amenities and services but focuses on providing a value experience while meeting travelers' expectations. The property can be expected to be clean, comfortable, and convenient.

Allow us to emphasize that we do not charge establishments for inclusion in our guides. We have no relationship with any of the businesses and attractions we list and act only as a consumer advocate. In essence, we do the investigative legwork so that you won't have to.

Keep in mind, too, that the hospitality business is ever-changing. Restaurants and lodgings—particularly small chains and stand-alone establishments—change management or even go out of business with surprising quickness. Although we make every effort to double-check information during our annual updates, we nevertheless recommend that you call ahead to make sure the place you've selected is still open and offers all the amenities you're looking for. We've provided phone numbers; when available, we also list fax numbers and Web site addresses.

We hope that your travels are enjoyable and relaxing and that our books help you get the most out of every trip you take. If any aspect of your accommodation, dining, or sightseeing experience motivates you to comment, please drop us a line. We depend a great deal on our readers' remarks, so you can be assured that we will read your comments and assimilate them into our research. General comments about our books are also welcome. You can write to us at Mobil Travel Guide, 7373 N Cicero Ave, Lincolnwood, IL 60712, or send an e-mail to info@mobiltravelguide.com.

Take your Mobil Travel Guide books along on every trip you take. We're confident that you'll be pleased with their convenience, ease of use, and breadth of dependable coverage.

Happy travels!

How to Use This Book

The Mobil Travel Guide Regional Travel Planners are designed for ease of use. Each state has its own chapter, beginning with a general introduction that provides a geographical and historical orientation to the state and gives basic statewide tourist information, from climate to calendar highlights to seatbelt laws. The remainder of each chapter is devoted to travel destinations within the state—mainly cities and towns, but also national parks and tourist areas—which, like the states, are arranged in alphabetical order.

The following sections explain the wealth of information you'll find about those travel destinations: information about the area, things to see and do there, and where to stay and eat.

Maps and Map Coordinates

At the front of this book in the full-color section, we have provided state maps as well as maps of selected larger cities to help you find your way around once you leave the highway. You'll find a key to the map symbols on the Contents page at the beginning of the map section.

Next to most cities and towns throughout the book, you'll find a set of map coordinates, such as C-2. These coordinates reference the maps at the front of this book and help you find the location you're looking for quickly and easily.

Destination Information

Because many travel destinations are close to other cities and towns where travelers might find additional attractions, accommodations, and restaurants, we've included cross-references to those cities and towns when it makes sense to do so. We also list addresses, phone numbers, and Web sites for travel information resources—usually the local chamber of commerce or office of tourism—as well as pertinent statistics and, in many cases, a brief introduction to the area.

Information about airports, ground transportation, and suburbs is included for large cities.

Driving Tours and Walking Tours

The driving tours that we include for many states are usually day trips that make for interesting side excursions, although they can be longer. They offer you a way to get off the beaten path and visit an area that travelers often overlook. These trips frequently cover areas of natural beauty or historical significance.

Each walking tour focuses on a particularly interesting area of a city or town. Again, these tours can provide a break from everyday tourist attractions. The tours often include places to stop for meals or snacks.

What to See and Do

Mobil Travel Guide offers information about nearly 20,000 museums, art galleries, amusement parks, historic sites, national and state parks, ski areas, and many other types of attractions. A white star on a black background ★ signals that the attraction is a must-see—one of the best in the area. Because municipal parks, public tennis courts, swimming pools, and small educational institutions are common to most towns, they generally are not mentioned.

Following an attraction's description, you'll find the months, days, and, in some cases, hours of operation; the address/directions, telephone number, and Web site (if there is one); and the admission price category. The following are the ranges we use for admission fees, based on one adult:

- ✪ **FREE**
- ✪ **$** = Up to $5
- ✪ **$$** = $5.01-$10
- ✪ **$$$** = $10.01-$15
- ✪ **$$$$** = Over $15

Special Events

Special events are either annual events that last only a short time, such as festivals and fairs, or longer, seasonal events such as horse racing, theater, and summer concerts. Our Special Events listings also include infrequently occurring occasions that mark certain dates or events, such as a centennial or other commemorative celebration.

Side Trips

We recognize that your travels don't always end where state lines fall, so we've included some side trips that fall outside the states covered in this book but that travelers frequently visit when they're in the region. Nearby national parks, major cities, and other prime tourist draws fall into this category. You'll find side trips for a particular state at the end of that state's section.

Listings

Lodgings, spas, and restaurants are usually listed under the city or town in which they're located. Make sure to check the related cities and towns that appear right beneath a city's heading for additional options, especially if you're traveling to a major metropolitan area that includes many suburbs. If a property is located in a town that doesn't have its own heading, the listing appears under the town nearest it, with the address and town given immediately after the establishment's name. In large cities, lodgings located within 5 miles of major commercial airports may be listed under a separate "Airport Area" heading that follows the city section.

LODGINGS

Travelers have different wants and needs when it comes to accommodations. To help you pinpoint properties that meet your particular needs, Mobil Travel Guide classifies each lodging by type according to the following characteristics.

Mobil Rated Lodgings

☼ **Limited-Service Hotel.** A limited-service hotel is traditionally a Mobil One-Star or Mobil Two-Star property. At a Mobil One-Star hotel, guests can expect to find a clean, comfortable property that commonly serves a complimentary continental breakfast. A Mobil Two-Star hotel is also clean and comfortable but has expanded amenities, such as a full-service restaurant, business

center, and fitness center. These services may have limited staffing and/or restricted hours of use.

☼ **Full-Service Hotel.** A full-service hotel traditionally enjoys a Mobil Three-Star, Mobil Four-Star, or Mobil Five-Star rating. Guests can expect these hotels to offer at least one full-service restaurant in addition to amenities such as valet parking, luggage assistance, 24-hour room service, concierge service, laundry and/or dry-cleaning services, and turndown service.

☼ **Full-Service Resort.** A resort is traditionally a full-service hotel that is geared toward recreation and represents a vacation and holiday destination. A resort's guest rooms are typically furnished to accommodate longer stays. The property may offer a full-service spa, golf, tennis, and fitness facilities or other leisure activities. Resorts are expected to offer a full-service restaurant and expanded amenities, such as luggage assistance, room service, meal plans, concierge service, and turndown service.

☼ **Full-Service Inn.** An inn is traditionally a Mobil Three-Star, Mobil Four-Star, or Mobil Five-Star property. Inns are similar to bed-and-breakfasts (see below) but offer a wider range of services, most significantly a full-service restaurant that serves at least breakfast and dinner.

Specialty Lodgings

Mobil Travel Guide recognizes the unique and individualized nature of many different types of lodging establishments, including bed-and-breakfasts, limited-service inns, and guest ranches. For that reason, we have chosen to place our stamp of approval on the properties that fall into these two categories in lieu of applying our traditional Mobil Star ratings.

☼ **B&B/Limited-Service Inn.** A bed-and-breakfast (B&B) or limited-service inn is traditionally an owner-occupied home or residence found in a residential area or vacation destination. It may be a structure of historic significance. Rooms are often individually decorated, but telephones, televisions, and private bathrooms may not be available in every room. A B&B typically serves only breakfast to its overnight guests, which is included in the room rate. Cocktails and refreshments may be served in the late afternoon or evening.

✪ **Guest Ranch.** A guest ranch is traditionally a rustic, Western-themed property that specializes in stays of three or more days. Horseback riding is often a feature, with stables and trails found on the property. Facilities can range from clean, comfortable establishments to more luxurious facilities.

Mobil Star Rating Definitions for Lodgings

✪ ★ ★ ★ ★ ★ : A Mobil Five-Star lodging provides consistently superlative service in an exceptionally distinctive luxury environment, with expanded services. Attention to detail is evident throughout the hotel, resort, or inn, from bed linens to staff uniforms.

✪ ★ ★ ★ ★ : A Mobil Four-Star lodging provides a luxury experience with expanded amenities in a distinctive environment. Services may include, but are not limited to, automatic turndown service, 24-hour room service, and valet parking.

✪ ★ ★ ★ : A Mobil Three-Star lodging is well appointed, with a full-service restaurant and expanded amenities, such as a fitness center, golf course, tennis courts, 24-hour room service, and optional turndown service.

✪ ★ ★ : A Mobil Two-Star lodging is considered a clean, comfortable, and reliable establishment that has expanded amenities, such as a full-service restaurant on the premises.

✪ ★ : A Mobil One-Star lodging is a limited-service hotel, motel, or inn that is considered a clean, comfortable, and reliable establishment.

Information Found in the Lodging Listings

Each lodging listing gives the name, address/location (when no street address is available), neighborhood and/or directions from downtown (in major cities), phone number(s), fax number, total number of guest rooms, and seasons open (if not year-round). Also included are details on business, luxury, recreational, and dining facilities at the property or nearby. A key to the symbols at the end of each listing can be found on the page following the "A Word to Our Readers" section.

For every property, we also provide pricing information. Because lodging rates change frequently, we list a pricing category rather than specific prices. The pricing categories break down as follows:

✪ **$** = Up to $150

✪ **$$** = $151-$250

✪ **$$$** = $251-$350

✪ **$$$$** = $351 and up

All prices quoted are in effect at the time of publication; however, prices cannot be guaranteed. In some locations, short-term price variations may exist because of special events, holidays, or seasonality. Certain resorts have complicated rate structures that vary with the time of year; always confirm rates when making your plans.

Because most lodgings offer the following features and services, information about them does not appear in the listings:

✪ Year-round operation

✪ Bathroom with tub and/or shower in each room

✪ Cable television in each room

✪ In-room telephones

✪ Cots and cribs available

✪ Daily maid service

✪ Elevators

✪ Major credit cards accepted

Although we recommend every lodging we list in this book, a few stand out—they offer noteworthy amenities or stand above the others in their category in terms of quality, value, or historical significance. To draw your attention to these special spots, we've included the magnifying glass icon to the left of the listing, as you see here.

SPAS

Mobil Travel Guide is pleased to announce its newest category: hotel and resort spas. Until now, hotel and resort spas have not been formally rated or inspected by any organization. Every spa selected for inclusion in this book underwent a rigorous inspection process similar to the one Mobil Travel Guide has been applying to lodgings and restaurants for more than four decades. After spending a year and a half researching more than 300 spas and performing exhaustive incognito inspections of more than 200 properties, we narrowed our list to the 48 best spas in the United States and Canada.

Mobil Travel Guide's spa ratings are based on objective evaluations of more than 450 attributes. Approximately half of these criteria assess basic expectations, such as staff courtesy, the technical proficiency and skill of the employees, and whether the facility is maintained properly and hygienically. Several standards address issues that impact a guest's physical comfort and convenience, as well as the staff's ability to impart a sense of personalized service and anticipate clients' needs. Additional criteria measure the spa's ability to create a completely calming ambience.

The Mobil Star ratings focus on much more than the facilities available at a spa and the treatments it offers. Each Mobil Star rating is a cumulative score achieved from multiple inspections that reflects the spa management's attention to detail and commitment to consumers' needs.

Mobil Star Rating Definitions for Spas

✪ ★ ★ ★ ★ ★ : A Mobil Five-Star spa provides consistently superlative service in an exceptionally distinctive luxury environment with extensive amenities. The staff at a Mobil Five-Star spa provides extraordinary service above and beyond the traditional spa experience, allowing guests to achieve the highest level of relaxation and pampering. A Mobil Five-Star spa offers an extensive array of treatments, often incorporating international themes and products. Attention to detail is evident throughout the spa, from arrival to departure.

✪ ★ ★ ★ : A Mobil Four-Star spa provides a luxurious experience with expanded amenities in an elegant and serene environment. Throughout the spa facility, guests experience personalized service. Amenities might include, but are not limited to, single-sex relaxation rooms where guests wait for their treatments, plunge pools and whirlpools in both men's and women's locker rooms, and an array of treatments, including at a minimum a selection of massages, body therapies, facials, and a variety of salon services.

✪ ★ ★ : A Mobil Three-Star spa is physically well appointed and has a full complement of staff to ensure that guests' needs are met. It has some expanded amenities, such as, but not limited to, a well-equipped fitness center, separate men's and women's locker rooms, a sauna or steam room, and a designated relaxation area. It also offers a menu of services that at a minimum includes massages, facial treatments, and at least one other type of body treatment, such as scrubs or wraps.

RESTAURANTS

All Mobil Star rated dining establishments listed in this book have a full kitchen and offer seating at tables; most offer table service.

Mobil Star Rating Definitions for Restaurants

✪ ★ ★ ★ ★ ★ : A Mobil Five-Star restaurant offers one of few flawless dining experiences in the country. These establishments consistently provide their guests with exceptional food, superlative service, elegant décor, and exquisite presentations of each detail surrounding a meal.

✪ ★ ★ ★ : A Mobil Four-Star restaurant provides professional service, distinctive presentations, and wonderful food.

✪ ★ ★ : A Mobil Three-Star restaurant has good food, warm and skillful service, and enjoyable décor.

✪ ★ : A Mobil Two-Star restaurant serves fresh food in a clean setting with efficient service. Value is considered in this category, as is family friendliness.

✪ ★ : A Mobil One-Star restaurant provides a distinctive experience through culinary specialty, local flair, or individual atmosphere.

Information Found in the Restaurant Listings

Each restaurant listing gives the cuisine type, street address (or directions if no address is available), phone and fax numbers, Web site (if available), meals served, days of operation (if not open daily year-round), and pricing category. Information about appropriate attire is provided, although it's always a good idea to call ahead and ask if you're unsure; the meaning of "casual" or "business casual" varies widely in different parts of the country. We also indicate whether the restaurant has a bar, whether a children's menu is offered, and whether outdoor seating is available. If reservations are recommended, we note that fact in the listing. When valet parking is available, it is noted in the description. In many cases, self-parking is available at the restaurant or nearby.

Because menu prices can fluctuate, we list a pricing category rather than specific prices. The pricing categories are defined as follows, per diner, and assume that you order an appetizer or dessert, an entrée, and one drink:

○ **$** = $15 and under

○ **$$** = $16-$35

○ **$$$** = $36-$85

○ **$$$$** = $86 and up

Again, all prices quoted are in effect at the time of publication, but prices cannot be guaranteed.

Although we recommend every restaurant we list in this book, a few stand out—they offer noteworthy local specialties or stand above the others in their category in terms of quality, value, or experience. To draw your attention to these special spots, we've included the magnifying glass icon to the left of the listing, as you see here.

SPECIAL INFORMATION FOR TRAVELERS WITH DISABILITIES

The Mobil Travel Guide ⓓ symbol indicates that an establishment is not at least partially accessible to people with mobility problems. When the ⓓ symbol follows a listing, the establishment is not equipped with facilities to accommodate people using wheelchairs or crutches or otherwise needing easy access to doorways and rest rooms. Travelers with severe mobility problems or with hearing or visual impairments may or may not find the facilities they need. Always phone ahead to make sure that an establishment can meet your needs.

AMERICA'S BYWAYS™

Mobil Travel Guide is pleased to announce a new partnership with the National Scenic Byways Program. Under this program, the US Secretary of Transportation recognizes certain roads as National Scenic Byways or All-American Roads based on their archaeological, cultural, historic, natural, recreational, and scenic qualities. To be designated a National Scenic Byway, a road must possess at least one of these six intrinsic qualities. To receive an All-American Road designation, a road must possess multiple intrinsic qualities that are nationally significant and contain one-of-a-kind features that do not exist elsewhere. The road or highway also must be considered a destination unto itself.

America's Byways are a great way to explore the country. From the mighty Mississippi to the towering Rockies to the Historic National Road, these routes take you past America's most treasured scenery and enable you to get in touch with America's past, present, and future. Bringing together all the nationally designated Byways in New England, this bonus section of the book is a handy reference whether you're planning to hop in the car tomorrow or you're simply looking for inspiration for future trips. Look for it at the end of the front section, before page 1.

Understanding the Symbols

What to See and Do

⭐	=	One of the top attractions in the area
$	=	Up to $5
$$	=	$5.01 to $10
$$$	=	$10.01 to $15
$$$$	=	Over $15

Lodgings

$	=	Up to $150
$$	=	$151 to $250
$$$	=	$251 to $350
$$$$	=	Over $350

Restaurants

$	=	Up to $15
$$	=	$16 to $35
$$$	=	$36 to $85
$$$$	=	Over $85

Lodging Star Definitions

★★★★★   A Mobil Five-Star lodging establishment provides consistently superlative service in an exceptionally distinctive luxury environment with expanded services. Attention to detail is evident throughout the hotel/resort/inn from the bed linens to the staff uniforms.

★★★★   A Mobil Four-Star lodging establishment is a hotel/resort/inn that provides a luxury experience with expanded amenities in a distinctive environment. Services may include, but are not limited to, automatic turndown service, 24-hour room service, and valet parking.

★★★   A Mobil Three-Star lodging establishment is a hotel/resort/inn that is well appointed, with a full-service restaurant and expanded amenities, such as, but not limited to, a fitness center, golf course, tennis courts, 24-hour room service, and optional turndown service.

★★   A Mobil Two-Star lodging establishment is a hotel/resort/inn that is considered a clean, comfortable, and reliable establishment, but also has expanded amenities, such as a full-service restaurant on the premises.

★   A Mobil One-Star lodging establishment is a limited-service hotel or inn that is considered a clean, comfortable, and reliable establishment.

Restaurant Star Definitions

★★★★★   A Mobil Five-Star restaurant is one of few flawless dining experiences in the country. These restaurants consistently provide their guests with exceptional food, superlative service, elegant décor, and exquisite presentations of each detail surrounding the meal.

★★★★   A Mobil Four-Star restaurant provides professional service, distinctive presentations, and wonderful food.

★★★   A Mobil Three-Star restaurant has good food, warm and skillful service, and enjoyable décor.

★★   A Mobil Two-Star restaurant serves fresh food in a clean setting with efficient service. Value is considered in this category, as is family friendliness.

★   A Mobil One-Star restaurant provides a distinctive experience through culinary specialty, local flair, or individual atmosphere.

Symbols at End of Listings

🔲	Facilities for people with disabilities not available	🎾	Tennis court(s) on premises
🐾	Pets allowed	🏊	Indoor or outdoor pool
⛷	Ski in/ski out access	🏋	Fitness room
⛳	Golf on premises	✈	Major commercial airport within 5 miles
		🏃	Business center

Making the Most of Your Trip

A few hardy souls might look back with fondness on a trip during which the car broke down, leaving them stranded for three days, or a vacation that cost twice what it was supposed to. For most travelers, though, the best trips are those that are safe, smooth, and within budget. To help you make your trip the best it can be, we've assembled a few tips and resources.

Saving Money

ON LODGING

Many hotels and motels offer discounts—for senior citizens, business travelers, families, you name it. It never hurts to ask—politely, that is. Sometimes, especially in the late afternoon, desk clerks are instructed to fill beds, and you might be offered a lower rate or a nicer room to entice you to stay. Simply ask the reservation agent for the best rate available. Also, make sure to try both the toll-free number and the local number. You may be able to get a lower rate from one than from the other.

Timing your trip right can cut your lodging costs as well. Look for bargains on stays over multiple nights, in the off-season, and on weekdays or weekends, depending on the location. Many hotels in major metropolitan areas, for example, have special weekend packages that offer leisure travelers considerable savings on rooms; they may include breakfast, cocktails, and/or dinner discounts.

Another way to save money is to choose accommodations that give you more than just a standard room. Rooms with kitchen facilities enable you to cook some meals yourself, reducing your restaurant costs. A suite might save money for two couples traveling together. Even hotel luxury levels can provide good value, as many include breakfast or cocktails in the price of a room.

State and city taxes, as well as special room taxes, can increase your room rate by as much as 25 percent per day. We are unable to include information about taxes in our listings, but we strongly urge you to ask about taxes when making reservations so that you understand the total cost of your lodgings before you book them.

Watch out for telephone-usage charges that hotels frequently impose on long-distance, credit-card, and other calls. Before phoning from your room, read the information given to you at check-in, and then be sure to review your bill carefully when checking out. You won't be expected to pay for charges that the hotel didn't spell out. Consider using your cell phone if you have one; or, if public telephones are available in the hotel lobby, your cost savings may outweigh the inconvenience of using them.

Here are some additional ways to save on lodgings:

- Stay in B&B accommodations. They're generally less expensive than standard hotel rooms, and the complimentary breakfast cuts down on food costs.

- If you're traveling with children, find lodgings at which kids stay free.

- When visiting a major city, stay just outside the city limits; these rooms are usually less expensive than those in downtown locations.

- Consider visiting national parks during the low season, when prices of lodgings near the parks drop by 25 percent or more.

- When calling a hotel, ask whether it is running any special promotions or if any discounts are available; many times reservationists are told not to volunteer these deals unless they're specifically asked about them.

- Check for hotel packages; some offer nightly rates that include a rental car or discounts on major attractions.

- Search the Internet for travel bargains. Web sites that allow for online booking of hotel rooms and travel planning, such as *www.mobiltravelguide.com,* often deliver lower rates than are available through telephone reservations.

ON DINING

There are several ways to get a less expensive meal at an expensive restaurant. Early-bird dinners are popular in many parts of the country and offer considerable savings. If you're interested in visiting a Mobil Four- or Five-Star establishment, consider going at lunchtime. Although the prices are probably still relatively high at midday, they may be half of those at dinner, and you'll experience the same ambience, service, and cuisine.

ON ENTERTAINMENT

Although many national parks, monuments, seashores, historic sites, and recreation areas may be visited free of charge, others charge an entrance fee and/or a usage fee for special services and facilities. If you plan to make several visits to national recreation areas, consider one of the following money-saving programs offered by the National Park Service:

○ **National Parks Pass.** This annual pass is good for entrance to any national park that charges an entrance fee. If the park charges a per-vehicle fee, the pass holder and any accompanying passengers in a private noncommercial vehicle may enter. If the park charges a per-person fee, the pass applies to the holder's spouse, children, and parents as well as the holder. It is valid for entrance fees only; it does not cover parking, camping, or other fees. You can purchase a National Parks Pass in person at any national park where an entrance fee is charged; by mail from the National Park Foundation, PO Box 34108, Washington, DC 20043-4108; by calling toll-free 888/467-2757; or at www.nationalparks.org. The cost is $50.

○ **Golden Eagle Sticker.** When affixed to a National Parks Pass, this hologram sticker, available to people who are between 17 and 61 years of age, extends coverage to sites managed by the US Fish and Wildlife Service, the US Forest Service, and the Bureau of Land Management. It is good until the National Parks Pass to which it is affixed expires and does not cover usage fees. You can purchase one at the National Park Service, the Fish and Wildlife Service, or the Bureau of Land Management fee stations. The cost is $15.

○ **Golden Age Passport.** Available to citizens and permanent US residents 62 and older, this passport is a lifetime entrance permit to fee-charging national recreation areas. The fee exemption extends to those accompanying the permit holder in a private noncommercial vehicle or, in the case of walk-in facilities, to the holder's spouse and children. The passport also entitles the holder to a 50 percent discount on federal usage fees charged in park areas, but not on concessions. Golden Age Passports must be obtained in person and are available at most National Park Service units that charge an entrance fee. The applicant must show proof of age, such as a driver's license or birth certificate (Medicare cards are not acceptable proof). The cost is $10.

○ **Golden Access Passport.** Issued to citizens and permanent US residents who are physically disabled or visually impaired, this passport is a free lifetime entrance permit to fee-charging national recreation areas. The fee exemption extends to those accompanying the permit holder in a private noncommercial vehicle or, in the case of walk-in facilities, to the holder's spouse and children. The passport also entitles the holder to a 50 percent discount on usage fees charged in park areas, but not on concessions. Golden Access Passports must be obtained in person and are available at most National Park Service units that charge an entrance fee. Proof of eligibility to receive federal benefits (under programs such as Disability Retirement, Compensation for Military Service-Connected Disability, and the Coal Mine Safety and Health Act) is required, or an affidavit must be signed attesting to eligibility.

A money-saving move in several large cities is to purchase a **CityPass.** If you plan to visit several museums and other major attractions, CityPass is a terrific option because it gets you into several sites for one substantially reduced price. Currently, CityPass is available in Boston, Chicago, Hollywood, New York, Philadelphia, San Francisco, Seattle, southern California (which includes Disneyland, SeaWorld, and the San Diego Zoo), and Toronto. For more information or to buy one, call toll-free 888/330-5008 or visit www.citypass.net. You can also buy a CityPass from any participating CityPass attraction.

Here are some additional ways to save on entertainment and shopping:

○ Check with your hotel's concierge for various coupons and special offers; they often have two-for-one tickets for area attractions and coupons for discounts at area stores and restaurants.

○ Purchase same-day concert or theater tickets for half-price through the local cheap-tickets outlet, such as TKTS in New York or Hot Tix in Chicago.

○ Visit museums on their free or "by donation" days, when you can pay what you wish rather than a specific admission fee.

○ Save receipts from purchases in Canada; visitors to Canada can get a rebate on federal taxes and some provincial sales taxes.

ON TRANSPORTATION

Transportation is a big part of any vacation budget. Here are some ways to reduce your costs:

○ If you're renting a car, shop early over the Internet; you can book a car during the low season for less, even if you'll be using it in the high season.

○ Rental car discounts are often available if you rent for one week or longer and reserve in advance.

○ Get the best gas mileage out of your vehicle by making sure that it's properly tuned up and keeping your tires properly inflated.

○ Travel at moderate speeds on the open road; higher speeds require more gasoline.

○ Fill the tank before you return your rental car; rental companies charge to refill the tank and do so at prices of up to 50 percent more than at local gas stations.

○ Make a checklist of travel essentials and purchase them before you leave; don't get stuck buying expensive sunscreen at your hotel or overpriced film at the airport.

FOR SENIOR CITIZENS

Always call ahead to ask if a discount is being offered, and be sure to carry proof of age. Additional information for mature travelers is available from the American Association of Retired Persons (AARP), 601 E St NW, Washington, DC 20049; phone 202/434-2277; www.aarp.org.

Tipping

Tips are expressions of appreciation for good service. However, you are never obligated to tip if you receive poor service.

IN HOTELS

○ Door attendants usually get $1 for hailing a cab.

○ Bell staff expect $2 per bag.

○ Concierges are tipped according to the service they perform. Tipping is not mandatory when you've asked for suggestions on sightseeing or restaurants or for help in making dining reservations. However, a tip of $5 is appropriate when a concierge books you a table at a restaurant known to be difficult to get into. For obtaining theater or sporting event tickets, $5 to $10 is expected.

○ Maids should be tipped $1 to $2 per day. Hand your tip directly to the maid, or leave it with a note saying that the money has been left expressly for the maid.

IN RESTAURANTS

Before tipping, carefully review your check for any gratuity or service charge that is already included in your bill. If you're in doubt, ask your server.

○ Coffee shop and counter service waitstaff usually receive 15 percent of the bill, before sales tax.

○ In full-service restaurants, tip 18 percent of the bill, before sales tax.

○ In fine restaurants, where gratuities are shared among a larger staff, 18 to 20 percent is appropriate.

○ In most cases, the maitre d' is tipped only if the service has been extraordinary, and only on the way out. At upscale properties in major metropolitan areas, $20 is the minimum.

○ If there is a wine steward, tip $20 for exemplary service and beyond, or more if the wine was decanted or the bottle was very expensive.

○ Tip $1 to $2 per coat at the coat check.

AT AIRPORTS

Curbside luggage handlers expect $1 per bag. Car-rental shuttle drivers who help with your luggage appreciate a $1 or $2 tip.

Staying Safe

The best way to deal with emergencies is to avoid them in the first place. However, unforeseen situations do happen, so you should be prepared for them.

IN YOUR CAR

Before you head out on a road trip, make sure that your car has been serviced and is in good working order. Change the oil, check the battery and belts, make sure that your windshield washer fluid is full and your tires are properly inflated (which can also improve your gas mileage). Other inspections recommended by the vehicle's manufacturer should also be made.

Next, be sure you have the tools and equipment needed to deal with a routine breakdown:

- Jack
- Spare tire
- Lug wrench
- Repair kit
- Emergency tools
- Jumper cables
- Spare fan belt
- Fuses
- Flares and/or reflectors
- Flashlight
- First-aid kit
- In winter, a windshield scraper and snow shovel

Many emergency supplies are sold in special packages that include the essentials you need to stay safe in the event of a breakdown.

Also bring all appropriate and up-to-date documentation—licenses, registration, and insurance cards—and know what your insurance covers. Bring an extra set of keys, too, just in case.

En route, always buckle up! In most states, wearing a seatbelt is required by law.

If your car does break down, do the following:

- Get out of traffic as soon as possible—pull well off the road.
- Raise the hood and turn on your emergency flashers or tie a white cloth to the roadside door handle or antenna.
- Stay in your car.
- Use flares or reflectors to keep your vehicle from being hit.

IN YOUR HOTEL

Chances are slim that you will encounter a hotel or motel fire, but you can protect yourself by doing the following:

- Once you've checked in, make sure that the smoke detector in your room is working properly.
- Find the property's fire safety instructions, usually posted on the inside of the room door.
- Locate the fire extinguishers and at least two fire exits.
- Never use an elevator in a fire.

For personal security, use the peephole in your room door and make sure that anyone claiming to be a hotel employee can show proper identification. Call the front desk if you feel threatened at any time.

PROTECTING AGAINST THEFT

To guard against theft wherever you go:

- Don't bring anything of more value than you need.
- If you do bring valuables, leave them at your hotel rather than in your car.
- If you bring something very expensive, lock it in a safe. Many hotels put one in each room; others will store your valuables in the hotel's safe.
- Don't carry more money than you need. Use traveler's checks and credit cards or visit cash machines to withdraw more cash when you run out.

For Travelers with Disabilities

To get the kind of service you need and have a right to expect, don't hesitate when making a reservation to question the management about the availability of accessible rooms, parking, entrances, restaurants, lounges, or any other facilities that are important to you, and confirm what is meant by "accessible."

The Mobil Travel Guide 🄳 symbol indicates establishments that are not at least partially accessible to people with special mobility needs (people using wheelchairs or crutches or otherwise needing easy access to buildings and rooms). Further information about these criteria can be found in the earlier section "How to Use This Book."

A thorough listing of published material for travelers with disabilities is available from the Disability Bookshop, Twin Peaks Press, Box 129, Vancouver, WA 98666; phone 360/694-2462; disabilitybookshop.virtualave.net. Another reliable organization is the Society for Accessible Travel & Hospitality (SATH), 347 Fifth Ave, Suite 610, New York, NY 10016; phone 212/447-7284; www.sath.org.

Border-Crossing Regulations

In addition to a photo ID, such as a driver's license or military ID, proof of citizenship—a passport or certified birth certificate—is required for travel into Canada for US citizens ages 18 and over. Children under age 18 traveling with their birth certificates are not required to have photo IDs, but it is highly recommended. A child under age 18 traveling to Canada without both legal guardians must have a notarized letter of consent from the nontraveling parent(s) granting permission for the child to travel. The notarized letter of consent is not waived even when the minor has his or her own passport.

For stays of up to 180 days, a visa is not required.

Each traveler may bring up to $800 worth of goods purchased in Canada back into the United States duty free. In addition, federal regulations permit each US citizen 21 years of age or older to bring back 1 liter of alcoholic beverage duty free in a 30-day period. Travelers are not permitted to bring in plants, fruits, or vegetables. State regulations vary, so check locally before entering Canada. New regulations may be issued at any time.

For more information about traveling to Canada, including safety information, look for the US State Department's Consular Information Sheet at travel. state.gov/canada.html, or request it by fax by calling 202/647-3000.

Important Toll-Free Numbers and Online Information

Hotels

Adams Mark 800/444-2326
www.adamsmark.com

AmericInn 800/634-3444
www.americinn.com

AmeriHost Inn 800/434-5800
www.amerihostinn.com

Amerisuites 800/833-1516
www.amerisuites.com

Baymont Inns 877/229-6667
www.baymontinns.com

Best Inns & Suites 800/237-8466
www.bestinn.com

Best Value Inn 888/315-2378
www.bestvalueinn.com

Best Western 800/780-7234
www.bestwestern.com

Budget Host Inn 800/283-4678
www.budgethost.com

Candlewood Suites 888/226-3539
www.candlewoodsuites.com

Clarion Hotels 800/252-7466
www.choicehotels.com

Comfort Inns and Suites 800/252-7466
www.comfortinn.com

Country Hearth Inns 800/848-5767
www.countryhearth.com

Country Inns & Suites 800/456-4000
www.countryinns.com

Courtyard by Marriott 800/321-2211
www.courtyard.com

Cross Country Inns (KY and OH) 800/621-1429
www.crosscountryinns.com

Crowne Plaza Hotels and Resorts 800/227-6963
www.crowneplaza.com

Days Inn 800/544-8313
www.daysinn.com

Delta Hotels 800/268-1133
www.deltahotels.com

Destination Hotels & Resorts 800/434-7347
www.destinationhotels.com

Doubletree Hotels 800/222-8733
www.doubletree.com

Drury Inn 800/378-7946
www.druryinn.com

Econolodge 800/553-2666
www.econolodge.com

Embassy Suites 800/362-2779
www.embassysuites.com

ExelInns of America 800/367-3935
www.exelinns.com

Extended StayAmerica 800/398-7829
www.extendedstayhotels.com

Fairfield Inn by Marriott 800/228-2800
www.fairfieldinn.com

Fairmont Hotels 800/441-1414
www.fairmont.com

Four Points by Sheraton 888/625-5144
www.fourpoints.com

Four Seasons 800/819-5053
www.fourseasons.com

Hampton Inn 800/426-7866
www.hamptoninn.com

Hard Rock Hotels, Resorts, and Casinos 800/473-7625
www.hardrock.com

Harrah's Entertainment 800/427-7247
www.harrahs.com

Hawthorn Suites 800/527-1133
www.hawthorn.com

Hilton Hotels and Resorts (US) 800/774-1500
www.hilton.com

Holiday Inn Express 800/465-4329
www.hiexpress.com

Holiday Inn Hotels and Resorts 800/465-4329
www.holiday-inn.com

Homestead Studio Suites 888/782-9473
www.homesteadhotels.com

Homewood Suites 800/225-5466
www.homewoodsuites.com

Howard Johnson 800/406-1411
www.hojo.com

Hyatt 800/633-7313
www.hyatt.com

Inns of America 800/826-0778
www.innsofamerica.com

InterContinental 888/567-8725
www.intercontinental.com

Joie de Vivre 800/738-7477
www.jdvhospitality.com

Kimpton Hotels 888/546-7866
www.kimptongroup.com

Knights Inn 800/843-5644
www.knightsinn.com

La Quinta 800/531-5900
www.laquinta.com

Le Meridien 800/543-4300
www.lemeridien.com

Leading Hotels of the World 800/223-6800
www.lhw.com

Loews Hotels 800/235-6397
www.loewshotels.com

MainStay Suites 800/660-6246
www.mainstaysuites.com

Mandarin Oriental 800/526-6566
www.mandarin-oriental.com

Marriott Hotels, Resorts, and Suites 800/228-9290
www.marriott.com

Microtel Inns & Suites 800/771-7171
www.microtelinn.com

Millennium & Copthorne Hotels 866/866-8086
www.millenniumhotels.com

Motel 6 . . . . 800/466-8356
www.motel6.com

Omni Hotels 800/843-6664
www.omnihotels.com

Pan Pacific Hotels and Resorts 800/327-8585
www.panpac.com

Park Inn & Park Plaza 888/201-1801
www.parkinn.com

The Peninsula Group . . . . Contact individual hotel
www.peninsula.com

Preferred Hotels & Resorts Worldwide 800/323-7500
www.preferredhotels.com

Quality Inn 800/228-5151
www.qualityinn.com

Radisson Hotels 800/333-3333
www.radisson.com

Raffles International Hotels and Resorts . . . 800/637-9477
www.raffles.com

Ramada Plazas, Limiteds, and Inns 800/272-6232
www.ramada.com

Red Lion Inns 800/733-5466
www.redlion.com

Red Roof Inns 800/733-7663
www.redroof.com

Regent International 800/545-4000
www.regenthotels.com

Relais & Chateaux 800/735-2478
www.relaischateaux.com

Renaissance Hotels 888/236-2427
www.renaissancehotels.com

Residence Inn 800/331-3131
www.residenceinn.com

Ritz-Carlton 800/241-3333
www.ritzcarlton.com

RockResorts 888/367-7625
www.rockresorts.com

Rodeway Inn 800/228-2000
www.rodeway.com

Rosewood Hotels & Resorts 888/767-3966
www.rosewoodhotels.com

Select Inn 800/641-1000
www.selectinn.com

Sheraton 888/625-5144
www.sheraton.com

Shilo Inns 800/222-2244
www.shiloinns.com

Shoney's Inn 800/552-4667
www.shoneysinn.com

Signature/Jameson Inns 800/822-5252
www.jamesoninns.com

Sleep Inn 877/424-6423
www.sleepinn.com

Small Luxury Hotels of the World 800/525-4800
www.slh.com

Sofitel 800/763-4835
www.sofitel.com

SpringHill Suites 888/236-2427
www.springhillsuites.com

St. Regis Luxury Collection 888/625-5144
www.stregis.com

Staybridge Suites 800/238-8000
www.staybridge.com

Summerfield Suites by Wyndham 800/833-4353
www.summerfieldsuites.com

Summit International 800/457-4000
www.summithotels.com

Super 8 Motels 800/800-8000
www.super8.com

The Sutton Place Hotels 866/378-8866
www.suttonplace.com

Swissôtel 800/637-9477
www.swissotel.com

TownePlace Suites 888/236-2427
www.towneplace.com

Travelodge 800/578-7878
www.travelodge.com

Vagabond Inns 800/522-1555
www.vagabondinns.com

W Hotels 888/625-5144
www.whotels.com

Wellesley Inn and Suites 800/444-8888
www.wellesleyinnandsuites.com

WestCoast Hotels 800/325-4000
www.westcoasthotels.com

Westin Hotels & Resorts 800/937-8461
www.westin.com

Wingate Inns. 800/228-1000
www.wingateinns.com
Woodfin Suite Hotels. 800/966-3346
www.woodfinsuitehotels.com
WorldHotels 800/223-5652
www.worldhotels.com
Wyndham Hotels & Resorts 800/996-3426
www.wyndham.com

Airlines

Air Canada. 888/247-2262
www.aircanada.ca
AirTran. 800/247-8726
www.airtran.com
Alaska Airlines. 800/252-7522
www.alaskaair.com
American Airlines. 800/433-7300
www.aa.com
America West. 800/235-9292
www.americawest.com
ATA. 800/435-9282
www.ata.com
Continental Airlines. 800/523-3273
www.continental.com
Delta Air Lines 800/221-1212
www.delta.com
Frontier Airlines. 800/432-1359
www.frontierairlines.com
Hawaiian Airways 800/367-5320
www.hawaiianair.com
Jet Blue Airlines. 800/538-2583
www.jetblue.com
Midwest Express 800/452-2022
www.midwestexpress.com

Northwest Airlines. 800/225-2525
www.nwa.com
Southwest Airlines. 800/435-9792
www.southwest.com
Spirit Airlines 800/772-7117
www.spiritair.com
United Airlines 800/241-6522
www.united.com
US Airways 800/428-4322
www.usairways.com

Car Rentals

Advantage 800/777-5500
www.arac.com
Alamo. 800/327-9633
www.goalamo.com
Avis 800/831-2847
www.avis.com
Budget 800/527-0700
www.budget.com
Dollar 800/800-4000
www.dollarcar.com
Enterprise 800/325-8007
www.enterprise.com
Hertz 800/654-3131
www.hertz.com
National. 800/227-7368
www.nationalcar.com
Payless 800/729-5377
www.paylesscarrental.com
Rent-A-Wreck.com. 800/535-1391
www.rent-a-wreck.com
Thrifty 800/847-4389
www.thrifty.com

Meet The Stars

Mobil Travel Guide 2006 *Five-Star* Award Winners

CALIFORNIA
Lodgings
The Beverly Hills Hotel, *Beverly Hills*
Chateau du Sureau, *Oakhurst*
Four Seasons Hotel San Francisco,
  San Francisco
Hotel Bel-Air, *Los Angeles*
The Peninsula Beverly Hills, *Beverly Hills*
Raffles L'Ermitage Beverly Hills, *Beverly Hills*
The Ritz-Carlton, San Francisco, *San Francisco*

Restaurants
Bastide, *Los Angeles*
The Dining Room, *San Francisco*
The French Laundry, *Yountville*
Gary Danko, *San Francisco*

COLORADO
Lodgings
The Broadmoor, *Colorado Springs*
The Little Nell, *Aspen*

CONNECTICUT
Lodging
The Mayflower Inn, *Washington*

DISTRICT OF COLUMBIA
Lodging
Four Seasons Hotel Washington, DC,
  Washington

FLORIDA
Lodgings
Four Seasons Resort Palm Beach, *Palm Beach*
The Ritz-Carlton Naples, *Naples*
The Ritz-Carlton, Palm Beach, *Manalapan*

GEORGIA
Lodgings
Four Seasons Hotel Atlanta, *Atlanta*
The Lodge at Sea Island Golf Club,
  St. Simons Island

Restaurants
The Dining Room, *Atlanta*
Seeger's, *Atlanta*

HAWAII
Lodging
Four Seasons Resort Maui at Wailea, *Wailea,*
  Maui

ILLINOIS
Lodgings
Four Seasons Hotel Chicago, *Chicago*
The Peninsula Chicago, *Chicago*
The Ritz-Carlton, A Four Seasons Hotel, *Chicago*

Restaurant
Charlie Trotter's, *Chicago*

MAINE
Restaurant
The White Barn Inn, *Kennebunkport*

MASSACHUSETTS
Lodgings
Blantyre, *Lenox*
Four Seasons Hotel Boston, *Boston*

NEW YORK
Lodgings
Four Seasons, Hotel New York, *New York*
The Point, *Saranac Lake*
The Ritz-Carlton New York, Central Park,
  New York
The St. Regis, *New York*

Restaurants
Alain Ducasse, *New York*
Jean Georges, *New York*
Masa, *New York*
per se, *New York*

NORTH CAROLINA
Lodging
The Fearrington House Country Inn, *Pittsboro*

PENNSYLVANIA
Restaurant
Le Bec-Fin, *Philadelphia*

SOUTH CAROLINA
Lodging
Woodlands Resort & Inn, *Summerville*

Restaurant
Dining Room at the Woodlands, *Summerville*

TEXAS
Lodging
The Mansion on Turtle Creek, *Dallas*

VERMONT
Lodging
Twin Farms, *Barnard*

VIRGINIA
Lodgings
The Inn at Little Washington, *Washington*
The Jefferson Hotel, *Richmond*

Restaurant
The Inn at Little Washington, *Washington*

Mobil Travel Guide has been rating establishments with its Mobil One- to Five-Star system since 1958. Each establishment awarded the Mobil Five-Star rating is one of the best in the country. Detailed information on each award winner can be found in the corresponding regional edition listed on the back cover of this book.

Four- and Five-Star Establishments in New England

Connecticut

★ ★ ★ ★ ★ Lodging
The Mayflower Inn, *Washington*

★ ★ ★ ★ Restaurant
Thomas Henkelmann, *Greenwich*

Maine

★ ★ ★ ★ Lodging
The White Barn Inn, *Kennebunkport*

★ ★ ★ ★ ★ Restaurant
The White Barn Inn Restaurant, *Kennebunkport*

Massachusetts

★ ★ ★ ★ ★ Lodgings
Blantyre, *Lenox*
Four Seasons Hotel Boston, *Boston*

★ ★ ★ ★ Lodgings
Charlotte Inn, *Martha's Vineyard*
The Ritz-Carlton, Boston, *Boston*
The Ritz-Carlton, Boston Common, *Boston*
The Wauwinet, *Nantucket Island*
XV Beacon, *Boston*

★ ★ ★ ★ Restaurants
Aujourd'hui, *Boston*
Hamersley's Bistro, *Boston*
L'Espalier, *Boston*
No. 9 Park, *Boston*
Rialto, *Cambridge*

Rhode Island

★ ★ ★ ★ Restaurant
Mill's Tavern, *Providence*

Vermont

★ ★ ★ ★ ★ Lodging
Twin Farms, *Barnard*

America's Byways™ are a distinctive collection of American roads, their stories, and treasured places. They are roads to the heart and soul of America. In this section, you'll find the nationally designated Byways in Maine.

Acadia Byway

MAINE

Fog is a common sight along this Byway, muting the landscape with its romantic gray mists. In the midday sun, the sea's bright blue surface is studded with colorful lobster buoys. Seen at sundown from Cadillac Mountain, the sea glows in soft pinks, mauves, and golds.

QUICK FACTS

Length: 40 miles.

Time to Allow: 3 hours.

Best Time to Drive: This Byway is excellent year-round, with beautiful foliage in autumn; hiking and cross-country skiing in winter; and bird-watching, hiking, and bicycling in spring. High season runs from late June though September; tourism is especially heavy on July 4 and Labor Day weekends.

Byway Travel Information: Bar Harbor Chamber of Commerce: phone 207/288-5103; Acadia National Park Service: phone 207/288-3888.

Special Considerations: Mount Desert Island now has a free seasonal bus service that visitors are encouraged to use; the central terminal is in downtown Bar Harbor. The buses stop at many of the hotels and campgrounds along the way. They also stop anywhere that offers adequate space to pull over. You can easily flag them down.

Restrictions: The Park Loop Road is closed from late November to mid-April. Other roads can be closed during extreme weather conditions. You must pay a car toll to get on Park Loop Road at the national park. This pass is good for three days.

Bicycle/Pedestrian Facilities: The Park Loop Road was designed around biking and walking recreational activities. It is a one-way road, and the right lane is specifically designated for both bikers and walkers. There are also plenty of other places to walk and bike along this Byway. For example, Acadia National Park alone boasts 120 miles of hiking trails and 45 miles of carriage roads.

As the name suggests, the Acadia area was French before it was American. French explorer Samuel Champlain sailed into Frenchman Bay in 1604, naming the area Mount Desert Island because of its landmark bare top. Today, the National Park Service owns approximately half of the island that makes up Acadia National Park. The island boasts lush forests, tranquil ponds, and granite-capped mountains, where exploring is made easy by an extensive system of carriage roads and hiking trails. This alternate transportation network provides access to all areas of the park for walkers, equestrians, bicyclists, and cross-country skiers.

Villages on Mount Desert present a variety of lifestyles on the island today. Bar Harbor offers many accommodations and amusements. Northeast Harbor shelters sailboats, both large and small, and a summer colony. Bass Harbor and Southwest Harbor retain more of a traditional flavor of Maine's coastal villages.

The Byway Story

The Acadia Byway tells archaeological, cultural, historical, natural, recreational, and scenic stories that make it a unique and treasured Byway.

ARCHAEOLOGICAL

Many aspects indicate Native American encampments, but prehistoric records are scant.

For example, deep shell heaps suggest Native American encampments dating back 6,000 years in Acadia National Park. The first written descriptions of Maine coast Native Americans were recorded 100 years after European trade contacts began. In these records, Native Americans were described as people who lived off the land by hunting, fishing, collecting shellfish, and gathering plants and berries.

The Wabanaki Indians called Mount Desert Island Pemetic, or "the sloping land." They built bark-covered conical shelters and traveled in delicately designed birch bark canoes. Archaeological evidence suggests that the Wabanaki wintered on the coast and summered inland in order to take advantage of salmon runs upstream in the winter and avoid harsh inland weather.

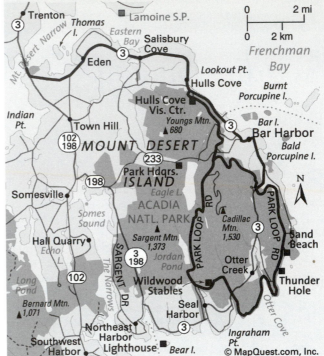

CULTURAL

While Maine is rich in culture, perhaps the best-known sights along the coast are the lobster traps and colorful buoys. Catching lobster has been a profitable activity in Maine since the 1840s. In fact, lobster was so plentiful during the age of elegant "cottages" in Acadia that the wealthy commonly fed their servants lobster because it was so inexpensive. Today, the sight of a lobsterman reeling in his trap is common.

Lobstermen use buoys to mark their trap sites, and every lobsterman has a different combination of colors to differentiate his buoys from someone else's. Often, one buoy is atop the wheelhouse of the lobster boat to display his colors. While the lobster boats are not the same wooden dories originally used, they are still a unique sight along the waters. They generally have a round bottom and a double wedge hull, ranging from 20 to 40 feet. The actual lobster traps come in various designs. Two of the best known are the parlor trap and the double-header trap, and they're set anywhere from 50 feet to miles apart. During the summer, lobster can be found in shallow waters (60 to 100 feet), but during the winter, lobster descend to depths of over 200 feet. You'll see lobstermen out hauling in their catch anytime weather permits and often when it does not.

HISTORICAL

Acadia's long history of settlement and colonization began with Samuel Champlain, who led the expedition that landed on Mount Desert on September 5, 1604. He wrote in his journal, "The mountain summits are all bare and rocky . . . I name it Isles des Monts Desert." Because Champlain, who made the first important contribution to the historical record of Mount Desert Island, visited 16 years before the

Pilgrims landed at Plymouth Rock, this land was known as New France before it became New England.

The land was in dispute between the French to the north and the English to the south for about 150 years. No one wanted to settle in the contested land until Antoine Laumet immigrated to New France in 1688 and bestowed upon himself the title Sieur de la Mothe Cadillac. He asked for, and received, 100,000 acres of land along the Maine Coast, including Mount Desert. He and his bride resided there for a time, but soon abandoned their enterprise of establishing a feudal estate in the new world.

After a century and a half of conflict, British troops triumphed at Quebec, ending French dominion in Acadia. Hence, lands along the Maine coast opened for English settlement. Soon, an increasing number of settlers homesteaded on Mount Desert Island. By 1820, farming and lumbering vied with fishing and shipbuilding as major occupations. Outsiders—artists and journalists—revealed and popularized the island to the world in the mid-1800s. Painters, called rusticators, inspired patrons and friends to flock to the island. Soon, tourism became a major industry.

For a handful of Americans, the 1880s and Gay Nineties meant affluence on a scale without precedent. Mount Desert, still remote from the cities of the east, became a retreat for prominent people of the times. The Rockefellers, Morgans, Fords, Vanderbilts, Carnegies, and Astors chose to spend their summers on the island. The families transformed the area with elegant estates, euphemistically called "cottages." For over 40 years, the wealthy held sway at Mount Desert until the Great Depression, World War II, and the fire of 1947 marked the end of such extravagance.

Although the wealthy came to the island to play, they also helped to preserve the landscape. George B. Dorr, in particular, was a tireless spokesman for conservation. He devoted 43 years of his life, energy, and family fortune to preserving Acadia. Dorr and others established the Hancock County Trustees of Public Reservations. This corporation's sole purpose was to preserve land for the perpetual use of the public, and it acquired some 6,000 acres by 1913. In 1916, the land became the Sieur de Monts National Monument, and in 1919 it became the first national park east of the Mississippi, with Dorr as the first park superintendent. In 1929, the park name changed to Acadia, and today the park encompasses 35,000 acres of land.

NATURAL

Acadia Byway runs right along Acadia National Park, where the sights are outstanding. Catching sight of an animal in its native environment will charm the casual visitor into an enthusiast, yet Acadia is home to a menagerie of wildlife that captivates the most experienced nature watcher. Whether you yearn to catch a glimpse of whales and seals or native and migratory birds, Acadia offers it all.

A variety of whales can be seen in the Gulf of Maine with antics that bring a smile, along with a sense of awe. Although finback, minke, and right whales can be seen, humpbacks are among the most playful of the whales. They are known for spy hopping (sticking their heads out of the water to look around), lobe tailing (throwing the lower half of their bodies out of the water), and tail slapping. To witness a humpback whale breaching (jumping completely out of the water) is a particularly amazing sight. Pay careful attention to the humpback's tail during its aerobatics—each whale's tail is unique.

After watching mammoth mammals in the water for a time, take a look above you. Acadia is an especially fertile area for bird sightings. In fact, 213 species—some migratory and some native—frequent the area. The peregrine falcon, once nearly extinct, can be seen winging overhead. They seem to circle lazily, but these raptors can attack prey at speeds of more than 100 miles per hour. They are most active at dawn and dusk in open areas. Puffins, also once nearly extinct, are making a comeback on islands along the Maine coast. Visitors may see this clown of the sea during offshore excursions.

RECREATIONAL

For outdoor recreation and fun, Acadia Byway is a dream come true. Relatively small at only 13 miles wide and 16 miles long, Acadia National Park offers a multitude of activities. Acadia maintains 45 miles of carriage roads for walking, riding, biking, and skiing and over 100 miles of trails just for hiking. Situated right along the coast, the area is perfect for boating, sailing, and kayaking. You can find an activity that best allows you to experience the tree-fringed lakes and streams, flower-filled meadows, or revitalizing sea breeze.

Hiking is one of the best ways to see all that Acadia has to offer. Trails that encourage meditation on the magnificence of nature crisscross the entire island. Take time to steal softly through a still forest, skip along the thundering coast, or meander through a swaying meadow. Up Cadillac Mountain is a particularly inspiring hike; its summit is the highest point on the Atlantic coast north of Rio de Janeiro. If you reach it before dawn and stand at the summit, you will be the first person in the continental United States to see the sun begin its journey across the sky and witness the beginning of a brand new day.

Want to see as much of the park as possible? Try cycling. Bicyclists experience the same closeness to nature as hikers but see more of the countryside and cover more ground. If you prefer paved roads, you'll find Acadia's smooth rides beckoning, while mountain bikers are in for a pleasant surprise: 45 miles of carriage roads wind around rippling lakes, through tunnels of leafy branches, over hills, and under a number of stone bridges. One ride that begins at Jordan Pond is a rolling 23 miles. This ride takes cyclists around the western portion of the eastern half of Mount Desert Island, between Somes Sound and Jordan Pond. If you enjoy flowering paths, two exquisite gardens along this ride bid you to stop and explore the sweet-smelling paths with a stunning view of the harbor.

For water enthusiasts, Acadia offers a number of alternatives. Ocean canoeing and kayaking are drawing new converts every day. The thrill of gliding on the surface of the rolling sea is an experience never to be forgotten. You can immerse yourself more fully in the ocean experience by swimming at one of the beaches, although water temperatures rarely exceed 55 degrees. Echo Lake Beach, a freshwater lake, is somewhat warmer. Take a trip on one of the schooners for a glimpse into sailing experiences of the late 1800s. Relax in the gentle breeze, try your hand at deep-sea fishing, or help the crew with the lines.

SCENIC

Acadia National Park preserves the natural beauty of Maine's coasts, mountains, and offshore islands. Acadia Byway takes you through a diverse area of scenery, from the seashore to the green vegetation inland. Park Loop Road, constructed specifically to take visitors through the variety of sights that Acadia has to offer, leads you along a path of breathtaking delight. Acadia's mountains are the highest rocky headlands on the Atlantic shore of the United States, and the views from these mountaintops encompass shadowy forests, gleaming lakes, hushed marshes, bold rocky shores, and coastal islands. The ocean, which surrounds Acadia on all sides, strongly influences the atmosphere of the park.

Travel along the Byway and stop to enjoy the tidepools along the beaches. Pockets in the rocky shore trap pools of water as the tide recedes, and remarkable plants and creatures grow and live in them, surviving the inhospitable world between tides. A little farther along, step into part of the woodlands where sunlight filters through the branches of spruce-fir, birch, aspen, and oak, leaving patches of light on your face and the sweet-smelling pine that crunches underfoot. Around another curve, a clear, shimmering freshwater lake appears. Filling a glacially carved valley, the solitude and peace the still water offers make the lakes in the interior of Acadia a place for reflection. At yet another place along the Byway, climb through the mountains and enjoy the stark beauty of the cliff faces and numerous plant species.

Highlights

While traveling this Byway, take your time. Because this route is on the coast and in a national park, you'll find no end to the brilliant views. Although the Byway runs just 40 miles, you can spend several days here.

Before you start out, pick up some hiking guides and other brochures and pamphlets at the visitor center, which is at the beginning of the Byway. If you're planning to hike, you'll want to know how difficult each of the hikes is so that you can plan according to your level of expertise. You'll also want to find out the cost of ferries if you plan to go out to the Cranberry Islands or go whale-watching.

○ **Day 1:** Spend a day in the city of Bar Harbor, soaking in the relaxed atmosphere, eating at a fine or charming local-flavor restaurant, and exploring a few of the hundreds of specialty shops. Some of the items the shops offer are so unique and distinctive that you'll never see their like again. You can seek out plenty of nightlife: bars, clubs, concerts, and specialty movie theaters (one is Art Deco; one has couches and pizza). You may even be able to catch one of the two annual music festivals, part of the annual film festival, or an opening night at an art gallery.

○ **Day 2:** Spend the day hiking around Dorr and Champlain Mountains and the Tarn. Explore off-road Acadia National Park on a mountain bike; take the 50+ miles of carriage roads that are safe, serene, gorgeous, and well maintained. You could even spend an overnighter in the park. There are plenty of places in Bar Harbor to pick up food and supplies if you need them.

○ **Day 3:** Make sure to hit Thunder Hole (and its associated historical ranger station). Otter Cliffs and the adjoining Otter Point are simply remarkable. You may want to don a jacket as you sit on the rocks and have a picnic lunch. Hop a ferry out to the Cranberry Islands to explore or take a ferry to whale-watch. You can see many other kinds of wildlife while whale-watching: bald eagles, puffins, and peregrine falcons (endangered). While out near the water, you can ocean kayak or canoe, deep-sea fish, or take a windjammer cruise. All of this equipment may be rented, and plenty of guides are available.

Connecticut

Connecticut is a state of beautiful hills and lakes and lovely old towns with white church steeples rising above green commons. It is also a state with a tradition of high technical achievement and fine machining. Old houses and buildings enchant the visitor; a re-creation of the life of the old sailing ship days at Mystic Seaport leads the traveler back to times long gone.

Adriaen Block sailed into the Connecticut River in 1614. This great river splits Massachusetts and Connecticut and separates Vermont from New Hampshire. It was the river by which Connecticut's first settlers, coming from Massachusetts in 1633, settled in Hartford, Windsor, and Wethersfield. These three towns created a practical constitution called the Fundamental Orders, through which a powerful "General Court" exercised both judicial and legislative duties. The Royal Charter of 1662 was so liberal that Sir Edmund Andros, governor of New England, tried to seize it (1687). To save it, citizens hid the charter in the Charter Oak, which once stood in Hartford.

Poultry, dairy products, and tobacco are the state's most important agricultural products; forest products, nursery stock, and fruit and vegetable produce follow in importance. Aircraft engines, helicopters, hardware, tools, nuclear submarines, and machinery are the principal manufactured products. The home offices of more than 40 insurance companies are located in the state.

When to Go/Climate

Connecticut's climate is the mildest of all the New England states. Coastal breezes help keep the humidity manageable, and mud season (between winter and spring, when topsoil thaws and lower earth remains frozen) is shorter here than in other New England states.

Population: 3,405,565

Area: 4,872 square miles

Elevation: 0-2,380 feet

Peak: Mount Frissel (Litchfield County)

Entered Union: Fifth of original 13 states (January 9, 1788)

Capital: Hartford

Motto: He who transplanted, still sustains

Nickname: Constitution State

Flower: Mountain Laurel

Bird: American Robin

Tree: White Oak

Time Zone: Eastern

Web Site: www.tourism.state.ct.us

Fun Facts:

- Connecticut is home to the oldest US newspaper still being published: *The Hartford Courant*, established in 1764.
- The world's first written constitution, the Fundamental Orders, was created in 1639 by English settlements that united to form the Connecticut Colony. That is why Connecticut is often referred to as the "Constitution State."

AVERAGE HIGH/LOW TEMPERATURES (° F)

Bridgeport

Jan 29/22	**May** 59/50	**Sept** 66/58
Feb 31/23	**June** 68/59	**Oct** 56/47
Mar 39/31	**July** 74/66	**Nov** 46/38
Apr 49/40	**Aug** 73/65	**Dec** 35/28

Hartford

Jan 25/16	**May** 60/48	**Sept** 64/52
Feb 28/19	**June** 69/57	**Oct** 53/41

Calendar Highlights

APRIL

Connecticut Storytelling Festival *(New London). Connecticut College. Phone 860/439-2764.* Nationally acclaimed artists; workshops, concerts.

MAY

Garlicfest *(Fairfield). Notre Dame Catholic High School. Phone 203/372-6521.* Vendors prepare international array of garlic-seasoned cuisine. Sales, entertainment.

International Festival of Arts and Ideas *(New Haven). Phone toll-free 888/278-4332.* Celebration of the arts and humanities.

Lobsterfest *(Mystic). Seaport. Phone 860/57-0711. www.visitmysticseaport.com.* Outdoor food festival.

JUNE

Barnum Festival *(Bridgeport). Phone toll-free 866/867-8495.* Commemorates the life of P. T. Barnum.

Taste of Hartford *(Hartford). Constitution Plz. Phone 860/920-5337. www.tasteofhartford.com.* Four-day event features specialties of more than 50 area restaurants; continuous entertainment.

JULY

Mark Twain Days *(Hartford). Phone 860/247-0998.* Celebration of Twain's legacy and Hartford's cultural heritage with more than 100 events. Concerts, riverboat rides, medieval jousting, tours of Twain House, entertainment.

Riverfest *(Hartford). Charter Oak Landing and Constitution Plz. Phone 860/713-3131.* Celebration of America's independence and the Connecticut River. Family entertainment, concerts, food, fireworks display over river.

AUGUST

Pilot Pen International Tennis Tournament *(New Haven). Connecticut Tennis Center, near Yale Bowl. Phone toll-free 888/997-4568.* Championship Series on the ATP Tour.

SEPTEMBER

Durham Fair *(Middletown). Fairgrounds, in Durham on Hwy 17. Phone 860/349-9495.* State's largest agricultural fair.

OCTOBER

Apple Harvest Festival *(Meriden). 3 miles S on Hwy 120, in Southington, on Town Green. Phone 860/628-8036.* Street festival celebrating local apple harvest. Carnival, arts and crafts, parade, road race, food booths, entertainment.

DECEMBER

Christmas Torchlight Parade *(Old Saybrook). Phone 860/388-3266.* More than 40 fife and drum corps march down Main Street.

Mar 38/28	**July** 74/62	**Nov** 42/33
Apr 49/38	**Aug** 72/60	**Dec** 30/21

Parks and Recreation

Water-related activities, hiking, riding, various other sports, picnicking and visitor centers, as well as camping, are available in designated areas. There are 32 state forests and 92 state parks inland and on the shore. A parking fee ($4-$12) is charged at many of these. Camping, mid-April-September; shore parks $15/site/night; inland parks with swimming $13/site/night; inland parks without swimming $11/site/night; additional charge per person for groups larger than four persons. Two- to three-week limit, mid-April-September; three-day limit, October-December. No camping January-mid-April; selected parks allow camping October-December. Forms for reservations for stays of more than two days may be obtained after January 15 by writing to the address in Hartford; these reservations should then be mailed to the park itself; no reservations by phone. Parks and forests are open all year, 8 am-sunset. Most shore parks allow all-night fishing (with permit). Inland swimming areas are open 8 am-sunset. No pets are allowed in state park campgrounds. For further information, reservations, and regulations contact the Department of Environmental Protection, Bureau of Outdoor Recreation, 79 Elm St, Hartford 06106; phone 860/424-3200.

FISHING AND HUNTING

Hunting license: nonresident, $42 (firearms). Archery permit (including big and small game): nonresident, $44. Deer permit: nonresident, $30 (firearms). Fishing license: nonresident, season, $25; three-day, $8. Combination firearm hunting, fishing license: nonresident, $55. Further information, including the latest regulations, can be obtained from Department of Environmental Protection, Licensing and Revenue, 79 Elm St, Hartford 06106; phone 860/424-3105.

Driving Information

Safety belts are mandatory for all persons in front seat of vehicle. Children under 4 years must be in approved passenger restraints anywhere in a vehicle: ages 1-3 may use regulation safety belts; under age 1 must use approved safety seats.

INTERSTATE HIGHWAY SYSTEM

The following alphabetical listing of Connecticut towns in this book shows that these cities are within 10 miles of the indicated interstate highways. A highway map, however, should be checked for the nearest exit.

Highway Number	Cities/Towns within 10 Miles
Interstate 84	Danbury, Farmington, Hartford, Manchester, Southbury, Stafford Springs, Vernon, Waterbury.
Interstate 91	Enfield, Hartford, Meriden, Middletown, New Haven, Wethersfield, Windsor, Windsor Locks.
Interstate 95	Branford, Bridgeport, Clinton, Fairfield, Greenwich, Groton, Guildford, Madison, Milford, Mystic, New Haven, New London, Norwalk, Old Saybrook, Stamford, Stonington, Stratford, Westport.
Interstate 395	Groton, New London, Norwich, Plainfield, Putnam.

Additional Visitor Information

Pamphlets, maps, and booklets, including the *Connecticut Vacation Guide*, are available to tourists by contacting the State of Connecticut, Department of Economic and Community Development, 505 Hudson St, Hartford 06106; phone toll-free 800/282-6863. In addition, *Connecticut*—a monthly magazine published by Communications International, 789 Reservoir Ave, Bridgeport 06606—gives a listing of activities around the state; available by subscription or at newsstands.

Connecticut tourism information centers also provide useful information: on I-95 southbound at North Stonington, northbound at Darien, northbound at Westbrook (seasonal); on I-84 eastbound at Danbury, eastbound at Southington (seasonal), westbound at Willington; on I-91 northbound at Middletown, southbound at Wallingford; on Merritt Parkway (Hwy 15) northbound at Greenwich (seasonal). Also, several privately operated tourism centers are located throughout the state.

A CLASSIC NEW ENGLAND ROAD TRIP

The town of Mystic (roughly halfway between New York and Boston on I-95) represents the state's top coastal lodgings/attractions hub. Mystic Seaport Museum, Mystic Aquarium, and a shopping mall in the shape of a New England village are popular attractions. Foxwoods Resort Casino, in nearby Ledyard, is the world's largest gambling casino; its complex includes lodging and a museum devoted to the Mashantucket Pequot, the tribe that owns the casino. From Mystic, take I-95 to Old Lyme, home of the Florence Griswold Art Museum and Rocky Neck State Park beach. Cross the bridge into Old Saybrook, and follow Highway 9 to Essex, a picturesque village with shops and restaurants. The Connecticut River Museum is located here, as is the departure point for the Valley Railroad, which runs along the river. (Railroad passengers can connect with a riverboat for a one-hour Connecticut River cruise.) Follow scenic Highway 154 to Chester, and take the country's oldest continuous ferry (it also carries cars) across to Gillette Castle in East Haddam. Or continue over the bridge to East Haddam for a great view of the Victorian Goodspeed Opera House, which stages American musicals and is a destination in its own right. You can return via Highway 9 (limited-access highway) or take the scenic way (country roads), Highway 82 to Highway 156 to I-95, back along the eastern side of the river. Continue west on I-95 to Hammonasset Beach State Park in Madison (the big beach in this area). Then head down Highway 1, past the town's classic historic homes, to Guilford (classic green), site of the Henry Whitfield State Museum. Get back on I-95 and follow it into New Haven. Another trip option from Mystic is to head east on I-95 to Stonington, a picturesque fishing village, and then to Watch Hill, a resort town with good beaches. From Stonington, it's a scenic 40-mile coastal drive along Highway 1, which passes the Rhode Island fishing resort towns of Charlestown and Narragansett (departure point for ferries to Block Island) and crosses to Jamestown Island in Newport, Rhode Island. **(Approximately 112 miles round-trip; approximately 124 miles round-trip from Mystic to Jamestown Island)**

Avon (D-3)

See also Bristol, Farmington, Hartford, Simsbury, Wethersfield

Population 13,937
Elevation 202 ft
Area Code 860
Zip 06001
Information Greater Hartford Tourism District, 234 Murphy Rd, Hartford 06114; phone 860/244-8181 or toll-free 800/793-4480
Web Site www.town.avon.ct.us

What to See and Do

Farmington Valley Arts Center. *25 Arts Center Ln, Avon (06001). Off Hwy 44. Phone 860/678-1867.* Twenty studios, located in a historic stone explosives plant, occupied by artists and artisans and open to the public at artist's discretion. Fisher Gallery and Shop featuring guest-curated exhibitions and a juried collection of handmade crafts, gifts, and artwork. (Jan-Oct: Wed-Sat, Sun afternoons; Nov-Dec: daily; closed holidays) **FREE**

Roaring Brook Nature Center. *70 Gracey Rd, Canton (06019). 1 1/2 miles N of Hwy 44. Phone 860/693-0263.* This 112-acre wildlife refuge has an interpretive building with seasonal natural history exhibits, wildlife observation area; 6 miles of marked trails. Gift shop. (Sept-June: Tues-Sun; rest of year: daily; closed holidays) **$$**

Ski Sundown. *126 Ratlum Rd, New Hartford (06057). 6 miles W via Hwy 44, then 1 1/2 miles NE on Hwy 219. Phone 860/379-9851. www.skisundown.com.* Three triple, double chairlift; Pomalift; snowmaking; school, patrol, rentals, half-day rate; bar, snack bar. Fifteen trails. Longest run 1 mile; vertical drop 625 feet. (Dec-Mar, daily) **$$$$**

Full-Service Hotel

★ ★ ★ **AVON OLD FARMS HOTEL.** *279 Avon Mountain, Avon (06001). Phone 860/677-1651; toll-free 800/836-4000; fax 860/677-0364. www.avonoldfarmshotel.com.* Guests can enjoy nature with walks to nearby parks and trails, or simply kick back and take in the hometown feel. 160 rooms, 3 story. Complimentary continental breakfast. Check-out noon. Restaurant. Fitness room. Outdoor pool. **$**

Restaurants

★ ★ ★ **AVON OLD FARMS INN.** *1 Nod Rd, Avon (06001). Phone 860/677-2818; fax 860/676-0280. www.avonoldfarmsinn.com.* Serving classic entrée favorites from the past, with a seasonally changing menu, this restaurant (a 1757 stagecoach stop) draws a local and tourist clientele. American menu. Lunch, dinner, Sun brunch. Bar. Children's menu. **$$**

★ ★ **DAKOTA.** *225 W Main St, Avon (06001). Phone 860/677-4311; fax 860/677-2872. www.dakotarestaurant.com.* Seafood, steak menu. Dinner. Bar. Children's menu. **$$**

Branford (E-3)

See also Guilford, Madison, Meriden, Milford, New Haven

Settled 1644
Population 27,603
Elevation 49 ft
Area Code 203, 860
Zip 06405
Information Connecticut River Valley & Shoreline Visitors Council, 393 Main St, Middletown 06457; phone 860/347-0028 or toll-free 800/486-3346
Web Site www.cttourism.org

Once a busy shipping center, Branford has become a residential and industrial suburb of New Haven. The community's bays and beaches attract many summertime vacationers. Branford's large green, dating from colonial days, is surrounded by public buildings.

What to See and Do

Harrison House. *124 Main St, Branford (06405). Phone 203/488-4828.* (Circa 1725) Classic colonial saltbox restored by J. Frederick Kelly, an early 20th-century architect; stone chimney, herb garden, period furnishings, and farm implements. (June-Sept, Thurs-Sat mid-late afternoon; also by appointment) **FREE**

Thimble Islands Cruise. *Thimble Island and Prospect Hill rds, Branford (06405). Departs from Stony Creek Dock. Phone 203/481-3345.* Legends of treasures hidden by Captain Kidd, along with picturesque shores and vegetation, have for more than 250 years lured people to these 20 to 30 rocky islets in Long Island Sound. Narrated tours (30-45 minutes) leave hourly aboard the *Volsunga III*. (May-Oct, Tues-Sun) Reservations required. **$$$**

Bridgeport (F-2)

See also Fairfield, Milford, Norwalk, Stratford, Westport

Settled 1639
Population 141,686
Elevation 20 ft
Area Code 203
Information Chamber of Commerce, 10 Middle St, 14th floor, 06604; phone 203/335-3800
Web Site www.brbcnet.com

An important manufacturing city, Bridgeport is home to dozens of well-known companies that produce a highly diversified array of manufactured products. The University of Bridgeport (1927) is also located in the city.

Bridgeport's most famous resident was probably P. T. Barnum. The city's most famous son was 28-inch Charles S. Stratton, who was promoted by Barnum as General Tom Thumb. There was a time when train passengers in and out of Bridgeport occasionally saw elephants hitched to plows; the elephants, of course, were from Barnum's winter quarters. As well as running the "Greatest Show on Earth," Barnum was for a time the mayor of Bridgeport.

What to See and Do

⭐ **Barnum Museum.** *820 Main St, Bridgeport (06604). Phone 203/331-1104. www.barnum-museum.org.* Houses memorabilia from P. T. Barnum's life and circus career, including artifacts relating to Barnum's legendary discoveries, General Tom Thumb and Jenny Lind; scale model of three-ring circus; displays of Victorian Bridgeport; changing exhibits; art gallery. (Tues-Sun; closed holidays) **$$**

Beardsley Zoological Gardens. *Beardsley Park, 1875 Noble Ave, Bridgeport (06604). Off I-95 exit 27A. Phone 203/394-6565.* This 30-acre zoo, the state's only, houses more than 200 animals; Siberian tiger exhibit; farmyard; concession; gift shop. (Daily; closed Jan 1, Thanksgiving, Dec 25) **$$$**

Captain's Cove Seaport. *1 Bostwick Ave, Bridgeport (06605). I-95 exit 26. Phone 203/335-1433.* Replica of the HMS *Rose*, the British warship that triggered the founding of the American Navy during the Revolutionary War. Marina; shops, restaurant, fish market. (Schedule varies)

Discovery Museum. *4450 Park Ave, Bridgeport (06604). Off Merritt Pkwy, exit 47. Phone 203/372-3521.* Planetarium; films; approximately 120 hands-on science and art exhibits; children's museum; Challenger Learning Center; changing art exhibits; lectures, demonstrations, and workshops. (Tues-Sun; closed Labor Day, Thanksgiving, Dec 25) **$$$**

Ferry to Port Jefferson, Long Island. Car and passenger service across Long Island Sound (1 hour, 20 minutes). (Daily)

Statue of Tom Thumb. *Mountain Grove Cemetery, North Ave and Dewey St, Bridgeport (06604).* Life-size statue on 10-foot base.

Special Event

Barnum Festival. *Main St and Fairfield, Bridgeport (06604). Phone toll-free 866/867-8495.* Commemorates the life of P. T. Barnum. Apr-July

Limited-Service Hotel

★ ★ **HOLIDAY INN.** *1070 Main St, Bridgeport (06604). Phone 203/334-1234; toll-free 800/465-4329; fax 203/367-1985. www.holiday-inn.com.* 234 rooms, 9 story. Pets accepted, some restrictions; fee. Check-in 3 pm, check-out noon. High-speed Internet access. Restaurant, bar. Fitness room. Indoor pool, outdoor pool. Airport transportation available. Business center. **$**

Full-Service Hotel

★ ★ ★ **MARRIOTT TRUMBULL MERRITT PARKWAY.** *180 Hawley Ln, Trumbull (06611). Phone 203/378-1400; toll-free 800/682-4095; fax 203/375-0632. www.marriott.com.* 320 rooms, 5 story. Check-in 4 pm, check-out noon. High-speed Internet access. Restaurant, bar. Fitness room. Indoor pool, outdoor pool, whirlpool. Business center. **$$**

Restaurant

★ **BLACK ROCK CASTLE.** *2895 Fairfield Ave, Bridgeport (06605). Phone 203/336-3990; fax 203/331-9325. www.blackrockcastle.com.* Irish menu. Lunch, dinner. Closed Jan 1, Dec 25. Children's menu. Valet parking. **$$**

Bristol (D-3)

See also Avon, Farmington, Litchfield, Meriden, New Britain, Waterbury, Woodbury

Settled 1727
Population 60,640
Elevation 289 ft
Area Code 860
Zip 06010
Information Greater Bristol Chamber of Commerce, 10 Main St; phone 860/584-4718. Litchfield Hills Visitors Bureau, PO Box 968, Litchfield 06759; phone 860/567-4506
Web Site www.bristol-chamber.org

Gideon Roberts began making and selling clocks here in 1790. Bristol has since been famous for clocks—particularly for Sessions and Ingraham. Today, Bristol is also the home of the Associated Spring Corporation; Dana Corporation/Warner Electric; Theis Precision Steel; and ESPN, the nation's first all-sports cable television network.

What to See and Do

American Clock and Watch Museum. *100 Maple St, Bristol (06010). Phone 860/583-6070.* More than 3,000 timepieces; exhibits and video show on history of clock and watch manufacturing located in historic house built 1801. Also award-winning sundial garden; bookshop. (Apr-Nov, daily; closed Thanksgiving) **$$**

Burlington Trout Hatchery. *34 Belden Rd, Burlington (06013). 10 miles N via Hwy 69, then approximately 1 mile E on Hwy 4 to Belden Rd. Phone 860/673-2340.* Hatchery building houses incubators and tanks; development of trout from egg to fish. (Daily) **FREE**

H. C. Barnes Memorial Nature Center. *175 Shrub Rd, Bristol (06010). 3 miles N on Hwy 69. Phone 860/589-6082.* Self-guiding trails through 70-acre preserve. Interpretive building features ecological and animal displays. (Sat, also Wed-Fri and Sun afternoons) Trails (daily; closed holidays). **$**

Lake Compounce Theme Park. *822 Lake Ave, Bristol (06010). Phone 860/583-3631. www.lakecompounce .com.* One of the oldest continuously operating amusement parks in the nation. Over 25 wet and dry attractions include roller coasters, whitewater raft ride, vintage trolley, bumper cars, and 1911 carou-

sel. Special events. (June-Aug, Mon, Wed-Sun; Sept, weekends) **$$$$**

Lock Museum of America. *230 Main St, Terryville (06786). 3 1/2 miles NW on Hwy 72, then W 3/4 mile on Hwy 6 to 130 Main St. Phone 860/589-6359.* Antique locks, displays on lock history and design. (May-Oct, Tues-Sun, limited hours) **$$** Two blocks west is

Eli Terry Jr. Waterwheel. *160 Main St, Terryville (06786).* Built in the early 1840s, this 20-foot diameter, rack-and-pinion, breast-type wheel is an excellent example of the type of waterwheel used to supply power to industrial buildings during this period.

New England Carousel Museum. *95 Riverside Ave, Bristol (06010). Phone 860/585-5411.* Displays more than 300 carved, wooden antique carousel figures, including two chariots. Restoration workshop on view. (Apr-Oct, daily; rest of year, Thurs-Sat, also Sun afternoons; closed holidays) **$$**

Special Events

Balloons Over Bristol. *Bristol Eastern High School, 632 King St, Bristol (06010). Phone 860/584-4718.* More than 60 hot air balloons from around the country gather to participate in this three-day event; carnival, crafts fair, food booths. Memorial Day weekend.

Chrysanthemum Festival. *130 Main St, Bristol (06010). Phone 860/584-4718.* Music, art, theater, hayrides, picking pumpkins, parades, and dances, Historical Society tours. Late Sept.

Specialty Lodging

The following lodging establishment is approved by Mobil Travel Guide, but due to its unique and individualized nature has not been given a traditional Mobil Star rating. Included in this listing you may find bed-and-breakfasts, limited-service inns, guest ranches, and other unique hotel properties.

CHIMNEY CREST MANOR. *5 Founders Dr, Bristol (06010). Phone 860/582-4219; fax 860/584-5903.* This historic (1930) Tudor-style bed-and-breakfast is located in the beautiful Federal Hill district of Bristol. The home features framed artwork and beamed ceilings. 6 rooms, 3 story. Closed Dec 24-25. Complimentary full breakfast. Check-in 3 pm, check-out 11 am. **$**

Clinton (E-4)

See also Essex, Guilford, Madison, New Haven, Old Saybrook

Settled 1663
Population 12,767
Elevation 25 ft
Area Code 860
Zip 06413
Information Chamber of Commerce, 50 E Main St, PO Box 334; phone 860/669-3889
Web Site www.clintonct.com

What to See and Do

Chamard Vineyards. *115 Cow Hill Rd, Clinton (06413). Phone 860/664-0299; toll-free 800/371-1609. www.chamard.com.* A 15-acre vineyard and winery offering chardonnay, pinot noir, merlot, and other varieties. Tours and tastings (Wed-Sat). **FREE**

Chatfield Hollow State Park. *381 Hwy 80, Killingworth (06419). 7 miles NW via Hwys 80 and 81, on N Branford Rd. Phone 860/663-2030.* Approximately 550 acres situated in a heavily wooded hollow with fine fall scenery and natural caves that once provided shelter for Native Americans. Pond swimming, fishing; hiking, ice skating, picnicking. **$$$**

Stanton House. *63 E Main St, Clinton (06413). Phone 860/669-2132.* (1789) Thirteen-room house connected to general store; original site of the first classroom of Yale University. Period furnishings; antique American and Staffordshire dinnerware; weapon collection; bed used by Marquis de Lafayette during 1824 visit. (June-Sept, Tues-Sun) **FREE**

Limited-Service Hotel

★ **CLINTON MOTEL.** *163 E Main St, Clinton (06413). Phone 860/669-8850; fax 860/669-3849.* 15 rooms. Check-out 11 am. Outdoor pool. **$**

Restaurant

★ **LOG CABIN RESTAURANT AND LOUNGE.** *232 Boston Post Rd, Clinton (06413). Phone 860/669-6253.* American, Italian menu. Lunch, dinner. Closed Dec 25. Bar. Children's menu. **$$**

Cornwall Bridge (D-1)

See also Kent, Lakeville, Litchfield, New Preston

Population 450
Elevation 445 ft
Area Code 860
Zip 06754
Information Litchfield Hills Visitors Bureau, PO Box 968, Litchfield 06759; phone 860/567-4506
Web Site www.litchfieldhills.com

The small central valley containing the villages of Cornwall, West Cornwall, and Cornwall Bridge was avoided by early settlers because its heavy stand of pine made the clearing of land difficult.

What to See and Do

Covered bridge. *West Cornwall. 4 miles N via Hwy 7 to Hwy 128 near West Cornwall, at Housatonic River.* Designed by Ithiel Town, in continuous service since 1837. **FREE**

Housatonic Meadows State Park. *Hwys 7 and 4, Cornwall Bridge (06754). 1 mile N on Hwy 7. Phone 860/927-3238.* A 452-acre park bordering the Housatonic River. Fishing, boating, canoeing; picnicking, camping (dump station). No pets. **FREE**

Mohawk Mountain Ski Area. *4 miles NE on Hwy 4, S on Hwy 128, on Great Hollow Rd in Mohawk Mountain State Park. Phone 860/672-6100 (snow conditions). www.mohawkmtn.com.* More than 20 trails and slopes, most with snowmaking; triple, four double chairlifts; patrol, school, rentals; cafeteria. Longest run 1 1/4 mile; vertical drop 650 feet. More than 40 miles of cross-country trails. Night skiing Mon-Sat. (Late Nov-early Apr, daily; closed holidays) **$$$$**

Sharon Audubon Center. *325 Cornwall Bridge Rd, Sharon (06069). Approximately 8 miles NW on Hwy 4. Phone 860/364-0520.* National Audubon Society wildlife sanctuary (684 acres) including nature center, 11 miles of walking trails, self-guided tours, herb and wildflower garden, gift/bookstore. Grounds (daily). Nature center, store (Tues-Sun; closed holidays). **$$**

Restaurant

★★ **CORNWALL INN.** *270 Kent Rd (Hwy 7), Cornwall Bridge (06754). Phone 860/672-6884.* American menu. Dinner. Bar. Casual attire. Outdoor seating. **$$**

Danbury (E-1)

See also Brewster, Ridgefield, Southbury, Woodbury

Settled 1685
Population 65,585
Elevation 378 ft
Area Code 203
Information Housatonic Valley Tourism District, 30 Main St, PO Box 406, 06810; phone 203/743-0546 or toll-free 800/841-4488
Web Site www.danbury.org

Danbury, originally settled by eight Norwalk families seeking fertile land, played an important role during the American Revolution as a supply depot and site of a military hospital for the Continental Army. After the war and until the 1950s, the community was the center of the hat industry. Zadoc Benedict is credited with the first factory in 1790, which made three hats a day.

What to See and Do

Candlewood Lake. *35 E Hayestown Rd, Danbury (06811). 2 miles NW on Hwy 37, then E on Hayestown Ave to E Hayestown Rd.* Connecticut's largest lake, more than 14 miles long and with more than 60 miles of shoreline, extends one finger into Danbury. Swimming, fishing, boating; picnicking, concession. Fees for some activities. On the west shore are Pootatuck State Forest and

Squantz Pond State Park. *178 Shortwoods Rd, New Fairfield (06812). 10 miles N on Hwys 37 and 39. Phone 203/797-4165.* More than 170 acres. Freshwater swimming, scuba diving, fishing, boating (7 1/2 hp limit), canoeing; hiking, biking, picnicking, concessions. **$$$**

Scott-Fanton Museum. *43 Main St, Danbury (06810). Phone 203/743-5200.* Includes Rider House (1785), period furnishings, New England memorabilia; Dodd Shop (circa 1790), historical display of hat industry; Huntington Hall, changing exhibits and research library. (Wed-Sun afternoons; closed holidays) **DONATION**

Special Events

Charles Ives Center for the Arts. *Mill Plain Rd, Danbury (06810). Phone 203/837-9226.* At Westside campus, Western Connecticut State University. Outdoor classical, country, folk, jazz, and pop concerts. Fri-Sun, July-Sept.

Taste of Greater Danbury. *Danbury Green, Green Ives and White sts, Danbury (06810). Phone 203/792-1711. www.citycenterdanbury.com.* Food vendors, live music, and children's games draw crowds together year after year. Sept.

Limited-Service Hotels

★ ★ **ETHAN ALLEN HOTEL.** *21 Lake Ave, Danbury (06811). Phone 203/744-1776; toll-free 800/742-1776; fax 203/791-9673. www.ethanalleninn.com.* 195 rooms, 6 story. Check-out noon. Restaurant, bar. Fitness room. Outdoor pool. Airport transportation available. Business center. **$**

★ ★ **HOLIDAY INN.** *80 Newtown Rd, Danbury (06810). Phone 203/792-4000; toll-free 800/465-4329; fax 203/797-0810. www.danburyholidayinn.com.* 114 rooms, 4 story. Pets accepted; fee. Check-in 2 pm, check-out noon. High-speed Internet access. Restaurant, bar. Outdoor pool. Airport transportation available. **$**

Full-Service Hotel

★ ★ ★ **SHERATON DANBURY HOTEL.** *18 Old Ridgebury Rd, Danbury (06810). Phone 203/794-0600; toll-free 800/325-3535; fax 203/830-5188. www.sheraton.com.* Conveniently located just 3 miles from Danbury Airport. 242 rooms, 10 story. Check-in 3 pm, check-out noon. Restaurant, bar. Fitness room. Indoor pool, whirlpool. Tennis. Business center. **$**

Specialty Lodging

The following lodging establishment is approved by Mobil Travel Guide, but due to its unique and individualized nature has not been given a traditional Mobil Star rating. Included in this listing you may find bed-and-breakfasts, limited-service inns, guest ranches, and other unique hotel properties.

THE HOMESTEAD INN. *5 Elm St, New Milford (06776). Phone 860/354-4080; fax 860/354-7046. www.homesteadct.com.* Inn built in 1853; many of the rooms are furnished with country antiques. 14 rooms, 2 story. Complimentary continental breakfast. Check-in 2 pm, check-out 11 am. **$**

Restaurants

★ ★ **CIAO CAFE AND WINE BAR.** *2B Ives St, Danbury (06810). Phone 203/791-0404; fax 203/730-1962.* Italian menu. Lunch, dinner, Sun brunch. Closed Labor Day, Dec 25. Bar. Reservations recommended. Outdoor seating. **$$**

★ **THE HEARTH.** *Hwy 7, Brookfield (06804). Phone 203/775-3360.* Seafood, steak menu. Lunch, dinner. Closed Mon; Thanksgiving, Dec 24-25; Feb. Bar. Children's menu. **$$**
🄳

★ ★ **TWO STEPS DOWNTOWN GRILLE.** *5 Ives St, Danbury (06810). Phone 203/794-0032; fax 203/730-1962.* American, Southwestern menu. Lunch, dinner, Sun brunch. Closed Labor Day, Dec 25. Bar. Children's menu. Outdoor seating. **$$**

East Haddam (E-4)

See also Essex, Middletown

Population 6,676
Elevation 35 ft
Area Code 860
Zip 06423
Information Connecticut River Valley & Shoreline Visitors Council, 393 Main St, Middletown 06457; phone 860/347-0028 or toll-free 800/486-3346
Web Site www.cttourism.org

The longest remaining swinging bridge in New England crosses the Connecticut River to Haddam.

What to See and Do

Amasa Day House. *Plains Rd, Moodus (06469). 4 miles N on Hwy 149 at junction Hwy 15. Phone 860/873-8144.* (1816) Period furnishings include some pieces owned by three generations of the Day family; stenciled floors and stairs. (June-Labor Day, Fri-Sun) **$$**

Camelot Cruises, Inc. *1 Marine Park, Haddam (06438). W on Hwy 82, across river at Marine Park. Phone 860/345-8591.* Offers Connecticut River cruises, Long Island cruises, Murder Mystery cruises, and evening music excursions. Long Island cruises (mid-June-Labor Day: daily; after Labor Day-mid-Oct: Sun). Murder Mystery cruises (Mar-Dec, Fri and Sat evenings). **$$$$**

Eagle Aviation. *Goodspeed Airport and Seaplane Base, Lumberyard Rd, East Haddam (06423). Phone 860/873-8568.* Scenic airplane rides over the Connecticut River Valley. (Daily; closed Dec 25-early Jan) **$$$$**

Gillette Castle State Park. *67 River Rd, East Haddam. 4 miles SE via local roads. Phone 860/526-2336.* The 184-acre park surrounds a 24-room castle built by turn-of-the-century actor and playwright William Gillette; medieval German design with dramatically decorated rooms. (Late May-mid-Oct: daily; mid-Oct-mid-Dec: Sat-Sun) You'll find picnicking and hiking trails in the surrounding park. **$$**

Goodspeed Opera House. *6 Main St, East Haddam (06423). On Hwy 82 at East Haddam Bridge. Phone 860/873-8668.* Home of the American Musical Theatre (1876). Performances of American musicals (Apr-Dec, Wed-Sun evenings, matinees Wed, Sat, and Sun) Guided tours (June-Sept, Mon and Sat; fee). **$**

Nathan Hale Schoolhouse. *33 Main St, East Haddam (06423). Main St (Hwy 149) at rear of St. Stephen's Church. Phone 860/873-9547 (church).* One-room school where the American Revolutionary patriot taught during the winter of 1773; period furnishings, memorabilia. Church has bell said to have been cast in Spain in AD 815. (Memorial Day-Labor Day, Sat-Sun, and holidays, limited hours) **FREE**

Specialty Lodging

The following lodging establishment is approved by Mobil Travel Guide, but due to its unique and individualized nature has not been given a traditional Mobil Star rating. Included in this listing you may find bed-and-breakfasts, limited-service inns, guest ranches, and other unique hotel properties.

BISHOPSGATE INN. *7 Norwich Rd, East Haddam (06423). Phone 860/873-1677; fax 860/873-3898. www.bishopsgate.com.* Near Connecticut River. 6 rooms, 2 story. Pets accepted, some restrictions. Children over 5 years only. Complimentary full breakfast. Check-in 2 pm, check-out 11 am. **$**
🐾

Enfield (C-3)

See also Holyoke, Springfield, Stafford Springs, Windsor, Windsor Locks

Settled 1680
Population 45,532

Elevation 150 ft
Area Code 860
Zip 06082
Information Connecticut's Heritage Valley North Central Tourism Bureau, 111 Hazard Ave; phone 860/763-2578 or toll-free 800/248-8283
Web Site www.cnctb.org

Located on the Connecticut River, Enfield was an important embarking point for flat-bottom boats transporting wares to Springfield, Massachusetts, in the 18th century. The Enfield Society for the Detection of Horse Thieves and Robbers was founded here over a century ago. Jonathan Edwards, a famous theologian, delivered his fire and brimstone sermon "Sinners in the Hands of an Angry God" here in 1741.

What to See and Do

Martha A. Parsons House. *1387 Enfield St, Enfield (06082). Phone 860/745-6064.* (1782) Constructed on land put aside for use by parsons or ministers, this house holds 180 years' worth of antiques collected by the Parsons family; tables brought from West Indies, George Washington memorial wallpaper. (May-Oct, Sun afternoons or by appointment) **FREE**

Old Town Hall (Purple Heart Museum). *1294 Enfield St, Enfield (06082). Phone 860/745-1729.* Includes inventions of the Shakers, a religious sect that observed a doctrine of celibacy, common property, and community living; medals and service memorabilia, 46-star flag; local historical displays and artifacts. (May-Oct, Sun afternoons or by appointment) **FREE**

Limited-Service Hotel

★ ★ **RADISSON HOTEL SPRINGFIELD.** *1 Bright Meadow Blvd, Enfield (06082). Phone 860/741-2211; fax 860/741-6917. www.radisson.com.* The 11-acre, country setting attracts a business clientele to this property. Outdoor recreation includes landscaped walking trails. 181 rooms, 6 story. Check-out 11 am. Restaurant, bar. Fitness room. Indoor pool, outdoor pool, whirlpool. Tennis. Airport transportation available. **$**

🏃 🖼 🎿

Essex (E-4)

See also Clinton, East Haddam, Middletown, Old Lyme, Old Saybrook

Population 5,904
Elevation 100 ft
Area Code 860
Zip 06426
Information Connecticut River Valley & Shoreline Visitors Council, 393 Main St, Middletown 06457; phone 860/347-0028 or toll-free 800/486-3346
Web Site www.cttourism.org

What to See and Do

Connecticut River Museum. *67 Main St, Essex (06426). At the foot of Main St at the river. Phone 860/767-8269.* Housed in the last remaining steamboat dock building on the Connecticut River. Presents exhibits celebrating the rich cultural heritage and natural resources of the river valley. Includes the only full-size, operating replica of the *Turtle*, America's first successful submarine, built along the Connecticut River during the Revolutionary War. (Tues-Sun; closed holidays) **$$**

Valley Railroad. *1 Railroad Ave, Essex (06426). Phone 860/767-0103.* Scenic 12-mile steam train excursion along Connecticut River to Chester; can opt to connect with a riverboat for one-hour Connecticut River cruise (additional fare). Cruise passengers are returned to Essex via later connecting trains. Turn-of-the-century equipment. (Early May-late Oct, days vary; also Christmas trips) **$$$$**

Special Event

Deep River Ancient Muster and Parade. *Devitt's Field, Main St, Deep River. 2 1/2 miles N via Hwy 9. Phone 860/526-0058.* Approximately 60 fife and drum corps recall the revolutionary War period; displays. Third Sat in July.

Full-Service Inns

★ ★ ★ **THE COPPER BEECH INN.** *46 Main St, Ivoryton (06442). Phone 860/767-0330; toll-free 888/809-2056. www.copperbeechinn.com.* Travelers looking for a romantic New England getaway will not want to miss this charming 1889 Victorian inn (once the residence of a prominent ivory importer) with sprawling wooded surroundings. This quaint country retreat will relax the mind and soul. 13 rooms, 2 story. Closed Dec 24-25; also first week in Jan. Children over 12 years only. Complimentary full breakfast. Check-in 4 pm, check-out noon. Restaurant. **$$**

The Best Small Town in America

The lower reaches of the Connecticut River are so unspoiled by development that about ten years ago, the Nature Conservancy named the area to its list of "Last Great Places" in the Western Hemisphere. Then in 1996, the riverfront town of Essex won honors as "The Best Small Town in America" in a much-publicized book by Norman Crampton. The village part of the town is ideal for walking and sightseeing; a loop that takes in the whole peninsula is just about a mile in length.

Start at the top of Main Street at Essex Square (street parking is free and easy to find), then walk south along Main. You'll pass dozens of appealing shops selling everything from clothing to antiques. The town's brick post office is next to Essex Park, a lovely swath of grass and trees overlooking Middle Cove. St. John's Episcopal Church is across the street in an imposing brownstone. Built in the late 1800s in the style of H. H. Richardson, the church is decades younger than many of the white clapboard houses that line Main Street. The older houses date to the mid-1700s, when Essex was a major ship-building center. Ships' captains and merchants built their houses close to what is now the Town Dock at the foot of Main. Today, some of these houses have been converted to delis, coffeehouses, and shops, but others are still private homes, decked with window boxes and encircled with blooming gardens.

The Griswold Inn (locally known as The Griz) is a landmark that has been offering travelers hospitality since 1776. It's famous for its Sunday morning English-style Hunt Breakfast. The Connecticut River Museum is housed in a former steamboat warehouse next to the Town Dock; it showcases the history of the river with memorabilia and ship models. Reversing direction, head north on Main, then turn right onto Ferry Street to the Dauntless Shipyard and Essex Island Marina. Turn left onto Pratt Street to return to the starting point at Essex Square.

★ ★ ★ **GRISWOLD INN.** *36 Main St, Essex (06426). Phone 860/767-1776; fax 860/767-0481. www.griswoldinn.com.* Located near the Connecticut River, this inn has been in operation since 1776. 31 rooms, 3 story. Complimentary continental breakfast. Check-in 2 pm, check-out 11 am. Restaurant. **$$**

Restaurants

★ ★ ★ **COPPER BEECH INN.** *46 Main St, Ivoryton (06442). Phone 860/767-0330. www.copper beechinn.com.* Dine in hearty, French country style with fresh flowers, sparkling silver, and soft candlelight. The atmosphere is pure romance and warm elegance. French menu. Dinner. Closed Mon-Tues (Jan-Mar); Jan 1, Dec 24-25. Bar. Jacket required. **$$$**

★ ★ ★ **GRISWOLD INN.** *36 Main St, Essex (06426). Phone 860/767-1776; fax 860/767-0481. www.griswoldinn.com.* This historic inn has been serving typical country fare since 1776. The continental specialties are sure to satisfy. American menu. Lunch, dinner, Sun brunch. Closed Dec 24-25. Bar. Children's menu. **$$**

★ ★ **SAGE AMERICAN BAR & GRILL.** *129 W Main St, Chester (06412). Phone 860/526-9898; fax 860/526-2201. www.sageamerican.com.* In converted 19th-century mill with wheels and belts overhead. Seafood, steak menu. Dinner. Children's menu. Outdoor seating. **$$**

★ ★ **STEVE CENTERBROOK CAFE.** *78 Main St, Centerbrook (06409). Phone 860/767-1277; fax 860/767-8326.* Victorian house. American menu. Dinner. Closed Mon. Bar. **$$**

Fairfield (F-4)

See also Bridgeport, Milford, Norwalk, Stamford, Stratford, Westport

Settled 1639
Population 53,418
Elevation 15 ft
Area Code 203
Information Chamber of Commerce, 1597 Post Rd, 06430; phone 203/255-1011
Web Site www.fairfieldchamber.com

A small band of colonists led by Roger Ludlowe settled Fairfield two years after the Pequot were subdued in the Great Swamp Fight. In 1779, British troops under

General Tyron marched into the area and requested that the people submit to royal authority. When this was refused, the village was put to the torch.

What to See and Do

Connecticut Audubon Society Birdcraft Museum and Sanctuary. *314 Unquowa Rd, Fairfield (06824). Phone 203/259-0416.* Established in 1914, this vest-pocket, 6-acre sanctuary houses a natural history museum with wildlife displays, dinosaur footprints, trails, ponds. (Tues-Sun) **FREE**

Connecticut Audubon Society Fairfield Nature Center and Larsen Sanctuary. *2325 Burr St, Fairfield (06824). Phone 203/259-6305.* Center features Connecticut wildlife and flora, solar greenhouse, natural history library, nature store. (Tues-Sat; also Sun in spring, fall; closed holidays; donation). Adjacent is 160-acre sanctuary with 6 miles of trails through woodlands, meadows, ponds, streams. (Daily) Trail for the disabled. **$**

Fairfield Historical Society. *636 Old Post Rd, Fairfield (06824). Phone 203/259-1598.* Museum with permanent displays of furniture, paintings, maritime memorabilia, dolls, toys, farm implements, clocks; changing exhibits of history, costumes, decorative arts; genealogical and research library. (Tues-Sun; closed holidays) **$$**

Ogden House. *1520 Bronson Rd, Fairfield (06824). Phone 203/259-1598.* (Circa 1750) Maintained by the Fairfield Historical Society, this 18th-century saltbox farmhouse, with authentic furnishings, has been restored to the time of its building by David and Jane Ogden; mid-18th-century kitchen garden. (Mid-May-mid-Oct, Thurs and Sun; other times by appointment) **$$**

Special Events

Chamber Arts & Crafts Festival. *On Sherman Green. Phone 203/255-1011.* Mid-June.

Dogwood Festival. *Greenfield Hill Congregational Church, 1045 Old Academy Rd, Fairfield (06824). Phone 203/259-5596.* Herbs, plants; arts and crafts; walking tours, music programs; food. Early or mid-May.

Garlicfest. *Notre Dame Catholic High School, 220 Jefferson St, Fairfield (06824). Phone 203/372-6521.* Vendors prepare international array of garlic-seasoned cuisine. Sales, entertainment. First weekend in May.

Limited-Service Hotel

★ ★ **FAIRFIELD INN.** *417 Post Rd, Fairfield (06430). Phone 203/255-0491; toll-free 800/347-0414; fax 203/255-2073.* 80 rooms, 2 story. Check-out 11 am. Restaurant, bar. Outdoor pool. **$**
🅿 ⊠

Farmington (D-3)

See also Avon, Bristol, Hartford, New Britain, Simsbury, Wethersfield

Settled 1640
Population 20,608
Elevation 245 ft
Area Code 860
Zip 06032
Information Greater Hartford Tourism District, 234 Murphy Rd, Hartford 06114; phone 860/244-8181 or toll-free 800/793-4480
Web Site www.farmington-ct.org

In 1802 and 1803, 15,000 yards of linen cloth were loomed in Farmington, and 2,500 hats were made in a shop on Hatter's Lane. There were silversmiths, tinsmiths, cabinetmakers, clockmakers, and carriage builders. Today, Farmington is a beautiful community—one of New England's museum pieces. It is also the home of Miss Porter's School (1844), a well-known private preparatory school for girls.

What to See and Do

Hill-Stead Museum. *35 Mountain Rd, Farmington (06032). Phone 860/677-9064.* (1901) Colonial Revival-style country house designed by Theodate Pope in collaboration with McKim, Mead, and White for industrialist A. A. Pope; contains Pope's collection of French impressionist paintings and decorative arts. Set on 152 acres, which include a sunken garden. One-hour tours. (Tues-Sun) **$$$**

Stanley-Whitman House. *37 High St, Farmington (06032). Phone 860/677-9222.* (Circa 1720) This is one of the finest early 18th-century houses in the United States; period furniture, local artifacts; changing displays; living history presentations; 18th-century herb and flower gardens. (May-Oct, Wed-Sun afternoons; Nov-Apr, Sun afternoons, also by appointment) **$$**

Special Event

Farmington Antiques Weekend. *Polo Grounds, Farmington (06032). Phone 860/871-7914.* One of the largest antique events in Connecticut; approximately 600 dealers. Early or mid-June.

Full-Service Hotel

★ ★ ★ **MARRIOTT HARTFORD FARMINGTON.** *15 Farm Springs Rd, Farmington (06032). Phone 860/678-1000; toll-free 800/228-9190; fax 860/677-8849. www.marriott.com.* Tucked away in suburban Farmington, guests will enjoy a relaxed atmosphere at this modern hotel that's just minutes from downtown Hartford. 381 rooms, 4 story. Check-in 4 pm, check-out noon. High-speed Internet access. Restaurant, bar. Fitness room. Indoor pool, outdoor pool, whirlpool. Tennis. Business center. **$**

Full-Service Inn

★ ★ ★ **THE FARMINGTON INN OF GREATER HARTFORD.** *827 Farmington Ave, Farmington (06032). Phone 860/677-2821; toll-free 800/648-9804; fax 860/677-8332. www.farmingtoninn .com.* 72 rooms, 2 story. Pets accepted, some restrictions. Complimentary continental breakfast. Check-out 11 am. **$**

Restaurants

★ ★ **APRICOT'S.** *1593 Farmington Ave, Farmington (06032). Phone 860/673-5405; fax 860/673-7138.* Converted trolley house. Seafood menu. Lunch, dinner, Sun brunch. Bar to 1 am. Children's menu. Reservations recommended. Outdoor seating. **$$**

★ **STONEWELL.** *354 Colt Hwy, Farmington (06032). Phone 860/677-8855; fax 860/674-9789.* Seafood, steak menu. Lunch, dinner, Sun brunch. Closed July 4, Dec 25. Bar. Children's menu. **$$**

Greenwich (F-1)

See also Norwalk, Stamford

Settled 1640
Population 58,441
Elevation 71 ft
Area Code 203

Information Chamber of Commerce, 21 W Putnam Ave, 06830; phone 203/869-3500
Web Site www.greenwichchamber.com

Greenwich (GREN-itch) is on the New York state line just 28 miles from Times Square. Behind the city's old New England façade, community leaders continue searching for ways to preserve 18th-century charm in the face of present-day economic, political, and social problems.

What to See and Do

Audubon Center in Greenwich. *613 Riversville Rd, Greenwich (06830). Phone 203/869-5272.* This 522-acre sanctuary includes a self-guided nature trail; interpretive building with exhibits. (Daily) **$$**

Bruce Museum. *1 Museum Dr, Greenwich (06830). Phone 203/869-0376.* Arts and sciences museum features exhibits, lectures, concerts, and educational programs. (Tues-Sun) **$$**

Bush-Holley House. *39 Strickland Rd, Cos Cob (06807). S off Hwy 1. Phone 203/869-6899.* (1732) Headquarters of the Historical Society of the Town of Greenwich. Residence of a successful 18th-century farmer, it became the site of the Cos Cob art colony at the turn of the century. Exhibits include late 18th-century Connecticut furniture; paintings by Childe Hassam, Elmer Livingston MacRae, John Henry Twachtman; sculptures by John Rogers; pottery by Leon Volkmar. (Tues-Fri and Sun, afternoons; closed holidays) **$$**

Putnam Cottage/Knapp Tavern. *243 E Putnam Ave, Greenwich (06830). Phone 203/869-9697.* (Circa 1690) Near this tavern, Revolutionary General Israel Putnam made a daring escape from the Redcoats in 1779; museum exhibits; rare scalloped shingles; herb garden, restored barn on grounds. (Wed, Fri, and Sun; also by appointment) **$**

Full-Service Hotel

★ ★ ★ **HYATT REGENCY GREENWICH.** *1800 E Putnam Ave, Old Greenwich (06870). Phone 203/637-1234; toll-free 800/633-7313; fax 203/637-2940. www.hyatt.com.* 374 rooms, 4 story. Check-in 3 pm, check-out noon. High-speed Internet access. Restaurant, bar. Fitness room. Indoor pool, whirlpool. Business center. **$$$**

Full-Service Inn

★ ★ ★ **HOMESTEAD INN.** *420 Field Point Rd, Greenwich (06830). Phone 203/869-7500; fax 203/869-7502. www.homesteadinn.com.* Secluded and romantic, elegant and sumptuous, this 1799 inn is just a short walk from the center of Greenwich. Purchased in 1997 by Thomas and Theresa Henkelmann, renovations were completed in 2001, and the historic New England Inn now stands as a tribute to Theresa's interior decorating skills and Thomas's magnificent cooking (the Thomas Henkelmann restaurant is off the lobby). Outside, the Homestead looks for all intents and purposes like a traditional, New England country inn. But step inside and you'll find an eclectic mix of antique furniture, imported pieces, and one-of-a-kind touches. The ground floor of the main house includes a backgammon room with fireplace, a cocktail lounge, and the restaurant Thomas Henkelmann (see); suites and rooms (or "chambers") are on the second and third floors. They are decorated with a mix of imported pieces from India, China, Bali, and Morocco combined with solid cherry bespoke furniture, Frette linens, and original artwork. And although there is a 24-hour concierge, there's no need to ring if you've forgotten your bedroom slippers. The bathroom floors are heated, of course. 19 rooms. Closed late Feb-early Mar. Children over 14 years only. Check-in 1 pm, check-out noon. Restaurant, bar. **$$$**

Specialty Lodgings

The following lodging establishments are approved by Mobil Travel Guide, but due to their unique and individualized nature have not been given a traditional Mobil Star rating. Included in this listing you may find bed-and-breakfasts, limited-service inns, guest ranches, and other unique hotel properties.

HARBOR HOUSE INN. *165 Shore Rd, Old Greenwich (06870). Phone 203/637-0145; fax 203/698-0943. www.hhinn.com.* 22 rooms, 3 story. Complimentary continental breakfast. Check-in 3 pm, check-out 11 am. **$**
🆔

STANTON HOUSE INN. *76 Maple Ave, Greenwich (06830). Phone 203/869-2110; fax 203/629-2116. www.shinngreenwich.com.* Built in 1900; antiques. 24 rooms, 3 story. Complimentary continental breakfast. Check-in 2 pm, check-out 11 am. Outdoor pool. **$$**
🆔 🏊

Restaurants

★ ★ ★ **JEAN-LOUIS.** *61 Lewis St, Greenwich (06830). Phone 203/622-8450; fax 203/622-5845. www.restaurantjeanlouis.com.* Sophisticated and elegant with professional service to match, this cozy restaurant in a small home has a menu grounded in the precision of French classicism. French menu. Lunch, dinner. Closed Sun. Casual attire. Reservations recommended. **$$$**
🆔

★ ★ ★ **L'ESCALE.** *200 Steamboat Rd, Greenwich (06830). Phone 203/661-4600.* Provence goes Yankee at L'Escale in tony Greenwich. The fine French restaurant earns its props for re-creating the Mediterranean on the North Atlantic shore, importing a stone fireplace and terra-cotta floors to warm the dining room and affixing light-filtering thatched bamboo to shade the patio. The solidly traditional menu from French expat Frederic Kieffer keeps pace with a salad of carmelized leeks and chanterelles; apple- and prune-paired foie gras; bouillabaisse; and crispy duck breast. Because it serves lunch as well as a substantial menu at the pewter-topped oak bar, L'Escale is gathering place for both locals and passers-through staying at the neighboring Delamar Hotel. French for "the port of call," L'Escale allows guests to yacht to dinner, tying up at its waterfront dock. French menu. Breakfast, lunch, dinner, brunch. Bar. Business casual attire. Reservations recommended. Valet parking. **$$$**

★ ★ **TERRA RISTORANTE ITALIANO.** *156 Greenwich Ave, Greenwich (06830). Phone 203/629-5222; fax 203/629-4354.* Italian menu. Lunch, dinner. Closed holidays. Bar. Casual attire. Outdoor seating. **$$$**
🆔

★ ★ **THAT LITTLE ITALIAN RESTAURANT.** *228-230 Mill St (Henry St), Greenwich (06830). Phone 203/531-7500.* Italian menu. Lunch, dinner. Closed Mon. Bar. Children's menu. Casual attire. Reservations recommended. Outdoor seating. **$$**
🆔

★ ★ ★ ★ **THOMAS HENKELMANN.** *420 Field Point Rd, Greenwich (06830). Phone 203/869-7500; fax 203/869-7502. www.thomashenkelmann.com.* You'll find the luxury-laden restaurant known as Thomas Henkelmann tucked inside the charming Homestead Inn (see), a 1799 Victorian manor house in Greenwich. Named for the gifted German-born, French-trained chef (and pastry chef) who founded the enchanted inn in 1997 with his wife, Theresa, Thomas Henkelmann epitomizes stylish French dining. The menu offers clever, but careful, modern takes on traditional French dishes, playing with delicate herbs and spices and the flawless ingredients of the season. The service is correct and formal, as you would expect in the company of such stunning fare and breathtaking surroundings. The heavenly wine list is delivered by the restaurant's wonderful sommelier; it is as impressive as the cuisine. Dining here is like watching *Casablanca*. It is a classic. You won't want it to end. And you'll probably cry (tears of joy, not regret) when it does. French menu. Lunch, dinner. Closed Jan 1; also the last week in Feb, first week in Mar. Bar. Reservations recommended. Valet parking (dinner). **$$$**

Groton (E-5)

See also Mystic, New London, Norwich, Stonington

Settled 1705
Population 9,837
Elevation 90 ft
Area Code 860
Zip 06340
Information Connecticut's Mystic & More, 470 Bank St, PO Box 89, New London 06320; phone 860/444-2206 or toll-free 800/863-6569 (outside CT)
Web Site www.town.groton.ct.us

Groton is the home of a huge US naval submarine base. It is also the place where the Electric Boat Division of the General Dynamics Corporation, the world's largest private builder of submarines, built the first diesel-powered submarine (1912) and the first nuclear-powered submarine, *Nautilus* (1955). Pfizer Incorporated operates one of the largest antibiotic plants in the world and maintains a research laboratory here.

What to See and Do

Charter fishing trips. *Phone toll-free 800/863-6569.* Several companies offer full- and 1/2-day saltwater fishing trips both for small and large groups.

Fort Griswold Battlefield State Park. *57 Fort St, Groton (06340). 1 1/2 miles S of Hwy 1. Phone 860/449-6877.* Includes a 135-foot monument to 88 Revolutionary soldiers slain here in 1781 by British troops under the command of Benedict Arnold. Park (daily). Monu-

ment and museum (Memorial Day-Labor Day: daily; Labor Day-Columbus Day: Sat-Sun).

Historic Ship *Nautilus* and Submarine *Force* Museum. *Naval Submarine Base New London, 1 Crystal Lake Rd, Groton (06349). 2 miles N on Hwy 12. Phone 860/694-3174; toll-free 800/343-0079.* Permanent home for *Nautilus*, the world's first nuclear-powered submarine. Self-guided, audio tour; museum exhibits depicting history of the US Submarine *Force*; working periscopes; authentic submarine control room; four mini-subs; mini-theaters. Picnicking. (Spring-fall, daily; winter, Mon, Wed-Sun; closed Jan 1, Thanksgiving, Dec 25, the first two weeks in May and the last two weeks in Oct) **FREE**

Oceanographic cruise. *Avery Point, 1084 Shennecossett Rd, Groton (06340). Phone 860/445-9007; toll-free 800/364-8472.* A 2 1/2-hour educational cruise on Long Island Sound aboard marine research vessels *Enviro-lab II* and *Enviro-lab III* (summer). Also board a Harbor Seal Watch on Long Island Sound (winter), or visit Ledge Lighthouse. Opportunity to use nets and scientific instruments to explore marine environment firsthand. (June-Aug) **$$$$**

Full-Service Hotel

★ ★ ★ **MARRIOTT MYSTIC HOTEL AND SPA.** *625 North Rd, Groton (06340). Phone 860/446-2600; toll-free 800/228-9290; fax 860/446-2601. www.marriott.com.* The Marriott Mystic Hotel and Spa is a perfect home-away-from-home for business or leisure travelers. Located just outside the historic seafaring town of Mystic, this full-service hotel is a perfect base for exploring the charming village, checking out the creatures at the renowned Mystic Aquarium, or gaming at nearby Foxwoods and Mohegan Sun casinos. A complete business center and accommodations fitted with business amenities put a smile on corporate visitors' faces. The guest rooms and suites are sophisticated and show off a continental flair. The centerpiece of the hotel is its Elizabeth Arden Red Door Spa, favored for its superior treatments and fine service. From aged steaks at Octagon and freshly brewed coffee at Starbucks to light cuisine at the Red Door Spa Café, this hotel has dining covered as well. 285 rooms, 6 story. Check-in 4 pm, check-out 11 am. High-speed Internet access. Restaurant, bar. Fitness room, spa. Indoor pool, whirlpool. Business center. **$$**

🄳 🏋 🛏 🏃

Restaurants

★ ★ ★ **OCTAGON.** *625 North Rd, Groton (06340).* *Phone 860/321-0360. www.octagonsteakhouse.com.* Steak menu. Dinner. Bar. Reservations recommended. Valet parking. **$$**

★★★**VINES AT OCTAGON.** *625 North Rd, Groton (06340). Phone 860/446-2600; fax 860/446-2601.* American menu. Breakfast, lunch, dinner. Bar. Children's menu. Casual attire. Reservations recommended. Valet parking. **$$**

Guilford (E-3)

See also Branford, Clinton, Madison, New Haven

Founded 1639
Population 19,848
Elevation 20 ft
Area Code 203
Zip 06437
Information Chamber of Commerce, 63 Whitfield St; phone 203/453-9677
Web Site www.guilfordct.com

Guilford was settled by a group of Puritans who followed Reverend Henry Whitfield here from England. One of the residents, Samuel Hill, gave rise to the expression "run like Sam Hill" when he repeatedly ran for political office.

What to See and Do

Henry Whitfield State Museum. *248 Old Whitfield St, Guilford (06437). 1/2 mile S. Phone 203/453-2457.* (1639) The oldest house in the state and among the oldest of stone houses in New England. Restored with 17th- and 18th-century furnishings; exhibits. Gift shop. (Apr-mid-Dec, Wed-Sun; closed holidays) **$$**

Hyland House. *84 Boston St, Guilford (06437). Phone 203/453-9477.* (1660) Restored and furnished in 17th-century period, herb garden; guided tours. (Early June-Oct, Tues-Sun) A map of historic houses in Guilford is available. **$**

Thomas Griswold House Museum. *171 Boston St, Guilford (06437). Phone 203/453-3176.* (Circa 1775) Fine example of a saltbox house; costumes of 1800s, changing historical exhibits, period gardens, restored working blacksmith shop. (Early June-Oct, Tues-Sun; winter by appointment) **$**

Limited-Service Hotel

★ **TOWER SUITES MOTEL.** *320 Boston Post Rd, Guilford (06437). Phone 203/453-9069; fax 203/458-2727.* 14 rooms, all suites. Check-out 11 am. **$**
🐕

Restaurant

★ ★ **SACHEM COUNTRY HOUSE.** *111 Goose Ln, Guilford (06437). Phone 203/453-5261; fax 203/453-4111. www.sachemhouse.com.* In 18th-century house; fireplace. Seafood menu. Dinner, Sun brunch. Children's menu. Reservations recommended. **$$**

Hartford (D-3)

See also Avon, Farmington, Manchester, Meriden, Middletown, New Britain, Riverton, Simsbury, Storrs, Vernon, Wethersfield, Windsor, Windsor Locks

Settled 1633
Population 139,739
Elevation 50 ft
Area Code 860
Information Greater Hartford Convention & Visitors Bureau, One Civic Center Plaza, Suite 300, 06103; phone 860/728-6789 or toll-free 800/446-7811 (outside CT)
Web Site www.enjoyhartford.com

The capital of Connecticut and a major industrial and cultural center on the Connecticut River, Hartford is headquarters for many of the nation's insurance companies.

Roots of American democracy are deep in Hartford's history. The city was made virtually independent in 1662 by Charles II, but an attempt was made by Sir Edmund Andros, governor of New England, to seize its charter. The document was hidden by Joseph Wadsworth in a hollow tree, since known as the Charter Oak. The tree was blown down in 1856; a plaque on Charter Oak Avenue marks the spot.

Hartford has what is said to be the oldest continuously published newspaper in the United States, the *Hartford Courant.* Founded in 1764, it became a daily in 1837. Trinity College (1823), the American School for the Deaf, the Connecticut Institute for the Blind, and the Institute of Living (for mental disabilities) are located in the city.

Public Transportation

Buses (Connecticut Transit), phone 860/525-9181.

Airport Hartford-Bradley International Airport. Cash machines, Terminal B, Concourse A.

Information Phone 860/627-3000

Lost and Found Phone 860/627-3340

What to See and Do

Bushnell Park. *Elm and Trinity sts, Hartford (06103). Downtown, between Jewell, Elm, and Trinity sts. Phone 860/246-7739. www.bushnellpark.org.* The 41-acre park contains 150 varieties of trees and a restored 1914 carousel (schedule varies; fee); concerts and special events (spring-fall). **FREE**

Butler-McCook Homestead and Main Street History Center. *396 Main St, Hartford (06103). Phone 860/522-1806.* (1782) Preserved house, occupied by four generations of one family (1782-1971), has possessions dating back 200 years; collection of Victorian toys; Japanese armor; Victorian garden. (Wed-Sun; closed holidays) **$$**

Center Church and Ancient Burying Ground. *60 Gold St, Hartford (06103). Phone 860/247-4080.* Church (1807) is patterned after London's St. Martin-in-the-Fields, with Tiffany stained-glass windows. Cemetery contains markers dating back to 1640.

Connecticut Audubon Society Holland Brook Nature Center. *1361 Main St, Hartford (06103). Phone 860/633-8402.* On 48 acres adjacent to the Connecticut River, the center features a variety of natural history exhibits and includes a discovery room. Many activities. (Tues-Sun; closed holidays) **$**

Connecticut Historical Society. *1 Elizabeth St, Hartford (06105). Phone 860/236-5621.* The library contains more than 3 million books and manuscripts. (Tues-Sat; closed holidays). The museum has nine galleries featuring permanent and changing exhibits on state history (Tues-Sun). **$$$**

Connecticut River Cruise. *152 River St, Deep River (06108). Departs from Charter Oak Landing. Phone 860/526-4954.* The *Silver Star*, a reproduction of an 1850s steam yacht, makes 1- to 2 1/2-hour trips on the Connecticut River. (Memorial Day-Labor Day, daily; after Labor Day-Oct, Sat-Sun) **$$$**

Elizabeth Park. *Prospect and Asylum aves, Hartford (06101). Phone 860/242-0017.* Public gardens feature 900 varieties of roses and more than 14,000 other plants; first municipal rose garden in country; greenhouses (all year). Outdoor concerts in summer; ice skating in winter. (Daily) **FREE**

Harriet Beecher Stowe Center. *77 Forest St, Hartford (06105). Phone 860/522-9258. www.harrietbeecher stowecenter.org.* (1871) The restored Victorian cottage of the author of *Uncle Tom's Cabin* contains original furniture and memorabilia. Tours. (Tues-Sat 9:30 am-4:30 pm, Sun noon-4:30 pm; also Mon from Memorial Day-Columbus Day and Dec) **$$**

Heritage Trails Sightseeing. *Departs from Hartford hotels. Phone 860/677-8867.* Guided and narrated tours of Hartford and Farmington. (Daily) **$$$$**

Mark Twain House. *351 Farmington Ave, Hartford (06105). Phone 860/247-0998.* (1874) *Tom Sawyer, Huckleberry Finn,* and other books were published while Samuel Clemens (Mark Twain) lived in this three-story Victorian mansion featuring the decorative work of Charles Comfort Tiffany and the Associated Artists; Tiffany-glass light fixtures, windows, and Tiffany-designed stencilwork in gold and silver leaf. Tours. (May-Oct and Dec, daily; rest of year, Mon, Wed-Sun; closed holidays) **$$$**

Noah Webster Foundation and Historical Society. *227 S Main St, West Hartford (06107). Phone 860/521-5362.* This 18th-century homestead was the birthplace of America's first lexicographer, writer of the *Blue-Backed Speller* (1783) and the *American Dictionary* (1828). Period furnishings, memorabilia; costumed guides; period gardens. (Mon, Thurs-Sun; closed holidays) **$$**

Old State House. *800 Main St, Hartford (06103). Phone 860/522-6766.* (1796) Oldest state house in the nation, designed by Charles Bulfinch; restored Senate chamber with Gilbert Stuart portrait of Washington; displays and rotating exhibitions. Tourist information center; museum shop. Guided tours by appointment. (Mon-Sat; closed holidays) **FREE**

Raymond E. Baldwin Museum of Connecticut History. *Connecticut State Library, 231 Capitol Ave, Hartford (06106). Opposite the Capitol. Phone 860/737-6535.* Exhibits include the Colt Collection of Firearms; Connecticut artifacts, including the original 1662 Royal Charter; portraits of Connecticut's governors. Library features law, social sciences, history, genealogy collections, and official state archives. (Daily; closed holidays) **FREE**

Science Center of Connecticut. *950 Trout Brook Dr, West Hartford (06119). Phone 860/231-2824.* Computer lab; UTC Wildlife Sanctuary; physical sciences discovery room; walk-in replica of sperm whale; "KaleidoSight," a giant walk-in kaleidoscope; planetarium shows; changing exhibits. (Tues-Sat, also Sun afternoons, Mon during summer; closed holidays) **$$$**

State Capitol. *210 Capitol Ave, Hartford (06106). Capitol Ave, at Trinity St. Phone 860/240-0222.* (1879) Guided tours (one hour) of the restored, gold-domed capitol building and the contemporary legislative office building (Mon-Fri; closed holidays, also Dec 25-Jan 1); includes historical displays. **FREE**

Talcott Mountain State Park. *8 miles NW via Hwy 44, off Hwy 185, near Simsbury. Phone 860/677-0662.* This 557-acre park features the 165-foot Heublein Tower, on a mountaintop 1,000 feet above the Farmington River, considered the best view in the state. Picnicking, shelters. (Late May-late Aug: Thurs-Sun 10 am-5 pm; Labor Day weekend-Oct: daily 10 am-5 pm)

University of Hartford. *200 Bloomfield Ave, West Hartford (06117). 4 miles W. Phone 860/768-4100. www.hartford.edu.* (1877) (6,844 students) Independent institution on 320-acre campus. Many free concerts, operas, lectures, and art exhibits. Located here is

Museum of American Political Life. *Harry Jack Gray Center, 200 Bloomfield Ave, West Hartford (06117). Phone 860/768-4090.* Exhibits include life-size mannequins re-creating political marches from the 1830s to the 1960s; 70-foot wall of historical pictures and images; political television commercials since 1952. (Tues-Sun afternoons; closed holidays) **FREE**

⭐ **Wadsworth Atheneum Museum of Art.** *600 Main St, Hartford (06103). Phone 860/278-2670.* One of the nation's oldest continuously operating public art museums with more than 40,000 works of art, spanning 5,000 years; 15th- to 20th-century paintings, American furniture, sculpture, porcelains, English and American silver, the Amistad Collection of African-American art; changing contemporary exhibits. (Tues-Sun; closed holidays) Free admission Thursday and Saturday mornings.

Special Events

Christmas Crafts Expo I & II. *1 Civic Center Plz, Hartford (06103). Phone 860/249-6333.* Exhibits and demonstrations of traditional and contemporary craft media. First and second weekends in Dec.

Mark Twain Days. *351 Farmington Ave, Hartford (06105). Phone 860/247-0998.* Celebration of Twain's legacy and Hartford's cultural heritage with more than 100 events. Concerts, riverboat rides, medieval jousting, tours of Twain House, entertainment. Mid-July.

Riverfest. *Charter Oak Landing and Constitution Plz, Hartford (06103). Phone 860/713-3131.* Celebration of America's independence and the Connecticut River. Family entertainment, concerts, food, fireworks display over river. Early July.

Taste of Hartford. *Constitution Plz, Hartford (06103). Phone 860/920-5337. www.tasteofhartford.com.* Four-day event features specialties of more than 50 area restaurants; continuous entertainment. June.

Limited-Service Hotels

★ ★ **CROWNE PLAZA.** *50 Morgan St, Hartford (06120). Phone 860/549-2400; toll-free 800/227-6963; fax 860/549-7844. www.crowneplaza.com.* 350 rooms, 18 story. Pets accepted, some restrictions; fee. Check-in 3 pm, check-out noon. Restaurant, bar. Fitness room. Outdoor pool. Airport transportation available. Business center. **$**
🔧 👤 🏊 🚶

★ ★ **HOLIDAY INN.** *363 Roberts St, East Hartford (06108). Phone 860/528-9611; toll-free 800/465-4329; fax 860/289-0270. www.holiday-inn.com.* 130 rooms, 5 story. Pets accepted; fee. Check-in 3 pm, check-out 11 am. High-speed Internet access, wireless Internet access. Restaurant, bar. Fitness room. Indoor pool. **$**
📠 🔧 👤 🏊

Full-Service Hotels

🔑 ★ ★ ★ **GOODWIN HOTEL.** *1 Haynes St, Hartford (06013). Phone 860/246-7500; toll-free 800/922-5006; fax 860/247-4576. www.goodwinhotel .com.* Visitors in the know stay at the sophisticated Goodwin Hotel. This luxury hotel is among Hartford's best, and its downtown location across from the Civic Center makes it a popular choice with business travelers. Built in 1881 for business tycoon J. P. Morgan, the red brick building was fashioned in the Queen Anne style. The rooms and suites have a masculine, clubby décor with mahogany furnishings, ruby red and hunter green colors, and striped patterns. The clubby appeal extends to the two restaurants, where patrons enjoy breakfast in the wood-paneled Pierpont's Restaurant and lunch and dinner in the casually elegant America's Cup Bar & Lounge. 124 rooms, 6 story. Pets accepted. Check-in 3 pm, check-out noon. Two restaurants, bar. Fitness room. **$$$**

★ ★ ★ **SHERATON HARTFORD HOTEL.** *100 E River Dr, East Hartford (06108). Phone 860/ 528-9703; toll-free 888/530-9703; fax 860/289-4728. www.sheraton.com.* 199 rooms, 8 story. Pets accepted, some restrictions; fee. Check-in 3 pm, check-out noon. Restaurant, bar. Indoor pool. **$$**

Restaurants

★ ★ **APP'S.** *451 Franklin Ave, Hartford (06114). Phone 860/296-2777. www.appshartford.com.* International menu. Lunch, dinner. Closed Mon. Bar. **$$$**

★ ★ **BUTTERFLY.** *831 Farmington Ave, West Hartford (06119). Phone 860/236-2816; fax 860/231-7911.* Chinese menu. Lunch, dinner, Sun brunch. Closed Thanksgiving. Bar. **$$**

★ ★ ★ **CARBONE'S.** *588 Franklin Ave, Hartford (06114). Phone 860/296-9646; fax 860/296-2785.* Italian, American menu. Lunch, dinner. Closed Sun; holidays. Bar. Casual attire. **$$$**

★ **HOT TOMATOES.** *1 Union Pl, Hartford (06103). Phone 860/249-5100; fax 860/524-8120.* Fusion menu. Lunch, dinner, late-night. Bar. Casual attire. Outdoor seating. **$$**

★ ★ ★ **MAX DOWNTOWN.** *185 Asylum St, Hartford (06103). Phone 860/522-2530; fax 860/246-5279. www.maxrestaurantgroup.com.* American menu. Lunch, dinner. Closed holidays. Bar. Children's menu. Casual attire. **$$$**

★ ★ **PASTIS.** *201 Ann St, Hartford (06103). Phone 860/278-8852; fax 860/278-8854. www.pastisbrasserie.com.* Guests can enjoy intimate dining at this authentic French-style bistro. French menu. Lunch, dinner. Closed Sun. Bar. Casual attire. Outdoor seating. **$$$**

★ ★ **PEPPERCORN'S GRILL.** *357 Main St, Hartford (06106). Phone 860/547-1714; fax 860/724-7612. www.peppercornsrestaurant.com.* Italian menu. Lunch, dinner, late-night. Closed Sun; holidays; two

weeks in summer. Bar. Children's menu. Casual attire. Outdoor seating. **$$**

★ **RESTAURANT BRICCO.** *78 LaSalle Rd, West Hartford (06903). Phone 860/233-0220; fax 860/233-7503. www.restaurantbricco.com.* Italian, Mediterranean menu. Lunch, dinner. Children's menu. Outdoor seating. **$$**

Kent (D-1)

See also Cornwall Bridge, New Preston

Population 2,918
Elevation 395 ft
Area Code 860
Zip 06757
Information Litchfield Hills Visitors Bureau, PO Box 968, Litchfield 06759; phone 860/567-4506
Web Site www.kentct.com

Kent, a small community near the western border of Connecticut, has become an art and antique center. Home to a large art colony, the surrounding area is characterized by massive hills that overlook the plain of the Housatonic River. The village of Kent was incorporated in 1738, after the tract of land was sold in a public auction. Although early development was based on agriculture, by the middle of the 19th century Kent was a booming industrial village with three iron furnaces operating in the area.

What to See and Do

Kent Falls State Park. *Hwy 7, Kent (06757). 5 miles N on Hwy 7. Phone 860/927-4100.* This 295-acre park is beautiful in spring when the stream is high and in fall when leaves are changing; 200-foot cascading waterfall. Stream fishing; hiking, picnicking. (Daily)

Macedonia Brook State Park. *159 Macedonia Brook Rd, Kent (06757). 2 miles E on Hwy 341, N on Macedonia Brook Rd. Phone 860/927-4100.* These 2,300 acres provide one of the state's finest nature study areas, as well as views of the Catskills and Taconic mountains. Trout-stocked stream fishing; hiking, picnicking, camping (late Apr-Sept) on 84 sites in open and wooded settings. (Daily) **FREE**

Sloane-Stanley Museum and Kent Furnace. *59 S Prospect St, Kent (06757). 1 mile N on Hwy 7. Phone 860/927-3849.* New England barn houses Eric Sloane's collection of Early American tools, re-creation of his studio, artifacts, works; on site of old Kent furnace (1826); video presentation. (Mid-May-Oct, Wed-Sun) **$$**

Special Event

Fall Festival. *Connecticut Antique Machinery Museum, Flanders Rd, Kent (06757). 1 mile N on Hwy 7. Phone 860/927-0050.* Exhibits include steam and traction engines, road roller (circa 1910), windmill; threshers; broom making, shingle sawing; antique cars, steamboats, tractors, and trucks. Late Sept.

Full-Service Inn

★ ★ ★ **FIFE 'N DRUM RESTAURANT & INN.** *53 N Main St, Kent (06757). Phone 860/927-3509; fax 860/927-4595. www.fifendrum.com.* 8 rooms. Check-in 2 pm, check-out 11 am. Restaurant, bar. **$$**

Restaurant

★ ★ ★ **FIFE 'N DRUM.** *53 N Main St, Kent (06757). Phone 860/927-3509; fax 860/927-4595. www.fifendrum.com.* Signed prints by the late, renowned artist Eric Sloane adorn the walls. American menu. Lunch, dinner, Sun brunch. Closed Tues; Dec 25. Bar. Children's menu. **$$**

Lakeville (C-1)

See also Cornwall Bridge, Norfolk

Settled 1740
Population 1,800
Elevation 764 ft
Area Code 860
Zip 06039
Information Litchfield Hills Visitors Bureau, PO Box 968, Litchfield 06759; phone 860/567-4506
Web Site www.litchfieldhills.com

Lakeville, located on Lake Wononscopomuc in the Litchfield Hills area, developed around a major blast furnace once owned by Ethan Allen. The furnace and nearby metals foundry cast many of the weapons used in the American Revolution as well as the guns for the USS *Constellation.* When the furnace was torn down in 1843, the first knife manufacturing factory was erected there. Nearby is the famous Hotchkiss School, a coed prep school.

What to See and Do

Holley House. *15 Millerton Rd, Lakeville (06039). Phone 860/435-2878.* Museums of 18th- and 19th-century history including 1768 iron-master's home with 1808 Classical Revival wing; Holley Manufacturing Company pocketknife exhibit from 1876; hands-on 1870s kitchen exhibit illustrating the debate over women's roles. 1876 Living History Tours (four tours daily). (Mid-June-mid-Oct, Sat-Sun, and holiday afternoons; also by appointment) Also here is

> **Salisbury Cannon Museum.** *15 Millerton Rd, Lakeville (06039). Phone 860/435-2878.* Hands-on exhibits illustrate contributions of local iron industry to American Revolution. Includes ice house, cutting tools, outhouse, 19th-century heritage gardens, and Nature's Medicine Cabinet exhibit. Same hours as Holley House. **FREE**

Special Events

Music Mountain Summer Music Festival. *Music Mountain Rd, Falls Village (06039). On Music Mountain, 5 miles NE via Hwy 44, 3 miles S on Hwy 126 to Falls Village, then 2 1/2 miles E on Hwy 126 to top of Music Mountain Rd. Phone 860/824-7126.* Performances by known ensembles and guest artists; also jazz series. Sat-Sun. Mid-June-early Sept.

Road Racing Classic. *497 Lime Rock Rd (Hwy 112), Lakeville (06039). 2 miles S on Hwy 41, then 4 miles E on Hwy 112, at junction Hwy 7. Phone toll-free 800/722-3577. www.limerock.com.* The Mohegan Sun Grand Prix and NASCAR Busch North 200 events are held the same weekend—racing fans should try to make time for this action-packed weekend of racing. Memorial Day weekend.

Limited-Service Hotel

★ ★ **INN AT IRON MASTERS.** *229 N Main St, Lakeville (06039). Phone 860/435-9844; fax 860/435-2254. www.innatironmasters.com.* 28 rooms. Pets accepted, some restrictions. Check-out 11 am. Restaurant, bar. Outdoor pool. **$**
🅳 🐾 ⊠

Full-Service Resort

★ ★ ★ **INTERLAKEN INN.** *74 Interlaken Rd, Lakeville (06039). Phone 860/435-9878; toll-free 800/222-2909; fax 860/435-2980. www.interlakeninn.com.* 80 rooms, 2 story. Pets accepted, some restrictions; fee.

Check-in 3 pm, check-out noon. Restaurant. Outdoor pool. Golf. Tennis. **$**

Specialty Lodging

The following lodging establishment is approved by Mobil Travel Guide, but due to its unique and individualized nature has not been given a traditional Mobil Star rating. Included in this listing you may find bed-and-breakfasts, limited-service inns, guest ranches, and other unique hotel properties.

WAKE ROBIN INN. *Hwy 41, Lakeville (06039). Phone 860/435-2515; fax 860/435-2000. www.wakerobininn.com.* 39 rooms, 2 story. Pets accepted, some restrictions; fee. Check-in 3 pm, check-out noon. **$$**

Litchfield (D-2)

See also Bristol, Cornwall Bridge

Settled 1720
Population 8,365
Elevation 1,085 ft
Area Code 860
Zip 06759
Information Litchfield Hills Visitors Bureau, PO Box 968; phone 860/567-4506
Web Site www.litchfieldhills.com

Litchfield, on a plateau above the Naugatuck Valley, has preserved a semblance of the 18th century through both its many early homes and its air of peace and quiet. Because the railroads laid their main lines below in the valley, industry largely bypassed Litchfield. The Reverend Henry Ward Beecher and his sister, Harriet Beecher Stowe, author of *Uncle Tom's Cabin,* grew up in Litchfield. Tapping Reeve established the first law school in the country here in the late 18th century.

What to See and Do

Haight Vineyard and Winery. *29 Chestnut Hill Rd, Litchfield (06759). Phone 860/567-4045.* First Connecticut winery; one of the few to grow vinifera grapes in New England. Tours, tastings; vineyard walk, picnic tables; gift shop. (Daily; closed holidays) **FREE**

Litchfield History Museum. *7 South St, Litchfield (06759). On the Green, at the junction of East and South sts. Phone 860/567-4501.* Houses an outstanding collection of American art and artifacts from the 18th-21st centuries; research library, changing exhibits, video presentation. (Mid-Apr-Nov, Tues-Sun; closed holidays) **$$**

Tapping Reeve House. *7 South St, Litchfield (06759). Phone 860/567-4501.* (1773) **And Law School** (1784). Introducing visitors to 19th-century Litchfield through the lives of the students who attended the Litchfield Law School and the Litchfield Female Academy; graduates include Aaron Burr and John C. Calhoun; garden. (Mid-Apr-Nov, Tues-Sun; closed July 4, Labor Day) **$**

Topsmead State Forest. *46 Chase Rd, Litchfield (06759). Phone 860/567-5694.* This 511-acre forest includes an English Tudor mansion overlooking a 40-acre wildlife preserve. Tours of the mansion (second and fourth weekends of June-Oct). **FREE**

White Memorial Foundation, Inc. *Hwy 202, Litchfield (06759). 2 1/2 miles W on Hwy 202. Phone 860/567-0857.* The 4,000-acre conservation area is contiguous with part of Bantam Lake shoreline (largest natural lake in the state), the Bantam River, and several small streams and ponds. Rolling woodland has wide variety of trees, flowers, ferns, mosses, 35 miles of trails; woodland birds, both nesting and in migration; and other woodland animals. The Conservation Center has displays and exhibits, extensive nature library with children's room (daily; fee). Swimming, fishing, boating; hiking trails, including a "trail of the senses," cross-country skiing, camping.

Special Event

Open House Tour. *39 Goshen Rd # B, Litchfield (06759). Phone 860/567-9423.* Tour of Litchfield's historic homes, special exhibits, tea, and luncheon. Early July. **$$$$**

Full-Service Inn

★ ★ ★ **LITCHFIELD INN.** *432 Bantam Rd, Litchfield (06759). Phone 860/567-4503; toll-free 800/499-3444; fax 860/567-5358. www.litchfieldinnct.com.* 32 rooms, 2 story. Complimentary continental breakfast. Check-in 3 pm, check-out 11 am. Restaurant, bar. **$**

Restaurants

★ **SEÑOR PANCHOS.** *7 Village Green Dr (Hwy 202), Litchfield (06759). Phone 860/567-3663. www.senor-panchos.com.* Mexican menu. Lunch, dinner. Casual attire. **$$**
🅳

★ ★ **VILLAGE RESTAURANT.** *25 West St, Litchfield (06759). Phone 860/567-8307; fax 860/567-8450.* American menu. Lunch, dinner, Sun brunch. Closed Dec 25. Bar. Children's menu. **$$**
🅳

★ ★ ★ **WEST STREET GRILL.** *43 West St, Litchfield (06759). Phone 860/567-3885; fax 860/567-1374.* Owner James O'Shea has created the improbable: a trendy hotspot that appeals to both second-home New Yorkers as well as local residents. American menu. Lunch, dinner. Closed Dec 25. Bar. Children's menu. Reservations recommended. **$$$**

Madison (E-3)

See also Branford, Clinton, Guilford, New Haven

Settled 1649
Population 15,485
Elevation 22 ft
Area Code 203
Zip 06443
Information Chamber of Commerce, 22 Scotland Ave, PO Box 706; phone 203/245-7394; Tourism Office, 22 School St; phone 203/245-5659
Web Site www.madisonct.com

What to See and Do

Allis-Bushnell House and Museum. *853 Boston Post Rd, Madison (06443). Phone 203/245-4567.* (Circa 1785) Period rooms with four-corner fireplaces; doctor's office and equipment; exhibits of costumes, dolls, household implements, farming, fishing and shipbuilding tools; original paneling; herb garden. (May-Oct, Wed, Fri-Sat, limited hours; other times by appointment) **DONATION**

Deacon John Grave House. *581 Boston Post Rd, Madison (06443). Phone 203/245-4798.* Frame garrison colonial house (1685). (Memorial Day-Labor Day, Tues-Sun; spring and fall, weekends only) **DONATION**

Hammonasset Beach State Park. *1288 Boston Post Rd, Madison (06443). 1 mile S of I-95, exit 62. Phone 203/245-2785.* More than 900 acres with a 2-mile long beach on Long Island Sound. Saltwater swimming, scuba diving, fishing, boating; hiking, picnicking (shelters), camping. Nature center.

Limited-Service Hotel

★ ★ **MADISON BEACH HOTEL.** *94 W Wharf Rd, Madison (06443-0546). Phone 203/245-1404; fax 203/245-0410. www.madisonbeachhotel.com.* 35 rooms, 4 story. Closed Jan-Feb. Pets accepted, some restrictions; fee. Complimentary continental breakfast. Check-in 2pm, check-out 11 am. Restaurant, bar. **$**
🐾

Restaurants

★ ★ ★ **CAFE ALLEGRE.** *725 Boston Post Rd, Madison (06443). Phone 203/245-7773; fax 203/245-6256. www.allegrecafe.com.* American menu. Lunch, dinner, Sun brunch. Closed Jan 1, Dec 25. Bar. Children's menu. Outdoor seating. **$$**

★ ★ **FRIENDS AND COMPANY.** *11 Boston Post Rd, Madison (06443). Phone 203/245-0462; fax 203/245-4396.* Seafood, steak menu. Lunch, dinner, Sun brunch. Closed Thanksgiving, Dec 25; last Mon in June. Bar. Children's menu. **$$**

Manchester (D-4)

See also Hartford, Storrs, Vernon, Windsor

Settled 1672
Population 51,618
Elevation 272 ft
Area Code 860
Zip 06040
Information Greater Manchester Chamber of Commerce, 20 Hartford Rd; phone 860/646-2223
Web Site www.manchesterchamber.com

The "city of village charm" has the peaceful air of another era, with great trees and 18th-century houses. Manchester, once the silk capital of the Western world, is still a major manufacturing center with more than 100 industries—many, more than a century old.

What to See and Do

Cheney Homestead. *106 Hartford Rd, Manchester (06040). Phone 860/643-5588.* (Circa 1780) Birthplace of the brothers that launched the state's once-promising silk industry; built by Timothy Cheney, clockmaker. Paintings and etchings, early 19th-century furniture; replica of schoolhouse. (Fri-Sun) **$**

Connecticut Firemen's Historical Society Fire Museum. *230 Pine St, Manchester (06040). Phone 860/649-9436.* Located in a 1901 firehouse, this museum exhibits antique firefighting equipment and memorabilia; leather fire buckets, hoses, and helmets, hand-pulled engines, horse-drawn hose wagon, old prints and lithographs. (Mid-Apr-mid-Nov, Fri-Sun) **DONATION**

Lutz Children's Museum. *247 S Main St, Manchester (06040). Phone 860/643-0949. www.lutzmuseum.org.* Houses participatory exhibits on natural and physical science, art, ethnology, and history; live animal exhibit. (Tues-Sun; closed holidays) **$$**

Oak Grove Nature Center. *Oak Grove St, Manchester (06040). Phone 860/647-3321.* More than 50 acres of woods, fields, stream, pond; trails. (Daily) **FREE**

Wickham Park. *1329 W Middle Tpke, Manchester (06040). Entrance on Hwy 44, off I-84 exit 60. Phone 860/528-0856.* More than 200 acres with gardens, including ornamental, woods, ponds; log cabin (refreshments weekends); playgrounds, picnic areas; nature center; aviary and small zoo; tennis courts, softball fields (Apr-Oct, daily). **$$**

Limited-Service Hotels

★ **BEST VALUE INN-MANCHESTER.** *400 Tolland Tpke, Manchester (06040). Phone 860/643-1555; toll-free 888/315-2378; fax 860/643-1881. www.bestvalueinn.com.* 31 rooms. Check-out 11 am. **$**
🅳

★ **CLARION HOTEL.** *191 Spencer St, Manchester (06040). Phone 860/643-5811; toll-free 800/992-4004; fax 860/646-3341. www.clarionsuites.com.* 104 rooms, 2 story, all suites. Pets accepted; fee. Complimentary full breakfast. Check-in 3 pm, check-out noon. Fitness room. Outdoor pool, whirlpool. Airport transportation available. **$**
🅳 🐾 🏋 ⚓

Restaurants

★ ★ ★ **CAVEY'S FRENCH RESTAURANT.** *45 E Center St, Manchester (06040). Phone 860/643-2751; fax 860/649-0344.* French menu. Dinner. Closed Sun-Mon; holidays. Bar. **$$$**
🅳

★ ★ ★ **CAVEY'S ITALIAN RESTAURANT.** *45 E Center St, Manchester (06040). Phone 860/643-2751; fax 860/649-0344.* Italian menu. Lunch, dinner. Closed Sun-Mon; holidays. Bar. **$$**

Meriden (E-3)

See also Branford, Bristol, Hartford, Middletown, New Britain, New Haven, Waterbury

Settled 1661
Population 59,479
Elevation 144 ft
Area Code 203
Zip 06450
Information Greater Meriden Chamber of Commerce, 5 Colony St, 06451; phone 203/235-7901
Web Site www.meridenchamber.com

Located in the heart of the central Connecticut Valley, Meriden was named after Meriden Farm in Warwickshire, England. Once called the "silver city of the world" because its principal business was the manufacture of silver products, Meriden now has a broad industrial base.

What to See and Do

Castle Craig Tower. *Hubbard Park, W Main St, Meriden. 2 miles W on I-691/Hwy 66.* Road leads to tower atop East Peak, site of Easter sunrise services. (May-Oct)

Mount Southington Ski Area. *Southington. Approximately 10 miles W, 1/2 mile W of I-84 exit 30, at Mount Vernon Rd. Phone 860/628-7669; toll-free 800/628-0954 or 800/628-7669. www.mountsouthington.com.* Triple, double chairlifts, two T-bars, two handle tows, J-bar; snowmaking, patrol, school, rentals; cafeteria, lounge. Fourteen trails; longest run approximately 1 mile; vertical drop 425 feet. Night skiing. (Dec-Mar, daily)

Solomon Goffe House. *677 N Colony St, Meriden (06489). Phone 203/634-9088.* (1711) Gambrel-roofed house features period furnishings, artifacts. Costumed guides. (July-Aug: Sat-Sun; rest of year: first Sun of month) **$**

Special Events

Apple Harvest Festival. *51 N Main St, Southington (06489). 3 miles S on Hwy 120, on Town Green. Phone 860/628-8036.* Street festival celebrating local apple harvest. Carnival, arts and crafts, parade, road race, food booths, entertainment. Seven days in early Oct.

Daffodil Festival. *Hubbard Park, W Main St, Meriden (06450). Phone 203/630-4259.* Approximately 500,000 daffodils in bloom; various events. Mid-Apr.

Limited-Service Hotels

★ ★ **FOUR POINTS BY SHERATON MERIDEN.** *275 Research Pkwy, Meriden (06450). Phone 203/238-2380; fax 203/238-3172. www.sheraton. com.* 150 rooms, 6 story. Check-in 3 pm, check-out noon. High-speed Internet access. Restaurant, bar. Fitness room. Indoor pool. Business center. **$**

★ **HAMPTON INN.** *10 Bee St, Meriden (06450). Phone 203/235-5154; toll-free 800/426-4329; fax 203/235-7139. www.hamptoninn.com.* 125 rooms, 4 story. Complimentary continental breakfast. Check-in 3 pm, check-out noon. High-speed Internet access. **$**

★ **HOLIDAY INN EXPRESS.** *120 Laning St, Southington (06489). Phone 860/276-0736; toll-free 800/465-4329; fax 860/276-9405. www.holiday-inn. com.* 122 rooms, 3 story. Complimentary continental breakfast. Check-in 3 pm, check-out 11 am. High-speed Internet access. Fitness room. Outdoor pool. **$**

Middletown (D-3)

See also East Haddam, Essex, Hartford, Meriden

Settled 1650
Population 42,762
Elevation 51 ft
Area Code 860
Zip 06457
Information Connecticut River Valley & Shoreline Visitors Council, 393 Main St; phone 860/347-0028 or toll-free 800/486-3346
Web Site www.cttourism.org

On the Connecticut River between Hartford and New Haven, Middletown was once an important shipping point for trade with the West Indies. The first official pistol-maker to the US Government, Simeon North, had his factory here in 1799. Today, Middletown boasts diversified industry and one of the longest and widest main streets in New England.

What to See and Do

Powder Ridge Ski Area. *99 Powder Hill Rd, Middlefield (06457). 5 miles SW off Hwy 147. Phone toll-free 877/754-7434. www.powderridgect.com.* Quad, three double chairlifts, handletow; patrol, school, rentals; snow-making; bar, restaurant, cafeteria; nursery. Fourteen trails; vertical drop 500 feet. (Nov-Apr, daily) **$$$$**

Wadsworth Falls State Park. *721 Wadsworth St, Middletown (06457). 3 miles SW off Hwy 66, on Hwy 157. Phone 860/566-2304.* These 285 acres surround Wadsworth Falls and lookout. Pond swimming, stream fishing; hiking along wooded area with mountain laurel display, picnicking. Beautiful waterfall with overlook.

Special Event

Durham Fair. *Fairgrounds, Jct of Hwys 68, 17 and 79, Durham (06422). Phone 860/349-9495.* State's largest agricultural fair. Last weekend in Sept.

Limited-Service Hotel

★ ★ **RADISSON CROMWELL HARTFORD SOUTH.** *100 Berlin Rd, Cromwell (06416). Phone 860/635-2000; fax 860/635-6970. www.radisson.com.* Located in the greater Hartford area, this is the area's premier hotel. 211 rooms, 4 story. Check-out noon. Restaurant, bar. Fitness room. Indoor pool, whirlpool. **$**

Milford (E-2)

See also Branford, Bridgeport, Fairfield, New Haven, Stratford

Settled 1639
Population 49,938
Elevation 89 ft
Area Code 203
Zip 06460
Information Milford Chamber of Commerce, 5 Broad

St; phone 203/878-0681
Web Site www.milfordct.com

What to See and Do

Milford Historical Society Wharf Lane Complex. *34 High St, Milford (06460). Phone 203/874-2664.* Three historical houses include Eells-Stow House (circa 1700), believed to be oldest house in Milford and featuring unusual "dog sled" stairway; Stockade House (circa 1780), first house built outside the city's early stockade; and Bryan-Downs House (circa 1785), two-story Early American structure housing more than 400 Native American artifacts spanning more than 10,000 years. (Memorial Day-Columbus Day, Sun; also by appointment) **$**

Special Event

Oyster Festival. *Milford town green. Phone 203/878-5363.* Arts and crafts exhibits, races, boat tours; games, food; entertainment. Mid-Aug.

Limited-Service Hotel

★ **HAMPTON INN.** *129 Plains Rd, Milford (06460). Phone 203/874-4400; toll-free 800/426-7866; fax 203/874-5348. www.hamptoninn.com.* 148 rooms, 3 story. Check-in 3 pm, check-out noon. High-speed Internet access. **$**

Restaurants

★ **ALDARIO'S.** *240 Naugatuck Ave, Milford (06460). Phone 203/874-6096; fax 203/874-5579. www.aldarios.com.* Italian menu. Lunch, dinner. Closed Mon; holidays. Bar. Children's menu. **$$**

★ ★ **THE GATHERING.** *989 Boston Post Rd, Milford (06460). Phone 203/878-6537; fax 203/876-2990. www.thegatheringrestaurant.com.* American menu. Dinner. Closed Dec 25. Bar. Children's menu. **$$**

★ ★ **SCRIBNER'S.** *31 Village Rd, Milford (06460). Phone 203/878-7019; fax 203/878-2238. www.scribners restaurant.com.* Seafood, steak menu. Lunch, dinner. Closed holidays. Bar. Children's menu. **$$**

Mystic (E-5)

See also Groton, New London, Norwich, Stonington

Settled 1654
Population 2,618
Elevation 16 ft
Area Code 860
Zip 06355
Information Tourist Information Center, Building 1D, Olde Mistick Village; phone 860/536-1641; or Connecticut's Mystic & More!, 470 Bank St, PO Box 89, New London 06320; phone 860/444-2206 or toll-free 800/863-6569 (outside CT)
Web Site www.mysticmore.com

The community of Mystic, divided by the Mystic River, was a shipbuilding and whaling center from the 17th to the 19th centuries. It derives its name from the Pequot, "Mistuket."

What to See and Do

Denison Homestead. *120 Pequotsepos Rd, Mystic (06355). 2 miles E of I-95 exit 90, on Pequotsepos Rd. Phone 860/536-9248.* (1717) Restored in the style of five eras (18th to mid-20th centuries); furnished with the heirlooms of 11 generations of a single family. Guided tour (mid-May-mid-Oct, Wed-Mon afternoons; rest of year, by appointment). **$$**

Denison Pequotsepos Nature Center. *109 Pequotsepos Rd, Mystic (06355). 2 miles NE of I-95 exit 90. Phone 860/536-1216.* An environmental education center and natural history museum active in wildlife rehabilitation. The 125-acre sanctuary has more than 7 miles of trails; family nature walks, films, lectures. (Daily; closed holidays) **$$**

Mystic Aquarium. *55 Coogan Blvd, Mystic (06355). Phone 860/536-3323. www.mysticaquarium.com.* The exhibits here feature more than 6,000 live specimens from all the world's waters. Demonstrations with dolphins, sea lions, and the only whales in New England delight young and old alike, as do Seal Island, an outdoor exhibit of seals and sea lions in natural settings, and the penguin pavilion. The facility also includes Dr. Robert Ballard's Institute for Exploration, which is dedicated to searching the deep seas for lost ships. The museum's Challenge of the Deep exhibit allows patrons to use state-of-the-art technology to re-create the search for the *Titanic* or explore the biology of undersea ocean vents. (Daily; hours vary by season; closed Jan 1, Thanksgiving, Dec 25) **$$$$**

⭐ **Mystic Seaport.** *75 Greenmanville Ave (Hwy 27), Mystic (06355). 1 mile S of I-95 exit 90. Phone 860/572-5315. www.visitmysticseaport.com.* This 17-acre complex is the nation's largest maritime museum, dedicated to preservation of 19th-century maritime history. Visitors may board the 1841 wooden whale-ship *Charles W. Morgan,* square-rigged ship *Joseph Conrad,* or fishing schooner *L.A. Dunton.* Collection also includes some 400 smaller vessels; representative seaport community with historic homes and water-front industries, some staff in 19th-century costume; exhibits, demonstrations, working shipyard; children's museum, planetarium (fee), 1908 steamboat cruises (May-Oct, daily; fee); restaurants; shopping; special events throughout the year. (Daily; closed Dec 25) **$$$$**

Olde Mistick Village. *Coogan Blvd and Hwy 27, Mystic (06355). Phone 860/536-4941.* More than 60 shops and restaurants in 1720s-style New England village, on 22 acres; duck pond, millwheel, waterfalls; entertainment, carillon (May-Oct, Sat-Sun). Village (daily). **FREE**

Special Event

Lobsterfest. *Mystic Seaport, 75 Greenmanville Ave, Mystic (06355). Phone 860/572-5315. www.visitmystic seaport.com.* Outdoor food festival. Late May.

Limited-Service Hotel

★ **COMFORT INN.** *48 Whitehall Ave, Mystic (06355). Phone 860/572-8531; toll-free 800/572-9339; fax 860/572-9358. www.comfortinn.com.* 120 rooms, 2 story. Complimentary continental breakfast. Check-in 3 pm, check-out 11 am. Fitness room. **$**
🏃

Full-Service Hotel

★ ★ ★ **HILTON MYSTIC.** *20 Coogan Blvd, Mystic (06355). Phone 860/572-0731; toll-free 800/774-1500; fax 860/572-0328. www.hilton.com.* Conveniently located on a side road close to Olde Mystic Village, just a block from I-95, this business-oriented hotel has a vaguely nautical theme. Several popular attractions, including the Mystic Seaport Museum, outlet shopping, and the Mystic Aquarium, are nearby. 182 rooms, 4 story. Check-in 3 pm, check-out 11 am. Restaurant, bar. Children's activity center. Fitness room. Indoor pool. **$$**
🏃 🏊

Full-Service Inns

★ ★ ★ **INN AT MYSTIC.** *Jct Hwy 1 and Hwy 27, Mystic (06355). Phone 860/536-9604; toll-free 800/*

237-2415; fax 860/572-1635. www.innatmystic.com. A variety of accommodations are available at this five-building property, the only inn in Connecticut that overlooks both Mystic Harbor and Long Island Sound. The Gatehouse, East Wing, and two modern hotels (collectively called the "Main House") are spread over the inn's 15 acres, but sitting like a jewel at the crest of the hill is the 1904 Classical Revival mansion that is known not just for its elegance, but also as the place where Lauren Bacall and Humphrey Bogart honeymooned. Mansion rooms are decorated with period furnishings and designer fabrics, have whirlpools, overlook the orchard and grounds, and are for adults only. The East Wing and Gatehouse, also for adults only, are similarly decorated, while the Main House, beautifully appointed with antiques or antique reproductions, has accommodations for couples and families. 67 rooms, 2 story. Pets accepted, some restrictions; fee. Check-in 3 pm, check-out 11 am. Restaurant, bar. Outdoor pool. Tennis. **$**
🐾 🏊 🎾

★ ★ ★ **WHALER'S INN.** *20 E Main St, Mystic (06355). Phone 860/536-1506; toll-free 800/243-2588; fax 860/572-1250. www.whalersinnmystic.com.* Homey, comfortable, and located in the heart of historic Mystic, the Whaler's Inn is designed for guests who want New England ambience with a bed-and-breakfast feel. You can almost see the sea captain rising from his rocking chair on the front porch of the 1865 colonial clapboard mansion as you approach, ready to greet you; inside, modern-day innkeepers take you to your guest room, where Waverly fabrics and wall coverings, a four-poster bed, wing-back chair, and large bath-room with pedestal sinks and whirlpool tub makes your stay cozy and comfortable. Each of the inn's eight guest rooms has a breathtaking view of the scenic Mystic River and bascule drawbridge. And that makes a decision about whether to leave that comfy chair on your veranda (most rooms have them) and go down to a bountiful breakfast or take a five-minute walk into town rather difficult. 49 rooms, 2 story. Complimentary continental breakfast. Check-in 2 pm, check-out 11 am. Restaurant. **$**

Specialty Lodging

The following lodging establishment is approved by Mobil Travel Guide, but due to its unique and individualized nature has not been given a traditional Mobil Star rating. Included in this listing you may find bed-and-breakfasts, limited-service inns, guest ranches, and other unique hotel properties.

THE OLD MYSTIC INN. *52 Main St, Old Mystic (06372). Phone 860/572-9422; fax 860/572-9954. www. oldmysticinn.com.* Built in 1794; early American décor. 8 rooms, 2 story. Check-in 2 pm, check-out 11 am. **$$** 🖵

Restaurants

★ ★ ★ **BRAVO BRAVO.** *20 E Main St, Mystic (06355). Phone 860/536-3228. www.whalersinnmystic .com.* Creative gourmet dining located in the Whaler's Inn (see). Lunch is served outdoors and dinner is served inside the beautifully decorated dining room at this local favorite. Italian menu. Lunch, dinner. Closed Mon. Bar. Casual attire. Reservations recommended. **$$$**

★ ★ **FLOOD TIDE.** *Jct Hwy 1 and Hwy 27, Mystic (06355). Phone 860/536-8140; fax 860/572-1635. www.innatmystic.com.* Complimentary hors d'oeuvres are served in the piano lounge. Gourmet dishes are impressive, and Sunday brunch is spectacular. American menu. Breakfast, dinner, Sun brunch. Closed ten days in Jan. Bar. Children's menu. Casual attire. Reservations recommended. Outdoor seating. **$$$**

★ ★ **GO FISH.** *Olde Mystic Village, Mystic (06355). Phone 860/536-2662; fax 860/536-4619.* Seafood menu. Lunch, dinner. Bar. Children's menu. Casual attire. Reservations recommended. **$$**

★ **MYSTIC PIZZA.** *56 W Main St, Mystic (06355). Phone 860/536-3700. www.mysticpizza.com.* Popular pizza parlor immortalized in the Julia Roberts film of the same name. Pizza. Lunch, dinner. Closed Easter, Thanksgiving, Dec 25. Bar. Casual attire. **$**

★ ★ **SEAMEN'S INNE.** *105 Greenmanville Ave, Mystic (06355). Phone 860/536-9649; fax 860/572-5304. www.seamensinne.com.* 19th-century sea captain's house décor; overlooks river. Seafood menu. Breakfast, lunch, dinner. Closed Dec 25. Bar. Children's menu. Casual attire. Outdoor seating. **$$**

New Britain (D-3)

See also Bristol, Farmington, Hartford, Meriden, Waterbury, Wethersfield

Settled 1686
Population 75,491
Elevation 179 ft

Area Code 860
Information Chamber of Commerce, 1 Court St, 06051; phone 860/229-1665; or the Central Connecticut Tourism District, 1 Grove St, 06053; phone 860/225-3901
Web Site www.newbritainchamber.com

This is the "hardware city." Production of sleigh bells and farm tools began about 1800, followed by locks and saddlery hardware. Many tool, hardware, and machinery manufacturers, including The Stanley Works, organized in 1843, are headquartered in New Britain.

What to See and Do

Central Connecticut State University. *1615 Stanley St, New Britain (06050). Phone 860/827-7000; toll-free 888/733-2278. www.ccsu.edu.* (1849) (14,000 students) On campus is Copernican Planetarium and Observatory, featuring one of the largest public telescopes in the United States; planetarium shows (Fri-Sat; children's shows Sat) **$$**

Hungerford Outdoor Education Center. *191 Farmington Ave, Berlin (06037). Approximately 3 miles S via Hwy 372. Phone 860/827-9064.* Outdoor animal areas, trails, gardens, pond, exhibits of regional and natural history, nutrition and energy; picnicking. (Apr-Oct: Tues-Sun; rest of year: Tues-Sat) **$**

New Britain Museum of American Art. *56 Lexington St, New Britain (06052). Phone 860/229-0257.* Works by outstanding American artists from 1740 to the present; works by Whistler, Church, Sargent, Wyeth; Thomas Hart Benton murals; Sanford Low Collection of American illustrations; Charles and Elizabeth Buchanan Collection of American impressionists. (Tues-Sun afternoons; closed holidays) **FREE**

New Britain Youth Museum. *30 High St, New Britain (06051). Phone 860/225-3020.* Exhibits of Americana, cultures of other nations, circus miniatures, dolls, hands-on displays. (Tues-Fri) **FREE**

Special Events

Baseball. *New Britain Stadium, 230 John Karbonic Way, New Britain (06051). Phone 860/224-8383. www.rockcats.com.* New Britain Rock Cats (AA team). Mid-Apr-Sept.

Dozynki Polish Harvest Festival. *8437 Valley Pike, New Britain (06053). Phone 860/225-3901.* Street dancing; polka bands; cultural displays; beer, singing, ethnic food; pony and hayrides; Polish arts and crafts. Third weekend in Sept.

Main Street, USA. *1 Grove St # 310, New Britain (06053). Phone 860/225-3901.* Street festival featuring wide variety of ethnic foods, entertainment, rides, arts and crafts. Second Sat in June.

Restaurant

★ **EAST SIDE.** *131 Dwight St, New Britain (06051). Phone 860/223-1188; fax 860/827-0327. www.eastside restaurant.com.* American, German menu. Lunch, dinner. Closed Mon; July 4, Dec 25. Bar. Children's menu. **$$**

New Canaan (F-1)

See also Norwalk, Ridgefield, Stamford

Founded 1801
Population 17,864
Elevation 300 ft
Area Code 203
Zip 06840
Information Chamber of Commerce, 111 Elm St; phone 203/966-2004
Web Site www.newcanaanchamber.com

New Canaan was settled in 1731 as Canaan Parish, a church society encompassing parts of Norwalk and Stamford. A quiet residential community situated on high ridges, New Canaan has retained its rural character despite its proximity to industrial areas.

What to See and Do

New Canaan Historical Society. *13 Oenoke Ridge Rd, New Canaan (06840). Phone 203/966-1776.* The First Town House (original town hall) has costume museum, library, and Cody Drugstore (1845), a restoration of the town's first pharmacy; on grounds of Hanford-Silliman House Museum (circa 1765) are a tool museum, hand press, one-room schoolhouse, and sculptor John Roger's studio and museum. Town House (Tues-Sat). Other buildings (Wed-Thurs, and Sun, limited afternoon hours; closed holidays). **$$**

New Canaan Nature Center. *144 Oenoke Ridge Rd, New Canaan (06840). Phone 203/966-9577.* More than 40 acres of woodland, ponds, and meadows; discovery center with hands-on exhibits; suburban ecology exhibits; solar greenhouse; cider house, and maple sugar shed; herb and wildflower gardens; trails; marsh boardwalk; animals. Grounds (daily). Buildings (Mon-Sat; closed holidays). **FREE**

Silvermine Guild Arts Center. *1037 Silvermine Rd, New Canaan (06840). Phone 203/966-5618 (programs).* Art center in rustic 6-acre setting has a school of the arts and three galleries with changing exhibits by member artists and artisans; invitational and juried exhibitions; many educational events and programs. (Tues-Sun; closed Jan 1, Thanksgiving, Dec 25) **FREE**

Full-Service Inn

★ ★ ★ **ROGER SHERMAN INN.** *195 Oenoke Ridge, New Canaan (06840). Phone 203/966-4541; fax 203/966-0503. www.rogershermaninn.com.* Built in 1740, this colonial landmark is top notch when it comes to attentive service. The guest rooms are romantic and the dining is superb. 18 rooms, 2 story. Complimentary continental breakfast. Check-in 2-6 pm, check-out 11 am. Restaurant. **$**

New Haven (E-3)

See also Branford, Clinton, Guilford, Madison, Meriden, Milford

Settled 1638
Population 130,474
Elevation 25 ft
Area Code 203
Information Greater New Haven Convention & Visitors Bureau, 59 Elm St, first floor, 06510; phone 203/777-8550 or toll-free 800/332-7829
Web Site www.newhavencvb.org or www.cityofnewhaven.com

New Haven is only 75 miles from New York City, but it is typical New England. Its colorful history is built into the stones and timbers of the area. Here, Eli Whitney worked out the principle of interchangeable parts for mass production. Around the corner, Nathan Hale roomed as a student, not far from where Noah Webster compiled the first dictionary. In addition to all this, Yale University puts New Haven on any list of the world's cultural centers.

Northwest of New Haven is a 400-foot red sandstone cliff called West Rock. In 1661 three Cromwellian judges, who had ordered Charles I beheaded, took refuge here from the soldiers of Charles II.

What to See and Do

Amistad Memorial. *165 Church St, New Haven (06510). In front of City Hall.* This 14-foot bronze relief sculpture is a unique three-sided form. Each side depicts a significant episode of the life of Joseph Cinque, one of 50 Africans kidnapped from Sierra Leone and slated for sale in Cuba in 1839. After secretly rerouting the slave ship to Long Island Sound, the battle for the would-be slaves' freedom ensued in New Haven. Two years later, their victory was complete. Ed Hamilton sculpted this important piece.

East Rock Park. *Orange and Cold Spring sts, New Haven (06511). 1 mile NE at foot of Orange St, on E Rock Rd. Phone 203/946-6086.* City's largest park includes Pardee Rose Gardens, bird sanctuary, hiking trails, athletic fields, tennis courts, picnic grounds. Excellent view of harbor and Long Island Sound. (Apr-Nov: daily; rest of year: Sat-Sun, and holidays) **FREE**

Fort Nathan Hale Park and Black Rock Fort. *36 Woodward Ave, New Haven (06510). Phone 203/946-8790.* Here, Federal guns kept British warships out of the harbor in 1812. Old Black Rock Fort, from Revolutionary War days, has been restored, and archaeological excavations are in progress. Fort Nathan Hale, from the Civil War era, also has been reconstructed. Both offer spectacular views of the harbor. Picnicking. Group guided tours (Memorial Day-Labor Day, daily).

The Green. *Church and Elm sts, New Haven (06510).* In 1638, these 16 acres were laid out, making New Haven the first planned city in America. On the town common are three churches—United (1813), Trinity Episcopal (1814), and Center Congregational (1813), which is one of the masterpieces of American Georgian architecture. **FREE**

Grove Street Cemetery. *227 Grove St, New Haven (06510).* First cemetery in the United States divided into family plots. Buried here are Noah Webster, Charles Goodyear, Eli Whitney, and many early settlers of the area. **FREE**

Lighthouse Point Park. *2 Lighthouse Rd, New Haven (06510). End of Lighthouse Rd, 5 miles SE off I-95, exit 50. Phone 203/946-8005.* This 82-acre park on Long Island Sound has a lighthouse built in 1840; restored antique carousel (fee); bird sanctuary. Beach, bathhouse, playfield, picnic facilities, boat ramp. (Daily) Parking fee (Memorial Day-Labor Day). **$$$**

New Haven Colony Historical Society Museum. *114 Whitney Ave, New Haven (06510). Phone 203/562-4183.* Museum of local history; special exhibits; also research library (fee). (Tues-Fri; closed holidays) **$**

Pardee-Morris House. *325 Lighthouse Rd, New Haven (06510). S of I-95 exit 50. Phone 203/772-7060.* (1750) Built in 18th century, burned by the British in 1779, then rebuilt in 1780 around surviving masonry; American period furnishings; kitchen garden. (June-Aug, Sat-Sun) **$**

Shore Line Trolley Museum. *17 River St, East Haven (06512). 5 miles E via I-95 exit 51 or 52. Phone 203/467-6927.* Collection of trolley, interurban, and rapid-transit cars from 15 states and Canada. A National Historic Site. Cars on display include pre-1900 trolleys (1893, 1899), the first commercially produced electric locomotive (1888), and a trolley parlor car. Exhibits on electric railways. Scenic trolley ride in authentic, restored cars; operator narrates on tour of display buildings and restoration shop; trolleys depart every 30 minutes (inquire for schedule). Picnic grove (May-Oct); gift shop; special events. (Memorial Day-Labor Day: daily; May, Sept-Oct, Dec: weekends and holidays; Apr and Nov: Sun only) **$$$**

Shubert Performing Arts Center. *247 College St, New Haven (06510). Phone 203/562-5666; toll-free 888/736-2663.* Full-service performing arts venue opened in 1914. Known as the "Birthplace of the Nation's Greatest Hits." Home to dance, musical, comedy, and dramatic performances. (Sept-June)

West Rock Nature Center. *1020 Wintergreen Ave, Hamden (06514). 1 mile N of Southern Connecticut State University. Phone 203/946-8016.* Nature center features native Connecticut wildlife in outdoor bird and mammal sections; indoor nature house with reptiles and other displays. Hiking trails; picnic areas. (Mon-Fri; closed holidays) **FREE**

★ **Yale University.** *149 Elm St, New Haven (06511). On N side of New Haven Green. Phone 203/432-2300. www.yale.edu.* (1701) (10,000 students) Founded by ten Connecticut ministers and named for Elihu Yale, an early donor to the school. In September, 1969, the undergraduate school became coeducational. Walking tours conducted daily by undergraduate students. Hear about Yale's rich 300-year history. See the school's distinctive architecture and visit both Sterling Memorial Library and the Beinecke Rare Book Library. Tours leave from Yale Visitor Center.

Weekdays 10:30 am, 2 pm; Sat-Sun 1:30 pm (free). Of special interest are

Beinecke Rare Book and Manuscript Library. *121 Wall St, New Haven (06511). Best approach is from College St via Cross Campus Walk, on High St. Phone 203/432-2977.* Exhibits of famous collections, Gutenberg Bible. (Sept-July, Mon-Sat; Aug, Mon-Fri; closed holidays) **FREE**

Collection of Musical Instruments. *15 Hillhouse Ave, New Haven (06511). Phone 203/432-0822.* Total holdings of 850 musical instruments; permanent displays and changing exhibits; lectures, concerts, special events. (Sept-June, Tues-Thurs afternoons; closed school holidays) Under 14 only with adult. **$**

Old Campus. *149 Elm St, New Haven (06511). Phone 203/432-2300.* Where Nathan Hale (class of 1773) roomed. One-hour guided walking tours (Mon-Fri, one tour morning, one tour afternoon; Sat-Sun, one tour afternoon). Inquire at Visitor Information Office. **FREE**

Peabody Museum of Natural History. *170 Whitney Ave, New Haven (06511). Whitney Ave at Sachem St. Phone 203/432-5050 (recording).* Exhibits on mammals, invertebrate life, Plains and Connecticut Native Americans, meteorites, minerals and rocks, birds of Connecticut; several life-size dinosaur exhibits include a brontosaurus (60-feet long) reconstructed from original fossil material; dioramas of North American flora and fauna; weekend films (free). (Daily; closed holidays) **$$**

Yale Art Gallery. *1111 Chapel St, New Haven (06511). Chapel St at York St. Phone 203/432-0600.* Collections include Italian Renaissance paintings, American paintings and decorative arts, ancient art, African sculpture, Near and Far Eastern art, and European paintings from the 13th-20th centuries. (Tues-Sat, also Sun afternoons; closed holidays) **FREE**

Yale Bowl. *Chapel and Yale sts, New Haven (06511). 2 miles W on Chapel St. Phone 203/432-4747.* An Ivy League football mecca.

Yale Center for British Art. *1080 Chapel St, New Haven (06511). Phone 203/432-2800.* British paintings, prints, drawings, sculpture, and rare books from Elizabethan period to present. Reference library and photo archive. Lectures, tours, films, concerts. (Tues-Sun; closed holidays) **FREE**

Special Events

International Festival of Arts and Ideas. *195 Church St, New Haven (06511). Phone toll-free 888/278-4332.* Celebration of the arts and humanities. Late June.

Long Wharf Theatre. *222 Sargent Dr, New Haven (06511). I-95 exit 46. Phone 203/787-4282.* Features new plays as well as classics. Sept-June.

New Haven Symphony Orchestra. *Woolsey Hall, College and Grove sts, New Haven (06511). Phone 203/776-1444.* Series of concerts by leading artists. Oct-May.

Pilot Pen International Tennis Tournament. *Connecticut Tennis Center, Central Ave, New Haven (06511). Near Yale Bowl. Phone toll-free 888/997-4568.* Championship Series on the ATP tour. Mid-Aug.

Yale Repertory Theater. *1120 Chapel St, New Haven (06511). Phone 203/432-1234; toll-free 800/833-8134. www.yale.edu/yalerep.* The Yale Repertory Theater prides itself on creating bold and passionate theatrical productions. The troupe successfully trains artistic leaders, proven by the fact that four of their productions have won the Pulitzer Prize. Mid-Sept-mid-May.

Limited-Service Hotels

★ ★ **THE COLONY.** *1157 Chapel St, New Haven (06511). Phone 203/776-1234; toll-free 800/458-8810; fax 203/772-3929. www.colonyatyale.com.* 86 rooms, 4 story. Check-out noon. Restaurant. Airport transportation available. **$**

★ ★ **COURTYARD BY MARRIOTT.** *30 Whalley Ave, New Haven (06511). Phone 203/777-6221; toll-free 800/228-9290; fax 203/772-1089. www.courtyard.com.* 160 rooms, 8 story. Check-in 3 pm, check-out 11 am. High-speed Internet access. Restaurant, bar. Outdoor pool. **$**

Full-Service Hotel

★ ★ ★ **OMNI NEW HAVEN HOTEL.** *155 Temple St, New Haven (06510). Phone 203/772-6664; toll-free 800/843-6664; fax 203/974-6777. www.omnihotels.com.* 306 rooms, 25 story. Check-in 3 pm, check-out noon. Restaurant, bar. Fitness room. Indoor pool, whirlpool. Business center. **$$**

Specialty Lodging

The following lodging establishment is approved by Mobil Travel Guide, but due to its unique and individualized nature has not been given a traditional Mobil Star rating. Included in this listing you may find bed-and-breakfasts, limited-service inns, guest ranches, and other unique hotel properties.

THREE CHIMNEYS. *1201 Chapel St, New Haven (06511). Phone 203/789-1201; toll-free 800/443-1554; fax 203/776-7363. www.threechimneysinn.com.* This lovely historic inn, built in the 1870s, is one block from Yale University. Guest rooms provide luxurious comfort featuring canopy beds with Edwardian bed drapes. 11 rooms, 3 story. Complimentary full breakfast. Check-in 3 pm, check-out 11 am. **$$**

Restaurants

★ ★ **500 BLAKE ST.** *500 Blake St, Westville (06515). Phone 203/387-0500. www.500blakestreetcafe .com.* American, Italian menu. Lunch, dinner, Sun brunch. Closed holidays. Bar. **$$$**

★ **INDOCHINE PAVILLION.** *1180 Chapel St, New Haven (06511). Phone 203/865-5033; fax 203/865-6495.* Vietnamese menu. Lunch, dinner. Closed Mon; holidays. Bar. **$$**

New London (E-5)

See also Groton, Mystic, Norwich, Old Lyme, Old Saybrook, Stonington

Settled 1646
Population 28,540
Elevation 33 ft
Area Code 860
Zip 06320
Information Connecticut's Mystic & More!, 470 Bank St, PO Box 89; phone 860/444-2206 or toll-free 800/863-6569
Web Site www.mysticmore.com

New London is a seagoing community and always has been; it has one of the finest deep-water ports on the Atlantic coast. From the first days of the republic into the 20th century, whalers brought fortunes home to New London. Townspeople still welcome all ships—submarines, cutters, yachts, cruisers. Today, the city's manufacturing industries include turbines, steel fabrication, high-tech products, medicines, electronics, and other products.

What to See and Do

Eugene O'Neill Theater Center. *305 Great Neck Rd, Waterford (06385). W via Hwy 1. Phone 860/443-5378. www.oneilltheatercenter.org.* Complex includes O'Neill Playwrights Conference, O'Neill Critics Institute, O'Neill Music Theater Conference, O'Neill Puppetry Conference, National Theater Institute. Staged readings of new plays and musicals during summer at Barn Theater, Amphitheater, and Instant Theater (June-Aug).

Ferries.

New London-Block Island, RI. *2 Ferry St, New London (06320). Phone 860/442-9553.* Auto ferry makes two-hour crossing; one round-trip (mid-June-Labor Day). **$$$$**

New London-Fishers Island, NY. *New London Pier, New London (06320). Phone 860/443-6851.* Auto ferries *Race Point* and *Munnatawket* make crossing to Fishers Island; several departures daily. Departs from New London Pier, foot of State Street. **$$$$**

New London-Orient Point, NY. *2 Ferry St, New London (06320). Phone 860/443-7394.* Five auto ferries make 90-minute trips across Long Island Sound. High-speed passenger ferry makes a 40-minute trip daily. (Daily; no trip Dec 25) Advance reservations required for vehicles. **$$$$**

Joshua Hempsted House. *11 Hempstead Ct, New London (06320). Phone 860/443-7949.* (1678) The oldest house in the city; restored, 17th- and 18th-century furnishings; Hempsted family diary detailing life in the house during colonial times. (Mid-May-mid-Oct, Tues-Sun afternoons) **$$** Admission includes

Nathaniel Hempsted House. *11 Hempstead Ct, New London (06320). Phone 860/443-7949.* (1759) One of two surviving examples of mid-18th-century cut-stone architecture in state. Stone exterior bake oven, seven rooms with period furnishings. (Mid-May-mid-Oct, Tues-Sun afternoons)

Lyman Allyn Art Museum. *625 Williams St, New London (06320). Phone 860/443-2545. www.lymanallyn .org.* Over 15,000 works of art. The collection includes Contemporary, Modern, and Early American fine arts; collection of dolls, doll houses; American and European paintings; Asian and primitive art. (Tues-Sat 10 am-5 pm, Sun 1-5 pm; closed holidays) **$$**

Monte Cristo Cottage. *325 Pequot Ave, New London (06320). Phone 860/443-0051.* Restored boyhood home of playwright and Nobel prize winner Eugene O'Neill; houses research library and memorabilia. Multimedia presentation. Literary readings. (Mid-June-late Oct, Tues-Sun) **$$**

Ocean Beach Park. *1225 Ocean Ave, New London (06320). 3 miles S on Ocean Ave, on Long Island Sound. Phone toll-free 800/510-7263.* Swimming in the ocean, Olympic-size pool, water slide; sheltered pavilion, boardwalk, picnic area, concessions, miniature golf, novelty shop, amusement arcade, entertainment. (Sat before Memorial Day-Labor Day, daily) **$$$**

Science Center of Eastern Connecticut. *33 Gallows Ln, New London (06320). N of I-95 exit 83. Phone 860/442-0391.* Regional science museum located on 415-acre Connecticut Arboretum with trees and shrubs native to the area (daily). Major exhibit on eastern Connecticut's natural and cultural history entitled "Time and the River: The Story of Land and People in the Thames River Basin"; workshops and courses; field trips, special programs; nature trail, herb garden; museum shop. (Tues-Sun; closed holidays) **$$**

Shaw Perkins Mansion. *305 Bank St, New London (06320). Phone 860/443-1209.* (1756) Naval head-quarters for state during Revolution; genealogical and historical library. Unique paneled cement fireplace walls. **$**

Sunbeam Fleet Nature Cruises. *15 1st St, Waterford (06385). Departs from dock near Niantic River bridge, W via I-95 exit 74, S on Hwy 161, left on Hwy 156 to first dock on left past bridge. Phone 860/443-7259.* Cruises to view bald eagles (Feb-Mar) and seals (Apr-May). Reservations suggested. **$$$$**

US Coast Guard Academy. *15 Mohegan Ave, New London (06320). 1 mile N on I-95 exit 83. Phone 860/444-8270.* (1876) 800 cadets. Visitors' Pavilion with multimedia show (May-Oct, daily). US Coast Guard Museum (daily; closed holidays). Cadet parade-reviews (fall, spring, usually Fri). Barque *Eagle,* 295 feet, open to visitors (Fri-Sun, when in port; limited hours); photography permitted. **FREE**

Ye Antientiest Burial Ground. *Huntington St, New London (06320).* (1653) **FREE**

Ye Olde Towne Mill. *Mill St and State Pier Rd, New London (06320). Under Gold Star Bridge.* (1650) Built for John Winthrop Jr, the founder of New London and Connecticut's sixth governor. The mill was restored in 1981; overshot waterwheel (closed to the public).

Special Events

Connecticut Storytelling Festival. *Connecticut College, New London (06320). Phone 860/439-2764.* Nationally acclaimed artists; workshops, concerts. Late Apr.

Sailfest. *New London City Pier, Bank St, New London (06320). Phone 860/443-1879. www.sailfest.org.* Arts and crafts and food vendors line the streets downtown while people of all ages browse, eat, and enjoy the three stages of entertainment. The largest fireworks show on the East Coast takes place on Saturday night. One weekend in July. **FREE**

Limited-Service Hotel

★ ★ **RADISSON HOTEL NEW LONDON.** *35 Governor Winthrop Blvd, New London (06320). Phone 860/443-7000; toll-free 800/333-3333; fax 860/443-1239. www.radisson.com.* Midway between Boston and New York, this hotel is convenient to nearby casinos and other area attractions. 120 rooms, 5 story. Check-out noon. Restaurant, bar. Indoor pool, whirlpool. Tennis. Airport transportation available. Business center. **$**

New Preston

See also Cornwall Bridge, Kent

Population 1,217
Elevation 700 ft
Area Code 860
Zip 06777
Information Litchfield Hills Visitors Bureau, PO Box 968, Litchfield 06759; phone 860/567-4506
Web Site www.litchfieldhills.com

What to See and Do

Historical Museum of Gunn Memorial Library. *5 Wykeham Rd, Washington (06793). 4 miles SW via Hwy 47 at junction Wykeham Rd, on the green. Phone 860/868-7756.* House built in 1781; contains collections and exhibits on area history; paintings, furnishings, gowns, dolls, dollhouses, and tools. (Thurs-Sun afternoons) **FREE**

⭐ **Institute for American Indian Studies.** *38 Curtis Rd, Washington (06793). 4 miles SW via CT 47 to CT 199 S, then 1 1/2 miles to Curtis Rd. Phone 860/868-0518.* A museum of Northeastern Woodland Indian artifacts with permanent exhibit hall. Exhibits include changing Native American art displays; also a replicated indoor longhouse, outdoor replicated Algonkian village, simulated archaeological site, and nature trail. Special programs. (Daily; closed holidays) **$$**

Lake Waramaug State Park. *30 Lake Waramaug Rd (Hwy 478), Kent (06777). 5 miles N. Phone 860/868-2592.* Swimming, fishing, scuba diving; field sports, hiking, ice skating, camping, picnicking.

Full-Service Inn

★ ★ ★ **BOULDERS INN.** *E Shore Rd (Hwy 45), New Preston (06777). Phone 860/868-0541; toll-free 800/455-1565; fax 860/868-1925. www.bouldersinn .com.* Enjoy country comforts in this quiet lakeside bed-and-breakfast. Guest rooms are homey and have canopy beds. 5 rooms, 2 story. Check-in 3 pm, check-out noon. Restaurant, bar. Beach. Tennis. **$$$$**

Specialty Lodging

The following lodging establishment is approved by Mobil Travel Guide, but due to its unique and individualized nature has not been given a traditional Mobil Star rating. Included in this listing you may find bed-and-breakfasts, limited-service inns, guest ranches, and other unique hotel properties.

HOPKINS INN. *22 Hopkins Rd, New Preston (06777). Phone 860/868-7295; fax 860/868-7464. www.thehopkins inn.com.* Established in 1847. Lake Waramaug opposite. 11 rooms, 3 story. Closed Jan-Mar. Check-in 1 pm, check-out 11 am. Restaurant, bar. Beach. **$**

Restaurants

★ ★ ★ **BOULDERS.** *E Shore Rd (Hwy 45), New Preston (06777). Phone 860/868-0541; fax 860/868-1925. www.bouldersinn.com.* Fine dining in a turn-of-the-century summer home overlooking crystalline Lake Waramaug. American menu. Dinner, Sun brunch. Closed Mon-Tues; Dec 25. Reservations recommended. Outdoor seating. **$$**

★ ★ **HOPKINS INN.** *22 Hopkins Rd, New Preston (06777). Phone 860/868-7295; fax 860/868-7464. www.thehopkinsinn.com.* In an old inn on a hill overlooking a lake. American menu. Lunch, dinner. Closed Mon; Jan-Mar. Bar. Children's menu. Outdoor seating. **$$**

★ ★ ★ **LE BON COIN.** *223 Litchfield Tpke, New Preston (06777). Phone 860/868-7763.* Serving classic French specialties with a light flair in an intimate, cozy atmosphere. French menu. Lunch, dinner. Closed Tues-Wed; Jan 1, Memorial Day, Dec 25. Bar. Children's menu. **$$**

Niantic

Restaurant

★ **CONSTANTINE'S.** *252 Main St, Niantic (06357). Phone 860/739-2848.* Seafood menu. Lunch, dinner. Closed Mon; Thanksgiving, Dec 25. Bar. Children's menu. **$$**

Norfolk (C-2)

See also Lakeville, Riverton

Founded 1758
Population 2,060
Elevation 1,230 ft
Area Code 860
Zip 06058
Information Litchfield Hills Visitors Bureau, PO Box 968, Litchfield 06759; phone 860/567-4506
Web Site www.litchfieldhills.com

What to See and Do

Campbell Falls. *Burr Pond State Park, 116 Mountain Rd, Winsted (06098). 6 miles N on Hwy 272. Phone 860/482-1817.* Winding trails through woodland composed of many splashing cascades; focal point is Campbell Falls. Fishing; hiking, picnicking. **FREE**

Dennis Hill. *Burr Pond State Park, 116 Mountain Rd, Winsted (06098). 2 miles S on Hwy 272. Phone 860/482-1817.* A unique summit pavilion (formerly a summer residence) is located at an elevation of 1,627 feet, providing a panoramic view of the Litchfield Hills and beyond. Picnicking, hiking, cross-country skiing. **FREE**

Hatstack Mountain. *Norfolk. 1 mile N on Hwy 272. Phone 860/482-1817.* A 34-foot-high stone tower at the summit, 1,716 feet above sea level, provides an excellent view of Long Island Sound, the Berkshires, and peaks in New York. A 1/2-mile trail leads from parking lot to tower. Picnicking; hiking.

Historical Museum. *13 Village Green, Norfolk (06058). On the green.* Phone 860/542-5761. Located in former Norfolk Academy (1840). Exhibits on the history of Norfolk include displays of a country store and post office as well as a children's room with an 1879 doll house. (Late May-mid-Oct: Sat-Sun; rest of year: by appointment) **FREE**

Special Event

Norfolk Chamber Music Festival. *E. B. Stoeckel Estate, Jct Hwy 44 and Hwy 272, Norfolk (06058).* Phone 860/542-3000 *(June-Oct)*. Musical performances Friday-Saturday evenings in acoustically superb 1906 Music Shed located on grounds of 19th-century estate; also picnicking, indoor performances, and art gallery before concerts; informal chamber music recitals Thurs and Sat. Mid-June-mid-Sept.

Norwalk (F-1)

See also Bridgeport, Fairfield, Greenwich, New Canaan, Pound Ridge, Ridgefield, Stamford, Stratford, Westport

Founded 1651
Population 78,331
Elevation 42 ft
Area Code 203
Information Coastal Fairfield County Convention & Visitors Bureau, 297 West Ave, 06850; phone 203/899-2799 or toll-free 800/866-7925
Web Site www.coastalct.com

Norwalk's growth was heavily influenced by Long Island Sound. The city evolved rapidly from an agriculturally based community to a major seaport, then to a manufacturing center known for high-fashion hats, corsets, and clocks. The sound still plays an important part in Norwalk's development, providing beauty, recreation and, of course, oysters.

What to See and Do

Charter fishing trips. Phone toll-free 800/866-7925. Several companies offer full- and 1/2-day saltwater fishing excursions. Contact the Coastal Fairfield County Tourism District for details.

Ferry to Sheffield Island Lighthouse. *132 Water St, 3rd floor, South Norwalk (06854).* Departs from Hope Dock, junction Washington and N Water Street. Phone 203/838-9444. Ferry through Norwalk Harbor to historic Sheffield lighthouse (1868) on 3-acre island. Tour. Picnicking. (Memorial Day-June, weekends; July-Labor Day, daily) **$$$$**

Historic South Norwalk (SoNo). *Washington and Water sts, South Norwalk (06854). 1 mile SE via I-95, exit 14 N/15 S.* Phone toll-free 800/866-7925. Nineteenth-century waterfront neighborhood on National Register featuring historical buildings, unique shops, art galleries, and restaurants.

Lockwood-Mathews Mansion Museum. *295 West Ave, Norwalk (06850).* Phone 203/838-9799. (1864-1868) Sixty-room Victorian mansion built by financier LeGrand Lockwood; 42-foot skylit rotunda, ornamented doors, and carved marble, inlaid woodwork throughout, period furnishings, musical boxes, and mechanical music exhibit; one-hour guided tour. Victorian Ice-Cream Social (mid-July) and Antiques Show (late Oct). (Mid-Mar-Dec: Wed-Sun; rest of year: by appointment only; closed holidays) **$$$**

Maritime Aquarium at Norwalk. *10 N Water St, Norwalk (06854). 2 miles S via I-95, exit 14 N or 15 S.* Phone 203/852-0700. Hands-on maritime museum featuring shark touch tank and harbor seal pool; 125 species, touch tanks, films on IMAX screen; boat building exhibit. Guided harbor study tours. (Daily; closed Thanksgiving, Dec 25) **$$$**

Mill Hill Historic Park. *2 E Wall St, Norwalk (06852).* Phone 203/846-0525. Complex of historic Early American buildings includes the Town House Museum (circa 1835), Fitch House Law Office (circa 1740), and schoolhouse (circa 1826); also old cemetery. (May-Oct, Sun) **FREE**

St. Paul's-on-the-Green. Phone 203/847-2806. This Gothic-style stone church contains the Seabury Altar; medieval stained glass; exquisite needlepoint. Antique organ. Also here is a colonial cemetery. (Daily by appointment)

WPA Murals. *125 East Ave, Norwalk (06851). City Hall (parking entrance, Sunset Hill Ave).* Phone 203/854-7900. America's largest collection of Works Progress Administration murals depict life in southeastern Fairfield County in the 1930s. (Mon-Fri; closed holidays) **FREE**

Special Events

International In-Water Boat Show. *Norwalk Cove*

Marina, Calf Pasture Beach Rd, Norwalk (06855). Phone 212/984-7000; toll-free 800/866-7925. www.boatshownorwalk.com. In addition to featuring more than 750 of the newest and most innovative crafts including performance boats, sailboats, and sailing yachts, guests at this waterside boat show can also try scuba diving, view a restored classic boat, or grab a drink at the Sand Bar. Sept. **$$$**

Norwalk Harbor Splash. *Phone 203/838-9444.* Regatta, harbor tours, music. Late May or early June.

Oyster Festival. *Veteran's Park, Seaview Ave, East Norwalk (06855). Phone toll-free 800/866-7925. www.seaport.org.* Featuring appearances from tall ships and vintage oyster boats, this festival has regularly drawn 60,000 visitors a year since it began in 1978. More than 3,000 volunteers make the festival possible each year, and many local nonprofit groups benefit. Norwalk is less than a two-hour drive from many of New England's larger cities, making it easy to attend the festival during a trip to New York or Hartford. Weekend after Labor Day. **$$**

Round Hill Highland Games. *Cranbury Park, Norwalk (06850). Phone toll-free 800/866-7925.* Heritage celebration with Highland dancing, pipe bands, caber tossing, clan tents, Scottish and American food. Late June or early July.

SoNo Arts Celebration. *Washington St, South Norwalk (06854). Phone toll-free 800/866-7925.* Juried crafts, kinetic sculpture race, entertainment, concessions, block party. In Historic South Norwalk. First weekend in Aug.

Limited-Service Hotels

★ ★ **DOUBLETREE HOTEL NORWALK.** *789 Connecticut Ave, Norwalk (06854). Phone 203/853-3477; toll-free 800/222-8733; fax 203/855-9404. www.doubletree.com.* Business travelers will appreciate this hotel located in the heart of Norwalk. Guests can enjoy the on-site bowling. 268 rooms, 8 story. Check-in 3 pm, check-out noon. High-speed Internet access, wireless Internet access. Restaurant, bar. Fitness room. Indoor pool. Business center. **$**
🏃 🏊 🏃

★ ★ **FOUR POINTS BY SHERATON.** *426 Main Ave, Norwalk (06851). Phone 203/849-9828; toll-free 800/329-7466; fax 203/846-6925. www.fourpoints.com.* 127 rooms, 4 story. Check-in 3 pm, check-out noon. Restaurant, bar. Fitness room. **$$**
🏃

Full-Service Inn

★ ★ ★ **THE SILVERMINE TAVERN.** *194 Perry Ave, Norwalk (06850). Phone 203/847-4558; fax 203/847-9171. www.silverminetavern.com.* 10 rooms, 2 story. Closed Dec 25; Tues (Sept-May). Complimentary continental breakfast. Check-in 3 pm, check-out 11 am. Restaurant, bar. **$$**
🄳

Restaurants

★ ★ **MESON GALICIA.** *10 Wall St, Norwalk (06850). Phone 203/866-8800; fax 203/899-0576.* Building once a trolley barn (1800s). Spanish menu. Lunch, dinner. Closed Mon; holidays. Bar. Reservations recommended. Outdoor seating. **$$**

★ ★ ★ **PASTA NOSTRA.** *116 Washington St, South Norwalk (06854). Phone 203/854-9700. www.pastanostra.com.* This former pasta retail store cooks with only the highest quality of ingredients. Italian menu. Dinner. Reservations recommended. **$$**

★ ★ **SILVERMINE TAVERN.** *194 Perry Ave, Norwalk (06850). Phone 203/847-4558; fax 203/847-9171. www.silverminetavern.com.* 18th-century colonial tavern overlooking mill pond; antiques. Country store opposite. Seafood menu. Lunch, dinner, Sun brunch. Closed Tues; Dec 25. Bar. Children's menu. Outdoor seating. **$$**
🄳

Norwich (E-5)

See also Groton, Mystic, New London, Plainfield, Stonington

Settled 1659
Population 37,391
Elevation 52 ft
Area Code 860
Zip 06360
Information Connecticut's Mystic and More!, 470 Bank St, PO Box 89, New London 06320; phone 860/444-2206 or toll-free 800/863-6569 (outside CT)
Web Site www.mysticmore.com

Norwich was one of the first cities chartered in Connecticut. Since the end of the 18th century, it has been a leader in the industrial development of the state. Here, the colony's first paper mill was opened in 1766, and the first cut nails in America were made in 1772. Cotton spinning began about 1790.

There are three distinct sections: Norwichtown to the northwest, a living museum of the past; the business section near the Thames docks; and a central residential section with many 19th-century homes.

What to See and Do

Indian Leap. *Yantic and Sachem sts, Norwich (06360). Yantic Falls off Yantic St. Phone 860/886-4683.* The falls was a favorite resort and outpost of the Mohegan. Legend has it that a band of Narragansetts, during the Battle of Great Plains in 1643, fled from pursuing Mohegans. As they came upon the falls, many were forced to jump off the cliffs and into the chasm below, hence the name. Can be viewed from the Monroe Street footbridge. **FREE**

Leffingwell Inn. *348 Washington St, Norwich (06360). Phone 860/889-9440.* (1675) Scene of Revolutionary War councils. Museum; period rooms. (Mid-May-Labor Day, Tues-Sun; rest of year, by appointment) **$$**

Mohegan Park and Memorial Rose Garden. *20 Park Center Rd, Norwich (06360). Entrances on Judd Rd and Rockwell St. Phone 860/823-3759.* Picnic and play area; swimming area (June-Labor Day, daily). Rose garden; best time to visit, June-Sept. (Daily) **FREE**

Native American Burial Grounds. *Sachem and Washington sts, Norwich (06360). Phone 860/886-4683.* The resting place of Uncas, chief of the Mohegans (more popularly known as the Mohicans), who gave the original land for the settlement of Norwich.

Old Burying Ground. *Cemetery Ln and E Town St, Norwich (06360). Entrance from E Town St; brochure available at Cemetery Ln entrance. Phone 860/886-4683.* Burial place of many Revolutionary War soldiers, including French soldiers; also Samuel Huntington, signer of the Declaration of Independence.

Slater Memorial Museum & Converse Art Gallery. *108 Crescent St, Norwich (06360). Approximately 1 mile N via I-395, exit 81 E, on campus of Norwich Free Academy. Phone 860/887-2506.* Roman and Greek casts; Vanderpoel Collection of Oriental Art; 17th to 20th-century American art and furnishings; changing exhibits. (Sept-June, daily; rest of year, Tues-Sun; closed holidays)

Tantaquidgeon Indian Museum. *1819 Norwich-New London Tpke, Uncasville (06382). 5 miles S on Hwy 32. Phone 860/848-9145.* Works of Mohegan and other New England tribes, past and present; also displays of Southeast, Southwest, and Northern Plains Native Americans. (May-Oct, Tues-Sun) **DONATION**

Special Events

Blue Grass Festival. *Strawberry Park, 42 Pierce Rd, Preston (06365). Phone 860/886-1944; toll-free 888/794-7944. www.strawberrypark.net/bluegrass.html.* You can either come for the day or make reservations for a campsite and enjoy four full days of bluegrass music. Past performers have included Rhonda Vincent, The Tim O'Brien Band, and The Waybacks. Late May-early June. **$$$$**

Chelsea Street Festival. *Chelsea district, Norwich (06360). Phone 860/887-2789.* Fine arts, entertainment, hayrides, children's events. Third Sat in May.

Harbor Day. *Brown Memorial Park, at waterfront, Norwich (06360). Phone 860/444-2206.* Raft race; boat rides; dunking booth; arts and crafts; entertainment. Late Aug.

Historic Norwichtown Days. *Norwichtown Green, Norwich (06360). Phone 860/444-2206.* Living history events, crafts, parade. Second weekend in Sept.

Rose-Arts Festival. *Broadway and Washington sts, Norwich (06360). Phone 860/444-2206.* Crowning of Rose Queen; arts and crafts shows; children's activities; entertainment; international food festival; flower competition; golf tournament; bicycle and road races. Ten days in late June-early July.

Full-Service Resort

★ ★ ★ **THE SPA AT NORWICH INN.** *607 W Thames St, Norwich (06360). Phone 860/886-2401; toll-free 800/275-4772; fax 860/886-9483. www.thespa atnorwichinn.com.* The Spa at Norwich Inn offers visitors the best of both worlds. Its historic country inn on 42 acres allows guests to take a step back in time, while its award-winning spa employs cutting-edge techniques and treatments to enhance relaxation and renewal. This is the place to come to truly unwind, with 32 treatment rooms dedicated to relieving stress and soothing tired souls. This spa's menu goes beyond the traditional facials and massages to include hydrotherapy, astrology, and energy work. From physical fitness and mind/body awareness to beautifying and pampering treatments, this spa offers the complete package. Dining is far from Spartan, although guests wishing to enjoy lighter spa cuisine appreciate the weight- and health-conscious menu. 65 rooms, 3 story. Check-out noon. Restaurant, bar. Fitness room. Indoor pool, outdoor pool, whirlpool. Tennis. Business center. **$**

Restaurant

★ ★ **KENSINGTON.** *607 W Thames St, Norwich (06360). Phone 860/886-2401.* American menu. Breakfast, lunch, dinner, Sun brunch. Bar. Outdoor seating. **$$$**

Old Lyme (E-4)

See also Essex, New London, Old Saybrook, Stonington

Settled 1665
Population 6,535
Elevation 17 ft
Area Code 860
Zip 06371
Information Connecticut's Mystic and More!, 470 Bank St, PO Box 89, New London 06320; phone 860/444-2206 or toll-free 800/863-6569
Web Site www.mysticmore.com

Once, long ago, they say a sea captain lived in every house in Old Lyme. Fortunately, a good many of the houses are still standing on the tree-lined streets of this sleepy old village. Named for Lyme Regis, England, it is a summer resort and an artists' colony, one of the first on the coast.

What to See and Do

Florence Griswold Museum. *96 Lyme St, Old Lyme (06371). 1 block W off CT Tpke exit 70. Phone 860/434-5542.* (1817) Stately late Georgian mansion that housed America's most celebrated art colony at the turn of the century. Paintings by Willard Metcalf, Childe Hassam, and other artists of the colony; exhibits of 18th- and 19th-century New England furnishings and decorative arts. (Jan-Mar, Wed-Sun; Apr-Dec, Tues-Sun)

Rocky Neck State Park. *244 W Main St, East Lyme (06371). 6 miles E via I-95, exit 72, on Hwy 156. Phone 860/739-5471.* Approximately 560 acres with 1/2-mile

frontage on Long Island Sound. Saltwater swimming, scuba diving, fishing; hiking, picnicking (shelters, concessions). Camping.

Full-Service Inns

★ ★ ★ **BEE AND THISTLE INN.** *100 Lyme St, Old Lyme (06371). Phone 860/434-1667; toll-free 800/622-4046; fax 860/434-3407. www.beeandthistleinn.com.* This 1756 inn has been rated as one of Connecticut's most romantic getaways. 11 rooms, 3 story. Closed two weeks in Jan. Children over 12 years only. Check-in 2 pm, check-out 11 am. Restaurant, bar. **$**

★ ★ ★ **OLD LYME INN.** *85 Lyme St, Old Lyme (06371). Phone 860/434-2600; toll-free 800/434-5352; fax 860/434-5352. www.oldlymeinn.com.* Located in the historic district of Old Lyme, this bed-and-breakfast (built in 1850) is close to Essex, Mystic Seaport, Mystic Aquarium, and art galleries. Guests can also enjoy outlet shopping and visiting the local museums. 13 rooms, 2 story. Pets accepted, some restrictions. Complimentary continental breakfast. Check-in 3-11 pm, check-out noon. Restaurant, bar. Business center. **$$**

Restaurants

★ ★ ★ **BEE AND THISTLE INN.** *100 Lyme St, Old Lyme (06371). Phone 860/434-1667; toll-free 800/622-4046; fax 860/434-3402. www.beeandthistleinn.com.* Romance and service are in full force here. Innovative American cuisine is prepared fresh by the staff. American menu. Breakfast, lunch, dinner, Sun brunch. Closed Tues; Dec 24 evening-Dec 25; two weeks in Jan. Bar. **$$$**

★ ★ ★ **OLD LYME INN.** *85 Lyme St, Old Lyme (06371). Phone 860/434-2600; toll-free 800/434-5352; fax 860/434-5352. www.oldlymeinn.com.* Located in the historic district, this restored 1850 home features three fireplaces, many antiques, and murals by a local artist. Superb desserts are made daily from scratch. American menu. Lunch, dinner. Bar. **$$$**

Old Saybrook (E-4)

See also Clinton, Essex, New London, Old Lyme, Stonington

Settled 1635
Population 9,552
Elevation 31 ft
Area Code 860
Zip 06475
Information Chamber of Commerce, 146 Main St, PO Box 625; phone 860/388-3266; or the Connecticut Valley Tourism Commission, 393 Main St, Middletown 06457; phone 860/347-0028
Web Site www.oldsaybrookct.com

Old Saybrook, at the mouth of the Connecticut River, is popular with summer vacationers. It is the third-oldest named community in Connecticut and is the oldest officially chartered town in the state. It was also the original site of Yale College until 1716.

What to See and Do

Fort Saybrook Monument Park. *On College St, at Saybrook Point.* Nearly 18-acre park with remains of Fort Saybrook, first military fortification in the state; picnicking. (Daily)

General William Hart House. *350 Main St, Old Saybrook (06475). Phone 860/388-2622.* (1767) Provincial Georgian-style, colonial residence of well-to-do New England merchant and politician; features include eight corner fireplaces, one of which is decorated with Sadler and Green transfer-print tiles illustrating *Aesop's Fables*; original wainscotting; Federal-style pieces, several of which are Hart family items; antique furniture, costumes, artifacts; on grounds are re-created colonial gardens, including award-winning herb garden. (Mid-June-mid-Sept, Fri-Sun, limited hours). **DONATION**

Special Events

Arts and Crafts Show. *Town Green, Main St, Old Saybrook (06475). Phone 860/388-3266.* More than 200 artists and craftspersons exhibiting. Last full weekend in July.

Christmas Torchlight Parade. *Main St, Old Saybrook (06475). Phone 860/388-3266.* More than 40 fife and drum corps march down Main Street. Second Sat in Dec.

Full-Service Resorts

★ ★ ★ **SAYBROOK POINT INN AND SPA.** *2 Bridge St, Old Saybrook (06475). Phone 860/395-3081; toll-free 800/243-0212; fax 860/388-1504. www.saybrookpointinn.com.* The charming coastal village of Old Saybrook is home to the exceptional Saybrook Point Inn and Spa. Warm interiors and courteous service define this seaside getaway, while views of Long Island Sound and the Connecticut River make for a scenic backdrop. The guest rooms and suites are classically styled with 18th-century period-style furnishings and accessories. Guests work out with a view of the sound in the comprehensive fitness center and luxuriate at the spa, where a complete menu of treatments tempts clients. The hotel's restaurant, Terra Mar Grille, wins rave reviews for its sophisticated cuisine matched only by the water views. The chef dazzles with contemporary American dishes, and spa cuisine is available for those guests watching their waistlines. 62 rooms, 3 story. Check-out noon. Restaurant, bar. Fitness room. Indoor pool, outdoor pool, whirlpool. **$$**

★ ★ ★ **WATER'S EDGE RESORT AND CONFERENCE CENTER.** *1522 Boston Post Rd, Westbrook (06498). Phone 860/399-5901; toll-free 800/222-5901; fax 860/399-6172. www.watersedge-resort.com.* This resort has a stunning view of Connecticut's Long Island Sound. Guests can enjoy such activities as softball, face painting, scavenger hunts, kite flying, football, horseshoes, and volleyball. 32 rooms, 3 story. Check-in 3 pm, check-out noon. Restaurant, bar. Children's activity center. Fitness room. Beach. Indoor pool, outdoor pool, whirlpool. Tennis. **$$**

Restaurant

★ ★ **DOCK AND DINE.** *College St, Old Saybrook (06475). Phone 860/388-4665; fax 860/536-0695.* Seafood, steak menu. Lunch, dinner. Closed Mon-Tues (mid-Oct-mid-Apr); Thanksgiving, Dec 24-25. Bar. Children's menu. **$$**

Plainfield (D-5)

See also Norwich, Putnam

Settled 1689
Population 14,363

Elevation 203 ft
Area Code 860
Zip 06374
Information Northeast Connecticut Visitors District, 13 Cantebury Rd, Suite 3, PO Box 145, Putnam 06260; phone 860/779-6383 or toll-free 888/628-1228
Web Site www.ctquietcorner.org

What to See and Do

Plainfield Greyhound Park. *137 Lathrop Rd, Plainfield (06374). Phone 860/564-3391.* Pari-mutuel betting. Concessions, bar. No minors. Races daily. (Daily) **$$**

Prudence Crandall House. *Hwys 14 and 169, Canterbury (06331). W on Hwy 14A at junction Hwy 169. Phone 860/546-9916.* Site of New England's first academy for African-American girls (1833-1834). Restored two-story frame building with changing exhibits, period furnishings; research library. Gift shop. (Wed-Sun; closed Thanksgiving; also mid-Dec-mid-Jan) **$**

Quinebaug Valley Trout Hatchery. *151 Trout Hatchery Rd, Plainfield (06374). Phone 860/564-7542.* A 1,200-acre hatchery for brook, brown, and rainbow trout. Exhibits and displays (daily). Fishing by permit only (Mar-May, weekends and holidays). **FREE**

Limited-Service Hotel

★ **BEST WESTERN PLAINFIELD YANKEE INN.** *55 Lathorp Rd, Plainfield (06374). Phone 860/564-4021; fax 860/564-4021.* 48 rooms, 2 story. Check-in 2 pm, check-out 11 am. **$**

Putnam (C-5)

See also Plainfield

Population 9,031
Elevation 290 ft
Area Code 860
Zip 06260
Information Northeast Connecticut Visitors District, 13 Canterbury Rd, Suite 3, PO Box 145; phone 860/779-6383 or toll-free 888/628-1228
Web Site www.ctquietcorner.org

Named for Revolutionary War hero Israel Putnam, this town is situated on four small hills. Because it was located at Cargill Falls on the Quinebaug River and a railroad station served as a connecting point between New York and Boston, Putnam at one time ranked eighth in New England in the volume of freight handled.

What to See and Do

⭐ **Roseland Cottage.** *556 Hwy 169, Woodstock (06281). 7 miles NW via Hwys 171 and 169. Phone 860/928-4074.* (1846) Influential abolitionist publisher Henry C. Bowen's summer home. One of the most important surviving examples of a Gothic Revival "cottage," complete with period furnishings. Located on Woodstock Hill with its bright pink exterior and picturesque profile, it stands in contrast to the otherwise colonial character of this New England village. Surrounded by original outbuildings, includes one of the oldest indoor bowling alleys in the country; aviary. Boasts one of the oldest parterre gardens in New England, edged by 1,800 feet of dwarf boxwood. Presidents Grant, Hayes, Harrison, and McKinley attended Bowen's celebrated Fourth of July parties here. (June-mid-Oct, Wed-Sun; closed holidays) **$$**

Limited-Service Hotel

★ **KINGS INN.** *5 Heritage Rd, Putnam (06260). Phone 860/928-7961; toll-free 800/541-7304; fax 860/963-2463.* 4 rooms, 2 story. Pets accepted. Complimentary continental breakfast. Check-out 11 am. Bar. Outdoor pool. **$**

Full-Service Inn

★ ★ ★ **INN AT WOODSTOCK HILL.** *94 Plaine Hill Rd, South Woodstock (6267). Phone 860/928-0528; fax 860/928-3236. www.woodstockhill.com.* Located on 14 acres, this inn (1815) is listed on the National Register of Historic Places. Guests can enjoy a stroll through the well-manicured lawns that adorn this property. 22 rooms, 3 story. Complimentary continental breakfast. Check-in 2 pm, check-out 11 am. Restaurant, bar. **$**

Ridgefield (E-1)

See also Danbury, New Canaan, Norwalk, Stamford

Settled 1709
Population 20,919
Elevation 749 ft
Area Code 203
Zip 06877

Information Chamber of Commerce, 9 Bailey Ave; phone 203/438-5992 or toll-free 800/386-1708; or Housatonic Valley Tourism Commission, Box 406, 30 Main St, Danbury 06810; phone 203/743-0546 or toll-free 800/841-4488 (outside CT)
Web Site www.ridgefieldchamber.org

Ridgefield is unusual among communities settled in the 19th century because it has a main street of boulevard width—99 feet lined with tree-shaded houses. On this street in 1777, Benedict Arnold (still a revolutionary) set up barricades and fought the Battle of Ridgefield against General Tyron.

What to See and Do

Aldrich Museum of Contemporary Art. *258 Main St, Ridgefield (06877). Phone 203/438-4519.* Changing exhibits; sculpture garden (daily; free). Museum (Tues-Sun afternoons). **$$**

Keeler Tavern. *132 Main St, Ridgefield (06877). Phone 203/438-5485.* Restored 18th-century tavern, stagecoach stop, home. Once Revolutionary patriot headquarters; British cannonball still embedded in wall. Summer home of architect Cass Gilbert. Period furnishings; gardens; tours; museum shop. (Wed, Sat-Sun afternoons; closed Jan) **$$**

Full-Service Inns

★ ★ ★ **THE ELMS INN.** *500 Main St, Ridgefield (06877). Phone 203/438-2541. www.elmsinn.com.* Open since 1799, this inn (built in the 1760s) is located in Ridgefield, which boasts much of the original architecture. Guests can visit the Community Center, which is the site of the Governor's Mansion (built in 1896), or stop by the town library. 23 rooms, 3 story. Complimentary continental breakfast. Check-in 3 pm, check-out noon. Restaurant, bar. **$$$**
🔊

★ ★ ★ **STONEHENGE INN.** *35 Stonehenge Rd, Ridgefield (6877). Phone 203/438-6511; fax 203/438-2478. www.stonehengeinn-ct.com.* This property is a lakeside colonial-style inn. The inn's elegant restaurant specializes in French cuisine. 16 rooms, 2 story. Complimentary continental breakfast. Check-in 3 pm, check-out 11 am. Restaurant, bar. **$$**

★ ★ ★ **WEST LANE INN.** *22 West Ln, Ridgefield (06877). Phone 203/438-7323; fax 203/438-7325. www.westlaneinn.com.* 18 rooms, 3 story. Complimentary continental breakfast. Check-in 2-10 pm, check-out 11 am. Restaurant. **$$**
🔊

Restaurants

★ ★ ★ **THE ELMS.** *500 Main St, Ridgefield (06877). Phone 203/438-9206. www.elmsinn.com.* Established in 1799, this is the oldest continuously-run inn in Ridgefield. American menu. Lunch, dinner. Closed Easter, Dec 25. Bar. Reservations recommended. Outdoor seating. **$$**
🔊

★ ★ ★ **STONEHENGE.** *35 Stonehenge Rd, Ridgefield (06877). Phone 203/438-6511; fax 203/438-2478. www.stonehengeinn-ct.com.* This restored home (circa 1853) is located near a pond. Tranquil scenery and attentive service make it a popular place. American menu. Dinner. Reservations recommended. Valet parking. **$$$**
🔊

★ **VENICE RESTAURANT.** *3 Danbury Rd, Ridgefield (06877). Phone 203/438-3333.* Italian menu. Lunch, dinner. Bar. Children's menu. Casual attire. Outdoor seating. **$$**

Riverton

See also Hartford, Norfolk

Population 500
Elevation 505 ft
Area Code 860
Zip 06065
Information Litchfield Hills Visitors Bureau, PO Box 968, Litchfield 06759; phone 860/567-4506
Web Site www.litchfieldhills.com

Lambert Hitchcock, one of America's greatest chair-makers, built his original chair factory here in 1826. His famous stenciled chairs and cabinet furniture are now prized pieces. The old factory is still in operation, and some antiques are on display. Today, the grand colonial houses and tree-lined streets of this New England village are filled with emporiums and shops.

What to See and Do

Hitchcock Museum. *Hwy 20, Riverton (06065). Center of village. Phone 860/738-4950.* Collection of original 18th-century furnishings by Hitchcock and others, displayed in historic church (1829). (Apr-Dec, Thurs-Sun) **DONATION**

Solomon Rockwell House. *225 Prospect St, Winsted (06098). 3 miles SW on Hwy 20, 2 miles S on Hwy 8. Phone 860/379-8433.* (1813) Antebellum house built by early industrialist; Hitchcock chairs, antique clocks, Revolutionary and Civil War memorabilia, wedding gown collection, melodeon. (June-Oct, Thurs-Sun afternoons) **$**

Special Event

Riverton Fair. *Hwy 20, Riverton (06065). Phone 860/ 567-4506.* 1800s country village fair, held since 1909; chopping, sawing, and pie-eating competitions; displays, art and crafts, entertainment. Second weekend in Oct.

Simsbury (D-3)

See also Avon, Farmington, Hartford

Settled 1660
Population 22,023
Elevation 181 ft
Area Code 860
Zip 06070
Information Simsbury Chamber of Commerce, 749 Hopmeadow St, PO Box 224; phone 860/651-7307
Web Site www.simsburycoc.org

Hopmeadow Street, in this characteristic New England village, is so named because hops were grown in the area to supply early distillers. Simsbury's handsome Congregational Church was built in 1830.

After it was founded, Simsbury developed steadily until 1676, when the settlers fled in terror during King Philip's War. Scouts returning three days later and found the settlement in ashes. Soon the village was reconstructed and activity was again stimulated by the discovery of copper at East Granby (then part of Simsbury).

What to See and Do

Phelps Tavern Museum. *800 Hopmeadow St, Simsbury (06070). Phone 860/658-2500.* Period rooms and interactive exhibition galleries interpret the use of the historic Captain Elisha Phelps house as an inn from 1786 to 1849. Three successive generations of the Phelps tavernkeepers are chronicled along with the social history of taverns in New England. Part of a 2-acre complex, which includes a museum store, research library, and award-winning period gardens. Group tours available. (Tues-Sat) **$$$**

Simsbury Farms. *100 Old Farms Rd, Simsbury (06070). Phone 860/658-3836.* Recreational facility covering 300 acres; swimming; picnicking, ice skating, tennis, golf, cross-country skiing, nature and family fitness trails, volleyball, paddle tennis. (Daily; some activities seasonal) Fees for most activities.

Limited-Service Hotel

★ **IRON HORSE INN.** *969 Hopmeadow St, Simsbury (06070). Phone 860/658-2216; toll-free 800/ 245-9938; fax 860/651-0822. www.ironhorseofsimsbury .com.* 27 rooms, 2 story. Pets accepted, some restrictions; fee. Complimentary continental breakfast. Check-out 11 am. Outdoor pool. **$**

Full-Service Hotel

★ ★ ★ **SIMSBURY INN.** *397 Hopmeadow St, Simsbury (06070). Phone 860/651-5700; toll-free 800/ 634-2719; fax 860/651-8024. www.simsburyinn.com.* This inn offers a true escape for the active traveler. 98 rooms, 4 story. Complimentary continental breakfast. Check-out 11 am. Restaurant, bar. Indoor pool, whirlpool. Tennis. Airport transportation available. **$$**

Specialty Lodging

The following lodging establishment is approved by Mobil Travel Guide, but due to its unique and individualized nature has not been given a traditional Mobil Star rating. Included in this listing you may find bed-and-breakfasts, limited-service inns, guest ranches, and other unique hotel properties.

SIMSBURY 1820 HOUSE. *731 Hopmeadow St, Simsbury (06070). Phone 860/658-7658; toll-free 800/879-1820; fax 860/651-0724. www.simsbury1820 house.com.* Built in 1820; antiques. 32 rooms, 3 story. Complimentary continental breakfast. Check-in 3 pm, check-out 11 am. Restaurant. **$**

Restaurant

★ **ONE-WAY FARE.** *4 Railroad St, Simsbury (06070). Phone 860/658-4477; fax 860/651-9087. www.onewayfare.org.* Old brick train station (1874);

train memorabilia. American menu. Lunch, dinner, Sun brunch. Closed Labor Day, Thanksgiving, Dec 25. Bar. Outdoor seating. **$$**

Southbury (E-2)

See also Danbury, Waterbury, Woodbury

Settled 1673
Population 15,818
Elevation 257 ft
Area Code 203
Zip 06488
Information Litchfield Hills Visitors Bureau, PO Box 968, Litchfield 06759; phone 860/567-4506
Web Site www.litchfieldhills.com

What to See and Do

Bullet Hill Schoolhouse. *215 Main St N, Southbury (06488). 1/2 mile E of I-84, exit 15, on Hwy 6. Phone 203/264-8781.* One of the oldest school buildings in the country, estimated to have been built in 1789, in use until 1942; some experts believe that it pre-dates the Revolutionary War. Early schooling exhibits. (Apr-May: limited hours; rest of year: by appointment) **DONATION**

Kettletown. *175 Quaker Farms Rd, Southbury (06488). 5 miles S via I-84, exit 15. Phone 203/264-5169.* The name of this park is derived from the time when settlers first arrived and purchased this tract of land from the Native Americans for one brass kettle. Swimming, fishing; hiking, sports field, picnicking, camping. Nature trail for the disabled.

Southford Falls. *175 Quaker Farms Rd, Southbury (06488). 4 miles SE via Hwys 67 and 188. Phone 203/264-5169.* Approximately 120 acres. Former site of Diamond Match Company. Stream and pond fishing; ice skating, bridle trail nearby, scenic hiking along Eight Mile River; picnicking. (Daily) **$**

Full-Service Hotel

★ ★ ★ **HILTON SOUTHBURY.** *1284 Strongtown Rd, Southbury (06488). Phone 203/598-7600; toll-free 800/774-1500; fax 203/598-7600. www.hilton.com.* Located in the Litchfield Hills area between Boston and New York, this property is sprawled in a country setting near numerous local antique centers and shops. The Quassy Amusement Park and several ski areas are also nearby. 198 rooms, 3 story. Pets

accepted, some restrictions. Check-in 3 pm, check-out noon. Restaurant, bar. Fitness room. Indoor pool, whirlpool. **$**

Restaurant

★ ★ **TARTUFO.** *900 Main St S, Southbury (06488). Phone 203/262-8001; fax 203/264-8657.* Italian menu. Lunch, dinner. Closed holidays. Bar. Children's menu. **$$**

Southington (D-3)

Restaurant

★ ★ **BRANNIGAN'S.** *176 Laning St, Southington (06489). Phone 860/621-9311; fax 860/628-0803. www.brannigans.com.* American menu. Lunch, dinner, Sun brunch. Closed Memorial Day, Dec 25. Bar. Children's menu. **$$**

Stafford Springs (C-4)

See also Enfield, Storrs, Windsor

Settled 1719
Population 4,100
Elevation 591 ft
Area Code 860
Zip 06076
Information Connecticut North Central Tourism & Visitors Bureau, 111 Hazard Ave, Enfield 06082; phone 860/763-2578 or toll-free 800/248-8283
Web Site www.cnctb.org

Stafford Springs is known for its production of woolen fabrics, printed circuits, and industrial filters.

What to See and Do

Civilian Conservation Corps Museum. *166 Chestnut Hill Rd (Hwy 190), Stafford Springs (06076). Phone 860/684-3430.* New Deal program devoted to state and national parks is commemorated. Video and photograph exhibits; equipment and uniforms; camp memorabilia. (Late May-Aug, afternoons) **DONATION**

Mineral Springs. *Hwy 190 and Spring St, Stafford Springs (06076). Spring St, between Grace Episcopal*

Church and the library. Located here are the springs that gave the town its name. In 1771, John Adams, future president of the United States, came to bathe in the springs after hearing of their healing effects. **FREE**

Special Event

Stafford Motor Speedway. *55 West St, Stafford Springs (06076). Hwy 140 W. Phone 860/684-2783.* A 1/2-mile paved oval track for stock car racing. Apr-Sept.

Stamford (F-1)

See also Fairfield, Greenwich, New Canaan, Norwalk, Ridgefield, Westport

Settled 1641
Population 108,056
Elevation 10 ft
Area Code 203
Information Chamber of Commerce, 733 Summer St, 06901; phone 203/359-4761
Web Site www.stamfordchamber.com

Stamford is a corporate headquarters, manufacturing and research center, as well as a residential suburb of New York City. More than 20 *Fortune* 500 corporations are located in this area. An assortment of marinas and beaches provide recreation on Long Island Sound.

What to See and Do

Bartlett Arboretum and Gardens. *151 Brookdale Rd, Stamford (06903). Off High Ridge Rd, 1 mile N of Merritt Pkwy (Hwy 15) exit 35. Phone 203/322-6971.* Collections of dwarf conifers, rhododendrons, azaleas, wildflowers, perennials, and witches brooms; ecology trails and swamp walk are within the natural woodlands surrounding the gardens. (Daily) **FREE**

First Presbyterian Church. *1101 Bedford St, Stamford (06905). Phone 203/324-9522.* (1958) Contemporary building shaped like a fish, designed by Wallace Harrison; glass by Gabriel Loire of Chartres, France; 56-bell carillon tower (1968), summer concerts (July, Thurs night). **FREE**

Special Event

Festival of Arts. *Mill River Park, Stamford (06901). Phone 203/359-4761.* Various exhibits of performing and visual arts. Late June.

Limited-Service Hotels

★ ★ **HOLIDAY INN.** *700 Main St, Stamford (06901). Phone 203/358-8400; toll-free 800/465-4329; fax 203/358-8872. www.holiday-inn.com.* 383 rooms, 10 story. Check-in 3 pm, check-out noon. High-speed Internet access, wireless Internet access. Restaurant, bar. Indoor pool. Business center. **$**
🏊 🏋

★ **STAMFORD SUITES HOTEL.** *720 Bedford St, Stamford (06901). Phone 203/359-7300; toll-free 866/394-4365; fax 203/359-7307. www.stamfordsuites.com.* 42 rooms, 8 story, all suites. Complimentary continental breakfast. Check-out 11 am. Business center. **$$**
🏋

Full-Service Hotels

★ ★ ★ **MARRIOTT STAMFORD.** *243 Tresser Blvd, Stamford (06901). Phone 203/357-9555; toll-free 800/732-9689; fax 203/324-6897. www.marriott.com.* Located across the street from the Stamford Town Center Mall, guests have access to over 130 stores. For those who don't enjoy shopping, there are other places to explore such as the Palace Theater, Playland Amusement Park, or the Whitney Museum. 506 rooms, 16 story. Check-in 3 pm, check-out noon. Restaurant, bar. Fitness room. Indoor/outdoor pool, whirlpool. Business center. **$$**
🏋 🏊 🏋

★ ★ ★ **SHERATON STAMFORD HOTEL.** *2701 Summer St, Stamford (06905). Phone 203/359-1300; toll-free 888/627-8315; fax 203/348-7937. www.sheraton.com.* This property is located 45 minutes from Manhattan and within the bustling corporate center of Connecticut's Gold Coast. 445 rooms, 5 story. Check-in 3 pm, check-out noon. Restaurant, bar. Fitness room. Indoor pool, whirlpool. Business center. **$**
🏋 🏊 🏋

★ ★ ★ **THE WESTIN STAMFORD.** *1 Stamford Pl, Stamford (06901). Phone 203/967-2222; toll-free 800/228-3000; fax 203/967-3475. www.westin.com.* 480 rooms, 10 story. Check-in 3 pm, check-out noon. Restaurant, bar. Fitness room. Indoor pool, whirlpool. Tennis. Business center. **$$**
🏋 🏊 🏋 🏋

Restaurants

★ **CRAB SHELL.** *46 Southfield Ave, Stamford (06902). Phone 203/967-7229; fax 203/967-7223. www.crabshell.com.* Seafood menu. Lunch, dinner. Bar. Children's menu. **$$$**

★ ★ **FIO'S RISTORANTE & PIZZERIA.** *299 Long Ridge Rd, Stamford (06902). Phone 203/964-9802.* Italian menu. Lunch, dinner. Bar. Casual attire. Reservations recommended. Outdoor seating. **$$$**
🅑

★ ★ **GIOVANNI'S.** *1297 Long Ridge Rd, Stamford (06903). Phone 203/322-8870; fax 203/322-7213.* Seafood, steak menu. Lunch, dinner. Closed Jan 1, Thanksgiving, Dec 25. Bar. Children's menu. **$$**

★ ★ **IL FALCO.** *59 Broad St, Stamford (06902). Phone 203/327-0002; fax 203/967-8315. www.ilfalco.com.* Italian menu. Lunch, dinner. Closed Sun; holidays. Bar. **$$$**

★ ★ **LA BRETAGNE.** *2010 W Main St (Hwy 1), Stamford (06902). Phone 203/324-9539; fax 203/961-9468. www.ctfrenchdining.com.* French menu. Lunch, dinner. Closed Sun; holidays. Bar. Children's menu. Reservations recommended. **$$$**

★ ★ **LA HACIENDA.** *222 Summer St, Stamford (06901). Phone 203/324-0577; fax 203/324-0177.* Mexican menu. Lunch, dinner. Closed Thanksgiving, Dec 25. Bar. Outdoor seating. **$$**

★ **MEERA INDIAN CUISINE.** *227 Summer St, Stamford (06901). Phone 203/975-0477; fax 203/323-9829.* Indian menu. Lunch, dinner. Bar. **$$**

Stonington (E-5)

See also Groton, Mystic, New London, Norwich, Old Lyme, Old Saybrook

Settled 1649
Population 16,919
Elevation 7 ft
Area Code 860
Zip 06378
Information Connecticut's Mystic and More!, 470 Bank St, PO Box 89, New London 06320; phone 860/444-2206 or toll-free 800/863-6569 (outside CT)
Web Site www.mysticmore.com

Until their defeat at Mystic Fort in 1637, the Pequot dominated the area around Stonington. In 1649, the first European settlers came here from Rehoboth, Massachusetts. Connecticut and Massachusetts both claimed ownership of the territory. In 1662, permanent control was granted to Connecticut by charter from King Charles II. Three years later the area was officially called Mystic, and in 1666 the name was changed to Stonington (which includes Stonington Borough).

The conclusion of the King Philip War in 1676 effectively ended the Native American threat in southern New England. The local economy, based on farming, shipping, and manufacturing, thrived. Prior to the Civil War, whaling and sealing expeditions left Stonington's port at regular intervals. After the war, maritime interests flourished as Stonington served as the connecting point for rail and steamer service to New York City. Today this maritime heritage is represented by a commercial fishing fleet and recreational boating.

What to See and Do

Old Lighthouse Museum. *7 Water St, Stonington (06378). Phone 860/535-1440 (summer).* First government-operated lighthouse in Connecticut (1823); exhibits include Stonington-made firearms, stoneware; ship models, whaling gear; China trade objects; folk art; local artifacts. Children's gallery. Visitors can climb the tower for a panoramic view of Long Island Sound. (May-June and Sept-Oct, Tues-Sun; July-Aug, daily; rest of year, by appointment) **$**

Specialty Lodging

The following lodging establishment is approved by Mobil Travel Guide, but due to its unique and individualized nature has not been given a traditional Mobil Star rating. Included in this listing you may find bed-and-breakfasts, limited-service inns, guest ranches, and other unique hotel properties.

RANDALL'S ORDINARY. *Hwy 2, North Stonington (06359). Phone 860/599-4540; toll-free 877/599-4540; fax 860/599-3308. www.randallsordinary.com.* Rural setting; 200 acres with barn and some farm animals. 15 rooms, 2 story. Check-in 2 pm, check-out 11 am. Restaurant. **$$**

Storrs (D-4)

See also Hartford, Manchester, Stafford Springs

Population 12,198
Elevation 600 ft
Area Code 860
Zip 06268
Information Northeast Connecticut Visitors District, 13 Cantebury Rd, Suite 3, PO Box 145, Brooklyn 06234; phone 860/779-6383 or toll-free 888/628-1228
Web Site www.ctquietcorner.org

What to See and Do

Ballard Institute and Museum of Puppetry. *6 Boum Pl, Storrs (06269). Phone 860/468-4605. www.bimp.uconn. edu.* Features changing exhibits from collection of more than 2,000 puppets. Gives visitors appreciation of puppetry as art form. (Mid-Apr-mid-Nov, Fri-Sat) **FREE**

Caprilands Herb Farm. *534 Silver St, Coventry (06238). 8 miles SW via Hwy 44. Phone 860/742-7244.* More than 30 different theme gardens using herbs, spices, and wild grasses; 18th-century farm building; lunchtime lectures (Apr-Dec; fee). Tea program (Sun). Basket and bookshops. (Daily) **FREE**

Nathan Hale Homestead. *2299 South St, Coventry (06238). 8 miles SW via Hwy 44. Phone 860/742-6917.* (1776) Country-Georgian-style structure built by Nathan's father, Richard. Restored; many original furnishings. (Mid-May-mid-Oct, afternoons) **$$**

University of Connecticut. *115 N Eagleville Rd, Storrs (06269). SE on I-84, exit 68, then S on Hwy 195. Phone 860/486-2000. www.uconn.edu.* (1881) (26,200 students) On campus are the state's largest public research library, art galleries, museums, animal barns, biological and floricultural greenhouses (tours; free). Also here are

    Connecticut State Museum of Natural History. *Wilbur Cross Building, 115 N Eagleville Rd, Storrs (06269). Phone 860/486-4460.* Exhibits on Native Americans, mounted birds of prey, honey bees, sharks, minerals. (Mon, Thurs-Sun, afternoons) **FREE**

    William Benton Museum of Art. *245 Glenbrook Rd, Storrs (06269). Phone 860/486-4520.* Permanent collection includes American and European paintings, sculpture, prints, and drawings; changing

exhibits. (Tues-Sun; closed holidays and between exhibitions) **FREE**

Special Event

Connecticut Repertory Theatre. *University of Connecticut, Harriet S. Jorgensen Theatre, 2132 Hillside Rd, Storrs (06269). Phone 860/486-4226.* Musicals, comedies, and dramas. Nightly. Feb-May, July, Sept-Dec.

Stratford (F-2)

See also Bridgeport, Fairfield, Milford, Norwalk

Settled 1639
Population 49,389
Elevation 25 ft
Area Code 203
Information Chamber of Commerce, 10 Middle St, PO Box 999, Bridgeport, 06601-0999; phone 203/335-3800

A fine port on the Housatonic River, Stratford has been a hub of shipbuilding and industry for more than three centuries.

What to See and Do

Boothe Memorial Park. *134 Main St, Stratford (06614). Phone 203/381-2068.* Former Boothe homestead (1663-1949) on 30 acres; unusual, historical buildings; Boothe home and carriage house (mid-May-late Oct, Tues-Sun), Americana Museum, blacksmith shop, architecturally eccentric "technocratic cathedral"; flower gardens, rose garden, picnicking, playgrounds. Park (daily). Other buildings (Memorial Day-late Oct, daily). **FREE**

Captain David Judson House. *967 Academy Hill, Stratford (06615). Phone 203/378-0630.* (Circa 1750) Restored and furnished colonial house; period furnishings and crafts, slave quarters, tool display; local history exhibits. (June-Oct, Wed, Sat-Sun; closed Memorial Day, July 4) **$** Admission includes

    Catharine B. Mitchell Museum. *967 Academy Hill, Stratford (06615). Connected to the Judson House. Phone 203/378-0630.* Changing and permanent exhibits depict the history of the Stratford area 1639-1830; local memorabilia. (Same hours as Judson House)

Limited-Service Hotels

★ **HONEYSPOT LODGE.** *360 Honeyspot Rd, Stratford (06497). Phone 203/375-5666; fax 203/378-1509.* 90 rooms, 2 story. Check-out noon. Indoor pool. **$**

★ ★ **RAMADA INN.** *225 Lordship Blvd, Stratford (06615). Phone 203/375-8866; toll-free 800/272-6232; fax 203/375-2482. www.ramada.com.* 145 rooms, 6 story. Check-in 3 pm, check-out noon. Restaurant, bar. Indoor pool. Airport transportation available. **$**

Restaurant

★ ★ ★ **PLOUF!** *14 Beach Dr, Stratford (06615). Phone 203/386-1477.* French bistro menu. Lunch, dinner. Bar. Casual attire. **$$**

Vernon (D-4)

See also Hartford, Manchester, Windsor

Population 29,841
Elevation 350 ft
Area Code 860
Zip 06066
Information Greater Hartford Tourism District, 234 Murphy Rd, Hartford 06114; phone 860/244-8181 or toll-free 800/793-4480
Web Site www.enjoyhartford.com

Limited-Service Hotel

★ ★ **QUALITY INN.** *51 Hartford Tpke, Vernon (06066). Phone 860/646-5700; toll-free 800/235-4667; fax 860/646-0202. www.qualityinn.com.* 127 rooms, 2 story. Check-in 3 pm, check-out 11 am. Restaurant, bar. Outdoor pool. Golf. **$**

Specialty Lodging

The following lodging establishment is approved by Mobil Travel Guide, but due to its unique and individualized nature has not been given a traditional Mobil Star rating. Included in this listing you may find bed-and-breakfasts, limited-service inns, guest ranches, and other unique hotel properties.

TOLLAND INN. *63 Tolland Green, Tolland (06084). Phone 860/872-0800; toll-free 877/465-0800; fax 860/870-7958. www.tollandinn.com.* New England inn built in 1800; handcrafted furniture. 7 rooms, 2 story. Children over 10 years only. Complimentary full breakfast. Check-in 4-9 pm, check-out 11 am. **$**

Restaurant

★ **REIN'S NEW YORK-STYLE DELI.** *435 Hartford Tpke, Vernon (06066). Phone 860/875-1344.* Deli menu. Breakfast, lunch, dinner. Bar. Children's menu. **$**

Washington

Area Code 860

Full-Service Inn

★ ★ ★ ★ ★ **THE MAYFLOWER INN.** *118 Woodbury Rd, Washington (06793). Phone 860/868-9466; fax 860/868-1497. www.mayflowerinn.com.* Just under two hours from New York City in Connecticut's verdant countryside, The Mayflower Inn is a pastoral paradise. Dating from the early 1900s, The Mayflower revives the great tradition of splendid country house hotels. The hotel is set within 28 acres of rolling hills, gurgling streams, stone walls, and lush gardens. Spread among three buildings, the guest rooms and suites bring to mind the English countryside. Four-poster, canopied beds and fireplaces enhance the romantic feel of The Mayflower Inn, perfect for a romantic getaway or a restorative retreat. The hotel's lovely grounds inspire poetry and instill serenity in visitors. The fitness center, pool, and tennis court provide diversions for active-minded guests, while others head straight for the area's well-known main streets lined with antique shops. Completing the heavenly experience is the restaurant, where fresh, local ingredients inspire the creative menu. 25 rooms, 3 story. Children over 12 years only. Check-in 3 pm, check-out 1 pm. Restaurant, bar. Fitness room, spa. Outdoor pool. Tennis. **$$$$**

Waterbury (D-2)

See also Bristol, Meriden, New Britain, Southbury, Woodbury

Settled 1674
Population 108,961

Elevation 290 ft
Area Code 203
Information Waterbury Region Convention & Visitors Bureau, 21 Church St, 06702-2106; phone 203/597-9527 or toll-free 888/588-7880 (outside CT)
Web Site www.wrcvb.com

Waterbury, the fourth-largest city in Connecticut, was once an important manufacturing center for brass-related products. Today, high-technology manufacturing and the banking industry dominate the economy. Waterbury's location near major highways provides quick and direct access to all Eastern cities.

What to See and Do

Brass Mill Center. *495 Union St, Waterbury (06702). I-84, exit 22 or 23. Phone 203/755-5003.* More than 1 million-square-foot indoor mall with many shops, food court, and 12-screen movie theater. (Daily)

Mattatuck Museum. *144 W Main St, Waterbury (06702). Phone 203/753-0381.* Industrial history exhibit, decorative arts, period rooms, paintings and prints by Connecticut artists. (July-Aug, Tues-Sat; rest of year, Tues-Sun; closed holidays) **$$**

Quassy Amusement Park. *2132 Middlebury Rd, Middlebury (06762). 5 miles W on I-84, exit 17, on Hwy 64. Phone 203/758-2913.* More than 30 different rides and activities set against Lake Quassapaug; beach, swimming, boating; miniature golf, picnicking, concession. (Late May-Labor Day, daily; Apr-late May, after Labor Day-Oct, weekends) **$$$$**

Full-Service Hotel

★ ★ ★ **CONNECTICUT GRAND HOTEL.** *3580 E Main St, Waterbury (06705). Phone 203/706-1000; toll-free 800/541-0469; fax 203/755-1555. www.sheraton.com.* 279 rooms, 4 story. Check-out noon. Restaurant, bar. Fitness room. Indoor pool, whirlpool. **$**
🅿 🏃 ⌷

Specialty Lodging

The following lodging establishment is approved by Mobil Travel Guide, but due to its unique and individualized nature has not been given a traditional Mobil Star rating. Included in this listing you may find bed-and-breakfasts, limited-service inns, guest ranches, and other unique hotel properties.

HOUSE ON THE HILL BED & BREAKFAST. *92 Woodlawn Terr, Waterbury (06710). Phone 203/757-9901. www.houseonthehill.biz.* This historic mansion, built in 1888, features a library, gardens, and many fireplaces. 4 rooms, 3 story. Complimentary full breakfast. Check-in 3-6 pm, check-out 11 am. **$$**
🅿

Westport (F-1)

See also Bridgeport, Fairfield, Norwalk, Stamford

Settled 1648
Population 24,410
Elevation 78 ft
Area Code 203
Information Westport/Weston Chamber of Commerce, 60 Church Ln, PO Box 30; phone 203/227-9234
Web Site www.westportchamber.com

Westport is a fashionable community on Long Island Sound 45 miles from New York City. Well-known writers and many successful actors, illustrators, and corporate and advertising executives make their homes here. Westport is surrounded by wooded hills and has three municipal beaches and a state park on the sound.

Special Events

Antique Dealers Outdoor Show and Sale. *180 Post Rd E, Westport (06880). Phone 203/227-9234.* Early Sept.

Levitt Pavilion for the Performing Arts. *Jesup Green, 260 Compo Rd S, Westport (06880). On the Saugatuck River. Phone 203/226-7600.* Nightly free outdoor performances of classical, jazz, pop, rock; dance, children's series. Late June-early Aug.

Westport Country Playhouse. *25 Powers Ct, Westport (06880). Phone 203/227-4177.* Broadway and pre-Broadway presentations by professional companies. Nightly Mon-Sat; matinees Wed and Sat; children's shows Fri. Mid-June-mid-Sept.

Westport Handcrafts Fair. *Staples High School Field House, 70 North Ave, Westport (06880). Phone 203/227-7844.* Features 100 crafts artisans. Memorial Day weekend.

Limited-Service Hotel

★ ★ **WESTPORT INN.** *1595 Post Rd E, Westport (06880). Phone 203/259-5236; toll-free 800/446-8997; fax 203/254-8439. www.westportinn.com.* 116 rooms, 2 story. Restaurant, bar. Fitness room. Indoor pool, whirlpool. **$**

Full-Service Hotel

★ ★ ★ **INN AT NATIONAL HALL.** *2 Post Rd W, Westport (06880). Phone 203/221-1351; toll-free 800/628-4255; fax 203/221-0276. www.innatnational hall.com.* Nestled along the banks of the Saugatuck River in Westport, within walking distance to shops, galleries, and the beach, The Inn at National Hall is perhaps one of the most distinctive properties in New England. Slightly quirky with an *Alice in Wonderland* quality to it, this 1873 Italianate inn has just 15 individually designed rooms gloriously decorated in vibrant colors. Each room lives up to its name, with themes such as the watermelon room and the equestrian suite. River views add an enchanting touch to many of the accommodations, and several chambers boast soaring two-story ceilings and crystal chandeliers. Rather like the house of a very well traveled but slightly eccentric relative, this inn surprises guests at each turn with whimsical accessories from around the world. Imaginations could truly run wild here, and even a ride in the elevator inspires creativity with its library-like murals and mysterious happenings. 15 rooms, 3 story. Complimentary continental breakfast. Check-in 3 pm, check-out 11:30 am. Restaurant. **$$$**

Specialty Lodging

The following lodging establishment is approved by Mobil Travel Guide, but due to its unique and individualized nature has not been given a traditional Mobil Star rating. Included in this listing you may find bed-and-breakfasts, limited-service inns, guest ranches, and other unique hotel properties.

THE INN AT LONGSHORE. *260 Compo Rd S, Westport (06880). Phone 203/226-3316; fax 203/227-5344. www.innatlongshore.com.* Overlooking Long Island Sound, this inn was built as a private estate in 1890. 12 rooms, 3 story. Complimentary continental breakfast. Check-in 3 pm, check-out noon. Restaurant. Outdoor pool. Golf. Tennis. **$**

Restaurants

★ ★ ★ **COBB'S MILL INN.** *12 Old Mill Rd, Weston (06880). Phone 203/227-7221; fax 203/226-1599. www.cobbsmillinn.com.* Excellent service with an elegant, historic ambience. Cuisine is beautifully presented. Seafood, steak menu. Lunch, dinner. Bar. Valet parking. **$$$**

★ ★ **NISTICO'S RED BARN.** *292 Wilton Rd, Westport (06880). Phone 203/222-9549; fax 203/222-8935. www.redbarnrestaurant.com.* American menu. Lunch, dinner, Sun brunch. Closed Dec 24-25. Children's menu. Valet parking. Outdoor seating. **$$$**

Wethersfield (D-3)

See also Avon, Farmington, Hartford, New Britain, Windsor

Settled 1634
Population 25,651
Elevation 45 ft
Area Code 860
Zip 06109
Information Wethersfield Historical Society, 150 Main St; phone 860/529-7656
Web Site www.wethhist.org

Wethersfield, "the most ancient towne in Connecticut," has a rich heritage. Settled by a group of Massachusetts colonists, it became the commercial center of the Connecticut River communities and an important post in the trade between the American colonies and the West Indies. Agriculture, especially corn, rye, and, later, the famous red onion, was the source of Wethersfield's trade. During the Revolutionary War years, notable figures, such as George Washington and Count de Rochambeau, came to Wethersfield and decided upon plans that became part of US history. Many existing buildings date from the Revolutionary War.

With the birth and development of the railroad and the shift of trade to the coastal villages, Wethersfield's importance as an industrial and commercial center declined.

What to See and Do

Buttolph-Williams House. *249 Broad St, Wethersfield (06109). Phone 860/529-0460.* (Circa 1700) Restored building contains fine collection of pewter, delft, fabrics, period furniture. (May-Oct, Wed-Mon, limited hours) **$**

⭐ **Dinosaur State Park.** *400 West St, Rocky Hill (06067). 3 miles S via I-91, exit 23, off West St. Phone 860/529-8423.* While excavating the site of a new building, a stone slab bearing the three-toed tracks of dinosaurs, which roamed the area 200 million years ago, was discovered. Construction was halted, and a 65-acre area was designated a state park. Eventually more than 2,000 prints were unearthed. A geodesic dome was set up over parts of the trackway to protect the find. Visitors are able to examine the crisscrossing tracks and view a skeletal cast and life-size models of the area's prehistoric inhabitants. Nature trails; picnicking. Exhibit center (Tues-Sun; closed Jan 1, Thanksgiving, Dec 25). Park (daily). **$**

First Church of Christ, Congregational United Church of Christ. *250 Main St, Wethersfield (06109). Phone 860/529-1575.* The church was established in 1635; the Meetinghouse (1761; restored 1973) is the third one to stand on or near this site. (Mon-Fri; also by appointment) **FREE**

Hurlburt-Dunham House. *212 Main St, Wethersfield (06109). Phone 860/529-7656.* Georgian house updated in Italianate style. Rich in decoration, includes original Rococo Revival wallpapers, painted ceilings, and a varied collection of furniture. (Mid-Mar-mid-May and mid-Oct-Dec 25, Sat-Sun) **$$**

Webb-Deane-Stevens Museum. *211 Main St, Wethersfield (06109). Phone 860/529-0612.* Consists of three 18th-century houses that stand at the center of old Wethersfield: the Joseph Webb house (1752), the Silas Deane house (1766), and the Isaac Stevens house (1789). The houses have been restored and are furnished with objects to reflect the different ways of life of their owners—a merchant, a diplomat, and a tradesman; also Colonial Revival garden. (May-Oct, Mon, Wed-Sun; rest of year, Sat-Sun) **$$$**

Wethersfield Museum. *Keeney Memorial Cultural Center, 200 Main St, Wethersfield (06109). Phone 860/529-7161.* Changing exhibit galleries; permanent Wethersfield exhibit. (Tues-Sun) **$**

Limited-Service Hotel

★ **BEST WESTERN CAMELOT INN.** *1330 Silas Deane Hwy, Wethersfield (06109). Phone 860/563-2311; toll-free 888/563-3930; fax 860/529-2974. www.bestwestern.com.* 112 rooms, 4 story. Pets accepted, some restrictions; fee. Complimentary continental breakfast. Check-out noon. Bar. **$**
🐾

Windsor (D-3)

See also Enfield, Hartford, Manchester, Stafford Springs, Vernon, Wethersfield, Windsor Locks

Settled 1633
Population 27,817
Elevation 57 ft
Area Code 860
Zip 06095
Information Chamber of Commerce, 261 Broad St, PO Box 9, 06095-0009; phone 860/688-5165; or the Heritage Valley North Central Tourism Bureau, 111 Hazard Ave, Enfield 06082; phone 860/763-2578
Web Site www.windsorcc.org

Windsor was first settled by members of an expeditionary group from the original Plymouth Colony. A farming center since the 17th century, it is only 9 miles north of Hartford. The village is divided by the Farmington River; there is a green and many colonial houses on each side of the river.

What to See and Do

Connecticut Trolley Museum. *58 North Rd, Windsor Locks. In East Windsor at 58 North Rd (Hwy 140); from Windsor Locks proceed NE on I-91 to exit 45, then 3/4 mile E on Hwy 140 (for clarification of directions, phone ahead). Phone 860/627-6540.* Exhibits include more than 50 antique trolley cars from 1894-1949; operating trolleys take visitors on 3-mile ride through countryside; electric passenger trains also operate some weekends. (Memorial Day-Labor Day, daily; rest of year, Sat, Sun, and holidays; closed Thanksgiving, Dec 25) **$$$** On grounds is

Connecticut Fire Museum. *58 North Rd, East Windsor (06088). Phone 860/623-4732.* Collection of fire engines and antique motorcoaches from 1856-1954. (June-Aug, daily; Apr-May and Sept-Oct, Sat-Sun) **$**

First Church in Windsor. *75 Palisado Ave, Windsor (06095). Phone 860/688-7229.* (1630) United Church of Christ Congregational. Classic Georgian-style architecture (1794); cemetery (1633) adjacent. Request key at church office, 107 Palisado Avenue. (Daily) **FREE**

Oliver Ellsworth Homestead. *778 Palisado Ave, Windsor (06095). Phone 860/688-8717.* (1781) Home of one of five men who drafted the Constitution; third Chief Justice of the United States and one of the first senators from Connecticut; Washington and Adams visited the house. Restored to period; many original Ellsworth furnishings. (May-Oct, Tues-Wed, Sat) **$$**

Windsor Historical Society. *96 Palisado Ave, Windsor (06095). Phone 860/688-3813.* Walking tours of the John and Sarah Strong House (1758) and the Dr. Hezekiah Chaffee House (1765); period costumes and furnishings; Puritan cemetery. (Tues-Sat) **$$**

Limited-Service Hotel

★ ★ **COURTYARD BY MARRIOTT.** *1 Day Hill Rd, Windsor (06095). Phone 203/683-0022; toll-free 800/321-2211; fax 203/683-1072. www.courtyard.com.* 149 rooms, 2 story. Check-in 3 pm, check-out noon. High-speed Internet access. Restaurant. Indoor pool, whirlpool. **$**

Windsor Locks (C-3)

See also Enfield, Hartford, Windsor; also see Springfield, MA

Population 12,358
Elevation 80 ft
Area Code 860
Zip 06096
Information Chamber of Commerce, PO Box 257; phone 860/623-9319
Web Site www.wmch.com

What to See and Do

New England Air Museum. *36 Perimeter Rd, Windsor Locks (06096). Adjacent to Bradley International Airport, 3 miles SW via I-91, exit 40, W on Hwy 20 to Hwy 75, follow signs. Phone 860/623-3305.* One of the largest and most comprehensive collections of aircraft and aeronautical memorabilia in the world. More than 80 aircraft on display including bombers, fighters, helicopters, and gliders dating from 1909-present era; movies; jet fighter cockpit simulator. (Daily; closed Jan 1, Thanksgiving, Dec 25) **$$$**

Noden-Reed House & Barn. *58 West St, Windsor Locks (06096). Phone 860/627-9212.* Housed in a 1840 house and a 1825 barn are an antique sleigh bed, 1871 taffeta evening dress, 1884 wedding dress, antique quilts, kitchen utensils, 1880s newspapers and periodicals. (May-Oct, Sun afternoons)

Old Newgate Prison. *115 Newgate Rd, East Granby (06026). 8 miles W on I-91 to exit 40; at junction Newgate Rd and Hwy 120. Phone 860/653-3563.* Site of a copper mine (1707) converted to Revolutionary prison for Tories (1775-1782) and a state prison (until 1827); self-guided tour of underground caverns where prisoners lived. (Mid-May-Oct, Wed-Sun) **$$**

Limited-Service Hotels

★ ★ **DOUBLETREE HOTEL.** *16 Ella Grasso Tpke, Windsor Locks (06096). Phone 860/627-5171; toll-free 800/222-8733; fax 860/627-7029. www.doubletree.com.* This hotel is located just 1 mile from Bradley International and minutes from Old Newgate Prison and Six Flags. 200 rooms, 5 story. Check-in 3 pm, check-out noon. Restaurant, bar. Fitness room. Indoor pool, whirlpool. Airport transportation available. **$**

★ **HOMEWOOD SUITES.** *65 Ella Grasso Tpke, Windsor Locks (06096). Phone 860/627-8463; toll-free 800/225-5466; fax 860/627-9313. www.homewoodsuites .com.* 132 rooms, 3 story, all suites. Pets accepted, some restrictions; fee. Complimentary continental breakfast. Check-in 3 pm, check-out noon. Fitness room. Outdoor pool. Airport transportation available. Business center. **$**

Full-Service Hotel

★ ★ ★ **SHERATON BRADLEY AIRPORT HOTEL.** *1 Bradley International Airport, Windsor Locks (06096). Phone 860/627-5311; toll-free 877/422-5311; fax 860/627-9348. www.sheraton.com/ bradleyairport.* 237 rooms, 8 story. Pets accepted. Check-in 3 pm, check-out noon. Restaurant, bar. Fitness room. Indoor pool. **$**

Woodbury (E-2)

See also Bristol, Danbury, Southbury, Waterbury

Population 1,290
Elevation 264 ft
Area Code 203
Zip 06798

Information Litchfield Hills Visitors Bureau, PO Box 968, Litchfield 06759; phone 860/567-4506
Web Site www.woodbury.org

What to See and Do

Flanders Nature Center. *5 Church Hill Rd, Woodbury (06798). Phone 203/263-3711.* Large conservation area with woodland hiking trails, wildlife marshes; wildflower trails. Self-guided tour; special events include maple syrup demonstration (Mar). (Daily) **FREE**

Glebe House and Gertrude Jekyll Garden. *Hollow Rd, Woodbury (06798). Off Hwy 6. Phone 203/263-2855. www.theglebehouse.org.* (Circa 1770) Minister's farmhouse or *glebe,* where Samuel Seabury was elected America's first Episcopal bishop in 1783; restored with 18th-century furnishings, original paneling; garden designed by Gertrude Jekyll. (Apr-Nov: Wed-Sun afternoons; rest of year: by appointment) **$**

Restaurants

★ ★ **CAROLE PECK'S GOOD NEWS CAFE.** *694 Main St S, Woodbury (06798). Phone 203/266-4663.* American menu. Lunch, dinner. Closed Tues; holidays. Bar. Outdoor seating. **$$**

★ **CURTIS HOUSE.** *506 Main St S, Woodbury (06798). Phone 203/263-2101; fax 203/263-6265. www.thecurtishouse.com.* American menu. Lunch, dinner. Closed holidays. Bar. Children's menu. **$$**

If you're in New England and you have a day or two to spare, you should make the roughly two-hour trek to New York City. The Big Apple must be seen and experienced to be believed. It offers some of the world's finest art museums, avant-garde galleries, electrifying neighborhoods, mouthwatering cuisine, beautiful parks, fantastic shopping, a lively music scene, and much, much more.

New York, NY

2 hours, 118 miles from Hartford, CT

Settled 1615
Population 8,008,278
Elevation 410 ft
Area Code 212, 646, 917
Information New York City Convention & Visitors Bureau, 810 Seventh Ave, New York, NY 10019; phone 212/484-1200
Web Site www.nycvisit.com

New York is the nation's most populous city, the capital of finance, business, communications, theater, and much more. It may not be the center of the universe, but it does occupy a central place in the world's imagination. Certainly, in one way or another, New York affects the lives of nearly every American. While other cities have everything that New York has—from symphonies to slums—no other city has quite the style or sheer abundance. Nowhere are things done in such a grandly American way as in New York City.

Giovanni da Verrazano was the first European to glimpse Manhattan Island (1524), but the area was not explored until 1609, when Henry Hudson sailed up the river that was later named for him, searching for a passage to India. Adriaen Block arrived here in 1613, and the first trading post was established by the Dutch West India Company two years later. Peter Minuit is said to have bought the island from Native Americans for $24 worth of beads and trinkets in 1626,

when New Amsterdam was founded—the biggest real estate bargain in history.

In 1664, the Dutch surrendered to a British fleet and the town was renamed New York in honor of the Duke of York. One of the earliest tests of independence occurred here in 1734 when John Peter Zenger, publisher and editor of the *New York Weekly Journal*, was charged with seditious libel and jailed for making anti-government remarks. Following the Battle of Long Island in 1776, the British occupied the city through the Revolution, until 1783.

On the balcony of Federal Hall at Wall Street, April 30, 1789, George Washington was inaugurated as the first president of the United States, and for a time New York was the country's capital.

When the Erie Canal opened in 1825, New York City expanded vastly as a port. It has since consistently maintained its leadership. In 1898, Manhattan merged with Brooklyn, the Bronx, Queens, and Staten Island. In the next half-century several million immigrants entered the United States here, providing the city with the supply of labor needed for its growth into a major focal point. Each wave of immigrants has brought new customs, culture, and life, which makes New York City the varied metropolis it is today.

New York continues to capitalize on its image as the Big Apple, attracting more than 39 million visitors each year, and its major attractions continue to thrive in style. These, of course, are centered in Manhattan; however, vacationers should not overlook the wealth of sights and activities the other boroughs have to offer. Brooklyn has Coney Island, the New York Aquarium, the superb Brooklyn History Museum, Brooklyn Botanic Garden, Brooklyn Children's Museum, and the famous landmark, Brooklyn Bridge. The Bronx is noted for its excellent Botanical Garden and Zoo and Yankee Stadium. Flushing Meadows-Corona Park, in Queens, was the site of two World's Fairs; nearby is Shea Stadium, home of the New York Mets. Uncrowded Staten Island has Richmond Town Restoration, a re-creation of 18th-century New York, rural farmland, beaches, salt marshes, and wildlife preserves.

New York Fun Facts

- Gennaro Lombardi opened the first pizzeria in the country in New York City in 1895.
- Babe Ruth hit his first home run in Yankee Stadium in the first game ever played there.
- The New York Stock Exchange began in 1792 when 24 brokers met under a buttonwood tree facing 68 Wall Street.
- As late as the 1840s, thousands of pigs roamed Wall Street to consume garbage—an early sanitation system.
- Downtown Manhattan was the nation's first capital.
- Macy's, the world's largest store, covers 2.1 million square feet of space and stocks over 500,000 different items.
- The nation's largest public Halloween parade is the Greenwich Village Halloween Parade.
- New York was the first state to require license plates on automobiles.
- There are 6,374.6 miles of streets in New York City.

Weather

The average mean temperatures for New York are 34° F in winter; 52° F in spring; 75° F in summer; and 58° F in fall. In summer the temperature is rarely above 90° F, but the humidity can be high. In winter the temperature is rarely lower than 10° F but has gone as low as -14° F. Average mean temperatures are listed from surveys taken at the National Weather Bureau station in Central Park.

Theater

New York is the theatrical headquarters of the United States, and theater here is an experience not to be missed. Broadway, a 36-square-block area (41st to 53rd streets and sixth to ninth avenues), offers standard full-scale plays and musicals, more than 30 of them on any particular evening. Off-Broadway, not confined to one area, is less expensive and more experimental, giving new talent a chance at exposure and established talent an opportunity to try new and different projects, such as the New York Shakespeare

Festival (see SEASONAL EVENTS). Even less expensive and more daring is off-off-Broadway, consisting of dozens of small theaters in storefronts, lofts, and cellars, producing every imaginable type of theater. There are a number of ways to obtain tickets, ranging from taking a pre-arranged package theater tour to walking up to the box office an hour before curtain for returned and unclaimed tickets. TicketMaster outlets (phone 212/307-7171), hotel theater desks, and ticket brokers will have tickets to several shows for the box office price plus a service charge. All Broadway theaters accept phone reservations charged to major credit cards. An On Stage Hotline can be reached at 212/768-1818. The Times Square Ticket Center (a booth with large banners proclaiming "TKTS") at 47th St and Broadway has same-day tickets at half-price for most shows (daily) and for matinees (Wed, Sat, Sun). There is also a downtown branch located at the South Street Seaport, open Mon-Sat, for same-day evening performances only. Same-day half-price tickets to music and dance events may be obtained at the Music & Dance Booth, at 42nd St and Avenue of the Americas in Bryant Park. *The New Yorker* and *New York* magazines carry extensive listings of the week's entertainment; the Friday edition of *The New York Times* also reports weekend availability of tickets.

Additional Visitor Information

Contact the New York Convention and Visitors Bureau, 810 Seventh Ave, 10019; phone 212/484-1222. The bureau has free maps, "twofers" to Broadway shows, bulletins, and brochures on attractions, events, shopping, restaurants, and hotels. For events of the week, visitors should get copies of *The New Yorker* and *New York* magazines and *The New York Times.*

Public Transportation

Subway and elevated trains, buses (New York City Transit Authority), phone 718/330-3322 or 718/330-1234. The subway system, which carries more than 4 million people on weekdays, covers every borough except Staten Island, which has its own transportation system. Maps of the system are posted at every station and on every car.

Airport Information

La Guardia, in Queens 8 miles northeast of Manhattan; **Kennedy International,** in Queens 15 miles southeast of Manhattan; **Newark International,** 16 miles southwest of Manhattan in New Jersey.

NEIGHBORHOODS

CHINATOWN

The only truly ethnic neighborhood still thriving in Manhattan, Chinatown is filled with teeming streets, jostling crowds, bustling restaurants, exotic markets, and prosperous shops. Once limited to a small enclave contained in the six blocks between the Bowery and Mulberry, Canal and Worth streets (now known as "traditional Chinatown"), it has burst these boundaries in recent years to spread north of Canal Street into Little Italy and east into the Lower East Side.

Chinatown is the perfect neighborhood for haphazard wandering. In traditional Chinatown, especially, every twist or turn of the small, winding streets brings mounds of shiny fish—live carp, eels, and crabs—piles of fresh produce—cabbage, ginger root, Chinese broccoli—or displays of pretty, colorful objects—toys, handbags, knickknacks. Bakeries selling everything from moon cakes and almond cookies to "cow ears" (chips of fried dough) and pork buns are everywhere, along with the justifiably famous Chinatown Ice Cream Factory (65 Bayard St, near Mott), selling every flavor of ice cream from ginger to mango.

Chinese men, accompanied by only a handful of women, began arriving in New York in the late 1870s. Many were former transcontinental railroad workers who came to escape the persecution they were experiencing on the West Coast. But they weren't especially welcomed on the East Coast either, and soon thereafter, the violent "tong wars" between criminal Chinese gangs helped lead to the Exclusion Acts of 1882, 1888, 1902, and 1924, forbidding further Chinese immigration. Chinatown became a "bachelor society," almost devoid of women and children—a situation that continued until the lifting of immigration quotas in 1965.

Today, Chinatown's estimated population of 100,000 is made up of two especially large groups—the well-established Cantonese community, who have been in New York for over a century, and the Fujianese community, a much newer and poorer immigration group who come from the Fujian Province on the southern coast of mainland China. The Cantonese own many of the prosperous shops and restaurants in traditional Chinatown, whereas the Fujianese have set up rice-noodle shops, herbal medicine shops, and outdoor markets along Broadway and neighboring streets between Canal Street and the Manhattan Bridge.

To learn more about the history of Chinatown, visit the Museum of Chinese in the Americas (70 Mulberry St, at Bayard). To get a good meal, explore almost any street, with Mott Street—the neighborhood's main thoroughfare—holding an especially large number. Pell Street is especially known for its barber and beauty shops and for its Buddhist Temple (4 Pell St). The neighborhood's biggest festival is the Chinese New Year, celebrated between mid-January and early February; then, the streets come even more alive than usual with dragon dances, lion dances, and fireworks.

TriBeCa

Short for *Triangle Below Canal*, **TriBeCa** is a former industrial district encompassing about 40 blocks between Canal, Chambers, and West streets, and Broadway. Like SoHo, its more fashionable cousin to the north, the neighborhood discarded its working-class roots years ago and now has its share of expensive restaurants and boutiques. Upper-middle-class residents have replaced factory workers, and avant-garde establishments have replaced sweatshops.

Nonetheless, TriBeCa is much quieter than SoHo—and many other sections of Manhattan—and, in parts, still retains its 19th-century feel, complete with cobblestone streets and dusty façades. After dark, especially, much of the area seems close to deserted.

TriBeCa's main thoroughfares are Broadway, West Broadway, and Church Street, three wide roads comfortable for strolling. West Broadway was originally built to relieve the congestion of Broadway and is home to a few art galleries, including the SoHo Photo Gallery (15 White St at W Broadway), a cooperative gallery featuring the work of 100-plus members. At Church and Walker streets reigns the sleek new TriBeCa Grand, the neighborhood's first upscale hotel.

Also well known is the TriBeCa Film Center, housed in the landmark Martinson Coffee Company warehouse (375 Greenwich St at Franklin St). The center was started in 1989 by actor Robert De Niro, who wanted to create a site where filmmakers could talk business, screen films, and socialize. Today, the center houses the offices of several major producers and the TriBeCa Grill, a chic eatery usually filled with more celebrity-watchers than celebrities. At Greenwich and Harrison streets stand the Harrison Houses, a group of nine restored Federal-style homes. Several were designed by John McComb, Jr., New York's first architect. East of the houses, at the northwest corner of Harrison and Hudson streets, find the former New York Mercantile Exchange. In this five-story building, complete with gables and a tower, $15,000 worth of eggs would change hands in an hour around the turn of the century. Today, TriBeCa is still the city's distribution center for eggs, cheese, and butter; a few remaining wholesalers cluster around Duane Park, one block south of the former exchange, between Hudson and Greenwich streets.

At the southern end of TriBeCa is Chambers Street, where you'll find the Borough of Manhattan Community College (199 Chambers St, near West St). At the western end of Chambers, cross over West Street via the TriBeCa Bridge to reach a public recreation center called Pier 25.

SoHo

Short for *South of Ho*uston (HOW-stun), SoHo is New York's trendiest neighborhood, filled with an impossible number of upscale eateries, fancy boutiques, of-the-moment bars, and, most recently, a few astronomically expensive hotels. Contained in just 25 blocks bounded by Houston and Canal streets, Lafayette, and West Broadway, SoHo attracts trend followers and tourists by the thousands, especially on weekend afternoons, when the place sometimes feels like one giant open-air bazaar.

From the late 1800s to the mid-1900s, SoHo was primarily a light manufacturing district, but starting in the 1960s, most of the factories moved out and artists—attracted by the area's low rents and loft spaces—began moving in. Soon thereafter, the art galleries arrived, and then the shops and restaurants. Almost overnight, SoHo became too expensive for the artists—and, more recently, the art galleries—who had originally settled the place, and a mecca for big-bucks shoppers from all over the world.

Nonetheless, SoHo still has plenty to offer art lovers. Broadway is lined with one first-rate museum after another, while Mercer and Greene streets, especially, boast a large number of galleries. Some top spots on Broadway include the Museum for African Art (593 Broadway), presenting an excellent array of changing exhibits and the New Museum for Contemporary Art (583 Broadway), one of the oldest, best-known, and most controversial art spaces in SoHo. To find out who's exhibiting what and where in SoHo, pick up a copy of the *Art Now Gallery Guide*, available at many bookstores and galleries.

SoHo is also home to an extraordinary number of luscious cast-iron buildings. Originally meant to serve as a cheap substitute for stone buildings, the cast-iron façades were an American invention, prefabricated in a variety of styles—from Italian Renaissance to Classical Greek—and bolted onto the front of iron-frame structures. Most of SoHo's best cast-iron gems can be found along Broadway; keep an eye out for the Haughwout Building (488 Broadway), the Singer Building (561 Broadway), and the Guggenheim Museum SoHo (575 Broadway).

Top thoroughfares for shopping include Prince and Spring streets, Broadway, and West Broadway. Numerous clothing and accessory boutiques are located along all these streets; West Broadway also offers several interesting bookstores. For antiques and furnishings, check out Lafayette Street; for craft and toy stores, try Greene and Mercer streets.

Restaurants and bars line almost every street in SoHo, but one especially lively nexus is the intersection of Grand Street and West Broadway. West Broadway itself is also home to a large number of eateries, some of which offer outdoor dining in the summer.

EAST VILLAGE

Once considered part of the Lower East Side, the East Village is considerably scruffier and more rambunctious than its better-known sister to the West. For years, it was the refuge of immigrants and the working class, but in the 1950s, struggling writers, actors, and artists—forced out of Greenwich Village by rising rents— began moving in. First came such well-known names as Willem de Kooning and W. H. Auden, followed by the beatniks, the hippies, the yippies, the rock groups, the punk musicians, and the fashion designers.

Only in the 1980s did the neighborhood start to gentrify, as young professionals moved in, bringing with them upscale restaurants and smart shops. Ever since, New York's continuously rising rents have forced out many of the younger, poorer, and more creative types that the East Village was known for just two decades ago. Nonetheless, the neighborhood has not completely succumbed and offers an interesting mix between the cutting edge and the mainstream.

The heart of the East Village is St. Mark's Place, an always-thronging thoroughfare where you'll find everything from punked-out musicians to well-heeled business types, leather shops to sleek bistros. Many of the street's noisiest addresses are between Third and Second avenues; many of its most appealing, farther east. At the eastern end of St. Mark's Place stretches Tompkins Square Park, once known for its drug dealers, now for its families and jungle gyms. Some of the best of the many interesting little shops that fill the East Village can be found on Avenue A near the park; others line Seventh and Ninth streets east of Second Avenue.

The neighborhood's second major thoroughfare, Second Avenue, was home to many lively Yiddish theaters early in the 20th century. All are gone now, but the landmark Second Avenue Deli (at 10th St)—known for its over-stuffed sandwiches—commemorates the street's past with stars in the sidewalk. At Second Avenue and East Tenth Street is St.-Mark's-in-the-Bowery, an historic church where Peter Stuyvesant—the last of the Dutch governors who ruled Manhattan in the 1600s—is buried. The church is also known for its poetry readings, performance art, and leftist politics.

On the western edge of the East Village sprawls Astor Place, home to Cooper Union—the city's first free educational institution, now a design school—and a huge cube sculpture oddly balanced on one corner. On Lafayette Street at the southern end of Astor Place reigns the Joseph Papp Public Theater, housed in an imposing columned building that was once the Astor Library. The theater is renowned for its first-run productions and for Shakespeare in the Park, a free festival that it produces every summer in Central Park.

GREENWICH VILLAGE

Although New York's fabled bohemian neighborhood has gone seriously upscale and more mainstream in recent decades, evidence of its iconoclastic past can still be found in its many narrow streets, off-Broadway theaters, cozy coffee shops, lively jazz clubs, and tiny bars. Stretching from 14th Street south to Houston Street, and from Broadway west to the Hudson River, Greenwich Village remains one of the city's best places for idle wandering, people watching, boutique browsing, and conversing over glasses of cabernet or cups of cappuccino.

Washington Square Park anchors the neighborhood to the east and, though it's nothing special to look at, is still the heart of the Village. On a sunny afternoon, everyone comes here: kids hot-dogging on skateboards, students strumming guitars, old men playing chess, and lovers entwined in each other's arms. Bordering the edges of the park are a mix of elegant townhouses and New York University buildings.

Just south and west of Washington Square, find Bleecker and MacDougal streets, home to coffee shops and bars once frequented by the likes of James Baldwin, Jack Kerouac, Allen Ginsberg, and James Agee. Le Figaro (corner of Bleecker and MacDougal) and the San Remo (93 MacDougal) were favorites back then and still attract crowds today, albeit mostly made up of tourists.

A bit farther west is Seventh Avenue South, where you'll find the Village Vanguard (178 Seventh Ave S, at 11th St)—the oldest and most venerable jazz club in the city. Also nearby are the Blue Note (131 West 3rd St, near 6th Ave), New York's premier jazz supper club, and Smalls (183 West 10th St near 7th Ave S), one of the best places to catch up-and-coming talent.

At the corner of Seventh Avenue South and Christopher Street stands Christopher Park, where a George Segal sculpture of two gay couples commemorates the Stonewall Riots, which marked the advent of the gay-rights movement. The Stonewall Inn, where the demonstration began in 1969, once stood directly across from the park at 51 Christopher, and Christopher Street itself is still lined with many gay establishments.

At the corner of Sixth Avenue and West 10th Street reigns the gothic towers and turrets of Jefferson Market Library, a stunning maroon-and-white building that dates to 1876. Across the street from the library is Balducci's (424 Sixth Ave), a famed gourmet food shop.

CHELSEA

Primarily middle-class residential and still somewhat industrial, Chelsea—stretching between 14th and 30th streets, from Sixth Avenue to the Hudson River—is not the most tourist-oriented of areas. However, the neighborhood does offer an exciting, avant-garde arts scene, as well as many lovely quiet blocks lined with attractive row houses and rustling trees. A new gay community has moved in recently, bringing with it trendy cafés, shops, and bars, while an enormous, state-of-the-art sports complex, the Chelsea Piers, beckons from the river's edge (between 18th and 22nd streets).

Most of Chelsea was once owned by Captain Thomas Clarke, whose grandson, Clement Charles Clarke, laid out the residential district in the early 1800s. Clement Charles was also a scholar and a poet who wrote the famous poem beginning with the line, "Twas the night before Christmas..." Another of Clement Charles's legacies is the General Theological Seminary, a peaceful enclave of ivy-covered buildings bounded by the block between Ninth and Tenth avenues and 20th and 21st streets.

Also on the western edge of Chelsea are many of the city's foremost art galleries, which began moving here in the early 1990s as rents in SoHo—their former home—began skyrocketing. An especially large number can be found on West 21st and 22nd streets between Tenth and Eleventh avenues; among them are the Paula Cooper Gallery (534 West 21st St), the Maximum Protech Gallery (511 West 22nd St), and the Dia Center for the Arts (548 West 22nd St). One of the pioneers of the area, the Dia Center is really more a museum than an art gallery and usually hosts a variety of eye-popping exhibits, along with an open-air sculpture garden on the roof.

Most of Chelsea's thriving shops, restaurants, and bars—some of which are predominantly gay, some not—stand along Sixth and Eighth avenues between 14th and 23rd streets. Some of the neighborhood's prettiest blocks, lined with elegant row houses, are West 20th, 21st, and 22nd streets between Eighth and Tenth avenues. Also, be sure to take a gander at the Chelsea Hotel (222 W 23rd St, near Eighth Ave), a maroon-colored landmark that has all-black gables, chimneys, and balconies. Built in 1884, the Chelsea has housed dozens of artists, writers, and musicians over the years, including Arthur Miller, Jackson Pollock, Bob Dylan, and Sid Vicious.

Just north of Chelsea lies the underground Pennsylvania Station (Seventh Ave at 32nd St), topped with circular Madison Square Garden, and the General Post Office (Eighth Ave, between 31st and 33rd sts)— a gorgeous building designed by McKim, Mead & White in 1913. The Garment District, centering on Seventh Avenue in the 30s, also begins here.

GRAMERCY PARK AND ENVIRONS

Largely residential, the East Side between 14th and 34th streets is home to two inviting squares—Gramercy Park at Irving Place between 20th and 21st streets, and Union Square at Broadway between 14th and 17th streets. A long line of trendy restaurants and bars beckon along Park Avenue between 17th and 23rd streets, while a bit farther north is Little India, centered on Lexington Avenue between 27th and 29th streets. The neighborhood lacks the vibrancy of some of Manhattan's better-known neighborhoods but has a quiet charm of its own, with residents ranging from young professionals to middle-class families to the upper middle class.

One of the most fashionable squares in the city, Gramercy Park is composed of elegant brownstones and townhouses surrounding an enclosed green to which only residents have the key. At the southern edge of the park stand two especially impressive buildings—the National Arts Club (15 Gramercy Park South) and the Players Club (16 Gramercy Park South). The National Arts Club was once home to New York governor Samuel Tilden, whereas the Players Club once belonged to the great thespian Edwin Booth, the brother of the man who assassinated Abraham Lincoln. Just east of Gramercy Park stands Theodore Roosevelt's Birthplace (28 East 20th St), a museum filled with the world's largest collection of Roosevelt memorabilia.

Farther south, find Union Square, a booming park surrounded by sleek megastores, upscale restaurants, and fashionable bars. The popular Farmers' Greenmarket operates in the park on Monday, Wednesday, Friday, and Saturday mornings, and free concerts and other events sometimes take place here during the summer. To the immediate east of the square are several excellent off-Broadway theaters.

Broadway between Union Square and Madison Square (between 23rd and 26th streets, Fifth and Madison avenues) was once known as the "Ladies Mile" because of the many fashionable department stores located here. Many were housed in extravagant cast-iron buildings, which still stand, now holding more modern emporiums.

At the corner of Broadway and 23rd Street is the famous 1902 Flatiron building, built in the shape of a narrow triangle and only 6 feet wide at its northern end. Meanwhile, reigning over Madison Park to the east are the enormous Art Deco Metropolitan Life Insurance Building (Madison Avenue, between 23rd and 25th streets) and the impossibly ornate Appellate Division of the New York State Supreme Court (Madison Avenue at 25th Street).

Still farther north and east lies Little India. Though not as thriving as it once was, it still houses a number of excellent Indian restaurants, sari shops, and spice stores, which attract shoppers from all over the city.

MIDTOWN

Stretching from 34th Street to 57th Street, the Harlem River to the East River, Midtown is the heart of Manhattan. Most of the city's skyscrapers are here, along with most of its offices, major hotels, famous shops, the Empire State Building, Times Square, the Broadway theaters, the Museum of Modern Art, Rockefeller Center, Grand Central Station, and the New York Public Library.

Fifth Avenue is the center of Midtown, dividing the city into east and west. Although nothing more than a line on a map as late as 1811, the thoroughfare had become New York's most fashionable address by the Civil War. It began to turn commercial in the early 1900s and is now lined with mostly shops and office buildings.

Towering over the southern end of Midtown is the Empire State Building (350 Fifth Ave, at 34th St), one of the world's most famous skyscrapers. Built in the early 1930s, the building took just 14 months to erect and remains an Art Deco masterpiece.

Forty-Second Street is lined with one major attraction after another. On the corner of Third Avenue soars the magnificent Chrysler Building, another Art Deco masterpiece; Grand Central Station, whose magnificent concourse was recently restored to the tune of $200 million, is at Lexington Avenue. At Fifth Avenue beckons the New York Public Library, behind which spreads Bryant Park, where many free events are held during the summer months.

West of Seventh Avenue along 42nd Street begins Times Square, which stretches north to 48th Street along the Seventh Avenue-Broadway nexus. The best time to come here is at night, when the huge state-of-the-art neon lights that line the square begin to shine. Much cleaned up in recent years, Times Square is also a good place to catch street performers and, of course, Broadway theater. Many of the city's most famous theaters are located on the side streets around Times Square.

North and a little east of Times Square, Rockefeller Center reigns as an Art Deco complex stretching between 48th and 51st streets, Sixth and Fifth avenues. Built by John D. Rockefeller during the height of the Depression, Rockefeller Center is home to the landmark Radio City Music Hall, the NBC Studios, and a famed skating rink filled with outdoor enthusiasts during the winter months.

Along Fifth Avenue just south and north of Rockefeller Center, find some of the city's most famous shops—Saks Fifth Avenue, Tiffany's, Steuben Glass, and Cartier, along with Trump Tower at 56th Street. Between 50th and 51st streets soars the Gothic Saint Patrick's Cathedral, the largest Roman Catholic cathedral in the United States; the Museum of Modern Art, a must-stop for any art lover, is on 53rd Street just west of Fifth.

UPPER EAST SIDE

Long associated with wealth, much of the Upper East Side—stretching from 57th Street north to 106th Street and Fifth Avenue east to the East River—is filled with elegant mansions and brownstones, clubs, and museums. Many of the city's most famous museums—including the Metropolitan Museum of Art—are located here, along with several posh hotels and Gracie Mansion, home to New York City's mayor.

But the neighborhood is about more than just wealth. Remnants of what was once a thriving German community can be found along the 86th Street-Second Avenue nexus, while a Puerto Rican and Latin community begins in the upper 80s, east of Lexington Avenue. At the corner of 96th Street and Third Avenue is a surprising sight—the Islamic Cultural Center, a modern, gold-domed mosque flanked by a skinny minaret.

Many of the Upper East Side's cultural institutions are located on Fifth Avenue, facing Central Park, along what is known as "Museum Mile." The Frick Collection, housing the private art collection of the former 19th-century industrialist Henry Clay Frick, marks the mile's southernmost end, at 70th Street. El Museo del Barrio, dedicated to the art and culture of Latin America, marks the northernmost end, at 104th Street. In between reign the grand Metropolitan Museum of Art (at 82nd St), huge flags flapping out front, and the circular, Frank Lloyd Wright-designed Guggenheim Museum (at 88th St)—to name just two.

The Plaza Hotel beckons from the southern end of the Upper East Side (Fifth Ave, between 58th and 59th sts). This magnificent French Renaissance-style edifice was built in 1907 and is now owned by Donald Trump. Directly across Fifth Avenue from the hotel, FAO Schwarz is an imaginative toy store that's as much fun for adults as it is for kids. Central Park is directly across 59th Street. Horse-drawn hansoms and their drivers congregate along the streets here, waiting hopefully for tourists interested in taking a clip-clopping tour. The small but state-of-the-art Central Park Zoo can be found in the park near Fifth Avenue and 65th Street.

Shoppers will want to take a gander at the many upscale boutiques lining Madison Avenue between 57th and 90th streets, or take a stroll over to Bloomingdale's (Lexington Ave at 59th St). Fifty-Seventh Street holds numerous world-famous galleries, including PaceWildenstein (32 E 57th St) and Andre Emmerich (41 E 57th St), as well as such popular tourist stops as Niketown (6 E 57th St). The infamous St. Patrick's Day Parade, attracting hordes of rowdy revelers, travels down Fifth Avenue from 86th Street to 44th Street every March 17th.

Harlem

Stretching from 110th to 168th streets, between the Harlem and Hudson rivers, Harlem is in the midst of a renaissance. After years of being known primarily for its grinding poverty, drugs, and despair, the historic African-American neighborhood is sprucing itself up, attracting mainstream businesses such as Starbucks and Ben & Jerry's, and becoming home once again to the middle class—African-American and white.

Harlem can be divided in two: west-central Harlem, which is primarily African-American, and east Harlem, home to many Latinos and a smaller number of Italians. Between 110th and 125th streets west of Morningside Park is Morningside Heights, where Columbia University is located. Washington Heights, north of 155th Street, is home to Fort Tyron Park and the Cloisters, which houses the medieval collection of the Metropolitan Museum of Art.

First a farming community and then an affluent white suburb, Harlem began attracting African-American residents after the construction of the IRT subway in 1901, and soon became the nation's premier African-American neighborhood. The Harlem Renaissance boomed during the 1920s and 1930s, attracting writers and intellectuals such as Langston Hughes and W. E. B. DuBois, and the streets were packed with nightclubs, dance halls, and jazz clubs. Everything changed, however, with the Depression, when poverty took a stronghold that continues in many parts of the neighborhood today. When exploring Harlem, it's best to stick to the main thoroughfares.

The heart of Harlem is 125th Street, where you'll find a new Magic Johnson Theater complex, several restaurants and sweet shops offering soul food and baked goods, and the famed Apollo Theater (253 W 125th St). Nearly every major jazz, blues, R&B, and soul artist to come along performed here, and the theater still presents its famed Amateur Night every Wednesday. Just down the street from the Apollo is the Studio Museum of Harlem (144 West 125th St), a first-class fine arts institution spread over several floors of a turn-of-the-century building.

Another Harlem landmark is the Schomburg Center for Research in Black Culture (Lenox Ave at 135th St), founded by Arthur C. Schomburg, a Puerto Rican of African descent who was told as a child that his race had no history. Although primarily a library, the center also houses a large exhibit area where a wide array of changing exhibits is presented.

Not far from Columbia University, which is centered on Broadway and 116th Street, the Cathedral of St. John the Divine (Amsterdam Ave at 112th St), is the world's largest Gothic cathedral, said to be big enough to fit both Notre Dame and Chartres inside. Another major attraction nearby is Grant's Tomb (122nd St at Riverside Dr), an imposing mausoleum sitting high on a bluff overlooking the Hudson.

BROOKLYN

The largest borough in population and second largest in area, Brooklyn was a city in its own right—separate from New York—up until 1898. Brooklyn had its own city hall, central park, downtown shops, and cultural attractions, which helps account for the unusual amount the borough has to offer the visitor today. Brooklyn is also home to multiple ethnic groups, socioeconomic groups, and neighborhoods, one of which—Coney Island—is world famous.

Brooklyn Heights and Williamsburg are located at the northern end of Brooklyn, closest to Manhattan. Brooklyn Heights is quiet, upper-middle-class, and dignified, filled with lovely brownstones, historic buildings, and the wide riverside Promenade, which offers magnificent views of the Manhattan skyline and New York Harbor. Williamsburg was once inhabited mostly by Jewish immigrants and is still home to the Satmarer Hasidim, a major orthodox sect. Today the area is better known for its large, young, arts-oriented population. Along Bedford Avenue, especially, find a plethora of lively, inexpensive restaurants, bars, art galleries, and shops.

Bordering Brooklyn Heights is downtown Brooklyn, home to a number of imposing government buildings that date back to the days when Brooklyn was a city in its own right. The Greek Revival Borough Hall, at the intersection of Joralemon, Fulton, and Court streets, was once Brooklyn's City Hall and is still filled with government offices. Not far away is the New York Transit Museum (Schermerhorn St at Boerum Pl), an excellent place to learn the story behind the New York subway.

Near the center of Brooklyn sprawls Prospect Park, one of the city's loveliest retreats. Spread out over 525 acres of forests and meadows, the park was designed by Frederick Law Olmsted and Calvert Vaux, the two men who also planned Central Park in Manhattan. Brooklyn's foremost cultural attractions—the Brooklyn Museum of Art (200 Eastern Pkwy, at Washington Ave) and the Brooklyn Botanic Gardens (1000 Washington Ave, near Eastern Pkwy)—are located on the eastern edge of the park. The northwestern edge is Park Slope, a genteel neighborhood filled with elegant Victorian brownstones, now mostly inhabited by urban professionals with young children.

At the far southern end of Brooklyn, you'll find three most unusual neighborhoods—Coney Island, Brighton Beach, and Sheepshead Bay. Once home to a famed amusement park, Coney Island still beckons with an idiosyncratic collection of creaky historic rides, tawdry newer ones, the first-rate Aquarium for Wildlife Conservation (West Eighth St, between the Boardwalk and Surf Ave), and a wide, windswept boardwalk that stretches along a beach. The popular Mermaid Parade, featuring eye-popping costumes, takes place here every June. Next door to Coney Island is Brighton Beach, home to a thriving a Russian community, and Sheepshead Bay, a tiny port filled with fishing boats, retirees, and seafood restaurants.

QUEENS

New York City's biggest borough, Queens is home to many large and vibrant ethnic neighborhoods as well as to some important cultural and historic gems. It also holds John F. Kennedy International and La Guardia airports and Shea Stadium, the ballpark of the New York Mets. At the western end of Queens stretch Long Island City and Astoria, both just a stop or two away from Manhattan on the subway.

Although largely an industrial area, Long Island City has recently become known for its burgeoning artistic community and holds a number of first-rate galleries and museums. Foremost among them are the Isamu Noguchi Garden Museum (32-37 Vernon Blvd, at 33rd Rd), containing many works of the late great sculptor, and the P.S.1 Contemporary Art Center (22-25 Jackson Ave, at 46th St), a premier showcase for art on the cutting edge.

Meanwhile, Astoria is home to a large Greek population, as well as to an increasing number of Pakistani, Italian, and Latino residents. Along 30th Avenue and Broadway between 31st and Steinway streets, you'll find many Greek restaurants, food shops, and bakeries; the American Museum of the Moving Image (34-12 36th St) is also nearby. Astoria was once the site of the Astoria Movie Studios, which produced such legends as Rudolf Valentino and Gloria Swanson; renovated and reopened in the late 1970s, the studios are now known as the Kaufman-Astoria Studios. Travel a bit farther east on the No. 7 subway line—the borough's main transportation artery—to find Jackson Heights. Nicknamed the "cornfield of Queens" in the early 1900s, Jackson Heights now holds large Colombian and Indian populations, as well as smaller Peruvian, Uruguayan, Filipino, and Thai populations. A number of excellent Colombian restaurants are located along Roosevelt Avenue near 82nd and 83rd streets; tasty Indian food can be sampled between 70th and 74th streets near Roosevelt Avenue and Broadway.

East of Jackson Heights, Flushing Meadows-Corona Park is an enormous green oasis that housed both the 1939 and 1964 World's Fairs. The park's Unisphere—a shining, 140-foot-high hollow globe—dates back to the 1964 fair, as do the buildings that now contain the Queens Museum of Art and the New York Hall of Science. The Queens Wildlife Center and Shea Stadium are also in the park.

Beyond the park, find Flushing, home to a clutch of historic buildings and large Asian communities. The historic buildings include the Bowne House (37-01 Bowne St), used for illegal Quaker meetings in the 1660s, and the 1785 Kingsland House (143-35 37th Ave), now the headquarters of the Queens Historical Society. The Asian community is centered on Main and Union streets; Asian restaurants serving delicious, authentic food are everywhere here.

THE BRONX

New York City's second-smallest borough both in size and population, the Bronx is also the only one attached to the mainland. In it you'll discover such legendary New York institutions as the Bronx Zoo, the New York Botanical Gardens, Yankee Stadium, and some of the city's biggest parks.

However, in the 1970s and 1980s, the borough also garnered a reputation for urban decay, as headlining stories involving murder, drugs, and arson seemed to come out of here daily. In more recent years, though, more than $1 billion in public funds has been spent on the South Bronx—where most of the decay occurred—and the place is in better shape now than it has been in years. Elsewhere in the borough, large residential neighborhoods have always flourished, most working- and middle-class (City Island, Co-Op City), a few quite exclusive (Riverdale, Fieldston).

First settled in 1644 by a Scandinavian named Jonas Bronck, the area soon became known as "The Broncks," and remained a predominantly agricultural community up until the late 1800s. But then the Third Avenue Elevated Railway arrived, and by 1900, the borough's population had soared to 200,000. During the 1920s and 1930s, grand Art Deco apartment buildings sprang up along the wide thoroughfare called the Grand Concourse—a considerably more dilapidated version of which still exists today.

The New York Botanical Garden and Bronx Zoo sit adjacent to each other in the heart of the Bronx. Since they're both enormous, however, it's hard to visit them both in one day. Instead, opt for one of the two, and then head to Belmont, an Italian community just west of the zoo. One of the city's older and more established ethnic neighborhoods, it is packed with Italian restaurants, pastry shops, bakeries, butcher shops, and food markets.

Also in the Bronx is Van Cortlandt Park, which, at 2 square miles, is one of the city's largest parks. In its northernmost section sits the Van Cortlandt House Museum, a charming 18th-century mansion that once belonged to a wealthy landowner.

Across Jerome Avenue from the park stretches Woodlawn Cemetery, a lush 19th-century burial ground filled with rolling hills, meandering walkways, mausoleums, and tombs. Author Herman Melville, financier Jay Gould, and musicians Duke Ellington and Miles Davis are all buried here.

At the northern end of the Bronx reigns City Island, one of New York City's more unusual communities. A sailor's haven that had once hoped to become an important port, City Island is still home to a small shipbuilding industry. The place had only one main street—City Island Avenue—which is lined with a number of fish restaurants ranging in style from simple to old-fashioned elaborate.

STATEN ISLAND

Significantly more rural and suburban than the four other New York City boroughs, Staten Island is also predominantly white, politically conservative, and mostly working-and middle-class. Many residents own their own homes here, complete with tidy front lawns and garages—something you don't see much in the rest of the city. Unless you have access to a car, Staten Island is also quite difficult to explore. Buses run much less frequently and have more ground to cover than they do elsewhere in the city, making travel a time-consuming affair.

At 14 miles long by 7 miles wide, Staten Island was originally settled by Native Americans who successfully fought off the Dutch until 1661. Later, it became a military camp for the British during the Revolutionary War and then remained predominantly rural throughout the 1800s and early 1900s. Even as late as 1964, when the Verrazano-Narrows Bridge was completed, connecting the borough to the rest of the city, Staten Island was largely undeveloped.

The Staten Island Ferry is the borough's biggest attraction, carrying about 3 1/2 million visitors back and forth every year, with few actually disembarking to explore the Staten Island side. Rides on the ferry are free, and the views they offer of Manhattan and New York Harbor are spectacular, especially at night.

The ferry docks at St. George, a small and often empty town with many deserted storefronts. About a mile away is the Snug Harbor Cultural Center (1000 Richmond Terrace; take the S40 bus), an odd complex of buildings that was once a home for retired sailors. Today, the center holds several galleries, a botanical garden, and a Chinese scholars' garden.

In the center of Staten Island stretches the Greenbelt, a 2,500-acre nature preserve made up of several tracts of woodlands, wetlands, and open fields, interspersed with a golf course, a nature center, a considerable amount of human settlement, and a few historic sites. A favorite stop for migrating birds, the Greenbelt also supports diverse flora, thanks to a wide variety of soils deposited here by glaciers about 10,000 years ago.

South of the Greenbelt, find the Jacques Marchais Museum of Tibetan Art (338 Lighthouse Ave; take the S74 bus), the housing what is said to be the largest collection of Tibetan art in the Western world. Within walking distance of the Tibetan is Historic Richmond Town (441 Clarke Ave), a re-crated historic village filled with 29 buildings, most moved here from elsewhere on the island.

Until recently, Staten Island was also the butt of many jokes, as the city's largest dump, the Fresh Kills land-fill, was located here. However, Fresh Kills was closed in early 2001.

UPPER WEST SIDE

Primarily residential, the Upper West Side has traditionally been known as the liberal-leaning home of writers, intellectuals, musicians, dancers, doctors, lawyers, and other upper-middle-class professionals. A mix of ornate 19th-century landmarks, pre-World War II apartment buildings, and tenement houses, the Upper West Side stretches from 57th Street north to 110th Street and from Fifth Avenue west to the Hudson River. At its eastern border, between Fifth Avenue and Central Park West and 59th and 110th streets, Central Park sprawls out in a vast and beautifully landscaped expanse of green.more rural and suburban than the four other New York City boroughs, Staten Island is also

Anchoring the neighborhood to the south is one of its best-known addresses—the Lincoln Center for the Performing Arts (Broadway, between 62nd and 66th streets), which presents about 3,000 cultural events a year. Centering on a large, circular fountain, the 14-acre complex is home to such renowned institutions as the Metropolitan Opera House and Avery Fisher Hall. Many free outdoor concerts are presented on the plaza during the summer.

Directly across from Lincoln Center beckons a row of attractive restaurants and cafés, many with outdoor seating in summer. The Museum of American Folk Art (Broadway, between 65th and 66th streets), one of the city's smaller and more unusual museums, is also here. Another dozen or so blocks farther north, the Museum of Natural History (Central Park West, at 79th St) is packed with everything from more than 100 dinosaur skeletons to artifacts from peoples around the world. Adjoining the museum on its north side is the state-of-the-art Rose Center for Earth and Space. Completed in 2000, the center is instantly recognizable for its unusual glass architecture revealing a globe within a triangle.

The Upper West Side didn't begin developing until the late 1800s, when a grand apartment building called the Dakota was built at what is now the corner of Central Park West and 72nd Street. At the time, the building was so far north of the rest of the city that New Yorkers said it was as remote as the state of Dakota—hence the name. Still standing today, the Dakota has been home to many celebrities, including Lauren Bacall, Gilda Radner, Boris Karloff, and John Lennon, who was fatally shot outside the building on December 8, 1980. In Central Park, directly across the street from the Dakota, is Strawberry Fields, a teardrop-shaped acre of land that Yoko Ono had landscaped in her husband's memory.

Central Park can be entered at major intersections all along Central Park West. Near the park's southern end, find Tavern on the Green (near Central Park West and 67th St), a glittering extravaganza of a restaurant packed with mirrors and chandeliers. A bit farther north, find an odd-shaped body of water simply known as "The Lake" (between 72nd and 77th streets); rowboats can be rented at the Loeb Boathouse at the lake's eastern edge.

MUSEUMS OF NEW YORK

New York is a city of museums. Almost everywhere you go, from the stately Upper East Side of Manhattan to the leafy reaches of Staten Island, you stumble upon them. Some are renowned worldwide: the Metropolitan Museum of Art, the Museum of Modern Art, the Museum of Natural History, the Guggenheim. Others are known only to enthusiasts: the Isamu Noguchi Garden Museum, the Tibetan Museum, the New York City Fire Museum, the Lower East Side Tenement Museum.

On these pages, find a guide to some of the city's most important, interesting, and/or offbeat museums, arranged by subject matter. If you're short on time, the must-sees are the Metropolitan Museum of Art, the Museum of Modern Art, and the American Museum of Natural History. Following not far behind are the Guggenheim, the Whitney, the Brooklyn Museum of Art, the Studio Museum in Harlem, the Cooper-Hewitt, the National Museum of the American Indian, and the Frick Collection.

Many of New York's major museums are packed with visitors on the weekends, especially in the afternoons or early evenings, because many are open late on Fridays and Saturdays. To avoid the crowds, come during the week or on weekend mornings.

MAJOR ART MUSEUMS

Any guide to the Big Apple's museums must start with that most venerable, enormous, and glorious of institutions, the **Metropolitan Museum of Art** (1000 Fifth Ave, at 82nd St; phone 212/535-7710). Housed behind an impressive Beaux Arts façade designed by Robert Morris Hunt, the museum holds collections of everything from Egyptian sarcophagi to contemporary American paintings. Equally important, it hosts at least two or three major temporary exhibits at any give time.

Founded in 1870, the Met centers on the Great Hall, a vast entrance room with a stately staircase leading to the second floor. Here you'll find the European Paintings galleries, one of the Met's most important collections. Housed in about 20 rooms are works by such masters as Rembrandt, Breughel, Rubens, Botticelli, Goya, and El Greco. Next door are the impressive 19th-century European Galleries, housing works by more modern masters such as van Gogh, Gauguin, Seurat, and Renoir.

Three sides of the Met's original buildings are flanked by modern glass wings. At the back is the Robert Lehman Collection, containing an exhibit of 19th-century French paintings, among other things. On the south side are the Rockefeller and Acheson Wings, the first holding a South Pacific collection—everything from totem poles to canoes—the second, 20th-century art. On the north side, find the Sacker Wing, best known for its 15th-century-BC Temple of Dendur, carved in faded hieroglyphics, and the American Wing, housing exhaustive galleries of decorative arts and paintings by the likes of Thomas Eakins and John Singer Sargent.

The Met's Egyptian collection is one of the largest in the world and a must-stop for history buffs. The Islamic art collection and the new South and Southeast Asian art collection are also among the world's finest. To see the museum's medieval collection, travel north to the **Cloisters** (Fort Tyron Park, 190th St at Overlook Terrace; phone 212/923-3700). Situated high on a hill with great views of the Hudson River, the Cloisters are housed in a reconstructed medieval monastery that incorporates the actual remains of four medieval cloisters.

The second stop for any serious art lover should be the **Museum of Modern Art** (11 W 53rd St, between Fifth and Sixth avenues; phone 212/708-9480; www.moma.org). After a major expansion that nearly doubled its size, the rejuvenated museum now sprawls more than 600,000 square feet. The six-story gallery building houses the main collection of more than 100,000 paintings, sculptures, drawings, prints, and photographs, as well as skylit galleries for temporary exhibits on the top floor. The eight-story education and research center holds an expanded library and archives, a reading room, and a 125-seat auditorium. Visitors can expect to find such masterpieces as Cézanne's *The Bather* and van Gogh's *Starry Night*, along with entire rooms devoted to Mondrian, Pollock, Matisse, and Monet's *Water Lilies* and a superb photography exhibit. The enlarged Abby Aldrich Rockefeller outdoor sculpture garden will include an outdoor patio for the museum's new restaurant.

Another essential stop for modern art lovers is the **Solomon R. Guggenheim Museum** (1071 Fifth Ave, at 88th St; phone 212/423-3500). Housed in a circular building designed by Frank Lloyd Wright in 1959, the main gallery is a gentle multileveled spiral circling around a central atrium. The exhibits, all major temporary shows featuring 20th- or 21st-century artists, start at the top of the spiral and wind their way down.

Next door to the main gallery is a rotunda, housing the small but stunning Justin K. Thannhauser Collection, which includes works by such artists as Picasso, Cézanne, Modigliani, and Seurat. A ten-story tower also abuts the main gallery to the back; here, find a mix of temporary and permanent exhibits and an outdoor sculpture garden.

Not far from the Guggenheim is the **Whitney Museum of American Art** (Madison Ave, at 75th Street; phone 212/570-3676). Most of the exhibits here are temporary and feature the work of one major American artist such as Edward Hopper, Jasper Johns, or Jean-Michel Basquiat. The museum is also known for its superb permanent collection

SMALLER ART MUSEUMS

In addition to the behemoths above, New York City is home to scores of smaller art museums, many of which are unique gems. No matter where your art interests lie, you're bound to find something that speaks to you.

Photography buffs won't want to miss the **International Center of Photography,** relocated from the Upper East Side to Midtown (1133 Sixth Ave, at 43rd St; phone 212/768-4682). In these spacious galleries, you'll find changing exhibits featuring everyone from Weegee (Arthur Fellig) to Annie Leibovitz.

Meanwhile, sculpture fans will want to visit the **Isamu Noguchi Garden Museum** in Long Island City, Queens (32-37 Vernon Blvd, at 33rd Rd; phone 718/204-7088), just a short trip from Manhattan. Housed in the sculptor's former studio, complete with an outdoor sculpture garden, the museum is filled with Noguchi stone, metal, and woodwork. The museum is open only from April through October, so you will have to time your visit accordingly.

In Murray Hill, find the **Pierpont Morgan Library** (29 E 36th St, at Madison Ave; phone 212/685-0610), housed in an elegant neoclassic mansion that was once financier John Pierpont Morgan's personal library and art museum. The library holds a priceless collection of illuminated manuscripts and Old Master drawings; compelling traveling exhibits are frequently on display as well.

In SoHo, the **New Museum of Contemporary Art** (583 Broadway, between Houston and Prince streets; phone 212/219-1222) hosts experimental and conceptual works by contemporary artists from all over the world. Also a premier center for art on the cutting edge is the **P.S.1 Contemporary Art Center** in Long Island City, Queens (22-25 Jackson Ave, at 46th St). On the Upper West Side, the **American Folk Art Museum** (45 W 53rd St; phone 212/595-9533) showcases everything from quilts and weathervanes to painting and sculpture; admission is always free.

HISTORY MUSEUMS

A good introduction to the history of the Big Apple can be found at the **Museum of the City of New York** (Fifth Ave, between 103rd and 104th streets; phone 212/534-1672), an eclectic establishment filled with a vast permanent collection of paintings and photographs, maps and prints, Broadway memorabilia, and old model ships. Housed in a sprawling neo-Georgian building, the museum also hosts an interesting series of temporary exhibits on such subjects as Duke Ellington or stickball.

Also devoted to the history of New York is the **New York Historical Society** (2 W 77th St, at Central Park West; phone 212/873-3400), which recently reawakened after years of inactivity due to financial troubles. Spread out over many high-ceilinged rooms, the society presents temporary exhibits on everything from the legendary Stork Club—frequented by everyone from Frank Sinatra to JFK—to the small African-American communities that once dotted Central Park.

To find out more about immigration history, visit the **Ellis Island Museum,** a trip that is usually made via ferry, in conjunction with a jaunt to the **Statue of Liberty** (for information, call the Circle Line Ferry at 212/269-5755; the ferries leave from Battery Park in Lower Manhattan). The primary point of entry for immigrants to the United States from 1892 to 1924, Ellis Island is a castlelike building, all red-brick towers and white domes, that now houses multiple exhibits on the immigrant experience, along with photographs, films, and taped oral histories. To avoid the crowds that flock here, especially during the summer, arrive first thing in the morning.

Related in theme to Ellis Island is the **Lower East Side Tenement Museum** (97 Orchard St, between Delancey and Broome streets; phone 212/431-0233; visits by guided tour only, reservations recommended). Deliberately dark and oppressive, the museum re-creates early immigrant life in Manhattan.

The **South Street Seaport Museum** is not so much a museum as it is an 11-block historic district, located in Lower Manhattan where Fulton Street meets the East River. A thriving port during the 19th century, the now-restored area is filled with commercial shops and restaurants, along with dozens of historic buildings—a boat-building shop, a former counting house—and a few historic sailing ships. The ships and some of the buildings require an entrance ticket that can be purchased at the Visitor Center (on Schermerhorn Row, an extension of Fulton Street; phone 212/748-8600).

In the East Village, find the **Merchant's House Museum** (29 E 4th St, near the Bowery; phone 212/777-1089). This classic Greek Revival home is furnished exactly as it was in 1835, when merchant Seabury Tredwell and his family lived here.

Near Gramercy Park presides **Theodore Roosevelt's Birthplace** (28 E 20th St, near Broadway; phone 212/260-1616), a handsome four-story brownstone that is an exact replica of the original. Now administered by the National Park Service, the museum houses the largest collection of Roosevelt memorabilia in the country.

CULTURAL MUSEUMS

As befits a city made up of many peoples, New York is home to a number of museums that focus on the culture of one country or area of the world. Some of these are major, professionally assembled institutions; others are small and homespun.

In lower Manhattan, find the George Gustav Heye Center of the **National Museum of the American Indian** (1 Bowling Green, at State St and Battery Pl; phone 212/668-6624), a branch of the Smithsonian Institution. Housed in a stunning 1907 Beaux Arts building designed by Cass Gilbert, the museum holds some of the country's finest Native American art and artifacts, ranging in date of origin from 3200 BC to the 20th century. Admission is always free.

Also in Lower Manhattan is the **Museum of Jewish Heritage** (18 First Pl, at Battery Park, Battery Park City; phone 212/968-1800), built in the shape of a hexagon, symbolic of the Star of David. Opened in 1997, the museum features thousands of moving photographs, cultural artifacts, and archival films documenting the Holocaust and the resilience of the Jewish community.

A second Jewish museum, this one devoted to the arts, culture, and history, can be found on the Upper East Side. Housed in a magnificent French Gothic mansion, the **Jewish Museum** (1109 Fifth Ave, at 92nd St, 212/423-3200) holds an outstanding permanent collection of ceremonial objects and artifacts while also hosting many major exhibits on everything from "The Dreyfus Affair" to painter Marc Chagall.

Also on the Upper East Side, find the **Asia Society** (502 Park Ave, at 59th St; phone 212/517-2742) and **El Museo del Barrio** (1230 Fifth Ave, between 104th and 105th streets; phone 212/831-7272). The former presents first-rate temporary exhibits, concerts, films, and lectures on various aspects of Asian culture and history. The latter features changing exhibits on both contemporary and historic subjects and houses a superb permanent collection of *Santos de Palo,* or carved wooden saints.

In Harlem is the **African American Wax Museum** (318 W 115th St, between Manhattan Avenue and Frederick Douglass Blvd; phone 212/678-7818; by appointment only), a tiny private place created and run by Haitian-born artist Raven Chanticleer. The museum is filled with wax figures of famous African Americans—Frederick Douglass, Josephine Baker, Nelson Mandela—as well as Chanticleer's own paintings and sculptures.

The **Museum of Chinese in the Americas** in Chinatown (70 Mulberry St, at Bayard St, second floor; phone 212/619-4785) is a small but fascinating place, filled with photographs, mementos, and poetry culled from nearly two decades of research in the community. Women's roles, religion, and Chinese laundries are among the subjects covered in the exhibits.

On Staten Island, find the **Jacques Marchais Museum of Tibetan Art** (338 Lighthouse Ave, at Windsor; phone 718/987-3500). Perched on a steep hill with views of the Atlantic Ocean, the museum houses the collection of Jacqueline Norman Klauber, who became fascinated with Tibet as a child. Highlights of the exhibit include a series of bright-colored masks and a large collection of golden *thangkas,* or religious images.

NATURAL HISTORY, SCIENCE, AND TECHNOLOGY MUSEUMS

The must-stop in this category is the enormous **American Museum of Natural History** (Central Park West at 79th St; phone 212/769-5100), one of the city's greatest museums. Always filled with hundreds of shouting, enthusiastic kids, the museum went through a major renovation in the late 1990s and is now filled with many state-of-the-art exhibits.

At the heart of the museum are approximately 100 dinosaur skeletons, some housed in the soaring, not-to-be-missed Theodore Roosevelt Memorial Hall. Other highlights include the Mammals Wing, the Hall of Human Biology and Evolution, the Hall of Primitive Vertebrates, and the museum's many dioramas and exhibits devoted to native peoples around the world. Adjoining the museum to the north is the spanking new **Rose Center for Earth and Science,** featuring a planetarium with a Zeiss sky projector capable of projecting 9,100 stars as viewed from Earth.

The city's top pure science museum is the **New York Hall of Science** (47-01 111th St; phone 718/699-0005), located in Flushing Meadows-Corona Park, Queens—best reached from Manhattan via the 7 subway. Housed in a dramatic building with undulating walls, the museum is packed with hands-on exhibits for kids and features a large Science Playground out back, where kids can learn about the laws of physics.

Docked at Pier 86 on the western edge of Manhattan is the **Intrepid Sea-Air-Space Museum** (West 46th St at 12th Ave; phone 212/245-0072). A former World War II aircraft carrier, the museum is now devoted to military history and includes lots of child-friendly hands-on exhibits. Small aircraft and space capsules are strewn here and there, and exhibits focus on such subjects as satellite communication and spaceship design.

Also in Midtown is the **Museum of Television and Radio** (25 W 52nd St, between Fifth and Sixth avenues; phone 212/621-6800), where you can watch your favorite old television show, listen to a classic radio broadcast, or research a pop-culture question. The museum also offers traditional exhibits on such subjects as the history of animation. Be sure to arrive early if you plan to visit on the weekend and want to use one of the museum's 96 semiprivate televisions or radio consoles.

MUSEUMS FOR KIDS

In addition to the natural history, science, and technology museums, children might also enjoy visiting the **Children's Museum of Manhattan** on the Upper West Side (212 W 83rd St, between Broadway and Amsterdam Ave; phone 212/721-1223) or the **Children's Museum of the Arts in SoHo** (182 Lafayette St, between Broome and Grand streets; phone 212/274-0986). In the former, aimed at ages 2 to 10, kids can draw and paint, play at being newscasters, or explore the ever-changing play areas; the latter features an "Artists' Studio," where youngsters can try their hand at sand painting, origami, sculpture, and beadwork.

Although not, strictly speaking, a children's museum, the **New York City Fire Museum** in SoHo (278 Spring St, between Varick and Houston; phone 212/691-1303) has great appeal for kids. Housed in an actual firehouse that was used up until 1959, the museum is filled with fire engines new and old, helmets and uniforms, hoses, and lifesaving nets. Retired firefighters take visitors through the museum, reciting fascinating tidbits of fire-fighting history along the way. This museum has been a particularly poignant stop since the terrorist attacks of 2001 reminded New Yorkers—and all Americans—what heroes firefighters are.

Older kids might enjoy a visit to the **Forbes Magazine Galleries** in Greenwich Village (62 Fifth Ave, near 12th St; phone 212/206-5548). Housing the collections of the idiosyncratic media tycoon Malcolm Forbes, the museum includes exhibits of more than 500 toy boats, 12,000 toy soldiers, about a dozen Fabergé eggs, and numerous historical documents relating to American history.

What to See and Do

Adventure on a Shoestring. *300 W 53rd St, New York (10019). Phone 212/265-2663.* Year-round walking tours of various neighborhoods, including SoHo, Haunted Greenwich Village, and Chinatown. **$**

African American Wax Museum. *318 W 115th St, New York (10026). Between Manhattan Ave and Frederick Douglass Blvd in Harlem. Phone 212/678-7818.* This tiny private place, created and run by Haitian-born artist Raven Chanticleer, is filled with wax figures of famous African Americans such as Frederick Douglass, Josephine Baker, and Nelson Mandela, as well as Chanticleer's own paintings and sculptures. (By appointment only) **DONATION**

American Bible Society Gallery/Library. *1865 Broadway, New York (10023). Phone 212/408-1200. www.americanbible.org/gallery.* Changing exhibits run the gamut from stained glass in American art and architecture to the impact of the Bible on the world to religious folk art in Guatemala. Special events include lectures, workshops, and symposia. Gallery (Mon-

Wed, Fri 10 am-6 pm; Thurs 10 am-7 pm; Sat 10 am-5 pm; closed holidays). Library (Mon-Fri 9 am-5 pm). **FREE**

American Folk Art Museum. *45 W 53rd St, New York (10019). Phone 212/265-1040. www.folkartmuseum.org.* Folk arts of all types, including paintings, sculptures, quilts, needlework, toys, weather vanes, and hand-made furniture. Changing exhibits; lectures and demonstrations. Café; museum shop. Admission is free on Friday evenings. (Wed-Thurs, Sat-Sun 10:30 am-5:30 pm, Fri to 7:30 pm; closed holidays) **$$**

Eva and Morris Feld Gallery. *2 Lincoln Sq, New York (10023). Phone 212/595-9533. www.folkartmuseum.org.* The original site of the American Folk Art Museum, reopened as a sister gallery, function space, and museum shop after renovations were completed in 2001. (Mon 11 am-6 pm, Tues-Sun 11 am-7:30 pm) **FREE**

⭐ **American Museum of Natural History.** *79th St and Central Park W, New York (10024). Phone 212/769-5100. www.amnh.org.* Kids love this behemoth of a museum. Among its 36 million specimens are at least 100 dinosaur skeletons, including a huge Tyrannosaurus rex whose serrated teeth alone measure 6 inches long. You may prefer to stroll through a roomful of free-flying butterflies or examine the 563-carat Star of India sapphire. Expect to be blown away by the 3-year-old Rose Center for Earth and Space and the Hayden Planetarium. The Planetarium Space Show is only 30 minutes long, but it's dazzling. Narrated by the likes of Tom Hanks and Harrison Ford, it uses the world's largest, most powerful projector, the Zeiss Mark IX, which was built to the museum's specifications. The show is one of unparalleled sophistication, accuracy, and excitement. Seating is limited, so choose a day for the museum and order tickets in advance. (Daily 10 am-5:45 pm; closed Thanksgiving, Dec 25). **$$$**

Angelika Film Center. *18 W Houston St, New York (10012). Phone 212/995-2000. www.angelikafilmcenter .com.* Get a taste of genuine SoHo living at this cultural institution that has attracted lovers of artsy movies for years. But the Angelika is even more than that. It is a special place—a world away from today's overcrowded, noisy multiplexes teeming with soccer moms and screaming kids. You'll find a generally urbane crowd at the independent films shown at the theater. And the Angelika Café in the lobby area is a great little place to grab a latte and a scone before the flick or a soda and a sandwich after the movie. On Sunday mornings, you'll find locals relaxing in the café, enjoying their coffee and *The New York Times.* Hang out here for a while and you'll feel more like a real New Yorker than a tourist. **$$**

Asia Society and Museum. *725 Park Ave, New York (10021). At 70th St. Phone 212/288-6400; fax 212/517-8315. www.asiasociety.org.* Masterpieces of Asian art, donated by founder John Rockefeller, make up most of this museum's permanent collection. Its works include sculptures, ceramics, and paintings from places like China, Korea, Japan, and India. In addition, the museum offers a schedule of films, performances, and lectures. The Asia Society also has a lovely indoor sculpture garden and café, which make for a nice stop on a hectic day of sightseeing. (Tues-Thurs, Sat-Sun 11 am-6 pm; Fri to 9 pm; closed holidays) **$$**

Astro Minerals Gallery of Gems. *185 Madison Ave, New York (10016). At 34th St. Phone 212/889-9000. www.astrogallery.com.* Display of minerals, gems, jewelry; primitive and African art. (Mon-Fri 10 am-7 pm, Sat 10 am-6 pm, Sun 11 am-6 pm; closed Jan 1, Thanksgiving, Dec 25) **FREE**

Bergdorf Goodman. *754 Fifth Ave, New York (10019). Phone 212/753-7300. www.bergdorfgoodman.com.* With its designer handbags that can set you back as much as $4,000, $700 swimsuits, and nightgowns that cost $500, Bergdorf Goodman is one of the city's grand-dame department stores. Ladies who lunch, yuppie professionals, and stylish Gen Xers with trust funds are equally at home in this shopping Mecca, located in the heart of the Midtown shopping district, which features a sophisticated selection of clothing, furs, jewelry, tableware, kitchenware, cosmetics, and lingerie. You can find items on sale, but this is not the place for bargain hunters. The selection of merchandise tends to appeal more to those whose taste borders on conservative. The sales staff is attentive and pleasant for those who need assistance in picking out just the right thing. Word to the wise: pack your platinum card. (Mon-Wed, Fri-Sat 10 am-7 pm, Thurs to 8 pm, Sun noon-6 pm)

Bloomingdale's. *1000 Third Ave, 59th St and Lexington Ave, New York (10022). Phone 212/705-2000; toll-free 800/472-0788. www.bloomingdales.com.* Everyone in New York knows the name Bloomingdale's and the famous Bloomie's shopping bags. This world-renowned department store, loved by locals and tourists alike, sells a mix of merchandise in a sleek, modern setting. You can find designer clothing for men and women, high-quality housewares, jewelry, cosmetics, and just about everything else. Although prices are high, you can find good sales. (Mon-Thurs 10 am-8:30 pm, Fri-Sat 9 am-10 pm, Sun 11 am-7 pm; closed Thanksgiving, Dec 25)

Blue Note. *131 W 3rd St, New York (10012). Phone 212/475-8592. www.bluenote.net.* For some of the world's best names in jazz, head downtown to Greenwich Village to the Blue Note. This bastion of fine jazz has played host over the years to many well-known jazz performers, as well as rising stars. Although the cover charge is higher here than at many other venues, the acts are worth it. Monday nights can be had for around $10, when the record companies promote new releases by their artists. The club also serves a variety of food and drinks if you want to grab dinner while listening to some cool tunes. (Daily) **$$$$**

Bowling Green. *Broadway and Whitehall St, New York (10004). At the Southern end of Broadway.* Originally a Dutch market, this is the city's oldest park, said to be the place where Peter Minuit purchased Manhattan for $24 worth of trinkets. The park fence dates from 1771. You'll also find *Charging Bull* here, a 7,000-pound bronze statue that stock market investors often rub for good luck.

Bowlmor Lanes. *110 University Pl, New York (10003). Phone 212/255-8188. www.bowlmor.com.* A New York landmark since 1938, this 42-lane, two-level "more than a bowling alley" features a restored retro bar and lounge with red booths, a yellow ceiling, and a DJ on Monday nights. Richard Nixon, Cameron Diaz, and the Rolling Stones have all bowled at these lanes, where a colorful Village crowd frequents the place until all hours. Munch on anything from nachos and hamburgers to fried calamari and grilled filet mignon in the restaurant, or have your meal brought straight to your lane. It's a funky, fun hangout, even if you don't bowl. Note that no one under 21 is admitted after 6 pm. (Daily) **$$$$**

Brooklyn Bridge. *Park Row near Municipal Building, New York (10002). Take the 4, 5, or 6 subway to the Brooklyn Bridge/City Hall station, or the N or R subway to the nearby City Hall stop.* For an awesome view of lower Manhattan, Brooklyn, and the New York Harbor, take a leisurely 40-minute stroll across downtown's historic Brooklyn Bridge, the first bridge to cross the East River (actually a tidal estuary between Long Island Sound and New York Harbor) to Brooklyn. Opened on May 24, 1883, the bridge was, and still is, seen as a monument to American engineering and creativity. Two massive stone pylons,

each pierced with two soaring Gothic arches, rise 272 feet to support an intricate web of cables. A particularly good time of day to take in the views is at sunset. Dress appropriately in cooler weather, since it can be very windy. At the Brooklyn end of the bridge is a lovely half-mile promenade with equally grand views. The bridge is also near the South Street Seaport (see), at the foot of Fulton Street and the East River. **FREE**

⭐ **Carnegie Hall.** *57th St and Broadway, New York (10019). Phone 212/247-7800. www.carnegiehall.org.* Completed in 1891, the celebrated auditorium has been home to the world's great musicians for more than a century. Guided one-hour tours ($$) (Oct-June: Mon-Fri 11:30 am, 2 pm, and 3 pm, performance schedule permitting). **$$$$**

Castle Clinton National Monument. *Battery Park, New York (10005). Phone 212/344-7220. www.nps.gov/cacl/.* (1811) Built as a fort, this later was a place of public entertainment called Castle Garden where Jenny Lind sang in 1850 under P. T. Barnum's management. In 1855, it was taken over by the state of New York for use as an immigrant receiving station. More than 8 million people entered the United States here between 1855 and 1890; Ellis Island was opened in 1892. The castle became the New York City Aquarium in 1896, which closed in 1941 and reopened at Coney Island in Brooklyn (see). The site has undergone modifications to serve as the visitor orientation/ferry departure center for the Statue of Liberty and Ellis Island. Ferry ticket booth; exhibits on Castle Clinton, Statue of Liberty, and Ellis Island; visitor center. (Daily 9 am-5 pm; closed Dec 25) **FREE**

Cathedral Church of St. John the Divine. *1047 Amsterdam Ave, New York (10025). At 112th St. Phone 212/316-7540. www.stjohndivine.org.* (Episcopal) Under construction since 1892. When completed, this will be the largest Gothic cathedral in the world, 601 feet long and 124 feet high. Bronze doors of the central portal represent scenes from the Old and New Testaments. The great rose window, 40 feet in diameter, is made up of more than 10,000 pieces of glass. A tapestry, painting, and sculpture collection is also housed here. The cathedral and five other buildings are on 13 acres with a park and garden areas, including the Biblical Garden. No parking provided. (Mon-Sat 7 am-6 pm, Sun 7 am-7 pm; tours Tues-Sat 11 am; also Sun at 1 pm, following last morning service; no tours religious holidays) **$$**

⭐ **Central Park.** *59th St and Fifth Ave (Grand Army Plaza Entrance), New York (10019). 59th to 110th* sts between Fifth Ave and Central Park West. Phone 212/360-3444 (recorded info). www.centralpark.org. Called "the lungs of New York," Central Park was reclaimed in 1858 from 843 acres of swampland that were used as a garbage dump and occupied by squatters. Landscape designer Frederick Law Olmsted's dream was to bring city dwellers the kind of refreshment found only in nature. A century-and-a-half later, the park still does that; today, it's a source of varied outdoor entertainment. Stop at the visitor's center, called The Dairy—mid-park at 65th Street—for a map and a calendar of events. If you're looking for active endeavors, you can jog around the Reservoir or rent ice skates at Wollman Rink or at Lasker Rink, which becomes a swimming pool in summer. If you're looking to have a Woody Allen moment on the Lake, rent a rowboat at Loeb Boathouse. Rent a kite from Big City Kites, at Lexington and 82nd Street, and walk over to the park to catch the breeze on the Great Lawn. If you have kids, visit one of the 19 themed playgrounds, the zoo and petting zoo, the Carousel, the raucous storytelling hour at the Hans Christian Andersen statue, and the Model Boat Pond, where serious modelers race their tiny remote-controlled boats on weekends. In summer, something's going on every night, and it's free! See Shakespeare in the Park at the Delacorte Theater. Get comfortable on the Great Lawn to hear the New York Philharmonic or the Metropolitan Opera under the stars. SummerStage brings well-known artists to Rumsey Playfield for jazz, dance, traditional, and contemporary musical performances. The Band Shell is the venue for classical concerts. Take advantage of Central Park. Amble through the forested Ramble. Stroll down the venerable, elm-lined Mall and past the bronze statues of Balto the dog, Alice in Wonderland, and forgotten poets. Bring a picnic! Also in the park are

Bicycle rentals at Loeb Boathouse. *Park Dr NE and 72nd St, New York (10023). Phone 212/517-2233. www.centralpark.org.* Central Park is an 843-acre oasis of calm in an otherwise chaotic city. Rent a bike for yourself and the kids and enjoy a ride through this sprawling mix of winding paths, meadows, lakes, and ponds. Take in the sight of dog walkers, kids playing softball, joggers—and an occasional homeless person. The park especially comes alive on the weekends in summer. (Mar-Oct, daily 10 am-7 pm) **$$$**

The Dairy. *64th St, mid-Park, New York (10019). In the park on 65th St, W of the Central Park Wildlife Conservation Center and the carousel. Phone 212/* 794-6564. Exhibition/Visitor Information Center. Video on history of the park; time-travel video; gift and book shop. (Tues-Sun 10 am-5 pm) **FREE**

Storytelling in the Park. *74th St and Fifth Ave, New York (10019). Phone 212/360-3444.* At Hans Christian Andersen statue in Central Park, near the model boat pond (June-Sept, Sat 11 am). Recommended for children 5 and older; also in certain playgrounds (July-Aug). **FREE**

Century 21. *22 Cortlandt St, New York (10007). Phone 212/227-9092. www.c21stores.com.* This is a can't-miss store if you want designer merchandise at rock-bottom prices and have time to look through aisles of items. The three-story department store sells men's, women's, and children's clothing; cosmetics; housewares; and electronics. The store's extended morning hours are a benefit for both New Yorkers who want to make purchases before work and for tourists who are early-birds. You won't be disappointed, and neither will your wallet or your wardrobe. But you may need to take a cab back to your hotel since you'll be so loaded down with shopping bags. (Mon-Wed, Fri 7:45 am-8 pm, Thurs to 8:30 pm, Sat 10 am-8 pm, Sun 11 am-7 pm; closed holidays)

Chelsea Piers Sports and Entertainment Complex. *24th St and West Side Hwy, New York (10011). Piers 59-62 on the Hudson River from 17th to 23rd sts. The entrance is at 23rd St. Take the C/E subway to 23rd St. Phone 212/336-6666. www.chelseapiers.com.* For the best in recreational activities all in one location, keep heading west until you hit Chelsea Piers. The 1.7-million-square-foot complex features an ice skating rink, a bowling alley, climbing walls, a driving range, basketball, in-line skating, and more. There also are pubs and restaurants where you can grab a meal after your busy day. Stop in for a cold one at the Chelsea Brewing Co., the state's largest microbrewery. Make a point to visit the complex at sundown to view the beautiful sunset off the river. Both kids and adults can spend a nice few hours at this mega sports center. (Mon-Fri 6 am-11 pm, Sat-Sun 8 am-9 pm)

Children's Museum of Manhattan. *The Tisch Building, 212 W 83rd St, New York (10024). On the Upper West Side, on 83rd between Broadway and Amsterdam. Phone 212/721-1234. www.cmom.org.* Hands-on exhibits for children ages 2-10; kids can draw and paint, learn crafts, play at being newscasters, listen to stories, or explore changing play areas. (Wed-Sun 10 am-5 pm; closed holidays) **$$**

⭐ **Chinatown.** *Bordered by Kenmore and Delancey streets on the north, East and Worth streets on the south, Allen street on the east, and Broadway on the west. Take the J, M, N, R, 6, or Z subway to Canal St. Phone 212/267-3510. www.chinatown-online.com.* How does the thought of 200 restaurants grab you? Or dozens of jewelry stores and gift shops? Or maybe you're into shops selling Asian antiques, feng shui items, and herbal remedies. Whatever you want to buy, from cheap and kitschy to pricey and unique, you'll find it in this noisy, crowded, and invigorating enclave of Lower Manhattan. And if you crave authentic Chinese food, you can visit this area over and over again to sample the flavorful mix of Cantonese, Szechwan, and Hunan dishes served up by mom-and-pop restaurateurs. Most of these eateries entice diners with massive meals that will suit even the most budget-conscious travelers. Tip: While many establishments close on Christmas Day, Chinatown's restaurants remain open and are usually filled with holiday diners.

Christie's Auctions. *20 Rockefeller Plz, New York (10020). At 49th St, between 5th and 6th aves. Phone 212/636-2000. www.christies.com.* Get a taste of high society at a Christie's auction. Whether you're just a spectator or you have lots of spare cash with which to purchase something wonderful, attending an auction at this institution is a thrilling, fast-paced experience. Items sold at auction at Christie's have included the "Master of Your Domain" script from the television show *Seinfeld,* gowns worn by the late Princess Diana, and a Honus Wagner baseball card (the most expensive card ever sold). Special departments are devoted to areas like wines, cameras, and cars. Publications like *New York* magazine and *The New York Times* contain listings of upcoming events. (Mon-Fri 9:30 am-5:30 pm; closed holidays) **FREE**

Chrysler Building. *405 Lexington Ave, New York (10174). At E 42nd St. Phone 212/682-3070.* New York's famous Art Deco skyscraper. The graceful pointed spire with triangular windows set in arches is lighted at night. The impressive lobby features beautiful jazz-age detailing. (Mon-Fri 8:30 am-5:30 pm) **FREE**

Circle Line Cruises. *Pier 83, W 42nd St and 12th Ave, New York (10036). All trains (subway) stop at 42nd St. Then transfer to westbound M42 bus to pier. Phone 212/563-3200. www.circleline.com.* Grab a seat on the port (left) side for a spectacular view of the skyline. Rest your feet and enjoy the sea air as you cruise around Manhattan. Narrated by knowledgeable, personable guides, these tours take you past the Statue of Liberty

and under the Brooklyn Bridge; if you opt for the three-hour cruise, you'll also see the New Jersey Palisades, a glorious sight in autumn. Food and drinks are available on board. (Closed Tues-Wed in Jan, Tues in Mar, Jan 1, Dec 25) **$$$$**

City Center. *131 W 55th St, New York (10019). 55th St between 6th and 7th aves. Phone 212/581-1212 (tickets); toll-free 877/581-1212 (tickets). www.citycenter.org.* This landmark theater hosts world-renowned dance companies, including the Alvin Ailey American Dance Theater, the Paul Taylor Dance Company, and Merce Cunningham Dance Company. It also presents American music and theater events. Downstairs, City Center Stages I and II host the Manhattan Theatre Club.

City College of New York. *138th St and Convent Ave, New York (10031). Phone 212/650-7000. www.ccny.cuny.edu.* (1847) (11,000 students) One of the nation's best-known municipal colleges and the oldest in the city university system. Alumni include eight Nobel laureates, Supreme Court Justice Felix Frankfurter, and authors Upton Sinclair, Paddy Chayefsky, and Bernard Malamud. Tours (Mon-Thurs, by appointment).

City Hall Park. *Broadway and Chambers St, New York (10007). Phone 212/788-3000.* Architecturally, City Hall is a combination of American Federalist and English Georgian, with Louis XIV detailing. It is built of marble and brownstone.

Claremont Riding Academy. *175 W 89th St, New York (10024). Phone 212/724-5100. www.potomachorse.com/clarmont.htm.* Come to the oldest continuously operated stable in the United States to take a private or group lesson, or rent a horse and go for an unescorted walk, trot, or canter on Central Park's bridle paths. Escorted rides also are available for those with riding experience. Book as early as you can. Viewing the action from atop a beautiful horse on a mild, sunny day in the park can be quite peaceful—and is quite popular. (Daily; closed Dec 25) **$$$$$**

⭐ **The Cloisters.** *In Fort Tryon Park, off Henry Hudson Pkwy, one exit N of George Washington Bridge. Phone 212/923-3700 (recording). www.metmuseum.org.* To escape the often frantic pace of the city, take the A train to Fort Tryon Park in upper Manhattan where The Cloisters, the medieval branch of the Metropolitan Museum, perches peacefully on a bluff overlooking the Hudson River. Funded in large part by John D. Rockefeller, Jr., The Cloisters houses an extraordinary collection of sculpture, illuminated manuscripts, stained glass, ivory, and precious metalwork, as well as the famed Unicorn tapestries. The architectural setting is as remarkable as its contents. Five cloisters (quadrangles enclosed by a roofed arcade), a chapter house, and chapels were taken from monasteries in France and Spain and reassembled stone by stone. In the Bonnefont Cloister, catch the spicy fragrance of the herb garden and take time to meditate; the sublime view of the Hudson Valley is always pristine. Donor Rockefeller also purchased the land across the river and restricted development there. (Tues-Sun 9:30 am-5:15 pm; until 4:45 pm Nov-Feb; closed Jan 1, Thanksgiving, Dec 25) **$$$**

Columbia University. *2960 Broadway, New York (10027). Phone 212/854-1754. www.columbia.edu.* (1754) (19,000 students) This Ivy League university was originally King's College; classes were conducted in the vestry room of Trinity Church. King's College still exists as Columbia College, with 3,000 students. The campus has more than 62 buildings, including Low Memorial Library, the administration building (which has the Rotunda and the Sackler Collection of Chinese Ceramics), and Butler Library, with more than 5 million volumes. The university numbers Alexander Hamilton, Gouverneur Morris, and John Jay among its early graduates and Nicholas Murray Butler, Dwight D. Eisenhower, and Andrew W. Cordier among its former presidents. Barnard College (1889) with 2,300 women, and the Teachers College (1887) with 5,000 students, are affiliated with Columbia. Multilingual guided tours available. (Mon-Fri except holidays and final exam period) **FREE**

Cooper Union. *Cooper Square, The Cooper Union for the Advancement, New York (10003). Third Ave at 7th St. Phone 212/353-4100. www.cooper.edu.* (1859) (1,000 students) All-scholarship college for art, architecture, and engineering. The Great Hall, where Lincoln spoke in 1861, is used as an auditorium for readings, films, lectures, and performing arts.

Dahesh Museum of Art. *IBM Building, 580 Madison Ave, New York (10022). Phone 212/759-0606. www. daheshmuseum.org.* This newer museum focuses on European art from the 19th and 20th centuries, by artists who came from the academic tradition. The permanent collection, the highlights of which include paintings by Rudolf Ernst, Edwin Long, and Maurice Leloir, was started by a prominent Lebanese writer for whom the museum is named. Museum shop, café. (Tues-Sun 11 am-6 pm; closed holidays) **$$**

The Dakota. *1 W 72nd St at Central Park W, New York (10024).* The first and most famous of the lavish apartment houses on Central Park West, The Dakota got its name because it was considered so far west that New Yorkers joked that it might as well be in the Dakotas. Planned as a turreted, chateaulike structure, it was then embellished with Wild West ornamentation. It has been the home of many celebrities, including Judy Garland, Boris Karloff, and John Lennon and Yoko Ono. On December 8, 1980, The Dakota earned its tragic claim to fame when Lennon was shot and killed by a crazed fan at its gate. Five years later, Yoko Ono—who still resides here—had a section of Central Park visible from The Dakota landscaped with foliage and a mosaic with the title of Lennon's song *Imagine.* Today, that area is known as Strawberry Fields.

Dean & DeLuca. *560 Broadway, New York (10012). At Prince St. Phone 212/226-6800. www.deandeluca.com.* From Portuguese cornbread to 80 percent pure cocoa and dark chocolate bars to a dozen kinds of gourmet mushrooms, Dean & DeLuca is a food lover's paradise. At this, the original outlet of the growing chain, the pastries and breads rival those of any bakery in Paris; the selection of salads, smoked fish, and meats is astounding; and the produce is so good that it puts the word *fresh* to shame. The personalized mini-cakes, available for any occasion, cost a bundle—but they're worth every fattening bite. Come early or late, because it can get very crowded (especially on weekends), and you want to spend your time browsing and stocking up on goodies as well as cookware and kitchen accessories. Forget about your budget and let your taste buds do the shopping. (Mon-Sat 9 am-8 pm, Sun 10 am-7 pm)

Dyckman Farmhouse Museum. *4881 Broadway, New York (10034). At 204th St. Phone 212/304-9422.* (Circa 1784) This is the only 18th-century Dutch farmhouse still on Manhattan Island. It was built by William Dyckman and refurnished with some original Dyckman pieces and others of the period. There is a replica of a British officers' hut on the landscaped grounds, a smokehouse, and a garden. (Tues-Sun 11 am-4 pm; closed holidays) Children only with adult. **FREE**

Ellis Island Immigration Museum. *Ellis Island, New York (10004). Boat from Castle Clinton on Battery to Statue of Liberty includes a stop at Ellis Island, which has been incorporated into the monument. Phone 212/363-3206. www.ellisisland.com.* The most famous port of immigration in the country. From 1892 to 1954, more than 12 million immigrants began their American dream here. The principle structure is the Main Building with its Great Hall, where the immigrants were processed; exhibits; 28-minute film; self-service restaurant. There is a fee for the round-trip ferry ride to the island. (Daily 9:30 am-5 pm, extended hours in the summer; closed Dec 25) **FREE**

Staten Island Ferry. *Whitehall Terminal, South Ferry Plz and Battery Park, New York (10301). Departs from the ferry terminal at the intersection of Whitehall, State, and South sts, just E of Battery Park. Phone 718/815-2628.* This famous ferry to St. George, Staten Island, offers passengers a close look at both the Statue of Liberty and Ellis Island, as well as extraordinary views of the lower Manhattan skyline. **FREE**

El Museo del Barrio. *1230 5th Ave, New York (10029). Phone 212/831-7272. www.elmuseo.org.* Dedicated to Puerto Rican and other Latin American art, this museum features changing exhibits on both contemporary and historic subjects and houses a superb permanent collection of *santos de palo,* or carved wooden saints. The museum also hosts films, theater, concerts, and educational programs. Inquire about bilingual tours. (Wed-Sun 11 am-5 pm; closed Jan 1, Thanksgiving, Dec 25) **$$**

⭐ **Empire State Building.** *350 5th Ave, New York (10118). Between 33rd and 34th sts. Phone 212/736-3100. www.esbnyc.com.* A beloved city symbol since it opened in 1931, the Empire State Building is where King Kong battled with airplanes in the movie classic and where visitors go for a panoramic view of Manhattan. Try going at night when the city lights compete with the stars. The slender Art Deco skyscraper is so popular that visitors are often greeted with a long line for tickets to the observation deck. Ordering them in advance from the Web site will save you time. (Daily 9:30 am-midnight) **$$$**

ESPN Zone. *1472 Broadway, New York (10036). Phone 212/921-3776. www.espnzone.com.* Want to have fun in the city on a rainy afternoon? Hang out at the ESPN Zone in the Theater District. This family-friendly restaurant, filled with huge TV screens, sells sports-related items and gives visitors the chance to view live ESPN broadcasts. The place is loud and boisterous and is a big draw for jocks and jock wannabes; kids get a real kick out of it, too. Have a beer, grab a burger or sandwich, buy a T-shirt or two, and just relax at this sports-lover's paradise. (Mon-Thurs 11:30 am-11 pm, Fri to midnight, Sat 11 am-midnight, Sun 11 am-11 pm)

FAO Schwarz. *767 Fifth Ave, New York (10153). At Fifth Ave and 58th St. Phone 212/644-9400. www.fao.com.* Children will instantly recognize the entrance to FAO Schwarz when they see the tall, brightly colored musical clock that guards the door. Inside, two floors are crowded with live clowns, chemistry sets, train sets, Madame Alexander dolls, giant stuffed animals, child-sized motorized cars, and all the latest electronic baubles in incredible profusion and magical, mechanical display. During the holidays, shoppers often have to stand in line just to get in. (Mon-Sat 10 am-9 pm, Sun 11 am-6 pm)

Federal Hall National Memorial. *26 Wall St, New York (10005). Phone 212/825-6888. www.nps.gov/feha.* (1842) Greek Revival building on the site of the original Federal Hall, where the Stamp Act Congress met (1765), George Washington was inaugurated (April 30, 1789), and the first Congress met (1789-1790). Originally a custom house, the building was for many years the sub-treasury of the United States. The JQA Ward statue of Washington is on the Wall Street steps. (Mon-Fri 9 am-5 pm; closed holidays) **FREE**

Federal Reserve Bank of New York. *33 Liberty St, New York (10045). Phone 212/720-6130. www.ny.frb.org.* Approximately 1/3 of the world's supply of gold bullion is stored here in a vault 80 feet below ground level; cash handling operation and historical exhibit of bank notes and coins. Tours (Mon-Fri at 9:30 am, 10:30 am, 11:30 am, 1:30 pm, and 2:30 pm; closed holidays). Sixteen years and older only; no cameras. Tour reservations required at least one week in advance. **FREE**

Food Tasting and Cultural Walking Tours. *95 Christopher St, New York (10014). Phone 212/239-1124. www.food.nyc.citysearch.com.* These two all-inclusive tours offer you a chance to sample a variety of food and drink while seeing historical sites and soaking up the city's atmosphere. The tour of the Chelsea Food Market and the Far West Village (also known as the Meatpacking District) includes tastings from Chelsea's nearly one-block-long indoor food market. This complex includes five bakeries and the largest produce shop in New York. Sample fresh milk from Hudson Valley dairies, buffalo mozzarella cheese flown in from Italy, homemade preserves, and seeded country French sourdough bread. The second tour of Greenwich Village's off-the-beaten-track sites includes stops at 15 unique food establishments, a 1920s speakeasy, and the narrowest house in the area. Tastings on this tour include homemade chocolates, Italian rice balls, Turkish falafel, and wine. All tastings are done on the go. Wear comfortable shoes and check the weather forecast before reserving a spot. (Tues-Sun) **$$$$**

Forbes Magazine Galleries. *60 Fifth Ave, New York (10011). At the corner of 12th St. Phone 212/206-5548. www.forbescollection.com.* Housing the collections of the idiosyncratic media tycoon Malcolm Forbes, this museum includes exhibits of more than 500 toy boats, 12,000 toy soldiers, about a dozen Fabergé eggs, and numerous historical documents relating to American history. (Tues-Wed, Fri-Sat 10 am-4 pm; closed holidays) **FREE**

Fordham University. *60th St and Columbus Ave, New York (10023). Across from St. Paul's Church. Phone 212/636-6000. www.fordham.edu.* Private Jesuit university founded in 1841. Other campuses are located in the Bronx and Tarrytown.

Fraunces Tavern Museum. *54 Pearl St, New York (10004). Phone 212/425-1778. www.frauncestavernmuseum.org.* (1907) The museum is housed in the historic Fraunces Tavern (1719) and four adjacent 19th-century buildings. It interprets the history and culture of early America through permanent collections of prints, paintings, decorative arts, and artifacts, changing exhibitions, and period rooms, one of which, the Long Room, is the site of George Washington's farewell to his officers at the end of the Revolutionary War (1783). The museum offers a variety of programs and activities, including tours, lectures, and films. Museum (Tues-Wed, Fri 10 am-5 pm, Thurs 10 am-7 pm, Sat 11 am-5 pm). Dining room (daily). **$**

The Frick Collection. *1 E 70th St, New York (10021). Between Madison and Fifth aves. Phone 212/288-0700. www.frick.org.* The mansion of Henry Clay Frick, wealthy tycoon, infamous strikebreaker, and avid collector of art, contains a remarkably diverse assemblage of paintings. The walls of one room are covered with large, frothy Fragonards depicting the "Progress of Love." In other rooms are masterworks by Bellini, Titian, Holbein, Rembrandt, El Greco, Turner, Degas, and many others. A superb collection in a superb setting. See it in one afternoon. (Tues-Thurs, Sat 10 am-6 pm, Fri 10 am-9 pm, Sun 1-6 pm; closed holidays) No children under 10; under 16 only with adult. **$$$**

The Garment District. *6th Ave to 8th Ave and from 34th St to 42nd St.* This crowded area, heart of the clothing industry in New York, has hundreds of small shops, factories, and streets jammed with trucks and hand-pushed delivery carts. Also in this area is Macy's.

General Grant National Memorial. *122nd St and Riverside Dr, New York (10027). Phone 212/666-1640. www.nps.gov/gegr.* The largest mausoleum in North America, the General Grant National Monument is the home of Ulysses S. Grant's tomb, along with that of his wife. When Grant died in 1885, he had led the North to victory in the Civil War and served two consecutive terms as President of the United States before retiring to New York City. General Grant was so popular that upon his death, more than 90,000 private citizens donated a total of $600,000 (the equivalent of over $11.5 million in today's dollars) to help in the building of his tomb. The tomb was dedicated on April 27, 1897, on the 75th anniversary of Grant's birth. Located near picturesque Columbia University, the monument draws more than 75,000 visitors annually. (Daily 9 am-5 pm; closed holidays)

The George Gustav Heye Center of the National Museum of the American Indian. *One Bowling Green St, New York (10004). Phone 212/668-6624. www.si.edu/nmai.* World's largest collection of materials of the native peoples of North, Central, and South America. (Sun-Wed, Fri-Sat 10 am-5 pm, Thurs 10 am-8 pm; closed Dec 25) **FREE**

Grand Central Station. *450 Lexington Ave, New York (10017). 42nd St, between Vanderbilt and Lexington. Phone 212/935-3960 (tour). www.grandcentralterminal.com.* (1913) Built in the Beaux Arts style and recently renovated for $200 million, this is one of New York's most glorious buildings. It has a vast 125-foot-high concourse, glassed-in catwalks, grand staircases, shops, restaurants, and a star-studded aquamarine ceiling. The Municipal Art Society offers tours on Wed ($$); meet at the information booth in the center of the concourse at 12:30 pm. Terminal (daily 5:30-1:30 am).

Gray Line. *777 Eighth Ave, New York (10019). Between 47th and 48th sts. Phone 212/397-2600; toll-free 800/669-0051. www.graylinenewyork.com.* Tours of Manhattan aboard glass-top motor coaches. Also day trips and tour packages. **$$$$**

Greenwich Village. *41 Bond St Frnt, New York (10012).* An area reaching from Broadway west to Greenwich Avenue between 14th Street on the north and Houston Street on the south. An extension of this area to the East River is known as the East Village. Perhaps most famous as an art and literary center, Greenwich Village was originally settled by wealthy Colonial New Yorkers wishing to escape to the country. Many Italian and Irish immigrants settled here in the late 19th century. Among the famous writers and artists who have lived and worked in this area are Tom Paine, Walt Whitman, Henry James, John Masefield (he scrubbed saloon floors), Eugene O'Neill, Edna St. Vincent Millay, Maximum Eastman, Arctic explorer-writer Vilhjalmur Stefansson, Franz Kline, e. e. cummings, John Dos Passos, and Martha Graham. It is a colorful area, with restaurants, taverns, book, print, art, and jewelry shops. Greenwich Village is a fashionable and expensive place to live, particularly in the vicinity of

Church of the Ascension. *12 W 11th St, New York (10011). Phone 212/254-8620. www.ascensionnyc .org.* (1840) Episcopal. English Gothic; redecorated 1885-1889 under the direction of Stanford White. John La Farge's mural, *"The Ascension of Our Lord,"* surmounts the altar; the sculptured angels are by Louis Saint-Gaudens. (Daily 9 am-5 pm)

Joseph Papp Public Theater. *425 Lafayette St, New York (10003). In the former Astor Library. Phone 212/260-2400. www.publictheater.org.* Complex of six theaters where Shakespeare, new American plays, new productions of classics, films, concerts, and poetry readings are presented.

H & M. *435 Seventh Ave, New York (10018). Phone 212/643-6955. www.hm.com.* If the notion of buying affordable versions of everything you couldn't afford on Madison Avenue appeals to your wallet, then H&M is the store for you. This fast-growing international chain, which sells stylish men's, women's, young adult's, and children's clothing, features its own brands at prices that suit most budgets. The shops are bright and airy, and each location has a slightly different mix of inventory. Currently there are five outlets in New York City: 435 Seventh Ave, 125 W 125th St, 1328 Broadway (34th and Herald Square), 640 Fifth Ave, and 558 Broadway (in SoHo). (Mon-Sat 10 am-9 pm, Sun 11 am-7 pm; closed Thanksgiving, Dec 25)

Hamilton Grange National Memorial. *287 Convent Ave, New York (10031). At W 141st St. Phone 212/283-5154. www.nps.gov/hagr.* (1802) Federal-style residence of Alexander Hamilton. Visitor information center and museum (Fri-Sun 9 am-5 pm). **FREE**

Harlem. *451 W 151st St, New York (10031). Phone 212/757-0425.* An area reaching from 110th Street to about 165th Street and from the Harlem River to Morningside Avenue. Spanish Harlem is toward the east, although Harlem and Spanish Harlem overlap. Harlem has been called "the black capital of America." Tours offered by Harlem Spirituals, 690 Eighth Ave, phone 212/391-0900.

⭐ **Hayden Planetarium at the Rose Center for Earth and Space.** *American Museum of Natural History, 79th St and Central Park W, New York (10024). Phone 212/769-5100. www.amnh.org/rose/haydenplanetarium .html.* Located in the four-block-long American Museum of Natural History, this exciting new planetarium will transport you to new galaxies. The planetarium is a huge sphere housed in a glass box several stories high. In the top part of the sphere is the Space Theater, which presents the awesome Space Show, a feat of sight and sound. The bottom part, called the Big Bang, re-creates the first moments of the universe in a multisensory format narrated by author and poet Maya Angelou. This is fun for the whole family that will leave everyone breathless. The admission price includes entrance to the Museum of Natural History and the rest of the Rose Center for Earth and Space, which features exhibits that cover cosmic evolution, discoveries in astrophysics, and the sizes of the universe's various heavenly bodies. (Mon-Thurs, Sat-Sun 10 am-5:45 pm, Fri 10 am-8:45 pm; closed Thanksgiving, Dec 25) **$$$$**

Henri Bendel. *712 Fifth Ave, New York (10019). Phone 212/247-1100.* The name Henri Bendel was synonymous with chic during the disco era. Today, the store still features hip, trendy women's designer clothes, hats, fragrances, handbags, and jewelry. Whether you're looking for a $1,200 dress or a $500 handbag, this is the shop for you. You may need to break the bank (or two!) to make a purchase, but you just may find yourself decked out in something that the girls back home wished they owned. (Mon-Wed, Fri-Sat 10 am-7 pm, Thurs to 8 pm, Sun noon-6 pm; closed Jan 1, Thanksgiving, Dec 25)

Hogs and Heifers Saloon. *859 Washington St, New York (10014). Phone 212/929-0655. www.hogsandheifers .com.* A biker bar with celebrities' bras hanging off deer antlers? Only in Manhattan. Located in the Meatpacking District (just north of Greenwich Village), this bar has hosted celebs like Julia Roberts and Drew Barrymore—who decided to leave their bras behind as eye candy for patrons. You never know who you'll run into on any given night at this wild place. In addition to downing cheap beer, you'll be treated to music and bar-top dancing. The bar also has a less-famous uptown location at 1843 First Ave, phone 212/722-8635. (Daily 11-4 am)

International Center of Photography. *1133 Avenue of the Americas, New York (10036). Phone 212/857-0000. www.icp.org.* Photography buffs won't want to miss the International Center for Photography, recently relocated from the Upper East Side to Midtown. In these spacious galleries, you'll find changing exhibits featuring everyone from Weegee (Arthur Fellig) to Annie Leibovitz. (Tues-Thurs 10 am-5 pm, Fri 10 am-8 pm, Sat-Sun 10 am-6 pm; closed July 4) **$$**

Intrepid Sea-Air-Space Museum. *Pier 86, 12th Ave and 46th St, New York (10036). Phone 212/245-0072. www.intrepidmuseum.org.* The famous aircraft carrier *Intrepid* has been converted into a museum with gallery space devoted to histories of the ship itself, the modern navy, and space technology. Also on display is a nuclear guided submarine and a Vietnam-era destroyer (available for boarding). Exhibits and film presentations. (Apr-late Sept: Mon-Fri 10 am-5 pm, Sat-Sun 10 am-6 pm; rest of year: Tues-Sun 10 am-5 pm; closed Thanksgiving, Dec 25) **$$$**

Jacob K. Javits Convention Center. *655 W 34th St, New York (10001). From 34th to 39th sts along the Hudson River, on 22-acre site SW of Times Square. Phone 212/216-2000. www.javitscenter.com.* One of the world's largest, most technically advanced exposition halls; 900,000 square feet of exhibit space and more than 100 meeting rooms can accommodate six events simultaneously. Designed by I. M. Pei, the center is easily recognized by its thousands of glass cubes that mirror the skyline by day.

Jewish Museum. *1109 5th Ave, New York (10128). At 92nd St. Phone 212/423-3200. www.jewishmuseum.org.* Devoted to Jewish art and culture, ancient and modern. Historical exhibits; contemporary painting and sculpture. (Sun-Wed 11 am-5:45 pm, Thurs 11 am-8 pm, Fri 11 am-3 pm; closed Jewish holidays) **$$**

Jewish Theological Seminary of America. *3080 Broadway, New York (10027). At 122nd St. Phone 212/678-8000. www.jtsa.edu.* Extensive collection of Judaica; rare book room; courtyard with sculpture by Jacques Lipchitz. Special programs. Kosher cafeteria. Tours available. (Mon-Thurs 8 am-9 pm, Fri 8 am-5 pm, Sun 9:30 am-9 pm; closed holidays)

Jivamukti Yoga Center. *404 Lafayette St, New York (10003). Phone 212/353-0214. www.jivamuktiyoga.com.* Relax and discover your inner peace at one of these soothing yoga classes (second location in Upper East Side at 853 Lexington Ave, New York, NY 10021; 212/396-4200). The reasonable rates, by New York standards, make it affordable for almost anyone to take a quick break from the hectic pace of sightseeing. Book evening classes as early as you can, since they can fill up fast. A little tip: be on the lookout for possible celebrity sightings. (Daily) **$$$**

Joyce Gold History Tours. *141 W 17th St, New York (10011). Phone 212/242-5762. www.nyctours.com.* Take a walk through time with a professional who knows endless stories, both serious and frivolous, about Manhattan and its people. Since 1976, Joyce Gold has led all tours personally, rain or shine. No reservations are necessary, and tours last from 2 to 2 1/2 hours. Stops include Grand Central Terminal, Harlem, the East Village, Chinatown, and Fifth Avenue. Check the Web site for specific subjects, dates, meeting places, and departure times. **$$$**

Kitchen Arts & Letters. *1435 Lexington Ave, New York (10128). Between 93rd and 94th sts. Phone 212/876-5550.* Great cooks and novices alike can spend hours in this store, which features more than 10,000 cookbooks from all over the world. You can find the hottest new books by the most popular chefs, as well as those that have been out of print for years. Whether you want to prepare complicated desserts or perfect the art of the grilled cheese sandwich, this store will have the right cookbook for you. (Mon-Fri 10 am-6:30 pm; closed holidays)

Lexington Avenue. *Take the 6 Lexington Ave subway to 28th St.* It may be only a three-block area just south of Murray Hill, but this neighborhood is brimming with the sights and sounds of India. Stores sell Indian and Pakistani spices, pastries, videos, cookware, saris, and fabrics. Restaurants cater to both Muslim and Hindu tastes, suiting both beefeaters and vegetarians. The low prices are a treat as well.

⭐ **Liberty Helicopter Tours.** *Downtown Manhattan Heliport, Pier 6 and the East River, New York (10004). Take the C/E subways to 34th St and Eighth Ave. Phone 212/967-6464; toll-free 800/542-9933. www.liberty helicopters.com.* See the grand sights of the city—-from the Empire State Building to Yankee Stadium to the Chrysler Building—all from the magnificent view that only a helicopter can offer. Liberty offers six different tours on its seven-passenger helicopters, which last from five minutes for those who are a bit nervous, to as long as 30 minutes for those who want to see everything. There's even a 30-minute package that enables you to design your own course ($275 per person) and a 15-minute romance package for reserving the entire helicopter ($849), perfect for a special occasion—-you even get a bottle of Champagne afterward. Just think, you can pop the question over the beautiful lights of Manhattan! A photo ID is required, and your bags will be screened. No carry-ons are allowed, except for cameras and video equipment. (Mon-Sat 9 am-6:30 pm, call for Sun tours) **$$$$**

⭐ **Lincoln Center for the Performing Arts.** *70 Lincoln Center Plz, New York (10023). At 66th St and Broadway. Phone 212/546-2656. www.lincolncenter.org.* The approach of curtain time at The Met is a glittering New York moment. People hurry across Lincoln Plaza and disappear under the ten-story marble arches that front the Opera House. The lobby empties, the director raises his baton, and the overture begins. The Metropolitan Opera House, at the heart of Lincoln Center, is home to one of the world's greatest opera companies and the renowned American Ballet. At the right side of the square is Avery Fisher Hall, where Lorin Maazel conducts the New York Philharmonic and an impressive roster of guest artists perform. The Philharmonic's Mostly Mozart Festival in August and frequent Young People's Concerts for children are perennial favorites. Opposite is the New York State Theater, shared by the New York City Opera and the New York City Ballet, especially famous for its beloved holiday classic, Balanchine's *The Nutcracker.* In addition to the three main buildings, the 14-acre campus contains a multitude of other venues, including the Vivian Beaumont Theater, which presents Broadway plays; Alice Tully Hall, home of the Chamber Music Society and the New York Film Festival; and the world-famous Juilliard School. Damrosch Park and its band shell offer many free summer programs, including folk, jazz, and classical concerts. To get the big picture, take a Lincoln Center Guided Tour (phone 212/875-5350), which includes stops at viewing booths when rehearsals are in session. (Daily; closed holidays) **$$$** Here is

> **New York Public Library for the Performing Arts.** *Dorothy and Lewis B. Cullman Center, 40 Lincoln Center Plz, New York (10023). Phone 212/870-1630. www.nypl.org/research/lpa/lpa.html.* Books, phonograph record collection; exhibits and research library on music, theater, and dance; concerts, films, dance recitals. **FREE**

The Lion King. *New Amsterdam Theater, 214 W 42nd St, New York (10036). Phone 212/307-4747. disney.go.com/disneytheatrical/thelionking.* Based on the Disney animated film of the same name, this wildly popular musical is a feast for the eyes, ears, and soul. It has action, adventure, amazing costumes, and inventive characters—with performers singing and dancing their hearts out. Even though it's a kid's story, adults of all ages have flocked to see this musical since it opened in 1998. Because the Tony Award winner is such a spectacle to see, it is worth splurging on expensive tickets to get the best seats available. Justify the price by skimping on dinner or lunch beforehand. Book as early as you can, since this show sells out at just about any time of the year. (Daily) **$$$$**

Live TV shows. *New York (10023).* For information regarding the availability of regular and/or standby tickets, contact NBC's ticket office at 30 Rockefeller Plaza, 10112 (phone 212/664-4000); CBS at 524 W 57th St, 10019 (phone 212/975-2476); or ABC at 77 W 66th St, 10023 (phone 212/456-7777). On the day of the show, the New York Convention and Visitors Bureau at 2 Columbus Circle often has tickets for out-of-town visitors on a first-come, first-served basis. Except for NBC productions, many hotels can get tickets for guests with reasonable notice. (To see an important production, write four to six weeks in advance; the number of tickets is usually limited.) Most shows are restricted to people over 18.

Loehmann's. *101 Seventh Ave, New York (10011). Phone 212/352-0856.* Women who are ravenous for famous brands of clothing at discount prices and are willing to do whatever it takes to take home the best items (near-fistfights have been witnessed) will love Loehmann's. This department store is well known to generations of New York women and still has a good reputation for bargains. The five-story store sells mostly women's clothing, jewelry, handbags, shoes, and accessories; it offers a smaller selection of men's apparel. (Mon-Sat 9 am-9 pm, Sun 11 am-7 pm)

Lower East Side. *Delancey and Essex sts, New York. Take the B or D subway to Grand St; J or M subway to Delancey St; or the F subway to Second Ave, Delancey/ Essex St, or East Broadway.* Formerly a Jewish ghetto in the 19th and early 20th centuries, The Lower East Side is an ethnically mixed neighborhood with a mishmash of mom-and-pop stores and trendy boutiques that will attract those looking for good deals on clothing, accessories, and housewares. The farther east you go, the dicier the area becomes. Because some stores are owned by Orthodox Jews, they aren't open Friday evening or on Saturday.

Lower East Side Tenement Museum. *90 Orchard St, New York (10002). Phone 212/431-0233; toll-free 800/ 965-4827 (tickets). www.tenement.org.* The highlight at this one-of-a-kind living history museum is the guided tour of an actual tenement inhabited by real Lower East Side immigrants from the late 19th and early 20th centuries. Three apartments have been restored to their original condition. (You will need reservations for any of the guided tours, of which several are offered.) The museum also offers walking tours around the Lower East Side itself, which give you a feel for the area and what its immigrant residents had to endure upon arriving in America in search of their dreams. (Mon-Fri 11 am-5:30 pm, Sat-Sun from 10:45 am) **$$**

Macy's Herald Square. *151 W 34th St, New York (10001). 34th St at Broadway. Phone 212/695-4400. www.macys.com.* "The world's largest store" has everything from international fashion collections for men and women to antique galleries. (Mon-Sat 10-8:30 pm, Sun 11 am-7 pm; closed Easter, Thanksgiving, Dec 25)

⭐ **Madison Avenue.** *Madison Ave and 57th St, New York. Take the 6 subway to the 77th St stop and walk south. Or take the 4, 5, or 6 subway to the 59th St stop or the N or R subway to the Lexington Ave stop and walk north.* If you are well schooled (or even a novice) in the fine art of window-shopping, this stretch of very exclusive brand-name stores along swanky Madison Avenue is calling your name. Top European designers have shops here, including Giorgio Armani (760 Madison Ave, 212/988-9191), Valentino (747 Madison Ave, 212/772-6969), and Prada (841 Madison Ave, 212/327-4200), to name a few. American designers such as Polo/Ralph Lauren (867 Madison Ave, 212/ 606-2100) and Calvin Klein (654 Madison Ave, 212/ 292-9000) also have stores along this chic Manhattan strip. Looking to buy something special for someone back home (or for yourself)? The salespeople in these light and airy stores are usually quite helpful, but don't expect to find anything remotely on the cheap side. On a mild, sunny day, window-shopping here makes for a very relaxing stroll.

Madison Square Garden. *4 Pennsylvania Plz, New York (10001). Phone 212/465-6741. www.thegarden.com.* The Garden has been the site of major sporting events, concerts, and other special events for well over a century. The present Garden, the fourth building bearing

that name, opened in 1968. (The original Garden was actually on Madison Square.) It is the home of the New York Knicks and Liberty basketball teams, and New York Rangers hockey club. The Garden complex includes the 20,000-seat arena and the Theater at Madison Square Garden, which features performances of the holiday classic *A Christmas Carol* every year.

Merchant's House Museum. *29 E 4th St, New York (10003). Phone 212/777-1089. www.merchantshouse .com.* This East Village home, dating back to the 1830s, offers a look into family life in the mid-19th century. The house has been totally preserved inside and out. Original furnishings, architectural details, and family memorabilia from retired merchant Seabury Tredwell and his descendants can be viewed here. The home was lived in until 1933, when it became a museum. Tours are available on weekends. (Thurs-Fri 1-5 pm, Sat-Mon from noon) **$$**

⭐ **Metropolitan Museum of Art.** *1000 Fifth Ave, New York (10028). At 82nd St. Phone 212/535-7710. www.metmuseum.org.* Vast, exhilarating, and a little unsettling to first-time visitors because of the number and diversity of its collections, the Metropolitan Museum of Art contains more than 2 million objects spanning a period of more than 5,000 years. Even with a map and an audio guide (for which you pay extra), getting lost is not difficult—it is also part of the experience. Finding the Rooftop Garden and its population of modern sculptures is easy. Stumbling across Michelangelo's sketch for the Sistine Chapel or the stunning state-of-the-art Costume Gallery may be a rewarding surprise. From the ancient Roman tomb, The Temple of Dendur, to a room designed by Frank Lloyd Wright in 1912, and from Picasso's powerful portrait of Gertrude Stein to the oddly sur-realistic wood panel, St. Anthony in the Wilderness by an unknown Italian master, the Met presents both familiar masterpieces and intriguing hidden treasures. You could spend days here. Plan to spend enough time to see what you'll most enjoy! Call ahead or ask at the Information Desk about free tours, concerts, lectures, and films. There are always special exhibits and children's programs, but strollers are not allowed on Sundays or at special exhibits. (Sun, Tues-Thurs 9:30 am-5 pm; Fri-Sat 9:30 am-9 pm; closed Jan 1, Thanksgiving, Dec 25) **$$$**

Metropolitan Opera Company. *Metropolitan Opera House, Lincoln Center, Broadway and 64th St, New York (10023). Take the 1 or 9 subway to the 66th Street stop. Phone 212/362-6000. www.metopera.org.* This is undoubtedly one of the world's leading opera companies. Some of the top performers can be seen on the massive, very impressive stage of the Metropolitan Opera House. Tickets go on sale in March for the upcoming season, so book in advance. While prices can be high, it is worth spending the money on the best seats you can get if you are a true opera aficionado. When the lights go down, the curtain opens, and the orchestra begins playing, you will feel like you have been transported to another world. Attending the Metropolitan Opera also gives you a chance to get really dressed up and feel like a star yourself. Add an elegant dinner beforehand at a nearby Upper West Side restaurant and drinks afterwards at a lounge or piano bar and you may have the perfect evening. (Sept-May) **$$$$**

Morris-Jumel Mansion. *Roger Morris Park, 65 Jumel Terrace, New York (10032). At 160th St and Edgecomb Ave. Phone 212/923-8008. www.morrisjumel.org.* (1765) Built by Colonel Roger and Mary Philipse Morris, this was George Washington's headquarters in 1776 and later became a British command post and Hessian headquarters. Purchased by French merchant Stephen Jumel in 1810, the house was the scene of the marriage of his widow, Madame Eliza Jumel, to former Vice-President Aaron Burr in 1833. The mansion is the only remaining colonial residence in Manhattan. Period furnishings. (Wed-Sun 10 am-4 pm; closed holidays) **$**

Movin' Out. *Richard Rodgers Theatre, 226 W 46th St, New York (10036). Phone 212/307-4100. www.movin outonbroadway.com.* If you love the music of everyone's favorite Piano Man, Billy Joel, and are equally enamored with dance performances, then this very different type of Broadway musical is for you. Based on the songs of Billy Joel, *Movin' Out* tells the saga of several friends' lives and the difficulties they face. The riveting dance numbers were conceived and choreographed by Twyla Tharp. The dancers are fantastic, the numbers are moving and passionate, and the music is brought to life by a wonderful singer with a style that is similar to Billy Joel's but still very much his own. This is not for theatergoers who are looking for the conventional, cookie-cutter musical. *Movin' Out* is its own breed of show that works great and is well worth spending the bucks to get the best seats in the house (if you can). (Tue-Sun) **$$$$**

Murray's Cheese Shop. *257 Bleecker St, New York (10014). At Cornelia St between Sixth and Seventh aves. Phone toll-free 888/692-4339. www.murrayscheese.com.*

For the best gourmet cheese selection in the city, pop into this 63-year-old New York institution in lower Manhattan. The shop will entice any discerning palate with its 250 varieties of domestic and imported cheeses, as well as a selection of breads, olives, antipasti, and personalized gift baskets. (Mon-Sat 8 am-8 pm, Sun 9 am-6 pm) Murray's also has a second, newer location in Midtown at 73 Grand Central Terminal.

Museum of Arts & Design. *40 W 53rd St, New York (10019). Between 5th and 6th aves. Phone 212/956-3535. www.americancraftmuseum.org.* Dedicated to the history of American crafts, including textiles, ceramics, and glasswork. Changing exhibits. (Daily 10 am-6 pm, Thurs to 8 pm; closed holidays) **$$**

Museum of Chinese in the Americas (MoCA). *70 Mulberry St, 2nd Floor, New York (10013). Phone 212/ 619-4785. www.moca-nyc.org.* This cultural and historical museum in Chinatown, also known as MoCA, is a small but fascinating place, filled with photographs, mementos, and poetry culled from nearly two decades of research in the community. Women's roles, religion, and Chinese laundries are among the subjects covered in the exhibits. Free admission on Friday. (Tues-Thurs, Sat-Sun noon-6 pm, Fri noon-7 pm) **$**

Museum of Jewish Heritage-A Living Memorial to the Holocaust. *Battery Park City, 36 Battery Pl, New York (10280). Phone 646/437-4200 (information). www.mjhnyc.org.* Opened in 1997, this museum features thousands of moving photographs, cultural artifacts, and archival films documenting the Holocaust and the resilience of the Jewish community. It's housed in a building the shape of a hexagon, symolic of the Star of David. The East Wing houses a theater, special-exhibit galleries, a memorial garden, and a café. (Sun-Tues, Thurs 10 am-5:45 pm, Wed 10 am-8 pm, Fri and the eve of Jewish holidays 10 am-3 pm; closed Sat, Jewish holidays, and Thanksgiving) **$$**

Museum of Television & Radio. *25 W 52nd St, New York (10019). Between Fifth and Sixth aves. Phone 212/621-6800. www.mtr.org.* William Paley, the former head of CBS, founded this museum to collect, preserve, and make available to the public the best of broadcasting. View special screenings or, at a private console, hear and see selections of your own choosing from the vast archive of more than 100,000 programs. From the comedy of Burns and Allen to the Beatles in America, and from a teary-eyed Walter Cronkite reporting on President Kennedy's assassination to a tireless Peter Jennings persevering through an endless 9/11, it's there for the asking. (Tues-Wed, Fri-Sun noon-6 pm, Thurs noon-8 pm; closed holidays) **$$**

Museum of the City of New York. *1220 Fifth Ave, New York (10029). At 103rd St. Phone 212/534-1672. www.mcny.org.* Explore unique aspects of the city in this Upper East Side mansion dating back to 1930. Displays include a toy gallery with dollhouses; collections of decorative arts, prints, and photographs; and an exhibit on Broadway, complete with costumes and set designs. Other exhibits feature slide shows, paintings, memorabilia, and sculptures, all dedicated to the fascinating history of the city up to the present day. (Wed-Sun 10 am-5 pm; closed holidays) **$$$**

New York City Fire Museum. *278 Spring St, New York (10013). In SoHo. Phone 212/691-1303. www.nycfire museum.org.* Although it isn't, strictly speaking, a children's museum, the New York City Fire Museum has great appeal for kids. Housed in an actual firehouse that was used until 1959, the museum is filled with fire engines new and old, helmets and uniforms, hoses and lifesaving nets. Retired firefighters take visitors through the museum, reciting fascinating tidbits of firefighting history along the way. (Tues-Sat 10 am-5 pm, Sun 10-am-4 pm) **DONATION**

New York Giants (NFL). *Giants Stadium, 50 Hwy 120, East Rutherford (07073). Phone 201/935-8111. www.giants.com.* The Giants had sporadic success throughout the 1980s and '90s (including winning two Super Bowls), and made an improbable run for the Super Bowl in 2000 before losing to the Baltimore Ravens.

New York Historical Society. *2 W 77th St at Central Park W, New York (10024). Phone 212/873-3400. www.nyhistory.org.* This monument to the history of the city recently reawakened after years of inactivity due to financial troubles. Spread out over many high-ceilinged rooms, the society presents temporary exhibits on everything from the legendary Stork Club—frequented by everyone from Frank Sinatra to JFK—to the small African-American communities that once dotted Central Park. The Henry Luce III Center for the Study of American culture features 40,000 objects, including George Washington's camp bed at Valley Forge to the world's largest collection of Tiffany lamps, as well as a nice collection of paintings, sculpture, furniture, and decorative objects. (Tues-Sun 11 am-6 pm) **$$**

New York Islanders (NHL). *Nassau Coliseum, 1255 Hempstead Tpke, Uniondale (11553). Phone 516/542-* 9348; toll-free 800/882-4753. www.newyorkislanders .com.* Pro hockey's Islanders were the dominant team of the early 1980s, winning three Stanley Cups in a row from 1980 to 1982.

New York Jets (NFL). *Giants Stadium, 50 Hwy 120, East Rutherford (07073). Phone 516/560-8200 (tickets). www.newyorkjets.com.* The Jets began their tenure in the NFL with a bang, when "Broadway Joe" Namath guaranteed victory over the Baltimore Colts in Super Bowl III and then pulled off the feat.

New York Knicks (NBA). *Madison Square Garden, 4 Pennsylvania Plz, New York (10121). Phone 212/465-5867 (tickets). www.nyknicks.com.* Knicks tickets are sometimes difficult to get because corporations and season ticket holders have snatched them up; call early to maximize your chances. Remember to be on the lookout for celebrities—Woody Allen and Spike Lee often attend games.

New York Liberty (WNBA). *Madison Square Garden, 4 Pennsylvania Plz, New York (10121). Phone 212/ 564-9622. www.nyliberty.com.* Professional women's basketball games.

⭐ **New York Mets (MLB).** *Shea Stadium, 123-01 Roosevelt Ave, Flushing (11368). Take the 7 subway to the Willets Point-Shea Stadium stop, or hop a leisurely ferry from Manhattan (phone toll-free 800/53-FERRY for information) to the stadium. Phone 718/507-6387. www.mets.com.* Although the Mets may not have as long and colorful a history as the Yankees, they are nonetheless a fun team to watch and offer any baseball lover a great spring or summer afternoon's or evening's experience. Tickets are usually easy to get for most games, except the annual match-up against the Bronx Bombers. Bring extra cash and do the game right by noshing on hot dogs and peanuts, loading up on souvenirs, and cheering loudly for your favorite players. Don't forget sunscreen, a hat, and sunglasses for day games. (Apr-Sept)

New York Public Library. *Fifth Ave and 42nd St, New York (10018). Phone 212/930-0501. www.nypl.org.* One of the best research libraries in the world, with more than 10 million volumes. Exhibits of rare books, art materials; free programs at branches. One-hour tours of central building (Tues-Sat), library tours at 11 am and 2 pm. Many interesting collections on display at the Central Research Library and The New York Public Library for the Performing Arts (also tours). **FREE**

New York Rangers (NHL). *Madison Square Garden, 4 Pennsylvania Plz, New York (10121). Phone 212/465-6741. www.newyorkrangers.com.* If you love the thrill of ice hockey—as well as the colorful fights that break out between players and the screaming, cursing fans on the sidelines—try to catch the popular New York Rangers in action. Because the team has done so well over the years, getting tickets has become very difficult. Buy yours months in advance if you can. Avoid the temptation to buy overpriced (or worse, counterfeit) tickets from the numerous scalpers who sell their wares in front of the Garden before each game. If you just can't get tickets but still want to experience live hockey while you're visiting New York, opt for a short commute to see either the New York Islanders (631/888-9000 for tickets) or the New Jersey Devils (201/935-6050 for tickets).

New York Stock Exchange. *20 Broad St, 3rd Fl, New York (10005). Phone 212/656-5165. www.nyse.com.* The world's largest securities trader. Currently, the New York Stock Exchange Interactive Education Center is closed indefinitely for all tours. Call for updated information.

New York University. *40 E 7th St, New York (10003). Phone 212/998-4524 (tours). www.nyu.edu.* (1831) (15,584 students) One of the largest private universities in the country, NYU is known for its undergraduate and graduate business, medical, and law schools, school of performing arts, and fine arts programs. The university has graduated a large number of "Fortune 500" company executives. Most programs, including the Graduate Business Center, are located on the main campus surrounding Washington Square Park; the medical and dental schools are on the East Side. Tours (Mon-Fri except holidays, from Admissions Office at 22 Washington Sq N). In the Main Building at the northeast corner of Washington Square is the Grey Art Gallery and Study Center, with paintings, drawings, sculpture, and changing exhibits (Tues-Sat). Renaissance musical instrument collection in Waverly Building (by appointment).

Police Museum. *100 Old Slip, New York (10005). Phone 212/480-3100. www.nycpolicemuseum.org.* Exhibits of police uniforms, badges, and equipment. (Tues-Sat 10 am-5 pm; closed holidays) **$**

The Producers. *St. James Theater, 246 W 44th St, New York (10036). Phone 212/239-5800. www.producersonbroadway.com.* This show has won the most Tony Awards ever, and it's truly worth all the accolades that it has received. Based on the hysterical Mel Brooks movie of the same name, this even funnier musical brings to life the story of two producers who try desperately to stage a Broadway flop. Take that wacky premise, add even wackier characters and very funny song and dance numbers, and you have a delightful night out for lovers of musical theater. You'll laugh from start to finish and even hum some of the catchy, irreverent tunes. This show is destined to be around for a long time. Book very early, since *The Producers* is always a sell-out with both locals and tourists. (Tues-Sun) **$$$$**

Riverside Park. *475 Riverside Dr, New York (10115). W 72nd St to W 158th St along the Hudson River. Phone 212/408-0264. www.nycgovparks.org.* This city park on the Upper West Side offers a pleasant, bucolic setting that's even more laid back than Central Park. The long, narrow, breezy park has a promenade for bike riders between West 72nd and West 110th streets designed for those who want to take a nice, easy ride at a slow pace. Bike rentals are available at the nearby Toga Bike Shop (110 West End Ave, phone 212/799-9625). For even more relaxation, the 79th Street Boat Basin (phone 212/496-2105) provides a quiet respite for walking on the river's edge. There's also a nearby café that's open in summer. The park offers some sightseeing in the way of Grant's Tomb, a towering granite tomb that is one of the world's largest mausoleums. It holds the remains of President Ulysses S. Grant and his wife, Julia—a must-see for Civil War history buffs. **FREE**

⭐ **Rockefeller Center.** *30 Rockefeller Plz, New York (10112). Fifth Ave to Ave of the Americas and beyond, 47th St to 51st St with some buildings stretching to 52nd St. Phone 212/632-3975. www.rockefellercenter.com.* Conceived of by John D. Rockefeller during the 1930s, Rockefeller Center is the largest privately owned business and entertainment complex in the world. Enter through the Channel Gardens (5th Avenue between 49th and 50th) and walk toward the central sunken plaza. Here, a golden statue of Prometheus sprawls benevolently beside a pool and an outdoor café that becomes an ice skating rink in winter. (Yes, you can rent skates.) The center is magical at Christmastime, when a 78,000-light tree towers over Prometheus. The backdrop of the scene is the core skyscraper, the GE Building, home to NBC Studios. You can take a studio tour (adults $17.50, seniors and children $15, no children under 6; phone 212/664-7174), or catch *The Today Show* being broadcast live through the street-level picture window at West 49th and Rockefeller Plaza. The 21-acre complex contains

19 buildings, most built of limestone with aluminum streamlining. But the Art Deco gem of the group is Radio City Music Hall, America's largest theater. Tour the theater or see a show—especially if the high-kicking Rockettes are performing (www.radiocity.com; phone 212/247-4777).

Schomburg Center for Research in Black Culture. *515 Malcolm X Blvd, New York (10037). Phone 212/491-2200. www.nypl.org/research/sc/sc.html.* The center's collection covers every phase of black activity wherever black people have lived in significant numbers. Books, manuscripts, periodicals, art, and audiovisual materials. (Tues-Sat) **FREE**

Serena. *222 W 23rd St, New York (10011). Phone 212/255-4646.* If you want to be a part of "the scene" and "be seen," Serena is the bar and lounge for you. It serves food and drinks and is known as an after-hours hangout for the chic and the hip. The place has a plush, dark look to it. But, look carefully, because you may see some celebrities sipping champagne off in a corner somewhere. (Daily)

The Slipper Room. *167 Orchard St, New York (10002). Phone 212/253-7246. www.slipperroom.com.* This club features a mix of offbeat shows and music. From quiz show nights to bawdy burlesque performances to up-and-coming bands, the Slipper Room is a fun, inexpensive place to act silly and party with your friends. The club gets a mixed late-night crowd and is the kind of place that attracts fun-loving night owls who like to party until dawn. (Tues-Sat; Sun, Mon special events only) **$**

Smithsonian Cooper-Hewitt, National Design Museum. *2 E 91st St, New York (10128). At Fifth Ave. Phone 212/849-8400. www.si.edu/ndm.* Once home to 19th-century industrialist Andrew Carnegie, this 64-room 1901 Georgian mansion is now a branch of the Smithsonian Institution dedicated to design and the decorative arts. The exhibits are temporary and focus on such subjects as ceramics, furniture, textiles, and metalwork. Out back is a romantic garden, where concerts are sometimes presented. (Tues-Thurs 10 am-5 pm, Fri 10 am-9 pm, Sat 10 am-6 pm, Sun noon-6 pm; closed holidays) **$$**

SOB's. *204 Varick St, New York (10014). Phone 212/243-4940. www.sobs.com.* Lovers of the Brazilian beat, as well as hip-hop, reggae, salsa, African music, and other kinds of international sounds, have flocked since 1982 to this venerable SoHo nightclub. SOB's—Sounds of Brazil—features new performers and

well-known stars who always get the crowd up and dancing. Monday nights are famous for Latin dance lessons, with an entrance fee of just $5 before 7 pm. Novices are most welcome to try out their dancing shoes during these classes. Saturday Night Samba features dancers and Brazilian performers. Every evening has a different theme and varied performers. For your dining pleasure, Latin and Brazilian cuisine are on the menu. While other clubs are quiet for the weekdays, SOB's continues to come alive. (Daily; hours vary) **$$$$**

SoHo Street Vendors. *South of Houston, New York (10012). The N/R subways stop at Canal or Prince St, or you can take the A/C/E subways to Canal St. Then wander around the general area, since street vendors change locations. Phone 212/369-6004.* Shopping from street vendors in this hip section of the city is a fun experience largely due to the haggling, which seems to come naturally to many native New Yorkers. If you're not comfortable doing this, bring along a buddy for moral support. Never accept a first offer, and don't look for authenticity. Just have fun with it. If you see something you like, grab it, because the same vendor may not be back at the same spot the next day. Vendors peddle a multitude of treasures, including trendy clothing, cool jewelry, and paintings, drawings, and other artwork. With so many items to choose from, you're sure to come away with something you haven't seen anywhere else before—or won't see until the trend hits your neck of the woods months later.

Solomon R. Guggenheim Museum. *1071 Fifth Ave, New York (10128). Between E 88th and 89th sts. Phone 212/423-3500. www.guggenheim.org.* Some say that the Guggenheim looks like a giant snail or an upside-down wedding cake. Few would deny that Frank Lloyd Wright's brilliant concept of ever-widening concrete circles around a central atrium provided an intriguing new way to display art—especially in 1959 when the museum opened. Take the elevator to the top and walk down the gently sloping spiral to view temporary exhibits that draw a diversity of viewers. Past shows have included "Centre Pompidou" from Paris, "Norman Rockwell: Pictures for the American People," and "Art of the Motorcycle." A smaller adjoining rotunda and tower hold a stunning permanent collection heavy in works by Wassily Kandinsky, Paul Klee, Francois Leger, and Marc Chagall, as well as by the French Impressionists. Pablo Picasso is well represented, especially in his early Blue Period, including *Woman Ironing,* the artist's well-known depiction of labor and fatigue. Free docent-led tours are scheduled daily at noon. (Sat-Wed 10 am-5:45 pm, Fri 10 am-8 pm; closed holidays) **$$**

Sotheby's Auctions. *1334 York Ave, New York (10021). Phone 212/606-7000. www.sothebys.com.* Get a taste of high society at a Sotheby's auction. Whether you're just a spectator or you have lots of spare cash with which to purchase something wonderful, attending an auction at this institution is a thrilling, fast-paced experience. Sotheby's has held auctions for items belonging to the Duke and Duchess of Windsor and other celebrities. It has fashion, book and manuscript, and vintage car departments, just to name a few. Sotheby's Arcade features more affordable items. Publications like *New York* magazine and *The New York Times* contain listings of upcoming events. (Closed holidays) **FREE**

South Street Seaport. *19 Fulton St, New York (10038). Fulton and Water sts, at the East River. Phone 212/732-7678. www.southstreetseaport.com.* This 12-block area was restored to display the city's maritime history, with an emphasis on South Street in the days of sailing vessels. The South Street Museum piers at South and Fulton streets now moor the *Ambrose*, a lightship (1908); the *Lettie G. Howard*, a Gloucester fishing schooner (1893); the fully-rigged *Wavertree* (1885); the *Peking*, a German four-masted barque (1911); and the *Pioneer*, a schooner (1885). Permanent and changing maritime exhibits include models, prints, photos, and artifacts. If history isn't your thing, this festival marketplace has more than 100 souvenir and mall-type stores, like Abercrombie & Fitch and The Body Shop, as well as 35 mostly casual restaurants. Don't miss the three-story glass and steel Pier 17 Pavilion, which extends into the East River and offers great views of the Brooklyn Bridge and New York Harbor.

South Street Seaport Museum. *South and Fulton sts, at the East River. Phone 212/748-8600. www.southstseaport.org.* This eleven-block area was restored to display the city's maritime history, with emphasis on South Street in the days of sailing vessels. The museum piers now moor the *Ambrose,* a lightship (1908); the *Lettie G. Howard,* a Gloucester fishing schooner (1893); the fully-rigged *Wavertree* (1885); the *Peking,* a German four-masted barque (1911); and the *Pioneer,* a schooner (1885). Permanent and changing maritime exhibits include models, prints, photos, and artifacts. Tours. Harbor excursions. Children admitted only when accompanied by adult. (Daily 10 am-5 pm; closed Jan 1, Thanksgiving, Dec 25) **$$**

St. Patrick's Cathedral. *460 Madison Ave, New York (10012). Between E 50th and 51st sts. Phone 212/226-8075. www.ny-archdiocese.org/pastoral/cathedral_about.html.* Irish immigrants and their descendents were largely responsible for the construction and dedication of St. Patrick's Cathedral, the largest Catholic cathedral in the United States. A standout on Fifth Avenue since 1859, the white marble and stone structure dominates the surrounding skyscrapers. Twin Gothic spires reach heavenward, and some of the stained glass windows were made in Chartres. Cool and calm within, the church bestows a palpable peace on visitors as well as those attending services. It is the resting place of New York's deceased archbishops; they are buried in tombs under the high altar, and their hats hang from the ceiling above. The steps of St. Pat's are a popular meeting place for New Yorkers. (Daily 7 am-9 pm) **FREE**

★ **Statue of Liberty National Monument.** *Liberty Island, New York (10004). Ferry tickets and departures from Castle Clinton National Monument in Battery Park. Phone 212/363-3200 (recording). www.nps.gov/stli.* This worldwide symbol of freedom is the first thing passengers see as their ships sail into New York Harbor. A gift from France in 1886 (her iron skeleton was designed by Gustave Eiffel, creator of Paris's Eiffel Tower), she stands 152 feet high on an 89-foot pedestal, indomitable and welcoming. Ellis Island, the most famous port of immigration in the United States, became part of the national monument in 1965. Between 1892 and 1954, 12 million immigrants first stepped on American soil at Ellis Island. When it closed in 1954, it had processed 40 percent of living American families. You can look for your ancestors' names on the Wall of Honor or visit the dramatic Immigrants' Living Theater and the cavernous Great Hall, where nervous immigrants awaited processing. Passing the Statue of Liberty on the return trip may prove to be a heart-stirring, thought-provoking experience. (Daily 9:30 am-5 pm; closed Dec 25) **$$** Located on the second floor in the pedestal of the Statue is

Statue of Liberty Exhibit. *52 Vanderbilt Ave, 4th Fl, New York (10017).* Photographs, artifacts, and history dioramas with light and sound effects depict the construction of the Statue of Liberty.

Studio Museum in Harlem. *144 W 125th St, New York (10027). Phone 212/864-4500. www.studiomuseuminharlem.org.* Founded in 1968, this museum is the "principal center for the study of Black art in

America," spread out over several well-lit floors of a turn-of-the-century building. The permanent exhibit features works by such masters as Romare Bearden, James VanDerZee, and Jacob Lawrence; temporary exhibits present a mixture of both world-renowned and emerging artists. The Studio is also known for its lively lecture and concert series, presented September through May. (Wed-Fri noon-6 pm, Sat 10 am-6 pm, Sun noon-6 pm; closed holidays) **$$**

Sullivan St Bakery. *73 Sullivan St, New York (10012). At Broome and Spring sts. Phone 212/334-9435. www. sullivanstreetbakery.com.* If bread is your passion, then enter these doors and take in the sights and smells of the Sullivan St Bakery. The bakery sells a variety of mouthwatering thin-crust Italian breads, Roman-style pizzas, biscotti, and tarts, as well as coffee to wash it all down. A second location is in Hell's Kitchen at 533 W 47th Street, phone 212/265-5580. (Daily 7 am-7 pm)

Temple Emanu-El. *1 E 65th St, New York (10021). Fifth Ave and 65th St. Phone 212/744-1400. www.emanuel nyc.org.* Largest Jewish house of worship in the world; Reform Congregation founded in 1845. Romanesque temple seats 2,500; Beth-El chapel seats 350. (Daily 10 am-5 pm; no visiting on High Holy Days) Tours (by appointment, upon written request).

Terence Conran Shop. *415 E 59th St, New York (10022). Phone 212/755-9079. www.conran.com.* This British-based retailer has come to the Big Apple, with a shop built right into a pavilion at the Queensboro Bridge. With international flair and a sense of style, the store sells fine—and sometimes unusual—home furnishings, kitchenware, and jewelry familiar to those who read *Wallpaper* and *British Elle Décor*. If you don't blow your budget on these irresistible, ultra-modern accessories, stop for a bite next door at Gustavino's, a French-American restaurant that is just as chic as the store. (Mon-Fri 11 am-8 pm, Sat 10 am-7 pm, Sun noon-6 pm)

Theodore Roosevelt Birthplace National Historic Site. *28 E 20th St, New York (10003). Between Broadway and Park Ave S. Phone 212/260-1616. www.nps.gov/thrb.* The reconstructed birthplace of the 26th president, who lived here from 1858 to 1872. Guided tours (every hour with the last tour at 4 pm) of five rooms restored to their 1865 appearance. Audiovisual presentation and special events. (Tues-Sat 9 am-5 pm; closed holidays) **$**

Times Square and the Theater District. *1560 Broadway, New York (10036). 6th to 8th aves and 40th to 53rd sts.* Entertainment center of the city and theatrical headquarters of the country offering plays, musicals, concerts, movies, and exotic entertainments; named for the Times Tower at One Times Square, originally the home of *The New York Times.*

TKTS Discount Theater Tickets. *Broadway at 47th St, New York (10036). www.tkts.com.* With the price of Broadway shows closing in at $100 for the best seats in the house, TKTS is a godsend to theater lovers. The more popular TKTS booth at Times Square (just look for lots of people standing on two lines) provides up to 50 percent discounted tickets on Broadway, off-Broadway, and some musical and dance events. Tickets are sold for the day of performance for matinees and evening shows. The downtown booth (199 Water St) sells tickets for evening day-of performance and for matinees one day in advance. Generally, you will not be able to get tickets for the hottest shows in town through TKTS, but usually for ones that have been playing for a while or are not doing as well. Lines are long and you are guaranteed nothing by waiting on line. Have a first, second, and third choice in mind. Only cash and traveler's checks are accepted. (Daily)

Trinity Church. *Broadway at Wall St, New York (10019). Broadway at Wall St. Phone 212/602-0800. www.trinity wallstreet.org.* (1846) The third building to occupy this site; the original was built in 1697. Its famous grave-yard, favorite lunchtime spot of workers in the financial district, contains the graves of Robert Fulton and Alexander Hamilton. The Gothic Revival brownstone church houses a museum. Parish center with dining room open to the public. Services (Mon-Fri 12:05 pm, Sun 9 am, 11:15 am). Church (daily 7 am-6 pm). Churchyard (weather permitting, daily 7 am-4 pm). **FREE** Also here is

St. Paul's Chapel. *211 Broadway, New York (10007). Phone 212/602-0874. www.saintpaulschapel.org.* A chapel of Trinity Church, this example of Georgian architecture, finished in 1766, is the oldest public building in continuous use on Manhattan Island. George Washington's pew is in the north aisle; chancel ornamentation by L'Enfant; Waterford chandeliers. Concerts (Mon and Thurs at noon). (Daily) **FREE**

Ukrainian Museum. *203 Second Ave, New York (10003). Between 12th and 13th sts. Phone 212/228-0110. www.ukrainianmuseum.org.* Changing exhibits of Ukrainian folk art, fine art, and history; workshops on weekends in folk crafts. (Wed-Sun 1-5 pm; closed holidays, Jan 7) **$$**

Union Square Greenmarket. *14th St and Broadway, New York (10001). The 4, 5, 6, N, and R subways stop at Union Square. Phone 212/477-3220. www.cenyc.org.* This bustling year-round farmers' market is located at Union Square between 14th and 17th streets and Broadway and Park Avenue. It's a chance to experience a bit of the country in the Big Apple, as farmers and other vendors sell fresh fruits, vegetables, cheeses, homemade pies, herbs, cut flowers, and potted plants. Plan to arrive early for the best selection. (Mon, Wed, Fri-Sat 8 am-6 pm; closed holidays)

United Nations. *First Ave at 46th St, New York (10017). First Ave from 42nd to 48th St. Phone 212/963-8687. www.un.org.* These four buildings, designed under the direction of Wallace K. Harrison, were completed between 1950 and 1952. Regular sessions of the General Assembly start on the third Tuesday in September. Tickets are occasionally available to certain official meetings on a first-come basis. The entrance is on First Avenue at 46th Street, at the north end of the General Assembly Building. An information desk and a ticket booth are in the lobby; the UN book and gift shops and the UN Post Office are in the basement, where one can mail letters bearing United Nations stamps. On the fourth floor is the UN Delegates Dining Room. The Conference Building is where the various UN Councils meet. The Secretariat Building is a 550-foot-high rectangular glass-and-steel building; here the day-to-day work of the UN staff is performed. The fourth building is the Dag Hammarskjold Library, open only to UN staff and delegations, or by special permission for serious research. Guided tours (45 minutes) leave the public entrance lobby at frequent intervals (daily; closed Thanksgiving and several days during year-end holiday season; also weekdays in Jan-Feb); no children under 5. Buildings (daily). **$$$**

Wall Street. *Between Broadway and South St.* New York's Wall Street stands for much more than an address: it is the symbol of American capitalism, known around the world. The street begins at Broadway, where you'll find Trinity Church (built in 1846 and a symbol of the city's strength when it survived the nearby September 11, 2001, terrorist attacks), and stretches east to the East River. If you walk the street's six or so blocks, you'll pass the Federal Hall National Monument, the site where George Washington took the Oath of Office and became the first President of the United States in 1789. Step inside the building to view the impressive rotunda and check out an exhibit on the Constitution. Just half a block south of Wall Street, on Broad Street, is the New York Stock Exchange, where fortunes are made and lost with every clang of the opening bell.

Washington Heights Museum Group. *Broadway and 155th St, New York (10032).* (Audubon Terrace) Clustered around a central plaza and accessible from Broadway, this group includes the American Geographical Society, the American Academy and Institute of Arts and Letters, the American Numismatic Society, and the Hispanic Society of America. Also here are the

> **American Numismatic Society.** *140 Williams St, New York (10032). Phone 212/234-3130. www.amnumsoc.org.* Society headquarters; numismatic library; "World of Coins" exhibit; changing exhibits. (Tues-Fri 9 am-4:30 pm; closed holidays) **FREE**

> **Hispanic Society of America.** *613 W 155th St, New York (10032). Between 155th and 156th sts. Phone 212/926-2234. www.hispanicsociety.org.* Art of the Iberian Peninsula from prehistoric times to the present. Paintings, sculpture, ceramics, drawings, etchings, lithographs, textiles, and metalwork. (Tues-Sat 10 am-4:30 pm, Sun 1-4 pm; closed holidays) **FREE**

Washington Square Park. *W 4th St and Waverly Pl, New York (10011). Many subways stop at nearby W 4th St.* For the ultimate in daytime people-watching, head downtown to the heart and soul of Greenwich Village. The bustling 9-acre park, dating back to 1827, serves up a cacophony of jugglers, street musicians, magicians, and countless students from nearby New York University. The park hosts outdoor art fairs in spring and fall, as well as jazz performances in summer. The north end of the park features the historic Washington Memorial Arch (14 Washington Square N). This marble structure was modeled after Paris' Arc de Triomphe and was erected in 1889. (Daily)

Whitney Museum of American Art. *945 Madison Ave, New York (10021). At E 75th St. Phone 212/570-3676; toll-free 800/944-8639. www.whitney.org.* Bauhaus-trained architect Marcel Breuer's museum is menacingly cantilevered toward Madison Avenue. Its bold, sculptural quality makes it a fitting home for modern and contemporary art. The impressive permanent collection takes American art from the early 20th century into the 21st, showing realistic works by Thomas Hart Benton, Edward Hopper, and Georgia O'Keeffe, as well as works by later artists such as Alexander Calder, Louise Nevelson, Robert Rauschenberg, and Jasper Johns. The controversial Whitney "Biennial" showcases the latest works of contemporary artists. (Wed-Thurs, Sat-Sun 11 am-6 pm, Fri 1-9 pm (6-9 pm pay-what-you-wish admission); closed Jan 1, Thanksgiving, Dec 25) **$$$** Branch museums include

Whitney Museum of American Art at Philip Morris. *120 Park Ave, New York (10017). At 42nd St.* Phone 917/663-2550. Gallery and sculpture court. Changing exhibits annually; free lectures, performances. Gallery talks (Mon, Wed, Fri). Gallery (Mon-Fri 11 am-6 pm, Thurs 11 am-7:30 pm). Sculpture court (Mon-Sat 7:30 am-9:30 pm, Sun and holidays 11 am-7 pm). **FREE**

Woolworth Building. *233 Broadway, New York (10279).* This neo-Gothic skyscraper by Cass Gilbert was the tallest building in the world (792 feet, 58 stories) when it was built. Frank W. Woolworth, the dime-store king, paid $13.5 million cash for his "cathedral of commerce" when it was completed in 1913.

World Financial Center. *200 Liberty St, New York (10281). West St between Liberty and Vesey sts.* Phone 212/945-0505. www.worldfinancialcenter.com. The center includes more than 40 shops and restaurants on and around the Winter Garden, a 120-foot-high, vaulted glass and steel atrium.

Yeshiva University. *Wilf Campus, 500 W 185th St, New York (10033).* Phone 212/960-5400. www.yu.edu. (1886) (6,300 students) America's oldest and largest university under Jewish auspices. Zysmon Hall, historic main building, has elaborate stone façade and Byzantine domes. The Mendel Gottesman Library houses many specialized collections (academic year, Mon-Fri, Sun; closed holidays, Jewish holidays; tours by appointment). Part of the university is

Yeshiva University Museum. *15 W 16th St, New York (10011).* Phone 212/294-8330. www.yu.edu/museum. This teaching museum devoted to Jewish art, architecture, history, and culture has permanent exhibits, including scale models of synagogues from the 3rd to 19th centuries; reproduction of frescoes from the Dura-Europos Synagogue; ceremonial objects, rare books; audiovisual presentations; theater; changing exhibits. (Academic year, Tues-Thurs, Sun 11 am-5 pm; closed holidays, Jewish holidays) **$$**

Zabar's. *2245 Broadway, New York (10024). At 80th St.* Phone 212/787-2000. www.zabars.com. Zabar's is one of those places that makes New York the yummy place that it is. This second-generation gourmet food market, considered sacred by those who enjoy fine eating, has graced Manhattan's Upper West Side since 1934. Occupying close to one city block and employing 250 people, Zabar's sells sinful breads and pastries, meats, cheeses, smoked fish, condiments, and cookware. The shop's babka (Russian coffee cake) makes life worth living. Since Zabar's is one of the rare establishments in New York that's open every day of the year, you can treat your taste buds anytime you like. Forget diets and just enjoy. (Mon-Fri 8 am-7:30 pm, Sat 8 am-8 pm, Sun 9 am-6 pm)

Special Events

Bryant Park Summer Film Festival. *42nd St between Fifth and Sixth aves, New York (10036).* Phone 212/512-5700. www.bryantpark.org. For a relaxing evening taking in the balmy breezes of summer, a picnic with your favorite foods, and an outdoor screening of a classic American film, park yourself on the lawn at Bryant Park for its weekly film showing. Hundreds come each Monday night to see a movie and hang out once the sun goes down. And you can't beat the price! Check the local newspapers to find out what's playing each week. Mon, June-Aug. **FREE**

Central Park Concerts. *72nd St and Fifth Ave, New York (10021).* Phone 212/360-3456. Free performances by the New York Philharmonic and the Metropolitan Opera Company on the Great Lawn, mid-park at 81st St. June-Aug.

Chinese New Year. *Mott and Pell sts, New York (10013).* Phone 212/226-1330. Parade with lions, dragons, costumes, firecrackers. Early-mid-Feb.

Christmas Star Show. *Hayden Planetarium, 79th St and Central Park W, New York (10024).* Phone 212/769-5920. Late Nov-early Jan.

Columbus Day Parade. *Fifth Ave between 45th and 86th sts, New York (10022).* Phone 212/484-1222. Oct.

Fleet Week. *Intrepid Sea-Air-Space Museum, 166 W 46th St, New York (10036).* Phone 212/245-0072. www.fleetweek.navy.mil. In a scene right out of the Gene Kelly, Navy-themed musical, *On the Town*, Navy and Coast Guard ships gather for a parade up the Hudson River that is a true spectacle of springtime in New York. After the ships dock by the museum, they are open to the public for tours. You can find some great photo opportunities here. Other fun sights for all ages include flyovers and 21-gun salutes. Expect to find Navy men all over the city, looking for a good time. Fleet Week is pure Americana that gives the city a real patriotic feeling. Late May.

Greenwich Village Halloween Parade. *Take almost any subway to W Fourth St and keep walking uptown into Chelsea. Phone 845/758-5519. www.halloween-nyc.com.* Straights, gays, men, women, kids, seniors, and everyone in between dress in the wildest of costumes for this annual Halloween tradition in the West Village. Strangers become instant friends and everyone gets into the fun spirit in what has become the largest Halloween parade in the United States. Although the crowd may get a bit wild, the event is usually quite safe due to the large police presence and general good feelings exuded by area residents. If you've ever wanted to let it all hang out and wear a costume that will shock everyone you know, this is the place to do it. Prepare to stay out late and enjoy some late-night partying at a local bar (unless you have the kids with you, of course). Late Oct.

Hispanic Day Parade. *Fifth Ave between 45th and 86th sts, New York (10036).* Mid-Oct.

Independence Day Harbor Festival. *East River and South St Seaport, New York (10044). Phone 212/494-4495.* This is the nation's largest July 4 celebration; fireworks; food; music. Weekend of July 4.

JVC Jazz Festival. *Park Row between Beekman and Ann sts, New York (10038). Phone 212/501-1390. www. festivalproductions.net/jvcjazz/newyork.htm.* World-famous musicians perform in Avery Fisher Hall, Carnegie Hall, Town Hall, and other sites throughout the city. Last two weeks in June.

Macy's Thanksgiving Day Parade. *34th and 72nd sts, New York (10001). Phone 212/494-5432.* If you have a child or you want to feel like a kid again yourself, spend Thanksgiving Day morning enjoying this wonderful and festive New York event. Amazing floats, cheerful clowns (who are all volunteers and are either Macy's employees or friends and families of Macy's employees), and celebrities are all part of the parade, which starts at 9 am and ends at around noon. The atmosphere is always jovial and will put you in the holiday spirit. Since you may spend most of the time standing, wear comfortable shoes, dress in layers, bring snacks, and duck into nearby eateries for hot drinks and bathroom breaks. Keep in mind that standing for several hours may be too tiring for

children under 5 (unless they spend most of the time perched atop your shoulders, which may be too tiring for you!). One of the best viewing spots is on Herald Square in front of Macy's.

The Meadowlands. *50 Hwy 120, East Rutherford (07073). Phone 201/935-8500; toll-free 888/445-6543. www.meadowlands.com.* Features sporting events at Giants Stadium, concerts at Continental Airlines Arena, and thoroughbred racing at the Meadowlands Racetrack.

New York Shakespeare Festival & Shakespeare in the Park. *81st St and Central Park W or 79th and Fifth Ave, New York (10024). Phone 212/539-8750. www.centralpark.org.* At the 2,000-seat outdoor Delacorte Theater in Central Park, near W 81st St. Tues-Sun. Free tickets are distributed on the day of the performance. June-Sept.

Ninth Avenue International Food Festival. *Ninth Ave between 37th and 57th sts, New York (10018). Take the A/C/E subway to 34th St and 8th Ave. Phone 212/581-7029.* This event epitomizes all the gastronomical diversity that is New York City. Taking place during the third weekend in May in the ethnically mixed Hell's Kitchen neighborhood, the two-day festival is a 20-block extravaganza of food booths and entertainment. From burritos to jerk chicken to curried chicken, you can find any kind of food imaginable in this ultimate of block parties. More than 1 million visitors have showed up in the past to this annual festival that's been going strong for 28 years, so prepare for crowds. Wear comfortable shoes and loose-fitting clothes so that you can pig out in total comfort. Late May.

The Nutcracker. *New York State Theater, 20 Lincoln Center, New York (10023). Phone 212/870-5570. www.nycballet.com.* Taking your child (and yourself!) to the New York City Ballet's performance of *The Nutcracker* is one of those magical events that both tourists and New Yorkers love to take in during the colorful, festive Christmas season. This fantasy story of the Mouse King and little Clara has delighted children for many years. The New York Ballet's version of this classic is sure to please, with renowned dancers, some of the most appealing young performers, beautiful music by Tchaikovsky, and luscious sets and costumes. No ballet lover should miss a performance of *The Nutcracker* while visiting New York City during Christmas. Dec.

NYC Marathon. *Staten Island side of the Verrazano-Narrows Bridge, New York (10024). Phone 212/423-*

2249 (marathon office). www.nyrrc.org. What event attracts more than 2 million spectators, 30,000 participants from every corner of the globe, and 12,000 volunteers? None other than the grueling 26.2-mile New York City Marathon. Whether you're an experienced runner or a diehard couch potato, to stand on the sidelines and cheer on these amazing men and women during the world's largest marathon is a thrilling and rewarding experience. The event begins on the Staten Island side of the Verrazano-Narrows Bridge, goes through all five boroughs of the city, and finishes up by Tavern on the Green restaurant in Central Park. Bring your camera, pack some bagels and coffee, and get ready to clap and holler. You'll feel really inspired afterward. First Sun in Nov.

Ringling Brothers and Barnum and Bailey Circus.

Madison Square Garden, Seventh Ave and 32nd St, New York (10001). Phone 212/465-6741. www.ringling.com. The kids will have a ball enjoying "the Greatest Show on Earth," which graces the city every spring. Expect the usual circus fare—elephants, trapeze artists, clowns, and the like. For a special treat, view the parade of circus people and animals from 12th Avenue and 34th Street to the Garden on the morning before the show opens. Mar-Apr.

San Gennaro Festival.

Little Italy, Mulberry St between Canal and Houston sts, New York (10013). Phone 212/768-9320. More than 75 years old, this giant street festival in Little Italy salutes the patron saint of Naples with a celebratory Mass and a candlelit procession of the Statue of the Saint. More than a million people descend on Little Italy over 11 days to feast on food from the old country, watch the parades, enjoy the live music, and compete for the title of cannoli-eating champion. Mid-Sept.

South Street Seaport Events.

Phone 212/732-8257. www.southstreetseaport.com. Throughout the year, concerts, festivals, and special events are staged in the seaport area; weather permitting, passengers are taken for a sail around the harbor aboard the *Pioneer*. The museum's Children's Center hosts a variety of special programs, workshops, and exhibits. In the fall, a fleet of classic sailing vessels is assembled to compete in a race for the Mayor's Cup.

St. Patrick's Day Parade.

Fifth Ave between 44th and 86th sts, New York (10017). www.saintpatricksday parade.com. New York's biggest parade; approximately 100,000 marchers.

Summer Events in Central Park.

14 E 60th St, New York (10022). Events held throughout the park and at Lincoln Center. Take the #1 or #9 subway to the 66th Street stop to get to Lincoln Center. Phone 212/310-6600 (Central Park Conservancy). www.centralpark.org. The city comes alive in summer with a plethora of wonderful, free cultural events that run the gamut and appeal to all ages. Central Park hosts a variety of musical performances by the New York Philharmonic and the Metropolitan Opera Co. In addition, its SummerStage (212/360-2777) attracts a mix of pop, blues, and rock stars. At nearby Lincoln Center, free concerts and dance performances are held during August at its Damrosch Park outdoor area. All these events, coupled with brunch or a casual picnic in the park, are a great, budget-conscious way to spend a warm, sunny day in the Big Apple. (Daily)

Washington Square Art Show.

LaGuardia Pl, between Bleecker and E 4th sts, New York (10021). Phone 212/982-6255. Outdoor art show. Weekends, late May-June and late Aug-early Sept.

Westminster Kennel Club Dog Show.

Madison Square Garden, 4 Pennsylvania Plz, New York (10001). Phone 212/465-6741; toll-free 800/455-3647. www.westminster kennelclub.org. Canine lovers unite! Nearly 3,000 top dogs and their owners take part in this two-day annual extravaganza leading up to the crowning of Best in Show on the second night of competition. Whether you love big or small dogs, you will surely find this event a delight. Here's a real insider's tip: arrive two hours early each night, at about 6 pm, and go to the huge backstage area. Here, you will be able to pet, play with, and nuzzle up to the dogs that vied for Best in Breed in competitions held earlier in the day. (Always ask the owner/handler for permission before petting an animal.) The owners and handlers welcome the public since they love showing off their pooches— they may even convince you to buy a future offspring of their show dogs. This is, by far, the best part of the show. Wear comfortable shoes, since this staging area is massive. Best in Group competitions for the seven groups run from 8-11 pm each night. You can buy tickets for one or both nights. For the best deal, purchase a general-admission, two-day pass. Mid-Feb.

Winter and Summer Restaurant Weeks.

www.restaurantweek.com. Many of the city's finest restaurants offer two- or three-course, fixed-price lunches at the bargain price of $20 a person during these two weeks in winter and summer. (Yes, for New York City, that is a bargain at a Four-Star restaurant.)

Actually, the exact price, if you want to get technical, corresponds to the year ($20.05 in 2005, $20.06 in 2006, etc.). This is a wildly popular promotion that natives can't wait to get their hands on. Check local newspapers at the beginning of your trip to see which restaurants are participating and make a reservation ASAP. This is a great way to experience top dining at great prices. Bon appétit! Second week in Jan, third week in June.

Limited-Service Hotels

★ ★ **ALGONQUIN HOTEL.** *59 W 44th St, New York (10036). Phone 212/840-6800; toll-free 800/555-8000; fax 212/944-1419. www.algonquinhotel.com.* Originally opened in 1902, this gracious hotel in the heart of Midtown became famous as a gathering spot for writers and theatrical performers. The legendary Algonquin Round Table, which formed after World War I, included such illustrious writers as Dorothy Parker and George S. Kaufman; additional regulars included Booth Tarkington, H. L. Mencken, and Gertrude Stein. That spirit lives on in the Oak Room, the Algonquin's supper club, where guests can catch well-known cabaret acts on Tuesday through Saturday evenings. Having undergone a historical restoration in the late 1990s, the hotel features beautifully detailed ironwork and the original marble staircase, with antique furnishings and rich tones to suit the period. Guest rooms combine historic elegance with 21st-century conveniences. 174 rooms, 12 story. Pets accepted, some restrictions. Check-in 3 pm, check-out noon. High-speed Internet access. Restaurant, bar. Fitness room. Business center. **$$**

★ ★ **AMERITANIA HOTEL.** *230 W 54th St, New York (10019). Phone 212/247-5000; toll-free 888/664-6835; fax 212/751-7868. www.nychotels.com/ameritania.html.* 219 rooms. Complimentary full breakfast. Check-in 3 pm, check-out noon. Restaurant, bar. **$$**

★ ★ **BENTLEY HOTEL.** *500 E 62nd St, New York (10022). Phone 212/644-6000; toll-free 888/664-6835; fax 212/751-7868.* 197 rooms, 21 story. Complimentary continental breakfast. Check-in 3 pm, check-out noon. Restaurant, bar. **$**

★ ★ **COURTYARD BY MARRIOTT TIMES SQUARE SOUTH.** *114 W 40th St, New York (10018). Phone 212/391-0088; toll-free 888/236-2427;* fax 212/391-6023. www.marriott.com. 244 rooms. Pets accepted, some restrictions. Check-in 3 pm, check-out noon. High-speed Internet access. Restaurant, bar. **$**

★ ★ **DAYS HOTEL NEW YORK CITY.** *790 8th Ave, New York (10019). Phone 212/581-7000; toll-free 800/544-8313; fax 212/974-0291. www.daysinn.com.* Just one block to Javits Convention Center and an easy walk to Times Square, this is a budget-friendly hotel in a busy commercial area. 367 rooms, 15 story. Check-in 3 pm, check-out noon. Restaurant, bar. **$**

★ **HAMPTON INN MANHATTAN CHELSEA.** *108 W 24th St, New York (10011). Phone 212/414-1000; fax 212/647-1511. www.hamptoninn.com.* 144 rooms. Complimentary continental breakfast. Check-in 3 pm, check-out noon. **$**

★ ★ **HOTEL BEACON.** *2130 Broadway at 75th St, New York (10023). Phone 212/787-1100; toll-free 800/572-4969; fax 212/724-0839. www.beaconhotel.com.* 241 rooms, 25 story. Check-in 2 pm, check-out noon. Restaurant, bar. Fitness room. **$$**

★ ★ **HOTEL WALES.** *1295 Madison Ave, New York (10128). Phone 212/876-6000; fax 212/860-7000.* Restored 1902 hotel; original fireplaces. 87 rooms, 10 story. Pets accepted, some restrictions; fee. Check-in 4 pm, check-out noon. Restaurant. Fitness room. **$$$**

★ **LYDEN GARDENS.** *215 E 64th St, New York (10021). Phone 212/355-1230; toll-free 800/637-8483; fax 212/758-7858. www.affinia.com.* 131 rooms, 13 story, all suites. Check-in 3 pm, check-out noon. Wireless Internet access. Fitness room. **$$$**

★ ★ **THE MANSFIELD.** *12 W 44th St, New York (10036). Phone 212/277-8700; toll-free 800/255-5167; fax 212/764-4477. www.mansfieldhotel.com.* 124 rooms, 13 story. Pets accepted. Check-in 3 pm, check-out noon. Restaurant, bar. **$$**

★ ★ **MAYFLOWER ON THE PARK.** *15 Central Park W, New York (10023). Phone 212/265-0060; toll-free 800/223-4164; fax 212/265-2026. www.mayflowerhotelny.com.* 365 rooms, 18 story. Pets accepted, some restrictions. Check-in 3 pm, check-out noon. Restaurant, bar. Fitness room. **$$**

★ ★ **RADISSON LEXINGTON HOTEL NEW YORK.** *511 Lexington Ave at 48th St, New York (10017). Phone 212/755-4400; toll-free 800/448-4471; fax 212/751-4091. lexingtonhotelnyc.com.* Near Grand Central Station. 705 rooms, 27 story. Check-in 3 pm, check-out noon. High-speed Internet access. Restaurant, bar. Fitness room. Business center. **$$**
🚶 🏃

★ **THE ROGER WILLIAMS.** *131 Madison Ave, New York (10016). Phone 212/448-7000; toll-free 888/448-7788; fax 212/448-7007. www.hotelrogerwilliams.com.* 187 rooms, 16 story. Complimentary continental breakfast. Check-out noon, check-out 3 pm. Fitness room. Business center. **$$**
🚶 🏃

★ ★ **ROOSEVELT HOTEL.** *45 E 45th St and Madison Ave, New York (10017). Phone 212/661-9600; toll-free 888/833-3969; fax 212/885-6161. www.theroosevelthotel.com.* 1,043 rooms, 19 story. Check-in 3 pm, check-out noon. High-speed Internet access. Restaurant, bar. Fitness room. Business center. **$$**
🚶 🏃

★ **SALISBURY HOTEL.** *123 W 57th St, New York (10019). Phone 212/246-1300; toll-free 888/692-5757; fax 212/977-7752. www.nycsalisbury.com.* 201 rooms, 17 story. Check-in 3 pm, check-out noon. **$$**

★ ★ **WARWICK HOTEL.** *65 W 54th St, New York (10019). Phone 212/247-2700; fax 212/247-2725. www.warwickhotelny.com.* 425 rooms, 33 story. Check-out 1 pm. Restaurant, bar. Fitness room. Business center. **$$$**
🚶 🏃

Full-Service Hotels

🔍 ★ ★ ★ **60 THOMPSON.** *60 Thompson St, New York (10012). Phone 212/431-0400; toll-free 877/431-0400; fax 212/431-0200. www.60thompson.com.* This SoHo boutique hotel features warm and inviting rooms and suites, done in brown and gray tones accented with dark woods and full-wall leather headboards. Frette linens, in-room spa products by Philosophy, and oversized showers pamper well-heeled guests. The accommodations will surely please high-tech aficionados, as they offer high-speed Internet connections, DVD players, and CD stereo systems. Matching this in hipness are decadent marble bathrooms with oversized showers. The hotel's Asian-influenced seafood restaurant, Thom, is popular with in-the-know locals. It also offers Thom's Bar, a clubby, intimate setting in which to relax and enjoy a drink. 100 rooms, 8 story. Check-in 3 pm, check-out noon. High-speed Internet access. Restaurant, bar. Business center. **$$$**
🏃

★ ★ ★ **THE AVALON.** *16 E 32nd St, New York (10016). Phone 212/299-7000; toll-free 888/442-8256; fax 212/299-7001. www.avalonhotelnyc.com.* Stately black marble columns and a pretty mosaic floor make an elegant first impression at this Murray Hill boutique hotel located near many area attractions. The elegant lobby is warm and inviting, with the look and feel of a mini European palace. Warm chestnut tones give the place a sense of grandeur, but in a smaller setting that is part of boutique intimacy. The guest rooms feature desk chairs designed for comfort and functionality, as well as Irish cotton linens and velour bathrobes. The Avalon bills itself as a home away from home: each room also comes with a signature body pillow. 100 rooms, 12 story. Complimentary continental breakfast. Check-in 3 pm, check-out noon. High-speed Internet access. Restaurant, bar. **$$**

★ ★ ★ **THE BENJAMIN.** *125 E 50th St, New York (10022). Phone 212/715-2500; toll-free 866/233-4642; fax 212/465-2525. www.thebenjamin.com.* Despite the fact that it's set in a classic 1927 building, this hotel has all the high-tech amenities a business traveler could want, including high-speed Internet access and Web TV. It offers comfortable accommodations in a sophisticated setting that features beige, silver, and brown tones throughout the property and in the marble and silver two-story lobby. A particularly nice amenity is the "pillow menu," which offers you a choice of ten different kinds of bed pillows and a guarantee of your money back if you do not wake well rested. The Benjamin's Woodstock Spa and Wellness Center offers many services and treatments with a holistic approach. 209 rooms. Pets accepted, some restrictions. Check-in 3 pm, check-out noon. High-speed Internet access. Restaurant, bar. Fitness room, spa. **$$**
🐾 🚶

★ ★ ★ **BRYANT PARK HOTEL.** *40 W 40th St, New York (10018). Phone 212/869-0100; toll-free 877/640-9300; fax 212/869-4446. www.bryantparkhotel.com.* In cents. Each room offers high-tech amenities like DSL Internet connections, making this hotel a good choice for people traveling on business. Every room has 400-thread-count linens, Tibetan rugs, Bose Wave radios, and cashmere throws, and some have deep soaking tubs. 149 rooms, 25 story. Check-in 3 pm, check-out noon. High-speed Internet access. Restaurant, bar. Fitness room. Business center. **$$$**

★ ★ ★ ★ **THE CARLYLE.** *35 E 76th St, New York (10021). Phone 212/744-1600; toll-free 800/227-5737; fax 212/717-4682. www.thecarlyle.com.* Discreetly tucked away on Manhattan's Upper East Side, The Carlyle has maintained the allure of being one of New York's best-kept secrets for more than 70 years. A favorite of many movie stars, presidents, and royals, The Carlyle feels like an exclusive private club with its white-glove service and impeccable taste. Its art collection is extraordinary, from Audubon prints and Piranesi architectural drawings to English country scenes by Kips. Art plays a significant role at The Carlyle, where all rooms are equipped with direct lines to Sotheby's. The rooms are completed in an Art Deco décor and are enhanced by striking antiques and bountiful bouquets. Populated by power brokers and socialites, The Carlyle Restaurant defines elegance. Bemelmans Bar proudly shows off its murals by *Madeline* creator Ludwig Bemelmans, while guests have been tapping their toes to the tunes of Bobby Short for more than 30 years in the Café Carlyle. 180 rooms, 35 story. Pets accepted, some restrictions. Check-in 3 pm, check-out noon. Restaurant, bar. Fitness room. **$$$$**

★ ★ ★ **CHAMBERS.** *15 W 56th St, New York (10019). Phone 212/974-5656; toll-free 866/204-5656; fax 212/974-5657. www.chambershotel.com.* Located just steps from some of New York's finest retail shops, the trendy hotel has a modern, open-air feel to it. The public spaces—including the soaring lobby with a double-sided fireplace—and the loftlike guest rooms feature original works of art, including pieces by film-maker John Waters. The spacious, high-tech rooms with hand-troweled cement walls offer amenities like slippers you can actually keep, umbrellas, Frette bathrobes, and flat-screen TVs. Baths are stocked with Bumble + Bumble amenities. Just off the lobby, Town restaurant (see) serves fine American cuisine accented with French and Asian influences; you can also enjoy a Town meal in the comfort of your room. Guests of the hotel receive complimentary passes to the New York Sports Club. 77 rooms, 30 story. Pets accepted, some restrictions. Check-in 3 pm, check-out noon. High-speed Internet access. Restaurant, bar. Business center. **$$$**

★ ★ ★ **CITY CLUB HOTEL.** *55 W 44th Street, New York (10036). Phone 212/921-5500; toll-free 877/367-2269; fax 212/944-5544. www.cityclubhotel.com.* 65 rooms. Pets accepted, some restrictions; fee. Check-in 3 pm, check-out noon. High-speed Internet access. Restaurant, bar. **$$**

★ ★ ★ **DOUBLETREE GUEST SUITES.** *1568 Broadway, New York (10036). Phone 212/719-1600; toll-free 800/222-8733; fax 212/921-5212. www.doubletree.com.* If you're looking for an all-suite hotel in Times Square, look no further; this hotel is located only steps away from the theater district. 458 rooms, 43 story, all suites. Check-in 3 pm, check-out noon. Restaurant, bar. Fitness room. **$$**

★ ★ ★ **DOUBLETREE METROPOLITAN HOTEL NEW YORK CITY.** *569 Lexington Ave, New York (10022). Phone 212/752-7000; toll-free 800/222-8733; fax 212/758-6311. www.doubletree.com.* Recently renovated, this East Side business traveler's hotel (formerly the Loews New York) has a casual elegance in its soft tones and king-bed rooms. The Lexington Avenue Grill serves contemporary American cuisine, and the popular Lexy Lounge features a signature cocktail called the Sexy Lexy that is a hit with locals. The business center offers everything from secretarial services to fax capabilities to workstation rentals. The premium business-class program includes a separate check-in and check-out area; private lounge with wine and cheese, continental breakfast, and snacks; and special in-room amenities like fax machines. 667 rooms, 20 story. Check-in 3 pm, check-out noon. Restaurant, bar. Fitness room. Airport transportation available. Business center. **$$**

★ ★ ★ **DYLAN HOTEL.** *52 E 41st St, New York (10017). Phone 212/338-0500; toll-free 866/553-9526; fax 212/338-0569. www.dylanhotel.com.* With a grand feeling throughout, the 1903 Beaux Arts-style building, with its ornate façade and spiraling marble staircase, used to be the home of the Chemists Club. The guest rooms are bright and airy, with 11-foot ceilings and elegant marble baths. The rooms' white and blue walls, deep amethyst and steel blue carpeting, and ebony-stained furniture give them a quiet, tailored look without being austere or cold. Situated on a quiet street, the hotel contains the Dylan restaurant, which serves basic fare like burgers and pastas, and a bar for relaxing with a drink. 107 rooms, 20 story. Check-in

3 pm, check-out noon. Restaurant, bar. Fitness room. Business center. **$$$**

★ ★ ★ **EASTGATE TOWER HOTEL.** *222 E 39th St, New York (10016). Phone 212/687-8000; toll-free 866/233-4642; fax 212/490-2634.* 188 rooms, 25 story, all suites. Pets accepted. Check-in 3 pm, check-out noon. Wireless Internet access. Restaurant, bar. Fitness room. **$$$**

★ ★ ★ ★ ★ **FOUR SEASONS HOTEL NEW YORK.** *57 E 57th St, New York (10022). Phone 212/758-5700; toll-free 800/819-5053; fax 212/758-5711. www.fourseasons.com.* The bustling world of 57th Street's designer boutiques and office towers awaits outside the doors of the Four Seasons Hotel New York, yet this temple of modern elegance provides a serene escape from city life. Designed by legendary architect I. M. Pei, the Four Seasons pays homage to the city's beloved skyscrapers as the tallest hotel in New York. The rooms and suites are testaments to chic simplicity with neutral tones, English sycamore furnishings, and state-of-the-art technology, but it's the service that defines the Four Seasons experience. The staff makes guests feel completely at ease in the monumental building, with ready smiles and generous spirit. The views are terrific, too; floor-to-ceiling windows showcase the dazzling city skyline or the quietude of Central Park. Some rooms offer furnished terraces so that guests can further admire the sights. Fifty Seven Fifty Seven, the hotel's restaurant, remains the place to see and be seen, while the bar and the Lobby Lounge provide perfect settings for lingering over drinks or casual fare. 368 rooms, 52 story. Pets accepted, some restrictions. Check-in 3 pm, check-out noon. High-speed Internet access, wireless Internet access. Two restaurants, two bars. Fitness room, fitness classes available, spa. Whirlpool. Airport transportation available. Business center. **$$$$**

★ ★ ★ **HILTON NEW YORK.** *1335 Avenue of the Americas, New York (10019). Phone 212/586-7000; toll-free 800/445-8667; fax 212/315-1374. www.hilton.com.* This large convention hotel has a bustling, urban charm. Several restaurants, shops, and services make it a convenient base from which to explore New York. 2,058 rooms, 44 story. Check-in 3 pm, check-out noon. High-speed Internet access. Two restaurants, two bars. Fitness room, spa. Airport transportation available. Business center. **$$**

★ ★ ★ **HOTEL ELYSEE.** *60 E 54th St, New York (10022). Phone 212/753-1066; toll-free 800/535-9733; fax 212/980-9278. www.elyseehotel.com.* Celebrities like Tennessee Williams, Joe Dimaggio, Ava Gardner, and Marlon Brando have called this historic hotel home over the years since it opened in the 1920s. This hotel is well-known for its library, and the Monkey Bar and Grill remains a thriving New York hotspot, serving American cuisine both in the restaurant and through hotel room service. The guest rooms have marble baths; some have terraces, solariums, or kitchenettes. 101 rooms, 14 story. Complimentary continental breakfast. Check-in 3 pm, check-out 1 pm. High-speed Internet access. Restaurant, bar. **$$$**

★ ★ ★ **HOTEL PLAZA ATHÉNÉE.** *37 E 64th St, New York (10021). Phone 212/734-9100; toll-free 800/447-8800; fax 212/772-0958. www.plaza-athenee.com.* Hotel Plaza Athénée is the perfect place to enjoy a little bit of France while visiting New York. Located between Park and Madison avenues in one of the city's most exclusive neighborhoods, this elegant hotel is a perfect hideaway with a decidedly residential feel. Celebrating its place among the boutiques of Madison Avenue, the townhouses and apartment buildings of Park Avenue, and the greenery of Central Park, the Plaza Athénée indeed feels like a home away from home for its guests. A palette of blues, golds, and reds creates the French contemporary décor of the rooms and suites. Some suites have dining rooms, while others have indoor terraces or outdoor balconies. The exotic flavor of the Bar Seine, with its vibrant colors and striking furnishings, transports guests to a faraway land, while Arabelle Restaurant combines gracious French style with delicious continental cuisine. 150 rooms, 17 story. Pets accepted, some restrictions. Check-in 3 pm, check-out 1 pm. Restaurant, bar. Fitness room. **$$$$**

★ ★ ★ **INTERCONTINENTAL THE BARCLAY NEW YORK.** *111 E 48th St, New York (10017). Phone 212/755-5900; toll-free 800/327-0200; fax 212/644-0079. new-york-barclay.intercontinental.com.* 603 rooms, 14 story. Check-in 3 pm, check-out noon. High-speed Internet access. Restaurant, bar. Fitness room. Airport transportation available. Business center. **$$$**

★ ★ ★ **THE IROQUOIS.** *49 W 44th St, New York (10036). Phone 212/840-3080; toll-free 800/332-7220; fax 212/398-1754. www.iroquoisny.com.* This hotel underwent a $10 million renovation several years ago, having been restored to its 1923 elegance. It has the feel of a European mansion, with French décor. The guest rooms are individually decorated with works of art reflecting New York themes such as Broadway, fashion, and museums and feature luxe Frette linens and Italian marble baths. A library provides a sitting area for perusing the hotel's collection of leather-bound editions of the classics. Triomphe restaurant features French cuisine, and the Burgundy Room offers breakfast and cocktails. 114 rooms, 12 story. Check-in 3 pm, check-out noon. High-speed Internet access. Restaurant, bar. Fitness room. **$$$**

★ ★ ★ **THE KIMBERLY HOTEL.** *145 E 50th St, New York (10022). Phone 212/702-1600; toll-free 800/683-0400; fax 212/486-6915. www.kimberlyhotel.com.* If you're looking for an elegant, spacious room designed in bold colors and warm wood furnishings that the whole family will feel comfortable in, the all-suite Kimberly Hotel is for you. The one- and two-bedroom suites feature living rooms, dining areas, and fully equipped separate kitchens. For extra comfort, the suites feature plush robes and goose down or aromatherapy pillows. Many suites also have private terraces with city views. Guests receive free use of the New York Health and Racquet Club. As an added bonus, guests can take a complimentary cruise on the hotel's 75-foot yacht on weekends from May through October. 185 rooms, 30 story, all suites. Check-in 3 pm, check-out noon. High-speed Internet access. Restaurant, bar. Indoor pool. **$$$**

★ ★ ★ **THE KITANO NEW YORK.** *66 Park Ave, New York (10016). Phone 212/885-7000; toll-free 800/548-2666; fax 212/885-7100. www.kitano.com.* This Japanese import located in Murray Hill features modern guest rooms with soft tones of beige and tan and soundproof windows that ensure peace and quiet. The rooms also feature Web TV, duvets, large desks, and Japanese teacups and green tea. Keeping with the Asian theme are an authentic Japanese tea room, gallery, and elegant shops located off the warm mahogany and marble lobby. Original works of art and sculptures are displayed throughout the hotel. The Nadaman Hakubai restaurant specializes in gourmet Japanese cuisine, and the sun-drenched Garden Café features contemporary continental cuisine. 149 rooms, 18 story. Check-in 3 pm, check-out 11 am. High-speed Internet access. Two restaurants, bar. Business center. **$$$$**

★ ★ ★ **LE PARKER MERIDIEN.** *118 W 57th St, New York (10019). Phone 212/245-5000; toll-free 800/543-4300; fax 212/307-1776. parkermeridien.com.* 730 rooms, 42 story. Pets accepted. Check-in 3 pm, check-out noon. High-speed Internet access. Three restaurants, bar. Fitness room, fitness classes available. Indoor pool. Business center. **$$$$**

★ ★ ★ **LIBRARY HOTEL.** *299 Madison Ave, New York (10017). Phone 212/983-4500; toll-free 877/793-7323; fax 212/499-9099. www.libraryhotel.com.* As the name suggests, this unique hotel was inspired by a library—the famous New York City Public Library located one block away. Each of the ten floors is dedicated to one of the ten categories of the Dewey Decimal System, which include languages, literature, history, the arts, and religion. Each guest room is furnished in a modern, sleek, yet warm and inviting décor and is stocked with books and art relevant to the floor's particular topic. In keeping with this theme, the hotel features a reading room and a poetry garden with terrace for relaxing and reading. 60 rooms, 10 story. Complimentary continental breakfast. Check-in 3 pm, check-out 1 pm. High-speed Internet access. Restaurant, bar. Business center. **$$$**

★ ★ ★ **THE LOMBARDY HOTEL.** *111 E 56th St, New York (10022). Phone 212/753-8600; toll-free 800/637-7200; fax 212/754-5683. www.lombardyhotel.com.* An elegant Midtown hotel, the Lombardy was built in the 1920s by William Randolph Hearst. This historic hotel has oversized rooms decorated in a classic, elegant, old-world style with comfortable couches and chairs. The marble baths have oversized showers and an array of upscale toiletries. Flowers, works of art, and crystal chandeliers are featured throughout the property. Above-and-beyond personal services include a seamstress and white-glove attendant service in the elevators. The hotel also has a fully equipped business center and is close to shopping, theaters, and Central Park. 115 rooms, 21 story. Closed Thanksgiving-Dec 25. Check-in 1 pm, check-out 1 pm. High-speed Internet access. Restaurant, bar. Fitness room. Business center. **$$$**

★ ★ ★ **THE LOWELL.** *28 E 63rd St, New York (10021). Phone 212/838-1400; toll-free 800/221-4444; fax 212/319-4230. www.lowellhotel.com.* Located in a landmark 1920s building in the historic district of the Upper East Side, The Lowell provides a refreshing change of pace. Its rooms and suites capture the essence of an elegant country house with a delightful blend of English prints, floral fabrics, and Chinese porcelains. Many suites boast wood-burning fireplaces—a rarity in Manhattan. All rooms are individually decorated, and The Lowell's specialty suites are a unique treat. The Garden Suite takes its inspiration from English country gardens and has two terraces, one complete with a rose garden and fountain. The glamour of the 1930s silver screen is recalled in the Hollywood Suite, while the Gym Suite, originally created for Madonna, is perfect for exercise buffs. The English influences extend to the Pembroke Room, where a proper tea is served, as are breakfast and brunch. Resembling a gentleman's club, the Post House (see), a well-respected New York steakhouse, is a paradise for carnivores. 70 rooms, 17 story. Pets accepted. Check-in 3 pm, check-out 1 pm. High-speed Internet access. Two restaurants, bar. Fitness room. Business center. **$$$$**

★ ★ ★ ★ **MANDARIN ORIENTAL, NEW YORK.** *80 Columbus Circle, New York (10023). Phone 212/805-8800; toll-free 866/801-8880; fax 212/805-8888. mandarinoriental.com.* One look through a window in the Mandarin Oriental, New York, could spoil guests for other New York City hotels forever. Part of the Time Warner Center, the first floor of the hotel sits high atop the city on the 35th floor of the building. Views of Central Park, the Hudson River, and the city skyline provide a dazzling backdrop to a luxurious experience. Though serene guest rooms make it tempting to laze about for hours on end, slip out to explore all that the hotel—and the Time Warner Center—has to offer. Take a swim in the surrounded-by-windows pool on the 36th floor. Indulge in a Balinese body massage or a foot and nail treatment with hot stones at the spa. Return to the room in the evening to find an orchid on the pillow. The hotel's Asian theme carries over into Asiate, which serves French and Japanese fusion cuisine, and MObar, which features drinks like the East Meets West, an innovative combination of pear and cinnamon-infused brandy, chilled champagne, and a sugar cube. Want to be dazzled by one of the world's best chefs? Call ahead to make reservations at one of the much talked-about restaurants that sit 33 floors below the hotel, including Thomas Keller's Per Se, Masa Takayama's Masa, or Jean-Georges Vongerichten's V. 251 rooms. Pets accepted. Check-in 3 pm, check-out noon. High-speed Internet access. Restaurant, two

bars. Fitness room, spa. Indoor pool, whirlpool. Airport transportation available. Business center. **$$$**

★ ★ ★ **THE MARK.** *25 E 77th St, New York (10021). Phone 212/744-4300; toll-free 800/843-6275; fax 212/744-2749. www.mandarinoriental.com.* Take a break from the shopping of Madison Avenue and the museums of the Upper East Side and enter the haven of The Mark New York, where style and comfort combine for an exceptional experience. Situated on a quiet tree-lined street, The Mark feels like an elegant private home. The hotel's eclectic décor perfectly blends the clean lines of Italian design with the lively spirit of English florals. Asian decorative objects and Piranesi prints complete the look in the hotel's rooms and suites. Sophisticated cuisine is highlighted at Mark's Restaurant, where the Master Sommelier also offers wine-tasting courses and themed dinners. Afternoon tea at The Mark is especially notable thanks to the Tea Master, who ensures that little bits of America and the Orient are brought to this British tradition. Mark's Bar, a jewel-toned bôite, is particularly popular with local denizens as well as hotel guests. 176 rooms, 16 story. Pets accepted, some restrictions. Check-in 3 pm, check-out 1 pm. High-speed Internet access. Restaurant, bar. Fitness room. **$$$**

★ ★ ★ ★ **THE MERCER.** *147 Mercer St, New York (10012). Phone 212/966-6060; toll-free 888/918-6060; fax 212/965-3838. www.mercerhotel.com.* Catering to a fashion-forward clientele in New York's SoHo, Mercer Hotel is a boutique hotel in the midst of one of the city's most exciting neighborhoods. This former artists' community stays true to its roots in its many cutting-edge boutiques and galleries. The loft-style Mercer Hotel epitomizes bohemian chic with its exposed brick, steel beams, and hardwood floors. Christian Liaigre, darling of the minimalist décor movement, has designed a sophisticated look for the hotel with simple furnishings and serene neutral colors. The uncluttered look extends to the bathrooms, with clean white tiles and luxurious two-person bathtubs or spacious showers with assorted spray fixtures. The lobby also serves as a lending library stocked with favorite books and videos, and the nearby trend-setting Crunch Gym is accessible to all guests. Mercer Kitchen (see) and Bar reign as hotspots on the local scene, for both their sensational food under the direction of Jean-Georges Vongerichten and their fabulous people-watching. 75 rooms, 6 story. Pets accepted. Check-in 3 pm, check-out noon. High-speed Internet access, wireless Internet access. Restaurant, bar. **$$$$**

★ ★ ★ **THE MICHELANGELO.** *152 W 51st St, New York (10019). Phone 212/765-0505; toll-free 800/237-0990; fax 212/581-7618. www.michelangelohotel.com.* If you are a lover of all things Italian, plan to stay at this ornate hotel during your next visit to New York. Special touches include opera music played in public spaces, Buon Di breakfast with cappuccino and Italian pastries, and Baci chocolates at turndown. The extra-large rooms are decorated in Art Deco, country French, or neoclassical style. Cherry wood furnishings have black accents and brass mounts. The rooms also feature woven fabrics from Italy. The hotel's upscale restaurant, Limoncello, serves Italian cuisine, and The Grotto offers more casual dining and a selection of fine cigars. 178 rooms, 7 story. Complimentary full breakfast. Check-in 3 pm, check-out 1 pm. High-speed Internet access. Restaurant, bar. Fitness room. **$$$**

★ ★ ★ **MILLENIUM HILTON.** *55 Church St, New York (10007). Phone 212/693-2001; toll-free 800/445-8667; fax 212/571-2316. www.hilton.com.* This tall, sleek Financial District hotel was built to match the skyscrapers around it. 565 rooms, 55 story. Check-in 3 pm, check-out noon. High-speed Internet access. Restaurant, bar. Fitness room. Indoor pool. Business center. **$$$**

★ ★ ★ **MILLENNIUM BROADWAY HOTEL NEW YORK.** *145 W 44th St, New York (10036). Phone 212/768-4400; toll-free 800/622-5569; fax 212/768-0847. www.millenniumhotels.com.* Colorful murals that evoke the 1930s adorn the lobby of this fine Midtown hotel. All Guest rooms are tastefully appointed and meet the needs of most travelers. 750 rooms, 52 story. Pets accepted, some restrictions. Check-in 4 pm, check-out noon. Restaurant, bar. Fitness room. Business center. **$$**

★ ★ ★ **MILLENNIUM UN PLAZA HOTEL.** *1 UN Plaza, New York (10017). Phone 212/758-1234; toll-free 866/866-8086; fax 212/702-5051. www.millenniumhotels.com.* Bright lights and big mirrors add glamour to the lobby of this hotel, just steps from the United Nations. 427 rooms, 40 story. Check-in 3 pm, check-

out noon. Restaurant, bar. Fitness room. Indoor pool. Tennis. Business center. **$$**

★ ★ ★ **MORGANS.** *237 Madison Ave, New York (10016). Phone 212/686-0300; toll-free 800/606-6090; fax 212/779-8352. www.morganshotel.com.* Another in Ian Schrager's collection of hotels, Morgans is so hip that the front door has no sign, and no address is even posted. The guest rooms are decorated in soft, muted tones; a contrasting black-and-white checkerboard design differentiates the ultra-sleek bathrooms. Added touches to make your stay more pleasant include down comforters and pillows, CD players, and fresh flowers in the rooms. Asia de Cuba restaurant attracts a hip air-kiss crowd. (You may see celebrities!) Complimentary breakfast and afternoon tea add to the value. 113 rooms, 19 story. Pets accepted, some restrictions; fee. Complimentary continental breakfast. Check-in 3 pm, check-out noon. Wireless Internet access. Restaurant, bar. **$$$**

★ ★ ★ **THE MUSE.** *130 W 46th St, New York (10036). Phone 212/485-2687; toll-free 877/692-6873; fax 212/485-2900. www.themusehotel.com.* A designers' dream, this hotel has restored its unique, triple-arched, limestone and brick façade to give it a dramatic feel. Adding to the drama is a 15-foot vaulted ceiling with a commissioned mural depicting the nine muses in the lobby. Original artwork celebrating the theater and the performing arts hangs in each room, decorated in a warm color scheme of rust, burgundy, pear green, and muted blue-green and cherry wood furniture. Custom linens and duvet-covered feather beds add to guests' comfort. Guest baths feature green marble with stone vanities. Other distinguishing features include in-room spa services, balconies, and DVD players. 200 rooms, 19 story. Pets accepted, some restrictions. Check-in 3 pm, check-out noon. High-speed Internet access. Restaurant, bar. Fitness room. Business center. **$$$**

★ ★ ★ **NEW YORK MARRIOTT FINANCIAL CENTER.** *85 West St, New York (10006). Phone 212/385-4900; toll-free 800/228-9290; fax 212/227-8136. www.marriott.com.* Walking distance to Wall St, ferry to Statue of Liberty. 508 rooms, 38 story. Check-in 4 pm, check-out 11 am. High-speed Internet access. Restaurant, bar. Indoor pool. Business center. **$$$**

★ ★ ★ NEW YORK MARRIOTT MARQUIS.

1535 Broadway, New York (10036). Phone 212/398-1900; toll-free 800/843-4898; fax 212/704-8930. www.marriott.com. 1,946 rooms, 49 story. Pets accepted, some restrictions. Check-in 3 pm, check-out noon. High-speed Internet access. Three restaurants, four bars. Fitness room. Business center. **$$$**

★ ★ ★ ★ THE NEW YORK PALACE.

455 Madison Ave, New York (10022). Phone 212/888-7000; toll-free 800/697-2522; fax 212/303-6000. www.newyorkpalace.com. Return to the Gilded Age at The New York Palace. Marrying the historic 1882 Villard Houses with a 55-story contemporary tower, The Palace brings the best of both worlds together under one roof. Directly across from St. Patrick's Cathedral, The Palace is convenient for sightseeing or conducting business. First impressions are memorable, and the grand entrance through the gated courtyard of twinkling lights is no exception. The glorious public rooms are masterfully restored and recall their former incarnations as part of the private residences of America's wealthiest citizens at the turn of the century. Set against the backdrop of New York City, The Palace's rooms and suites are a blend of contemporary flair or period décor. The Villard Bar & Lounge captures the imagination of its patrons with its Victorian design. Home to Le Cirque 2000 (see), one of the world's most famous restaurants, The New York Palace is in its own class. 896 rooms, 55 story. Pets accepted, some restrictions. Check-in 3 pm, check-out noon. High-speed Internet access. Three restaurants, two bars. Fitness room. Business center. **$$$$**

★ ★ ★ OMNI BERKSHIRE PLACE.

21 E 52nd St at Madison Ave, New York (10022). Phone 212/753-5800; toll-free 800/843-6664; fax 212/754-5018. www.omnihotels.com. A soaring atrium with a wood-burning fireplace is the focal point of the lobby of this understated hotel. The rooms are designed with an Asian aesthetic, and business travelers will find all they need for a hassle-free stay. 396 rooms, 21 story. Pets accepted, some restrictions; fee. Check-in 3 pm, check-out noon. Wireless Internet access. Restaurant, bar. Fitness room. Business center. **$$$**

★ ★ ★ PARAMOUNT NEW YORK.

235 W 46th St, New York (10036). Phone 212/764-5500; toll-free 888/956-3542; fax 212/354-5237. www.solmelia.com. Ian Schrager does it again. One-of-a kind, funky but comfortable furniture (such as a wood chair upholstered with a large silkscreen image of a growling dog) dots the lobby. Guest rooms are decorated in white tones, with ultra-modern furniture and Scottish lambswool throws. The Mezzanine Restaurant features a Latin-inspired tasting and tapas menu. For foodies, the hotel has a Dean & Deluca takeout shop that offers mouthwatering items you can enjoy back in your room. 610 rooms, 19 story. Pets accepted, some restrictions. Check-in 3 pm, check-out noon. Wireless Internet access. Restaurant, bar. Fitness room. Business center. **$$**

★ ★ ★ ★ THE PENINSULA NEW YORK.

700 5th Ave, New York (10019). Phone 212/956-2888; toll-free 800/262-9467; fax 212/903-3949. www.peninsula.com. Situated on Fifth Avenue in Midtown, The Peninsula is a perfect location for exploring the sights and sounds of New York City, whether you're heading for the stores, catching a concert at nearby Carnegie Hall or Radio City, or relaxing in Rockefeller Center. The lobby is magnificent with its sweeping staircase carpeted in crimson. Bellhops in crisp white uniforms escort guests to rooms and suites, where lush fabrics and warm tones create a sensual ambience. The Peninsula is known for setting standards in the industry, which is evident in the fact that guests are able to regulate the temperature, lighting, and entertainment systems from their beds with a simple touch. The fitness center, overlooking the city, brings new meaning to "exercise high," while the hotel's lively mood is celebrated in its bars and restaurants. With its staggering views above the city, the Pen-Top Terrace & Bar should not be missed, regardless of the prices of cocktails, which are as high as the tower itself. 239 rooms, 23 story. Pets accepted. Check-in 3 pm, check-out 12 pm. High-speed Internet access, wireless Internet access. Restaurant, two bars. Fitness room, fitness classes available, spa. Indoor pool, whirlpool. Business center. **$$$$**

★ ★ ★ ★ THE PIERRE NEW YORK, A FOUR SEASONS HOTEL.

2 E 61st St, New York (10021). Phone 212/838-8000; toll-free 800/545-4000; fax 212/826-0319. www.fourseasons.com. Regal and esteemed, The Pierre New York is the definition of a grand old hotel. Relishing its location across from Central Park on Fifth Avenue, The Pierre has been a city landmark since 1930. Owned by Charles Pierre and John Paul Getty, among others, The Pierre is now managed by Four Seasons, which carefully maintains the integrity of this historic building while imparting its signature service levels with mixed success. Guests linger for hours in the impressive lobby, soaking up the ambience of old-world Europe. The rooms and suites are traditional with floral prints and antique reproductions. The Rotunda, where breakfast, light lunch, and afternoon tea are served, is a magical place where the cares of the world disappear under a ceiling of *trompe l'oeil* murals. Influenced by Renaissance paintings, the murals depict pastoral scenes of mythological figures intertwined with icons of the 1960s, including Jacqueline Kennedy Onassis. 202 rooms, 41 story. Pets accepted. Complimentary continental breakfast. Check-in 3 pm, check-out noon. High-speed Internet access. Restaurant, bar. Fitness room. Airport transportation available. Business center. **$$$$**

★ ★ ★ **THE REGENCY.** *540 Park Ave, New York (10021). Phone 212/759-4100; toll-free 800/233-2356; fax 212/688-2898. www.loewshotels.com/hotels/newyork.* Home of the original power breakfast, where deals are sealed and fortunes are made, The Regency consistently ranks as one of New York's top hotels. Combining the appearance of a library and a private club, The Regency provides attentive service that extends above and beyond the ordinary to create a memorable stay. International design influences create a warm atmosphere throughout the well-appointed rooms, while the fitness and business centers cater to guests with specific goals in mind. Creature comforts abound in the luxurious rooms and suites, from the Frette linens to the "Did You Forget" closet stocked with items often left at home. Pets are even welcomed in grand style with room service designed exclusively for man's best friend, as well as dog-walking services and listings of pet-friendly establishments. Unwind at Feinstein's, where Grammy-nominated Michael Feinstein entertains nightly, or savor a delectable meal at 540 Park or The Library. 351 rooms, 20 story. Pets accepted. Check-in 3 pm, check-out 1 pm. High-speed Internet access. Two restaurants, bar. Fitness room. Business center. **$$$**

★ ★ ★ **RENAISSANCE NEW YORK HOTEL TIMES SQUARE.** *714 7th Ave, New York (10036). Phone 212/765-7676; toll-free 800/468-3571; fax 212/765-1962. www.renaissancehotels.com.* You'll find many conveniences at this business hotel located just north of Times Square. The lobby, located three floors above the street, has an appealing Art Deco theme that carries into the comfortable guest rooms. 305 rooms,

26 story. Pets accepted, some restrictions; fee. Check-in 4 pm, check-out noon. Restaurant, two bars. Fitness room. Business center. **$$$**

★ ★ ★ **RIHGA ROYAL HOTEL.** *151 W 54th St, New York (10019). Phone 212/307-5000; toll-free 866/656-1777; fax 212/765-6530. www.rihgaroyalny.com.* 500 rooms, all suites. Check-in 3 pm, check-out 12 pm. Restaurant, bar. Fitness room. Airport transportation available. Business center. **$$**

★ ★ ★ ★ **THE RITZ-CARLTON NEW YORK BATTERY PARK.** *2 West St, New York (10004). Phone 212/344-0800; toll-free 800/241-3333; fax 212/344-3801. www.ritzcarlton.com.* Watch the world from The Ritz-Carlton New York, Battery Park. While only a 5-minute walk from Wall Street and the Financial District, The Ritz-Carlton feels light years away with its staggering views of the Hudson River, the Statue of Liberty, and Ellis Island from its location on the southern tip of Manhattan. This 38-story glass and brick tower is a departure from the traditional Ritz-Carlton European style, from the contemporary glass artwork bestowed upon the public and private spaces to the modern furnishings in rooms and suites. The service is distinctly Ritz-Carlton, however, with exceptional concierge service and Bath Butlers who create special concoctions for bath time. The view is omnipresent throughout the hotel, whether you're gazing through a telescope in a harbor view room, enjoying a cocktail while at Rise, the 14th-floor bar, or savoring a delicious meal at 2 West. 298 rooms, 39 story. Pets accepted, some restrictions; fee. Check-in 3 pm, check-out noon. High-speed Internet access. Restaurant, bar. Fitness room. Business center. **$$$$**

★ ★ ★ ★ ★ **THE RITZ-CARLTON NEW YORK, CENTRAL PARK.** *50 Central Park S, New York (10019). Phone 212/308-9100; toll-free 800/241-3333; fax 212/207-8831. www.ritzcarlton.com.* Rising above Central Park and flanked by prestigious Fifth Avenue and fashionable Central Park West, The Ritz-Carlton New York, Central Park has one of the most coveted locations in town. This genteel hotel is exquisite down to every last detail, from the priceless antiques and artwork to the bountiful floral displays. The light-filled rooms and suites are a pastel-hued paradise, with sumptuous fabrics and plush furnishings. No detail is overlooked; rooms facing the park include telescopes for closer viewing. The distinguished ambience and white-glove service make this a top choice of well-heeled travelers. The hotel's restaurant, Atelier (see), garners praise from top critics for its modern French cuisine. Dedicated to excellence in all areas, the hotel includes an outpost of the renowned European La Prairie Spa. 277 rooms, 15 story. Pets accepted, some restrictions. Check-in 3 pm, check-out noon. High-speed Internet access, wireless Internet access. Restaurant, bar. Fitness room, fitness classes available, spa. Airport transportation available. Business center. **$$$$**

★ ★ ★ **ROYALTON.** *44 W 44th St, New York (10036). Phone 212/869-4400; toll-free 800/606-6090; fax 212/869-8965. www.royalton.com.* Join the "in" crowd at this Ian Schrager hotel. Designed by Philippe Starck, the Royalton raised the bar on hipness when it opened a decade ago. Every detail is just so, from the stylish vodka bar to the lobby lounge where guests recline on cushioned steps to the small, minimalist guest rooms with modern, custom-made beds. The cream-colored rooms feature fresh flowers, down comforters and pillows, VCRs, CD players, and subtle lighting. The bathrooms are right out of the future, with stainless steel and glass fixtures. Some rooms have fireplaces and round tubs for two. The lobby also has a steely, minimalist look that is clean and sleek. The restaurant 44 is popular with local movers and shakers. 169 rooms, 16 story. Pets accepted, some restrictions. Check-in 3 pm, check-out noon. Wireless Internet access. Restaurant, bar. Fitness room. **$$**

★ ★ ★ **SAN CARLOS HOTEL.** *150 E 50th St, New York (10022). Phone 212/755-1800; toll-free 800/722-2012; fax 212/688-9778. www.sancarloshotel.com.* 147 rooms. Check-in 3 pm, check-out noon. High-speed Internet access. Fitness room. Airport transportation available. Business center. **$$**

★ ★ ★ **SHERATON NEW YORK HOTEL AND TOWERS.** *811 7th Ave, New York (10019). Phone 212/581-1000; fax 212/262-4410. www.sheraton.com.* This large, comfortable hotel is one of Sheraton's flagships—good for business or pleasure. Close to the theater district, the rooms are large by New York standards and the service is friendly. 1,750 rooms, 50 story. Pets accepted, some restrictions. Check-in 3 pm, check-out noon. High-speed Internet access. Restaurant, bar. Fitness room. Business center. **$$**

★ ★ ★ **THE SHOREHAM HOTEL.** *33 W 55th St, New York (10019). Phone 212/247-6700; toll-free 800/553-3347; fax 212/765-9741. www.shorehamhotel.com.* Renovated hotel built in 1930. 174 rooms, 11 story. Pets accepted. Check-in 3 pm, check-out noon. High-speed Internet access, wireless Internet access. Restaurant, bar. Business center. **$$**

★ ★ ★ **SOFITEL NEW YORK.** *45 W 44th St, New York (10036). Phone 212/354-8844; toll-free 877/565-9240; fax 212/354-2480. www.sofitel.com.* 398 rooms, 30 story. Pets accepted. Check-in 3 pm, check-out 12 pm. High-speed Internet access. Restaurant, bar. Fitness room. **$$$**

★ ★ ★ **SOHO GRAND HOTEL.** *310 W Broadway, New York (10013). Phone 212/965-3000; toll-free 800/965-3000; fax 212/965-3200. www.sohogrand.com.* Calculated cool is the best way to describe this trendy downtown hotel. The second-floor lobby doubles as a popular lounge. The guest rooms are simple in design, with tones of black and white and clean, uncluttered baths. All rooms have stereos, and some have rocking chairs. The lobby provides a comfortable gathering place, with high ceilings, couches, and exotic plants. Each floor also features a pantry with complimentary coffee, tea, and espresso. The Grand Bar & Lounge serves a mix of dishes, from macaroni and cheese to lobster tea sandwiches to chickpea-fried rock shrimp. The lounge also features music and DJs—a good place to hang out after a day of sightseeing. 367 rooms, 17 story. Pets accepted. Check-in 3 pm, check-out noon. Restaurant, bar. Fitness room. **$$$**

★ ★ ★ ★ ★ **THE ST. REGIS.** *2 E 55th St, New York (10022). Phone 212/753-4500; toll-free 888/759-7550; fax 212/787-3447. www.starwoodhotels.com.* Located just steps off Fifth Avenue in the heart of Manhattan, The St. Regis reigns as New York's grande dame. Opened in 1904, guests glide past the revolving doors of this Beaux Arts landmark to enter the rarefied world of old New York. The St. Regis defines elegance with its gleaming marble, glittering gold leafing, and sparkling chandeliers. The guest rooms are elegantly decorated in soft pastel colors with Louis XVI-style furnishings, while personal butlers cater to every whim 24 hours a day. Set under a ceiling of magical clouds that casts a dreamlike spell over its patrons, the Astor Court is the perfect place to enjoy traditional afternoon tea. Renowned for its famous

Red Snapper cocktail and bewitching Maxfield Parrish mural, the King Cole Bar is a favorite of hotel guests and locals alike. 315 rooms, 20 story. Pets accepted, some restrictions; fee. Complimentary continental breakfast. Check-in 3 pm, check-out noon. High-speed Internet access. Restaurant, bar. Fitness room, fitness classes available, spa. Airport transportation available. Business center. **$$$$**

★ ★ ★ **SURREY HOTEL.** *20 E 76th St, New York (10021). Phone 212/288-3700; toll-free 800/637-8483; fax 212/628-1549. www.affinia.com.* Like staying at the home of a rich great-aunt, this hotel has the understated grandeur of a faded residence. You'll see old-world charm upon entering the lobby, with its 18th-century English décor, wood-paneled elevators, and leather sofas. The studio, one-bedroom, and two-bedroom suites have a similar look, with molded ceilings, beveled-glass mirrors, and antique accents. Some have kitchenettes, and others have full kitchens. Suites also offer Web TV, Nintendo, VCRs, and bathrobes—all the comforts of home. The hotel's best feature is its restaurant—world-renowned chef Daniel Boulud's Café Boulud serves up gourmet French cuisine (at prices to match). 131 rooms, 16 story. Pets accepted, some restrictions. Check-in 3 pm, check-out noon. High-speed Internet access. Restaurant, bar. Fitness room. **$$**

★ ★ ★ **SWISSOTEL THE DRAKE, NEW YORK.** *440 Park Ave and 56th St, New York (10022). Phone 212/421-0900; toll-free 800/637-9477; fax 212/371-4190. www.swissotel.com.* This hotel is popular with business travelers who need easy access to Midtown's many corporate offices. For vacationers, it's within walking distance of Fifth Avenue shopping and Central Park. 495 rooms, 21 story. Pets accepted, some restrictions; fee. Check-in 3 pm, check-out noon. High-speed Internet access. Restaurant, bar. Fitness room, spa. Business center. **$$$**

★ ★ ★ **TRIBECA GRAND HOTEL.** *2 6th Ave, New York (10013). Phone 212/519-6600; toll-free 800/965-3000; fax 212/519-6700. www.tribecagrand.com.* 203 rooms. Pets accepted, some restrictions. Check-in 3 pm, check-out noon. Restaurant. Fitness room. **$$$**

★ ★ ★ ★ **TRUMP INTERNATIONAL HOTEL & TOWER.** *One Central Park W, New York (10023).* Phone 212/299-1000; toll-free 888/448-7867; fax 212/299-1150. www.trumpintl.com. Occupying an enviable site across from Central Park on Manhattan's Upper West Side, the 52-story Trump International Hotel & Tower makes guests feel like they are on top of the world. The lobby's warm brass tones and polished marble welcome visitors to the world of Trump, where attention to detail results in perfection and everyone feels like a tycoon. The guest rooms and suites are elegantly decorated with a contemporary European flavor, while the floor-to-ceiling windows focus attention on the mesmerizing views of Central Park framed by the impressive skyline. The Personal Attaché service ensures that all guests are properly coddled, while the extensive fitness center caters to exercise enthusiasts. All suites and most rooms come complete with kitchens, and in-room chefs are available to craft memorable dining experiences. Room service is world-class and created by one of New York's top chefs, Jean-Georges Vongerichten, whose restaurant, Jean Georges (see), is located here. 176 rooms, 52 story. Pets accepted, some restrictions; fee. Check-in 4 pm, check-out noon. High-speed Internet access, wireless Internet access. Restaurant, bar. Fitness room, spa. Indoor pool. Business center. **$$$$**

★ ★ ★ **W NEW YORK.** *541 Lexington Ave, New York (10022). Phone 212/755-1200; toll-free 888/625-5144; fax 212/319-8344. www.whotels.com.* The chic lobby has the air of an urban ski lodge, with a sunken lobby bar that has tree trunk end tables and colorful rugs. The guest rooms have an organic feel with natural cotton linens and neutral tones. 713 rooms, 18 story. Pets accepted, some restrictions; fee. Check-in 3 pm, check-out 12 pm. High-speed Internet access. Restaurant, two bars. Fitness room, spa. Airport transportation available. Business center. **$$$**

★ ★ ★ **W NEW YORK - TIMES SQUARE.** *1567 Broadway, New York (10036). Phone 212/930-7400; fax 212/930-7500. www.whotels.com.* 509 rooms. Pets accepted, some restrictions; fee. Check-in 3 pm, check-out noon. High-speed Internet access. Restaurant, bar. Fitness room. Business center. **$$**

★ ★ ★ **W NEW YORK - UNION SQUARE.** *201 Park Ave S, New York (10003). Phone 212/253-9119; toll-free 888/625-5144; fax 212/253-9229. www.whotels.com.* The Union Square outpost of this hip hotel chain pampers both business and leisure travelers (and their pooches, too). Its setting in the 1911 Guardian Life Building, a lovely Beaux Arts-style structure, brings a historic touch to this thoroughly modern hotel. It's one of few hotels on Union Square, which offers shops, restaurants, bars, theaters, and the famous Greenmarket. Inside, you'll find hotspots Olives (see), chef Todd English's Mediterranean restaurant, and Underbar, owned by Rande Gerber. Guest rooms, done in shades of purple, feature the W's signature feather beds with pillowtop mattresses, large work desks, and Aveda bath products. If you can't find something to satisfy your cravings in the W munchie box, room service is available 24 hours a day. 270 rooms, 25 story. Pets accepted, some restrictions; fee. Check-in 3 pm, check-out noon. High-speed Internet access. Restaurant, bar. Fitness room. Business center. **$$$$**

★ ★ ★ **THE WALDORF-ASTORIA.** *301 Park Ave, New York (10022). Phone 212/355-3000; toll-free 800/ 925-3673; fax 212/872-7272. www.waldorfastoria.com.* Enjoy a taste of old New York at this lodging landmark. The 1931 Art Deco hotel has played host to US presidents and other luminaries and features a grand lobby that is not to be missed. It has murals, mosaics, elaborate design work, and a piano that once belonged to Cole Porter. The rooms are individually decorated, elegant, and traditional in style. The Bull & Bear steakhouse has a 1940s feel and attracts the powerful and wealthy. The ultra-exclusive Waldorf Towers, from floor 28 and above, is even more upscale and private. 1,425 rooms, 42 story. Check-in 3 pm, check-out 12 pm. Restaurants, bar. Fitness room, spa. Business center. **$$**

★ ★ ★ **WESTIN ESSEX HOUSE ON CENTRAL PARK.** *160 Central Park S, New York (10019). Phone 212/247-0300; toll-free 800/937-8461; fax 212/315-1839. www.essexhouse.com.* An elegant hotel on Central Park South, one of the more fabulous locations in New York City, the Essex House is full of wealth and history. The Art Deco hotel boasts many luxurious touches, as well as large rooms and spectacular views of Central Park. Don't miss the stunning elevator doors and the terrific gift shop on the ground floor. Dining options include the casual Cafe Botanica and the haute cuisine of Alain Ducasse (see). 601 rooms, 19 story. Pets accepted, some restrictions. Check-in 3 pm, check-out noon. High-speed Internet access. Two restaurants, bar. Fitness room (fee), spa. Business center. **$$$**

★ ★ ★ **THE WESTIN NEW YORK AT TIMES SQUARE.** *270 W 43rd St, New York (10036). Phone 212/201-2700; toll-free 866/837-4183; fax 212/201-2701. www.westinny.com.* 863 rooms. Pets accepted, some restrictions. Check-in 3 pm, check-out noon. High-speed Internet access. Restaurant, two bars. Fitness room. Airport transportation available. Business center. **$$$**

Full-Service Inn

★ ★ ★ **INN AT IRVING PLACE.** *56 Irving Pl, New York (10003). Phone 212/533-4600; toll-free 800/ 685-1447; fax 212/533-4611. www.innatirving.com.* Step back in time to 19th-century New York in this intimate, romantic brownstone hideaway located in a row of 1830s townhouses just south of Gramercy Park. The high-ceilinged guest rooms feature antiques, four-poster beds, and cozy couches and chairs without sacrificing modern amenities like remote climate control and Internet access. Enjoy breakfast in bed or take it in the elegant guest parlor. Continental breakfast and afternoon high tea are served at a leisurely pace in this elegant country-style inn. The staff can arrange any special services you need, such as an in-room massage or the booking of theater tickets. 12 rooms, 3 story. Children over 12 years only. Complimentary continental breakfast. Check-in 3 pm, check-out noon. **$$$$**

Spas

★ ★ ★ ★ **FOUR SEASONS HOTEL NEW YORK SPA.** *57 E 57th St, New York (10022). Phone 212/758-5700. www.fourseasons.com.* Elegant, yet far from fussy, the spa at the Four Seasons mirrors the hotel's commitment to contemporary chic. Blonde woods, soothing accent colors, and black-and-white photography create a serene escape from the city streets, and the treatment rooms are stylish cocoons. The spa's dedication to complete surrender is easily discovered on its treatment menu, where modern technology meets aromatherapy and Asian traditions. Awaken the body with the coffee blossom treatment, or heal the skin with an omega body elixir, which uses a propolis moisturizing lotion created by honeybees in the rainforest. The Four Seasons in One treatment celebrates the seasons with a cooling scrub symbolizing winter, a floral body wrap for spring, a medley of massages for summer, and a soothing scalp treatment for fall. Let your troubles drift away during the floating sensory experience, where a heated flotation bed makes for a delightfully relaxing treatment. In addition to shiatsu, aromatherapy, and reflexology, the Four Seasons offers a full range of unique massage therapies. From the Thai ceremony massage, which uses heated herbal mushroom packs to soothe muscles, and acupressure with walking bars, where a therapist uses his or her body weight to deliver relief, to the Asian Scentao hot stone massage, a definitive Asian influence is found here. Facials harness the power of modern technology with microcurrent lifting, oxygen cellular renewal, and DNA molecular regeneration.

★ ★ ★ ★ **MANDARIN ORIENTAL NEW YORK.** *80 Columbus Circle, New York (10019).* This sleek hotel marries Asian sensibilities with New York panache, and its 14,500-square-foot spa is the piece-de-la-resistance. Bamboo and natural stone are used throughout, creating a temple of serenity in this most frenetic of world capitals. Chinese, Ayurvedic, Balinese, and Thai healing therapies are the highlight of a visit to this facility, where guests are encouraged to book blocks of time, known as Time Rituals, for a comprehensive relaxation experience. The spa menu is far-reaching, offering a wide array of massage therapies, body treatments, and facials designed to purify, nurture, balance, and rejuvenate visitors. Signature therapies celebrate the spa's Eastern heritage with Lomi Lomi massage, Chakra balancing, and Ama releasing Abhyanga. This bastion of blissful quietude is capped off by a state-of-the-art fitness center, complete with a magnificent pool where swimmers can lap up the city skyline views.

★ ★ ★ ★ **THE PENINSULA SPA AT THE PENINSULA NEW YORK.** *700 Fifth Ave, New York (10019). Phone 212/903-3910; toll-free 800/262-9467. www.peninsulaspa.com.* The Peninsula Spa is the embodiment of the urban oasis. It is defined by its city skyline views, and sleek styling adds to the cosmopolitan atmosphere. Fitness and wellness programming are a large part of The Peninsula Spa experience. Personal trainers are available in addition to group classes, including yoga, Pilates, and ballet, tap, or jazz dance classes. Water aerobics and one-on-one swim instruction are offered at the pool. The spa features a wide range of skin care, massage, and body treatments. The facial menu includes deep-cleansing, aromatherapy, and sensitive skin treatments, while the specialty facials include signature therapies using June Jacobs or Valmont products. Microdermabrasion

targets lifeless skin, and the back treatment pays special attention to this often-neglected region. The body treatments are among the most appealing offerings, with treatments such as the papaya hydrating body mask, chai soy mud mask, and body champagne, which uses heated seaweed and other ingredients to give the body a bubbly sensation. Stressed-out executives head straight for the massage table to enjoy a Swedish, shiatsu, sports, deep-tissue, or aromatherapy massage. Couples and pregnancy massages are also featured here.

Restaurants

★ ★ ★ **21 CLUB.** *21 W 52nd St, New York (10019). Phone 212/582-7200; fax 212/974-7562. www.21club.com.* This one-time speakeasy is now one of New York City's most celebrated spots for lunch, dinner, and lots of drinks—at least for the well-heeled Wall Street, media, and superstar regulars who frequent its best tables. Chef Erik Blauberg turns out stellar, seasonal American-French fare, with standards that shine and inventive twists that delight. The restaurant has a distinguished air to it, with a clubby, brass-railed bar (often the sight of dealmakers clinking martini glasses), luxurious linen-lined tables, golden lighting, antique oil paintings, and old photos hung on wood-paneled walls. The deep wine list explores the world at large and works well to complement the cuisine. American menu. Lunch (Mon-Fri in the Bar Room), dinner. Closed Sun; holidays. Bar. Jacket required in Upstairs at 21. Reservations recommended. **$$$**
🅟

★ **2ND AVENUE DELI.** *156 Second Ave, New York (10003). Phone 212/677-0606; fax 800/228-3354. www.2ndavedeli.com.* Pastrami, chopped liver, and matzo brie are the kinds of things you'll find on the menu at this classic kosher delicatessen, which has been serving traditional Jewish delicacies since 1954. Tongue and corned beef are cured on the premises. If you'd like to re-create the experience after you leave New York, you can order by mail (phone toll-free 800/692-3354). Kosher deli menu. Breakfast, lunch, dinner, late-night. Closed Jewish holidays. Casual attire. **$$**
🅟

★ **88 PALACE.** *88 E Broadway, New York (10002). Phone 212/941-8886.* If you are craving dim sum, or a perfect Chinese tea luncheon, consider stopping at 88 Palace, a bustling Chinese restaurant featuring a delicious and authentic selection of dim sum and house-made soups, fish, meats, and rice dishes. The restaurant is a favorite among Chinatown's locals, and many of the staff don't speak much English, but no matter. The point-to-order method works well. Chinese, Dim Sum. Breakfast, lunch, dinner. **$**

★ ★ **@SQC.** *270 Columbus Ave, New York (10023). Phone 212/579-0100; fax 212/579-3288. www.sqcnyc.com.* The Upper West Side traditionally has not been known as a culinary destination, but the one draw for years has been chef/owner Scott Campbell's wonderful creative American fare. Now at his own joint, he continues to offer locals and travelers his delicious brand of stylish seasonal fare like diver scallops wrapped in bacon, pork chops with cheddar grits, and lots of terrific daily specials. The restaurant has an easy, chic vibe that allows for lots of people-watching thanks to floor-to-ceiling sidewalk windows. A Valrhona hot chocolate and walnut tart for dessert should keep you smiling long after you leave. American menu. Breakfast, lunch, dinner, Sat-Sun. Bar. Casual attire. **$$$**

★ ★ ★ **AL BUSTAN.** *827 Third Ave, New York (10022). Phone 212/759-5933.* If you've ever wondered what Lebanese cuisine is like, head to Al Bustan and discover a world of aromatic and exquisite food. Many have already made the discovery, which means that Al Bustan is very popular, especially at lunch, as its Midtown location makes it a nice choice for dealmakers. But when the sun sets, Al Bustan becomes an elegant respite for dinner, offering guests a luxurious upscale Lebanese dining experience that includes some of the best bread in the city, served with a magnificent array of mezze, not to mention a full menu of authentic Lebanese dishes. Middle Eastern menu. Lunch, dinner. Casual attire. Reservations recommended. **$$$**

★ ★ ★ ★ ★ **ALAIN DUCASSE.** *155 W 58th St, New York (10019). Phone 212/265-7300; fax 212/265-5200. www.alain-ducasse.com.* When word came that the famed French wizard of gastronomy, Alain Ducasse, was opening a restaurant in New York, the city's food world began salivating. And while the excess, such as the choice of half a dozen pens to sign the bill, drew some criticism at its opening, people started to embrace the restaurant once they experienced Ducasse firsthand. Ducasse has superhuman culinary powers; food doesn't taste this way anywhere else, and it sure doesn't arrive at a table this way anywhere else. Elegant to the point of being regal, Ducasse is a restaurant designed to please every one of the senses: sight, sound, smell, taste, and touch. The room frequently fills with attractive diners. Hours later, when dinner is over and you attempt to get up and walk to the door, you receive a gift for

breakfast the next morning: a gift-wrapped buttery, fruit-laced brioche that will make you swoon. If you manage not to dig into it in the cab on the way back to your hotel, you have a will of steel. But divine excess does not come without its price. Dinner at Ducasse will set you back several pretty pennies, but really, isn't paying your mortgage a dull way to spend your money? French menu. Dinner. Closed Sun; holidays; Mon in August. Jacket required. Reservations recommended. **$$$$**

★ ★ **ALFAMA.** *551 Hudson St, New York (10014). Phone 212/645-2500; fax 212/645-1476. www.alfama restaurant.com.* The wonderful seaside cuisine of Alfama, an ancient village in Portugal, is on the menu at this namesake bistro decorated with authentic blue and white Portuguese tiles in Manhattan's West Village. Bacalau (salt cod) is one of the most common ingredients in Portuguese cooking, and it shows up here mixed in a dish with potatoes and peppers that is alive with robust flavors. Cooking in a cataplana—a sort of open-mouth clamshell pot made from copper—is another tradition in Portugal. The cataplana is filled with fish, scallops, and shrimp and studded with chorizo, potatoes, and tomatoes—a Hungry Man-style bouillabaisse that is complemented by an incredible selection of Portuguese wines. To keep things like they are in the old country, soulful Fado singers perform on Wednesday nights. Portuguese menu. Lunch Mon-Sat, dinner Mon-Sat, Sun brunch. Bar. Casual attire. Reservations recommended. Outdoor seating. **$$$**

★ ★ **ALPHABET KITCHEN.** *171 Avenue A, New York (10009). Phone 212/982-3838.* Located on a now bustling block of Avenue A, Alphabet Kitchen is a warm, cozy respite from the grind of city life. This intimate restaurant is all aglow with candles and gets its rustic warmth from wooden tables, a long dark-wood bar, an open kitchen, and a serene garden with a waterfall trickling down a stone wall. The menu has a Spanish flair to it and features inspired tapas and Iberian dishes like paella, chorizo, grilled shrimp, and a succulent and bold braised lamb shank with grilled polenta. To wash it all down, Alphabet Kitchen serves a mean sangria. Fruity yet balanced, this is one beverage that should be ordered by the pitcher. Spanish, tapas menu. Dinner, late-night. Casual attire. Outdoor seating. **$$**
🄳

★ ★ **AMMA.** *246 E 51st St, New York (10022). Phone 212/644-8330.* At Amma, an elegant, petite Midtown spot serving excellent Indian fare, you'll find tables jammed with eager curry lovers kvelling over dishes of Goan shrimp, piles of toothsome bhel puri, and plates of frizzled okra with tomatoes and onions. This is not your ordinary curry house, though. Amma is stylish and serene, and the service is efficient and fine. The chef, formerly of Tamarind (see), knows his way around the tandor oven, and you should by all means order several tandoori dishes like stuffed chicken breasts, crisp and spiced shrimp, or the succulent yogurt-infused lamb chops. Save room for dessert; the rasmalai dumplings are a showstopper. Indian menu. Lunch, dinner. Children's menu. Casual attire. **$$**

★ ★ ★ **AMUSE.** *108 W 18th St, New York (10011). Phone 212/929-9755; fax 212/989-2203.* Amuse is a unique restaurant, which is quite an accomplishment in the scheme of New York City dining. The kitchen offers a clever menu of different-sized plates—$5, $15, or $20 each, depending on portion size—for tasting, sharing, passing, and, above all, enjoying. The menu spans the globe and features lots of full-flavored snacks, appetizers, and entrée-type plates from comfort food favorites to inventive haute creations. This design-your-own-dinner formula fits seamlessly with the slick cocktail-crazed crowds that come in for the scene as much as the terrific and, as the restaurant's name promises, fun food. American, Seafood menu. Lunch, dinner, Sat brunch. Closed Sun. Bar. Casual attire. Reservations recommended. **$$$**

★ ★ ★ **ANNISA.** *13 Barrow St, New York (10014). Phone 212/741-6699.* At Annisa, a cozy, off-the-beaten-path gem in Greenwich Village, chef/partner Anita Lo and partner Jennifer Scism (who runs the front of the house) bring a bit of Asia and a lot of flavor and savvy style to the contemporary American table. With the restaurant's golden glow and elegant, sheer-white curtains draped along the tall walls, it's easy to feel like you're dining somewhere very close to heaven. The simple, approachable menu helps keep you in the celestial mood. An array of wines by the glass and a strong sommelier make pairing wine with dinner a no-brainer. American menu. Dinner. Closed Sun. Casual attire. Reservations recommended. **$$$**

★ ★ **AOC BEDFORD.** *14 Bedford St, New York (10014). Phone 212/414-4764.* Located on a quiet, tree-lined street in the West Village, AOC Bedford is a stylish yet rustic retreat that welcomes you in with its exposed brick walls and wood-beamed ceilings. The restaurant derives its name from the term *appellation d'origine contrôlée,* the official French designation for food products of the highest quality. The menu is not exclusively French, though. In fact, much of it has a Spanish flare, like the house specialty of suckling pig, served Iberian style (with the bone-in) and accompanied by a pile of dates, or the grand paella, stocked with cockles, clams, shrimp, and squid—all ingredients that shine easily. Italian, Spanish menu. Dinner. Closed Mon. Bar. Casual attire. **$$**

★ ★ ★ **AQUAGRILL.** *210 Spring St, New York (10012). Phone 212/274-0505; fax 212/274-0587.* When the sun is out and a warm breeze is in the air, you'll find the city's hip locals lounging outside at Aquagrill, a perennial favorite for swimmingly fresh seafood (and great dry-aged steak). With its tall French doors sprung open to the street, Aquagrill has a European elegance and calm to it that makes it an irresistible spot to settle in, even if only for a glass of sparkling wine and a dozen (or two) shimmering oysters. Although the warmer months are the most fun, when there is a nip in the air, the dining room wraps you up, making you feel cozy in an instant. Seafood menu. Dinner, brunch. Closed Mon; holidays; also the first week in July. Bar. Casual attire. Reservations recommended. Outdoor seating. **$$$**

★ ★ ★ **AQUAVIT.** *13 W 54th St, New York (10019). Phone 212/307-7311; fax 212/265-8584. www.aquavit.org.* Chef/partner (and culinary heartthrob) Marcus Samuelsson introduced New York to his splashy brand of modern Scandinavian cuisine a decade ago at Aquavit, an elegant two-story restaurant housed in a historic Midtown townhouse, just a stone's throw from the Museum of Modern Art and the shops of Fifth Avenue. After ten years and a facelift, the restaurant still has a sleek, sophisticated vibe, and the cuisine is even more spectacular. While ingredients like herring, lamb, salmon, caviar, and dill show up with regularity on this Scandinavian-inspired menu, the food here is more uniquely Samuelsson than anything else. What this means is that every dazzling plate achieves a startlingly delicious harmony as the result of the chef's careful and creative combination of textures, flavors, temperatures, ingredients, and the cooking styles of France, Asia, and Sweden. A shot of smooth, citrus-tinged aquavit complements dinner nicely, as does a selection from the impressive wine list. Scandanavian menu. Lunch, dinner. Closed holidays. Bar. Casual attire. **$$$$**

★ ★ **ARTISANAL.** *2 Park Ave, New York (10016).* *Phone 212/725-8585; fax 212/481-5455.* Say cheese! Artisinal is chef/owner Terrance Brennan's ode to the stuff, and it is a glorious tribute at that. (Brennan is also chef/owner of Picholine—see also.) In addition to one of the best cheese selections this side of the Atlantic, you'll find lovely brasserie standards like moules frites, gougères (warm, cheese-filled brioche puffs that melt in your mouth and are impossible to stop eating), frisée au lardons, and of course, cheese fondue—the house specialty. If you are more inclined to eat a meal at the bar, Artisinal's is a terrific spot to hunker down and sample some of the best cheeses from the United States and around the world, not to mention wines, all 120 of which are available by the glass. Located in the east 30s, this is also just about the best place to eat before or after a Madison Square Garden event. French bistro menu. Lunch, dinner, brunch. Bar. Casual attire. **$$**

★ ★ ★ **ASIATE.** *80 Columbus Circle, New York (10023). Phone 212/805-8800; fax 212/805-8888. www.mandarinoriental.com.* French-Asian cuisine has been given a bad name, and deservedly so. Too often, the fusion of such wide-ranging traditions results in flavors unpleasantly smushed together rather than heightened. But at its best, contact between cultures can produce unique dishes of subtlety and depth that transcend their origins. At Asiate, chef Nori Sugie challenges customers' palates. There's his "Caesar salad soup," for example, and pan-roasted branzino with green papaya salad. Or Wagyu beef, the US version of high-end beef from Japan, served with smoked potato puree and oxtail sauce. Desserts also borrow from the two traditions—raspberry clafoutis comes with a sake cheesecake foam and Thai basil ice cream. This is rich food served in a rich setting. At 35 floors up, in a plush room designed by Tony Chi, the elegance and exclusivity add to the appreciation of what's on the plate. French, Japanese menu. Breakfast, lunch, dinner, brunch. Bar. Business casual attire. Reservations recommended. Valet parking. **$$$$**

★ ★ ★ ★ **ATELIER.** *50 Central Park S, New York (10019). Phone 212/521-6125; fax 212/207-8831. www.ritzcarlton.com.* This is no run-of-the-mill hotel restaurant. This is the restaurant at The Ritz-Carlton New York, Central Park (see). Executive Chef Gabriel Kreuther, originally from Alsace, began his restaurant training at age 12 by helping out around his uncle's hotel and restaurant. Now he is considered one of America's top young chefs. Before taking over the kitchen at Atelier in early 2002, Kreuther was the chef

de cuisine at the much-lauded Jean Georges. From signature dishes, including bluefin tuna and diver scallop tartare seasoned with Iranian Osetra caviar, to the exclusive china pattern made by Bernardaud, Atelier's staff takes incredible care to make sure the experience is most memorable. Even the restaurant's restrooms, featuring the same plush hand towels hotel guests enjoy, have won awards. Gentle harp, piano, or recorded music doesn't drown out voices. If the conversation flags at dinner, quick inspiration is available by looking out the restaurant windows on the horse drawn carriages that slowly roll in and out of the park. A meal at Atelier calls for a handsomely knotted tie or beautiful new outfit; those who don't dress the part risk being upstaged by the elegant setting. French bistro menu. Breakfast, lunch, dinner, brunch Sun. Bar. Jacket required. Reservations recommended. **$$$$**

★ ★ ★ ★ **AUREOLE.** *34 E 61st St, New York (10021). Phone 212/319-1660; fax 212/755-3126. www.charliepalmer.com/aureole_ny/home.html.* Hidden away inside a lovely brownstone on Manhattan's Upper East Side, Aureole is inviting and warm and feels like a special place to dine. The waitstaff's gracious hospitality ensures that you continue to feel that way throughout your meal. The luxurious space is bathed in cream tones and warm lighting, and is furnished with overstuffed wine-colored banquettes. (An enclosed courtyard garden opens for warm-weather dining.) Diners at Aureole are generally here to celebrate something, as it is one of New York's most impressive eateries. The crowd is mostly middle-aged and from the upper echelon of New York society, although Aureole is not a stuffy place. It is friendly and cozy and well suited for just about any occasion, from couples looking for romance to colleagues looking to have a delightful business dinner together. Owner and celebrity chef Charlie Palmer offers his guests the delicious opportunity to dine on a wonderfully prepared menu of what he calls "Progressive American" fare. But it doesn't really matter what label you give it, because it's all great. There are always two tasting menus—one vegetarian and another inspired from the market—in addition to a parade of terrific à la carte selections. The extensive and celebrated wine program includes bold wines from California, Spain, and Italy. American menu. Lunch, dinner. Closed Sun; holidays. Bar. Jacket required. Reservations recommended. **$$$$**

★ ★ **AVRA.** *141 E 48th St, New York (10017). Phone 212/759-8550; fax 212/751-0894. www.avrany.com.* At this terrific, airy, and elegant estiatorio, you can eat like they do on the Greek islands, feasting on fresh fish (priced by the pound) simply grilled with lemon, herbs, and olive oil; salads of fresh briny feta and tomato; and loaves of fluffy, warm pita to dip into assorted garlicky mezze like hummus and tzatziki. Save room for dessert, as the sticky-sweet honey-soaked baklava is not to be missed. Greek menu. Lunch, dinner, brunch. Bar. Casual attire. Reservations recommended. Outdoor seating. **$$$**

★ ★ **AZUL BISTRO.** *152 Stanton St, New York (10002). Phone 646/602-2004.* Located on a sleepy corner of Stanton Street in the now hip 'hood known as the Lower East Side, Azul Bistro is a seductive corner spot with raw wood accents and low lighting. Serving South American fare to the soft rhythms of tango music, Azul makes a nice substitute for a trip to Buenos Aires. While the menu focuses on Argentinean cuisine, you'll also find Latin American dishes like ceviche and empanadas. Grilled meats are a specialty, like the lamb and the juicy steak dotted with chimichurri sauce (think garlicky pesto). The watermelon sangria should get the night going on the right foot, no matter what you order. Latin American menu. Dinner, late-night. Bar. Casual attire. **$$**
🖻

★ ★ ★ **BABBO.** *110 Waverly Pl, New York (10011). Phone 212/777-0303; fax 212/777-3365. www.babbonyc.com.* Dressed in his signature orange clogs and shorts, Mario Batali is the king of rustic authentic Italian cuisine on television's Food Network. But before he was a star of the small screen, he was a cook—and he is one celebrity chef who still is. Here in New York, you'll find him at Babbo, a charming Greenwich Village carriage house-turned-stylish duplex hotspot where celebrities, foodies, VIPs, and supermodels fill tables (and every nook of space) for the chance to feast on Batali's unique brand of robust and risky Italian fare. The man is known for serving braised pigs' feet, warm lamb tongue, and testa (head cheese). Cult-status signature pastas like beef cheek ravioli and mint love letters—spicy lamb sausage ragu soothed with mint and wrapped in envelopes of fresh pasta—are lick-lipping delicious and demonstrate that some culinary risks are worth taking. Italian menu. Dinner. Bar. Casual attire. **$$$**

★ ★ ★ **BALTHAZAR.** *80 Spring St, New York (10012). Phone 212/965-1785; fax 212/966-2502.* *www.balthazarny.com.* If you don't know what all the hype surrounding Balthazar is about, you most certainly should. Keith McNally's super-fabulous replica of a Parisian brasserie is one of those rare spots that actually deserves the buzz. From the attractive crowds at the bar to the stunning folks who squeeze into the restaurant's tiny tables (you'll be seated as close to a stranger as is possible without becoming intimate), Balthazar is a dazzling, dizzying, wonderfully chaotic destination that sports a perfect menu of delicious brasserie standards like frisee au lardons, pan bagnat, steak frites, and a glistening raw bar built for royalty, not to mention the fresh-baked bread from the Balthazar bakery next door. To feel like a true New Yorker, pick up a bag of croissants, a couple of baguettes, and a dozen tarts on your way out for breakfast or lunch the next day. Balthazar is fun and loud and, in its own electric way, flawless. French menu. Breakfast, lunch, dinner, late-night, brunch Sat-Sun. Bar. Casual attire. Reservations recommended. **$$$$**

★ ★ **BAO 111.** *111 Avenue C, New York (10009). Phone 212/254-7773. www.bao111.com.* This sleek little spot on Avenue C gets major snaps for its contemporary brand of Vietnamese fare. Drawing an eclectic crowd of stilettoed babes and overly coiffed men, as well as those without a care about fashion, Bao 111 is an alluring space, marked by amber lighting and wood banquettes littered with embroidered pillows. The menu is authentic Vietnamese, tweaked for a trendy New York palate. Expect dishes like the signature short ribs skewered with lemongrass, spring rolls with mint and basil, five-spice quail, and crab and shrimp soup with noodles. Vietnamese menu. Dinner, late-night. Bar. Casual attire. **$$**
🖻

★ **BAR JAMON.** *125 E 17th St, New York (10003). Phone 212/253-2773.* Mario Batali is turning Spanish on us. After mastering the art of simple Italian fare at Babbo, Lupa, Otto (see all three), and Esca, he is taking on the Iberian Peninsula with Bar Jamon. Yes folks, a ham and wine bar set adjacent to Casa Mono (see), where he serves up a menu of Catalan small plates in a convivial setting straight out of Barcelona. A miniature spot with dark wood accents and a marble bar, this crowded watering hole features all sorts of Spanish jamon (pronounced *haah-mon*), cheeses (manchego, queso de tetilla, valdeon, calabres), and olives. More exciting plates include smoked trout salad with olives and cava-soaked grapes and classics like tortilla d'Espana—all perfectly suited to

Spanish wine and sherry. Spanish, tapas menu. Lunch, dinner, late-night. Casual attire. **$$**

★ ★ ★ **BAR MASA.** *10 Columbus Circle, New York (10019). Phone 212/823-9800; fax 212/823-9809. www.masanyc.com.* Japanese, sushi menu. Lunch, dinner. Closed Sun. Bar. Business casual attire. Reservations recommended. **$$$$**

★ ★ **BARBETTA.** *321 W 46th St, New York (10036). Phone 212/246-9171; fax 212/246-1279. www.barbetta restaurant.com.* Barbetta is the grand old dame of the theater district. This classic Italian restaurant opened its doors in 1906 and is still owned by the same loving family, the Maioglios. Located in a pair of historic early-19th-century townhouses, this restaurant is a classic charmer that's all about super-elegant, old-world dining. The menu doesn't aim anywhere other than where its heart is—Italy—but don't expect just pasta. The kitchen offers a great selection of seafood, poultry, and beef prepared with seasonal ingredients and lively flavors. The tree-lined outdoor garden is an enchanted spot to unwind over dinner or drinks. Italian menu. Lunch, dinner. Closed Sun, outdoor seating. **$$$**

★ **BARNEY GREENGRASS.** *541 Amsterdam Ave, New York (10024). Phone 212/724-4707. www.barney greengrass.com.* If you don't mind lines that rival opening day of *The Lord of the Rings,* then you'll be fine at Barney Greengrass, an Upper West Side institution for brunch since 1908. The restaurant, still decked out like a vintage New York soda fountain, features a simple menu of eggs, waffles, pancakes, and assorted heavenly platters of smoked fish and bagels. From the menu to the waiters to the décor, Barney Greengrass hasn't really changed a whole lot in its century of doing business, and that is part of its distinct old-world charm. Deli menu. Breakfast, lunch, brunch. Closed Mon. Casual attire. No credit cards accepted. **$$**

★ ★ ★ **BAYARD'S.** *1 Hanover Sq, New York (10004). Phone 212/514-9454; fax 212/514-9443. www.bayards.com.* Fresh flowers, a rare Buddha collection, crafted ship models, stately antiques, fine china, mahogany double staircases, and hand-carved working fireplaces are just some of the charming details you will encounter at Bayard's—an exquisite French-American restaurant located in the India House, a historic landmark building located at One Hanover Square, near Wall Street. To match the surroundings, executive chef Eberhard Müller delivers a magnificent menu that showcases the seasons. Indeed, most of the menu's fruits and vegetables are hand-harvested from Satur Farms—the 50-acre family farm chef Müller and his wife own in the North Fork of Long Island—making every bite a delicious discovery of the land. Signatures include Fisher's Island oysters, served warm with champagne sauce and osetra caviar, Maine lobster with black trumpet mushrooms and pea shoots, and dry-aged New York strip steak with cipolini onions, creamed spinach, and fingerling potatoes. American, French menu. Dinner. Closed Sun. Bar. Casual attire. **$$$**

★ ★ **BECCO.** *355 W 46th St, New York (10036). Phone 212/397-7597; fax 212/977-6738. www.becconyc. com.* Becco, a charming Italian restaurant in the Theater District, is a delightful place to relax over a delicious Italian supper before or after the theater, or at lunch for a business meeting. Becco offers great food, gracious service, and a lovely, airy atmosphere. The pre-theater special for which it has become famous offers authentic homemade pastas in an all-you-can-eat format. You choose three pastas, and they keep dishing them out until you say "Uncle!" or until you can't rise from the table, whichever comes first. Italian menu. Lunch, dinner. Closed Dec 25. Casual attire. Reservations recommended. **$$$**

★ ★ ★ **BEN BENSON'S STEAKHOUSE.** *123 W 52nd St, New York (10019). Phone 212/581-8888; fax 212/581-1170. www.benbensons.com.* At this popular Midtown testosterone-infused steakhouse, you'll find yourself elbow to elbow with celebrities, politicians, sports stars, and the city's financial elite. As you might expect from a power steak spot, the menu is as big as the egos in the room and includes solid standards like salads, poultry, and seafood that are simply and impeccably prepared. But the magnetic pull here is the restaurant's signature selection of USDA dry-aged prime beef, served in the form of about a dozen cuts and portion sizes. The huge steaks are matched in size by lobsters the size of small pets. Don't miss the house's signature crispy hashed browns. When the sun is shining, grab a seat outside in the sidewalk dining room, appointed in the same style as the indoor space with deep armchairs, formal white linens, and green-and-white wainscoted planters—an ideal alfresco setting. Steak menu. Lunch, dinner. Closed holidays. Bar. Casual attire. Outdoor seating. **$$$**

★ ★ **BEPPE.** *45 E 22nd St, New York (10010). Phone 212/982-8422.* Walk into Chelsea's Beppe, and you may feel yourself leaving the city of New York and entering the lovely land of Italy. At this warm, weathered eatery filled with all the charm of an Italian farmhouse kitchen, you can sample some of chef/owner Cesare Cassella's earthy and divine pasta; a terrific selection of Tuscan-style wood-fired seafood, meat, and game; and a wine list that focuses on gems from Tuscany and Italy's lesser-known regions. Italian menu. Lunch, dinner. Closed Sun. Bar. Casual attire. **$$$**

★ ★ **BEYOGLU.** *1431 Third Ave, New York (10028). Phone 212/650-0850. www.beyoglunyc.com.* There is much to love about this family-run Turkish restaurant on the Upper East Side. From the service, which is warm and friendly, to the dining room, a spacious, stylish, low-lit space, to the easygoing crowd of neighborhood folks, Beyoglu beckons you back as soon as you enter. The real star here is the food, which includes delicious warm pita bread drizzled with olive oil to start and moves on to a terrific variety of mezze and a heavenly spiced selection of fragrant rice and assorted kabobs that will leave you in want of a ticket to Istanbul ASAP. Mediterranean, Turkish menu. Lunch, dinner. Bar. Casual attire. Outdoor seating. **$$**

★ ★ ★ **THE BILTMORE ROOM.** *290 Eighth Ave, New York (10001). Phone 212/807-0111. www.thebiltmoreroom.com.* Located on a nondescript block of Chelsea, The Biltmore Room appears like a mirage in the desert, its magnificent façade marked by guilded gates and marble columns that make the entranceway feel like an old palace. Once inside, the design continues to please the eye, with marble floors; a long, sexy bar; high ceilings; and loveseat-style banquettes set around the dining room like an elegant old-world parlor. The bar, where the impressive cocktails are made from the freshest ingredients, draws the beautiful people crowd, a mix of sophisticated foodies and hipsters in scant dress. As if the design and the drinks weren't enough, the food, by chef/partner Gary Robbins, is already creating legions of fans. The menu features a savvy fusion style of American and Asian flavors with dishes accented with chiles, mango, lime, sweet spices, fresh mint, basil, and other savory herbs. The Biltmore Room is the rare spot that lacks pretension despite its fabulous food and design, which makes it a perfect spot for drinks, a special occasion, or a night out with friends. American, pan-Asian menu. Dinner. Closed Sun. Bar. Business casual attire. Reservations recommended. **$$$$**

★ ★ ★ **BLUE FIN.** *1567 Broadway, New York (10036). Phone 212/918-1400; fax 212/918-1300. www.brguestrestaurants.com/restaurants/blue_fin/ index.php.* Located in the heart of Times Square in the swanky W Times Square Hotel, Blue Fin is restaurateur Steve Hanson's (Blue Water Grill, Dos Caminos—see both) most elaborate seafood palace. On two levels, with a breathtaking aquatic-themed design, Blue Fin features high-end fish dishes and a stunning array of sushi, sashimi, and maki. The bar on the ground floor is always packed to the gills with suits sipping tall, cool cocktails, while the upstairs bar is more mellow but may still be a struggle for intimate conversation at peak times. Blue Fin offers terrific food in a stylish and slick setting that makes it a great spot for pre-theater, a dinner with a large group, or a business lunch. American, seafood, sushi menu. Breakfast, lunch, dinner, late-night, Sat-Sun. Bar. Children's menu. Casual attire. Outdoor seating. **$$$**

★ ★ ★ **BLUE HILL.** *75 Washington Pl, New York (10011). Phone 212/539-1776; fax 212/539-0959. www.bluehillnyc.com.* Blue Hill is a rare and lovely restaurant offering gracious hospitality, extraordinary seasonal American fare, and a stellar wine list in a warm, cozy, contemporary space that feels just right, like a page out of an upscale Pottery Barn catalog. Chocolate tones, soft lighting, and serene service make this restaurant a luxurious experience perfect for special occasions, and the truly wonderful menu by chef/owner Dan Barber ensures a delicious evening. American menu. Dinner. Bar. Casual attire. Reservations recommended. Outdoor seating. **$$$** 🅱

★ ★ **BLUE RIBBON.** *97 Sullivan St, New York (10012). Phone 212/274-0404.* Brothers Bruce and Eric Bromberg opened Blue Ribbon on a quiet block in SoHo some ten years ago, and it is as packed today as it was on day one. The tiny, low-lit bistro oozes fabulousness (models, moguls, and musicians are regulars) and features an eclectic menu of New York and French staples, like an icy raw bar stocked with oysters, deliriously good fried chicken (served with honey), and a perfect, meaty, and intensely flavored steak tartare garnished with cornichons, onion, egg, and coarse mustard. Blue Ribbon's notoriety comes from its late-night crowd that inevitably includes superstar chefs unwinding after a night of cooking or a night on the town. American, French menu. Dinner, late-night. Closed holidays. Bar. Casual attire. **$$$**

★ ★ **BLUE RIBBON BAKERY.** *35 Downing St, New York (10014). Phone 212/337-0404; fax 212/242-1086. www.blueribbonrestaurants.com/bakery_about.html.* The brothers Bromberg first brought New

Yorkers a taste of their creative culinary genius with Blue Ribbon, their hip late-night bistro. With Blue Ribbon Bakery, a rustic, wood-beamed, windowed corner spot in the West Village, they took on the task of baking bread (delicious bread) and decided to offer a menu of salads, small plates, and fresh seasonal entrées to boot. Whether for lunch, brunch, dinner, or an afternoon pick-me-up, Blue Ribbon Bakery is the perfect spot for a casual and always tasty bite. American menu. Lunch, dinner, brunch Sat-Sun. Bar. Children's menu. Casual attire. **$$**

★ ★ **BLUE SMOKE.** *116 E 27th St, New York (10016). Phone 212/447-7733; fax 212/576-2561. www.bluesmoke.com.* With elegant restaurants like Union Square Cafe and Gramercy Tavern (see both) in his repertoire, Danny Meyer might come as a surprise as the man behind Blue Smoke, a sleek, casual barbecue joint packed nightly with a loud and boisterous crowd. But Meyer hails from St. Louis, and barbecue has been his longtime passion. This love of 'cue shines through in saucy, meaty ribs; pulled pork sandwiches; and fried catfish, paired with super sides like smoky bacon-laced pit beans, messy slaw, and, for dessert, a perfect banana cream pie. Barbecue menu. Lunch, dinner, late-night. Bar. Children's menu. Casual attire. **$$**

★ ★ **BLUE WATER GRILL.** *31 Union Sq W, New York (10003). Phone 212/675-9500; fax 212/331-0354. www.brguestrestaurants.com.* Overlooking Union Square Park, Blue Water Grill is a buzzing shrine to seafood, with a raw bar and an extensive menu of fresh fish prepared with global accents and a terrific array of sushi, sashimi, and creative maki rolls. The dining room is massive and magnificent, with marble columns and floors, and sky-high ceilings. The crowds are always here because the food is tasty, inventive, and fun, which means the vibe is spirited and lively. Be warned that conversation may be difficult to conduct above the roar at peak times. American, seafood menu. Lunch, dinner, Sun brunch. Bar. Casual attire. Outdoor seating. **$$**
🅑

★ ★ **BOATHOUSE RESTAURANT.** *72nd St and Park Dr N, New York (10028). Phone 212/517-2233; fax 212/517-8821. www.thecentralparkboathouse.com.* Central Park is one of the most wonderful places to spend a day in Manhattan. It really doesn't matter what the season. The same can be said of the Boathouse Cafe, an open, airy, and romantic New York icon/restaurant with views of the rowboaters

making their way across the unfortunately green Central Park pond. Sure, summer is the ideal time to settle in for cocktails on the patio under the cherry blossoms, but this restaurant is equally idyllic in the winter, when snow blankets the park in a soft hush. The menu at the Boathouse is New American, with steak, fish, pasta, and salads sure to please any and all culinary desires. Brunch in warmer months is a winner here, but the lines are long, so call ahead for a table. American menu. Lunch, dinner, brunch. Bar. Children's menu. Casual attire. Reservations recommended. Outdoor seating. **$$$**

★ ★ **BOLO.** *23 E 22nd St, New York (10010). Phone 212/228-2200; fax 212/228-2239. www.bolorestaurant.com.* Chef, restaurateur, Food Network star, and author Bobby Flay is one busy celebrity chef. Lucky for us, fame hasn't gone to his head. The food at Bolo, the Spanish restaurant he opened a decade ago, keeps getting better. Since taking trips to Barcelona, Flay has reinvented the menu at Bolo, adding a delicious menu of tapas (and a nice list of sherries) to his lively, contemporary Spanish menu. While the food continues to excite, the room at Bolo could use a facelift and feels worn at the seams. Nevertheless, the bar is still alive with regulars, and the restaurant has a warm energy that makes it a wonderful place to dine. Spanish, tapas menu. Lunch, dinner. Closed Dec 25. Bar. Casual attire. **$$$**
🅑

★ ★ ★ **BOND STREET.** *6 Bond St, New York (10012). Phone 212/777-2500; fax 212/777-6530.* High-art sushi and sashimi are the calling cards of Bond Street, a hotspot and hipster hangout disguised as a modern Japanese restaurant. Famous fashionistas, celebrities, and supermodels are the typical guests at the white-washed, airy restaurant, and down in the dark and sexy lower-level bar you'll find more of the same. For all the hype, though, Bond Street serves excellent sushi and sashimi, and the extensive and inventive modern Japanese-influenced menu stands up to the scene with impressive resolve. Japanese, sushi menu. Dinner, late-night. Closed holidays. Bar. Casual attire. **$$$$**
🅑

★ ★ **BOOM.** *152 Spring St, New York (10012). Phone 212/431-3663; fax 212/431-3643.* Located in the heart of SoHo, Boom is a popular spot for European expats living (and shopping) in New York. The stylish crowds give Boom a hotspot vibe, but it's really just a simple, cozy bistro, with wood floors, candles burning, and, through open windows, a great view of the hipsters strolling by on Spring Street. The kitchen is not breaking any culinary ground but manages to turn out a respectable and eclectic menu of tasty global dishes. International menu. Lunch, dinner, brunch. Bar. **$**

★ ★ ★ ★ **BOULEY.** *120 W Broadway, New York (10013). Phone 212/964-2525. www.bouley.net.* Acclaimed chef David Bouley is the talent behind the stoves at this temple of haute French gastronomy. Housed in the renovated and impeccably decorated space that was once his more casual bistro, Bouley Bakery, Bouley appeals to Manhattan's most discerning and divine diners. The elegant and oh-so-civilized place is packed with well-heeled foodies, fashionistas, political pundits, and celebs who understand that a night in Bouley's care is nothing short of miraculous. Bouley delivers on every front: the service is charming, the seasonal ingredients are stunning, the French technique is impeccable, and his kitchen magic is nothing short of brilliant. American menu. Lunch, dinner. Closed the first week of Sept. Business casual attire. **$$$$**

★ ★ **BRASSERIE.** *100 E 53rd St, New York (10022). Phone 212/751-4840; fax 212/751-8777. www.restaurant associates.com.* As you enter Brasserie, you may feel all eyes on you, which is probably because they are. The dining room is set down a level, and when you enter, you must walk down a futuristic glass staircase, a dramatic walkway that calls all eyes up. In case the folks at the backlit bar and seated along the long, luxurious banquettes are too busy feasting on the tasty brasserie fare (like duck cassoulet, frisée aux lardons, onion soup, escargots, or goujonettes of sole) to look up and catch your entrance, 15 video screens broadcast images of incoming diners; you'll be captured on film for repeat viewing later. It's best just to get over your stage fright and relax, because it's so easy to enjoy a meal here. French, American menu. Breakfast, lunch, dinner, Sun brunch. Bar. Casual attire. **$$$**

★ ★ ★ **BRASSERIE 8 1/2.** *9 W 57th St, New York (10019). Phone 212/829-0812; fax 212/829-0821. www.brasserie8andahalf.com.* Located in the sleek, Gordon Bunshaft-designed "9" building in the heart of West 57th Street, Brasserie 8 1/2 is the perfect spot for all sort of plans. It's a great pick for a power lunch or for shimmering cocktails after work. The long, backlit bar is a mecca for stylish men and women in search of one another. It's also a wise choice for pre-theater dinner and a terrific selection for those who want to relax in a slick, modern setting and enjoy a

leisurely meal of updated brasserie classics tweaked to modern attention. The kitchen incorporates accents from Asia and the Mediterranean into these classic dishes, varying each dish just enough from its original base. Be warned that the spacious banquettes are so soft and comfortable that you may never want to get up. French menu. Lunch, dinner, Sun brunch. Bar. Jacket required. Reservations recommended. **$$$**

★ ★ **BRICK LANE CURRY HOUSE.** *306-308 E 6th St, New York (10003). Phone 212/979-2900.* Brick Lane Curry House is a standout in Curry Row, a stretch of East 6th Street in the East Village that's lined with Indian restaurants. Named for London's Little India dining district, Brick Lane opened to instant raves for its stunning well-spiced Indian cuisine and stylish, hip setting. Some of the dishes, like the phaal curry, are so fiery that the house will buy you a beer if you can finish it. May the force be with you. Indian menu. Lunch, dinner, late-night. Bar. Casual attire. Reservations recommended. Outdoor seating. **$$**
🅳

★ ★ **BRYANT PARK GRILL.** *25 W 40th St, New York (10018). Phone 212/840-6500; fax 212/840-8122. www.arkrestaurants.com.* Located behind the New York Public Library in the leafy tree-lined Bryant Park, the Bryant Park Grill is an airy, vaulted, and stylish spot to relax over dinner or hammer out a complex business transaction over lunch. The simple American menu features salads, steaks, fish, sandwiches, and pasta on a straightforward, seasonal menu. The bar is a zoo in the summertime, so if mingling with happy hour crowds is your thing, make Bryant Park Grill your destination. American menu. Lunch, dinner. Bar. Children's menu. Casual attire. Outdoor seating. **$$$**
🅳

★ ★ ★ **BULL AND BEAR STEAKHOUSE.** *49th St and Lexington Ave, New York (10022). Phone 212/ 872-4900; fax 212/486-5107. www.waldorfastoria.com.* Located in the stately Waldorf-Astoria Hotel in Midtown (see), the Bull and Bear Steakhouse is a testosterone-heavy, meat-eater's haven. The street-level dining room is elegant in a clubby, macho sort of way, and the steaks, all cut from certified aged Black Angus, are fat, juicy, and the way to go, even though the menu does offer a wide variety of other choices, including chicken, lamb, pot pie, and assorted seafood. Classic steakhouse sides like creamed spinach, garlic mashed potatoes, and buttermilk fried onion rings are sinful and match up well with the rich beef on the plate. A terrific selection of red wine will complete your meaty meal nicely. American menu. Lunch, dinner. Bar. **$$$**

★ ★ **CAFETERIA.** *119 Seventh Ave, New York (10011). Phone 212/414-1717.* This Chelsea restaurant is a hotspot late at night—and at all times in between—for its easy-to-love American menu in a minimalist whitewashed setting. Cafeteria is a sleek, ramped-up diner with good food, fun cocktails, and lots of fabulous attitude that makes it a second home to lots of size 2 babes, metrosexuals, and buff Chelsea boys. American menu. Breakfast, lunch, dinner, late-night, brunch. Bar. Children's menu. Casual attire. Outdoor seating. **$$**

★ ★ ★ **CAFÉ BOULUD.** *20 E 76th St, New York (10021). Phone 212/772-2600; fax 212/772-7755. www.danielnyc.com.* Daniel Boulud is one very committed chef. So committed, in fact, that he is the chef-king of a little empire of French restaurants in New York City. Café Boulud is his less formal version of his haute temple of French gastronomy, Daniel (see). But less formal is a relative term. Café Boulud is a majestic space, perfect for quiet conversation and intimate dining. The service is helpful and unobtrusive. The chef is a whiz at pleasing the palate and offers a choice of four à la carte menus: La Tradition (French Classics and Country Cooking), La Saison (The Rhythm of the Seasons), Le Potager (Vegetarian Selections from the Farmers' Market), and Le Voyage (a menu inspired from a changing international destination—Mexico, Morocco, etc.). The wine program is ambitious, and the staff is unintimidating and eager to assist with pairings, making the total dining experience like a little slice of French heaven. French menu. Lunch, dinner. Bar. Jacket required. Reservations recommended. Outdoor seating. **$$$$**

★ ★ ★ **CAFÉ DES ARTISTES.** *1 W 67th St, New York (10023). Phone 212/877-3500; fax 212/877-7754. www.cafenyc.com.* Café des Artistes is a timeless New York City classic. Originally fashioned after the English Ordinary, a cozy bistro with a limited menu based on food available in the market, the Café was a regular meeting place where local artists in the neighborhood would come together to discuss their creative works. Today, the restaurant remains an old-guard favorite for its luxurious, sophisticated setting, impeccable service, and menu of up-to-the-minute, yet approachable, seasonal, French bistro fare. While elegant in its art-filled décor, the restaurant's menu does not try too hard, over-flourish, or over-think things. The kitchen stays true to its roots. French

bistro menu. Lunch, dinner, brunch Sat-Sun. Closed Dec 25. Bar. **$$$**
🅳

★ ★ **CAFE FIORELLO'S.** *1900 Broadway, New York (10023). Phone 212/595-5330; fax 212/496-2471. www.cafefiorello.com.* If you find yourself taking in a ballet or an opera at Lincoln Center and you don't want to break the bank on dinner because you've just spent your last dime on those tough-to-get tickets, Fiorello's is a great choice for a reasonable, casual, and tasty meal. The convivial restaurant has a large outdoor patio for summertime seating and people-watching, while the indoor room is warm and welcoming, making it equally charming in the winter months. The menu offers a delicious selection of antipasti, pasta, meat, and fish prepared in the tradition of a Roman osteria, along with classic desserts like a creamy tiramisu. Italian menu. Lunch, dinner, late-night, brunch. Closed Dec 25. Bar. Casual attire. Reservations recommended. Outdoor seating. **$$$**

★ **CAFÉ HABANA.** *17 Prince St, New York (10012). Phone 212/625-2001.* It's safe to say that if you don't see a crowd of models, musicians, and assorted other super-fabulous people strewn out on the sidewalk outside Café Habana, it is closed. Indeed, as soon as this Cuban diner opens, the crowds are there, like metal to a magnet. The space is decked out in vintage chrome, with a food bar and way-cool retro booths, but the draw here is the flawless menu of cheap, straight-up Cuban grub, like rice and beans, terrific hangover-curing egg dishes, fried plantains, and divine plates of classic ropa vieja. Cuban menu. Breakfast, lunch, dinner, late-night. Casual attire. **$**

★ ★ **CAFÉ LOUP.** *105 W 13th St, New York (10011). Phone 212/255-4746; fax 212/255-2022.* Café Loup is a neighborhood favorite for simple but stylish French fare. This spacious, airy restaurant has a soothing vibe and is adorned with fresh flowers, lithographs, and photographs. If you are in the mood for attitude and a scene, head somewhere else, as this is an easy place to feel comfortable and to enjoy dinner. French bistro menu. Lunch, dinner, Sun brunch. Bar. Casual attire. **$$**
🅳

★ **CAFÉ SABARSKY.** *1048 Fifth Ave, New York (10028). Phone 212/288-0665; fax 212/645-7127. www.wallse.com.* Located in the Neue Galerie, facing the magnificent Central Park on Fifth Avenue, Café Sabarsky offers a taste of Austria in a spectacular

New York City setting. With sky-high ceilings, marble pillars, crystal chandeliers, and elegant brocade banquettes, Café Sabarsky feels like a royal chateau in the Austrian Alps. The divine menu, prepared by wonder-chef Kurt Gutenbrunner of Wallse, includes delicious and authentic Viennese pastries and savory Austrian dishes. The wine list is extensive and includes wonderful Austrian red and white varietals. Austrian menu. Breakfast, lunch, dinner. Closed Tuesday. Bar. Casual attire. **$$**

★ ★ **CANDELA RESTAURANT.** *116 E 16th St, New York (10003). Phone 212/254-1600; fax 212/614-8626. www.candelarestaurant.com.* Located near Union Square Park, Candela is an ideal choice for a romantic dinner, a large gathering of friends, or a light bite and a drink at the long, inviting, low-lit bar. Candela, as the name suggests, is filled with ivory-pillared candles of varying sizes, giving the large dining room dressed in dark wood a sexy, amber glow. The space gets its medieval vibe from heavy hanging tapestries, beamed ceilings, and dark oak-planked floors. The menu is sort of like the Gap, offering something for everyone at reasonable prices. Expect a nice selection of Mediterranean, Italian, and Asian dishes like garlicky hummus, lobster and corn ravioli, and sushi dishes like a tempura-battered spicy tuna roll or black cod with a rich miso glaze. International/Fusion menu. Dinner, Sun brunch. Bar. Casual attire. Reservations recommended. **$$**
⊡

★ ★ **CANTEEN.** *142 Mercer St, New York (10012). Phone 212/431-7676. www.canteennyc.com.* The creation of restaurateur John MacDonald (Merc Bar), Canteen is a bright, mod, super-hip playground for scensters and their fearless fashionista leaders. Decked out in day-glo orange, this subterranean cafeteria-style space is located underneath the flagship Prada store in SoHo, which does much to explain the super-tall, super-thin, super-fabulous folks pretending to eat here. The contemporary American menu, though, is truly worth digging into with zeal. Dishes like salmon with a fiery wasabi crust and pork chops with roasted corn pudding and bacon ragout are spirited and approachable. American menu. Lunch, dinner. Bar. Casual attire. **$$**
⊡

★ ★ ★ **CAPSOUTO FRERES.** *451 Washington St, New York (10013). Phone 212/966-4900; fax 212/925-5296. www.capsoutofreres.com.* As its name suggests, Capsouto Freres is owned by the Capsouto brothers.

What you may not get from its name is that this is a lovely choice for a special night on the town. Set in a restored 1891 factory in TriBeCa, it has an understated elegance, with original beam floors, exposed brick walls, magnificent open windows, and sunny floral arrangements. The restaurant is a neighborhood institution, having survived for years in this once deserted and now hip part of town. The eclectic menu features an impressive variety of choices, from calf's liver in sherry vinegar sauce to cassoulet, salmon with green herb sauce, and wild Scottish venison. If you are wandering around downtown on a Sunday, the brunch here is a great choice, with omelets and excellent French toast at reasonable prices. French menu. Lunch (Tues-Fri), dinner, brunch. Bar. Casual attire. Outdoor seating. **$$$**
⊡

★ **CARMINE'S.** *2450 Broadway, New York (10024). Phone 212/362-2200; fax 212/362-0742. www.carminesnyc.com.* If you have an aversion to garlic, do yourself a favor and stay far away from Carmine's, a loud, frenetic, oversized Italian spot in the theater district. Garlic, a prominent ingredient here, reeks from the walls. But if you crave hearty portions of zesty, family-style, red-sauced Italian food at reasonable prices, this is your place. Conversation is difficult as the noise level rivals a jet engine at close range. The dining room, originally a hotel ballroom, is a re-creation of a 1940s neighborhood Italian restaurant. Italian menu. Lunch, dinner. Bar. Outdoor seating. **$$**

★ **CARNEGIE DELI.** *854 Seventh Ave, New York (10019). Phone 212/757-2245; fax 212/757-9889. www.carnegiedeli.com.* Sandwiches are the specialty of Carnegie Deli, and by sandwich we mean at least a pound of freshly sliced meat, cheese, cole slaw, and assorted condiments stuffed between two slices of rye bread. Take note—this is not a place for dainty eaters. The Carnegie Deli is a loud, hectic, and chaotic whirlwind of a place with a bustling lunch crowd that is equally crazy in the evenings, when the old-fashioned booths fill up with eager sandwich lovers. Deli menu. Breakfast, lunch, dinner, late-night. **$$**
⊡

★ ★ **CASA MONO.** *52 Irving Pl, New York (10003). Phone 212/253-2773.* With Casa Mono (which means "monkey house"), a snug little restaurant on the corner of 17th and Irving Place, Mario Batali has stepped off of familiar Italian earth and onto the culinary and fashion hotbed known as Barcelona. Grab a seat in this cozy restaurant and watch as the chefs in the open kitchen deliver a menu that excites and invigorates in its simplicity. Popular picks include the sepia a la plancha (grilled squid), quail with quince, and oxtail-stuffed piquillo peppers. This is the sort of place that makes you smile until your face hurts. Claim your sliver of real estate and be patient. You'll soon be rewarded. Spanish menu. Lunch, dinner. Casual attire. **$$$**

★ ★ **CENTOLIRE.** *1167 Madison Ave, New York (10028). Phone 212/734-7711.* Fashionable Upper East Siders use Pino Luongo's Centolire as their elegant dining room and watering hole. The space, soothing and all aglow in ultra-flattering light, has a serene vibe with an air of money and power subtly floating in the background. This is not to say that Centolire is pretentious, it's not. The service is gracious and the Italian menu of simple, well articulated flavors is wonderful. However, if you are used to a downtown crowd, you may feel out of place among all the glitzy guests. Italian menu. Lunch, dinner. Bar. Casual attire. **$$$**

★ ★ ★ **'CESCA.** *164 W 75th St, New York (10024). Phone 212/787-6300. www.cescanyc.com.* Chef Tom Valenti is like Santa Claus for the Upper West Side—bringing culinary treats for all the good neighbors strolling along Columbus Avenue totting lattes and H&H Bagels. The follow-up to his slam hit Ouest, 'Cesca is an earthy and lively restaurant specializing in rustic, authentic, and often slow-cooked Italian fare like the oven-baked pasta with meat ragu and a Fred Flintstone-sized braised pork shank. If at all possible, go with an empty tummy so it can be filled all the way up. And while a reservation is nice, the warm, chocolate-toned bar, decked out in dark wood with amber lighting, is a perfect place to sit awhile, drink some wine, and nosh (read: pig out). Italian menu. Dinner. Bar. Jacket required. Reservations recommended. **$$$**

★ ★ **CHANGO.** *239 Park Ave S, New York (10003). Phone 212/477-1500.* Mexican menu. Lunch, dinner, late-night. Bar. Casual attire. **$$**

★ ★ ★ **CHANTERELLE.** *2 Harrison St, New York (10013). Phone 212/966-6960; fax 212/966-6143. www.chanterellenyc.com.* Long hailed as one of the most romantic restaurants in New York City, Chanterelle has been the scene of many bent-knee, velvet-box-in-hand proposals. Indeed, this restaurant is a New York dining icon. But Chanterelle, located on a sleepy corner in TriBeCa, offers much more than romance. Husband-and-wife owners David and Karen Waltuck (he is the chef, she works the room) have been serving brilliant, unfussy, modern French fare for more than 20 years. The menu, handwritten each week, reflects the best products available from local greenmarkets and regional farmers, and the award-winning wine list makes meals here even more memorable. French menu. Lunch Tues-Sat, dinner. Closed Sun; holidays; also the first week of July, first two weeks of July for lunch. Reservations recommended. **$$$$**

★ **CHAT'N'CHEW.** *10 E 16th St, New York (10003). Phone 212/243-1616; fax 212/243-2895.* Walk by Chat'n'Chew on a Saturday afternoon and you'll walk straight into a line of twentysomethings, married couples with strollers, and red-eyed partiers waiting to get inside to feast on one of the best and most reasonably priced brunch menus in the city. Filled with vintage décor and thrift store restaurant finds, this crowded Union Square diner is about quantity (portions are giant) and comfort food. There's roast turkey with gravy, mac 'n' cheese, and hearty breakfast fare like eggs, hash browns, French toast, and pancakes. It's not fancy, it's inexpensive, and it's all good. American menu. Lunch, dinner, brunch Sat-Sun. Casual attire. Outdoor seating. **$**

★ ★ **CHELSEA BISTRO AND BAR.** *358 W 23rd St, New York (10011). Phone 212/727-2026; fax 212/727-2180.* Chelsea Bistro and Bar is a lovely neighborhood bistro that goes beyond the call of the average local spot. Warm service, a charming atmosphere, wonderful food, and romantic lighting make this an ideal choice for almost any type of evening plans. A bite at the bar makes you feel like a regular even if you are from miles away. French bistro menu. Dinner. Bar. **$$**

★ **CHIKALICIOUS.** *203 E 10th St, New York (10003). Phone 212/995-9511.* Children are always fantasizing about skipping supper and just having dessert for dinner, and secretly, adults crave the same indulgence. With Chikalicious, the dream of an all-dessert-all-the-time meal has come true. At this quaint and sweetly decorated East Village cake, cupcake, cookie, brownie, and muffin depot, you can enjoy haute treats while watching the pastry chefs in action. Chikalicious opens at 3 pm, the perfect time for an afternoon snack, or for breaking the ultimate rule—having dessert before dinner. American menu. Dinner. Children's menu. Casual attire. **$$** 🅳

★ ★ **CHOW BAR.** *230 W 4th St, New York (10014). Phone 212/633-2212.* Asian fusion menu. Dinner, late-night. Bar. Casual attire. Reservations recommended. **$$**

★ ★ **CHURRASCARIA PLATAFORMA.** *316 W 49th St, New York (10019). Phone 212/245-0505; fax 212/974-8250. www.churrascariaplataforma.com.* Succulent Brazilian barbecue is served in delicious abundance at Churrascaria Plataforma, a loud, high-energy eatery in the theater district. This authentic Riodizio offers grilled and skewered beef, pork, chicken, sausage, lamb, and fish in all-you-can-eat portions (you give your server the green light by flipping the small disc at your place setting, indicating "Go!"), accompanied by intoxicating caiparinas—tangy, lime-soaked cocktails made from cachaca, a potent alcohol similar to rum. Brazilian menu. Lunch, dinner. Closed Dec 25. Bar. Casual attire. Reservations recommended. **$$$**

★ ★ ★ **CITE.** *120 W 51st St, New York (10020). Phone 212/956-7100; fax 212/956-7157. www.cite restaurant.com.* Located in the heart of Midtown, Cité is an elegant, civilized spot for wining and dining. The restaurant is known for its wonderful prix fixe meals paired with four complimentary wines, making this power spot a meat and wine lover's paradise. The signature tender prime filet mignon (piled high with golden French fries) is a dish made for the restaurant's bold reds from France, Spain, and around the world. Seafaring diners, fret not: you too can rejoice in lobster, salmon, and meaty crab cakes, with lots of crisp whites to complement them. American, French menu. Lunch, dinner. Closed holidays. Bar. Casual attire. **$$$**

★ **CITY BAKERY.** *3 W 18th St, New York (10003). Phone 212/366-1414.* Maury Rubin, the owner and creator of City Bakery, would probably have a warrant taken out on him if he ever closed City Bakery. Literally, New Yorkers would revolt and hunt him down. This hall of out-of-this-world baked goods is perpetually jammed with trendy locals craving his rich and creamy hot chocolate with house-made marshmallows, and his signature try-and-stop-at-one pretzel croissants. Aside from his selection of baked goods, he offers a dreamy buffet stocked with sandwiches, salads, antipasti, and soups made from the freshest seasonal ingredients. Just try and leave

without loosening your belt buckle. American menu. Breakfast, lunch, dinner. Casual attire. **$** 🅳

★ ★ **COCO PAZZO.** *23 E 74th St, New York (10021). Phone 212/794-0205; fax 212/794-0208. www.cocopazzo.com.* For more than a decade, Pino Luongo has been serving the wonderful cuisine of his native Tuscany in this sunny, airy space on the Upper East Side. Your senses will be seduced upon entry by tables crowded with Italian cheeses and roasted vegetable displays. After you're seated, dense home-made breads arrive, along with vibrant green olive oil. Try to save some room for dinner, though. The kitchen masters classics like tomato bruschetta, spaghetti with meatballs, and osso bucco, and also excels in modern dishes like a seasonal salad made from goat cheese, brussels sprouts, pumpkin, and endive. Italian menu. Lunch, dinner. Closed holidays. Bar. Jacket required. Reservations recommended. **$$$**

★ **CORNER BISTRO.** *331 W 4th St, New York (10014). Phone 212/242-9502.* Corner Bistro is known far and wide for one thing and one thing only: burgers. They are good, but the hype is a bit out of control these days. The place, a run-down little tavern with quite a bit of "character," is located, as its name suggests, on a nice little corner of the West Village, and the space is far from glamorous. In a word, it's a dive, but a friendly one, that serves tasty burgers on cardboard plates topped with cheese, bacon, or, if you're splurging on the Bistro Burger, bacon, raw onions, lettuce, tomato, and cheese. The Corner Bistro formula is simple: it's beer, burgers, and if you're lucky, some napkins. If you want anything more, you'd better go elsewhere. American menu. Lunch, dinner, late-night. Bar. Casual attire. No credit cards accepted. **$**

★ ★ ★ **CRAFT.** *43 E 19th St, New York (10003). Phone 212/780-0880; fax 212/780-0580.* Chef/owner Tom Colicchio's Craft (Colicchio is also a partner and the executive chef at Gramercy Tavern—see also) is a restaurant for two types of people: inventive, adventurous sorts who like to build things and gourmets who appreciate perfectly executed portions of meat, fish, fowl, and vegetables. Why these two sorts of folks? Because at Craft, lovers of Legos delight in creating dinner from the listlike menu of meat, fish, vegetables, mushrooms, and condiments. You choose what two delicious morsels should come together on your plate. (Those who prefer to defer to the chef may opt for a preplanned menu.) Dinner at Craft is a unique, interactive, exciting, and delicious adventure that should be experienced at least once, with like-minded builders. American menu. Dinner. Closed holidays. Bar. Casual attire. **$$$$**

★ ★ **CRAFTBAR.** *900 Broadway, New York (10003). Phone 212/780-0880; fax 212/598-1859.* After the runaway success of Craft (see), chef/owner Tom Colicchio's magnificent temple to the season's best ingredients, it was only a matter of time before he opened a smaller, more intimate and casual off-shoot. Located right next door to its fancier sibling, craftbar is part wine bar, part Italian trattoria, and part American eatery, serving small plates like the signature fried, stuffed sage leaves and crisp fried oysters with preserved lemon, alongside beautiful salads, soups, crusty panini, game, fish, and the most extraordinary veal ricotta meatballs in the country, if not the world. The wine list is extensive, and a meal at the bar is a great way to go if you can't score a table. American, Mediterranean menu. Lunch, dinner. Bar. Casual attire. Reservations recommended. **$$**

★ ★ **CRISPO.** *240 W 14th St, New York (10011). Phone 212/229-1818.* Named after its chef/owner Frank Crispo, this newcomer to West 14th Street is already considered a staple for fans of rustic, Italian-accented cuisine, like plates of delicious hand-sliced prosciutto di Parma, simple yet stellar pastas, grilled chops, and seasonal salads. The warm, exposed-brick room gets crowded early on, so plan to reserve a table ahead of time or wait at the bar (not a bad option at all, although the bar area is small) for one of the coveted tables to open up. Italian, Mediterranean menu. Dinner. Closed Sun. Bar. Casual attire. Reservations recommended. Outdoor seating. **$$**

★ ★ **CUB ROOM CAFE.** *131 Sullivan St, New York (10012). Phone 212/677-4100; fax 212/228-3425. www.cubroom.com.* The Cub Room was one of the first hotspots to open in SoHo, and it has stood the test of time thanks to chef-owner Henry Meer, who keeps the seasonal Mediterranean-accented menu fresh and fun, offering the perfect brand of upscale fare for the lively bunch that frequents this popular destination. In the chic, living room-style lounge with vintage fabric-covered sofas and a long, serpentine bar, a gregarious and gorgeous crowd sips chilly cocktails, while inside the rustic, country-style dining room, big groups and whispering couples feast on Meer's solid cooking. American menu. Lunch, dinner, Sat-Sun brunch. Closed Dec 25. Bar. Casual attire. **$$**

★ ★ ★ **DA SILVANO.** *260 Sixth Ave, New York (10014). Phone 212/982-2343; fax 212/982-2254.* If one thing is certain about a meal at Da Silvano, it is that before you finish your Tuscan dinner, you will have spotted at least one actor, model, musician, or other such celebrity. Da Silvano is a scene, and a great one at that. With such a loyal and fabulous following, the food could be mediocre, but the kitchen does not rest on its star-infested laurels. This kitchen offers wonderful, robust, regional Italian fare, like home-made pasta, meat, fish, and salad. The sliver of a wine bar next door, Da Silvano Cantinetta, offers Italian-style tapas paired with a wide selection of wines by the glass. But perhaps the best way to experience Da Silvano is on a warm day, where a seat at the wide, European-style sidewalk café offers prime people-watching. Italian menu. Lunch, dinner. Closed Dec 25. Casual attire. Outdoor seating. **$$$**

★ ★ ★ **DANIEL.** *60 E 65th St, New York (10021). Phone 212/288-0033; fax 212/396-9014.* Daniel Boulud is one of those chefs who could make scrambled eggs taste like manna from heaven. He has a magic touch that warms you from the inside out. For this reason, Daniel is a dining experience. It is not dinner. The experience starts when you enter the palatial front room, continues as you sip an old-fashioned cocktail in the romantic, low-lit lounge, and is taken to new heights when you take a seat at your table, your home for the hours you will spend as the fortunate culinary guest of Boulud. French food at other restaurants is good. With Boulud facing the stove, it is sublime. Potato-crusted sea bass is a signature. The crisp, golden coat, fashioned from whisper-thin slices of potatoes, protects the fish while it cooks and seals in its juices so that it melts on the tongue. It is wonder-ful. Wine service is another perk. Friendly and helpful, the staff wants you to learn and wants to help you choose the right wine for your meal and your wallet. You will have a new favorite wine before leaving. After dessert, you will think that you're free to go, but not so fast. There are petit fours, of course, and then the pièce de resistance: madeleines. Daniel is famous for these delicate, fluffy, lemony little cakes served warm, just seconds out of the oven. When you are finally free to go, you may not want to. French menu. Dinner. Closed Sun. Bar. Jacket required. Reservations recommended. **$$$$**

★ ★ ★ **DANUBE.** *30 Hudson St, New York (10013). Phone 212/791-3771; fax 212/267-1526. www.bouley.net.* Danube is the creation of David Bouley, the inspired and famed chef who has created many notable New York establishments. It is a stunning place to spend an evening. It has the feel of an old Austrian castle, with dark wood; deep, plush banquettes; and soft, warm lighting. It repeatedly draws a glamorous crowd that craves Bouley's masterful technique and creativity. Bouley's regal, majestic restaurant celebrates the cuisine of Austria within the framework of a New York restaurant. On the menu, you'll find a couple of Austrian-inspired dishes interspersed with lighter, modern, and truly exciting seasonal New American dishes. Bouley has a rare talent, and his food is spectacular, though not for those who are fearful of taking some risks at dinner. This is not a creamed-corn-and-roast-chicken place. The staff offers refined service, and the wine list is eclectic and extensive. As you would expect, it includes some gems from Austria. The cocktail lounge at Danube is a perfect spot to relax and get cozy before or after dinner. It is low-lit and romantic, and the bartenders serve delicious, perfectly balanced cocktails. American, Austrian menu. Dinner. Bar. Business casual attire. Reservations recommended. **$$$$**

★ ★ **DAWAT.** *210 E 58th St, New York (10022). Phone 212/355-7555; fax 212/355-1735. www.restaurant.com/dawat.* Located on the eastern edge of Midtown, just a stone's throw from Bloomingdale's, Dawat is one of the city's first (and best) high-end Indian restaurants. Serving elegant haute cuisine in a posh, hushed townhouse setting, Dawat is one of the most popular destinations for seekers of upscale, authentic Indian cuisine, including curries, rice dishes, poori, naan, and chutneys. Indian menu. Lunch, dinner. Casual attire. Reservations recommended. **$$**

★ ★ ★ **DB BISTRO MODERNE.** *55 W 44th St, New York (10036). Phone 212/391-2400; fax 212/391-1188.* This cool, sexy, ultra-stylish bistro in Midtown is Daniel Boulud's most casual restaurant. But he succeeds in making it a hotspot for foodies and moguls of all sorts without making it ordinary. For Boulud, making a regular restaurant is simply not possible. It's like asking Frank Sinatra to hum a simple tune. In many dishes, Boulud has a magic touch, transforming simple into spectacular with ease. His signature DB Burger is an excellent example of his creative interpretations. He builds the fattest, juiciest round of beef and stuffs it with short ribs and sinful amounts of foie gras and truffles. He serves it on a homemade Parmesan brioche bun, with house-stewed tomato confit (instead of ketchup) and a great big vat of fries. Don't think that this will be too much food

for you to eat alone—you'll regret offering to share after the first bite. American, French bistro menu. Lunch, dinner, late-night. Closed holidays. Casual attire. Reservations recommended. **$$$**

★ ★ **DELEGATES DINING ROOM.** *UN General Assembly Bldg, New York (10017). Phone 212/963-7625; fax 212/963-2025.* The United Nations may not be the first place you think of in terms of dining options, but the Delegates Dining Room offers a rotating buffet of international cuisine, often prepared by chefs who are visiting America from their native lands. Expect exotic menus from far-off places like Thailand, Korea, and India, as well as more traditional spots like Italy, Greece, and France. The restaurant is an elegant place to dine, and with its floor-to-ceiling windows, it provides some of the city's most captivating, panoramic views of the East River. International menu. Lunch. Closed Sat-Sun; holidays. Jacket required. Reservations recommended. Photo identification is required. **$$**

★ **DIM SUM GO GO.** *5 E Broadway, New York (10038). Phone 212/732-0797; fax 212/964-3149.* Looking for a chic little spot to have a quick bite of inventive Chinese fare? Dim Sum Go Go is your place. This super-mod, super-hip, minimalist spot sports a terrific menu of Chinese snacks like fresh soybeans with pickled vegetables, as well as homemade noodles and bigger dishes like the Garlicky Go Go roast chicken, with a taut golden skin. On weekends, you can sample fresh steamed dumplings with fillings like shark fin and crunchy white sea fungus. Come on, live a little. Dim Sum, Chinese menu. Lunch, dinner. Casual attire. **$**
🄳

★ ★ **DIWAN.** *148 E 48th St, New York (10017). Phone 212/593-5425; fax 212/593-5732. www.diwan restaurant.com.* Indian cuisine may not seem glamorous, but it is at Diwan—one of the city's most acclaimed Indian restaurants, serving amazing, upscale dishes in a swanky, newly remodeled setting smack dab in the center of Midtown. The lunchtime hour finds Diwan packed with businesspeople leaning in over tables to seal deals, while dinner is more relaxed and intimate, with an extensive menu of Bombay-inspired dishes that will satisfy your strongest craving for great Indian cuisine. Indian menu. Lunch, dinner. Casual attire. **$$**

★ ★ **DO HWA.** *55 Carmine St, New York (10014). Phone 212/414-1224.* Do Hwa is always crowded with Village trendsetters. It's one of those perpetually hot restaurants, mostly due to the menu, which features spicy, authentic Korean food at reasonable prices. Sure, there are more elegant, refined places to dine in the city, but Do Hwa is not trying to be anything other than what it is—a warm and lively restaurant that focuses on food and does it very well. Korean menu. Dinner, late-night. Bar. Casual attire. Reservations recommended. **$$**

★ ★ **DOS CAMINOS.** *373 Park Ave S, New York (10016). Phone 212/294-1000.* Steve Hanson has built a New York City restaurant empire with Blue Water Grill (see), Ruby Foo's (see), and Fiamma. With Dos Caminos, he has introduced the regional cuisines of Mexico to his winning formula of hip scene, cool bar, and crowd-pleasing eats. Dos Caminos is loud and always crowded, so don't plan on intimate dining, but certainly plan on tasty food. The menu reflects the diverse regions of Mexico, including guacamole made tableside to your desired level of spiciness; warm homemade tacos filled with chile-rubbed shrimp, steak, or pulled pork; and snapper steamed in banana leaves. To wash it all down, margaritas are potent and tasty. Mexican menu. Lunch, dinner. Bar. Casual attire. **$$$**

★ ★ **EAST POST.** *92 Second Ave, New York (10003). Phone 212/387-0065.* Italian menu. Lunch, dinner, late-night. Bar. Casual attire. Outdoor seating. **$$**

★ ★ **THE ELEPHANT.** *58 E 1st St, New York (10003). Phone 212/505-7739.* Located on the burgeoning restaurant row known as 1st Street in the East Village, The Elephant is a local hipster's hang-out, perpetually crowded with trendy twenty- and thirtysomethings who pile in to fill this sexy bistro's cramped tables and experience the cool, dressed-down vibe as well as the Thai-French bistro fare. The Elephant is loud, it has a great buzz, and everyone is fashionably underweight. You get the picture. Thai, French menu. Lunch, dinner. Bar. Casual attire. **$$**

★ **ELEPHANT AND CASTLE.** *68 Greenwich Ave, New York (10011). Phone 212/243-1400; fax 212/989-9294.* Elephant and Castle feels like a bit of London here in the Big Apple. This pub, styled like those found in rainy England, is low-lit and narrow, with dark wood paneling that gives the place a warm vibe that feels welcoming and cozy. The menu is straightforward and includes easy-to-love New York-style fare like Caesar salads, omelets, burgers, and top-notch sandwiches. The beer list is impressive as well. American menu. Breakfast, lunch, dinner, Sat-Sun brunch. Casual attire. **$**

★ ★ ★ **ELEVEN MADISON PARK.** *11 Madison Ave, New York (10010). Phone 212/889-0905; fax 212/889-0918. www.elevenmadisonpark.com.* Located across from the leafy, historic Madison Square Park, Danny Meyer's grand New American restaurant is a wonderful, soothing spot to take respite from the frenetic pace of a day in New York City. The magnificent dining room boasts old-world charm with vaulted ceilings, clubby banquettes, giant floor-to-ceiling windows, and warm, golden lighting. The crowd is equally stunning: a savvy blend of sexy, suited Wall Street types and chic, fashion-forward New Yorkers. The contemporary seasonal menu features updated American classics as well as a smart selection of dishes that borrow accents from Spain, France, and Asia. Meyer, who also owns Gramercy Tavern and Union Square Cafe (see both), continues to offer his gracious brand of warmth and hospitality at Eleven Madison Park. You will feel at home in an instant. American menu. Lunch, dinner. Closed Jan 1, Labor Day, Dec 24-25. Bar. Casual attire. **$$$**

★ ★ **ELMO.** *156 Seventh Ave, New York (10011). Phone 212/337-8000. www.elmorestaurant.com.* Located in the heart of Chelsea, Elmo is a convivial American eatery with a bustling bar serving comfort food that has been tweaked a bit for a fashionable New York City crowd. There are dishes as retro as Alphabet Soup with fluffy, dill-accented chicken dumplings; a hearty mac and cheese; and easy-to-love Hungry Man-type meals featuring meat and potatoes. There's even a Duncan Hines devil's food cake for dessert. Mom would be proud. American menu. Lunch, dinner, brunch. Bar. Casual attire. Outdoor seating. **$$**

★ ★ **ESSEX RESTAURANT.** *120 Essex St, New York (10002). Phone 212/533-9616; fax 212/533-7413. www.essexnyc.com.* Located on the Lower East Side, one of Manhattan's hippest 'hoods, Essex is a warm, inviting, minimalist space marked by skylights, white-washed brick, and sleek black tables. This is a perfect place for cocktails or a dinner date. The menu is as eclectic as the neighborhood, with dishes that pay tribute to the diverse local population—like a potato cake napoleon (a haute version of the knish), the Essex cubano sandwich, a scallop and mango ceviche, and kasha varnishkes. Late-night, the place turns into a loud and lively DJ party, the perfect prelude to the $12 brunch with all-you-can-drink Bloody Marys, mimosas, or screwdrivers. International/Fusion menu. Dinner, late-night, brunch. Closed Mon. Bar. Casual attire. **$$**

★ ★ ★ **ESTIATORIO MILOS.** *125 W 55th St, New York (10019). Phone 212/245-7400; fax 212/245-4828. www.milos.ca.* Milos, as it's called for short (try saying "Estiatorio" over and over again and you'll understand why), is a luxurious, cavernous, whitewashed eatery decorated with umbrella-topped tables and seafood market-style fish displays. Showcasing simple, rustic Greek cooking, this elegant, airy restaurant takes you from the hustle of Midtown to the shores of the Mediterranean in the whirl of a revolving door. Seafood is priced by the pound and is prepared either perfectly grilled over charcoal or in the Greek style called *spetsiota*—filleted and baked with tomatoes, onions, herbs, and olive oil. Greek, Seafood menu. Lunch, dinner. Closed Jan 1, Dec 25. Bar. Casual attire. **$$$$**

★ **FANELLI'S CAFE.** *94 Prince St, New York (10012). Phone 212/431-5744.* This classic SoHo eatery dressed in dark wood, with a long, tavern-style bar up front, has been around for a dog's age (since 1872). It remains one of the neighborhood's best hideaways for honest and hearty American meals like mac and cheese, big bowls of hot chili, juicy burgers, and thick steaks. Some things are better for not changing with the times; Fanelli's is one of them. American menu. Lunch, dinner, late-night. Bar. Casual attire. **$$**

★ ★ ★ **FELIDIA.** *243 E 58th St, New York (10022). Phone 212/758-1479; fax 212/935-7687. www.lidiasitaly.com.* Celebrated chef and TV personaity Lidia Bastianich is the unofficial matriarch of Italian-American cuisine. Her restaurant, Felidia (she and son Joe are partners in Becco (see), Babbo (see), and Esca as well), is warm and elegant and draws an elite New York crowd, although it remains free of pretense. The lovely dining room is bathed in golden, amber light and decorated with rich wood-paneled walls, hardwood floors, magnificent flowers, and seasonal vegetable and fruit displays. The menu focuses on a wide array of Italian dishes that you would discover if you journeyed throughout the country's varied culinary regions. Diners are expected to eat as they do in Italy, so you'll start with a plate of antipasti or a bowl of *zuppe* (soup), move on to a fragrant bowl of fresh pasta and then to a grilled whole fish, and finally have a bit of dolci for dessert. The Italian wine list is extra-special, so be sure to pair your meal with a few glasses. Italian menu. Lunch, dinner. Closed Sun; holidays. Bar. Jacket required. **$$$**

★ ★ **FELIX.** *340 W Broadway, New York (10013). Phone 212/431-0021; fax 212/343-0278. www.felixnyc.com.* Located on a busy stretch of West Broadway in SoHo (more of a mall these days than its former renegade artsy self), Felix is one of those perfect French bistros for moules frites, steak frites, or just about anything with frites. At this beautiful people scene, you'll find statuesque lovelies sipping cocktails and nibbling on salad greens while chiseled men recline and admire them. Felix is really more about the scene than the food, but if you need a place to rest after shopping, you'll do just fine with this menu of decent bistro standards. French bistro menu. Lunch, dinner, brunch. Casual attire. Outdoor seating. **$$**

★ ★ ★ **FIAMMA OSTERIA.** *206 Spring St, New York (10012). Phone 212/653-0100; fax 212/653-0101. www.brguestrestaurants.com.* This upscale and stylish spot for refined Italian fare in SoHo is the first chef-driven restaurant from Stephen Hanson, the owner of hip, casual eateries like Blue Water Grill and Dos Caminos (see both). For this project, Hanson pulled out all the stops, creating one of the best Italian dining experiences in New York City. From homemade pastas to silky fish and tender grilled meats to the all-Italian cheese course to the massive wine list, this is a place to mark for impressing business associates and loved ones alike. Italian menu. Lunch, dinner. Bar. Casual attire. Reservations recommended. **$$$**

★ ★ ★ **FIFTY SEVEN FIFTY SEVEN.** *57 E 57th St, New York (10022). Phone 212/758-5757; fax 212/758-5711. www.fourseasons.com.* A power spot to meet for (at least two) martinis, Fifty Seven Fifty Seven, at the über-civilized Four Seasons Hotel on the magnificent shopping mile of 57th Street, is indeed a hotspot for the city's movers and shakers. This is not to say that mere mortals can't sit down for dinner. Despite the moneyed crowd at the bar, the 22-foot coffered-ceiling dining room remains an oasis of calm, with glossy maple floors and bronzed chandeliers. The gifted crew in the kitchen dresses up classic American fare to suit a demanding urban sensibility. The restaurant also boasts an award-winning international wine list in addition to a fantastic selection of martinis and other perfectly shaken and stirred classic cocktails. American menu. Breakfast, lunch, dinner, brunch. Bar. Business casual attire. Valet parking. **$$$$**

★ ★ ★ **FIREBIRD.** *365 W 46th St, New York (10036). Phone 212/586-0244; fax 212/957-2983. www.firebirdrestaurant.com.* Firebird is an ode to the

glamour and gluttony of St. Petersburg, sometime around its heyday in 1912. Set in a lavish, double townhouse, this restaurant and cabaret is furnished like a majestic Russian palace, with ornate antique furniture, intricate china and etched glass, old-world oil paintings, and 19th-century photographs. The extravagance extends to the food, with Russian classics like blinis with sour cream and caviar, *zakuska* (the Russian equivalent of tapas), borscht made with pork and dill, and sturgeon baked in puff pastry. Vodka flows like water in a fast-running stream, and the wine list is deep as well. Russian menu. Dinner. Closed Mon; holidays. Bar. Outdoor seating. **$$$$**
🄳

★ ★ ★ **FLEUR DE SEL.** *5 E 20th St, New York (10003). Phone 212/460-9100; fax 212/460-8319. www.fleurdeselnyc.com.* Located on a sleepy block of East 20th Street, Fleur de Sel sneaks up on you like a ray of sunshine through the clouds. This lovely butter-cup-colored cottage-like restaurant is one of the most enchanted hideaways in the city, serving sophisticated French-American fare in a serene dining room deco-rated with sheer curtains, soothing creamy walls, and precious bouquets of fresh flowers. It is, quite simply, a lovely setting to enjoy a dinner of stunningly pre-sented, delicate, and deliciously prepared food. French menu. Lunch, dinner. Bar. Casual attire. Reservations recommended. **$$$**
🄳

★ ★ **FLORENT.** *69 Gansevoort St, New York (10014). Phone 212/989-5779; fax 212/645-2498. restaurantflorent.com.* Florent is a late-night reveler's institution. Located in the now-hip Meatpacking District, Florent has been there for decades. It opened way back in the day when the neighborhood was filled with seedy, unsavory characters, not haute, savory meals. It is still a hotspot, serving its menu of simple, brasserie-style French fare 24-7. You can feast on boudin with caramelized onions, steak frites, eggs, and fat, juicy burgers. The best part of Florent is strolling in after a long night of partying and sitting down to a cup of coffee, a good hot meal, and a whole lot of people-watching. You'll see drag queens, truckers, supermodels, Chelsea boys, and just about every other walk of life sitting side by side, smiling, and enjoy-ing the wonderful world that is New York. French, American menu. Breakfast, lunch, dinner, late-night, brunch. Closed Dec 25. Bar. Children's menu. Casual attire. **$$**

★ ★ ★ ★ **FOUR SEASONS RESTAURANT.** *99 E 52nd St, New York (10022). Phone 212/754-9494; fax 212/754-1077. www.fourseasonsrestaurant.com.* The Four Seasons is truly a New York classic. Since 1959, it has been the de facto dining room of media powerhouses, financial movers and shakers, publish-ing hotshots, legal dealmakers, and the generally fabulous crowd that follows them. Lunch can be an exercise in connect-the-famous-faces, as is the bar, a must for a pre-dinner cocktail or a quick bite. As for what you'll eat when you take a break from gawking at the stars, the food at The Four Seasons is simple but well prepared and takes its cues from around the world. You'll find classic French entrées as well as more contemporary American fare accented with flavors borrowed from Asia, Morocco, and Latin America. Guests at The Four Seasons are often some of the highest rollers, and the room has an energetic buzz that epitomizes the life and breath of the city that never sleeps. It is a scene. Dining here is fun, especially at lunch, if only to be a fly on the wall as deals are made and fortunes are won and lost. American menu. Breakfast, lunch, dinner. Closed holidays. Bar. Jacket required. Reservations recommended. **$$$$**

★ **FRANK.** *88 Second Ave, New York (10003). Phone 212/420-0202; fax 212/420-0699. www.frankrestaurant.com.* Do you love simple, rustic Italian food? Do you love reasonable prices and a cool downtown vibe? If you answered yes to these questions, you will fall in love with Frank in an instant, for the same reason that throngs of East Villagers are already swooning over this cramped, thrift-store-furnished spot for southern Italian cuisine. You'll find great food, cheap prices, and a happening crowd that doesn't mind waiting over an hour to get inside and sit elbow to elbow. Italian menu. Breakfast, lunch, dinner. Bar. Casual attire. Outdoor seating. No credit cards accepted. **$$**

★ ★ **GABRIEL'S.** *11 W 60th St, New York (10023). Phone 212/956-4600; fax 212/956-2309. www.gabriels barandrest.com.* Gabriel's is the creation of owner Gabriel Aiello, a charming host who knows how to make guests feel at home in this elegant Lincoln Center area spot for sumptuous Tuscan fare like tortelloni filled with lamb and tossed in a shiitake mushroom tomato sauce, artichoke Lasagna, and a daily house-made risotto. The restaurant is elegantly dressed with contemporary art cloaking the warm saffron-toned walls; wide, sleep-worthy green felt banquettes; well-spaced tables; soothing indirect lighting; and a 35-foot-long mahogany bar. While Gabriel's may look like a see-and-be-scene hotspot, the restaurant is warm and welcoming, without pretension, making an evening here a delight from start to finish. Italian menu. Lunch, dinner. Closed Sun; holidays. Bar. Casual attire. **$$$**

★ **GABRIELA'S.** *685 Amsterdam Ave, New York (10025). Phone 212/961-0574; fax 212/961-0576. www.gabrielas.com.* From the people who brought you the large-scale Italian fare at Carmine's (see) comes Gabriela's, a breezy, colorful Mexican cantina that offers family-style portions of zesty south-of-the-border cuisine, without leaving you broke. The menu of spicy and fresh fare includes savory plates like shredded, spice-infused pork with rice and black beans, and fat burritos with vibrant sides of guacamole. Mexican menu. Lunch, dinner, brunch. Bar. Casual attire. **$**
🔁

★ ★ **GALLAGHER'S.** *228 W 52nd St, New York (10019). Phone 212/245-5336; fax 212/245-5426. www.gallaghersnysteakhouse.com.* The theater district has some great longtime restaurant hotspots to choose from, and Gallagher's is one of its brightest stars. This steakhouse is a New York City landmark and former speakeasy, and remains decorated as it was the day it opened in November 1927, with plain-planked floors, red-checked tablecloths, and dark wood-paneled walls covered in old photos. Specializing in dry-aged beef, the kitchen stays true to simple American fare rather than straying off course for global flourishes that have no place in such a comfortable, back-to-basics establishment. The tried-and-true formula is winning; after all these years, Gallagher's is a perennial favorite on Theater Row. American, steak menu. Lunch, dinner. Bar. Casual attire. **$$$**
🔁

★ ★ **GASCOGNE.** *158 Eighth Ave, New York (10011). Phone 212/675-6564; fax 212/627-3018. www.gascognenyc.com.* At this charming neighborhood restaurant, the robust regional cuisine of Gascogne fills the air. Paying tribute to the southwest of France, the kitchen offers heavenly plates of fill-in-the-blank confit, Armagnac-soaked prunes and foie gras terrine, cassoulet, and monkfish casserole, and a lovely list of wines to match. This is a spot for romance, as the dining room is intimate and candlelit, and the garden out back makes you feel like you are miles from the city. French menu. Lunch, dinner. Closed holidays. Bar. Casual attire. Outdoor seating. **$$**
🔁

★ ★ ★ **GEISHA.** *33 E 61st St, New York (10021). Phone 212/813-1113.* Set in a modern, posh townhouse in the east 60s, Geisha is seafood whiz kid Eric Ripert's inspired translation of Japanese cuisine. While he is still manning the stoves at Le Bernardin (see), here at Geisha, his love affair with Asian-tinged seafood is in full bloom. The food at Geisha delivers Zen enlightenment in plates of coconut-marinated fluke with coconut ponzu, lime vinaigrette, and orange essence; bowls of tiger shrimp dumplings with toasted pumpkin in a green curry broth; and dishes of dayboat cod with warm pepper and snow pea salad in soy ginger butter, not to mention gorgeous platters of sushi, sashimi and signature rolls prepared by a pair of seriously skilled sushi chefs. Japanese tea and an extensive sake list will keep you well hydrated and spiritually centered. Japanese menu. Lunch, dinner. Bar. Casual attire. **$$$**
🔁

★ ★ **GHENET RESTAURANT.** *284 Mulberry St, New York (10012). Phone 212/343-1888. www.ghenet.com.* Featuring the fragrant dishes of Ethiopia, Ghenet is a charming spot to explore a new and delicious cuisine. The menu reads like a wonderful textbook, with great explanations of all the menu items, many of which are savory rice dishes and lamb or beef stews to be mopped up with Frisbee-size rounds of homemade flatbread. Owned by a husband-and-wife team, this family-run establishment is all about hospitality, and you will feel like family when you leave. Ethiopian menu. Lunch, dinner. Bar. Casual attire. **$$**
🔁

★ ★ **GIGINO TRATTORIA.** *323 Greenwich St, New York (10013). Phone 212/431-1112; fax 212/226-3855. www.giginony.com.* Gigino Trattoria has been a local favorite for Italian fare since 1983. Owned by Phil Suarez and Bob Giraldi (partners in Patria and Jean-Georges), this TriBeCa gem offers casual, comfortable dining and the tasty, home-style cooking of an authentic Italian trattoria. Generous bowls of pasta, brick-oven pizzas, seasonal produce, game, fish, and meats round out the appealing menu. Italian menu. Lunch, dinner. Closed Jan 1, Memorial Day, Dec 25. Bar. Casual attire. Outdoor seating. **$$$**
🔁

★ ★ ★ **GOTHAM BAR & GRILL.** *12 E 12th St, New York (10003). Phone 212/620-4020; fax 212/627-7810.* Alfred Portale, the chef and owner of Gotham Bar & Grill, is an icon in New York's hallowed culinary circles. The leader of the tall-food movement and a passionate advocate of seasonal Greenmarket ingredients, he has been a gastronomic force from behind the stoves at his swanky, vaulted-ceilinged Gotham Bar & Grill for more than a decade. The room is loud, energetic, and packed with a very stylish crowd at both lunch and dinner. The lively bar also draws a regular crowd of black-clad after-work revelers. You'll have no problem finding a dish with your name on it at Gotham. The menu offers something for everyone—salad, fish, pasta, poultry, beef, and game—and each dish is prepared with a bold dose of sophistication. Portale is an icon for a reason. Under his care, simple dishes are taken to new heights. And while the food isn't as tall as it used to be, size really doesn't matter. His food is just terrific. American menu. Lunch, dinner. Bar. Casual attire. **$$$$**

★ ★ ★ ★ **GRAMERCY TAVERN.** *42 E 20th St, New York (10003). Phone 212/477-0777; fax 212/477-1160. www.gramercytavern.com.* Dining at Gramercy Tavern is for people who don't have trouble being very well taken care of. Owner Danny Meyer's perpetually bustling New York eatery oozes warmth and charm without a smidgen of pretension. Chef/co-owner Tom Colicchio delivers on the food in much the same way. While his menu is inventive, it is not overfussed. Pristine, seasonal, locally sourced ingredients shine, and every bite allows the flavors to converse quietly yet speak individually as well. Though formal and elegant in tone, Gramercy Tavern is a fun place to dine. Colicchio's food is so good that you can't help but have a great time, and the waitstaff's enthusiasm for the chef's talent shows, adding to the appeal. In the glorious main room, you can choose from a pair of seasonal tasting menus or a wide array of equally tempting à la carte selections. And if you don't have a reservation, don't fret. Meyer is a fan of democracy and accepts walk-ins in the front Tavern Room. Stroll in, put your name on the list, and you'll have the chance to sample Colicchio's spectacular food (the menu is different than in the main dining room but just as wonderful) and rub elbows with the city's sexy locals. There's a terrific house cocktail list as well, so make a nice toast while you're there. American menu. Lunch, dinner. Bar. Casual attire. **$$$$**

★ **GREAT NY NOODLETOWN.** *28 Bowery, New York (10013). Phone 212/349-0923.* It would be impossible to pass NY Noodletown off as your own private discovery. Anointed years ago by rave reviews, this bright corner spot continues to draw crowds all day and late into the night. Press in and enjoy the

bustle. This is not the place for complicated dishes. Treat NY Noodletown like a Chinese version of your local coffee shop: avoid preparations that have more than two ingredients and you'll do well. The roast meats are top-notch, particularly the crisp-skinned baby pig. Greens are basic and fresh, and perfectly cooked noodles, naturally, are a strong point. When summer comes, the salt-baked soft-shell crab is a must, juicy and tasting of the sea, as much of a New York ritual as a trip to Coney Island. Chinese menu. Lunch, dinner. Casual attire. No credit cards accepted. **$**

★ ★ **GUASTAVINO'S.** *409 E 59th St, New York (10022). Phone 212/980-2455; fax 212/980-2904. www.guastavinos.com.* Located under the Queensborough Bridge, a marvelous structure built by Guastavino, this cavernous and awesome restaurant is home to chef/owner Daniel Orr's stunning New American brasserie. The downstairs bar and lounge serves as watering hole to hundreds of sexy singles, all well dressed in swanky business attire and ready for after-work reveling. Beyond the bar, in the gorgeous, marble-arched dining room, you'll discover terrific seasonal American fare in a magnificent and alluring setting. For drinks or dinner, Guastavino's is visually mesmerizing and gastronomically pleasing. American menu. Lunch, dinner, brunch. Bar. Children's menu. Casual attire. Outdoor seating. **$$$**

★ ★ ★ **HAKUBAI.** *66 Park Ave, New York (10016). Phone 212/885-7111; fax 212/885-7095. www.kitano.com.* Located in the posh Kitano Hotel (see), Hakubai offers authentic Japanese fare in a tranquil, Zen-like space. The menu features a myriad of traditionally prepared seafood dishes like *ika shiokara* (chopped salted squid), *karuge-su* (vinegar-marinated jellyfish), and *karei* (fried, grilled, or simmered flounder). For a special treat, call ahead and reserve a private room for the multicourse chef's choice menu ($120 to $150), or, to savor a simpler meal, choose from the restaurant's swimming selection of sushi, sashimi, and maki rolls, as well as udon and soba noodle dishes. Japanese menu. Lunch, dinner. Casual attire. **$$$$**

★ ★ ★ **THE HARRISON.** *355 Greenwich St, New York (10013). Phone 212/274-9310; fax 212/274-9376. www.beanstalkrestaurants.com.* With its amber lighting, hardwood floors, wainscoting, and inviting bar, The Harrison is one of those restaurants that makes you feel like never leaving. Owned by Jimmy Bradley and Danny Abrams, the savvy team behind The Red Cat and the Mermaid Inn (see both), this Mediterranean-accented restaurant is a charming neighborhood hotspot with a chic clientele. The signature fried clams with fried slivered rounds of lemon are a must have, whether seated at the happening bar or at one of the well-spaced, linen-topped tables. American menu. Dinner. Bar. Casual attire. Outdoor seating. **$$$**

★ ★ ★ **HARRY CIPRIANI.** *781 Fifth Ave, New York (10022). Phone 212/753-5566; fax 212/308-5653. www.cipriani.com.* If you are searching for a place to see and be seen by some of New York's most moneyed crowds, Harry's is your spot. Located across the street from Central Park, this posh restaurant has not been renovated in a while and could use a facelift, but perhaps because many of its patrons have already had work done, the owners don't feel as obligated to make over the room. The menu is Italian, the prices are high, the service is gracious, and the entire experience very old-world charming. Be prepared to hear the word "daaahhling" with alarming regularity. Italian menu. Breakfast, lunch, dinner. Bar. Jacket required. Reservations recommended. **$$$$**

★ **HEARTLAND BREWERY.** *35 Union Square W, New York (10003). Phone 212/645-3400. www.heartland .citysearch.com.* American menu. Lunch, dinner, late-night. Bar. Casual attire. Outdoor seating. **$$**

★ **THE HOG PIT.** *22 Ninth Ave, New York (10014). Phone 212/604-0092.* Located in the Meatpacking District, the Hog Pit is a down-home barbecue spot with a roadside dive flare. This is the sort of place where licking your fingers is a must, and manners are not necessary. The menu at this rough-and-tumble watering hole includes soul food and barbecue dishes like baby-back pork ribs, and meatloaf served with sides of hush puppies, black-eyed peas, collard greens, and creamy mac and cheese. Barbecue menu. Dinner. Bar. Casual attire. **$**

★ ★ **HOME.** *20 Cornelia St, New York (10014). Phone 212/243-9579; fax 212/647-9393. www.recipes fromhome.com.* Owned by husband-wife team David Page (he is also executive chef) and Barbara Shin, Home is one of those rare and wonderful restaurants that wraps you in warmth, hospitality, grace, and delicious cuisine. Tucked away on a sleepy block of the West Village, Home offers diners home-style American meals made from the season's best in-gredients. The restaurant has a charming outdoor garden (heated in winter) and boasts one of the most extensive all-New York State wine lists around town. (The couple's own wine, Shin Merlot, made in the

North Fork of Long Island was added to the list in 2004.) This gem of a restaurant should be shared with someone as special as it is. American menu. Lunch, dinner, brunch. Closed Dec 25. Casual attire. Outdoor seating. **$$**

★ ★ ★ **HONMURA AN.** *170 Mercer St, New York (10012). Phone 212/334-5253; fax 212/334-6162.* New Yorkers who are over the lines at Nobu and the crowds at Yama flock to Honmura An, a delightful, serene escape in SoHo where spectacular just-made soba and udon noodles are the house specialty. Bring an appetite, because aside from the noodles, the kitchen has an in for some of the most delicious fish in the city—sashimi, sushi, and maki rolls that will force you to order more even if you have reached maximum food capacity. Japanese menu. Lunch Wed-Sat, dinner. Closed Mon. Casual attire. **$$$**

★ ★ **HUE.** *91 Charles St, New York (10014). Phone 212/691-4170; fax 212/691-4380. www.huenyc.com.* Hue (pronounced "hway"), a Vietnamese-inspired Zen den for trendsetters and foodies alike, is a sexy lounge that blends elements of earth, wind, water, and fire in its sultry and serene design. The menu, emblematic of the fare served in this region of Vietnam, is spicy and spirited, heavy on chiles, lemongrass, mint, and sugar cane. The cocktail list is impressive as well, so make sure to imbibe a bit before, during, and after dinner. French, Vietnamese menu. Dinner. Closed Sun. Bar. Casual attire. **$$$**

★ ★ ★ **I TRULLI.** *122 E 27th St, New York (10016). Phone 212/481-7372.* i Trulli envelops you with warmth, whether in the winter with its hearth-style, wood-burning fireplace, or in the summer when the lovely outdoor courtyard garden opens up for dining under the stars. This is a true neighborhood place, with charming service that features the rustic Italian cuisine of the Apulia region. Favorites include ricotta-stuffed cannelloni, orchiette with veal ragu, and fantastically fat calzones made by hand and baked to a golden brown in the wood-burning oven. Italian menu. Lunch, dinner. Bar. Casual attire. Reservations recommended. Outdoor seating. **$$$**

★ ★ **IL BUCO.** *47 Bond St, New York (10012). Phone 212/533-1932; fax 212/533-3502. www.ilbuco.com.* While the Italian food here is some of the most honest and well executed of its kind in the city, Il Buco is all about atmosphere. The place is low-lit and warm, filled with antiques (many for sale) and sturdy farmhouse tables that give the restaurant the soft, inviting charm of an out-of-the-way farmhouse somewhere in the mountains. Romance is always a big draw, but even if you aren't in love, go with friends. You'll have a great meal, and you'll leave feeling all warm and fuzzy inside. Italian, Mediterranean menu. Lunch Tues-Sat, dinner. Bar. Casual attire. **$$$**

★ ★ **IL CORTILE.** *125 Mulberry St, New York (10013). Phone 212/226-6060; fax 212/431-7283. www.ilcortile.com.* Il Cortile has been a pillar of Italian cuisine in Little Italy since 1975. This neighborhood tratorria, located amid the bustling streets of Little Italy and Chinatown, offers heaps of authentic Italian fare—antipasti, pasta, fish, poultry, and beef, prepared with love and with a nod to the traditions of the old country. The restaurant has a sunny indoor garden room that makes you feel like you are dining somewhere on the Mediterranean. Italian menu. Lunch, dinner. Closed Thanksgiving, Dec 24-25. Bar. Casual attire. Reservations recommended. **$$$**

★ ★ ★ **IL MULINO.** *86 W 3rd St, New York (10012). Phone 212/673-3783; fax 212/673-9875. www.ilmulinonewyork.com.* If Tony Soprano were having dinner out in New York City, chances are he'd love Il Mulino. It's a dark relic of an Italian spot where the service is excellent and the rich, heavy food is read from long lists of specials and served in huge portions (the herb-crusted lamb chops are built for Fred Flintstone). Tableside theatrics like making a Caesar salad and filleting a whole fish give guests even more of a show. Il Mulino is a boys' club with lots of loud, brash eaters who tend to drink one too many bottles of wine. Italian menu. Lunch, dinner. Closed Sun. Bar. Reservations recommended. **$$$$**

★ **INO.** *21 Bedford St, New York (10014). Phone 212/989-5769.* Jason Denton honed his skills at Mario Batali's first hit restaurant, Po, and decided to branch off on his own and open a little nook of a wine and panini bar in the West Village. Lucky for us. His itty-bitty Italian wine bar is open from breakfast until late at night, serving a mouthwatering selection of pressed sandwiches and an extensive and reasonably priced list of Italian wines by the glass. Don't miss the signature truffled egg toast, a delicious snack anytime of the day. Deli menu. Breakfast, lunch, dinner, late-night. Bar. Casual attire. **$**

★ **'INOTECA.** *98 Rivington St, New York (10002). Phone 212/614-0473.* From Jason and Joe Denton, the owners of the tiny and irresistible wine bar 'ino comes 'inoteca, a rustic, wood-beamed Italian wine bar in the super-hip Lower East Side. The wine list is all Italian, all the time—and the wonderful staff is ready, willing, and able to help walk you through it. The simply delicious menu of Italian snacks includes platters of cured meats and cheeses, panini, antipasti, and the house signature truffled egg toast. Although the fashionable crowds gather here in full force on a regular basis, the place is surprisingly attitude free. Be sure to bring your patience, because the waiting is the hardest part. Italian menu. Lunch, dinner, late-night. Bar. Casual attire. **$$**

★ **JACKSON HOLE.** *1611 Second Ave, New York (10028). Phone 212/737-8788; fax 212/737-8621. www.jacksonholeburgers.com.* If you crave a thick, juicy burger and don't mind a loud crowd and a fast-paced, sometimes frenetic setting, then Jackson Hole is the place for you. This is a top spot to feast on burgers offered in various sizes and weights with an almost infinite variety of toppings. All are served with piles of steak fries and thick slices of red onion and ripe tomatoes. Jackson Hole restaurants are fun joints where cold beer and great beef burgers are the draw. American, Hamburgers, Mexican menu. Breakfast, lunch, dinner, late-night, brunch Sat-Sun. Closed Thanksgiving, Dec 25. Bar. Outdoor seating. **$**

★ ★ ★ ★ ★ **JEAN GEORGES.** *One Central Park W, New York (10023). Phone 212/299-3900; fax 212/299-3914. www.jean-georges.com.* Perfection is a word that comes to mind when speaking of meals at Jean-Georges. Heaven is another word and divine yet another. Located in the Trump International Hotel & Tower (see) across from Central Park, Jean-Georges is a shrine to haute cuisine. Drawing influences from around the world, the menu is conceived and impeccably executed by celebrity chef/owner (and author) Jean-Georges Vongerichten. Vongerichten is a man of meticulous discipline, and it shows on the plate. Nothing is present that shouldn't be there. Under Vongerichten's direction, ingredients shine, flavors spark, and the mouth trembles. Suffice it to say that you will be in heaven within minutes of the meal's commencement. The room is sophisticated and stunning, yet remains comfortable. You'll find that it's filled nightly with well-known names, high-powered financial moguls, actors, models, and local New Yorkers who are lucky enough to score reservations. Call well in advance. It is worth the time it may take you to get through. If you can't manage to secure a table, try your luck at Nougatine, the popular café in the outer bar area. It has a simpler menu but will give you a taste of what Vongerichten is capable of. The bar is also a lovely place to meet for an aperitif or a cocktail before dinner or a walk through the park. French menu. Dinner. Bar. Jacket required. Reservations recommended. Valet parking. Outdoor seating. **$$$$**

★ ★ ★ **JEWEL BAKO.** *239 E 5th St, New York (10003). Phone 212/979-1012.* This is one restaurant that sounds like its name—it is a shoebox-sized jewel of a place, serving precious, glorious sushi and sashimi as well as more traditional Japanese meals. The tiny, intimate, and chic East Village sliver of a space is owned by a husband-wife team who make it their mission to ensure that your experience is marked by warm service and gracious hospitality. The restaurant's small size and popular following make reserving a table ahead of time a good plan. Japanese menu. Dinner. Closed Sun; also one week in Aug. Casual attire. Reservations recommended. **$$$**
🅳

★ **JING FONG.** *20 Elizabeth St, New York (10013). Phone 212/964-5256.* Jing Fong is a dim sum lover's paradise. This vast banquet hall offers mountains of delicious dim sum from carts, but also allows those too hungry to wait for a cart to hover by the kitchen to snatch up plates of fresh morsels—dumplings, buns, rolls—as they are cooked. In addition, you can opt for a feast from a buffet of raw seafood and have it cooked to order. Don't leave without sampling one of the tiny white mochi desserts—coconut shells filled with black sesame paste that tastes like peanut butter. Dim Sum, Asian menu. Breakfast, lunch, dinner. Casual attire. **$**

★ **JOHN'S PIZZERIA.** *278 Bleecker St, New York (10014). Phone 212/935-2895.* For many pizza aficionados, John's is the beginning, the middle, and the end. There simply is no other. This decades-old standard, located on a congested block of Bleecker Street in Greenwich Village, is almost a dive in terms of décor, but no matter; the pizza—gorgeous, piping hot, bubbling mozzarella-topped pies—is divine. To wash it down, there are carafes of wine, pitchers of beer, and not much else, but what else do you really need? Pizza. Lunch, dinner. Children's menu. Casual attire. **$**

★ ★ ★ **JOJO.** *160 E 64th St, New York (10021). Phone 212/223-5656; fax 212/755-9038. www.jean-georges.com.* Located in a charming old townhouse, Jo Jo was one of the first restaurants from acclaimed star-chef and restaurateur Jean-Georges Vongerichten. It was recently renovated and given a turn-of-the-century feel, with deep jewel tones, velvet and silk fabrics, and 17th-century terra-cotta tiles. While the dining room has been made over, the menu has stayed much the same, with dishes that highlight Vongerichten's French-Asian style, such as goat cheese and potato terrine with chive oil, roast chicken with chickpea fries, and tuna spring rolls with soybean coulis. Jo Jo is a wonderful spot for elegant, restful, special-occasion dining. French menu. Lunch, dinner. Closed holidays. Bar. Casual attire. **$$$$**
🅳

★ ★ ★ ★ **KAI.** *822 Madison Ave, New York (10021). Phone 212/988-7277.* Take respite from the city streets at KAI, a restaurant and teahouse on the second floor of renowned tea merchant ITO EN. Located in one of New York City's toniest shopping areas, KAI offers instant transport to the peace and serenity of Japan's best teahouses. Bamboo, stone, slate, and traditional Japanese pottery are the main design elements of the spare yet elegant restaurant. Along with an afternoon tea featuring many of ITO EN's premium teas and sweets like black sesame and green tea layered cake, the restaurant is open for lunch and dinner. At lunch, diners delight in flavors and textures of soups and dishes made with noodles, tea-scented rice, vegetables, seafood, or beef. Bento boxes or sashimi lunches are also popular choices. At dinner, order à la carte or a tasting menu such as the nine-course Iron Goddess, which features dishes like chilled puree of lily bulb soup and "live" unagi with seasonal vegetables and spicy miso. Make the experience last by purchasing favorite teas at ITO EN. Japanese menu. Lunch, dinner. Closed Sun; holidays. Casual attire. **$$$**
🅳

★ **KELLEY & PING.** *127 Greene St, New York (10012). Phone 212/228-1212.* This trendy pan-Asian eatery has been filling up with slinky hipsters since the day it opened. The menu of fiery fare served at this exposed-brick, wood-paneled teashop, noodle bar, and Asian grocery reflects many regions of Asia, including China, Vietnam, Korea, and Thailand. For those who can't make a decision about what to eat first, the menu offers combination platters that include spring rolls, chicken satay, dumplings, and duck pancakes. Pan-Asian menu. Lunch, dinner. Children's menu. Casual attire. **$$**

★ ★ **KINGS' CARRIAGE HOUSE.** *251 E 82nd St, New York (10028). Phone 212/734-5490. www.kings carriagehouse.com.* Located on a tree-lined block of the Upper East Side, Kings' Carriage House is an exquisite and intimate restaurant with all the comforts of an antique-filled Irish manor house. Owned by former food stylist Elizabeth King and her husband, Paul Farell, a native of Dublin, this is indeed one of Manhattan's most enchanted and personal restaurants. Special treats include Sunday afternoon tea and the Sunday roast dinner, but the everyday menu with dishes like shrimp bisque and Irish smoked salmon is winning as well. Irish, English menu. Lunch, dinner. Closed Dec 25. Bar. Reservations recommended. **$$$**

★ ★ **KITCHEN 22.** *36 E 22nd St, New York (10010). Phone 212/228-4399; fax 212/228-4612.* At this low-lit neighborhood bistro in the Flatiron neighborhood, you'll be treated to a three-course prix fixe menu of seasonal American fare for an unbelievably affordable price of $25 for dinner. This Charlie Palmer restaurant provides a winning formula for hip locals who crowd in for drinks and delicious meals in a dark, sexy setting. The crowded bar up front is a popular spot for regulars to gather and sip martinis in style. American menu. Dinner. Closed Sun. Bar. Casual attire. **$$**

★ ★ **KOMODO.** *186 Avenue A, New York (10009). Phone 212/529-2658.* Located on a busy stretch of Avenue A, Komodo offers smart, flavorful Asian fusion cuisine in a chic, low-lit, Zenlike space. Expect a sexy crowd and inspired dishes—heavy on the fish— accented with Asian and Latin ingredients like soy, chiles, ginger, cilantro, garlic, and miso. Sake is a wise choice for pairing. Mexican, Asian menu. Dinner. **$$**

★ ★ ★ **KURUMA ZUSHI.** *7 E 47th St, New York (10017). Phone 212/317-2802; fax 212/317-2803.* Kuruma Zushi is New York's most secreted sushi spot. Located on the second floor of a less-than-impressive Midtown building, with only a tiny sign to alert you to its presence, it is tough to find but well worth the search. Fresh, supple, mouthwatering fish is served with freshly grated wasabi and bright, fiery shavings of ginger. This sushi temple has quite a following, among them Ruth Reichl, the former *New York Times* restaurant critic and current editor of *Gourmet* magazine, who is vocal about her love of the restaurant's spectacular fish. You will be dreaming about this fish for weeks after your meal has ended. While many consider this the pinnacle of sushi, it does come with quite an insane price tag. Dinner per person can easily hit the $100 mark, which may be why the restaurant,

an earth-colored, minimalist room, is most popular with business people on expense accounts and true devotees. Japanese, Sushi menu. Lunch, dinner. Closed Sun. **$$$$**

★ ★ **L'EXPRESS.** *249 Park Ave, New York (10003). Phone 212/254-5858.* Open 24 hours a day for omelettes, frisee au lardons, steak frites, and other traditional bistro fare, L'Express is a perfect choice for an off-hour snack, a late-night meal, or a quiet breakfast of eggs, coffee, and a newspaper. At prime lunch and dinner hours, this replica of a French brasserie can get a bit frenetic, but if you don't mind the hustle and bustle, you'll have yourself a nice Parisian-style meal. French bistro menu. Breakfast, lunch, dinner, late-night. Bar. Casual attire. **$$**

★ ★ ★ **L'IMPERO.** *45 Tudor City Pl, New York (10017). Phone 212/599-5045.* L'Impero arrived on the New York City dining scene in 2002, and with it, the landscape of elegant Italian cuisine was permanently changed. Chef/partner Scott Conant takes you to new heights with his interpretation of the Italian cucina. There are simple plates of pasta, like a gorgeous bowl of perfect handmade spaghetti garnished with fresh tomato and basil that will renew your love of a dish tossed aside long ago. His signature capretto (that would be goat) is moist-roasted until fork-tender and saturated with rich, delicious flavors. His takes on crudo (raw, brightly accented sashimi-style dishes of fish) are luminous. The service is flawless, the wine list is an Italian encyclopedia, and the décor is serene and civilized, warmed with chocolate and blue tones. L'Impero is a must-visit for a special occasion or for a well-deserved renewal of a love affair with Italian food. Italian menu. Lunch, dinner. Closed Sun. Bar. Casual attire. Outdoor seating. **$$$**

★ **LA BONNE SOUPE.** *48 W 55th St, New York (10019). Phone 212/586-7650; fax 212/765-6409. www.labonnesoupe.com.* La Bonne Soupe is one of those restaurants that fits like an old shoe, in the best sense of the word. Comfortable and easy, the room feels like a Parisian bistro with checked tablecloths, long banquettes, and lovely French waitresses. The menu keeps the illusion of Paris alive with dishes like fluffy quiche, an excellent bouillabaisse, and of course, a delicious French onion soup capped with a thick and gooey blanket of melting Gruyère cheese. For a pre-theater meal, keep this gem in mind. French bistro menu. Lunch, dinner, Sun brunch. Closed holidays. Bar. Children's menu. Casual attire. Outdoor seating. **$**

★ ★ ★ **LA GRENOUILLE.** *3 E 52nd St, New York (10022). Phone 212/752-1495; fax 212/593-4964. www.la-grenouille.com.* Yes, frogs' legs are on the menu at La Grenouille, whose name literally means "The Frog." This stunning Midtown restaurant is the epitome of a classic. If you're craving some sort of fusion hotspot with a loud crowd and a lengthy cocktail list that contains the word "cosmopolitan," you won't be happy here. La Grenouille is elegant and conservative in style and substance. The room is quiet, lovely, and modest; the kitchen serves authentic, sophisticated French cuisine at its finest; and the staff offers service that is refined and seemingly effortless. Now back to those frogs' legs, which appropriately are the restaurant's signature. They are served sautéed, Provençal style, and are a must for adventurous diners who have never indulged in them. This is certainly the place to have your first experience with them, although it may spoil you for life. The wine list is mostly French, although some American wines have managed to make the cut as well. Indulging in a cheese course is a nice way to finish your meal, as it is in France. The restaurant is popular at lunch and is frequently crowded with well-preserved businesspeople on lunch hour, being in the heart of Midtown. It is also a wonderful spot to take a civilized siesta from hours of shopping along Fifth Avenue and recharge your batteries for the afternoon ahead. French menu. Lunch, dinner. Closed Sun-Mon; also Aug. Bar. Reservations recommended. **$$$$**
🅳

★ ★ **LA MANGEOIRE.** *1008 Second Ave, New York (10022). Phone 212/759-7086; fax 212/759-6387. www.lamangeoire.com.* La Mangeoire is a perfect place for a business lunch or a quiet, intimate dinner. The warm dining room is charming and cozy, and the menu offers enough of a selection of contemporary French fare—escargots, Provençal fish soup, and the caramelized onion tart are signatures—to please even the most high-maintenance diners. The staff is gracious, and hospitality flows effortlessly. French menu. Lunch, dinner, Sun brunch. Closed holidays. Casual attire. Reservations recommended. **$$$**

★ ★ **LA METAIRIE.** *189 W 10th St, New York (10014). Phone 212/989-0343; fax 212/989-0810. www.lametairie.com.* So you're looking for a quiet, romantic restaurant without hype or a scene? La Metairie fits the bill perfectly. Aside from a large dose of irresistible charm (the restaurant resembles an old French farmhouse with wood-beamed ceilings,

dried flowers, and stacks of firewood), this hospitable bistro tucked into the West Village serves a delicious menu of French-Mediterranean fare with flavorful and satisfying dishes like roasted rack of lamb, a lovely Provençal-style vegetable tart, and a nice selection of wines to match. French menu. Lunch, dinner, brunch. Casual attire. **$$$**

★ ★ **LA PAELLA.** *214 E 9th St, New York (10003). Phone 212/598-4321.* La Paella is a lively Iberian hotspot that seems tailor made for large, loud groups of friends who are on a budget. While the room could seem claustrophobic to some, with gaggles of couples and hordes of singles sitting at candlelit tables, somehow it seems cozy and quaint. The specialty is—shocker—paella, and it is offered in five different varieties, in addition to a dozen or so hot and cold tapas. Spanish, tapas menu. Lunch, dinner. Casual attire. **$$**

★ ★ **LA PALAPA.** *77 St. Marks Pl, New York (10003). Phone 212/777-2537.* In Mexico, when the blazing afternoon sun beats down on the beach, locals flock to palapas—palm-thatched shelters where icy cervezas wash down spicy fish tacos. The seaside palapa now exists in New York City, thanks to chef/owner Barbara Sibley and her partner Margaritte Malfy, who opened La Palapa, a hacienda-style urban shelter in the East Village featuring tearfully good authentic Mexican home cooking. Expect strong, tart margaritas and plates piled high with chile-rich regional signatures like masa pockets stuffed with chicken in chipotle and grilled muscovy duck breast in a wild raspberry and ancho chile mole. Mexican menu. Lunch, dinner. Bar. Children's menu. Casual attire. Outdoor seating. **$$**

★ **LA PARISIENNE.** *910 Seventh Ave, New York (10019). Phone 212/765-4590.* American menu. Breakfast, lunch, dinner. Casual attire. **$**
🅳

★ ★ ★ **LAFAYETTE GRILL & BAR.** *54 Franklin St, New York (10013). Phone 212/732-5600; fax 212/732-4144. www.lafgrill.com.* Mediterranean menu. Lunch, dinner, late-night. Closed Sun. Bar. Casual attire. Reservations recommended. **$$**

★ ★ ★ ★ **LE BERNARDIN.** *155 W 51st St, New York (10019). Phone 212/554-1515; fax 212/554-1100. www.le-bernardin.com.* If you crave the fruits of the sea, if you dream of lush, shimmering plates of pristine, perfectly prepared seafood, if you are a fan of soft, sinking seats, if your idea of paradise is a long, luxurious meal, you will be very happy at Le Bernardin. The restaurant, born in Paris in 1972, has been impressing foodies and novices alike since it moved across the ocean to Manhattan in 1986. After you experience the food and service, it's easy to see why. Le Bernardin is elegant everything—elegant service, elegant food, elegant crowd. It's all very civilized and sophisticated, and it's not the type of place to go for a quick bite. This is real dining at its finest. The sauces are light, aromatic, and perfectly balanced. The ingredients are seasonal and stunning. The presentations are museum-worthy in their perfection. All these elements combined with flawless service make dinner at Le Bernardin an experience that will stay with you for days, even months. The food is thoughtful and innovative, yet simple and approachable. It is the sort of menu that makes you want to try new things. But those craving beef need not enter. Seafood is the star at this distinguished, elegant New York restaurant, and the menu reflects the kitchen's passion for this food. Mind-altering fish first courses are divided between "Simply Raw" and "Lightly Cooked." Equally stellar entrées are completely from the sea, with a reluctant addition of meat at the end, in a section entitled "Upon Request." This is not the strength of the talented kitchen. Enjoy all courses of that which once swam when you're at Le Bernardin, and you won't regret it. French, Seafood menu. Lunch, dinner. Closed Sun; holidays. Bar. Jacket required. **$$$$**

★ ★ ★ ★ **LE CIRQUE 2000.** *455 Madison Ave, New York (10022). Phone 212/303-7788; fax 212/303-7712. www.lecirque.com.* Located in the stunning New York Palace (see), Le Cirque has set the standard for New York City dining. The restaurant, designed by Adam Tihany, combines old-world charm with modern design. Bright swirls of neon lights and bold, primary-colored banquettes evoke a playful, 21st-century circus theme, while mahogany walls, vintage carpets, and crown moldings maintain the elegance of the original palace-like space. The kitchen does a wonderful job of balancing old and new as well, creating meals (both prix fixe and à la carte) that challenge yet feel safe, and manage to satisfy every taste and appetite. The à la carte menu is divided into several sections: Appetizers, Pasta, Main Courses, Classics, and From the Grill. Desserts are wonderful, showy, artistic creations and should not be turned down. They are worth any added inches on the hips. An extensive wine list and a menu of caviar accent the meal and bring the dining experience into another

realm of luxury. Le Cirque is perpetually crowded and with an eclectic mix of socialites, tourists, fashion-forward New Yorkers, influential visitors, and other elite. It is constantly buzzing, yet the energy is not overwhelming. Quite the opposite. The place makes you feel alive and giddy, like a kid in a toy store. French menu. Lunch, dinner. Bar. Jacket required. Reservations recommended. Outdoor seating. **$$$$**

★ ★ **LE COLONIAL.** *149 E 57th St, New York (10022). Phone 212/752-0808; fax 212/752-7534. www.lecolonialnyc.com.* Serving sophisticated French-Vietnamese fare, Le Colonial is a Midtown favorite for lunch and dinner. The room feels like colonial Saigon come to life, with tall bamboo, spinning ceiling fans, lazy palms, and soft lighting. The menu offers the vibrant chile-tinged signature dishes of the region and includes such treats as glossy spring rolls filled with shrimp, pork, and mushrooms; tender ginger-marinated duck with a tamarind dipping sauce; and grilled loin of pork paired with a lively mango and jicama salad. Vietnamese, French menu. Lunch, dinner. Closed July 4, Thanksgiving, Dec 25. Bar. Casual attire. **$$$**

★ ★ ★ **LE PERIGORD.** *405 E 52nd St, New York (10022). Phone 212/755-6244; fax 212/486-3906. www.leperigord.com.* Le Perigord is one of New York's old-time favorites for sophisticated French dining. The menu of classic dishes, including the restaurant's signature game selection (in season), is geared for diners who define luxury in terms of impeccable, attentive service; elegant furnishings; inspired haute cuisine of the nouvelle French variety; and the quiet of a dining room filled with people enjoying a civilized meal. The food here is delicate and serene, in perfect harmony with the peaceful and majestic dining room. French menu. Lunch, dinner. Bar. Jacket required. **$$$**
🄳

★ ★ ★ **LE REFUGE.** *166 E 82nd St, New York (10021). Phone 212/861-4505; fax 212/736-0384. www.lerefugeinn.com.* Located within walking distance of the Metropolitan Museum of Art and the lush greenery of Central Park, Le Refuge is a classically charming French restaurant that offers a small slice of Paris in New York, without the smoking, of course. Aside from the lack of cigarette smoke, the difference between the two is negligible. The upper crust of society gathers at Le Refuge for its Parisian elegance and its impressive wine list that pairs up perfectly with the selection of simple, bistro-style fare, like farm-raised duck with fresh fruit and filet mignon with peppercorn sauce. French menu. Lunch, dinner, brunch. Closed holidays. Casual attire. Outdoor seating. **$$$**

★ ★ **LE SOUK.** *47 Avenue B, New York (10009). Phone 212/777-5454.* The fragrant and seductive foods of Morocco and Egypt are served with warm hospitality at this East Village hideaway. Amber lighting and hookah pipes lend an opium den quality to the dining room that doubles as a stage for belly dancers. The menu includes Moroccan specialties like chicken cooked in a tagine, moulekaya—a rich and savory Egyptian stew—and toasty pita bread with assorted mezze (think Middle Eastern tapas like stuffed grape leaves, hummus, baba ghanoush, and the like). A tray of deserts arrives in show-and-tell style, and the selection includes everything from chocolate mousse cake to baklava. Moroccan menu. Dinner. Bar. Casual attire. Outdoor seating. **$$**

★ ★ ★ **LENOX ROOM.** *1278 Third Ave, New York (10021). Phone 212/772-0404; fax 212/772-3229. www.lenoxroom.com/lenox.* Restaurateur Tony Fortuna has managed to bring a bit of slick, downtown style to this quiet, residential (some might say culinarily comatose) neighborhood on the Upper East Side. Thanks to Fortuna, the vibrant life inside Lenox Room more than makes up for the lack of a pulse beating at nearby eateries. At Lenox, you will find a sexy bar and lounge with cool cocktails and inventive tiers of cocktail cuisine, and a swanky, intimate dining room offering a smart New American menu. Lenox is a sure thing for a business lunch, a ladies-only cocktail outing, or a spirited dinner with friends. Not only will the food win you over, but Fortuna's gracious hospitality will have you scheduling your next visit before you leave. American menu. Lunch, dinner, Sun brunch. Closed holidays. Bar. **$$$$**

★ ★ **LES HALLES.** *411 Park Ave S, New York (10016). Phone 212/679-4111. www.leshallesny.citysearch.com.* Chef Anthony Bourdain (author of behind-the-scenes memoir *Kitchen Confidential*) brought Les Halles into the culinary limelight a few years back. Despite all the hype, this brasserie remains a genuine star for amazing cuts of steak and terrific takes on pork, chicken, moules, and, of course, lots of frites. The front serves as a French-style butcher shop, while the crowded bistro-style dining room feels like it just fell out of some super-fabulous arrondisement

in Paris. French menu. Lunch, dinner, brunch. Bar. Casual attire. **$$**

★ ★ **LES HALLES DOWNTOWN.** *15 John St, New York (10038). Phone 212/285-8585.* French, kosher, steak menu. Lunch, dinner. Bar. Children's menu. Casual attire. **$$**

★ ★ **LESHKO'S.** *111 Avenue A, New York (10009). Phone 212/777-2111.* This diner in the East Village is home to some of the best pierogies and Eastern European comfort food in town. Blintzes, borsht, goulash, dumplings, and the like fill out the authentic menu. The space, which feels like a fancy, sleek diner, fills up quickly with a trendy crowd that craves the restaurant's simple, warm, home-style fare. Eastern European menu. Dinner. **$**

★ **LOMBARDI'S.** *32 Spring St, New York (10012). Phone 212/941-7994; fax 212/941-4159. www.lombardispizza.com.* Arguably the best pizza in the city is served at Lombardi's, a decades-old institution in Little Italy. Straight from the coal-fired oven, these pies are served piping hot and smoky from the coal's char, with thin, crispy crusts and fresh toppings. The service can be lazy but is always friendly, and the tables are tight, but who cares? This is not Mobil Four-Star dining, but Four-Star eating, and when you crave pizza and a bottle of red, nothing is better. Pizza. Lunch, dinner. Casual attire. Outdoor seating. No credit cards accepted. **$**

★ ★ **LUCKY STRIKE.** *59 Grand St, New York (10013). Phone 212/941-0479.* Lucky Strike was one of the first downtown hotspots from Keith McNally, the king of the distressed Parisian chic brasserie—think Balthazar (see), Pastis, and the latest entry, Schiller's Liquor Bar (see). Filled with smoky mirrors and a dressed-down vintage French vibe, Lucky Strike is still a super-cool spot to slink down into a sexy banquette and feast on perfect bistro standards like steak frites, frisée and goat cheese salad, steamed mussels, and juicy roast chicken. French, American menu. Lunch, dinner, late-night. Bar. Casual attire. **$$**

★ ★ **LUPA.** *170 Thompson St, New York (10012). Phone 212/982-5089; fax 212/982-5490. www.luparestaurant.com.* There are several sure things about Lupa, celebrity chef Mario Batali's wonderfully rustic, Roman osteria: the line for a table will wind its way down Thompson Street. The heavenly spaghettini with spicy cauliflower ragout (chef/partner Mark Ladner's signature dish since he opened the place in

1999) will leave you wondering how you ever hated cauliflower. The antipasti board—a massive butcher block piled high with house-made cured meats and sausages—will leave you unable to eat these heavenly pork products anywhere else. For all these reasons and more (like wine, atmosphere, service, and style), Lupa is, hands-down, one of the most beloved spots for earthy and satisfying Roman fare. It's worth the wait. Italian menu. Lunch, dinner. Bar. Casual attire. Outdoor seating. **$$**

★ ★ **LUSARDI'S.** *1494 Second Ave, New York (10021). Phone 212/249-2020; fax 212/585-2941. www.lusardis.com.* This well-established neighborhood staple is a favorite among Upper East Siders craving reliable Italian fare in a modest, warm setting. The menu sticks to the things Italian restaurants do best—lavish plates of antipasti, fresh composed salads, hearty bowls of pasta, olive oil-grilled fish, and tender slow-cooked meats braised in red wine. This is a lovely restaurant with a gracious staff and a wonderful wine list to complement the cuisine. Italian menu. Lunch, dinner. Closed holidays. Bar. Casual attire. Reservations recommended. **$$$**

★ ★ ★ **MALONEY & PORCELLI.** *37 E 50th St, New York (10022). Phone 212/750-2233; fax 212/750-2252. www.maloneyandporcelli.com.* Named for the restaurant owners' attorneys, Maloney & Porcelli is an easy, smart choice for an urban business lunch or a simple dinner out with a group of friends who favor simple, well-executed cuisine served in a classic, clubby environment without fuss or pretense. The New American menu offers straight-ahead choices like a raw bar, thin-crust pizza, and filet mignon from consulting chef David Burke. The wine list contains some real gems as well, making Maloney & Porcelli a favorite for Midtown dining. American menu. Lunch, dinner, brunch. Closed Jan 1, Dec 25. Bar. **$$$**

★ ★ ★ **MAMLOUK.** *211 E 4th St, New York (10009). Phone 212/529-3477.* At Mamlouk, a cozy Middle Eastern spot in the East Village, you are taken away to an Arabic land filled with sitar music and warm, fragrant spiced meals of Middle Eastern fare. Mamlouk is an experience, from the gentle rhythmic music to the tables named "Beirut" and "Jerusalem," to the hostess who addresses everyone as "darling." While hookah smoking is now banned by New York City law, Mamlouk still manages to spirit you off to a star-filled night by the Nile. Dinner at Mamlouk is always six courses, with dishes like zatter, a flat bread topped with a paste of sesame seeds, olive oil, and thyme; vegetarian moussaka; and mjadarra, a sweet spice-flecked lentil puree served with tender grilled chicken. Middle Eastern menu. Dinner. Closed Mon. Bar. Casual attire. Outdoor seating. **$$**

★ ★ ★ ★ **MARCH.** *405 E 58th, New York (10022). Phone 212/754-6272; fax 212/838-5108. www.marchrestaurant.com.* Many people have issues with indulgence. Chef/owner Wayne Nish is not one of them. He believes that his guests should be indulged from the moment they enter his jewellike, turn-of-the-century-townhouse restaurant to the moment they sadly must part. And a meal at March is just that—pure, blissful indulgence-from start to finish. For this reason (and because it's one of the most romantic spots in New York City), it is truly a special-occasion place, and reservations should be secured well in advance. Nish's menu, of what he calls "New York City Cuisine," is fabulous. Dishes focus on fresh, seasonal products sparked to attention with luxurious ingredients from around the world. Choose from three-, four-, five-, or six-course tasting menus; each is available with or without wine pairings. Go for the wine. Co-owner Joseph Scalice is a gifted wine director, so you're in for a treat. Alfresco dining on the townhouse's rooftop terrace and mezzanine is magical in warm months. American menu. Lunch, dinner. Closed holidays. Jacket required. Reservations recommended. Outdoor seating. **$$$$**

★ ★ **MARKT.** *401 W 14th St, New York (10014). Phone 212/727-3314; fax 212/255-8515.* Located in the Meatpacking District, the new land of the hip and fabulous set, Markt offers a taste of Belgium in a festive brasserie setting. The specialty of the house, as you might expect from a Belgian restaurant, is mussels, served in a variety of ways with crispy vats of golden fries, a nice dish to pair with one of the dozens of international beers on tap. Outdoor seating in the warmer months makes this place sizzle. Belgian menu. Lunch, dinner, Sat-Sun. Bar. Casual attire. Reservations recommended. Outdoor seating. **$$**

★ ★ **MARY'S FISH CAMP.** *64 Charles St (W 4th St), New York (10014). Phone 646/486-2185; fax 646/486-6703. www.marysfishcamp.com.* Mary Redding, chef/owner of this downscale neighborhood seafood shack, is a smart woman. She knows that even people who don't live in New England crave that simple style of food—fat, sweet steamers; meaty lobster rolls; salt-crusted shrimp; and all sorts of daily-catch specials. At her bustling, minimalist, forever-crowded West

Village restaurant, the vibe is fun and casual and the fish is swimming-fresh and delicious. Don't mind the wait—it is so worth it. Seafood menu. Lunch, dinner. Closed Sun. Bar. Casual attire. **$$**

★ ★ ★ ★ ★ **MASA.** *10 Columbus Circle, New York (10019). Phone 212/823-9800.* You need deep, deep, deep pockets to indulge at Masa, or at least a healthy expense account. It's the high rollers table for gourmands, given the starting bid is $300 before you've had a drink, tacked on the 8.625 percent tax, or made your gratuity donation. A meal can easily hit the $1,000 mark for two, without excessive sake consumption. Dinner in Tokyo doesn't cost this much. And in New York, a city renowned for having some of the best sushi on the planet, it takes hubris to come out and say that your fish and the way you treat it is better than all other fish prepared everywhere else. But it is. Chef/owner Masa Takayama offers an omakase, or chef's tasting, that does, indeed, provide a glimpse of the spirituality of living things available to us for consumption. This feast includes more toro in one seating than seems fair, given all the other toro-less dinners one will have to endure in life. The ingredients that Takayama uses are precious, and his ability to present them in a simplified form is artistic. A mere shitake mushroom is raised to shrine-worthy status, attended to as if it were the last pearl of caviar from the Caspian. Every detail presented to you is aesthetically exquisite, from the tasteful sake glasses to the unusual ceramic ware. Pass on a table for this meal and perch yourself at the bar where the chefs will serve you course by course and you can benefit from the calmness of their passionate devotion. Eating at Masa is theatre, and if you accept that the sticker price includes a mesmerizing display of true talent and commitment, the bite may sting a bit less. Sushi menu. Lunch, dinner. Closed Sun. Business casual attire. Reservations recommended. **$$$$**

★ **MAX.** *51 Avenue B, New York (10009). Phone 212/539-0111.* Delicious and cheap are two words commonly used to describe Max, a no-frills joint for terrific red sauce, pasta, lasagna, and all sorts of dishes whose names end in parmagiana. Other words you might be tempted to throw into the mix include crowded, loud, and no reservations, all of which means that you'd better be prepared to wait, and to shout to be heard. But that's part of Max's charm, and the food makes it worthwhile. Pizza. Lunch, dinner. Casual attire. Outdoor seating. No credit cards accepted. **$**

★ ★ ★ **MAYA.** *1191 First Ave, New York (10021). Phone 212/585-1818; fax 212/734-6579. www.modernmexican.com/mayany.* A native of Mexico City, Maya's chef/owner Richard Sandoval knows authentic Mexican cuisine. His popular Upper East Side outpost is perpetually packed with smart, sexy neighborhood locals who understand that Mexico does more than just refried beans and cheesy enchiladas. At Maya, you'll find a soothing hacienda-style room—wood-paneled walls accented with native art, and terra-cotta tiled floors—a comfortable, stylish place to relax for dinner. And speaking of dinner, you'll be treated to a thrilling menu of authentic regional Mexican dishes like Cordero en Mole Verde—lamb shank braised in mole verde with pan-roasted potatoes, chayote squash, and baby carrots, and the house Mariscada—a mammoth bowl bobbing with sea scallops, shrimp, mussels, and clams, served with black rice and a coriander seed-red pepper emulsion. The food goes down almost as easily as the terrific selection of one hundred tequilas and mezcals. Take two aspirin before bed. Mexican menu. Dinner. Closed Jan 1, Dec 25. Bar. Casual attire. Reservations recommended. **$$$**

★ ★ **MERCER KITCHEN.** *99 Prince St, New York (10012). Phone 212/966-5454; fax 212/965-3855.* Located in the ultra-chic Mercer Hotel in SoHo, this exposed-brick, subterranean hotspot is constantly teeming with celebrities and those who believe that they are celebrities merely because they are dining in their glow. The Asian-influenced American menu, under the talented direction of chef/owner Jean-Georges Vongerichten, is as swanky as the crowd, with signatures like raw tuna and wasabi pizza and yellow-tail carpaccio with lime, coriander, and mint. If you haven't the slightest appetite, head over to the sexy bar, where hipsters sip martinis with abandon. American menu. Lunch, dinner, brunch. Closed holidays. Bar. Casual attire. **$$**

★ ★ **MERMAID INN.** *96 Second Ave, New York (10003). Phone 212/674-5870.* Jimmy Bradley (of The Red Cat and The Harrison—see both) has opened another easy-to-love restaurant with The Mermaid Inn, located in the East Village. The restaurant will take you away to the bluffs of a windswept seashore with its dark wainscoting, hurricane lamps, vintage nautical maps, and big, icy raw bar. The menu here is all seafood, all the time. The signature lobster sandwich—a sort of lobster roll gone burger—is a mess of sweet, fat, juicy lobster meat, held together by just the right bit of mayo, that is served on a wide, puffy, golden brioche bun with a mountain of skinny, crispy fries dusted with Old Bay seasoning. Bradley also offers more global takes on seafood, like a flaky, moist skate, sautéed until golden and set in a nutty puddle of white gazpacho sauce made from almonds. Mermaid has a great neighborhood vibe that makes it perfect for a first date, a last date, or dinner with the girls, the guys, your parents, or heck, even your enemies. Seafood menu. Dinner, late-night. Bar. Casual attire. Outdoor seating. **$$**

★ ★ **MESA GRILL.** *102 Fifth Ave, New York (10011). Phone 212/807-7400; fax 212/989-0034. www.mesagrill.com.* In the more than ten years since the Southwestern haven known as Mesa Grill opened its tall blond-wood doors and chef/owner Bobby Flay reached stardom on cable TV's Food Network, he has, impressively, managed to keep his creative eye on this, his first restaurant. The vaulted, lively room remains a popular spot for margarita-soaked happy hours, as well as a top choice for superb Southwestern-inspired American fare. The vibrant menu changes with the seasons, but famous plates include the cotija-crusted quesadilla stuffed with goat cheese, basil, and red chiles, topped with a charred corn salsa; and the 16-spiced chicken with mango garlic sauce and cilantro-pesto mashed potatoes. Flay's food is not shy, so keep a cold margarita handy to soothe the heat. Southwestern menu. Lunch, dinner. Closed Dec 25. Bar. Casual attire. **$$$**

★ ★ **MI COCINA.** *57 Jane St, New York (10014). Phone 212/627-8273; fax 212/627-0174. www.micocinanyc.com.* Authentic regional Mexican cuisine is featured at Mi Cocina, a cozy, colorful, and lively West Village favorite for outstanding dishes of our neighbor to the south. The menu offers easy-to-love dishes like crisp, savory quesadillas and soft tacos fashioned from fresh corn tortillas filled with ancho-rubbed pulled pork, as well as vibrant regional specialties like the rich, chocolate moles of Oaxaca and the lime- and chile-marinated fish from the seaside region of Veracruz. Margaritas are wonderfully tart with lots of fresh lime juice and, of course, quite a bit of tequila. This restaurant is all about fun. Mexican menu. Lunch, dinner, brunch. Closed Dec 24-25; also two weeks in Aug. Bar. Children's menu. Casual attire. Outdoor seating. **$$**

★ **MICKEY MANTLE'S.** *42 Central Park S, New York (10019). Phone 212/688-7777; fax 212/751-5797. www.theswearingens.com/mick/mmrest.htm.* Located on Central Park South, Mickey Mantle's is an easy and smart choice when you want to catch a game and have a good meal minus the roar of a crowded sports bar. This elegant dining room is a good option if you're wandering around Central Park and get hungry for straightforward, tasty American fare. Burgers, steaks, seafood, and pastas are on the menu, and in season, the Yankees are always on TV here. As you'd expect, you'll also find a nice collection of baseball memorabilia and sports-themed art on the walls. American menu. Lunch, dinner. Bar. Children's menu. Outdoor seating. **$$**

★ ★ ★ **MIX NEW YORK.** *68 W 58th St, New York (10019). Phone 212/583-0300. www.mixny.com.* After startling New Yorkers with sky-high prices at his flagship restaurant, Alain Ducasse (see), Mix New York is Ducasse's latest attempt at wooing the city's finicky dining public, and by all indications, it's working. A sleek, high-styled, modern space in Midtown, Mix offers French and American comfort food created from stunning ingredients and presented with whimsical style. Macaroni and cheese takes on a glamorous cast, plated on fine china and topped with artisanal cheese, while more elegant takes on duck confit, tuna niçoise, and roast chicken grand mere make your head swirl with delight. All meals start with homemade peanut butter and jelly for your table's bread, and end with Madelines straight from the oven served with Nutella—the perfect way to end a meal. American, French menu. Lunch, dinner. Bar. Business casual attire. Reservations recommended. **$$$**

★ ★ ★ **MOLYVOS.** *871 Seventh Ave, New York (10019). Phone 212/582-7500; fax 212/582-7502. www.molyvos.com.* Located just steps from Carnegie Hall and City Center, Molyvos is a great choice for before or after a dance or concert, with a wonderful menu of modern Greek specialties like assorted mezze served with warm, puffy pita; grilled whole fish; stunning takes on lamb; and an impressive international wine list. The restaurant feels like it fell from the shores of the Mediterranean, with blue and white tiles and sturdy wooden tables. The lively bar and front room is ideal if you're in the mood for a light bite and a glass of wine before a show, while the more refined dining room offers leisurely diners a place to unwind without rushing. Greek menu. Lunch, dinner. Bar. Casual attire. Reservations recommended. **$$$**

★ ★ ★ **MONTRACHET.** *239 W Broadway, New York (10013). Phone 212/219-2777; fax 212/274-9508. myriadrestaurantgroup.com/montrachet.* Montrachet is

the first restaurant from restaurateur Drew Nieporent. (He also owns Nobu and Tribeca Grill, among others.) While the restaurant is pushing 20, it is still one of the most prized and romantic dining experiences to be had in New York City. The seasonal, modern French-American menu and the warm, attentive service remain as fresh and inspired as they were on day one. Montrachet's wine list has been met with critical acclaim and marries well with the sophisticated fare, making for delightful dining. French, American menu. Lunch (Fri), dinner. Closed Sun; holidays. Bar. Casual attire. Reservations recommended. **$$$**
🅓

★ ★ ★ **MORTON'S, THE STEAKHOUSE.** *551 Fifth Ave, New York (10017). Phone 585/972-3315; fax 585/972-0018. www.mortons.com.* This steakhouse chain, which originated in Chicago in 1978, appeals to serious meat lovers. With a selection of belt-busting carnivorous delights (like the house specialty, a 24-ounce porterhouse), as well as fresh fish, lobster, and chicken entrées, Morton's rarely disappoints. If you just aren't sure what you're in the mood for, the tableside menu presentation may help you decide. Here, main course selections are placed on a cart that's rolled to your table, where servers describe each item in detail. Steak menu. Lunch, dinner. Closed holidays. Bar. Jacket required. Reservations recommended. **$$$**

★ ★ ★ **MR. K'S.** *570 Lexington Ave, New York (10022). Phone 212/583-1668; fax 212/583-1620.* In general, most movers and shakers in the world of finance, media, and power know of Mr. K's—it is their daily cafeteria for grease-less, elegant Chinese food. Forget what you may have ever thought about Chinese food, because Mr. K's breaks all the rules, bringing New Yorkers wonderful, upscale, exotic dishes from the various regions of China and serving them in an ultra-elegant, posh setting filled with fresh flowers, plush cushioned banquettes, and most notably, waiters who know the meaning of service. The restaurant, which is a clone of the DC original, is a wonderful choice for a big party to celebrate a special occasion, even if it's just being able to share a dazzling meal at Mr. K's together. Chinese menu. Lunch, dinner. Casual attire. Reservations recommended. **$$$**

★ ★ **NAM.** *110 Reade St, New York (10013). Phone 212/267-1777; fax 212/267-3781. www.namnyc.com.* The fresh, spicy flavors of Vietnam are on the menu at Nam, a chic, breezy, bamboo-accented restaurant in TriBeCa. Giving a city-slicker kick to this Asian cuisine, Nam offers Vietnamese classics like noodle dishes, soups, spring rolls, green papaya salads, and simply magnificent seafood dishes. The crispy whole red snapper is slathered in chile and lime and served with steamed jasmine rice, while the steamed sea bass is a fleshy, sweet dish, accompanied by stewed tomatoes. Vietnamese menu. Lunch, dinner. Bar. Casual attire. **$$**

★ **NHA TRANG CENTRE.** *148 Centre St, New York (10013). Phone 212/941-9292; fax 212/941-6034.* New Yorkers who are forced to serve jury duty look forward to it for one reason and one reason only—not their chance to serve their community, but because the courthouses are near Nha Trang, a frenetic, fast-paced, cafeteria-style spot serving some of the best authentic Vietnamese fare going. The place is generally chaotic, especially at lunch (be prepared to share your table with people you don't know), but the experience is a great one nonetheless, considering that you can feast on excellent bowls of pho (noodle soup), spicy spring rolls banh xeo, crispy yellow rice-flower pancakes wrapped around sautéed mushrooms, shrimp, and sprouts. Vietnamese menu. Lunch, dinner. Casual attire. **$**

★ **NICE.** *35 E Broadway, New York (10002). Phone 212/406-9510.* In classic Chinatown form, Nice, a Cantonese restaurant with a following, serves loads of delicious steaming dim sum out of traditional trolley carts. The crowds come out in numbers on the weekends, making this massive place feel a tad scary, so try to sneak in during the week or be prepared to feel claustrophobic. Chinese menu. Lunch, dinner. Casual attire. **$**

★ ★ ★ **NOBU.** *105 Hudson St, New York (10013). Phone 212/219-0500; fax 212/219-1441.* There is a place in New York where folks have been known to cry when they eat because the food is so good. That place is Nobu. The lively room is decorated with seaweed-like wall coverings and bamboo poles and has a serene vibe despite the high-energy, high-fashion crowd that packs in nightly for some of famed chef Nobu Matsuhisa's simply spectacular sushi and unique brand of Asian-Latin-inspired seafood. Lime, soy, chiles, miso, cilantro, and ginger are flavors frequently employed to accent many of the chef's succulent creations. A signature dish is black cod with miso, and it's a signature for good reason. The fish is coated in a sweet miso glaze, and once it enters your mouth, it slowly vaporizes, melting away like ice over a flame. The omakase ("chef's choice") menu is an option for those with an adventurous palate. If you can't get a reservation (call well in advance and be prepared for many busy signals), you can always try to sneak in at the sushi bar. Be warned, though; once you eat sushi here, it's hard to eat it anywhere else. Japanese menu. Lunch, dinner. Closed holidays. Casual attire. Reservations recommended. **$$$$**

★ **NYONYA.** *194 Grand St, New York (10013). Phone 212/334-3669.* Serving some of the best Malaysian fare in town, Nyonya is a slightly chaotic spot with a vibrant and authentic menu. While the atmosphere is not exactly elegant (it feels like a diner), this restaurant is an ideal place for a group of friends to sit down to dinner and taste the variety of refreshing Malaysian dishes on the menu. But be sure to come on an empty stomach, as the food is too good not to lick plates clean. Malaysian menu. Lunch, dinner. Casual attire. Reservations recommended. No credit cards accepted. **$**
🄳

★ ★ ★ **OCEANA.** *55 E 54th St, New York (10022). Phone 212/759-5941; fax 212/759-6076. www.oceana restaurant.com.* Oceana has been one of New York's most lauded seafood spots for more than a decade. Although ten years could have derailed the restaurant, it has stayed a steady course and its mission is as clear as ever: stunning, just-shy-of-swimming seafood tinged with subtle, precise flavors from around the globe. You'll find practically every glorious fish in the sea on the menu, from halibut to tuna, dorade to turbot. Scallops, lobster, and glistening oysters are also on the menu. But there's a nod to the issue of overfishing here as well. Oceana is known for serving only sustainable seafood that is not in danger of becoming extinct. The service is warm and efficient, and the cream-colored, nautical-themed room (portholes dot the walls) is peaceful and comfortable, making Oceana a perennial favorite for power lunchers and pre-theater diners. The wine list is impressive, with a good number of seafood-friendly options at a variety of price points. A signature selection of American caviar from sturgeon, paddlefish, and rainbow trout makes a strong argument for forgoing osetra, beluga, and sevruga. American, Seafood menu. Lunch, dinner. Closed Sun; holidays. Jacket required. Reservations recommended. **$$$$**
🄳

★ ★ **THE ODEON.** *145 W Broadway, New York (10013). Phone 212/233-0507; fax 212/406-1962. www .theodeonrestaurant.com.* Odeon is the original hipster diner. This sleek, retro space, located in TriBeCa, has been serving delicious brasserie fare like perfect frisée

au lardons, thick and juicy burgers, and steak frites to the masses of fabulous locals for almost two decades. Brunch is a must, but if you are in the area late at night, it is also a hotspot to grab a bite to tide you over until morning. Celebrities of the Robert De Niro caliber are bound to be tucked into booths, so keep an eye out. American, French menu. Lunch, dinner, late-night, Sat-Sun brunch. Bar. Children's menu. Casual attire. Outdoor seating. **$$**

★ ★ ★ **OLIVES.** *201 Park Ave S, New York (10003). Phone 212/353-8345; fax 212/353-9592. www.todd english.com.* Celebrity chef-restaurateur Todd English's New York debut is a branch of his mega-successful Boston-based bistro. Located in the swanky W Union Square Hotel, the inviting and bustling restaurant has an open kitchen, with buttery walls, an open hearth fireplace, and deep, oval banquettes for luxurious relaxation all night long. The menu stars English's standard (but delicious) Mediterranean formula: boldly flavored, luxurious dishes that are impeccably prepared and artfully presented on the plate. His signature tart filled with olives, goat cheese, and sweet caramelized onions is a winner, but the menu offers a dish for every taste, including lamb, fish, homemade pastas, and pizzas from the wood oven. Mediterranean menu. Breakfast, lunch, dinner, brunch. Bar. Casual attire. Outdoor seating. **$$$**

★ ★ ★ **ONE IF BY LAND, TWO IF BY SEA.** *17 Barrow St, New York (10014). Phone 212/228-0822. www.oneifbyland.com.* This classic French restaurant, set in a restored, turn-of-the-century carriage house in Greenwich Village that was once owned by Aaron Burr, is one of New York's most cherished spots for romance and other love-related special occasion dining: anniversaries, engagements, and the like. Dark and elegant, the hushed, candlelit, two-story dining room is richly appointed with antique sconces, heavy velvet drapes, oriental carpets, and blazing fireplaces. The menu here is straight-ahead French, with seasonal accompaniments and modern flourishes that add sparkle to the plate. French menu. Dinner. Closed holidays. Bar. Casual attire. Reservations recommended. **$$$$**

★ ★ **OSTERIA AL DOGE.** *142 W 44th St, New York (10036). Phone 212/944-3643; fax 212/944-5754. www.osteria-doge.com.* Osteria al Doge is a warm restaurant that feels like a seaside town near Venice. The room is decorated warmly with blue, green, and yellow and has a balcony overlooking the main dining area. The kitchen is not breaking culinary ground, but it doesn't really need to. This restaurant is a solid standby for Venetian-inspired seafood dishes like whole branzino with cherry tomatoes, olives, and potatoes; a bouillabaisse-style seafood stew; and house-made trenette pasta with crabmeat. Those craving more substantial meals can dig into veal, poultry, and beef. A good choice for pre-theater dining. Italian menu. Lunch, dinner. Closed Jan 1, Dec 25. Bar. **$$**

★ ★ **OSTERIA DEL CIRCO.** *120 W 55th St, New York (10019). Phone 212/265-3636; fax 212/265-9283. www.osteriadelcirco.com.* Owned by Sirio Maccioni of Le Cirque 2000 (see), Osterio del Circo carries on his signature brand of homespun hospitality in a more casual, yet no less spirited, atmosphere. The rustic menu of Italian fare includes delicious homemade pastas made from Maccioni Mama Egi's lick-your-plate-clean recipes, as well as thin Tuscan-style pizzas, classic antipasti, and signature main courses like salt-baked Mediterranean seabass and brick-pressed chicken. Because it's located near Carnegie Hall and City Center, it's a great place to stop by before or after the theater. Italian menu. Lunch, dinner. Closed holidays. Bar. Casual attire. **$$$**

★ ★ **OTTO.** *1 Fifth Ave, New York (10003). Phone 212/995-9559.* With Otto, celebrity chef Mario Batali has veered into casual territory, offering New Yorkers a taste of an authentic Italian pizzeria in the style of an old-fashioned European train station. Decorated with tall marble bars and dark wainscoting, this high-energy eatery is always filled with a stylish crowd that comes in for wonderful antipasti (the mussels with chile flakes is delish), can't-stop-at-one-slice prosciutto di Parma, and an amazing array of magnificent thin-crust pizzas. Gelatos are extra-special, especially the one made from olive oil that tastes like a very creamy version of heaven. Pizza. Lunch, dinner. Bar. Casual attire. **$$**

★ ★ **OUR PLACE.** *1444 Third Ave, New York (10028). Phone 212/288-4888; fax 212/744-3620.* Our Place could be mistaken for just another neighborhood Chinese joint, but once you try their sophisticated cuisine, you'll agree it's a notch or two above. The dining room and staff are so pleasant and professional it's worth dining in, but if you must stay at home it's by far the highest-quality Chinese delivery on the Upper East Side. On weekends, don't miss their dim sum brunch for a fun change from the usual brunch destinations. Chinese menu. Lunch, dinner, brunch. Closed Thanksgiving. Bar. **$$$**

★ ★ **OYSTER BAR.** *Grand Central Terminal, Lower Level, New York (10017). Phone 212/490-6650; fax 212/949-5210. www.oysterbarny.com.* Chaos has never been more fun than at the Oyster Bar. Packed to the gills at lunch and dinner daily, this Grand Central Station icon is one of the best places to gorge on all sorts of seafood. The room makes you feel as though you have gone back in time, with vaulted subway-tiled ceilings and waiters who have been working here since Nixon was in the White House. As for the grub, there are more than two dozen varieties of oysters to choose from, as well as all sorts of chowders, fish sandwiches, fish entrées, and, well, you get the idea. If it swims or even sits in water, it's on the menu. If you're on the run, don't worry: grab a seat at the bar or at one of the old-fashioned lunch counters for a quick lunch. Seafood menu. Lunch, dinner. Closed Sun; holidays. Bar. Casual attire. **$$**

★ ★ ★ **PARK AVENUE CAFE.** *100 E 63rd St, New York (10021). Phone 212/644-1900; fax 212/688-0373. www.parkavenuecafe.com.* Sophisticated and savvy New Yorkers head to Park Avenue Cafe for luxurious lunch meetings, intimate dinners, and large party outings. The warm, blond-wooded room is bright and airy and feels easy and comfortable. The menu of inspired seasonal dishes uses clean, simple flavors that please the palate. Desserts whipped up by famed pastry chef Richard Leach make you feel like a kid again; finger-licking may be necessary. American menu. Lunch, dinner, brunch. Closed Jan 1, Dec 25. Bar. Casual attire. **$$$$**

★ **PAT PONG.** *97 E 7th St, New York (10009). Phone 212/505-6454.* Located in the East Village, Pat Pong serves a need in the local community for reasonably priced and very tasty Thai cuisine. The restaurant is spare and bright, with a variety of authentic dishes on the menu, including beef, pork, shrimp, and many vegetarian options. Thai menu. Lunch, dinner. Casual attire. **$**

★ ★ ★ **PATROON.** *160 E 46th St, New York (10017). Phone 212/883-7373; fax 212/883-1118. www.patroonrestaurant.com.* Owner Ken Aretsky's popular, clubby, low-lit Patroon is more than a boys' club for juicy steaks. You'll also find women feasting at Patroon, as his American restaurant has that edge that other steakhouses don't—a terrific kitchen with talent for more than just beef (although the beef is fabulous). Of the USDA Prime selections, Steak Diana (named for Aretsky's wife) is a house specialty and is prepared tableside with brown butter, shallots, and wine for an arresting visual presentation. The kitchen also gussies things up with hearty dishes like pork shanks, short ribs, and lighter fare like oysters, shrimp, lump crab, and a slew of stunning seafood. A wide rooftop deck makes summertime fun with great grilled fare and chilly cocktails. American, Steak menu. Lunch, dinner. Closed Sat-Sun; holidays. Bar. Casual attire. Outdoor seating. **$$$**

★ **PATSY'S PIZZERIA.** *2287-91 First Ave, New York (10035). Phone 212/534-9783.* Folks in New York take their pizza seriously, and with a pizza joint on what seems like every corner, the competition is fierce. But Patsy's remains a favorite among pie connoisseurs, consistently serving wonderful pizza with thin, crisp but chewy crusts, with an array of toppings for every appetite. Patsy's original location in Harlem is an easy, casual place, with gingham tablecloths, wood floors, and a welcoming, seasoned waitstaff. Pizza. Lunch, dinner. Casual attire. No credit cards accepted. **$**

★ ★ ★ **PAYARD PATISSERIE AND BISTRO.** *1032 Lexington Ave, New York (10021). Phone 212/717-5252; fax 212/717-0986. www.payard.com.* Willpower must be left outside of Payard. Aside from the great selection of sandwiches, salads, and Parisian bistro staples served in this lovely, butter-yellow French pastry shop, the desserts are as tempting as they come. But this should come as no surprise considering that the baker in question is François Payard, a master of sweets and treats. While lunch and dinner are good choices, Payard's afternoon tea is a wonderful way to get acquainted with his talents. French menu. Lunch, dinner. Closed Sun; holidays. **$$$**

★ **PEARL OYSTER BAR.** *18 Cornelia St, New York (10014). Phone 212/691-8211. www.pearloysterbar.com.* Rebecca Charles, who cooked for many years in New England, offers up the steamy, rustic ocean cuisine of the Atlantic Coast to New Yorkers at her newly expanded restaurant, Pearl Oyster Bar. Named for Charles's grandmother, Pearl is known for its luscious lobster rolls, fat steamers, and fresh fried fish sandwiches. While this warm, upscale New England diner-style place is always packed, it is worth the madness. If tables are taken, the warm and friendly bar is a super place to grab a fresh fish bite with a cold ale. Seafood menu. Lunch, dinner. Closed Sun. Casual attire. **$$**

★ **PEARSON'S TEXAS BARBECUE.** *170 E 81st St, New York (10028). Phone 212/288-2700. www.pearsonsbbq.com.* Now more conveniently located on the Upper East Side, Pearson's claims to serve the most authentic barbecue this side of the Mississippi. Once you step inside, it sure feels like a roadside BBQ stand, with gingham-checked tablecloths, memorabilia galore, and smoky smells wafting through the dining room. The menu of ribs, pulled pork, beans, slaw, onion rings, and sausages offers something for everyone, and the casual staff makes this an easy choice for families and groups. Expect to have to wait for a table, as Pearson's does not take reservations and has developed a loyal following over the years. Barbecue menu. Lunch, dinner. Children's menu. Casual attire. Outdoor seating. **$$**

★ **PENANG MALAYSIAN.** *109 Spring St, New York (10012). Phone 212/274-8883; fax 212/925-8530. www.penangnyc.com.* Crowds flock to Penang like ants to a picnic, so if you are not up for the masses, go elsewhere. Then again, the hordes of people dining here have to be coming for something, and it's not the atmosphere, which is dim and a bit cramped. It is the food, which is authentic Malaysian and spectacular. Expect bright, invigorating flavors in dishes like Kari Ayam (chicken and potatoes seasoned with red curry in a coconut milk) and Masak Nenas (chicken or beef sautéed with fresh pineapple chunks, lemongrass, mint, and red onion in a fiery curry served in a pineapple shell). Malaysian menu. Lunch, dinner. Bar. Casual attire. **$$**

★ ★ ★ **PERIYALI.** *35 W 20th St, New York (10011). Phone 212/463-7890; fax 212/924-9403. www.periyali.com.* Offering authentic Greek fare in a soothing Mediterranean-accented setting, Periyali is a wonderful place to experience the delicious seaside cuisine of Athens and beyond. Classics on the menu include octopus marinated in red wine, sautéed sweetbreads with white beans, grilled whole fish, and mezze like taramosalata (caviar mousse), melitzanosalata (grilled-eggplant mousse), and spanakopita (spinach and cheese pie). Periyali has been around for a while, but the restaurant's popularity has not waned. You'll find it full of regulars most days at lunch, although at night the pace is calmer, making it a great choice for a leisurely dinner. Greek menu. Lunch, dinner. Closed Sun. Casual attire. Reservations recommended. **$$$**

★ ★ ★ ★ ★ **PER SE.** *1 Time Warner Center, New York (10019). Phone 212/823-9335. www.frenchlaundry.com/perse.* Thomas Keller, the chef at Yountville, California's The French Laundry, calls his new restaurant in the Time Warner Center Per Se because "it's not exactly The French Laundry, per se." What's missing is the bucolic setting of the Napa Valley, but in its place are the finest views of any restaurant in Manhattan, a new level of urban sophistication in service and ambience, and food so pure in flavor that every meal is memorable. The best way to enjoy Per Se is to order a tasting menu and then sit back for three hours of culinary epiphanies exemplified by small dishes such as truffles and custard in an eggshell and foie gras accompanied by various salts. The kitchen excels in its use of high-end ingredients, but attention to detail is also evident in the regard given to vegetables and legumes. The quality of dining at Per Se is so superior to what is typical, even in a luxury restaurant, that Keller and his team have established the gold standard. American menu. Lunch, dinner. Bar. Business casual attire. Reservations recommended. **$$$$**

★ ★ **PETROSSIAN.** *182 W 58th St, New York (10019). Phone 212/245-2214; fax 212/245-2812. www.petrossian.com.* Caviar, caviar, and caviar are the first three reasons to head to Petrossian, an elegant restaurant in Midtown featuring, you guessed it, caviar, served on perfect blinis and crème fraiche. In addition to the great salty roe, you'll find an ultra-luxurious brand of Franco-Russian cuisine that includes classics like borscht, assorted Russian *zazuska* (tapas) like smoked salmon (served with cold shots of vodka—ask for Zyr, one of the best from Russia), and other glamorous plates, including foie gras prepared several different ways and, of course, beef Stroganoff. But don't miss the caviar. Russian menu. Lunch, dinner, late-night, brunch. Bar. Casual attire. Reservations recommended. **$$$$**
🅳

★ ★ ★ **PICHOLINE.** *35 W 64th St, New York (10023). Phone 212/724-8585; fax 212/875-8979.* Located on Manhattan's Upper West Side, Picholine is a great choice for dinner if you happen to be attending an opera, ballet, or play at Lincoln Center. Don't feel like you need to be heading over to Lincoln Center in order to dine here, though; chef/owner Terrance Brennan's lovely, serene restaurant is easy to enjoy all by itself, which is probably why Picholine is often pleasantly packed with a savvy set of New Yorkers at both lunch and dinner, with no ticket stubs to be found. The menu changes with the seasons, and the chef uses organic and local ingredients as much as possible. Picholine is a safe bet for both adventurous diners and conservative eaters and for vegetarians and meat lovers

alike. The menu runs the gamut from the exotic to the familiar, offering a wide selection of dishes from the land and the sea. Folks with a weakness for cheese are in the right place, as well. The cheese list (not to mention the great wine list) is one of the best in the city, and room must be saved to indulge in several types. The wine list, though seriously priced, offers a variety of selections to match all courses. Mediterranean menu. Lunch, dinner. Closed holidays. Bar. Jacket required. Reservations recommended. **$$$$**
🅳

★ **PIE BY THE POUND.** *124 Fourth Ave, New York (10003). Phone 212/475-4977.* At Pie, a slick little pizza joint in the East Village, pizza by the slice is taboo. Ditto for pizza by the round pie. The pizzas at Pie are long and rectangular, with scissors used to slice off just the amount you want. You can have your very own pizza party by selecting a variety of pizzas topped with fresh and tasty ingredients like crispy potato, tallegio, and walnuts or pillowy mozzarella, tomato, and basil. Once you make your selections, your slices are weighed, and you pay by the pound, not by the slice. Pizza. Lunch, dinner. Children's menu. Casual attire. Outdoor seating. No credit cards accepted. **$**

★ ★ **PIG HEAVEN.** *1540 Second Ave, New York (10028). Phone 212/744-4887; fax 212/744-2853. www.pigheaven.biz.* The name may be intimidating but they're not guilty of false advertising one bit. The spare ribs, roast pork, and suckling pig are some of the best found outside Chinatown. The roast duck is fantastic as well and after a delightful renovation a few years ago, Pig Heaven is just as much for dining out as for dining in. Nancy Lee, the well-known hostess, will make sure you enjoy the best food Pig Heaven has to offer. Chinese menu. Lunch, dinner, late-night. Bar. Reservations recommended. **$$**

★ ★ **PING'S.** *22 Mott St, New York (10013). Phone 212/602-9988; fax 212/602-9992.* Be sure to pack your sense of culinary adventure when you go to Ping's, a Chinatown favorite for dim sum and gorgeous live seafood cooked up to order. The room is usually filled to capacity with Chinese families and lawyers on break from arguing at the nearby courthouses, but do not be deterred by the crowds. The steamed pork buns alone make Ping's worth the wait. Chinese menu. Lunch, dinner. Casual attire. **$$**
🅳

★ ★ **PIPA.** *38 E 19th St, New York (10003). Phone 212/677-2233.* Pipa, a lively and sultry restaurant and tapas bar in the Flatiron District, serves up some of the most delicious modern Spanish food in the city in a sexy, candlelit, antique-filled setting worthy of a designer's dream. The eclectic flea market décor should come as no surprise, as the restaurant occupies the ground floor of ABC Carpet & Home, one of the city's swankiest furniture and accessories stores, making it the perfect shopping pit stop. Spanish menu. Lunch, dinner. Bar. Casual attire. Reservations recommended. Outdoor seating. **$$$**

★ ★ ★ **POST HOUSE.** *28 E 63rd St, New York (10021). Phone 212/935-2888; fax 212/371-9265. www.theposthouse.com.* New York has many steak-houses, and The Post House is one of the power lunch club's favorites. The comfortable dining room, with a long bar, has an easy feel thanks to polished parquet floors, wooden wainscoting, and leather armchair seating. The menu sports a super selection of salads, signature appetizers like cornmeal-fried oysters, and a shimmering raw bar in addition to entrées like grilled chicken, rack of lamb, and meat-eater delights like prime rib, filet mignon, and the signature "Stolen Cajun Rib Steak." An extensive wine list emphasizes California wines and some rare gems from Burgundy and Bordeaux. Steak menu. Lunch, dinner. Closed Jan 1, Thanksgiving, Dec 25. Bar. Casual attire. **$$$**
🅳

★ ★ **PRAVDA.** *281 Lafayette St, New York (10012). Phone 212/226-4944; fax 212/226-5052. www.pravda ny.com.* Vodka is the main theme at Pravda, a sexy, subterranean bar and lounge in SoHo. As for the menu, it pretty much matches what might be served at a Russian vodka bar: caviar, blinis, assorted smoked fish, and black bread—perfect nibbles for late-night revelers of the waif, supermodel, or straight-ahead European expatriate variety. Pravda is dark and luxuriously decadent, and it's all about the vodka. Russian menu. Dinner, late-night. Closed Sun July-Aug. Bar. Casual attire. **$$**
🅳

★ ★ **PROVENCE.** *38 MacDougal St, New York (10012). Phone 212/475-7500; fax 212/674-7876. www.provence.citysearch.com.* Located on a sleepy block in SoHo, Provence offers a taste of this sunny French region right here in the concrete jungle. It is a wonderfully charming restaurant, decorated with antiques and fresh flowers and warmed by delicate, soft lighting. In summer, don't miss out on the charming garden. Even in winter, this place is a simple delight, offering homey French dishes like steak au poivre, bouillabaisse, and bourrides. The menu is authentic

Provençal, and all meals start with warm, crusty bread and are complemented by a terrific wine list. French menu. Lunch, dinner, Sat brunch. Closed holidays. Casual attire. Reservations recommended. **$$**
🅳

★ ★ **PRUNE.** *54 E 1st St, New York (10003). Phone 212/677-6221.* Prune is one of those neighborhood restaurants that immediately seduces you. The distressed décor—very Left Bank chic—is irresistible. The American bistro menu, devised by chef/owner Gabrielle Hamilton, is a list of guilty pleasures, from her signature Triscuit and canned sardine appetizer to more labor-intensive dishes like slow-cooked lamb shanks to her leftover dish of bread heels and pulled chicken. This is one of the most popular restaurants in New York for a reason. Although the tables are too close together and the waits are too long, the food is delicious, and the vibe is casual but fierce. Brunch on Sundays is a must, even if you go just for the Bloody Marys. International/Fusion menu. Lunch, dinner, brunch. Bar. Casual attire. Reservations recommended. **$$**

★ ★ **RADIO PERFECTO.** *190 Avenue B, New York (10009). Phone 212/477-3366; fax 212/477-4336. www.radioperfecto.com.* This hip, retro eatery in the East Village is known for its terrific juicy rotisserie chicken, but it also keeps hordes of locals happy with its spicy blend of Mexican fusion cuisine like steak with tequila mushroom sauce and kickin' chile-rubbed pulled pork. This is a lively joint to hang with friends. Lines can get long, so be prepared to wait—with a killer margarita in hand. American, Mexican menu. Dinner, Sun brunch. Bar. Casual attire. Outdoor seating. **$$**

★ ★ **RAGA.** *433 E 6th St, New York (10009). Phone 212/388-0957.* Located on Curry Row in the East Village, Raga sets itself apart with its dark, sexy décor and truly innovative Indian menu. While you'll find straight-ahead classics, the kitchen serves a few more contemporary plates as well. Vegetable curries share menu space with ambitious dishes like roasted lamb sirloin with cranberry beans, mussels steeped in lemongrass, and wildly flavorful house samosas. The kitchen is not afraid of being fresh and innovative, making eating here an exciting and delicious experience. Indian menu. Dinner. Closed Mon. Casual attire. **$$$**
🅳

★ ★ **RAOUL'S.** *180 Prince St, New York (10012). Phone 212/966-3518; fax 212/966-0205. www.raouls restaurant.com.* Raoul's is one of the most French and

most romantic restaurants in the city. Opened in the mid-1970s, this intimate little bistro has managed to retain its popularity, meaning that it is constantly packed, so reservations are a must. (Specify which room you'd like to be seated in—the downstairs main dining room is dark and sultry, while the upstairs has a bit more light and feels more civilized.) Seafood dishes are especially good here, although peppercorn steak frites will not disappoint carnivores. House pâté and frisée with cambozola cheese are also lovely menu items. French menu. Dinner, late-night. Bar. Casual attire. Reservations recommended. Outdoor seating. **$$$**
🅑

★ ★ **THE RED CAT.** *227 Tenth Ave, New York (10011). Phone 212/242-1122. www.theredcat.com.* Jimmy Bradley, chef/owner of The Red Cat, is one of those restaurateurs who knows exactly what New Yorkers are looking for in a dining experience: a cool, hip scene? Check. An innovative and exciting menu? Check. A solid international wine list with lots by the glass and a tempting selection of sexy house cocktails? Check, check. Indeed, Bradley delivers it all at his West Chelsea haunt for inspired Mediterranean-accented fare set in a New England-chic space trimmed with white-and-red wainscoting, hurricane lamps, and deep, long banquettes. This is one place you will want to return to, even if it's just to figure out how to replicate his formula in your own town. American menu. Dinner. Closed Jan 1, Dec 24-25. Bar. Casual attire. **$$$**
🅑

★ ★ **REDEYE GRILL.** *890 Seventh Ave, New York (10019). Phone 212/541-9000; fax 212/245-6840. www.redeyegrillgroup.com.* You can't miss the bright red entrance to Redeye Grill, which sits just 50 feet from Carnegie Hall. Its name comes from the dreaded overnight flight linking the West and East coasts, and that link is exactly what inspires its seafood-heavy menu and its design. The soaring dining room features Mission-style furnishings and is anchored by a shrimp, sushi, and smoked fish bar, flanked by giant bronze shrimp sculptures. Nightly jazz on the balcony keeps diners' toes tapping. American menu. Lunch, dinner, late-night, brunch. Bar. Casual attire. Outdoor seating. **$$$**
🅑

★ ★ **REMI.** *145 W 53rd St, New York (10019). Phone 212/581-4242; fax 212/581-7182.* The cuisine of Venice is the focus of the menu at Remi, an airy, lofty

restaurant decorated with ornate Venetian blown-glass lights and murals of the Italian city's romantic canals. Remi has long been a favorite for local businesspeople to dish over lunch, but also makes a terrific choice for drinks, dinner, or a visit before or after a theater show. The kitchen's specialty is brilliant handmade pastas, but the menu also features contemporary Mediterranean takes on fish, beef, poultry, and game. A *ciccetti* menu of Venetian tapas is also available at the bar for nibbling while working through the restaurant's impressive Italian wine list. Italian menu. Lunch, dinner. Closed holidays. Casual attire. Reservations recommended. Outdoor seating. **$$**
🅑

★ ★ **RENE PUJOL.** *321 W 51st St, New York (10019). Phone 212/246-3023; fax 212/245-5206. www.renepujol.com.* René Pujol is a theater district charmer, offering Gallic cuisine updated with a modern sensibility. The restaurant is warm and convivial, with butter-colored walls, a brick hearth, and snug, cozy tables. The menu offers refined takes on French dishes that are hearty and savory, like the lamb shanks with white beans, a house specialty. French menu. Lunch, dinner. Closed Mon; holidays. Jacket required. **$$$**
🅑

★ **REPUBLIC.** *37 Union Sq W, New York (10003). Phone 212/627-7172; fax 212/627-7010. www.thinknoodles.com.* Located on Union Square West, Republic is perpetually packed with trendy locals who seek out the restaurant's signature Asian noodle dishes. Be ready to sit on communal picnic tables and shout above the din, but the decibels and the less-than-comfy seating vanish when the steaming bowls arrive, brimming with Thai, Japanese, and other East Asian recipes for all sorts of delicious noodles. Asian menu. Lunch, dinner. Closed Memorial Day, Dec 25. Bar. Casual attire. Outdoor seating. **$**

★ ★ **RHONE.** *63 Ganesvoort St, New York (10014). Phone 212/367-8440. www.rhonenyc.com.* Located in the city's hipster haven known as the Meatpacking District, Rhone is an airy, chic restaurant, lounge, and wine bar that features the wines of its namesake region in France. Sitting in Rhone, with its wide, floor-to-ceiling windows thrown open to the street, you'll feel transported. With about 100 bottles and 30 glasses of Rhone varietals on the list, you'll have no problem finding a match for the ambitious French menu, which includes dishes like potato-crusted seabass and braised lamb shank. Those craving lighter fare may pair their vino with a cheese plate or caviar. French menu. Dinner. Closed Sun. Casual attire. **$$$**

★ ★ ★ **RIINGO.** *205 E 45th St, New York (10017). Phone 212/867-4200. riingo.com.* Marcus Samuelsson, the heartthrob, boy-wonder chef behind the very popular contemporary Scandinavian spot Aquavit (see), is the man behind Riingo, a white-hot Asian restaurant in Midtown's Alex Hotel. Japanese for apple, Riingo is a sleek and sexy bilevel space featuring dark ebony woodwork and bamboo floors, and luxurious banquettes that swallow you up in warmth. It's tough not to feel fabulous here, seated in magnificent surroundings while nibbling on Samuelsson's inventive brand of Japanese-American fare. This stylish restaurant comes equipped with the requisite swanky lounge, an extensive house-infused sake list, full sushi bar, and look-at-me crowds. Riingo is the perfect apple for the Big Apple. American, Japanese, Sushi menu. Lunch, dinner, brunch. Business casual attire. Valet parking. **$$$**

★ ★ ★ ★ **RM.** *33 E 60th St, New York (10022). Phone 212/319-3800; fax 212/319-4955.* After almost a decade at the helm at Oceana, chef Rick Moonen decided to set off on a ship of his own in 2002. At RM, his namesake eatery, seafood remains the star attraction. Moonen has a gift with the ocean's bounty, and with the new space, he has found new inspiration and a source of revitalization. The New American menu at RM sets off sparks, focusing on the freshest catches and perfectly blending seasonal ingredients with vibrant global flavors. The sophisticated dining room is dressed in soothing neutral tones, with lots of blond wood and warm, golden lighting, lending the restaurant a Zen vibe. Despite the high-income power crowds that fill the restaurant for business lunches and civilized, exquisite dinners, the dining room remains a serene retreat from Manhattan stress. Seafood menu. Lunch, dinner. Closed Sun. Reservations recommended. **$$$$**

★ ★ **ROCK CENTER CAFE.** *20 W 50th St, New York (10020). Phone 212/332-7620; fax 212/332-7677. www.restaurantassociates.com.* Located in Rockefeller Center, this American restaurant is an ideal place to relax under blue summer skies with cool cocktails, or to grab a seat and watch the ice skaters slip, slide, and crash all winter long under the twinkling Christmas tree. The Rock Center Café is one of those places that never fails to satisfy with a broad menu of terrific salads, sandwiches, burgers, and generously sized

seasonal American entrées. American menu. Breakfast, lunch, dinner, brunch. Outdoor seating. **$$**

★ ★ **ROSA MEXICANO.** *61 Columbus Ave, New York (10023). Phone 212/977-7700; fax 212/397-0999. www.rosamexicano.com.* One of the first restaurants to introduce New Yorkers to authentic Mexican cuisine, Rosa Mexicano was founded by chef Josefina Howard in the early '80s and today remains an essential stop for anyone who craves strong, chilly, perfectly mixed margaritas (frozen or on the rocks), and bright, fresh, vibrant bowls of guacamole mixed tableside to your desired level of heat (mild to scorching). The menu is a beautiful tribute to the regional home-cooking of Mexico—steamy pork tamales, chicken in a rich savory blanket of mole, terra-cotta cazuelas brimming with shrimp, tomatoes, garlic, and chiles, and a long-time entrée signature—budin Azteca, a wonderful tortilla casserole with layers of shredded chicken and cheese. Expect a crowd with as much spice and attitude as the food. Mexican menu. Lunch, dinner, late-night. Bar. Casual attire. **$$$**

★ ★ ★ **SAKAGURA.** *211 E 43rd St, New York (10017). Phone 212/953-7253; fax 212/557-5205. www.sakagura.com.* At this subterranean hideaway in Midtown, you'll find one of the most extensive sake collections in the city, as well as a talented knife-wielding team of sushi chefs turning out some of the most delicious sashimi you've ever tasted. (There is no sushi here, as it is forbidden to serve rice with sake.) Sakagura may be a bit tough to find—you enter through the lobby of an office building and follow a small gold sign that points you toward this buried basement space. But once you have found it, you will be hesitant to leave. The space is very Zen/minimalist and is leanly decorated with bamboo plants and paper lanterns. Between the soothing atmosphere and the potent sake, you'll sleep like a baby after your evening here. Japanese menu. Lunch, dinner. Bar. Casual attire. Reservations recommended. **$$**

★ ★ ★ **SAN DOMENICO.** *240 Central Park S, New York (10019). Phone 212/265-5959; fax 212/397-0844. www.sandomenicony.com.* Tony May's San Domenico is like an Armani suit—classic, elegant, and perfect for every occasion. Located on Central Park South with views of the horse-drawn carriages lined up along the edge of Central Park just outside, San Domenico is one of city's most well regarded restaurants for sophisticated, contemporary Italian cuisine. Pasta, fish, and meat dishes manage to feel rustic yet updated, as the chef teams new-world ingredients and twists with authentic old-world recipes and style. An impressive wine list from the motherland of Italy enriches every bite. Italian menu. Lunch, dinner, Sunday brunch (fall-spring). Closed Jan 1, Thanksgiving, Dec 25. Bar. Casual attire. **$$$$**

★ ★ ★ **SAN PIETRO.** *18 E 54th St, New York (10022). Phone 212/753-9015; fax 212/371-2337. www.sanpietro.net.* San Pietro is one of the restaurants where you walk in a customer and leave a part of the family. Located on a busy Midtown street, San Pietro is owned and run by the three Bruno brothers, who grew up on a family farm along the Amalfi Coast in the southern Italian region of Campagna. At San Pietro, the brothers pay homage to their homeland by serving traditional dishes—antipasti, pasta, poultry, fish, veal, and beef—accented with seasonal ingredients and lots of Italian charm. The wine list contains a knockout selection of southern Italian wines to complete the experience. Italian menu. Lunch, dinner. Closed Sun; holidays. Bar. Jacket required. Reservations recommended. Outdoor seating. **$$$**

★ ★ **SARABETH'S WEST.** *423 Amsterdam Ave, New York (10024). Phone 212/496-6280; fax 212/787-9655. www.sarabeth.com.* Sarabeth's is known for some of the most delicate and delicious pastries, scones, and muffins in the city, so brunch here is a must for anyone who craves buttery cakes with coffee in the morning. Aside from the pastry arena, Sarabeth's offers a wonderful brunch of wild berry pancakes, brioche French toast, and plates of fluffy eggs, as well as a seasonal American menu for dinner nightly. Don't forget to pick up some baked goods for the next morning on your way out. American menu. Breakfast, lunch, dinner, brunch. Closed Dec 25. Bar. Casual attire. Reservations recommended. Outdoor seating. **$$**

★ ★ **SARDI'S.** *234 W 44th St, New York (10036). Phone 212/221-8440; fax 212/302-0865. www.sardis.com.* This icon in the theater district, established in 1921, is one of those old-time favorites that seems to stay the same year after year. For some places, though, no change is a good thing. Sardi's still serves as a cafeteria of sorts for many theater celebrities, and still offers hearty Italian signatures like stuffed cannelloni (veal, beef, or sausage), serviceable antipasti (this is not the restaurant's strong suit), and solid simple dishes like rotisserie roasted chicken and grilled filet mignon. Yes, the brilliant baked Alaska is still on the menu, and it's still a monster—a tasty one at that. Italian menu. Lunch, dinner, late-night. Closed Mon. Bar. Casual attire. Reservations recommended. **$$$**

★ ★ **SAVORE.** *200 Spring St, New York (10012). Phone 212/431-1212; fax 212/343-2605.* Located on a lovely block in SoHo, Savore is a quiet little gem that offers Tuscan dining in a relaxed and authentic countryside setting. At Savore, you'll feel like you are dining in Europe. Meals are not rushed, service is leisurely, and the food is simple and delicious—the menu features earthy pastas, grilled whole fish, braised meats, and fresh salads. All you crave after dinner is a ticket to Italy. Italian menu. Lunch, dinner. Closed Dec 25. Bar. Casual attire. Outdoor seating. **$$$**

★ ★ ★ **SAVOY.** *70 Prince St, New York (10012). Phone 212/219-8570; fax 212/334-4868.* Peter Hoffman, the chef and an owner of Savoy, a comfortable, urban dining spot in SoHo, has been a proponent of Greenmarket cooking style for more than ten years. You'll find him with his tricycle-pulled wagon at the local farmers' markets several times a week, picking produce for his inspired menu of global fare—dishes taken from Spain, Latin America, France, Morocco, and Greece, as well as America's various regions—brought to life with simple, brilliant ingredients. The intimate dining room upstairs features an open fireplace where many of Hoffman's rustic dishes are cooked right before your eyes in the blazing hearth. American, Mediterranean menu. Lunch, dinner. Closed holidays. Bar. Casual attire. **$$$**

★ ★ **SCHILLER'S LIQUOR BAR.** *131 Rivington St, New York (10002). Phone 212/260-4555.* The latest hipster haunt from Keith McNally, the king of the distressed vintage Parisian brasserie, Schiller's Liquor Bar is already bursting at its authentic subway-tiled seams with the most up-to-the-minute stars and scene-seekers. It's safe to say that this formerly grungy corner of Rivington and Norfolk has never seen so much Prada and Paul Smith. American, Mediterranean menu. Breakfast, lunch, dinner, brunch. Bar. Casual attire. **$$**

★ ★ **THE SEA GRILL.** *19 W 49th St, New York (10020). Phone 212/332-7610; fax 212/332-7677. www.restaurantassociates.com/theseagrill.* The Sea Grill is home to some of the most delicious seafood in the city. This lavish, ocean-blue restaurant dressed up in aquamarine and off-white tones sports a slick bar and prime wintertime views of ice skaters twirling (and crashing) on the rink under the twinkling Christmas tree at Rockefeller Plaza. Summertime brings alfresco dining and lots of icy cool cocktails to pair up with veteran chef Ed Brown's fantastic contemporary seafood menu. Crab cakes are his signature, and they deserve to be ordered at least once. Other dishes—salmon, cod, halibut, skate, you name it—are just as special, as Brown infuses his cooking with techniques and flavors from Asia and the world at large. Seafood menu. Lunch, dinner. Closed Sun; holidays. Bar. Casual attire. Reservations recommended. Valet parking. Outdoor seating. **$$$**

★ ★ **SERAFINA FABULOUS PIZZA.** *1022 Madison Ave, New York (10021). Phone 212/734-2676.* At this mini-chain of velvet-roped pizza joints, you can start the evening off with a simple meal of tasty Italian fare like wood-fired pizzas, salads, antipasti, pasta, seafood, and meat and then stay and hang out in the bar to sip cool cocktails and listen to the DJs spinning tunes. Serafina is casual but hip, with a generally young and gorgeous European crowd that comes in more for the see-and-be-scene vibe than the terrific pizzas. Pizza. Lunch, dinner, late-night. **$$**

★ **SERENDIPITY 3.** *225 E 60th St, New York (10022). Phone 212/838-3531; fax 212/688-4896. www.serendipity3.com.* Most restaurants rest on their savory menus. Not at Serendipity 3, a loud, kid-in-a-candy-store sort of a place that is fashioned after a vintage soda parlor. Decorated with Tiffany lamps and stained-glass windows, with a fun boutique up front, this is one restaurant where desserts rule the roost. Sure, you can grab sandwiches, burgers, salads, and the like, but really, this is one place to have dessert for dinner. Monster-sized sundaes, gooey chocolate layer cake, mountain-size cheesecake, and the signature frozen hot chocolate—a birdbath-sized chocolate seducer—are great dinner dishes. Who needs protein? American menu. Lunch, dinner. Closed Dec 25. Reservations recommended. **$$**
🄳

★ ★ **SHAAN.** *57 W 48th St, New York (10020). Phone 212/977-8400; fax 212/977-3069. www.shaanofindia.com.* Shaan offers traditional northern Indian cuisine of the distinctly delicious variety. The restaurant is located just a stone's throw from Rockefeller Center, so it makes a great pit stop during holiday shopping and skating. Shaan offers dishes from the clay tandoor oven, as well as savory vegetarian, lamb, chicken, and fish dishes served with steaming bowls of fragrant rice. A heavenly selection of breads, like naan, poori, and roti, makes mopping up the wonderfully aromatic sauces easy work. On Friday and Saturday nights, the restaurant usually hosts classical Indian musicians for a transporting evening. Indian menu. Lunch, dinner. Closed holidays. Bar. Casual attire. **$$$**

★ ★ **SHUN LEE CAFE.** *43 W 65th St, New York (10023). Phone 212/595-8895; fax 212/799-3598.* You won't find typical white-carton options at this urban Chinese outpost with an eclectic menu. The drama is evident in the décor and on the plates—from the white ceramic monkeys hanging off the bar to the specialty sweetbreads with black mushrooms. Chinese menu. Lunch, dinner. Closed Thanksgiving. Bar. Casual attire. Reservations recommended. **$$$**
🄳

★ ★ ★ **SHUN LEE PALACE.** *155 E 55th St, New York (10022). Phone 212/371-8844; fax 212/752-1936. www.shunleepalace.com.* The lovely, swirling décor of the Adam Tihany-designed dining room should tell you that something special awaits you at Shun Lee Palace. The large space is perfect for business luncheons or family get-togethers. Restaurateur Michael Tong's extensive haute Chinese menu makes this spot a New York favorite—so much so that a second location has opened on the West Side. Guest chefs visit frequently from Hong Kong, and the special prix fixe lunch is a deal. Chinese menu. Lunch, dinner, late-night. Closed Thanksgiving. Bar. Casual attire. Reservations recommended. **$$$**

★ **SIAM GRILL.** *592 Ninth Ave, New York (10036). Phone 212/307-1363; fax 212/265-5383.* At this warm and cozy Thai grill in the theater district, you'll find that it's easy to kick back and relax for dinner. The service is pleasant and prompt, and the menu is filled with tasty traditional Thai dishes like pad Thai and Bammee curry and house specialties like crispy duck in red curry and steamed fish in ginger and bean threads. The prices seem high for the fare, but considering its location, they aren't out of line. Thai menu. Lunch, dinner. Closed holidays. **$$**
🄳

★ ★ ★ **SMITH & WOLLENSKY.** *797 Third Ave, New York (10022). Phone 212/753-1530; fax 212/751-5446. www.smithandwollensky.com.* The original after which the national chain was modeled, this 390-seat, wood-paneled dining room is known for sirloin steaks and filet mignon, but also offers lamb and veal chops.

Sides are huge and straightforward, with the likes of creamed spinach and hash browns. Good wines and personable service complete the experience. American menu. Lunch, dinner, late-night. Closed Jan 1, Thanksgiving, Dec 25. Bar. Casual attire. **$$$**
🅳

★ **SNACK TAVERNA.** *63 Bedford St, New York (10014). Phone 212/920-3499.* This West Village clone of Snack in SoHo offers the same authentic Greek cuisine in a cozy corner eatery decorated with hardwood floors, wide-open windows, soft candlelight, bistro tables, and vintage tin ceilings. The menu offers great pita, mezze, and lots of wonderful lamb dishes. For those who want to taste something new, different, and delicious, the wine list is all Greek. Greek menu. Lunch, dinner. Bar. Casual attire. **$**
🅳

★ ★ **SOBA-YA.** *229 E 9th St, New York (10003). Phone 212/533-6966.* Located in the East Village, Soba-Ya is a tiny, serene space that is the neighborhood's perennial favorite for Japanese noodle dishes. Noodles come both hot and cold, plus you can watch the soba and udon noodles being cut and hung to dry like in an old laundry house. Although the noodles make the best impression, the rest of the menu deserves attention as well, like tempura vegetables with spicy curry sauce and an excellent assortment of sakes, organized on the menu to pair up with the food. Japanese menu. Lunch, dinner. Closed holidays. Casual attire. **$$**
🅳

★ ★ **SOHO STEAK.** *90 Thompson St, New York (10012). Phone 212/226-0602.* This longtime standard in SoHo is a classic neighborhood bistro. Tables are crowded together, waiters are charming, wine flows from old-fashioned glass carafes, and the food consists of easy-to-devour diner fare like steak frites, moules, cassoulet, and omelettes. In the summer, the French doors open up to the street, and in winter it feels just as lively, like a warm and bustling Paris bistro. French bistro menu. Lunch, dinner, brunch. Closed holidays. Bar. Casual attire. Outdoor seating. **$$**

★ ★ ★ **SPARKS STEAK HOUSE.** *210 E 46th St, New York (10017). Phone 212/687-4855; fax 212/557-7409. www.sparkssteakhouse.com.* This temple of beef is one of the standard spots for meat-seekers in New York City. The cavernous dining room has a classic old-world charm to it, with oil paintings, etched glass, and dark wood paneling, and the large bar feels like home as soon as you wrap your fingers around the stem of your martini glass. Sparks is a serious

American chophouse, and only serious appetites need apply for entry. There are no dainty portions here, so come ready to feast on thick, juicy steaks, burgers, roasts, racks, and fish (if you must). Seafood, steak menu. Lunch, dinner. Closed Sun; holidays. Bar. Casual attire. Reservations recommended. **$$**
🅳

★ ★ **SPICE MARKET.** *403 W 13th St, New York (10014). Phone 212/675-2322; fax 212/675-4551. www.jean-georges.com.* Spice Market, the first project from dynamic chef duo Jean-Georges Vongerichten and Gray Kunz, is like something out of the Kasbah—an authentic jewel-toned Moroccan wonderland with raw, color-stained wood panels and benches flown in from India and waitresses decked out in saris and backless silk halter tops. As for the fare, you are in for magic on the plate. Out of the 60-foot-long open kitchen (complete with its own sultry food bar) comes fragrant, exotically spiced, family-style dishes inspired by Morocco and the Far East—satays and summer rolls, dosa and pho, and fragrant pulled-oxtail hot pots with coriander chutney and kumquats. Filled with the most fabulous crowds reclining on stunning banquettes in the amber glow of candles and lanterns, Spice Market is easily a contender for New York's hottest and tastiest scene. International, Pacific-Rim/Pan-Asian menu. Lunch, dinner. Business casual attire. **$$$**

★ **STAGE DELI.** *834 Seventh Ave, New York (10019). Phone 212/245-7850; fax 212/245-7957. www.stagedeli.com.* Stage Deli is one of New York's most favored between-the-bread restaurants, offering lovely sandwiches crafted from rye bread, pastrami, tongue, brisket, mustard, mayo, and half-sour pickles, as well as comforting standards like chicken noodle soup. This is a hectic and bustling deli, with a ton of energy that exemplifies life in the Big Apple. Deli menu. Breakfast, lunch, dinner, late-night. Children's menu. Casual attire. **$$**
🅳

★ ★ **STEAK FRITES.** *9 E 16th St, New York (10003). Phone 212/463-7101; fax 212/627-2760. www.steakfritesnyc.com.* Located down the block from the Union Square Greenmarket, Steak Frites is the perfect rest stop after shopping for the season's best produce. Open for Saturday and Sunday brunch, it is popular on weekends, when locals grab outdoor tables and people-watch. At night, the restaurant is lively and has a rich European flair, decorated with vintage posters and long leather banquettes. This is a fun restaurant to hang out in and just have drinks, but it's also an ideal spot to hunker down over a dinner of the signature steak frites with a bold red wine. The menu also offers a great selection of fish, pastas, and salads. French bistro menu. Lunch, dinner, Sat-Sun brunch. Closed Jan 1, Dec 25. Bar. Casual attire. Outdoor seating. **$$**

★ ★ ★ **STRIP HOUSE.** *13 E 12th St, New York (10003). Phone 212/328-0000; fax 212/337-0233. www.theglaziergroup.com.* If you can get over the fact that you're eating in a restaurant called Strip House (no dollar bills needed here other than to tip the folks in coat check), you will be in for some of the best beef in the city. The low-lit restaurant, swathed in deep red fabric and decorated with old black-and-white photos of burlesque stars, has a great vibe in a bordello-chic sort of way. It is sexy; tawdry it is not. The kitchen does a great job with its selection of steakhouse favorites (a half-dozen steaks and chops cooked to chin-wiping perfection) and adds some inspired sides, like truffle-scented creamed spinach, goosefat potatoes, and mixed heirloom tomatoes in season. Steak menu. Dinner. Bar. Casual attire. **$$$$**

★ ★ **SUEÑOS.** *311 W 17th St, New York (10011). Phone 212/243-1333; fax 212/243-1333. www.suenosnyc.com.* Walk by Sueños and you will most likely spy a crowd of people gathered on the sidewalk, looking through a large rectangular window, drooling. The porthole gives sidewalk voyeurs a bird's eye view of the kitchen, where Mexican-cuisine diva (chef/owner) Sue Torres executes orders of her addictive modern regional Mexican cuisine. There are fat, steamy empanadas filled with fava beans and drunken goat cheese, heavenly pork tamales steamed in banana leaves and plated in a fiery lather of ancho beurre blanc, and tortilla-crusted Chilean sea bass with a chile rajas tamale. The restaurant is lively and hip, decorated in bright colors and filled with the sweet smell of fresh corn tortillas, which are made by hand in the main dining room. The margaritas are a must. Mexican menu. Dinner. Bar. Casual attire. Reservations recommended. **$$$**

★ ★ ★ **SUGIYAMA.** *251 W 55th St, New York (10019). Phone 212/956-0670; fax 212/956-0671.* If you're searching for an oasis of calm in the center of Midtown Manhattan, head to Sugiyama and your blood pressure will drop upon entry. The dining room is warm and tranquil and has a Zen air to it. The spare, warm room fills up quickly at lunch with strikingly well-appointed businesspeople on expense accounts. But even filled to capacity, it maintains a soothing energy. Sugiyama's specialties are prix fixe kaiseki-style meals. Those who are not well suited to culinary adventures should search for calm somewhere else. It's not worth the visit to order only sushi. Kaiseki are multicourse meals that were originally part of elaborate, traditional Japanese tea ceremonies, but at Sugiyama they have evolved into a procession of precious little plates, holding petite portions that are as tasty as they are appealing to the eye. Lead by head chef and owner Nao Sugiyama, the chefs here have a talent for presentation—every dish is a work of art. Meals are tailored to suit your appetite and preferences and start with sakizuke (an amuse bouche) followed by a seasonal special (zensai), soup, sashimi, sushi, salad, and beef or seafood cooked over a hot stone (ishiyaki), among other sumptuous Japanese delicacies. Soups are Nao's specialty, and warm broths have never been so dynamic and exciting. Dining at Sugiyama is an unexpected adventure. The chef's enthusiasm and energy are contagious, and you can't help departing with a giant grin knowing that you've just had an experience like no other. Japanese menu. Lunch, dinner. Closed Sun-Mon. **$$$$**

★ ★ ★ **SUMILE.** *154 W 13th St, New York (10011). Phone 212/989-7699; fax 212/989-0421.* There are some restaurants that try to please everyone, and then there are restaurants that dance to the beat of their own drum. Sumile, a spare, windowless, and soothing Zen space, is of the latter category. Filled with leggy lovelies reclining on pillowed banquettes next to assorted men in waiting, Sumile feels like a space out of a movie set with star-quality guests to match. The menu is a celebration of Japanese ingredients and contrasting textures, temperatures, and flavors. Josh DeChellis, the young avant-garde chef, dares to be true to his own culinary vision in the face of populist trends. His menu features innovative plates like sweet braised gulf shrimp in horseradish consommé, poached hamachi with pickled melon and nori salt, and seared duck in a frothy foie gras mousse blended with aged sake. This is not a place for timid eaters. Bring your sense of adventure, or stay home. Japanese, pan-Asian menu. Dinner. Closed Mon-Sun. Bar. Casual attire. Reservations recommended. **$$$**

★ ★ **SURYA.** *302 Bleecker St, New York (10014). Phone 212/807-7770; fax 212/337-0695.* Surya is a sleek, low-lit restaurant and boîte that offers the most stylish setting in the city for contemporary Indian cuisine. The lounge is a chic place to stop in for a cocktail, like the house tajmapolitan (a cosmopolitan with cinnamon). After that drink, you might want to move into the sultry dining room for dinner (beef-free), featuring a wonderful list of inspired vegetable dishes like birianyi—basmati rice perfumed with sweet spices and served with raita—and urulakilangu katrika koze, spiced potatoes and eggplant served with paratha (griddle-fried bread). In warm weather, you can dine outside in the restaurant's lovely leafy garden. Indian menu. Lunch, dinner. Bar. Casual attire. Reservations recommended. Outdoor seating. **$$**

★ ★ **SUSHI OF GARI.** *402 E 78th St, New York (10021). Phone 212/517-5340.* Sushi of Gari is one of those spots frequented by New Yorkers in the know. Nobu's divine, sure, but Sushi of Gari stays true to Japanese fare rather than infusing Latin ingredients. The problem is that, like Nobu, Sushi of Gari is always packed to capacity with sushi-seeking trendsetters, and at times, it's hard to hear yourself order, let alone have a conversation. But try to keep your ears tuned to other tables as they order, since many regulars come in and order amazing dishes that are not on the menu. Either eavesdrop or feel free to ask your neighbors for their recommendations—New Yorkers love to talk about food. If you're sticking to the basics, the raw fish—like the kanpachi (Japanese yellowtail) and the toro (fatty tuna)—is silky and luscious. Japanese menu. Dinner. Closed Mon. Casual attire. Reservations recommended. **$$$**

★ **SWEET AND TART.** *20 Mott St, New York (10013). Phone 212/964-0380; fax 212/571-7696. www.sweetandtart.com.* In the heart of Chinatown, you will find Sweet and Tart, an authentic Hong Kong-style Chinese restaurant that offers enough variety to please an army of eaters. The space has three levels: the upper level is crowded with families, while the ground floor soda-fountain diner is more for Gen Xers. The menu sticks to impeccably prepared Cantonese classics and delicious dim sum, and also offers dishes from Thailand and Japan. Chinese menu. Lunch, dinner, late-night. Casual attire. **$**
🅳

★ ★ ★ **TABLA.** *11 Madison Ave, New York (10010). Phone 212/889-0667; fax 212/889-0914. www.tablany.com.* Tabla is the Indian-inspired culinary star from restaurant tour de force Danny Meyer (Gramercy Tavern, Union Square Cafe—see both). Chef/partner Floyd Cardoz cleverly peppers his menu with the intoxicating flavors of India—sweet and savory spices, chutneys, meats from a tandoor oven, and soft rounds of pillowy, handmade

breads. The result is a delicious introduction to the sumptuous flavors of India, not a crash course that hits you over the head. The stunning, bilevel dining room has an almost mystical quality to it, with its muted jewel-toned accents, rich redwood floors, and soaring windows that face Madison Square Park. American, Indian menu. Lunch, dinner. Bar. Reservations recommended. **$$$**

★ ★ ★ **TAMARIND.** *41-43 E 22nd St, New York (10010). Phone 212/674-7400; fax 212/674-4449. www.tamarinde22.com.* The fragrant cuisine of India is served at Tamarind, an elegant restaurant in the Flatiron District with a lively bar and a serene and beautiful dining room. The attraction here is a menu of dishes showcasing perfect-pitch flavors—spicy, sweet, sour, and hot play together wonderfully on the plate. The kitchen serves stunning samosas, naan, pouri, chutneys, and traditional curries, alongside more contemporary dishes that play to the sophisticated New Yorker crowd. Indian menu. Lunch, dinner. Bar. Casual attire. Reservations recommended. **$$$**

★ ★ **TASTING ROOM.** *72 E 1st St, New York (10003). Phone 212/358-7831; fax 212/358-8432. www.thetastingroomnyc.com.* The Tasting Room, a charming shoebox-sized East Village restaurant, features a seasonal American menu with dishes in two sizes—tasting (appetizer size) and sharing (entrée size), allowing you to sample many of the gifted chef's wonderful seasonal dishes. Chef/owner Colin Alevras is dedicated to shopping from local organic producers, and his passion for local products extends to the all-American, 300-bottle wine list. Colin's wife, Renee, runs the petite dining room, making you feel like you are at home in an instant. The Tasting Room is truly a jewel of a spot, perfect for intimate evenings. American menu. Dinner. Closed Sun-Mon. Casual attire. **$$$**
🅳

★ ★ **TAVERN ON THE GREEN.** *Central Park at W 67th St, New York (10023). Phone 212/873-3200; fax 212/580-4265. www.tavernonthegreen.com.* Ornate, over the top, and brash, Tavern on the Green is the Cher of the New York restaurant scene. Like the one-name singer, it's still popular after all these years, it's had a lot of work done, and it's tacky but loved anyway. If you're in the mood for a serviceable meal and extra-high prices, go for it; otherwise, you may want to steer clear of this tourist trap. The food is straightforward and fine, and the view of Central Park is romantic, but the restaurant has morphed into more of a theme park than a serious dining destination. American menu. Lunch, dinner, brunch. Bar. Valet parking. **$$$**

★ ★ ★ **TERRACE IN THE SKY.** *400 W 119th St, New York (10027). Phone 212/666-9490; fax 212/666-3471.* Set high in the sky on the top floor of a prewar Upper West Side building, Terrace in the Sky offers breathtaking panoramic views of the city and a rich selection of eclectic fare to match. The haute menu of seared sweetbreads, foie gras torchon, smoked salmon, lobster, and caviar make dining here seem very posh. If you have love on your mind, this is *the* place to go. Terrace in the Sky is ideal for romance with its elegant linen-topped tables, soft candlelit ambience, and views that are truly beyond compare. French, Mediterranean menu. Lunch, dinner, brunch Sun. Closed Mon. Bar. Casual attire. Reservations recommended. Outdoor seating. **$$$**

★ ★ ★ **TOCQUEVILLE.** *15 E 15th St, New York (10003). Phone 212/647-1515. www.tocqueville restaurant.com.* Owned by husband Marco Moreira (chef) and wife Jo-Ann Makovitsky (front-of-house manager), Tocqueville is a little slice of paradise in the form of a restaurant. This is the sort of place that will calm you from the moment you walk through the tall blond doors into the petite, elegant room warmed with golden light, butter-yellow walls, and stunningly appointed tabletops. The cuisine is as magical as the space. Chef Moreira offers impeccably prepared, inventive New American fare crafted with care from pristine seasonal ingredients hand-picked from local farmers and the nearby Greenmarket. Intimate and soothing, Tocqueville is a perfect spot for those seeking quiet conversation and luxurious food. American, French menu. Lunch, dinner. Bar. Casual attire. **$$$$**

★ ★ ★ **TOWN.** *15 W 56th St, New York (10019). Phone 212/582-4445. www.chambershotel.com.* Located in the swanky Chambers Hotel (see), Town is an oasis of hipness, featuring a white-hot, low-lit lounge and bar with some of the most inventive and well-made cocktails in the city. Move downstairs to the sexy, oversized-banquetted, David Rockwell-designed dining room, and you'll find it filled edge to edge with high-powered media and fashion folks digging into chef/owner Geoffrey Zakarian's brilliant high-styled, modern American fare. American menu. Lunch, dinner. Bar. Casual attire. Reservations recommended. **$$$**

★ ★ ★ **TRATTORIA DELL'ARTE.** *900 Seventh Ave, New York (10019). Phone 212/245-9800; fax 212/265-3296. www.trattoriadellarte.com.* Trattoria dell'Arte is the perfect choice if Carnegie Hall or a performance at City Center is on your list. Owned by Shelly Fireman, this lively and popular restaurant offers easy, approachable Italian cuisine in a comfortable, neighborly setting. The scene here is festive, so expect it to be loud with diners who are clearly enjoying the generous plates of homemade pastas, selections from the spectacular antipasti bar, seafood, and meats, all prepared in simple Mediterranean style. Italian menu. Lunch, dinner, brunch. Closed Thanksgiving, Dec 25. Bar. Casual attire. Reservations recommended. **$$$**

★ ★ ★ **TRIBECA GRILL.** *375 Greenwich St, New York (10013). Phone 212/941-3900; fax 212/941-3915. www.myriadrestaurantgroup.com/tribecagrill.* This New York icon from super-restaurateur Drew Nieporent (Nobu, Montrachet—see both) and partner Robert De Niro is a shining example of what a restaurant should offer. First, hospitality—the service is warm, attentive, and knowledgeable without an ounce of pretension. Second, atmosphere—the Grill is a comfortable, urban dining room with exposed brick walls, oil paintings by Robert De Niro, Sr., and a magnificent cherry wood, wraparound bar that looks like it fell off the set of *Cheers.* Third, food—the kitchen features an approachable, contemporary, seasonal American menu with dishes for every type of diner, from wild foodies to simple roast chicken eaters. Finally, wine—TriBeCa Grill offers an impressive and diverse wine program led by David Gordon, who has earned the restaurant much praise and admiration near and far. TriBeCa Grill, which is more than 10 years old, remains a winner on all counts. American menu. Lunch, dinner, late-night, Sun brunch. Closed holidays. Bar. Casual attire. Reservations recommended. **$$$**

★ ★ **TURKISH KITCHEN.** *386 Third Ave, New York (10016). Phone 212/679-1810.* Be prepared to enjoy your food at this bustling Murray Hill outpost for authentic Turkish fare. The restaurant specializes in the well-spiced cuisine of this beautiful country, with dishes of tender lamb, beef, and chicken, as well as lots of warm bread for ripping off and dipping in assorted mezze. Stained a deep red, the walls and the Arabic décor give the room a warm feeling. The only draw back is the service, which is very friendly and very knowledgeable, but can be slow. Turkish menu. Lunch, dinner. Children's menu. Casual attire. Reservations recommended. **$$**

★ ★ **TUSCAN SQUARE.** *16 W 51st St, New York (10020). Phone 212/977-7777; fax 212/977-3144. www.tuscansquare.com.* Restaurateur Pino Luongo is a native Italian whose airy, comfortable Tuscan Square restaurant brings his idyllic homeland to life, warding off all cases of homesickness here in the big, boisterous city. Located in Rockefeller Center, Tuscan Square is a great place to relax and unwind at lunch or dinner. It offers a taste of the Italian countryside with a sunny, frescoed dining room and impressive antipasti and homemade pastas, as well as more robust regional specialties that match up well with the deep selection of Chianti, Barbaresco, Barolo, montepulciano, Orvieto, and pinot grigio. Italian menu. Lunch, dinner. Closed Sun; holidays. Casual attire. **$$$**

★ ★ ★ **UNION SQUARE CAFE.** *21 E 16th St, New York (10003). Phone 212/243-4020; fax 212/627-2673.* Union Square Cafe is the first restaurant from the man who brought New York Gramercy Tavern, Eleven Madison, Tabla, and Blue Smoke (see all): Danny Meyer. This bright, warm, cheery, bilevel restaurant and bar is still packing in locals and wooing tourists with Meyer's signature hospitality, chef Michael Romano's divine New American fare, and an award-wining wine list. While the menu changes with the seasons and often features produce from the Greenmarket across the way, the chef's succulent signature grilled tuna burger should not be considered optional. If a table doesn't seem possible (reservations are tough to score), a seat at the bar is a fabulous—and more authentic New Yorker—alternative. American menu. Lunch, dinner. Closed holidays. Bar. Casual attire. Reservations recommended. **$$$**
🅟

★ **UNITED NOODLES.** *349 E 12th St, New York (10003). Phone 212/614-0155.* At this narrow, modestly priced, ultramodern noodle house in the East Village, the menu is all about noodles—think soba and udon—spiced with an assortment of pan-Asian accents. The room, a bit space-aged in design, feels like it belongs aboard the *Starship Enterprise,* and it fills up fast with regulars who love the terrific cheap eats. Thai menu. Breakfast, lunch, dinner, brunch. Casual attire. **$**
🅟

★ ★ ★ **VERITAS.** *43 E 20th St, New York (10003). Phone 212/353-3700; fax 212/353-1632. www.veritas-nyc.com.* If a passion for wine runs through your veins, then a visit to Veritas should be considered mandatory. At this stylish Gramercy Park gem, you'll find a magnificent wine list that, at last count, was 2,700 bottles long. Despite its intimidating length, wine neophytes should not be deterred. There is no fear factor here. The staff is friendly and knowledgeable and all too happy to help you find a suitable wine to match your meal and budget. Bottles range from $20 to $1,300. While wine is the primary draw for Veritas, the food gives the wine a run for its money. It is specifically created with wine in mind and perfectly complements the beverage of focus. The full menu is available at the sleek bar, which is a nice option if you want a quick bite and some (or lots of) wine. Whether you're seated at the bar or tucked into a snug and intimate booth, the restaurant's contemporary American menu is easy to love. Robust flavors, seasonal ingredients, and a light hand in the kitchen make for magical meals. Veritas is a perfect place to explore wine and food alike. American menu. Dinner. Bar. **$$$$**

★ ★ **VESPA CIBOBUONO.** *1625 2nd Ave, New York (10028). Phone 212/472-2050; fax 212/472-7566. www.barvespa.com.* Italian menu. Lunch Fri-Sun, dinner. Closed holidays. Bar. Casual attire. Outdoor seating. **$$**

★ ★ **VICTOR'S.** *236 W 52nd St, New York (10019). Phone 212/586-7714.* Long before the mojito became as popular as the cosmopolitan, these minty rum drinks from Cuba were the cocktail of choice at Victor's, a popular theater district restaurant that feels like an elegant throwback to Havana, decorated with tall palm trees and filled with the rhythmic sounds of Cuban jazz. Aside from the terrific cocktails, Victor's is a festive place to feast on top-notch contemporary Cuban cuisine, like roasted marinated pork with rice and beans, picadillo, fried plantains, and tostones. Cuban menu. Lunch, dinner. Bar. Casual attire. **$$**

★ **VIRGIL'S REAL BARBECUE.** *152 W 44th St, New York (10036). Phone 212/921-9494; fax 212/921-9631. www.virgilsbbq.com.* While everyone has an opinion about barbecue, most will agree that Virgil's is a super choice. Manners are thrown to the wind at Virgil's, a sprawling hog pit where ribs, juicy chicken, tomato-based pulled pork, Memphis pit beans, and spicy collard greens are gobbled up in record time. The noise can be deafening, but there really isn't time to talk once the food arrives. The warm, fluffy buttermilk biscuits usually quiet everyone down rather quickly. Barbecue menu. Lunch, dinner, late-night. Closed Dec 25. Bar. Children's menu. Casual attire. **$$**

★ ★ ★ **VONG.** *200 E 54th St, New York (10022). Phone 212/486-9592; fax 212/980-3745. www.jean-georges.com.* When Jean-Georges Vongerichten, Alsatian-born wonder chef, opened a Thai restaurant called Vong, people weren't sure what to make of it. But doubts were soon dispelled as diners began to experience his exciting and exotic French riffs on fiery Thai classics, incorporating spices and flavors of the East with a New York sensibility. The restaurant feels like a wild and mystical night in the Orient, decorated with long, deep banquettes covered with silk pillows in brilliant jewel tones, walls painted crimson red and accented with gold leaf, and a long table showcasing a Buddha altar. It's a journey for all of the senses. Thai, French menu. Dinner. Closed holidays. Bar. Casual attire. **$$$**

★ ★ ★ **WALLSE.** *344 W 11th St, New York (10014). Phone 212/352-2300. www.wallserestaurant.com.* Enter this charming restaurant, tucked in a sleepy corner of the West Village, and you are instantly transported to Vienna. Decorated with contemporary art and filled with close, square tables; antique furnishings; deep blue banquettes; and a long, romantic stretch of rich mahogany bar (where the cocktails are stellar), chef Kurt Gutenbrunner's Wallse is a personal and delicious ode to the hearty yet delicate cuisine of his homeland, Austria. The thin, golden-crusted Wiener schnitzel should not be missed. A terrific selection of Austrian wines complements the meal, and a nice slice of strudel will send you off on a sweet note. Austrian menu. Dinner. Bar. Casual attire. Reservations recommended. **$$$**

🅿

★ ★ **THE WATER CLUB.** *500 E 30th St, New York (10016). Phone 212/683-3333; fax 212/696-4009. www.thewaterclub.com.* Special occasions were made for The Water Club, a lovely restaurant with romantic, panoramic views of the East River. The shiplike space features soothing, nightly live piano and an intimate, clubby lounge, perfect for relaxing before or after dinner. While poultry and beef are on the menu, The Water Club is known for its seafood. In addition to a gigantic raw bar, you'll find an impressive selection of lobster, scallops, cod, tuna, salmon, and whatever else looks good at the fish markets. On a sunny day, you can't beat brunch out on the deck with a fiery Bloody

Mary in hand, watching the ships go by, feeling like you're far away from it all. American, Seafood menu. Lunch, dinner, Sun brunch. Bar. Jacket required. Reservations recommended. Valet parking. Outdoor seating. **$$$**

🅿

★ ★ ★ **WOO LAE OAK.** *148 Mercer St, New York (10012). Phone 212/925-8200; fax 212/925-8232.* If you're searching for a lively spot to gather a large group for some very tasty and authentic Korean food, Woo Lae Oak is the place. This sleek, cavernous multiplex-style space offers some of the best Korean barbecue in the city. Guests grill marinated meats and seafood to a savory char on wicked-cool smoke-less grill tables. The food is traditional; novices in the arena of Korean fare should seek assistance from one of the restaurant's très chic yet very friendly waiters. Meltingly creamy black cod simmered in a sweet-hot, garlicky soy sauce is a one of the restaurant's most famous plates, but there isn't a bad choice on the menu. Korean menu. Lunch, dinner. Bar. Casual attire. **$$$$**

★ ★ **ZARELA.** *953 Second Ave, New York (10022). Phone 212/644-6740; fax 212/980-1073. www.zarela.com.* This colorful and spirited Mexican eatery in Midtown is renowned for its killer margaritas (be careful with these) and delicious regional Mexican fare. Loud and lively, the bar is always packed with a rowdy after-work crowd that lingers well into the evening. Upstairs, in the more intimate yet still boisterous dining room, you'll feast on some of chef/owner Zarela Martinez's vibrant dishes, from rich enchiladas to luxuriously savory moles. Mexican menu. Lunch, dinner. Closed holidays. Bar. Casual attire. **$$**

🅿

★ ★ **ZOE.** *90 Prince St, New York (10012). Phone 212/966-6722; fax 212/966-6718. www.zoerest.com.* Thalia and Stephen Loffredo opened Zoë smack in the heart of SoHo more than ten years ago, and they have managed to maintain its chic yet comfortable American bistro vibe and, better yet, to keep the kitchen inspired. The menu is still in sync with the demanding and fickle New York palate, offering creative, sophisticated American standards painted with global accents and seasonal flourishes and an extensive, heavily American wine list. There is also a terrific cocktail list and a tempting menu of bar snacks to match, all of which makes Zoë an ideal restaurant for brunch, lunch, dinner, or just wine and a bite at the inviting bar. American menu. Lunch, dinner, brunch. Closed Mon; also July 4, Dec 25. Bar. Casual attire. **$$$**

Bronx, NY

1 hour 47 minutes, 103 miles from Hartford, CT

Area Code 718
Information Chamber of Commerce, 2885 Schley Ave, 10465; phone 718/829-4111

Jonas Bronck, a Swedish settler, bought 500 acres of land from the Dutch in 1639, lending his name to the future borough. Locally it is always referred to as "the Bronx," never simply "Bronx." It is the only borough in New York City on the North American continent (the others are all on islands).

What to See and Do

Bronx Museum of the Arts. *1040 Grand Concourse, Bronx (10456). At 165th St. Phone 718/681-6000. www.bxma.org.* Changing exhibits focus on contemporary art and current cultural subjects pertaining to the Bronx. Concerts, family workshops, and special events. (Wed noon-9 pm, Thurs-Sun noon-6 pm) Free admission Wed. **DONATION**

Bronx Zoo. *Fordham Rd and Bronx River Pkwy, Bronx (10460). Liberty Lines runs an express bus to the zoo gates. Catch the BXM11 Bus at designated stops on Madison Ave. Phone 718/652-8400 for the stop nearest you. Phone 718/367-1010. www.bronxzoo.com.* See the endangered snow leopards, come nose to nose with a gorilla, and encourage your kids to ride a camel at the imaginative, exciting Children's Zoo. And don't miss the Bengali Express, a 25-minute monorail ride over forests and plains that are populated by elephants, lions, tigers, and other prowling, playing wildlife. This is the largest urban zoo in the United States, the heart of the Wildlife Conservation Society's efforts to save animals and wild places. The superb and cutting-edge exhibits re-create naturalistic habitats for many of the zoo's more than 4,000 animals. Be sure to see the Congo Gorilla Forest and the new habitat, Tiger Mountain. (Daily) **$$$**

City Island. *Island off the SE coast of the Bronx mainland, Bronx (10464). E of Hutchinson River Pkwy, through Pelham Bay Park, via City Island Bridge. Phone 718/829-4111. www.cityisland.com.* Referred to as "a bit of New England in the city," City Island is devoted to shipping and shipbuilding. Seafood restaurants; City Island Historical Nautical Museum (Sun).

Edgar Allan Poe Cottage. *E Kingsbridge Rd and Grand Concourse, Bronx (10458). Phone 718/881-8900.* (1812) Poe wrote *Annabel Lee, The Bells,* and *Ulalume* while living here (1846-1849). Period furniture; exhibits about the poet and his wife. Films, tours (Sat and Sun). **$$**

Fordham University. *441 E Fordham Rd, Bronx (10458). In North Bronx. Phone 718/817-4000. www.fordham.edu.* (1841) (15,000 students). All four original Gothic structures of the Rose Hill campus are designated landmarks: University Chapel (St. John's Church), St. John's Residence Hall, Administration Building, and Alumni House. A second campus is at 60th and Columbus Ave, across from the Lincoln Center for the Performing Arts.

The Hall of Fame for Great Americans. *University Ave and W 181st St, Bronx (10453). Hall of Fame Terrace, on the campus of Bronx Community College. Phone 718/289-5161.* A 630-foot, open-air colonnade provides the framework for bronze busts of great Americans; exhibits. **FREE**

Museum of Bronx History. *3266 Bainbridge Ave, Bronx (10467). At E 208th St. Phone 718/881-8900.* Valentine-Varian House (1758), site of Revolutionary War activities; exhibits on Bronx history. (Sat 10 am-4 pm and Sun 1-5 pm; tours by appointment on weekdays) **$**

The New York Botanical Garden. *200th St and Kazimiroff Blvd, Bronx (10458). Bronx Park, entrance on Southern Blvd, S of Moshulu Pkwy. Phone 718/817-8700. www.nybg.org.* One of the largest and oldest in the country, this botanical garden consists of 250 acres of natural terrain and 48 gardens. The garden also has the last 40 acres of the forest that once covered New York City. The Enid A. Haupt Conservatory has 11 distinct plant environments with changing exhibits and permanent displays, including the Fern Forest, Palm Court, and Desert Houses. Tours. Education courses. (Tues-Sun 10 am-6 pm; to 5 pm from Nov-Mar; closed Thanksgiving, Dec 25) **$$**

⭐ **New York Yankees (MLB).** *Yankee Stadium, 161st St and River Ave, Bronx (10451). Take the B/D/4 subway to 161st St—Yankee Stadium stop, or hop a leisurely ferry from Manhattan (800/533-3779 for information) to the stadium. Phone 718/293-6000 (tickets). www.yankees.com.* If you're at all a baseball fan and you are visiting New York City during the summer, you owe it to yourself to catch a Yankees game in the house that Babe Ruth built. Watching the Bronx Bombers is the quintessential New York experience. Get tickets as early as you can, since these legendary pinstripers are popular with locals and tourists alike. The annual games between the Yankees and the New York Mets are always a very early sellout. **$$$$**

North Wind Undersea Museum. *610 City Island Ave, Bronx (10464). Phone 718/885-0701.* (Daily)

Pelham Bay Park. *E of the Hutchinson River, Bronx (10475). Hutchinson River and Hutchinson River Pkwy (W); the city's northern limits; Pelham Pkwy, Burr Ave, Bruckner Expy, and Watt Ave (S); and Eastchester Bay and Long Island Sound (E) at NE corner of the Bronx. Phone 718/430-1832.* The city's largest park (2,764 acres) has Orchard Beach, 13 miles of shoreline, fishing, two golf courses (18-hole), a wildlife refuge, an environmental center, a nature trail, a visitor center, tennis courts, ball fields, a running track, riding stables and bridle paths, and picnicking. Also here near southern boundary is

The Bartow-Pell Mansion Museum. *895 Shore Rd, Bronx (10464). In Pelham Bay Park. Phone 718/885-1461. www.bartowpellmansionmuseum.org.* Greek Revival stone mansion (circa 1840) furnished in the Empire period; gardens (seasonal); carriage house. (Wed, Sat-Sun noon-4 pm; closed holidays) Guided tours and luncheon tours (by appointment). **$**

Van Cortlandt Golf Course. *Van Cortlandt Park S and Bailey Ave, Bronx (10463). Phone 718/543-4595.* This affordable course in the New York area has a subway stop only a block from its entrance. Former New York mayor Rudy Giuliani appropriated some $4 million in the late 1990s, which helped create 20 new tee boxes and contributed to the overall renovation of a course that was run down from heavy play. Now, it's a conversation starter like it was when course architect Tom Bendelow conceived it in the late 1800s. With two par-fives of more than 600 yards each, bring your driver and swing away! **$$$$**

Van Cortlandt House Museum. *Broadway and 246th St, Bronx (10025). In Van Cortlandt Park. Phone 718/543-3344. www.vancortlandthouse.org.* (1748) Georgian house is furnished in the 18th-century Dutch-English manner. (Tues-Fri 10 am-3 pm, Sat-Sun 11 am-4 pm; closed holidays) **$**

Wave Hill. *675 W 252nd St, Bronx (10471). 249th St and Independence Ave. Phone 718/549-3200. www.wavehill.org.* This Hudson River estate was, at various times, home to such notables as Mark Twain and Arturo Toscanini; it's now a public garden and cultural center featuring Wave Hill House (1843), gardens, four greenhouses, nature trails, woods, and meadows. The grounds consist of 28 acres overlooking the Hudson. Special events include concerts, dance programs, art exhibits, and education and nature workshops. (Spring-summer Tues-Sun 9 am-5:30 pm, Wed until 9 pm; fall-winter Tues-Sun 9 am-4:30 pm; closed holidays) Free admission Tues, also Sat mornings. **$**

Full-Service Inn

★ ★ ★ **LE REFUGE INN.** *620 City Island Ave, Bronx (10464). Phone 718/885-2478; fax 718/885-1519.* Located on Long Island Sound with views of Manhattan, this Victorian house (1880) features individually decorated rooms with many antiques. 7 rooms, 3 story. Check-in 1:30 pm, check-out 11 am. Restaurant, bar. **$**

Restaurants

★ **BLACK WHALE.** *279 City Island Ave, Bronx (10464). Phone 718/885-3657. www.dineatblackwhale .com.* American menu. Lunch, dinner, Sun brunch. Bar. Children's menu. Casual attire. **$$**

★ **CHARLIE'S INN.** *2711 Harding Ave, Bronx (10465). Phone 718/931-9727.* This classic old-timer has been around since the 1930s and is still serving authentic German fare and one of the heartiest all-you-can-eat Sunday brunches in the Bronx, if not the entire city. While the menu includes stomach-filling fare like sauerbraten, Wiener schnitzel, and sausages, it is also stocked with lighter continental dishes like pasta, baked clams, fish, and chicken. In the summer, the restaurant opens its outdoor beer garden on Sundays, giving you the perfect excuse to be lazy all day long. American, German menu. Lunch, dinner, Sun brunch. Closed Mon. Bar. Children's menu. Casual attire. Outdoor seating. **$$**

★ ★ **EMILIA'S.** *2331 Arthur Ave, Bronx (10458). Phone 718/367-5915; fax 718/367-1483. arthuravenuebronx.com/emilia's.htm.* The Bronx is certainly not short on Italian food, but Emilia's takes traditional fare and makes it shine, without breaking the bank. Lunch specials are the reason many locals flock here, but dinner is also a sure thing, with a generous menu of pastas, fish, and meat. Emilia's serves a killer tiramisu with a healthy dose of alcohol in the sponge

Arthur Avenue

Old-world charm abounds in this charming section of the Bronx, which has been the home of generations of Italian families for more than a century. Seven square blocks make up the Arthur Avenue Retail Market, an Italian-American food oasis. One of the last indoor markets in New York, opened by Mayor Fiorello LaGuardia in the 1940s, it thrives to this day as a bustling cacophony of sights, sounds, and smells. Shoppers entering through the rickety doors can only think of the possibilities lined up before them as they begin to scan the stands. Perhaps some roasted peppers? What about some cardoon fritters? It is a mecca for serious cooks. The crowded storefronts of mom-and-pop shops sell everything from fine Italian wines and homemade pastas to imported cheeses and meats to gifts and cookware.

And then there are the mouthwatering restaurants, pizza parlors, and pastry shops—some dating to the 1920s—to entice your palate. Have a blast with the two greengrocer brothers whose stand dominates the southern end of the market. Their knowledge of produce and preparation techniques equals any high-priced culinary education. If you are lucky enough to have a garden and are looking for heirloom seed varieties, see Joe Liberatore's Garden of Plenty (2344 Arthur Ave, phone 718/733-7960) located inside the market. They carry seeds ideal for the Italian kitchen, difficult to find elsewhere. Do not miss the fresh, locally made (farm and production in Pennsylvania) cheeses and velvety ricotta at S. Calandra & Sons (2314 Arthur Ave, phone 718/365-7572), or the pungent scent that welcomes you at Calabria Pork Store (2338 Arthur Ave, phone 718/367-5145). Be sure to look up at the gems hanging from the ceiling! The bread sold at

Terranova Bakery (691 E 187th St, phone 718/733-3827) is a feast in itself. Marie's Roasted Coffee (2378 Arthur Ave, phone 718/295-0514) will make you disdain any other espresso blend. Get a pound, put it in the car, and no matter how long it takes you to get home, that fresh-ground coffee smell will be overwhelming.

Forget calories when shopping here, as the Mediterranean diet is often an excellent health benefit, and you won't break the bank in these reasonably priced eateries and shops. Many of the nearly 200 shops around this densely packed area do not take credit cards, so have plenty of cash on hand. If all the shopping and snooping has made you hungry, one of the best restaurants to enjoy an Italian-American meal is Roberto's (632 E 186th St, phone 718/733-9503). And if you desire a little culture with your stuffed tummy, there's even a small repertory theater, the Belmont Playhouse, dedicated to works by Italian writers. Additionally, the Italian Cultural Center, part of the New York Library, has an amazing collection of Italian books, newspapers, and films. Go ahead and poke your head in; the staff is always helpful.

What is most fascinating about the evolution of this historic market is that although the products sold and the dishes served are primarily consumed by Americans of Italian descent, the area serves a non-distinct community. Fordham University students prowl at all hours for sustenance; families coming from or going to the nearby Bronx Zoo or Botanical Garden come by to stock up on tasty morsels for their picnics or for their dining tables back in Manhattan. And any foodie in the area worth his or her salt makes a regular pilgrimage.

cake that will make you want to return and have dessert for dinner. Italian menu. Lunch, dinner. Closed Mon; Dec 25. Bar. **$$**

★ **FEEDING TREE.** *892 Gerard Ave, Bronx (10452). Phone 718/293-5025.* Feeding Tree is one of New York's most beloved Jamaican restaurants, located within a home run's distance from Yankee Stadium. At this friendly and lively joint, a steel drum plays in the background, and you can almost feel the Caribbean

sun on your face. This is the sort of spot to tuck a napkin into your collar and fill up on jerk chicken, stewed kingfish, oxtails, curried goat, and crisp golden patties filled with spiced meat—the perfect snack to grab before a game. Caribbean menu. Breakfast, lunch, dinner. Children's menu. Casual attire. **$$**

★ ★ **JIMMY'S BRONX CAFE.** *281 W Fordham Rd, Bronx (10468). Phone 718/329-2000.* This legendary Bronx restaurant and bar from the venerable

Jimmy Rodriguez has a cult following, and is especially nutty when the Yankees are playing. This is one of the few velvet rope joints in the Bronx, with a boisterous bar and a cavernous 450-seat restaurant jammed with sports, music, and celebrities. The Caribbean-Latin menu is an ode to Rodriguez's Latin-American heritage, and the kitchen turns out impressively tasty and flavorful food. Don't expect a peaceful night here; aside from the din of the crowds and the thumping beat of the music, the place is also a sports bar and boasts more than 15 televisions. Caribbean, Latin menu. Lunch, dinner, late-night. Bar. Casual attire. **$$**

★ ★ ★ **LE REFUGE INN.** *620 City Island Ave, Bronx (10464). Phone 718/885-2478.* Le Refuge Inn is, as its name suggests, a refuge. This 19th-century Victorian manor house on historic City Island is a cozy chalet of warmth, peace, and romance—perfect for melting away stress. Surrounded by the waters of the Long Island Sound, you will instantly be transported to the French countryside once tucked inside the elegant antique-filled dining room and treated to a menu of wonderful classics like bouillabaisse and duck à l'orange. French menu. Dinner. Closed Mon. Bar. Children's menu. Jacket required. Reservations recommended. Outdoor seating. **$$**
🄳

★ ★ **LOBSTER BOX.** *34 City Island Ave, Bronx (10464). Phone 718/885-1952; fax 718/885-3232. www.lobsterbox.com.* The Lobster Box is a historic City Island landmark that, true to its name, offers its specialty, fresh lobster, any way you like it. Choices include broiled, steamed, stuffed, fra diavolo, or marinara, and every preparation is delicious. Pasta is also on the menu, many laden with meaty bits of lobster meat, like the lobster ravioli with sun-dried tomatoes and basil cream sauce. The Lobster Box is an easy-to-love place where the portions are generous and the expansive river views are mesmerizing. Seafood menu. Lunch, dinner. Bar. Casual attire. Valet parking. **$$**

★ ★ **ROBERTO'S TRATTORIA.** *632 Crescent Ave, Bronx (10458). Phone 718/733-9503.* Set in the Italian enclave of the Bronx, Roberto's Trattoria is not high on décor or elegant atmosphere, but it is filled with terrific food prepared in the Positano style. The kitchen is sure-handed and sends out home-style dishes like grilled calamari and assorted pastas, as well as heartier fare like tender short ribs. For a real treat, ask the kitchen to prepare the house specialty, a four-course meal with dishes from Roberto's native Amalfi

coast that will bring applause to your table. Italian menu. Lunch, dinner. Closed Mon. Casual attire. Outdoor seating. **$$**

★ **VENICE RESTAURANT AND PIZZERIA.** *772 E 149th St, Bronx (10455). Phone 718/585-5164.* Old-school pizza and pasta are what you'll find at Venice, a little short on décor but long on value and honest Italian-American food. Founded more than 50 years ago, this restaurant has a menu that focuses on seafood but also offers whole thin-crust pies. Italian menu, pizza. Lunch, dinner. Children's menu. Casual attire. **$$**

★ **VERNON'S NEW JERK HOUSE.** *987 E 223rd St, Bronx (10466). Phone 718/655-8348.* As the name suggests, Caribbean fare is the specialty of the house at Vernon's New Jerk House, a lively spot in the Bronx with an easy vibe and a loyal community following. Dinner here can mean a ginger beer and a bowl of curried goat, or a plate of sweet-spiced jerk chicken with rice and beans. Take this advice: if you have never tried jerk, make a special trip; it doesn't get much better than this, at least without a plane ticket. Caribbean menu. Lunch, dinner. Bar. Casual attire. No credit cards accepted. **$**
🄳

Brooklyn, NY

2 hours 15 minutes, 122 miles from Hartford, CT

Area Code 718
Information Brooklyn Historical Society, 128 Pierrepont St, 11201, phone 718/254-9830; or the NYC Convention & Visitors Bureau, phone 212/484-1200.

Many of the novels, plays, films, and television shows about New York City—ranging from *Death of a Salesman* to *The Honeymooners*—are set in Brooklyn rather than Manhattan, perhaps because of the widely differing characters of these two boroughs. While Manhattan is world-class in sophistication and influence, Brooklyn is famous for such things as the hot dogs on Coney Island, and always has been quintessentially American.

Yet there is much more to Brooklyn than the popular stereotype. Manhattanites flock to performances at the renowned Brooklyn Academy of Music, and the Egyptology collection at the Brooklyn Museum compares with those in London and Cairo. Brooklyn's beautiful Prospect Park was designed by Olmsted and

Vaux, who considered it more beautiful than another park they designed—Central Park in Manhattan.

As the most heavily populated borough, Brooklyn handles about 40 percent of New York City's vast shipping industry. It was pieced together from 25 independent villages and fought valiantly before allowing itself to be taken into New York City in 1898.

What to See and Do

Brooklyn Academy of Music. *30 Lafayette Ave, Brooklyn (10007). Fort Greene/Clinton Hill. Phone 718/636-4100. www.bam.org.* (1907) Founded in 1859, BAM is the oldest performing arts center in America, presenting original productions in contemporary performing arts in the Next Wave Festival each fall, noted national and international theater, dance, and opera companies, and classical and contemporary music programs.

Brooklyn Children's Museum. *145 Brooklyn Ave, Brooklyn (11213). At St. Mark's Ave. Phone 718/735-4400. www.bchildmus.org.* Founded in 1899, this is the world's oldest children's museum, featuring interactive exhibits, workshops, and special events. "The Mystery of Things" teaches children about cultural and scientific objects, and "Music Mix" welcomes young virtuosos. (Wed-Fri 2-5 pm, Sat-Sun 10 am-5 pm; also school holidays) **$$**

Brooklyn Heights Promenade. *The R subway goes to the nearby City Hall stop. Phone 718/965-8900.* For a peaceful stroll and a great view of Manhattan, visit this 1/3-mile-long waterfront area, stretching from Orange Street on the north to Remsen Street on the south. Pack a lunch, claim a bench, and enjoy the sights of the city skyline, Ellis Island, and Statue of Liberty. The promenade is lined with lovely homes and is a popular outdoor hangout for Brooklyn Heights yuppies during the summer. If you're in town over Independence Day weekend, this is usually a great place to view the Fourth of July fireworks. (Daily)

Brooklyn Historical Society. *128 Pierrepont St, Brooklyn Heights (11201). At the corner of Clinton and Pierrepont. Phone 718/222-4111. www.brooklynhistory.org.* This terra-cotta and pressed-brick building, designed by noted architect George Post, has been the headquarters of the Brooklyn Historical Society since 1881. Permanent and changing exhibits deal with Brooklyn history; the major exhibition, Brooklyn Works: 400 Years of Making a Living in Brooklyn, combines re-created stage set environments, authentic personal narratives, historic primary documents, and interactive media and games. Programs include performances, readings, lectures, and activities for children. (Wed-Thurs, Sat 10 am-5 pm; Fri 10 am-8 pm; Sun noon-5 pm; closed holidays) **$$**

Coney Island. *1208 Surf Ave, Brooklyn (11224). Phone 718/372-5159. www.coneyisland.com.* Although it's become a bit frayed, you can still experience a bit of old New York along Coney Island's beachfront boardwalk. Take a ride on the legendary Cyclone roller coaster at **Astroland Amusement Park** (1000 Surf Ave, 718/372-0275, www.astroland.com; open on weekends in Apr, seven days a week June-Labor Day). Afterward, grab the perfect hot dog, waffle fries, and a lemonade at Nathan's Famous. For some really cheesy thrills, experience the nearby circus sideshow shown on weekends in summer. **FREE**

Discovery Tour of Brooklyn. *49 W 45th St, Brooklyn (10036). Phone 212/397-2600.* Six-hour bus tour to many of Brooklyn's sites and neighborhoods. Departs from Gray Line Bus Terminal in Manhattan. (May-Oct, Thurs and Sat) **$$$$**

Dyker Beach Golf Course. *86th St and 7th Ave, Brooklyn (11228). Phone 718/836-9722.* Easily accessible via public transit, Dyker Beach is inexpensive and should be playable for almost any golfer. It's open year-round and can be busy, but there aren't many trees, and the course offers a few nice views. Dyker Beach was built just before the turn of the 20th century and was redesigned in the 1930s. New Yorkers will tell you that it's a must to play at some point if you live in close proximity to the city. **$$$$**

Gateway National Recreation Area. *Kings Hwy and Flatbush Ave, Brooklyn (11234). Phone 718/338-3338. www.nps.gov/gate/.* One of the nation's first two urban national parks. A barrier peninsula across Rockaway Inlet from Coney Island via Flatbush Ave and the Marine Pkwy Bridge. This sprawling, urban recreation area consists of approximately 26,000 acres of land and water in two states—New York and New Jersey: Floyd Bennett Field in Brooklyn (Jamaica Bay in Brooklyn and Queens), Breezy Point on the Rockaway Peninsula in Queens, Miller Field, and Great Kills Park on southeastern Staten Island and the Sandy Hook Unit in New Jersey. Jamaica Bay Wildlife Refuge in Broad Channel, Queens (9,000 acres) offers wildlife observation and hiking trails. Floyd Bennett Field has nature observation opportunities. Jacob Riis Park in Queens, with a mile-long boardwalk, offers beach

Brooklyn Heights

Brooklyn Heights and Atlantic Avenue provide a wonderful combination of historic Brooklyn (dating to when it was an independent city), fantastic Manhattan skyline views, and some of New York City's best ethnic food and shops.

The best start is to walk from Manhattan over the Brooklyn Bridge—about a 20-minute journey. Started in 1869 and completed in 1883, it was (at that time) the longest suspension bridge in the world (1,600 feet). It is now the oldest existing suspension bridge in America.

Coming off the bridge, follow the right-hand sidewalks onto Adams Street and Cadman Plaza. Walk the length of the Plaza onto Court Street to Brooklyn Borough Hall, a remarkable Beaux Arts building circa 1848. Free tours are offered on Tuesdays at 1 pm. Leave Borough Hall, walking back the way you came, and turn left onto Montague Street. This neighborhood was Manhattan's first "suburb." Montague is the neighborhood's main street, and it holds a potpourri of restaurants, businesses, and shops. At Clinton Street stands St. Ann's Church. The building contains 60 stained-glass windows, the first ever produced in the United States. Follow Clinton one block to Pierrepont Street, turn left, and stop in at the Brooklyn Historical Society (28 Pierrepont). This landmark building houses exhibits on the borough's past, as well as venues for performances and art exhibits.

At the end of Montague walk up onto the Promenade, the tour's highlight. It stretches north for about six blocks and offers fabulous Manhattan views. Exit the Promenade at Pineapple Street. Turn left onto Columbia Heights and walk to Fulton Landing at its end, once a ferry terminal and now the site of Barge Music, classical concerts staged on a barge moored in the river. Turn right onto Old Fulton Street. At 19 Fulton Street, right under the Brooklyn Bridge, is Patsy Grimaldi's, a.k.a. Patsy's Pizza, a family operation that serves what many have called the city's best pizza.

Continue on Old Fulton, which becomes Cadman Plaza West, and turn right on Henry Street. At this point, feel free to wander among the grid of streets—Clinton, Henry, Hicks, Willow, Cranberry, Orange, and Pineapple—to take in the townhouses and wood-framed buildings. More than half of Brooklyn Heights' structures predate the Civil War. On Henry Street, note the St. George Hotel (100 Henry St), a landmark built in 1884. Henry runs some 11 blocks before it intersects Atlantic Avenue. Turn left on Atlantic and enter a frenetic and fascinating world of Middle Eastern stores and restaurants. Be sure to visit Sahadi (187 Atlantic) for a huge choice of fruits, nuts, candies, olives, feta cheese, and grains by the pound; La Bouillabaisse (145 Atlantic) for great seafood; the Moroccan Star (205 Atlantic) for fine Middle Eastern fare; the Waterfront Ale House (155 Atlantic) for microbrew; and, for dessert, either the Damascus Bakery (195 Atlantic)—fantastic pita bread and spinach pies and baklava—or Pete's Ice Cream (185 Atlantic), a shop with superb homemade ice cream and baked goods. For one last place to visit, turn left on Boerum Place and walk two blocks to Schermerhorn Street to the Transit Museum, which explores the city's subway and mass-transit system.

and waterfront activities. Fort Tilden in Queens offers exhibits, nature walks, guided and self-guided tours of old defense batteries, sporting events, and fishing. Canarsie Pier in Brooklyn offers free weekend summer concerts and restaurants. The Staten Island Unit offers hiking trails, organized athletic programs, and recreational activities. Concession services at some units. **FREE**

New York Aquarium. *W 8th St and Surf Ave, Brooklyn (11224). Phone 718/265-3474. www.nyaquarium.org.* A varied collection of marine life that includes sharks, beluga whales, seals, seahorses, jellyfish, penguins, sea otters, and walruses. Dolphin feedings (Apr-Oct, outdoors); sea lion shows. Restaurant. (Opens daily at 10 am; closing times vary by season) **$$$**

New York Transit Museum. *Boerum Pl at Schermerhorn St, Brooklyn Heights (11201). Phone 718/243-8601. www.mta.nyc.ny.us/museum.* Exhibits on the history of the New York City transit system displayed within a 1930s subway station. Subway cars on display, including a 1903 "El" car. Photographs, maps, antique turnstiles. (Tues-Sun; closed holidays) **$$**

Prospect Park. *211 9th Ave, Brooklyn (11215). Bounded by Parkside Ave, Ocean Ave, Flatbush Ave, and Prospect Park W and SW. Phone 718/438-0100. www.prospectpark.org.* Planned by Olmsted and Vaux, designers of Central Park, its 526 acres include the impressive Grand Army Plaza with Memorial Arch (N end of park), the 90-acre Long Meadow, and a 60-acre lake. The Boathouse Visitor Center has information on park history and design; art shows (Apr-Nov). Ball fields, boating, ice rink, bridle paths, tennis courts, bandshell, historic carousel, and the Lefferts Homestead, a 1783 Dutch colonial farmhouse. Directly across Flatbush Ave is

Brooklyn Botanic Garden. *1000 Washington Ave, Brooklyn (11225). Phone 718/623-7200. www.bbg .org.* For a peaceful respite away from Manhattan, hop the 1 or 2 subway to Eastern Parkway in Brooklyn and enjoy a natural wonder: the 52-acre Brooklyn Botanic Garden. It features a gorgeous Japanese garden; the Steinhardt onservatory, which has several greenhouses filled with a variety of plants; and the Fragrance Garden, designed specifically for the blind. There are rose gardens, the annual cherry blossom festival, and many other beautiful sights to behold as well. (Apr-Sept: Tues-Fri 8 am-6 pm, Sat-Sun from 10 am; Oct-Mar: Tues-Fri 8 am-4:30 pm, Sat-Sun from 10 am; closed Jan 1, Thanksgiving, Dec 25) **$**

Brooklyn Museum of Art. *200 Eastern Pkwy, Brooklyn (11238). Phone 718/638-5000. www.brooklynart.org.* Although it's often overlooked by tourists, the Brooklyn Museum of Art is one of the city's foremost art institutions. Similar to the Metropolitan in some ways, it is housed in a lovely Beaux Arts building, with collections spanning virtually the entire history of art. Highlights include a large Egyptian wing, a superb Native American collection, and a major permanent assemblage of contemporary art. In addition to staging some of the more unusual and controversial exhibits in town, the museum also hosts a "First Saturday" series (the first Saturday of every month, 5-11 pm) featuring free concerts, performances, films, dances, and dance lessons. The sculpture garden, with architectural orna-ments from buildings demolished in the New York City area, is a lovely spot. (Wed-Fri 10 am-5 pm, Sat-Sun 11 am-6 pm; closed Jan 1, Thanksgiving, Dec 25) **$$**

Sheepshead Bay. *2575 Coney Island Ave, Brooklyn (11223). Just E and slightly N of Coney Island via Ocean Pkwy or Shore Pkwy. Phone 718/627-6611.* This area has all the requisites of an ocean fishing community: seafood restaurants, clam bars, tackle shops, fishing boats, and some lovely views.

Full-Service Hotel

★ ★ ★ **MARRIOTT BROOKLYN BRIDGE NEW YORK.** *333 Adams St, Brooklyn (11201). Phone 718/246-7000; toll-free 888/436-3759; fax 718/246-0563. www.brooklynmarriott.com.* 376 rooms, 7 story. Check-in 4 pm, check-out 11 am. High-speed Internet access. Restaurant, bar. Indoor pool. Business center. **$$$**

Restaurants

★ ★ **360.** *360 Van Brunt St, Brooklyn (11231). Phone 718/246-0360.* The restaurant 360 is an off-the-beaten-path neighborhood spot that may take a bit of effort to find, but those who persevere will be rewarded. The dining room is marked by artisan woodwork as well as by partner Arnaud Erhart's charming ways that welcome you inside, help you make a wine selection from the mostly organic list, and ensure that your night here is memorable. But the charm doesn't just come from the dining room; the kitchen also doles out the goods in the form of a three-course prix fixe menu that changes daily, with dishes like roasted scallops with leek fondue, hanger steak, and à la carte, wine-friendly bites like oysters and charcuterie. French menu. Dinner. Closed Mon-Wed. Bar. Casual attire. Reservations recommended. Outdoor seating. No credit cards accepted. **$$**

★ **A TABLE.** *171 Lafayette Ave, Brooklyn (11238). Phone 718/935-9121.* A Table offers a charming slice of the Mediterranean just a stone's throw from the Brooklyn Academy of Music in the heart of Fort Greene. Sunny, sponge-painted walls and wide windows (with nooks to curl up in and have a morning snack) give the place breezy warmth, and the communal farmhouse table lends a charming, convivial feel. The menu offers something for everyone, like Argentine shell steak, slow-roasted lamb shank, foie gras, a raw bar, and fish dishes like sea bass. Mediterranean menu. Breakfast, lunch, dinner. Closed Mon. Bar. Casual attire. Reservations recommended. **$$**

★ ★ **AL DI LA TRATTORIA.** *248 Fifth St, Brooklyn (11215). Phone 718/636-8888. www.aldilatrattoria.com.* Al Di La is a charming neighborhood trattoria decorated with antiques and crowded with candlelit tables of locals laughing and inhaling the delicious Venetian cuisine. It is owned by a husband-wife team (he runs the room, she is in the kitchen) who have amassed a strong fan base, making lines inevitable. But patience will pay off, as the daily changing menu from chef Anna Klinger (Lespinasse and San Francisco's La Folie) includes stunning antipasti like grilled sardines with fennel; magnificent pastas like poppy-seeded sweet beet ravioli; and savory main courses like braised rabbit over polenta and roasted monkfish with lemon-rosemary escarole. Italian menu. Dinner. Closed Sun. Bar. Casual attire. Reservations recommended. Valet parking. **$$$**
🅳

★ ★ **ALMA.** *187 Columbia St, Brooklyn (11231). Phone 718/643-5400.* After many years as chef at Zarela (see), one of Manhattan's most popular authentic Mexican restaurants, chef Gary Jacobson dcided to take his soulful chile-laden fare to Brooklyn. At Alma, a bilevel restaurant and bar with a stunning lantern-lit roof deck for dining by skyline, you will find his food has remained as good as it was on Second Avenue. Guacamole; tortillas filled with braised duck; sweet, warm tamales; and tender seafood ceviche make up some of the best appetizers while generous entrées include dishes like ancho chile rellenos stuffed with shredded pork, raisins, and green olives. Mexican menu. Dinner, brunch. Bar. Business casual attire. Reservations recommended. Valet parking. Outdoor seating. **$$**

★ ★ **BLUE RIBBON BROOKLYN.** *280 Fifth Ave, Brooklyn (11215). Phone 718/840-0404.* Set in a former grocery store in Park Slope, Blue Ribbon Brooklyn is a sleek, bustling and expansive, brick-colored bistro with a well-stocked raw bar—just like its next door sibling, Blue Ribbon Sushi (see). But in addition, this branch also offers the owners' (brothers Bruce and Eric Bromberg) signature overly ambitious menu filled with all sorts of deliciously comforting dishes—marrow bones, chicken liver, variations on surf and turf, famous fried chicken, and plates of golden fries piled sky-high. Like the New York branch, the restaurant is open until 4 am to satisfy all those late-night hunger pangs. American menu. Breakfast (Sun), dinner, late-night. Children's menu. Casual attire. **$$**

★ ★ **BLUE RIBBON SUSHI.** *278 Fifth Ave, Brooklyn (11215). Phone 718/840-0408.* Blue Ribbon Sushi is the beloved Brooklyn sibling of the brothers Bromberg's Blue Ribbon Sushi in the city. Located on a thriving strip of Fifth Avenue in Park Slope, this lively wood-accented restaurant and sushi bar offers the same winning formula the Brombergs offer in Manhattan—just to larger crowds, thanks to easier access to real estate. Expect the best raw fish in town, warm and knowledgeable service, and a tremendous selection of sake—but not a table after 7 pm without a wait. Japanese, sushi menu. Dinner, late-night. Closed Mon. Children's menu. Casual attire. **$$$**

★ ★ **BONITA.** *338 Bedford Ave, Williamsburg (11211). Phone 718/384-9500.* Although Bonita can get very crowded, you will still be happy you came to this happenin' little eatery that serves top-notch authentic Mexican fare in a lively diner-esque setting. Owned by the folks who own Diner (see), also in the youthful hipster land of Williamsburg, Bonita serves spot-on tapas-style Mexican fare including a vibrant, chile-studded guacamole, a hefty torta, and a mean mole. The vibe is cool and slick yet the service is friendly and efficient with no 'tude. Mexican menu. Lunch, dinner. Closed Mon. Bar. Casual attire. Valet parking. **$$**
🅳

★ ★ **CHESTNUT.** *271 Smith St, Brooklyn (11231). Phone 718/243-0049.* Chestnut, a cozy newcomer to Cobble Hill's restaurant row (Smith Street), is already winning fans from the 'hood and from Manhattan. With its wide French doors, high blond chestnut-beamed ceilings, and raw slate-tiled walls, the restaurant is a warm, lively gathering place that makes you feel like staying a long while. The talented kitchen turns out a menu of honest and delicious food with ingredients that shine, and plates that are filled with smart, creative, and well-articulated flavors. The menu features rustic dishes like chicken liver and apple toast as well as more elegant dishes like tea-smoked scallops with fingerling potatoes and sweet-hot mustard, and comforting plates like roasted organic chicken with artichokes and soft polenta. American menu. Dinner. Closed Mon. Bar. Casual attire. Reservations recommended. Outdoor seating. **$$**

★ ★ **CHICKENBONE CAFÉ.** *177 S 4th St, Williamsburg (11211). Phone 718/302-2663.* Chickenbone Café, a slickly rustic, inviting, wood-paneled hang in Williamsburg, is constantly buzzing from the moment it opens early in the evening to the

minute it closes in the early hours of the morning (when it is still bursting at the seams with young, sexy, and hip locals). The reason for its mass appeal is the irresistible, modestly priced, international menu of small plates, sandwiches, salads, soups, and sweets made from sustainably-grown, local ingredients. This is the sort of tasty fare that you'll want to feast on every day. There's a Vietnamese sausage sandwich that gives sweet and hot taste buds a thrilling twister ride, a tartiflette that clogs arteries with delight, and a slab of cashmere-like foie gras tourchon that brings a calm sense of bliss to the whole body. American menu. Dinner, late-night. Bar. Casual attire. Valet parking. **$$**
🄳

★ ★ **CONVIVIUM OSTERIA.** *68 Fifth Ave, Brooklyn (11217). Phone 718/857-1833.* Convivium Osteria is a local gem serving some of the most soul-satisfying Mediterranean fare in the borough, if not all of New York City. With a setting straight out of a hillside in Tuscany, the restaurant is all aglow in candlelight and a rustic, distressed vintage design that makes you feel like it's been here forever. The menu is stocked with country-style dishes from Spain, Portugal, and Italy that focus on robust flavors in casseroles, as well as earthy pastas, slow-cooked meats, and plentiful amounts of preserved, cured, and smoked ingredients—think salt cod and lots of delicious pig parts. Mediterranean menu. Dinner. Casual attire. Outdoor seating. **$$**

★ ★ ★ **CUCINA.** *256 Fifth Ave, Brooklyn (11215). Phone 718/230-0711; fax 718/230-0124. www.cucina restaurant.com.* Cucina was one of the first restaurants to brave the Brooklyn neighborhood of Park Slope, and years later it is still wooing neighborhood regulars and Manhattanites alike with its warm and elegant setting and refined menu of sumptuous Italian fare. The restaurant is decorated with old-world tapestries and warm ocher walls, giving it a sort of Italian Renaissance-styled elegance. While the menu features outstanding pasta, the kitchen is also savvy with seafood—like salt cod and salmon—and features a lengthy and wonderful list of antipasti to make the wait for the main courses quite enjoyable, indeed. Italian menu. Dinner. Closed Mon; Thanksgiving, Dec 25. Bar. Children's menu. Reservations recommended. Valet parking. **$$$**
🄳

★ **DIFARA'S PIZZERIA.** *1424 Avenue J, Brooklyn (11230). Phone 718/392-1222.* Heading out to the recesses of Brooklyn may not be on your list of things to do for something as seemingly ordinary as a slice of pizza, but DiFara's pizza is the one of those handmade slices that warrants a visit. Tucked into a residential stretch of Avenue J, you'll find pizza-man Dominick DeMarco flipping his signature Neapolitan pies as he has been for decades. He tops them with basil grown in the window, a drizzle of extra-virgin olive oil, tomato sauce, and gooey lumps of mozzarella. A dusting of hand-grated Parmesan is the final touch on the masterpiece that is DiFara's Pizza. Pizza. Lunch, dinner. Bar. Casual attire. **$**
🄳

★ **DINER.** *85 Broadway, Williamsburg (11211). Phone 718/486-3077.* Williamsburg hipsters flock to Diner like ants to a picnic. Indeed, this place often feels like a zoo for young, thrift-store clad locals. Set in a loungy, refurbished dining car, this bar and restaurant is a mess hall for struggling writers, actors, musicians, and the like. The menu is a fun selection of contemporary American dishes including juicy burgers, platters of charcuterie, fresh salads, crisp and golden fries, and hearty sandwiches stuffed with seasonal ingredients. American menu. Lunch, dinner, late-night, brunch. Casual attire. **$$**

★ **GRIMALDI'S PIZZERIA.** *19 Old Fulton St, Brooklyn (11201). Phone 718/858-4300.* In Brooklyn, Grimaldi's is synonymous with pizza. And not just any old pizza by the slice, but thin-crusted, piping hot pizza pies layered with milky house-made mozzarella, bright tomato sauce, and vibrant strips of zingy basil. The restaurant is decorated in casual pizzeria style with gingham-printed tablecloths and the requisite Sinatra soundtrack playing in the background. Aside from the basic tomato, mozzarella, and basil pies, you can choose your own mess of toppings from a wide list that includes spicy sausage, house-roasted peppers, spinach, and mushrooms. Pizza. Lunch, dinner. Bar. Children's menu. Casual attire. **$**
🄳

★ ★ ★ **THE GROCERY.** *288 Smith St, Brooklyn (11231). Phone 718/596-3335.* When husband-wife team Charlie Kiely and Sharon Patcher—chef-veterans of the New York restaurant scene—opened The Grocery, an intimate spot on Smith Street with a leafy back patio and yard, they had no idea that they would inspire a cult following. This stylish, earth-toned dining room has a serene vibe, and the delicious food coming out of the tiny kitchen makes the 13-table space all the more exquisite, with dishes that mirror the seasons. There's not a plate on the menu that won't make your mouth water. Seasons dictate the menu, but star dishes include brook trout with spinach and bacon-flecked spaetzle, ratatouille-stuffed squid, roasted beets with goat cheese ravioli, duck confit with roasted quince sauce, and pork loin with sweet potatoes and roasted pears. Get ready to fall in love with dining in Brooklyn. American menu. Dinner. Closed Sun. Bar. Casual attire. Outdoor seating. **$$$**

★ ★ M SHANGHAI BISTRO & DEN. *138 Havemeyer St, Brooklyn (11211). Phone 718/384-9300.* M Shanghai is not your average Chinese restaurant. Decorated in a slinky style, with chocolate brown banquet tables, brick walls, and a moody soundtrack, M is a lovely den of design and food, graciously presided over by owner May Liu. The menu also sets itself apart from the fray with vibrant dishes of steamed dumplings and puffy pork buns, and deliciously flavored main courses like shredded pork with bean curd and salmon with smooth and well-seasoned tofu sauce. Once you are through with dinner, head down to the hopping downstairs lounge. Chinese menu. Dinner, late-night. Closed Mon. Bar. Casual attire. **$$**

★ ★ MISS WILLIAMSBURG DINER. *206 Kent Ave, Williamsburg (11211). Phone 718/963-0802.* This vintage 1940s boxcar diner is a charming old-timer with brushed aluminum siding, distressed leather banquettes, and swivel stools under a Formica counter. The place feels like something out of an old movie and transports you back in time. The menu takes its cues from Italy, and owner Max Bartoli presents a reasonably priced, market-driven menu of Mediterranean-inspired small plates like fontina bruschetta with zucchini puree, as well as hearty plates like grilled pork chops, and gorgeous pastas like beet ravioli with lemon sauce and lasagna oozing with a sinfully hearty ragu. Italian menu. Dinner. Closed Mon. Bar. Casual attire. Reservations recommended. **$$**

★ ★ PATOIS. *255 Smith St, Brooklyn (11231). Phone 718/855-1535.* Restaurant Row in Cobble Hill is Smith Street, and Patois is one of this hopping street's original destinations for flavorful French fare served in a warm bistro setting. Patois overflows with charm from its saffron-colored walls, open kitchen, and delightful Provençal-style garden. The menu is

classic French (think steak frites), with a little bit of Morocco thrown in for good measure in dishes like lamb sausage with couscous and nectarine chutney. The weekend brunch is a zoo, so grab a mimosa or an espresso and get ready to wait in line. French menu. Dinner, Sun brunch. Closed Mon. Casual attire. Outdoor seating. **$$**

★ ★ ★ PETER LUGER STEAK HOUSE. *178 Broadway, Brooklyn (11211). Phone 718/387-7400; fax 718/387-3523. www.peterluger.com.* Peter Luger Steak House is the stuff legends are made of. This landmark restaurant has been serving juicy porterhouse steaks since 1887 and is still one of the city's top tables. Don't expect elegant surroundings with your expertly charred dry-aged slab of beef, though. This place is bare bones, with exposed beamed ceilings, worn tables and chairs, and waiters that are as well seasoned as the beef. In addition to the gorgeously marbled steaks, you can dig into sides like German-fried potatoes and creamed spinach. If you make it over for lunch you can wrap your hands around New York's best burger, made from fresh ground beef and served with slices of tearjerker raw onion and a thick beefsteak tomato. Steak menu. Lunch, dinner. Bar. Casual attire. Reservations recommended. **$$$$**

★ PIER 116. *116 Smith St, Brooklyn (11201). Phone 718/260-8900.* Pier 116 is a great neighborhood seafood pub that instantly transports you to the windswept New England Coast. Come inside and you'll feel immediately at home amongst the crowds of happy families sitting elbow to elbow with vintage-clad locals. The menu serves up that sand-in-your-toes feeling all year long, with fat, sea-salty steamers served in pails; succulent, meaty lobster rolls; crunchy buttermilk fried chicken; and meaty, flavorful baby-back ribs. To prevent choking on all this lip-licking seashore grub, the Pier keeps a terrific selection of ice-cold brews on tap like Dogfish Head Indian Brown Ale, Old Speckled Hen, and Stone Smoked Porter. American, seafood menu. Lunch, dinner. Bar. Casual attire. Outdoor seating. **$$**

★ ★ RELISH. *225 Wythe Ave, Brooklyn (11211). Phone 718/963-4546.* At Relish, a sleek, refurbished railcar diner, you can dig into contemporary Southern fare in style. This former dining car is now a bright, stylish, windowed hang, offering regional comfort food like macaroni and cheese, hearty cheeseburgers, and rich, smoked pork loin with spiced mango

chutney. Relish is also quite the popular spot on weekends, when the crowds line up for the eggs with Serrano ham and cheddar grits. American menu. Lunch, dinner. Bar. Casual attire. **$$**

★ ★ ★ **RIVER CAFE.** *1 Water St, Brooklyn (11201). Phone 718/522-5200; fax 718/875-0037. www.rivercafe.com.* If romance is on the evening's agenda, The River Café should be as well. Located on the Brooklyn waterfront, with the an unmatched view of the East River and the twinkling Manhattan skyline, this elegant old-timer has always been a favorite for celebrating special occasions and for creating reasons to celebrate new ones. The kitchen is skilled at sophisticated New American fare like lobster, rack of lamb, and duck, artistically plated so as to inspire oohs and aaahs. The wine list is award winning, the service is graceful and unobtrusive, and is practiced at staying away when not needed, so as to let the romance bloom. American menu. Lunch, dinner. Bar. Jacket required. Reservations recommended. Valet parking. Outdoor seating. **$$$$**

★ ★ **SAUL.** *140 Smith St, Brooklyn (11201). Phone 718/935-9844.* Restaurant Saul is one of those truly inviting spots that every neighborhood craves. Known for its terrific New American fare—courtesy of chef/owner Saul Bolton—Saul is urbane in décor, with warm, sandy tones and exposed brick walls. The modest menu reflects Bolton's training at Le Bernardin (see); expect plates adorned with stunning seasonal ingredients and simple, flavorful preparations of everything from diver scallops, to leg of lamb, duck confit, and foie gras. Don't forget to have dessert; Saul is known for its sweets, especially the classic baked Alaska. American menu. Dinner, Sun brunch. Bar. Casual attire. **$$**

★ ★ **SEA.** *114 N 6th St, Brooklyn (11211). Phone 718/384-8850.* Sea is known just as much for its wild Zen-inspired disco décor (complete with an in-ground pool watched over by a golden Buddha) as it is for its fiery Thai fare. Often crowded and loud, with fast servers who are interested in turning tables, Sea is not a peaceful place to dine, but it is a tasty one. The menu includes dishes like whole red snapper, rice paper-wrapped spring rolls, and a fun list of desserts like the crispy banana with green tea ice cream. The cocktail list guarantees a hangover with easy-to-imbibe drinks like the spicy pineapple-ginger martini. Thai menu. Lunch, dinner, late-night. Bar. Casual attire. Reservations recommended. **$$**

★ ★ **SUPERFINE.** *126 Front St, Brooklyn (11201). Phone 718/243-9005.* Located in DUBMO, Superfine is a casual neighborhood eatery with a warm, earthy vibe marked by brick walls, high ceilings, stunning flower arrangements, and views of the Manhattan Bridge. The kitchen boasts some serious skills, turning out robust Texas-style fare like seared duck breast with rutabaga and sliced shiitake mushrooms, and grilled pork chops with mashed potatoes and bitter greens. The menu of easy-to-love eats has the place packed with kids and families and hot crop of locals. On Sundays, brunch gets a pick-me-up from a bluegrass band and burritos laced with eggs, refried beans, and zesty salsa. American menu. Lunch, dinner, Sun brunch. Closed Mon. Bar. Casual attire. **$$**

Queens, NY

2 hours, 112 miles from Hartford, CT

Area Code 718

By far the largest borough geographically, Queens occupies 121 square miles of Long Island. Like Brooklyn, it was assembled from a number of small towns, and each of these neighborhoods has retained a strong sense of identity. Parts of the borough are less densely settled than Brooklyn, and the majority of Queens's population are homeowners. Many manufacturing plants, warehouses, and shipping facilities are in the portion called Long Island City, near the East River. Forest Hills, with its West Side Tennis Club, at Tennis Place and Burns Street, is a world-famous center for tennis. Flushing Meadows Corona Park has been the site of two world's fairs; many facilities still stand.

Public Transportation

Subway and elevated trains, buses (New York Transit Authority), phone 718/330-3322 or 718/330-1234.

Airports LaGuardia. Information 718/476-5000; lost and found 718/533-3988; cash machines, upper level Main Terminal, Finger 4, Delta Terminal. **Kennedy.** Information 718/656-4444; lost and found 718/244-3225.

Web Sites LaGuardia www.panynj.gov/aviation/lagframe.HTM; Kennedy www.panynj.gov/aviation/jfkframe.HTM

Airlines LaGuardia. Air Canada, Air China, Air Tran Airways, American, American Eagle, ATA, Colgan, Comair, Continental, Continental Express, Delta, Delta Connection, Delta Shuttle, Frontier Airlines, Midwest, Northwest, Song, Spirit, United, United Express, US Airways, US Airways Express, US Airways Shuttle. **Kennedy.** Aer Lingus, Aeroflot, Aerolineas Argentinas, Aeromar, Aero Mexico, AeroSvit, Air Canada, Air China, Air France, Air India, Air Jamaica, Air MaltaAir Plus Comet, Air Santo Domingo, Alitalia, Allegro, America West, Asiana Austrian Airlines, Avianca, Biman Bangladesh, British Airways, BWIA, Cathay Pacific, China Airlines, Continental, Continental Express, Corsair, Czech Airlines, Delta Air Lines, Delta Connection, Delta Express, Egyptair El Al, Finnair, Ghana Airways, Iberia, Icelandair, Japan Airlines, jetBlue KLM Royal Dutch, Korean Air, Kuwait Airways, Lacsa, Lan Chile, Lan Ecuador Lan Peru, Lot Polish, Lufthansa, Malev Hungarian, Miami Air (charter), North American, Northwest, Olympic, PACE Airlines, Pakistan International Airlines Qantas, Royal Air Maroc, Royal Jordanian, Saudi Arabian Airlines, Song, South African Airways, Sun Country, Swiss International Air Lines, TACA International, TACV Cabo Verde, Tarom Romanian, Thai Airways International, Turkish, United Airlines, Universal, Uzbekistan, VARIG, Virgin Atlantic.

What to See and Do

American Museum of the Moving Image. *35th Ave and 36th St, Astoria (11106). Phone 718/784-0077. www.ammi.org.* On the site of historic Astoria Studios, where many classic early movies were filmed. Museum is devoted to the art and history of film, television, and video and their effects on American culture. Permanent and changing exhibitions; two theaters with film and video series (screenings weekends). (Wed-Thurs noon-5 pm, Fri to 8 pm, Sat-Sun 11 am-6:30 pm; closed holidays). **$$**

Astoria. *At the NW tip of Queens. Phone 718/286-2667. www.queens.nyc.us.* Experience your own Big Fat Greek Wedding in this Hellenic community, just 15 minutes from Midtown Manhattan, which offers the best Greek food this side of Athens. Astoria has an estimated Greek population of 70,000—the largest community outside of Greece—which means that the area is alive with music, culture, and melt-in-your mouth saganaki and baklava. Food markets, gift shops, bakeries, restaurants, and intimate cafés await your shopping and dining pleasure. Finish your excursion by relaxing on a nice, sunny day with a cup of Greek

coffee in nearby Astoria Park and take in a great view of upper Manhattan. If you want to combine this Greek experience with other area attractions, the **American Museum of the Moving Image** (phone 718/784-0077) and the historic **Kaufman Astoria Motion Picture Studios** (phone 718/392-5600) are located in Astoria. This fun neighborhood proves that there *is* life in the outer boroughs of New York City.

Bowne House. *37-01 Bowne St, Flushing (11354). Phone 718/359-0528.* (1661) One of the oldest houses in New York City was built by John Bowne, a Quaker who led a historic struggle for religious freedom under Dutch rule; 17th- to 19th-century furnishings. (Tues, Sat, and Sun afternoons; closed Easter and mid-Dec-mid-Jan) Under 12 admitted only with adult. **$**

Clearview Golf Course. *202-12 Willets Point Blvd, Flushing (11360). Phone 718/229-2570.* Clearview is recognized as a good course for beginners in the New York area, and because of this it's very popular. You can expect your round to take a little longer than normal, but the price won't break the bank. The rough is deep, but if you can keep your shots straight, you can avoid it. A par-70 course, Clearview plays just over 6,200 yards from the back tees, but that belies the challenge of the narrow fairways. Enjoy an inexpensive round of golf with your friends, as you'll have some time to chat while you wait for the group ahead of you. **$$$$**

Flushing Meadows-Corona Park. *Flushing and Metropolitan aves, Flushing (11368). Grand Central Pkwy to Van Wyck Expy and Union Tpke to Northern Blvd. Phone 718/217-6034.* Originally a marsh, this 1,255-acre area became the site of two World's Fairs (1939-1940 and 1964-1965). It is now the home of the United States Tennis Association National Tennis Center, where the US Open is held annually (phone 718/760-6200). The park is also the site of some of the largest cultural and ethnic festivals in the city. Facilities include an indoor ice rink, carousel, 87-acre Meadow Lake, and the Playground for All Children, designed for disabled and able-bodied children. Park rangers conduct occasional weekend tours. Also on the grounds are

> **New York Hall of Science.** *47-01 111th St, Flushing (11368). 111th St and 48th Ave. Phone 718/699-0005. www.nyhallsci.org.* Exhibition hall with hands-on science and technology exhibits. (Sept-June: Tues-Thurs 9:30 am-2 pm, Fri to 5 pm, Sat-Sun noon-5 pm; July-Aug: Mon 9:30 am-2 pm,

Tues-Fri to 5 pm, Sat-Sun 10:30 am-6 pm; closed holidays) Free admission Thurs and Fri afternoons. **$$$**

The Queens Museum of Art. *New York Building, 25th Ave and 76th St, Flushing (11368). Phone 718/592-9700. www.queensmuseum.org.* Interdisciplinary fine arts presentations, major traveling exhibitions; permanent collection includes 9,000-square-foot panorama of New York City, the world's largest three-dimensional architectural model. (Sept-June: Wed-Fri 10 am-5 pm, Sat-Sun from noon, Jul-Aug: Wed-Sun 1-8 pm; closed holidays) **$**

Shea Stadium. *126th St and Roosevelt Ave, Flushing (11368). Phone 718/507-6387. www.mets.com.* Home of the New York Mets. **$$$$**

Isamu Noguchi Garden Museum. *36-01 43rd Ave, Long Island City (11101). Phone 718/204-7088. www.noguchi.org.* Sculpture fans will want to visit the Isamu Noguchi Museum, just a short trip from Manhattan. Housed in the sculptor's former studio, complete with an outdoor sculpture garden, the museum is filled with Noguchi stone, metal, and woodwork. (Apr-Nov; Mon, Thurs, Fri 10 am-5 pm; Sat-Sun 10 am-6 pm; closed Tues, Wed) **DONATION**

P. S. 1 Contemporary Art Center. *22-25 Jackson Ave, Long Island City, L.I. (11101). At 46th Ave. Phone 718/784-2084. www.ps1.org.* A premier center for art on the cutting edge; specializes in the avant-garde, conceptual, and experimental; housed in a newly renovated, four-story building that was once a public school; changing exhibits. (Mon, Thurs-Sun; closed holidays) **$$**

Queens Botanical Garden. *43-50 Main St, Flushing (11355). Phone 718/886-3800. www.queensbotanical.org.* Collections include large rose, herb, Victorian wedding, bee, woodland, and bird gardens and an arboretum. (Tues-Sun) **DONATION**

Union Street. *Union and Main sts, Flushing (11367). Take the 7 subway to Main Street, the last stop.* This section of Flushing, located one long block past Main Street, is home a large, culture-rich Korean community. Tiny shops feature American and Korean clothing and wedding gowns from both cultures. Gift shops sell miniature collectibles, and food markets offer exotic foods and spices. Korean restaurants serve traditional barbecue dishes and other items. In addition to being easy on the wallet, many eateries are open 24 hours a day to satisfy late-night cravings.

Special Events

Aqueduct. *11000 Rockaway Blvd, South Ozone Park (11420). Take the A train to the Aqueduct stop. Phone 718/641-4700. www.nyra.com/aqueduct.* Yes, people actually do take the A train! Hop on the subway for a short ride out to Queens for an afternoon of thoroughbred races, held from late October through early May. Races take place Wednesday through Sunday and begin at 1 pm. The track also has pretty lawns and gardens that come alive in spring. You can't beat the cheap admission price, so splurge a little and place some bets. Gates open at 11 am. **$**

Belmont Park. *2150 Hempstead Tpke, Elmont (11003). Just outside of Queens in Nassau County, on Cross Island Pkwy via Hempstead Tpke and Plainfield Ave. Phone 516/488-6000. www.nyra.com/belmont.* This 430-acre racetrack is the home of the third jewel in horse racing's Triple Crown, the Belmont Stakes. This major spectacle is held in June and attracts gamblers, horse lovers, and spectators from all walks of life. It's one of the oldest annual sporting events in the nation, so make your plans in advance and reserve seats early. Hopefully, you will get a good-weather day on which to enjoy this event. The regular season racing at Belmont Park is from May through July and from September through October. Sundays are Family Fun Days; kids can play in the playground in the Backyard area. (Wed-Sun, May-July and Sept-Oct) **$**

P. S. 1 Contemporary Art Center—Warm Up Music Series. *22-25 Jackson Ave, Long Island City (11101). Phone 718/784-2084. www.ps1.org.* This new-wave community arts center in Queens attracts the hippest of DJs and crowds to its Saturday afternoon/evening outdoor dance parties in its courtyard. You won't see dance parties like these anywhere else. All ages are welcome. You'll see a variety of social butterflies and some pretty good dancers here. The center is a short subway or cab ride from Manhattan, and you can't beat the price—so join in the fun. July-Aug; Sat evenings. **$$**

US Open Tennis. *Flushing Meadows-Corona Park, USTA National Tennis Center, Flushing (11351). Take the 7 subway to the Willets Point-Shea Stadium stop. Phone 718/760-6200. www.usopen.org.* Tennis fans from near and far flock to the US Open tennis tournament each September. You can see your favorite players, the stars of tomorrow, and a host of celebrities in the audience at this upper-crust sporting event. Tickets go on sale in late May or by the beginning of June, and those matches held closer to the finals sell out first. Purchase tickets as early as possible. Buying a ticket to the Arthur Ashe Stadium, the main court, gives you admission to all the other courts on the grounds. However, these seats tend to be more in the back, since the better seats go to corporate sponsors. Bring a pad to keep your own score, binoculars, sunscreen, and sunglasses for day games. Late Aug-early Sept.

Limited-Service Hotel

★ ★ **HOLIDAY INN.** *14402 135th Ave, Jamaica (11436). Phone 718/659-0200; toll-free 800/692-5359; fax 718/322-2533. www.holiday-inn.com.* 360 rooms, 12 story. Check-out noon. Restaurant, bar. Fitness room. Indoor pool, whirlpool. Airport transportation available. **$$**

Full-Service Hotel

★ ★ ★ **CROWNE PLAZA HOTEL NEW YORK-LAGUARDIA AIRPORT.** *104-04 Ditmars Blvd, East Elmhurst (11369). Phone 718/457-6300; toll-free 800/ 227-6963; fax 718/899-9768. www.crowneplaza.com.* 358 rooms, 7 story. Check-in 4 pm, check-out noon. Restaurant, bar. Fitness room. Indoor pool. **$$**

Restaurants

★ ★ **CAVO.** *4218 31st Ave, Astoria (11103). Phone 718/721-1001.* Joining the ranks of the non-Greek restaurants in Astoria, Cavo is a sprawling Mediterranean spot with a stone patio and a wonderful, wide garden that will leave you wanting to set up camp in the backyard and never leave. The menu features all the wonders of the Mediterranean, from assorted savory pastas to whole fish with lemon and herbs, rack of lamb, and assorted mezze to start. Cavo attracts a local crowd but also pulls in guests from the city, giving new meaning to "Bridge and Tunnel." Mediterranean menu. Dinner, late-night. Bar. Casual attire. Reservations recommended. Outdoor seating. **$$**

★ ★ **CHRISTOS HASAPO-TAVERNA.** *41-08 23rd Ave, Astoria (11105). Phone 718/726-5195. www.christossteakhouse.com.* Christos Hasapo is a restaurant with dual personalities, and both are wonderful. By day, locals crowd into this butcher shop to purchase their day's beef. But at night, the shop turns into a Greek steakhouse, serving Astoria's finest selection of beef, prepared simply and perfectly every time. This lovely Greek taverna makes you feel like you are in Athens, and the wine list is surprisingly terrific, making a trip from the city a great idea. Greek menu. Lunch, dinner. Bar. Casual attire. Outdoor seating. **$$$**

★ ★ **CINA.** *45-17 28th Ave, Astoria (11103). Phone 718/956-0372.* If you've ever wondered what sort of dinners people have in Romania, this Romanian bistro, with a lively staff and a convivial vibe, will answer all your questions. First on the menu would be steak—and lots of it—grilled to juicy perfection. Then there might be some polenta topped with sour cream and perhaps some grated feta. Cina features both of these dishes and more, like sausages, spicy stuffed cabbage, and, for fearless eaters, a deep-fried Cornish hen. And if you thought American donuts were good, try the papanasi—fried lumps of yeasty dough topped with, you guessed it, sour cream. Romanian menu. Lunch, dinner. Casual attire. Reservations recommended. **$$**

★ ★ **COOKING WITH JAZZ.** *12-01 154th St, Whitestone (11357). Phone 718/767-6979. www.cwj.net.* Cooking with Jazz is a spirited restaurant that brings a bit of New Orleans to the modest hamlet known as Queens. From the vibrant and festive décor to the enthusiastic and well-informed staff to the creative Cajun menu, this homey freestanding restaurant is bursting with energy and robust cooking. The chef/owner is a Paul Prudhomme protégé, and his training shows in classics like chicken jambalaya, a rich and smoky stew stocked with blackened chicken and meaty Andouille sausage. If you're feeling adventurous, try some alligator, which can be found in fritters or in sausage. Cajun/Creole menu. Dinner. Closed Sun-Mon. Casual attire. No credit cards accepted. **$$**

★ **ELIAS CORNER.** *24-02 31st St, Astoria (11102). Phone 718/932-1510.* Elias Corner is not easy on the eyes. The restaurant, a cult favorite, is a bit garish, decked out in all turquoise, and is far from subtle in the décor department. But the blinding color scheme does not seem to deter the herds of folks who come here to feast on the restaurant's standout Greek fare. If you can stand the wait (the line is usually out the door), you will be treated to a wonderful meal, cooked from whatever is in the refrigerated deli case at the front of the restaurant. Usually, that includes some sort of fish, lamb, and, of course, a selection of mezze with warm, puffy pita. Greek menu. Dinner. Casual attire. Outdoor seating. No credit cards accepted. **$$**

★ ★ **IL TOSCANO.** *42-05 235th St, Douglaston (11363). Phone 718/631-0300; fax 718/225-5223.* Italian menu. Dinner. Closed Mon, Dec 25. Bar. Casual attire. Reservations recommended. Valet parking. **$$$**

★ **JACKSON DINER.** *37-47 74th St, Jackson Heights (11372). Phone 718/672-1232.* Bright, open, and airy, the Jackson Diner has been a Queens favorite for years, serving authentic Indian cuisine in a bright and casual setting. The enormous buffet lunch is a steal, and the à la carte dinner menu is a terrific taste of the kitchen's talents: yogurt-marinated lamb chops, assorted dosas, and tasty appetizers to share among the table, like coconut-flecked chicken, fried fish, and flaky samosas. Indian menu. Lunch, dinner. Casual attire. No credit cards accepted. **$**

★ **KABAB CAFE.** *25-12 Steinway St, Astoria (11103). Phone 718/728-9858.* Kabab Café may not look like much from the outside, but on the inside, it's a different story. For instance, it takes your basic mezze trio—baba ganoush, hummus, and tahini—and makes them shine. Creamy, spicy, zesty, and ridiculously good, the mezze here are truly remarkable, reaching beyond the ordinary trio to more exotic treats like eggah (an Egyptian omelette), foul (a white bean salad with puréed tomatoes, lemon juice, spices, and olive oil), and a crunchy fava bean falafel. In addition to the stellar spreads (served with delicious fresh-from-the-oven bread), you can feast on larger dishes like slow-cooked lamb shank and sautéed calf's liver. Middle Eastern menu. Lunch, dinner. Closed Mon. Casual attire. No credit cards accepted. **$**

★ **KHAO HOMM.** *39-28 61st St, Woodside (11377). Phone 718/205-0080; fax 718/205-0048.* This fresh and fun Thai restaurant comes complete with a spirited menu, a talented and accommodating kitchen, gracious service, karaoke machines, and a loyal clientele. What sets Khao Homm apart, though, is perhaps its willingness to cook dishes that are not on the menu. But more than likely, you won't have to bother the kitchen, as the menu offers tasty options like fried whole fish topped with papaya, roasted cashews, and a sweet-and-sour vinegar sauce and pad kee mao—broad noodles coated in chiles and basil. Thai menu. Lunch, dinner. Casual attire. **$**

★ **KUM GANG SAN.** *138-28 Northern Blvd, Flushing (11354). Phone 718/461-0909.* Kum Gang San, a Korean barbecue, sushi, and seafood stalwart, never closes. If you'd like to perform your own *Survivor,* try to stay for all 24 hours. You could spend part of the day hanging out by the indoor waterfall while having a lunch of blistering barbecue, crisped scallion and seafood pancakes, and pungent kimchi. Then you could move over to the sushi bar for an afternoon snack, and for dinner, take a stab at plates of panchan—Korean-style tapas-like crab claw with hot pepper and soy-marinated shortribs. And in the wee hours, you might join the late-night revelers and watch the fresh fish coming in from the seafood markets. Korean menu. Lunch, dinner, late-night. Casual attire. **$$**

★ ★ **MANDUCATIS.** *13-27 Jackson Ave, Long Island City (11101). Phone 718/729-4602; fax 718/361-0411.* Sure, Manhattan boasts some fairly impressive Italian eateries, but one of the best-hidden treasures is located in Queens. Owned by Vicenzo Cerbone, Manducatis is a family-run operation serving the home-style dishes of Italy's best mamas. The terra-cotta room has an earthy, countryside appeal, as does the menu. Expect delicate homemade pastas topped with soft pillows of milky mozzarella. The kitchen also turns out lovely fish and meat dishes and has an extensive wine list that includes many rare wines from small producers. In the winter, grab a seat by the blazing fireplace and you will be transported to the mountains of Tuscany. Italian menu. Lunch, dinner. Closed holidays; also the last two weeks in Aug. Bar. **$$**

★ ★ **MOMBAR.** *2522 Steinway St, Astoria (11103). Phone 718/726-2356.* Mombar is a warm, family-owned Egyptian restaurant with a big heart. Owned by artist and chef Moustafa El Sayed and run by his wife and family, the restaurant is decorated with his stunning handmade tile work, mix-and-match wooden tables, and comfy, pillow-filled banquettes. El Sayed is there all the time, to cook, to chat, and to guide you through a meal you will never forget. While his menu changes daily, you can't go wrong with the mezze plate or any of his clay pot stews: Moulekaya, an aromatic stew made from Egyptian greens with braised rabbit or chicken, or the fragrant, soft lamb pulled from a tagine filled with a messy stew of raisins, almonds, and olives. Meals end with tea—served in old-world tea glasses—and dense little powdered sugar-coated nut cookies. Middle Eastern menu. Dinner. Closed Mon. Children's menu. Casual attire. No credit cards accepted. **$$**

★ ★ **PARK SIDE.** *107-01 Corona Ave, Corona (11368). Phone 718/271-9274; fax 718/271-2454.* If you try to imagine what *My Big Fat Greek Wedding* would have been like with an Italian family, you'll get an idea of what dinner is like at Park Side, a lively, boisterous restaurant in Queens that serves hearty portions of Italian food. The waiters give the place an old-school vibe, all dressed in black suits, while the dining room feels like an ornate catering hall filled with large parties and the occasional celebrity. The menu is straight-ahead and delicious Italian—think spicy red sauce, big steaks, giant orders of fill-in-the-blank-parmigiana, and heaping bowls of risotto, in addition to a superb hot and cold antipasti selection. Italian menu. Lunch, dinner. Bar. Valet parking. Outdoor seating. **$$**

★ ★ ★ **PICCOLA VENEZIA.** *42-01 28th Ave, Astoria (11103). Phone 718/721-8470; fax 718/721-2110. www.piccola-venezia.com.* There are only a few reasons to leave the island of Manhattan. One is baseball. (Yankees and Mets games both require a trip through a bridge or tunnel.) Another is Piccola Venezia, an old-world trattoria offering authentic northern Italian fare in the humble borough of Queens. Located in Astoria since 1973, Piccola Venezia is a family-run operation that features delicious homemade pastas and a generous menu of salads, antipasti, seafood, meat, and game prepared with imported ingredients and a strong nod to the wonderful culinary traditions of northern Italy. Italian menu. Lunch, dinner. Closed Tues; Jan 1, Dec 25; also late July-late Aug. Valet parking. **$$$**

★ ★ **PING'S SEAFOOD.** *83-02 Queens Blvd, Elmhurst (11373). Phone 718/396-1238.* This old-time favorite for Chinese cuisine is a straightforward spot to dine on fresh fish infused with the bright flavors of Asia. As you might expect, Ping's specializes in fish, but not just any old fish. Bring along a sense of culinary adventure if you decide to dine here, as the restaurant features tanks filled with all sorts of wild sea creatures for you to experiment with at dinner. The restaurant also offers dim sum, including steamed pork buns and shrimp dumplings. Chinese menu. Lunch, dinner. Closed Sun. **$$**

🅿

★ ★ **RESTAURANT 718.** *35-01 Ditmars Blvd, Astoria (11105). Phone 718/204-5553.* While Astoria was once all about Greek restaurants, the recent influx of Manhattanites fleeing rent hikes has brought about a shift in the culinary landscape.

Restaurant 718 marks the official arrival of the French bistro to the Big Fat Greek scene. This sweet, cozy Parisian bistro offers standards like duck terrine and steak frites, but also features Spanish-accented plates like grilled tuna with chorizo and soy-cherry sauce, roasted duck with Serrano ham, and, in a respectful nod to the neighborhood, tzatziki with endive. French menu. Dinner, brunch. Bar. Casual attire. Reservations recommended. **$$**

★ **S'AGAPO TAVERNA.** *34-21 34th Ave, Astoria (11106). Phone 718/626-0303.* At this neighborhood taverna, a taste of the Greek Isles is served up with charm every night of the week. The service is warm and welcoming, as you would expect from a local gathering place. The restaurant specializes in swimmingly fresh grilled seafood as well as classic mezze like tangy, garlicky tzatziki. The only potential downside to S'Agapo is that the place can get cramped at times, as tables are snuggled up right next to one another. But if you don't mind cozy dining, you should be fine. Greek menu. Lunch, dinner. Casual attire. **$$**

★ ★ **SICHUAN DYNASTY.** *135-32 40th Rd, Flushing (11354). Phone 718/961-7500.* If you are one of those people who has trouble deciding what to order, do not go to Sichuan Dynasty. The menu contains some 60 items and will stymie even the most decisive of eaters. The key to dining here may be to go with a large group that can handle lots of fiery fare so that no dish will be left off your evening's menu. The selections run the gamut from your basic kung pao chicken and whole fish to more *Fear Factor*-style dishes like kidney in sesame oil. The setting is bright and comfortable, with colorful tabletops, wide booths, and an upper-deck bar stocked with a decent selection of California wines. Chinese menu. Lunch, dinner. Casual attire. **$$**

★ **SRIPRAPHAI.** *64-13 39th Ave, Woodside (11377). Phone 718/899-9599.* Sripraphai serves the sort of food you might get in Thailand. But instead of hopping a jet plane, all you have to do is grab the number 7 train out to Queens. The only problem is that you may have to wait in the line that stretches out the door to get your table. The menu is filled with authentic Thai dishes like noodle bowls, green papaya salad, chile-rubbed pork, and fire-breathing dishes of green curry that will set your mouth ablaze with spice. If you have issues with heat, make sure to let your waiter know. Thai menu. Lunch, dinner. Closed Wed. Casual attire. Outdoor seating. No credit cards accepted. **$**

★ ★ **TOURNESOL.** *50-12 Vernon Blvd, Long Island City (11109). Phone 718/472-4355. tournesolny.com.* Tournesol is a sunny little French bistro just across the river from Manhattan in Long Island City that could have fallen off any old charming *rue* in Paris. Filled to the gills with trappings of Paris—romantic music, a sidewalk café, bistro tables and chairs, floor-to-ceiling French doors, and vintage tin ceilings—this cheery local favorite offers up friendly service and a rustic menu of classic French standards like rabbit stew, braised beef cheeks, frisée au lardons, and country pâté. Tournesol is a sweet little gem of a restaurant that offers all the romance of Paris without the hassle of transcontinental travel. French menu. Lunch, dinner, brunch. Casual attire. Reservations recommended. Outdoor seating. **$$**

★ **UBOL'S KITCHEN.** *24-42 Steinway St, Astoria (11103). Phone 718/545-2874.* This neighborhood Thai restaurant gets consistent "wows" from locals who head over for vibrant fare with a generous amount of heat. The menu includes many standard curry and noodle dishes, but also makes an effort to woo vegetarians with dishes like mock duck. In a neighborhood that is inundated with a slew of ubiquitous Thai restaurants of the same formula, Ubol's remains a spicy favorite. Thai menu. Lunch, dinner. Casual attire. **$**
🄳

★ ★ **WATER'S EDGE.** *44th Dr at the East River, Long Island City (11101). Phone 718/482-0033; fax 718/937-8817. www.watersedgenyc.com.* On the riverfront opposite the United Nations complex; views of the New York City skyline. Seafood menu. Lunch, dinner. Closed Sun. Bar. Reservations recommended. Valet parking. Outdoor seating. Complimentary riverboat transportation to and from Manhattan. **$$**

Staten Island, NY

2 1/2 hours, 140 miles from Hartford, CT

Area Code 718
Information Staten Island Chamber of Commerce, 130 Bay St, 10301; phone 718/727-1900; or the NYC Convention & Visitors Bureau

Staten Island, twice the size of Manhattan with only one twenty-fourth the population, is the most removed, in distance and character, from the other boroughs. At one time, sightseers on the famous Staten Island Ferry rarely disembarked to explore the almost rural character of the island. The completion of the Verrazano Bridge to Brooklyn, however, brought growth and the beginning of a struggle between developers and those who would preserve the island's uncrowded appeal.

What to See and Do

Conference House. *7455 Hylan Blvd, Staten Island (10307). Phone 718/984-6046.* Built in the mid-1680s by an English sea captain, this was the site of an unproductive meeting on Sept 11, 1776, between British Admiral Lord Howe, Benjamin Franklin, John Adams, and Edward Rutledge to discuss terms of peace to end the Revolutionary War. The meeting helped to produce the phrase the "United States of America." Rose, herb gardens; open-hearth cooking; spinning and weaving demonstrations. (Apr-Nov, Fri-Sun). **$**

The Greenbelt/High Rock. *200 Nevada Ave, Egbertville. 7 miles from Verrazano Bridge via Richmond Rd. Phone 718/667-2165.* An 85-acre nature preserve in a 2,500-acre park. Visitor center, trails. Environmental programs, workshops. Self-guided tours. Urban park ranger-guided tours (by appointment). (Daily) No picnicking or camping. **FREE**

Historic Richmond Town. *441 Clarke Ave, Staten Island (10306). Phone 718/351-1611. www.historicrichmond town.org.* This outdoor museum complex depicts three centuries of history and culture of Staten Island and the surrounding region. Daily life and work of a rural community is shown in trade demonstrations and tours of shops and buildings. Among the restoration's 27 historic structures are the Historic Museum; Voorlezer's House (circa 1695), the oldest surviving elementary school in the United States; general store; and trademen's shops. Special events and demonstrations. (Wed-Sun afternoons; extended hours July-Aug; closed Jan 1, Thanksgiving, Dec 25) **$$**

Jacques Marchais Museum of Tibetan Art. *338 Lighthouse Ave, Staten Island (10306). Between New Dorp and Richmondtown. Phone 718/987-3500. www.tibetanmuseum.com.* Perched on a steep hill with views of the Atlantic Ocean, this museum houses the collection of Jacqueline Norman Klauber, who became fascinated with Tibet as a child. Highlights of the exhibits include a series of bright-colored masks and a large collection of golden *thangkas,* or religious images, plus terraced sculpture gardens and a koi pond. (Wed-Sun 1-5 pm) **$**

Snug Harbor Cultural Center. *1000 Richmond Terrace, Staten Island (10301). Phone 718/448-2500. www.snug-harbor.org.* Founded in 1833 as a seamen's retirement home, Snug Harbor is now a performing and visual arts center with 28 historic buildings featuring Greek Revival and Victorian architecture; art galleries (Wed-Sun, fee); children's museum (Tues-Sun afternoons); botanical garden, sculpture, 83 acres of parkland. (Daily; closed Thanksgiving, Dec 25)

Staten Island Zoo. *614 Broadway, W New Brighton (10310). Barrett Park, between Broadway and Clove Rd. Phone 718/442-3100. www.statenislandzoo.org.* Maintained by the Staten Island Zoological Society. Large collection of native and exotic reptiles, varied species of rattlesnakes, amphibians, marine reef fishes, mammals, birds. Children's center includes a miniature farm. (Daily; closed Jan 1, Thanksgiving, Dec 25) Free admission on Wed afternoon, inquire for hours. **$$**

Maine

Here are the highest tides (28 feet in Passamaquoddy Bay), the tastiest potatoes, and the tartest conversation in the country. Flat Yankee twang and the patois of French Canadians make Maine's speech as salty as its sea. Hunters, anglers, canoeists, and campers appreciate its 6,000 lakes and ponds, and summer vacationers enjoy its 3,500 miles of seacoast even though the water is a bit chilly.

Downeasters brag about the state's temperature range from -46° F to 105° F, as well as its famous lobsters. Paper and allied products are the chief manufactured products; machine tools, electronic components, and other metal products are important. Food canning and freezing are major industries. Potatoes, blueberries, poultry, eggs, dairy products, and apples are leading farm crops.

Maine's first settlement (1604) was on St. Croix Island; it lasted one winter. Another early settlement was established near Pemaquid Point. The short-lived Popham Colony, at the mouth of the Kennebec River, built America's first transatlantic trader, the *Virginia,* in 1607. Until 1819, Maine was a part of Massachusetts. It was admitted to the Union in 1820.

Most of Maine's 17.6 million acres of forestland is open to public recreational use, including more than 580,000 acres owned by the state. For more information about recreational use of public and private forestland, contact the Maine Bureau of Public Lands, phone 207/287-3061, or the Maine Forest Service at 207/287-2791.

When to Go/Climate

Maine is a large state affected by several different weather patterns. Coastal temperatures are more

Population: 1,227,928
Area: 30,995 square miles
Elevation: 0-5,268 feet
Peak: Mount Katahdin (Piscataquis County)
Entered Union: March 15, 1820 (23rd state)
Capital: Augusta
Motto: I Lead
Nickname: Pine Tree State
Flower: Pine Cone and Tassel
Bird: Chickadee
Tree: Eastern White Pine
Fair: August in Skowhegan
Time Zone: Eastern
Web Site: www.visitmaine.com
Fun Facts:
• Nearly 90 percent of the nation's lobster supply is caught off the coast of Maine.
• Maine has over 5,000 miles of coastline, which is more than California.

moderate than inland temperatures, and fog is common in spring and fall. In general, winters are cold and snowy. Summers are filled with warm, sunny days and cool, clear nights. Fall's famous "nor'easters" can bring high tides, gale-force winds, and huge amounts of rain to the coastal areas.

AVERAGE HIGH/LOW TEMPERATURES (° F)

Caribou

Jan 19/-2	**May** 62/40	**Sept** 64/43
Feb 23/7	**June** 72/49	**Oct** 52/34
Mar 34/15	**July** 77/55	**Nov** 38/24
Apr 47/29	**Aug** 74/52	**Dec** 42/6

Portland

Jan 45/34	**May** 67/47	**Sept** 75/52
Feb 51/36	**June** 74/53	**Oct** 64/45
Mar 56/39	**July** 80/57	**Nov** 53/40
Apr 61/41	**Aug** 80/57	**Dec** 46/35

Calendar Highlights

FEBRUARY

Kennebunk Winter Carnival (*Kennebunk*). *Phone 207/985-6890*. Snow sculpture contests, snow palace moonwalk, magic show, ice-skating party, chili and chowder contests, children's events.

MAY

Maine State Parade (*Lewiston and Auburn*). *Downtown Lewiston and Auburn. Phone Androscoggin County Chamber of Commerce, 207/783-2249*. Maine's largest parade; more than 30,000 people represent 60 communities.

JUNE

Great Whatever Family Festival Week (*Augusta*). *Kennebec Valley Chamber of Commerce. Phone 207/623-4559*. More than 60 events include tournaments, carnival, barbecue, parade, and fireworks. Festivities culminate with the canoe and kayak regatta on the Kennebec River between Augusta and Gardiner. There are also canoe and kayak races.

Windjammer Days (*Boothbay Harbor*). *Phone 207/633-2353*. Old schooners that formerly sailed the trade routes and now cruise the Maine coast sail en masse into the harbor. Waterfront food court, entertainment, street parade, children's activities.

JULY

Bangor State Fair (*Bangor*). *Phone 207/947-5555. www.bangorstatefair.com*. One of the country's oldest fairs. Horse racing, exhibits, stage shows.

Festival de Joie (*Lewiston and Auburn*). *Central Maine Civic Center. Androscoggin County Chamber of Commerce. Phone 207/782-6231. www.festivaldejoie.org*. A celebration of Lewiston and Auburn's Franco-American heritage. Features ethnic songs, dances, cultural activities, and traditional foods.

Schooner Days & North Atlantic Blues Festival (*Rockland*). *Phone 207/596-0376*. A three-day festival celebrating Maine's maritime heritage; features Parade of Schooners, arts, entertainment, concessions, fireworks; blues bands and club crawl.

AUGUST

Maine Lobster Festival (*Rockland*). *Phone 207/596-0376 or toll-free 800/562-2529*. A five-day event centered around Maine's chief marine creature, with a huge tent cafeteria serving lobster and other seafood. Parade, harbor cruises, maritime displays, bands, entertainment.

Skowhegan State Fair (*Skowhegan*). *Phone 207/474-2947*. One of the oldest fairs in the country (1818). Mile-long midway, stage shows, harness racing; contests, exhibits.

DECEMBER

Christmas by the Sea (*Camden*). *Phone 207/236-4404*. A celebration of the holiday season with musical entertainment, horse-drawn wagon rides, Holiday House Tour, Santa's arrival by lobsterboat.

Parks and Recreation

Water-related activities, hiking, biking, various other sports, picnicking and visitor centers, as well as camping, are available in many of Maine's state parks. Most state parks and historic sites are open seasonally from 9 am-sunset; Popham Beach, John Paul Jones Memorial, and Reid are open year-round. Most areas have day-use and/or parking fees, $1.50-$3 per person; annual pass, $40/vehicle, $20/individual. Camping May-October (areas vary), nonresidents $11-$17 per site, residents $9-$13 per site; reservations fee $2 a night. Camping reservations may be made by mail to the Bureau of Parks and Lands, Station #22, Augusta 04333, Attention Reservation Clerk; in person at the office of the Bureau of Parks and Lands in Augusta; by phone, 207/287-3824 or toll-free 800/332-1501 (ME). Maine historic sites fee $2.50-$3. Pets on leash only in most parks. No dogs on beaches or at Sebago Lake campground. For more information, contact the Bureau of Parks and Lands, Maine Department of Conservation, 286 Water Street, Key Bank Plaza, Augusta 04333, phone 207/287-3821.

THE COASTAL ROUTE

Most tourists stick to coastal Route 1 when it splits from Interstate 95 at Brunswick, home of the Bowdoin College museums, the Joshua Chamberlain Museum, and outstanding summer music and theater. Bath is worth a stop to see the Maine Maritime Museum and Shipyard. Traffic streams down a peninsula to Boothbay Harbor, a resort village with a footbridge across its harbor that is a departure point for numerous excursion boats. Rockland is the next must-see stop on Route 1. Visit the Farnsworth Art Museum and Wyeth Center, Owls Head Transportation Museum, or the Maine Lighthouse Museum. Maine Windjammers and ferries to Vinalhaven and North Haven depart from here. Next on our route is Camden, a town backed by hills and filled with inns, restaurants, and shops. Camden Hills State Park offers spectacular views of the coast, as well as hiking, camping, and picnic facilities. Belfast, another interesting old port, is a departure point for excursion boats and for the Belfast & Moosehead Lake Railroad Company excursion train. Continue up coastal Route 1 to Ellsworth, then turn down Route 3 to Mount Desert Island, site of Acadia National Park. The big tourist town here is Bar Harbor (the park is the big draw, also many excursion boats). Return the same way, perhaps taking the ferry to Yarmouth, Nova Scotia, for an interesting side trip. Another option is to continue north on Route 1 past Ellsworth (the turnoff for Bar Harbor). Here Route 1 changes, becoming far quieter, especially after the turnoff for Schoodic Point, which is part of Acadia National Park. The obvious next stop is in Machias, where the Burnham Tavern Museum tells the area's revolutionary history. Take a detour at the cliffside walking trails of Quoddy Head State Park (the easternmost point in the United States). Then continue on to Lubec and over the bridge to Campobello Island (New Brunswick, Canada) to see the Roosevelt Campobello International Park with Franklin D. Roosevelt's summer home as its centerpiece. The park also includes a golf course and extensive hiking trails. Return to Bar Harbor along the same route. **(Approximately 306 miles; add 128 miles if continuing on to Lubec)**

FISHING AND HUNTING

Nonresident fishing license: $51; 12-15 years, $8; 15-day license, $39; seven-day license, $35; three-day license, $22; one-day license, $10. Nonresident hunting license for birds and animals except deer, bear, turkey, moose, bobcat, and raccoon: $56; includes all legal game species: $86. These fees do not include agent fees, which range from $1-$2. Detailed information about the state's regulations is available in the brochures *Maine Hunting and Trapping Laws* and *Maine Open Water Fishing Laws* from the Maine Fish and Wildlife Department, Station 41, 284 State Street, Augusta 04333; phone 207/287-8000.

Driving Information

Every person must be in an approved passenger restraint anywhere in a vehicle; children under age 4 must use approved safety seats. For further information, phone 207/871-7771.

INTERSTATE HIGHWAY SYSTEM

The following alphabetical listing of Maine towns in this book shows that these cities are within 10 miles of the indicated interstate highway. Check a highway map for the nearest exit.

Highway Number	Cities/Towns within 10 Miles
Interstate 95	Augusta, Bangor, Bath, Biddeford, Brunswick, Freeport, Houlton, Kennebunk, Kittery, Lincoln, Millinocket, Newport, Ogunquit, Old Orchard Beach, Orono, Portland, Saco, Scarborough, Waterville, Wells, Yarmouth, York.

Additional Visitor Information

The pulp and paper industry mills throughout Maine offer tours of their woodlands and manufacturing facilities at various times of the year. For further information, contact the Maine Pulp & Paper Association Information Office, 104 Sewall Street, PO Box 5670, Augusta 04332; phone 207/622-3166.

There are eight official information service centers in Maine. Visitors who stop by will find information and brochures helpful in planning stops to points of interest. Their locations are as follows: in Bethel, on Highway 2; at Kittery, between Interstate 95 and Highway 1; in Fryeburg (summer only), on Highway 302; in Calais, on Union Street, off Highway 1; in Hampden, on Interstate 95 N at mile marker 169; on Interstate 95 S between mile markers 171 and 172; in Houlton, on Ludlow Road; in Yarmouth, between Interstate 95, exit 17 and Highway 1.

Acadia National Park (E-3)

See also Bar Harbor, Northeast Harbor, Southwest Harbor

Web Site www.nps.gov/acad

On Mount Desert Island, south and west of Bar Harbor; entrance off Highway 3.

Waves crashing against a rocky coastline, thick woodlands abundant with wildlife, and mountains scraping the sky—Acadia National Park is the Maine of storybooks. Occupying nearly half of Mount Desert Island, with smaller areas on Isle au Haut, Little Cranberry Island (see CRANBERRY ISLES), Baker Island, Little

Moose Island, and part of the mainland at Schoodic Point, Acadia amazes visitors. It is a sea-lashed granite coastal area of forested valleys, lakes, and mountains, all created by the force of the glaciers. At 40,000 acres, Acadia is small compared to other national parks; however, it is one of the most visited national parks in the United States and the only national park in the northeastern United States. A 27-mile loop road connects the park's eastern sights on

Mount Desert Island, and ferry services take travelers to some of the smaller islands. Visitors can explore 1,530-foot Cadillac Mountain, the highest point on the Atlantic Coast of the United States; watch waves crash against Thunder Hole, creating a thunderous boom; or swim in the ocean at various coastal beaches. A road to the summit of Cadillac provides views of Frenchman, Blue Hill, and Penobscot bays.Mount Desert Island was named by the French explorer Samuel de Champlain in 1604. Shortly thereafter, French Jesuit missionaries settled here until driven off by an armed vessel from Virginia. This was the first act of overt warfare between France and England for control of North America. Until 1713, the island was a part of French Acadia. It was not until after the Revolutionary War that it was settled extensively. In 1916, a portion of the area was proclaimed Sieur de Monts National Monument. It was changed to Lafayette National Park in 1919, and finally, in 1929, it was enlarged and renamed Acadia National Park.

Like all national parks, Acadia is a wildlife sanctuary. Fir, pine, spruce, many hardwoods, and hundreds of varieties of wildflowers thrive. Nature lovers will be delighted with the more than 120 miles of trails; park rangers take visitors on various walks and cruises, pointing out and explaining the natural, cultural, and historical features of the park. Forty-five miles of carriage roads offer bicyclists scenic rides through Acadia. Copies of ranger-led programs and trail maps are available at the visitor center.

There is saltwater swimming at Sand Beach and freshwater swimming at Echo Lake. Snowmobiles are allowed in some areas, and cross-country skiing is available. Most facilities are open Memorial Day-September; however, portions of the park are open year-round, and the picnic grounds are open May-October. Limited camping is available at two park campgrounds: Blackwoods, open year-round, requires reservations from mid-June-mid-September; and Seawall, open late May-late September, is on a first-come, first-served basis. The park headquarters, 2 1/2 miles west of Bar Harbor (see) on Highway 233, provides visitor information (Nov-Apr, daily; closed Jan 1, Thanksgiving, Dec 24-25). For further information, contact the Superintendent, PO Box 177, Bar Harbor 04609; phone 207/288-3338. Golden Eagle, Golden Age, and Golden Access passports are accepted (see MAKING THE MOST OF YOUR TRIP).

What to See and Do

Auto Tape Tours. *Mount Desert Island.* A scenic, 56-mile self-guided tour gives a mile-by-mile description of the points of interest, history, and geology of the park. Tapes are available May-October at the visitor center. Cassette player and tape rental, deposit required; or tape may be purchased. **$$$$**

Ferry Service. *Northeast Harbor. Phone 207/244-3575.* Connects Islesford, Great Cranberry Island, and Northeast Harbor on a regular schedule all year. **$$**

Isle au Haut (EEL-oh-HO). *Isle au Haut.* Mountains rise more than 540 feet on this island of forested shores and cobblestone beaches; hiking trails; small primitive campground (advance mail reservations; phone 207/288-3338 for reservation form). A ferry from Stonington (see DEER ISLE) takes visitors on the 45-minute trip to the island (Mon-Sat; closed holidays; fee).

Islesford Historical Museum. *Islesford. On Little Cranberry Island; 2 miles S of Seal Harbor.* A 30-minute boat trip from Northeast Harbor. (See Cranberry Isles) **FREE**

Naturalist Sea Cruises. *Northeast Harbor.* Marine life and history of the area are explained. Cruises visit Frenchman Bay (phone 207/288-3322), Islesford (phone 207/276-5352), and Baker Island (phone 207/276-3717). (Daily during summer season, schedules vary; phone for fees)

Park Tours. *Main St, Bar Harbor (04609). Phone 207/288-3327.* Narrated sightseeing trips through the park. Buses leave Main Street, in Bar Harbor. (June-early Oct) For tickets and information about tour schedules and fees, contact Testa's Cafe, 53 Main Street, Bar Harbor. **$$**

Visitor Center. *Rte 3, Hulls Cove (04644). 3 miles NW of Bar Harbor at Hulls Cove.* (May-Oct, daily)

Allagash Wilderness Waterway

See also Fort Kent

In 1970, the Allagash River was designated a national wild river. Stretching 95 miles through 200,000 acres of lakes, rivers, and timberland in Maine's northern wilderness, this waterway is a favorite of canoeists. A good put-in point is Chamberlain Thoroughfare at the junction of Chamberlain and Telos lakes. The trip ends at Allagash Village, 8 miles north of Allagash Falls, near the Canadian border, where the Allagash flows into the St. John River. Some canoe experience is necessary before attempting the entire trip as high winds can be a problem on the lakes and, depending on the level of the Allagash, the rapids can be dangerous.

Registration is required upon entering and leaving the waterway; rangers are at Allagash Lake, Chamberlain Thoroughfare, Eagle Lake, Churchill Dam, Long Lake Thoroughfare, and the Michaud Farm. Supplies and canoes must be brought in; gasoline is not available. There are restrictions regarding the size of parties using the waterway, as well as watercraft permitted. Numerous primitive campsites accessible only by water are scattered along the waterway (mid-May-mid-Oct). Campsite fee per person, per night ($).

For further information and rules, contact the Bureau of Parks & Lands, Maine Department of Conservation, Northern Regional Office, BMHI Complex, Building H, 106 Hogan Road, Bangor, 04401; phone 207/941-4014.

Auburn (E-1)

See also Lewiston, Poland Spring

Settled 1797
Population 24,309
Elevation 188 ft
Area Code 207
Information Androscoggin County Chamber of Commerce, 179 Lisbon St, PO Box 59, Lewiston 04243-0059; phone 207/783-2249
Web Site www.androscoggincounty.com

Auburn, together with its sister city, Lewiston, make up an important manufacturing center. In 1836, the first organized shoe company was started here. The Minot Shoe Company prospered, selling more than $6 million in shoes by 1900, and becoming the fifth-largest shoe company in the United States by 1920. When the depression hit, the company suffered a severe blow. The city continued to expand, however, and today Auburn is one of the largest cities in the state.

What to See and Do

Androscoggin Historical Society Library and Museum. *County Building, 2 Turner St, Auburn (04210). Turner St at Court St.* Phone 207/784-0586. Exhibits trace local, county and state history. (Wed-Fri; closed holidays) Museum; library. **FREE**

Lost Valley Ski Area. *200 Lost Valley Rd, Auburn (04210). Follow signs off Hwy 11.* Phone 207/784-1561. *www.lostvalleyski.com.* Two double chairlifts, T-bar; snowmaking; patrol, school, rentals; bar, lounge, restaurant. (Dec-mid-Mar, daily) **$$$$**

Norlands Living History Center. *290 Norlands Rd, Livermore (04523). 25 miles N just off Hwy 4.* Phone 207/897-4366. *www.norlands.org.* Life as it was lived a century ago; clothing, customs. Year-round working farm with oxen, horses, cows, crops, and seasonal activities. Features 19th-century Victorian home of Washburn family; school, library, church, farmer's cottage, barn. Tours (July-Sept, daily). Picnicking. (See SPECIAL EVENTS) **$$**

Special Events

Autumn Celebration. *Norlands Living History Center, 290 Norlands Rd, Livermore (04523).* Phone 207/897-4366. Cider pressing, hayrides, and building tours are some of the activities at this traditional harvest festival. Sept.

Maple Days. *Norlands Living History Center, 290 Norlands Rd, Livermore (04523).* Phone 207/897-4366. Mid-Mar.

Augusta (E-2)

See also Waterville

Settled 1628
Population 21,325
Elevation 153 ft

Area Code 207
Information Kennebec Valley Chamber of Commerce, 21 University Dr, PO Box 676, 04332-0192; phone 207/623-4559
Web Site www.augustamaine.com

Augusta, the capital of Maine, began in 1628 when men from Plymouth established a trading post on the site of Cushnoc, a Native American village. From there, Fort Western was built in 1754 to protect settlers against Native American raids, and the settlement grew. Today, 39 miles from the sea, Augusta is at the head of navigation on the Kennebec River; some of the town's leading industries include steel and food processing and service-related industries.

What to See and Do

Old Fort Western. *City Center Plaza, 16 Cony St, Augusta (04330).* Phone 207/626-2385. *www.oldfortwestern.org.* Fort complex built in 1754 by Boston merchants; main house and reproduction blockhouse, watchboxes, and palisade. Costumed staff interprets 18th-century life on the Kennebec River. (Memorial Day-Labor Day: daily; after Labor Day-Columbus Day: Sat-Sun, limited hours)

State House. *83 State House Station, Augusta (04330). State and Capitol sts.* Phone 207/287-2301. (1829-1832) The original design for this impressive building was by Charles Bulfinch (architect of the Massachusetts State House). Remodeled and enlarged (1909-1910), it rises majestically above Capitol Park and the Kennebec River. On its 185-foot dome is a statue, designed by W. Clark Noble, of a classically robed woman bearing a pine bough torch. (Mon-Fri; closed holidays) **FREE** Also here is

Blaine House. *State and Capitol sts, Augusta (04330).* Phone 207/287-2301. (1833) House of James G. Blaine, Speaker of the US House of Representatives and 1884 presidential candidate. Since 1919, this 28-room house has been the official residence of Maine's governors. Originally built in Federal-style, it was remodeled several times and today appears semicolonial. Tours (Tues-Thurs, limited hours; closed holidays). **FREE**

Maine State Museum. *83 State House Station, Augusta (04330).* Phone 207/287-2301. Exhibits of Maine's natural environment, prehistory, social history, and manufacturing heritage. "This Land Called Maine" features five natural history scenes as well as a presentation of 40 spectacular gems and gem minerals found in Maine. "Made in Maine" presents 19th-century products and manufacturing technologies and includes a water-powered woodworking mill, a two-story textile factory, and more than 1,000 Maine-made objects. Other exhibits examine the early economic activities of agriculture, fishing, granite quarrying, ice harvesting, lumbering, and shipbuilding. Also featured are a display of military, political, and geographical artifacts relating to the formation of the state of Maine as well as an exhibition on Maine glass. Gift shop. (Daily; closed holidays) **FREE**

Special Event

Great Whatever Family Festival Week. *21 University Dr, Augusta (04330). Augusta/Gardiner area. Phone 207/623-4559.* More than 60 events include tournaments, carnival, barbecue, parade, and fireworks. Festivities culminate with the canoe and kayak regatta on the Kennebec River between Augusta and Gardiner. There are also canoe and kayak races. Contact Chamber of Commerce. Ten days in late June-early July.

Limited-Service Hotels

★ **BEST INN.** *65 Whitten Rd, Augusta (04330). Phone 207/622-3776; toll-free 800/237-8466; fax 207/622-3778. www.bestinn.com.* 58 rooms, 2 story. Complimentary continental breakfast. Check-out 11 am. Outdoor pool. **$**

★ **COMFORT INN.** *281 Civic Center Dr, Augusta (04330). Phone 207/623-1000; toll-free 800/808-1188; fax 207/623-3505. www.comfortinn.com.* 99 rooms, 3 story. Pets accepted. Complimentary continental breakfast. Check-in 3 pm, check-out 11 am. Restaurant, bar. Fitness room. Indoor pool. **$**

Full-Service Resort

★ ★ ★ **BEST WESTERN SENATOR INN & SPA.** *284 Western Ave, Augusta (04330). Phone 207/622-5804; toll-free 877/772-2224; fax 207/622-8803. www.senatorinn.com.* 124 rooms, 2 story. Pets accepted, some restrictions; fee. Complimentary full breakfast. Check-in 3 pm, check-out noon. High-speed Internet access, wireless Internet access. Restaurant, bar. Children's activity center. Fitness

room, fitness classes available, spa. Indoor pool, outdoor pool, whirlpool. **$$**

Specialty Lodging

The following lodging establishment is approved by Mobil Travel Guide, but due to its unique and individualized nature has not been given a traditional Mobil Star rating. Included in this listing you may find bed-and-breakfasts, limited-service inns, guest ranches, and other unique hotel properties.

WINGS HILL INN. *Rte 27, Augusta (04918). Phone 207/495-2400; toll-free 866/495-2400; fax 207/495-3400. www.wingshillinn.com.* Renovated farmhouse built in 1800; antique quilts. 8 rooms, 2 story. Complimentary full breakfast. Check-in 3-9 pm, check-out 11 am. **$**

Bailey Island (E-2)

See also Brunswick

Elevation 20 ft
Area Code 207
Zip 04003
Information Chamber of Commerce of the Bath-Brunswick Region, 59 Pleasant St, Brunswick 04011; phone 207/725-8797
Web Site www.midcoastmaine.com

At the terminus of Highway 24, along the northern shore of Casco Bay, lies Bailey Island, the most popular of the 365 Calendar Islands. Together with Orr's Island, to which it is connected by a cribstone bridge, Bailey is a resort and fishing center. Originally called Newwaggin by an early trader from Kittery, Bailey Island was renamed after Deacon Timothy Bailey of Massachusetts, who claimed the land for himself and banished early settlers. Bailey Island and Orr's Island partially enclose an arm of Casco Bay called Harpswell Sound—the locale of John Whittier's poem "The Dead Ship of Harpswell" and of Harriet Beecher Stowe's "Pearl of Orr's Island."

What to See and Do

Bailey Island Cribstone Bridge. *On Hwy 24 S, over Will Straits.* Unique construction of uncemented granite blocks laid honeycomb fashion, allowing the tides to flow through. **FREE**

Giant Staircase. *Washington St, Bailey Island.* Natural rock formation dropping 200 feet in steps to ocean. Scenic overlook area. **FREE**

Specialty Lodging

The following lodging establishment is approved by Mobil Travel Guide, but due to its unique and individualized nature has not been given a traditional Mobil Star rating. Included in this listing you may find bed-and-breakfasts, limited-service inns, guest ranches, and other unique hotel properties.

LOG CABIN ISLAND INN. *5 Log Cabin Ln, Bailey Island (04003). Phone 207/833-5546; fax 207/833-7858. www.logcabin-maine.com.* Log cabin; panoramic view of bay, islands. 8 rooms. Closed Nov-Mar. Complimentary full breakfast. Check-in 3 pm, check-out 11 am. Restaurant. **$**
🅿

Restaurant

★ **COOK'S LOBSTER HOUSE.** *Garrison Cove Rd, Bailey Island (04003). Phone 207/833-2818; fax 207/833-5851. www.cookslobsterhouse.com.* Dockage. Seafood, steak menu. Lunch, dinner. Bar. Children's menu. Outdoor seating. **$$$**

Bangor (D-3)

See also Bucksport

Settled 1769
Population 33,181
Elevation 61 ft
Area Code 207
Zip 04401
Information Bangor Convention and Visitors Bureau, PO Box 1938, 04402; phone 207/947-5205
Web Site www.bangorcvb.org

In 1604, Samuel de Champlain sailed up the Penobscot River to the area that was to become Bangor and reported that the country was "most pleasant and agreeable," the hunting good, and the oak trees impressive. As the area grew, these things remained true. Begun as a harbor town, as did many of Maine's coastal areas, Bangor turned to lumber when the railroads picked up much of the shipping business. In 1842, it became the second-largest lumber port in the country.

Bangor received its name by mistake. An early settler, Reverend Seth Noble, was sent to register the new town under its chosen name of Sunbury; however, when officials asked Noble for the name, he thought they were asking him for the name of a tune he was humming, and replied "Bangor" instead. Today, the city is the third largest in Maine and a trading and distribution center.

What to See and Do

Bangor Historical Museum. *159 Union St, Bangor (04401). At High St. Phone 207/942-5766.* (Thomas A. Hill House, 1834) Tour of the first floor of a Greek Revival house; a second-floor gallery features changing exhibits. (June-Dec, Tues-Sat) **$**

Cole Land Transportation Museum. *405 Perry Rd, Bangor (04401). Phone 207/990-3600. www.cole museum.org.* The Cole Museum takes great pride in depicting the history of transportation in the American Northeast. The museum houses one of the largest collections of snow removal equipment found in one place anywhere in the country, as well as a cache of military vehicles. A great place to take children, more than 20,000 visitors go through the turnstiles each year to see the museum's permanent collection including local railroad pieces and cars and trucks, uniquely designed to traverse the streets of Bangor. Historic photographs of Maine are also on display. (Daily 9 am-5 pm) **$$**

Monument to Paul Bunyan. *Bass Park, Main St, Bangor.* A 31-foot-tall statue commemorating the legendary lumberjack. **FREE**

Special Events

Band concerts. *Paul Bunyan Park, 647 Main St, Bangor (04401). Phone 207/947-1018.* Grab a blanket or lawn chair and enjoy an hour of music performed by the Bangor Band. Tues evenings, June-Aug.

Bangor State Fair. *100 Dutton St, Bangor (04401). Phone 207/947-5555. www.bangorstatefair.com.* One of the country's oldest fairs. Horse racing, exhibits, stage shows. Late July-first week in Aug.

Kenduskeag Stream Canoe Race. *647 Main St, Bangor (04401). Phone 207/947-1018.* Sixteen and a half mile canoe race over flat water and white water through Six Mile Falls and the Shopping Cart rapids, into the downtown of Bangor, and the final stop at the Penobscot River. Mid-Apr.

Limited-Service Hotels

★ **FAIRFIELD INN.** *300 Odlin Rd, Bangor (04401). Phone 207/990-0001; toll-free 800/228-2800; fax 207/990-0917. www.fairfieldinn.com.* 153 rooms, 3 story. Complimentary continental breakfast. Check-out noon. Fitness room. Indoor pool, whirlpool. **$**

★ ★ **HOLIDAY INN.** *500 Main St, Bangor (04401). Phone 207/947-8651; toll-free 800/799-8651; fax 207/942-2848. www.holiday-inn.com/bangor-civic.* Opposite Civic Center. 121 rooms, 4 story. Pets accepted, some restrictions. Check-out noon. Restaurant, bar. Outdoor pool. Airport transportation available. **$**

Specialty Lodging

The following lodging establishment is approved by Mobil Travel Guide, but due to its unique and individualized nature has not been given a traditional Mobil Star rating. Included in this listing you may find bed-and-breakfasts, limited-service inns, guest ranches, and other unique hotel properties.

THE LUCERNE INN. *Rte 1A Bar Harbor Rd, Holden (04429). Phone 207/843-5123; toll-free 800/325-5123; fax 207/843-6138. www.lucerneinn.com.* Colonial-style farmhouse and connecting stable, established as an inn in 1814. 30 rooms, 3 story. Complimentary continental breakfast. Check-in 2 pm, check-out 11 am. Restaurant. Outdoor pool. **$$**

Restaurants

★ **CAPTAIN NICK'S SEAFOOD HOUSE.** *1165 Union St, Bangor (04401). Phone 207/942-6444; fax 207/947-8630.* Seafood menu. Lunch, dinner. Closed Thanksgiving, Dec 25. Bar. Children's menu. **$$**

★ ★ **MILLER'S.** *427 Main St, Bangor (04401). Phone 207/942-6361. www.millersrestaurant.com.* American menu. Lunch, dinner, Sun brunch. Closed Dec 25. Children's menu. **$$**

Bar Harbor (E-3)

See also Acadia National Park, Blue Hill, Cranberry Isles, Ellsworth, Northeast Harbor, Southwest Harbor

Population 2,768
Elevation 20 ft

Area Code 207
Zip 04609
Information Chamber of Commerce, 93 Cottage St, PO Box 158; phone 207/288-5103
Web Site www.barharborinfo.com

Bar Harbor, the largest village on Mount Desert Island, has a summer population of as many as 20,000 and is headquarters for the surrounding summer resort area. The island, which includes most of Acadia National Park, is mainly rugged granite, forested and flowered, with many bays and inlets where sailing is popular. In the mid-1800s, socially prominent figures, including publisher Joseph Pulitzer, had elaborate summer cottages built on the island. The era of elegance ebbed, however, with the Great Depression, World War II, and the "Great Fire of 1947," which destroyed many of the estates and scorched more than 17,000 acres. As a result, the forests in the area now have younger, more varied trees bearing red, yellow, and orange leaves instead of just evergreens.

What to See and Do

Abbe Museum. *26 Mount Desert St, Bar Harbor (04609). Rte 3 S to Sieur de Monts exit. Phone 207/288-3519. www.abbemuseum.org.* This museum holds an extensive collection of Native American artifacts. (Daily 9 am-5 pm; closed Thanksgiving, Dec 25; also Jan) The original location in Acadia National Park, open Memorial Day-mid-October, now houses exhibits on the archaeology of Maine and the history of the Abbe. **$$**

Bar Harbor Historical Society Museum. *33 Ledgelawn Ave, Bar Harbor (04609). Jesup Memorial Library. Phone 207/288-0000. www.barharborhistorical.org.* Collection of early photographs of hotels, summer cottages, and Green Mountain cog railroad; hotel registers from the early to late 1800s; maps, scrapbook of the 1947 fire. (Mid-June-Oct, Mon-Sat 1-4 pm; closed holidays) **FREE**

Bar Harbor Whale Watch Company. *39 Cottage St, Bar Harbor (04609). 1 mile N on Hwy 3. Phone 207/288-2386; toll-free 800/942-5374. www.whalesrus.com.* Offers a variety of cruises aboard catamarans *Friendship V* or *Helen H* to view whales, seal, puffin, osprey, and more. Also nature cruises and lobster and seal-watching. Cruises vary in length and destination. (May-Oct, daily) Depart from Bluenose Ferry Terminal.

Ferry service to Yarmouth, Nova Scotia. *121 Edens St, Bar Harbor (04609). Phone toll-free 888/249-7245. www.catferry.com.* Passenger and car carrier *Cat* Ferry makes three-hour trips. **$$$$**

Fishing. Fresh water in many lakes and streams (check regulations, obtain license). Salt water off coast; commercial boat operators will arrange trips.

The Jackson Laboratory. *600 Main St, Bar Harbor (04609). 2 miles S on Hwy 3. Phone 207/288-6049.* An internationally known mammalian genetics laboratory conducting research relevant to cancer, diabetes, AIDS, heart disease, blood disorders, birth defects, aging, and normal growth and development. Audiovisual and lecture programs (early June-late Aug, Wed afternoons; closed one week in late July and one week in mid-Aug). **FREE**

Natural History Museum. *109 Eden St, Bar Harbor (04609). In the historic Turrets Building on the College of the Atlantic waterfront campus. Phone 207/288-5015. www.coamuseum.org.* More than 50 exhibits depicting animals in their natural settings; 22-foot Minke whale skeleton. Interpretive programs; evening lectures in summer (Wed). (June-Labor Day: Mon-Sat; rest of year: Fri-Sun; closed Thanksgiving-mid-Jan, last two weeks in Mar) **$**

Oceanarium-Bar Harbor. *Rte 3, Bar Harbor (04609). 9 miles N on Hwy 3. Phone 207/288-5005.* An extension of the Mount Desert Oceanarium in Southwest Harbor (see); features include salt-marsh walks, viewing tower; also lobster museum with hands-on exhibits. (Mid-May-mid-Oct, Mon-Sat) **$$** Also included is the

Lobster Hatchery. *1 West St, Bar Harbor (04609). Phone 207/288-2334.* Young lobsters are hatched from eggs to 1/2 inch in length, then returned to the ocean to supplement the supply; guides narrate process. (Mid-May-mid-Oct, Mon-Sat)

Special Events

Art Exhibit. *Village Green, Bar Harbor (04069). Phone 207/288-5103.* Third weekend in July and Aug.

Celebrate Bar Harbor. *Phone 207/288-5103.* Mid-June.

Limited-Service Hotels

★ **ACADIA INN.** *98 Eden St, Bar Harbor (04609). Phone 207/288-3500; toll-free 800/638-3636; fax 207/288-8424. www.acadiainn.com.* 95 rooms, 3 story.

Closed mid-Nov-Mar. Complimentary continental breakfast. Check-out 11 am. Outdoor pool, whirlpool. **$$**

★ ★ **BAR HARBOR INN.** *Newport Dr, Bar Harbor (04609). Phone 207/288-3351; toll-free 800/248-3351; fax 207/288-5296. www.barharborinn.com.* This inn is located on 8 acres of nicely groomed gardens and lawns, directly on Frenchman Bay. There are three guest buildings featuring rooms with patios or balconies overlooking the ocean or grounds. A large selection of recreational activities are nearby. Pier; sailing cruises on 19th-century replica schooner. 153 rooms, 2 story. Complimentary continental breakfast. Check-in 2 pm, check-out 11 am. Restaurant, bar. Fitness room. Outdoor pool. Beach. **$$**

★ **BAR HARBOR MOTEL.** *100 Eden St (Rte 3), Bar Harbor (04609). Phone 207/288-3453; toll-free 800/388-3453; fax 207/288-3598. www.barharbormotel.com.* 70 rooms. Closed mid-Oct-mid-May. Check-out 11 am. Outdoor pool. **$**

★ **BEST WESTERN INN.** *Rte 3, Bar Harbor (04609). Phone 207/288-5823; toll-free 800/780-7234; fax 207/288-9827. www.bestwesterninn.com.* 70 rooms. Closed Nov-Apr. Complimentary continental breakfast. Check-out 11 am. Outdoor pool. **$$**

★ ★ **HARBORSIDE HOTEL & MARINA.** *55 West St, Bar Harbor (04609). Phone 207/288-5033; toll-free 800/328-5033; fax 207/288-3661. www.theharborsidehotel.com.* 88 rooms, 2 story. Closed Nov-Mar. Complimentary continental breakfast. Check-out 11 am. Restaurant, bar. Whirlpool. **$$**

★ ★ **HOLIDAY INN.** *123 Eden St, Bar Harbor (04609). Phone 207/288-9723; toll-free 800/465-4329; fax 207/288-3089. www.barharborholidayinn.com.* This inn is located close to the Hancock County Airport and 50 miles from Bangor International Airport. The restaurant specializes in local seafood and features a lovely view. The Edenfield lounge serves cocktails until late evening. 221 rooms, 4 story. Closed Nov-Apr. Check-out noon. Restaurant, bar. Children's activity center. Fitness room. Outdoor pool. Tennis. **$$**

★ **QUALITY INN.** *40 Kebo St, Bar Harbor (04609). Phone 207/288-5403; toll-free 800/282-5403; fax*

207/288-5473. www.qualityinn.com. 77 rooms, 2 story. Closed Nov-mid-Apr. Check-out 11 am. Outdoor pool, whirlpool. **$$**

★ ★ **WONDER VIEW INN.** *50 Eden St, Bar Harbor (10801). Phone 207/288-3358; toll-free 888/439-8439; fax 207/288-2005. www.wonderviewinn.com.* 79 rooms, 2 story. Closed Nov-Apr. Check-out 11 am. Restaurant, bar. Outdoor pool. **$$**

Full-Service Hotel

★ ★ ★ **BAR HARBOR HOTEL - BLUENOSE INN.** *90 Eden St, Bar Harbor (04609). Phone 207/288-3348; toll-free 800/445-4077; fax 207/288-2183. www.bluenoseinn.com.* From its hilltop location on Mount Desert Island, this hotel offers breathtaking views of Frenchman Bay. Rooms and suites are spread between the Mizzentop and Stenna Nordica buildings. Guests can explore nearby Acadia National Park or walk down to the dock and catch the *Cat Ferry* for a day trip to Yarmouth, Nova Scotia. Enjoy gourmet dining in the Rose Garden Restaurant. 97 rooms, 4 story. Closed Nov-Mar. Check-in 3 pm, check-out 11 am. Restaurant, bar. Fitness room. Indoor pool, whirlpool. **$$**

Full-Service Inn

★ ★ ★ **THE BAYVIEW.** *111 Eden St, Bar Harbor (04609). Phone 207/288-5861; toll-free 800/356-3585; fax 207/288-3173. www.barharbor.com/bayview.* This 8-acre inn is close to shopping, restaurants, the town pier, the historical district, and Acadia National Park. 33 rooms, 3 story. Closed Nov-mid-May. Complimentary full breakfast. Check-out 11 am. Restaurant, bar. Whirlpool. Airport transportation available. **$$**

Specialty Lodgings

The following lodging establishments are approved by Mobil Travel Guide, but due to their unique and individualized nature have not been given a traditional Mobil Star rating. Included in this listing you may find bed-and-breakfasts, limited-service inns, guest ranches, and other unique hotel properties.

BALANCE ROCK INN. *21 Albert Meadow, Bar Harbor (04609). Phone 207/288-2610; toll-free 800/*

753-0494. www.barharborvacations.com. 23 rooms. Closed late Oct-early May. Complimentary full breakfast. Check-in 4 pm, check-out 11 am. **$$**

BAR HARBOR GRAND HOTEL. *269 Main St, Bar Harbor (04609). Phone toll-free 888/766-2529. www.barharborgrandhotel.com.* 70 rooms. Closed Dec -Apr. Complimentary continental breakfast. Check-in 3 pm, check-out noon. **$$**

BLACK FRIAR INN. *10 Summer St, Bar Harbor (04609). Phone 207/288-5091; fax 207/288-4197. www.blackfriarinn.com.* Victorian décor. 7 rooms, 3 story. Children over 12 years only. Complimentary full breakfast. Check-in after 4 pm, check-out 11 am. **$**

CASTELMAINE. *39 Holland Ave, Bar Harbor (04609). Phone 207/288-4563; toll-free 800/338-4563; fax 207/288-4525. www.castlemaineinn.com.* Tucked away on a quiet side street, this inn is a rambling, Victorian-style house (1886) located 1 mile from Acadia National Park and within walking distance of the ocean. It was once the summer residence of the Austro-Hungarian ambassador. 17 rooms, 3 story. Closed Nov-Apr. Complimentary continental breakfast. Check-in 2 pm, check-out 11 am. **$**

CLEFTSTONE MANOR. *92 Eden St, Bar Harbor (04609). Phone 207/288-4951; toll-free 888/288-4951; fax 207/288-2089. www.cleftstone.com.* This Victorian inn (1894) is set on a hill of terraced grounds and is located less than 1 mile from downtown Bar Harbor and only a few minutes from Acadia National Park. The inn was once owned by the Blair family of Washington DC. 16 rooms, 3 story. Closed Nov-Apr. Children over 8 years only. Complimentary full breakfast. Check-in 3 pm, check-out 11 am. **$**

INN AT BAY LEDGE. *150 Sand Point Rd, Bar Harbor (04609). Phone 207/288-4204 (summer); fax 207/288-5573. www.innatbayledge.com.* This inn (1907) is located at the top of an 80-foot cliff on Mount Desert Island near Acadia National Park. It offers the mixture of luxury and rustic Maine living and is beautifully decorated with antiques. Guests can view eagles and dolphins as they enjoy the lavish breakfast on the deck overlooking Frenchman's Bay and nearby mountains. 10 rooms, 2 story. Closed late Oct-Apr. Children over 15 years only. Complimentary full breakfast. Check-in 3 pm, check-out 11 am. **$$$**

MANOR HOUSE INN. *106 West St, Bar Harbor (04609). Phone 207/288-3759; toll-free 800/437-0088; fax 207/288-2974. www.barharbormanorhouse.com.* This is a restored historic Victorian mansion (1887). 18 rooms, 3 story. Children over 12 years only. Complimentary full breakfast. Check-in 3 pm, check-out 10:30 am. **$$**
🅳

MIRA MONTE INN & SUITES. *69 Mount Desert St, Bar Harbor (04609). Phone 207/288-4263; toll-free 800/553-5109; fax 207/288-3115. www.miramonte.com.* This restored Victorian home (1864) is on 2 1/2 acres; wraparound porch, period furnishings. 16 rooms, 2 story. Closed mid-Oct-Apr. Complimentary full breakfast. Check-in 3 pm, check-out 11 am. **$$**
🅳

STRATFORD HOUSE INN. *45 Mt Desert St, Bar Harbor (04609). Phone 207/288-5189; fax 207/288-4184. www.stratfordinn.com.* This inn was built by the publisher of Louisa May Alcott's *Little Women* (1900). Its English Tudor design was modeled after Shakespeare's house in Stratford-on-Avon; it features original Jacobean furniture. 10 rooms, 3 story. Closed mid-Oct-mid-May. Complimentary continental breakfast. Check-in 1 pm, check-out 11 am. **$**
🅳

THORNHEDGE INN. *47 Mount Desert St, Bar Harbor (04609). Phone 207/288-5398; toll-free 877/288-5398. www.thornhedgeinn.com.* This Queen Anne-style inn is located in the Historic Corridor District of Bar Harbor, close to many shops, galleries, and restaurants. It was built by the publisher of Louisa May Alcott's *Little Women* as a summer cottage (1900). 13 rooms, 3 story. Check-in noon, check-out 11 am. **$**
🅳

Restaurants

★ ★ **124 COTTAGE STREET.** *124 Cottage St, Bar Harbor (04609). Phone 207/288-4383.* This reastaurant is located in a restored, turn-of-the-century cottage. American menu. Dinner. Closed Nov-May. Bar. Children's menu. Outdoor seating. **$$**
🅳

★ **FISHERMAN'S LANDING.** *35 West St, Bar Harbor (04609). Phone 207/288-4632.* Built over water. Seafood menu. Lunch, dinner. Closed Oct-May. Bar. Outdoor seating. **$**

★ **FREDDIE'S ROUTE 66.** *21 Cottage St, Bar Harbor (04609). Phone 207/288-3708.* American menu. Dinner. Closed mid-Oct-mid-May. Bar. Children's menu. **$$**

★ ★ ★ **GEORGE'S.** *7 Stephens Ln, Bar Harbor (04609). Phone 207/288-4505. www.georgesbarharbor.com.* This restaurant, located in a restored mid-1800s home near the ocean, has perfected its Mediterranean-inspired menu. Creative tastes and unique flavors appear throughout the dishes, and adventurous guests do not leave disappointed. Mediterranean menu. Dinner. Closed Nov-late May. Bar. Children's menu. Outdoor seating. **$**
🅳

★ ★ **MAGGIE'S CLASSIC SCALES.** *6 Summer St, Bar Harbor (04609). Phone 207/288-9007.* Seafood menu. Dinner. Closed mid-Oct-late June. Bar. **$$**
🅳

★ ★ **MAMA'S BOY BISTRO.** *Newman and Main sts, Winter Harbor (04693). Phone 207/963-2365. www.mamasboybistro.com.* American menu. Dinner. Casual attire. Reservations recommended. Outdoor seating. **$$**
🅳

★ **MIGUEL'S MEXICAN.** *51 Rodick St, Bar Harbor (04609). Phone 207/288-5117.* Mexican menu. Dinner. Closed mid-Nov-Mar. Bar. Children's menu. Outdoor seating. **$$**

★ ★ ★ **READING ROOM.** *Newport Dr, Bar Harbor (04609). Phone 207/288-3351; fax 207/288-5296. www.barharborinn.com.* Seafood menu. Breakfast, dinner, Sun brunch. Closed mid-Nov-Easter. Bar. Children's menu. Valet parking. **$$**

Bath (E-2)

See also Boothbay Harbor, Brunswick, Freeport, Wiscasset

Population 9,799
Elevation 13 ft
Area Code 207
Zip 04530
Information Chamber of Commerce of the Bath-Brunswick Region, 45 Front St; phone 207/443-9751
Web Site www.midcoastmaine.com

For more than two centuries, Bath has been a ship-building center on the west bank of the Kennebec

River. The Bath Iron Works, which dates to 1833, began building ships in 1889. It has produced destroyers, cruisers, a battleship, pleasure craft, and steamers, and now also produces patrol frigates. Altogether, Bath has launched more than 4,000 ships from its shores, and launching a ship today is still a great event.

Many fine old mansions, built when Bath was a great seaport, still stand. A restored 19th-century business district, waterfront park, and public landing are also part of the city.

What to See and Do

Fort Popham Memorial. *Popham Beach. 16 miles S on Hwy 209. Phone 207/389-1335.* Construction of the fort began in 1861. Never finished, it was garrisoned in 1865-1866 and remains an impressive masonry structure with gun emplacements. Picnic tables (no garbage receptacles). (May-Sept, daily)

Maine Maritime Museum. *243 Washington St, Bath (04530). 2 miles S of Hwy 1, located on Kennebec River. Phone 207/443-1316. www.mainemaritimemuseum.org.* Maritime History Building has exhibits of maritime art and artifacts, shipmodels and paintings. Tours of original shipyard buildings, demonstrations of seafaring techniques (seasonal); waterfront picnic area and playground. Museum store. (Daily; closed Jan 1, Thanksgiving, Dec 25) **$$$**

Popham Beach State Park. *10 Perkins Farm Ln, Bath (04562). 12 miles S on Hwy 209. Phone 207/389-1335.* Swimming, tidal pools (mid-Apr-Nov), surfing; fishing; picnicking. (Daily) **$**

Popham Colony. *16 miles S on Hwy 209 on Sabino Head.* A picturesque drive. In 1607, the first American vessel, the *Virginia,* was built here by colonists who shortly thereafter returned to England, many of them in the ship they had built. On the hilltop nearby is Fort Baldwin, built during World War I. A 70-foot tower offers a panoramic view of the coast and the Kennebec River. **FREE**

Reid State Park. *Seguinland Rd, Georgetown (04548). 1 mile E on Hwy 1 to Woolwich, then 13 miles SE on Hwy 127 to Georgetown, then SE. Phone 207/371-2303.* Swimming, saltwater lagoon, bathhouse, fishing; picnic facilities, concession. (Daily) **$**

Limited-Service Hotel

★ ★ **HOLIDAY INN.** *139 Richardson St, Bath (04530). Phone 207/443-9741; toll-free 800/465-4329; fax 207/442-8281. www.holiday-inn.com.* 141 rooms, 4 story. Pets accepted, some restrictions. Check-out noon. Restaurant, bar. Fitness room. Outdoor pool, whirlpool. **$**

Specialty Lodging

The following lodging establishment is approved by Mobil Travel Guide, but due to its unique and individualized nature has not been given a traditional Mobil Star rating. Included in this listing you may find bed-and-breakfasts, limited-service inns, guest ranches, and other unique hotel properties.

GALEN C. MOSES HOUSE. *1009 Washington St, Bath (04530). Phone 207/442-8771; toll-free 888/442-8771; fax 207/442-0808. www.galenmoses.com.* This inn, built in 1874, is a lovely plum, pink, and teal house, which is on the National Register of Historic Houses. It features a Victorian interior and stained-glass windows. All the rooms are tastefully decorated with antiques. Guests can take leisurely walks along the waterfront, visit antiques stores, and enjoy many fine restaurants in the area. 4 rooms. Children over 12 years only. Complimentary full breakfast. Check-in 3-8 pm, check-out 11 am. **$$**

Restaurants

★ ★ **KRISTINA'S.** *160 Centre St, Bath (04530). Phone 207/442-8577; fax 207/443-5498.* American menu. Breakfast, lunch, dinner, brunch. Closed Mon (off-season); Thanksgiving, Dec 25; Jan. Bar. Children's menu. Outdoor seating. **$$**

★ **TASTE OF MAINE.** *Hwy 1, Woolwich (04579). Phone 207/443-4554; fax 207/443-6394. www.tasteofmaine.com.* Seafood, steak menu. Lunch, dinner. Children's menu. Outdoor seating. **$$**

Baxter State Park

See also Millinocket

18 miles NW of Millinocket via park roads.

While serving as a legislator and as governor of Maine, Percival P. Baxter urged creation of a wilderness park around Mount Katahdin—Maine's highest peak (5,267 feet). Rebuffed but not defeated, Baxter bought the land with his own money and deeded to the state of Maine a 201,018-acre park "to be forever left in its natural, wild state." The park can be reached from Greenville via paper company roads, from Millinocket via Hwy 157, or from Patten via Hwy 159.

The Park Authority operates the following camp-grounds: Katahdin Stream, Abol and Nesowadnehunk, Roaring Brook (Roaring Brook Road), Chimney Pond (by trail 3.3 miles beyond Roaring Brook), Russell Pond (Wassataquoik Valley, 7 miles by trail beyond Roaring Brook), South Branch Pond (at outlet of Lower South Branch Pond), Trout Brook Farm (Trout Brook Crossing). There are cabins ($17/person/night) at Daicey Pond off Nesowadnehunk Road and at Kidney Pond. All areas except Chimney, Kidney, and Daicey ponds have tent space, and all areas except Trout Brook Farm, Kidney, and Daicey ponds have lean-tos ($6/person/night), water (unprotected, should be purified), and primitive facilities (no indoor plumbing, no running water; some springs); bunk-houses ($7/night) at some campgrounds. Under age 7 free throughout the park.

Reservations should be made by mail (and paid in full) in advance. For detailed information, contact the Reservation Clerk, Baxter State Park, 64 Balsam Drive, Millinocket 04462. Swimming, fishing, canoes for rent at Russell Pond, South Branch Pond, Daicey Pond, Kidney Pond, and Trout Brook farm.

The park is open for camping mid-May-mid-October. No pets or motorcycles are permitted. Vehicles exceeding 7 feet wide, 9 feet high, or 22 feet long will not be admitted. For further information, contact Park Manager, 64 Balsam Drive, Millinocket 04462. Nonresident vehicle fee **$$**

Belfast (E-3)

See also Bucksport, Camden, Searsport

Settled 1770
Population 6,355
Elevation 103 ft
Area Code 207
Zip 04915
Information Chamber of Commerce, 17 Main St, PO Box 58; phone 207/338-5900
Web Site www.belfastmaine.org

Belfast, named for the city in Northern Ireland, was settled in 1770 by Irish and Scottish immigrants. An old seaport on the west shore of Penobscot Bay, Belfast, is also a hub of small boat traffic to the bay islands. It is the seat of Waldo County, with sardine canneries, potato processing, window making, and printing as its major industries.

What to See and Do

Lake St. George State Park. *Liberty. 19 miles W on Hwy 3, near Montville. Phone 207/589-4255.* More than 360 acres. Swimming, bathhouse, lifeguard, fishing, boating (ramp, rentals); snowmobiling permitted, picnicking, camping. (Mid-May-mid-Oct)

Special Event

Belfast Bay Festival. *City Park, 1 Main St, Belfast (04915). Phone 207/338-5719.* Parade, concerts, carnival. July.

Limited-Service Hotel

★ **BELFAST HARBOR INN.** *91 Searsport Ave, Belfast (04915). Phone 207/338-2740; toll-free 800/545-8576; fax 207/338-5205. www.belfastharborinn.com.* Overlooks Penobscot Bay. 61 rooms, 2 story. Pets accepted, some restrictions; fee. Complimentary continental breakfast. Check-out 11 am. Restaurant. Outdoor pool. **$**

Specialty Lodging

The following lodging establishment is approved by Mobil Travel Guide, but due to its unique and individualized nature has not been given a traditional Mobil Star rating. Included in this listing you may find bed-and-breakfasts, limited-service inns, guest ranches, and other unique hotel properties.

BELFAST BAY MEADOWS INN. *192 Northport Ave, Belfast (04915). Phone 207/338-5715; toll-free 800/335-2370. www.baymeadowsinn.com.* This turn-of-the-century country inn overlooks the bay. 19 rooms, 3 story. Pets accepted; fee. Complimentary full breakfast. Check-in 3:30-6:30 pm, check-out 11 am. **$$**

Restaurants

★ ★ **DARBY'S.** *155 High St, Belfast (04915). Phone 207/338-2339; fax 207/338-5521.* International/Fusion menu. Lunch, dinner. Closed Easter, Dec 25. Bar. Children's menu. **$$**

★ **YOUNG'S LOBSTER POND.** *Mitchell Rd, Belfast (04915). Phone 207/338-1160; fax 207/338-5652.* Seafood menu. Breakfast, lunch, dinner. Outdoor seating. **$$**
🅓

Bethel (E-1)

See also Rumford

Settled 1774
Population 2,329
Elevation 700 ft
Area Code 207
Zip 04217
Information Chamber of Commerce, PO Box 1247; phone 207/824-2282 or toll-free 800/442-5826
Web Site www.bethelmaine.com

Bethel, on both banks of the winding Androscoggin River, is built on the rolling Oxford Hills and is backed by the rough foothills of the White Mountains. In addition to being a year-round resort, it's an educational and wood products center. One of Maine's leading preparatory schools, Gould Academy (founded in 1836), is located here.

What to See and Do

Carter's X-Country Ski Center. *420 Main St, Bethel (04270). Phone 207/539-4848. www.cartersxcski.com.* One thousand acres with 55 kilometers of groomed cross-country trails. Rentals, lessons; lounge, shop; two lodges. (Nov-Mar, daily 9 am-4:30 pm) **$$$**

Dr. Moses Mason House Museum. *10 Broad St, Bethel (04217). In the National Historic District. Phone 207/824-2908.* (1813) Restored home of prominent congressman who served during administration of Andrew Jackson. Antique furnishings, Early American murals. (July-Labor Day: Sat-Sun afternoons; rest of year: Mon-Fri, also by appointment) **$**

Grafton Notch State Park. *Approximately 9 miles NW via Hwy 2, Hwy 26. Phone 207/824-2912.* The Appalachian Trail passes through the notch;

interpretive displays, scenic view, picnicking; fishing. (Mid-May-mid-Oct) **$**

Sunday River Ski Resort. *Sunday River Rd, Bethel (04217). 6 miles NE on Hwy 2. Phone 207/824-3000; toll-free 800/543-2754 (reservations). www.sundayriver.com.* Nine quad, four triple, two double chairlifts (including four high-speed detachables and one surface lift); patrol, school, rentals, ski shop; snowmaking; cafeterias, restaurants; bars. 127 runs; longest run 3 miles; vertical drop 2,340 feet. (Early Oct-mid-May, daily) 100 cross-country trails adjacent. Mountain biking (May-Labor Day: daily; Labor Day-late Oct: weekends). **$$$$**

Swimming, picnicking, camping, boating, fishing. *E on Hwy 26.* Songo Lake in Bethel; Christopher Lake in Bryant Pond; North and South ponds in Locke Mills; Littlefield beaches and Stony Brook campgrounds.

White Mountain National Forest. *Phone 603/528-8721. www.fs.fed.us/r9/white.* (See NEW HAMPSHIRE) More than 49,000 acres of this forest extend into Maine southwest of here. Birches and sugar maples turn fall into a season of breathtaking color. Fishing; hiking, rock hounding, camping (fee). For more information, contact the Supervisor, 719 Main St, PO Box 638, Laconia, NH 03247.

Limited-Service Hotel

★ **NORSEMAN INN.** *134 Mayville Rd, Bethel (04217). Phone 207/824-2002; fax 207/824-0640. www.norsemaninn.com.* 31 rooms, 2 story. Complimentary continental breakfast. Check-out 10:30 am. **$$**

Full-Service Resort

★ ★ ★ **BETHEL INN & COUNTRY CLUB.** *On the Common, Bethel (04217). Phone 207/824-2175; toll-free 800/654-0125; fax 207/824-2233. www.bethelinn.com.* 60 rooms. Pets accepted, some restrictions; fee. Check-in 2 pm, check-out 11 am. Restaurant, bar. Children's activity center. Fitness room. Outdoor pool, whirlpool. Golf. Tennis. **$$**
🐾 🏋 🏊 🏌 🖼

Full-Service Inn

★ ★ ★ **BRIAR LEA INN & RESTAURANT.** *150 Mayville Rd, Bethel (04217). Phone 207/824-4717; toll-free 877/311-1299; fax 207/824-7121. www.briarleainnrestaurant.com.* Built in the 1850s; farmhouse atmosphere. 6 rooms. Pets accepted, some restrictions; fee. Complimentary full breakfast. Check-in 4 pm, check-out 11 am. Restaurant. **$**

Restaurant

★ **MOTHER'S.** *43 Main St, Bethel (04217). Phone 207/824-2589.* American menu. Lunch, dinner. Closed Thanksgiving, Dec 24-25. Children's menu. Outdoor seating. **$$**

Bingham (D-2)

See also Skowhegan

Settled 1785
Population 1,071
Elevation 371 ft
Area Code 207
Zip 04920

What to See and Do

Wilderness Expeditions. *1 Birches Dr, Rockwood (04478). Phone 207/534-7305; toll-free 800/825-9453.* Guided raft trips on the Kennebec, Penobscot, and Dead rivers; also canoe outfitting, guided kayaking and ski tours. (May-Sept, daily) **$$$$**

Limited-Service Hotel

★ **BINGHAM MOTOR INN & SPORTS COMPLEX.** *Rte 201, Bingham (04920). Phone 207/672-4135; fax 207/672-4138. www.binghammotorinn.com.* 20 rooms. Pets accepted, some restrictions. Check-out 10 am. Outdoor pool. **$**

Blue Hill (E-3)

See also Bar Harbor, Ellsworth

Settled 1722
Population 1,941
Elevation 40 ft
Area Code 207
Zip 04614
Information Blue Hill Peninsula Chamber of Commerce, PO Box 520; phone 207/374-3242
Web Site www.bluehillme.com

Named for a nearby hill that gives a beautiful view of Mount Desert Island, Blue Hill changed from a thriving seaport to a summer colony known for its crafts and antiques. Mary Ellen Chase, born here in 1887, wrote about Blue Hill in *A Goodly Heritage* and *Mary Peters.*

What to See and Do

Holt House. *Water St, Blue Hill (04614). Phone 207/326-8250.* One of the oldest houses in Blue Hill; now home of the Blue Hill Historical Society. Memorabilia. (Tues, Thurs, Sat afternoons; closed holidays) For further information contact the town clerk. **$**

Jonathan Fisher House. *Hwy 15, Blue Hill (04862). Phone 207/374-2844.* (1814) House designed and built by town's first minister, who also made most of his own furniture and household articles; paintings and woodcuts by the minister; memorabilia. (June-Oct, Mon-Sat afternoons) **$$**

Rackliffe Pottery. *138 Elsworth Rd, Blue Hill (04614). Phone 207/374-2297.* Family manufactures wheel-thrown dinnerware from native red-firing clay. Open workshop. (July-Aug: daily; rest of year: Mon-Sat; closed holidays) **FREE**

Rowantrees Pottery. *84 Union St, Union (04862). Phone 207/374-5535.* Manufactures functional pottery and wheel-thrown handcrafted dinnerware. (June-Sept: daily; rest of year: Mon-Fri; closed holidays) **FREE**

Wooden Boat School. *Naskeag Rd, Brooklin (04616). Naskeag Rd and Brooklyn. Phone 207/359-4651.* (Daily)

Special Event

Blue Hill Fair. *Phone 207/374-3701.* Sheep dog trials, agriculture and livestock exhibits; midway, harness racing, crafts. Five days over Labor Day weekend.

Limited-Service Hotel

★ **HERITAGE INN.** *Ellsworth Rd, Blue Hill (04614). Phone 207/374-5646. www.bhheritagemotorinn.com.* On hillside, overlooking bay. 23 rooms, 2 story. Check-out 11 am. **$$**

Full-Service Inn

★ ★ ★ **BLUE HILL INN.** *Union St, Blue Hill (04614). Phone 207/374-2844; toll-free 800/826-7415; fax 207/374-2829. www.bluehillinn.com.* This federal-style home has provided bed-and-breakfast amenities at the tip of the bay since 1840 and is on the National Register of Historic Houses. Choose one of the quaint guest rooms or the adjacent Cape House suite for a more private retreat. 12 rooms, 3 story. Check-in 2-5 pm, check-out 10:30 am. Restaurant. Airport transportation available. **$$**

Boothbay Harbor (E-2)

See also Bath, Damariscotta, Monhegan Island, Wiscasset

Population 1,267
Elevation 16 ft
Area Code 207
Zip 04538
Information Boothbay Harbor Region Chamber of Commerce, PO Box 356; phone 207/633-2353 or toll-free 800/266-8422
Web Site www.boothbayharbor.com

Native Americans were paid 20 beaver pelts for the area encompassing Boothbay Harbor. Today, its protected harbor, a haven for boatmen, is the scene of well-attended regattas several times a summer. Boothbay Harbor, on the peninsula between the Sheepscot and Damariscotta rivers, shares the peninsula and adjacent islands with a dozen other communities, including Boothbay (settled 1630), of which it was once a part.

What to See and Do

Balmy Days Boat Trips. *Pier 8, Commercial St, Boothbay Harbor (04538). Phone 207/633-2284.* Makes trips to Monhegan Island (see) with four-hour stopover. (June-Sept, daily)

Boothbay Railway Village. *Hwy 27, Boothbay (04537). 1 mile N of Boothbay Center on Hwy 27. Phone 207/633-4727.* Historical Maine exhibits of rural life, railroads, and antique autos and trucks. Rides on a coal-fired, narrow-gauge steam train to an antique vehicle display. Also on exhibit on 8 acres are displays of early fire equipment, a general store, a one-room schoolhouse, and two restored railroad stations. (Mid-June-mid-Oct, daily) **$$**

Boothbay Region Historical Society Museum. *72 Oak St, Boothbay Harbor (04538). Phone 207/633-0820. www.boothbayhistorical.org.* Artifacts of Boothbay Region. (July-Labor Day: Wed, Fri- Sat; rest of year: Sat only) **DONATION**

Cap'n Fish's Boat Trips and Deep Sea Fishing. *Pier 1, 65 Atlantic Ave, Boothbay Harbor (04538). Phone 207/633-3244.* Boats make varied excursions: 1 1/4- to 3-hour trips; puffin, seal, and whale watches; scenic, sunset, and cruises; fall foliage and Kennebec River trips; charters. (Mid-May-Oct; days vary) **$$$$**

Fishing. In inland waters, Golf Course Brook, Adams, West Harbor and Knickerbocker ponds in Boothbay; Meadow Brook in East Boothbay. Ocean fishing from harbor docks. Boat rentals, deep-sea fishing.

Novelty Boat Trips. *Pier 8, Commercial St, Boothbay Harbor (04538). Phone 207/633-2284.* One-hour harbor cruises with stop at Squirrel Island; Night Lights cruises (July-Aug, Tues-Sat). Harbor cruises (Apr-Oct, Daily).

Picnicking. *99 Atlantic Ave, Boothbay Harbor (04538). Phone 207/633-5160.* Boothbay Region Lobstermen's Cooperative, Atlantic Avenue. Lobsterman's Wharf, East Boothbay. Robinson's Wharf, Highway 27 at bridge, Southport. Boiled lobsters and steamed clams, snacks available.

Special Events

Fall Foliage Festival. *Phone 207/633-4743.* Foliage drives, harvest suppers, boat trips, country fair. Columbus Day weekend.

Fisherman's Festival. *Phone 207/633-2353.* Celebration of the rich fishing heritage of the region includes a fish relay race, a lobster trap hauling competition, a lobster crate race, and lobster trap running. Other events include the Shrimp Princess Pageant, a pancake breakfast, arts and crafts show, old-fasioned fish fry, church suppers, dockside dancing, lighthouse tours, and tall tales as only fishermen can tell them. Mid-Apr.

Harbor Lights Festival. *192 Townsend Ave, Boothbay Harbor (04538). Phone 207/633-2353.* Craft fair, lighted boat parade. First Sat in Dec.

Windjammer Days. *192 Townsend Ave, Boothbay Harbor (04538). Phone 207/633-2353.* Old schooners that formerly sailed the trade routes and now cruise the Maine coast sail en masse into harbor. Waterfront food court, entertainment, street parade, children's activities. Late June.

Limited-Service Hotels

★ ★ **BROWN'S WHARF MOTEL.** *105 Atlantic Ave, Boothbay Harbor (04538). Phone 207/633-5440; toll-free 800/334-8110. www.brownswharfinn.com.* This marina property overlooks the ocean directly on inner Boothbay Harbor and has both guest rooms and efficiencies overlooking the water. Brown's Wharf Restaurant features delicious seafood dinners, and there is a comfortable rustic bar and lounge. Visit downtown Boothbay via the footbridge from the motel. 70 rooms, 3 story. Closed Nov-Apr. Check-out 11 am. Restaurant, bar. **$**

★ ★ **FISHERMAN'S WHARF INN.** *22 Commercial St, Boothbay Harbor (04538). Phone 207/633-5090; toll-free 800/628-6872; fax 207/633-5092. www.fishermanswharfinn.com.* 54 rooms, 3 story. Closed Nov-mid-May. Complimentary continental breakfast. Check-out 11 am. Restaurant, bar. **$**

★ **TUGBOAT INN.** *80 Commercial St, Boothbay Harbor (04538). Phone 207/633-4434; toll-free 800/248-2628. www.tugboatinn.com.* 64 rooms, 2 story. Closed Dec-mid-Mar. Check-out 11 am. Restaurant, bar. **$**

Full-Service Resort

★ ★ ★ **SPRUCE POINT INN.** *Atlantic Ave, Boothbay Harbor (04538). Phone 207/633-4152; toll-free 800/553-0289; fax 207/633-7138. www.sprucepointinn.com.* Located on 15 secluded acres of a quiet peninsula on the Atlantic ocean, this beautiful retreat is the perfect getaway. 45 rooms, 3 story. Closed mid-Oct-mid-May. Check-in 3 pm, check-out 11 am. Restaurant, bar. Fitness room. Two outdoor pools, whirlpool. Tennis. **$**

Specialty Lodgings

The following lodging establishments are approved by Mobil Travel Guide, but due to their unique and individualized nature have not been given a traditional Mobil Star rating. Included in this listing you may find bed-and-breakfasts, limited-service inns, guest ranches, and other unique hotel properties.

1830 ADMIRAL'S QUARTERS INN. *71 Commercial St, Boothbay Harbor (04538). Phone 207/633-2474; fax 207/633-5904. www.admiralsquartersinn.com.* Built in 1830. 7 rooms. Closed mid-Dec-mid-Feb. Children over 12 years only. Complimentary full breakfast. Check-in 2-6 pm, check-out 11 am. **$$**

ANCHOR WATCH BED & BREAKFAST. *9 Eames Rd, Boothbay Harbor (04538). Phone 207/633-7565; fax 207/633-5319. www.anchorwatch.com.* 5 rooms, 3 story. Children over 9 years only. Complimentary full breakfast. Check-in 2 pm, check-out 11 am. **$$**

FIVE GABLES INN. *107 Murray Hill Rd, East Boothbay (04544). Phone 207/633-4551; toll-free 800/451-5048. www.fivegablesinn.com.* This inn, built in 1890, features Victorian décor. 15 rooms, 3 story. Children over 11 years only. Complimentary full breakfast. Check-in 2 pm, check-out 11 am. **$**

HARBOUR TOWNE INN ON WATERFRONT. *71 Townsend Ave, Boothbay Harbor (04538). Phone 207/633-4300. www.harbourtowneinn.com.* On harbor. 12 rooms, 3 story. Complimentary continental breakfast. Check-in 3:30 pm, check-out 10 am. **$$**

HOWARD HOUSE LODGE. *347 Townsend Ave, Boothbay Harbor (04538). Phone 207/633-3933; toll-free 800/466-6697; fax 207/633-6244. www.howardhouselodge.com.* Country, chalet-style building in wooded area. 14 rooms, 2 story. Complimentary full breakfast. Check-in 3 pm, check-out 11 am. **$**

KENNISTON HILL INN. *Wiscasset Rd (Hwy 27), Boothbay (04537). Phone 207/633-2159; toll-free 800/992-2915. www.kennistonhillinn.com.* Restored Colonial-style farmhouse (1786); antiques. 10 rooms, 2 story. Children over 10 years only. Complimentary full breakfast. Check-in 3 pm, check-out 11 am. **$$**

Restaurants

★ **CHINA BY THE SEA.** *96 Townsend Ave, Boothbay Harbor (04538). Phone 207/633-4449; fax 207/633-7044. www.chinabythesea.com.* Chinese menu. Lunch, dinner. Closed Thanksgiving, Dec 25. Outdoor seating. **$$**

★ **EBB TIDE.** *43 Commercial St, Boothbay Harbor (04538). Phone 207/633-5692.* Seafood menu. Breakfast, lunch, dinner. Closed Dec 25. Children's menu. **$$**

★ ★ **FISHERMAN'S WHARF INN.** *22 Commercial St, Boothbay Harbor (04538). Phone 207/633-5090. www.fishermanswharfinn.com.* Scenic murals. Seafood menu. Lunch, dinner. Closed mid-Oct-mid-May. Bar. Valet parking. Outdoor seating. **$$$**

★ **HARBORSIDE.** *12 Bridge St, Boothbay Harbor (04538). Phone 207/633-4074.* Seafood menu. Breakfast, lunch, dinner. Closed mid-Oct-Apr. Children's menu. **$$**

Bridgton (E-1)

See also Poland Spring, Sebago Lake

Population 2,195
Elevation 494 ft
Area Code 207
Zip 04009
Information Bridgton Lakes Region Chamber of Commerce, PO Box 236; phone 207/647-3472
Web Site www.mainelakeschamber.com

Primarily a resort, this community between Long and Highland lakes is within easy reach of Pleasant Mountain (2,007 feet), a recreational area that offers skiing as well as a magnificent view of 50 lakes. Bridgton also has many unique craft and antiques shops located within a 2-mile radius of the town center.

What to See and Do

Gibbs Avenue Museum. *44 Gibbs Ave, Bridgton (04009). Phone 207/647-3699.* Headquarters of Bridgton Historical Society. Permanent exhibits include narrow-gauge railroad memorabilia; Civil War artifacts; Sears "horseless carriage" (1911). Special summer exhibits. Genealogy research facility includes Bridgton and Saw River railroad documents. (Sept-June: Tues and Thurs; rest of year: Tues-Fri; closed holidays) **$**

Shawnee Peak Ski Area. *734 Mountain Rd, Bridgton (04009). 6 miles W, off Hwy 302. Phone 207/647-8444. www.shawneepeak.com.* Quad, two triple, double chairlift; snowmaking, school, rentals, patrol; nursery; restaurant, cafeteria, bar. Longest run 1 1/2 miles; vertical drop 1,350 feet. Night skiing. (Dec-Mar, daily)

Special Event

Quilt Show. *Town hall, Bridgton (04009). Phone 207/647-3472.* New and old quilts; demonstrations. Contact Chamber of Commerce. Mid-July.

Full-Service Inn

★ ★ ★ **THE INN AT LONG LAKE.** *Lake House Rd and Hwy 302, Naples (04055). Phone 207/693-6226; toll-free 800/437-0328. www.innatlonglake.com.* The colonial styling of this Lakes Region inn (1906) fits right in with the ambience of historic Naples Village. Amenities include country breakfasts, cozy common rooms, and a landscaped backyard. 16 rooms, 4 story. Closed Jan-Mar. Complimentary continental breakfast. Check-in 3 pm, check-out 11 am. **$$**
🄳

Restaurant

★ **BLACK HORSE TAVERN.** *8 Portland St, Bridgton (04099). Phone 207/647-5300; fax 207/647-5310.* In restored homestead. Seafood, steak menu. Lunch, dinner, Sun brunch. Closed Thanksgiving, Dec 25. Bar. Children's menu. **$$**

Brunswick (E-2)

See also Bailey Island, Bath, Freeport, Yarmouth

Settled 1628
Population 20,906
Elevation 67 ft
Area Code 207
Zip 04011
Information Chamber of Commerce of the Bath-Brunswick Region, 59 Pleasant St; phone 207/725-8797
Web Site www.midcoastmaine.com

Once a lumbering center and later a mill town, Brunswick is now mainly concerned with trade, health care, and education; it is the home of Bowdoin College and Brunswick Naval Air Station. The city lies northeast of a summer resort area on the shores and islands of Casco Bay. Magnificent Federalist mansions along Federal Street and Park Row remind visitors of Brunswick's past.

What to See and Do

Bowdoin College. *1 College St, Brunswick (04011). Phone 207/725-3000.* (1794)(1,500 students) Nathaniel Hawthorne, Henry Wadsworth Longfellow, Robert Peary, Franklin Pierce, and Joan Benoit Samuelson graduated from here. Tours.

Museum of Art. *Walker Art Building, Bowdoin College, Upper Park Row and Bath Rd, Brunswick (04011). Phone 207/725-3275.* Portraits by Stuart, Feke, and Copley; paintings by Homer and Eakins; Greek and Roman vases and sculpture. (Tues-Sun; closed holidays) **FREE**

Peary-MacMillan Arctic Museum. *Hubbard Hall, Bowdoin College, 9500 College Station, Brunswick (04011). Phone 207/725-3416.* Exhibits relating to Arctic exploration, ecology, and Inuit (Eskimo) culture. (Tues-Sun; closed holidays) **FREE**

Pejepscot Historical Society Museum. *159 Park Row, Brunswick (04011). Phone 207/729-6606.* Regional historical museum housed in an 1858 sea captain's home; changing exhibits, research facilities. (Tues-Sat; closed holidays) **FREE** The Society also operates

Joshua L. Chamberlain Museum. *226 Maine St, Brunswick (04011).* Former residence of Maine's greatest Civil War hero, four-term Governor of Maine, and president of Bowdoin College. Guided tours. (June-mid-Oct, Tues-Sat; closed holidays)

Skolfield-Whittier House. *161 Park Row, Brunswick (04011).* An 18-room Victorian structure last occupied in 1925; furnishings and housewares of three generations. Guided tours. (June-mid-Oct, Tues-Sat; closed holidays) **$$$**

Thomas Point Beach. *29 Meadow Rd, Brunswick (04011). Off Hwy 24, at Cook's Corner. Phone 207/725-6009.* Swimming, lifeguard. Picnicking, tables, fireplaces. Snack bar; gift shop, arcade, playground; camping (fee). (Memorial Day-Labor Day, daily)

Special Events

Bluegrass Festival. *Thomas Point Beach, 29 Meadow Rd, Brunswick (04011). Phone 207/725-8797.* Many bluegrass bands perform at this 85-acre park, where the music meets the sea. Labor Day weekend.

Bowdoin Summer Music Festival and School. *Brunswick High School and Bowdoin College campus, 116 Maquoit Rd, Brunswick (04011). Phone 207/373-1400.* Chamber music, concert series. Fri evenings, late June-Aug.

Maine State Music Theater. *Pickard Theater, Bowdoin College campus, 14 Maine St, Brunswick (04011). Phone 207/725-8769.* Broadway musicals by professional cast. Tues-Sat evenings; Wed, Fri, Sun matinees. Mid-June-Aug.

Music on the Mall. *Downtown, 59 Pleasant St, Brunswick (04011). Phone 207/725-8797.* Free outdoor family concert series. Wed evenings, July and Aug.

Topsham Fair. *Phone 207/725-8797.* N via Hwy 24 in Topsham. Entertainment, arts and crafts. Seven days in early Aug.

Limited-Service Hotels

★ **COMFORT INN.** *199 Pleasant St, Brunswick (04011). Phone 207/729-1129; toll-free 800/228-5150; fax 207/725-8310. www.comfortinn.com.* 80 rooms, 2 story. Complimentary continental breakfast. Check-out 11 am. **$**

★ **SUPER 8.** *224 Bath Rd, Brunswick (04011). Phone 207/725-8883; toll-free 800/800-8000; fax 207/729-8766. www.super8.com.* 71 rooms. Complimentary continental breakfast. Check-out 11 am. **$**

Full-Service Inn

★ ★ ★ **CAPTAIN DANIEL STONE INN.** *10 Water St, Brunswick (04011). Phone 207/725-9898; fax 207/527-5858. www.captaindanielstoneinn.com.* This 1819 inn has been elegantly restored in an old-world charm but comes equipped with many of today's plusses. Most rooms come equipped with TVs and VCRs. Relax in classic ambience while feasting in the restaurant featuring marvelous New England flavor with an international flair. 34 rooms, 3 story. Complimentary continental breakfast. Check-in 4 pm, check-out 11 am. Restaurant, bar. **$$**

Restaurant

★ **GREAT IMPASTA.** *42 Maine St, Brunswick (04011). Phone 207/729-5858; fax 207/729-8576. www.thegreatimpasta.com.* Italian menu. Lunch, dinner. Closed Sun; Thanksgiving, Dec 25. **$$**

Bucksport (D-3)

See also Bangor, Belfast, Ellsworth, Searsport

Settled 1762
Population 4,825
Elevation 43 ft
Area Code 207
Zip 04416
Information Bucksport Chamber of Commerce, PO Box 1880; phone 207/469-6818
Web Site www.allmaine.com/bucksport

Although originally settled in 1762, the Penobscot Valley town of Bucksport was so thoroughly burned by the British in 1779 that it was not resettled until 1812. On the east bank of the Penobscot River, Bucksport is a shopping center for the area, but is primarily an industrial town with an emphasis on paper manufacturing. The Waldo Hancock Bridge crosses the Penobscot to Verona Island.

What to See and Do

Accursed Tombstone. *Buck Cemetery, Main and Hinks sts, Bucksport (04416). Near Verona Island Bridge.* Granite obelisk over grave of founder Jonathan Buck bears an indelible mark in the shape of a woman's leg—said to have been put there by a witch whom he had hanged. **FREE**

Fort Knox State Park. *S on Hwy 1 across Waldo Hancock Bridge. Phone 207/469-7719.* The park consists of 124 acres around a huge granite fort started in 1844 and used as a defense in the Aroostook War. The structure includes spiral staircases. Hiking, picnicking. Interpretive displays. Tours (Aug-Sept). (May-Oct)

Fort Point State Park. *8 miles S on Hwy 1. Phone 207/469-6818.* Ocean view. Fishing; picnicking. (Memorial Day-Labor Day)

Northeast Historic Film. *379 Main St, Bucksport (04416). Phone 207/469-0924.* The Alamo Theatre (1916) houses a museum, theater, store, and archives of northern New England film and video. Exhibits present 100 years of moviegoing, from nickelodeons to mall cinemas. Video and film presentations interpret regional culture. (Mon-Fri) **FREE**

Wilson Museum. *107 Perkins St, Castine (04421). 18 miles S via Hwy 175, 166. Phone 207/326-9247.* Prehistoric, historic, geologic, and art exhibits (Late May-Sept, Tues-Sun, also holidays). On grounds are John Perkins House (1763-1783), Hearse House, Blacksmith Shop (July-Aug, Wed and Sun). **$$**

Specialty Lodgings

The following lodging establishments are approved by Mobil Travel Guide, but due to their unique and individualized nature have not been given a traditional Mobil Star rating. Included in this listing you may find bed-and-breakfasts, limited-service inns, guest ranches, and other unique hotel properties.

CASTINE INN. *Main St, Castine (04421). Phone 207/326-4365; fax 207/326-4570. www.castineinn.com.* Built in 1898. 19 rooms, 3 story. Closed Nov-Apr. Children over 8 years only. Complimentary full breakfast. Check-in 3 pm, check-out 11 am. Restaurant, bar. **$$** 🄳

PENTAGOET INN. *26 Main St, Castine (04421). Phone 207/326-8616; toll-free 800/845-1701; fax 207/326-9382. www.pentagoet.com.* Victorian main building (1894) with smaller, colonial annex (circa 1770); library/sitting room, antiques, period furnishings. 16 rooms, 3 story. Closed Nov-Apr. Complimentary full breakfast. Check-in 2-6 pm, check-out 10:30 am. Restaurant, bar. **$** 🄳

Calais (D-4)

Settled 1770
Population 3,963
Elevation 19 ft
Area Code 207
Zip 04619
Information Calais Regional Chamber of Commerce, 16 Swan St, PO Box 368; phone 207/454-2308 or toll-free 888/422-3112
Web Site www.visitcalais.com

International cooperation is rarely as warm and helpful as it is between Calais (KAL-iss) and St. Stephen, New Brunswick, just across the St. Croix River in Canada. Because of an early closing law in St. Stephen, Canadians stroll over to the United States for a nightcap, and fire engines and ambulances cross the International Bridge in both directions as needed. (For Border Crossing Regulations, see MAKING THE MOST OF YOUR TRIP.) *Note:* New Brunswick is on Atlantic Time, one hour ahead of Eastern Standard Time.

Calais has a unique distinction—it is located exactly halfway between the North Pole and the equator. The 45th Parallel passes a few miles south of town; a marker on Highway 1 near Perry indicates the spot. Bass, togue, trout, and salmon fishing is available in many lakes and streams in Calais, and there is swimming at Meddybemps Lake, 13 miles north on Highway 191.

What to See and Do

Moosehorn National Wildlife Refuge. *4 miles N via Hwy 1, on Charlotte Rd. Contact Refuge Manager, PO Box 1077. Phone 207/454-7161.* Glacial terrain with forests, valleys, lakes, bogs, and marshes. Abundant wildlife. Fishing; hiking, hunting, cross-country skiing, bird-watching. (Daily) **FREE**

St. Croix Island International Historic Site. *8 miles S via Hwy 1, opposite Red Beach in St. Croix River; accessible only by boat. Phone 207/288-3338.* In 1604, French explorers Pierre Duguaf and Samuel de Champlain, leading a group of approximately 75 men, selected this as the site of the first attempted European settlement on the Atlantic Coast north of Florida. Information shelter; no facilities. (Daily)

Special Event

International Festival Week. *Phone toll-free 888/422-3112.* Celebration of friendship between Calais and St. Stephen, New Brunswick; entertainment, concessions, contests, fireworks, parade. Early Aug.

Restaurant

★ **WICKACHEE.** *282 Main St, Calais (04619). Phone 207/454-3400.* Seafood, steak menu. Breakfast, lunch, dinner. Closed Dec 25. Children's menu. **$$**

Camden (E-3)

See also Belfast, Rockland

Population 5,060
Elevation 33 ft
Area Code 207
Zip 04843
Information Camden-Rockport-Lincolnville Chamber of Commerce, Public Landing, PO Box 919; phone 207/236-4404
Web Site www.camdenme.org

Camden's unique setting—where the mountains meet the sea—makes it a popular four-season resort area. Recreational activities include boat cruises and boat rentals, swimming, fishing, camping, hiking, and picnicking, as well as winter activities. The poet Edna St. Vincent Millay began her career in Camden.

What to See and Do

Camden Hills State Park. *280 Belfast, Camden (04843). 2 miles NE on Hwy 1. Phone 207/236-3109.* Maine's third-largest state park, surrounding 1,380-foot Mount Megunticook. Road leads to Mount Battie (800 feet). Spectacular view of coast. Hiking, picnic

facilities, camping (dump station). (Memorial Day-Columbus Day)

Camden Snow Bowl. *S on Hwy 1 to John St to Hosmer Pond Rd. Phone 207/236-3438. www.camdensnowbowl.com.* Double chairlift, two T-bars; patrol, school, rentals; toboggan chute and rentals; snowboarding; snowmaking; snack bar, lodge. (Mid-Dec-mid-Mar, daily)

Conway Homestead-Cramer Museum. *Hwy 1 and Conway Rd, Camden (04843). Phone 207/236-2257.* Authentically restored 18th-century farmhouse. Collection of carriages, sleighs, and farm implements in old barn; blacksmith shop, privy, and herb garden. Mary Meeker Cramer Museum contains paintings, ship models, quilts; costumes, documents, and other memorabilia; changing exhibits. (July-Aug, Tues-Fri) **$**

Kelmscott Farm. *Hwy 52 Green Acres and Vancycle Rd, Lincolnville (04849). N on Hwy 52. Phone 207/763-4088.* Working farm established to conserve rare and endangered breeds of farm livestock, including Cotswold sheep, Ancient White Park cattle, American Cream Draft horse, Suffolk Punch horse, Kerry cattle, and Gloucestershire Old Spots pigs. Educational demonstrations. Farm tours (Labor Day-Memorial Day, by appointment). Museum and gift shop. Picnic area. Special events throughout the year. (Tues-Sun) **$$**

Maine State Ferry Service. *McKay St and Hwy 1, Lincolnville Beach (04849). 6 miles N on Hwy 1. Phone 207/789-5611.* 20-minute trip to Islesboro (Dark Harbor) on *Margaret Chase Smith.* (Mid-May-late Oct: weekdays, nine trips; Sun, eight trips; rest of year: six trips daily) **$$**

Sailing trips. Old-time schooners leave from Camden and Rockport Harbors for half- to six-day trips along the coast of Maine. (May-Oct) For further information, rates, schedules, or reservations, contact the individual companies.

Angelique. *Public Landing, Camden (04843). Phone toll-free 800/282-9989.*

Appledore. *Hwy 1 and Bayview, Camden (04843). Phone 207/236-8353.*

Maine Windjammer Cruises. *46 John St, Camden (04843). Phone 207/236-2938.*

Olad and Northwind. *PO Box 432, Camden (04843). Phone 207/236-2323.*

Schooner *Lewis R. French*. *Public Landing, Camden (04843). Phone toll-free 800/469-4635.*

Schooner *Mary Day*. *Public Landing, Camden (04843). Phone toll-free 800/992-2218.*

Schooner *Roseway*. *Hwy 1 and Bayview, Camden (04843). Phone toll-free 800/255-4449.*

Schooner *Surprise*. *Camden (04843). Phone 207/236-4687.*

Schooner *Timberwind*. *PO Box 247, Rockport (04856). Phone 207/236-3639; toll-free 800/759-9250.*

Schooner Yacht *Wendameen*. *PO Box 252, Rockport (04856). Phone 207/594-1751.*

Sightseeing cruises on Penobscot Bay. *Phone 207/236-4404.* Cruises (one to four hours) leave from public landing. Contact Chamber of Commerce.

Special Events

Bay Chamber Concerts. *Central St, Rockport (04856). Rockport Opera House.Phone 207/236-2823 (for schedule and ticket information).* Classical music performances by Vermeer Quartet and guest artists (July-Aug, Thurs-Fri evenings). Jazz musicians perform Sept-June (one show each month).

Camden Opera House. *29 Elm St, Camden (04843). Phone 207/236-7963.* Elm St. Theater with musical and theatrical performances and concerts. July-Aug.

Christmas by the Sea. *Phone 207/236-4404.* Celebration of the holiday season with musical entertainment, horse-drawn wagon rides, Holiday House Tour, Santa's arrival by lobster boat. First weekend in Dec.

Garden Club Open House Day. *Hwy 1 and Bayview, Camden (04843). Phone 207/236-6375.* Tour of homes and gardens (fee). Third Thurs in July.

Windjammer Weekend. *Phone 207/236-4404.* Celebration of windjammer industry; fireworks. Labor Day weekend.

Limited-Service Hotels

★ **BEST WESTERN CAMDEN RIVERHOUSE HOTEL.** *11 Tannery Ln, Camden (04843). Phone 207/236-0500; toll-free 800/757-4837; fax 207/236-4711. www.camdenmaine.com.* 35 rooms, 4 story. Complimentary continental breakfast. Check-out

11 am. Fitness room. Indoor pool, whirlpool. **$$**
🏃 ⛱

★ ★ **CEDAR CREST MOTEL.** *115 Elm St, Camden (04845). Phone 207/236-4859; toll-free 800/422-4964. www.cedarcrestmotel.com.* 37 rooms, 2 story. Closed Nov-Apr. Check-out 11 am. Restaurant. Outdoor pool. **$**
🅳 ⛱

Full-Service Inns

★ ★ ★ **BLUE HARBOR HOUSE, A VILLAGE INN.** *67 Elm St, Camden (04843). Phone 207/236-3196; toll-free 800/248-3196; fax 207/236-6523. www.blueharborhouse.com.* Built in 1768 as the home of the first Camden settler, James Richards, this property now offers guest rooms filled with quilts and antiques. Enjoy a hearty breakfast before hiking Camden Hills State Park or taking a Penobscot Bay boat ride. 11 rooms, 2 story. Complimentary full breakfast. Check-in 3-6 pm, check-out 11 am. **$$**
🅳

★ ★ ★ **DARK HARBOR HOUSE.** *117 Getty Rd, Camden (04848). Phone 207/734-6669; fax 207/734-6938. www.darkharborhouse.com.* Built in 1896, this island inn represents Georgian Revival architecture and is listed on the National Register of Historic Places. Visitors will be impressed by the grand double staircase in the entrance foyer and hilltop location overlooking Dark Harbor. 11 rooms, 3 story. Closed Nov-Apr. No children allowed. Complimentary full breakfast. Check-in 1:30 pm, check-out 11 am. Restaurant, bar. **$$**
🅳

Specialty Lodgings

The following lodging establishments are approved by Mobil Travel Guide, but due to their unique and individualized nature have not been given a traditional Mobil Star rating. Included in this listing you may find bed-and-breakfasts, limited-service inns, guest ranches, and other unique hotel properties.

CAMDEN WINDWARD HOUSE. *6 High St, Camden (04843). Phone 207/236-9656; toll-free 877/492-9656; fax 207/230-0433. www.windwardhouse.com.* This 1854 inn is located in the center of Camden's historic district, walking distance to many restaurants, shops, and Camden Harbor. Mount Battie and Camden Hills State Park are nearby. 8 rooms, 3 story.

Children over 12 years only. Complimentary full breakfast. Check-in 3 pm, check-out 11 am. **$$**
🄳

ELMS BED & BREAKFAST. *84 Elm St, Camden (04843). Phone 207/236-6250; toll-free 800/755-3567; fax 207/236-7330. www.elmsinn.net.* This Federal-style home, built in 1806, features a lighthouse theme. 7 rooms, 3 story. Children over 5 years only. Complimentary full breakfast. Check-in 3-6 pm, check-out 10:30 am. **$$**

HAWTHORN INN. *9 High St, Camden (04843). Phone 207/236-8842; fax 207/236-6181. www.camden hawthorn.com.* This 1894 Victorian inn is conveniently located for guests to tour Camden and the surrounding area. The rooms all have private baths, and some have fireplaces, whirlpools, and private decks with harbor views. In Camden, you can explore the many galleries, shops, restaurants, and the Camden docks. 10 rooms, 3 story. Closed Jan. Children over 12 years only. Complimentary full breakfast. Check-in 3 pm, check-out 11 am. **$$**
🄳

INN AT OCEAN'S EDGE. *Hwy 1, Camden (04843). Phone 207/236-0945; fax 207/236-0609. www.innatoceansedge.com.* This contemporary inn (circa 1999) overlooks Penobscot Bay. Spacious contemporary rooms feature reproduction four-poster king beds. Most rooms have an ocean view. 15 rooms, 3 story. Complimentary full breakfast. Check-out 11 am. Fitness room. **$$**
🛉

INN AT SUNRISE POINT. *Hwy 1, Fireroad 9, Camden (04849). Phone 207/236-7716; toll-free 800/435-6278; fax 207/236-0820. www.sunrisepoint.com.* This 4-acre oceanfront hideaway is just minutes from Camden Harbor with its old windjammers and modern yachts. Guests can choose to stay at a restored 1920s Maine-style cottage or in the main house and listen to the soothing sound of waves breaking at shore. Breakfast is served in the conservatory and hors d'oeuvres are available in the library in the afternoons. 13 rooms, 2 story. Children over 14 years only. Complimentary full breakfast. Check-in 3 pm, check-out 11 am. Whirlpool. **$$$**

THE LODGE AND COTTAGES AT CAMDEN HILLS. *Hwy 1, Camden (04843). Phone 207/236-8478; toll-free 800/832-7058; fax 207/236-7163. www.thelodge atcamdenhills.com.* View of bay. 23 rooms. Check-in 3 pm, check-out 11 am. **$$**

MAINE STAY BED & BREAKFAST. *22 High St, Camden (04843). Phone 207/236-9636; fax 207/236-0621. www.mainestay.com.* Farmhouse built in 1802; barn and carriage house. Antiques include a 17th-century samurai chest. 8 rooms, 3 story. Children over 12 years only. Complimentary full breakfast. Check-in 3 pm, check-out 11 am. **$$**
🄳

NORUMBEGA INN. *61 High St, Camden (04843). Phone 207/236-4646; fax 207/236-0824. www.norumbegainn.com.* This stone castle-by-the-sea was designed and built by the investor of duplex telegraphy and is located near Penobscot Bay with a panoramic view of the ocean. The property has been fully restored and is furnished with modern conveniences. Close by are the windjammers and yachts, shops, restaurants, and galleries. Each room has a king bed, private bath, and evening turndown service is provided. 13 rooms, 4 story. Children over 7 years only. Complimentary full breakfast. Check-in 3 pm, check-out 11 am. **$$**
🄳

THE VICTORIAN BY THE SEA. *Sea View Dr, Lincolnville (04843). Phone 207/236-3785; toll-free 800/382-9817; fax 207/236-0017. www.victorianbythe sea.com.* This Victorian summer cottage was built in 1881. 7 rooms, 3 story. Children over 12 years only. Complimentary full breakfast. Check-in 3 pm, check-out 11 am. **$$**
🄳

WHITEHALL INN. *52 High St, Camden (04843). Phone 207/236-3391; toll-free 800/789-6565; fax 207/236-4427. www.whitehall-inn.com.* Spacious old resort inn (1834); poet Edna St. Vincent Millay gave a reading here in 1912. 50 rooms, 3 story. Closed mid-Oct-mid-May. Check-in 3 pm, check-out 11 am. Restaurant, bar. Tennis. **$$**
🛋

Restaurants

★ ★ **CORK RESTAURANT.** *51 Bayview St, Camden (04843). Phone 207/230-0533; fax 207/236-7431. www.corkrestaurant.com.* Seafood, steak menu. Dinner. Closed Sun-Mon. **$$$**
🄳

★ ★ **THE HELM.** *RR 1, Camden Rd, Rockport (04856). Phone 207/236-4337.* American, French menu. Lunch, dinner. Closed mid-Dec-early Apr. Bar. Children's menu. **$$**

★ ★ **LOBSTER POUND.** *Hwy 1, Lincolnville (04849). Phone 207/789-5550; fax 207/789-5656.* Lobster tanks. Seafood menu. Lunch, dinner. Closed Nov-Apr. Children's menu. Outdoor seating. **$$$**

★ ★ **PETER OTT'S.** *16 Bayview St, Camden (04843). Phone 207/236-4032; fax 207/236-3836.* Seafood, steak menu. Dinner. Closed Mon (off-season); Jan 1, Dec 25. Bar. Children's menu. **$$**

★ ★ **WATERFRONT.** *40 Bayview St, Camden (04843). Phone 207/236-3747; fax 207/236-3815.* On harbor. Seafood menu. Lunch, dinner. Closed Thanksgiving, Dec 25. Bar. Children's menu. Outdoor seating. **$$**

★ ★ **WHITEHALL DINING ROOM.** *52 High St (Hwy 1), Camden (04843). Phone 207/236-3391; fax 207/236-4427. www.whitehall-inn.com.* Located in the quaint Whitehall Inn (see), the dining room attracts not only overnight guests but also local residents. There are several fresh seafood entrées offered daily, and when blueberries are in season, the chef finds many ways to feature them on the menu. American menu. Breakfast, dinner. Closed mid-Oct-mid-June. Bar. Children's menu. **$$**

Cape Neddick

Restaurants

★ ★ ★ **CAPE NEDDICK INN.** *1233 Hwy 1, Cape Neddick (03902). Phone 207/363-2899; fax 207/363-4780.* Simple, satisfying cuisine with elegant flourishes is the nature of this cozy restaurant, which despite its name, is not attached to an inn. American menu. Dinner. Closed Dec 25. Bar. **$$$**

★ ★ ★ **CLAY HILL FARM.** *226 Clay Hill Rd, Cape Neddick (03907). Phone 207/361-2272. www.clayhillfarm.com.* This dining establishment, set in a historic farmhouse (1780), is situated on 30 acres of protected woodlands and is certified by the National Wildlife Association as a wildlife habitat and bird sanctuary. Enjoy fresh local seafood and game, or one of the vegetarian dishes of the week. Seafood menu. Dinner. Closed Mon-Wed (Nov-Apr). Bar. Valet parking. **$$$**

Caribou (A-4)

See also Presque Isle

Population 9,415
Elevation 442 ft
Area Code 207
Zip 04736
Information Chamber of Commerce, 24 Sweden St, Suite 101; phone toll-free 800/722-7648
Web Site www.cariboumaine.net

Caribou, the nation's northeasternmost city, is primarily an agricultural area but has become diversified in manufacturing. Located here are a food processing plant, a paper bag manufacturing plant, and an electronics manufacturing plant. Swimming, fishing, boating, camping, and hunting are available in the many lakes located 20 miles northwest on Highway 161.

What to See and Do

Caribou Historical Center. *Hwy 1, Caribou (04736). 3 miles S on Hwy 1. Phone 207/498-2556.* Museum housing history of northern Maine. (June-Aug: Thurs-Sat; rest of year: by appointment) **DONATION**

Nylander Museum. *393 Main St, Caribou (04736). 1/4 mile S on Hwy 161. Phone 207/493-4209.* Fossils, rocks, minerals, butterflies, and shells collected by Olof Nylander, Swedish-born geologist and naturalist; early man artifacts; changing exhibits. Gift shop. (Memorial Day-Labor Day: Wed-Sun; rest of year: weekends and by appointment)

Rosie O'Grady's Balloon of Peace Monument. *Main St, Caribou (04736). 2 miles S on S Main St.* Honoring Colonel Joe W. Kittinger Jr., who in 1984 was the first balloonist to fly solo across the Atlantic Ocean, breaking the distance record set earlier by the *Double Eagle II* flight.

Special Event

Winter Carnival. *111 High St, Caribou (04736). Phone toll-free 800/722-7648.* Snow sculptures, ski jumping, and family fun slide are just a few of the events held at Teague Park. Feb.

Limited-Service Hotel

★ ★ **CARIBOU INN & CONVENTION CENTER.**
*19 Main St, Caribou (04736). Phone 207/498-3733;
toll-free 800/235-0466. www.caribouinn.com.* 73 rooms,
3 story. Check-out 11 am. Restaurant, bar. Indoor
pool, whirlpool. Airport transportation available. **$**
🌊

Restaurants

★ **JADE PALACE.** *Skyway Plz, Caribou (04736).
Phone 207/498-3648.* American, Chinese menu.
Lunch, dinner. Closed Thanksgiving. Bar. **$$**

★ **RENO'S.** *117 Sweden St, Caribou (04736). Phone
207/496-5331; fax 207/492-1612.* American, Italian
menu. Breakfast, lunch, dinner. Closed Memorial Day,
Thanksgiving, Dec 25. Children's menu. **$**

Center Lovell

Population 100
Elevation 532 ft
Area Code 207
Zip 04016

This community on Kezar Lake is close to the New
Hampshire border and the recreational opportuni-
ties of the White Mountain National Forest (see New
Hampshire). The surrounding region is rich in gems
and minerals.

Full-Service Resort

★ ★ **QUISISANA LODGE.** *Pleasant Point Rd,
Center Lovell (04016). Phone 207/925-3500; fax 207/
925-1004. www.quisisanaresort.com.* 16 rooms. Closed
Sept-May. Check-in 2 pm, check-out 11 am. Restaurant.
Private sand beaches. Tennis. **$$$**
🔲🎿

Specialty Lodgings

The following lodging establishments are approved
by Mobil Travel Guide, but due to their unique and
individualized nature have not been given a traditional
Mobil Star rating. Included in this listing you may
find bed-and-breakfasts, limited-service inns, guest
ranches, and other unique hotel properties.

ADMIRAL PEARY HOUSE. *9 Elm St, Fryeburg
(04037). Phone 207/935-3365; toll-free 800/237-8080.*

www.admiralpearyhouse.com. Located in the oldest
village in the White Mountains of western Maine, this
bed-and-breakfast named after the renowned discov-
erer of the North Pole, sits on 10 acres of landscaped
lawns and gardens. 6 rooms, 3 story. Complimentary
full breakfast. Check-in 4 pm, check-out 11 am.
Whirlpool. Tennis. Airport transportation available. **$**
🔲🎿

OXFORD HOUSE INN. *105 Main St, Fryeburg
(04037). Phone 207/935-3442; toll-free 800/261-
7206; fax 207/935-7046. www.oxfordhouseinn.com.*
Historic house (1913); veranda. 4 rooms, 3 story.
Complimentary full breakfast. Check-in 2 pm,
check-out 11 am. Restaurant. **$**
🔲

Restaurant

★ ★ **OXFORD HOUSE INN.** *105 Main St,
Fryeburg (04037). Phone 207/935-3442; toll-free
800/261-7206. www.oxfordhouseinn.com.* Seafood
menu. Dinner. Closed Dec 24-25; also Mon-Wed in
winter and spring. Bar. Children's menu. Reservations
recommended. Outdoor seating. **$$**
🔲

Chebeague Islands

Population 300
Elevation 40 ft
Area Code 207
Zip 04017

Little Chebeague (sha-BEEG) and Great Chebeague
islands, off the coast of Portland in Casco Bay, were
at one time a favorite camping spot of various tribes.
The Native Americans had a penchant for clams; the
first European settlers thus found heaps of clamshells
scattered across the land. Those shells were later used
to pave many of the islands' roads, some of which still
exist today.

Great Chebeague, 6 miles long and approximately 3
miles wide, is connected to Little Chebeague at low
tide by a sandbar. There are various locations for
swimming. Additionally, both islands lend themselves
well to exploring on foot or bicycle. At one time, Great
Chebeague was home to a bustling fishing and ship-
building community, and it was a quarrying center in
the late 1700s. Today, it welcomes hundreds of visitors
every summer.

What to See and Do

Casco Bay Lines. *56 Commercial St, Portland (04101). Phone 207/774-7871.* From Portland, Commercial, and Franklin streets; one-hour crossing. (Daily) **$$$**

Chebeague Transportation. *Phone 207/846-3700.* From Cousins Island, near Yarmouth; 15-minute crossing. (Daily) Off-site parking with shuttle to ferry. **$$$**

Cranberry Isles

See also Bar Harbor, Northeast Harbor, Southwest Harbor

Population 189
Elevation 20 ft
Area Code 207
Zip 04625

The Cranberry Isles, named because of the rich, red cranberry bogs that once covered Great Cranberry Isle, lie off the southeast coast of Mount Desert Island. There are five islands in the group: Little and Great Cranberry, Sutton, Bear, and Baker. Great Cranberry, the largest, covers about 900 acres. Baker Island is part of Acadia National Park, and Sutton is privately owned. In 1830, the islands petitioned the state to separate from Mount Desert Island. In the late 1800s, the area was a thriving fishing community.

What to See and Do

Islesford Historical Museum. *Main St and Sand Beach Rd, Cranberry Isles (04625).* Islesford, on Little Cranberry Island. *Phone 207/244-9224.* Exhibits on local island history from 1604. (July-Aug: daily; Sept: by appointment) **FREE**

Damariscotta (E-2)

See also Boothbay Harbor, Monhegan Island, Wiscasset

Settled 1730
Population 1,811
Elevation 69 ft
Area Code 207
Zip 04543
Information Chamber of Commerce, PO Box 13; phone 207/563-8340
Web Site www.damariscottaregion.com

Damariscotta, whose name is an Abenaki word meaning "river of many fishes," has a number of colonial, Greek Revival, and pre-Civil War houses. With the neighboring city of Newcastle across the Damariscotta River, this is a trading center for a seaside resort region extending to Pemaquid Point and Christmas Cove.

What to See and Do

Chapman-Hall House. *Main and Church sts, Damariscotta (04543).* (1754) Restored house with original whitewash kitchen, period furniture; local shipbuilding exhibition. (July-early Sept, Mon-Sat) **$**

Colonial Pemaquid State Memorial. *Colonial Pemaquid Rd, New Harbor (04554). 14 miles S via Hwy 130. Phone 207/677-2423.* Excavations have uncovered foundations of a jail, tavern, and private homes. Fishing, boat ramp; picnicking; free parking. (Memorial Day-Labor Day, daily) Also here is

Fort William Henry State Memorial. Reconstructed 1692 fort tower; museum contains relics, portraits, maps, and copies of Native American deeds (fee).

⭐ **Pemaquid Point Lighthouse Park.** *Pemaquid Lighthouse, New Harbor (04554). 15 miles S at end of Hwy 130 on Pemaquid Point. Phone 207/677-2494.* Includes a 1827 lighthouse that towers above the pounding surf (not open to public); Fishermen's Museum housed in old lightkeeper's dwelling (donation); art gallery; some recreational facilities. Fishermen's Museum (Memorial Day-Columbus Day: daily; rest of year: by appointment). **$**

St. Patrick's Church. *W to Newcastle, then 2 miles N off Hwy 1. Phone 207/563-3240.* (1808) Early Federal architecture; Revere bell in steeple; one of the oldest surviving Catholic churches in New England.

Swimming. *Pemaquid Beach, N of lighthouse.*

Full-Service Inns

★ ★ ★ **THE BRADLEY INN.** *3063 Bristol Rd, New Harbor (04554). Phone 207/677-2105; toll-free 800/942-5560; fax 207/677-3367. www.bradleyinn.com.* This inn, built by a sea captian for his new bride in 1880, is located at the tip of Pemaquid Peninsula, near Johns Bay and the Pemaquid Lighthouse. It is a lovely country property with nicely appointed guest rooms. Guests can sit or walk on the well-groomed grounds and enjoy a fantastic view of the ocean. Nearby activities include golfing, fishing, boating, walks on the beach, a winery, nature area, and fine restaurants.

16 rooms, 3 story. Complimentary full breakfast. Check-in 2 pm, check-out 11 am. Restaurant. **$$$**

★ ★ ★ **NEWCASTLE INN.** *60 River Rd, Newcastle (04553). Phone 207/563-5685; toll-free 800/832-8669; fax 207/563-6877. www.newcastleinn.com.* Overlooking lupine gardens and the Damariscotta river, this Federal-style inn (1850) provides guests with many relaxing options. Reading a book or lounging outside on an Adirondack chair are just two of them. Some of the inn's rooms and suites have four-poster or canopy beds, while others have sitting areas or fireplaces. A four-course dinner preceded by complimentary hors d'oeuvres, is served in one of the two dining rooms. 15 rooms, 3 story. Children over 12 years only. Check-in 3 pm, check-out 11 am. Restaurant, bar. **$$**

Specialty Lodgings

The following lodging establishments are approved by Mobil Travel Guide, but due to their unique and individualized nature have not been given a traditional Mobil Star rating. Included in this listing you may find bed-and-breakfasts, limited-service inns, guest ranches, and other unique hotel properties.

BRANNON-BUNKER INN. *349 Hwy 129, Walpole (04573). Phone 207/563-5941; toll-free 800/563-9225.* World War I memorabilia. On river. 8 rooms, 2 story. Complimentary continental breakfast. Check-in 2 pm, check-out 11 am. **$$**

DOWN EASTER INN. *218 Bristol Rd, Damariscotta (04543). Phone 207/563-5332.* This Greek Revival farmhouse (1785) was built by a ship chandler whose ancestors were among the first settlers of Bristol. 22 rooms, 2 story. Closed Nov-mid-May. Complimentary continental breakfast. Check-in 2 pm, check-out 11 am. Restaurant. **$**

Restaurant

★ ★ **BACKSTREET LANDING.** *Elm St Plz, Damariscotta (04543). Phone 207/563-5666.* Seafood menu. Lunch, dinner. Closed Wed (Nov-Apr); Jan 1, Thanksgiving, Dec 25. Bar. Children's menu. **$$**

Deer Isle

Settled 1762
Population 1,829
Elevation 23 ft

Area Code 207
Zip 04627
Information Deer Isle/Stonington Chamber of Commerce, PO Box 459, Stonington 04681; phone 207/348-6124 (in season)
Web Site www.deerisle.com

A bridge over Eggemoggin Reach connects these islands with the mainland. There are two major villages here—Deer Isle (the older) and Stonington. Lobster fishing and tourism are the backbone of the economy, and Stonington also cans sardines. Fishing, sailing, tennis, and golf are available in the area.

What to See and Do

Isle au Haut. *Phone 207/367-5193.* (EEL-oh-HO) Reached by ferry from Stonington. Much of this island—with hills more than 500 feet tall, forested shores, and cobblestone beaches—is in Acadia National Park (see).

Isle au Haut Ferry Service. *Seabreeze Ave, Stonington (04681). Phone 207/367-5193.* Service to the island and excursion trips available.

Limited-Service Hotel

★ ★ **GOOSE COVE LODGE.** *Goose Cove Rd, Sunset (04683). Phone 207/348-2508; toll-free 800/728-1963; fax 207/348-2624. www.goosecovelodge.com.* 23 rooms. Closed mid-Oct-Apr. Check-in 3 pm, check-out 10:30 am. Children's activity center. **$**

Full-Service Inn

★ ★ ★ **PILGRIMS INN.** *20 Main St, Deer Isle (04627). Phone 207/348-6615; fax 207/348-6615. www.pilgrimsinn.com.* This restored, historic wood frame building was built in 1793 and has eight-foot-wide fireplaces. For families or guests with pets, there are two housekeeping units on property. Nearby are art galleries and a famous art school. The chef prepares meals from local seafood, produce, and fresh-grown ingredients from the garden. 15 rooms, 4 story. Closed Nov-mid-May. Check-in 1-5 pm, check-out 11 am. Restaurant. **$$**

Eastport (D-5)

See also Lubec

Settled 1780
Population 1,965
Elevation 60 ft
Area Code 207
Zip 04631
Information Chamber of Commerce, PO Box 254; phone 207/853-4644
Web Site www.eastport.net

At the southern end of Passamaquoddy Bay, Eastport is a community with 150-year-old houses and ancient elms. The average tide at Eastport is approximately 18 feet, but tides up to 25 feet have been recorded here. Eastport was the site of one of the country's first tide-powered electric generating projects, and though never completed, it resulted in the construction of two tidal dams. The city also boasts of being the nation's salmonid aquaculture capital, where millions of salmon and trout are raised in pens in the chilly off-shore waters.

What to See and Do

Barracks Museum. *74 Washington St, Eastport (04631).* This 1822 building once served as the officers' barracks for a nearby fort, which was held by British troops during the War of 1812. Museum. (Memorial Day-Labor Day, Tues-Sat afternoons) **FREE**

Ferry to Deer Island, New Brunswick. A 20-minute trip; camping, picnicking on Deer Island. (June-Sept, daily) For schedules, fees inquire locally. (For border crossing regulations, see MAKING THE MOST OF YOUR TRIP.) **$$**

Fishing. Pollock, cod, flounder, and others caught from wharves. Charter boats available for deep-sea fishing in sheltered waters.

Old Sow Whirlpool. *Between Dog and Deer islands.* One of largest in the Western Hemisphere; most active three hours before high tide.

Passamaquoddy Indian Reservation. *Hwy 190, Perry (04667). About 5 miles N on Hwy 190 at Pleasant Point. Phone 207/853-2551.* Champlain, in 1604, was the first European to encounter members of this Algonquin tribe. Festivals and ceremonies throughout the year (see SPECIAL EVENTS). **FREE**

Whale-watching trips. Boat excursions during the summer to view whales in the bay.

Special Events

Indian Festival. *Passamaquoddy Indian Reservation, Eastport (04631). Phone 207-853-4644.* Ceremonies, fireworks, traditional celebrations. Second weekend in Aug.

Salmon Festival. *78 Water St, Eastport (04631). Phone 207/853-4644.* Tours of aquaculture pens; music, crafts, educational displays; farm-raised Atlantic salmon dinners. Sun after Labor Day.

Specialty Lodgings

The following lodging establishments are approved by Mobil Travel Guide, but due to their unique and individualized nature have not been given a traditional Mobil Star rating. Included in this listing you may find bed-and-breakfasts, limited-service inns, guest ranches, and other unique hotel properties.

TODD HOUSE. *1 Capen Ave, Eastport (04631). Phone 207/853-2328.* This authentic New England Cape once housed soldiers during the War of 1812. It is near the ocean and features a view of the bay. 6 rooms, 2 story. Pets accepted, some restrictions. Complimentary continental breakfast. Check-in 2 pm, check-out 11 am. **$**
🔊

WESTON HOUSE BED & BREAKFAST. *26 Boyton St, Eastport (04631). Phone 207/853-2907; toll-free 800/853-2907; fax 207/853-0981. www.westonhouse-maine.com.* Restored 19th-century residence; sitting room with tin ceiling. 3 rooms. Complimentary full breakfast. Check-in 1 pm, check-out 11 am. **$**
🖻

Ellsworth (D-3)

See also Bar Harbor, Blue Hill, Bucksport

Settled 1763
Population 5,975
Elevation 100 ft
Area Code 207
Zip 04605
Information Chamber of Commerce, 163 High St, PO Box 267; phone 207/667-5584
Web Site www.ellsworthchamber.org

This is the shire town and trading center for Hancock County—which includes some of the country's choicest resort territory, including Bar Harbor. In the beginning of the 19th century, Ellsworth was the second-largest lumber shipping port in the world. Its business district was destroyed by fire in 1933, but was handsomely rebuilt, contrasting with the old residential streets.

What to See and Do

Lamoine State Park. *Lamoine Rd, Lamoine (04605). 8 miles SE on Hwy 184. Phone 207/667-4778.* A 55-acre recreation area around beach on Frenchman Bay. Fishing; boating (ramp); picnicking, camping. (Memorial Day-mid-Oct, daily) **$**

Stanwood Sanctuary (Birdsacre) and Homestead Museum. *289 High St, Ellsworth (04605). On Bar Harbor Rd (Hwy 3). Phone 207/667-8460.* Trails, ponds, and picnic areas on 130-acre site. Collections include mounted birds, nests, and eggs. Wildlife rehabilitation center with shelters for injured birds, including hawks and owls. Museum was home of pioneer ornithologist, photographer and writer Cordelia Stanwood (1865-1958). Sanctuary and rehabilitation center (daily; free); museum (mid-June-mid-Oct, daily). Gift shop. **$$**

Limited-Service Hotel

★ ★ **HOLIDAY INN.** *215 High St, Ellsworth (04605). Phone 207/667-9341; toll-free 800/465-4329; fax 207/667-7294. www.holidayinnellsworth.com.* 103 rooms, 2 story. Pets accepted, some restrictions; fee. Check-out noon. Restaurant, bar. Fitness room. Indoor pool, whirlpool. Tennis. **$**

🐾 🚶 ⊠ ⊠

Restaurants

★ ★ **ARMANDO'S.** *Hwy 1, Hancock (04640). Phone 207/422-3151.* Italian, seafood menu. Dinner. Closed Sun-Thurs in winter; Jan 1, Easter, Dec 25. Bar. **$$**
🅑

★ **HILLTOP HOUSE.** *317 High St, Ellsworth (04605). Phone 207/667-9368; fax 207/667-4834.* American menu. Lunch, dinner. Closed Jan 1, Thanksgiving, Dec 25. Bar. Children's menu. **$$**

Fort Kent (A-3)

See also Allagash Wilderness Waterway

Settled 1829
Population 4,268
Area Code 207
Zip 04743
Information Chamber of Commerce, PO Box 430; phone 207/834-5354 or toll-free 800/733-3563

Fort Kent, at the northern end of famous Highway 1 (the other end is at Key West, Florida), is the chief community of Maine's "far north." A bridge across the St. John River leads to Clair, New Brunswick. (For border crossing regulations, see MAKING THE MOST OF YOUR TRIP.) The town is a lumbering, farming, hunting, and fishing center, and canoeing, downhill and cross-country skiing, and snowmobiling are popular here. A campus of the University of Maine is located here.

What to See and Do

Canoeing. Fort Kent is the downstream terminus of the St. John-Allagash canoe trip, which starts at East Seboomook on Moosehead Lake, 156 miles and six portages away. (See ALLAGASH WILDERNESS WATERWAY)

Cross-country skiing. Fort Kent has 11 1/2 miles of scenic intermediate and advanced trails. **FREE**

Fishing. Guides, boats, and gear available for short or long expeditions up the Fish River chain of lakes for salmon or trout; St. John or Allagash rivers for trout.

Fort Kent Block House. *N edge of town. Phone 207/834-3866.* Built in 1839, during the Aroostook Bloodless War with Britain, used for training exercises and as a guard post. Restored; antique hand tools in museum; interpretive displays. Picnicking. (Memorial Day-Labor Day, daily)

Fort Kent Historical Society Museum and Gardens. *54 W Main St, Fort Kent (04743). For further information contact the Chamber of Commerce.* Former Bangor and Aroostook railroad station, built in early 1900s, now houses historical museum. (Usually last two weeks in June-first week in Aug, Tues-Sat)

Lonesome Pine Trails. *Forest Ave, Fort Kent (04743). Phone 207/834-5202.* Thirteen trails, 2,300-foot slope with 500-foot drop; beginners slope and tow; rope tow, T-bar; school, patrol, rentals; lodge, concession. (Dec-Apr: Wed and Fri-Sun, also holidays) **$$$$**

Special Event

Can Am Crown Sled Dog Races. *W Main St, Fort Kent (04743). Phone 207/834-3312; toll-free 800/733-3563. can-am.sjv.net.* Three races (30-, 60-, and 250-mile) begin on Main Street and finish at the Lonesome Pine Ski Lodge. Late Feb-early Mar.

Freeport (E-2)

See also Bath, Brunswick, Yarmouth

Population 6,905
Elevation 130 ft
Area Code 207
Zip 04032
Information Freeport Merchants Association, Hose Tower Information Center, 23 Depot St, PO Box 452; phone 207/865-1212 or toll-free 800/865-1994
Web Site www.freeportusa.com

It was in Freeport that legislators signed papers granting Maine independence from Massachusetts and, eventually, its statehood. The town is home to the renowned L. L. Bean clothing and sporting goods store; its major industries include retail, tourism, crabbing, and crabmeat packing.

What to See and Do

Atlantic Seal Cruises. *South Freeport. Depart from Town Wharf, foot of Main St in South Freeport, 2 miles S on S Freeport Rd. Phone 207/865-6112.* Cruises aboard 40-foot, 28-passenger vessel on Casco Bay to Eagle Island and Robert E. Peary house museum; also seal- and bird-watching trips, fall foliage sightseeing cruises. (Schedules vary) Tickets must be purchased at Main Street office, South Freeport.

⭐ **Factory outlet stores.** *42-28 Main St, Freeport (04032). Phone toll-free 800/865-1994.* Freeport is home to more than 120 outlet stores and centers that offer brand-name merchandise at discounted prices, including the famous L. L. Bean clothing and sporting goods store, which stays open 24 hours a day. For a list of outlet stores, contact the Freeport Merchants Association.

Mast Landing Sanctuary. *20 Gilsland Farm Rd, Falmouth (04105). Upper Mast Landing Rd, 1 1/2 miles*

E. *Phone 207/781-2330.* A 140-acre area maintained by the Maine Audubon Society. Hiking, cross-country skiing. (Daily) **FREE**

Winslow Memorial Park. *Staples Point, Freeport. 5 miles S off Hwy 1, I-95. Phone 207/865-4198.* Campground with swimming, boating (fee), cross-country skiing; picnicking. (Schedule varies) **$**

Limited-Service Hotels

⭐ ⭐ **BEST WESTERN FREEPORT INN.** *31 Hwy 1, Freeport (04032). Phone 207/865-3106; toll-free 800/780-7234; fax 207/865-6364. www.bestwestern.com.* On 25 acres; river; canoe. 80 rooms, 3 story. Pets accepted, some restrictions. Check-out 11 am. Restaurant. Two outdoor pools. **$**

🐾 ⚊

⭐ **CASCO BAY INN.** *107 Hwy 1, Freeport (04032). Phone 207/865-4925; toll-free 800/570-4970; fax 207/865-0696. www.cascobayinn.com.* 45 rooms, 2 story. Closed mid-Dec-mid-Apr. Check-out 11 am. **$**

Full-Service Inn

⭐ ⭐ **HARRASEEKET INN.** *162 Main St, Freeport (04032). Phone 207/865-9377; toll-free 800/342-6423; fax 207/865-1684. www.harraseeketinn.com.* This inn is located just two blocks from L. L. Bean and more than 170 stores. It features rooms filled with antiques. Each afternoon complimentary tea is served in the paneled drawing room. Guest rooms feature Colonial Revival décor and many have working fireplaces. The inn consists of three structures: Federalist house (1798), early Victorian house (1850) modern, colonial-style inn. 84 rooms, 3 story. Complimentary full breakfast. Check-in 3 pm, check-out 11 am. Restaurant, bar. Indoor pool. Airport transportation available. **$$$**

⚊

Specialty Lodgings

The following lodging establishments are approved by Mobil Travel Guide, but due to their unique and individualized nature have not been given a traditional Mobil Star rating. Included in this listing you may find bed-and-breakfasts, limited-service inns, guest ranches, and other unique hotel properties.

THE BAGLEY HOUSE. *1290 Royalsborough Rd, Durham (04222). Phone 207/865-6566; toll-free 800/765-1772; fax 207/353-5878. www.bagleyhouse.com.*

Restored country inn (1772); hand-hewn wood beams, wide pine floors, original beehive oven. 8 rooms, 2 story. Complimentary full breakfast. Check-in 3 pm, check-out 11 am. **$$**

BREWSTER HOUSE BED & BREAKFAST. *180 Main St, Freeport (04032). Phone 207/865-4121; toll-free 800/865-0822; fax 207/865-4221. www.brewsterhouse.com.* Built in 1888. 7 rooms, 3 story. Children over 8 years only. Complimentary full breakfast. Check-in 3 pm, check-out 11 am. **$$$** 🛅

FREEPORT CLIPPER INN. *181 Main St, Freeport (04032). Phone 207/865-1226; toll-free 800/235-9750. www.freeportclipperinn.com.* This restored Greek Revival Cape home (circa 1840) features colonial furnishings. 7 rooms, 2 story. Children over 14 years only. Complimentary full breakfast. Check-in 3-7 pm, check-out 11 am. Outdoor pool. **$** 🛅 ⛱

KENDALL TAVERN B&B. *213 Main St, Freeport (04032). Phone 207/865-1338; toll-free 800/341-9572; fax 207/865-3544. www.kendalltavern.com.* Restored New England farmhouse (circa 1850). 7 rooms, 3 story. Complimentary full breakfast. Check-in 3 pm, check-out 11 am. **$$** 🛅

WHITE CEDAR INN. *178 Main St, Freeport (04032). Phone 207/865-9099; toll-free 800/853-1269. www.whitecedarinn.com.* Former home of Arctic explorer Donald MacMillan. 7 rooms, 2 story. Children over 8 years only. Complimentary full breakfast. Check-in 3 pm, check-out 11 am. **$** 🛅

Restaurants

★ **CORSICAN.** *9 Mechanic St, Freeport (04032). Phone 207/865-9421.* American, Italian menu. Lunch, dinner. Closed Jan 1, Thanksgiving, Dec 25. **$$** 🛅

★ **GRITTY MCDUFF'S.** *187 Lower Main St, Freeport (04032). Phone 207/865-4321. www.grittys. com.* Seafood menu. Lunch, dinner. Bar. Children's menu. Outdoor seating. **$$**

★ ★ **JAMESON TAVERN.** *115 Main St (Hwy 1), Freeport (04032). Phone 207/865-4196; fax 207/865-6769.* Historic tavern (1779); final papers separating Maine from the Commonwealth of Massachusetts were signed here. Seafood, steak menu. Lunch, dinner. Closed Dec 25. Bar. Children's menu. Outdoor seating. **$$**

★ **LOBSTER COOKER.** *39 Main St (Hwy 1), Freeport (04032). Phone 207/865-4349; fax 207/865-3883.* Historic building (1816). Seafood menu. Lunch, dinner. Outdoor seating. **$$**

★ ★ ★ **THE MAINE DINING ROOM.** *162 Main St, Freeport (04032). Phone 207/865-1085; fax 207/865-1684. www.harraseeketinn.com.* This restaurant, located in the Harraseeket Inn (see), has a very cozy atmosphere, which is enhanced by two wood-burning fireplaces. American menu. Dinner. Bar. Children's menu. Outdoor seating. **$$$**

Greenville (C-2)

See also Moosehead Lake

Settled 1824
Population 1,884
Elevation 1,038 ft
Area Code 207
Zip 04441
Information Moosehead Lake Region Chamber of Commerce, PO Box 581; phone 207/695-2702 or toll-free 888/876-2778
Web Site www.mooseheadlake.org

Greenville is a starting point for trips into the Moosehead Lake region (see). Until it was incorporated in 1836, it was known as Haskell, in honor of its founder Nathaniel Haskell.

What to See and Do

Lily Bay State Park. *8 miles N via local roads, near Beaver Cove. Phone 207/695-2700 (seasonal).* A 924-acre park on Moosehead Lake. Swimming, fishing, boating (ramp); picnicking, camping (dump station). (Mid-May-mid-Oct) Snowmobiling permitted.

Moosehead Marine Museum. *N Main St, Greenville (04441). In the center of town behind the Fleet Bank, across the street from Shaw Public Library. Phone 207/695-2716.* On steamboat *Katahdin*, berthed in East Cove. Exhibits of the steamboat era and the Kineo Hotel; cruises available. (July-Columbus Day: daily; June: Sat-Sun) **$$$$**

Moosehead Resort on Big Squaw Mountain. *Hwy 15, Greenville (04441). 5 miles NW on Hwy 6/15, then 2* miles W on access road. *Phone toll-free 800/940-2112.* Double, triple chairlifts, T-bar, pony lift; novice-to-expert trails; rentals, school, patrol, snowmaking; cafeteria, restaurant, bar; nursery; lodge. Longest run 2 1/2 miles; vertical drop 1,750 feet. (Late Nov-Apr, daily) cross-country trails. Chairlift rides (June-mid-Oct; fee). For further information contact the Chamber of Commerce.

Special Event

MooseMainea. *Various locations around Greenville. Phone 207/695-2702.* Celebration honoring the moose. Canoe race, rowing regatta, fly-fishing championship, Tour de Moose bike race. Family Fun Day with parade, crafts, entertainment. Moose-sighting tours. Mid-May–mid-June.

Limited-Service Hotels

★ **CHALET MOOSEHEAD LAKEFRONT MO-TEL.** *Birch St, Greenville (04441). Phone 207/695-2950; toll-free 800/290-3645. www.mooseheadlodging.com.* 27 rooms, 2 story. Pets accepted, some restrictions; fee. Check-out 10 am. **$**

🐾

★ **INDIAN HILL.** *S Main St, Greenville (04441). Phone 207/695-2623; toll-free 800/771-4620; fax 207/695-2950. www.mooseheadlodging.com.* 15 rooms. Check-out 10:30 am. **$**

Specialty Lodgings

The following lodging establishments are approved by Mobil Travel Guide, but due to their unique and individualized nature have not been given a traditional Mobil Star rating. Included in this listing you may find bed-and-breakfasts, limited-service inns, guest ranches, and other unique hotel properties.

GREENVILLE INN. *40 Norris St, Greenville (04441). Phone 207/695-2206; toll-free 888/695-6000; fax 207/695-0335. www.greenvilleinn.com.* 6 rooms, 3 story. Complimentary continental breakfast. Check-in 3 pm, check-out 11 am. Restaurant (May-Oct), bar. **$$**

🔲

THE LODGE AT MOOSEHEAD LAKE. *Lily Bay Rd, Greenville (04441). Phone 207/695-4400; fax 207/695-2281. www.lodgeatmooseheadlake.com.* This romantic nature retreat offers lodge rooms and adjacent carriage house suites each with charming rustic interiors including hand-carved poster beds, twig tables, and woodsy fabrics. Most guest rooms afford dramatic sunset views over the water and Squaw Mountain. Explore nearby Lily Bay State Park or take part in the year-round recreations of the lake and surrounding wilderness. 5 rooms, 2 story. Children over 14 years only. Complimentary full breakfast. Check-in 3 pm, check-out 11 am. **$$$$**

Houlton (B-4)

Settled 1805
Population 6,613
Elevation 366 ft
Area Code 207
Zip 04730
Information Greater Houlton Chamber of Commerce, 109 Main St; phone 207/532-4216
Web Site www.greaterhoulton.com

Houlton prospered first from lumber, then from the famous Maine potatoes. It is young by New England standards, but was the first town settled in Aroostook County. Industries include woodworking and wood chip and waferboard factories. It is 2 miles from the Canadian border and a major port of entry. Swimming is available at Nickerson Lake. Fishing is available in several nearby lakes. (For border crossing regulations, see MAKING THE MOST OF YOUR TRIP.)

What to See and Do

Aroostook Historical and Art Museum. *109 Main St, Houlton (04730). Phone 207/532-4216.* Pioneer exhibits, local historical items include model and artifacts from Hancock Barracks, memorabilia from the now closed Ricker College. (Memorial Day-Labor Day, Mon-Fri) **FREE**

Hancock Barracks. *Garrison Hill, Houlton (04730). 1 mile E on Hwy 2.* Second-northernmost Federal outpost in the country; manned by troops from 1828-1846. **FREE**

Market Square Historic District. *Main and Broadway sts, Houlton (04730).* These historic 1890s buildings show a high degree of design artistry. Contact the Chamber of Commerce for walking tour maps. **FREE**

Museum of Vintage Fashions. *Sherman and Main sts, Houlton (04730). 25 miles SW via Hwy 2 to Island Falls, on Sherman St. Phone 207/463-2404.* Contains 17 rooms of men's, women's, and children's vintage fashions. Dressmaker's shop, hat boutique, bridal room, haberdashery. (June-early Oct: Mon-Thurs, also Fri-Sun by appointment only) **DONATION**

Special Events

Houlton Fair. *Community Park, Randall Ave, Houlton (04730). Phone 207/532-4216.* Entertainment, concessions, rides. Early July.

Houlton Potato Feast Days. *Phone 207/532-4216.* Events held throughout the city. Last full weekend in Aug.

Meduxnekeag River Canoe Race. *7 Bird St, Houlton (04730). Phone 207/532-4216.* Late Apr.

Limited-Service Hotels

★ **IVEYS MOTOR LODGE.** *Hwy 1 and I-95, Houlton (04730). Phone 207/532-4206; toll-free 800/ 244-4206. www.houlton.com/iveys.htm.* 24 rooms. Check-out 11 am. Bar. **$**

★ **SCOTTISH INN.** *239 Bangor St, Houlton (04730). Phone 207/532-2236; fax 207/532-9893.* 43 rooms. Pets accepted, some restrictions; fee. Check-out 11 am. **$**
🅳 🐾

★ **SHIRETOWN MOTOR INN.** *282 North St at I-95, Houlton (04730). Phone 207/532-9421; toll-free 800/441-9421; fax 207/532-3390. www.shiretownmotorairport.com.* 51 rooms. Check-out 11 am. Restaurant, bar. Fitness room. Indoor pool. Tennis. **$**
🅳 🧍 ⛱ 🎿

Kennebunk (F-1)

See also Kennebunkport, Ogunquit, Old Orchard Beach, Portland, Saco, Wells

Settled 1650
Population 8,004
Elevation 50 ft
Area Code 207
Zip 04043
Information Chamber of Commerce, 17 Western Ave, Hwy 9-Lower Village, PO Box 740; phone 207/967-0857
Web Site www.kkcc.maine.org

The original settlement that was to become Kennebunk was at one time a part of Wells. When Maine separated from Massachusetts in 1820, Kennebunk separated from Wells. Once a shipbuilding communi-

ty on the Mousam and Kennebunk rivers, Kennebunk today is the principal business center of a summer resort area that includes Kennebunkport (see) and Kennebunk Beach.

What to See and Do

Brick Store Museum. *117 Main St, Kennebunk (04043). Hwy 1, opposite library. Phone 207/985-4802.* A block of restored 19th-century buildings including William Lord's Brick Store (1825); exhibits of fine and decorative arts, historical and maritime collections. (Wed-Fri; closed holidays) **$$**

Taylor-Barry House. *24 Summer St, Kennebunk (04043). Phone 207/985-4802.* (Circa 1803) Sea captain's Federal period house with furniture, stenciled hallway; 20th-century artist's studio. (June-Sept, Tues-Fri afternoons) **$$**

Special Event

Winter Carnival. *1 Summer St, Kennebunk (04043). Phone toll-free 800/982-4421.* Snow sculpture contests, snow palace moonwalk, magic show, ice-skating party, chili and chowder contests, children's events. Feb.

Limited-Service Hotel

★ **THE SEASONS INN OF THE KENNEBUNK.** *55 York St, Kennebunk (04043). Phone 207/985-6100; toll-free 800/336-5634; fax 207/985-4031. www.the seasonsinnofthekennebunks.com.* 44 rooms, 2 story. Complimentary continental breakfast. Check-out 11 am. Outdoor pool. **$**
⛱

Specialty Lodgings

The following lodging establishments are approved by Mobil Travel Guide, but due to their unique and individualized nature have not been given a traditional Mobil Star rating. Included in this listing you may find bed-and-breakfasts, limited-service inns, guest ranches, and other unique hotel properties.

ARUNDEL MEADOWS INN. *Hwy 1, Kennebunk (04046). Phone 207/985-3770. www.arundelmeadowsin n.com.* Restored farmhouse (1827); artwork, antiques, garden. 7 rooms, 2 story. Children over 12 years only. Complimentary full breakfast. Check-in 2 pm, check-out 11 am. Outdoor pool. **$**
🅳 ⛱

THE BEACH HOUSE. *211 Beach Ave, Kennebunk Beach (04043). Phone 207/967-3850; fax 207/967-4719. www.beachhseinn.com.* This inn (circa 1890) is located on Kennebunk Beach, which is just 2 miles from Kennebunkport. The inn is a few minutes from the Port Village, where guests can visit many boutiques, shops, galleries, and restaurants. Guests may also partake in deep-sea fishing, whale-watching, or visit the Rachel Carson Wildlife Refuge. 34 rooms, 4 story. Complimentary continental breakfast. Check-in 3 pm, check-out 11 am. **$$$$**

THE KENNEBUNK INN. *45 Main St, Kennebunk (04043). Phone 207/985-3351; fax 207/985-8865. www.thekennebunkinn.com.* Built in 1799; turn-of-the-century décor. 24 rooms, 3 story. Pets accepted, some restrictions. Complimentary continental breakfast. Check-in 3 pm, check-out 11 am. Restaurant. **$**

Restaurants

★ ★ ★ **GRISSINI.** *27 Western Ave, Kennebunk (04043). Phone 207/967-2211.* Grissini offers Italian/Tuscan cooking in an airy, loftlike setting. The restaurant is decorated with Italian posters, vases filled with flowers, and bread baskets. Italian menu. Dinner. Closed Thanksgiving. Bar. Children's menu. Outdoor seating. **$$**

★ ★ **THE KENNEBUNK INN.** *45 Main St, Kennebunk (04043). Phone 207/985-3351. www.the kennebunkinn.com.* Inn built in 1799; stained-glass windows. American menu. Dinner. Closed Dec 25. Bar. Children's menu. Outdoor seating. **$$**

★ ★ ★ **WINDOWS ON THE WATER.** *12 Chase Hill Rd, Kennebunk (04043). Phone 207/967-3313; fax 207/967-5377. www.windowsonthewater.com.* American menu. Lunch, dinner. Closed Dec 24-25. Children's menu. Outdoor seating. **$$$**

Kennebunkport (F-1)

See also Kennebunk, Old Orchard Beach, Portland, Saco

Settled 1629
Population 3,356
Elevation 20 ft
Area Code 207
Zip 04046
Information Chamber of Commerce, 17 Western Ave,

Hwy 9-Lower Village, PO Box 740, Kennebunk 04043; phone 207/967-0857
Web Site www.kkcc.maine.org

At the mouth of the Kennebunk River, this coastal town is a summer and winter resort, as well as an art and literary colony. It was the home of author Kenneth Roberts and the scene of his novel *Arundel*. During the Bush administration, the town achieved fame as the summer residence of the 41st president.

What to See and Do

Architectural Walking Tour. *Phone 207/985-4802.* Tours of historic district (June-Sept, Wed, Fri). **$$**

The Nott House. *8 Maine St, Kennebunkport (04046). Phone 207/967-2751.* (1853) Greek Revival house with original wallpaper and furnishings from the Perkins-Nott family. Tours. (June-mid-Oct, Tues-Fri afternoons) **$$**

School House. *135 North St, Kennebunkport (04046). Phone 207/967-2751.* (1899) Headquarters of the Kennebunkport Historical Society. Houses collections of genealogy, photographs, maritime history, and many artifacts and documents on Kennebunkport's history. (Wed-Fri afternoons) **FREE**

Seashore Trolley Museum. *Log Cabin Rd, Kennebunkport (04046). 3 1/2 miles N on Log Cabin Rd (North St). Phone 207/967-2800.* Approximately 200 antique streetcars from the United States and abroad; special events. (Late May-mid-Oct, daily) **$$$**

Swimming. *6 Community House Way, Kennebunkport (04046).* Colony Beach and Goose Rocks Beach.

Limited-Service Hotels

★ **RHUMB LINE MOTOR LODGE.** *Ocean Ave, Kennebunkport (04046). Phone 207/967-5457; toll-free 800/337-4862; fax 207/967-4418. www.rhumblinemaine .com.* This secluded woodland location is on the trolley route. 59 rooms, 3 story. Complimentary continental breakfast. Check-out 11 am. Bar. Fitness room. Indoor pool, outdoor pool, whirlpool. **$**

★ ★ **THE SCHOONERS INN.** *127 Ocean Ave, Kennebunkport (04046). Phone 207/967-5333; fax 207/ 967-2040. www.schoonersinn.com.* 17 rooms, 3 story. Complimentary continental breakfast. Check-out 11 am. Restaurant. **$$$**

Full-Service Hotels

★ ★ ★ **THE COLONY HOTEL.** *140 Ocean Ave, Kennebunkport (04046). Phone 207/967-3331; toll-free 800/552-2363; fax 207/967-8738. www.thecolonyhotel .com/maine.* Located on a rock promontory overlooking the Atlantic Ocean and the mouth of the Kennebunk River, this hotel provides guests with many activities. There is a heated saltwater pool, beach, and gardens on the premises, and nearby are golf, tennis, kayaking, bicycling, boating, shopping, and touring of art galleries. Maine lobster and local seafoods are the featured cuisine, and afternoon tea is served daily. 125 rooms, 4 story. Closed Nov-mid-May. Pets accepted; fee. Check-in 3 pm, check-out 11 am. Restaurant, bar. Beach. Outdoor pool. **$$**

★ ★ ★ **KENNEBUNKPORT INN.** *1 Dock Sq, Kennebunkport (04046). Phone 207/967-2621; toll-free 800/248-2621; fax 207/967-3705. www.kennebunkport inn.com.* A Victorian mansion (1899), conveniently located at the heart of the historic seaport of Kennebunkport, Maine, the inn is an easy walk to the harbor and all the shops and galleries of Dock Square. Many of the inn's rooms have antiques and four-poster beds, several have gas fireplaces, and all have private baths. This inn is also known for creative cuisine served in the dining room. The house was built by a wealthy tea and coffee merchant and was renovated to an inn in 1926. 34 rooms, 3 story. Check-in 3 pm, check-out 11 am. Restaurant, bar. Outdoor pool. **$**

Full-Service Resort

★ ★ ★ **NONANTUM RESORT.** *95 Ocean Ave, Kennebunkport (04046). Phone 207/967-4050; toll-free 800/552-5651; fax 207/967-8451. www.nonantumresort.com.* Located in the picturesque, historic town of Kennebunkport with fine shops, art galleries, and historic landmarks, the guest rooms are in two buildings and all have air-conditioning, cable, and private baths. Guests can walk to a nearby beach or to the summer home of former President Bush to view the rocky coast of Maine or take a swim or lounge by the outdoor heated pool and whirlpool. Maine seafood is featured on the cuisine side. This is one of the oldest operating inns in the state. 116 rooms, 4 story. Closed Dec-Mar. Check-out 11 am. Restaurant, bar. Outdoor pool. **$**

Full-Service Inn

★ ★ ★ ★ **THE WHITE BARN INN.** *37 Beach Ave, Kennebunkport (04046). Phone 207/967-2321; fax 207/967-1100. www.whitebarninn.com.* The White Barn Inn is a picture-perfect New England hideaway. This cluster of cottages, restored barns, and 1860s homestead offers its guests a leisurely change of pace. Maine's craggy coastline is only a short walk away, as is the quaint town of Kennebunkport, where guests wander in and out of antique and specialty stores. Period furnishings, wall coverings, and antiques capture the essence of colonial New England in the charming rooms and suites. Warm and inviting, the rooms are topped off by wood-burning fireplaces, whirlpool tubs, and stunning views of the countryside. Simple pleasures, like relaxing by the stone infinity pool or riding a bike along the coast, are the draw here. Composed of two converted barns, the Inn has one of the region's most acclaimed restaurants (see THE WHITE BARN INN RESTAURANT). The haute cuisine of the four-course dinner and the romantic, candlelit setting are perfectly suited for a tête-à-tête. 29 rooms, 3 story. Children over 12 years only. Complimentary full breakfast. Check-in 3 pm, check-out 11 am. Restaurant, bar. Outdoor pool. **$$$$**

Specialty Lodgings

The following lodging establishments are approved by Mobil Travel Guide, but due to their unique and individualized nature have not been given a traditional Mobil Star rating. Included in this listing you may find bed-and-breakfasts, limited-service inns, guest ranches, and other unique hotel properties.

BUFFLEHEAD COVE. *Bufflehead Cove Ln, Kennebunkport (04046). Phone 207/967-3879. www.buffleheadcove.com.* This secluded Victorian inn is hidden away in the woods, on the Kennebunk River. The inn is spacious, old-fashioned, and close to downtown Kennebunkport. Guests can leisurely explore the local beaches, or visit the numerous restaurants, art galleries, antique shops, and old bookstores. 5 rooms, 2 story. Children over 11 years only. Complimentary full breakfast. Check-in 3 pm, check-out 11 am. **$$$**

CAPE ARUNDEL INN. *208 Ocean Ave, Kennebunkport (04046). Phone 207/967-2125; fax 207/967-1199. www.capearundelinn.com.* This Victorian-style inn (1890) features turn-of-the-century décor and overlooks the seacoast. 13 rooms. Closed mid-Dec-mid-Apr. Complimentary continental breakfast. Check-out 11 am. Restaurant. **$$**

CAPTAIN FAIRFIELD INN. *8 Pleasant St, Kennebunkport (04046). Phone 207/967-4454; toll-free 800/322-1928; fax 207/967-8537. www.captainfair field.com.* This Federal-style historic bed-and-breakfast (1813) is in the heart of the seaport resort of Kennebunkport. It is surrounded by towering trees, gardens, and overlooks the river and harbor. It is within walking distance to shops and art galleries, as well as the ocean and a variety of restaurants. Guest rooms are decorated with antique and period furniture and each has its own private bath and sitting area. 9 rooms, 2 story. Children over 6 years only. Complimentary full breakfast. Check-in 3 pm, check-out 11 am. **$$**
🅱

THE CAPTAIN JEFFERDS INN. *5 Pearl St, Kennebunkport (04046). Phone 207/967-2311; toll-free 800/839-6844; fax 207/964-0721. www.captainjefferds inn.com.* This historic inn, built in 1804, has been restored and is furnished with antiques and period reproductions. All rooms have private baths, fresh flowers, down-filled comforters, fireplaces, porches, CD players, and whirlpools. A three-course breakfast is included as well as afternoon refreshments. 16 rooms, 3 story. Closed last two weeks in Dec. Pets accepted, some restrictions; fee. Children over 8 years only. Complimentary full breakfast. Check-in 3 pm, check-out 11 am. **$$$**
🅱 🐾

THE CAPTAIN LORD MANSION. *6 Pleasant St, Kennebunkport (04046). Phone 207/967-3141; fax 207/967-3172. www.captainlord.com.* The Captain Lord Mansion is the kind of place that mandates repeat visits. Indeed, this bewitching bed-and-breakfast rewards its guests with an engraved stone in the delightful Memory Garden upon their tenth arrival. Set on an acre of blooming gardens, this inn wholeheartedly welcomes visitors to the charming village of Kennebunkport on the southern coast of Maine. From the gentle-mannered innkeepers to the mouthwatering morning feasts, the experience is exceptional. The interiors represent a departure from the traditional country inn style, with an opulent and worldly mix of unique touches, period furnishings, and even several items belonging to the original Lord family. Each guest room is distinguished by a different theme, yet all feel luxurious. 16 rooms, 3 story. Children over 12

years only. Complimentary full breakfast. Check-in 3 pm, check-out 11 am. **$$**
🅱

ENGLISH MEADOWS INN. *141 Port Rd, Kennebunkport (04043). Phone 207/967-5766; toll-free 800/272-0698; fax 207/967-3868. www.englishmeadows inn.com.* Victorian farmhouse (1860) and attached carriage house. 12 rooms, 3 story. Closed Jan. Complimentary full breakfast. Check-in 3 pm, check-out 11 am. **$**
🅱

THE INN AT HARBOR HEAD. *41 Pier Rd, Kennebunkport (04046). Phone 207/967-5564; fax 207/967-1294. www.harborhead.com.* This 100-year-old shingled farmhouse is intimate and informal, with uniquely decorated, romantic guest rooms filled with antiques, books, chintz, and paddle fans. Stop by the ocean-view breakfast room for a morning meal, then head to nearby Goose Rocks Beach, or just sit on the dock and watch the day pass. The inn overlooks picturesque Cape Porpoise Harbor. 4 rooms, 2 story. Closed Nov-Apr. Children over 12 years only. Complimentary full breakfast. Check-in 3 pm, check-out 11 am. **$$$**
🅱

MAINE STAY INN & COTTAGES AT THE MELVILLE WALKER HOUSE. *34 Maine St, Kennebunkport (04046). Phone 207/967-2117; toll-free 800/950-2117; fax 207/967-8757. www.mainestayinn .com.* This 19th-century bed-and-breakfast (1860) is located in the residential area of Kennebunkport's historic district. It is near the harbor and beach. 17 rooms, 2 story. Complimentary full breakfast. Check-in 3 pm, check-out 11 am. **$$$**
🅱

OLD FORT INN. *8 Old Fort Ave, Kennebunkport (04046). Phone 207/967-5353; toll-free 800/828-3678; fax 207/967-4547. oldfortinn.com.* This inn, located just one block from the Atlantic Ocean, has guest rooms in a turn-of-the-century carriage house built of red brick and local stone. There is a tennis court and heated freshwater pool on the premises and nearby guests can explore boutiques and art galleries or the beaches and rugged coastline. 16 rooms, 2 story. Closed mid-Dec-mid-Apr. Complimentary full breakfast. Check-in 3-8 pm, check-out 11 am. Outdoor pool. Tennis. **$$$$**
🅱 🏊 🎾

TIDES INN BY THE SEA. *252 Kings Hwy, Kennebunkport (04046). Phone 207/967-3757; fax 207/967-5183. www.tidesinnbythesea.com.* Built as an inn in 1899. Original guest book on display; signatures include Theodore Roosevelt and Arthur Conan Doyle. 22 rooms, 3 story. Closed mid-Oct-mid-May. Complimentary continental breakfast. Check-in 3 pm, check-out 10:30 am. Restaurant. **$$$**
🔊

YACHTSMAN LODGE & MARINA. *Ocean Ave, Kennebunkport (04046). Phone 207/967-2511; fax 207/ 967-5056. www.yachtsmanlodge.com.* 30 rooms. Closed Nov-Apr. Complimentary continental breakfast. Check-out 11 am. **$**

Restaurants

★ **ALISSON'S.** *11 Dock Sq, Kennebunkport (04046). Phone 207/967-4841; fax 207/967-2532. www.alissons.com.* Seafood menu. Lunch, dinner. Closed Thanksgiving, Dec 25. Bar. Children's menu. **$$**

★ **BARTLEY'S DOCKSIDE DINING.** *Western Ave, Kennebunkport (04046). Phone 207/967-5050; fax 207/985-3655. www.int-usa.net/bartley.* Seafood menu. Lunch, dinner. Bar. Children's menu. Outdoor seating. **$$**

★ ★ **THE BELVIDERE ROOM.** *252 Kings Hwy, Kennebunkport (04046). Phone 207/967-3757; fax 207/967-5183. www.tidesinnbythesea.com.* In historic inn (see TIDES INN BY THE SEA). American menu. Dinner. Closed mid-Oct-mid-May. Bar. Children's menu. **$$$**
🔊

★ **MABEL'S LOBSTER CLAW.** *124 Ocean Ave, Kennebunkport (04046). Phone 207/967-2562.* Seafood menu. Lunch, dinner. Closed early Nov-Apr. Children's menu. Outdoor seating. **$$**

★ ★ ★ **SEASCAPES.** *77 Pier Rd, Cape Porpoise (04046). Phone 207/967-8500; fax 207/967-8559. www.seascapesrestaurant.com.* Specializing in the cuisines of the Pacific Rim and the Mediterranean, this seaside restaurant offers incredible views of the Atlantic Ocean. The flavors are creative and exciting, and the presentations are unique. True to its location, the seafood dishes are a must. Mediterranean, Pacific Rim menu. Lunch, dinner. Closed Nov-mid-Apr. **$$**
🔊

★ ★ ★ ★ **THE WHITE BARN INN RESTAURANT.** *37 Beach Ave, Kennebunkport (04046). Phone 207/967-2321. www.whitebarninn.com.* A pair of restored barns dating to the 1860s now houses The White Barn Inn and its restaurant. A New England classic, this charming candlelit space, filled with fresh flowers, white linen-topped tables, and beautiful pastoral views, is a perfect place for a relaxed but elegant dining experience. The specialty of the house is, as you might expect, contemporary New England cuisine; the chef offers delicious regional dishes expertly accented with a European flair. The four-course prix fixe menu changes weekly, highlighting seafood from Maine's icy waters as well as native game and poultry. An ant-loving picnic menu is available in summer months for dining under the sun or stars. The vast wine selection perfectly complements the cuisine, and a rolling cheese cart offers some of the best local artisans' products to savor after your meal. In addition to the cozy vibe and mouthwatering menu, The White Barn Inn Restaurant offers exemplary service. The end result is an overwhelming urge to snuggle in and never leave. American menu. Breakfast, dinner. Closed three weeks in Jan. Bar. Jacket required. Reservations recommended. Outdoor seating. **$$$$**
🔊

Kingfield (D-1)

Population 1,114
Elevation 560 ft
Area Code 207
Zip 04947

On a narrow intervale in the valley of the Carrabassett River, Kingfield once had several lumber mills. The town was named after William King, Maine's first governor, and was the birthplace of F. E. and F. O. Stanley, the twins who developed the Stanley Steamer. There is good canoeing, hiking, trout fishing, and hunting in nearby areas.

What to See and Do

Carrabassett Valley Ski Touring Center. *Sugarloaf Access Rd, Kingfield (04947). 15 miles N via Hwy 16/27. Phone 207/237-2000. www.sugarloaf.com.* Approximately 50 miles of ski touring trails. Center offers lunch (daily); school, rentals; skating rink (fee), rentals; trail information area; shop. (Early Dec-late Apr, daily) Half-day rates. **$$$$**

Sugarloaf/USA Ski Area. *Sugarloaf Access Rd, Kingfield (04947). 15 miles N on Hwy 16/27. Phone 207/237-2000; toll-free 800/843-5623 (reservations only). www.sugarloaf.com.* Two quad, triple, eight double chairlifts; T-bar; school, patrol, rentals; snowmaking; lodge; restaurants, coffee shop, cafeteria, bars; nursery; bank, health club, shops. Six Olympic runs, 45 miles of trails; longest run 3 1/2 miles; vertical drop 2,820 feet. 65 miles of cross-country trails. (Early Nov-May, daily). **$$$$**

Limited-Service Hotels

★ ★ **THE HERBERT GRAND HOTEL.** *Main St, Kingfield (04947). Phone 207/265-2000; toll-free 800/843-4372; fax 207/265-4597.* Built in 1917; elaborate fumed oak woodwork. On river. 33 rooms, 3 story. Pets accepted; fee. Complimentary continental breakfast. Check-in noon, check-out 11 am. Restaurant. **$**
🐾

★ ★ **SUGARLOAF INN.** *Hwy 27, Kingfield (04947). Phone 207/237-3768. www.sugarloaf.com.* 42 rooms, 4 story. Check-in 4 pm, check-out 11 am. Restaurant, bar. Indoor pool, outdoor pool, whirlpool. Golf. Tennis. Ski in/ski out. **$**
🐾🏊🍴🎿🏂⬇

Full-Service Resort

★ ★ ★ **GRAND SUMMIT RESORT HOTEL.** *Hwy 1, Kingfield (04947). Phone 207/237-2222; toll-free 800/527-9879; fax 207/237-2874. www.sugarloaf.com.* Each room in this hotel has a view of the mountains and features oak furniture and brass fixtures, television with a VCR, and a coffee maker. Guests can enjoy skiing, golfing, or can just relax and enjoy the mountain scenery. The hotel is located at the base of the slopes. 120 rooms, 6 story. Check-out 10 am. Restaurant, bar. Fitness room. Whirlpool. Golf, 18 holes. Tennis. Ski in/ski out. **$**
🎿🍴🎿⬇

Restaurant

★ ★ **LONGFELLOW'S.** *Main and Kingfield sts, Kingfield (04947). Phone 207/265-4394.* One of town's oldest buildings (1860s). American, seafood menu. Lunch, dinner. Children's menu. Outdoor seating. **$**

Kittery (F-1)

See also Ogunquit, York

Settled 1623
Population 9,372
Elevation 22 ft
Area Code 207
Zip 03904
Information Greater York Region Chamber of Commerce, 1 Stonewall Ln; phone 207/363-4422
Web Site www.yorkme.org

This old sea community has built ships since its early days. Kittery men built the *Ranger,* which sailed to France under John Paul Jones with the news of Burgoyne's surrender. Across the Piscataqua River from Portsmouth, New Hampshire, Kittery is the home of the Portsmouth Naval Shipyard, which sprawls over islands on the Maine side of the river.

What to See and Do

Factory Outlet Stores. *Hwy 1, Kittery (03904).* Approximately 120 outlet stores can be found throughout Kittery. For a complete listing, contact the Chamber of Commerce.

Fort Foster Park. *NE via Hwy 103 to Gerrish Island. Phone 207/439-3800.* A 92-acre park with picnicking, pavilion; beach; baseball field; fishing pier. Cross-country skiing in winter. (June-Aug: daily; May and Sept: Sat-Sun) Entrance fee per individual and per vehicle.

Fort McClary Memorial. *Kittery Point (03905). 3 1/2 miles E of Hwy 1.* Restored hexagonal blockhouse on site of 1809 fort. Interpretive displays; picnicking. (Memorial Day-Labor Day, daily) For further information, contact the Chamber of Commerce.

Hamilton House. *Vaughan Ln, South Berwick (03908). N on I-95 to Hwy 236, then approximately 10 miles NW to Vaughan Ln. Phone 207/384-5269.* (Circa 1785) This Georgian house, situated overlooking the Salmon Falls River, was redecorated at the turn of the century with a mixture of antiques, painted murals, and country furnishings to create an interpretation of America's colonial past. Perennial garden, flowering trees and shrubs, and garden cottage. Tours. (June-mid-Oct: Tues, Thurs, Sat-Sun afternoons) **$$**

John Paul Jones State Memorial. *River bank, E side of Hwy 1 at entrance to Kittery. Phone 207/384-5160.* Memorial to the sailors and soldiers of Maine. (Daily) **FREE**

Kittery Historical and Naval Museum. *Hwy 1 and Rogers Rd, Kittery (03904). Rogers Rd, off Rte 1 by Rotary at Hwy 236. Phone 207/439-3080.* Exhibits portray history of US Navy and Kittery—Maine's oldest incorporated town—as well as southern Maine's maritime heritage. (June-Oct: Tues-Sat; rest of year: Fri and by appointment) **$$**

Sarah Orne Jewett House. *5 Portland St, South Berwick (03908). N on I-95 to Hwy 236, then approximately 10 miles NW. Phone 207/384-2454.* (1774) Novelist Sarah Orne Jewett spent most of her life in this fine Georgian residence. Interior restored to re-create the appearance of the house during her time (1849-1909). Contains some original 18th- and 19th-century wallpaper; fine paneling. Her own bedroom-study has been left as she arranged it. (June-mid-Oct, Wed-Sun) **$$**

Limited-Service Hotel

★ **COACHMAN INN.** *380 Hwy 1, Kittery (03904). Phone 207/439-4434; toll-free 800/824-6183; fax 207/439-6757. www.coachmaninn.net.* 43 rooms, 2 story. Complimentary continental breakfast. Check-in 3 pm, check-out 11 am. Outdoor pool. **$**
🌊

Restaurants

★ **CAPTAIN SIMEON'S GALLEY.** *90 Pepperell Rd (Hwy 103), Kittery Point (03905). Phone 207/439-3655.* Original hand-hewn beams from 17th-century boathouse; views of pier, lighthouses. Seafood menu. Lunch, dinner, Sun brunch. Closed Tues (off-season); Thanksgiving, Dec 25. Bar. **$$**

★ ★ **WARREN'S LOBSTER HOUSE.** *11 Water St, Kittery (03904). Phone 207/439-1630; fax 207/439-8821. www.lobsterhouse.com.* Seafood menu. Lunch, dinner, Sun brunch. Closed Jan 1, Dec 24-25. Bar. Children's menu. Outdoor seating. **$**

Lewiston (E-1)

See also Auburn

Settled 1770
Population 39,757

Elevation 210 ft
Area Code 207
Information Androscoggin County Chamber of Commerce, 179 Lisbon St, PO Box 59, 04243-0059; phone 207/783-2249
Web Site www.androscoggincounty.com

Maine's second-largest city is 30 miles up the Androscoggin River from the sea, directly across the river from its sister city of Auburn (see). Known as the Twin Cities, both are strong manufacturing and service-oriented communities. Lewiston was the first of the two cities to harness the water power of the Androscoggin Falls; however, both cities have benefited from the river.

What to See and Do

Bates College. *56 Campus Ave, Lewiston (04240). Phone 207/786-6255.* (1855) (1,600 students) New England's oldest and the nation's second-oldest co-educational institution of higher learning; originally the Maine State Seminary, it was renamed after a prominent Boston investor. Liberal arts and sciences. On its well-landscaped campus are the Edmund S. Muskie Archives (1936 alumnus and former Senator and US Secretary of State) and a beautiful chapel containing a hand-crafted tracker-action organ. Also on campus are

Mount David. A 340-foot rocky hill offering a view of Lewiston, the Androscoggin Valley, and the Presidential Range of the White Mountains to the west.

Olin Arts Center. *College St and Campus Ave, Lewiston (04240). Phone 207/786-6158 (museum).* Multilevel facility overlooking campus lake houses a concert hall and a Museum of Art that contains a variety of changing and permanent exhibits (Tues-Sun; closed holidays). **FREE**

Special Events

Festival de Joie. *190 Birch St, Lewiston (04240). Phone 207/782-6231. www.festivaldejoie.org.* Celebration of Lewiston and Auburn's Franco-American heritage. Features ethnic song, dance, cultural activities, and traditional foods. Late July-early Aug.

Lewiston-Auburn Garden Tour. *215 Lisbon St, Lewiston (04240). Phone 207/782-1403.* Tour of six gardens in the area. Ticket purchase required. July.

Maine State Parade. *215 Lisbon St #1A, Lewiston (04240). Downtown Lewiston and Auburn.Phone 207/783-2249.* Maine's largest parade; more than 30,000 people representing 60 communities. Televised statewide. First weekend in May.

Limited-Service Hotel

★ ★ **RAMADA INN.** *490 Pleasant St, Lewiston (04240). Phone 207/784-2331; toll-free 800/272-6232; fax 207/784-2332. www.ramadamaine.com.* 117 rooms, 2 story. Complimentary continental breakfast. Check-out 11 am. Restaurant, bar. Fitness room. Indoor pool, whirlpool. Business center. **$**

Lincoln (C-3))

Population 5,587
Elevation 180 ft
Area Code 207
Zip 04457
Information Lincoln Lakes Region Chamber of Commerce, 75 Main St, PO Box 164; phone 207/794-8065 or toll-free 800/794-8065
Web Site www.lincolnmechamber.org

What to See and Do

Mount Jefferson Ski Area. *Lee (04455). 12 miles NE via Hwy 6. Phone 207/738-2377.* Novice, intermediate, and expert trails; two T-bar, rope tow; patrol, school, rentals; lodge, concession. Longest run 0.7 miles, vertical drop 432 feet. (Jan-Mar: Tues-Thurs, Sat-Sun; daily during school vacations)

Limited-Service Hotel

★ **BRIARWOOD MOTOR INN.** *Outer West Broadway, Lincoln (04457). Phone 207/794-6731. www.angelfire.com/me4/briarwood.* 24 rooms, 2 story. Pets accepted; fee. Check-out 11 am. **$**

Lubec (D-5)

See also Eastport, Machias

Population 1,853
Elevation 20 ft
Area Code 207
Zip 04652

Quoddy Head State Park, the easternmost point in the United States, is located in Lubec. There is a lighthouse here, as well as the Franklin D. Roosevelt Memorial Bridge, which stretches over Lubec Narrows to Campobello Island. Herring smoking and sardine packing are local industries.

What to See and Do

Roosevelt Campobello International Park. *459 Hwy 774, New Brunswick. 1 1/2 miles E off Hwy 189 on Campobello Island. Phone 506/752-2922. www.nps.gov/roca.* Canadian property jointly maintained by Canada and United States. Approximately 2,800 acres includes the 11-acre estate where Franklin D. Roosevelt had his summer home and was stricken with poliomyelitis. Self-guided tours of 34-room house, interpretive guides available; films shown in visitor center; picnic sites in natural area; observation platforms and interpretive panels at Friar's Head; vistas. No camping. (Sat before Memorial Day-Oct 31, daily) **FREE**

Specialty Lodgings

The following lodging establishments are approved by Mobil Travel Guide, but due to their unique and individualized nature have not been given a traditional Mobil Star rating. Included in this listing you may find bed-and-breakfasts, limited-service inns, guest ranches, and other unique hotel properties.

HOME PORT INN. *45 Main St, Lubec (04652). Phone 207/733-2077; toll-free 800/457-2077; fax 207/733-2950. www.homeportinn.com.* Built in 1880. 7 rooms, 2 story. Closed mid-Oct-late May. Complimentary continental breakfast. Check-in 2 pm, check-out 10 am. Restaurant. **$**

OWEN HOUSE. *11 Welshpool Rd, Campobello Island (E0G 3H0). Phone 506/752-2977. www.owenhouse.ca.* 9 rooms, 3 story. Closed mid-Oct-mid-May. Complimentary continental breakfast. Check-in 3 pm, check-out 11 am. Built by son of first settler of Campobello Island. **$**

Restaurant

★ ★ **HOME PORT INN.** *45 Main St, Lubec (04652). Phone 207/733-2077; fax 207/733-2950. www.homeportinn.com.* Seafood menu. Dinner. Closed mid-Oct-May. **$**

Machias (D-4)

See also Lubec

Settled 1763
Population 2,569
Elevation 70 ft
Area Code 207
Zip 04654
Information Machias Bay Area Chamber of Commerce, PO Box 606; phone 207/255-4402
Web Site www.nemaine.com/mbacc

For almost a hundred years before 1750, Machias (muh-CHY-as) was the headquarters for a number of pirates including Samuel Bellamy, called the Robin Hood of Atlantic pirates. After pirating abated, Machias became a hotbed of Revolutionary fervor. Off Machiasport, downriver, the British schooner *Margaretta* was captured (June 1775) in the first naval engagement of the war. Today, the area is noted particularly for hunting, fishing, and nature trails. Bear, deer, puffin, salmon, and striped bass abound nearby. The University of Maine has a branch in Machias.

What to See and Do

Burnham Tavern Museum. *Main St, Machias (04654). Just off Hwy 1 on Hwy 192.* Phone 207/255-4432. (1770) Memorabilia from 1770-1830. (June-Sept, Mon-Fri; rest of year, by appointment) **$**

Cobscook Bay State Park. *20 miles NE on Rte 1, near Whiting.* Phone 207/726-4412. Fishing, boating (ramp); hiking, picnicking, snowmobiling permitted, camping (dump station). (Mid-May-mid-Oct, daily) **$**

Fort O'Brien State Historic Site. *5 miles E on Hwy 92.* Phone 207/941-4014. The remains of a fort commanding the harbor, commissioned by George Washington in 1775. Hiking, picnicking. (Memorial Day-Labor Day, daily) **FREE**

Roque Bluffs. *145 Schoppee Point Rd, Machias (04654). 7 miles S, off Hwy 1.* Phone 207/255-3475. Oceanfront pebble beach; freshwater pond. Swimming, fishing; picnicking. (Mid-May-mid-Oct, daily) **$**

Ruggles House. *Columbia Falls (04623). 20 miles S on Hwy 1, then 1/4 mile off Hwy 1.* Phone 207/483-4637. (1820) This home exhibits Adam-style architecture and unusual "flying" staircase. Intricate wood carving; period furnishings. (June-mid-Oct, daily) **$**

Special Event

Wild Blueberry Festival. *Downtown area, Machias (04654).* Phone 207/255-4402. www.machiasblueberry.com. Located in Washington County, which produces 85 percent of the world's blueberries, this festival's activities include a children's parade, pancake breakfast, craft fair, and pie-eating contest. Third weekend in Aug.

Millinocket (C-3)

See also Baxter State Park

Population 6,956
Elevation 350 ft
Area Code 207
Zip 04462
Information Katahdin Area Chamber of Commerce, 1029 Central St; phone 207/723-4443
Web Site www.katahdinmaine.com

Limited-Service Hotels

★ ★ BEST VALUE HERITAGE MOTOR INN-MILLINOCKET. *935 Central St, Millinocket (04462).* Phone 207/723-9777. 49 rooms, 2 story. Pets accepted. Complimentary continental breakfast. Check-out 11 am. Restaurant, bar. Fitness room. **$**

★ KATAHDIN INN. *740 Central St, Millinocket (04462).* Phone 207/723-4555; toll-free 877/902-4555; fax 207/723-6480. www.katahdininn.com. 82 rooms, 3 story. Pets accepted, some restrictions. Complimentary continental breakfast. Check-out noon. Bar. Fitness room. Indoor pool, children's pool, whirlpool. **$**

★ ★ PAMOLA MOTOR LODGE. *973 Central St, Millinocket (04462).* Phone 207/723-9746; fax 207/723-9746. www.pamolamotorlodge.com. 29 rooms, 2 story. Complimentary continental breakfast. Check-out 11 am. Restaurant, bar. Outdoor pool, whirlpool. **$**

The Fragile Beauty of Monhegan Island

Just 1 square mile in area, Monhegan is one of Maine's best known islands because it is spectacularly beautiful. No roads are paved, and there are 17 miles of walking trails. They lead through woods and over rocky ledges, along some of the highest ocean cliffs along the coast of Maine. Less than 20 percent of the island is inhabited.

Ideally, visitors should spend at least a night or two on Monhegan, but most come for just a few hours. The following loop offers a sense of the island's variety with time to still make the boat. (*Note:* Wear sensible shoes and appropriate weather gear. Respect the fragile beauty of the island and do not litter or pick flowers.)

The Lupine Gallery near the ferry wharf is the logical first stop because it showcases the work of the many artists who work on the island and hold open studios. Turn right on the single village street and follow it past Swim Beach and Fish Beach to the first and only intersection. Turn left here at

Monhegan House and walk up Horn Hill. Note the island's only public restrooms (behind the hotel) and the small signs indicating open artists' studios. At a Y in the path, follow the main path to the left as it climbs steeply up to Burnt Head, a cliff that rises a sheer 140 feet above the open ocean. It's the obvious spot for a picnic or at least to catch your breath and take in the beauty of the rocks, fir trees, and flowers. The narrow path continues along the cliffs, dipping between unusual rock formations at Gull Cove, and on to more cliffs at White Head and Little White Head. Turn onto the Whitehead Trail and follow it across the island to Monhegan Island Light, built in 1850, automated in 1959. The former keeper's cottage is now the Monhegan Museum, with a spellbinding display on local flora and fauna, art, and history. A separate art museum offers special exhibits. One of the most memorable along the entire coast, the view of the village from the lighthouse appears in numerous art museums. Walk back down to the main road and turn left toward the dock.

Monhegan Island (E-2)

See also Boothbay Harbor, Damariscotta, Rockland

Settled 1720
Population 88
Elevation 50 ft
Area Code 207
Zip 04852

Monhegan Plantation, 9 miles out to sea, approximately 2 miles long and 1 mile wide, is profitably devoted to lobsters and summer visitors. Rockwell Kent and Milton Burns were among the first of many artists to summer here. Today, the warm-weather population is about 20 times the year-round number. There is more work in winter: by special law, lobsters may be trapped in Monhegan waters only from January to June. This gives them the other six months to fatten. Monhegan lobsters thus command the highest prices.

Leif Ericson may have landed on Monhegan Island in AD 1000. In its early years, Monhegan Island was a landmark for sailors, and by 1611 it was well known as a general headquarters for European fishermen, traders, and explorers. For a time, the island was a pirate den. Small compared to other Maine islands, Monhegan is a land of contrasts. On one side of the island, sheer cliffs drop 150 feet to the ocean below, while on the other side, Cathedral Woods offers visitors a serene haven.

What to See and Do

Ferry from Port Clyde. *Main St, Port Clyde (04855). Foot of Hwy 131. Phone 207/372-8848. www.monheganboat.com. Laura B* makes an 11-mile journey (1 hour, 10 minutes) from Muscongus Bay. (Memorial Day-Columbus Day, three trips daily; no trips holidays) No cars permitted; reservations required. **$$$$**

⭐ **Monhegan Lighthouse.** Historic lighthouse has been in operation since 1824; automated since 1959. Magnificient views. **FREE**

Trips from Boothbay Harbor. *5 Eames Rd, Monhegan Island (04538). Phone 207/633-2284. Balmy Days* makes trips from the mainland (see BOOTHBAY HARBOR). (June-Sept, daily) **$$$$**

Moosehead Lake

See also Greenville, Rockwood

Web site www.mooseheadlake.org

N of Greenville; approximately 32 miles E of Jackman.

The largest of Maine's countless lakes, Moosehead is also the center for the state's wilderness sports. The source of the Kennebec River, Moosehead Lake is 40 miles long and 20 miles wide, with many bays, islands, ponds, rivers, and brooks surrounding it. Its waters are good for ice fishing in the winter, and trout, landlocked salmon, and togue can be caught in the summer. The lake is located in the heart of Maine's North Woods. Here is the largest moose population in the continental United States. Moose can best be seen in the early morning or at dusk. Being placid creatures, the moose allow watchers plenty of time to snap pictures. It is possible to hunt moose in northern Maine in season, but only by permit granted through a lottery.

Greenville (see), at the southern tip of the lake, is the headquarters for moose-watching, hunting, fishing, camping, whitewater rafting, canoeing, hiking, snowmobiling, and cross-country and alpine skiing. The town has an airport with two runways, one 3,000 feet long. Other communities around Moosehead Lake include Rockwood, Kokadjo, and Greenville Junction.

Newport (D-2)

See also Skowhegan

Population 3,036
Elevation 202 ft
Area Code 207
Zip 04953

Specialty Lodging

The following lodging establishment is approved by Mobil Travel Guide, but due to its unique and individualized nature has not been given a traditional Mobil Star rating. Included in this listing you may find bed-and-breakfasts, limited-service inns, guest ranches, and other unique hotel properties.

BREWSTER INN. *37 Zions Hill Rd, Dexter (04930). Phone 207/924-3130; fax 207/924-9768. www.brewsterinn.com.* Built in 1935; original fixtures.

10 rooms, 2 story. Complimentary full breakfast. Check-in 3 pm, check-out 11 am. **$**

Restaurant

★ **LOG CABIN DINER.** *Hwy 2, East Newport (04953). Phone 207/368-4551.* Seafood, steak menu. Breakfast, lunch, dinner. Closed Dec-Mar. Children's menu. **$$**

Northeast Harbor (E-3)

See also Acadia National Park, Bar Harbor, Cranberry Isles

Population 650
Elevation 80 ft
Area Code 207
Zip 04662

This coastal village is located on Mount Desert Island, a land of rocky coastlines, forests, and lakes. The island is reached from the mainland by a short bridge.

What to See and Do

Ferry Service. *33 Main St, Cranberry Isles (04679). Phone 207/244-3575.* Connects Northeast Harbor with the Cranberry Isles (see); 3-mile, 30-minute crossing. (Summer: daily; rest of year: schedule varies) **$$$**

Woodlawn Museum (The Black House). *172 Surrey Rd, Northeast Harbor (04605). Phone 207/667-8671. www.woodlawnmuseum.com.* (Circa 1820) Federal house built by a local landowner; antiques. Garden; carriage house with old carriages and sleighs. (June-Sept, Tues-Sun) **$$**

Full-Service Inn

★ ★ ★ **ASTICOU INN.** *Asticou Way, Northeast Harbor (4662). Phone 207/276-3344; toll-free 800/258-3373; fax 207/276-3373. www.asticou.com.* Renovated country inn (1883). At head of harbor, public dock adjacent. 31 rooms. Closed mid-Sept-mid-June. Check-in 3 pm, check-out 11 am. Restaurant, bar. Outdoor pool. Tennis. **$$$**

Specialty Lodging

The following lodging establishment is approved by Mobil Travel Guide, but due to its unique and individualized nature has not been given a traditional Mobil Star rating. Included in this listing you may find bed-and-breakfasts, limited-service inns, guest ranches, and other unique hotel properties.

MAISON SUISSE INN. *Main St, Northeast Harbor (04662). Phone 207/276-5223; toll-free 800/624-7668. www.maisonsuisse.com.* This restored, single-style summer cottage (1892) was once a speakeasy during Prohibition. 15 rooms, 2 story. Closed Nov-Apr. Complimentary full breakfast. Check-in 3-7 pm, check-out 11 am. **$$$**

Restaurant

★ **DOCKSIDER.** *14 Sea St, Northeast Harbor (04662). Phone 207/276-3965.* Seafood menu. Lunch, dinner. Closed mid-Oct-mid-May. Children's menu. Outdoor seating. **$$**

Norway (E-1)

See also Poland Spring

Population 4,754
Elevation 383 ft
Area Code 207
Zip 04268
Information Oxford Hills Chamber of Commerce, 213 Main St, South Paris 04281; phone 207/743-2281
Web Site www.oxfordhillsmaine.com

What to See and Do

Pennesseewasee Lake. *W of town.* This 7-mile-long lake, covering 922 acres, received its name from the Native American words meaning "sweet water." Swimming, beaches, water-skiing; fishing for brown trout, bass, and perch; boating (marina, rentals, launch). Ice skating. Contact Chamber of Commerce. **FREE**

Full-Service Inn

★ ★ ★ **WATERFORD INN.** *258 Chadbourne Rd, Waterford (04088). Phone 207/583-4037; fax 207/583-4037. www.waterfordinn.com.* This 19th-century (1825), eight-room farmhouse is surrounded by fields and woods and is furnished with both the old and the new. A pond, an old red barn, and hundreds of birds are outside, and inside are antiques, art, barnwood, and brass as well as pewter and a library. 8 rooms, 2

story. Pets accepted; fee. Complimentary full breakfast. Check-in 2 pm, check-out 11 am. Restaurant. **$**

Restaurant

★ ★ **MAURICE RESTAURANT FRANCAIS.** *109 Main St, South Paris (04281). Phone 207/743-2532; fax 207/743-5810. www.mauricerestaurant.com.* French menu. Lunch, dinner, Sun brunch. Closed Thanksgiving, Dec 24-25. Bar. **$$**

Ogunquit (F-1)

See also Kennebunk, Kittery, Wells, York

Population 974
Elevation 40 ft
Area Code 207
Zip 03907
Information Chamber of Commerce, PO Box 2289; phone 207/646-2939
Web Site www.ogunquit.org

Here Maine's "stern and rockbound coast" becomes a sunny strand—a great white beach stretching 3 miles, with gentle (though sometimes chilly) surf. The Ogunquit public beach is one of the finest on the Atlantic. Marine views, with the picturesque little harbor of Perkins Cove, have attracted a substantial art colony.

What to See and Do

Marginal Way. A beautiful and unusual walk along the cliffs overlooking the ocean, with tidepools at the water's edge.

Ogunquit Museum of American Art. *183 Shore Rd, Ogunquit (03907). At Narrow Cove. Phone 207/646-4909.* Twentieth-century American sculpture and painting. Museum overlooks the ocean and sculpture gardens. (July-mid-Sept, daily) **$$**

Special Event

Ogunquit Playhouse. *10 Hwy 1, Northeast Harbor (03907). 1 mile S on Hwy 1.Phone 207/646-2402.* Established in the early 1930s. Top plays and musicals with professional actors. Late June-Labor Day weekend.

Limited-Service Hotels

★ **THE BEACHMERE INN.** *12 Beachmere Pl, Ogunquit (03907). Phone 207/646-2021; toll-free 800/336-3983; fax 207/646-2231. www.beachmereinn.com.* Victorian-style inn (1889). 54 rooms, 3 story. Closed mid-Dec-Apr. Complimentary continental breakfast. Check-out 11 am. **$$**

★ ★ **GORGES GRANT HOTEL.** *449 Main St, Ogunquit (03907). Phone 207/646-7003; toll-free 800/646-5001; fax 207/646-0660. www.ogunquit.com.* This year-round smoke-free property offers a variety of guest rooms each with full bath, refrigerator, and television. It is located in the heart of Ogunquit within easy walking distance of the shops and galleries, and guests can relax and enjoy the heated pool and lounge area either indoors or outside. 81 rooms. Closed mid-Dec-Mar. Check-out 11 am. Restaurant. Fitness room. Indoor pool, outdoor pool, whirlpool. **$**

★ ★ **THE GRAND HOTEL.** *108 Shore Rd, Ogunquit (03907). Phone 207/646-1231; toll-free 800/806-1231. www.thegrandhotel.com.* 28 rooms, 3 story. Closed mid-Nov-mid-Apr. Complimentary continental breakfast. Check-out 11 am. Indoor pool. **$**

★ **JUNIPER HILL INN.** *336 Main St, Ogunquit (3907). Phone 207/646-4501; toll-free 800/646-4544; fax 207/646-4595. www.ogunquit.com.* 100 rooms, 2 story. Check-out 11 am. Fitness room. One indoor pool, two outdoor pools, two whirlpools. **$**

★ ★ **MEADOWMERE.** *Hwy 1, Ogunquit (03907). Phone 207/646-9661; toll-free 800/633-8718; fax 207/646-6952. www.meadowmere.com.* On trolley route. 145 rooms, 2 story. Closed mid-Oct-mid-Apr. Complimentary continental breakfast. Check-out 11 am. Indoor pool, outdoor pool. **$$**

★ **THE MILESTONE.** *687 Main St, Ogunquit (03907). Phone 207/646-4562; toll-free 800/646-6453; fax 207/646-1739. www.ogunquit.com.* 70 rooms, 3 story. Closed Nov-Mar. Fitness room. Outdoor pool, whirlpool. **$**

★ **RIVERSIDE.** *159 Shore Rd, Ogunquit (03907). Phone 207/646-2741; fax 207/646-0216. www.riversidemotel.com.* Overlooks Perkins Cove.

38 rooms, 2 story. Closed Nov-mid-Apr. Complimentary continental breakfast. Check-out 11 am. **$**

Full-Service Resorts

★ ★ ★ **ANCHORAGE BY THE SEA.** *133 Shore Rd, Ogunquit (03907). Phone 207/646-9384; fax 207/646-6256. www.anchoragebythesea.com.* This property has a sensational location directly on the ocean. The rooms are nicely decorated and appointed and have wonderful views of the ocean. A short walk will take guests to a 3-mile stretch of beach for pure relaxation or a visit to the galleries and shops located in Ogunquit Village. On trolley route. 212 rooms, 3 story. Complimentary continental breakfast. Check-out 11 am. Restaurant. Indoor pool, outdoor pool, children's pool, whirlpool. **$**

★ **THE TERRACE BY THE SEA.** *23 Wharf Ln, Ogunquit (3907). Phone 207/646-3232. www.terracebythesea.com.* 36 rooms, 2 story. Closed Nov-Apr. Complimentary continental breakfast. Check-out 11 am. Outdoor pool. **$**

Specialty Lodgings

The following lodging establishments are approved by Mobil Travel Guide, but due to their unique and individualized nature have not been given a traditional Mobil Star rating. Included in this listing you may find bed-and-breakfasts, limited-service inns, guest ranches, and other unique hotel properties.

HARTWELL HOUSE. *118 Shore Rd, Ogunquit (03907). Phone 207/646-7210; toll-free 800/235-8883; fax 207/646-6032. www.hartwellhouseinn.com.* Located in the countryside of Maine, this bed-and-breakfast is only minutes from a summer resort. It is open year-round, and each room is furnished with Early American and English antiques. Most of the rooms have French doors leading to terraces or balconies that overlook the gardens. A complimentary full gourmet breakfast and afternoon tea are served daily. The lily pond is home to exotic fish, flowering plants, and a small waterfall providing a great retreat. 16 rooms, 2 story. Children over 14 years only. Complimentary full breakfast. Check-in 3 pm, check-out 11 am. **$$**

THE PINE HILL INN. *14 Pine Hill Rd S, Ogunquit (03907). Phone 207/361-1004; fax 207/361-1815. www.pinehillinn.com.* Turn-of-the-century cottage with sun porch. 6 rooms, 2 story. Children over 12 years only. Complimentary full breakfast. Check-in 4-6 pm, check-out 11 am. **$**

Restaurants

★ ★ ★ **ARROW'S.** *Berwick Rd, Ogunquit (03907). Phone 207/361-1100; fax 207/361-1183. www.arrowsrestaurant.com.* Co-owners and co-chefs, Clark Frasier and Mark Gaier, have made this idyllic restaurant in an 18th-century farmhouse a seasonsal dining destination. They bake their own breads, grow their own organic vegetables, and devise a creative, elegant menu that reflects their diverse backgrounds and passion for travel. American menu. Dinner. Closed Mon; also late Nov-Dec, mid-Apr. Bar. Valet parking. **$$$$**

★ **BARNACLE BILLY'S.** *Perkins Cove, Ogunquit (03907). Phone 207/646-5575; fax 207/646-1219. www.barnbilly.com.* Lobster tank. Seafood menu. Lunch, dinner. Closed late Oct, mid-Apr, and early May. Bar. Valet parking. Outdoor seating. **$$**

★ ★ **BILLY'S ETC.** *Oarweed Cove Rd, Ogunquit (03907). Phone 207/646-4711; fax 207/646-1219. www.barnbilly.com.* Seafood, steak menu. Lunch, dinner. Closed Nov-early May. Bar. Children's menu. Valet parking. Outdoor seating. **$$**

★ ★ **GYPSY SWEETHEARTS.** *30 Shore Rd, Ogunquit (03907). Phone 207/646-7021. www.gypsysweethearts.com.* This converted early-1800s home features original décor, perennial gardens, and an enclosed sunporch. American menu. Dinner. Closed Nov-early Apr. Bar. Children's menu. **$$**

★ ★ **HURRICANE.** *111 Perkins Cove Rd, Ogunquit (03907). Phone 207/646-6348; fax 207/646-7282. www.hurricanerestaurant.com.* American menu. Lunch, dinner, Sun brunch. Closed Dec 25. Bar. Reservations recommended. **$$**

★ ★ ★ **JONATHAN'S.** *92 Bourne Ln, Ogunquit (03907). Phone 207/646-4777; fax 207/646-4526. www.jonathansrestaurant.com.* This is a great place to enjoy live entertainment while vacationing in Ogunquit. Don't miss the unique offerings from JJ's Oyster Bar—oysters prepared in an international style including Japanese, Greek, French, and Russian oysters on the half shell. American, seafood menu. Dinner. Bar. Children's menu. Piano Sat. **$$**

★ **OARWEED COVE.** *Perkins Cove Rd, Ogunquit (03907). Phone 207/646-4022; fax 207/646-1525. www.oarweed.com.* Seafood menu. Lunch, dinner. Closed mid-Oct-mid-Apr. Children's menu. Outdoor seating. **$$**

★ **OGUNQUIT LOBSTER POUND.** *504 Main St, Ogunquit (03907). Phone 207/646-2516; fax 207/646-4713.* Seafood menu. Dinner. Closed mid-Oct-Apr. Bar. Outdoor seating. **$$**

★ ★ ★ **OLD VILLAGE INN.** *30 Main St, Ogunquit (03907). Phone 207/646-7088; fax 207/646-7089. www.oldvillageinn.com.* Located in a mid-19th-century inn (1883), this cozy restaurant has an understated elegant atmosphere. The dining room is intimate, a perfect choice for a romantic meal. Guest rooms are available. Seafood menu. Breakfast, dinner. Closed Dec 25. Bar. Children's menu. **$$**

★ ★ **POOR RICHARD'S TAVERN.** *331 Shore Rd, Ogunquit (03907). Phone 207/646-4722. www.poorrichardstavern.com.* American menu. Dinner. Closed Sun; Dec-Mar. Bar. Valet parking. **$$**

★ ★ ★ **PROVENCE.** *262 Shore Rd, Ogunquit (03907). Phone 207/646-9898; fax 207/641-8786. www.98provence.com.* This country French restaurant is located in a small clapboard house with comfortable décor. French, seafood menu. Dinner. Closed Tues; mid-Dec-mid-Apr. Bar. **$$**

Old Orchard Beach (F-1)

See also Kennebunk, Kennebunkport, Portland, Saco

Settled 1630
Population 7,789
Elevation 40 ft
Area Code 207
Zip 04064
Information Chamber of Commerce, PO Box 600; phone 207/934-2500 or toll-free 800/365-9386
Web Site www.oldorchardbeachmaine.com

This popular beach resort, 12 miles south of Portland, is one of the long-time favorites on the Maine Coast. It has a crescent beach 7 miles long and about 700 feet wide—which in rocky Maine is a good deal of beach. In summer, it is the vacation destination of thousands.

What to See and Do

Palace Playland. *1 Old Orchard St, Old Orchard Beach (04064). Off Hwy 5, on beachfront. Phone 207/934-2001.* Amusement park featuring restored 1906 carousel, arcade, games, rides, water slide; concessions. (Late June-Labor Day: daily; Memorial Day-late June: weekends) Fee for individual attractions or one-price daily pass. **$$$$**

The Pier. Extends 475 feet into the harbor; features shops, boutiques, restaurant. (May-Sept, daily)

Limited-Service Hotels

★ **THE EDGEWATER.** *57 W Grand Ave, Old Orchard Beach (04064). Phone 207/934-2221; toll-free 800/203-2034; fax 207/934-3731. www.janelle.com.* 35 rooms, 2 story. Closed mid-Nov-mid-Mar. Check-out 11 am. Outdoor pool. **$**

★ **THE GULL MOTEL INN & COTTAGES.** *89 W Grand Ave, Old Orchard Beach (04064). Phone 207/934-4321; toll-free 877/662-4855; fax 207/934-1742. www.gullmotel.com.* 25 rooms, 2 story. Closed mid-Oct-Apr. Check-out 10 am. Outdoor pool. **$**

★ **HORIZON.** *2 Atlantic Ave, Old Orchard Beach (04064). Phone 207/934-2323; toll-free 888/550-1745; fax 207/934-3215. www.horizonmotel.com.* 14 rooms, 3 story, all suites. Closed Nov-Mar. Check-out 10 am. **$**

★ **ROYAL ANCHOR RESORT.** *203 E Grand Ave, Old Orchard Beach (04064). Phone 207/934-4521; toll-free 800/934-4521. www.royalanchor.com.* 40 rooms, 3 story. Closed mid-Oct-Apr. Complimentary continental breakfast. Check-out 10:30 am. Outdoor pool. Tennis. **$**

Specialty Lodging

The following lodging establishment is approved by Mobil Travel Guide, but due to its unique and individualized nature has not been given a traditional Mobil Star rating. Included in this listing you may find bed-and-breakfasts, limited-service inns, guest ranches, and other unique hotel properties.

ATLANTIC BIRCHES INN. *20 Portland Ave, Old Orchard Beach (04064). Phone 207/934-5295; toll-free 888/934-5295; fax 207/934-3781. www.atlanticbirches.com.* Restored Victorian house. 10

rooms, 3 story. Complimentary continental breakfast. Check-in 3-7 pm, check-out 11 am. Outdoor pool. **$**

Orono (D-3)

Settled 1774
Population 10,573
Elevation 80 ft
Area Code 207
Zip 04473
Information Bangor Region Chamber of Commerce, 519 Main St, PO Box 1443, Bangor 04401; phone 207/947-0307
Web Site www.bangorregion.com

The Penobscot River flows through this valley town, which was named for a Native American chief called Joseph Orono (OR-a-no). The "Maine Stein Song" was popularized here in the 1930s by Rudy Vallee.

What to See and Do

University of Maine-Orono. *5703 Alumni Hall, Orono (04469). Phone 207/581-1341. www.umaine.edu.* (1865) (11,500 students) This is the largest of seven campuses of the University of Maine system. On campus is Jordan Planetarium. Also on campus is

Hudson Museum. *5746 Maine Center for Arts, Orono (04469). Phone 207/581-1901.* Exhibits relating to history and anthropology. (Tues-Sun) **FREE**

Restaurant

★ ★ **MARGARITA'S.** *15 Mill St, Orono (04473). Phone 207/866-4863; fax 207/866-3023.* Mexican menu. Dinner. Bar. Children's menu. **$**

Poland Spring (E-1)

See also Auburn, Bridgton, Norway, Sebago Lake

Settled 1768
Population 200
Elevation 500 ft
Area Code 207
Zip 04274

The Poland Spring Inn, once New England's largest private resort (5,000 acres), stands on a rise near the mineral spring that has made it famous since 1844. Actually, the hotel had even earlier beginnings with the Mansion House, built in 1794 by the Ricker brothers. In 1974, the original inn burned and was replaced by a smaller hotel.

What to See and Do

⭐ **Shaker Museum.** *707 Shaker Rd, Poland Spring (04274). 1 mile S on Hwy 26. Phone 207/926-4597.* Shaker furniture, folk and decorative arts, textiles, tin and woodenware; Early American tools and farm implements displayed. Guided tours of buildings in this last active Shaker community includes Meetinghouse (1794), Ministry Shop (1839), Boys' Shop (1850), Sisters' Shop (1821), and Spin House (1816). Workshops, demonstrations, concerts, and other special events. Extensive research library (Tues-Thurs, by appointment only). (Memorial Day-Columbus Day, Mon-Sat) **$$**

Portland (F-1)

See also Kennebunk, Kennebunkport, Old Orchard Beach, Saco, Scarborough, Yarmouth

Settled 1632
Population 64,358
Elevation 50 ft
Area Code 207
Information Convention & Visitors Bureau of Greater Portland, 305 Commercial St, 04101; phone 207/772-5800
Web Site www.visitportland.com

Maine's largest city is on beautiful Casco Bay, dotted with islands popular with summer visitors. Not far from the North Atlantic fishing waters, it leads Maine in this industry. Shipping is also important. It is a city of fine elms, stately old homes, historic churches, and charming streets.

Portland was raided by Native Americans several times before the Revolution. In 1775, it was bombarded by the British, who afterward burned the town. Another fire, in 1866, wiped out large sections of the city. Longfellow remarked that the ruins reminded him of Pompeii.

What to See and Do

Boat trips. Cruises along Casco Bay, some with stops at individual islands or other locations; special charters also available. Most cruises (May-Oct). For further information, rates, schedules, or fees, contact the individual companies.

Bay View Cruises. *Fisherman's Wharf, 184 Commercial St, Portland (04101). Phone 207/761-0496.*

Casco Bay Lines. *56 Commercial St, Portland (04101). Phone 207/774-7871.*

Eagle Tours Inc. *19 Raybon Rd Extension, York (03909). Phone 207/774-6498.*

M/S *Scotia Prince*. *Phone 207/775-5616; toll-free 800/341-7540 or 800/482-0955 (ME).* A 1,500-passenger cruise ferry leaves nightly for an 11-hour crossing to Yarmouth, Nova Scotia. (May-Oct) Staterooms available.

Olde Port Mariner Fleet, Inc. *170 Commercial St, Portland (04104). Phone 207/775-0727.* A 1,500-passenger cruise ferry leaves nightly for 11-hour crossing to Yarmouth, Nova Scotia. (May-Oct) Staterooms available.

Children's Museum of Maine. *142 Free St, Portland (04101). Phone 207/828-1234.* Hands-on museum where interactive exhibits allow children to become a Maine lobsterman, storekeeper, computer expert, or astronaut. (Daily) **$$**

Crescent Beach. *66 Two Lights Rd, Cape Elizabeth (04107). 10 miles SE on Hwy 77. Phone 207/799-5871 (seasonal).* Swimming, sand beach, bathhouse, fishing; picnicking, playground, concession. (Memorial Day-mid-Oct)

Maine Historical Society. *489 Congress St, Portland (04101). Phone 207/774-1822.* Research library for Maine history and genealogy. (Tues-Sat; closed holidays)

Maine History Gallery. *489 Congress St, Portland (04101). Phone 207/774-1822.* Features Museums Collection with more than 2,000 paintings, prints, and other original works of art, and approximately 8,000 artifacts. Collection includes costume and textiles, decorative arts, Native American artifacts and archaeological material, political items, and military artifacts. Changing programs and exhibits trace the history of life in Maine. Gallery talks and hands-on workshops also offered. (June-Oct: daily; Dec-May: Tues-Sat) **$$**

Old Port Exchange. *Congress and Exchange sts, Portland (04101). Between Exchange and Pearl sts,* *extending five blocks from waterfront to Congress St.* A charming collection of shops and restaurants located in 19th-century brick buildings built after the fire of 1866.

Portland Head Lighthouse Museum. *1000 Shore Rd, Cape Elizabeth (04107). Phone 207/799-2661.* (1791) Said to be first lighthouse authorized by the United States and oldest lighthouse in continuous use; erected on orders from George Washington. (June-Oct: daily; Nov-Dec and Apr-May: weekends) **$**

Portland Museum of Art. *7 Congress Sq, Portland (04101). Phone 207/775-6148. www.portlandmuseum. org.* Collections of American and European painting, sculpture, prints, and decorative art; State of Maine Collection with works by artists from and associated with Maine; John Whitney Payson Collection (Renoir, Monet, Picasso, and others). Free admission Friday evenings. (May-Oct: daily; Nov-Apr: Tues-Sun; closed holidays) **$$**

Portland Observatory. *138 Congress St, Portland (04101). Phone 207/772-5561.* (1807) This octagonal, shingled landmark is the last surviving 19th-century signal tower on the Atlantic. There are 102 steps to the top. (June-Oct, daily)

Research Library. *489 Congress St, Portland (04101). Phone 207/774-1822.* World's most complete collection of Maine history materials. Includes 125,000 books and newspapers, 3,500 maps, 70,000 photos, 500 pamphlets, over 2,000,000 manuscripts, and 100,000 architectural and engineering drawings. Also Fogg collection of autographs and rare original copy of Dunlap version of the Declaration of Independence. (Tues-Sat; closed holidays) **$$$$**

Southworth Planetarium. *96 Falmouth St, Portland (04103). Phone 207/780-4249.* Astronomy programs, laser light concerts, children's shows. (Fri-Sat; additional shows summer months) **$$$**

Tate House. *1270 Westbrook St, Portland (04102). Phone 207/774-9781.* (1755) Georgian structure built by George Tate, mast agent for the British Navy. Furnished and decorated in the period of Tate's residence, 1755-1800; 18th-century herb gardens. (July-mid-Sept: Tues-Sun; mid-May-June and mid-Sept-mid-Oct: by appointment only; closed July 4, Labor Day) **$$**

Two Lights. *66 Two Lights Rd, Cape Elizabeth (04107). 9 miles SE off Hwy 77. Phone 207/799-5871.*

Approximately 40 acres along Atlantic Ocean. Fishing; picnicking. (Mid-Apr-Nov)

University of Southern Maine. *Portland campus, off I-295 exit 6; Gorham campus, junction Hwy 25 and College Ave. Phone 207/780-4500 (special events). www.usm.maine.edu.* (1878) (11,000 students) One of the seven units of the University of Maine system. Special shows are held periodically in the university planetarium and in the art gallery. Also theatrical and musical events.

Victoria Mansion. *109 Danforth St, Portland (04101). At Park St. Phone 207/772-4841.* (1858) One of the finest examples of 19th-century architecture surviving in the United States. Opulent Victorian interior includes frescoes, carved woodwork, and stained and etched glass. (May-Oct, Tues-Sun; closed holidays) **$$**

Wadsworth-Longfellow House. *489 Congress St, Portland (04101). Phone 207/772-1807.* (1785) Boyhood home of Henry Wadsworth Longfellow. Built by the poet's grandfather, General Peleg Wadsworth, it is maintained by the Maine Historical Society. Contains furnishings, portraits, and personal possessions of the family. (June-mid-Oct, Tues-Sat; closed July 4, Labor Day) **$$**

Special Events

New Year's Eve Portland. *582 Congress St, Portland (04101). Phone 207/772-5800.* Fifteen indoor and many outdoor locations. More than 90 performances, mid-afternoon to midnight; a citywide, nonalcoholic celebration with parade and fireworks. Dec 31.

Old Port Festival. *400 Congress St #100, Portland (04101). Phone 207/772-6828.* Celebration of Portland's restored waterfront district between Commercial Street and Congress Street, is the host of this one-day event; it features a parade, entertainment and food. Early June.

Sidewalk Art Show. *1 Congress Sq, Portland (04101). Phone 207/772-5800.* Exhibits extend along Congress Street from Congress Square to Monument Square. Third Sat in Aug.

Limited-Service Hotels

★★BEST WESTERN MERRY MANOR INN.
700 Main St, South Portland (04106). Phone 207/ 774-6151; toll-free 800/780-7234; fax 207/871-0537. www.bestwestern.com. 151 rooms, 3 story. Pets accepted, some restrictions. Check-out 11 am. Restaurant. Indoor pool, outdoor pool, children's pool. **$**

★ ★ **EASTLAND PARK HOTEL.** *157 High St, Portland (04101). Phone 207/775-5411; toll-free 888/ 671-8008; fax 207/775-2872. www.eastlandparkhotel .com.* 204 rooms, 12 story. Check-out noon. Restaurant, bar. Fitness room. Airport transportation available. Business center. **$**

★ ★ **EMBASSY SUITES.** *1050 Westbrook St, Portland (04102). Phone 207/775-2200; toll-free 800/ 362-2779; fax 207/775-4052. www.embassysuitesport land.com.* This hotel is located close to the Portland jetport and has an indoor pool, sauna, whirlpool, and fitness area. In addition to complimentary transportation to and from the airport, there is free parking, a complimentary newspaper, a gift shop, and a great spot for Sunday brunch. 119 rooms, 6 story, all suites. Complimentary full breakfast. Check-out noon. Restaurant, bar. Fitness room. Indoor pool, whirlpool. Airport transportation available. **$$**

★ **HAMPTON INN.** *171 Philbrook Ave, South Portland (04106). Phone 207/773-4400; toll-free 800/ 426-7866; fax 207/773-6786. www.portlandhamptoninn .com.* 117 rooms, 4 story. Complimentary continental breakfast. Check-out noon. High-speed Internet access. Airport transportation available. **$**

★ ★ **HOLIDAY INN.** *88 Spring St, Portland (04101). Phone 207/775-2311; toll-free 800/345-5050; fax 207/ 761-8224. www.innbythebay.com.* Some rooms over-look harbor. 239 rooms, 14 story. Check-out noon. Restaurant, bar. Fitness room. Indoor pool. Airport transportation available. **$**

Full-Service Hotels

★ ★ ★ **MARRIOTT PORTLAND AT SABLE OAKS.** *200 Sable Oaks Dr, South Portland (04106). Phone 207/871-8000; toll-free 800/228-9290; fax 207/ 871-7971. www.marriott.com.* This hotel is located on a hill close to historic downtown Portland. Rooms are specifically designed for the business traveler with a spacious work desk, two-line phone, speaker phone, voice mail, and data ports. Nearby is golf, jogging, tennis, a spa, and the beach. 227 rooms, 6 story. Pets accepted, some restrictions; fee. Check-out noon. Restaurant, bar. Fitness room. Indoor pool, whirlpool. **$**

★ ★ ★ **PORTLAND HARBOR HOTEL.** *468 Fore St, Portland (04101). Phone 207/775-9090; toll-free 888/798-9090; fax 207/775-9990. www.portlandharbor hotel.com.* 97 rooms. Pets accepted; fee. Check-in 3 pm, check-out noon. High-speed Internet access. Restaurant, bar. Fitness room. Airport transportation available. Business center. **$$**

★ ★ ★ **PORTLAND REGENCY HOTEL.** *20 Milk St, Portland (04101). Phone 207/774-4200; fax 207/775-2150.* This small, European-style hotel is located in the center of Portland's historic district and is surrounded by galleries, shops, and restaurants. Attractions include Casco Bay, the Portland Museum of Art, and the symphony orchestra. Amenities include turndown service, room service, honor bar, and complimentary coffee served with wakeup notice. The health club is a complete fitness area including Cybex equipment, whirlpool, steamroom, sauna, massage therapy, and tanning. 95 rooms, 4 story. Check-out noon. Restaurant, bar. Fitness room. Airport transportation available. **$$**

Full-Service Resort

★ ★ ★ **INN BY THE SEA.** *40 Bowery Beach Rd, Cape Elizabeth (04107). Phone 207/799-3134; toll-free 800/888-4287; fax 207/799-4779. www.innbythesea .com.* This all-suite resort property is located close to the historic city of Portland on the coast. Every guest room has a porch or deck with a view of the ocean. Recreational activities include an outdoor pool, tennis, shuffleboard, walking or jogging, and volleyball. Amenities for guests include terry robes and turndown service with 24-hour business and concierge service. 43 rooms, 3 story, all suites. Pets accepted. Check-out noon. Restaurant. Outdoor pool. Tennis. **$$**

Full-Service Inn

★ ★ ★ **BLACK POINT INN.** *510 Black Point Rd, Portland (04074). Phone 207/883-2500; toll-free 800/ 258-0003; fax 207/883-9976. www.blackpointinn.com.* This seaside resort is located on a hill at the tip of Prouts Neck with the natural rugged beauty of the Maine coast on three sides. There are numerous rooms and many cottages which were former sea captains' homes. Each room has fine furnishing, period wallpaper, Martha Washington bedspreads, and both porcelain and crystal lamps. Terry robes and turndown service are just a few of the amenities offered guests. 65 rooms. Closed Dec-Apr. Check-in 3 pm, check-out noon. Restaurant, bar. Fitness room. Beach. Indoor pool, outdoor pool, whirlpool. Airport transportation available. **$$$**

Specialty Lodgings

The following lodging establishments are approved by Mobil Travel Guide, but due to their unique and individualized nature have not been given a traditional Mobil Star rating. Included in this listing you may find bed-and-breakfasts, limited-service inns, guest ranches, and other unique hotel properties.

INN AT SAINT JOHN. *939 Congress St, Portland (04102). Phone 207/773-6481; toll-free 800/636-9127; fax 207/756-7629. www.innatstjohn.com.* Built in 1896; European motif, antiques. 32 rooms, 4 story. Pets accepted, some restrictions. Complimentary continental breakfast. Check-out 11 am. Airport transportation available. **$**

INN ON CARLETON. *46 Carleton St, Portland (04102). Phone 207/775-1910; toll-free 800/639-1779. www.innoncarleton.com.* This brick townhouse was built in 1869. 7 rooms, 3 story. Children over 8 years only. Complimentary full breakfast. Check-in 4 pm, check-out 10 am. **$$**

POMEGRANATE INN. *49 Neal St, Portland (04102). Phone 207/772-1006; toll-free 800/356-0408; fax 207/773-4426. www.pomegranateinn.com.* This inn (house built in 1884) is small yet sophisticated and located in the Western Promende historic neighborhood. There are antiques and art throughout the property, and a lovely urban garden awaits guests. It is a short walk to the midtown arts district and there are museums, art galleries, boat rides, fine restaurants, and recreational activities nearby. 8 rooms, 3 story. Children over 16 years only. Complimentary full breakfast. Check-in 4-6 pm, check-out 11 am. **$$**

Restaurants

★ ★ **BACK BAY GRILL.** *65 Portland St, Portland (04101). Phone 207/772-8833; fax 207/874-0451. www.backbaygrill.com.* Located in downtown Portland in a restored pharmacy (1888), this local favorite offers innovative cuisine in a comfortably elegant bistro-style atmosphere. Don't miss the "chicken and dumplings" prepared with a nine-herb stuffing; tomato petals and pearl onions and a zinfandel/pancetta demi-glace. Seafood menu. Dinner. Closed Sun; holidays. Bar. **$$$**

★ ★ **BOONE'S.** *6 Custom House Wharf, Portland (04112). Phone 207/774-5725.* Fishing port atmosphere; built on wharf. Established in 1898. Seafood menu. Lunch, dinner. Closed Thanksgiving, Dec 25. Bar. Children's menu. Outdoor seating. **$**

★ ★ **DI MILLO'S FLOATING RESTAURANT.** *25 Long Wharf, Portland (04101). Phone 207/772-2216; fax 207/772-1081. www.dimillos.com.* Seafood, steak menu. Lunch, dinner. Closed Thanksgiving, Dec 25. Bar. Children's menu. Outdoor seating. **$$**

★ ★ **F. PARKER REIDY'S.** *83 Exchange St, Portland (04101). Phone 207/773-4731.* Originally Portland Savings Bank (1866). Seafood, steak menu. Lunch, dinner, Sun brunch. Closed July 4, Thanksgiving, Dec 25. Bar. Children's menu. **$$**

★ ★ **FORE STREET.** *288 Fore St, Portland (04101). Phone 207/775-2717; fax 207/772-6778.* The James Beard Society's best chef of the Northeast in 2004, Sam Hayward runs the unpretentious and acclaimed Fore Street in the Old Port district of Portland. Foodies call weeks in advance for a reservation at the destination eatery where Hayward, who strongly supports local farmers, works regional foodstuffs into recipes that aficionados claim are both honest and magical. Wood-fired ovens and rotisseries manage most of the menu highlighted by wood-grilled Vermont quail with hasty corn pudding and roast plums, oven-roasted Maine mussels, and Maine-raised rabbit with wild mushrooms. The down-to-earth restaurant dressed in salvaged wood floors and recycled metal tables displays its vegetable cooler near the front door, underscoring Fore Street's farm-fresh philosophy. Seafood, steak menu. Dinner. Closed Thanksgiving. Bar. Children's menu. **$$$**

★ **NEWICK'S SEAFOOD.** *740 Broadway, South Portland (04106). Phone 207/799-3090; fax 207/799-3619. www.newicks.com.* Seafood menu. Lunch, dinner. Closed Mon; Thanksgiving, Dec 25. Bar. Children's menu. **$$**

★ ★ **RIBOLITA.** *41 Middle St, Portland (04101). Phone 207/774-2972.* Italian menu. Dinner. Closed Sun; holidays. Children's menu. Outdoor seating. **$$**

★ ★ **THE ROMA.** *769 Congress St, Portland (04102). Phone 207/773-9873; fax 207/756-6768. www.theromacafe.com.* Located in a Victorian mansion (circa 1885), this restaurant specializes in seafood, lobster, and Italian dishes. Fireplaces add warmth and comfort to the already charming atmosphere. Italian, seafood menu. Lunch, dinner. Closed Memorial Day, Labor Day, Dec 25; also Sun in Dec-May. Bar. Children's menu. **$$**

★ ★ **STREET & CO.** *33 Wharf St, Portland (04101). Phone 207/775-0887.* Housed in a 19th-century commercial building with original floor woodwork. Mediterranean, seafood menu. Dinner. Closed Jan 1, Thanksgiving, Dec 24-25. Bar. Outdoor seating. **$$**

★ ★ **VILLAGE CAFE.** *112 Newbury St, Portland (04101). Phone 207/772-5320; fax 207/772-5652. www.villagecafe.baweb.com.* American, Italian menu. Lunch, dinner. Closed Thanksgiving, Dec 25. Bar. Children's menu. **$$**

★ ★ **WALTER'S CAFE.** *15 Exchange St, Portland (04101). Phone 207/871-9258; fax 207/871-1018. www.walterscafe.com.* Mid-1800s commercial building with much original interior; three dining areas on two levels. American menu. Lunch, dinner. Closed Jan 1, Dec 25; also first Sat in May. Bar. **$$**

Presque Isle (B-4)

See also Caribou

Settled 1820
Population 10,550
Elevation 446 ft
Area Code 207
Zip 04769
Information Presque Isle Area Chamber of Commerce, PO Box 672; phone 207/764-6561 or toll-free 800/764-7420
Web Site www.pichamber.com

Commercial and industrial center of Aroostook County, this city is famous for its potatoes. A deactivated air base nearby is now a vocational school and industrial park.

What to See and Do

Aroostook Farm—Maine Agricultural Experiment Station. *59 Houlton Rd, Presque Isle (04769). 2 miles S on Hwy 1. Phone 207/762-8281.* Approximately 375 acres operated by University of Maine; experiments to improve growing and marketing of potatoes and grain. (Mon-Fri; closed holidays) **FREE**

Aroostook State Park. *87 State Park Rd, Presque Isle (04769). 4 miles S on Hwy 1, then W. Phone 207/768-8341.* 577 acres. Swimming, bathhouse, fishing, boating (rentals, ramp on Echo Lake); hiking, cross-country trails, picnicking, camping. (Mid-May-mid-Oct, daily) Snowmobiling permitted.

Double Eagle II Launch Site Monument. *Spragueville Rd, Presque Isle (04769). 4 miles S on Hwy 1, then W.* Double Eagle II, the first balloon to travel across the Atlantic Ocean, was launched from this site in 1978. **FREE**

University of Maine at Presque Isle. *181 Main St, Presque Isle (04769). Phone 207/768-9400.* (1903) (1,500 students) During the summer there is the Pioneer Playhouse and an Elderhostel program. In winter, the business breakfast program, theater productions, and a number of other cultural and educational events are open to the public.

Special Events

Northern Maine Fair. *84 Machane St, Presque Isle (04769). Phone 207/764-6561.* Midway, harness racing, entertainment. Late July-early Aug.

Spudland Open Amateur Golf Tournament. *Presque Isle Country Club, 35 Parkhurst Siding Rd, Presque Isle (04769). Phone 207/769-7431.* Held for more than 30 years, this is one of Maine's major amateur golf tournaments. Mid-July.

Limited-Service Hotel

★ **NORTHERN LIGHTS.** *72 Houlton Rd, Presque Isle (04769). Phone 207/764-4441; fax 207/769-6931. www.northernlightsmotel.com.* 13 rooms. Pets accepted. Check-out 11 am. **$**

Rangeley (D-1)

Settled 1825
Population 1,063
Elevation 1,545 ft
Area Code 207
Zip 04970
Information Rangeley Lakes Chamber of Commerce,

PO Box 317; phone 207/864-5364 or toll-free 800/685-2537 (reservations)
Web Site www.rangeleymaine.com

Within 10 miles of Rangeley, there are 40 lakes and ponds. The six lakes that form the Rangeley chain—Rangeley, Cupsuptic, Mooselookmeguntic, Aziscoos, Upper Richardson, and Lower Richardson—spread over a wide area and give rise to the Androscoggin River. Some of Maine's highest mountains rise beside the lakes. The development of ski and snowmobiling areas has turned this summer vacation spot into a year-round resort.

What to See and Do

Camping. Several designated public camp and picnic sites; wilderness sites on islands.

Fishing. Boats for rent; licensed guides. The lakes are stocked with square-tailed trout and landlocked salmon.

Rangeley Lake State Park. *S Shore Dr, Rangeley (04970). 4 miles S on Hwy 4, then 5 miles W via local road. Phone 207/864-3858.* More than 690 acres on Rangeley Lake. Swimming, fishing, boating (ramp, floating docks); snowmobiling permitted, picnicking, camping (dump station). (May-Oct)

Saddleback Ski & Summer Lake Preserve. *7 miles E off Hwy 4. Phone 207/864-5671. www.saddlebackskiarea.com.* Two double chairlifts, three T-bars; rentals, school, patrol; snowmaking; cafeteria, bar; nursery, lodge. Longest run 2.5 miles; vertical drop 1,830 feet. (Late Nov-mid-Apr, daily) Cross-country trails.

Swimming, boating. Several public beaches and docks on lakefront. Rangeley Lakeside Park on lakeshore has public swimming, picnicking areas.

Wilhelm Reich Museum. *19 Dodge Pond Rd, Rangeley (04970). 4 miles W off Hwy 4. Phone 207/864-3443.* Unusual stone building housing scientific equipment, paintings, and other memorabilia of this physician-scientist; slide presentation, nature trail, discovery room. (July-Aug: Tues-Sun; Sept: Sun only) **$$**

Special Events

Logging Museum Field Days. *123 Main St, Rangeley (04970). Phone 207/864-5595.* Logging competitions, Miss Woodchip contest, parade, logging demonstrations. Last weekend in July.

Sled Dog Race. *Main St and Rangeley Inn, Rangeley (04970). Phone 207/864-5364.* Teams from eastern United States and Canada compete in this 20-mile race. First weekend in Mar.

Limited-Service Hotel

★ ★ **COUNTRY CLUB INN.** *1 Country Club Dr, Rangeley (04970). Phone 207/864-3831. www.countryclubinnrangeley.com.* 10 rooms, 2 story. Closed Apr, Nov. Check-in 1 pm, check-out 10:30 am. Restaurant, bar. Outdoor pool. Airport transportation available. **$$**
🄳 ⊡

Full-Service Inn

★ ★ ★ **RANGELEY INN.** *51 Main St (Hwy 4), Rangeley (4970). Phone 207/864-3341; toll-free 800/666-3687; fax 207/864-3634. www.rangeleyinn.com.* This restored inn is located within the mountain lake wilderness of the Longfellow mountains of western Maine. This year-round resort offers skiing and snowmobiling in the winter and swimming and boating in the summer. Moose can be spotted here, and loons can be both seen and heard. Check-out 11 am. Restaurant, bar. **$**

Restaurants

★ **PEOPLE'S CHOICE.** *Main St (Hwy 4), Rangeley (04970). Phone 207/864-5220; fax 207/864-2178.* Chainsaw-carved lumberjack on display. Seafood menu. Breakfast, lunch, dinner. Closed Thanksgiving, Dec 25. Bar. Children's menu. **$$**

★ ★ ★ **RANGELEY INN.** *51 Main St, Rangeley (04970). Phone 207/864-3341; fax 207/864-3634. www.rangeleyinn.com.* This romantic inn has been in operation for more than ninety years, and the dining room still showcases an ornate tin ceiling and glittering chandeliers. Enjoy an elegant dinner in the main dining room and then retire to the pub that has a crackling fire in the fireplace and local microbrews on tap. American, seafood menu. Breakfast, dinner. Closed Dec 25; also Apr-May. Bar. Children's menu. Outdoor seating. **$**

Rockland (E-3)

See also Camden, Monhegan Island

Settled 1770
Population 7,972

Elevation 35 ft
Area Code 207
Zip 04841
Information Rockland-Thomaston Area Chamber of Commerce, PO Box 508; phone 207/596-0376 or toll-free 800/562-2529
Web Site www.therealmaine.com

This town on Penobscot Bay is the banking and commercial center of the region and seat of Knox County. It is also the birthplace of the poet Edna St. Vincent Millay. Its economy is geared to the resort trade, but there is commercial fishing and light industry. It is the railhead for the whole bay. Supplies for boats, public landing, and guest moorings are here.

What to See and Do

Coasting schooners *Isaac H. Evans, American Eagle,* and *Heritage.* *Phone 207/594-8007; toll-free 800/648-4544 (except ME).* Four- and six-day cruises (Late May-mid-Oct).

Farnsworth Art Museum and Wyeth Center. *325 Main St, Rockland (04841). Phone 207/596-6457.* Cultural and educational center for the region. Collection of more than 10,000 works of 18th- to 20th-century American art. Center houses personal collection of Wyeth family art and archival material. (June-Sept: daily; rest of year: Tues-Sun) **$$$** Included in admission and adjacent is

> **Farnsworth Homestead.** *356 Main St, Rockland (04841). Phone 207/596-6457.* A 19th-century Victorian mansion with period furniture. (June-Sept, daily)

Fisherman's Memorial Pier and Chamber of Commerce. *Public landing, Harbor Park.*

Maine State Ferry Service. *517A Main St, Rockland (04841). Phone 207/596-2202.* Ferries make a 15-mile (1 hour, 15 minute) trip to Vinalhaven and a 12 1/2-mile (1 hour, 10 minute) trip to North Haven. (All year, two to three trips daily) Also a 23-mile (2 hour, 15 minute) trip to Matinicus Island once a month.

Owls Head Transportation Museum. *Hwy 73 and Museum Dr, Owls Head (04854). 2 miles S via Hwy 73. Phone 207/594-4418.* Working display of antique cars, airplanes, and 100-ton steam engine. (Daily) **$$**

Schooner *J. & E. Riggin.* *Phone 207/594-1875; toll-free 800/869-0604.* Three-, four-, five-, and six-day cruises (May-Oct).

Schooner *Stephen Taber* and Motor Yacht *Pauline.* *Rockland. Phone 207/236-3520; toll-free 800/999-7352.* Three- and six-day cruises through Penobscot, Casco, Blue Hill, and Frenchman bays. (Late May-mid-Oct)

Windjammers. Old-time schooners sail out for three to six days following the same basic route through Penobscot Bay, into Blue Hill and Frenchman's Bay, stopping at small villages and islands along the way. Each ship carries an average of 30 passengers. (Memorial Day-Columbus Day) For further information, rates, schedules, or reservations, contact the individual companies.

> ***Nathaniel Bowditch.*** *Phone toll-free 800/288-4098.*

> ***Victory Chimes.*** *120 Tillson Ave, Rockland (04841). Phone toll-free 800/745-5651.*

Special Events

Maine Lobster Festival. *Harbor Park, or at the public landing, Rockland (04841). Phone 207/596-0376; toll-free 800/562-2529.* A five-day event centered on Maine's chief marine creature, with a huge tent cafeteria serving lobster and other seafood. Parade, harbor cruises, maritime displays, bands, entertainment. First weekend in Aug.

Schooner Days & North Atlantic Blues Festival. *Phone 207/596-0376.* Three-day festival celebrating Maine's maritime heritage, featuring Parade of Schooners, arts, entertainment, concessions, fireworks; blues bands and club crawl. Weekend after July 4.

Limited-Service Hotel

★ **GLEN COVE MOTEL.** *Hwy 1, Glen Cove (04846). Phone 207/594-4062; toll-free 800/453-6268. www.glencovemotel.com.* Overlooks Penobscot Bay. 34 rooms, 2 story. Closed Feb. Check-out 11 am. Outdoor pool. **$**
🖼

Full-Service Resort

★ ★ ★ **SAMOSET RESORT.** *220 Warrenton St, Rockport (04856). Phone 207/594-2511; toll-free 800/341-1650; fax 207/594-0722. www.samoset.com.* Named for the chief of the Pemaquid Indians who greeted the Pilgrims, this inn has welcomed guests since 1889. It is a year-round resort set on 230 oceanside acres of the rugged coast of Maine. 178 rooms, 4 story. Check-in after 3 pm, check-out noon. Restaurant, bar. Children's activity center. Fitness room. Indoor pool, outdoor pool, whirlpool. Tennis. **$$**

Full-Service Inn

★ ★ ★ CAPTAIN LINDSEY HOUSE INN.

5 Lindsey St, Rockland (04841). Phone 207/596-7950; toll-free 800/523-2145; fax 207/596-2758. www.lindseyhouse.com. This inn (built in 1830) is located in downtown Rockland, close to galleries, shops, and the waterfront. The guest rooms have furnishings from around the world. There are four museums nearby and many shops and restaurants to explore. 9 rooms, 3 story. Children over 10 years only. Complimentary continental breakfast. Check-in 3 pm, check-out 11 am. Restaurant. **$$**

Specialty Lodgings

The following lodging establishments are approved by Mobil Travel Guide, but due to their unique and individualized nature have not been given a traditional Mobil Star rating. Included in this listing you may find bed-and-breakfasts, limited-service inns, guest ranches, and other unique hotel properties.

CRAIGNAIR INN. *5 Third St, Spruce Head (04859). Phone 207/594-7644; toll-free 800/320-9997; fax 207/596-7124. www.craignair.com.* Built in 1930, this boarding house was converted to an inn in 1947. 20 rooms, 3 story. Pets accepted; fee. Complimentary full breakfast. Check-in 3 pm, check-out 11 am. Restaurant. **$**

LAKESHORE INN. *184 Lakeview Dr, Rockland (04841). Phone 207/594-4209; toll-free 866/540-8800; fax 207/596-6407. www.lakeshorebb.com.* This Colonial New England farmhouse was built in 1767. 4 rooms, 2 story. Children over 12 years only. Complimentary full breakfast. Check-in 3 pm, check-out 11 am. Whirlpool. **$$**

Restaurants

★ **HARBOR VIEW.** *Thomaston Landing, Thomaston (04861). Phone 207/354-8173; fax 207/354-0036.* Seafood menu. Lunch, dinner. Closed Sun-Mon (Nov-Apr); Thanksgiving, Dec 25. Bar. Outdoor seating. **$$**

★ ★ ★ **PRIMO.** *2 S Main St, Rockland (04841). Phone 207/596-0770; fax 207/596-5938. www.primorestaurant.com.* Chef Melissa Kelly has helped moved Maine from the state known for lobster rolls onto serious foodie maps with Primo. An ardent supporter of sustainable agriculture, Kelly uses mostly local, organic produce—much of it grown on the restaurant's farm—and makes vegetables distinct contributors even to meat dishes. The menu, which changes weekly, draws on coastal Italy and France, resulting in asparagus soup with goat cheese, olive oil-poached salmon with bitter greens and beets, wood-roasted oysters, grilled calamari with house-made cavatelli pasta, and ham-wrapped roast monkfish. Co-owner and pastry chef Price Kushner contributes equally savory desserts. Primo's location in a restored Victorian home, with five dining rooms downstairs and a bar upstairs, contributes to the warmth seeded by the chefs' passions. Mediterranean menu. Dinner. Closed Tues. Bar. **$$**

Rockwood (C-2)

See also Moosehead Lake

Population 190
Elevation 1,050 ft
Area Code 207
Zip 04478

What to See and Do

Northern Outdoors, Inc. *Martins Pond and Hwy 201, Rockwood (04478). Phone 207/663-4466; toll-free 800/765-7238.* Specializes in outdoor adventures including whitewater rafting on Maine's Kennebec, Penobscot, and Dead rivers (May-Oct). Also snowmobiling (rentals), hunting, and resort facilities. Rock climbing, freshwater kayak touring. **$$$$**

Wilderness Expeditions, Inc. *Phone 207/534-2242; toll-free 800/825-9453.* Whitewater rafting on the Kennebec, Penobscot, and Dead rivers; also canoe trips and ski tours. (May-Sept, daily) **$$$$**

Limited-Service Hotel

★ ★ **MOOSEHEAD MOTEL.** *Hwy 15, Rockwood (04478). Phone 207/534-7787. www.maineguide.com/moosehead/motel.* 27 rooms, 2 story. Check-out 11 am. Restaurant. **$**

Rumford (D-1)

See also Bethel

Settled 1774
Population 7,078
Elevation 505 ft
Area Code 207
Zip 04276
Information River Valley Chamber of Commerce, 34 River St; phone 207/364-3241
Web Site www.rivervalleychamber.com

This papermill town is located in the valley of the Oxford Hills, where the Ellis, Swift, and Concord rivers flow into the Androscoggin. The spectacular Penacook Falls of the Androscoggin are right in town. Rumford serves as a year-round resort area.

What to See and Do

Mount Blue State Park. *Weld (04285). 4 miles E on Hwy 2 to Dixfield, then 14 miles N on Hwy 142. Phone 207/585-2347.* Recreation areas on Lake Webb include swimming, bathhouse, lifeguard, fishing, boating (ramp, rentals); hiking trail to Mount Blue, cross-country skiing, snowmobiling permitted, picnicking, camping (dump station). (Memorial Day-Labor Day)

Limited-Service Hotels

★ **BLUE IRIS MOTOR INN.** *Hwy 2, Rumford (04276). Phone 207/364-4495; toll-free 800/601-1515. www.sundayriveronline.com/BlueIrisMotorInn.* On river. 14 rooms. Check-out 10 am. Outdoor pool. **$**
🅑 🏊

★ ★ **MADISON RESORT INN.** *Hwy 2, Rumford (04276). Phone 207/364-7973; toll-free 800/258-6234; fax 207/369-0341. www.madisoninn.com.* 60 rooms, 2 story. Pets accepted, some restrictions. Check-out 11 am. Restaurant, bar. Fitness room. Outdoor pool, whirlpool. **$**
🐾 🏋 🏊

Saco (F-1)

See also Kennebunk, Kennebunkport, Old Orchard Beach, Portland

Settled 1631
Population 15,181

Elevation 60 ft
Area Code 207
Zip 04072
Information Biddeford/Saco Chamber of Commerce, 110 Main St, Suite 1202; phone 207/282-1567
Web Site www.biddefordsacochamber.com

Saco, on the east bank of the Saco River, facing its twin city Biddeford, was originally called Pepperellboro, until its name was changed in 1805. The city has diversified industry, including a machine and metal-working plant. Saco is only 4 miles from the ocean.

What to See and Do

Aquaboggan Water Park. *980 Portland Rd, Saco (04072). 4 miles N on US 1. Phone 207/282-3112. www.aquaboggan.com.* More than 40 acres of water and land attractions, including five water slides, wave pool, children's pool, "aquasaucer," games, miniature golf, bumper boats, race cars. Picnicking. (May-Sept, daily) **$$$$**

Dyer Library & York Institute Museum. *371 Main St, Saco (04072). On Hwy 1 Phone 207/283-3861.* Public library has arts and cultural programs. Museum features local history, decorative and fine art; American paintings, ceramics, glass, clocks, and furniture; changing exhibits. (Mon-Sat)

Ferry Beach State Park. *Hwy 9, Saco (04072). 3 1/2 miles N via Hwy 9. Phone 207/283-0067.* Beach, swimming, picnicking, nature and cross-country trails. (Memorial Day-Labor Day, daily)

Funtown USA. *774 Portland Rd, Saco (04072). 2 miles NE on Hwy 1. Phone 207/284-5139.* Theme park featuring adult and kiddie rides; log flume ride; Excalibur wooden roller coaster; Grand Prix Racers; games. Picnicking. (Mid-June-Sept: daily; early May-mid-June: weekends) **$$$$**

Restaurant

★ ★ **CASCADE INN.** *941 Portland Rd (Hwy 1), Saco (04072). Phone 207/283-3271; fax 207/282-3271. www.cascadeinn.com.* American, Italian menu. Breakfast, lunch, dinner, Sun brunch. Bar. Children's menu. **$**

Scarborough (F-1)

See also Portland

Population 12,518
Elevation 17 ft
Area Code 207
Zip 04074
Information Convention & Visitors Bureau of Greater Portland, 305 Commercial St, Portland 04101; phone 207/772-5800
Web Site www.visitportland.com

Scarborough contains some industry, but it is primarily a farming community and has been for more than 300 years. It is also a bustling tourist town during the summer months as vacationers flock to nearby beaches and resorts. The first Anglican church in Maine is here, as is painter Winslow Homer's studio, now a national landmark.

What to See and Do

Scarborough Marsh Nature Center. *Phone 207/883-5100.* Miles of nature and waterway trails through marshland area; canoe tours, special programs (fee). (Mid-June-Labor Day, daily) **FREE**

Sebago Lake State Park. *11 Park Access Rd, Scarborough (04015). 2 miles S of Naples off Hwy 11/114. Phone 207/693-6231.* A 1,300-acre area. Extensive sand beaches, bathhouse, lifeguards; fishing, boating (rentals, ramps); picnicking, concession, camping (dump station). No pets. (May-mid-Oct, daily)

Special Event

Harness racing. Scarborough Downs. *Hwy 1, Scarborough (04074). ME Tpke, exit 6. Phone 207/883-4331.* Evenings and matinees. Apr-Nov.

Limited-Service Hotels

★ **FAIRFIELD INN.** *2 Cummings Rd, Scarborough (04074). Phone 207/883-0300; toll-free 800/228-2800; fax 207/883-0572. www.fairfieldinn.com.* 120 rooms, 3 story. Complimentary continental breakfast. Check-out noon. Outdoor pool. **$**
🌊

★ **TOWNEPLACE SUITES BY MARRIOTT PORTLAND SCARBOROUGH.** *700 Roundwood Dr, Scarborough (04074). Phone 207/883-6800; toll-free 800/257-3000; fax 207/883-6866. www.towneplacesuites .com.* 95 rooms, 3 story. Pets accepted, some restrictions; fee. Check-in 3 pm, check-out noon. Fitness room. Outdoor pool. **$**
🅟 🔌 🛬 🌊

Searsport (D-3)

See also Belfast, Bucksport

Settled 1770
Population 2,603
Elevation 60 ft
Area Code 207
Zip 04974
Information Chamber of Commerce, Main St, PO Box 139; phone 207/548-6510

On the quiet upper reaches of Penobscot Bay, this is an old seafaring town. In the 1870s, at least ten percent of the captains of the US Merchant Marines lived here. Sea terminal of the Bangor and Aroostook Railway, Searsport ships potatoes and newsprint. This village abounds with antiques shops and is sometimes referred to as the "antique capital of Maine."

What to See and Do

Fishing, boating on bay. Town maintains wharf and boat landing, beachside park.

Penobscot Marine Museum. *5 Church St, Searsport (04974). Off Hwy 1. Phone 207/548-2529.* Old Town Hall (1845), Merithew House (circa 1860), Fowler-True-Ross House (1825), Phillips Library, and Carver Memorial Gallery. Ship models, marine paintings, American and Asian furnishings. (Memorial Day weekend-mid-Oct, daily) **$$$**

Specialty Lodging

The following lodging establishment is approved by Mobil Travel Guide, but due to its unique and individualized nature has not been given a traditional Mobil Star rating. Included in this listing you may find bed-and-breakfasts, limited-service inns, guest ranches, and other unique hotel properties.

BRASS LANTERN INN BED & BREAKFAST. *81 W Main St, Searsport (04974). Phone 207/548-0150; toll-free 800/691-0150; fax 207/548-0304. www.brass lanternmaine.com.* This captain's house was built in 1850. 5 rooms, 2 story. Children over 11 years only.

Complimentary full breakfast. Check-in 4 pm, check-out 11 am. **$$**

Sebago Lake (E-1)

See also Bridgton, Poland Spring

Second largest of Maine's lakes, this is perhaps the most popular, partly because of its proximity to Portland. About 12 miles long and 8 miles wide, it lies among wooded hills. Boats can run a total of more than 40 miles from the south end of Sebago Lake, through the Songo River to the north end of Long Lake. Numerous resort communities are hidden in the trees along the shores. Sebago, home of the landlocked salmon *(Salmo sebago),* is also stocked with lake trout.

What to See and Do

The Jones Museum of Glass and Ceramics. *35 Douglas Mountain Rd, Sebago Lake (04029). 5 miles NW via Hwy 114 and 107 on Douglas Hill.* Phone 207/787-3370. A decorative arts museum significant for its collection of both glass and ceramics. More than 7,000 pieces from early times to present. Changing exhibits; gallery tours, library, museum shop. (Mid-May-mid-Nov, daily) **$$**

Marrett House and Garden. *Hwy 25, Standish (04084). Approximately 2 miles S on Rte 25 to center of Standish.* Phone 207/642-3032. (1789) Built in Georgian-style, but later enlarged and remodeled in the Greek Revival fashion; period furnishings; farm implements. Coin from Portland banks was stored here during the War of 1812, when it was thought that the British would take Portland. Perennial and herb garden. Tours (mid-June-Aug: Tues, Thurs, Sat-Sun). **$$**

Full-Service Resort

★ ★ ★ **MIGIS LODGE.** *Off Hwy 302, South Casco (04077).* Phone 207/655-4524; fax 207/655-2054. *www.migis.com.* This property is set on more than 100 acres of wooded land and on the shore of a lake. A gift shop sells crafts from Maine. Wood for the fireplace in each guest room is delivered daily and there are handmade quilts on every bed and fresh flowers in the room. Sunsets are beautiful. 58 rooms, 2 story. Closed mid-Oct-May. Check-out noon. Restaurant, bar. Children's activity center. Fitness room. Beach. Tennis. Airport transportation available. **$$$**

Restaurants

★ ★ **BARNHOUSE TAVERN RESTAURANT.** *61 Hwy 35, Windham (04062).* Phone 207/892-2221; fax 207/892-6704. Authentically restored post-and-beam barn and farmhouse (1872); country atmosphere, loft dining. Seafood, steak menu. Lunch, dinner. Closed Dec 25. Bar. Outdoor seating. **$$**

★ ★ ★ **OLDE HOUSE.** *Hwy 85, Raymond (04071).* Phone 207/655-7841; fax 207/655-3247. This restaurant is located in a historic home, which dates to 1790. American menu. Dinner. Children's menu. **$$**

Skowhegan (D-2)

See also Bingham, Newport, Waterville

Settled 1771
Population 8,725
Elevation 175 ft
Area Code 207
Zip 04976
Information Chamber of Commerce, 23 Commercial St; phone 207/474-3621 or toll-free 888/772-4392
Web Site www.skowheganchamber.com

Skowhegan, on the Kennebec River, is surrounded by beautiful lakes. Shoes, paper pulp, and other wood products are made here. In the village's center stands a 12-ton, 62-foot-high Native American carved of native pine by Bernard Langlais. Skowhegan is the birthplace of Margaret Chase Smith, who served three terms in the US House of Representatives and four terms in the Senate.

What to See and Do

History House. *2 Coburn Ave, Skowhegan (04976).* Phone 207/474-6632. (1839) Old household furnishings; museum contains books, china, dolls, and documents. (Mid-June-mid-Sept, Tues-Fri afternoons) **$**

Special Events

Skowhegan Log Days. *10 Russell St, Skowhegan (04976).* Phone 207/474-3621. Parade, fireworks, pig roast, lobster bake, golf tournament, amateur and professional competitions, bean dinner. Commemorates last log drive on Kennebec River. Last full week in Aug.

Skowhegan State Fair. *Madison Ave Fairgrounds, Skowhegan (04976).* Phone 207/474-2947. One of oldest in country (1818). One-mile-long midway, stage shows, harness racing; contests, exhibits. Aug.

Restaurant

★ ★ **HERITAGE HOUSE.** *182 Madison Ave, Skowhegan (04976). Phone 207/474-5100.* Restored home; oak staircase. Seafood, steak menu. Lunch, dinner. Closed July 4, Dec 25. Bar. Children's menu. **$$**

Southwest Harbor (E-3)

See also Acadia National Park, Bar Harbor, Cranberry Isles

Population 1,952
Elevation 50 ft
Area Code 207
Zip 04679
Information Chamber of Commerce, PO Box 1143; phone 207/244-9264 or toll-free 800/423-9264
Web Site www.acadia.net/swhtrcoc

This is a prosperous, working seacoast village on Mount Desert Island. There are lobster wharves, where visitors can watch about 70 fishermen bring in their catch, and many shops where boats are constructed. Visitors may rent sail and power boats in Southwest Harbor to explore the coves and islands; hiking trails and quiet harbors offer relaxation.

What to See and Do

Cranberry Cove Boating Company. *Phone 207/244-5882.* Cruise to Cranberry Islands. See native wildlife and learn island history. Six departures daily. (Mid-June-mid-Sept, daily) Departs from Upper Town Dock. **$$**

Ferry service. *33 Main St, Southwest Harbor (04679). Phone 207/244-3575.* Ferry connects Little Cranberry and Great Cranberry with Northeast Harbor (see) on Mount Desert Island; 3-mile, 30-minute crossing. (Summer: daily; rest of year: varied schedule) **$$$**

Maine State Ferry Service. *Grandville Rd, Bass Harbor (04653). 4 miles S on Hwy 102 and Hwy 102A. Phone 207/244-3254 (Bass Harbor).* Ferry makes 6-mile (40-minute) trip to Swans Island and 8 1/4-mile (50-minute) trip to Frenchboro (limited schedule). Swans Island (all-year, one to six trips daily).

Mount Desert Oceanarium. *172 Clark Point Rd., Southwest Harbor (04679). Phone 207/244-7330.* More than 20 tanks with Gulf of Maine marine creatures. Touch tank permits animals to be picked up. Exhibits on tides, seawater, plankton, fishing gear, weather. Inquire for information on special events. (Mid-May-mid-Oct, Mon-Sat)

Wendell Gilley Museum. *4 Herrick Rd, Southwest Harbor (04679). Phone 207/244-7555.* Art and natural history museum featuring a collection of bird carvings by local artist Wendell Gilley; changing exhibits of local and historical art; films. (June-Oct: Tues-Sun; May and Nov-Dec: Fri-Sun) **$$**

Specialty Lodgings

The following lodging establishments are approved by Mobil Travel Guide, but due to their unique and individualized nature have not been given a traditional Mobil Star rating. Included in this listing you may find bed-and-breakfasts, limited-service inns, guest ranches, and other unique hotel properties.

THE CLARK POINT INN. *109 Clark Point Rd, Southwest Harbor (04679). Phone 207/244-9828; fax 207/244-9924. www.clarkpointinn.com.* Captain's house (1857); deck with harbor view. 5 rooms, 2 story. Closed mid-Oct-Apr. Children over 8 years only. Complimentary full breakfast. Check-in 2-6 pm, check-out 10:30 am. **$$**
🄳

KINGSLEIGH INN 1904. *373 Main St, Southwest Harbor (04679). Phone 207/244-5302; fax 207/244-7691. www.kingsleighinn.com.* Built in 1904, wraparound porch. 8 rooms, 3 story. Children over 12 years only. Complimentary full breakfast. Check-in 3 pm, check-out 11 am. **$**
🄳

Restaurants

★ **BEAL'S LOBSTER PIER.** *Clark Point Rd, Southwest Harbor (04679). Phone 207/244-3202; fax 207/244-9479.* Lobsters boiled to order; self-service. All seating is outdoors on a working wharf overlooking the Southwest Harbor. Seafood menu. Breakfast, lunch, dinner. Closed July 4. Outdoor seating. **$$**

★ **SEAWALL DINING ROOM.** *566 Seawall Rd, Southwest Harbor (04679). Phone 207/244-9250; fax 207/244-0299. www.seawallmotel.com.* Seafood menu. Lunch, dinner. Closed Dec-Apr. Children's menu. **$$**

Waterville (D-2)

See also Augusta, Skowhegan

Settled 1754
Population 17,173
Elevation 113 ft
Area Code 207
Information Mid-Maine Chamber of Commerce, One Post Office Sq, PO Box 142, 04903; phone 207/873-3315
Web Site www.mid-mainechamber.com

A large Native American village once occupied the west bank of the Kennebec River where many of Waterville's factories now stand. An important industrial town, Waterville is the center of the Belgrade and China lakes resort area. Manufactured goods include men's and women's shirts, paper and molded pulp products, and woolens.

What to See and Do

Colby College. *4601 Mayflower Hill Dr, Waterville (04901). 2 miles W, 1/2 mile E of I-95. Phone 207/872-3000.* (1813) (1,700 students) This 714-acre campus includes an art museum in the Bixler Art and Music Center (daily; closed holidays; free); a Walcker organ designed by Albert Schweitzer in Lorimer Chapel; and books, manuscripts, and letters of Maine authors Edwin Arlington Robinson and Sarah Jewett in the Miller Library (Mon-Fri; closed holidays; free).

Old Fort Halifax. *Winslow. 1 mile E on Hwy 201, on Bay St in Winslow, on E bank of Kennebec River.* (1754) Blockhouse. Bridge over Kennebec gives view of Ticonic Falls. (Memorial Day-Labor Day, daily)

Redington Museum. *62 Silver St, Waterville (04901). Phone 207/872-9439.* (1814) Waterville Historical Society collection includes 18th- and 19th-century furnishings, manuscripts, Civil War and Native American relics; historical library; children's room; apothecary museum. (Mid-May-Sept, Tues-Sat) **$$**

Two-Cent Footbridge. *Front St, Waterville (04901).* One of the few remaining former toll footbridges in the United States. **FREE**

Special Event

New England Music Camp. *8 Goldenrod Ln, Augusta (04330). 5 miles W on Hwy 137 to Oakland, then 4 miles S on Hwy 23. Phone 207/465-3025.* Faculty and student concerts, Sun; faculty concerts, Wed; student recitals, Fri. Late June-late Aug.

Limited-Service Hotels

★ ★ **BEST WESTERN WATERVILLE INN.** *356 Main St, Waterville (04901). Phone 207/873-3335; toll-free 800/780-7234; fax 207/873-3335. www.best western.com.* 86 rooms, 2 story. Pets accepted, some restrictions; fee. Check-out noon. Restaurant, bar. Outdoor pool. **$**

★ ★ **HOLIDAY INN.** *375 Main St, Waterville (04901). Phone 207/873-0111; toll-free 800/785-0111; fax 207/872-2310. www.holiday-inn.com.* 138 rooms, 3 story. Pets accepted, some restrictions. Check-out noon. Restaurant, bar. Fitness room. Indoor pool, whirlpool. **$**

Restaurants

★ **BIG G'S DELI.** *Outer Benton Ave, Winslow (04901). Phone 207/873-7808.* Deli menu. Breakfast, lunch, dinner. Children's menu. **$**

★ ★ **JOHN MARTIN'S MANOR.** *54 College Ave, Waterville (04901). Phone 207/873-5676; fax 207/877-9158. www.johnmartinsmanor.com.* American menu. Lunch, dinner. Closed Dec 25. Bar. Children's menu. **$**

★ **WEATHERVANE.** *470 Kennedy Memorial Dr, Waterville (04901). Phone 207/873-4522; fax 207/859-9846.* Seafood menu. Lunch, dinner. Closed Thanksgiving, Dec 24-25. Children's menu. **$$**

Wells (F-1)

See also Kennebunk, Ogunquit, York

Settled 1640
Population 7,778
Elevation 70 ft
Area Code 207
Zip 04090
Information Chamber of Commerce, PO Box 356; phone 207/646-2451
Web Site www.wellschamber.org

One of the oldest English settlements in Maine, Wells includes Moody, Wells Beach, and Drake's Island. It was largely a farming center, with some commercial fishing, until the resort trade began in the 20th century. Charter boats, surfcasting, and pier fishing attract anglers; 7 miles of beaches entice swimmers.

What to See and Do

⭐ **Rachel Carson National Wildlife Refuge.** *3 miles NE on Hwy 9.* Phone 207/646-9226. Approximately 5,000 acres of salt marsh and coastal edge habitat; more than 250 species of birds may be observed during the year. Visitor center; 1-mile interpretive nature trail. (All year, sunrise-sunset)

Wells Auto Museum. *1181 Post Rd, Wells (04090).* Phone 207/646-9064. Approximately 80 antique cars dating to 1900 trace progress of the automotive industry. Also displayed is a collection of nickelodeons, picture machines, and antique arcade games to play. (Memorial Day-Columbus Day, daily) **$$**

Wells Natural Estuarine Research Reserve. *342 Laudholm Farm Rd, Wells (04090). 1 1/2 miles N of Wells Corner on Hwy 1.* Phone 207/646-1555. Approximately 1,600 acres of fields, forest, wetlands, and beach. Laudholm Farm serves as visitor center. Programs on coastal ecology and stewardship, exhibits, and tours. Reserve (daily). Visitor center (May-Oct: daily; rest of year; Mon-Fri). **FREE**

Limited-Service Hotels

⭐ **GARRISON SUITES.** *1099 Post Rd (Hwy 1), Wells (04090).* Phone 207/646-3497; toll-free 800/646-3497. www.garrisonsuites.com. 60 rooms. Closed Nov-Apr. Check-out 11 am. Outdoor pool, whirlpool. **$**

⭐ ⭐ **VILLAGE BY THE SEA.** *Hwy 1 S, Wells (04090).* Phone 207/646-1100; toll-free 800/444-8862; fax 207/646-1401. www.vbts.com. Located between Kennebunkport and Ogunquit on Maine's southern coast, this 11-acre property is near Wells Beach and the Rachel Carson Wildlife Preserve. 73 rooms, 4 story, all suites. Check-out 10 am. Indoor pool, outdoor pool. **$$**

Restaurants

⭐ ⭐ **GREY GULL.** *475 Webhannet Dr, Wells (04090).* Phone 207/646-7501; fax 207/646-0938. www.thegreygullinn.com. This restaurant is located in a 19th-century inn on the ocean. American, seafood menu. Dinner, Sun brunch. Closed Wed-Thurs in winter.

Bar. Children's menu. Valet parking (in season). **$$**

⭐ **HAYLOFT.** *Hwy 1, Moody (04054).* Phone 207/646-4400. Seafood menu. Lunch, dinner. Closed week before Dec 25. Bar. Children's menu. **$**

⭐ ⭐ **LITCHFIELD'S.** *2135 Post Rd (Hwy 1), Wells (04090).* Phone 207/646-5711; fax 207/646-0594. Seafood, steak menu. Lunch, dinner, Sun brunch. Closed Dec 25. Bar. Children's menu. **$$$**

⭐ ⭐ **LORD'S HARBORSIDE.** *352 Harbor Rd, Wells (04090).* Phone 207/646-2651; fax 207/646-0818. Seafood menu. Lunch, dinner. Closed Tues; mid-Oct-Apr. Children's menu. **$$**

⭐ **MAINE DINER.** *2265 Post Rd, Wells (04090).* Phone 207/646-4441; fax 207/641-8470. www.mainediner.com. Seafood menu. Breakfast, lunch, dinner. Closed Thanksgiving, Dec 25. Children's menu. **$$**

⭐ ⭐ **STEAKHOUSE.** *1205 Post Rd (Hwy 1), Wells (04090).* Phone 207/646-4200; fax 207/646-0835. Seafood, steak menu. Dinner. Closed Mon; mid-Dec-Mar. Children's menu. **$$**

Wiscasset (E-2)

See also Bath, Boothbay Harbor, Damariscotta

Settled 1653
Population 3,339
Elevation 50 ft
Area Code 207
Zip 04578

Many artists and writers live here in beautiful old houses put up in the golden days of clipper ship barons and sea captains. Chiefly a summer resort area centered around its harbor, Wiscasset is half as populous as it was in 1850. Its pictorial charm is extraordinary even on the picturesque Maine coast. A noted sight in Wiscasset are the remains of two ancient wooden schooners, which were hauled into the harbor in 1932.

What to See and Do

Lincoln County Museum and Old Jail. *133 Federal St, Wiscasset (04578).* Phone 207/882-6817. First penitentiary built in the District of Maine (1809-1811). Jailer's house has changing exhibits, relics of Lincoln County. (July-Aug, Tues-Sun)

Maine Art Gallery. *In Old Academy Building (1807), Warren St, Wiscasset (04578).* Phone 207/882-7511. Exhibits by Maine artists. (Mid-May-early-Oct: Tues-Sun; rest of year: Thurs-Sun) **DONATION**

Musical Wonder House-Music Museum. *18 High St, Wiscasset (04578).* Phone 207/882-7163; toll-free 800/336-3725. (1852) Talking machines, antique musical boxes, player pianos shown and played in historical settings; antique furnishings; gift shop. (Late May-mid-Oct, daily) **$$$$**

Nickels-Sortwell House. *121 Main St, Wiscasset (04578).* At Federal St. Phone 207/882-6218. (1807) Classic Federal-style elegance. Built for a shipmaster in the lumber trade, William Nickels, it was used as a hotel between 1820 and 1900. The mansion was then bought by Mayor Alvin Sortwell of Cambridge, Massachusetts, as a private home. Graceful elliptical stairway; many Sortwell family furnishings; restored garden. (June-mid-Oct, Wed-Sun) **$$**

Pownalborough Courthouse. *Dresden. 8 miles N on Hwy 27, then 3 miles S on Hwy 128, bordering Kennebec River.* Phone 207/882-6817. (1761) Oldest pre-Revolutionary courthouse in Maine. Three-story building houses furnished courtroom, judges' chambers, spinning room, tavern, bedrooms, parlor, and kitchen. Nature trails along river; picnic areas; Revolutionary cemetery. (Wed-Sat; July-Aug also Sun afternoon) **$$**

Specialty Lodgings

The following lodging establishments are approved by Mobil Travel Guide, but due to their unique and individualized nature have not been given a traditional Mobil Star rating. Included in this listing you may find bed-and-breakfasts, limited-service inns, guest ranches, and other unique hotel properties.

COD COVE INN. *22 Cross Rd, Edgecomb (4556).* Phone 207/882-9586; toll-free 800/882-9586; fax 207/882-9294. www.codcoveinn.com. Located high on a hill, this New England-style inn overlooks the Sheepscott River and the harbor. Amenities for guests include a flowering garden with gazebo and outdoor swimming pool and whirlpool. Area activities include lighthouse touring, antique shopping, whale-watching or dining on lobster. 30 rooms, 2 story. Complimentary continental breakfast. Check-out 11:30 am. Outdoor pool, whirlpool. **$**
🏊

SQUIRE TARBOX INN. *1181 Main Rd, Westport Island (04578).* Phone 207/882-7693; fax 207/882-7107. www.squiretarboxinn.com. Restored 18th-century farmhouse situated on working dairy goat farm. 11 rooms, 2 story. Closed Jan-Mar. Complimentary full breakfast. Check-in 2 pm, check-out 11 am. Restaurant. **$$**
🔲

Restaurant

★ ★ **LE GARAGE.** *Water St, Wiscasset (04578).* Phone 207/882-5409; fax 207/882-6370. American, seafood menu. Lunch, dinner. Closed holidays; Jan. Bar. **$$**

Yarmouth (E-1)

See also Brunswick, Freeport, Portland

Settled 1636
Population 7,862
Elevation 100 ft
Area Code 207
Zip 04096
Information Chamber of Commerce, 158 Main St; phone 207/846-3984
Web Site www.yarmouthmaine.org

Yarmouth is a quaint New England village 10 miles north of Portland (see) on Highway 1. There are many well-maintained older homes and specialty shops. It is linked by a bridge to Cousins Island in the bay.

What to See and Do

Eartha. *2 DeLorme Dr, Yarmouth (04096). I-95, exit 17.* Phone 207/846-7000. www.delorme.com. World's largest globe. Three stories high, Eartha is the largest printed image of the Earth ever created and spins in the lobby of the DeLorme Map Company. (Daily) **FREE**

Yarmouth Historical Society Museum. *215 Main St, Yarmouth (04096). Third floor, Merrill Memorial Library.* Phone 207/846-6259. Two galleries with changing exhibits of local and maritime history, fine and decorative arts. Local history research room; historical lecture series. (July-Aug: Mon-Fri afternoons; rest of year: Tues-Sat) **FREE**

Old Ledge School. *215 Main St, Yarmouth (04096). Phone 207/846-6259.* (1738) Restored one-room schoolhouse. (By appointment) **FREE**

Special Event

Clam Festival. *158 Main St, Yarmouth (04096). Phone 207/846-3984. www.clamfestival.com.* Celebration of soft-shelled clams. Arts and crafts, entertainment, parade, fireworks. Third weekend in July.

Restaurant

★ ★ **ROYAL RIVER GRILLHOUSE.** *106 Lafayette St, Yarmouth (04096). Phone 207/846-1226; fax 207/846-0920. www.royalrivergrillhouse.com.* American menu. Lunch, dinner, Sun brunch. Closed Thanksgiving, Dec 25. Bar. Children's menu. Outdoor seating. **$$**

York (F-1)

See also Kittery, Ogunquit, Wells

Settled 1624
Population 9,818
Elevation 60 ft
Area Code 207
Zip 03909
Information Greater York Region Chamber of Commerce, 1 Stonewall Ln, PO Box 417; phone 207/363-4422
Web Site www.yorkme.org

Originally named Agamenticus by the Plymouth Company, which settled the area in 1624, the settlement was chartered as a city—the first in America—in 1641 and renamed Gorgeanna. Following a reorganization in 1652, the "city" in the wilderness took the name York. The present-day York area includes York Village, York Harbor, York Beach, and Cape Neddick.

What to See and Do

⭐ **Old York Historical Society.** *140 Lindsay Rd, York (03909). Phone 207/363-4974.* Tours of seven buildings dating to the early 1700s. (Mid-June-Sept, Tues-Sun) Visitor orientation and tickets at Jefferds Tavern. Administration Office houses museum offices (Mon-Fri) and historical and research library. **$**

Elizabeth Perkins House. Turn-of-the-century summer house on the banks of the York River, at Sewall's Bridge. Former home of a prominent York preservationist. The furnishings reflect the Colonial Revival period.

Emerson-Wilcox House. *York and Lindsey rds, York (03909). Phone 207/363-4422.* Built in 1742, with later additions. Served at various times as a general store, tavern, and post office, as well as the home of two of the town's prominent early families. Now contains a series of period rooms dating to 1750; antique furnishings.

George Marshall Store. *Lindsay Rd, York (03909). At the York River.* Mid-19th-century general store houses local art exhibits.

Jefferds Tavern and Schoolhouse. Built by Captain Samuel Jefferds in 1750 and furnished as a tavern in coastal Maine in the late 18th century; used as an orientation center and educational facility. Schoolhouse adjacent is probably the state's oldest surviving one-room schoolhouse; contains exhibit on one-room schooling in Maine.

John Hancock Warehouse. *York and Lindsey rds, York (03909). Phone 207/363-4974.* Owned by John Hancock until 1794, this is one of the earliest surviving customs houses in Maine. Used now to interpret the maritime history of this coastal village.

Old Gaol. *Lindsay Rd, York. On Hwy 1A at the York River.* Built in 1719 with 18th-century additions. One of the oldest English public buildings in the United States, it was used as a jail until 1860. Has dungeons and cells for felons and debtors, as well as galleries of local historical artifacts, late 1800s photography exhibit.

Sayward-Wheeler House. *79 Barrell Ln, York Harbor (03909). 2 miles S. Phone 207/436-3205.* (1718) Home of the 18th-century merchant and civic leader Tory Jonathan Sayward. Tours. (June-mid-Oct, Sat-Sun) **$$**

Special Event

Harvest Fest. *Hwy 95, York (03909). Exit 4, last exit before the toll. Phone 207/363-4422.* Juried crafts, ox roast, colonial theme. Mid-Oct.

Limited-Service Hotel

★ ★ **ANCHORAGE MOTOR INN.** *265 Long Beach Ave, York Beach (03910). Phone 207/363-5112; fax 207/363-6753. www.anchorageinn.com.* 179 rooms, 3 story.

Check-out 11 am. Bar. Fitness room. Two indoor pools, outdoor pool, whirlpool. **$**

Full-Service Resort

★ ★ ★ **STAGE NECK INN.** *22 Stage Neck Rd, York Harbor (03911). Phone 207/363-3850; toll-free 800/340-1130; fax 207/363-2221. www.stageneck.com.* This inn is located on an ocean-bound peninsula in York Harbor. The resort offers a beach and is also close to the Kittery outlet malls, antiques shops, art galleries, and historic attractions of York. 60 rooms, 3 story. Check-out 11 am. Restaurant, bar. Fitness room. Beach. Indoor pool, outdoor pool, whirlpool. Tennis. **$$**

Specialty Lodgings

The following lodging establishments are approved by Mobil Travel Guide, but due to their unique and individualized nature have not been given a traditional Mobil Star rating. Included in this listing you may find bed-and-breakfasts, limited-service inns, guest ranches, and other unique hotel properties.

DOCKSIDE GUEST QUARTERS. *Harris Island Rd, York (03909). Phone 207/363-2868; toll-free 800/270-1977; fax 207/363-1977. www.docksidegq.com.* 25 rooms. Closed weekdays Nov-Apr. Check-in 3 pm, check-out 11 am. Restaurant. **$$**

EDWARDS HARBORSIDE INN. *Stage Neck Rd, York Harbor (03911). Phone 207/363-3037; fax 207/363-1544. www.edwardsharborside.com.* Turn-of-the-century house with period furnishings. 12 rooms, 3 story. Children over 12 years only. Complimentary continental breakfast. Check-in 3-8 pm, check-out 11 am. **$$$**

YORK HARBOR INN. *Coastal Hwy 1A, York Harbor (03911). Phone 207/363-5119; toll-free 800/343-3869; fax 207/363-7151. www.yorkharborinn.com.* 47 rooms, 2 story. Complimentary continental breakfast. Check-in 2:30 pm, check-out 11 am. Restaurant. Whirlpool. **$$**

Restaurants

★ ★ **DOCKSIDE.** *Harris Island Rd, York (03909). Phone 207/363-2722; fax 207/363-1977. www.docksidegq.com.* Seafood menu. Lunch, dinner. Closed Mon; Nov-Memorial Day. Bar. Children's menu. Outdoor seating. **$$**

★ ★ **FAZIO'S ITALIAN.** *38 Woodbridge Rd, York (03909). Phone 207/363-7019; fax 207/363-8473. www.fazios.com.* Mural of Italian street market; photos from the '30s and '40s. Italian menu. Dinner. Closed holidays. Bar. Outdoor seating. **$**

★ ★ ★ **YORK HARBOR INN.** *Hwy 1A, York Harbor (03911). Phone 207/363-5119; fax 207/363-7151. www.yorkharborinn.com.* The menu at this seaside inn features local seafood, much of it caught close to the restaurant. Seafood menu. Lunch, dinner, Sun brunch. Closed Mon-Thurs (Jan-mid-May). Bar. Children's menu. **$$**

Massachusetts

Leif Ericson—or even a French or Spanish fisherman—may have originally discovered the Cape Cod coast. However, the first recorded visit of a European to Massachusetts was that of John Cabot in 1497. Not until the Pilgrims landed at Provincetown and settled at Plymouth was there a permanent settlement north of Virginia. Ten years later, Boston was founded with the arrival of John Winthrop and his group of Puritans.

Native American wars plagued Massachusetts until the 1680s, after which the people experienced a relatively peaceful period combined with a fast-growing, mostly agricultural economy. In the 1760s, opposition to British taxation without representation exploded into the American Revolution. It began in Massachusetts, and from here, the American tradition of freedom and justice spread around the world. The Constitution of Massachusetts is the oldest written constitution still in effect. The New England town meeting, a basic democratic institution, still governs most of its towns. The state had a child labor law in 1836, a law legalizing trade unions in 1842, and the first minimum wage law for women and children.

Massachusetts proved to be fertile ground for intellectual ideas and activities. In the early 19th century, Emerson, Thoreau, and their followers expounded the Transcendentalist theory of the innate nobilty of man and the doctrine of individual expression, which exerted a major influence on American thought, then and now. Social improvement was sought through colonies of idealists, many of which hoped to prove that sharing labor and the fruits of labor were the means to a just

society. Dorothea Dix crusaded on behalf of the mentally disturbed, and Horace Mann promoted universal education. In 1831, William Lloyd Garrison, an ardent abolitionist, founded his weekly, *The Liberator.* Massachusetts was the heartland of the Abolitionist movement, and her soldiers fought in the Civil War because they were convinced it was a war against slavery.

Massachusetts was also an important center during the Industrial Revolution. After the Civil War, the earlier success of the textile mills, like those in Lowell, generated scores of drab, hastily built, industrial towns. Now these mills are being replaced by modern plants with landscaped grounds. Modern industry is as much a part of Massachusetts as the quiet sandy beaches of Cape Cod with their bayberry and beach plum bushes.

Population: 6,016,425

Area: 7,826 square miles

Elevation: 0-3,491 feet

Peak: Mount Greylock (Berkshire County)

Entered Union: Sixth of original 13 states (February 6, 1788)

Capital: Boston

Motto: By the Sword We Seek Peace, but Peace Only Under Liberty

Nickname: Bay State

Flower: Mayflower

Bird: Chickadee

Tree: American Elm

Time Zone: Eastern

Web Site: www.mass-vacation.com

Fun Facts:

- James Naismith invented basketball in Springfield in 1891. He taught physical education and wanted an indoor sport for his students during the winter months.
- Harvard University, the nation's oldest college, was chartered in Cambridge in 1636.

Calendar Highlights

APRIL

Boston Marathon (Boston). *Phone 617/236-1652. www.bostonmarathon.org.* Famous 26-mile footrace from Hopkinton to Boston.

Daffodil Festival *(Nantucket Island). Siasconset Village. Phone Chamber of Commerce, 508/228-1700. www.nantucket.net.* The Daffodil festival celebrates the budding of millions of daffodils on the main roads of Nantucket. Parade of antique cars, open houses, garden tours, and entertainment.

Reenactment of Battle of Lexington and Concord *(Lexington). Massachusetts Ave. Phone Lexington Historical Society, 781/862-1703.* Reenactment of opening battle of American Revolution; parade.

JUNE

Green River Music and Balloon Festival *(Greenfield). Phone 413/733-5463.* Hot air balloon launches, craft show, musical entertainment, food.

Harborfest *(Boston). Hatch Shell on the Esplande. Phone 617/227-1528.* Concerts, chowder fest, children's activites, Boston Pops Orchestra, fireworks.

La Festa *(North Adams). Phone 413/663-3782.* Ethnic festival, food, entertainment, events.

SEPTEMBER

The "Big E" *(Springfield). Phone 413/737-2443. www.thebige.com.* Largest fair in the Northeast; entertainment, exhibits, historic Avenue of States, Storrowton Village; hores show, agricultural events, "Better Living Center" exhibit.

OCTOBER

Haunted Happenings *(Salem). Various sites. Phone Salem Halloween Office, 978/744-0013.* Psychic festival, historical exhibits, haunted house, costume parade, contests, dances.

NOVEMBER

Thanksgiving Week *(Plymouth). Phone 508/747-7525 or toll-free 800/872-1620.* Programs for various events may be obtained by contacting Destination Plymouth.

DECEMBER

Stockbridge Main Street at Christmas *(Stockbridge and West Stockbridge). Phone 413/298-5200.* Events include a re-creation of Norman Rockwell's painting. Holiday marketplace, concerts, house tour, silent auction, sleigh/hayrides, caroling.

Massachusetts has also been home to several generations of the politically prominent Kennedy family. John F. Kennedy, 35th president of the United States, was born in the Boston suburb of Brookline, as was his younger brother, Senator Robert Kennedy.

The Bay State offers mountains, ocean swimming, camping, summer resorts, freshwater and saltwater fishing, and a variety of metropolitan cultural advantages. No other state in the Union can claim so much history in so small an area, for in Massachusetts each town or city has a part in the American story.

When to Go/Climate

Massachusetts enjoys a moderate climate with four distinct seasons. Cape Cod and the Islands offer milder temperatures than other parts of the state and rarely have snow, while the windchill in Boston (the windiest city in the United States) can make temperatures feel well below zero, and snow is not uncommon.

AVERAGE HIGH/LOW TEMPERATURES (° F)

Boston

Jan 36/22	**May** 67/50	**Sept** 73/57
Feb 38/23	**June** 76/60	**Oct** 63/47
Mar 46/31	**July** 82/65	**Nov** 52/38
Apr 56/40	**Aug** 80/64	**Dec** 40/27

Worcester

Jan 31/15	**May** 66/45	**Sept** 70/51
Feb 33/17	**June** 75/54	**Oct** 60/41
Mar 42/25	**July** 80/60	**Nov** 47/31
Apr 54/35	**Aug** 77/59	**Dec** 35/20

Parks and Recreation

Water-related activities, hiking, riding, various other sports, picnicking and visitor centers, as well as camping, are available in many state parks. Day-use areas (approximately Memorial Day-Labor Day, some areas all year): $5/car. Camping (approximately mid-April-October, schedule may vary, phone ahead; two-week maximum, last Saturday in May-Saturday before Labor Day at many parks): campsites $10-$15/day; electricity $5/day. Pets on leash only; no pets in bathing areas. Information available from the Department of Environmental Management, Division of Forests & Parks, phone 617/727-3180.

FISHING AND HUNTING

Deep-sea and surf fishing are good; boats are available in most coastal towns. For information on saltwater fishing, contact the Division of Marine Fisheries, phone 617/727-3193. Inland fishing is excellent in more than 500 streams and 3,000 ponds. Nonresident fishing license $40.50; three-consecutive-day nonresident license $25.50. Nonresident hunting license: small game $75.50; big game $110.50. Inquire for trapping licenses. Fees subject to change. Licenses issued by town clerks, selected sporting good stores, or from the Division of Fisheries and Wildlife, phone 617/727-3151 or toll-free 800/275-3474. Information on freshwater fishing, regulations, and a guide to stocked trout waters and best bass ponds are also available from the Division of Fisheries and Wildlife.

Driving Information

Safety belts are mandatory for all persons. Children under 13 years must be in federally approved child safety seats or safety belts anywhere in a vehicle: it is recommended that children 40 pounds and under use federally approved child safety seats and be placed in the back seat. For more information, phone 617/624-5070 or toll-free 800/227-7233 (MA).

INTERSTATE HIGHWAY SYSTEM

The following list shows that these cities are within 10 miles of the indicated interstate highways. Check a highway map for the nearest exit.

Highway Number	Cities/Towns within 10 Miles
Interstate 90	Boston, Cambridge, Framingham, Great Barrington, Holyoke, Lee, Lenox, Natick, Newton, Pittsfield, Springfield, Stockbridge and West Stockbridge, Sturbridge, Sudbury Center, Waltham, Wellesley, Worcester.
Interstate 91	Amherst, Deerfield, Greenfield, Holyoke, Northampton, Springfield.
Interstate 93	Andover, Boston, Lawrence, Lowell.
Interstate 95	Bedford, Boston, Burlington, Concord, Danvers, Dedham, Foxboro, Framingham, Lexington, Lynn, Lynnfield, Natick, Newton, Saugus, Sudbury Center, Waltham, Wellesley.

Additional Visitor Information

The Massachusetts Office of Travel and Tourism, phone 617/727-3201, has travel information. For a free *Massachusetts Getaway Guide,* phone toll-free 800/447-6277.

Many properties of the Society for the Preservation of New England Antiquities (SPNEA) are located in Massachusetts and neighboring states. For complete information on these properties, contact SPNEA Headquarters, 141 Cambridge St, Boston 02114; phone 617/227-3956. For information regarding the 71 properties owned and managed by the Trustees of Reservations, contact 527 Essex St, Beverly, MA 01905, phone 508/921-1944.

Massachusetts has many statewide fairs, though none is considered the official state fair; contact the Massachusetts Department of Agriculture, Division of Fairs, phone 617/727-3037.

To the Berkshires!

Two major limited-access highways link Boston with the Berkshires, traversing the width of Massachusetts. The older, slower, more scenic Route 2 runs across the state's hilly northern tier; the Massachusetts Turnpike (I-90) is the quick way home. Begin on Route 2 in Cambridge. To explore Revolutionary War battle sites, take exit 56 (Waltham Street) into the center of Lexington and turn left on Route 2A for Battle Green. Continue west on Route 2A, stopping at the Battle Road Visitors Center and moving on to Concord's Minute Man National Historical Park sights. Pick up Route 2 west again in Concord. In Harvard, take exit 38A to the hilltop Fruitlands Museums with its paintings, Shaker furnishings, and local Indian artifacts. This is the Nashoba Valley, known for its orchards, served by the Johnny Appleseed information center just west of exit 35. Wachusett Mountain in Princeton (exit 25) is a popular ski area; there is also a state reservation with a road to its summit. Templeton (exit 21), just off the highway, is a classic old village with interesting shops and a local historical museum.

For a sense of central Massachusetts' countryside, detour south on Route 32 (exit 17) to the handsome old ridge town of Petersham. South of the village, turn west on Route 122, skirting the Quabbin Fervor, said to be one of the largest reservoirs in the world. Rejoin the highway in the town of Orange. Here, Route 2 officially becomes "The Mohawk Trail" because it's said to shadow an old Indian trail through the hills. (Note the information center at the junction of Reservoir 2, I-91, and Route 5.) Take a detour to Old Deerfield and its many historic house museums, located 12 miles south on Route 5. Or continue on Route 2 as it climbs steeply from Greenfield out of the Connecticut River Valley and into the Berkshire Hills. The vintage 1930s lookout towers and Indian trading posts along this stretch are relics from when this was the state's first scenic "auto touring" route.

The village of Shelburne Falls, just off Route 2, is known for its Bridge of Flowers, shops, and restaurants. The "trail" continues through the Deerfield River Valley, threads the heavily wooded Mohawk Trail Forest (camping, swimming), and finally plunges down a series of hairpin turns into the Hoosac Valley and through the town of North Adams, site of MASS MoCA, the country's largest center for contemporary art. The Western Gateway Heritage State Park here tells the story of Hoosac Railroad Tunnel construction beneath the mountains you have just crossed.

Williamstown, 126 miles from Boston, marks the state's northwest corner. It's home to Williams College and two outstanding art museums, the Clark Art Institute and the Williams College Museum of Art. This is an obvious stop for food and lodging.

If you have more than one day, continue south on Route 7 from Williamstown. In Lanesborough, note the main access road to Mount Greylock, the highest mountain in the state. Pittsfield, site of the Berkshire Museum, is also the turnoff point for the Hancock Shaker Village (5 miles west on Route 20). Continue down Route 7 to Lenox, site of the Tanglewood summer music festival, summer Shakespeare productions, several museums, and ample lodging. Take Route 7A south to Stockbridge and through the village to the Norman Rockwell Museum. Return on Route 102 to the entrance to the Massachusetts Turnpike (Route 90) at Lee, the quick way back to Boston. Stop at Sturbridge (exit 9) to tour Old Sturbridge Village. **(Approximately 290 miles)**

Several visitor centers are located in Massachusetts; they are located on the MA Turnpike (daily, 9 am-6 pm) at Charlton (eastbound and westbound), Lee (eastbound), and Natick (eastbound); also I-95 at Mansfield, between exits 5 and 6 (northbound); and on Highway 3 at Plymouth (southbound).

Amesbury (A-7)

See also Haverhill, Newburyport

Settled 1654
Population 16,450
Elevation 50 ft
Area Code 978

Zip 01913
Information Alliance for Amesbury, 5 Market Sq,
01913-2440; phone 978/388-3178
Web Site www.amesburymass.com

In 1853, Jacob R. Huntington, "the Henry Ford of
carriage-making," began a low-cost, high-quality carriage industry that became the economic backbone of
Amesbury.

What to See and Do

Amesbury Sports Park. *12 Hunt Rd, Amesbury
(01913). Off Hwy 495, exit 54. Phone 978/388-5788.
www.goslide.com.* Winter snow tubing, summer
go-carts, golf range, miniature golf, bumper boats,
volleyball park. Restaurant; lounge. (Tues-Fri 4-10 pm,
Sat-Sun 9 am-10 pm; closed Easter, Thanksgiving,
Dec 25) **$$$$**

Bartlett Museum. *270 Main St, Amesbury (01913).
Phone 978/388-4528.* (1870) Houses memorabilia
of Amesbury's history dating from prehistoric days
to the settlement and beyond. The Native American
artifact collection, consisting of relics of local tribes,
is considered one of the finest collections in the state.
(Memorial Day-Labor Day, Wed-Sun afternoons;
Labor Day-Columbus Day, Sat-Sun) **$**

John Greenleaf Whittier Home. *86 Friend St, Amesbury
(01913). Phone 978/388-1337.* John Greenleaf Whittier
lived here from 1836 until his death in 1892; six rooms
contain books, manuscripts, pictures, and furniture;
the Garden Room, where he wrote *Snow-Bound,* and
many other works, remains unchanged. (May-Oct,
Tues-Sat) **$$**

Limited-Service Hotel

★ **FAIRFIELD INN.** *35 Clarks Rd, Amesbury
(01913). Phone 978/388-3400; toll-free 800/228-2800;
fax 978/388-9850. www.fairfieldinn.com.* Convenient
to I-95 and I-495 and across the street from a family
restaurant, this motel gets quite a bit of traffic noise,
but the guest rooms are large and comfortable. Guest
laundry facilities are available. 105 rooms, 4 story.
Complimentary continental breakfast. Check-in 3 pm,
check-out noon. Wireless Internet access. Outdoor
pool. **$**

Amherst (B-4)

See also South Hadley

Founded 1759
Population 34,874
Elevation 320 ft
Area Code 413
Zip 01002
Information Chamber of Commerce, 409 Main St;
phone phone 413/253-0700
Web Site www.amherstchamber.com

Amherst College, founded in 1821 to educate
"promising but needy youths who wished to enter the
Ministry," has educated several of the nation's leaders,
including Calvin Coolidge and Henry Ward Beecher.
Amherst is also the seat of the University of Mas-
sachusetts and of Hampshire College. This attractive,
academic town was the home of three celebrated
American poets: Emily Dickinson, Eugene Field,
and Robert Frost; Noah Webster also lived here and
apparently completed A-K of his famous dictionary in
Amherst.

What to See and Do

Amherst College. *100 Boltwood Ave, Amherst (01002).
Phone 413/542-2000. www.amherst.edu.* (1821) (1,550
students) On the tree-shaded green in the middle of
town. The Robert Frost Library owns approximately
half of Emily Dickinson's poems in manuscript and
has a Robert Frost collection, as well as materials of
Wordsworth, Eugene O'Neill, and others. Also on
campus are

Mead Art Museum. *Phone 413/542-2335.
www.amherst.edu/~mead.* A notable art collection
of nearly 14,000 works is housed here. (Sept-May,
Tues-Sun 10 am-4:30 pm) **FREE**

Amherst History Museum. *67 Amity St, Amherst
(01002). Phone 413/256-0678. www.amhersthistory.org.*
In the circa-1750 Strong House, which reflects chang-
ing tastes in local architecture and interior decoration,
this museum boasts an extensive collection of 18th-
and 19th-century textiles and artifacts. Gallery. (June-
early Dec, Wed and Sat afternoons) 18th-century herb
and flower gardens to the east of Strong House are
open to the public (spring-summer). **$$**

Emily Dickinson Museum: the Homestead and the Evergreens. *280 Main St, Amherst (01002). Phone 413/542-8161. www.emilydickinsonmuseum.org.* (1813) The Homestead was the birthplace and home of poet Emily Dickinson; the Evergreens housed her brother and his family. Selected rooms are open for tours on a first-come, first-served basis. (Apr-May, Sept-Oct: Wed-Sat 1-5 pm; June-Aug: Wed-Sat 10 am-5 pm, Sun 1-5 pm; Mar, Nov-mid-Dec: Wed, Sat 1-5 pm) **$$**

Eric Carle Museum of Picture Book Art. *125 W Bay Rd, Amherst (01002). Phone 413/658-1100. www. picturebookart.org.* This 40,000-square-foot facility opened in 2002 as the first museum in the United States exclusively devoted to children's picture book art. Its founder, Eric Carle, has illustrated more than 70 picture books, including *The Very Hungry Caterpillar,* which has been published in more than 30 languages and has sold more than 18 million copies. Nestled within a 7.5-acre apple orchard adjacent to the campus of Hampshire College, the museum features three galleries and a hands-on art studio, along with an auditorium, library, and café. A past exhibit celebrated the picture book art of Maurice Sendak, author and illustrator of such classics as *Where the Wild Things Are.* (Tues-Sat 10 am-4 pm, Sun noon-4 pm; closed holidays) **$**

Hadley Farm Museum. *208 Middle St, Hadley (01035). 5 miles SW at junction Hwys 9, 47. www. hadleyonline.com/farmmuseum.* A restored 1782 barn houses agricultural implements, tools, and domestic items dating from the 1700s; broom-making machines, spinning wheels, cobblers' benches, and other historic artifacts. (May-Oct, Tues-Sat 10 am-4:30 pm, Sun 1:30-4:30 pm) **FREE**

Jones Library. *43 Amity St, Amherst (01002). Phone 413/256-4090. www.joneslibrary.org.* Amherst's public library houses collections of the local authors, including a Robert Frost collection and an Emily Dickinson room with some of Dickinson's personal articles, manuscripts, and a model of her bedroom. Historical collection (Mon-Sat); library (Sept-May: daily; rest of year: Mon-Sat; closed holidays). **FREE**

National Yiddish Book Center. *893 West St, Amherst (01002). Hwy 116, on the campus of Hampshire College. Phone 413/256-4900. yiddishbookcenter.org.* This 37,000-square-foot nonprofit facility was founded by Aaron Lansky to preserve Yiddish literature and its history and to ensure its lasting legacy. Book Repository houses a core collection of 120,000 Yiddish books—the largest in the world—and 150,000

folios of rare Yiddish and Hebrew sheet music. The Book Processing Center, shipping and receiving area, and Bibliography Center are all open for viewing as rare books are catalogued and shipped to libraries across the country. The vistor center includes three exhibit halls, a kosher dairy kitchen, and educational story rails that introduce visitors to the books and the Center's important work. Reading Room, Yiddish Resource Center, Yiddish Writers Garden. Also galleries for print, spoken, and performing arts. Bookstore; gift shop. (Mon-Fri 10 am-3:30 pm, Sun 11 am-4 pm; closed holidays) **FREE**

University of Massachusetts. *Massachusetts Ave and N Pleasant St, Amherst (01002). N edge of town on Hwy 116. Phone 413/545-4237. www.umass.edu.* (1863) (24,000 students) The state's major facility of public higher education. More than 150 buildings on a 1,450-acre campus. Tours (daily). Also here is

Fine Arts Center and Gallery. *Phone 413/545-3670. www.umass.edu/pac.* A variety of nationally and internationally known performances in theater, music, and dance. Art galleries (daily). Performances (Sept-May).

Special Event

Maple sugaring. *Mount Toby Sugar House, Amherst. NW via Hwy 116 to Sunderland, then 2 miles N on Hwy 47. Phone 413/253-0700.* Visitors are welcome at maple camps, daily. (Late Feb-Mar)

Limited-Service Hotel

★ **HOWARD JOHNSON.** *401 Russell St, Hwy 9, Hadley (01035). Phone 413/586-0114; fax 413/584-7163. www.hojo.com.* 100 rooms, 3 story. Pets accepted, some restrictions; fee. Complimentary full breakfast. Check-out noon. Fitness room. Outdoor pool. **$**
🔖 ⫯ ⛱

Specialty Lodgings

The following lodging establishments are approved by Mobil Travel Guide, but due to their unique and individualized nature have not been given a traditional Mobil Star rating. Included in this listing you may find bed-and-breakfasts, limited-service inns, guest ranches, and other unique hotel properties.

ALLEN HOUSE VICTORIAN INN. *599 Main St, Amherst (01002). Phone 413/253-5000. www.allenhouse.com.* Queen Anne-style house built in

1886; many antiques. 7 rooms, 2 story. Children over 8 years only. Complimentary full breakfast. Check-in noon, check-out 11 am. **$**

LORD JEFFERY INN. *30 Boltwood Ave, Amherst (01002). Phone 413/253-2576; toll-free 800/742-0358; fax 413/256-6152. www.lordjeffreyinn.com.* 48 rooms, 4 story. Check-in 3 pm, check-out 11 am. Two restaurants, bar. **$**

Andover and North Andover (A-7)

Settled circa 1643
Population 31,247
Elevation 164 ft
Area Code 978
Zip Andover: 01810; North Andover: 01845
Information Merrimack Valley Chamber of Commerce, 264 Essex St, Lawrence 01840-1496; phone 978/686-0900
Web Site www.merrimackvalleychamber.com

An attempt was made in Andover in the 19th century to surpass Japan's silk industry by growing mulberry trees on which silkworms feed. But Andover has had to be content with making electronic parts and woolen and rubber goods instead. Its true fame rests on Phillips Academy, the oldest incorporated school in the United States, founded in 1778 by Samuel Phillips.

What to See and Do

Amos Blanchard House. *97 Main St, Andover (01810). Phone 978/475-2236.* (1819) **Barn Museum** (1818) Also **Research Library** (1978). House features period rooms; special local history exhibits; 17th- to 20th-century themes. Barn Museum features early farm equipment; household items; hand-pumped fire wagon. Library houses local history, genealogy, and special collections. Guided tours (by appointment). (Tues-Fri, also by appointment; closed holidays) **$$**

Phillips Academy. *180 Main St, Andover (01810). Hwy 28. Phone 978/749-4000. www.andover.edu.* (1778) (1,065 students) A coed residential school for grades 9-12. Notable alumni include photographer Walker Evans, poet Oliver Wendell Holmes, child-rearing expert Benjamin Spock, and actor Humphrey Bogart. The campus sits on 450 acres with 170 buildings,

many of historical interest. The Cochran Sanctuary, a 65-acre landscaped area, has walking trails, a brook, and two ponds. (Daily) Also on the grounds are

Addison Gallery of American Art. *Phone 978/749-4016. www.andover.edu/addison.* More than 12,000 works, including paintings, sculpture, and photography. Changing exhibits. A ship model collection traces the history of American sailing vessels. (Sept-July, Tues-Sat 10 am-5 pm, Sun 1-5 pm; closed holidays) **FREE**

Peabody Museum. *175 Main St, Andover (01810). Phone 978/749-4490. www.andover.edu/rspeabody.* This Native American archaeological museum has exhibits on the physical and cultural evolution of man and the prehistoric archaeology of New England, the Southwest, Mexico, and the Arctic. (Mon-Fri 9 am-5 pm, by appointment only) **FREE**

Stevens-Coolidge Place. *137 Andover St, North Andover (01845). Phone 978/682-3580. www.the trustees.org/stevens-coolidgeplace.cfm.* House and extensive gardens are maintained as they were in the early 20th century by diplomat John Gardener Coolidge and his wife, Helen Stevens Coolidge, who summered here. Collection of Chinese porcelain, Irish and English cut glass, linens, and clothing. Early American furnishings. House (late Apr-Oct, Sun 1-5 pm; also Wed 2-4 pm in July-Aug). Gardens (daily dawn-dusk; free). **$**

Limited-Service Hotels

★ ★ **ANDOVER WYNDHAM HOTEL.** *123 Old River Rd, Andover (01810). Phone 978/975-3600; fax 978/975-2664. www.wyndham.com.* 293 rooms, 5 story. Pets accepted; fee. Check-in 3 pm, check-out noon. Restaurant, bar. Fitness room. Indoor pool, whirlpool. Airport transportation available. **$$**

★ ★ **TAGE INN ANDOVER.** *131 River Rd, Andover (01810). Phone 978/685-6200; toll-free 800/322-8243; fax 978/794-9626. www.tageinn.com.* 185 rooms, 3 story. Complimentary continental breakfast. Check-out noon. Restaurant. Fitness room. Indoor pool, whirlpool. Tennis. **$**

Full-Service Inn

★ ★ ★ **ANDOVER INN.** *10 Chapel Ave, Andover (01810). Phone 978/475-5903; toll-free 800/242-5903;*

fax 978/475-1053. *www.andoverinn.com.* Located on the campus of Philips Andover Academy, this neo-Georgian country inn was built in 1930 to provide lodging for visiting parents and alumni. 29 rooms, 3 story. Check-out noon. Restaurant, bar. Business center. **$**

⌖

Restaurant

★ **CHINA BLOSSOM.** *946 Osgood St, North Andover (01845). Phone 978/682-2242; fax 978/685-1268.* Chinese menu. Lunch, dinner. Closed Thanksgiving. Bar. **$$**

Bedford (B-7)

Population 12,595
Elevation 135 ft
Area Code 781
Zip 01730

Limited-Service Hotel

★ ★ **BEST WESTERN SOVEREIGN HOTEL.** *340 Great Rd, Bedford (01730). Phone 781/275-6700; toll-free 800/602-9876; fax 781/275-3011. www.sovereignhotels.com.* In a busy suburban commercial area, this 99-room hotel underwent a major renovation completed in 2004. The unadorned brown stucco exterior belies a much more attractive interior, with spacious guest rooms arranged around a three-story atrium housing a large indoor pool. 99 rooms, 3 story. Complimentary full breakfast. Check-in 2 pm, check-out noon. Wireless Internet access. Restaurant, bar. Fitness room. Indoor pool. **$**

⌖ ⌦

Full-Service Hotels

★ ★ ★ **RENAISSANCE BEDFORD HOTEL.** *44 Middlesex Tpke, Bedford (01730). Phone 781/275-5500; toll-free 888/236-2427; fax 781/275-8956. www.renaissancehotels.com.* Nestled in a corporate office park area on 24 attractively landscaped acres, this contemporary hotel is great for business travelers and group functions. Indoor tennis courts with equipment and a pro available, as well as a glass-enclosed lap pool, sand volleyball court, and basketball court, offer lots of options for leisure travelers, too. Guests also enjoy complimentary shuttle service to public transportation, area businesses, and nearby recreational destinations, such as the Burlington Mall. 284 rooms, 3 story. Complimentary continental breakfast. Check-in 3 pm, check-out 1 pm. High-speed Internet access. Restaurant, bar. Fitness room. Indoor pool, whirlpool. Tennis. Business center. **$**

⌖ ⌦ ⌖ ⌖

★ ★ ★ **WYNDHAM BILLERICA HOTEL.** *270 Concord Rd, Bedford (01821). Phone 978/670-7500; fax 978/670-8898. www.wyndham.com.* 210 rooms, 8 story. Check-in 4 pm, check-out noon. Restaurant, bar. Fitness room. Indoor pool, whirlpool. Business center. **$**

◫ ⌖ ⌦ ⌖

Berkshire Hills

Web site www.berkshire.org

This western Massachusetts resort area is just south of Vermont's Green Mountains, but has neither the ruggedness nor the lonesomeness of the range to its north. The highest peak, Mt. Greylock (elevation: 3,491 feet), is cragless and serene. Farms and villages dot the landscape. The area is famous for its variety of accommodations, culture, and recreation. There are also countless summer homes and camps for children by the lakes, ponds, and brooks.

Berkshire County is about 45 miles long from north to south, and half that from east to west. It has 90 lakes and ponds, 90,000 acres of state forest, golf courses, ski areas, ski touring centers, numerous tennis facilities, and campsites. The area first became famous when Nathaniel Hawthorne wrote *Tanglewood Tales,* and it has since become distinguished for its many summer cultural activities, including the Tanglewood Music Festival at Tanglewood (see LENOX) and the Berkshire Theatre Festival (see STOCKBRIDGE and WEST STOCKBRIDGE).

Beverly (B-8)

See also Danvers, Salem

Settled 1626
Population 39,862
Elevation 26 ft
Area Code 978
Zip 01915
Information North Shore Chamber of Commerce, 5 Cherry Hill Dr, Danvers 01923; phone 978/774-8565
Web Site www.northshorechamber.org

When George Washington commissioned the first US naval vessel, the schooner *Hannah,* on September 5, 1775, at Glover's Wharf in Beverly, the town was already well established. In 1693, the local Puritan minister's wife, Mistress Hale, was accused of witchcraft. She was so far above reproach that the charge—and the hysteria—collapsed. Today, Beverly is a popular summer resort area. Saltwater fishing, boating, and scuba diving are available near Glover's Wharf.

What to See and Do

Balch House. *448 Cabot St, Beverly (01915). Phone 978/922-1186. www.beverlyhistory.com.* (17th century) One of the two oldest wood-frame houses in America. Born in 1579, John Balch came to America in 1623 as one of the first permanent settlers of Massachusetts Bay. (Mid-May-mid-Oct, Wed-Sun; closed holidays) Inquire about combination ticket (includes Hale and Cabot houses). **$$**

Cabot House. *117 Cabot St, Beverly (01915). Phone 978/922-1186. www.beverlyhistory.com.* (1781) Headquarters of the Beverly Historical Society. Brick mansion of Revolutionary War privateer John Cabot, built a year after it was written that "the Cabots of Beverly are now said to be by far the most wealthy in New England." Changing exhibits. (Wed-Sat) Inquire about combination ticket (includes Hale and Balch houses). **$$**

Hale House. *39 Hale St, Beverly (01915). Phone 978/ 922-1186. www.beverlyhistory.com.* (1694) Built by the Reverend John Hale, who was active in the witchcraft trials and whose own wife was accused of witchcraft. Rare wallpaper and furnishings show changes through the 18th and 19th centuries. (July-Aug, Sat afternoons; closed holidays) Inquire about combination ticket (includes Cabot and Balch houses). **$$**

"Le Grand David and His Own Spectacular Magic Company." *Cabot Street Cinema Theatre (1920), 286 Cabot St, Beverly (01915). Phone 978/927-3677.* Resident stage magic company, New England's longest running theatrical attraction. This 2 1/4-hour stage magic production features magic, music, comedy, and dance. Five hundred costumes, two dozen sets and backdrops; 50 magic illusions. (Sun) Additional performances at Larcom Theatre (1912), 13 Wallis Street. Advance tickets recommended. **$$$$**

Wenham Museum. *132 Main St, Wenham (01984). 2 1/2 miles N on Hwy 1A. Phone 978/468-2377. wenhammuseum.org.* The Wenham's doll collection, comprised of more than 5,000 dolls, represents cultures from 1500 BC to the present. The toy room houses British lead soldiers, board games and puzzles, and 20th-century mechanical toys. The Claflin-Richards House (circa 1690) contains collections of quilts, costumes, and fans, along with period furniture. The Winslow Shoe Shop has displays on the history of shoemaking, early ice-cutting tools, and a research library. Changing arts, crafts, and antique exhibits. (Tues-Sun 10 am-4 pm; closed holidays) **$**

Special Events

Band Concerts. *Lynch Park, 55 Ober St, Beverly (01915). Phone 978/774-8565.* Lynch Park Bandshell Sun evening; downtown Ellis Square, Thurs evening. (Late June-mid-Aug)

North Shore Music Theatre. *62 Dunham Rd, Beverly (01915). At Hwy 128 N exit 19. Phone 978/922-8500.* Broadway musicals and plays; children's musicals; celebrity concerts. (Late Apr-late Dec)

Restaurant

★ **BEVERLY DEPOT.** *10 Park St, Beverly (01915). Phone 978/927-5402; fax 978/927-9897. www.barnsider restaurants.com.* In 1800s train depot. Seafood, steak menu. Dinner. Bar. Children's menu. **$$**

Boston (B-7)

See also Braintree, Cambridge, Ipswich, Lynn, Marblehead, Newton, Quincy, Saugus, Sudbury Center, Waltham, Wellesley

Founded 1630
Population 589,141
Elevation 0-330 ft
Area Code 617
Information Greater Boston Convention & Visitors Bureau, 2 Copley Pl, Suite 105, 02116; phone 617/536-4100 or toll-free 888/733-2678
Web Site www.bostonusa.com
Surburbs Braintree, Burlington, Cambridge, Dedham, Framingham, Lexington, Lynn, Newton, Quincy, Saugus, Waltham, Wellesley. (See individual alphabetical listings.)

Greater Boston is a fascinating combination of old and new. It consists of 83 cities and towns in an area of 1,057 square miles with a total population of more than 3 million people. Boston proper is the hub of this busy complex, which many Bostonians still believe is the hub of the universe.

Boston is a haven for walkers; in fact, strolling along its streets is advised to get a true sense of this most European of all American cities. If you drive, a map is invaluable. Traffic is heavy. The streets (many of them narrow and one-way) run at odd angles and express-way traffic speeds.

Boston's wealth of historic sights makes it a must for all who are interested in America's past. John Winthrop and 800 colonists first settled in Charlestown, just north of the Charles River, and moved to Boston in 1630. Arriving too late to plant crops, 200 colonists died during the first winter, mostly of starvation. In the spring, a ship arrived with provisions, and the new Puritan commonwealth began to thrive and grow. Fisheries, fur trapping, lumbering, and trading with Native Americans were the foundation of Boston's commerce. The port is still viable, with 250 wharves along 30 miles of berthing space.

The Revolutionary War began here in 1770. British troops fired on an angry mob, killing five in what has since been called the "Boston Massacre." In 1773, the Boston Tea Party dumped East Indian tea into the bay in a dramatic protest against restriction of colonial trade by British governors. Great Britain closed the port in retaliation. The course of history was set.

In April 1775, British General Thomas Gage decided to march on Concord to capture military supplies and overwhelm the countryside. During the night of April 18-19, Paul Revere, William Dawes, and Samuel Prescott spread the news to Lexington and Concord in a ride immortalized, somewhat inaccurately, by Henry Wadsworth Longfellow. The Revolutionary War had begun in earnest; the Battle of Bunker Hill followed the battles of Lexington and Concord. On March 17, 1776, General William Howe, commander of the British forces, evacuated the city.

Boston's list of distinguished native sons includes John Hancock, Samuel Adams, Paul Revere, Henry Ward Beecher, Edward Everett Hale, Ralph Waldo Emerson, William Lloyd Garrison, Oliver Wendell Holmes (father and son), and hundreds of others.

Mention Boston, and many people automatically think of the gentry of Beacon Hill, with their elegant homes and rigid social code. However, the Irish have long had a powerful influence in Boston's politics and personality, while a stroll through an Italian neighborhood in the North End will be like stepping back to the old country.

Boston today manages to retain its heritage and charm while thriving in the modern age. Urban renewal and increased construction have reversed an almost 40-year slump that plagued Boston earlier in the 20th century. With more than 100 universities, colleges, and trade and vocational schools in the area, Boston is a city as full of vigor and promise for the future as it is rich with the past.

Public Transportation

Buses, subway, and elevated trains (Massachusetts Bay Transportation Authority), visitor pass available, phone 617/722-3200. Information phone toll-free 800/235-6426

Airport Logan International Airport; weather 617/936-1234; cash machines in Terminals A, B, C

Information Phone 617/561-1800 or toll-free 800/235-6426.

Lost and found Phone 617/561-1714

Airlines Aer Lingus, Air Canada/Air Canada Jazz, Air France, Air Jamaica, AirTran, Alaska Airlines, Alitalia, America West, American, American Eagle, ATA, British Airways, Cape Air, Continental, Delta Air Lines, Delta Connection/Atlantic Coast, Delta Connection/Com Air, Delta Shuttle (LaGuardia.), Delta Shuttle/Comair (Washington, DC), Icelandair KLM, Lufthansa, Midwest, Northwest, Qantas, SATA, Song, Swiss, TACA, United, United Express/Atlantic Coast, US Airways Shuttle (LaGuardia & DC), US Airways, US Airways Express, Virgin Atlantic

What to See and Do

Bay State Cruise Company. *Commonwealth Pier, World Trade Center, 184 High St, Boston (02110). Phone 617/748-1428. www.boston-ptown.com.* All-day sail to Provincetown and Cape Cod from Commonwealth Pier. The 2 1/2- and 3 1/2-hour harbor and island cruises aboard *Spirit of Boston* highlight adventure and history. (May-Columbus Day, daily) Contact Bay State Cruise Company. **$$$$**

Bean Pot Hockey. *Fleet Center, Boston.* The Bean Pot refers to games between four Boston-based teams: Boston College, Boston University, Harvard

University, and Northeastern University. Attending a hockey game between any two of the four is sure to be an intense experience, because all four teams compete vigorously for the Bean Pot each year. If you like to see body checking up close, get the lowest seats you can afford at any of the four corners of the rink. (Oct-Apr) **$$$$**

Berklee Performing Center at Berklee College of Music. *136 Massachusetts Ave, Boston (02115). Take the Green Line ("T") to the Hynes Convention Center/ICA stop. Exit left onto Massachusetts Ave and cross Boylston St. The Berklee Performance Center is about 30 yards from the corner. Phone 617/747-2261. www.berkleebpc.com.* The Berklee Performance Center is the performing arm of the Berklee College of Music, a prestigious Boston institution. Housed in a 1,200-seat renovated theater, this state-of-the-art venue hosts both student performances and national concerts, most notably featuring jazz and pop musicians. Ticket prices for nationally known performers are higher than admission fees for student performances. **$$**

Bernard Toale Gallery. *450 Harrison Ave, Boston (02118). Phone 617/482-2477. www.bernardtoalegallery .com.* The Bernard Toale Gallery offers you an opportunity to view (and buy, if you're so inclined) paintings, drawings, photographs, and sculptures from some of today's hottest artists. Both established artists and select up-and-comers display works at the gallery, so you get a chance to take in cutting-edge works that have not yet made their way into contemporary art museums. Look for occasional readings, videos, and fashion shows, too. Allow one or two hours. (Tues-Sat; Aug by appointment only; closed Sat in July) **FREE**

Bible Exhibit. *Belvidere St, Boston (02115). Opposite the Prudential Center.* Nondenominational exhibit; audiovisual activities; rare Biblical treasures; historical timeline; large Plexiglas wall-map with lighted journeys of six Biblical figures; historic editions; children's story corner; exploring center for reference; film and slide program on the hour. (Wed-Sun; closed Jan 1, Thanksgiving, Dec 25)

Blue Hills Reservation. *1904 Canton Ave, Milton (02186). Phone 617/698-1802. www.state.ma.us/mdc/ blue.htm.* Blue Hills offers more than 200 miles of trails in the 6,500-acre reservation, about a third of which are set aside for mountain biking, making the other two-thirds ideal for hiking, bird-watching, and sightseeing. Climb Summit Road (which is paved) 635 feet to get to Great Blue Hill and the stunning view that rewards you there. In winter, the reservation opens for downhill skiing. (Wed-Sun) **FREE** On reservation is the

Blue Hills Trailside Museum. *Phone 617/333-0690. www.massaudbon.org/Nature_Connection/ Sanctuaries.* Visitor center for the 7,000-acre Blue Hills Reservation. Deer, turkeys, otters, snakes, owls, and honeybees. Exhibit hall with natural science/history displays, including a Native American wigwam; viewing tower. Activities include hikes, films, and animal programs. Special events include maple sugaring (March), Hawks Weekend (September), and Honey Harvest (October). Visitor center and buildings (Wed-Sun 10 am-5 pm) **$**

Blue Man Group. *74 Warrenton St, Boston (02116). Phone 617/931-2787 (tickets). www.blueman.com.* Blue Man Group is a percussion (drums) band and performance group that's literally blue—all three members cover themselves in blue body paint. The group performs by thumping on drums, banging on barrels, and pounding on pipes. The heart-pounding, entertaining, dramatic performance includes audience members (although no one is forced to participate against his will); if you so choose, you may even get painted, too! Performances last just over two hours. (Closed Mon-Tues) **$$$$**

Boston African American National Historic Site. *46 Joy St, Boston (02114). Smith Ct, off Joy St on Beacon Hill. Phone 617/742-5415. www.nps.gov/boaf.* Includes **African Meeting House.** Part of the Museum of Afro-American History. Built by free black Bostonians in 1806, the building was an educational and religious center and site of the founding of the New England Anti-Slavery Society in 1832. (May-Sept, daily; rest of year, Mon-Sat) Thirty-minute tour (Memorial Day-Labor Day: Mon-Sat; rest of year: by appointment) of Meeting House by museum staff. **FREE** Meeting house is the starting point for

Black Heritage Trail. *Boston. Phone 617/742-5415.* Marked walking tour conducted by the National Park Service, past sites in the Beacon Hill section that relate the history of 19th-century black Boston. Brochure and maps are at National Park Visitor Center. Two-hour guided tours by National Park Service (by appointment). **FREE**

Boston Ballet. *270 Tremont St, Boston (02116). Phone 617/695-6955. www.bostonballet.com.* A delight for children and adults, the Boston Ballet offers classic and more contemporary performances by a company of some of the finest dancers in the world. If you're visiting Boston in late November or December, don't miss *The Nutcracker,* performed annually before more than 140,000 people, the largest audience for a ballet production in the world. (Performances held Oct-May) **$$$$**

Boston Beer Museum. *30 Germania St, Jamaica Plain (02130). Take the Orange Line ("T") to the Stony Brook stop. Phone 617/522-9080.* Take a tour of the Boston Beer Museum (formerly the Haffenreffer Brewery) and discover the critical details of the brewing process. And check out all the museum's artifacts, which span two centuries of brewing. At the end of the tour, you're offered a sampling of Samuel Adams beers, the host company of the museum. (Tours Thurs-Sat) **$**

Boston Breakers. *Boston University, 200 Highland Ave, 4th Floor, Needham (02494). Harry Agganis Way at Commonwealth Ave. Take the Green Line B to the Pleasant St stop. Phone 617/931-2000 (tickets). www.bostonbreakers.com.* The professional women's soccer team in the Boston area plays at Nickerson Field at Boston University. Unlike some professional sports that pay extraordinary base salaries that can lead to isolation among players, Breakers players are extremely accessible, offering autographs, appearing at youth soccer clinics and camps, and spending time in the community to promote the sport. (Closed Apr-Sept)

Boston Bruins (NHL). *Fleet Center, One Fleet Center Pl, Boston (02114). Take the Green/Orange Line (the "T") to North Station. Phone 617/624-1000. www.bostonbruins.com.* The Bruins are one of the great hockey traditions in the NHL; in fact, the team was one of the original six teams in the league. In the early 1940s, the Bruins won back-to-back Stanley Cup championships, and the team won the Cup again 30 years later, when Bobby Orr scored a game-winning goal in overtime. Today, you can spend an exciting evening of Bruins hockey with family or friends; if you like to see a lot of body checking, try to get a seat as close to the ice as you can afford on one of the four corners of the rink. If you can manage the high price tag, pick up a Bobby Orr game sweater at the Bruins gift shop. **$$$$**

Boston by Little Feet. *1 Faneuil Hall Sq, Boston (02114). Phone 617/367-2345. www.bostonbyfoot.com.* Designed especially for 6- to 12-year-olds (accompanied by an adult), Boston by Little Feet is a 60-minute walking tour that follows the Freedom Trail and explores local architecture and history. You can

take the tour regardless of the weather, but be sure to bring rain boots and an umbrella during inclement weather. Every young walker gets a free Explorer's Map and Guide. (May-Oct, Sat-Mon; closed Nov-Apr) **$$**

Boston Celtics (NBA). *Fleet Center, One Fleet Center Pl, Boston (02114). Take the Green/Orange Line (the "T") to North Station. Phone 617/624-1000. www.nba.com/celtics.* The Celtics were more of a must-see tourist attraction when they played in Boston Garden. Today, playing at the Fleet Center, the Celts seem less impressive. Still, with 16 NBA championships notched in its belt, the team boasts more NBA titles than any other franchise. (Oct-June). **$$$$**

Boston College. *140 Commonwealth Ave, Chestnut Hill (02467). (1863) (14,500 students)* On campus is

Bapst Library. *Phone 617/552-3200.* English Collegiate Gothic building with fine stained glass. Rare books display; changing exhibits. (Summer, Mon-Fri; rest of year, daily)

Boston College Football. *At Alumni Stadium. Phone 617/552-3000.* Although Boston College hasn't won a national championship since 1940, as the only Division I-A football team in the area, BC football remains a fall tradition in Boston. Tickets can be difficult to obtain as game day nears, so plan to buy your tickets online ahead of time. Keep yourself entertained before the game by spotting the BC superfans—students and alums who paint their bodies, wear multicolored wigs, and carry in-your-face signs meant for TV cameras. (Weekends in fall) **$$$$**

Boston Common. *Beacon and Tremont sts, Boston (02108). Take the Red or Green Line ("T") to Park St.* As the oldest public park in the United States, Boston Common is steeped in history. Established in 1640, Bostonians used the Common as a pasture for grazing their cattle; later, the colonial militia used it to train soldiers, and it even served as a British military camp. Colonists gathered to hear speeches, witness public hangings, and watch spirited fencing duels. Today, the Common's 45 acres are still a vibrant center of the city—a perfect place to stroll, in-line skate, play Frisbee, catch a free concert, or enjoy a picnic (watch out for dog droppings, however). The park is a perfect place to begin walking the Freedom Trail; the park itself is loaded with signs, plaques, and monuments, most notably that of Robert Gould Shaw, who led the Union Army's 54th Massachusetts Colored Regiment, the first all-black army unit in the United States. (Daily) **FREE** Also here are

Boston Common Frog Pond Rink. *Phone 617/635-2120.* Ice skating abounds each winter in Boston, with outdoor rinks spread throughout the city. Frog Pond, the largest of these rinks, is a natural mud pond on Boston Common during spring, summer, and fall. From November to March, however, the city transforms the wading pool into an enormous outdoor skating rink and maintains it all winter, regardless of the weather. At the rink, you can rent skates ($), get the feeling back in your toes by standing in the warming room, and use the public rest room. Other skating rinks in the area—all of which are free—include Bajko Memorial Rink (Boston), Turtle Pond Parkway, phone 617/364-9188; Devine Memorial Rink (Boston), Morrissey Blvd, phone 617/436-4356; Porazzo Memorial Rink (Boston), Constitution Beach, phone 617/567-9571; and Simoni Memorial Rink (Cambridge), Gore St, phone 617/354-9523. (Mid-Nov-mid-Mar daily; closed in spring, summer, and fall) **$**

Central Burying Ground. *Boylston and Tremont sts, Boston (02116).* The grave of Gilbert Stuart, the painter, is here; technically not a part of the Common, although it's in it.

Swan Boats/Boston Public Garden. *Arlington, Boylston, Charles, and Beacon sts, Boston (02108). Take the Green Line to Arlington Station. Phone 617/522-1966. www.swanboats.com.* The launching point for the swan boats is the Boston Public Garden (daily), the first botanical garden in the United States, with 24 acres featuring a splendid variety of flowers and ornamental shrubs that bloom from early April until mid-October. Entry to the Public Garden is free. Each swan boat, so named because it's decorated with a larger-than-life swan, operates by pedal power (the driver's, not yours) for a 15-minute ride around the Public Garden Lagoon. (Daily) **$**

Boston Harbor Islands National Recreation Area. *Building 45, 349 Lincoln St, Hingham (02043). 45 minutes from downtown Boston via ferry. Phone 781/740-1605. www.state.ma.us/dem/parks/bhis.htm.* The Boston Harbor Islands national park area encompasses several islands in Boston Harbor. Take the ferry to Georges Island (phone 617/227-4321); from there, a free water taxi sails you to Lovells, Peddocks, Gallops, Grape, and Bumpkin islands. The islands

boast sand dunes, a freshwater pond, and unique wildlife habitats. Camp on Lovells Island (the only island that allows swimming) and Peddocks Island (the largest at 134 acres) by petitioning in writing for a permit from the Metropolitan District Commission; write to MDC Reservations and Historic Sites, 98 Taylor St, Dorchester, MA 02122. Note that sites don't have electricity; you must carry in your own fresh water; and you're responsible for carrying out your trash when you leave. (May-mid-Oct) **FREE**

Boston Massacre Monument. *206 Washington St, Boston (02109).* Commemorates this 1770 event, which has been called the origin of the Revolution.

Boston Public Library. *700 Boylston St, Boston (02116). Phone 617/536-5400. www.bpl.org.* (1895) This Italian Renaissance building by Charles McKim includes a central courtyard and fountain. Mural decorations, bronze doors, sculpture. Contemporary addition (1972), by Philip Johnson, houses large circulating library, recordings, and films. Film and author programs; exhibits. Central Library (Mon-Thurs 9 am-9 pm; Fri-Sat 9 am-5 pm)

Boston Red Sox (MLB). *Fenway Park, 4 Yawkey Way, Boston (02215). Near Brookline Ave; take the Green Line (the "T" or subway) to Kenmore or Fenway. Phone 617/482-4769 (tickets). www.redsox.mlb.com.* Going to Fenway isn't just about watching men play baseball; it's about steeping yourself in the tradition of one of the finest ball clubs in history. Fenway, built in 1901, is home of the Green Monster, the 37-foot, left-field wall where balls disappear in blazing green reflections. Cy Young pitched a perfect game at Fenway in 1904, and in 1914, young Babe Ruth came to play for the Sox. Since the Red Sox first began wearing numbers on their uniforms in 1931, the team has retired the uniforms of five players: Joe Cronin, Ted Williams, Bobby Doerr, Carl Yastremski, and Carlton Fisk. (Mar-Oct) **$$$$**

Boston Symphony Orchestra/Boston Pops. *301 Massachusetts Ave, Boston (02115). Phone 617/266-1492. www.bso.org.* Symphony Hall, with its perfect acoustics, is home to both the Boston Symphony Orchestra (BSO) and the Boston Pops (a livelier version of the symphony), both of which are world-class orchestras. If the pricey tickets (up to $120) are an obstacle, stop by the box office at 9 am Friday or 5 pm Tuesday or Thursday—you may be able to pick up a special ticket for just $8, although it certainly won't be the best seat in the house. The Boston Pops also give free outdoor concerts in the Hatch Shell Amphitheater on the Esplanade during Harborfest on the Fourth of July. If you're not in town while either orchestra is playing, find out which musical act is playing at Symphony Hall so that you can appreciate its terrific design. (BSO performances Oct-Apr; Pops performances May-early July, mid- to late Dec) **$$$$**

Boston Tea Party Ship and Museum. *300 Congress St, Boston (02210). Between Congress St Bridge and Northern Ave Bridge, opposite Fan Pier. Phone 617/338-1773. www.bostonteapartyship.com.* The Boston Tea Party Ship is a replica of one of the three tea ships docked in the harbor the night of the Boston Tea Party; dumping the tea overboard from these ships was one of the triggers of the Revolutionary War. Note that the Boston Tea Party Ship and Museum suffered serious fire damage in 2001 and, as of this writing, had not yet reopened. Continue checking the museum's Web site for updates. (Daily; closed Thanksgiving, Dec-late Feb) **$$**

Boston Tours from Suburban Hotels. *56 Williams St, Waltham (02453). Phone 781/899-1454 (reservations, schedule, and fee information).* Escorted bus tours departing from suburban hotels and motels along I-95/Hwy 128. Also departures from metrowest suburban hotels in Natick/Framingham area. Tours follow the Freedom Trail and include stops at Old North Church, "Old Ironsides," Faneuil Hall Marketplace, and Cambridge. Six-hour tour (daily). **$$$$**

Boston University. *595 Commonwealth Ave, Boston (02115). Phone 617/353-2300 (tours). www.bu.edu.* (1839) (28,000 students) The information center is located at 771 Commonwealth Avenue in the George Sherman Union. Also located here is the George Sherman Union Gallery. Mugar Memorial Library houses papers of Dr. Martin Luther King Jr., as well as those of Robert Frost, Isaac Asimov, and other writers and artists. Boston University Art Gallery exhibits at the School for the Arts, 855 Commonwealth Avenue. Campus tours from the Admissions Office, 121 Bay State Road.

BostonWalks. *Phone 617/489-5020. bostonwalks.tripod .com.* Although several groups offer guided tours of Boston, those arranged by BostonWalks are among the most unique. Nearly every guided-tour company, including BostonWalks, offers historical tours, but where else can you find walking and biking tours of churches and synagogues, unique ethnic areas, universities, medical areas, high-tech areas, and Boston's delightful neighborhoods? Groups must include 15

to 55 participants, and tours last two to three hours. **$$$$**

Boston Women's Heritage Trail. *22 Holbrook St, Boston (02130). Phone 617/522-2872. www.bwht.org.* Women played an essential role in Boston's rich history, yet their contributions were often overlooked. The Boston Women's Heritage Trail (BWHT) leads you through Boston's historical, cultural, religious, and scientific sites, highlighting the critical part that women played in each. To walk the entire trail may take several days, but you can walk a portion of the trail and visit only the sites that interest you in just an hour or two. **FREE**

Brush Hill Tours. *14 Charles St S, Boston (02116). Phone 781/986-6100.; toll-free 800/343-1328. www.brushhilltours.com.* Fully lectured three-hour bus tours of Boston/Cambridge (late Mar-mid-Nov); 1/2-day tours of Lexington/Concord, Salem/Marblehead (mid-June-Oct), and Plymouth (May-Oct); full-day tours of Cape Cod (includes Provincetown) and Newport, Rhode Island (June-Sept). Also 1 1/2-hour tours along Freedom Trail aboard the Beantown Trolleys. Departures from major downtown hotels, Copley Square, and Boston Common (daily). **$$$$**

Charles River Pathway (the Esplanade). *Take the Red Line ("T") to the Charles/MGHT stop.* The Charles River Pathway, a flat, smooth asphalt surface, extends

---

Boston Fun Facts

- Boston boasts the nation's first subway, built in 1897.

- The Boston University Bridge (on Commonwealth Avenue) is the only place in the world where a boat can sail under a train driving under a car driving under an airplane.

- Boston Common became the first public park in 1634.

- The first post office, free public school, and public library were all founded in Boston.

---

18 miles along the Charles River, connecting Boston and Cambridge and ending in Watertown. The view of the Charles River is stunning, and at certain times of the year you may see university crew teams training. Use the trail to run or walk, joining the hundreds

of Bostonians who train there daily. To bike the path, rent a bike at Back Bay Bikes & Boards (Boston), 336 Commonwealth Ave, phone 617/247-2336, www.backbaybicycles.com; Community Bicycle Supply (Boston), 496 Tremont St, phone 617/542-8623, www.communitybicycle.com; Cambridge Bicycle (Cambridge), 259 Massachusetts Ave, phone 617/876-6555; or Ata Cycle (Cambridge), 1773 Massachusetts Ave, phone 617/354-0907, www.atabike .com. The trail is also perfect for in-line skating, even if you're a novice. Rent blades at Beacon Hill Skate Shop (Boston), 135 Charles St, phone 617/482-7400; or Blades Board & Skate, with locations in Boston and Cambridge, phone 617/437-6300, www.blades.com. (Always open) **FREE**

⭐ **Children's Museum of Boston.** *300 Congress St, Boston (02110). Phone 617/426-8855. www.bostonkids .org.* Advertised as "Boston's best place for kids 0-10," the Children's Museum lives up to its billing with interactive exhibits that highlight science, technology, art, and culture. Exhibitions range from re-creations of favorite kids' stories, a kid-size construction site, and a messy artist studio to performances on Kid-Stage, a Latin American supermarket, a real loom and weaving area, a full-size wigwam, and a rock climbing area. Offerings change periodically, and three or four are always housed outdoors in the Science Playground. Each Friday from 3 to 5 pm and Saturday and Sunday from 2 to 4 pm, take the ZOOMSci challenge at the ZOOM Zone within the museum: you solve puzzles and work through a variety of math challenges. Note that admission is just $1 on Fridays from 5 to 9 pm. Plan on at least half a day. (Sat-Thurs 10 am-5 pm, Fri 10 am-9 pm; closed Thanksgiving, Dec 25) **$$**

Community Boating, Inc. *21 David Mugar Way, Boston (02114). Embankment Rd on the Charles River Esplanade between the Hatch Shell and the Longfellow Bridge. Phone 617/523-7406. www.community-boating.org.* Whether you're an experienced sailor or have always wanted to learn, you can spend a day or two sailing while in Boston. Community Boating runs the largest and oldest public sailing program in the country. Purchasing a two-day membership allows you unlimited use of boats and sailing instruction, along with windsurfing and kayaking. Also check out Boston Sailing Center, Lewis Wharf, phone 617/227-4198, www.bostonsailingcenter.com, which is more expensive but is open year-round, even in the chilliest weather. (Apr-Nov, daily; closed Dec-Mar) **$$$$**

Copley Place. *100 Huntington Ave, Boston (02116). Phone 617/369-5000. www.shopcopleyplace.com.* With more than 100 stores and a glass atrium in a beautiful setting, Copley Place is all about upscale, including names like Neiman Marcus, Louis Vuitton, Christian Dior, and Gucci. If you're looking for dinner and a movie, Copley Place fills that bill, too, with ten restaurants and an 11-screen theater. (Daily)

Duck Tours. *790 Boylston St, Boston (02199). Phone toll-free 800/226-7442. www.bostonducktours.com.* Boston Duck Tours take you from land to sea in a World War II half-boat, half-truck vehicle known as a Duck. Your conDUCKtor starts the 80-minute tour on land, leading you past Boston Common, the golden-domed State House, Public Gardens, the Big Dig, Faneuil Hall Marketplace, Boston's North End, Government Center, Copley Square, Prudential Tower, Newbury Street, Bunker Hill, and the Fleet Center. The Duck then transforms into an amphibious vehicle and dives into the Charles River for more sightseeing. (Apr-Nov; on the hour from 9 am to one hour before sunset) **$$$$**

Fenway Park Tours. *Fenway Park, 4 Yawkey Way, Boston (02215). Phone 617/236-6666. boston.redsox. mlb.com.* Take a tour of Fenway Park, not only the oldest park in Major League Baseball but also the most charming. Soak in over 100 years of Red Sox history and tradition as you stroll next to the famous Green Monster (Fenway's 37-foot left-field wall that obscures even the easiest pop-ups), take a tour of the press box, and stand on the warning track. The brick stadium is aging by today's standards—views are obstructed, seats are small, and plush boxes are rare—so it, too, will likely be torn down to make way for a new one. Take a tour while you still can. (Daily 9 am-4 pm) **$$$**

Filene's Basement. *426 Washington St, Boston (02108). Take the Red or Orange Line ("T") to the Downtown Crossing stop. Phone 617/348-7974. www.filenesbasement.com.* Located directly beneath Filene's Department Store, the Basement is famous for its automatic markdowns: after two weeks at full price, merchandise falls by percentages until, five weeks later, it's 75 percent off. (Any unsold merchandise is then given to charity.) Filene's Basement is also the site of an annual wedding gown sale—brides-to-be race each other to racks in the hopes of finding the right dress for a fraction of its retail price. (Mon-Fri 9:30 am-8 pm, Sat 9 am-8 pm, Sun 11 am-7 pm; closed Easter, Thanksgiving, Dec 25)

Franklin Park Golf Course (William J. Devine Golf Course). *1 Circuit Dr, Dorchester (02121). Take the Orange Line ("T") to Forest Hills Station and board the #16 bus, which has a stop right along the parking lot. Phone 617/265-4084. www.sterlinggolf.com.* This 6,009-yard, par-70 golf course lies within Boston's city limits and is the second-oldest public golf course in the United States. Rates are reasonable, especially for kids under 18, and club rentals are just $10. The course is wide open but demanding, with some steep hills. Gram Slam winner Bobby Jones practiced at Franklin Park when he was a student at Harvard. (Daily dawn-dusk; closed for snow and inclement weather) **$$$$**

Franklin Park Zoo. *1 Franklin Park Rd, Dorchester (02121). S on Jamaicaway, E on Hwy 203. Phone 617/541-5466. www.zoonewengland.org.* "Bird's World" indoor/outdoor aviary complex with natural habitats; African tropical forest; hilltop range with camels, antelopes, zebras, mouflon; children's zoo. (Daily; closed Jan 1, Thanksgiving, Dec 25) **$$**

Frederick Law Olmsted National Historic Site. *99 Warren St, Brookline (02445). Phone 617/566-1689. www.nps.gov/frla.* Former home and office of the founder of landscape architecture in America. Site archives contain documentation of the firm's work. Also here are landscaped grounds designed by Olmsted. Guided tours of historic offices. (Fri-Sun)

⭐ **Freedom Trail.** *Phone 617/242-5642. www.the freedomtrail.org.* This two- or three-hour walking tour takes you past Boston's most famous historical sites while also meandering through the city's vibrant neighborhoods. The Freedom Trail begins at Boston Common (see) and ends at the Bunker Hill Monument, with more than a dozen sites in between. Red bricks or red paint mark the trail, which you can follow on your own (free brochures are available) or with guided assistance. Purchase the official Freedom Trail Guidebook ($$) as your step-by-step guide, travel with earphones and take an audio tour ($$$), or take a guided tour that's led by historic characters in costume ($$$). Dress appropriately—the weather in Boston can change rapidly. **FREE**

State House. *24 Beacon St, Boston (02114). Phone 617/727-3676. www.state.ma.us/sec/trs.* The Massachusetts State House (which replaced the Old State House, next to the site of the Boston Massacre) is an architectural marvel. As you travel around Boston, you can't miss the golden dome (sheathed in 23-carat gold leaf) of the state house that replaced the original copper. Designed by

Charles Bulfinch and built on land owned by John Hancock, patriot Paul Revere, and Governor Samuel Adams laid the cornerstone on July 4, 1795. Tours are free. (Mon-Fri 10 am-3:30 pm; closed state holidays) **FREE**

Park Street Church. *1 Park St, Boston (02108). Phone 617/523-3383. www.parkstreet.org.* (1809) Often called "Brimstone Corner" because brimstone for gunpowder was stored here during the War of 1812. William Lloyd Garrison delivered his first antislavery address here in 1829. (mid-June-Aug, limited hours; Sun services all year)

Granary Burying Ground. *Tremont and Bromfield sts, Boston (02108). Take the "T" to Park St, walk 1 block on Tremont St. Phone 617/635-4505.* Although Granary is Boston's third-oldest cemetery, it is, perhaps, its most famous. Revolutionary War patriots Paul Revere, John Hancock, Samuel Adams, and Peter Faneuil (whose headstone is marked "Peter Funal") all lie here. The name stems from a grain storage building (called a granary) that used to sit nearby. (Daily 9 am-7 pm) **FREE**

King's Chapel and Burying Ground. *58 Tremont St, Boston (02108). Phone 617/227-2155. www.kings-chapel.org.* King's Chapel, started by the Massachusetts Royal Governor who had no desire to worship in a Puritan church, has held church services at its location longer than any other church in the United States. When the congregation outgrew the church in 1754, a new building was erected around the old, which was then dismantled. The Burying Ground next door is the oldest cemetery in Boston. Stop in for concerts on Tuesdays at 12:15 pm and Sundays at 5 pm. (Daily; closed Sun-Fri in winter) **FREE**

Site of the first US free public school. *School St at City Hall Ave, Boston (02108). Blue or Orange Line.* A mosaic in the sidewalk marks the site of the first free US public school. The original building was demolished to make room for the expansion of King's Chapel. The school, now known as the Boston Latin School, was moved across the street.

Statue of Benjamin Franklin. *School St at City Hall Ave, Boston (02108).* This, Boston's first portrait statue, was created by Richard S. Greenough in 1856.

Old South Meeting House. *310 Washington St, Boston (02108). Corner of Washington and Milk sts. Phone 617/482-6439. www.oldsouthmeetinghouse*

.org. Built as a Puritan meeting house (or church), colonists congregated at the Old South Meeting House each year from 1771 to 1775 to mark the death of those killed in the Boston Massacre and listen to speeches by prominent colonists. The most important date in Old South's history, however, is December 16, 1773, when 5,000 colonists gathered at the church to protest the British tax on tea and decide on a course of action. From there, men dressed as Native Americans, snuck onto three ships laden with tea on Griffin's Wharf, and dumped all the tea overboard. Restored in 1997, the church no longer has an active congregation but is still a gathering place for political debate. An interactive exhibit called Voices of Protest recalls the Old South Meeting House's historic legacy. (Daily; closed Jan 1, Thanksgiving, Dec 24-25) **$**

Old State House/Site of Boston Massacre. *206 Washington St, Boston (02108). Phone 617/720-1713. www.bostonhistory.org.* The Old State House (not to be confused with the golden-dome new State House) was originally built as the headquarters of the British government in Boston and is Boston's oldest surviving public building. Inside, the Bostonian Society operates a museum that reflects the prominent role the Old State House played in the American Revolution. The Massachusetts Assembly met there and debated political issues in front of all citizens who wanted to observe. After these issues were decided, politicians read summaries—including the Declaration of Independence on July 18, 1776—from the House's balcony. The balcony hovers above the spot where the Boston Massacre occurred in 1770, when British troops shot into a crowd that had gathered to hear a proclamation. There, in a small triangle surrounded by dense city traffic, the site of the massacre is marked with a circle of paving stones. Plan on one hour for a tour. (Daily 9 am-5 pm; closed Jan 1, Thanksgiving, Dec 25) **$**

Faneuil Hall Marketplace. *4 S Market Bldg, 5th Fl, Boston (02109). Take the Blue or Green Line ("T") to Government Center, then walk across the plaza, down the long set of stairs, and across busy Congress St. Phone 617/523-1300. www.faneuilhallmarketplace.com.* Faneuil Hall Marketplace offers the best variety of shops and kiosks in Boston, housed in five buildings and several plazas. The central building, Quincy Market, is filled with dining options, from coffee to seafood and everything in between; many are open earlier and later than the shops.

Look for delightful street performers even in winter months, and especially the rest of the year. Faneuil Hall (pronounced FAN-yal or FAN-yoo-ul) is more than just a shopping center: it has operated as a local marketplace since 1742, when wealthy merchant Peter Faneuil built and donated the marketplace to the city. The Hall is remembered as the site of town meetings that produced the policy of "no taxation without representation." Listen to a historical talk every half hour from 9:30 am to 4:30 pm in the second-floor auditorium. (Daily; closed Thanksgiving, Dec 25)

Paul Revere House. *19 North Sq, Boston (02113). Phone 617/523-2338. www.paulreverehouse.org.* Built in 1680 and well preserved today, the Paul Revere House is Boston's oldest building and includes authentic furnishings from the Revere family. This historical landmark offers a rare glimpse at colonial life, because few other houses from the period survived remodeling, fire damage, and demolition. At his house, Paul Revere plied his silversmith trade and sold his wares, often in exchange for food or livestock when case-strapped colonists couldn't pay. Although a staunch patriot, Revere was largely undistinguished among Sam Adams, John Hancock, and Ben Franklin. However, Revere's successful ride to Lexington and Concord on April 18, 1775, to warn of the approaching British army—a feat immortalized in Henry Wadsworth Longfellow's poem, "The Midnight Ride of Paul Revere"—made him one of the best-known American historic figures. (Mid-Apr-late Oct: daily 9:30 am-5:15 pm; early Nov-mid-Apr: daily 9:30 am-4:15 pm; closed Jan 1, Thanksgiving, Dec 25, Mon in Jan-Mar) **$**

Old North Church. *193 Salem St, Boston (02113). Phone 617/523-6676. www.oldnorth.com.* Old North Church is the oldest church in Boston and continues today as Christ Church, with an Episcopal congregation of 150 members. On April 18, 1775, in the steeple of Old North Church, church sexton Robert Newman hung two lanterns to signal that the British Army was heading up the Charles River to Cambridge in order to march to Lexington and take possession of weapons stored there. When Paul Revere saw the signal, he jumped on his horse and rode to Lexington to warn the militia. The next day, the "shot heard 'round the world" was fired on Lexington Green, officially beginning the Revolutionary War. Sit in one of the box pews and listen to the ten-minute talk about the history of the church; it's free, although donations are gladly accepted. Behind-the-scenes tours and other presentations are available by appointment for a fee. (Daily; closed holidays) **FREE**

Copp's Hill Burying Ground. *Hull and Snow Hill sts, Boston (02113). Take Causeway St to North Washington St. When North Washington becomes Commercial St, walk 2 more blocks, turn right, and climb the hill. Phone 617/635-4505.* Copp's Hill Burying Ground, named after William Copp, who owned the land, is the second-oldest burying ground in Boston. Robert Newman, who hung the lanterns in the steeple of Old North Church, is buried at Copp's Hill, as are the Mather family of Puritan ministers and a host of African Americans from the nearby New Guinea Community, who lie in unmarked graves. (Daily) **FREE**

Bunker Hill Monument. *Monument Sq, Charlestown (02129). Phone 617/242-5641.* Standing 221 feet high (that's 294 steps, with no elevator), the Bunker Hill Monument marks the site of the first major battle of the Revolutionary War on June 17, 1775. It was here that American Colonel William Prescott ordered his troops not to "fire until you see the whites of their eyes," so that no bullets would be wasted. The British won the battle but suffered heavy casualties, and that limited success encouraged the colonists to continue the fight. (Daily) **FREE**

USS *Constitution.* *Charlestown Navy Yard, Boston National Historical Park, Constitution Rd, Boston (02129). I-93 northbound exit 25 and follow signs across Charlestown bridge; southbound, exit 28 to Sullivan Sq and follow signs. Phone 617/426-1812. www.ussconstitutionmuseum.org.* The USS *Constitution*, the oldest commissioned warship in the world, got the nickname "Old Ironsides" during the War of 1812. Some 600 miles off the coast of Boston, it engaged the British HMS *Guerriere* in battle; while the *Guerriere* was so badly damaged that it had to be sunk and its crew rescued, cannonballs merely bounced off the *Constitution's* sides, as if they were "made of iron," although they were actually made of three layers of oak. In 1830, the ship was saved from the scrap heap because of public response to Oliver Wendell Holmes's poem "Old Ironsides." It was restored in 1925 and today is available for daily tours. The museum next door offers hands-on exhibits, historic displays, and

reenactments. (May-September: daily 9 am-6 pm, Oct-Apr: daily 10 am-5 pm)

Gibson House Museum. *137 Beacon St, Boston (02116). Phone 617/267-6338. www.thegibsonhouse.org.* Victorian townhouse with period furnishings. Tours (Wed-Sun afternoons; closed holidays). **$$**

Guided Walking Tours. Boston by Foot. *77 N Washington St, Boston (02113). Hull and Snow Hill sts. Phone 617/367-2345.* Ninety-minute architectural walking tours includes the heart of the Freedom Trail (daily); Beacon Hill (daily, departures vary); Victorian Back Bay Tour (Fri-Sun); North End (Fri-Sat); children's tour (daily); downtown Boston (Sun). All tours (May-Oct). Tour of the month each fourth Sun; custom tours. **$$$**

Guild of Boston Artists. *162 Newbury St, Boston (02116). Phone 617/536-7660.* Changing exhibits of paintings, graphics, and sculpture by New England artists. (Tues-Sat 10:30 am-5:30 pm; closed Jan 1, Thanksgiving, Dec 25) **FREE**

Harborwalk. *www.bostonharborwalk.com.* A blue line guides visitors from the Old State House to the New England Aquarium, ending at the Boston Tea Party Ship and Museum, forming a walking tour with many stops in between.

Harrison Gray Otis House. *141 Cambridge St, Boston (02114). Enter from Lynde St. Phone 617/227-3956.* (1796) Otis, a lawyer and statesman, built this first of three houses designed for him by Charles Bulfinch. A later move to Beacon Hill left this house as a rooming house for 100 years. Restored to reflect Boston taste and decoration of 1796-1820. Some family furnishings are present. The house reflects the proportion and delicate detail Bulfinch introduced to Boston, strongly influencing the Federal style in New England. Museum. The headquarters for the Society for the Preservation of New England Antiquities is located here. Tours (Wed-Sun 11 am-4:40 pm). **$$**

Harvard Medical Area. *Huntington and Longwood aves, Cambridge (02115). Phone 617/432-1000.* One of the world's great centers of medicine.

Haymarket. *Blackstone St, off I-93, Boston (02109). Around the corner from Faneuil Hall Marketplace; take the Orange or Green line to the Haymarket stop.* Rain or shine, winter or summer, Bostonians flock to Haymarket for the freshest fruits, vegetables, and seafood you've ever seen. If you do your shopping in a grocery store back home, you won't believe the differences in price (far lower) and quality (much higher) here. The market is bustling with lively scents and sounds, including languages from around the world. Haggling is the norm and remains friendly—you'll want three yellow peppers for $1, and the vendor will want to sell you six for $2. Start your day at Haymarket, buying a few pieces of fruit to snack on, and then meander through the city or walk the Freedom Trail. (Fri-Sat) **FREE**

Institute of Contemporary Art. *955 Boylston St, Boston (02115). Opposite Prudential Center. Phone 617/266-5152. www.icaboston.org.* The Institute of Contemporary Art offers some of the world's finest modern art exhibits. Because no collection is permanent, every trip to the Institute is likely to be different from the last. Note that museum admission is free every Thursday after 5 pm, as is the *Viewpoints* series, held at 6:30 pm on certain Thursdays, in which artists, staff members, and others speak to visitors about particular works of art. Allow two to four hours for a visit. (Tues-Sun; closed Mon, Thanksgiving, Dec 25, Jan 1, between exhibitions) **$$**

Isaac Royall House. *15 George St, Medford (02155). 3/4 mile S off I-93. Phone 781/396-9032.* (1637) Originally built as a four-room farmhouse by John Winthrop, first governor of the Bay State Colony; enlarged in 1732 by Isaac Royall. Example of early Georgian architecture; examples of Queen Anne, Chippendale, and Hepplewhite furnishings. (May-Sept, Wed-Sun) **$$**

Isabella Stewart Gardner Museum. *280 The Fenway, Boston (02115). Take the Green Line E ("T") to the Museum stop; walk 2 blocks straight ahead. Phone 617/566-1401. www.gardnermuseum.com.* The Gardner Museum is housed in the 19th-century home of Isabella Stewart Gardner that itself is a work of art. The collections include masterpieces from around the world—both paintings and sculptures—that are displayed year-round, and special exhibits are installed from time to time. You can spend from two hours to half a day at the museum. On weekends in fall, winter, and spring, look for free afternoon concerts. (Tues-Sun; concerts late Sept-May; closed Thanksgiving, Dec 25) **$$$**

Kitchen Arts. *161 Newbury St, Boston (02116). Phone 617/266-8701.* Dubbed "a hardware store for cooks," Kitchen Arts isn't just any cooking store: it's the best-stocked cooking store you'll likely ever find—an absolute foodie's paradise. You'll find everything you see in ordinary culinary stores—pots and pans, mixing bowls, appliances, kitchen tools, knives, measur-

ing cups, cutting boards, spatulas—but a greater variety and a much wider selection than anywhere else. (Mon-Sat 10 am-6 pm, Sun noon-5 pm; closed holidays)

L'Arte Di Cucinare. *6 Charter St, Boston (02113). Take the Green Line ("T") to Haymarket Station and walk beneath the Expressway to Salem St. Phone 617/523-6032; fax 617/367-2185. www.cucinare.com.* Michele Topor, a 30-year resident of the North End and a passionate gourmet chef herself, takes you on a 3 1/2-hour tour of the North End markets, where you taste a delicious variety of local foods in a historic setting (the North End is Boston's oldest neighborhood). You're introduced to shopkeepers and chefs throughout your tour and hear fascinating recipes and ideas for food selection. You can also arrange for special tours: 2 hours instead of 3 1/2, a morning tour with cappuccino and pastries, an olive-oil and balsamic-vinegar-tasting tour, an Italian regional dinner tour at North End restaurants, or anything else you can dream up. Reservations are required, and each tour is limited to 13 people. (Wed, Fri-Sat) **$$$$**

Louis Boston. *234 Berkeley St, Boston (02116). Phone 617/262-6100; toll-free 800/225-5135. www.louisboston.com.* Louis Boston is about as upscale as upscale gets; in fact, this men's and women's clothing store is considered among the finest in the world. The 140-year-old building is an architectural delight: it once housed the New England Museum of Natural History. Although Louis Boston has been at the location only since 1989, the company dates back to the late 1800s. The building also houses a café and a salon. (Mon-Wed 10 am-6 pm, Thurs-Sat 10 am-7 pm; closed Thanksgiving, Dec 25)

Louisburg Square. *Beacon Hill, Boston.* This lovely little residential square with its central park is the ultimate in traditional Boston charm. Louisa May Alcott, William Dean Howells, and other famous Bostonians have lived here. It is one of the most treasured spots in Boston. Christmas caroling is traditional here.

Make Way for Ducklings Tour. *99 Bedford St, Boston (02111). Phone 617/426-1885. www.historic-neighborhoods.org.* When Robert McCloskey wrote *Make Way for Ducklings* in 1940, he described two duck parents, Mr. and Mrs. Mallard, trying to find the perfect spot in which to raise their family. After the fictional duck family toured Boston's well-known sites, they settled in Boston's Public Garden, and Bostonians have been in love with this Caldecott-winning children's book ever since. Now you can re-create the duck's route via the Make Way for Ducklings tour, although you must make reservations in advance. Take advantage of other duckling events, such as the fancy and expensive Ducklings Day Tea held in April (reservations required) and the Ducklings Day Parade that begins at 1 pm on Mother's Day at Boston Common—children come to the parade dressed as their favorite characters from the story. **$$**

MDC Memorial Hatch Shell. *On the Charles River, between Storrow Dr and the water. www.mass.gov/dcr/ hatch_events.htm.* Packing as much as possible into the three months of the summer tourist season, the MDC Memorial Hatch Shell offers free entertainment nearly every night of the week. Offerings range from dance performances to rock concerts by big-name bands to a Boston Pops concerts sometime around the Fourth of July. Enjoy Free Friday Flicks throughout the summer; although the offerings are those that you'd find on DVD (either recent releases or classics), the movies somehow look better on the big screen. Bring a blanket to sit on, a picnic dinner to munch on, and a sweater to ward off cool river breezes. (Early June-early Sept) **FREE**

Minuteman Commuter Bikeway. *Begins near Alewife ("T") station, goes through Lexington and Arlington, and ends at Bedford (note that you can't bring a bike on the "T" during rush hour) www.minutemanbikeway.org.* This 11-mile bike path looks like a miniature highway (but without the cars, of course), complete with on- and off-ramps, a center line, and traffic signs. The trail mimics portions of Paul Revere's famous ride, so you can stop off for a break from riding at the battleground at Battle Green and historic park at Lexington Center. The path mingles with the Great Meadows Wildlife Refuge for a time. In winter, the bikeway opens for cross-country skiing. (Daily) **FREE**

Mother Church, the First Church of Christ, Scientist. *Christian Science Center, Huntington and Massachusetts aves, Boston (02115). Phone 617/450-3793. www.tfccs.com.* (Daily; closed holidays) Adjacent is

> **Christian Science Publishing Society.** *175 Huntington Ave, Boston (02115). Phone 617/450-3793. (The Christian Science Monitor)* Mapparium, a walk-through stained-glass globe, is here. Call ahead.

⭐ **Museum at the John Fitzgerald Kennedy Library.** *5 miles SE on I-93, off exit 15, at University of*

Massachusetts Columbia Point campus (02125). Phone 617/514-1600; toll-free 866/535-1960. www.jfklibrary.org. Designed by I. M. Pei, the library is considered one of the most beautiful contemporary works of architecture in the country. The library tower houses a collection of documents from the Kennedy administration as well as audiovisual programs designed to re-create the era. (Daily 9 am-5 pm; closed Jan 1, Thanksgiving, Dec 25) Picnic facilities on oceanfront. **$$**

Museum of Afro American History/Black Heritage Trail. *46 Joy St, Boston (02108). The self-guided trail begins at the Robert Gould Shaw/45th Massachusetts Regiment Memorial on Beacon Hill. Phone 617/725-0022. www.afroammuseum.org.* The Museum of Afro American History (MAAH) preserves and exhibits the contributions of African-American Bostonians and New Englanders during colonial settlement and the Revolutionary War. The museum also features workshops for kids and adults, a public lecture series, storytelling for children, and poet and author visits. The Black Heritage Trail explores stops on the Underground Railroad; Phillip's School, one of Boston's first integrated public schools; African American churches, in which, unlike other churches in the area, members could sit on the main level during services and participate in church business; and historic homes of prominent African-American leaders. Guided walking tours are offered daily throughout the summer and at other times by request. (Mon-Sat 10 am-4 pm; closed Jan 1, Thanksgiving, Dec 25) **FREE**

Museum of Fine Arts. *465 Huntington Ave, Boston (02115). Take the Green Line E. Phone 617/267-9300. www.mfa.org.* The Museum of Fine Arts (MFA) is a rare treasure, even if art museums have never been your favorite tourist spots. The vast number of collections are unique, combining classic and contemporary art with ancient artifacts. To see everything the museum has to offer takes from a half to a full day. If the museum seems intimidating, try taking a free guided tour before heading off to see what interests you. If you're hoping to see a particular exhibit, check the Web site before leaving on your trip. Note that from 4 pm to closing on Wednesdays, admission is free, although a $14 contribution is suggested. Also on Wednesday evenings throughout the summer, the MFA hosts courtyard concerts. (Mon-Tues and Sat-Sun 10 am-4:45 pm, Wed-Fri to 9:45 pm) **$$$**

Museum of Science. *Science Park, Charles River Dam and Storrow Dr, Boston (02114). Take the Lechmere Green Line to the Science Park stop. Phone 617/723-2500. www.mos.org.* The Museum of Science blends science with entertainment that the whole family can enjoy. Exhibitions range from a T. Rex model (complete with 58 teeth), presentations with live animals at the Wright Theater, a chick hatchery, and a beautiful lighthouse that explains light, optics, and color. One exhibit, called "Where in the world are you?" allows visitors to enter clue-filled geographic areas and make educated guesses about where they are. Another exhibit, Cahner's ComputerPlace, features a gallery of the most effective software for kids. While visiting Boston, the city of Ben Franklin's youth, visit the museum's Theater of Electricity for presentations about lightning and electrical currents. The museum also sponsors a Community Solar System, a scale-model solar system that includes a model of Mercury in the museum and one of Pluto all the way across Boston at the Riverside T stop. You can easily spend half a day at this museum. (Sat-Thurs 9 am-5 pm, Fri to 9 pm; closed Thanksgiving, Dec 25) **$$$** Also here is

> **Charles Hayden Planetarium.** *Phone 617/523-6664.* Shows are approximately 50 minutes. (Same hours as museum) Children under 4 years not admitted. **$$$**

Newbury Street. *1-361 Newbury St, Boston (02116). www.newbury-st.com.* If you're a shop-a-holic, Newbury Street's eight blocks between Arlington Street and Massachusetts Avenue are a must-stop during your Boston vacation. Shops and galleries—from clothing to antiques to art galleries—tend to be pricey, so you may want to plan to window-shop only. Special finds include the Society of Arts and Crafts (glassware, jewelry), Simeon Pearce (glassware), Kitchen Arts (gourmet kitchen supplies), and the Avenue Victor Hugo Bookshop. In fair weather, get a bite to eat at a café with outdoor seating and people-watch for an afternoon. Also consider visiting at Christmas, when the street lights up with decorations, music, and food.

New England Aquarium. *Central Wharf, Boston (02110). Near Faneuil Hall Marketplace. Phone 617/973-5200. www.neaq.org.* Boston's Central Wharf houses the New England Aquarium, which boasts a colorful array of dolphins, sea lions, penguins, turtles, sharks, eels, harbor seals, and fish from around the world. You can't miss the bright-red Echo of the Waves sculpture that rotates high above the expansive Aquarium plaza, or the 187,000-gallon Giant Ocean

Tank inside. The Aquarium has an educational and research bent, so ecological and medical exhibits abound, but all the aquatic sights will captivate your entire family. Every 90 minutes, sea lions perform. Kids and adults alike will marvel at aquatic films offered at the Simons IMAX Theater ($$). To get a hands-on look at marine life in Boston Harbor—including taking water samples and hauling in lobster traps—take the Science at Sea harbor tour ($$$), which operates daily except in winter. Plan to spend from a few hours to a full day. (Mon-Fri 9 am-5 pm, Sat-Sun, holidays to 6 pm; closed Thanksgiving, Dec 25) **$$$**

New England Aquarium Whale Watches. *Central Wharf, Boston (02110). Phone 617/973-5206. www.neaq.org/visit/ww.tickets.html.* Stellwagen Bank, 25 miles from Boston, is a terrific area for whale-watching. From Boston, the New England Aquarium's tour takes you out to see to the feeding grounds of a variety of whales, many of which are endangered, and you may see dolphins as well. The tour emphasizes education—it puts naturalists on board to teach about whale behavior, allows kids and adults to experiment with hands-on exhibits, and shows films about whale history. Allow four to five hours round-trip. Purchase tickets in advance. Boston Harbor Cruises (phone 617/227-4321; www.bostonharborcruises.com) and Beantown Whale Watch (phone 617/542-8000; www.beantownwhalewatch.com) also operate whale cruises in Boston. (mid-Apr-late Oct; closed Thanksgiving, Dec 25) **$$$$**

Nichols House Museum. *55 Mt. Vernon St, Boston (02108). Phone 617/227-6993. www.nicholshouse museum.org.* (1804) Typical domestic architecture of Beacon Hill from its era; one of two homes on Beacon Hill open to the public. Attributed to Charles Bulfinch; antique furnishings and art from America, Europe, and the Orient from the 17th to early 19th centuries. Collection of Rose Standish Nichols, landscape designer and writer. (May-Oct, Tues-Sat noon-4 pm; Nov-Apr, Thurs-Sat noon-4 pm). **$$**

Old South Church. *645 Boylston St, Boston (02116). Phone 617/536-1970. www.oldsouth.org.* Operating continuously as a church community since 1669, Old South Church began when colonists objected to Massachusetts's requirement that religious dissenters join the First Church of Boston and formed Third Church of Boston (later Old South Church) in protest. The current building—sometimes referred to as New Old South Church—was completed in 1875 in a medieval architectural style that boasts impressive mosaics, stained glass, and cherry woodwork. (Worship held Sun)

Peter L. Stern. *55 Temple Pl, Boston (02111). Phone 617/542-2376. www.abebooks.com/home/plsabe.* Peter L. Stern stocks rare and antique books, including many first editions of 19th- and 20th-century literature, and a full offering of mystery books. If you've never stepped foot inside a rare bookstore before, Stern is a great place to start. Seeing books that have remained intact for nearly 200 years makes a terrific connection with the past, especially in this historic city. (Mon-Fri 9 am-5:30 pm, Sat 9 am-4 pm; closed holidays)

Reel Pursuit Fishing Charters. *28 Constitution Rd, Charlestown (02129). On the Freedom Trail near the Bunker Hill Monument. Phone 617/731-1172. www.bostonfishing.com.* Jump aboard the *Reel Pursuit*, a 34-foot fishing boat that comfortably seats six passengers for a memorable day of fishing striped bass, bluefish, cod, and tuna. You can charter the *Reel Pursuit* for four hours, six hours, an entire day, or a nighttime excursion. The captain and his first mate are seasoned veterans who'll even bait your hook for you, if fishing is new to you, and are more than willing to clean and fillet your catch. Wear boat shoes or other white-soled shoes so as not to scuff the deck, and pack a bag with warm clothes, rain gear, sunscreen, sunglasses, and a hat. **$$$$**

Shirley-Eustis House. *33 Shirley St, Boston (02119). Phone 617/442-2275. www.shirleyeustishouse.org.* (1747) This Georgian-style home, one of only four remaining in the country, was built for British Royal Governor William Shirley and restored to the style of the period when Governor William Eustis lived here from 1818 to 1825. Tours (June-Sept, Tues-Sun; also by appointment)

The Shops at the Pru. *800 Boylston St, Boston (02199). Take the Green Line E ("T") to the Prudential stop. Phone toll-free 800/746-7778. www.prudentialcenter .com.* The presence of Saks Fifth Avenue as the mall's anchor may lead you to believe that The Shops at the Pru are expensive, but they're actually midpriced and very much like those in your local mall at home. The mall connects to Copley Place (see), which is far more upscale. The Prudential Center also boasts the Skywalk ($$), which offers you a panoramic view of the city from the 50th floor. (Daily; closed Jan 1, Easter, Thanksgiving, Dec 25)

Shreve, Crump & Low. *330 Boylston St, Boston (02116). Phone 617/267-9100; toll-free 800/324-0222. www. shrevecrumpandlow.com.* Any store that's more than 200 years old is worth a visit, and Shreve's is no exception. For two centuries, this jewelry store has been selling engagement rings, watches, silver gifts, and estate jewelry. Now the oldest jeweler in the United States, the store also includes the country's oldest antique shop and oldest bridal registry. (Mon-Sat 10 am-5:30 pm, Thurs until 7 pm; closed Sun, holidays)

Suffolk Downs. *111 Waldemar Ave, East Boston (02128). Take the Blue Line (the "T" or subway) to Suffolk Downs station, and then take a shuttle bus or walk for ten minutes. Phone 617/567-3900. www.suffolkdowns.com.* Suffolk Downs, which opened its doors in 1935, is steeped in horse racing history; in fact, Seabiscuit once won at Suffolk. The track offers pari-mutuel betting, which, unlike casino gambling, doesn't involve betting against the house, only against other spectators. The minimum wager per race is $2, and you can place as many bets as you'd like. Even if your horse doesn't come in first, you can still win: simply bet to win (first), place (second), show (third), and so on. Check out the Suffolk Downs Web site (www.suffolkdowns.com) to perfect your horse betting jargon before you go. (Daily; closed Dec 25) **$**

Symphony Hall. *301 Massachusetts Ave, Boston (02115). Huntington and Massachusetts aves. Phone 617/266-1492.* Home of Boston Symphony (late Sept-early May) and Boston Pops (May-mid-July, Tues-Sun).

Tealuxe. *108 Newbury St, Boston (02116). Phone 617/927-0400. www.tealuxe.com.* Tealuxe, a tea lover's utopia, offers more than 100 varieties of tea in its café. The interior architecture is reminiscent of a British estate, and jazz music plays in the background. You can also purchase teas to take home, along with teapots, teacups and mugs, and other tea paraphernalia. Don't let the historical significance of a tea shop in Boston escape you. Also check out a second location at Zero Brattle Street in Cambridge. (Daily; closed Thanksgiving, Dec 25)

Trinity Church. *206 Clarendon St, Boston (02116). Phone 617/536-0944. www.trinitychurchboston.org.* This Henry Hobson Richardson building is the noblest work of the architect. It was inspired by Phillips Brooks, the ninth rector of Trinity Church, and author of the Christmas carol, "O Little Town of Bethlehem." The church combines Romanesque design with beautiful frescos, Craftsman-style stained glass, and ornate carvings. Trinity still serves as an Episcopal church today, with services at 8 am, 9 am, 11 am, and 6 pm. On Fridays at 12:15 pm, stop in for a free organ recital and take a guided or unguided tour. (Daily) **$**

Wang Theater/The Shubert Theater. *265 and 270 Tremont St, Boston (02116). Phone 617/482-9393. www.wangcenter.org.* Broadway shows, theater productions, dance and opera companies, and musical performers appear at the 3,600-seat Wang Theater, which is a world-class venue for the performing arts. Formerly called the Metropolitan Theater, The Wang Theater was designed to look like a French palace and has been completely restored to its original grandeur and beauty. The Shubert Theater across the street hosts an impressive array of quality local theater, dance, and opera productions, many of which appeal to children. **$$$$**

"Whites of Their Eyes." *Bunker Hill Pavilion, 55 Constitution Rd, Charlestown (02129). Just W of the USS Constitution. Phone 617/241-7575.* This specially designed pavilion houses a multimedia reenactment of the Battle of Bunker Hill using life-size figures and eyewitness narratives. Audience "viewpoint" from atop Breed's Hill. Continuous 30-minute shows. (Apr-Nov, daily; closed Thanksgiving)

Wonderland Greyhound Park. *190 VFW Pkwy, Revere (02151). 5 miles north of historic downtown Boston on Hwy 1A N. Phone 781/284-1300. www.wonderland greyhound.com.* Open since 1935, Wonderland offers greyhound racing and pari-mutuel betting, which means that you're betting against other people at the track, not against the house. The minimum wager per race is $2, you can place at many bets as you'd like, and your dog doesn't have to come in first for you to win. (See the list of betting terms on Wonderland's Web site.) Wonderland hosts two annual premier events: the Grady Memorial Sprint and the Wonderland Derby. Note that Massachusetts voters frequently put dog-racing referendums on the ballot; before planning to attend Wonderland, check its Web site (www.won derlandgreyhound.com) to ensure that voters haven't approved a greyhound-racing ban. (Daily; closed Thanksgiving, Dec 25) **$**

Special Events

Boston Kite Festival. *Franklin Park, Bluehill Ave and Circuit Dr, Dorchester (02121). Phone 617/635-4505.* Bring your kite when you visit Boston in mid-May and visit the annual Boston Kite Festival. If you don't have a kite, don't let that stop you—festivities include kite-making clinics, face painting, live music, and kite-flying competitions. See thousands of kites, from beautiful and elaborate to simple, homemade varieties. Mid-May. **FREE**

Boston Marathon. *Starts in Hopkington, MA, and finishes at Copley Square, in front of the Boston Public Library. The Copley Square "T" stop is closed on Marathon day; take the Green Line C to any stop on Beacon St to see the finish. Phone 617/236-1652. www.bostonmarathon.org.* What separates the Boston Marathon from other marathons around the United States is that every person running the race has run another marathon in a fast enough time to qualify for this one. Qualifying standards, which are based on a combination of a previous marathon finish time, sex, and age, are tough—some people train for a lifetime to make the standard and run in this race. Because the course is notoriously hilly and difficult, few elite runners are able to run record times, and because the fast and flat London Marathon is held at about the same time of year as Boston, elite runners as a whole aren't as prevalent here as they once were. Still, Boston is one of the world's best marathons, so you won't find a single spot along the course where you're not in a crowd. Try to find a shady area in which to cheer on the runners. Third Mon in Apr. **FREE**

Bunker Hill Day. *Charlestown. Phone 617/536-4100.* Mid-June.

Charles River Regatta. *Harvard and Mass Ave bridges, Boston (02115). Phone 617/868-6200; toll-free 888/733-2678. www.hocr.org.* Third weekend in Oct.

Chowderfest. *1 City Hall Plz, Boston (02201). Phone 617/227-1528. www.bostonharborfest.com/chowderfest.* During Harborfest, an event that begins a few days before July 4 and ends a few days after, Boston's finest restaurants compete to have their *chowda* called "Boston's Best Chowder." More than 2,000 gallons of New England clam chowder (you won't find that tomatoey Manhattan variety here) are yours to sample and judge in this enjoyable annual event. Early July.

Esplanade Concerts. *Hatch Shell, Charles River Esplanade, Boston (02114). Phone 617/536-4100; toll-free 888/733-2678.* Musical program by the Boston Pops in the Hatch Shell on the Esplanade on the Fourth of July.

First Night Boston. *Phone 617/542-1399. www.first night.org.* First Night is Boston's alternative to traditional New Year's Eve celebrations. This alcohol-free celebration begins with a Mardi Gras-style Grand

Procession and features more than 250 performances in both indoor and outdoor venues. You'll be entertained with concerts, films (on seven screens), tango dancing, stand-up comedy, orchestral music, Boston Rock Opera, a magic show, puppets, and ice sculptures. The evening literally ends with a bang: a fireworks display at midnight. A badge gives you entrance to every event, and badges are for sale at retail outlets throughout the city. If you hang onto your badge after the event, it gets you discounts throughout the city later in the spring. After 8 pm on First Night, MTBA offers free transportation service. Keep in mind that Boylston Street and adjoining streets close in the afternoon for the Grand Procession; Atlantic Avenue and adjoining streets close later in the evening for the fireworks displays. Dec 31. **$$$**

Harborfest. *Hatch Shell, Charles River Esplanade, Boston (02114). Phone 617/227-1528. www.boston harborfest.com.* Boston Pops Orchestra, fireworks. Six days over July 4.

Patriot's Day Celebration. *City Center, Boston (02108). Phone 617/536-4100.* Third Mon in Apr.

Limited-Service Hotels

★ BEST WESTERN ROUNDHOUSE SUITES.
891 Massachusetts Ave, Boston (02118). Phone 617/ 989-1000; toll-free 888/468-3562; fax 617/541-9588. www.bestwestern.com. A decent lodging at a good price if you have your own wheels, this new-construction hotel inside the shell of a former railroad roundhouse is convenient to the Southeast Expressway, the Massachusetts Turnpike, and Boston City Hospital. But it's far from downtown and nearly a mile from the nearest subway stop (there is frequent bus service, however). Guest rooms are large for the price and the mini-fridges are handy, especially since you're not going to run out at night for a snack. 92 rooms. Pets accepted. Complimentary continental breakfast. Check-in 3 pm, check-out 11 am. Fitness room. Airport transportation available. Business center. **$**

★ ★ DOUBLETREE GUEST SUITES.
400 Soldiers Field Rd, Boston (02134). Phone 617/783-0090; toll-free 800/222-8733; fax 617/783-0897. www.doubletree.com. Alternately described as being in Boston or in Cambridge, this highway-side high-rise sits at the Allston-Cambridge exit from the Massachusetts Turnpike. Regular shuttles to Harvard Square ameliorate the awkward location, and you get a lot of room in a bright and spacious open-atrium hotel. Besides the suite design—a bedroom separate from the office/living area—the best reason to stay here might be Scullers Jazz Club, one of the top venues in the Northeast for touring jazz headliners. The Doubletree Guest Suites is also a good bet for drivers leery of coping with urban traffic. 308 rooms, 15 story, all suites. Pets accepted; fee. Check-in 3 pm, check-out noon. Restaurant, bar. Fitness room. Indoor pool, whirlpool. Business center. **$**

★ ★ HARBORSIDE INN OF BOSTON.
185 State St, Boston (02109). Phone 617/723-7500; toll-free 888/ 723-7565; fax 617/670-6015. www.harborsideinn boston.com. Now that the Big Dig construction project has almost concluded and Boston's elevated highway has been removed, this 1858 brick and granite spice warehouse building has an enviable location next to Faneuil Hall Marketplace and literally steps from the waterfront. The modestly priced boutique hotel features exposed-brick walls, hardwood floors, Turkish rugs, Federal-style cherry furniture, and reproductions of paintings from the Museum of Fine Arts. Limited off-site parking is available for a fee; make sure to arrange for this when reserving your room. 54 rooms, 8 story. Check-in 3 pm, check-out noon. Restaurant, bar. **$**

★ ★ HOLIDAY INN SELECT-GOVERNMENT CENTER.
5 Blossom St, Boston (02114). Phone 617/ 742-7630; toll-free 800/465-4329; fax 617/742-4192. www.holiday-inn.com. The institutional décor and floral-print fabrics don't exactly scream "chic," but recent renovations to this urban renewal-era tower near Massachusetts General Hospital and the Government Center have created a road warrior's dream, with large workspaces and "Executive Edition" floors where rooms are equipped almost as offices. Frequent specials make the hotel a good deal, and although the immediate surroundings are unattractive, Beacon Hill is literally just across the street. 303 rooms, 14 story. Check-in 4 pm, check-out noon. Restaurant, bar. Fitness room. Outdoor pool. **$$**

★ RAMADA INN.
800 Morrissey Blvd, Boston (02122). Phone 617/287-9100; fax 617/265-9287. www.bostonhotel.com. 177 rooms, 5 story. Pets accepted, some restrictions. Check-in 3 pm, check-out noon. Outdoor pool. **$**

Full-Service Hotels

★ ★ ★ **BOSTON HARBOR HOTEL.** *70 Rowes Wharf, Boston (02110). Phone 617/439-7000; toll-free 800/752-7077; fax 617/330-9450. www.bhh.com.* Privileged guests rest their weary heads at the Boston Harbor Hotel. Boston's rich heritage comes alive here at Rowes Wharf, once home to revolutionaries and traders. Occupying an idyllic waterfront location, the hotel is across the street from the financial district and three blocks from the Freedom Trail and Faneuil Hall Marketplace. Guests enjoy an especially civilized lifestyle here. They need not worry about the snarls of traffic, thanks to the hotel's fantastic airport ferry service. This full-service hotel takes care of every possible amenity, ensuring satisfaction and comfort. Rooms and suites are beautifully appointed in rich colors; to pay a few dollars more for one with a view is well worth it. The views of the harbor are sensational, whether enjoyed in the privacy of a guest room or in one of the public spaces. Meritage presents diners with an inventive menu and an extensive wine list in striking contemporary surroundings. In the summer, the hotel hosts live music and dancing, along with an outdoor movie night. 230 rooms, 8 story. Pets accepted. Check-in 3 pm, check-out 1 pm. High-speed Internet access. Three restaurants, three bars. Fitness room. Indoor pool, whirlpool. Business center. **$$$**

★ ★ ★ **THE COLONNADE HOTEL.** *120 Huntington Ave, Boston (02116). Phone 617/424-7000; toll-free 800/962-3030; fax 617/424-1717. www.colonnadehotel.com.* One of Back Bay's more family-friendly hotels, the Colonnade boasts the city's only outdoor rooftop swimming pool. The pool is an attraction for Bostonians as well as hotel guests, and there's often a lively singles scene at the poolside bar. A subway stop of the Green Line's E branch is just outside the door, making the Colonnade convenient for getting downtown or out to the major museums. The hotel often hosts meetings and small conferences. The street-level restaurant, Brasserie Jo (see), is a popular after-work watering hole for Back Bay professionals. 285 rooms, 1 story. Pets accepted. Check-in 3 pm, check-out noon. High-speed Internet access, wireless Internet access. Restaurant, bar. Fitness room. Outdoor pool. Business center. **$$**

★ ★ **COPLEY SQUARE HOTEL.** *47 Huntington Ave, Boston (02116). Phone 617/536-9000; toll-free 800/225-7062; fax 617/267-3547. www.copleysquare hotel.com.* Location, location, location—this older hotel stands across Huntington Avenue from the Copley Place shopping center and the complex of conference meeting rooms associated with the nearby Westin, Marriott, Sheraton, and Hilton hotels. It's typically cheaper than those conference hotels, with smaller guest rooms and less posh furniture, but it does have a "home away from home" feel. It's very popular with European budget travelers, so you might meet some interesting people in the elevator. Amenities are limited here, but guests receive complimentary access to the fitness center at the nearby Lenox Hotel. 143 rooms, 7 story. Check-in 3 pm, check-out noon. Two restaurants. **$$**

★ ★ ★ **THE ELIOT HOTEL.** *370 Commonwealth Ave, Boston (02215). Phone 617/267-1607; toll-free 800/443-5468; fax 617/536-9114. www.eliothotel.com.* This 95-room European-style hotel is located just off the Mass Turnpike in the Back Bay area, convenient to the Hynes Convention Center and various shopping, entertainment, and cultural sites. A quiet elegance pervades the lobby, which is richly furnished; a superb faux finish on the walls mimics the look of stone. Most of the accommodations are spacious suites, which feature pull-out sofas, French doors to the bedrooms, Italian marble baths, and down comforters. Surrounded by lush greenery, the hotel has no fitness room of its own, but guests have complimentary use of the health club around the corner. The Eliot is also home to the critically acclaimed Clio restaurant (see), serving contemporary French-American cuisine. 95 rooms, 9 story. Pets accepted, some restrictions. Check-in 3 pm, check-out noon. High-speed Internet access. Two restaurants, bar. Fitness room. Business center. **$$$**

★ ★ ★ **THE FAIRMONT COPLEY PLAZA BOSTON.** *138 St. James Ave, Boston (02116). Phone 617/267-5300; toll-free 800/441-1414; fax 617/267-7668. www.fairmont.com.* Ideally situated in the heart of the theater district, this landmark hotel was built in 1925 and is considered by many as the grande dame of Boston. Named after the great American painter John Singleton Copley, this traditional lodging offers elegant surroundings. The lobby flaunts an exquisite high-domed ceiling with beautiful ornate furnishings, as well as dramatic marble pillars and remarkable imported rugs. Recently remodeled guest rooms are furnished with top-quality materials and sport crown moldings. Lending a personal touch is Katie Copley, the resident black Lab, who's happy to be petted or even taken for walks by hotel guests. 383 rooms, 7 story. Pets accepted. Check-in 3 pm, check-out noon. Restaurant, bar. Fitness room. Business center. **$$$**

★ ★ ★ ★ **FOUR SEASONS HOTEL BOSTON.** *200 Boylston St, Boston (02116). Phone 617/338-4400; toll-free 800/330-3442; fax 617/423-0154. www.fourseasons.com.* The Four Seasons Hotel would make any Boston Brahmin proud. Discriminating travelers are drawn to this refined hotel where the finer things in life may be enjoyed. The Four Seasons offers its guests a prime location overlooking Beacon Hill's Public Garden and the State Capitol. All of Boston is easily explored from here, and the hotel makes it carefree with courtesy town car service. The contemporary lobby, complete with a dramatic yellow marble and black granite floor in a startling geometric pattern, absolutely gleams. Antiques, fine art, sumptuous fabrics, and period furniture create a magnificent setting in the guest rooms and suites, while impeccable and attentive service heightens the luxurious experience. Aquatic workouts with a view are available at the indoor pool with floor-to-ceiling windows overlooking the city, and the fitness center keeps guests in tip-top shape. Aujourd'hui (see) is an epicurean's delight with its sensational New American cuisine and distinguished dining room. The Bristol presents diners with a casually elegant alternative. 272 rooms, 15 story. Pets accepted, some restrictions. Complimentary continental breakfast. Check-in 3 pm, check-out noon. High-speed Internet access. Two restaurants, bar. Fitness room. Indoor pool, whirlpool. Business center. **$$$**

★ ★ ★ **HILTON BOSTON BACK BAY.** *40 Dalton St, Boston (02115). Phone 617/236-1100; toll-free 800/445-8667; fax 617/867-6104. www.hilton.com.* Built in the age of glass-box towers, the Hilton Back Bay is a premium conference and convention hotel across the street from the Hynes Convention Center at the western edge of Back Bay. A recent update reconfigured the hotel to make the guest rooms larger and furnish them with the kind of dark wood, plush-fabric ambience that visitors expect in Back Bay. Business travelers make up the bulk of the clientele, so you can count on excellent desks, a top-notch fitness center, and a business center that's open around the clock. The location is also ideal for sightseeing. Newbury Street boutiques are a block away, and the Hynes/Auditorium subway stop is just outside. It's even a convenient stroll to Symphony Hall. 385 rooms, 26

story. Check-in 3 pm, check-out noon. Restaurant, two bars. Fitness room. Indoor pool. Business center. **$$**

★ ★ ★ **HILTON BOSTON LOGAN AIRPORT.** *85 Terminal Rd, Boston (02128). Phone 617/568-6700; toll-free 800/445-8667; fax 617/568-6800. www.hilton.com.* The 599-room Hilton is the most convenient and plushest lodging at Boston's airport. A skybridge provides pedestrian access to and from the terminals, and the hotel runs free shuttles to the airport subway stop and water taxi dock for quick transport to downtown. There's something comfortingly familiar for road warriors about the ruddy wood of Hilton's furnishings and its attention to the needs of business travelers who might have to crank out a report overnight, make conference calls, or just kick back with in-room entertainment while waiting for tomorrow's flight home. 599 rooms, 10 story. Pets accepted, some restrictions. Check-in 3 pm, check-out noon. High-speed Internet access. Two restaurants, bar. Fitness room. Indoor pool. Business center. **$$**

★ ★ ★ **HOTEL COMMONWEALTH.** *500 Commonwealth Ave, Boston (02215). Phone 617/933-5000; toll-free 866/784-4000; fax 617/266-6888. www.hotelcommonwealth.com.* The Commonwealth functions as Boston University's elegant lodging to host visiting scholars, trustees, and parents who can afford full tuition. Constructed in the heart of once-funky Kenmore Square, its architecture suggests the mansard-roofed Victorian structures it replaced, but the Victoriana is really a conservative skin on a thoroughly contemporary deluxe hotel. Gestures of grace and stateliness abound—oversized writing desks with French Empire lines, heavy draperies that slide back to reveal large windows, a plethora of dark wood, and earth- and forest-tone carpets, wall coverings, and upholstery. Fenway Park is around the corner, and the Boston University campus begins a few yards up the street. Great Bay, one of the hotel's restaurants, has made a name for itself with upscale and innovative seafood. 150 rooms. Pets accepted, some restrictions; fee. Check-in 3 pm, check-out noon. High-speed Internet access. Restaurant, bar. Fitness room. Airport transportation available. Business center. **$$$**

★ ★ ★ **HYATT HARBORSIDE.** *101 Harborside Dr, Boston (02128). Phone 617/568-1234; toll-free 800/233-1234; fax 617/567-8856. www.hyatt.com.* Located adjacent to Logan Airport, this elegant hotel has a friendly staff, spacious guest rooms, and a meeting facility designed with the business traveler in mind. For leisure activities, guests can enjoy the indoor lap pool or the premier health and fitness center, both with views of the scenic waterfront and Boston skyline. 277 rooms, 15 story. Check-in 3 pm, check-out noon. Restaurant, bar. Fitness room. Indoor pool, whirlpool. Airport transportation available. Business center. **$$**

★ ★ ★ **HYATT REGENCY BOSTON FINANCIAL DISTRICT.** *1 Ave de Lafayette, Boston (02111). Phone 617/912-1234; toll-free 800/233-1234; fax 617/422-5422. www.hyatt.com.* Hyatt took over this former Swissôtel and wisely kept much of the elegant décor as well as the policy of running frequent discount packages on weekends. Principally a business hotel, it sits a block off Boston Common at the intersection of the financial and theater districts. Public areas suggest old-world refinement with antique furniture, marble floors, and Waterford crystal chandeliers. Many upper-level corner suites have breathtaking views of either Boston Common or downtown architecture. The hotel's pedestrian entrance from Avenue de Lafayette subjects everyone coming or going to the close scrutiny of the staff—a reminder that the hotel was a pioneer in the city's now nearly vanished red-light district. Today, the trendy restaurants and nightclubs of the Ladder District are just a few steps away. 500 rooms, 22 story. Pet accepted, some restrictions. Check-in 4 pm, check-out noon. High-speed Internet access. Two restaurants, bar. Fitness room. Indoor pool, whirlpool. Airport transportation available. Business center. **$$**

★ ★ ★ **THE LANGHAM BOSTON.** *250 Franklin St, Boston (02110). Phone 617/451-1900; toll-free 800/791-7781; fax 617/423-2844. www.langhamhotels.com.* Just a stone's throw from Faneuil Hall, the Freedom Trail, and other historic sites, the elegant Langham Hotel (formerly Le Meridien) is a perfect base for retracing the steps of famous patriots. A sense of old-world Europe is felt throughout the Langham, from the discreet façade with its signature red awnings to the magnificent lobby done in jewel tones. The guest rooms are equally delightful, and many offer wonderful views of the gardens of Post Office Square. Extra touches are provided to ensure exceedingly comfortable visits. The remarkable French cuisine at Julien is only the beginning, where sparkling chandeliers and glittering gold leaf details will

make any guest feel like royalty. Once the Governor's Reception Room of Boston's Federal Reserve Bank, the Julien Bar is a sensational place, while the Mediterranean dishes of Café Fleuri have universal appeal. 326 rooms, 9 story. Pets accepted, some restrictions; fee. Check-in 3 pm, check-out 1 pm. Two restaurants, bar. Fitness room. Indoor pool, whirlpool. Airport transportation available. **$$**

★ ★ ★ **LENOX HOTEL.** *61 Exeter St, Boston (02116). Phone 617/536-5300; toll-free 800/225-7676; fax 617/267-1237. www.lenoxhotel.com.* This 214-room replica of a classic European hotel is centrally located in the heart of Boston. Although it isn't much to look at on the outside, this Boston landmark welcomes guests with a beautiful lobby and mezzanine—notice the lovely ceilings with ornate gridworks of gilded mouldings. Charmingly appointed guest rooms exude a level of elegance and style that stand up to even the most discriminating travelers' expectations. 214 rooms, 11 story. Check-in 3 pm, check-out noon. Two restaurants, bar. Fitness room. **$$$**

★ ★ ★ **MARRIOTT BOSTON COPLEY PLACE.** *110 Huntington Ave, Boston (02116). Phone 617/236-5800; toll-free 877/901-2079; fax 617/236-5885. www.copleymarriott.com.* With a prime location in the heart of Back Bay, the 1,147-room Marriott is a family-friendly hotel offering lots of amenities. An enclosed walkway connects the hotel to a large mall with many shops and restaurants, as well as to the Hynes Convention Center. Just minutes from the Museum of Fine Arts and Newbury Street shops, the hotel boasts one of the largest ballrooms in New England and offers a variety of dining options, including a sushi bar. 1,147 rooms, 38 story. Check-in 4 pm, check-out noon. High-speed Internet access. Four restaurants, two bars. Children's activity center. Fitness room. Indoor pool, whirlpool. Business center. **$$$**

★ ★ ★ **MARRIOTT BOSTON LONG WHARF.** *296 State St, Boston (02109). Phone 617/227-0800; toll-free 800/228-9290; fax 617/227-2867. www.marriott.com.* Adjacent to Faneuil Hall and near the Fleet Center, this mid-20th-century hotel was a generation ahead of its time in anticipating the cleanup of Boston's downtown shores. The harborfront finally caught up with the hotel, and in 2001, Marriott gave each of the 402 guest rooms a complete makeover that realized the tremendous potential of the site. Most rooms have stunning harbor or city skyline views, and you need only walk out the door to catch the ferry to the harbor islands park, a whale-watching boat, or a water taxi to anywhere on the harbor. The hotel's public spaces capitalize on the nautical theme as well, featuring enormous murals of fishermen at work on Long Wharf and a railing system that mimics the levels on a cruise ship. Summertime nirvana is a bucket of steamed clams and a bottle of cold beer on the outdoor patio of the hotel's casual restaurant, Tia's on the Waterfront. 402 rooms, 7 story. Check-in 4 pm, check-out noon. High-speed Internet access. Restaurant, bar. Children's activity center. Fitness room. Outdoor pool, whirlpool. Business center. **$$$**

★ ★ ★ **MARRIOTT COURTYARD BOSTON TREMONT HOTEL.** *275 Tremont St, Boston (02116). Phone 617/426-1400; toll-free 800/ 321-2211; fax 617/482-6730. www.marriott.com.* This sophisticated 322-room hotel is located in the Western Promenade historic neighborhood, across the street from the Wang Center for the Performing Arts and not far from the Boston Garden. The midtown Arts District is a short walk away, and museums, art galleries, boat rides, fine restaurants, and recreational activities are nearby. Antiques and artwork are found throughout the hotel, and the lobby is punctuated with abundant marble and rich hanging tapestries. 322 rooms, 15 story. Check-in 3 pm, check-out noon. High-speed Internet access, wireless Internet access. Restaurant, bar. Fitness room. Business center. **$$**

★ ★ ★ **MARRIOTT PEABODY.** *8A Centennial Dr, Peabody (01960). Phone 978/977-9700; toll-free 800/228-9290; fax 978/977-0297. www.marriott.com.* 260 rooms, 6 story. Check-in 3 pm, check-out noon. Restaurant, bar. Fitness room. Indoor pool, whirlpool. Business center. **$**

★ ★ ★ **MILLENNIUM BOSTONIAN HOTEL.** *26 North St, Boston (02109). Phone 617/523-3600; toll-free 800/343-0922; fax 617/523-2454. www.millennium hotels.com.* It's hard to believe that this spacious and modern luxury hotel was able to squeeze into one of the oldest neighborhoods in Boston without disturbing the ambience. Good soundproofing provides a serene sanctuary from the bustle of Faneuil Hall Marketplace next door—a location that makes the Millennium ideal for tourists (although the hotel caters mainly to business travelers given its proximity to

the Government Center). Because the hotel was constructed around some older buildings, guest rooms vary from tiny to palatial; be sure to inquire carefully when booking. The hotel's restaurant (see SEASONS) was a pioneer in introducing contemporary upscale cuisine to Boston 30 years ago and remains one of the poshest dining spots in town. City Hall is nearby, so plenty of local business gets accomplished in the lobby bar. 201 rooms, 7 story. Check-in 3 pm, check-out noon. Restaurant, bar. Fitness room. Business center. **$$**

★ ★ ★ **NINE ZERO HOTEL.** *90 Tremont St, Boston (02108). Phone 617/772-5800; toll-free 866/646-3937; fax 617/772-5810. www.ninezero.com.* This midtown hotel is located on the famed Boston Freedom Trail, a short walk from the financial district and top attractions such as Faneuil Hall, Back Bay, and Beacon Hill. A red brick and limestone façade contrasts with the inner décor-a contemporary mix of nickel, chrome, stainless steel, and glass with accents of color and wood finishes. Rooms marry comfort and technology for business and leisure travelers. Luxe trappings include Frette linens, goose-down comforters and pillows, CD stereo sound systems, and Mario Russo bath products. In-room personal offices feature task lighting, high-performance desk chairs, printers, complimentary high-speed Internet access, and dual-in cordless telephones with speaker capabilities. 189 rooms, 19 story. Pets accepted. Check-in 3 pm, check-out noon. High-speed Internet access. Restaurant, bar. Fitness room. Business center. **$$**

★ ★ ★ **OMNI PARKER HOUSE.** *60 School St, Boston (02108). Phone 617/227-8600; toll-free 800/843-6664; fax 617/742-5729. www.omnihotels.com.* The Parker House, which gave the world its eponymous dinner rolls and the Boston cream pie, is the oldest hotel in the United States in continuous operation (part of the building dates from 1856). The plush lobby and dining room, which date from just before World War I, are breathtaking examples of Edwardian excess. The $70 million renovation in 2001 brought the guest rooms up to a modern standard, although some are quite compact. The location, just beneath the peak of Beacon Hill and in the midst of downtown shopping, is marvelously convenient. Great history is attached to the hotel—from the literary dinners with Emerson and Longfellow playing host to Dickens to the stories about JFK, who made this his political headquarters. 551 rooms, 15 story. Pets accepted, some restrictions; fee. Check-in 3 pm, check-out noon. Three restaurants, two bars. Fitness room. **$$**

★ ★ ★ ★ **THE RITZ-CARLTON, BOSTON.**
15 Arlington St, Boston (02117). Phone 617/536-5700; toll-free 800/241-3333; fax 617/536-1335. www.ritzcarlton.com. Distinguished and refined, The Ritz-Carlton is unquestionably the grande dame of Boston. This lovely hotel, faithfully restored to its 1920s splendor, has been a cherished city landmark for many years. Located across from the Public Garden, this aristocratic hotel opens its doors to a rarefied world of genteel manners and distinguished surroundings. With its intricate "wedding cake" ceiling detail, elaborate mouldings, lavish carpets and upholstery, and graceful marble staircases, the lobby is a truly elegant space. The guest rooms are a celebration of traditional style; luxurious marble bathrooms encourage soothing soaks. Suites include wood-burning fireplaces, and the hotel even offers a considerate fireplace butler service. The sun-filled Café is an ideal place for shoppers to take a break from the boutiques of Newbury Street, while a proper afternoon tea can be enjoyed in the Lounge. The Bar has a fascinating history, having survived Prohibition, and its wood-paneled walls and roaring fireplace exude a clubby feel. Even pets are pampered here; a special treat bag is presented on a silver tray, and food and water bowls are provided, along with a dog tag engraved with the hotel's name on one side and the dog's name on the other. 273 rooms, 17 story. Pets accepted; fee. Check-in 3 pm, check-out noon. High-speed Internet access. Restaurant, two bars. Fitness room. Business center. **$$$$**

★ ★ ★ ★ **THE RITZ-CARLTON, BOSTON COMMON.** *10 Avery St, Boston (02111). Phone 617/574-7100; toll-free 888/709-2027; fax 617/574-7200. www.ritzcarlton.com.* While only a short skip across the park from its sister property, The Ritz-Carlton, Boston Common is a world apart from its traditional counterpart with its modern sensibility of clean lines, neutral tones, and hip atmosphere. This contemporary construction attracts the fashionable set seeking the high levels of service synonymous with Ritz-Carlton properties. Flanked by the financial and theater districts, The Ritz-Carlton, Boston Common is convenient for business and leisure travelers alike. In the inviting lobby, a dramatic arched ceiling is lit for effect, while leather seating beside a black marble fireplace encourages conversation. The guest rooms and

suites have a distinctly serene feel with muted tones of taupe, cream, and celadon and polished woods. JER-NE Restaurant is a feast for the tongue and the eyes with its inventive creations and sensational décor. An open kitchen enables guests to watch the talented chefs in action, while the bar has a vibrant scene. After a night of indulgence, Ritz-Carlton guests often head to the massive Sports Club/LA, a veritable temple of fitness. Dogs are welcomed in style with the Pampered Pet Package, consisting of bowls, biscuits, and a personalized dog tag. 193 rooms, 4 story. Pets accepted; fee. Check-in 3 pm, check-out noon. High-speed Internet access. Restaurant, bar. Indoor pool. Business center. **$$$**

★ ★ ★ **SEAPORT HOTEL.** *1 Seaport Ln, Boston (02210). Phone 617/385-4000; toll-free 877/732-7678; fax 617/385-4001. www.seaporthotel.com.* Looking a bit like a beached ocean liner, the Seaport is joined to the World Trade Center by an overhead walkway and serves as a base hotel for many conferences, conventions, and sales events. The ship metaphor only goes so far: the soothing, modern-styled rooms are much larger and better appointed than most staterooms. The surrounding area will be a bustling part of the city by 2010, or so developers promise, but the Seaport is currently a bit removed from the downtown action. Frequent shuttles to South Station and the financial district help ease the sense of isolation, as will a soon-to-be-completed train line. The health club is large and well equipped, and the restaurant is one of Boston's best for upscale seafood dining. The Seaport is also convenient to many casual fish restaurants near Fish Pier and to the summertime concert pavilion on the harbor. Canine guests are registered just like humans, and the lucky ones munch on dog treats from guest-room minibars. 426 rooms, 18 story. Pets accepted, some restrictions. Check-in 3 pm, check-out noon. High-speed Internet access. Two restaurants, bar. Fitness room, fitness classes available, spa. Indoor pool. Business center. **$$**

★ ★ ★ **SHERATON BOSTON HOTEL.** *39 Dalton St, Boston (02199). Phone 617/236-2000; toll-free 800/325-3535; fax 617/236-1702. www.sheraton.com/boston.* Ideally located in the historic Back Bay and adjacent to the Hynes Convention Center, this hotel offers guests attentive service along with an elegant atmosphere. 1,215 rooms, 29 story. Pets accepted, some restrictions. Check-in 3 pm, check-out noon. High-speed Internet access.

Restaurant, bar. Fitness room. Indoor pool, outdoor pool, whirlpool. Airport transportation available. Business center. **$$$**

★ ★ ★ **WESTIN COPLEY PLACE.** *10 Huntington Ave, Boston (02116). Phone 617/262-9600; toll-free 800/937-8461; fax 617/424-7483. www.westin.com/copleyplace.* This grand, contemporary hotel is located in the heart of historic Back Bay and boasts some of the largest guest rooms in Boston, along with panaromic views of the city. Conveniently connected by skybridge to the Hynes Convention Center and elite shopping at Copley Place, the hotel is frequented by business travelers but also welcomes vacationing families with its Westin Kids Club. Pets, too, are greeted warmly here, and are given their own Heavenly Beds and snack menu. An immaculate fitness facility and spa and salon tempt guests to enjoy a rigorous workout and then to treat themselves to some pampering. 803 rooms, 36 story. Pets accepted, some restrictions. Check-in 3 pm, check-out noon. High-speed Internet access, wireless Internet access. Five restaurants, bar. Fitness room. Indoor pool, whirlpool. Airport transportation available. Business center. **$$$$**

★ ★ ★ ★ **XV BEACON.** *15 Beacon St, Boston (02108). Phone 617/670-1500; toll-free 877/982-3226; fax 617/670-2525. www.xvbeacon.com.* Dazzling and daring, XV Beacon is the hipster's answer to the luxury hotel. This turn-of-the-century Beaux Arts building in Beacon Hill belies the sleek décor found within. This highly stylized, seductive hotel flaunts a refreshing change of pace in traditional Boston. Decidedly contemporary, XV Beacon employs whimsical touches, like the plaster busts found at reception, to wink at the city's past. (Sam Adams is buried next door, and Thomas Jefferson lived around the corner.) Original artwork commissioned specifically for the hotel by well-known artists decorates the walls of both public and private spaces. The guest rooms and suites are furnished in an eclectic style in a palette of rich chocolate browns, blacks, and creams. Rooms feature canopy beds with luxurious Italian linens and gas fireplaces covered in cool stainless steel. Completed in crisp white with simple fixtures, the bathrooms are a modernist's dream. The nouvelle cuisine at The Federalist (see) is delicious and fresh, thanks to the chef's rooftop garden and in-kitchen fish tanks. 60 rooms, 10 story. Pets accepted, some restrictions.

Check-in 3 pm, check-out noon. Restaurant, bar. Fitness room. **$$$$**

Specialty Lodgings

The following lodging establishments are approved by Mobil Travel Guide, but due to their unique and individualized nature have not been given a traditional Mobil Star rating. Included in this listing you may find bed-and-breakfasts, limited-service inns, guest ranches, and other unique hotel properties.

CHARLES STREET INN. *94 Charles St, Boston (02114). Phone 617/314-8900; toll-free 877/772-8900; fax 617/371-0009. www.charlesstreetinn.com.* Step into the past without sacrificing modern conveniences at this utterly charming inn, which occupies a building constructed as a showcase of architectural styles of the 1880s. Guest rooms are large and regal enough to qualify as decadent, although the street-level reception and staircases are rather tight. Expect to find working fireplaces, massive antique armoires, and heavily draped canopy beds, along with period artwork. The location is perfect for exploring Beacon Hill, downtown, or Back Bay on foot—a good thing, since parking is limited. There's no dining room, so a bounteous continental breakfast is delivered to your door. Guest rooms are themed to artists and writers associated with Boston, such as Louisa May Alcott. What would Henry James have made of the sub-zero refrigerator and high-speed Internet access? 9 rooms, 5 story. Pets accepted, some restrictions; fee. Complimentary continental breakfast. Check-in 3 pm, check-out 11 am. High-speed Internet access. **$$$**

GRYPHON HOUSE. *9 Bay State Rd, Boston (02215). Phone 617/375-9003; toll-free 877/375-9003; fax 617/425-0716. www.gryphonhouseboston.com.* More a luxury B&B than a hotel, this circa-1895 brownstone townhouse stands at the juncture of Back Bay and Fenway. It's one of the more architecturally distinctive residential neighborhoods in Boston, and the Gryphon House stands up nicely to its neighbors. The rooms are huge—each about the size of a studio apartment and individually decorated in an array of Victorian styles. Each room has a working gas fireplace and wet bar as well as remote-controlled air conditioning. The Kenmore subway stop and Fenway Park are just a brief saunter away, and Boston University begins just a few doors down on Bay State

Road. 8 rooms. Complimentary full breakfast. Check-in 3 pm, check-out 11 am. **$$**

NEWBURY GUEST HOUSE. *261 Newbury St, Boston (02116). Phone 617/437-7666; toll-free 800/437-7668; fax 617/670-6100. www.hagopianhotels.com.* A string of residences along upper Newbury Street was linked with indoor staircases and hallways to create this pioneer among Back Bay B&Bs. Rooms tend to be on the small side, in part because bathrooms stole space from bedrooms when the conversions were made. The décor is eclectic, with a bias toward the kind of furniture that Granny jettisoned when she bought her recliner. The B&B offers good value for the location, but ask for a room on the back side to escape weekend street noise. 32 rooms, 4 story. Complimentary continental breakfast. Check-in 3 pm, check-out noon. Restaurant. **$**

Restaurants

★ ★ **ABE & LOUIE'S.** *793 Boylston St, Boston (02116). Phone 617/536-6300; fax 617/437-6291. www.bbrginc.com/al.* Fittingly situated at the Convention Center end of Back Bay, this New York-style steakhouse satisfies by fulfilling expectations. The clubby décor of dark wooden booths and a flickering fireplace is a perfect match for the high-protein menu of charred steaks and grilled fish. The dessert trolley even features New York cheesecake. Atkins dieters can pass on the extra carbs, like the side of mashed potatoes. Seafood, steak menu. Lunch, dinner. Bar. Casual attire. Outdoor seating. **$$$**

★ ★ ★ **AQUITAINE.** *569 Tremont St, Boston (02118). Phone 617/424-8577; fax 617/424-0249. www.aquitaineboston.com.* An offshoot of fellow South End restaurant Metropolis (both are owned by Seth Woods), this French bistro wavers between classical and nouveau. Regulars rave about the steak frites; there's also an intriguing wine list as well as a helpful staff. French bistro menu. Dinner, Sat-Sun brunch. Closed holidays. Valet parking. **$$$**

★ ★ ★ ★ **AUJOURD'HUI.** *200 Boylston St, Boston (02116). Phone 617/338-4400; fax 617/423-0154. www.fourseasons.com.* With floor-to-ceiling windows overlooking Boston's famed Public Garden, Aujourd'hui is a beautiful spot for a business lunch or an intimate dinner. Brimming with old-world charm, this spacious and elegant dining room, located in the Four Seasons, is lined with rich oak paneling and decorated with tall potted palms and oil paintings. The tables are set with Italian damask linens and decorated with antique plates and lovely fresh flowers. The kitchen aims to please here, and it succeeds with an innovative selection of seasonal modern French fare prepared with regional ingredients and global flavors. The predominantly American wine list complements the kitchen's talent. A lighter menu of more, shall we say, nutritionally responsible dishes (read: low salt, low fat, low cholesterol) is also available. The service at Aujourd'hui enhances the dining experience. Like the restaurant, it is formal yet charming. French menu. Dinner, Sun brunch. Bar. Children's menu. Jacket required. Reservations recommended. Valet parking. **$$$$**

★ ★ **B & G OYSTERS LTD.** *550 Tremont St, Boston (02116). Phone 617/423-0550.* The Maine lobster roll at B & G Oysters costs over $20, fried Ipswich clams are close behind, and raw oysters are $2 each, but customers line up day and night to spend barrels of cash at James Beard award-winning chef Barbara Lynch's latest enterprise. Why? Lynch and business partner Garrett Hasker are using ingredients fresh enough to remind you of summers spent by the sea. The quality is so superior that dishes can be presented simply. Flavors are pure: raw items are briny and fried dishes crisp. The atmosphere is urban chic—in a cellar, a noisy, well-informed crowd dines casually on food that is the antithesis of casual. Lynch and Hasker have used the old-fashioned concept of a New England seafood and fish shack to create a restaurant that's closer to what you find on coastal France than on the coast of Maine. Nostalgia has a price. Seafood menu. Lunch, dinner. Valet parking. **$$**

★ ★ ★ **BLU.** *4 Avery St, Boston (02111). Phone 617/375-8550; fax 617/375-8551. www.blurestaurant.com.* Located in the ladder district, Blu is a sleek, sharp American restaurant owned by the folks who created Rialto in Cambridge (see). With glass walls, chrome accents, and a hip crowd to match, Blu is an edgy addition to this neighborhood. If you feel like a taste of the briny waters, start with the Out of the Blu raw bar sampler—an easy fix for anyone with a sushi, sashimi, or shellfish fetish. The kitchen turns out a whimsical and delicious menu of upscale comfort food-ish dishes like seared foie gras on cornbread and stylish, seasonal American plates like roasted chicken with autumn vegetable hash. For a business lunch, a hot date, or just a night out with friends, Blu is a sure thing. Lunch, dinner. Bar. Children's menu. Casual attire. Valet parking. Outdoor seating. **$$**

★ ★ **BOB THE CHEF'S.** *604 Columbus Ave, Boston (02118). Phone 617/536-6204; fax 617/536-0907. www.bobthechefs.com.* Owner Daryl Settles serves a lightened version of American soul food—cornbread, collard greens, ribs, chicken, barbecue, and fried corn—with a healthy side of live jazz, often played by students from nearby Berklee College of Music. The Sunday jazz brunch is an institution in the South End. Don't let the cuisine fool you into dressing down—Bob the Chef's is a stylish joint. Southern/Soul menu. Lunch (Fri-Sat), dinner, Sun brunch. Closed holidays. Bar. Business casual attire. **$$**

★ ★ **BRASSERIE JO.** *120 Huntington Ave, Boston (02116). Phone 617/424-7000; fax 617/425-1717. www.colonnadehotel.com.* Like its sister French brasserie in Chicago, this restaurant serves authentic French, or more specifically Alsatian, cuisine with the usual flair of the Lettuce Entertain You group. Shoppers and theater attendees will delight in its location: the Colonnade Hotel (see) next to Copley Place. French bistro menu. Breakfast, lunch, dinner. Bar. Children's menu. Casual attire. Outdoor seating. **$$**

★ ★ **BROWN SUGAR CAFE.** *129 Jersey St, Boston (02215). Phone 617/266-2928. www.brownsugarcafe.com.* A steady crowd of Thai-hungry folks fills the Brown Sugar Cafe, a cramped spot for terrific traditional and contemporary dishes of this lemongrass-tinged Southeast Asian land. The airy room is filled to capacity most of the time, yet there is an easiness to the service and the pace of the place; every table is set with a pot of brown sugar, an ode to the restaurant's sweet name. The menu offers a lengthy list of reasonably priced rice and noodle dishes, prepared to your preferred level of scorch. A selection of fresh fish and meats balances out the voluminous number of vegetarian plates. Thai menu. Lunch, dinner. Closed Jan 1, July 4, Thanksgiving. Bar. Casual attire. Outdoor seating. **$$**

★ ★ **THE BUTCHER SHOP.** *552 Tremont St, Boston (02118). Phone 617/423-4800; fax 617/423-4820. www.thebutchershopboston.com.* The Butcher Shop is a lot like the wine bars in Paris, Madrid, and Venice. At the front, a long bar offers a variety of terrific wines by the glass from small growers around the globe. Chef Barbara Lynch pairs the wines with flavorful, French-inspired dishes like marrow with toast, sea salt, and haricots verts; pork rillettes; a torchon of duck foie gras; or a selection of house-cured meats. The wine and small plates of upscale bar food have a calming effect on the palate. What's also fun about this informal restaurant is the ease with which guests are induced to slow down and savor life. In that sense, it has captured what travelers to Europe enjoy: a rhythm that eschews a race to the finish line. When it's time to leave this oasis, you can buy products from its retail section. European menu. Lunch, dinner. **$$**

★ **CAFE MARLIAVE.** *10 Bosworth St, Boston (02108). Phone 617/423-6340; fax 617/542-1133.* Tucked into a nook near the downtown section of the Freedom Trail, Cafe Marliave has a long history of its own. Established in 1875, it was one of Boston's first red-sauce Italian-American restaurants, and the tin walls and minuscule booths supply a romantic atmosphere. Portions are generous, as if a nonna were peering out from the kitchen, exhorting "Mangia! Mangia!" Italian menu. Lunch, dinner. Closed Sun, holidays. Bar. **$$**

★ ★ **CAFFE UMBRA.** *1395 Washington St, Boston (02118). Phone 617/867-0707. www.caffeumbra.com.* Located in Boston's South End neighborhood, Caffe Umbra treats diners to inventive Italian and French country cooking. The creative dishes are best enjoyed with a selection from the restaurant's extensive wine list, featuring vintages from some of the lesser-known regions of Italy and France. A warm atmosphere pervades the restaurant, where exposed-brick walls, a large cherry bar, and windows framing views of the Cathedral of the Holy Cross make this a particularly inviting spot for urban sophisticates. French, Italian menu. Dinner. Closed Mon. Bar. Casual attire. Valet parking. **$$**

★ ★ ★ **THE CAPITAL GRILLE.** *359 Newbury St, Boston (02115). Phone 617/262-8900; fax 617/262-9449. www.thecapitalgrille.com.* The Capital Grille is a man's man sort of restaurant. Sporting dark wainscoted walls and an extensive single-malt Scotch list, this high-roller steakhouse is heavy with testosterone, beef, and a bold dash of big-time expense account. Indeed, The Capital Grille has all the bells and whistles you'd expect from a steakhouse, including a stunning raw bar and generous portions of well-marbled steak, served any and every way you want it. The house specialty is the gargantuan dry-aged porterhouse. Weighing in at 24 juicy, bold ounces, it should come with its own defibrillator. If you're feeling gluttonous, finish off dinner with a slice of cheesecake. Steak menu. Dinner. Closed July 4. Bar. Valet parking. **$$$$**

★ ★ **CARMEN.** *33 North Sq, Boston (02113). Phone 617/742-6421.* The handful of tables and exposed-brick walls of the narrow room make Carmen about as intimate and romantic a trattoria as you'll find in the North End, yet it's easy to locate because the Freedom Trail stripe runs past the door. (The Paul Revere House is a neighbor.) For tapas-style snacking, sit at the bar, sip a nebbiola d'Alba, and enjoy olives marinated with cherry peppers and orange or a plate of grilled squid. Among the full dinner entrées, seared scallops fit the bill for light eaters, while hearty cre-spelle stuffed with wild mushrooms and topped with a meaty Bolognese sauce can stave off the strongest hunger pangs. Mediterranean menu. Lunch, dinner. Closed Mon. Bar. Casual attire. **$$**
🅳

★ ★ **CASA ROMERO.** *30 Gloucester St, Boston (02115). Phone 617/536-4341; fax 617/536-6191. www.casaromero.com.* For more than three decades, chef/owner Leo Romero has been serving a taste of traditional Mexican cooking to Back Bay residents and visitors. Decorated with exposed brick and colorful Talavera tiles from Puebla, Casa Romero is a hidden gem, secreted in an alleyway between Newbury Street and Commonwealth Avenue. You will be hard-pressed to find a burrito on the menu, but you will find lots of authentic regional Mexican dishes, like huitla-coche folded into spinach tortillas, pork tenderloin marinated in oranges and smoked chipotle peppers, and mole poblano, accompanied by potent and tart margaritas. In the balmy weather, have dinner in the charming courtyard garden. Mexican menu. Dinner, Sun brunch. Closed Jan 1, July 4, Dec 25. Bar. Outdoor seating. **$$$**

★ ★ **CHAU CHOW CITY.** *83 Essex St, Boston (02111). Phone 617/338-8158.* The top floor of this three-level Chinatown institution is Boston's most adventurous dim sum venue. Even on weekday morn-ings, the rolling carts proffer a range of dishes worthy of a Hong Kong dim sum emporium. For a full meal on the other levels, stick to the kitchen's seafood specialties, including such delicacies as clams in black bean sauce or crab with ginger and scallion. Chinese, Hong Kong, dim sum menu. Breakfast, lunch, dinner, late-night. Casual attire. **$**

★ **CHEERS.** *84 Beacon St, Boston (02108). Phone 617/227-9605; fax 617/723-1898. www.cheersboston .com.* Life imitates art imitating life. Well, if not art, then television. Born as The Bull & Finch, this neigh-borhood watering hole was the model for TV's *Cheers.* The fame of its progeny eclipsed the charm of the original, but even if nobody knows your name, you can get a decent burger and a draft—once you get in the door. American menu. Lunch, dinner. Closed Dec. 25. Children's menu. Casual attire. **$$**

★ ★ **CIAO BELLA.** *240A Newbury St, Boston (02116). Phone 617/536-2626; fax 617/437-7585. www.ciaobella.com.* In the summer, the sidewalk tables at this townhouse restaurant on the corner of Fairfield and Newbury are some of the most coveted people-watching and flirting seats in town. The menu is a curious blend of steakhouse (robust veal chops, planks of swordfish) and Italian-American (specials like egg-plant ravioli). Many professional athletes hang here with their best buddies. Italian menu. Lunch, din-ner. Closed Thanksgiving, Dec 25. Bar. Casual attire. Reservations recommended. Valet parking. Outdoor seating. **$$$**
🅳

★ **CLAREMONT CAFE.** *535 Columbus Ave, Boston (02118). Phone 617/247-9001; fax 617/437-0062. www. claremontcafe.com.* This friendly neighborhood bistro specializes in American fare with Mediterranean touches. At breakfast, you'll find omelets, French toast, and breakfast sandwiches. Lunch brings burgers (in-cluding traditional as well as chicken, crab, and porto-bello), as well as entrées like steamed mussels and goat cheese ravioli. Dinnertime crowds find a wide variety of tapas, plus hearty roast chicken, Peruvian paella, and flavorful salads, along with seasonal daily specials. In warm weather, diners especially enjoy the outdoor patio. Mediterranean, American menu. Lunch, dinner, brunch. Closed Mon; holidays. Valet parking. Outdoor seating. **$$**

★ ★ **CLARKE'S TURN OF THE CENTURY.** *21 Merchants Row, Boston (02109). Phone 617/227-7800.* American menu. Lunch, dinner, late-night. Bar. Casual attire. **$$**

★ ★ ★ **CLIO.** *370 Commonwealth Ave, Boston (02215). Phone 617/536-7200; fax 617/578-0394. www.cliorestaurant.com.* Once you dine at Clio, you may want to write to chef/owner Ken Oringer and ask him to clone his Modern American restaurant and open one in your neighborhood. Picture-perfect plates arrive and practically glisten with attention to detail. The presentations are so intricate that you may want to photograph rather than eat. Ingredients are treated like notes in a melody; each one complements the next, and the result is a culinary symphony. Fresh fish plays a big role on the menu, and for those who prefer their seafood raw, Clio has a separate sashimi bar that features a pricey selection of rare fish that Oringer has flown in from around the world. With food this global and attentive service to match, the room is jammed nightly with a who's who of Boston's media and financial elite. The energy of the room gives Clio a steady buzz of Bostonian social electricity, and the food coming out of the kitchen gives you reason to return. American, French menu. Breakfast, dinner. Closed Mon. Bar. Business casual attire. Reservations recommended. Valet parking. **$$$$**

★ ★ **DAVIDE.** 326 Commercial St, Boston (02109). Phone 617/227-5745; fax 617/227-8976. www.davide ristorante.com. Named for Michelangelo's *David*, this North End Italian restaurant has been a standard favorite for handmade pastas, prime meats and seafood, and a terrific list of grappas for over two decades. The intimate subterranean dining room is set in a restored 18th-century church, and it has the worn, but warm, feel of a treasure from long ago and far away. Lovers of veal scaloppine can take comfort in knowing that chef/owner Franco Caritano's is one of the best in the city, while fans of Caesar salad, mixed tableside, will applaud this rich and creamy version. Pastas are wonderful as well, so be sure to come with an appetite. In short, dinner at Davide is delicious and uncomplicated, and sometimes that is all you need. Italian menu. Dinner. Bar. Valet parking. **$$**
🅳

★ ★ ★ **DAVIO'S.** 75 Arlington St, Boston (02116). Phone 617/357-4810; fax 617/357-1997. www.davios.com. Italian menu. Lunch, dinner. Bar. Children's menu. Casual attire. **$$**

★ **DURGIN PARK.** 340 Faneuil Hall Marketplace, Boston (02109). Phone 617/227-2038; fax 617/720-1542. www.durgin-park.com. While the menu runs the gamut from fish chowder to chicken pot pie, prime rib is the specialty at Durgin Park (established in 1826), a loud, fun, kitschy, red-and-white-checked-tablecloth spot in Faneuil Hall that's packed with good cheer nightly. Like the crowds, the food is unpretentious. The theme here is simple, honest home cookin'. Durgin Park is on two levels. Go upstairs if you feel like sitting elbow-to-elbow at communal-style tables and sharing a wilder time, and downstairs if you need privacy and a table of your own. American menu. Lunch, dinner. Closed Dec 25. Bar. Children's menu. Casual attire. Outdoor seating. **$$**

★ ★ **EXCELSIOR.** 272 Boylston St, Boston (02116). Phone 617/426-7878. www.excelsiorrestaurant.com/

home. Celebrity chef Lydia Shire has done it again with Excelsior, which breathes new life into one of Boston's famed locations. This dramatic restaurant pleases both the palate and the eye, even if its price comes as a bit of a shock. A "see and be seen" ambience defines this modern and sophisticated setting crafted by the darling of the design world, Adam Tihany, and its location in one of the city's landmarks overlooking Beacon Hill's Public Garden makes it a natural choice for celebrating special occasions. Everything is over the top here, from the 7,000-bottle wine cellar to the decadent meals. American menu. Dinner, late-night. Bar. Casual attire. **$$$**

★ ★ ★ **THE FEDERALIST.** 15 Beacon St, Boston (02108). Phone 617/670-2515; fax 617/670-2525. www.xvbeacon.com. This much-acclaimed-before-it-opened restaurant is becoming one of Boston's "to be seen" places. Its clubby, tongue-in-cheek salute to old Boston, with faux crumbling columns and plaster busts of colonial luminaries, continues on to the menu, where you can find updated versions of Yankee classics. Seafood menu. Breakfast, lunch, dinner. **$$$**

★ ★ **FILIPPO.** 283 Causeway St, Boston (02114). Phone 617/742-4143; fax 617/742-4245. www.filippo ristorante.com. The movie *Big Night* comes to mind at Filippo, a full-throttle Italian eatery with all the bells and whistles—mirrors, marble, and murals. Located in the North End, Filippo is known for its gargantuan portions and matching larger-than-life prices, but the cuisine is far more subtle and tasteful than the room might suggest. Although it's a far cry from haute cuisine, you'll find nicely done grilled meats and fish along with a delicious selection of pastas. Italian menu. Lunch, dinner. Closed Mon-Tues, Thanksgiving, Dec 25. Bar. Children's menu. Valet parking. **$$$**

★ ★ **FRANKLIN CAFE.** 278 Shawmut Ave, Boston (02118). Phone 617/350-0010. www.franklincafe.com. The Franklin stands on an ungentrified street, and the neo-Beatnik, all-black décor can scare off casual browsers. But there's usually a wait for tables as South End twentysomethings on a budget and smart foodies with a yen for Dave Du Bois's no-nonsense cooking fill the place. Each simple dish has an original twist, such as a grilled double-thick pork chop served on apple-sage bread pudding with bourbon gravy. The whole menu is available until 1 am. American menu. Dinner, late-night. Bar. Casual attire. **$$**
🅳

★ ★ **GINZA.** 16 Hudson St, Boston (02111). Phone 617/338-2261; fax 617/426-3563. Packed with Japanese patrons, Chinatown's first Japanese restaurant, Ginza, feels like a scene out of Tokyo. Waitresses are decked out in beautiful kimonos, and Japanese pop music fills the room as sushi chefs focus on their intricate craft, constructing maki at the speed of sound, their sushi knives flying in a blur of steel. The menu offers several house maki that tend to be gigantic, like an overstuffed roll filled with fried soft-shell crab, cucumber, avocado, flying fish roe, and spicy mayo; but it also includes more traditional Japanese (that is, normal-sized) sushi rolls and authentic barbecue and hot pot meals. Japanese menu. Lunch, dinner. **$$$**

★ **GRAND CHAU-CHOW.** *45 Beach St, Boston (02111). Phone 617/292-5166; fax 617/292-4646.* Authentic Cantonese cuisine is the star of the show at Grand Chau-Chow, a fast-paced restaurant featuring fresh fish brought straight from the tank to the flame to your plate, as well as traditional fare like spicy, fried, salted squid; steamed flounder; and clams in black bean sauce. The only issue with Grand Chau-Chow may be the fact that it seems to have a beat-the-clock mentality when it comes to serving you your meal. Expect to feel rushed, but good food has its price. Chinese menu. Lunch, dinner, late-night. **$$**

★ ★ ★ **GRILL 23 & BAR.** *161 Berkeley St, Boston (02116). Phone 617/542-2255; fax 617/542-5114. www.grill23.com.* The restaurant market is filled with formulaic steakhouse concepts: lots of beef paired with lots of testosterone, served up in a dark wood-paneled boys' club of a room. Grill 23 may serve lots of beef (seven juicy cuts are available, and each is dry-aged USDA Prime sirloin) and indeed houses its share of testosterone (hoards of handsome men in suits line the buzzing bar), but this high-energy beefeater's heaven is formulaic in no other way. Set in the historic Salada Tea Building in Boston's Back Bay, Grill 23 & Bar is a vast and stunning space, with original sculptured ceilings, massive Corinthian columns, mahogany paneling, and hardwood and marble floors that give the space a sense of history and warmth. In addition to the terrific selection of USDA Prime sirloin prepared in the restaurant's grand exhibition kitchen, the menu offers exciting and decidedly nonsteakhouse dishes as well. The "Fruits of the Sea" section includes tastings from the shimmering raw bar—lobster, shrimp, and clams—as well as caviar, sashimi, and assorted fish tartare, while entrées offer inventive American fare: roasted and grilled fish, poultry, lamb shanks, and the like. In colder months, the upstairs lounge is the place to be with its blazing fire

and cozy seating. Seafood, steak menu. Dinner. Closed holidays. Bar. Jacket required. Valet parking. **$$$$**

★ ★ ★ ★ **HAMERSLEY'S BISTRO.** *553 Tremont St, Boston (02116). Phone 617/423-2700; fax 617/423-7710. www.hamersleysbistro.com.* Buttercup walls, mile-deep plush banquettes, authentic farmhouse wood-beamed ceilings, and a warm amber glow give Hamersley's Bistro the air of home. The food coming out of chef/owner Gordon Hamersley's lively open kitchen (Hamersley is usually on the line, cooking in a baseball hat) makes you realize that you are, in fact, not at home. If the food were this good at your home, it is doubtful that you would ever bother leaving. The house specialty, chicken roasted with garlic, lemon, and parsley, is the perfect example of how simple food can shine. The bird has a crisp, taut, golden skin, and its flesh is moist, succulent, and saturated with flavor. While the menu centers on hearty American bistro fare, do not take this to mean that the food here is boring, dull, or tired. Standards are expertly prepared with care and skill, and the kitchen is not afraid to bring in eclectic global flavors to create inventive dishes for guests who have been dining here for more than a decade. The kitchen also offers a weekly vegan special that could turn on the most ardent of carnivores. Hamersley's eclectic wine list changes with the seasons, as does the menu, and the restaurant's warm staff is more than happy (and very able) to help guide you to the right selection for your meal. French menu. Dinner. Closed holidays. Bar. Casual attire. Reservations recommended. Valet parking. Outdoor seating. **$$$**

★ ★ **THE HUNGRY I.** *71 Charles St, Boston (02114). Phone 617/227-3524; fax 617/227-0237.* Romantic, but drafty in the winter (perhaps better for snuggling up next to that special someone), The Hungry I specializes in intimate, cozy, candlelit dining in a historic 1840s house. If you are planning an evening of gazing across the table, this is a good choice. The menu is old-school French, so expect dishes like frogs' legs, rabbit, venison, and pheasant, dressed in classic sauces thickened with decadent amounts of butter. The specials are always a treat, especially the tomato and garlic soup. French menu. Lunch Thurs-Fri, dinner, Sun brunch. Closed July 4, Thanksgiving, Dec 25. Bar. Casual attire. Outdoor seating (Sun brunch only). **$$$**
🅱

★ ★ ★ **ICARUS.** *3 Appleton St, Boston (02116). Phone 617/426-1790; fax 617/426-2150. www.icarus*

restaurant.com. Located in the South End in a converted 1860s building, Icarus is one of those rare restaurants where the evening is over way too soon. The intimate bar serves tasty cocktails and delicious homemade rosemary breadsticks, while the lovely, serene dining room (there's live jazz every Friday evening) is an easy place to relax and enjoy chef/owner Chris Douglas's flavorful seasonal New American menu, with whimsical dishes like slow-roasted tomato soup with Timson cheese panini, polenta with braised exotic mushrooms, and duck in a show-stopping cider and bourbon sauce. It's tough to fit dessert in, but it's worth loosening the belt—the chocolate molten cake with homemade vanilla bean ice cream and raspberry sauce is a necessary evil. American menu. Dinner. Closed holidays. Bar. Valet parking. **$$$$**

★ **JASPER WHITE'S SUMMER SHACK.** *50 Dalton St, Boston (02115). Phone 617/867-9955. www.summershackrestaurant.com.* Celebrate the fun-loving spirit of summer year-round at Jasper White's Summer Shack. This casual and lively joint, styled after the classic clam shacks of the New England coast, brings the best of the beach to the heart of the city. Armed with large appetites, diners come in groups to strap on bibs and dig into heaping portions of fresh and delicious seafood served broiled, boiled, grilled, fried, or raw. Live music and a bustling bar add to the Summer Shack's inimitable gregarious atmosphere. Seafood menu. Lunch, dinner. Bar. Children's menu. Casual attire. **$$**

★ ★ **JIMMY'S HARBORSIDE.** *242 Northern Ave, Boston (02210). Phone 617/423-1000; fax 617/451-0669. www.jimmysharborside.com.* A recent makeover transformed Jimmy's from a faded waterfront lounge into a retro icon of summer, adding outdoor seating with stupendous harbor views and devoting a portion of the extended dining area to a clam-shack menu. The split personality works—Dad with his martini and crumb-crusted scrod, Junior with his bucket of steamers and pitcher of beer. American, seafood menu. Lunch, dinner. Closed Dec 25. Bar. Children's menu. Casual attire. Valet parking. Outdoor seating. **$$**

★ ★ **KASHMIR.** *279 Newbury St, Boston (02116). Phone 617/536-1695; fax 617/536-1598. www.kashmirspices.com.* Kashmir is a sophisticated local spot for extra-special Indian cuisine. Located in the Back Bay, Kashmir is not your typical Indian all-you-can-eat restaurant. While it does offer an exten-

sive daily buffet (a culinary paradise for lovers of this savory, spiced cuisine), Kashmir is a soothing, cozy space, swathed in off-white and turquoise, with lovely, deep banquettes. If the buffet is too overwhelming, stick to the dinner menu, where you'll find wonderful standards like mulligatawny, samosas, and a tandoori mixed grill. Indian menu. Lunch, dinner. Jacket required. Valet parking. Outdoor seating. **$$$**

★ ★ ★ **L'ESPALIER.** *30 Gloucester St, Boston (02115). Phone 617/262-3023; fax 617/375-9297. www.lespalier.com.* Housed in a charming 19th-century townhouse, L'Espalier makes it easy to slip into another era. The restaurant feels like a Merchant-Ivory film come to life. Luxuriously appointed with vintage drapes framing tall bay windows, fresh flowers, fine linens, and antique china adorning each table, L'Espalier is a decidedly sophisticated venue for a decadent and delicious dining experience. The menu is prepared with impeccable French technique and a nod to New England's regional ingredients and comfortable style. The chef prepares prix fixe and tasting menus as well as a Degustation of Caviar—each of five courses is prepared with caviar—for those feeling very indulgent. At L'Espalier, you'll find that your first bite tastes as good as your last. The kitchen consistently wows, sending out one extraordinary dish after another. A glorious monster of a wine list offers an amazing variety of wines and vintages, with a wide enough price range to allow for great choices under $50. American menu. Dinner, Sat tea. Closed Sun; holidays. Business casual attire. Reservations recommended. Valet parking. **$$$$**

★ ★ **LALA ROKH.** *97 Mt. Vernon St, Boston (02108). Phone 617/720-5511. www.lalarokh.com.* If you've never tasted Persian cuisine, you simply must, and Lala Rokh is the perfect place to experiment with the authentic, home-style dishes of this exotic region of the Middle East. Fragrant pots of silky rice make up the base of almost every meal, topped with a variety of stews made with slow-cooked, fork-tender beef or with lamb, stewed with aromatics like saffron or dill and intense traditional flavors like sumaq and preserved lemon. The restaurant prides itself on its hospitality, which it delivers with grace, ensuring that every diner leaves feeling pampered and with a happy, full belly. Persian menu. Lunch, dinner. Closed holidays. Casual attire. Valet parking. **$$**

★ ★ **LES ZYGOMATES.** *129 South St, Boston (02111). Phone 617/542-5108; fax 617/482-8806. www.winebar.com.* Mixing French cuisine with select Mexican and Italian dishes, Les Zygomates is a comfortable Paris bistro that's right at home in Boston's old leather district. Six nights per week, enjoy live jazz performed by local and national musicians while you top off your meal with a decadent chocolate dessert. French bistro menu. Lunch, dinner, late-night. Closed Sun. Casual attire. Valet parking. **$$**

★ ★ ★ **LOCKE-OBER.** *3 Winter Pl, Boston (02108). Phone 617/542-1340; fax 617/542-6452. www.lockeober.com.* Established in 1875, Boston's famed Locke-Ober restaurant is a classic's classic. This glitzy, turn-of-the-(previous)-century dining landmark buzzes with electricity as the room fills to the seams with assorted foodies, superstars, financiers, and celebrity political types. Under the skilled leadership of chef/co-owner Lydia Shire, traditional American fare feels fresh and exciting and makes a persuasive case for eating nothing that flirts with fusion ever again. The menu speaks in simple yet spectacular terms, featuring classic plates from America's past, like beef Stroganoff with hand-cut egg noodles, as well as old French standards like duck l'orange and onion soup gratinée. The Indian pudding is a signature dessert, as is the fresh strawberry shortcake, when in season. American menu. Lunch, dinner. Closed Sun; holidays. Bar. Jacket required. Valet parking. **$$$**

★ ★ **LUCIA.** *415 Hanover St, Boston (02113). Phone 617/523-9148; fax 617/367-8952. www.luciaboston.com.* Lucia, a North End favorite since 1977, remains a steady choice for regional Italian fare. Owned by the Frattaroli family, the restaurant is marked by over-the-top and very large floor-to-ceiling murals, while the menu is most noted for the robust dishes of Italy's Abruzzi region, like Granasso d'Italia (a light dish of veal, peas, artichokes, prosciutto, pine nuts, eggplant, and mozzarella), and Gnocchi d'Abruzzo (with pesto), as well as a bold selection of country-style meat dishes. There's also a second location in Winchester. Italian menu. Lunch, dinner. Closed Thanksgiving, Dec 25. Bar. Children's menu. Valet parking. **$$**

★ ★ ★ **MAMMA MARIA.** *3 North Sq, Boston (02113). Phone 617/523-0077; fax 617/523-4348. www.mammamaria.com.* Located in North Square, Mamma Maria is one of Boston's most beloved Italian restaurants. Filled nightly with celebrities and savvy locals, this romantic spot, set in an early 19th-century brick townhouse, serves an elegant New American and contemporary Italian menu that features seasonal ingredients and steers clear of heavy, cheesy, red-sauced pastas. This is the sort of restaurant that easily impresses diners, from its impeccable service to its delicious menu, so if you're out to, say, meet the parents for the first time, this would be a good choice. Italian menu. Dinner. Closed holidays. Bar. Casual attire. Valet parking. **$$$**

★ ★ ★ **MANTRA.** *52 Temple Pl, Boston (02111). Phone 617/542-8111; fax 617/542-8666. www.mantrarestaurant.com.* Chef/owner Thomas John has created a jewel of a restaurant with Mantra, a low-lit, sexy restaurant set in a stunning turn-of-the-century former bank in Boston's über-hip ladder district. Decked out in raw silk upholstery, with chainmail drapery and red crushed suede banquettes, Mantra is an exotic space that makes you feel wildly beautiful. The menu is a perfect blend of French technique and Indian accents like saffron, cumin, tamarind, and cloves, and the kitchen delivers aromatic dishes marked by exciting, deliciously bold flavor pairings. Desserts are wonderful and include such delights as vanilla bean kulfi, an Indian ice cream that has a delicate, dreamy creaminess. Indian, French menu. Lunch, dinner, late-night. Closed Sun. Bar. Casual attire. Reservations recommended. **$$$**

★ ★ ★ **MASA.** *439 Tremont St, Boston (02116). Phone 617/338-8884; fax 617/338-6019. www.masarestaurant.com.* Southwestern menu. Dinner, late-night, Sun brunch. Bar. Casual attire. Outdoor seating. **$$$**

★ **MIKE'S CITY DINER.** *1714 Washington St, Boston (02118). Phone 617/267-9393.* Mike's serves breakfast and lunch only, but it's worth getting up early for the corned-beef hash or the fat Belgian waffles. A survivor from the era of real diners, it has a patina that no imitation can match. Customers range from construction workers to artsy loft dwellers, but watch out when politicians are in town—they love the place for photo ops. American menu. Breakfast, lunch. Casual attire. **$**

★ ★ ★ **MISTRAL.** *223 Columbus Ave, Boston (02116). Phone 617/867-9300; fax 617/351-2601. www.mistralbistro.com.* Although the vaulted ceilings and sophisticated décor may scream glam central, chef/owner Jamie Mammanno's creative yet uncomplicated cuisine departs from those kinds of expectations. Menu items such as tuna tartare, grilled thin-crust pizzas, and skillet-roasted Cornish game hen are complemented by a superb wine list. French, Mediterranean menu. Dinner, late-night. Closed Thanksgiving, Dec 25. Bar. Reservations recommended. Valet parking. **$$$**

★ ★ ★ ★ **NO. 9 PARK.** *9 Park St, Boston (02108). Phone 617/742-9991; fax 617/742-9993.* In the shadow of the Massachusetts State House in historic Beacon Hill, you will find No. 9 Park, a 19th-century mansion turned elegant dining salon. Inside, you'll find a kitchen that serves some of the most wonderful European country-style cuisine in the region. Many of the ingredients on the seasonal menu are identified by farm; chef/owner Barbara Lynch makes an effort to support top-of-the-line small producers of sustainable agriculture. Perfectly prepared with a healthy dose of flavor and style, Lynch's sophisticated, tempting menu of modern European fare runs the gamut from beef to fish to venison and pheasant, depending on the season. After dinner, stop at the beautifully appointed bar for a cognac or port, and give yourself some more time to relax before you go back to the real world. No. 9 Park is a magical sort of place that you just won't want to leave. Mediterranean menu. Lunch, dinner. Closed Sun; holidays. Bar. Casual attire. Valet parking. **$$$$**

★ ★ ★ **THE OAK ROOM.** *138 St. James Ave, Boston (02116). Phone 617/267-5300; fax 617/247-6681. www.fairmont.com.* This old-world steakhouse, located in the Fairmont Copley Plaza Boston Hotel (see), is steeped in Edwardian charm, with a restored carved-plaster ceiling, baroque woodwork, and garnet-red draperies. Drawing a boisterous crowd of twenty- and thirtysomethings and more sophisticated, mature audiences alike, The Oak Room's mass appeal is attributed to its stunning slabs of grilled fish and beef tenderloin, and classics like chateaubriand (for two), oysters Rockefeller, and clams casino. American, seafood, steak menu. Breakfast, lunch, dinner. Bar. Business casual attire. Reservations recommended. Valet parking. **$$$**

★ ★ ★ **OLIVES.** *10 City Sq, Charlestown (02129). Phone 617/242-1999. toddenglish.com.* Some celebrity chefs rest on their laurels while their restaurants unravel at the culinary seams. Not so for Todd English. Olives, his first restaurant, has remained a destination for wildly good, boldly flavored Mediterranean fare. While the food is a big reason to dine here, the atmosphere may not be for everyone. The rustic European décor and large windows overlooking the square add appeal, but tables tend to be full nightly, which can make the dining room a bit cramped—this may not be the best choice for quiet conversation. But who really needs to talk when mouths are filled with such good food? Mediterranean menu. Dinner. Closed holidays. Bar. Valet parking. **$$$**

★ ★ ★ **THE PALM.** *200 Dartmouth St, Boston (02116). Phone 617/867-9292; fax 617/867-0789. www.thepalm.com.* "Let them eat meat!" might be an apt phrase to hang on a wall at The Palm, a boys' club of a steakhouse located in the Westin Copley Place (see). This branch of the New York City favorite attracts local celebrities, financial moguls, and out-of-town dealmakers looking to talk shop over copious amounts of perfectly seared prime beef. The service is efficient and knowledgeable, and the kitchen is expert at making sure that your beef is cooked to specification every time. In addition to the carnivorous menu items, you'll find fat, fillerless crab cakes, lobsters the size of small pets, and Italian fare like veal marsala. Of course, no steakhouse would be complete without sides, and the creamed spinach here, laced with Parmesan, is an absolute pinup. Steak menu. Lunch, dinner. Closed holidays. Bar. Valet parking. **$$$**

★ ★ **PARKER'S.** *60 School St, Boston (02108). Phone 617/227-8600; fax 617/742-5729. www.omnihotels.com.* JFK's grandfather made Parker's the de facto headquarters of Massachusetts pols, Ho Chi Minh worked in the kitchen, and Charles Dickens ate here with Ralph Waldo Emerson whenever he was in town. It's the birthplace of Parker House rolls and Boston cream pie, and one of the oldest dining rooms in the nation—though lovingly updated. Parker's is Boston's first choice for pomp and history—and the roast beef's not bad either. American menu. Breakfast, lunch, dinner. Bar. Children's menu. Valet parking. **$$$**

★ **PEKING TOM'S.** *25 Kingston St, Boston (02111). Phone 617/482-6282. www.pekingtom.com.* Peking Tom's resurrects the whole package of 1950s Chinese glamour dining: food with glazes, electric-colored drinks, and hostesses in shiny silk dresses. The sushi bar is the culinary star, as the regular menu is filled with the retro likes of crab rangoon (made with cream cheese) and tamarind-glazed spareribs. The bar is a hot singles spot. Chinese menu. Lunch, dinner. Bar. Casual attire. **$$**

★ ★ **PERDIX.** *560 Tremont St, Boston (02118). Phone 617/338-8070; fax 617/338-2201. www.*

perdixrestaurant.com. After a successful run with just ten tables in Boston's Jamaica Plain neighborhood, chef/owner Tim Partridge has moved into a South End space big enough for lots of people to enjoy. His family bistro cooking produces food with visual and sensual punch—a nori roll of tuna, scallions, and flash-fried radishes, or monkfish with roasted fresh tomatoes. The entrée list is short, but specials abound. For romance, ask for a greenhouse table. American menu. Dinner, Sun brunch. Closed Mon. Bar. Casual attire. Outdoor seating. **$$**

★ ★ **PHO REPUBLIQUE.** *1415 Washington St, Boston (02118). Phone 617/262-0005.* While an old-country version of pho (the noodle soup that's the national dish of Vietnam) reigns supreme here, chef Didi Emmons also conjures up French-Vietnamese food for hipsters with great taste but modest budgets. The crowd tends to be young and multiethnic; the food, such as shrimp and sweet potato nests, tends to be bright and sassy. Several vegetarian and vegan options are available. Vietnamese menu. Dinner, late-night. Bar. Casual attire. **$$**

★ ★ ★ **RADIUS.** *8 High St, Boston (02110). Phone 617/426-1234; fax 617/426-2526. www.radius restaurant.com.* Chef/partner Michael Schlow is a man who understands what people are looking for in a dining experience. First, there's atmosphere. Radius is a stunningly chic, slick, modern space decked out in silver and garnet red. Crowded with some of Boston's most stylish residents, you will step inside and instantly feel like you're on the set of *Sex and the City.* Second, there's the food. Schlow offers diners a chance to taste some truly inspired modern French cooking. There is an emphasis on the seasons here, so the menu changes often, but what doesn't change is the quality of the ingredients and the care with which the kitchen assembles each magnificent dish. Schlow doesn't like to overload the plate (or the belly) with heavy sauces. This is refined, light-handed cooking using infused oils, emulsions, juices, vegetable purées, and reductions to heighten flavors and add texture and balance to every dish. Dining here is a wonderful feast for all the senses. French menu. Lunch, dinner. Closed Sun. Bar. Reservations recommended. Valet parking. **$$$**

★ ★ **THE RED FEZ.** *1222 Washington St, Boston (02118). Phone 617/338-6060; fax 617/338-6666. www.theredfez.com.* First opened in 1940, The Red Fez celebrates the foods of the Middle East and the Mediterranean. The menu is heavy on salads and hot and cold mezze but also offers a variety of grilled meats and skewers. Small, tasty plates of marinated olives, grape leaves, and savory lamb and tomato pie are great for sharing. You'll also find a nice selection of international beers and wines. The lively dining room features tall windows, exposed-brick walls, and cheerful blue glassware. Middle Eastern menu. Dinner, late-night, Sun brunch. Bar. Casual attire. Outdoor seating. **$$**

★ ★ **RISTORANTE TOSCANO.** *47 Charles St, Boston (02114). Phone 617/723-4090; fax 617/720-4280. www.ristorantetoscano.com.* Toscano is one of Beacon Hill's hottest destinations for rustic Italian fare. The exposed-brick dining room is just a few blocks from the State House, so it's often filled with political movers and shakers, but it's also home to many locals who come in several times a week for their fix of chef/owner Vinicio Paoli's country-style dishes, like braised lamb, roast pork, grilled beef, and homemade pasta. The heavenly ricotta pie is a must for dessert. Italian menu. Lunch, dinner. Closed Sun, holidays. Bar. Valet parking. **$$$**

★ ★ ★ **SAGE.** *69 Prince St, Boston (02113). Phone 617/248-8814; fax 617/248-1879. www.sageboston.com.* Great things do indeed come in small packages, and Boston's Sage is one such small but precious thing. At a mere 35 seats (reserve ahead), Sage is a petite but perfect stage for chef/owner Anthony Susi's beautiful modern American fare, including a stunning selection of handmade pastas like gnocchi and ravioli that are as light as air, but rich in flavor. If you can't decide, the pasta sampler is a wonderful way to try a few. American menu. Dinner. Closed Sun. Reservations recommended. **$$$**

★ ★ **SAVANNAH GRILL.** *233A Elm St, Somerville (02144). Phone 617/666-4200.* American, Mediterranean, vegetarian menu. Lunch, dinner. Casual attire. Outdoor seating. **$$**

★ ★ ★ **SEASONS.** *26 North St, Boston (02109). Phone 617/523-4119; fax 617/523-2593. www. millenniumhotels.com.* Set in the Millennium Bostonian Hotel (see), with views of Faneuil Hall, Seasons is a sophisticated destination for romantic, charming dining. While the delicious, if pricey, fusion menu features a global mix of dishes from Asia, Italy, France, and America, the wine list is 100 percent American, a nice tribute to our domestic wineries. Seasons is a lovely place to spend an evening, especially if you believe that conversation should be heard without the need to yell, that service should be gracious, and that dinner should never be rushed. American menu. Breakfast, lunch, dinner. Closed holidays. Bar. Children's menu. Valet parking. **$$$**

★ ★ **SISTER SOREL.** *647 Tremont St, Boston (02118). Phone 617/266-4600. www.tremont647.com.* Snuggled up to the lauded Tremont 647, Sister Sorel is a trendy wine bar and café that is most often used as a holding pen for those looking to dig into the full, bold flavors of Tremont's chef/owner Andy Husbands. Also the chef/owner of Sister Sorel, he turns out the same arrestingly robust cuisine at this café, only in smaller portions and at smaller prices. The modest menu includes spit-roasted chicken; salt-and-pepper fried skirt steak; and the Burger Daddy, a gorgeous pup infused with smoke and topped with chipotle mustard. American menu. Dinner. Bar. Casual attire. Outdoor seating. **$$**

★ ★ **SONSIE.** *327 Newbury St, Boston (02115). Phone 617/351-2500; fax 617/351-2565. www.sonsieboston.com.* Chic shoppers in need of sustenance head for Newbury Street's favorite sidewalk café, Sonsie. A stylish clientele flocks to this delightful restaurant, where open-air tables and French doors create a Parisian feel. The fusion menu is matched only by the superior people-watching. Since it can be a bit of a scene, those in the know arrive early to avoid the long lines and snag a table in the front for better viewing. Sunday brunch is a best bet, offering consistently good meals and value. American menu. Breakfast, lunch, dinner, late-night, brunch. Bar. Casual attire. Reservations recommended. Outdoor seating. **$$**

★ ★ **TAPEO.** *266 Newbury St, Boston (02116). Phone 617/267-4799; fax 617/267-1602. www.tapeo.com.* Tapeo is a Back Bay charmer with a singular Spanish vision. Serving all things from this Iberian land, expect a long menu of hot and cold authentic tapas, including shrimp sizzling in garlic and classic tortilla d'Espana, and an all-Spanish wine and sherry list. The restaurant is low-lit, romantic, and extremely popular with locals for people-watching, tasty fare, and pitchers of fruity sangria with a good kick. Spanish menu. Lunch, dinner. Closed holidays. Bar. Outdoor seating. **$$**

★ ★ **TARANTA.** *210 Hanover St, Boston. Phone 617/720-0052; fax 617/507-0492. www.tarantarist.com.* Chef/owner Jose Duarte hails from Peru, got started cooking among Italian immigrants in Venezuela, and has had a steady hit on his hands since opening the North End's only Peruvian-Italian fusion

restaurant. His signature shrimp ravioli in a pesto of pine nuts and Peruvian black mint demonstrates the easy cohibitation of the two cuisines, as does his substitution of quinoa for rice in the saffron "risotto" accompanying braised veal shanks. The piquant lift to many of Duarte's sauces comes from his careful use of the rocoto pepper, another Peruvian native, but the new-world fillips never overwhelm what is essentially old-world comfort food prepared with flair and served with style. Peruvian, Italian menu. Dinner. Closed July 4, Thanksgiving. Casual attire. **$$$**

★ ★ **TERRAMIA.** *98 Salem St, Boston (02113). Phone 617/523-3112. www.terramiaristorante.com.* Located in the North End, Terramia is a lovely Italian restaurant with a warm and charming atmosphere that makes you feel at home in an instant. The menu is of the modern trattoria genre—a great selection of meats, pastas, and salads that may sound straightforward in style, but in substance rise above and beyond. Dishes that could be run-of-the-mill are freshened up by quality seasonal ingredients and by the skill of co-owner and chef Mario Nocera. The restaurant's culinary reputation is well known around town, so be sure and reserve in advance if possible. Italian menu. Dinner. Closed holidays. Children's menu. Reservations recommended. **$$$**

★ ★ ★ **TOP OF THE HUB.** *800 Boylston St, Boston (02199). Phone 617/536-1775; fax 617/859-8298. www.topofthehub.net.* If sweeping, awesome views are your thing, Top of the Hub should make it onto your short list while you're in Boston. Located in the trendy Back Bay area, this special-occasion spot specializes in elegant and romantic, yet decidedly comfortable, dining. The New American menu takes some chances but for the most part stays true to the seasons, featuring a wide selection of fish, game, pork, and beef. Main courses are ample, like the slow-roasted pork tenderloin (enough to feed a family of four) and a plate of supple slices of seared yellowfin tuna with fragrant coconut-jasmine rice. American menu. Lunch, dinner. Closed Dec 25. Bar. **$$$**

★ ★ ★ **TORCH.** *26 Charles St, Boston (02114). Phone 617/723-5939. www.bostontorch.com.* Torch is an intimate, warm, family-operated bistro serving classic French fare. Chef/co-owner Evan Deluty offers his happy guests many easy ways to enjoy dinner, including a wonderfully buttery hanger steak, a terrific duck confit, wildly rich smashed potatoes, desserts that contain one's body weight in butter, and a great cheese course. The crowd is casual, but hip, and seems intent on doing nothing more than dining leisurely and simply, with good food, good friends, lots of laughter, and lots of wine. French menu. Dinner. Closed Mon. Casual attire. Reservations recommended. Valet parking. **$$$**

★ ★ ★ **TROQUET.** *140 Boylston St, Boston (02116). Phone 617/695-9463.* The marriage of food and wine is the focus of this authentic Back Bay bistro. Owned by Chris and Diane Campbell (who used to own Uva), Troquet pairs wine with food, with wine running the show. For instance, a flight of Sauvignon Blanc would require you start with a fresh, tangy goat cheese coated in nuts and deep-fried over an arugula salad. If you are craving a jammy Merlot, you'll have to deal with a leg of lamb. (It's a nice problem to have.) The couplings work well for the most part and will teach you a thing or two about relationships that are worth continuing and those that really aren't worth it. American, French menu. Dinner. Closed Sun-Mon. Bar. Casual attire. Reservations recommended. **$$$**

★ ★ ★ **UNION BAR AND GRILLE.** *1357 Washington St, Boston (02118). Phone 617/423-0555. www.unionrestaurant.com.* With sleek leather banquettes and blazingly white tablecloths, Union Bar and Grille caps the gentrification process of Washington Street. Stephen Sherman, the Culinary Institute of America-trained chef, produces a seasonally shifting menu that nods to trendy dishes (tuna with grilled fennel) but leans heavily on updated New England classics, such as lobster meat tossed with corn and chanterelle mushrooms and a succulent rack of lamb drizzled with fig sauce. The wine list is as aggressively new world as the menu, pulling in a lot of Californian meritage bottles along with New Zealand whites. Pastry chef Joshua Steinberg's dessert menu seems to have a spot of chocolate on almost every plate. American menu. Dinner, Sun brunch. Bar. Casual attire. Valet parking. **$$$**

★ ★ **UNION OYSTER HOUSE.** *41 Union St, Boston (02108). Phone 617/227-2750; fax 617/227-6401. www.unionoysterhouse.com.* This popular 1826 oyster bar and tavern, decorated in old-fashioned Federalist style, has served such dignitaries as John F. Kennedy and Bill Clinton. But not to worry—they'll serve you too. This crowded hotspot attracts hordes of businessmen, ties tucked behind white shirts, slurping down hearty bowls of chowder and slipping chilled oysters out of their shells. The menu also caters to lovers of fresh fish, prepared perfectly every time.

Seafood menu. Lunch, dinner. Closed Thanksgiving, Dec 25. Bar. Children's menu. Valet parking. **$$**

★ ★ ★ **VIA MATTA.** *79 Park Plz, Boston (02116). Phone 617/422-0008; fax 617/422-0014. www.viamattarestaurant.com.* Michael Schlow, Christopher Myers, and Esti Benson, the savvy team behind Radius (see), are the folks you can thank for opening Via Matta, a trendy spot for authentic Italian fare located across the street from the Park Plaza Hotel. You have several choices of where to dine here—the bustling, stylish dining room; the cozy, softly lit bar; or the casual café—but fret not about your decision. Regardless of where you decide to sit, you will feast happily on chef Schlow's gorgeous traditional Italian dishes. Plates are alive with flavor and fitted with the highest-quality ingredients. Hearty appetites should be required here, as the menu lists close to a dozen antipasti, followed by several pasta selections, and a half-dozen entrées. But empty stomachs will be rewarded, as the food here is truly an inspiration. From the simple spaghetti aglio e olio to pan-roasted chicken, dishes are simple and perfectly executed. To get from course to course without being parched, check out the all-Italian wine list that showcases rare winemakers. Italian menu. Lunch, dinner, late-night. Closed Sun. Bar. Casual attire. **$$**

Bourne (Cape Cod) (D-8)

See also Sandwich

Settled 1627
Population 18,721
Elevation 19 ft
Area Code 508
Zip 02532
Information Cape Cod Chamber of Commerce, Hwys 6 and 132, PO Box 790, Hyannis 02601-0790; phone 508/362-3225 or toll-free 888/332-2732
Web Site www.capecodchamber.org

Named for Jonathan Bourne, a successful whaling merchant, this town has had a variety of industries since its founding. Originally a center for herring fishing, the town turned to manufacturing stoves, kettles, and later, freight cars. Bourne's current prosperity is derived from cranberries and tourism.

What to See and Do

Aptucxet Trading Post. *24 Aptucxet Rd, Bourne (02532). Off Shore Rd, 1/2 mile W of Bourne Bridge. Phone 508/759-9487.* A replica of a 1627 trading post that may have been the first of its kind in America. Native American artifacts; rune stone believed to be proof of visits to the area by the Phoenicians in 400 BC; artifacts in two rooms. On grounds are herb garden, site of original spring, saltworks; railroad station built for President Grover Cleveland for use at his Gray Gables home, his summer White House; Dutch-style windmill; picnic area adjacent to Cape Cod Canal. (July-Aug, daily; last two weekends in May-June and Sept-mid-Oct, Tues-Sun) **$**

Bourne Scenic Park. *375 Scenic Hwy, Bourne (02532). North bank of Cape Cod Canal. Phone 508/759-7873.* Playground, picnicking; bike trails; swimming pool, bathhouse; recreation building; camping (fee); store. (Apr-May: weekends; June-Oct: daily) **$$**

Pairpoint Crystal Company. *851 Sandwich Rd (Hwy 6), Sagamore (02561). Phone 508/888-2344.* (Established in 1837) Handmade lead crystal ware, glassblowing demonstrations. Viewing (Mon-Fri). Store (daily). **FREE**

Braintree (C-7)

See also Boston

Settled 1634
Population 33,828
Elevation 90 ft
Area Code 781
Zip 02184
Information South Shore Chamber of Commerce, 36 Miller Stile Rd, Quincy 02169; phone 781/479-1111
Web Site www.southshorechamber.org

What to See and Do

Abigail Adams House. *North and Norton sts, Weymouth (02188). 2 miles E. Phone 781/335-1849.* Birthplace of Abigail Smith Adams (1744), daughter of a local clergyman, wife of President John Adams, mother of President John Quincy Adams. Period furnishings. (July-Labor Day, Tues-Sun) **$$**

Gilbert Bean Museum. *786 Washington St, Braintree (02184). Phone 781/848-1640.* (1720) Thayer, a soldier and educator, served as fifth Superintendent of West Point, 1817-1833. House contains 17th- and 18th-

century furnishings, military exhibits, and local historical displays. (Tues-Wed, Sat-Sun) **$$** Adjacent is a

Reconstructed 18th-Century Barn. Houses farm equipment, ice-cutting and wood tools; costumes; research library and genealogical records. (Tues-Wed, Sat-Sun) **$**

Limited-Service Hotels

★ ★ **HOLIDAY INN.** *1374 N Main St, Randolph (02368). Phone 781/961-1000; toll-free 800/465-4329; fax 781/963-0089. www.holiday-inn.com.* 158 rooms, 4 story. Pets accepted. Check-in 3 pm, check-out noon. Restaurant, bar. Outdoor pool. **$**

★ **HOLIDAY INN EXPRESS.** *909 Hingham St, Rockland (02370). Phone 781/871-5660; toll-free 800/465-4329; fax 781/871-7255. www.hiexpress.com/rocklandma.* 76 rooms, 2 story. Complimentary continental breakfast. Check-in 3 pm, check-out 11 am. **$**

Full-Service Hotel

★ ★ ★ **SHERATON BRAINTREE HOTEL.** *37 Forbes Rd, Braintree (02184). Phone 781/848-0600; toll-free 800/325-3535; fax 781/843-9492. www.sheraton.com/braintree.* The Sheraton is located 12 miles from the Logan International Airport and near the JFK library and Bayside Exposition Center. Rooms were designed and furnished with a guest's needs in mind. Relax in the indoor or outdoor pool, sauna and steamrooms, or enjoy an invigorating workout at the extensive health club with racquetball, aerobics, and Nautilus machines. 396 rooms, 6 story. Check-in 3 pm, check-out noon. Restaurant, bar. Fitness room. Indoor pool, outdoor pool. **$**

Restaurant

★ ★ **CAFFE BELLA.** *19 Warren St, Randolph (02368). Phone 781/961-7729; fax 781/961-3681.* Italian menu. Dinner. Closed Sun; holidays. Bar. **$$$**

Brewster (Cape Cod) (D-9)

Settled 1656
Population 10,094
Elevation 39 ft
Area Code 508
Zip 02631
Information Cape Cod Chamber of Commerce, Hwys 6 and 132, PO Box 790, Hyannis 02601-0790; phone 508/362-3225 or toll-free 888/332-2732
Web Site www.capecodchamber.org

This quiet community on Cape Cod Bay is dominated by its miles of beautiful saltwater beaches, where the tides have caused the water to recede by more than a mile, creating an expanse of sand and tidepools. The New England Fire and History Museum is located here, as are plentiful opportunities to shop for crafts and antiques. The outstanding Chillingsworth is a standout among both lodgings and restaurants here.

What to See and Do

Cape Cod Museum of Natural History. *869 Hwy 6A, Brewster (02631). Phone 508/896-3867; toll-free 800/479-3867.* Exhibits on wildlife and ecology of the area; art exhibits; library; lectures; nature trails; field walks; trips to Monomoy Island. Gift shop. (Daily; closed holidays) **$$**

Cape Cod Repertory Theater Company. *3379 Hwy 6A, Brewster (02631). Phone 508/896-1888. www.caperep.org.* Boasting both an indoor and outdoor theater, the Cape Cod Repertory Theater offers a children's theater two mornings per week (Tues and Fri) in July and August. In addition, you'll find productions for the whole family in the outdoor theater, which sits back in the beautiful woods near Nickerson State Park and is open in fair weather. The indoor theater offers plays and musicals year-round. **$$$**

⭐ **New England Fire & History Museum.** *1439 Main St, Brewster (02631). 1/2 mile W of Hwy 137 on Hwy 6A. Phone 508/896-5711.* This six-building complex houses an extensive collection of fire-fighting equipment and includes the Arthur Fiedler Memorial Fire Collection; diorama of Chicago fire of 1871; engines dating from the Revolution to the 1930s; world's only 1929 Mercedes Benz fire engine; life-size reproduction of Ben Franklin's firehouse; 19th-century blacksmith shop; largest apothecary shop in the country contains 664 gold-leaf bottles of medicine; medicinal herb gardens; library; films; theater performances. Guided tours. Picnic area. (Memorial Day weekend-mid-Sept: daily; mid-Sept-Columbus Day: weekends) **$$$**

Nickerson State Park. *3488 Hwy 6A, Brewster (02631). Phone 508/896-3491. www.state.ma.us/dem/parks/nick.htm.* Nickerson State Park offers an unusual experience on Cape Cod: densely wooded areas that show no signs of the marshy areas that abound on the Cape. Nickerson offers camping, challenging hiking trails, an 8-mile bike path that connects to the Cape Cod Rail Trail (a 25-mile paved bike trail), fishing, swimming, canoeing, and bird-watching. Also consider areas on the Cape that offer similar activities: Green Briar Nature Center in Sandwich, Lowell Holly Reservation in Mashpee, Ashumet Holly and Wildlife Sanctuary in East Falmouth, Great Island Trail in Wellfleet, Coatue-Coksata-Great Point on Nantucket. (Daily) **FREE**

Ocean Edge Golf Course. *2660 Hwy 6A, Brewster (02631). Phone 508/896-9000. www.oceanedge.com.* This beautiful golf course, just a stone's throw from the ocean, offers 6,665 yards of manicured green, plus five ponds for challenging play. Play during the week in the off-season, and you'll pay extremely reasonable greens fees. Lessons from PGA pros are available. The course is part of a resort that offers accommodations, tennis courts and lessons, a private beach, and 26 miles of paved bike trails (bike rentals are available). (Daily; closed for snow and inclement weather) **$$$$**

Stoney Brook Mill. *830 Stoney Brook Rd, Brewster (02631). Old Gristmill in West Brewster, on site of one of first gristmills in America. Phone 508/896-1734.* Museum upstairs includes historical exhibits, weaving. Corn grinding (July-Aug, Thurs-Sat afternoons). **FREE**

Full-Service Resort

⭐⭐⭐ **OCEAN EDGE RESORT.** *2907 Main St, Brewster (02631). Phone 508/896-9000; toll-free 800/343-6074; fax 5/088-9627. www.oceanedge.com.* Ideally situated on the charming Cape Cod Bay and surrounded by lush gardens, this charming English country manor offers guests an oasis of comfort and privacy while being surrounded by understated elegance and superb service. Discover the charm and character of this 19th-century mansion and carriage house. From the quiet elegance of their luxurious guest rooms to the championship 18-hole golf course, 11 tennis courts, and premiere health and fitness center, this resort offers timeless tranquility and complete relaxation for a romantic weekend or a quiet business retreat. 406 rooms, 2 story. Check-in 3 pm, check-out 11 am. Restaurant, bar. Children's activity center. Fitness room. Two indoor pools, four outdoor pools, whirlpool. Golf. Tennis. Airport transportation available. Business center. **$$**

Specialty Lodgings

The following lodging establishments are approved by Mobil Travel Guide, but due to their unique and individualized nature have not been given a traditional Mobil Star rating. Included in this listing you may find bed-and-breakfasts, limited-service inns, guest ranches, and other unique hotel properties.

BRAMBLE INN. *2019 Main St, Brewster (02631). Phone 508/896-7644; fax 508/896-9332. www.brambleinn.com.* Family owned and operated, this attractive inn, with its pine floors, lovely antiques, and charmingly appointed guest rooms, offers guests a truly delightful stay. 8 rooms, 2 story. Closed Jan-Apr. Children over 8 years only. Complimentary full breakfast. Check-in 2 pm, check-out 11 am. Restaurant. **$**

BREWSTER FARMHOUSE INN. *716 Main St, Brewster (02631). Phone 508/896-3910; toll-free 800/892-3910; fax 508/896-4232. www.brewsterfarm houseinn.com.* Get away from it all, rejuvenate, and relax at this charming and elegant inn. Built in 1846 and set amidst a country-like setting, this inn has been charmingly restored and offers guests a delightful stay. 8 rooms, 2 story. Children over 16 years only. Complimentary full breakfast. Check-in 3 pm, check-out 11 am. Outdoor pool, whirlpool. **$**

CAPTAIN FREEMAN INN. *15 Breakwater Rd, Brewster (02631). Phone 508/896-7481; toll-free 800/843-4664; fax 508/896-5618. www.captainfreem aninn.com.* 12 rooms, 3 story. Children over 10 years only. Complimentary full breakfast. Check-in 2 pm, check-out 11 am. Outdoor pool. Airport transportation available. **$**

ISAIAH CLARK HOUSE. *1187 Main St, Brewster (02631). Phone 508/896-2223; toll-free 800/822-4001; fax 508/896-2138. www.isaiahclark.com.* Former sea captain's house (1780). 7 rooms, 2 story. Children over 10 years only. Complimentary full breakfast. Check-in 2-5 pm, check-out 11 am. **$**

THE OLD MANSE INN. *1861 Main St, Brewster (02631). Phone 508/896-3149. www.oldmanseinn.com.* 9 rooms. Complimentary full breakfast. Check-in 4 pm, check-out 11 am. **$$**

OLD SEA PINES INN. *2553 Main St, Brewster (02631). Phone 508/896-6114; fax 508/896-7387. www.oldseapinesinn.com.* On 3 1/2 acres. Founded in 1907 as School of Charm and Personality for Young Women. 24 rooms, 3 story. Children over 8 years only (except in family suites). Complimentary full breakfast. Check-in 2 pm, check-out 11 am. **$**

RUDDY TURNSTONE. *463 Main St, Brewster (02631). Phone 508/385-9871; toll-free 800/654-1995; fax 508/385-5696. www.ruddyturnstone.com.* Early 19th-century Cape Cod house; antique furnishings. 5 rooms, 2 story. Children over 10 years only. Complimentary full breakfast. Check-in 1 pm, check-out 11 am. **$**

Restaurants

★ ★ ★ **BRAMBLE INN.** *2019 Main St, Brewster (02631). Phone 508/896-7644; fax 508/896-9332. www.brambleinn.com.* This restaurant is located in the charming Bramble Inn (built in 1861), in the heart of Brewster's historic district. Chef/owner Ruth Manchester delights guests with creative cuisine and heartwarming hospitality. The four quaint dining rooms, including an enclosed porch, make the Bramble Inn a perfect choice for a romantic dinner. International/Fusion menu. Dinner. Closed Mon-Wed in the off-season; also Jan-Apr. Reservations recommended. **$$$**

★ ★ **BREWSTER FISH HOUSE.** *2208 Main St, Brewster (02631). Phone 508/896-7867.* Those with sophisticated palates who enjoy a good meal in an unstuffy atmosphere rave about the Brewster Fish House. Seafood is prepared in a variety of innovative ways here, with meat and vegetarian options rounding out the menu. Consistently crowded, this restaurant often sees long lines—and for good reason. American, seafood menu. Lunch, dinner. Closed Dec-Apr. **$$$**

★ BREWSTER INN AND CHOWDER HOUSE.

1993 Main St, Brewster (02631). Phone 508/896-7771. The Brewster Inn and Chowder House is a Cape Cod institution, feeding hungry souls for over a century. Diners are attracted by the promise of deliciously prepared, unfussy seafood in an unpretentious setting. As the name suggests, clam chowder is a signature dish here, and the thick, tasty soup is not to be skipped. American, seafood menu. Lunch, dinner. Bar. Children's menu. Casual attire. Outdoor seating. **$$**

★ ★ ★ CHILLINGSWORTH.

2449 Main St, Brewster (02631). Phone 508/896-3640; fax 508/896-7540. www.chillingsworth.com. The grand 300-year-old Chillingsworth Foster estate sprawls along the edge of the King's Highway. For the last 30 years, Chillingsworth has been synonymous with epicurean dining on Cape Cod. The formal main dining rooms, furnished in fine antiques, are spread through the central house, while the more casual bistro occupies a glassed-in porch and greenhouse. The seven-course table d'hôte dinner offers a contemporary interpretation of classic French cuisine—seared veal steak with truffle risotto, for example, or lobster with sautéed spinach and fennel. It's a dressy, ceremonial meal that takes all evening. Quicker, lighter fare is available à la carte in the bistro. French menu. Lunch, dinner, Sun brunch. Bar. Reservations recommended. **$$$**

★ ★ ★ OLD MANSE INN AND RESTAURANT.

1861 Main St, Brewster (02631). Phone 508/896-3149; fax 508/896-1546. www.oldmanseinn.com. The Old Manse Inn, a historic 19th-century sea captain's home, inn, and Brewster landmark, successfully bridges the gap between past and present in its well-received restaurant. This dining room respects tradition while shaking things up on its New American menu. Run by two graduates of the Culinary Institute of America, the restaurant's riffs on classic dishes mesmerize diners. And if you're too stuffed to drive home, guest rooms are available at the inn. American menu. Dinner. Closed Mon; also Jan-Apr. **$$**

★ ★ SPARK FISH.

2671 Main St, Brewster (02631). Phone 508/896-1067. Simple, uncomplicated food takes center stage at Spark Fish. This mellow spot serves dinner to a casual crowd who come here for the wood-fired grill specialties. The menu focuses on seafood, but there are plenty of meat and chicken selections for non-fish eaters. Seating on the outdoor deck is highly coveted during the summer months.

American, seafood menu. Lunch, dinner. Bar. Casual attire. Outdoor seating. **$$**

Brockton (C-7)

Settled 1700
Population 94,304
Elevation 112 ft
Area Code 508
Information Metro South Chamber of Commerce, 60 School St, 02301; phone 508/586-0500
Web Site www.metrosouthchamber.com

Half of the Union Army in the Civil War marched in Brockton-made shoes. Known as the nation's shoe capital until the 20th century, diverse manufacturing and service industries contribute to the city's economic base today. Brockton was home of boxing champions Rocky Marciano and "Marvelous" Marvin Hagler.

What to See and Do

Brockton Historical Society Museums. *216 N Pearl St, Brockton (02301). Phone 508/583-1039.* The Heritage Center, the main building of the complex, consists of the Shoe Museum, Fire Museum, and "The Homestead," an early Brockton shoemaker's home. "The Homestead" features exhibits on Thomas Edison, who electrified the first shoe factory in the world in Brockton in 1883, and former local shoemaker and undefeated world champion boxer, Rocky Marciano. (First and third Sun afternoon of each month or by appointment) **$**

Fuller Museum of Art. *455 Oak St, Brockton (02301). On Porter's Pond. Phone 508/588-6000.* Permanent exhibits of 19th- and 20th-century American art; children's gallery; changing exhibits; lectures, gallery talks, and tours. Museum (Tues-Sun afternoons; closed holidays). **$$**

Special Event

Brockton Fair. *Fairgrounds on Belmont St, Brockton (02301). Phone 508/586-8000.* Midway, agricultural exhibits, entertainment. (Early July)

Limited-Service Hotels

★ ★ BEST WESTERN CARLTON HOUSE.

1005 Belmont St, Brockton (02301). Phone 508/588-3333; toll-free 800/780-7234; fax 508/588-3333. www.bestwestern.com. 69 rooms, 2 story. Check-in

3 pm, check-out 11 am. Restaurant, bar. Outdoor pool. **$**

★ ★ **RADISSON HOTEL BROCKTON.** *195 Westgate Dr, Brockton (02301). Phone 508/588-6300; fax 508/580-4384.* 186 rooms, 3 story. Check-out noon. Restaurant, bar. Fitness room. Indoor pool, whirlpool. **$**

Restaurant

★ **CHRISTOS.** *782 Crescent St, Brockton (02402). Phone 508/588-4200; fax 508/583-6946.* Greek, steak menu. Lunch, dinner. Closed Thanksgiving, Dec 25. Bar. **$$**

Brookline (B-7)

Established 1705
Population 57,107
Area Code 617
Zip 02445, 02446
Web Site www.townofbrooklinemass.com

This booming commuter suburb to the east of Boston has a history dating to the 1630s. Having started out as a rural community, it developed into a residential area in the 1800s, when wealthy merchants and politicians began purchasing farms and turning them into summer estates. Landscape architect Frederick Law Olmstead was among its 19th-century residents and served on its planning board; a National Historic Site remembers his achievements today. Its major attraction for travelers is the John F. Kennedy National Historic Site, the president's birthplace and boyhood home. Foodies will enjoy the Brookline Farmers' Market in the Center Street parking lot, where area growers come to sell their fresh fruits, vegetables, herbs, cut flowers, and more.

What to See and Do

John F. Kennedy National Historic Site. *83 Beals St, Brookline (02446). Phone 617/566-7937. www.nps.gov/jofi.* The birthplace and early childhood home of the nation's 35th president is restored in appearance to 1917, the year of his birth. Ranger-guided tours. (May-Oct, Wed-Sun 10 am-4:30 pm; closed holidays) Golden Eagle Passport accepted (see MAKING THE MOST OF YOUR TRIP). **$**

Restaurants

★ ★ ★ **THE FIREPLACE.** *1634 Beacon St, Brookline (02446). Phone 617/975-1900; fax 617/975-1600. www.fireplacerest.com.* Situated in a section of Brookline heavily populated with young professionals, The Fireplace can seem like a cross between *Friends* and *Cheers,* where everyone knows everyone and half the diners are just stopping off for a glass of Sancerre and a small plate of duck sausage and mashed turnips. But the wood-fired oven, the rotisserie, and the kitchen's own smoke box make Jim Solomon's neighborhood bistro a fine destination for a hearty meal of braised brisket or grilled halibut. Desserts (such as gingerbread pudding with burnt lemon sauce) are rich, dark, and treacly. The eponymous hearth provides the welcome tang of woodsmoke in cold weather. American, seafood menu. Lunch, dinner. Children's menu. Casual attire. **$$**

★ **RUBIN'S KOSHER DELICATESSEN.** *500 Harvard St, Brookline (02446). Phone 617/731-8787; fax 617/566-3354. www.rubinskosher.com.* Since 1927, central and eastern European immigrants have made Rubin's their kitchen away from home. The full-service deli sells all the classics, from chopped liver (chicken or beef) to lean pastrami, pickled herring, countless varieties of latkes, and both potato and sweet potato kugel. Most customers stop in to stock the larder at home, but for those too hungry to wait, the staff behind the counter will make sandwiches or heat up cooked dishes to eat at the few small tables. Deli menu. Lunch, dinner. Closed Sat; Jewish holidays. **$**

★ ★ **WASHINGTON SQUARE TAVERN.** *714 Washington St, Brookline (02446). Phone 617/232-8989.* Chef/owner Paul Hathaway accommodates late and early diners alike at his classic neighborhood tavern by offering a choice between inexpensive hearty sandwich plates (grilled chicken with Gruyère cheese and onion jam, for example) and more refined New American entrées, such as pan-roasted cod with sautéed potatoes. The single large room gets boisterous as the night progresses, in part a tribute to the smartly chosen and reasonably priced wine list. Unfortunately, there are no desserts on the menu. American menu. Lunch, dinner. Bar. Casual attire. **$$**

Burlington (B-7)

Settled 1641
Population 22,876
Elevation 218 ft
Area Code 781
Zip 01803

Limited-Service Hotel

★ **HAMPTON INN.** *315 Mishawum Rd, Woburn (01801). Phone 781/935-7666; fax 781/933-6899. www.hamptoninn.com.* 99 rooms, 5 story. Complimentary continental breakfast. Check-out noon. **$**

Full-Service Hotel

★ ★ ★ **MARRIOTT BOSTON BURLINGTON.** *1 Mall Rd, Burlington (01803). Phone 781/229-6565; toll-free 800/371-3625; fax 781/229-7973. www. marriott.com.* 423 rooms, 9 story. Check-in 4 pm, check-out noon. Restaurant, bar. Fitness room. Indoor, outdoor pool; whirlpool. **$**

Restaurant

★ **DANDELION INN.** *90 Burlington Mall Rd, Burlington (01803). Phone 781/273-1616; fax 781/273-5426. www.barnsiderestaurants.com.* Seafood, steak menu. Lunch, dinner. Closed holidays. Bar. Children's menu. **$$$**

Cambridge (B-7)

See also Boston

Settled 1630
Population 101,355
Elevation 40 ft
Area Code 617
Information Chamber of Commerce, 859 Massachusetts Ave, 02139; phone 617/876-4100
Web Site www.cambcc.org

The city of Cambridge—academically inclined, historically rich, internationally flavored—occupies an enviable geographic position alongside the northern banks of the Charles River. It is home to two of the nation's most prestigious institutions of higher learning, Harvard University and the Massachusetts Institute of Technology (MIT). The Radcliffe Institute for Advanced Study and Lesley University can also be found here. It should come as no surprise that one-fourth of Cambridge's 95,000 residents are students and that one-sixth of the city's jobs are in higher education.

A group of approximately 700 Puritans set sail from England in 1630, making their way across the Atlantic Ocean to the Massachusetts Bay Colony, where they settled in the area now known as Cambridge. The nation's oldest university, Harvard, was founded six years later. At the time of the American Revolution, Cambridge existed as a quiet farming village, its population comprised mainly of descendants of the original Puritans. Over the course of the 18th century, an increasing number of immigrants, mostly Irish, arrived. The immigration trend continued into the 20th century, with Italians, Portuguese, and Russians seeking a better life in this hamlet to the immediate northwest of Boston. Today, Cambridge is well known for its diversity and multiculturalism, a reputation underscored by the fact that 80 different nations are represented by the children attending the city's public schools.

Cambridge offers a vibrant nightlife, with numerous restaurants, theaters, and clubs surrounding the city's squares: Central Square, Harvard Square, and Inman Square. Some of the best entertainment can be enjoyed on the city's sidewalks, where street performers—ranging from illusionists to musicians to puppeteers—often draw large crowds. Like most college towns, Cambridge has plenty of bookshops. One of the most popular is Curious George Goes to WordsWorth, a two-story bookshop housing more than 20,000 children's titles.

What to See and Do

Cambridge Antique Mall. *201 Msgr O'Brien Hwy, Cambridge (02140). Take the Green Line ("T") to the Lechmere stop. Phone 617/868-9655. www.marketantique.com.* Stroll through five floors of antique furniture, books, artwork, toys, clothing, and more. More than 150 dealers offer up antiques here, which seems most appropriate in this historic town. Although no one's making any promises, you can't help but wonder whether a dresser or rocking chair once sat prominently in John Hancock's house or Paul Revere's workshop. (Tues-Sun; closed holidays)

Christ Church. *Garden and Mason sts, Cambridge (02138). At the Common. Phone 617/876-0200. www.cccambridge.org.* (1759) Episcopal. The oldest church building in Cambridge. A fine Georgian colonial building designed by Peter Harrison that was used as a colonial barracks during the Revolution. (Daily) **FREE**

Dance Complex. *536 Massachusetts Ave, Cambridge (02139). Take the Red Line to the Central Square MBTA station, exit toward Pearl St/Main St. Phone 617/547-9363.* Ready to dance the night away but need to first brush up on your skills? Sashay into The Dance Complex, a not-for-profit dance studio that offers drop-in classes in everything from salsa to hip-hop. With more than 60 teachers on staff, you're sure to find a class to fit your needs. After you're ready to rumba, check out www.havetodance.com for links to some of the best dancing venues in Boston. (Daily) **$$$**

Formaggio Kitchen. *244 Huron Ave, Cambridge (02138). Phone 617/354-4750. www.formaggiokitchen .com.* Whether you consider yourself a *gourmet* or a *gourmand*, you'll easily lose yourself in this culinary playground. With a selection of 200 artisanal cheeses, the finest pastas, chocolates from Italy, France, and the United States, as well as a variety of exotic spices, mouthwatering snacks, and Italian coffees, the famed Formaggio Kitchen is a food-lover's dream. While you're here, pick up some professional-quality cutlery or select one of the many gift baskets for a foodie friend back home. A second location has opened in South Boston at 268 Shawmut Avenue.

Fresh Pond Golf Course. *691 Huron Ave, Cambridge (02138). Phone 617/349-6292. www.freshpondgolf.com.* This nine-hole, par-35 course lies next to the Fresh Pond Reservoir, creating a few challenging water hazards. However, this course plays gently and is a perfect starting point for beginners. More experienced players will appreciate Fresh Pond's quick play, which means that you'll have time to get back to more sightseeing around Boston. (Daily dawn-dusk; closed for snow and inclement weather) **$$$**

Grolier Poetry Book Shop. *6 Plympton St, Cambridge (02138). Take the Red Line ("T") to Harvard Square. Phone 617/547-4648. www.grolierpoetrybookshop.com.* With more than 15,000 volumes of poetry, Grolier's is a gathering place for poets and those who delight in poetry books and readings. The shop holds weekly readings on Tuesdays, Fridays, or Sundays. Founded in 1927, it is the oldest continuously operating poetry bookshop in the United States. (Mon-Sat; closed Sun, holidays)

⭐ **Harvard University.** *24 Quincy St, Cambridge (02138). Harvard Square.* (18,179 students) This magnificent university, America's oldest, was founded in 1636. Two years later, when a minister named John Harvard died and left half his estate and his considerable personal library, it was named for him. Includes Harvard and Radcliffe colleges as well as ten graduate and professional schools. Harvard Yard, as the original campus is called, is tree-shaded and occupied by stately red-brick buildings. In and around the yard are

Harvard Museum of Natural History. *26 Oxford St, Cambridge (02138). Phone 617/495-3045. www.hmnh.harvard.edu.* The Harvard Museum of Natural History (HMNH) combines three museums in one: a botanical museum that examines the study of plants, the museum of zoology that examines the study of animals, and a geological museum that examines the study of rocks and minerals. All three explore the evolution of science and nature throughout time. A collection of glass models of plants—more than 3,000 plant lookalikes rendered carefully in glass—is the only exhibit of its kind in the world. (Daily; closed holidays) **$$**

Harvard University Art Museums. *32 Quincy St, Cambridge (02138). Phone 617/495-9400. www. artmuseums.harvard.edu.* Three museums make up the Harvard Art Museums: the Fogg Art Museum (including wide-ranging collections of paintings and sculpture), the Busch-Reisinger Museum (which features mostly German art), and the Arthur M. Sackler Museum (offering ancient art, plus Asian and Islamic collections). Admission to one museum covers all three; allow a half day for all. Entry to the museums is free on Wednesdays and Saturdays until noon. (Daily; closed holidays) **$$**

Houses of Harvard-Radcliffe. Between Harvard Square and the Charles River, and northeast of Harvard Yard between Shepard and Linnaean streets.

Information Center. *1350 Massachusetts Ave, Cambridge (02138). Phone 617/495-1573.* Provides maps, brochures. (June-Aug, daily; rest of year, Mon-Sat) Student-guided tours begin here.

John F. Kennedy School of Government. *79 JFK St, Cambridge (02138). On the banks of the Charles*

River. (1978) Contains a library, classrooms, and a public affairs forum for lectures.

Massachusetts Hall. *24 Quincy St, Cambridge (02138).* Oldest building (1720) and architectural inspiration for the campus. **FREE**

Peabody Museum of Archaeology and Ethnology. *11 Divinity Ave, Cambridge (02138). Phone 617/ 496-1027. www.peabody.harvard.edu.* Anthropology and ethnology are sciences that record how humans develop culturally. The Peabody Museum, one of the oldest anthropology museums in the world, traces human cultural history in the Western Hemisphere with four major exhibits. In addition, the museum sponsors interactive programs for kids, public lectures, and summer science camps. (Daily; closed holidays) **$$**

University Hall. *Harvard Yard, Cambridge (02138). Phone 617/495-0450.* (1813-1815) Designed by Charles Bulfinch, made of Chelmsford granite in contrast to the surrounding brick, and one of the Yard's most handsome buildings. **FREE**

Widener Library. *1329 Massachusetts Ave, Cambridge (02138). S side of Harvard Yard. Phone 617/495-4166.* (1915) Has an enormous Corinthian portico; more than 3 million books. Near it are Houghton, with a fine collection of rare books, and Lamont, the first undergraduate library in America. **FREE**

House of Blues. *96 Winthrop St, Cambridge (02138). Take the Red line ("T") to Harvard. Phone 617/491-2583. www.hob.com.* This isn't any old chain version of House of Blues, but the original location that drips with hipness. Concerts include performers from Etta James and James Taylor to Norah Jones and John Mayer (**$$$$**). The food is southern and bluesy, too, so stop off for dinner on the way. On Sunday mornings, catch the roof-raising Gospel Sunday Brunch (**$$$$**) at 10 am, noon, or 2 pm. (Daily) **$$$**

Longfellow National Historic Site. *105 Brattle St, Cambridge (02138). 1/2 mile from Harvard. Phone 617/876-4491.* This Georgian-style house, built in 1759, was Washington's headquarters during the 1775-1776 siege of Boston, and Henry Wadsworth Longfellow's home from 1837 until his death in 1882. Longfellow taught at Harvard, and his books are located here. (Daily; closed Jan 1, Thanksgiving, Dec 25) **$$**

Massachusetts Institute of Technology. *77 Massachusetts Ave, Cambridge (02139). Phone 617/*

253-4795. www.mit.edu. (1861) (9,500 students) One of the greatest science and engineering schools in the world. On the Charles River, the campus includes 135 acres of impressive neoclassic and modern buildings. Information center in the lobby of the main building; guided tours, two departures (Mon-Fri). On campus are

Hart Nautical Galleries. *55 Massachusetts Ave, Cambridge (02139).* Shows ship and marine engineering development through displays of rigged merchant and naval ship models; changing exhibits. (Daily) **FREE**

List Visual Arts Center at MIT. *Wiesner Building, 20 Ames St, Cambridge (02139).* Changing exhibits of contemporary art. (Oct-June, daily; closed holidays; free) The MIT campus also has an outstanding permanent collection of outdoor sculpture, including works by Calder, Moore, and Picasso, and significant architecture, including buildings by Aalto, Pei, and Saarinen. Walking tour map at information center.

MIT Museum. *265 Massachusetts Ave, Cambridge (02139). Phone 617/253-4444.* Collections and exhibits that interpret the Institute's social and educational history, developments in science and technology, and the interplay of technology and art. (Tues-Sun; closed Mon, holidays) **$$**

Radcliffe College's Schlesinger Library Culinary Collection. *10 Garden St, Cambridge (02138). Take the Red Line ("T") to the Harvard Square station. Walk through Harvard Square, down Brattle St; Radcliffe Yard is 3 blocks away, at the corner of Brattle and James sts. Phone 617/495-8647. www.radcliffe.edu/schles.* Through Radcliffe's culinary collection, you'll have access to more than 9,000 cookbooks and other culinary texts. Although you can't borrow from the library, you can conduct culinary research by tapping into the books of some of the world's greatest chefs, including Samuel Narcisse Chamberlain, Julia Child, and Sophie Coe. (Mon-Fri; closed holidays, Dec 25-Jan 1) **FREE**

The Radcliffe Institute for Advanced Study. *8 Garden St, Cambridge (02138). Admissions office. Phone 617/ 495-8601.* (1879) (2,700 women) Coordinate institution with Harvard. Unique women's educational and scholarly resources including the Arthur and Elizabeth Schlesinger Library on the History of Women in America (at 3 James St). More than 850 major collections of history of women from 1800 to present.

Special Event

Head of the Charles Regatta. *2 Gerry's Landing Rd, Cambridge (02138). The race starts on the Charles, near Boston University. Take the Green Line B to Boston University and walk to the BU Bridge. Phone 617/ 868-6200. www.hocr.org.* The Head of the Charles Regatta is a 3-mile rowing race that involves 7,000 athletes, 1,470 rowing shells, and 300,000 spectators. Oarspeople, including Olympic and World champions, Olympic medalists, and national champions from around the world, race the Charles River, from Boston to Cambridge and under the Charles Eliot Bridge to the finish line. In addition, after the close of the Head of the Charles Regatta, you can watch the Charles Schwab Championship sprint at 5 pm Sunday, when the top three rowers from the preceding day's Championship Single take to their shells for a 550-meter dead sprint along the Charles, from River Street Bridge to the Weeks Footbridge. Late Oct. **FREE**

Limited-Service Hotels

★ ★ **BEST WESTERN HOTEL TRIA.** *220 Alewife Brook Pkwy, Cambridge (02138). Phone 617/491-8000; toll-free 800/491-4914; fax 617/491-4932. www.bestwestern.com.* Boutique room design has filtered down to value-priced lodging at this completely overhauled (as of 2004) property 2 miles outside Harvard Square on a busy traffic circle. The interior belies its strip setting, with luxurious mattresses, hip but soothing design, snappy contemporary furniture (including ergonomic desk chairs), and free high-speed Internet access (both wired and wireless) throughout. The walk to the Alewife subway stop is short but crosses a busy highway. If the TV show *Divine Design* took on a circa-1963 roadside hotel, this might be the result. 69 rooms, 4 story. Pets accepted; fee. Complimentary continental breakfast. Check-out noon. High-speed Internet access. Restaurant, bar. Indoor pool, whirlpool. **$**

★ ★ **HOLIDAY INN.** *30 Washington St, Somerville (02143). Phone 617/628-1000; toll-free 800/465-4329; fax 617/628-0143. www.holiday-inn.com.* 184 rooms, 9 story. Check-out noon. Restaurant, bar. Fitness room. Indoor pool, whirlpool. **$$**

★ ★ **THE INN AT HARVARD.** *1201 Massachusetts Ave, Cambridge (02138). Phone 617/491-2222; toll-free 800/458-5886; fax 617/491-6520. www.theinnat harvard.com.* Apart from private clubs, there's hardly a lodging in greater Boston quite like The Inn at Harvard. Acclaimed postmodernist Cambridge architect Graham Gund showed great restraint in creating this neoclassical structure at the edge of Harvard Square and within a block of Harvard University's art museums. Guest rooms have a casual, homey feel, but the most important feature is the four-story atrium that turns the reception area into a soaring library and lounge that works equally well for relaxing with a good book, sipping afternoon tea, or dining in the evening. Harvard frequently books many of the rooms for visiting scholars and dignitaries. It's especially hard to find a vacancy during commencement, homecoming, or alumni weekend. 113 rooms, 4 story. Check-out noon. Wireless Internet access. Restaurant, bar. **$$**

Full-Service Hotels

★ ★ ★ **CHARLES HOTEL.** *1 Bennett St, Cambridge (02138). Phone 617/864-1200; fax 617/864-5715.* This upscale hotel just off Harvard Square on the Charles River defines luxury lodging in Cambridge. For that reason, it attracts celebrities and other high-profile guests, as well as the wealthy parents of Harvard students. Its guest rooms mix Shaker-inspired design with a multitude of modern amenities—duvets, three two-line phones, Bose Wave radios, televisions in the bathrooms, and more. Dine in either of its two restaurants, and be sure to tune into the sweet sounds of jazz at the Regattabar, where swingin' national bands hit the stage. The hotel also has an on-site athletic center with indoor pool, a day spa, and indoor parking. 293 rooms, 10 story. Pets accepted, some restrictions; fee. Check-in 3 pm, check-out noon. High-speed Internet access. Two restaurants, two bars. Fitness room, spa. Indoor pool, whirlpool. **$$**

★ ★ ★ **HOTEL MARLOWE.** *25 Edwin H Land Blvd, Cambridge (02141). Phone 617/868-8000; fax 617/868-8001. www.hotelmarlowe.com.* It's rare to find a luxury hotel with a sense of whimsy in its design, but the Marlowe sets itself apart from the other East Cambridge lodgings with a bold palette of crimson red, deep blue, and bright gold and a variety of subtle nautical references, such as carpets with a compass rose and painted nautical banners. It shares the once-industrial Lechmere canal with luxury condos and an upscale shopping mall—all less than a block from the Museum of Science and its subway stop. Some hotels tolerate pets; the Marlowe caters to them (the concierge can even order Rover a birthday cake from the Polka Dog Bakery). Amenities are top of the line (Frette linens, Aveda bath products), and the Sony PlayStation in every room wins youngsters over. 236 rooms. Pets accepted. Check-in 3 pm, check-out noon. High-speed Internet access. Restaurant, bar. Fitness room. Business center. **$$$**

★ ★ **HYATT REGENCY CAMBRIDGE.** *575 Memorial Dr, Cambridge (02139). Phone 617/492-1234; toll-free 800/633-7313; fax 617/491-6906. www.hyatt.com.* Ideally situated along the picturesque Charles River and with views of the alluring Boston skyline, guests are offered a level of style and comfort that's expected from Hyatt. From the lavishly appointed lobby and spacious guest rooms, as well as the charming gazebo nestled in the well-maintained courtyard, guests will immediately feel relaxed and welcomed. 479 rooms, 16 story. Check-in 4 pm, check-out noon. Restaurant, bar. Fitness room. Indoor pool, whirlpool. Business center. **$**

★ ★ ★ **MARRIOTT BOSTON CAMBRIDGE.** *2 Cambridge Ctr, Cambridge (02142). Phone 617/494-6600; toll-free 800/228-9290; fax 617/494-0036. www.marriott.com.* Nestled in the heart of the Cambridge Business Community and only a few short miles from Logan International Airport, this hotel offers guests all the comforts of home. Rooms are spacious and have been equipped with guests' needs in mind. Guests can relax in the indoor pool or enjoy a invigorating workout in the well-maintained health club. Nearby attractions include downtown Boston, Harvard Square, and the Museum of Science. 444 rooms, 26 story. Check-in 4 pm, check-out noon. High-speed Internet access. Restaurant, bar. Fitness room. Indoor pool, whirlpool. Business center. **$**

★ ★ ★ **ROYAL SONESTA HOTEL BOSTON.** *5 Cambridge Pkwy, Cambridge (02142). Phone 617/806-4200; fax 617/806-4232.* Perched along the Charles River, this magnificent hotel offers guests panaromic Boston views, handsomely appointed and spacious guest rooms, as well as a state-of-the-art health spa featuring massage therapists, reflexology, and an indoor and outdoor pool with a retractable roof and sun deck. This luxury hotel is ideally situated across from the waterfront shopping area and next door to the Museum of Science. 421 rooms, 10 story. Check-in

3 pm, check-out noon. Restaurant, bar. Fitness room. Indoor pool, outdoor pool. **$$**

★ ★ ★ **UNIVERSITY PARK HOTEL @ MIT.** *20 Sidney St, Cambridge (02139). Phone 617/577-0200; toll-free 800/774-1500; fax 617/551-0444. www.univparkhotel.com.* This high-tech-themed hotel identifies closely with the Massachusetts Institute of Technology, even incorporating printed circuit boards as a design motif in the bedroom furniture. Predictably, the hotel is wired every which way, with Internet access about ten times faster than so-called broadband and Sony PlayStations in all guest rooms. The hotel functions as a conference and meeting center for cutting-edge companies in media, biotech, robotics, and computing as well as a venue for purely academic meetings. Sidney's Grill continues the spirit of innovation with a contemporary Mediterranean menu. Central Square, with a Red Line subway stop, is a ten-minute walk away. This hotel is part of the Doubletree Hotel chain. 210 rooms. Check-in 3 pm, check-out noon. High-speed Internet access. Restaurant, bar. Airport transportation available. Business center. **$$$**

Specialty Lodging

The following lodging establishment is approved by Mobil Travel Guide, but due to its unique and individualized nature has not been given a traditional Mobil Star rating. Included in this listing you may find bed-and-breakfasts, limited-service inns, guest ranches, and other unique hotel properties.

A CAMBRIDGE HOUSE BED AND BREAKFAST INN. *2218 Massachusetts Ave, Cambridge (02140). Phone 617/491-6300; toll-free 800/232-9989; fax 617/868-2848. www.ucambridgehouse.com.* Despite its location in metro Boston, about 1 1/2 miles from Harvard Square, this cozy inn offers couples the perfect setting for a romantic getaway. Many of the guest rooms in this turn-of-the-century, three-story frame house have heavenly four-poster beds lavishly dressed with fine linens and pillows, and most have gas-log fireplaces. In warm weather, the lovely backyard garden adds even more charm. The nightly rate includes a hearty breakfast buffet and hors d'oeuvres and pasta in the evening. 15 rooms. Complimentary full breakfast. Check-in 2 pm, check-out noon. **$$**

Restaurants

★ ★ **ARGANA.** *1287 Cambridge St, Cambridge (02139). Phone 617/868-1247. www.arganarestaurant .com.* Humphrey Bogart would have loved Argana, a *Casablanca*-style Moroccan bistro with a warm vibe and a fragrant, exotic menu of well-spiced fare. Set in Inman Square, Argana has a swanky little bar that opens up to the street to reveal a lively crowd comfortably reclining on cushy banquettes. The menu here is North African and Moroccan, with plates of mezze like zaalouk, an eggplant spread heavy with cumin, for sharing. Entrées are also rich with sweetness and spice, like duck with plum port sauce and couscous and a chicken tagine accented with preserved lemon. Moroccan menu. Lunch, dinner, brunch. Bar. Casual attire. **$$**

★ ★ **BARAKA CAFE.** *80 1/2 Pearl St, Cambridge (02139). Phone 617/868-3951.* Menu descriptions only hint at the subtlety of the North African dishes in this tiny, cash-only neighborhood restaurant outside Central Square. The warm and bright cuisine laced with saffron, star anise, and cinnamon is perhaps best exemplified in the vegetarian couscous (often with luscious bites of melon). Reserve your dessert before the kitchen runs out: one of the co-owners worked for many years as a classic French pastry chef. Call ahead for groups of more than five. Mediterranean menu. Lunch, dinner. Closed Mon. Casual attire. No credit cards accepted. **$$**

★ ★ **BLUE ROOM.** *One Kendall Sq, Cambridge (02139). Phone 617/494-9034. www.theblueroom.net.* The Blue Room's Sunday buffet brunch is one of the most popular in Cambridge, a veritable United Nations of flavors that can range from Moroccan chicken thighs to quesadillas with avocado and pepper jack cheese. The equally cosmopolitan dinner menu, drawing extensively from Latin American and Mediterranean inspirations, relies heavily on a huge wood grill. Part of the fun is watching the ballet of the cooks in the open kitchen. American menu. Dinner, Sun brunch. Closed July 4, Thanksgiving, Dec 24-25. Bar. Outdoor seating. **$$**
🅳

★ ★ **CASABLANCA.** *40 Brattle St, Cambridge (02138). Phone 617/876-0999; fax 617/661-1373. www.casablanca-restaurant.com.* You can always count on a great burger in the bar of this landmark Harvard Square hangout. Befitting its name, the front dining room also explores the North African side of Mediterranean bistro cooking, jumping between Moroccan and French dishes. The cassoulet, redolent of duck confit, rarely seems to go off the menu, and almost anything with preserved lemon is a great bet. Murals from the classic Bogart movie provide the atmosphere. Mediterranean menu. Lunch, dinner. Bar. Casual attire. Reservations recommended. **$$**

★ ★ **CHEZ HENRI.** *1 Shepard St, Cambridge (02138). Phone 617/354-8980; fax 617/441-8784.* Brassy as a trumpet solo, Chez Henri puts a Cuban shake on French bistro cooking. Chef/owner Paul O'Connell maintains a lively bar scene (the only place to get his acclaimed Cubano sandwiches) while simultaneously offering a warm but more formal dining room that's a favorite with Harvard professors and graduate students looking for a big night out. Such upscale dishes as grilled marlin in a macadamia nut crust and steak frites with hot pepper-dusted fries could make you think you're in South Beach. Even the bistro classic of roast chicken makes a pass through the Caribbean, arriving at the table with yucca fries. Chez Henri's wine list is commendably French and features many obscure finds; the restaurant is also celebrated for its mojitos and caipirinhas. Cuban, French menu. Dinner. Closed Memorial Day, July 4. **$$$**

★ ★ **CRAIGIE STREET BISTROT.** *5 Craigie Cir, Cambridge (02138). Phone 617/497-5511. www.craigie streetbistrot.com.* This tiny, very French bistro in the basement of an apartment building a couple of blocks outside Harvard Square is something of a local secret. Chef/owner Tony Maws trained with the best in the United States, but his heart belongs to Lyon. His French bistro cooking is lovingly old-fashioned: he grinds and blends his own mustard, makes terrines and pates for appetizers and garnishes, and puts up his own duck confit. The menu is in constant flux, truly depending on what the market yields. Trust his delicate way with whatever fish looked best at the morning market. Vegetarian entrées, such as wild mushrooms on cheese-enriched polenta, are feasts rather than afterthoughts. French bistro menu. Dinner. Closed Mon-Tues. Casual attire. Reservations recommended. **$$**

★ ★ **DALI RESTAURANT AND TAPAS BAR.** *415 Washington St, Somerville (02143). Phone 617/661-3254; fax 617/661-2813. www.dalirestaurant.com.* Dalí defines Spanish cuisine for the Boston area, offering 45 tapas and five entrées each night, as well as a long list of sherries, ports, and Spanish table wines. Choices range from earthy Andalusian bar food (like potatoes in a garlic-caper mayonnaise) to fresh fish baked in coarse salt in the style of Cadiz. No reservations are taken, so be ready to balance a plate on your wine glass while waiting for a table. Spanish menu. Lunch, dinner. Closed holidays; also Dec 31. Bar. Business casual attire. **$$$**

★ ★ **EAST COAST GRILL & RAW BAR.** *1271 Cambridge St, Cambridge (02139). Phone 617/491-6568; fax 617/868-4278. www.eastcoastgrill.net.* Guests should plan to wait during peak hours at this local favorite—strong margaritas, fresh dishes, and friendly staff keep guests coming back. Although the menu focuses on seafood, vegetarians will delight in the "All Vegetable Experience of the Day." Barbecue, Caribbean, seafood menu. Dinner. Closed Dec 25. **$$**

★ ★ **THE ELEPHANT WALK.** *2067 Massachusetts Ave, Cambridge (02140). Phone 617/492-6900. www.elephantwalk.com/cambridge.* Two distinct menus tempt diners at The Elephant Walk. Rather than offering fusion cuisine, this sophisticated establishment entices guests to mix and match from its authentic and delicious French and Cambodian menus—diners may choose a French appetizer and a Cambodian entrée. Tradition blends with creativity here, where classic favorites are offered in addition to inventive dishes. Stylish interiors with a tropical-meets-Asian urban feel and an award-winning wine list prove that ethnic dining need not be basic and uninspiring. Cambodian, French menu. Dinner. Bar. Children's menu. Casual attire. **$$**

★ ★ **FLORA.** *190 Massachusetts Ave, Arlington. Phone 781/641-1664.* American menu. Dinner. Closed Mon. Bar. Casual attire. **$$**

★ ★ **HARVEST.** *44 Brattle St, Cambridge (02138). Phone 617/868-2255; fax 617/868-5422.* This restaurant has returned under new ownership, the same three partners who own Grill 23 & Bar (see BOSTON), and offers American dishes enhanced by classic techniques. Guests will enjoy the open kitchen, great bread, and large number of seafood choices, as well as the nightly risotto special. American menu. Lunch, dinner. Children's menu. Outdoor seating. **$$$**

★ ★ **HELMAND.** *143 1st St, Cambridge (02142). Phone 617/492-4646; fax 617/497-6507.* The East Cambridge location can be a little hard for out-of-towners to find, but this first and finest of the region's Afghan restaurants makes the search worthwhile. The cuisine comes from the historic overland spice trade route between South Asia and Europe, and Helmand's dishes are rich with the characteristic cardamom, coriander, cinnamon, and turmeric. Lamb dishes are among the menu's stars. Afghan menu. Dinner. Closed Jan 1, Thanksgiving, Dec 25. **$$**

★ ★ ★ **OLEANA.** *134 Hampshire St, Cambridge (02139). Phone 617/661-0505.* Menus that roam the perimeter of the Mediterranean are nothing new in the Boston area, but few chefs coax out the Arabic influences on Mediterranean bistro fare as well as Oleana's chef/owner Ana Sortun. To create a luscious, complex style, Sortun gleefully matches Arabic almonds to the herbs of Provence in a chicken dish. The food is always comforting, yet often as surprising as a Basque-influenced venison with caramelized turnip or a rabbit and mushroom paella salad. Regulars would revolt if she removed the scallops with basmati-pistachio pilaf from the menu. The fireplace offers cozy comfort in the winter, while an outdoor patio beckons in the summertime. Mediterranean menu. Dinner. Bar. Casual attire. Outdoor seating. **$$**

★ **REDBONES.** *55 Chester St, Somerville (02144). Phone 617/628-2200; fax 617/625-5909. www.redbonesbbq.com.* Not since the 1960 presidential ticket of JFK and LBJ has there been such a strong Boston-Austin connection. Redbones keeps things simple by offering little more than great Texas roadhouse barbecue executed with near perfection. The upstairs dining room is family-friendly, while the downstairs bar carries through the roadhouse vibe with a sweeping selection of beers, both on tap and in the bottle. Barbecue menu. Lunch, dinner. Closed Thanksgiving, Dec 25. Bar. Casual attire. **$$**

★ ★ ★ ★ **RIALTO.** *1 Bennett St, Cambridge (02138). Phone 617/661-5050; fax 617/234-8093. www.rialto-restaurant.com.* Located in the Charles Hotel (see), Rialto is home to chef/owner Jody Adams's distinctive brand of boldly flavored Mediterranean-inspired fare. Adams's approach to food is honest and straightforward, paying homage to the seasons and to fresh, locally grown fruits and vegetables. This approach allows her to create stellar up-to-the-minute dishes from the varying culinary regions of France, Italy, and Spain. If you'd like to actually enjoy your dinner, try not to fill up on the basket of incredible home-baked breads beforehand. A complementary wine list features more than 100 bottles from Spain, Italy, France, and the United States. The sunny room is filled with deep, dramatic, high-backed banquettes; flower-topped tables; and richly colored hardwood floors and is lined with soaring floor-to-ceiling windows equipped with vintage wooden shutters. The effect is a sophisticated yet immensely comfortable urban space—a room that seduces you into lingering over dessert, cheese, and after-dinner drinks. Mediterranean menu. Dinner. Closed holidays. Bar. Children's menu. Casual attire. **$$$**

★ ★ **ROKA.** *1001 Massachusetts Ave, Cambridge (02138). Phone 617/661-0344.* The panache of this Osaka-style Japanese restaurant midway between Harvard and Central squares belies its below-street-level digs in a district of furniture stores. Sushi is the main attraction, and many patrons gravitate to the te-maki combination plate, which includes sheets of nori and all the fixings to roll your own crab stick, shrimp, tuna, and squid rolls. The tempura is especially light, and Roka boasts an extensive selection of Japanese beers and sakes. Japanese menu. Lunch, dinner. Casual attire. **$$**

★ ★ ★ **SALTS.** *798 Main St, Cambridge (02139). Phone 617/876-8444; fax 617/876-8569.* This newcomer to Central Square is a tiny neighborhood place with mustard-colored walls and purple wainscoting that has people all over town talking. The simple food has a slight Eastern European accent, and the atmosphere is quiet and elegant. American menu. Dinner. Closed Mon. **$$**

★ ★ **SANDRINE'S.** *8 Holyoke St, Cambridge (02138). Phone 617/497-5300; fax 617/497-8504. www.sandrines.com.* Chef/owner Raymond Ost has created a little oasis of his native Alsace in the heart of Harvard Square. The bar around the restaurant's hearth oven is a favorite gathering spot to snack on Ost's signature flammekueche, a flatbread topped with fromage blanc, smoked bacon, and caramelized onions. The dinner menu features such hearty dishes as a classic choucroute of homemade sauerkraut studded with sausages, grilled smoked pork, and bacon. French menu. Lunch, dinner. Closed Jan 1, Labor Day, Dec 25. Bar. Children's menu. Casual attire. **$$**

Cape Cod

See also Bourne, Brewster, Cape Cod National Seashore, Chatham, Dennis, Eastham, Falmouth, Harwich, Hyannis and Barnstable, Orleans, Provincetown, Sandwich, Truro and North Truro, Wellfleet, Yarmouth

The popularity of the automobile changed Cape Cod from a group of isolated fishing villages, large estates, and cranberry bogs into one of the world's prime resort areas. The Cape's permanent population of about 201,000 witnesses this change each year with the arrival of nearly 500,000 summer visitors.

A great many hotels and motels have sprung up since World War II, and cottages line the beaches in some areas. Yet the villages have remained virtually unchanged. The long main streets of villages like Yarmouthport and Brewster are still lined with old houses, some dating from the 17th century. The sea wind still blows across the moors below Truro and the woods of the Sandwich Hills.

The Cape is about 70 miles long and bent like an arm with its fist upraised. Buzzards Bay and the Cape Cod Canal are at the shoulder, Chatham and Nauset beach are at the elbow, and Provincetown is the fist. Because the Cape extends so far out toward the warm Gulf Stream (about 30 miles), its climate is notably gentler than that of the mainland; summers are cooler and winters are milder. It has almost 560 miles of coastline, most of which is gleaming beach—the Cape being composed of sand rather than bedrock. As if to please every taste, many towns on the Cape have two coasts—the Nantucket Sound beaches with warm, calm waters; the Atlantic Ocean beaches with colder water and high breakers; or Cape Cod Bay with cool, calm waters. Inland woods are dotted with 365 clear freshwater ponds known as kettle ponds.

Surf casting (day and night) and small-boat and deep-sea fishing are major sports along the entire Cape coastline. At least a dozen varieties of game fish are found, including giant tuna.

The current summer gaiety belies the Cape's hardy pioneer history. It was in Provincetown harbor that the Mayflower first set anchor for the winter and the first party of Pilgrims went ashore. Eighteen years earlier, in 1602, Cape Cod was named by the English explorer Bartholomew Gosnold after the great schools of fish he saw in the bay.

The following towns, villages, and special areas on Cape Cod are included in the Mobil Travel Guide. For information about any of them, see the individual alphabetical listing: Bourne, Brewster, Cape Cod National Seashore, Chatham, Dennis, Eastham, Falmouth, Harwich, Hyannis and Barnstable, Orleans, Provincetown, Sandwich, Truro & North Truro, Wellfleet, and Yarmouth.

Cape Cod National Seashore

This recreation area consists of 44,600 acres, including submerged lands located offshore along the eastern part of Barnstable County. Headquarters are at South Wellfleet. Exhibits, interpretive programs at the Salt Pond Visitor Center in Eastham (mid-Feb-Dec, daily; Jan-mid-Feb weekends only), phone 508/255-3421; Province Lands Visitor Center on Race Point Rd in Provincetown (mid-Apr-Nov, daily), phone 508/487-1256. Numerous private homes are within park boundaries. Swimming, lifeguards at designated areas (late June-Labor Day), fishing; hunting, bicycle trails, self-guided nature trails, guided walks, and evening programs in summer. Parking at beaches (fee); free after Labor Day. Buttonbush Trail has Braille trail markers. For further information, contact the Superintendent, 99 Marconi Site, Wellfleet 02667.

Chatham (Cape Cod) (D-10)

Settled 1656
Population 6,625
Elevation 46 ft
Area Code 508
Zip 02633
Information Chamber of Commerce, PO Box 793; phone toll-free 800/715-5567; or the Cape Cod Chamber of Commerce, Hwys 6 and 132, PO Box 790, Hyannis 02601-0790; phone 508/362-3225 or toll-free 888/227-3263
Web Site www.capecodchamber.org

Chatham is among the Cape's fashionable shopping centers. Comfortable estates in the hilly country nearby look out on Pleasant Bay and Nantucket Sound. Monomoy Island, an unattached sand bar, stretches 10 miles south into the sea. It was once a haunt of "moon-cussers"—beach pirates who lured vessels aground with false lights and then looted the wrecks.

What to See and Do

Chatham Light. *Bridge and Main sts, Chatham (02633). Phone 508/862-0700.* Chatham Light is a quintessential Cape Cod lighthouse: gleaming white, with a charming keeper's house attached. Originally built with two towers to distinguish the signal from a single lighthouse farther north, the first pair—built of wood—decayed three decades later. A second pair, made of brick, fell to the beach far below when bad weather eroded the cliff on which they were built. A third pair was built inland, and one was moved to Nauset Beach and forever disconnected from her Chatham sister. Today, the lighthouse offers a superb view of the Atlantic and seals on the beach below, and the Coast Guard uses the keeper's house as its station. (Daily) **FREE**

Clambake Celebrations. *1223 Main St, Chatham (02633). Phone 508/945-7771. www.clambake-to-go.com.* For the easiest clam and lobster takeout on the Cape, visit Clambake Celebrations for simple packages that you steam and eat. You can also pick up complete meals with complementary side dishes, utensils, and bibs. If, after you leave, you need to taste fresh seafood again, you can have a meal for two or four people FedExed to you anywhere in the United States. (Mon-Sat 9 am-3 pm; closed Sun, Jan 1, July 4, Dec 25)

Gristmill. *Shattuck Pl, off Cross St, Chatham (02633). W shore of Mill Pond in Chase Park. Phone 508/945-5158.* (1797) (Daily) **FREE**

Monomoy National Wildlife Refuge. *Monomoy Island, Chatham (02633). Take Hwy 6 E to Hwy 137 S to Hwy 28 E to the Coast Guard Station. Take the first left after the Chatham Lighthouse, and then take the first right. Follow signs for the refuge, which is on your left off Morris Island Rd. Phone 508/945-0594.* The Monomoy National Wildlife Refuge is 2,750 acres of birdlover's paradise. You'll spot a wealth of shorebirds all year 'round, although the spectacle is greatest in spring, when birds exhibit bright plumage while breeding. Also visit Sandy Neck Recreation Area in Barnstable, Wellfleet Bay/Audubon Sanctuary in Brewster, Crane

Reservation in Mashpee, and Beech Forest in Provincetown. **FREE**

Old Atwood House. *347 Stage Harbor Rd, Chatham (02633). 1/2 mile off Hwy 28. Phone 508/945-2493.* (1752) Chatham Historical Society. Memorabilia of Joseph C. Lincoln, Cape Cod novelist. Shell collection, murals by Alice Stallknecht, "Portrait of a New England Town." China trade collection. Maritime collection. (Mid-June-Sept, Tues-Fri afternoons; Sat mornings; schedule may vary) **$$**

Railroad Museum. *Depot Rd and Main St, Chatham (02633). Phone 508/945-5199.* Restored "country railroad depot" houses scale models, photographs, railroad memorabilia, and relics; restored 1910 New York Central caboose. (Mid-June-mid-Sept, Tues-Sat) **DONATION**

Top Rod and Cape Cod Charters. *1082 Orleans Rd, Chatham (02650). Next to Ryders Cove. Phone 508/945-2256. www.capefishingcharters.com.* Captain Joe Fitzback takes you to Cape Cod's prime saltwater fishing areas, providing tackle, bait, and anything else you need to bring in the big one. Although a day's adventure will cost you a bundle, each additional person adds little to the cost, so plan on bringing a group and splitting the fee. (May-Oct by reservation; closed Nov-Apr) **$$$$**

Special Events

Band Concerts. *Kate Gould Park, Main St, Chatham (02633). Phone 508/362-3225.* Fri evenings. Late June-early Sept.

Monomoy Theatre. *776 Main St, Chatham (02633). Phone 508/945-1589.* Ohio University Players in comedies, musicals, dramas, classics. Late June-late Aug.

Limited-Service Hotels

★ **THE CHATHAM MOTEL.** *1487 Main St, Chatham (02633). Phone 508/945-2630; toll-free 800/770-5545. www.chathammotel.com.* In pine grove. 32 rooms. Closed Nov-Apr. Check-out 11 am. Outdoor pool. **$**

★ **CHATHAM SEAFARER.** *2079 Main St, Chatham (02633). Phone 508/432-1739; toll-free 800/786-2772; fax 508/432-8969. www.chatham seafarer.com.* 20 rooms. Check-out 11 am. **$**

★ ★ **DOLPHIN OF CHATHAM INN AND MOTEL.** *352 Main St, Chatham (02633). Phone 508/945-0070; toll-free 800/688-5900; fax 508/945-5945. www.dolphininn.com.* 38 rooms. Check-out 10 am. Restaurant. Outdoor pool, whirlpool. **$$**

Full-Service Resorts

★ ★ ★ **CHATHAM BARS INN.** *297 Shore Rd, Chatham (02633). Phone 508/945-0096; toll-free 800/527-4884; fax 508/945-5491. www.chathambarsinn.com.* Built in 1814, this grand and elegant Cape Cod landmark has managed to maintain all of the historic charm of a bygone era. Beauty and allure are reflected in the charmingly appointed guest rooms, some of which offer private decks along with breathtaking views of Pleasant Bay. With well-maintained gardens and a private beach just steps away, guests can not help but find serenity and peace of mind amidst the luxurious setting. 205 rooms, 3 story. Check-in 3 pm, check-out 11 am. Restaurant, bar. Children's activity center. Fitness room. Beach. Outdoor pool. Tennis. **$$**

★ ★ ★ **PLEASANT BAY VILLAGE RESORT.** *1191 Orleans Rd, Chatham (02633). Phone 508/945-1133; toll-free 800/547-1011; fax 508/945-9701. www.pleasantbayvillage.com.* From the exquisitely arranged rock garden, where a waterfall bravely cascades its way down into a stone-edged pool and offers guests a delighted view of colorful and flashing koi, to the lavishly appointed gardens, this woodland retreat welcomes guests to a place of timeless tranquility. 58 rooms. Closed mid-Oct-mid-May. Check-out 11 am. Restaurant. Outdoor pool. **$$**

★ ★ ★ **WEQUASSETT INN.** *On Pleasant Bay, Chatham (02633). Phone 508/432-5400; fax 508/430-3131.* The Wequassett Inn is the perfect place for those who like the charm of a country inn with the amenities of a resort. Situated on 22 acres overlooking Pleasant Bay and the Atlantic Ocean in the picturesque seafaring village of Chatham, this full-service resort is the last word in country chic. The rooms and suites are decorator showpieces with a cosmopolitan slant on country décor. From golf privileges at the prestigious Cape Cod National Golf Club to on-site tennis and water sports at the private beach, this resort entitles its guests to a world of recreational opportunities. Sophisticated palates seek refuge at the sensational twenty-eight atlantic, while more casual fare is served at Thoreau's tavern and the poolside cafés. 98 rooms, 2 story. Closed mid-Nov-mid-Apr. Check-in 3 pm, check-out 11 am. Restaurant. Children's activity center. Fitness room. Outdoor pool. Tennis. Airport transportation available. Business center. **$$**

Full-Service Inns

★ ★ ★ **THE BRADFORD OF CHATHAM.** *26 Cross St, Chatham (02633). Phone 508/945-1030; toll-free 888/242-8426; fax 508/945-9652. www.bradfordinn.com.* 38 rooms. Complimentary full breakfast. Check-in 4 pm, check-out 11 am. Outdoor pool, whirlpool. **$$**

★ ★ ★ **CHATHAM WAYSIDE INN.** *512 Main St, Chatham (02633). Phone 508/945-5550; toll-free 800/242-8426; fax 508/945-1884. www.waysideinn.com.* 57 rooms. Check-in 3 pm, check-out 11 am. Restaurant. **$$**

★ ★ ★ **CRANBERRY INN.** *359 Main St, Chatham (02633). Phone 508/945-9232; toll-free 800/332-4667; fax 508/945-3769. www.cranberryinn.com.* Built in 1830, and nestled in the heart of the historic district, this elegant inn offers guests all the comforts of home. Relax in one of the charming guest rooms, or enjoy the picturesque view of a windmill while lazing away in one of the Kennedy rocking chairs set along the expansive front porch. 18 rooms, 2 story. Children over 12 years only. Complimentary full breakfast. Check-in 2 pm, check-out 11 am. **$**

★ ★ ★ **QUEEN ANNE INN.** *7 Queen Anne Rd, Chatham (02633). Phone 508/945-0394; toll-free 800/545-4667; fax 508/945-0113. www.queenanneinn.com.* Built in 1840. Rooms feature antique furniture. 34 rooms, 3 story. Closed Jan. Complimentary continental breakfast. Check-in 3 pm, check-out 11 am. Restaurant. Outdoor pool, whirlpool. Tennis. **$**

Specialty Lodgings

The following lodging establishments are approved by Mobil Travel Guide, but due to their unique and individualized nature have not been given a traditional Mobil Star rating. Included in this listing you may find bed-and-breakfasts, limited-service inns, guest ranches, and other unique hotel properties.

CAPTAIN'S HOUSE INN. *369-377 Old Harbor Rd, Chatham (02633). Phone 508/945-0127; toll-free 800/315-0728; fax 508/945-0866. www.captainshouseinn .com.* Once a sea captain's estate, this charming inn was built in 1839 and features exquisite period wallpapers, Williamsburg antiques, and elegantly refined Queen Anne chairs. Some of the charmingly guestrooms are named after the ships the captain skippered. 16 rooms, 2 story. Complimentary full breakfast. Check-in 2 pm, check-out 11 am. Outdoor pool. **$$**

CHATHAM TOWN HOUSE INN. *11 Library Ln, Chatham (02633). Phone 508/945-2180; toll-free 800/242-2180; fax 508/945-3990. www.chathamtown house.com.* This former sea captain's estate has undergone many transformations over the years, yet has still maintained the elegance and style of yesterday. Guests will find some of the old hemlock floors as well as original woodwork characterizing the harpoon and oar motifs still in place. The attractively furnished guest rooms offer picturesque water or garden views, as well as romantic canopies and private balconies. 29 rooms, 2 story. Complimentary full breakfast. Check-in 3 pm, check-out noon. Outdoor pool, whirlpool. **$**

MOSES NICKERSON HOUSE INN. *364 Old Harbor Rd, Chatham (02633). Phone 508/945-5859; toll-free 800/628-6972; fax 508/945-7087. www.moses nickersonhouse.com.* Built in 1839. 7 rooms, 2 story. Children over 14 years only. Complimentary full breakfast. Check-in 2:30 pm, check-out 10:30 am. **$**

OLD HARBOR INN. *22 Old Harbor Rd, Chatham (02633). Phone 508/945-4434; toll-free 800/942-4434; fax 508/945-7665. www.chathamoldharborinn.com.* Built in 1933; former residence of prominent doctor. Renovated and furnished with a blend of antiques and modern conveniences. 8 rooms, 2 story. Children over 14 years only. Complimentary full breakfast. Check-in 3 pm, check-out 11 am. **$**

PORT FORTUNE INN. *201 Main St, Chatham (02633). Phone 508/945-0792; toll-free 800/750-0792. www.portfortuneinn.com.* Built in 1910. 12 rooms, 2 story. Children over 8 years only. Complimentary continental breakfast. Check-in 2 pm, check-out 11 am. **$$**

Restaurants

★ ★ **CHATHAM SQUIRE.** *487 Main St, Chatham (02633). Phone 508/945-0945; fax 508/945-4708. www.thesquire.com.* The Squire represents the salty side of Chatham, where it's possible to belly up to the bar with the fishermen for a bowl of Monomoy mussels or a rack of barbecued ribs, or sit down with the police chief or the mayor over scallops meunière. The Squire also does a bustling lunch business with hearty sandwiches and fried fish. Seafood menu. Lunch, dinner. Bar. Children's menu. Casual attire. **$$**

★ ★ **CHRISTIAN'S.** *443 Main St, Chatham (02633). Phone 508/945-3362; fax 508/945-9058. www.christiansrestaurant.com.* Tucked inside a former sea captain's home (built in 1819) in the center of town, Christian's is a Chatham favorite. Floral wallpaper and Shaker-style furnishings define the traditional New England décor in the dining room, where an extensive menu caters to the tastes of all diners. Lighter fare is served in the mahogany-paneled bar and in the upstairs sunroom. Seafood menu. Lunch, dinner. Bar. Outdoor seating. **$$**

★ ★ **IMPUDENT OYSTER.** *15 Chatham Bars Ave, Chatham (02633). Phone 508/945-3545; fax 508/945-9319.* One of Chatham's liveliest casual bars for much of the day, the Oyster becomes a serious restaurant at mealtimes, specializing in the catch that comes ashore daily at this busy fishing port. Some of the zestiest dishes, such as cataplana (pork and clams) are, like the fishermen, Portuguese by background. During off-peak hours, the lower-level bar in back serves a limited tavern menu that includes good calamari and clam chowder. Seafood menu. Lunch, dinner. Bar. Children's menu. Reservations recommended. **$$**

★ ★ **PATE'S.** *1260 Main St, Chatham (02633). Phone 508/945-9777.* Pate's ignites diners' thrill for the grill with its wide variety of tasty steaks, chops, and seafood. Sear marks are a sign of good things to come at this clubby restaurant, where even first-time visitors feel like regulars. The relaxed atmosphere and friendly service also make Pate's a favorite of families. American menu. Dinner. Bar. Children's menu. Casual attire. **$$**

★ ★ **VINING'S BISTRO.** *595 Main St, Chatham (02633). Phone 508/945-5033. www.viningsbistro.com.* This mom-and-pop bistro with attitude occupies the upstairs rooms of a small shopping center. Even marooned in the heart of town, it exudes the carefree ambience of a beachside establishment for sailors who've been around the world and just want to kick back with a good meal. The menu borrows wildly from spicy cuisines from around the globe, such as jerk chicken tossed with fettucine ("rasta pasta") and braised lamb shanks rubbed with hot-pepper harissa. International/Fusion menu. Dinner. Casual attire. **$$**

Concord (B-6)

See also Lexington, Sudbury Center

Settled 1635
Population 16,993
Elevation 141 ft
Area Code 978
Zip 01742
Information Concord Chamber of Commerce, 105 Everett St, phone 978/369-3120

This town shares with Lexington the title of Birthplace of the Republic. But it was Ralph Waldo Emerson who saw to it that the shot fired "by the rude bridge" was indeed heard 'round the world.

The town's name arose because of the "peace and concord" between the settlers and the Native Americans in the 17th century. The famous Concord grape was developed here in 1849 by Ephraim Bull.

The town of Lincoln, adjoining Concord on the east, was the scene of a running battle with the Redcoats on their withdrawal toward Boston. Here the harassing fire of the Minutemen was perhaps most effective.

What to See and Do

Codman House. *Codman Rd, Lincoln (01773). 5 miles S of Hwy 2 via Bedford Rd. Phone 781/259-8843.* (Circa 1740) Originally a two-story, L-shaped Georgian mansion. In 1797-1798, it was more than doubled in size by Federal merchant John Codman to imitate an English country residence. Family furnishings. Grounds have many unusual trees and plants; formal Italian garden. (June-mid-Oct, Wed-Sun afternoons) **$$**

Concord Free Public Library. *129 Main St, Concord (01742). Main St at Sudbury Rd. Phone 978/318-3300.* Modern public library, historical collections of famous Concord authors. On display is a mantelpiece from the US Capitol (circa 1815). Also statues of Emerson and others by Daniel Chester French. (Nov-May: daily, limited hours Sun; rest of year: Mon-Sat) **FREE**

Concord Museum. *200 Lexington Rd, Concord (01742). Phone 978/369-9609.* Period rooms and galleries of domestic artifacts and decorative arts chronicling history of Concord from Native American habitation to present. Exhibits include Ralph Waldo Emerson's study, Henry David Thoreau's belongings used at Walden Pond, and Revolutionary War relics, including Paul Revere's signal lantern. Self-guided tours. (Daily; closed Easter, Thanksgiving, Dec 25) **$$$**

DeCordova Museum & Sculpture Park. *51 Sandy Pond Rd, Lincoln (01773). SE on Sandy Pond Rd. Phone 781/259-8355. www.decordova.org.* The DeCordova Museum exhibits an eclectic and delightful collection of paintings, posters, photography, sculpture, and media. The Sculpture Park, which is free, displays large contemporary sculptures throughout its 35 wooded acres. In early June—rain or shine—the museum sponsors the Annual Art in the Park Festival and Art Sale ($$), featuring musical performers, terrific food, and extraordinary art exhibitions, many of which are for sale. You can easily make the DeCordova an all-day event. (Tues-Sun) **$$**

Drumlin Farm Education Center. *201 S Great Rd, Lincoln (01773). 2 1/2 miles S on Hwy 126, then E on Hwy 117 (S Great Rd). Phone 781/259-9807.* Demonstration farm with domestic and native wild animals and birds; gardens; hayrides; special events. (Tues-Sun and Mon holidays; closed Jan 1, Thanksgiving, Dec 25) **$$$**

Fruitlands Museums. *102 Prospect Hill Rd, Harvard (01451). 15 miles W via Hwy 2, exit 38A. Phone 978/456-9028. www.fruitlands.com.* Four museums, including the Fruitlands Farmhouse, the scene of Bronson Alcott's experiment in community life, which contains furniture, books, and memorabilia of the Alcott family and the Transcendentalists; Shaker Museum, formerly in the Harvard Shaker Village, with furniture and handicrafts; Picture Gallery, with American primitive portraits and paintings by Hudson River School artists; American Indian Museum, with prehistoric artifacts and Native American art. Hiking trails with views west to Mount Wachusett and north to Mount Monadnock. Tearoom; gift shop. (Mid-May-mid-Oct, Tues-Sun and Mon holidays) **$$$**

Great Meadows National Wildlife Refuge. *Lincoln St and Weir Hill Rd, Sudbury Center (01776). Office and visitor center off Lincoln Rd, 20 miles W of Boston. Phone 978/443-4661.* Great Meadows combines terrific dirt trails with a wildlife refuge that attracts more than 200 species of birds, including the magnificent great blue heron and other heron species. As you hike near the marsh, you'll see nesting boxes for wood ducks and lodges built by muskrats, who will come out to take a peek at you near nightfall. (Daily dawn-dusk) **FREE**

Gropius House. *68 Baker Bridge Rd, Lincoln (01773). SE in Lincoln. Phone 781/259-8843.* (1937-1938) Family home of architect Walter Gropius. First building he designed upon arrival in the United States in 1937; blends New England traditions and Bauhaus principles of function and simplicity with New England's building materials and environment. Original furniture, artwork. (June-mid-Oct: Fri-Sun afternoons; rest of year: Sat-Sun first full weekend of each month) **$$**

Minute Man National Historical Park. *174 Liberty St, Concord (01742). From I-95, take Hwy 2A W. The park is 1 mile west off the ramp. Phone 978/369-6993. www.nps.gov/mima.* The Minute Man National Historical Park consists of 900 acres along the Battle Road between Lexington and Concord. Walk the 5 1/2 mile Battle Road Trail, stop at Hartwell Tavern to see reenactments of colonial life, and continue to North Bridge, site of the first battle of the Revolutionary War (the "shot heard 'round the world"). Your visit can last from a couple hours to all day, depending on how much you hike and how many sites you visit within the park. Note that some of the attractions are open only seasonally. While at the park, take advantage of multimedia programs, a lecture series, and workshops. (Spring, summer, fall: daily; winter: Sat-Sun) **FREE**

Old Manse. *269 Monument St, Concord (01742). Monument St at the North Bridge. Phone 978/369-3909.* (1770) Parsonage of Concord's early ministers, including Reverend William Emerson, Ralph Waldo Emerson's grandfather. Nathaniel Hawthorne lived here for a time and made it the setting for *Mosses from an Old Manse*. Original furnishings. (Mid-Apr-Oct, Mon-Sat, also Sun afternoons) **$$$**

Orchard House. *399 Lexington Rd, Concord (01742). Phone 978/369-4118.* Here Louisa May Alcott wrote *Little Women*. Alcott memorabilia. Guided tours. (Open year-round, hours vary seasonally) **$$$**

Ralph Waldo Emerson House. *28 Cambridge Tpke, Concord (01742). At Lexington Rd (Hwy 2A). Phone 978/369-2236.* Ralph Waldo Emerson's home from 1835 to 1882. Original furnishings and family memorabilia; 30-minute guided tours. (Mid-Apr-late Oct, Thurs-Sun, limited hours Sun) **$$$**

Sleepy Hollow Cemetery. *Bedford St, NE of square.* The Alcotts, Ralph Waldo Emerson, Nathaniel Hawthorne, Margaret Sidney, Daniel Chester French, and Henry David Thoreau are buried here.

⭐ **Walden Pond State Reservation.** *915 Walden St, Concord (01742). 1/2 mile S of Hwy 2 on Hwy 126. Phone 978/369-3254.* Henry David Thoreau, the American writer and naturalist you probably studied in tenth grade, made Walden Pond famous when he lived near the pond in a rustic cabin for two quiet years (minus a few evenings here and there, when he went to Ralph Waldo Emerson's place for dinner). The cabin still stands and is part of the park's collection. A 1 1/2 mile trail circles the pond—perfect for hiking, running, or a guided tour from the park staff. You can also fish or swim in Walden Pond; a bathhouse by the beach offers rest rooms. Visitors are limited to 1,000 or 350 cars, whichever comes first; in the summer, you'll need to arrive before 11 am to gain entry. (Daily) **FREE**

Wayside. *455 Lexington Rd (MA 2A), Concord (01742). Phone 978/369-6975.* Well-known 19th-century authors Nathaniel Hawthorne, the Alcotts, and Margaret Sidney, author of the *Five Little Peppers* books, lived here. Orientation program; 45-minute tours (May-Oct)

Special Event

Patriots Day Parade. *Phone 978/369-3042; toll-free 888/733-2678.* Patriot's Day commemorates the Battle of Lexington and Concord, which marked the beginning of the Revolutionary War on April 18 and 19, 1775. Schools and many businesses close, and the entire city celebrates. Watch parades and reenactments of the night of Paul Revere's famous ride (including one actor hanging two lanterns in Old North Church and two others riding to Lexington before meeting up with a third riding actor who finishes in Concord). At noon, the famous Boston Marathon begins in Hopkington and ends on Boylston Street. Because the historical significance of the day centers around Lexington and Concord, those two cities begin festivities the weekend preceding Patriot's Day (see www.battleroad.org/patday.htm for details). (Third Mon in Apr, one-day-only event) **FREE**

Limited-Service Hotels

★ **BEST WESTERN AT HISTORIC CONCORD.** *740 Elm St, Concord (01742). Phone 978/369-6100; toll-free 800/780-7234; fax 978/371-1656. www.bestwestern.com.* 106 rooms, 2 story. Pets accepted; fee. Complimentary continental breakfast. Check-in 2 pm, check-out noon. Fitness room. Outdoor pool, whirlpool. **$**
🍴 🏋 🏊

★ ★ **HOLIDAY INN.** *242 Adams Pl, Boxborough (01719). Phone 978/263-8701; fax 978/263-0518. www.holiday-inn.com.* 143 rooms, 3 story. Check-out noon. Restaurant, bar. Fitness room. Indoor pool. **$**
🏋 🏊

Full-Service Inn

★ ★ ★ **COLONIAL INN.** *48 Monument Sq, Concord (01742). Phone 978/369-9200; toll-free 800/370-9200; fax 978/371-1533. www.concordscolonialinn.com.* Historically prominent guests noted have stayed at this inn. Walden Pond is 2 miles away. 56 rooms. Check-in 3 pm, check-out 11 am. Wireless Internet access. Restaurant, bar. **$$**

Specialty Lodging

The following lodging establishment is approved by Mobil Travel Guide, but due to its unique and individualized nature has not been given a traditional Mobil Star rating. Included in this listing you may find bed-and-breakfasts, limited-service inns, guest ranches, and other unique hotel properties.

HAWTHORNE INN. *462 Lexington Rd, Concord (01742). Phone 978/369-5610; fax 978/287-4949. www.concordmass.com.* 7 rooms, 2 story. Complimentary continental breakfast. Check-in 3 pm, check-out 11 am. **$$**
🔲

Restaurant

★ ★ **COLONIAL INN.** *48 Monument Sq, Concord (01742). Phone 978/369-2373; fax 978/371-1533. www.concordscolonialinn.com.* Henry David Thoreau's house. Built in 1716. American menu. Breakfast, lunch, dinner, Sun brunch. Bar. Children's menu. Casual attire. Reservations recommended. Outdoor seating. **$$**

Danvers (A-7)

See also Beverly, Salem

Settled 1636
Population 25,212
Elevation 48 ft
Area Code 978
Zip 01923
Information North Shore Chamber of Commerce, 5 Cherry Hill Dr; phone 978/774-8565
Web Site www.northshorechamber.org

This small industrial town was once Salem Village—a community started by settlers from Salem looking for more farmland. In 1692, Danvers was the scene of some of the most severe witchcraft hysteria; 20 persons were put to death.

What to See and Do

Glen Magna Farms. *Ingersoll St, Danvers. 2 miles N on Hwy 1, then 1/4 mile E via Centre St to Ingersoll St. Phone 978/774-9165.* A 20-room mansion; 1790-1890 furnishings; Chamberlain gardens. Derby summer house was built by Samuel McIntire (1794); on the roof are two life-size carvings (reaper and milkmaid) by the Skillin brothers; reproduction of 1844 gazebo. Various special events and programs. (June-Sept, Tues and Thurs; closed holidays; also by appointment) **$$**

Rebecca Nurse Homestead. *149 Pine St, Danvers (01923). Phone 978/774-8799.* The house (circa 1680), an excellent example of the New England saltbox, was the homestead of Rebecca Nurse, a saintly woman accused of and executed for witchcraft during the hysteria of 1692. House includes restored rooms with furnishings from 17th and 18th centuries; outbuildings, a reproduction of the 1672 Salem Village Meetinghouse and exhibit areas. (Mid-June-mid-Sept: Tues-Sun; mid-Sept-Oct: weekends; rest of year: by appointment; closed holidays) **$$**

Witchcraft Victims Memorial. *176 Hobart St, Danvers (01923).* Memorial includes names of those who died, as well as quotes from eight victims.

Special Event

Danvers Family Festival. *Phone 978/774-8565.* Exhibits, fireworks, races, music. Late June-early July.

Limited-Service Hotels

★ **DAYS INN.** *152 Endicott St, Danvers (01923). Phone 978/777-1030; toll-free 800/329-7466; fax 978/777-0264. www.daysinn.com.* 129 rooms, 2 story. Complimentary continental breakfast. Check-out 11 am. Outdoor pool. **$**

★ ★ **COURTYARD BY MARRIOTT.** *275 Independence Way, Danvers (01923). Phone 978/777-8630; toll-free 800/321-2211; fax 978/777-7341. www.courtyard.com.* 120 rooms, 3 story. Check-in 3 pm, check-out noon. High-speed Internet access. Restaurant, bar. Fitness room. Outdoor pool. **$**

Full-Service Hotel

★ ★ ★ **SHERATON FERNCROFT RESORT.** *50 Ferncroft Rd, Danvers (01923). Phone 978/777-2500; toll-free 800/325-3535; fax 978/750-7959. www.sheraton.com.* This hotel boasts luxurious guest rooms, world class dining, and a distinctive, state-of-the-art, and fully-staffed business center. For the leisure traveler, guests can pamper themselves at the salon and day spa, enjoy a game of golf on the 18-hole Robert Trent Jones-designed golf course, or luxuriate in the indoor pool. 367 rooms, 8 story. Check-in 3 pm, check-out 11 am. High-speed Internet access. Restaurant, bar. Fitness room. Indoor pool, whirlpool. Golf. Tennis. Airport transportation available. Business center. **$$**

Restaurant

★ ★ **THE HARDCOVER.** *15-A Newbury St, Danvers (01923). Phone 978/774-1223; fax 978/777-5038. www.barnsiderrestaurants.com.* Seafood, steak menu. Dinner. Bar. Children's menu. **$$$**

Dedham (B-7)

Settled 1635
Population 23,464
Elevation 120 ft
Area Code 781
Zip 02026
Information Neponset Valley Chamber of Commerce, 190 Vanderbilt Ave, Suite 1, Norwood 02062-5047; phone 781/769-1126
Web Site www.nvcc.com

What to See and Do

Dedham Historical Society. *612 High St, Dedham (02026). Phone 781/326-1385. www.dedhamhistorical .org.* Small but important collection of 16th- to 19th-century furniture; collection of work by silversmith Katharine Pratt; world's largest public collection of Dedham and Chelsea pottery; changing exhibits. Also 10,000-volume historical and genealogical library. (Tues-Fri, some Sat; closed holidays) **$**

Fairbanks House. *511 East St, Dedham (02026). At Eastern Ave, off Hwy 1. Phone 781/326-1170.* (1636) One of the oldest frame houses still standing in the United States. Fine example of 17th-century architecture, furnished with Fairbanks family heirlooms; guided tours. (May-Oct, Tues-Sat, also Sun afternoons) **$$**

Limited-Service Hotel

★ ★ **HOLIDAY INN.** *55 Ariadne Rd, Dedham (02026). Phone 781/329-1000; toll-free 800/465-4329; fax 781/329-0903. www.holiday-inn.com.* 203 rooms, 8 story. Check-in 3 pm, check-out noon. High-speed Internet access. Restaurant. Fitness room. Indoor pool. **$**
🚶 🛌

Full-Service Hotel

★ ★ ★ **HILTON BOSTON/DEDHAM.** *25 Allied Dr, Dedham (02026). Phone 617/329-7900; toll-free 800/345-6565; fax 617/329-5552. http://www.boston dedham.hilton.com.* Located just 20 minutes from downtown Boston, this hotel's focus is to ensure that guests are offered all of the services and facilities needed to make their trip pleasurable. Make sure to take time and enjoy the outdoor jogging trail or the state-of-the-art fitness center. 254 rooms, 4 story. Check-in 3 pm, check-out noon. Restaurant, bar. Fitness room. Indoor pool, whirlpool. Tennis. Business center. **$**
🚶 🛌 🏌 🚶

Deerfield (B-3)

Settled 1669
Population 4,750
Elevation 150 ft
Area Code 413
Zip 01342
Information Historic Deerfield, Inc, PO Box 321; phone 413/774-5581

Web Site www.historic-deerfield.org

Twice destroyed by French and Native American attacks when it was the northwest frontier of New England, and almost forgotten by industry, Deerfield is noted for its unspoiled meadowland, beautiful houses, and nationally famous boarding schools (Deerfield Academy, 1797, a coeducational preparatory school; the Bement School, a coeducational school; and Eaglebrook School for boys).

In 1675, the Bloody Brook Massacre (King Philip's War) crippled the settlement, which was then a struggling frontier outpost. In 1704 (Queen Anne's War), half of the resettled town was burned. Forty-nine inhabitants were killed and more than 100 were captured and taken to Canada.

The village boasts that it has one of the most beautiful streets in America, known just as "The Street," a mile-long stretch of 80 houses, many dating from the 18th and early 19th centuries.

What to See and Do

⭐ **Historic Deerfield.** *Hwys 5 and 10, Deerfield (01342). Phone 413/774-5581.* Maintains 14 historic house museums (fee) furnished with collections of antique furniture, silver, ceramics, textiles. A 28,000-square-foot Collections Study Center features changing exhibits and study-storage displays of portions of the museum's collections. Daily walking tours, meadow walk, antique forums and workshops, special events weekends. Information Center is located at Hall Tavern, The Street. (Daily; closed Thanksgiving, Dec 24-25) **$$$$**

Memorial Hall Museum. *10 Memorial St, Deerfield (01342). Phone 413/774-7476.* (1798) The first building of Deerfield Academy; contains colonial furnishings, Native American relics. (May-Oct, daily) **$$**

Full-Service Inn

★ ★ ★ **DEERFIELD INN.** *81 Old Main St, Deerfield (01342). Phone 413/774-5587; toll-free 800/ 926-3865; fax 413/775-7221. www.deerfieldinn.com.* There is a tavern in this historic 1884 inn, and elegant sitting parlors with authentic period wallpaper and antiques, and it is filled with nooks and alcoves where you can sink in and relax. This is a classic New England inn, one of the few originals still in operation, where its first guests arrived by stagecoach and then trolleys. Today, the main building has ten rooms, and the new wing, built to resemble a barn, has 13. While the accommodations have modern bathrooms, they also have four-poster beds and period furniture, each room unique and named after a historical figure with a local connection. But beware: it is said there are a couple of ghosts wandering the premises—clearly figures who can't bring themselves to leave the inn's warmth and charm. 23 rooms, 2 story. Closed Dec 24-Dec 26, Pets accepted, some restrictions; fee. Complimentary full breakfast. Check-in 2 pm, check-out noon. Two restaurants, bar. **$$**

Restaurants

★ ★ ★ **DEERFIELD INN.** *81 Old Main St, Deerfield (01342). Phone 413/774-5587; toll-free 800/826-3865; fax 413/775-7221. www.deerfieldinn.com.* This warm and elegant dining room is located in a quintessential New England country inn that is nestled among a street full of historic houses. The menu features New England cuisine and changes seasonally. American menu. Breakfast, dinner. Closed Dec 24-26. Bar. Children's menu. Business casual attire. Reservations recommended. **$$**

★ ★ ★ **SIENNA.** *6B Elm St, Deerfield (01373). Phone 413/665-0215; fax 413/665-6644. www.siennarest.com.* Chef Richard Labonte changes the menu to take advantage of seasonal ingredients. His creative American cuisine is enhanced by flavors from many other cuisines. American menu. Dinner. Closed Mon-Tues. **$$**

Dennis (Cape Cod) (D-9)

Settled 1639
Population 15,973
Elevation 24 ft
Area Code 508
Zip 02638
Information Chamber of Commerce, 242 Swan River Rd, phone 508/398-3568
Web Site www.dennischamber.com

Dennis heads a group, often called "the Dennises," that includes Dennisport, East Dennis, South Dennis, West

Dennis, and Dennis. It was here, in 1816, that Henry Hall developed the commercial cultivation of cranberries. Swimming beaches are located throughout the area.

What to See and Do

Jericho House and Historical Center. *Old Main St and Trotting Park Rd, West Dennis (02670). Phone 508/394-6114.* (1801) Period furniture. Barn museum contains old tools, household articles, model of salt works, photographs. (July-Aug, Wed and Fri) **DONATION**

Josiah Dennis Manse. *77 Nobscusset Rd, Dennis (02638). Phone 508/385-3528.* (1736) and **Old West School House** (1770). Restored home of minister for whom town was named; antiques, Pilgrim chest, children's room, spinning and weaving exhibit, maritime wing. (July-Aug, Tues and Thurs) **DONATION**

Sand Bar Club and Lounge. *4 Lighthouse Rd, West Dennis (02670). Phone 508/398-7586. www.lighthouseinn.com.* Local talent Philo Rockwell King, better known as Rock King, has been performing musical and comedy acts at the Sand Bar for nearly 40 years and is still going strong—catch his act Wednesdays through Saturdays. Other acts include jazz musicians, singers, comedians, and more. Check the Web site for performance schedules. The Sand Bar is on the grounds of The Lighthouse Inn, a country inn that offers outstanding entertainment for children.

Special Events

Cape Playhouse. *820 Main St, Dennis (02638). Phone 508/385-3911. www.capeplayhouse.com.* The Cape Playhouse offers opportunities to watch both established Broadway stars and up-and-coming actors for two-week runs of musicals, comedies, and other plays. Putting on performances since 1927, the Playhouse is the oldest professional summer theater in the United States—you can sometimes take a backstage tour of this historic facility. On Friday mornings during summer, attend the special children's performance that includes puppetry, storytelling, and musicals. The Playhouse complex also houses the Cape Museum of Fine Arts, the Playhouse Bistro, and the Cape Cinema. (Late June-Labor Day) **$$$$**

Festival Week. *Phone 508/398-3568.* Canoe and road races, antique car parade, craft fair, antique show. (Late Aug)

Limited-Service Hotels

★ **COLONIAL VILLAGE RESORT.** *426 Lower County Rd, Dennisport (02639). Phone 508/398-2071; toll-free 800/287-2071; fax 508/398-2071.* 49 rooms, 2 story. Closed mid-Oct-mid-May. Check-out 11 am. Beach. Indoor pool, outdoor pool, whirlpool. **$**
🅳 ⌨

★ **EDGEWATER BEACH RESORT.** *95 Chase Ave, Dennisport (02639). Phone 508/398-6922; fax 508/760-3447. www.edgewatercapecod.com.* 86 rooms, 2 story. Closed mid-Nov-mid-Mar. Check-out 11 am. Fitness room. Indoor pool, outdoor pool, whirlpool. **$**
🅳 🏃 ⌨

★ **HUNTSMAN MOTOR LODGE.** *829 Main St (Hwy 28), West Dennis (02670). Phone 508/394-5415; toll-free 800/628-0498. www.thehuntsman.com.* 25 rooms, 2 story. Closed Nov-mid-Apr. Check-out 11 am. Outdoor pool. **$**
🅳 ⌨

★ **SESUIT HARBOR.** *1421 Main St, East Dennis (02641). Phone 508/385-3326; toll-free 800/359-0097; fax 508/385-3326. www.sesuitharbormotel.com.* 20 rooms, 2 story. Complimentary continental breakfast. Check-out 10:30 am. Outdoor pool. **$**
🅳 ⌨

★ ★ **SOUNDINGS SEASIDE RESORT.** *79 Chase Ave, Dennisport (02639). Phone 505/394-6561; fax 508/374-7537. www.thesoundings.com.* 100 rooms, 2 story. Closed mid-Oct-late Apr. Check-in 3 pm, check-out 11 am. Restaurant. Beach. Indoor pool, outdoor pool. **$**
🅳 ⌨

★ ★ **THREE SEASONS MOTOR LODGE.** *421 Old Wharf Rd, Dennisport (02639). Phone 508/398-6091; fax 508/398-3762. www.threeseasonsmotel.com.* 61 rooms, 2 story. Closed Nov-late May. Check-out 11 am. Restaurant. Beach. **$**
🅳

Full-Service Resort

★ ★ **LIGHTHOUSE INN.** *1 Lighthouse Rd, West Dennis (02670). Phone 508/398-2244; fax 508/398-5658. www.lighthouseinn.com.* 63 rooms. Closed mid-Oct-late May. Check-out 11 am. Restaurant, bar. Children's activity center. Beach. Outdoor pool. Tennis. Business center. **$$**
⌨ 🎿 🏃

Specialty Lodgings

The following lodging establishments are approved by Mobil Travel Guide, but due to their unique and individualized nature have not been given a traditional Mobil Star rating. Included in this listing you may find bed-and-breakfasts, limited-service inns, guest ranches, and other unique hotel properties.

BY THE SEA GUESTS. *57 Chase Ave, Dennisport (02639). Phone 508/398-8685; toll-free 800/447-9202; fax 508/398-0334. www.bytheseaguests.com.* 12 rooms, 3 story. Complimentary continental breakfast. Check-in 2 pm, check-out 11 am. Beach. **$**

CORSAIR AND CROSS RIP OCEANFRONT. *41 Chase Ave, Dennisport (02639). Phone 508/398-6600; fax 508/760-6681.www.corsaircrossrip.com.* 46 rooms. Closed late Oct-mid-Apr. Complimentary continental breakfast. Check-in 3 pm, check-out 11 am. Wireless Internet access. Children's activity center. Beach. Indoor pool, two outdoor pools, children's pool, whirlpool. **$$**
⌨

FOUR CHIMNEYS INN. *946 Main St, Dennis (02638). Phone 508/385-6317; toll-free 800/874-5502; fax 508/385-6285. www.fourchimneysinn.com.* 8 rooms, 3 story. Complimentary full breakfast. Check-in 3 pm, check-out 11 am. **$**
🅳

ISAIAH HALL BED AND BREAKFAST INN. *152 Whig St, Dennis (02638). Phone 508/385-9928; toll-free 800/736-0160; fax 508/385-5879. www.isaiahhallinn.com.* Farmhouse built in 1857. 10 rooms, 2 story. Closed Nov-mid-Apr. Children over 7 years only. Complimentary continental breakfast. Check-in 2 pm, check-out 2-9:30 pm. **$**
🅳

ROSE PETAL BED & BREAKFAST. *152 Sea St, Dennisport (02639). Phone 508/398-8470. www.rose petalofdennis.com.* 3 rooms. Complimentary full breakfast. Check-in 3 pm, check-out 11 am. **$**

Restaurants

★ **BOB'S BEST SANDWICHES.** *613 Main St (Hwy 28), Dennisport (02639). Phone 508/394-8450.* The owner wakes early to bake his own bread at Bob's Best Sandwiches, and the crusty, delicious result is worth the wake-up call. Roast turkey and roast beef are this sandwich shop's two most requested selections, and the breakfasts of savory French toast and fluffy omelets are noteworthy. Deli menu. Lunch. Children's menu. Casual attire. Outdoor seating. No credit cards accepted. **$**

[D]

★ ★ **CHRISTINE'S.** *581 Main St (Hwy 28), West Dennis (02670). Phone 508/394-7333; fax 508/394-9112. www.christinesofcapecod.com.* This sizable family-owned restaurant has been around for more than 20 years, and for good reason: the Jamiels pride themselves on top-quality ingredients and reasonable prices. The menu features spicy dishes from their native Lebanon in addition to typical American fare and Italian plates. Live entertainment is a fixture here later in the evenings. American, Lebanese menu. Lunch, dinner, Sun brunch. Bar. Children's menu. **$$**

★ ★ **CLANCY'S.** *8 Upper County Rd, Dennisport (02639). Phone 508/394-6661; fax 508/394-6074. www.clancysrestaurant.com.* Lunch, brunch, and dinner come with a view at the country clublike setting of Clancy's. This likable restaurant enjoys one of the most scenic locations in the area, nestled alongside the Swan River. From chicken and steak to pasta and fish, the menu truly has something for everyone, and Sunday brunch here is outstanding. American, seafood menu. Lunch, dinner, Sun brunch. Closed Thanksgiving, Dec 25. Bar. Children's menu. Casual attire. Valet parking. Outdoor seating. **$$**

★ ★ **GINA'S BY THE SEA.** *134 Taunton Ave, Dennis (02638). Phone 508/385-3213.* Gina's by the Sea whips up Italian food just like your grandmother used to make—if your grandmother happened to be Italian. Located in Dennis's Little Italy neighborhood right near the beach, this casual restaurant has been a culinary landmark since 1938. Bring a hearty appetite along with a bit of patience, since Gina's doesn't take reservations. Italian menu. Dinner. Closed Dec-Mar. Casual attire. **$$**

★ ★ **LA SCALA.** *106 Depot St, Dennisport (02639). Phone 508/398-3910.* Diners sing praises for the food at La Scala. This recently transformed restaurant once known as the Captain William's House features American and Italian cuisine. Generous portions of tasty meals that are easy on the wallet make this a popular choice for families. Takeout is also available here. Italian, American menu. Dinner. Closed Jan-Mar. Bar. Children's menu. **$$**

★ **MARSHSIDE.** *28 Bridge St, East Dennis (02641). Phone 508/385-4010.* Good home cooking and a waterside location make Marshside a true find. This East Dennis diner earns a loyal following among locals and visitors alike for its reliable, reasonably priced meals and freshly baked desserts. Its location at Sesuit Creek with views extending to the harbor makes this restaurant a visitor's dream come true. Seafood menu. Breakfast, lunch, dinner. Closed Thanksgiving, Dec 25. Children's menu. **$**

★ ★ ★ **RED PHEASANT INN.** *905 Main St, Dennis (02638). Phone 508/385-2133; toll-free 800/480-2133; fax 508/385-2112. www.redpheasantinn.com.* The Red Pheasant Inn is the very essence of country charm. Housed within a 200-year-old barn, this gourmet restaurant delights romantics and gourmands alike with its quaint surroundings and fine food. The American menu consists of fish and meat specialties, with lamb and game offerings changing nightly. A 300-bottle wine list is sure to please the most demanding connoisseurs. The dining room is lovely during the winter months with two blazing fireplaces, while the gardens provide an enchanting setting in summer. American menu. Dinner. Bar. Valet parking. **$$$**

★ ★ **SCARGO CAFE.** *799 Main St, Dennis (02638). Phone 508/385-8200; fax 508/385-6977. www.scargocafe.com.* Located across from the Cape Playhouse (the nation's oldest stock company theater) and the Cape Cinema, Scargo serves a hearty menu of grilled steaks and chops and a full range of Cape Cod seafood. The house special is an inventive "seafood strudel," a pot pie of crab, shrimp, and scallops in Newburg sauce with a flaky pastry crust. For a romantic tête-à-tête, ask for the table for two beneath the stairs. International/Fusion menu. Lunch, dinner. Closed Thanksgiving, Dec 25. Bar. Children's menu. **$$$**

★ **SWAN RIVER SEAFOOD.** *5 Lower County Rd, Dennisport (02639). Phone 508/394-4466; fax 508/398-3201. www.swanriverseafoods.com.* Fish doesn't get any fresher. Local fishermen unload their catch here at the restaurant and fish market that sits at the marshy mouth of the Swan River. While deep-fried treatments make up a good part of the menu, the kitchen also knows how to grill, broil, and sauté, resulting in such treats as fresh fillets poached in garlic broth and grilled swordfish and shark encrusted in black pepper. Seafood menu. Lunch, dinner. Closed mid-Sept-late May. Bar. Children's menu. **$$**

Eastham (Cape Cod) (D-10)

See also Orleans

Settled 1644
Population 5,453
Elevation 48 ft
Area Code 508
Zip 02642
Information Chamber of Commerce, PO Box 1329; phone 508/240-7211 or 508/255-3444 (summer only); or visit the Information Booth at Hwy 6 and Fort Hill
Web Site www.easthamchamber.com

On the bay side of the Cape, in what is now Eastham town, the *Mayflower* shore party met their first Native Americans. Also in the town is a magnificent stretch of Nauset Beach, which was once a graveyard of ships. Nauset Light is an old friend of mariners.

What to See and Do

Eastham Historical Society. *190 Samoset Rd, Eastham (02642). Just off Hwy 6. Phone 508/255-0788.* 1869 schoolhouse museum; Native American artifacts; farming and nautical implements. (July-Aug, Mon-Fri afternoons) **DONATION** The society also maintains the

> **Swift-Daley House.** *Phone 508/255-1766.* (1741) Cape Cod house contains period furniture, clothing, original hardware. (July-Aug, Mon-Fri afternoons or by appointment) **FREE**

Eastham Windmill. *Windmill Green, Eastham (02642). In town center. Phone 508/240-7211.* Oldest windmill on the Cape (1680); restored in 1936. (Late June-Labor Day, daily) **DONATION**

Limited-Service Hotels

★ **CAPTAIN'S QUARTERS.** *Hwy 6, North Eastham (02651). Phone 508/255-5686; toll-free 800/327-7769; fax 508/240-0280. www.captains-quarters.com.* 75 rooms. Closed mid-Nov-mid-Apr. Complimentary continental breakfast. Check-out 11 am. Outdoor pool. Tennis. **$**
🏊 🎿

★ ★ **FOUR POINTS BY SHERATON.** *3800 Hwy 6, Eastham (02642). Phone 508/255-5000; toll-free*

800/533-3986; fax 508/240-1870. www.fourpoints.com. 107 rooms, 2 story. Check-in 3 pm, check-out 11 am. Restaurant, bar. Fitness room. Indoor pool, outdoor pool, whirlpool. Tennis. **$$**
🧍 🏊 🎿

Specialty Lodgings

The following lodging establishments are approved by Mobil Travel Guide, but due to their unique and individualized nature have not been given a traditional Mobil Star rating. Included in this listing you may find bed-and-breakfasts, limited-service inns, guest ranches, and other unique hotel properties.

OVERLOOK INN OF CAPE COD. *3085 County Rd (Hwy 6), Eastham (02642). Phone 508/255-1886; fax 508/240-0545. www.overlookinn.com.* 10 rooms, 3 story. Complimentary full breakfast. Check-in 2 pm, check-out 11 am. **$$**
🅳

THE PENNY HOUSE INN. *Hwy 6, North Eastham (02651). Phone 508/255-6632; toll-free 800/554-1751; fax 508/255-4893. www.pennyhouseinn.com.* 12 rooms, 2 story. Children over 8 years only. Complimentary full breakfast. Check-in 3 pm, check-out 11 am. **$$**
🅳

THE WHALEWALK INN. *220 Bridge Rd, Eastham (02642). Phone 508/255-0617; toll-free 800/440-1281; fax 508/240-0017. www.whalewalkinn.com.* 16 rooms. Complimentary full breakfast. Check-in 3 pm, check-out 11 am. **$$$**

Fall River (D-7)

See also New Bedford; also see Providence, RI

Settled 1656
Population 91,938
Elevation 200 ft
Area Code 508
Information Fall River Area Chamber of Commerce, 200 Pocasset St, 02721; phone 508/676-8226
Web Site www.fallriverchamber.com

The city's name, adopted in 1834, was translated from the Native American "quequechan." In 1892, Fall River was the scene of one of the most famous murder trials in American history—that of Lizzie Borden, who was acquitted of the ax murders of her father and stepmother. Water power and cotton textiles built Fall

River into one of the largest cotton manufacturers in the world, but its industry is now greatly diversified.

What to See and Do

⭐ **Battleship Cove.** *5 Water St, Fall River (02721). At jct Hwy 138, I-195. Phone 508/678-1100.* Five historic naval ships of the World War II period. The submarine *Lionfish*, a World War II attack sub with all her equipment intact, and the battleship USS *Massachusetts* are open to visitors. The *Massachusetts*, commissioned in 1942, was active in the European and Pacific theaters of operation in the Second World War and now houses the state's official World War II and Gulf War Memorial; on board is a full-scale model of a Patriot missile. Also here are *PT Boat 796, PT Boat 617,* and the destroyer USS *Joseph P. Kennedy Jr.,* which saw action in both the Korean and Vietnam conflicts and the Cuban missile blockade. The PT boats may be viewed from walkways. A landing craft (LCM) exhibit is located on the grounds. Gift shop; snack bar. (Daily; closed Jan 1, Thanksgiving, Dec 25) **$$$**

Factory Outlet District. *638 Quequechan St, Fall River (02721). Phone 508/677-4949.* Fall River is an extensive factory outlet area.

Fall River Heritage State Park. *100 Frontage Rd, Fall River (02720). Davol St. Phone 508/675-5759.* Nine acres on the riverfront; sailing. Visitor center (daily) has multimedia presentation on how Fall River developed into the greatest textile producer in the country; tourist information. (Daily; closed Jan 1, Dec 25) **FREE**

Fall River Historical Society. *451 Rock St, Fall River (02720). Phone 508/679-1071.* Historical displays in 16-room Victorian mansion. Exhibits of Fall River Steamship Line, dolls, fine art, glassware, costumes; artifacts relating to the Lizzie Borden trial. Gift shop. (Apr-May, Oct-Nov, Tues-Fri; June-Sept, Tues-Sun; Dec, Mon) **$$**

Marine Museum. *70 Water St, Fall River (02720). Phone 508/674-3533.* More than 100 ship models on display, including a 28-foot, 1-ton model of the *Titanic,* trace the growth of maritime steam power from the early 1800s to 1937; paintings, photographs, artifacts. (Daily; closed Jan 1, Thanksgiving, Dec 25) **$$**

St. Anne's Church and Shrine. *818 Middle St, Fall River (02721). S Main St, facing Kennedy Park. Phone 508/674-5651.* (1906) Designed by Canadian architect Napoleon Bourassa, the upper church is constructed of Vermont blue marble; the lower church is of solid granite. In the upper church are stained-glass windows produced by E. Rault in Rennes, France, a "Casavant Freres" organ, and exceptional oak wood ornamentation in the vault of the ceiling. The shrine is in the lower church.

Limited-Service Hotels

★ **HAMPTON INN.** *53 Old Bedford Rd, Westport (02790). Phone 508/675-8500; toll-free 800/426-7866; fax 508/675-0075. www.hamptoninn.com.* 133 rooms, 4 story. Complimentary continental breakfast. Check-in 3 pm, check-out noon. Fitness room. Whirlpool. Tennis. Airport transportation available. **$** 🧑 🛫

★ **QUALITY INN.** *1878 Wilbur Ave, Somerset (02725). Phone 508/678-4545; toll-free 800/228-5151; fax 508/678-9352. www.qualityinn.com.* 107 rooms, 2 story. Pets accepted, some restrictions. Complimentary continental breakfast. Check-in 3 pm, check-out noon. Fitness room. Indoor pool. **$** 🐾 🧑 🏊

Restaurant

★ ★ **WHITE'S OF WESTPORT.** *66 Hwy 6, Westport (02790). Phone 508/675-7185; fax 508/679-9324. www.lafrancehospitality.com.* Seafood, steak menu. Lunch, dinner. Closed Dec 25. Bar. Children's menu. **$$**

Falmouth (Cape Cod) (D-8)

See also Martha's Vineyard

Settled circa 1660
Population 32,660
Elevation 10 ft
Area Code 508
Zip 02540
Information Cape Cod Chamber of Commerce, Hwys 6 and 132, PO Box 790, Hyannis 02601-0790; phone 508/362-3225 or toll-free 888/227-3263
Web Site www.capecodchamber.org

Falmouth, at the southwest corner of the Cape, boasts a whopping 68 miles of coastline, with 12 public beaches. Its pride and joy is the Woods Hole Oceanographic Institution, a research facility dedicated to marine science—the largest independent oceanographic institution in the world. In East Falmouth is the Cape Cod Winery, which grows six varieties of grapes.

What to See and Do

Ashumet Holly & Wildlife Sanctuary. *Ashumet and Currier rds, Falmouth (02540). Just N of Hwy 151.* Phone 508/362-1426. (Massachusetts Audubon Society) A 45-acre wildlife preserve with holly trail; herb garden; observation beehive. Trails open dawn to dusk. (Tues-Sun) **$$**

Bradley House Museum. *573 Woods Hole Rd, Woods Hole (02543). Phone 508/548-7270.* Model of Woods Hole Village (circa 1895); audiovisual show of local history; restored spritsail sailboat; model ships. Walking tour of village. (July-Aug: Tues-Sat; June and Sept: Wed, Sat; schedule may vary) **FREE**

Cape Cod Canal Cruises. *Onset Town, Onset (02558). 3 miles W via Hwys 6 and 28. Phone 508/295-3883.* Cruises with historical narration. Also evening cocktail and entertainment cruises. (June-Oct, daily; May, Sat-Sun) **$$$$**

⭐ **Cape Cod Kayak.** *676 N Falmouth Hwy, Hwy 28A, North Falmouth (02556). Phone 508/563-9377. www.capecodkayak.com.* Guided kayak tours on area lakes, rivers, harbors, and coves last from three hours to a full day. Guides are happy to teach you kayaking basics before you set out, so even if you've never kayaked before, you'll enjoy this unique way to see Cape Cod. If you're an experienced kayaker and know the area, rent a kayak for a day, weekend, or entire week. (Mar-Nov; closed Dec-Feb) **$$$$**

Car/Passenger Boat Trips. *509 Falmouth Rd, Woods Hole (02649). Phone 508/477-8600.* Woods Hole, Martha's Vineyard Steamship Authority conducts trips to Martha's Vineyard (all year). Schedule may vary. **$$$$**

Falmouth Historical Society Museums. Julia Wood House. *55 Palmer Ave, Falmouth (02540). Phone 508/548-4857.* (1790) and **Conant House** (circa 1740). Whaling collection; period furniture; 19th-century paintings; glassware; silver; tools; costumes; widow's walk; memorial park; colonial garden. (Mid-June-mid-Sept: Mon-Thurs; rest of year: by appointment) Katharine Lee Bates exhibit in Conant House honors

author of "America the Beautiful." (Mid-June-mid-Sept, Mon-Thurs) On village green. **$$**

Island Queen. *Phone 508/548-4800.* Passenger boat trips to Martha's Vineyard; 600-passenger vessel. (Late May-mid-Oct)

Porter's Thermometer Museum. *49 Zarahemla Rd, Onset (02532). Just E of the junction of I-495 and I-195. Phone 508/295-5504.* Heralded as the only museum of its kind in the world, the Porter Thermometer Museum in tiny Onset houses some 2,600 distinct specimens. Varieties include those used by astronauts, ones that can be worn as earrings, and temperature-telling instruments from around the world. One thermometer from Alaska can accurately record temperatures all the way down to -100 degrees! Run by former high school science teacher Richard Porter out of his house, the museum is free, as long as you call ahead. Make sure to admire the world's largest thermometer out front, which can be read from as far as a mile. **FREE**

Special Events

Arts & Crafts Street Fair. *Main St, Falmouth (02540). Phone 508/548-8500.* On a midsummer Wednesday each year in Falmouth, more than 200 painters, weavers, glassworkers, woodworkers, potters, and others artisans set up booths along Main Street. The Arts & Crafts Street Fair is a classic summer festival, with food and entertainment for the entire family. The Falmouth Artists Guild also hosts a fundraising art auction during the fair. Mid-July. **FREE**

Barnstable County Fair. *1220 Nathan Ellis Hwy, Falmouth (02536). 8 miles N on Hwy 151. Phone 508/563-3200.* Horse and dog shows, horse-pulling contest; exhibits. Last week in July.

College Light Opera Company at Highfield Theatre. *Depot Ave, Hwy 28, Falmouth (02540). Phone 508/548-2211.* Nine-week season of musicals and operettas with full orchestra. Mon-Sat. Late June-Labor Day.

Falmouth Road Race. *790 E Main St (race headquarters), Falmouth (02540). Phone 508/540-7000. www.falmouthroadrace.com.* Starting in scenic Woods Hole and winding back into Falmouth Heights, this hilly and hot course takes you past some of the best scenery in the country. This 7.1-mile race has been called the "Best USA Road Race" by *Runner's World* magazine. The entry is a lottery, which means that far more people try to enter than are allowed in. Your best bet is to join the over 70,000 spectators who line the course. If you want to race and don't get in, check the Internet for at least a dozen other summer road races on Cape Cod. Third Sun in Aug. **$$$**

Music on the Green. *Peg Noonan Park, Main St, Falmouth (02540). Phone 508/362-0066. www.arts foundationcapecod.org.* Professional musicians from the Cape Cod area take part in the Music on the Green series, held on the town green in Falmouth. You'll enjoy rock, swing, marches, and folk music, all performed in the breezy park, and you're encouraged to bring a picnic and beach chair or blanket. The town of Hyannis also offers a Jazz by the Sea concert in early August on its town green. Early July-late Aug. **FREE**

Limited-Service Hotels

★ ★ **INN ON THE SQUARE.** *40 N Main St, Falmouth (02540). Phone 508/457-0606; toll-free 888/ 744-5394. www.innonthesquare.com.* 72 rooms, 2 story. Check-out 11 am. Restaurant, bar. Indoor pool. **$**
🏊 📶

★ **NAUTILUS MOTOR INN.** *539 Woods Hole Rd, Woods Hole (02543). Phone 508/548-1525; toll-free 800/654-2333; fax 508/457-9674. www.nautilusinn.com.* 54 rooms, 2 story. Closed late Oct-mid-Apr. Check-out 11 am. Outdoor pool. Tennis. **$**
📶 🏊 🎿

★ **RED HORSE INN.** *28 Falmouth Hts Rd, Falmouth (02540). Phone 508/548-0053; toll-free 800/ 628-3811; fax 508/540-6563. www.redhorseinn.com.* 22 rooms, 2 story. Check-out 11 am. Outdoor pool. **$**
🏊

Full-Service Resorts

★ ★ ★ **NEW SEABURY RESORT AND CONFERENCE CENTER.** *Rock Landing Rd, New Seabury (02649). Phone 508/477-9111; toll-free 800/999-9033; fax 508/477-9790. www.newseabury.com.* This resort, conference center, and residential community sits on 2,300 recreation-filled acres and offers rentals from early March to early January. The resort's villa development began in 1962 and consists of two golf courses, 16 tennis courts, and private beaches. 160 rooms. Check-in 4 pm, check-out 10 am. Restaurant, bar. Children's activity center. Fitness room. Outdoor pool, children's pool. Golf. Tennis. Airport transportation available. Business center. **$**
🧍 🏊 🏌 🎿 🚶

★ ★ **SEA CREST RESORT.** *350 Quaker Rd, North Falmouth (02556). Phone 508/540-9400; toll-free 800/ 225-3110; fax 508/540-7602. www.seacrest-resort.com.* 266 rooms, 3 story. Check-in 3 pm, check-out 11 am. Restaurant, bar. Children's activity center. Fitness room. Beach. Indoor pool, outdoor pool, whirlpool. Tennis. Business center. **$$**
🧍 🏊 🎿 🚶

Full-Service Inn

★ ★ ★ **COONAMESSETT INN.** *311 Gifford St, Falmouth (02540). Phone 508/548-2300.* 28 rooms. Check-in 3 pm, check-out 11 am. High-speed Internet access. Restaurant, bar. **$**

Specialty Lodgings

The following lodging establishments are approved by Mobil Travel Guide, but due to their unique and individualized nature have not been given a traditional Mobil Star rating. Included in this listing you may find bed-and-breakfasts, limited-service inns, guest ranches, and other unique hotel properties.

BEACH HOUSE AT FALMOUTH HEIGHTS. *10 Worcester Ct, Falmouth (02540). Phone 508/457-0310; toll-free 800/351-3426; fax 508/548-7895. www.cape codbeachhouse.com.* 8 rooms, 2 story. Closed Nov-May. Children over 12 years only. Complimentary continental breakfast. Check-in 3-6 pm, check-out 11 am. Outdoor pool. **$**
📶 🏊

CAPT. TOM LAWRENCE HOUSE. *75 Locust St, Falmouth (02540). Phone 508/540-1445; toll-free 800/ 266-8139; fax 508/457-1790. www.captaintom lawrence.com.* Vaulted ceilings, hardwood floors, and a spiral staircase add to the romantic, old-world charm of this intimate inn located within walking distance of the town's historic main street. Built in 1861, it is a former whaling captain's home. 7 rooms, 2 story. Closed Jan. Complimentary full breakfast. Check-in 3 pm, check-out 11 am. **$$**
📶

ELM ARCH INN. *26 Elm Arch Way, Falmouth (02540). Phone 508/548-0133. www.elmarchinn.com.* This former private residence of a whaling captain was built in 1810. It was attacked by the British in 1814, and the hole where the cannonball hit can still be seen in the dining area. 24 rooms, 2 story. Check-in noon, check-out 11 am. Outdoor pool. **$**

GRAFTON INN. *261 Grand Ave S, Falmouth (02540). Phone 508/540-8688; toll-free 800/642-4069; fax 508/540-1861. www.graftoninn.com.* This former home of a sea captain was built in 1850 and is located on Nantucket Sound. 10 rooms, 3 story. Children over 16 years only. Complimentary full breakfast. Check-in 2-6 pm, check-out 11 am. **$$**

INN ON THE SOUND. *313 Grand Ave, Falmouth (02540). Phone 508/457-9666; toll-free 800/564-9668; fax 508/457-9631. www.innonthesound.com.* Built in 1880. Overlooking Vineyard Sound. 10 rooms, 2 story. Children over 16 years only. Complimentary full breakfast. Check-in 3-6 pm, check-out 11 am. **$$**

MOSTLY HALL. *27 Main St, Falmouth (02540). Phone 508/548-3786; fax 508/548-5778. www.mostly hall.com.* This 1849 plantation-style house, which is the only one of its kind on Cape Cod, offers a secluded location in the heart of the town's historic district. 6 rooms, 3 story. Closed Nov-mid-May. Children over 16 years only. Complimentary full breakfast. Check-in 3 pm, check-out 11 am. **$**

THE PALMER HOUSE INN. *81 Palmer Ave, Falmouth (02540). Phone 508/548-1230; toll-free 800/ 472-2632; fax 508/540-1878. www.palmerhouseinn .com.* Perched at the upper end of Cape Cod, this 1901 Queen Anne-style inn and guesthouse welcomes visitors year-round. Beaches, the Shining Sea Bikeway, and ferries to the islands are all nearby. 16 rooms, 3 story. Complimentary full breakfast. Check-in 3-9 pm, check-out 11 am. **$$**

WILDFLOWER INN. *167 Palmer Ave, Falmouth (02540). Phone 508/548-9524; toll-free 800/294-5459; fax 508/548-9524. www.wildflower-inn.com.* Built in 1898. Conveniently located near Martha's Vineyard, guests will enjoy the relaxing and peaceful atmosphere offered at this bed-and-breakfast. 6 rooms, 3 story. Complimentary full breakfast. Check-in 3-6 pm, check-out 11 am. **$$**

Restaurants

★ **BETSY'S DINER.** *457 Main St, Falmouth (02540). Phone 508/540-4446.* Save a few coins for the jukebox when visiting Betsy's Diner. Reminiscent of the diners of the 1950s, this place knows how to satisfy a hungry appetite with all-day breakfast and good old American comfort food, including meat loaf and turkey dinners. Always bustling, Betsy's high-spirited atmosphere is part of its charm. American menu. Breakfast, lunch, dinner. Children's menu. Casual attire. **$**

★ **THE FLYING BRIDGE.** *220 Scranton Ave, Falmouth (02540). Phone 508/548-2700; fax 508/457-7675. www.capecodrestaurants.org.* Bring the whole family to The Flying Bridge. Fronting Falmouth Harbor with views of Martha's Vineyard, this restaurant's location is superb. A nautical feel permeates the place, from the three hopping bars to the dockside seating. A seafood-centric menu also includes steaks and lighter bar food. Seafood menu. Lunch, dinner. Bar. Children's menu. Valet parking. Outdoor seating. **$$**

★ ★ **LANDFALL.** *2 Luscombe Ave, Woods Hole (02543). Phone 508/548-1758. www.woodshole.com/ landfall.* Like many restaurants on Cape Cod, Landfall exists to serve fresh seafood in a lovely setting. Perched directly over Woods Hole Harbor, this 60-year-old restaurant (regulars know that it's been in the same family since it opened) was constructed of wood from wrecked ships and old buildings, giving it a gently weathered look and a deep sense of the area's history. Articles inside the dining room, like the Grecian urn that hangs from the rafters, were rescued from the sea. American, seafood menu. Lunch, dinner, Sun brunch. Closed Dec-Mar. Bar. Children's menu. Outdoor seating. **$$**

★ **THE NIMROD.** *100 Dillingham Ave, Falmouth (02540). Phone 508/540-4132. www.thenimrod.com.* The Nimrod offers delicious lunch and dinner fare at great prices, but the entertainment and atmosphere are what draw people there. Musical choices range from live jazz performances to singalongs at the piano bar to big band dancing. American menu. Lunch, dinner. Bar. Children's menu. Casual attire. Outdoor seating. **$$**

Foxborough (C-7)

Settled 1704
Population 16,246
Elevation 280 ft
Area Code 508
Zip 02035
Information Neponset Valley Chamber of Commerce, 190 Vanderbilt Ave, Suite 1, Norwood 02062; phone 781/769-1126
Web Site www.nvcc.com

What to See and Do

New England Patriots (NFL). *60 Washington St, Foxboro (02035). Take I-93 S (SE Expressway) to I-95 S; take I-95 S to exit 9 (Wrentham) onto Hwy 1 S. Follow Hwy 1 S approximately 3 miles to Gillette Stadium (on the left). Phone toll-free 800/543-1776. www.patriots.com.* The 2002 and 2004 Super Bowl Champion Patriots are exciting to watch, but games at the new Gillette Stadium are more expensive to view. If you go, enjoy the Patriot tailgating experience; if you don't want to hang out with your hibachi in the parking lot, head over the End Zone (or Picnic Zone) Plaza, which features picnic tables. (Closed Feb-July) **$$$$**

New England Revolution (MLS). *60 Washington St, Foxboro (02035). 45 miles S of Boston (halfway between Boston and Providence, RI). Phone toll-free 877/438-7387. www.revolutionsoccer.net.* The New England Revolution is the men's soccer team in the Northeast. To make a game even more memorable, consider renting the Revolution Netside Terrace, a special café and seating area located in the South End of Gillette field, directly behind the net. The $300 price tag includes free parking and a meal and beverage for four people. At the gift shop, the team's unique logo is well worth the price of a T-shirt. (Closed Oct-Mar) **$$$$**

Limited-Service Hotels

★ ★ **COURTYARD BY MARRIOTT.** *35 Foxborough Blvd, Foxborough (02035). Phone 508/543-5222; toll-free 800/321-2211; fax 508/543-0445. www.courtyard.com.* 161 rooms, 3 story. Check-in 3 pm, check-out noon. High-speed Internet access. Restaurant, bar. Fitness room. Indoor pool, whirlpool. **$**

★ ★ **HOLIDAY INN.** *31 Hampshire St, Mansfield (02048). Phone 508/339-2200; toll-free 800/465-4329; fax 508/339-1040. www.holiday-inn.com/bos-mansfield.* 202 rooms, 3 story. Check-in 3 pm, check-out 11 am. Restaurant, bar. Fitness room. Indoor pool. Tennis. **$**

Restaurant

★ ★ **LAFAYETTE HOUSE.** *109 Washington St (Hwy 1), Foxborough (02035). Phone 508/543-5344; fax 508/543-0773. www.lafayettehouse.com.* Historic colonial tavern built in 1784. Seafood menu. Lunch, dinner. Bar. Children's menu. **$$**

Framingham (B-6)

Settled 1650
Population 66,910
Elevation 165 ft
Area Code 508
Zip 01701

Framingham is an industrial, commercial, and residential community. Framingham Centre, the original town, was bypassed by the railroad in the 19th century and is 2 miles north of downtown.

What to See and Do

Danforth Museum of Art. *123 Union Ave, Framingham (01702). Phone 508/620-0050.* Six galleries, including a children's gallery; changing exhibits, special events; art reference library. (Closed holidays) **$$**

Garden in the Woods. *180 Hemenway Rd, Framingham (01701). Phone 508/877-6574 (recording).* A 45-acre botanical garden and sanctuary. Largest landscaped collection of wild flowers in northeast. Exceptional collection of wildflowers and other native plants; variety of gardens and habitats. Headquarters of New England Wildflower Society. (Mid-June-Oct: Tues-Sun; mid-Apr-mid-June: daily) Guided walks (daily). Visitor center; museum shop. **$$$**

Full-Service Hotels

★ ★ ★ **SHERATON FRAMINGHAM HOTEL.** *1657 Worcester Rd, Framingham (01701). Phone 508/879-7200; toll-free 800/277-1150; fax 508/875-7593. www.sheraton.com.* The brick façade of this property in Metrowest Boston is styled after a 17th-century

Irish castle. 373 rooms, 6 story. Check-in 3 pm, check-out noon. Restaurant, bar. Fitness room. Indoor pool, outdoor pool, whirlpool. Business center. **$**

🏃 🛏 🏃

★ ★ ★ WYNDHAM WESTBOROUGH HOTEL.

5400 Computer Dr, Framingham (01581). Phone 508/366-5511; toll-free 877/999-3223; fax 508/870-5965. www.wyndham.com. 223 rooms, 4 story. Check-in 4 pm, check-out noon. Restaurant, bar. Fitness room. Indoor pool, whirlpool. Business center. **$$**

🅿 🏃 🛏 🏃

Gloucester (A-8)

See also Ipswich

Settled 1623
Population 30,273
Elevation 50 ft
Area Code 978
Zip 01930
Information Cape Ann Chamber of Commerce, 33 Commercial St; phone 978/283-1601 or toll-free 800/321-0133
Web Site www.capeannvacations.com

It is said that more than 10,000 Gloucester men have been lost at sea in the last three centuries, which emphasizes how closely the community has been linked with seafaring. Today, it is still a leading fishing port—although the fast schooners made famous in *Captains Courageous* and countless romances have been replaced by diesel trawlers. Gloucester is also the center of an extensive summer resort area that includes the famous artists' colony of Rocky Neck.

What to See and Do

Beauport, the Sleeper-McCann House. *75 Eastern Point Blvd, Gloucester (01930). Phone 978/283-0800.* (1907-1934) Henry Davis Sleeper, early 20th-century interior designer, began by building a 26-room house, continually adding rooms with the help of Halfdan Hanson, a Gloucester architect, until there were 40 rooms; 25 are now on view, containing extraordinary collections of antique furniture, rugs, wallpaper, ceramics, and glass; American and European decorative arts. Many artists, statesmen, and businessmen were entertained here. (Mid-May-mid-Sept: Mon-Fri; mid-Sept-mid-Oct: daily) **$$$**

Cape Ann Historical Museum. *27 Pleasant St, Gloucester (01930). Phone 978/283-0455.* Paintings by Fitz Hugh Lane; decorative arts and furnishings; Federal-style house (circa 1805). Emphasis on Gloucester's fishing industry; fisheries/maritime galleries and changing exhibitions depict various aspects of Cape Ann's history. (Tues-Sat; closed holidays, also Feb) **$$**

Gloucester Fisherman. *On Stacy Blvd on the harbor.* Bronze statue by Leonard Craske, a memorial to anglers lost at sea.

Hammond Castle Museum. *80 Hesperus Ave, Gloucester (01930). Off Hwy 127. Phone 978/283-2081.* (1926-1929) Built like a medieval castle by inventor Dr. John Hays Hammond Jr., the museum contains a rare collection of art objects. The great Hall contains a pipe organ with 8,200 pipes; concerts (selected days throughout the year). (Memorial Day-Labor Day: daily; after Labor Day-Columbus Day: Thurs-Sun; rest of year: Sat-Sun; closed Jan 1, Thanksgiving, Dec 25) Schedule may vary. **$$**

Sargent House Museum. *49 Middle St, Gloucester (01930). Phone 978/281-2432.* Late 18th-century Georgian residence, built for Judith Sargent, an early feminist writer and sister of Governor Winthrop Sargent; also the home of her second husband, John Murray, leader of Universalism. Period furniture, china, glass, silver, needlework, Early American portraits, and paintings by John Singer Sargent. (Memorial Day-Columbus Day, Mon, Fri-Sun; closed holidays) **$**

Special Events

Schooner Festival. *33 Commercial St, Gloucester (01930). Phone 978/283-1601.* Races and a parade of sail and maritime activities. Labor Day weekend.

St. Peter's Fiesta. *Phone 978/283-1601.* A four-day celebration with sports events, fireworks; procession; Blessing of the Fleet. Last weekend in June.

Waterfront Festival. *33 Commercial St, Gloucester (01930). Phone 978/283-1601.* Arts and crafts show, entertainment, food. Third weekend in Aug.

Whale-watching. *33 Commercial St, Gloucester (01930). Phone 978/283-1601.* Half-day trips, mornings and afternoons. May-Oct.

Limited-Service Hotels

★ BEST WESTERN BASS ROCKS OCEAN

INN. *107 Atlantic Rd, Gloucester (01930). Phone 978/283-7600; toll-free 800/780-7234; fax 978/281-6489. www.bestwestern.com/bassrocksoceaninn.* 48 rooms, 2 story. Closed Dec-Mar. Complimentary full breakfast. Check-out noon. Outdoor pool. **$$**
🅳 🌊

★ **THE MANOR INN.** *141 Essex Ave, Gloucester (01930). Phone 978/283-0614; fax 978/283-3154. www.themanorinnofgloucester.com.* Victorian manor house. 10 rooms. Closed Nov-Mar. Pets accepted, some restrictions; fee. Complimentary continental breakfast. Check-in 2 pm, check-out 11 am. **$**
🅳 🐾

Full-Service Resort

★ ★ **OCEAN VIEW INN AND RESORT.** *171 Atlantic Rd, Gloucester (01930). Phone 978/283-6200; toll-free 800/315-7557; fax 978/283-1852. www.oceanviewinnandresort.com.* Several buildings have accommodations, including a turn-of-the-century English manor house. 62 rooms, 3 story. Pets accepted, some restrictions. Check-in 2 pm, check-out 11 am. Restaurant. Two outdoor pools. **$**
🅳 🐾 🌊

Restaurant

★ ★ **GLOUCESTER HOUSE RESTAURANT.** *7 Seas Wharf, Gloucester (01930). Phone 978/283-1812; fax 978/281-0369. www.lobster-express.com.* Seafood menu. Lunch, dinner. Closed Thanksgiving, Dec 25. Bar. Children's menu. Outdoor seating. **$$**

Great Barrington (C-2)

Settled 1726
Population 7,527
Elevation 721 ft
Area Code 413
Zip 01230
Information Southern Berkshire Chamber of Commerce, 362 Main St; phone 413/528-1510 or 413/528-4006
Web Site www.greatbarrington.org

As early as 1774, the people of Great Barrington rose up against the King, seizing the courthouse. Today, Great Barrington is the shopping center of the southern Berkshire resort country. Writer, professor, and lawyer James Weldon Johnson, cofounder of the NAACP, and W. E. B. du Bois, black author and editor, lived here. Another resident, the poet William Cullen Bryant, was the town clerk for 13 years.

What to See and Do

Beartown State Forest. *Blue Hill Rd, Monterey (01245). Approximately 5 miles E on Hwy 23.* Phone 413/528-0904. Swimming, fishing; hunting; boating, bridle and hiking trails, snowmobiling, picnicking, camping.

Catamount Ski Area. *7 miles W on Hwy 23.* Four double chairlifts, tow, J-bar; patrol, school, rentals; snowmaking; cafeteria, bar; nursery. Longest run 2 miles; vertical drop 1,000 feet. Night skiing. (Dec-Mar, daily) Half-day rates.

Colonel Ashley House. *117 Cooper Hill Rd, Sheffield (01257). 9 miles S via Hwys 7 and 7A to Ashley Falls, then 1/2 mile on Rannapo Rd to Cooper Hill Rd.* Phone 413/229-8600. (1735) Elegance of the home reflects Colonel Ashley's prominent place in his society. One political meeting he held here produced the Sheffield Declaration, forerunner to the Declaration of Independence. Period furnishings. Adjacent to Bartholowmew's Cobble. (July-Aug: Wed-Sun; Memorial Day-June and Sept-Columbus Day: weekends; open Mon holidays) **$$**

Otis Ridge. *159 Monterey Rd, Otis (01253). 16 miles E on Hwy 23.* Phone 413/269-4444. www.otisridge.com. Double chairlift, T-bar, J-bar, three rope tows; patrol, school, rentals; snowmaking; cafeteria. Night skiing (Tues-Sun). Longest run 1 mile; vertical drop 400 feet. (Dec-Mar, daily) **$$$$**

Ski Butternut. *1 1/2 miles E on Hwy 23.* Phone 413/528-2000; toll-free 800/438-7669. www.butternutbasin.com. Quad, triple, four double chairlifts; Pomalift; rope tow; patrol, school, rentals, snowmaking; nursery (weekends and holidays after Dec 26); cafeterias; wine room; electronically timed slalom race course. Longest run approximately 1 1/2 miles; vertical drop 1,000 feet. Also 7 miles of cross-country trails; rentals. (Dec-Mar, daily) **$$$$**

Special Event

Berkshire Craft Fair. *Monument Mountain Regional High School, 600 Stockbridge Rd, Great Barrington (01230). Phone 413/528-3346.* Juried fair with more than 100 artisans. Early Aug.

Limited-Service Hotel

★ **MONUMENT MOUNTAIN MOTEL.** *249 Stockbridge Rd, Great Barrington (01230). Phone 413/ 528-3272; fax 413/528-3132. www.monument mountainmotel.com.* 18 rooms. Check-out 11 am. Outdoor pool. Tennis. **$**

Specialty Lodgings

The following lodging establishments are approved by Mobil Travel Guide, but due to their unique and in-dividualized nature have not been given a traditional Mobil Star rating. Included in this listing you may find bed-and-breakfasts, limited-service inns, guest ranches, and other unique hotel properties.

THE EGREMONT INN. *10 Sheffield Rd, South Egremont (01258). Phone 413/528-2111; toll-free 800/ 859-1780; fax 413/528-3284. www.egremontinn.com.* 20 rooms, 4 story. Complimentary continental breakfast. Check-in 3 pm, check-out 11 am. Restaurant. Outdoor pool. Tennis. **$**

RACE BROOK LODGE. *864 S Undermountain Rd, Sheffield (01257). Phone 413/229-2916; toll-free 888/725-6343; fax 413/229-6629. www.rblodge.com.* 32 rooms, 3 story. Pets accepted, some restrictions; fee. Complimentary full breakfast. Check-in 2-3 pm, check-out 11 am. Bar. **$$**

THORNEWOOD INN & RESTAURANT. *453 Stockbridge Rd, Great Barrington (01230). Phone 413/ 528-3828; toll-free 800/458-1008; fax 413/528-3307. www.thornewood.com.* 15 rooms, 2 story. Children over 12 years only. Complimentary full breakfast. Check-in 3 pm, check-out 11:30 am. Restaurant. Outdoor pool. **$$**

WINDFLOWER INN. *6845 S Egremont Rd, South Egremont (01258). Phone 413/528-2720; toll-free 800/ 992-1993; fax 413/528-5147. www.windflowerinn.com.* On 10 acres of Berkshire hillside, this white clap-board, country inn is classically New England with its screened porch and 13 antique-filled rooms. The estate dates back to the 1850s and is near year-round recreation including Tanglewood music center. 13 rooms. Complimentary full breakfast. Check-in 2 pm, check-out 11 am. Outdoor pool. **$$**

Restaurants

★ ★ ★ **CASTLE STREET CAFE.** *10 Castle St, Great Barrington (01230). Phone 413/781-7111; fax 413/731-8932. www.castlestreetcafe.com.* Chef/owner Michael Ballon delights guests of the Berkshires with his creative cooking and hospitable service. Enjoy live entertainment several nights of the week and relax in the comfortable Celestial Bar. American menu. Dinner. Closed Tues; Thanksgiving, Dec 25. Bar. **$$**

★ ★ **JOHN ANDREW'S RESTAURANT.** *Hwy 23, South Egremont (01258). Phone 413/528-3469; fax 413/528-2535.* American menu. Dinner. Closed Wed in Sept-June. Bar. Children's menu. Outdoor seating. **$$**

★ ★ **THE OLD MILL.** *53 Main St (Hwy 23), South Egremont (01258). Phone 413/528-1421; fax 413/528-0007.* Built in 1978. In gristmill. American menu. Dinner. Closed Mon; Thanksgiving, Dec 25. Bar. Children's menu. **$$**

★ ★ ★ **SPENCER'S.** *453 Stockbridge Rd, Great Barrington (01230). Phone 413/528-3828; fax 413/528-3307. www.thornewood.com.* This restaurant is located in the turn-of-the-century Thornewood Inn (see). The fresh produce is provided by the inn's gardens. Guests will feel like family at this cozy establishment, especially when they learn the restaurant is named after the owners' grandson. American menu. Dinner, Sun brunch. Closed Tues; Jan 1; also Mon, Wed in Sept-mid-June. Bar. Outdoor seating. **$$**

Greenfield (A-3)

See also Brattleboro, VT

Settled 1686
Population 18,168
Elevation 250 ft
Area Code 413
Zip 01301
Information Franklin County Chamber of Commerce, 395 Main St, PO Box 898; phone 413/773-5463
Web Site www.co.franklin.ma.us

The center of a prosperous agricultural area, Greenfield is also the home of many factories and a center for winter and summer sports, hunting, and fishing. The first cutlery factory in America was estab-lished in Greenfield in the early 19th century.

What to See and Do

Northfield Mountain Recreation and Environmental Center. *99 Miller's Falls Rd, Northfield (01360). Hwy 63. Phone 413/659-3714.* On the site of Northeast Utilities Hydro Electric Pump storage plant. Hiking, camping, riverboat ride, and picnicking. (Dec-Mar: Mon-Fri; May-Oct: Wed-Sun) Fee for some activities.

Special Events

Franklin County Fair. *89 Wisdom Way, Greenfield (01301). Phone 413/774-4282.* Four days starting first Thurs after Labor Day.

Green River Music & Balloon Festival. *Phone 413/773-5463.* Hot air balloon launches, craft show, musical entertainment, food. July.

Specialty Lodging

The following lodging establishment is approved by Mobil Travel Guide, but due to its unique and individualized nature has not been given a traditional Mobil Star rating. Included in this listing you may find bed-and-breakfasts, limited-service inns, guest ranches, and other unique hotel properties.

BRANDT HOUSE. *29 Highland Ave, Greenfield (01301). Phone 413/774-3329; toll-free 800/235-3329; fax 413/772-2908. www.brandthouse.com.* This turn-of-the-century Colonial Revival mansion offers contemporary creature comforts. The owner is an interior decorator and has given each room its own personality. Antiques, fresh flowers, and feather beds allow guests to bask in comfort. 8 rooms, 3 story. Pets accepted, some restrictions; fee. Complimentary full breakfast. Check-in 2 pm, check-out 11 am. Golf. Tennis. **$$**
🖥 ♠ 🏌️ 🐾

Restaurants

★ ★ **BELLA-NOTTE.** *199 Huckle Hill Rd, Bernardston (01337). Phone 413/648-9107; fax 413/648-0217.* Italian menu. Dinner. Closed Dec 24-25. Bar. **$$**

★ ★ **FAMOUS BILL'S.** *30 Federal St, Greenfield (01301). Phone 413/773-9230; fax 413/774-3671.* Seafood, steak menu. Lunch, dinner. Bar. Children's menu. **$$**

Harwich (Cape Cod)

Settled circa 1670
Population 12,386
Elevation 55 ft
Area Code 508
Zip 02646
Information Harwich Chamber of Commerce, PO Box 34; phone 508/432-1600; or the Cape Cod Chamber of Commerce, Hwys 6 and 132, PO Box 790, Hyannis 02601-0790, phone 508/362-3225 or toll-free 888/227-3263
Web Site www.capecodchamber.org

Harwich, whose namesake in England was dubbed "Happy-Go-Lucky Harwich" by Queen Elizabeth, is one of those towns made famous in New England literature. It is "Harniss" in the Joseph C. Lincoln novels of Cape Cod. A local citizen, Jonathan Walker, was immortalized as "the man with the branded hand" in Whittier's poem about helping escaped slaves; Enoch Crosby of Harwich was the Harvey Birch of James Fenimore Cooper's novel *The Spy.* Today, summer residents own three-quarters of the land.

What to See and Do

Brooks Free Library. *Harwich Center, 739 Main St, Harwich (02646). Phone 508/430-7562.* Houses 24 John Rogers's figurines. (Mon-Sat; closed holidays) **FREE**

⭐ **Cape Cod Baseball League.** *11 North Rd, Harwich (02645). Phone 508/432-3878. www.capecodbaseball.org.* The Cape Cod Baseball League is baseball as you remember it: local, passionate, affordable, and played only with wooden bats. The ten teams are all drawn from college players from around the country, who live with host families for the summer, visit schools to interact with kids, and host a summer baseball clinic. Spectators sit on wooden benches, pack a picnic lunch or dinner, and cheer for their favorite players during each of the 44 games played each season at venues throughout Cape Cod. (Mid-June-mid-Aug) **FREE**

Harwich Historical Society. *80 Parallel St, Harwich (02645). At Sisson Rd, in Harwich Center. Phone 508/432-8089.* Includes Brooks Academy Building and Revolutionary War Powder House. Native American artifacts, marine exhibit, cranberry industry articles, early newspapers and photographs. Site of one of the first schools of navigation in United States. (Usually mid-June-mid-Sept, Tues-Fri; schedule may vary) **DONATION**

Red River Beach. *Deep Hole and Uncle Venies rds, South Harwich (02646). Off Hwy 28, S on Uncle Venies Rd.* A fine Nantucket Sound swimming beach (water 68° F to 72° F in summer). Sticker fee per weekday.

Saquatucket Municipal Marina. *715 Main St, Harwich (02646). Off Hwy 28. Phone 508/432-2562.* Boat ramp for launching small craft. (May-mid-Nov) **$$$**

Special Events

Cranberry Harvest Festival. *Hwy 58 N and Rochester Rd, Harwich (02645).* Family Day, antique car show, music, arts and crafts, fireworks, carnival, parade. One weekend in mid-Sept.

Harwich Junior Theatre. *105 Division St, West Harwich (02671). Phone 508/432-2002.* Plays for the family and children through high school age. Reservations required. (July-Aug, daily; Sept-June, monthly)

Limited-Service Hotels

★ ★ **THE COMMODORE INN.** *30 Earle Rd, West Harwich (02671). Phone 508/432-1180; toll-free 800/368-1180; fax 508/432-3263. www.commodoreinn.com.* 27 rooms. Closed Nov-Apr. Complimentary continental breakfast. Check-in 2 pm, check-out 11 am. Restaurant, bar. Outdoor pool. **$**

★ **THE SANDPIPER BEACH INN.** *16 Bank St, Harwich Port (02646). Phone 508/432-0485; toll-free 800/433-2234. www.sandpiperbeachinn.com.* 20 rooms. Check-in 3 pm, check-out 11 am. Beach. **$**

★ **SEADAR INN.** *Bank St Beach, Harwich Port (02646). Phone 508/432-0264; toll-free 800/888-5250; fax 508/430-1916. www.seadarinn.com.* Main building is an old colonial house (1789). Early American décor; some rooms with bay windows. 20 rooms, 2 story. Closed mid-Oct-late May. Complimentary continental breakfast. Check-out 11 am. Near beach. **$**

Specialty Lodgings

The following lodging establishments are approved by Mobil Travel Guide, but due to their unique and in-

dividualized nature have not been given a traditional Mobil Star rating. Included in this listing you may find bed-and-breakfasts, limited-service inns, guest ranches, and other unique hotel properties.

AUGUSTUS SNOW HOUSE. *528 Main St, Harwich Port (02646). Phone 508/430-0528; toll-free 800/320-0528; fax 508/432-6638. www.augustussnow .com.* Built in 1901; Victorian décor. 5 rooms, 2 story. Children over 12 years only. Complimentary full breakfast. Check-in 2 pm, check-out 11 am. Beach. Airport transportation available. **$$**

CAPE COD CLADDAGH INN. *77 Main St, West Harwich (02671). Phone 508/432-9628; toll-free 800/356-9628; fax 508/432-6039. www.capecodcladdaghinn .com.* Former Baptist parsonage (circa 1900). 9 rooms, 3 story. Closed Jan-Mar. Pets accepted, some restrictions. Complimentary full breakfast. Check-in 2 pm, check-out 10:30 am. Restaurant. Outdoor pool. **$**

COUNTRY INN. *86 Sisson Rd, Harwich Port (02646). Phone 508/432-2769; toll-free 800/231-1722; fax 508/430-1455. www.countryinncapecod.com.* 6 rooms, 2 story. Complimentary continental breakfast. Check-in 2 pm, check-out noon. Restaurant. Beach. Outdoor pool. **$**

DUNSCROFT BY THE SEA. *24 Pilgrim Rd, Harwich Port (02646). Phone 508/432-0810; toll-free 800/432-4345; fax 508/432-5134. www.dunscroftbythe sea.com.* Guests will enjoy the white sand beach, just steps away, as well as such nearby activities as shopping, miniature golf, fishing, water sports, clambakes, and whale-watching. 8 rooms, 2 story. Children over 12 years only. Complimentary full breakfast. Check-in 2 pm, check-out 11 am. Whirlpool. **$$**

Restaurants

★ **400 EAST.** *1421 Orleans Rd, Harwich (02645). Phone 508/432-1800.* Large crowds waiting for tables pack 400 East. This popular restaurant is recognized for its good food and good fun. A thriving bar scene makes this nouveau tavern a great place to kick back with a beer. Sandwiches, burgers, pasta, and pizzas round out the comprehensive menu, and the daily specials are a source of pride. American menu. Lunch, dinner. Bar. Children's menu. Casual attire. **$**

★ ★ **AY! CARAMBA CAFE.** *703 Main St, Harwich (02645). Phone 508/432-9800; fax 508/432-9977. www.aycarambacafe.com.* The authentic flavors of Mexico shine at Ay! Caramba Café. This standout packs a punch with its tasty dishes and festive, easygoing atmosphere. The kitchen takes great pride in using original recipes and top-quality ingredients. Brightly colored walls decorated with scenes of the Mexican seaside add a kitschy charm. Mexican menu. Lunch, dinner. Casual attire. Outdoor seating. **$**

★ ★ **L'ALOUETTE.** *787 Main St, Harwich Port (02646). Phone 508/430-0405; fax 508/430-0975. www.capecodmenu.com.* The romance of the French countryside comes alive at L'Alouette. Owners Danielle and Jean-Louis Bastres, a husband-and-wife team, originally from France, show off their hometown pride with a series of well-executed, classic dishes, such as chateaubriand and rack of lamb. The dining room, with its Provençal furnishings, is especially cozy. French menu. Dinner. Closed Mon; Dec 25; also Feb. Reservations recommended. **$$$**

Haverhill (A-7)

See also Amesbury

Settled 1640
Population 58,969
Elevation 27 ft
Area Code 978
Information Chamber of Commerce, 87 Winter St, 01830; phone 978/373-5663
Web Site www.haverhillchamber.com

Haverhill is a thriving manufacturing and commercial center located along the Merrimack River. Long known for its role in the manufacturing of women's shoes, Haverhill now boasts a highly diversified high-tech industrial base. The city features fine neighborhoods of early 19th-century homes. The Quaker poet John Greenleaf Whittier was born here.

A statue at Winter and Main Streets commemorates the remarkable Hannah Dustin, who, according to legend, was kidnapped by Native Americans in March 1697, and escaped with the scalps of ten of her captors.

What to See and Do

Haverhill Historical Society. *240 Water St, Haverhill (01830). Hwy 97. Phone 978/374-4626.* Located in

The Buttonwoods, an early 19th-century house. Period furnishings, china, glass, Hannah Dustin relics, memorabilia from turn-of-the-century theaters, Civil War artifacts, and archaeological collection. Also on grounds is the John Ward House (1641), furnished with colonial items; and an 1850s shoe factory with displays. Guided tours. (Wed-Thurs, also Sat-Sun afternoons) **$$**

John Greenleaf Whittier Birthplace. *305 Whittier Rd, Haverhill (01830). I-495 exit 52, 1 mile E on Hwy 110. Phone 978/373-3979.* Whittier family homestead since the 17th century, this is the setting of his best-known poems, including "Snow-Bound," and "Barefoot Boy." His writing desk and mother's bedroom, built over a rock too large to move, are here. The house is furnished with original pieces and arranged as it would have appeared in his childhood. Grounds (69 acres) still actively farmed. (Tues-Sun; closed Jan 1, Thanksgiving, Dec 25; limited hours in winter) **$**

Limited-Service Hotels

★ **BEST WESTERN MERRIMACK VALLEY.** *401 Lowell Ave, Haverhill (01832). Phone 978/373-1511; toll-free 888/645-2025; fax 978/373-1517. www.bestwestern.com.* 127 rooms, 3 story. Pets accepted, some restrictions; fee. Complimentary continental breakfast. Check-in 3 pm, check-out noon. High-speed Internet access. Indoor pool, whirlpool. Airport transportation available. Business center. **$**

★ **COMFORT SUITES.** *106 Bank Rd, Haverhill (01832). Phone 978/374-7755; fax 978/521-1894.* 131 rooms, 4 story, all suites. Complimentary continental breakfast. Check-in 3 pm, check-out noon. Fitness room. Whirlpool. **$**

Holyoke (C-3)

See also South Hadley, Springfield; also see Enfield, CT

Settled 1745
Population 39,838
Elevation 270 ft
Area Code 413
Zip 01040
Information Greater Holyoke Chamber of Commerce, 177 High St; phone 413/534-3376
Web Site www.holycham.com

Captain Elizur Holyoke explored the Connecticut Valley as early as 1633. His name is preserved in the industrial city made possible with the development of the great river by an unusual set of power canals.

What to See and Do

Holyoke Heritage State Park. *221 Appleton St, Holyoke (01040). Phone 413/534-1723. www.state.ma.us/dem/ parks/hhsp.htm.* At this canalside park, the visitor center features cultural, environmental, and recreational programs; a slide show; and exhibits on the region and on Holyoke's history as a planned city, its canals, industries, and people. The restored antique Holyoke Merry-Go-Round is also here (Sat-Sun afternoons; expanded summer hours). (Wed-Sun afternoons; schedule may vary) **FREE** Also on the site and adjacent is

> **Children's Museum.** *444 Dwight St, Holyoke (01040). Phone 413/536-5437.* Participatory museum. Exhibits include paper-making, sand pendulum, bubble making, TV studio, two-story climbing structure, tot lot, "Cityscape," and other changing exhibits. (Daily except Mon) **$$**

Wistariahurst Museum. *238 Cabot St, Holyoke (01040). Phone 413/534-2216. www.holyoke.org.* Victorian mansion, family home of noted silk manufacturer William Skinner. House highlights include interior architectural detail unique to late 19th and early 20th centuries, including a leather-paneled room, conservatory and music hall; period furniture, decorative arts. Textile and archival collections available for research scholars. Changing exhibits. (Wed, Sat-Sun afternoons; schedule may vary) **DONATION**

Limited-Service Hotel

★ ★ **HOLIDAY INN.** *245 Whiting Farms Rd, Holyoke (01040). Phone 413/534-3311; toll-free 800/ 465-4329; fax 413/533-8443. www.holiday-inn.com.* At a busy commercial intersection off I-91, this 216-room hotel is a Holidome property, which means that it has lots to offer active families. A large atrium at the back of the hotel houses a pool, whirlpool, sauna, video arcade, and shuffleboard court, along with foosball, air hocky, and pool tables. A New England tradition for ice cream and tuna melts, Friendly's serves as the hotel's restaurant. If the kids tire of all this, the large and upscale Holyoke Mall is just down the street, and Six Flags New England is 12 miles away. For adults, the hotel also has a huge sports bar and

a ballroom for group functions. 216 rooms, 4 story. Check-in 3 pm, check-out noon. High-speed Internet access. Restaurant, bar. Fitness room. Indoor pool, whirlpool. Business center. **$**
⬆ 🏊 🚶

Restaurants

★ ★ ★ **DELANY HOUSE.** *Hwy 5 at Smith's Ferry, Holyoke (01040). Phone 413/532-1800; fax 413/ 539-9761. www.delaney-house.com.* This charming restaurant is located in picturesque Smith's Ferry. The American menu features the freshest of ingredients and the atmosphere is casually elegant. Seafood menu. Dinner. Closed Jan 1, Dec 25. Bar. Children's menu. Valet parking. Outdoor seating. **$$**

★ ★ **YANKEE PEDLAR.** *1866 Northhamptons St, Holyoke (01040). Phone 413/532-9494; fax 413/536-8877. www.yankeepedlarinn.com.* American menu. Lunch, dinner, Sun brunch. Closed Mon; Dec 25. Bar. Outdoor seating. **$$**

Hyannis and Barnstable (Cape Cod) (D-9)

See also Centerville, Martha's Vineyard, Nantucket Island, Yarmouth

Settled 1639
Population 14,120
Elevation 19 ft
Area Code 508
Zip 02601
Information Chamber of Commerce, 1481 Hwy 132; phone 508/362-5230 or toll-free 877/492-6647
Web Site www.hyannis.com

Hyannis is the main vacation and transportation center of Cape Cod. Recreational facilities and specialty areas abound, including tennis courts, golf courses, arts and crafts galleries, theaters, and antique shops. There are libraries, museums, and the Kennedy Memorial and Compound. Candle-making tours are available. Scheduled airliners and Amtrak stop here, and it is also a port for boat trips to Nantucket Island and Martha's Vineyard. More than 6 million people visit the village every year, and it is within an hour's drive of the many attractions on the Cape.

What to See and Do

Auto Ferry/Steamship Authority. *Ocean St, Hyannis (02601). Phone 508/477-8600. www.steamshipauthority .com.* Woods Hole, Martha's Vineyard, and Nantucket Steamship Authority conduct trips to Nantucket from Hyannis (year-round); depart from South Street dock.

Beaches. *Phone 508/790-6345.* **Craigville Beach.** Basset Ln. SW of town center. **Sea St Beach.** Sea St. Overlooking Hyannis Port harbor, bathhouse. **Kalmus Park.** Ocean St, bathhouse. **Veteran's Park.** Ocean St. Picnicking at Kalmus and Veteran's parks. There is a parking fee at all beaches.

Cape Cod Art Association Gallery. *3480 Hwy 6A, Barnstable (02630). Phone 508/362-2909.* Changing exhibits, exhibitions by New England artists; demonstrations, lectures, classes. (Apr-Nov: daily, limited hours; rest of year: inquire for schedule) **FREE**

Cape Cod Crusaders. *35 Winter St, Hyannis (02601). Games are played at Dennis-Yarmouth High School. Take Hwy 6 to exit 8, turn right off the ramp, and the stadium is about 2 miles down on your left. Phone 508/ 790-4782. www.capecodcrusaders.com.* If you want to see a professional sports team on Cape Cod, the Crusaders are the only team to watch. As members of the USISL (United States Independent Soccer League), the Crusaders play about 12 home games throughout late spring and summer. The Crusaders are the farm team for the New England Revolution, which means that Crusaders' players are often recruited from around the world and start out in Cape Cod. **$$**

Cape Cod Melody Tent. *21 W Main St, Hyannis (02601). Phone 508/775-9100. www.melodytent.com.* Looking for top-notch musical acts? The Cape Cod Melody Tent draws top musicians from around the country—mostly easy listening and country music—plus comedians. The venue is a huge white tent that's been hosting concerts on Cape Cod for more than 50 years. Wednesday mornings in July and August bring theater and musical productions for kids. Call, or visit the Web site for all concert dates and times, and if you want to be sure you get tickets, purchase them the day they go on sale. You may be able to pick up tickets left behind by no-shows just before performances begin. (Late May-mid-Sept)

Cape Cod Pathways. *3225 Hwy 6A, Barnstable (02630). Phone 508/362-3828. www.capecodcommission .org/pathways.* This network of walking and hiking trails is composed of a perfect mix of dirt, sand, and gravel, and when completed will link all the towns in Cape Cod. The Cape Cod Commission oversees the trails and produces a detailed map, yours for the asking by calling or writing. Don't miss the Cape Walk in early June, in which hearty souls hike from one end of the cape to another, or the Walking Weekend in late October, when trail guides lead walks and hikes of varying lengths. (Daily) **FREE**

⭐ **Cape Cod Potato Chip Company.** *100 Breed's Hill Rd, Hyannis (02601). Phone 508/775-7253. www.capecodchips.com.* Cape Cod Potato Chips, which are now sold all over the world, may be Cape Cod's most recognizable food product (although Nantucket Nectars, a local brand of juices available on the island and around the world, may take issue with that assessment). Perhaps the best part about taking the ten-minute self-guided tour of the facility is tasting the free samples, although seeing the unique kettles in which these crunchy chips are cooked is a close second. (Mon-Fri 9 am-5 pm, also Sat 10 am-4 pm July-Aug; closed holidays) **FREE**

Centerville Historical Society Museum. *513 Main St, Centerville (02632). Phone 508/775-0331.* Houses 14 exhibition rooms interpreting Cape Cod's history, art, industry, and domestic life. Displays include Early American furniture, housewares, quilts; dolls, costumes; Crowell carved birds, Sandwich glass collection, marine room, tool room, research library. (June-mid-Sept, Wed-Sun; winter by appointment) **$$**

Donald G. Trayser Memorial Museum. *Old Custom House and Post Office, 3353 Main St, Barnstable (02630). In Old Custom House and Post Office, Main St on Cobb's Hill, Rte 6A (02630). Phone 508/362-2092.* Marine exhibits, scrimshaw, Barnstable silver, historic documents. (July-mid-Oct, Tues-Sat afternoons)

Hyannis *Whale Watcher* Cruises. *Barnstable Harbor, 269 Mill Way, Barnstable (02630). Phone 508/362-6088.* View whales aboard the *Whale Watcher*, a 297-passenger super-cruiser, custom designed and built specifically for whale-watching. Naturalist on board will narrate. Café on board. (Apr-Oct, daily) Reservations necessary. **$$$$**

Hyannis-Nantucket or Martha's Vineyard Day Round-Trip. *Hy-Line, Pier #1, Ocean St Dock, Hyannis (02601). Phone 508/778-2600.* (May-Oct) Also hourly sightseeing trips to Hyannis Port (late Apr-Oct, daily); all-day or half-day deep-sea fishing excursions (late Apr-mid-Oct, daily).

John F. Kennedy Hyannis Museum. *397 Main St, Hyannis (02601). In Old Town Hall. Phone 508/790-*

3077. Photographic exhibits and a seven-minute video narrated by Walter Cronkite focus on President Kennedy's relationship with Cape Cod. (Mid-Apr-Oct: Mon-Sat 9 am-5 pm, Sun and holidays noon-5 pm; rest of year: Thurs-Sat 10 am-4 pm, Sun and holidays noon-4 pm) **$**

John F. Kennedy Memorial. *Ocean St, Hyannis (02601).* This 12-foot-high circular fieldstone wall memorial with presidential seal, fountain, and small pool honors the late president, who grew up nearby.

Mill Way Fish and Lobster Market. *276 Mill Way, Barnstable (02630). Phone 508/362-2760. www.millwayfish.com.* Mill Way is both a restaurant that specializes in seafood and vegetarian dishes, and a take-out market, offering fried and grilled dishes, pastas, cod cakes, salads, and other on-the-go meals. Try the unique shellfish sausage that's stuffed with shrimp, lobster, and scallops. (Tues-Sun 10 am-8 pm)

Osterville Historical Society Museum. *155 W Bay Rd, Osterville (02655). 3 miles SW, at junction West Bay and Parker rds. Phone 508/428-5861.* Sea captain's house with 18th- and 19th-century furnishings; Sandwich glass, Chinese porcelain, majolica and Staffordshire pottery; doll collection. Special events throughout the summer. Boat-building museum, ship models; catboat *Cayugha* is on display. Restored Cammett House (circa 1730) is on grounds. (Mid-June-Sept, Thurs-Sun afternoons; other times by appointment) **$$**

Pufferbellies Entertainment Complex. *183 Rear Iyanough Rd, Hyannis (02601). Phone 508/790-4300; toll-free 800/233-4301. www.pufferbellies.com.* Pufferbellies is a unique collection of nightclubs and places to eat and drink. On four separate dance floors, you'll dance the night away to swing, disco, country, and Top 40 music. If you have two left feet, be sure to take an on-site dance lesson. The sports bar entertains you with three big-screen TVs, dart boards, pool tables, and basketball machines, and a beach volleyball court in the Jimmy Buffet Parrothead Bar extends the fun outdoors in the summer months. (Fri-Sun; hours and activities vary by season) **$$**

Sturgis Library. *3090 Main St, Barnstable (02630). Phone 508/362-6636.* Oldest library building (1644) in United States has material on the Cape, including maritime history; genealogical records of Cape Cod families. Research fee for nonresidents. (Mon-Sat; closed holidays; limited hours) **$$**

West Parish Meetinghouse. *2049 Meetinghouse Way, West Barnstable (02668). Jct Hwys 6, 149. Phone 508/362-4385.* (1717) Said to be the oldest Congregational church in the country; restored. Congregation established in London, 1616. Regular Sunday services are held here all year. **FREE**

Special Events

Cape Cod Oyster Festival. *20 Independence Dr, Hyannis (02601). Phone 508/778-6500. www.cape codoysterfestival.com.* What you get at the Cape Cod Oyster Festival is oysters—as many as you care to eat—accompanied by wine from local vineyards. Sample raw, baked, and roasted oysters, and also taste oyster stew. Held at the Naked Oyster restaurant under a big tent, the Oyster Festival draws locals and tourists alike. Late Oct. **$$$$**

Figawi Sailboat Race and Charity Ball. *70 Jobys Ln, Osterville (02655). Phone 508/778-6100. www.figawi.com.* The Figawi Sailboat Race (the East Coast's largest) features 200 sailboats racing from Hyannis to Nantucket on Saturday—and back again in a fun Return Race on Monday. Don't miss the Clam Bake on Nantucket Sunday afternoon and numerous cocktail parties, too. The annual Charity Ball (black-tie optional) precedes the event by one week. Held in Hyannis and featuring live bands, dancing, and a feast prepared by local restaurants, the Charity Ball is a major social event on Cape Cod. Memorial Day weekend. **FREE**

Fleet Pops by the Sea. *Town Green, Hyannis (02601). Phone 508/362-0066. www.artsfoundationcapecod.org.* In early August, the Boston Pops makes its way from Boston to Cape Cod for a once-a-year concert on the Hyannis Town Green. You'll enjoy classics, pops, and Sousa marches. Each year brings a new celebrity guest conductor, from actors to poets to famous chefs. The performance serves as a fundraiser that supports the Arts Foundation of Cape Cod. **$$$$**

Hyannis Harbor Festival. *On the waterfront at Bismore Park. Phone 508/362-5230.* Coast Guard cutter tours, sailboat races, marine displays, food, entertainment. Weekend in early June.

Willowbend Children's Charity Pro-Am. *100 Willowbend Rd, Mashpee (02649). Phone 508/539-5000. www.willowbendproam.com.* The biggest names in professional golf pair up with celebrities for this annual charity golf event on Willowbend's beautiful course. Although numerous spectators attend, you still get a chance to see your favorite players up close. The fee ($20) is among the lowest you can pay to watch professional golf, and the proceeds benefit a variety of children's charities on Cape Cod. Early July. **$$$$**

Limited-Service Hotels

★ **ANCHOR-IN.** *1 South St, Hyannis (02601). Phone 508/775-0357; fax 508/775-1313. www.anchorin.com.* 43 rooms. Complimentary continental breakfast. Check-in 3 pm, check-out noon. Beach. Outdoor pool, whirlpool. **$**

★ ★ **CAPE CODDER RESORT & SPA.** *1225 Iyanough Rd, Hyannis (02601). Phone 508/771-3000; toll-free 888/297-2200; fax 508/771-6564. www.cape codderresort.com.* 258 rooms, 2 story. Check-in 3 pm, check-out 11 am. High-speed Internet access. Restaurant, bar. Fitness room, spa. Indoor pool, whirlpool. Tennis. Airport transportation available. Business center. **$**

★ **CENTERVILLE CORNERS MOTOR LODGE.** *1338 Craigville Beach Rd, Centerville (02632). Phone 508/775-7223; toll-free 800/242-1137; fax 508/775-4147. www.centervillecorners.com.* 48 rooms, 2 story. Closed Dec-Apr. Pets accepted, some restrictions; fee. Complimentary continental breakfast. Check-out 11 am. Indoor pool. **$**

★ ★ **COURTYARD BY MARRIOTT.** *707 Hwy 132, Hyannis (02601). Phone 508/775-6600; toll-free 800/321-2211; fax 508/790-0119. www.marriott.com.* 120 rooms. Check-in 3 pm, check-out noon. High-speed Internet access. Indoor pool. Business center. **$**

★ ★ **HERITAGE HOUSE HOTEL.** *259 Main St, Hyannis (02601). Phone 508/775-7000; toll-free 800/352-7189; fax 508/778-5687. www.heritagehousehotel .com.* 143 rooms, 3 story. Check-out 11 am. Restaurant. Indoor, outdoor pool; whirlpool. **$**

★ ★ **INTERNATIONAL INN.** *662 Main St, Hyannis (02601). Phone 508/775-5600; toll-free 877/588-3353; fax 508/775-3933. www.cuddles.com.* With a trademark like "cuddle and bubble," it's obvious romance is the distinguishing feature of this Cape Cod hotel conveniently located within walking distance of town and ferries. Geared toward couples, each room or suite has

a Jacuzzi built for two. 141 rooms, 2 story. Check-out 11 am. Restaurant, bar. Indoor pool, outdoor pool. **$**

Full-Service Resort

★ ★ ★ **FOUR POINTS BY SHERATON HYANNIS RESORT.** *West End Cir, Hyannis (02601). Phone 508/775-7775; fax 508/778-6423.* The property is conveniently located at the island's center, and is within walking distance of shops and restaurants. 224 rooms, 2 story. Check-in 4 pm, check-out 11 am. Restaurant, bar. Children's activity center. Fitness room, spa. Indoor pool, outdoor pool, whirlpool. Golf. Tennis. Airport transportation available. Business center. **$**

Specialty Lodgings

The following lodging establishments are approved by Mobil Travel Guide, but due to their unique and individualized nature have not been given a traditional Mobil Star rating. Included in this listing you may find bed-and-breakfasts, limited-service inns, guest ranches, and other unique hotel properties.

ACWORTH INN. *4352 Old King's Hwy, Hwy 6A, Barnstable (02637). Phone 508/362-3330; toll-free 800/362-6363; fax 508/375-0304. www.acworthinn.com.* Whether guests come here to relax and unwind or for a romantic getaway, this bed-and-breakfast has everything one needs for both. Guests can enjoy a day of sightseeing, mountain biking, or golf and then return to enjoy a nice cozy evening in the gathering room. 5 rooms, 2 story. Children over 12 years only. Complimentary full breakfast. Check-in 3-7 pm, check-out 11 am. **$**

ADAM'S TERRACE GARDENS INN. *539 Main St, Centerville (02632). Phone 508/775-4707. www.adamsterrace.com.* 5 rooms, 2 story. Complimentary full breakfast. Check-in 3-6 pm, check-out 11 am. **$**

ASHLEY MANOR. *3660 Main St, Barnstable (02630). Phone 508/362-8044; toll-free 888/535-2246; fax 508/362-9927. www.ashleymanor.net.* A lovely garden and gazebo adorn this beautiful inn. Guests can unwind with a book in the library or with afternoon tea in front of the fire. Some activities available to guests include whale-watching, biking, and even off-

Cape excursions. 6 rooms, 2 story. Children over 14 years only. Complimentary full breakfast. Check-in 2 pm, check-out 11 am. Tennis. **$**

BEECHWOOD INN. *2839 Main St, Barnstable (02630). Phone 508/362-6618; toll-free 800/609-6618; fax 508/362-0298. www.beechwoodinn.com.* Situated near Barnstable Village, guests can enjoy biking, whale-watching, and golf. The guest who prefers a relaxing vacation may sit on the porch and enjoy an iced tea or lemonade while rocking on the gliders. 6 rooms, 3 story. Complimentary full breakfast. Check-in 2 pm, check-out 11 am. **$**

HONEYSUCKLE HILL B&B. *591 Old King's Hwy, Hwy 6A, West Barnstable (02668). Phone 508/362-8418; toll-free 800/444-5522; fax 508/362-8386. www.honeysucklehill.com.* Built in 1810. Restored Victorian décor. 5 rooms, 2 story. Children over 12 years only. Complimentary full breakfast. Check-in 3 pm, check-out 11 am. **$**

SEA BREEZE INN. *270 Ocean Ave, Hyannis (02601). Phone 508/771-7213; fax 508/862-0663. www.seabreezeinn.com.* Near beach; some rooms with ocean view. 14 rooms, 2 story. Complimentary continental breakfast. Check-in 2 pm, check-out 10:30 am. **$**

SIMMONS HOMESTEAD INN. *288 Scudder Ave, Hyannis Port (02647). Phone 508/778-4999; toll-free 800/637-1649; fax 508/790-1342. www.simmonshome steadinn.com.* Restored sea captain's home built in 1820; some canopied beds. 14 rooms, 2 story. Pets accepted, some restrictions; fee. Complimentary full breakfast. Check-in 1 pm, check-out 11 am. **$$**

Restaurants

★ ★ **BARNSTABLE TAVERN AND GRILLE.** *3176 Main St, Barnstable (02630). Phone 508/362-2355; fax 508/362-9012.* The Barnstable has been an inn and tavern since 1799. Seafood menu. Lunch, dinner. Closed Dec 24-25. Bar. Children's menu. Outdoor seating. **$$**

★ ★ **DOLPHIN RESTAURANT.** *3250 Main St, Barnstable (02630). Phone 508/362-6610. www.the dolphinrestaurant.com.* From the pale gray clapboards outside to the maple captain's chairs and ship's wheel inside, the Dolphin is the quintessential Cape Cod townie restaurant, where folks stop off for burgers, lobster rolls, and club sandwiches at lunch and return in the evening for pan-fried sole. Some modern twists enliven the plate as well, like an orange-scallion sauce to dress up broiled codfish. American, seafood menu. Lunch, dinner. Bar. Children's menu. Casual attire. Reservations recommended. **$$**

★ **EGG & I.** *521 Main St, Hyannis (02601). Phone 508/771-1596; fax 508/778-6385.* Breakfast lovers rejoice at the Egg & I restaurant. This delightful place celebrates the first meal of the day like no other, and diners enjoy the friendly service and unfussy atmosphere. Diner. American menu. Breakfast. Closed Dec-Feb; weekends only in Mar, Nov. Children's menu. **$**

★ ★ **FIVE BAYS BISTRO.** *825 Main St, Osterville (02655). Phone 508/420-5559. www.fivebaysbistro.com.* This polished storefront bistro offers some nice twists on traditional Cape fare. Rare tuna is paired with lo mein noodles and wasabi soy, while from-the-land options like veal medallions and grilled chicken risotto please those in the mood for something other than fish and shellfish. The bar serves up a selection of martinis and wines by the glass, including grappa and port, and homemade desserts satisfy a sweet tooth. American menu. Dinner. Bar. Casual attire. **$$$**

★ **HARRY'S.** *700 Main St, Hyannis (02601). Phone 508/778-4188.* Harry's lets the good times roll. Belly-busting tastes from the Bayou are the inspiration behind this rollicking joint. From crawdaddies and shrimp Creole to jambalaya, the fiery flavors of the South come alive here. This place rocks year-round, with some of the area's best R&B and blues music performed here nightly. Cajun/Creole menu. Lunch, dinner. Bar. Casual attire. Outdoor seating. **$$**

★ **MARKETPLACE RAW BAR.** *Popponesset Marketplace, Mashpee (02649). Phone 508/539-4858.* Seafood menu. Lunch, dinner. Closed late Oct-Apr. Casual attire. **$$**

★ **MILL WAY FISH AND LOBSTER.** *275 Mill Way, Barnstable (02630). Phone 508/362-2760.* Mill Way may look like a simple harborside fish shack with a few picnic tables sitting on the deck by the order window, but looks are deceiving. Chef/owner Ralph Binder runs the Upper Cape's top gourmet-to-go shop with takeout treats that range from homemade seafood sausage to tubs of bouillabaisse and clam chowder. The mostly fried quick food (too good to be called fast food) features giant portions of the local catch. Seafood menu. Lunch, dinner. Closed Oct-Mar. Casual attire. Outdoor seating. **$$**

★ ★ **NAKED OYSTER.** *20 Independence Dr, Hyannis (02601). Phone 508/778-6500. www.naked oyster.com.* Raw-seafood cravings meet their match at Naked Oyster, a bistro and raw bar near the Cape Cod Mall. The Chilled Seafood Tower—a selection of clams, oysters, shrimp, lobster, and tuna sashimi—makes for a fun cocktail hour; add a bottle of Veuve Cliquot for an extra-special celebration. On the menu, you'll also find a variety of dressed oysters and seafood and steak entrées, along with a nice selection of wines by the glass. Seafood menu. Lunch, dinner. Closed Sun. Bar. Casual attire. **$$**

★ **ORIGINAL GOURMET BRUNCH.** *517 Main St, Hyannis (02601). Phone 508/771-2558; fax 508/778-6052. www.theoriginalgourmetbrunch.com.* Hungry diners come armed with large appetites to Hyannis's beloved Original Gourmet Brunch. This country-casual restaurant does breakfast like none other, with more than 100 different omelet choices available. Eggs are a large part of the menu here, but those with a sweet tooth dig into fluffy Belgian waffles and savory French toast. American menu. Breakfast, lunch. Closed Thanksgiving, Dec 25. Casual attire. **$**

★ ★ **THE PADDOCK.** *W Main St Rotary, Hyannis (02601). Phone 508/775-7677; fax 508/771-9517. www.paddockcapecod.com.* Elegant Victorian surroundings, fine wine, and exceptional food make for a winning combination at The Paddock restaurant. Pressed linens and abundant flowers add to the sophistication, yet children are welcomed here. The menu pays tribute to the region with a variety of seafood dishes, although poultry, steak, and pasta also present enticing choices. The wine list is award winning for its well-priced selections. American menu. Lunch, dinner. Closed Nov-Apr. Bar. Children's menu. Casual attire. Valet parking. **$$**

★ ★ ★ **THE REGATTA OF COTUIT.** *4631 Falmouth Rd, Cotuit (02635). Phone 508/428-5715; fax 508/428-5742. www.regattaofcotuit.com.* Refined piano music provides the background for diners in eight intimate, candlelit rooms in this circa-1790 stagecoach inn. Chef Heather Allen makes culinary music of her own with variations on French, American, and Asian themes. Her lacquered duck is a neatly Americanized version of Peking duck, and the tempura dish of Vietnamese-style fish and chips with vegetable slaw

varies daily, depending on what the local fishermen catch and what's harvested from local gardens. Owners Wendy and Branz Bryan have accrued a nearly legendary wine list over the last three decades, making The Regatta a must-stop for oenophiles visiting Cape Cod. From October to May, The Regatta offers an alluring early-bird special of three courses for the price of an entrée. American menu. Dinner, Sun brunch (in the off-season). Bar. Business casual attire. Reservations recommended. **$$**

★ ★ **ROADHOUSE CAFE.** *488 South St, Hyannis (02601). Phone 508/775-2386; fax 508/778-1025. www.roadhousecafe.com.* The Roadhouse Cafe jazzes up the American standards. This tasteful restaurant, located in a 1903 house, is cherished by locals for its consistent food, elegant surroundings, and fabulous entertainment. The menu is well rounded, with a large variety of Italian-influenced seafood, poultry, and meat dishes. The vintage piano bar is among the best in town for enjoying live entertainment on the weekends. International/Fusion menu. Dinner. Closed Dec 24-25. Bar. Valet parking. **$$**

★ **SAM DIEGO'S.** *950 Hyannis Rd (Hwy 132), Hyannis (02601). Phone 508/771-8816. www.cape restaurantassociation.com.* Sam Diego's is fun for the entire family. This Tex-Mex spot shares a playful attitude with guests. From its whimsical décor to its Texas iced teas served in boot-shaped glasses, this restaurant puts a smile on everyone's face. Standard Mexican fare includes burritos and tacos, while baby back ribs show off the Texan influence. Mexican menu. Lunch, dinner. Closed Easter, Thanksgiving, Dec 25. Bar. Children's menu. Outdoor seating. **$**

★ **STARBUCKS.** *668 Hwy 132, Hyannis (02601). Phone 508/778-6767; fax 508/790-0036. www.starbucks capecod.com.* Mexican menu. Dinner. Closed Dec 25. Bar. Children's menu. Outdoor seating. **$$**

★ **YING'S.** *59 Center St, Hyannis (02601). Phone 508/790-2432.* Asian menu. Lunch, dinner. Casual attire. Reservations recommended. Outdoor seating. **$$**

Ipswich (A-8)

See also Boston, Gloucester

Settled 1633
Population 12,987
Elevation 50 ft
Area Code 978
Zip 01938

Information Ipswich Visitors Center-Hall Haskell House, 36 S Main St, next to Town Hall; phone 978/356-8540

Ipswich is a summer resort town and home of the Ipswich clam; it has beaches nearby and a countryside of rolling woodland. Historically, Ipswich claims to have been the nation's first lacemaking town, the birthplace of the US hosiery industry, and of the American independence movement. In 1687, the Reverend John Wise rose in a meeting and denounced taxation without representation. His target was the hated Sir Edmund Andros, the British Colonial governor.

Andros and the lace are gone, but Ipswich retains the aura of its past. Besides a fine green, it has nearly 50 houses built before 1725, many from the 17th century.

What to See and Do

Crane Beach. *290 Argilla Rd, Ipswich (01938). End of Argilla Rd, on Ipswich Bay. Phone 978/356-4354.* Among the best on the Atlantic coast; 5 miles of beach; lifeguards, bathhouses, refreshment stand, trail. (Daily)

The John Whipple House. *53 S Main St, Ipswich (01938). On Hwy 1A. Phone 978/356-2811.* (1640) Contains 17th- and 18th-century furniture; garden. (May-mid-Oct, Wed-Sat, Sun afternoons; closed holidays) **$$$** Opposite is

> **John Heard House.** *40 S Main St, Ipswich (01938).* (1795) Bought as memorial to Thomas F. Waters, house has Chinese furnishings from the China sea trade. (Schedule same as Whipple House) **$$**

Special Event

Old Ipswich Days. *Phone 978/356-8540.* Arts and crafts exhibits, games, clambakes, entertainment. Late July.

Limited-Service Hotel

★ COUNTRY GARDEN INN AND MOTEL. *101 Main St, Rowley (01969). Phone 978/948-7773; toll-free 800/287-7773; fax 978/948-7947. www.countrygardenmotel.com.* 24 rooms, 3 story. Check-in after 2 pm, check-out 10 am. Fitness room. Outdoor pool, whirlpool. **$**

Specialty Lodging

The following lodging establishment is approved by Mobil Travel Guide, but due to its unique and individualized nature has not been given a traditional Mobil Star rating. Included in this listing you may find bed-and-breakfasts, limited-service inns, guest ranches, and other unique hotel properties.

MILES RIVER COUNTRY INN B&B. *823 Bay Rd, Hamilton (01936). Phone 978/468-7206; fax 978/468-3999. www.milesriver.com.* This 200-year-old, rambling colonial is set on 30 acres that adjoin meadows, woodlands, and marshes. Guests enjoy strolls on woodland walkways and exploring the gardens and ponds on the property. 6 rooms, 3 story. Complimentary full breakfast. Check-in 3 pm, check-out 11 am. **$**

Restaurant

★ ★ ★ 1640 HART HOUSE. *51 Linebrook Rd, Ipswich (01938). Phone 978/356-1640; fax 978/356-8847. www.1640harthouse.com.* This restored property was built 20 years after the Pilgrims landed in the town of Ipswich. The original room has since been sold to the Metropolitan Museum of Art. American menu. Lunch, dinner. Closed Mon; Dec 25. Bar. Children's menu. Reservations recommended. **$$**

Lawrence (A-7)

Founded 1847
Population 72,043
Elevation 50 ft
Area Code 978
Information Chamber of Commerce, 264 Essex St, 01840; phone 508/686-0900
Web Site www.merrimackvalleychamber.com

Lawrence was founded by a group of Boston financiers to tap the water power of the Merrimack River for the textile industry. As textiles moved out, diversified industries have been attracted to the community.

What to See and Do

Lawrence Heritage State Park. *1 Jackson St, Lawrence (01840). Canal St. Phone 978/794-1655.* Twenty-three acres in the city center includes the restored Campagnone Common, canal and riverside esplanades. The visitor center in a restored workers' boardinghouse has participatory exhibits on the workers' experiences with industry in Lawrence and their contribution to the city's vitality. (Daily; closed Jan 1, Thanksgiving, Dec 25) **FREE**

Limited-Service Hotel

★ **HAMPTON INN.** *224 Winthrop Ave, Lawrence (01843). Phone 978/975-4050; toll-free 800/426-7866; fax 978/687-7122. www.hamptoninn.com.* 126 rooms, 5 story. Pets accepted. Complimentary continental breakfast. Check-in 3 pm, check-out noon. High-speed Internet access. Fitness room. **$**

Lee *(B-2)*

Founded 1777
Population 5,985
Elevation 1,000 ft
Area Code 413
Zip 01238

Lee's major industry has been papermaking since the first years of the 19th century. Today, it is also a summer and ski resort area.

What to See and Do

October Mountain State Forest. *317 Woodland Rd, Lee (01238). I-90 exit 2, Hwy 20 W. Phone 413/243-1778.* Fine mountain scenery overlooking 16,000 acres. Hiking, hunting; snowmobiling. Camping on west side of forest.

Santarella Museum & Garden. *75 Main Rd, Tyringham (01238). 4 miles SE. Phone 413/243-3260.* Former studio of sculptor Sir Henry Kitson, creator of the *Minuteman* statue in Lexington. Built in the early 1920s, the house's major element is the roof, which was designed to look like thatching and to represent the rolling hills of the Berkshires in autumn; the fronting rock pillars and the grottoes between them are fashioned after similar edifices in Europe; Santarella Sculpture garden. Exhibits include ceramics, glass, paintings, graphics; also changing exhibits. Sculpture garden with lily pond. (Late May-Oct, daily) **$**

Special Event

Jacob's Pillow Dance Festival. *George Carter Rd, Becket (01223). 8 miles E via Hwy 20. Phone 413/243-* 0745 (box office). Ted Shawn Theatre and Doris Duke Theatre. America's oldest and most prestigious dance festival includes performances by international dance companies. Performances Tues-Sat, some Sun. Late June-Aug.

Limited-Service Hotel

★ ★ **BEST WESTERN BLACK SWAN INN.** *435 Laurel St; Hwy 20 W, Lee (01238). Phone 413/243-2700; toll-free 800/876-7926; fax 413/637-0798. www.bestwestern.com.* 52 rooms, 2 story. Check-in 3 pm, check-out 11 am. Restaurant, bar. Outdoor pool. Business center. **$**

Specialty Lodgings

The following lodging establishments are approved by Mobil Travel Guide, but due to their unique and individualized nature have not been given a traditional Mobil Star rating. Included in this listing you may find bed-and-breakfasts, limited-service inns, guest ranches, and other unique hotel properties.

APPLEGATE. *279 W Park St, Lee (01238). Phone 413/243-4451; toll-free 800/691-9012; fax 413/243-9832. www.applegateinn.com.* Built in the 1920s, this Georgian Colonial is a charming bed-and-breakfast. Each guest room is individually decorated, and guests can enjoy strolls through the 6 acres of rose gardens, perennial beds, and apple trees. 11 rooms, 2 story. Children over 12 years only. Complimentary full breakfast. Check-in 2 pm, check-out 11 am. Outdoor pool. **$**

CHAMBERY INN. *199 Main St (Hwy 20 W), Lee (01238). Phone 413/243-2221; toll-free 800/537-4321; fax 413/243-0039. www.berkshireinns.com.* This property was originally built as the county's first parochial school. The owners saved the building from destruction and restored it, keeping the unique structure and even the original blackboards. Guests enjoy the "menu selected" breakfasts, delivered to the guest room door in a charming country basket. 9 rooms, 3 story. Children over 16 years only. Check-in 2 pm, check-out 11 am. **$$**

DEVONFIELD INN. *85 Stockbridge Rd, Lee (01238). Phone 413/243-3298; toll-free 800/664-0880; fax 413/243-1360. www.devonfield.com.* Located in the heart of the Berkshires, this Federal-era manor house offers a comfortable and fun experience. 10 rooms, 3 story.

Children over 10 years only. Complimentary full breakfast. Check-in 3 pm, check-out 11 am. Outdoor pool. Tennis. **$$**

FEDERAL HOUSE INN. *1560 Pleasant St (Hwy 102), South Lee (01260). Phone 413/243-1824; toll-free 800/243-1824; fax 413/243-1828. www.federalhouseinn.com.* Originally built in 1824, this inn is nestled beside the Housatonic River and at the base of Beartown State Forest. The guest rooms have a casual, country-style décor and all include golf and tennis privileges at nearby Stockbridge Country Club. 10 rooms, 2 story. Children over 12 years only. Complimentary full breakfast. Check-in 3 pm, check-out 11 am. Bar. **$$**

HISTORIC MERRELL INN. *1565 Pleasant St (Hwy 102), South Lee (01260). Phone 413/243-1794; toll-free 800/243-1794; fax 413/243-2669. www.merrell-inn.com.* Listed on the National Register of Historic Places, this old-stagecoach inn sits on 2 acres of picturesque, Housatonic River-front property. All rooms have private baths, include a country breakfast, and offer a location full of recreations during all Berkshire Mountain seasons. 10 rooms, 3 story. Complimentary full breakfast. Check-in 2 pm, check-out 11 am. **$**

MORGAN HOUSE. *33 Main St, Lee (01238). Phone 413/243-3661; toll-free 877/571-0837; fax 413/243-3103. www.morganhouseinn.com.* Built in 1817. Stagecoach inn (1853); antiques; country-style décor. 11 rooms, 3 story. Complimentary full breakfast. Check-in 1 pm, check-out 11 am. Restaurant, bar. **$**

Restaurants

★ ★ **CORK N' HEARTH.** *Hwy 20 W, Lee (01238). Phone 413/243-0535; fax 413/637-1945.* Three dining rooms. Seafood, steak menu. Dinner. Closed Mon; Thanksgiving, Dec 24-25. Bar. Children's menu. **$$**

★ ★ **SULLIVAN STATION RESTAURANT.** *109 Railroad St, Lee (01238). Phone 413/243-2082.* American menu. Lunch, dinner. Closed Thanksgiving, Dec 25; also two weeks in late Feb-early Mar. Bar. Outdoor seating. **$$**

Lenox (B-2)

See also Pittsfield, Stockbridge and West Stockbridge

Settled circa 1750
Population 5,985
Elevation 1,200 ft
Area Code 413
Zip 01240
Information Chamber of Commerce, 65 Main St, PO Box 646; phone 413/637-3646
Web Site www.lenox.org

This summer resort became world-famous for music when the Boston Symphony began its Berkshire Festival here in 1939. Nearby is Stockbridge Bowl, one of the prettiest lakes in the Berkshires.

What to See and Do

⭐ **Edith Wharton Restoration (The Mount).** *2 Plunkett St, Lenox (01240). Plunkett St at S junction of Hwys 7 and 7A. Phone 413/637-1899.* Edith Wharton's summer estate; was planned from a book she coauthored in 1897, *The Decoration of Houses,* and built in 1902. This Classical Revival house is architecturally significant; ongoing restoration. On 49 acres, with gardens. Tour of house and gardens (early June-early Nov, daily). (See SPECIAL EVENTS) **$$$$**

Pleasant Valley Wildlife Sanctuary. *472 Mountain Rd, Lenox (01240). On West Mountain Rd, 1 1/2 miles W of Hwy 7/20. Phone 413/637-0320.* Sanctuary of the Massachusetts Audubon Society. 1,500 acres with 7 miles of trails; beaver colony; office. No dogs. (Mid-June-Columbus Day) **$$**

⭐ **Tanglewood.** *197 West St, Lenox (02140). On West St, 1 1/2 miles SW on Hwy 183. Phone 413/637-1600 (summer).* Where Nathaniel Hawthorne lived and wrote. Here he planned *Tanglewood Tales.* Many of the 526 acres, developed into a gentleman's estate by William Aspinwall Tappan, are in formal gardens. Well known today as the summer home of the Boston Symphony Orchestra and the Tanglewood Music Center, the symphony's training academy for young musicians. (See SPECIAL EVENTS) Grounds (daily; free except during concerts).

Chamber Music Hall. *197 West St, Lenox (02140).* Small chamber music ensembles, lectures, seminars, and large classes held here. Designed by Eliel Saarinen, who also designed the

Formal Gardens. *197 West St, Lenox (02140).* Manicured hemlock hedges and lawn, tall pine. Picnicking.

Hawthorne Cottage. *197 West St, Lenox (02140).* Replica of the "Little Red House" where Hawthorne lived 1850-1851, now contains music studios, Hawthorne memorabilia. (Open before each festival concert.)

Koussevitzky Music Shed. *197 West St, Lenox (02140).* (1938) The so-called "Shed," where Boston Symphony Orchestra concerts take place; holds 5,121.

Main Gate Area. *197 West St, Lenox (01240).* Friends of Tanglewood, box office, music and bookstore; cafeteria; gift shop.

Maron House. *197 West St, Lenox (02140).* Original mansion, now the Boston Symphony Orchestra Visitors Center and the Community Relations Office. Excellent view of Lake Mahkeenac, Monument Mountain.

Seiji Ozawa Concert Hall. *197 West St, Lenox (02140).* (1941) Festival chamber music programs, Tanglewood Music Center activities; seats 1,200.

Special Events

Apple Squeeze Festival. *65 Main St, Lenox (01240). Phone 413/637-3646.* Celebration of apple harvest; entertainment, food, music. Usually the third weekend in Sept.

Shakespeare & Company. *70 Kemble St (box office), Lenox (01240). Phone 413/637-3353 (box office).* Professional theater company performs plays by Shakespeare and Edith Wharton, as well as other events. Four stages, one outdoor. Late May-Dec, Tues-Sun.

Tanglewood Music Festival. *1277 Main St, Springfield (02115). Phone 617/266-1200.* Tanglewood Boston Symphony Orchestra. Concerts performed on Friday and Saturday evenings and Sunday afternoons. Inquire for other musical events. July-Aug.

Limited-Service Hotel

★ **YANKEE INN.** *461 Pittsfield Rd, Lenox (01240). Phone 413/499-3700; toll-free 800/835-2364; fax 413/499-3634. www.yankeeinn.com.* 96 rooms, 2 story. Complimentary continental breakfast. Check-out 11 am. Indoor pool. Business center. **$**
🏊 🚶

Full-Service Hotels

★ ★ ★ ★ ★ **BLANTYRE.** *16 Blantyre Rd, Lenox (01240). Phone 413/637-3556; fax 413/637-4282. www.blantyre.com.* Listen closely and you can still hear the laughter of Gilded Age garden parties at Blantyre. A private home in the early 1900s, this Tudor-style mansion set on 100 acres in the Berkshire Mountains now welcomes guests seeking to live out a splendid pastoral fantasy. Blantyre's rooms maintain a decidedly British country style of floral fabrics and overstuffed furniture. Fireplaces are available in many rooms to warm the often-chilly evenings. Country pursuits like croquet, tennis, and swimming entice many, while the cultural festivals of Tanglewood and Jacob's Pillow attract others. Dining at Blantyre is a special occasion, whether you're lingering over breakfast in the conservatory or enjoying the romantic ambience of a candlelit dinner. The chef even packs gourmet picnics for lazy summer afternoons that guests spend lounging within Blantyre's grounds or exploring the beautiful countryside. 25 rooms, 2 story. Closed early Nov-early May. Children over 12 years only. Complimentary continental breakfast. Check-in 3 pm, check-out noon. Restaurant. Outdoor pool, whirlpool. Tennis. Airport transportation available. **$$$**
🅿 🏊 🎿

★ ★ ★ **CRANWELL RESORT SPA AND GOLF CLUB.** *55 Lee Rd, Lenox (01240). Phone 413/637-1364; fax 413/637-0571.* This historic 100-year-old country hotel is set on a hill and has a 60-mile view of the southern Berkshires. Situated on 380 acres, the property has a fantastic 18-hole championship golf course that is host to Beecher's golf school. 105 rooms, 3 story. Complimentary continental breakfast. Check-out 11 am. Restaurant, bar. Fitness room. Indoor pool. Golf. Tennis. **$$**
🚶 🏊 ⛳ 🎿

★ ★ ★ **WHEATLEIGH.** *Hawthorne Rd, Lenox (01240). Phone 413/637-0610; fax 413/637-4507. www.wheatleigh.com.* Wheatleigh is a country house hotel of the finest order. This 19th-century Italianate palazzo is gloriously set on 22 acres of rolling hills and lush gardens in the Berkshire Mountains. The magical estate shares in the grand Gilded Age heritage of this celebrated region. This bucolic retreat, with a

Frederick Law Olmstead-designed private park as its backyard, maintains an urbane spirit. The interiors present a crisp, contemporary approach to classic sensibilities. Lacking the formality of the past and avoiding the starkness of modern style, the guest rooms are comfortably elegant. Details make the difference here, from the dazzling Tiffany windows to the ornate fireplace in the Great Hall. The restaurant is a great source of pride, and its updated French dishes draw gourmets. 19 rooms, 2 story. Children over 9 years only. Check-in 3 pm, check-out noon. Restaurant. Outdoor pool. Tennis. **$$**

Specialty Lodgings

The following lodging establishments are approved by Mobil Travel Guide, but due to their unique and individualized nature have not been given a traditional Mobil Star rating. Included in this listing you may find bed-and-breakfasts, limited-service inns, guest ranches, and other unique hotel properties.

APPLE TREE INN. *10 Richmond Mountain Rd, Lenox (01240). Phone 413/637-1477; fax 413/637-2528. www.appletree-inn.com.* Built in 1885; situated on 22 hilltop acres. 35 rooms, 3 story. Complimentary continental breakfast. Check-in 2 pm, check-out 11:30 am. Restaurant. Outdoor pool. Tennis. **$**

BIRCHWOOD INN. *7 Hubbard St, Lenox (01240). Phone 413/637-2600; toll-free 800/524-1646; fax 413/637-4604.* Built in 1767; many antiques, gardens. 12 rooms, 3 story. Children over 12 years only. Complimentary full breakfast. Check-in 2 pm, check-out 11:30 am. **$**

BROOK FARM INN. *15 Hawthorne St, Lenox (01240). Phone 413/637-3013; toll-free 800/285-7638; fax 413/637-4751. www.brookfarm.com.* The interior of this Victorian inn has a very literary feel perfectly suited to its historic location. Visit nearby cultural venues, including Tanglewood Music Center, or curl up with a treasure from the impressive library of poetry, fiction, and history. 12 rooms, 3 story. Children over 15 years only. Complimentary full breakfast. Check-in 3 pm, check-out 11 am. Outdoor pool. **$$**

CANDLELIGHT INN AND RESTAURANT. *35 Walker St, Lenox (01240). Phone 413/637-1555; toll-free 800/428-0580. www.candlelightinn-lenox.com.* 8

rooms, 3 story. Children over 10 years only. Complimentary continental breakfast. Check-in 2 pm, check-out 11 am. Restaurant, bar. **$$**

THE GABLES INN. *81 Walker St, Lenox (01240). Phone 413/637-3416; toll-free 800/382-9401. www.gableslenox.com.* Built in the Queen Anne style in 1885, and once the home of writer Edith Wharton, this classic Berkshire home is 1 mile from Tanglewood Music Center. The owners' collection of artwork and rare books and manuscripts lends an authentic touch to the charming rooms and suites. 19 rooms, 3 story. Children over 12 years only. Complimentary full breakfast. Check-in 2 pm, check-out noon. Indoor pool. Tennis. **$**

GARDEN GABLES INN. *135 Main St, Lenox (01240). Phone 413/637-0193; fax 413/637-4554. www.lenoxinn.com.* This bed-and-breakfast has been welcoming guests since the late 1940s. Originally built as a private estate in 1780, the inn now offers main-house rooms and cottages and is just 1 mile from Tanglewood Music Center. 18 rooms, 2 story. Children over 12 years only. Complimentary full breakfast. Check-in 2 pm, check-out 11 am. Outdoor pool. Business center. **$$**

GATEWAYS INN. *51 Walker St, Lenox (01240). Phone 413/637-2532; toll-free 888/492-9466; fax 413/637-1432. www.gatewaysinn.com.* Restored mansion (1912). 12 rooms, 2 story. Children over 12 years only. Complimentary continental breakfast. Check-in 1 pm, check-out 11 am. Restaurant. **$**

HARRISON HOUSE. *174 Main St, Lenox (01240). Phone 413/637-1746; fax 413/637-9957. www.harrison-house.com.* The circular drive and immaculate porch of this country inn are directly across from Kennedy Park and overlook Tanglewood. Rooms vary in size and décor. 7 rooms, 2 story. Children over 12 years only. Complimentary continental breakfast. Check-in 2 pm, check-out 11 am. **$**

KEMBLE INN. *2 Kemble St, Lenox (01240). Phone 413/637-4113; toll-free 800/353-4113. www.kembleinn.com.* Located on 3 acres in the center of historic Lenox, this inn features magnificent views of the Berkshire Mountains. The guest rooms are named after American authors. 15 rooms, 3 story.

Children over 12 years only. Complimentary continental breakfast. Check-in 2 pm, check-out 11 am. **$$**

ROOKWOOD INN. *11 Old Stockbridge Rd, Lenox (01240). Phone 413/637-9750; toll-free 800/223-9750; fax 413/637-1532.* Victorian inn (1885) furnished with English antiques. 20 rooms, 3 story. Complimentary full breakfast. Check-in 3 pm, check-out 11 am. **$**

THE SUMMER WHITE HOUSE. *17 Main St, Lenox (01240). Phone 413/637-4489; toll-free 800/382-9401. www.summerwhitehouse.com.* Located in the heart of historic Lenox, only 1 mile from Tanglewood, this inn is an original Berkshire cottage built in 1885. Guest rooms feature private baths and air conditioning. 7 rooms. Closed Nov-Apr. Children over 16 years only. Complimentary continental breakfast. Check-in 2 pm, check-out 11 am. **$$**

THE VILLAGE INN. *16 Church St, Lenox (01240). Phone 413/637-0020; toll-free 800/253-0917; fax 413/637-9756. www.villageinn-lenox.com.* Has been an inn since 1775. 32 rooms, 3 story. Check-in 1 pm, check-out 11 am. Restaurant, bar. **$**

WHISTLER'S INN. *5 Greenwood St, Lenox (01240). Phone 413/637-0975; fax 419/637-2190. www.whistlersinnlenox.com.* Tudor-style mansion built in 1820. 14 rooms, 2 story. Complimentary full breakfast. Check-in 3 pm, check-out noon. **$**

Restaurants

★ ★ **APPLE TREE.** *10 Richmond Mountain Rd, Lenox (01240). Phone 413/637-1477; fax 413/637-2528. www.appletree-inn.com.* American menu. Dinner, brunch. Closed Mon-Wed in the off-season. Bar. Outdoor seating. **$$**

★ ★ ★ **BISTRO ZINC.** *56 Church St, Lenox (01240). Phone 413/637-8800.* French menu. Lunch, dinner. Bar. Children's menu. Casual attire. **$$**

★ ★ ★ **BLANTYRE.** *16 Blantyre Rd, Lenox (01240). Phone 413/637-3556; fax 413/637-4282. www.blantyre.com.* Dining at this 1902 mansion is a special experience. Antique glassware and place settings, candlelight, and harp music all combine for a romantic atmosphere. French menu. Lunch, dinner. Closed Mon; also Nov-Apr. Jacket required. Reservations recommended. Valet parking. Outdoor seating (lunch). **$$$**

★ ★ **CAFE LUCIA.** *80 Church St, Lenox (01240). Phone 413/637-2640; fax 413/243-9161.* Italian menu. Dinner. Closed Mon; Easter, Thanksgiving, Dec 25; also Sun in Nov-June. Outdoor seating. **$$$**

★ **CAROL'S.** *8 Franklin St, Lenox (01240). Phone 413/637-8948.* American menu. Breakfast, lunch. Closed Thanksgiving, Dec 25; Tues-Wed in Sept-June. Children's menu. **$**

★ ★ **CHURCH STREET CAFE.** *65 Church St, Lenox (01240). Phone 413/637-2745; fax 413/637-2050.* American menu. Lunch, dinner. Closed Jan 1, Thanksgiving, Dec 25; also Sun-Mon in Nov-May. Bar. Outdoor seating. **$$**

★ ★ ★ **GATEWAYS INN.** *51 Walker St, Lenox (01240). Phone 413/637-2532; fax 413/637-1432. www.gatewaysinn.com.* The restaurant at this charming inn features Italian and American cuisine with international influences. The chefs use locally grown produce and dairy products, and the menu changes seasonally. Choose to sit in the main room that has French doors and terra cotta painted walls, or, for a more private experience, dine in the Rockwell Room. American, Italian menu. Dinner. Closed Mon-Tues in winter. Outdoor seating. **$$**

★ ★ ★ **LENOX 218 RESTAURANT.** *218 Main St, Lenox (01240). Phone 413/637-4218. www.lenox218.com.* A convenient place to dine when visiting Tanglewood, this contemporary restaurant specializes in Italian and American dishes and can handle banquets for up to 100 people. Don't miss the incredible Sunday brunch. American, Italian menu. Dinner, brunch. Bar. Children's menu. Casual attire. **$$**

★ **PANDA HOUSE CHINESE RESTAURANT.** *506 Pittsfield Rd, Lenox (01240). Phone 413/499-0660; fax 413/499-0786.* Chinese menu. Lunch, dinner, Sun brunch. Closed Thanksgiving, Dec 25. Bar. **$$**

★ ★ ★ **WHEATLEIGH.** *Hawthorne Rd, Lenox (01240). Phone 413/637-0610; fax 413/637-4507. www.wheatleigh.com.* Polished mahogany doors lead to this historic hotel's elegant restaurant. The dining room's design is just as regal as the building itself, which was modeled in 1893 after a 16th-century Florentine palazzo. Guests dine on contemporary French cuisine in a beautiful sun-drenched room filled with oil paintings, hand-carved Chippendale chairs, and sparkling crystal chandeliers. French menu. Dinner, Sun brunch. Reservations recommended. Valet parking. **$$$$**

★ ★ ★ **THE WYNDHURST RESTAURANT.**
55 Lee Rd, Lenox (01240). Phone 413/637-1364; fax 413/637-4364. www.cranwell.com. The dining room of the Cranwell Resort is situated on the main floor of the 100-year-old Tudor mansion. Large windows offer vistas of the Berkshire Hills. The cuisine highlights local produce, including game and cheeses. American menu. Dinner. Bar. Children's menu. **$$$**

Leominster (B-5)

Settled 1653
Population 41,303
Area Code 978
Zip 01453
Information Johnny Appleseed Visitor Center, 110 Erdman Way; phone 978/840-4300
Web Site www.leominster-ma.gov

Leominster (LEMMINst'r) has retained the pronunciation of the English town for which it was named. Known at one time as "Comb City," in 1845 Leominster housed 24 factories manufacturing horn combs. It is the birthplace of "Johnny Appleseed"—John Chapman (1774-1845)—a devout Swedenborgian missionary who traveled throughout America on foot, planting apple orchards and the seeds of his faith. The National Plastics Center and Museum is located here.

Limited-Service Hotels

★ ★ **FOUR POINTS BY SHERATON.** *99 Erdman Way, Leominster (01453). Phone 978/534-9000; fax 978/534-0891. www.fourpoints.com.* 187 rooms, 7 story. Complimentary continental breakfast. Check-in 3 pm, check-out noon. Restaurant, bar. Indoor pool, whirlpool. Business center. **$**

★ ★ **WACHUSETT VILLAGE INN.** *9 Village Inn Rd, Westminster (01473). Phone 978/874-2000; toll-free 800/342-1905; fax 978/874-1753. www.wachusett villageinn.com.* Situated on 100 acres near the Wachusett Mountain ski area, this inn's 3,000 square feet of meeting space and retreat-like setting attract group clientele. Take a wintertime sleigh ride then retreat to the casual, American restaurant for a bite to

eat. 74 rooms, 2 story. Check-out 11 am. Restaurant. Fitness room. Indoor pool, outdoor pool. Tennis. **$**

Lexington (B-7)

See also Concord

Settled circa 1640
Population 30,355
Elevation 210 ft
Area Code 781
Zip 02173
Information Chamber of Commerce Visitors Center, 1875 Massachusetts Ave; phone 781/862-1450. The center, open daily, offers a diorama depicting the Battle of Lexington and has a walking tour map.

Lexington is called the birthplace of American liberty. On its Green, April 19, 1775, eight Minutemen were killed in what is traditionally considered the first organized fight of the War for Independence. However, in 1908, the US Senate recognized the counterclaim of Point Pleasant, West Virginia, as the first battle site. It is still possible to visualize the Battle of Lexington. Down the street came the British, 700 strong. To the right of the Green is the tavern the militia used as headquarters. It was here that 77 Minutemen lined up near the west end of the Green, facing down the Charlestown road. Nearby is a boulder with a plaque bearing the words of Captain John Parker, spoken just before the Redcoats opened fire: "Stand your ground. Don't fire unless fired upon. But if they mean to have a war, let it begin here!" It did—the fight then moved on to Concord.

What to See and Do

Battle Green. *At the center of town.* The Old Monument, the *Minuteman* statue, and the Boulder mark the line of the Minutemen, seven of whom are buried under the monument.

Lexington Historical Society. *1331 Massachusetts Ave, Lexington (02421). Phone 781/862-1703.* Revolutionary period houses. Guided tours. **$$$**

Buckman Tavern. *1 Bedford St, Lexington (02420). Facing the Battle Green. Phone 781/862-1703.* (1709) Minutemen assembled here before the battle. Period furnishings, portraits. (Mid-Apr-Oct, daily; Nov, weekends only)

Hancock-Clarke House. *36 Hancock St, Lexington (02420). Phone 781/862-1703.* (1698) Here John Hancock and Samuel Adams were awakened by Paul Revere's alarm on April 18, 1775. Furniture, portraits, utensils; small museum. Fire engine exhibit in barn (by appointment). (Mid-Apr-Oct, daily)

Munroe Tavern. *1332 Massachusetts Ave, Lexington (02420). Phone 781/862-1703.* (1695) British hospital after the battle. George Washington dined here in 1789. Period furnishings, artifacts. (Mid-Apr-Oct, daily)

National Heritage Museum. *33 Marrett Rd (Hwy 2A), Lexington (02421). At junction Massachusetts Ave. Phone 781/861-6559.* Museum features exhibits on American history and culture, from its founding to the present; also history of Lexington and the Revolutionary War. (Daily) **FREE**

Special Event

Reenactment of the Battle of Lexington and Concord. *Massachusetts Ave, Lexington (02173). Phone 781/862-1450.* Reenactment of the opening battle of the Revolutionary War; parade. Patriots Day. Mon nearest Apr 19.

Limited-Service Hotel

★ **HOLIDAY INN EXPRESS.** *440 Bedford St, Lexington (02420). Phone 781/861-0850; toll-free 800/465-4329; fax 781/861-0821. www.holiday-inn.com.* 204 rooms, 2 story. Complimentary continental breakfast. Check-out noon. Outdoor pool, whirlpool. **$**
🛏

Full-Service Hotel

★ ★ ★ **SHERATON LEXINGTON INN.** *727 Marrett Rd, Lexington (02421). Phone 781/862-8700; fax 781/863-0404. www.sheraton.com.* Centrally located in a historical town 15 miles from Boston, this inn has 5,000 square feet of meeting space and an outdoor pool. Cracker Barrel Restaurant and Tavern is on-site for traditional, New-England-style dining. 121 rooms, 2 story. Check-in 3 pm, check-out noon. Restaurant, bar. Fitness room. Outdoor pool. **$**
🧍 🛏

Lowell (A-6)

Settled 1655
Population 105,167
Elevation 102 ft
Area Code 978
Information Greater Lowell Chamber of Commerce, 77 Merrimack St, 01852; phone 978/459-8154
Web Site www.greaterlowellchamber.org

In the 19th century, the powerful Merrimack River and its canals transformed Lowell from a handicraft center to a textile industrial center. The Francis Floodgate, near Broadway and Clare Streets, was called "Francis's Folly" when it was built in 1848, but it saved the city from flood in 1936. Restoration of the historic canal system is currently in progress.

What to See and Do

American Textile History Museum. *491 Dutton St, Lowell (01854). Phone 978/441-0400. www.athm.org.* Permanent exhibit, "Textiles in America," features 18th- to 20th-century textiles, artifacts, and machinery in operation, showing the impact of the Industrial Revolution on labor. Collections of cloth samples, books, prints, photographs, and preindustrial tools may be seen by appointment. Tours; activities. Library; education center. Restaurant; museum store. (Tues-Sun; closed Jan 1, Thanksgiving, Dec 25) **$$**

Lowell Heritage State Park. *246 Market St, Lowell (01852). Phone 978/453-0592.* Six miles of canals and associated linear parks and 2 miles of park on the bank of Merrimack River offer boating, boathouse; concert pavilion, interpretive programs. (Schedule varies) **FREE**

Lowell National Historical Park. *Visitor Center, 246 Market St, Lowell (01852). Phone 978/970-5000.* Established to commemorate Lowell's unique legacy as the most important planned industrial city in America. The nation's first large-scale center for the mechanized production of cotton cloth, Lowell became a model for 19th-century industrial development. Park includes mill buildings and a 5 1/2-mile canal system. Visitor center at Market Mills includes audiovisual show and exhibits (daily; closed Jan 1, Thanksgiving, Dec 25). Free walking and trolley tours (Mar-Nov). Tours by barge and trolley (May-Columbus Day weekend; fee), reservations suggested. Located here are

Boott Cotton Mills Museum. *400 Foot of John St, Lowell (01852).* Phone 978/970-5000. Industrial history museum with operating looms (ear plugs supplied). Interactive exhibits, video presentations. (Daily; closed Jan 1, Thanksgiving, Dec 24-25) **$$**

Patrick J. Mogan Cultural Center. *40 French St, Lowell (01852).* Restored 1836 boarding house of the Boott Cotton Mills including a re-created kitchen, keeper's room, parlor, and mill girls' bedroom; exhibits on working people, immigrants, and labor history; also local history. (Daily)

New England Quilt Museum. *18 Shattuck St, Lowell (01852). Phone 978/452-4207. www.nequiltmuseum .org.* Changing exhibits feature antique, traditional, and contemporary quilts. Museum shop. (Tues-Sat; closed holidays) **$**

University of MA-Lowell. *1 University Ave, Lowell (01854). Phone 978/934-4000.* (15,500 students) State-operated university formed by the 1975 merger of Lowell Technological Institute (1895) and Lowell State College (1894). Music ensembles at Durgin Hall Performing Arts Center.

Whistler House Museum of Art. *243 Worthen St, Lowell (01852). Phone 978/452-7641. www.whistlerhouse.org.* Birthplace of the painter James Abbott McNeill Whistler. Exhibits include several of his etchings. Collection of 19th- and early 20th-century American art. (Wed-Sun; closed holidays) **$**

Special Events

Lowell Celebrates Kerouac Festival. *PO Box 1111, Lowell (01852). Phone toll-free 877/537-6822. lckorg. tripod.com.* Tours, music, poetry competition, book signings, and panel discussions. First weekend in Oct.

Lowell Folk Festival. *246 Market St, Lowell (01852). Phone 978/970-5000.* Concerts, crafts, and demonstrations, ethnic food, street parade. Last full weekend in July.

Limited-Service Hotels

★ **BEST WESTERN CHELMSFORD INN.** *187 Chelmsford St, Chelmsford (01824). Phone 978/256-7511; toll-free 888/770-9992; fax 978/250-1401. www.bestwestern.com/chelmsfordinn.* 120 rooms, 5 story. Check-in 3 pm, check-out noon. High-speed Internet access. Fitness room. Outdoor pool, whirlpool. **$**

★ ★ **COURTYARD BY MARRIOTT.** *30 Industrial Ave E, Lowell (01852). Phone 978/458-7575; toll-free 888/236-2427; fax 978/458-1302. www.courtyard.com.* Large rooms with free, high-speed Internet access, two phone lines, a TV with cable, and an all-news channel are in each room. Fax, copying, and printing services are available, and a rental car desk is on-site. While there is no doubt that this hotel is designed for business travelers, there are also conveniences for those who are here for pleasure. There is, for instance, shuttle service into Lowell for those who want to stroll the streets of this historic little town at the confluence of the Concord and Merrimack rivers, while others stroll the hallways of the myriad of businesses and corporations within a 5-mile radius. In addition to an on-site fitness room and outdoor pool for working out after-hours kinks, guests have privileges at a nearby health club. But you can't miss the relaxation element of this contemporary brick hotel. Part of its common area is designed as a library, filled with bookcases and a sitting area nestled around a large fireplace and flat-screen TV. A small, casual dining area sits at the opposite end of the room. 120 rooms, 3 story. Check-in 3 pm, check-out noon. High-speed Internet access. Restaurant. Fitness room. Outdoor pool. **$**

★ ★ **DOUBLETREE HOTEL.** *50 Warren St, Lowell (01852). Phone 978/452-1200; toll-free 800/876-4586; fax 978/453-4674. www.doubletree.com.* It's hard to find a more ideal location. This is the closest hotel to the UMass Lowell campus, and it's just across the canal from Middlesex Community College. This modern, nine-story hotel is also in the heart of downtown, where old brick mill structures have been turned into multiuse buildings of shops and restaurants. Many of the Doubletree's 252 rooms, as well as its River's Edge restaurant, overlook the city's scenic canals, and guests have easy access to the popular and historic Canal Walk. Brass sconces, marble bathroom floors, and contemporary décor with natural touches of copper and wood make this a soothing place to come home to at the end of a day of work or play. 252 rooms, 9 story. Check-in 3 pm, check-out noon. High-speed Internet access, wireless Internet access. Restaurant, bar. Fitness room. Indoor pool, outdoor pool, whirlpool. **$**

Full-Service Hotels

★ ★ **RADISSON HOTEL AND SUITES CHELMSFORD.** *10 Independence Dr, Chelmsford*

(01824). *Phone 978/256-0800; toll-free 800/333-3333; fax 978/256-0750. www.radisson.com.* 194 rooms, 5 story. Check-in 2 pm, check-out 11 am. Restaurant, bar. Fitness room. Indoor pool. **$**

★ ★ **WESTFORD REGENCY INN AND CONFERENCE CENTER.** *219 Littleton Rd, Westford (01886). Phone 978/692-8200; toll-free 800/543-7801; fax 978/692-7403. www.westfordregency.com.* Take in the joys of New England at this inn and conference center with 20,000 square feet of meeting space. Every Thursday from June through August, there's a classic lobster boil and clambake hosted outdoors under a 6,000-square-foot tent. 193 rooms, 4 story. Pets accepted, some restrictions; fee. Check-out noon. Restaurant, bar. Fitness room. Indoor pool, whirlpool. **$$**

Full-Service Inn

★ ★ ★ **STONEHEDGE INN.** *160 Pawtucket Blvd, Tyngsboro (01879). Phone 978/649-4400; fax 978/649-9256. www.stonehedgeinn.com.* This contemporary inn is an American imitation of an English country manor. It has an intimate feel, and the staff is eager to meet guests' needs. Large, comfortable guest rooms feature spacious bathrooms and heated towel racks. Set on the grounds of a horse farm, this out-of-the-way inn is perfect for a romantic rendezvous or a corporate retreat. 30 rooms, 2 story. Check-in 3 pm, check-out noon. Restaurant, bar. Fitness room. Indoor pool, outdoor pool, whirlpool. Golf. Tennis. **$$**

Restaurants

★ ★ **COBBLESTONES.** *91 Dutton St, Lowell (01852). Phone 978/970-2282; fax 978/970-0266. www.cobblestonesoflowell.com.* For guests who appreciate the wilderness, this restaurant is sure to please. Seasonal game dishes include ostrich, antelope, and kangaroo, and the property is set within the Lowell National Historic Park. For dessert, be sure to try the bananas flambé. American menu. Lunch, dinner. Closed Sun; holidays. Bar. **$$$**

★ ★ ★ **LA BONICHE.** *143 Merrimack St, Lowell (01852). Phone 978/458-9473.* Though the food is upscale, the dress is casual at this fine restaurant. French

menu. Lunch, dinner. Closed Sun-Mon; holidays. Bar. Children's menu. **$$$**

★ ★ ★ **SILKS.** *160 Pawtucket Blvd, Tyngsboro (01879). Phone 978/649-4400; fax 978/649-9256. www.stonehedgeinn.com.* If you are searching for a little hideaway in the country for dinner and are hoping to find a place that happens to have one of the world's most impressive wine caves, schedule a visit to Silks. Secreted away in 36 acres of New England horse country, Silks is located in the Stonehedge Inn (see), a charming old English-style manor house. This enchanted spot has not only an incredible international wine collection (there are over 90,000 bottles in the cave, with about 2,000 wines offered daily), but also a talented team of chefs in the kitchen cooking up a spectacular selection of very French, very haute cuisine. Although the food plays second fiddle to the wine, the menu offers exciting, modern riffs on classic French dishes. Herbs and spices are borrowed from around the globe, successfully bringing flavor, style, and flair to the extensive selection of cold and hot appetizers, fish, and meats. The green and burgundy room is warm, comfortable, and romantic. Considering the size of the wine list, several toasts should be made; this is a great spot for a special occasion. While the service is impeccable and European in style, it is free from pretension. French menu. Breakfast, lunch, dinner, Sun brunch. Closed Mon. Outdoor seating. **$$$**

Lynn (B-7)

See also Boston, Salem

Settled 1629
Population 89,050
Elevation 30 ft
Area Code 781
Information Chamber of Commerce, 100 Oxford St, Suite 416, 01901; phone 781/592-2900
Web Site www.lynnareachamber.com

Shoe manufacturing began as a home craft in Lynn as early as 1635. Today, Lynn's industry is widely diversified. Founded here in 1883, General Electric is the biggest single enterprise. Lynn also has more than 3 miles of sandy beaches.

What to See and Do

Grand Army of the Republic Museum. *58 Andrew St, Lynn (01901). Phone 781/477-7085.* Features

Revolutionary War, Civil War, Spanish-American War, and World War I weapons, artifacts, and exhibits. (Mon-Fri by appointment; closed holidays) **DONATION**

Horizon's Edge Casino Cruises. *76 Marine Blvd, Lynn (01905). Take Hwy 1A N to the Lynnway. Proceed 1 mile past the General Edwards Bridge, and see Horizon's Edge entrance on right onto Marine Blvd. Phone 781/581-7733. www.horizonsedge.com.* "Horizon's Edge takes its 500-passenger cruise ship 3 miles into international waters, where casino-style gambling is legal. On board, you'll find blackjack, Caribbean stud poker, three-card poker, let it ride, roulette, craps, slot machines, and bingo. (Note that you must be 21 to board.) Your admission fee includes a buffet in the ship's nonsmoking restaurant, and Horizon's Edge provides live musical entertainment. (Daily; closed Dec-mid-Apr) **$$$$**

Lynn Heritage State Park. *590 Washington St, Lynn (01901). Phone 781/598-1974.* Five-acre waterfront park and marina. (Daily; closed Jan 1, Dec 25) The visitor center (590 Washington St) has museum-quality exhibits from past to present, from hand-crafted shoes to high-tech items; inquire for hours. **FREE**

Lynn Woods Reservation. *106 Pennybrook Rd, Lynn (01905). 10 miles N of Boston. Phone 781/598-4000. www.lynndpw.com/woods/lynnwood.htm.* Situated on 2,200 acres, Lynn Park is a mountain biker's paradise and also offers excellent cross-country ski trails. The park boasts single tracks of gravel and dirt, many with steep hills, sheer ledges, and large boulders. Head up the hills to look down on Walden Pond or the Boston city skyline. Hardwood forests offer protection to a variety of bird species, making this site a good spot for bird-watching as well. (Daily dawn-dusk) **FREE**

Mary Baker Eddy Historical Home. *12 Broad St, Lynn (01902). Phone 781/593-5634.* Restored house where the founder of Christian Science lived from 1875 to 1882. Call for tour days and times. **FREE**

Specialty Lodging

The following lodging establishment is approved by Mobil Travel Guide, but due to its unique and individualized nature has not been given a traditional Mobil Star rating. Included in this listing you may find bed-and-breakfasts, limited-service inns, guest ranches, and other unique hotel properties.

DIAMOND DISTRICT BREAKFAST INN. *142 Ocean St, Lynn (01902). Phone 781/599-4470; toll-free 800/666-3076; fax 781/599-5122. www.diamond districtinn.com.* Located just minutes away from Boston and only steps away from the water, this Georgian-style inn (built in 1911) offers a great l ocation on a quiet block of town. Guest rooms are named for types of shoes or shoe parts. 11 rooms, 3 story. Pets accepted, some restrictions. Complimentary full breakfast. Check-in 3 pm, check-out 11 am. **$$**
🐾 🦮

Lynnfield (B-7)

Settled 1639
Population 11,542
Elevation 98 ft
Area Code 781
Zip 01940

Full-Service Hotel

★ ★ ★ **SHERATON COLONIAL HOTEL AND GOLF CLUB BOSTON NORTH.** *1 Audubon Rd, Wakefield (01880). Phone 781/245-9300; toll-free 800/325-3535; fax 781/245-0842. www.sheraton.com.* Fifteen miles from downtown Boston, this 220-acre golf resort offers an 18-hole PGA course. For more outdoor recreation, Lake Quannapowitt is nearby. 280 rooms, 11 story. Check-in 3 pm, check-out noon. High-speed Internet access. Restaurant. Fitness room. Indoor pool, whirlpool. Golf. Tennis. **$**
🏃 🏊 🏌 🎾

Restaurant

★ ★ **KERNWOOD.** *55 Salem St, Lynnfield (01940). Phone 781/245-4011; fax 781/255-3530.* New England menu. Lunch, dinner. Closed July 4, Dec 25. Bar. Children's menu. **$$**
🐾

Marblehead (B-8)

See also Boston, Salem

Settled 1629
Population 20,377
Elevation 65 ft
Area Code 781
Zip 01945
Information Chamber of Commerce, 62 Pleasant St,

PO Box 76; phone 781/631-2868
Web Site www.marbleheadchamber.org

A unique blend of old and new, Marblehead is situated on a peninsula 17 miles north of Boston. Named Marble Harbor for a short time, the town was settled in 1629 by hardy fishermen from England's West counties. It now boasts a beautiful harbor and a number of busy boatyards. Pleasure craft anchor in this picturesque port each summer, and a record number of modern racing yachts participate in the annual Race Week. Beaches, boating, fishing, art exhibits, antique and curio shops—all combine to offer a choice of quiet relaxation or active recreation.

What to See and Do

Abbot Hall. *188 Washington St, Marblehead (01945). Abbot Hall, Washington Sq. Phone 781/631-0000.* Displays the original "Spirit of '76" painting and deed to town (1684) from the Nanepashemet. Museum, Marine Room. Gift shop. (Last weekend in May-last weekend in Oct: daily; rest of year: Mon-Fri; closed winter holidays) **DONATION**

Jeremiah Lee Mansion. *161 Washington St, Marblehead (01945). Phone 781/631-1069.* (1768) Marblehead Historical Society. Where Generals Glover, Lafayette, and Washington were entertained. Opulent Georgian architecture and interiors; Marblehead history; antiques of the period, rare original hand-painted wallpaper. (June-mid-Oct, daily; closed holidays) **$$**

King Hooper Mansion. *8 Hooper St, Marblehead (01945). Phone 781/631-2608.* (1728) Restored house with garden. Art exhibits. (Tues-Sat afternoons; closed Jan 1, Dec 25) **FREE**

Special Event

Sailing races. *Boston Yacht Club, 1 Front St, Marblehead (01945). Phone 781/631-3100.* May-Oct, Wed evening and weekends. Race week third week in July.

Specialty Lodgings

The following lodging establishments are approved by Mobil Travel Guide, but due to their unique and individualized nature have not been given a traditional Mobil Star rating. Included in this listing you may find bed-and-breakfasts, limited-service inns, guest ranches, and other unique hotel properties.

HARBOR LIGHT INN. *58 Washington St, Marblehead (01945). Phone 781/631-2186; fax 781/631-2216. www.harborlightinn.com.* Plenty of shops, galleries, and restaurants are near this bed-and-breakfast in the historic harbor district. All rooms have fireplaces, romantic canopied beds, and Jacuzzi baths. Continental breakfast and afternoon, fresh-baked cookies are served in the colonial dining room. 21 rooms. Complimentary continental breakfast. Check-in 1 pm, check-out 11 am. Outdoor pool. Airport transportation available. **$**
🐾 🏊

MARBLEHEAD INN. *264 Pleasant St, Marblehead (01945). Phone 781/639-9999; toll-free 800/399-5843; fax 781/639-9996. www.marbleheadinn.com.* Victorian inn (1872) near beach. 10 rooms, 3 story. Children over 10 only. Complimentary continental breakfast. Check-in 3 pm, check-out 11 am. **$$**
🐾

SEAGULL INN. *106 Harbor Ave, Marblehead (01945). Phone 781/631-1893; fax 781/631-3535. www.seagullinn.com.* Built in 1880; turn-of-the-century atmosphere. 6 rooms, 2 story. Pets accepted; fee. Complimentary continental breakfast. Check-in 2 pm, check-out 11 am. **$$**
🐾 🐾

SPRAY CLIFF ON THE OCEAN. *25 Spray Ave, Marblehead (01945). Phone 781/631-6789; toll-free 800/626-1530; fax 781/639-4563. www.spraycliff.com.* Built in 1910. 7 rooms, 3 story. No children allowed. Complimentary continental breakfast. Check-in 3 pm, check-out 11 am. **$$**
🐾

Restaurants

★ ★ **MARBLEHEAD LANDING.** *81 Front St, Marblehead (01945). Phone 781/631-1878; fax 781/631-8439. www.thelandingrestaurant.com.* Seafood menu. Lunch, dinner, Sun brunch. Closed Thanksgiving, Dec 25. Bar. Children's menu. Outdoor seating. **$$**

★ ★ **PELLINO'S.** *261 Washington St, Marblehead (01945). Phone 781/631-3344; fax 781/777-5920. www.pellinos.com.* Italian menu. Dinner. Closed Jan 1, Easter, Dec 25. Bar. Reservations recommended. **$$**
🐾

Martha's Vineyard (E-8)

See also Falmouth, Hyannis and Barnstable, Nantucket Island

Settled 1642
Population 12,690
Elevation 0-311 ft
Area Code 508
Information Chamber of Commerce, Beach Rd, PO Box 1698, Vineyard Haven 02568; phone 508/693-0085
Web Site www.mvy.com

This triangular island below the arm of Cape Cod combines moors, dunes, multicolored cliffs, flower-filled ravines, farmland, and forest. It is less than 20 miles from west to east and 10 miles from north to south.

There was once a whaling fleet at the island, but Martha's Vineyard now devotes itself almost entirely to being a vacation playground, with summer houses that range from small cottages to elaborate mansions. The colonial atmosphere still survives in Vineyard Haven, the chief port; Oak Bluffs; Edgartown; West Tisbury; Gay Head; and Chilmark.

Gay Head is one of the few Massachusetts towns in which many inhabitants are of Native American descent.

What to See and Do

★ **Aquinnah Cliffs.** *State Rd, Aquinnah (02535).* These cliffs—a national landmark—are the most popular and most photographed tourist attraction on Martha's Vineyard because of the stunning view they offer. The 150-foot, brilliantly colored cliffs were formed over millions of years by glaciers; today, the cliffs are owned by the Wampanoag Indians, who hold them sacred. (Previous names of the cliffs include Dover Cliffs, so named by settlers in 1602, and Gay Head Cliffs, a name that originated from British sailors. Gay Head was the official name of this part of Martha's Vineyard until 1998.) On top of the Cliffs stands Aquinnah Light lighthouse, which was commissioned by President John Adams in 1798 and rebuilt in 1844 to protect ships from the treacherous stretch of sea below and built with clay from the cliffs. (Apr-Nov)

Black Dog Bakery. *Water St, Vineyard Haven (02568). Near Steamship Authority parking lot. Phone 508/693-4786. www.theblackdog.com.* The Black Dog is more than just a bakery: it's a cultural phenomenon. Everywhere you look, you see the Black Dog logo (a black Labrador retriever) on T-shirts, hats, mugs, and so on. The Black Dog General Store (with four locations on Martha's Vineyard) sells these souvenirs, along with special treats for your dog. The bakery, which sits just in front of one of the stores, is a great place to start your day, serving coffee, pastries, torts, truffles, and other human treats. Also visit the Black Dog Tavern (see) for tasty seafood and other dishes in an ideal location right on the harbor. (Daily 5:30 am-5 pm, to 7 pm in summer; closed Dec 25)

Chicama Vineyards. *Stoney Hill Rd, West Tisbury (02545). Phone 508/693-0309. www.chicamavineyards.com.* Martha's Vineyard was once awash in winemaking; today Chicama Vineyards is reviving the practice. The European grapes are used to produce a variety of wines, including merlot, chardonnay, and cabernet. You'll also find other foodstuffs for sale, including vinegars and salad dressings, mustards and chutneys, and jams and jellies. Tours and wine tastings are available, but hours vary with the day and season. (Hours vary; call ahead) **FREE**

East Beach. *Chappaquiddick Rd, Chappaquiddick Island (02539). Take your four-wheel drive car on the On Time ferry from Martha's Vineyard to Chappaquiddick Island. From the ferry dock, take Chappaquiddick Road until a sharp right turn, where the road becomes Dike Bridge Road. Park near the bridge or obtain an oversand vehicle permit to drive on the beach. Phone 508/627-7689.* East Beach is the popular name for two adjoining beaches: Wasque Reservation and Cape Pogue Wildlife Refuge. You'll go to a lot of trouble to get to this rustic beach that has no restrooms or concessions, but the quiet, beautiful stretch of shoreline makes the preparation and trip worthwhile. Chances are you'll have this stunning beach all to yourself. (Daily) **$$**

Featherstone Meeting House For the Arts. *Barnes Rd, Oak Bluffs (02568). Phone 508/693-1850. www.featherstonearts.org.* This unique arts center offers tourists the hourly use of artists' studios and also features classes in photography, woodworking, pottery, weaving, and stained glass. Nestled on a former horse farm on 18 acres, the Meeting House also includes a gallery of works from local artists. Call for details about a summer art camp for kids. (Daily; call for studio availability)

Felix Neck Sanctuary. *Edgartown-Vineyard Haven Rd, Vineyard Haven (02569). 3 miles from Edgartown off Edgartown-Vineyard Haven Rd. Phone 508/627-4850. www.massaudubon.org/Nature_Connection/Sancturaries/Felix_Neck.* This 350-acre wildlife preserve is a haven for kids and bird lovers alike. Six miles of trails (guided or self-guided) meander through the sanctuary's meadows, woods, salt marshes, and beaches. The visitors center offers unique exhibits along with a more traditional gift shop. In the summer, consider enrolling the kids in Fern & Feather Day Camp at the Sanctuary. Park (daily dawn-7 pm). Visitor Center (8 am-4 pm; closed Mon in Oct-May). **$**

Flying Horse Carousel. *33 Circuit Ave, Oak Bluffs (02557). Circuit and Lake aves. Phone 508/693-9481.* Whether you're traveling with a youngster who loves horses (but is too young to ride them for real) or want to hop on for yourself, Flying Horse Carousel is a treat not to be missed. This carousel, the oldest in the country and a national historic landmark, looks nothing like modern carousels you may have seen in malls or shopping centers. Instead, Flying Horse features gorgeous, hand-carved, lifelike horses that glide to festive music. Try to grasp the brass ring in the center to earn your next ride free.

Hyannis-Martha's Vineyard Day Round-Trip. *Phone 508/778-2600.* Passenger service from Hyannis (May-Oct).

Menemsha Fishing Village. *North St, Menemsha (02552). Take a shuttle bus or bike ferry from Aquinnah.* Menemsha is a picturesque fishing village, which means you'll see plenty of cedar-sided fishing shacks, fishermen in waterproof gear, and lobster traps strewn about. The movie *Jaws* was filmed here, and if you saw it, you may have haunting flashbacks while you're here! You'll find quaint shopping areas in the village, as well.

Mytoi. *Dike Rd, Chappaquiddick (02539). Phone 508/693-7662.* Although Martha's Vineyard may not be a logical location for a Japanese garden, Mytoi has won praises for its breathtaking mix of azaleas, irises, dogwood, daffodils, rhododendron, and Japanese maple for nearly 50 years. You'll spy goldfish and koi swimming in a pond that's the centerpiece of the garden; you can visit the small island at the pond's center via the ornamental bridge. Take an easy 1-mile hike that weaves through the gardens and into forested area

and salt marshes. Allow from an hour to a half day. (Daily) **FREE**

Oak Bluffs. In 1835, this Methodist community served as the site of annual summer camp meetings for church groups. As thousands attended these meetings, the communal tents gave way to family tents, which in turn became wooden cottages designed to look like tents. Today, visitors to the community may see these "Gingerbread Cottages of the Campground."

Recreation. Swimming. *Martha's Vineyard. Phone 508/693-3057.* Many sheltered beaches, among them public beaches at Menemsha, Oak Bluffs, Edgartown, and Vineyard Haven. Surf swimming on south shore. **Tennis.** Public courts in Edgartown, Oak Bluffs, West Tisbury, and Vineyard Haven. **Boat rentals** at Vineyard Haven, Oak Bluffs, and Gay Head. **Fishing.** Good for striped bass, bonito, bluefish, weakfish. **Golf** at Farm Neck Club.

Steamship Authority. *1494 E Rodney French Blvd, Mashpee (02744). Phone 508/477-8600. www.steamshipauthority.com.* New Bedford-Martha's Vineyard Ferry. Daily passenger service (mid-May-mid-Sept) to New Bedford. Same-day round-trips available. Also bus tours of the island. Schedule may vary. **$$$$**

⭐ **Vincent House.** *Pease's Point Way, Edgartown (02539). Phone 508/627-4440.* The oldest known house on the island, built in 1672, has been carefully restored to allow visitors to see how buildings were constructed 300 years ago. Original brickwork, hardware, and woodwork. (June-early Oct, daily; rest of year, by appointment) **FREE** Also on Main Street is

> **Old Whaling Church.** *89 Main St, Edgartown (02539). Phone 508/627-4442.* Built in 1843, this is a fine example of Greek Revival architecture. Now a performing arts center with seating for 500.

Vineyard Haven and Edgartown Shopping. *Phone 508/693-0085. www.mvy.com.* Vineyard Haven is where most of Martha's Vineyard's year-round residents live, so its shops are a bit less upscale than those in ritzy Edgartown, where you could spend an afternoon or even an entire day. In both areas, you'll find clothing (both casual and upscale), books, jewelry, home-decorating items, and goodies to eat (fudge, candy, and jams). Vineyard Haven is perhaps best known as the location of the Black Dog General Store (along with the Black Dog Bakery and Black Dog Tavern) that sell T-shirts and other goods bearing the logo of its now-famous black Lab. Edgartown is home to an astounding number of art galleries.

Vineyard Museum. *8 Cooke St, Edgartown (02539). Phone 508/627-4441.* Four buildings dating back to pre-Revolutionary times join together to form the Vineyard Museum. Thomas Cooke House, a historic colonial home, specializes in antiques and folk art; Foster Gallery displays exhibits from the whaling industry; Pease Galleries specializes in Native American exhibits, and Gale Huntington Library is a useful tool for genealogy. A Cape Cod museum wouldn't be complete without displaying a huge Fresnel (lighthouse) lens—view it just outside the front doors. **$**

Woods Hole, Martha's Vineyard & Nantucket Steamship Authority. *Phone 508/477-8600. www.steamshipauthority.com.* Conducts round-trip service to Martha's Vineyard (all year, weather permitting).

The Yard. *Middle Rd, Chilmark (02535). Phone 508/645-9662.* For 30 years, The Yard has hosted dance performances throughout the summer. The theater is intimate, with just 100 seats available, and makes its home in a renovated barn nestled in the Chilmark woods. The Yard also offers community dance classes, and free performances for children and senior citizens. (Mid-Oct-mid-June) **$$$**

Special Events

Martha's Vineyard Windsurfing Challenge. *Joseph Sylvia State Beach, Beach Rd, Oak Bluffs (02557). On Beach Rd between Oak Bluffs and Edgartown. Phone 508/696-8609. www.mvchallenge.com.* Windsurfing (sometimes called sailboarding) is a combination of sailing and surfing: You stand up on a surfboard and guide a sail that's attached to the board. The Martha's Vineyard Windsurf Challenge is an awesome display of some of the best athletes in this sport, which is largely amateur but no less intense than many pro sports. On windy days, the race is especially fun to watch, as windsurfers zoom along the 30 mile-per-hour winds. Mid- to late Sept. **FREE**

Striped Bass & Bluefish Derby. *1A Dock St, Edgartown (02539). Phone 508/693-0085. www.mvderby.com.* Just after midnight on the first day of the Derby, fishing enthusiasts seek out their favorite fishing holes and cast off, hoping to land the big one during the following month. Whenever contestants haul in striped bass, bluefish, bonito, or false albacore, the catch is weighed and measured at Edgartown Harbor. Prizes are awarded daily for the largest fish; a grand prize awaits the contestant who nets the largest fish caught during the tournament. Watching the weighing in at the Harbor is a unique Cape Cod treat. Mid-Sept-mid-Oct.

Limited-Service Hotels

★ ★ **MANSION HOUSE HOTEL & HEALTH CLUB.** *9 Main St, Vineyard Haven (02568). Phone 508/693-2200; toll-free 800/332-4112. www.mvmansionhouse.com.* 32 rooms. Check-in 3 pm, check-out noon. High-speed Internet access. Restaurant, bar. Fitness room. Indoor pool. Business center. **$$**

★ **THE NASHUA HOUSE HOTEL.** *30 Kennebec Ave, Oak Bluffs (02557). Phone 508/693-0043. www.nashuahouse.com.* 16 rooms. Check-in 2 pm, check-out 11 am. **$**

Full-Service Hotels

★ ★ ★ **HARBOR VIEW HOTEL.** *131 N Water St, Edgartown (02539). Phone 508/627-7000; fax 617/742-1042.* Built in 1891, this resort is a prime example of the heritage of Martha's Vineyard. Overlooking Egartown Harbor, guests can relax in a rocking chair on one of the verandas, stroll among the beautifully maintained gardens, enjoy a swim in the heated outdoor pool, or practice their backhand at a game of tennis. 124 rooms, 4 story. Check-out 11 am. Restaurant, bar. Outdoor pool. Tennis. **$**

★ ★ ★ **KELLEY HOUSE.** *23 Kelley St, Edgartown (02539). Phone 508/627-7900; toll-free 800/225-6005; fax 508/627-8142. www.kelley-house.com.* 53 rooms, 3 story. Complimentary continental breakfast. Check-out 11 am. Restaurant. Outdoor pool. **$$**

Full-Service Resorts

★ ★ **ISLAND INN.** *Beach Rd, Oak Bluffs (02557). Phone 508/693-2002; toll-free 800/462-0269; fax 508/693-7911. www.islandinn.com.* 51 rooms, 2 story. Check-out 11 am. Restaurant, bar. Outdoor pool. Tennis. Beach. **$**

★ ★ ★ **THE WINNETU INN & RESORT.** *31 Dunes Rd, Edgartown (02539). Phone 508/627-3663. www.winnetu.com.* 52 rooms. Check-in 3 pm, check-out noon. Restaurant, bar. Children's activity center. Fitness room, fitness classes available. Outdoor pool, whirlpool. **$$**

Full-Service Inns

★ ★ ★ **BEACH PLUM INN.** *50 Beach Plum Ln, Menemsha (02552). Phone 508/645-9454; toll-free 877/ 645-7398; fax 508/645-2801. www.beachpluminn.com.* Built in 1890 from the salvage of a shipwreck, this Martha's Vineyard inn sits on a hilltop overlooking the ocean and boasts one of the island's most well-regarded restaurants. A stone drive and gardenlike path lead to the main house, and several other cottages dot the 7-acre property. 11 rooms, 2 story. Complimentary full breakfast. Check-in 2 pm, check-out 11 am. Restaurant. Tennis. **$$**

★ ★ ★ ★ **CHARLOTTE INN.** *27 S Summer St, Edgartown (02539). Phone 508/627-4751; fax 508/627-6452. www.relaischateaux.com.* The Charlotte Inn extends open arms to guests seeking the quintessential New England experience. This charming inn enjoys a central location among Edgartown's quaint streets and stately sea captains' homes. Convenient to the village, the Charlotte Inn is the perfect place to enjoy the many delights of Martha's Vineyard. A wrought-iron fence stands guard over the manicured grounds of this irresistible colonial inn. Inside, a romantic English country style dominates the public and private rooms. Artwork, antiques, and other decorative objects lend a hand in creating a historical flavor in the bedrooms. Individually designed, some rooms feature luxurious canopy beds. Spread throughout the main house, carriage house, and coach house, the rooms and suites are simply delightful. Light French cuisine enhanced by American and French wine is served in the restaurant, where candlelit dinners are particularly unforgettable. 25 rooms. Children over 14 years only. Restaurant. **$$$**

Specialty Lodgings

The following lodging establishments are approved by Mobil Travel Guide, but due to their unique and individualized nature have not been given a traditional Mobil Star rating. Included in this listing you may find bed-and-breakfasts, limited-service inns, guest ranches, and other unique hotel properties.

THE ARBOR INN. *222 Upper Main St, Edgartown (02539). Phone 508/627-8137; toll-free 888/748-4383. www.mvy.com/arborinn.* 10 rooms, 2 story. Closed Nov-Apr. Children over 12 years only. Complimentary continental breakfast. Check-in 2 pm, check-out 11 am. **$$**

ASHLEY INN. *129 Main St, Edgartown (02539). Phone 508/627-9655; toll-free 800/477-9655; fax 508/ 627-6629.* 10 rooms, 3 story. Children over 12 years only. Complimentary continental breakfast. Check-in 2 pm, check-out 11 am. **$**

COLONIAL INN OF MARTHA'S VINEYARD. *38 N Water St, Edgartown (02539). Phone 508/627-4711; toll-free 800/627-4701; fax 508/627-5904. www.colonialinnmvy.com.* 43 rooms, 4 story. Closed Jan-mid-Apr. Complimentary continental breakfast. Check-out 11 am. Restaurant. **$**

DAGGETT HOUSE. *59 N Water St, Edgartown (02539). Phone 508/627-4600; fax 508/627-4611. www.mvweb.com/daggett.* Restaurant. Open hearth, antiques in dining room, part of a historic tavern (1660). 31 rooms, 2 story. Check-in 3 pm, check-out 11 am. **$$**

DOCKSIDE INN. *Circuit Ave Ext, Oak Bluffs (02557). Phone 508/693-2966; toll-free 800/245-5979; fax 508/ 696-7293. www.vineyard.net/inns.* This gingerbread-style inn overlooks the harbor in the seaside village of Oak Bluffs and is walking distance to many attractions, miles of beaches, and shopping areas. 22 rooms, 3 story. Closed Dec-Mar. Complimentary continental breakfast. Check-in 2-7 pm, check-out 11 am. **$**

THE EDGARTOWN INN. *56 N Water St, Edgartown (02539). Phone 508/627-4794; fax 508/627-9420. www.edgartowninn.com.* Historic (1798) sea captain's home. Inn since 1820; colonial furnishings and antiques in rooms. 12 rooms, 3 story. Closed Nov-Mar. Check-in 2 pm, check-out 11 am. Restaurant. **$**

GREENWOOD HOUSE. *40 Greenwood Ave, Vineyard Haven (02568). Phone 508/693-6150; toll-free 866/693-6150; fax 508/696-8113. www.greenwoodhouse.com.* 5 rooms, 3 story. Complimentary full breakfast. Check-in 2 pm, check-out 10 am. **$$**

THE HANOVER HOUSE. *28 Edgartown Rd, Vineyard Haven (02568). Phone 508/693-1066; toll-free 800/339-1066; fax 508/696-6099. www.hanoverhouseinn.com.* Set on a half acre of land, this cozy bed-and-breakfast is walking distance to the ferry, shopping, restaurants, and the library. Shuttles are available for travel to Edgartown and Oak Bluffs. 15 rooms, 2 story. Complimentary continental breakfast. Check-in 2 pm, check-out 10 am. **$$**

HOB KNOB INN. *128 Main St, Edgartown (02539). Phone 508/627-9510; toll-free 800/696-2723; fax 508/627-4560. www.hobknob.com.* Welcoming guests with a warm country atmosphere and personalized service, this remarkable inn offers timeless tranquility. Charmingly furnished guest rooms, fireplaces that ensnare guests with their warmth, and fine food add to the historic ambience. 16 rooms, 3 story. Complimentary full breakfast. Check-in 2 pm, check-out 11 am. Fitness room. **$$**

LAMBERT'S COVE COUNTRY INN. *Lambert's Cove Rd, Vineyard Haven (02568). Phone 508/693-2298; fax 508/693-7890. www.lambertscoveinn.com.* 15 rooms, 2 story. Complimentary full breakfast. Check-in 2 pm, check-out 11 am. Restaurant (public by reservation). Tennis. **$$**

MARTHA'S PLACE B&B. *114 Main St, Vineyard Haven (02568). Phone 508/693-0253. www.marthas place.com.* This restored Greek Revival mansion built in 1840 offers the perfect location: across from Owen Park Beach overlooking Vineyard Haven Harbor and just one block from the ferry, restaurants, and shops. All guest rooms feature down comforters and Egyptian cotton linens. 7 rooms, 2 story. Complimentary continental breakfast. Check-in noon, check-out 10 am. **$$**

THE OAK HOUSE. *Seaview and Pequot aves, Oak Bluffs (02557). Phone 508/693-4187; fax 508/696-7385. www.vineyard.net/inns.* Opposite beach. 10 rooms, 3 story. Closed mid-Oct-mid-May. Children over 10 years only. Complimentary continental breakfast. Check-in 4 pm, check-out 11 am. **$$**

OUTERMOST INN. *171 Lighthouse Rd, Chilmark (02535). Phone 508/645-3511; fax 508/645-3514. www.outermostinn.com.* Picture windows provide excellent views of Vineyard Sound and Elizabeth Islands. 7 rooms, 2 story. Children over 12 years only.

Complimentary full breakfast. Check-in 2 pm, check-out 11 am. Restaurant. **$$**

PEQUOT HOTEL. *19 Pequot Ave, Oak Bluffs (02557). Phone 508/693-5087; toll-free 800/947-8704; fax 508/696-9413. www.pequothotel.com.* 29 rooms, 3 story. Closed Nov-Apr. Complimentary continental breakfast. Check-in 3 pm, check-out 11 am. **$**

SHIRETOWN INN. *44 N Water St, Edgartown (02539). Phone 508/627-3353; fax 508/627-8478. www.shiretowninn.com.* 18th-century whaling house. 35 rooms, 3 story. Closed mid-Oct-Apr. Complimentary continental breakfast. Check-in 2 pm, check-out 11 am. Restaurant, bar. **$**

THORNCROFT INN. *460 Main St, Vineyard Haven (02568). Phone 508/693-3333; toll-free 800/332-1236; fax 508/693-5419. www.thorncroft.com.* Secluded on a tree-lined, 3-acre peninsula, this charming, white-shuttered home houses romantic guest rooms, some with hot tubs and fireplaces. A full country breakfast can be enjoyed in the dining room or requested for breakfast-in-bed delivery. 14 rooms, 2 story. Complimentary full breakfast. Check-in 3-9 pm, check-out 11 am. **$$$**

Restaurants

★ ★ ★ **ALCHEMY.** *71 Main St, Edgartown (02539). Phone 508/627-9999.* A smart, casual crowd frequents Edgartown's popular Alchemy. This American bistro offers upscale dining in a relaxed setting. The New American menu leans heavily toward seafood, and the dishes are artfully prepared. The happening bar and stylish dining room make this restaurant one of the best places to see and be seen. American menu. Lunch, dinner. Closed three weeks in Jan. Bar. Casual attire. Outdoor seating. **$$$**

★ ★ **THE AQUINNAH SHOP.** *State Rd, Aquinnah (02535). Phone 508/645-3142.* The heavenly smell of freshly baked pies lures diners to The Aquinnah Shop. This casual establishment serves some of the best comfort food around, and many of the dishes seem to come straight from grandma's kitchen. The prices are right at this friendly place, and its fantastic Gay Head Cliffs location makes it an ideal spot to enjoy magnificent sunsets. American menu. Breakfast, lunch, dinner. Closed mid-Oct-Easter. Children's menu. Casual attire. Outdoor seating. **$$**

★ ★ ★ **BALANCE.** *57 Circuit Ave, Oak Bluffs (02557). Phone 508/696-3000.* Balance is the "in" place in Oak Bluffs. This restaurant brings a bit of contemporary splash to Martha's Vineyard, and the flavors that come from the kitchen are as bold as the spirit here. The chef is something of a local celebrity, and his touch of whimsy is evident in his creative dishes. The thriving bar scene attracts fashionable A-listers. American menu. Dinner. Bar. Casual attire. **$$**

★ ★ ★ **BEACH PLUM INN RESTAURANT.** *50 Beach Plum Ln, Menemsha (02552). Phone 508/645-9454.* Every table comes with an ocean view at The Beach Plum Inn Restaurant, making it one of the most romantic places on the island. Seafood accounts for many of the main courses on the regionally influenced menu. A four-course prix fixe menu is offered in addition to à la carte specialties. American menu. Dinner. Closed Jan-early May. Casual attire. Outdoor seating. **$$$**

★ ★ **BLACK DOG TAVERN.** *33 Beach St, Vineyard Haven (02568). Phone 508/693-9223; toll-free 800/626-1991. www.theblackdog.com.* The Black Dog Tavern is a Martha's Vineyard institution, with a highly recognizable Labrador logo to match. Weathered and filled with nautical memorabilia, this restaurant is an old salt's dream, and its location at the Coastwise Wharf on the Vineyard Haven Harbor is one of the island's best. For more than 30 years, this restaurant has been serving up fine food accompanied by amiable service that makes everyone feel like a regular. American menu. Breakfast, lunch, dinner. Casual attire. **$$**

★ ★ **CAFE MOXIE.** *Main and Center sts, Vineyard Haven (02568). Phone 508/693-1484. www.cafemoxie.com.* Cafe Moxie is a Vineyard Haven favorite. The traditional saltbox exterior belies the funky interior, where the works of local artists grace the walls. This bistro-style setting makes for a cozy ambience, while the upscale New American menu pleases the most demanding palates. Open for dinner only, this trendy spot is BYOB, making the check as palatable as the meal. American menu. Dinner. Closed fall-winter. Casual attire. **$$$**

★ ★ ★ **COACH HOUSE.** *131 N Water St, Edgartown (02539). Phone 508/627-7000; fax 508/627-8417. www.harbor-view.com.* Casual refinement is the calling card of the Coach House. This breezily elegant restaurant situated right on Edgartown Harbor is the picture of contemporary coastal living. Large windows let the magnificent ocean views inside, where an up-

dated take on the classics defines the tasteful space. An upscale crowd comes here for modern twists on old standbys at breakfast and lunch, while fresh seafood and shellfish dominate the dinner menu. The wine list is comprehensive, providing the perfect complement to an exceptional meal, and desserts are not to be missed. American menu. Breakfast, lunch, dinner, Sun brunch. Bar. Children's menu. **$$$**

★ **ESPRESSO LOVE CAFE.** *17 Church St, Edgartown (02539). Phone 508/627-9211.* International/Fusion menu. Breakfast, lunch, dinner. Children's menu. Casual attire. Reservations recommended. Outdoor seating. **$$**

★ ★ **HOME PORT.** *512 North Rd, Menemsha (02552). Phone 508/645-2679; fax 508/645-3119.* Calling the quaint fishing village of Menemsha home, the Home Port is just the spot for seafood lovers. This family-friendly restaurant has been grilling, frying, and broiling fish since the 1930s. A fun, nautical-themed interior is filled with fishing nets and other memorabilia. Takeout is available for guests to enjoy on the lawn or the dock fronting the harbor. Seafood menu. Dinner. Closed mid-Oct-mid-Apr. Children's menu. Reservations recommended. **$$$**

★ ★ **JIMMY SEA'S.** *32 Kennebec Ave, Oak Bluffs (02557). Phone 508/696-8550.* Reservations are not accepted at Jimmy Sea's, but islanders and well-versed visitors know to arrive early. This restaurant's garlic-laden seafood dishes and Italian favorites attract a loyal following to the somewhat kitschy yet charming restaurant. Italian menu. Dinner. Casual attire. Outdoor seating. **$$**

★ ★ ★ **L'ETOILE.** *27 S Summer St, Edgartown (02539). Phone 508/627-5187.* The Charlotte Inn (see), one of the island's finest lodgings, is home to the much-heralded L'Etoile. This elegant restaurant speaks to special occasions with its classic French menu and stunning glass-enclosed dining room. The wine list, though pricey, features great selections from Europe and California, and the service is appropriately attentive. French menu. Dinner. Closed Jan. Jacket required. Reservations recommended. **$$$$**

★ **LATTANZI'S PIZZERIA.** *Old Post Office Sq, Edgartown (02539). Phone 508/627-9084.* Pizza takes on a whole new meaning at Lattanzi's. This Edgartown pizzeria makes an art form out of brick-oven pizzas. From the classics, such as pepperoni and mushroom, to the more exotic, including white clams, the toppings add panache to these appealing pies. The entire family can enjoy this relaxed restaurant, where pastas and gelato also tempt diners. Italian, pizza menu. Dinner. Closed Nov. Children's menu. Casual attire. Reservations recommended. Outdoor seating. **$**

★ ★ **LE GRENIER FRENCH RESTAURANT.** *82 Main St, Vineyard Haven (02568). Phone 508/693-4906; fax 508/693-5008. www.legrenierrestaurant.com.* Situated in the heart of Vineyard Haven, Le Grenier has been attracting a loyal following of Francophiles and gourmets for more than 30 years. Diners visit this charming restaurant for its classically French dishes, including such favorites as frogs' legs, steak au poivre, and fondue. The candlelit dining room and casual elegance lure sophisticated diners. French menu. Dinner. **$$$**
🅳

★ **LINDA JEAN'S.** *34 Circuit Ave, Oak Bluffs (02568). Phone 508/693-4093.* Those weary of eclectic fusion cuisine head over to Linda Jean's. This traditional diner offers an antidote to the overpriced restaurant with heaping portions of good food at a great price. Breakfast is served throughout the day at this no-frills establishment, adored by locals for its laid-back attitude. American menu. Breakfast, lunch, dinner. Children's menu. Casual attire. Outdoor seating. **$**

★ ★ **LOLA'S SOUTHERN SEAFOOD.** *Beach Rd, Oak Bluffs (02557). Phone 508/693-5007; fax 508/696-6071. www.lolassouthernseafood.com.* Lola's Southern Seafood promises a rollicking good time. Leave the calorie counters at home when tucking in to this restaurant's heaping portions of zesty, Cajun-spiced seafood and signature dishes, including jambalaya. Entertainment is an integral part of the experience here, from the nightly dance parties to the gospel Sunday brunch. American, seafood menu. Lunch, dinner, late-night, Sun brunch. Closed Tues-Wed. Bar. Casual attire. **$$**

★ **LOOKOUT TAVERN.** *8 Seaview Ave, Oak Bluffs (02557). Phone 508/696-9844.* On the water across from the Steamship Terminal, the Lookout Tavern lives up to its name. Complementing the views is a full seafood menu, including a raw bar, clam bar, steamers, lobster, and sushi. Seafood menu. Lunch, dinner. Closed Nov-Apr. Bar. Casual attire. Outdoor seating. **$$**

★ ★ **LURE.** *31 Dunes Rd, Edgartown (02539). Phone 508/627-3663; fax 508/627-4749. www.winnetu.com.* Executive chef Ed Gannon came to the Winnetu Inn

from Aujourd'hui, the Four Seasons Hotel Boston's anchor restaurant, so he knows a thing or two about fine dining. Befitting its location, the menu at Lure focuses on simple but flavorful preparations of fresh seafood, including raw bar items. If you wish, hop on the complimentary sunset water taxi from Edgartown and take a few minutes to stroll through the historic Vineyard Art Gallery before or after your meal. Seafood menu. Dinner. Closed Dec-mid-Apr. **$$$**

★ ★ **THE NAVIGATOR.** *2 Lower Main St, Edgartown (02539). Phone 508/627-4320; fax 508/627-3544.* Guests in search of the taste and feel of authentic New England sail over to The Navigator. Situated right on Edgartown Harbor, this nautical-themed restaurant pays tribute to the island's whaling history in its décor. Seafood is the major draw here, with lobster and the much-loved quahog chowder among the many selections. Live entertainment on the weekends adds to the upbeat atmosphere. Seafood menu. Lunch, dinner. Closed mid-Oct-mid-May. Bar. Children's menu. Outdoor seating. **$$$**

★ ★ ★ **OUTERMOST INN.** *Lighthouse Rd, Aquinnah (02535). Phone 508/645-3511. www.outermostinn.com.* From its serene clifftop location with picture-perfect ocean views to its relaxed elegance, the Outermost Inn is like a breath of fresh air. This refined bed-and-breakfast's restaurant is open to the public for dinner only, and reservations are a must. Fresh herbs and vegetables grown on the property influence the creative prix fixe menu. If you enjoy wine with dinner, plan to buy a bottle ahead of time, as the inn is strictly BYOB. American menu. Dinner. Closed Mon-Tues; also mid-May-Columbus Day. Reservations recommended. **$$$**

★ ★ **SEASONS EATERY.** *19 Circuit Ave, Oak Bluffs (02568). Phone 508/693-7129.* Vacationers beat a path to Seasons Eatery. This casual restaurant in Oak Bluffs turns out consistently good American pub food in a casual setting. The bar offers a large selection of microbrewed beers, and the Eatery's juicy burgers and delicious sandwiches win praise. Live acoustic music is played here most summer nights, providing terrific entertainment. American menu. Lunch, dinner. Bar. Children's menu. Casual attire. **$**

★ ★ **SQUARE RIGGER.** *225 State Rd, Edgartown (02539). Phone 508/627-9968; fax 508/627-4837.* Tucked inside a historic whaling captain's home, Square Rigger epitomizes New England charm. This traditional seafood restaurant is adored by locals and visitors alike for its tempting preparations of fresh seafood. Grilled selections and broiled specialties are well liked, and lobster is prepared in a variety of tantalizing ways. Seafood menu. Dinner. Bar. Children's menu. **$$**

★ ★ **SWEET LIFE CAFE.** *63 Circuit Ave, Oak Bluffs (02557). Phone 508/696-0200.* The Sweet Life Cafe offers its guests a taste of the good life. This refined restaurant, located within a quaint Victorian house, delights diners with its innovative takes on regional seafood. Those who prefer a more formal setting choose the antique-filled dining room, while the candlelit garden is an elegantly casual and romantic alternative. Seafood menu. Dinner. Closed Jan-Mar. Reservations recommended. Outdoor seating. **$$**

★ ★ **THEO'S AT THE INN AT BLUEBERRY HILL.** *74 North Rd, Chilmark (02535). Phone 508/645-3322; toll-free 800/356-3322; fax 508/645-3799. www.blueberryinn.com.* Theo's at the Inn at Blueberry Hill offers diners a perfect blend of health conscious, yet surprisingly indulgent, cuisine. The chef's loyalty to the island's many farms comes shining through in the innovative menu, which changes daily based on the freshest available ingredients. The bucolic setting on more than 50 acres of former farmland is certainly worth the drive. American menu. Dinner. Casual attire. **$$**

★ ★ **THE WHARF PUB & RESTAURANT.** *Lower Main St, Edgartown (02539). Phone 508/627-9966.* Across from the harbor in Edgartown, The Wharf Pub & Restaurant goes beyond typical pub fare to include a host of favorite dishes. From burgers, sandwiches, and chowder to fish and chips, lobster rolls, and fried clams, this likable restaurant has something for everyone. More sophisticated fare includes steaks and pasta, and while the selection is large, the price is right. Seafood menu. Lunch, dinner. Closed Thanksgiving, Dec 24-25. Bar. Children's menu. **$$**

Nantucket Island (E-9)

See also Hyannis and Barnstable, Martha's Vineyard

Settled 1659
Population 6,012
Elevation 0-108 ft
Area Code 508
Zip 02554
Information Chamber of Commerce, 48 Main St; phone 508/228-1700. General information may also be obtained at the Information Bureau, 25 Federal St;

phone 508/228-1700.
Web Site www.nantucketchamber.org

Nantucket is not just an island; it is an experience. Nantucket Island is at once a popular resort and a living museum. Siasconset (SCON-set) and Nantucket Town remain quiet and charming despite heavy tourism. With 49 square miles of lovely beaches and green moors inland, Nantucket is south of Cape Cod, 30 miles at sea. The island was the world's greatest whaling port from the late 17th century until New Bedford became dominant in the early 1800s. Whaling prosperity built the towns; tourism maintains them.

There is regular car ferry and passenger service from Hyannis. If you plan to take your car, make an advance reservation with the Woods Hole, Martha's Vineyard & Nantucket Steamship Authority, PO Box 284, Woods Hole 02543; phone 508/477-8600. Keep in mind, though, that traffic has become severe. Bicycles and public transportation may be better alternatives.

What to See and Do

Actors Theatre of Nantucket. *2 Centre St, Nantucket (02554). Phone 508/228-6325. www.nantucket theatre.com.* The Actors Theatre of Nantucket has staged comedies, dramas, plays, and dance concerts since 1985. Both professionals and amateurs make up the company, which offers between six and ten performances during the summer. When purchasing tickets, ask whether family matinees are offered for that performance. **$$$$**

Altar Rock. *Off Polpis Rd, Nantucket (02554). To the S on unmarked dirt road.* Climb up Altar Rock, which rises 90 feet above sea level, and you're afforded stunning views of Nantucket and the surrounding Cape. Go at dawn or dusk for the best views. The Moors surrounding Altar Rock offer a chance to hike on the trails or two-track dirt roads. Few tourists make the trek, which makes for unexpected solitude on Nantucket.

Barrett's Tours. *Phone 508/228-0174.* Offers 1 1/2-hour bus and van tours (Apr-Nov).

Bartlett's Ocean View Farm. *33 Bartlett Farm Rd, Nantucket (02584). Phone 508/228-9403. www. bartlettsoceanviewfarm.com.* Nurturing Nantucket's largest farm, the Bartlett family has tilled this land for nearly 200 years. Stop by for fresh vegetables, milk, eggs, cheese, freshly baked bread, and cut flowers. If you're looking for prepared dishes, taste the farm kitchen's salads, entrées (including several that are vegetarian), pies, snacks, jams, chutneys, and other farm delights. Also visit the East Coast Seafood market, less than a mile away, for fresh fish and seafood to complete your meal. (Daily 8 am-6 pm)

Bass Hole Boardwalk and Gray's Beach. *End of Centre St, Nantucket (02675). Take Route 6A to Church St. Bear left onto Centre St and follow to the end.* This honest-to-goodness elevated boardwalk—stretching 860 feet—offers delightful scenery as it meanders through one of Cape Cod's finest marshes to the beach. Kids enjoy playing on the beach or adjoining playground; the whole family can walk the beach and into the bay at low tide.

Boat trips. Hyannis-Nantucket Day Round-Trip. *22 Channel Point Rd, Nantucket (02601). Phone 508/778-2600.* Summer passenger service from Hyannis. **$$$$**

Cisco Brewers. *5 Bartlett Farm Rd, Nantucket (02584). Phone 508/325-5929. www.ciscobrewers.com.* If you enjoy beer, visit Cisco Brewers and taste the delicious locally made brews. From Whale's Tales Pale Ale and Bailey's Ale to Moor Porter, Cap'n Swain's Extra Stout, Summer of Lager, and Baggywrinkle Barleywine, just about every variety of beer is represented at Cisco. Stop by for the daily guided tour ($10; times vary) that includes a walk through the brewery (including taste testing), as well as a tour of the Triple Eight Distillery and Nantucket Vineyard next door. Allow 1 1/2 hours for the entire tour. (Summer: Mon-Sat 10 am-6 pm; fall-spring: Sat 10 am-5 pm) **FREE**

Claire Murray. *11 S Water St, Nantucket (02554). Phone 508/228-1913. www.clairemurray.com.* Even if you've seen Claire Murray's delightful rug designs elsewhere in the country, visit the store where she got her start. Nantucket winters don't bring many visitors, and Claire Murray, who used to run a bed-and-breakfast, started hooking rugs to pass the time during these months. She soon began designing and selling rugs full-time around the world. Today, her store in Nantucket sells both finished rugs and kits and also offers classes. Around the Cape, look for other locations in West Barnstable, Osterville, Mashpee, and Edgartown (on Martha's Vineyard). (Mon-Sat 10 am-9 pm, Sun 11 am-7 pm)

★ **Endeavor Sailing Adventures.** *Straight Wharf, Nantucket (02554). Phone 508/228-5585. www.endeavorsailing.com.* US Coast Guard Captain James Genthner built his sloop, named the *Endeavor*, and has been sailing it for over 20 years. Take a 90-minute sail around Nantucket Sound and let the good captain and his wife, Sue, acquaint you with Nantucket's sights, sounds, and history. No sailing experience is necessary, and you can bring a picnic lunch. A special one-hour kids' tour sails at 11:30 am daily. (May-Oct; closed Nov-Apr) **$$$$**

First Congregational Church & View. *62 Centre St, Nantucket (02554). Phone 508/228-0950.* Also called Old North Church, the First Congregational Church offers Nantucket's best view of the island and surrounding ocean. Climb 94 steps to the 120-foot-tall steeple, and you're amply rewarded with a view from the top of the world. While you're at the church, take in the historical display that shows photos of the church as it has looked throughout its long history. (Mon-Sat, mid-June-mid-Oct) **$**

Gail's Tours. *Tours depart from Information Center at Federal and Broad sts. Phone 508/257-6557.* Narrated van tours (approximately 1 3/4 hours) of area. Three tours daily. Reservations recommended.

Jetties Beach. *Bathing Beach Rd, Nantucket (02554). Take North Beach Rd to Bathing Beach Rd; from there, take a shuttle bus (mid-June-Labor Day), walk, or bike, the distance (just over a mile) to the beach.* You won't find better amenities for families with kids than Jetties Beach. Besides the convenient rest rooms, showers, changing rooms, and snack bar, the beach employs life guards, offers chairs for rent, provides a well-equipped playground, maintains volleyball and tennis courts, and offers a skateboarding park. You can also rent kayaks, sailboards, and sailboats through Nantucket Community Sailing (phone 508/228-5358), which maintains an office at the beach. Look for occasional concerts and a July 4 fireworks display. (Daily)

The Lifesaving Museum. *158 Polpis Rd, Nantucket (02554). Phone 508/228-1885. www.nantucketlifesavingmuseum.com.* The building that houses the museum is a recreation of the original 1874 lifesaving station that was built to assist mariners from the oft-times deadly seas. Museum exhibits include lifesaving surfboats, large and intricate lighthouse lenses, historical objects from the *Andrea Doria* (which sank off the coast of Nantucket Island), demonstrations, stories of rescues, and action photos. **$**

Loines Observatory. *59 Milk St, Nantucket (02554). Phone 508/228-8690. www.mmo.org.* Part of the Maria Mitchell Association (MMA)—named for the first professional female astronomer—the Loines Observatory gives you a chance to peek through a fine old telescope and view the magnificent, star-filled Cape Cod skies. Also visit the MMA's other observatory on Vestal Street, which includes an outdoor true-to-scale model of the solar system, an astronomy exhibit, and a sundial. Kids may prefer the attractions at The Vestal Street Observatory, which is noted for its work with young scientists. (Mon, Wed, Fri evenings in summer, Sat evenings year-round; closed Tues, Thurs, Sun in summer, Sun-Fri year-round) **$$**

⭐ **Main Street.** Phone 508/228-1894. www.nantucket.com. Paved with cobblestones, lined with elegant houses built by whaling merchants, and shaded by great elms, this is one of New England's most beautiful streets. The Nantucket Historical Association maintains the following attractions (June-Oct: daily; spring and fall: limited hours).

1800 House. Mill and Pleasant sts, Nantucket Island (02554). Phone 508/228-1894. Home of the sheriff, early 19th century. Period home and furnishings; large, round cellar; kitchen garden.

Folger-Franklin Seat & Memorial Boulder. Nantucket Island (02554). Madaket Rd, 1 mile from W end of Main St. Birthplace site of Abiah Folger, mother of Benjamin Franklin.

Hadwen House. Main and Pleasant sts, Nantucket Island (02554). (1845) Greek Revival mansion; furnishings of whaling period; gardens. **$$**

⭐ **Jethro Coffin House (Oldest House).** 16 Sunset Hill Ln, Nantucket Island (02554). N on North Water to West Chester, left to Sunset Hill. Phone 508/228-1894. Built in 1686, Oldest House is, true to its name, one of the oldest houses you'll ever visit in the United States, and the oldest on Nantucket. The house was a wedding present given to the children of two feuding families (the Gardners and the Coffins) by their in-laws, who reconciled after the happy event. In 1987, after lightning struck Oldest House, it was fully restored to its original beauty. This colonial saltbox and its spare furnishings exude classic Nantucket style and charm. (Seasonal; call for dates and times) **$**

Museum of Nantucket History (Macy Warehouse). 2 Whalers Ln, Nantucket Island (02554). Straight Wharf. Phone 508/228-1894. Exhibits related to Nantucket history; diorama; craft demonstrations. **$$**

Old Fire Hose Cart House. Gardner and Main sts, Nantucket Island (02554). (1886) Old-time fire-fighting equipment. **FREE**

Old Gaol. Vestal St, Nantucket Island (02554). Phone 508/228-1894. (1805) Unusual two-story construction; used until 1933. **FREE**

Old Mill. South Mill and Prospect sts, Nantucket (02554). Phone 508/228-1894. This Dutch-style windmill is impressive in its beauty and sheer size (50 feet high), but it was built for function—to grind grain brought by local farmers—and it remains functional today. Believed to be the oldest windmill in the United States, it was built in 1746 with salvaged oak that washed up on shore from shipwrecks and after many owners, eventually came to belong to the Nantucket Historical Society. (June-Aug, daily; call for off-season hours) **$**

Research Center. Broad St, Nantucket (02554). Next to Whaling Museum. Phone 508/228-1655. Ships' logs, diaries, charts, and Nantucket photographs; library. (Mon-Fri)

Whaling Museum. 12 Broad St, Nantucket Island (02554). Near Steamboat Wharf. Phone 508/228-1736. Outstanding collection of relics from whaling days; whale skeleton, tryworks, scrimshaw, candle press. **$$**

Miacomet Golf Course. 12 W Miacomet Rd, Nantucket (02554). Phone 508/228-9764. Nantucket's only public golf course offers nine holes—including two par-five holes—that you can play twice for a par-74 round. Winds off the ocean make for interesting play. Reserve a tee time at least a week in advance; your chances of playing without a reservation are zero during the summer. (Daily) **$$$$**

Murray's Toggery. 62 Main St, Nantucket (02554). Phone 508/228-0437. www.nantucketreds.com. Murray's Toggery was the first store in Nantucket to sell Nantucket Reds—casual red pants that eventually fade to a decidedly pink hue—a product that defines both Cape Cod and the preppy look. Murray's also sells oxford shirts, sweaters, shoes, hats, coats, and jackets for both men and women. (Mon-Sat 9 am-7 pm, Sun 10 am-6 pm; winter: Mon-Sat 9 am-5 pm; closed Sun in winter)

Nantucket Gourmet. 4 India St, Nantucket (02554). Phone 508/228-4353. www.nantucketgourmet.com. Nantucket Gourmet offers a well-balanced blend of cookware and other culinary tools, and condiments to take back home with you (including marmalades, jams, mustards, and vinegars), and ready-to-eat deli foods for your lunch on the island. You'll find great gifts for any food-lover. (Summer: daily 10 am-6 pm; winter: Mon-Fri 10 am-4 pm; closed holidays)

Nantucket Maria Mitchell Association. *1 Vestal St, Nantucket Island (02554). Phone 508/228-9198.* The birthplace of the first American woman astronomer; memorial observatory (1908). The scientific library has Nantucket historical documents, science journals, and Mitchell family memorabilia. Natural science museum with local wildlife. Aquarium is at 28 Washington Street. Combination ticket available for museum, birthplace, and aquarium. (Mid-June-Aug, Tues-Sat; library also open rest of year, Wed-Sat; closed July 4, Labor Day) **$$**

Nantucket Town. *The areas between Main, Broad, and Centre sts. Phone 508/228-1700. www.nantucket chamber.org/directory/merchants.* Nantucket Town is a shopper's dream, with narrow cobblestone streets that wind past hundreds of shops. You'll find items for your home (furniture, rugs, throws and blankets, baskets, prints, soaps, and so on), your boat (including all manner of weather-predicting equipment), and yourself (from preppy and upscale clothing, hats, shawls, jewelry, and everything in between). In about 20 stores, you'll find the famous Nantucket baskets (also called lightship baskets), which are handmade through a time-consuming process. You'll also come across numerous art galleries, antiques shops, and craft stores.

Nantucket Whaling Museum. *13 Broad St, Nantucket (02554). Phone 508/228-1894. www.nha.org.* To really understand Nantucket, you have to understand whaling, the industry that put Nantucket on the map. The Nantucket Whaling Museum—housed in a former factory that produced candles from whale oil—shows you a fully rigged whale boat (smaller than you may think), rope and basket collections, scrimshaw (whalebone carving) exhibits, a huge lighthouse Fresnel lens, a skeleton of a finback whale, and maritime folk art. Enjoy one of three daily lectures offered by the museum staff. Visit in December to see the Festival of Trees, which includes 50 decorated Christmas trees. **$$**

Rafael Osona Auctions. *21 Washington St, Nantucket (02554). At the American Legion Hall. Phone 508/228-3942.* If you like antiques, you'll love Rafael Osona. The auctioneers host estate auctions on selected weekends (call for exact dates and times) that feature treasured pieces from both the United States and Europe.

If an auction isn't planned while you're in town, visit the two dozen other antique stores on the island, plus many more around Cape Cod. (Late May-early Dec)

Siasconset Village. *E end of Nantucket Island.* The Siasconset Village lies 7 miles from Nantucket Town, and can be traveled by bicycle or shuttle bus. This 18th-century fishing village features quaint cottages, grand mansions, restaurants, a few shops, and a summer cinema. Visit Siasconset Beach and the paved biking path that meanders through the area.

Something Natural. *50 Cliff Rd, Nantucket (02554). Phone 508/228-0504. www.somethingnatural.com.* If you're looking for a casual breakfast or lunch—perhaps even one to take with you on a bike ride or island hike—check out Something Natural for healthy sandwiches, breads and bagels, salads, cookies, and beverages. The eatery has also established a second location at 6 Oak Street (phone 508/228-6616). (May-Oct)

The Straight Wharf. *Straight Wharf, Nantucket (02554). On the harbor, next to the ferry.* Built in 1723, the Straight Wharf is Nantucket's launching area for sailboats, sloops, and kayaks, but it's also a great shopping and eating area. Loaded with restaurants and quaint one-room cottage shops selling island fare, the wharf also features an art gallery, a museum, and an outdoor concert pavilion.

Strong Wings Summer Camp. *PO Box 2884, Nantucket (02584). Phone 508/228-1769. www.strongwings.org.* Open for just one month every year, the Strong Wings Summer Camp offers more excitement and activity for kids than you're likely to find anywhere else on the Cape. Kids ages 5 to 15 attend three-day or five-day sessions, where they explore the natural attributes of the area, mountain bike, hike, kayak, snorkel, rock climb, and boogie board (as appropriate for each age group). Older kids even learn search-and-rescue techniques. (Late June-late Aug, daily) **$$$$**

The Sunken Ship. *12 Broad St, Nantucket (02554). Phone 508/228-9226. www.sunkenship.com.* The Sunken Ship is a full-service dive shop that offers lessons and rentals. When the *Andrea Doria* sank off the coast of Nantucket in the middle of the last century, the area invited divers from around the world to investigate the sunken ship, hence the name of this shop. The general store offers an eclectic array of dive and maritime goods. (Daily; call for closures) **$$$$**

Windswept Cranberry Bog. *Polpis Rd, Siasconset (02554).* Cranberries are an important industry to

Nantucket; in town, you can purchase jars of cranberry honey, and Northland Cranberries harvests berries from Nantucket to make its well-known juices. To see how cranberries are grown and harvested, visit this 200-acre cranberry bog during the fall harvest (late September through October from dawn to dusk), when bogs are flooded so that machines can shake off and scoop up the individual berries. (Mid-October also brings the Nantucket Cranberry Festival.) Even at other times of year, the bog is peaceful and beautiful—a good place to walk and bike and spend half a day. Another nearby cranberry bog is the **Milestone Bog** (off Milestone Rd west of Siasconset). (Daily dawn-dusk)

Special Events

Christmas Stroll. *Phone 508/228-1700.* First weekend in Dec.

Daffodil Festival. *Siasconset Village, Nantucket Island (02564). Phone 508/228-1700. www.nantucket.net/ daffy.* The Daffodil Festival celebrates the budding of millions of daffodils on the main roads of Nantucket. A parade of antique car classics kicks off the well-attended event, which also includes open houses, garden tours, and a lively picnic that offers great food and live entertainment. Late Apr. **FREE**

Harborfest. *Phone 508/228-1700.* Early June.

Nantucket Arts Festival. *Various venues. Phone 508/325-8588.* This week-long festival celebrates a full range of arts on the island: films, poetry and fiction readings, acting, dance performances, and exhibits of paintings, photography, and many other art forms. Look for the wet-paint sale in which you can bid on works completed just that day by local artists. Early Oct. **FREE**

Nantucket County Fair. *Tom Nevers Navy Base, Nantucket (02554). Phone 508/325-4748.* Looking for an old-fashioned county fair? Head to Nantucket for down-home family fun and entertainment. At the Nantucket County Fair, an event that began over 150 years ago, you'll find pies, breads, pastries, jams, jellies, fresh fall fruits, and concessions of all types. You'll also see and experience tractor displays and rides, a petting zoo and pet show, a flea market, quilt displays and sales, hay rides, concerts, and square dancing. Third weekend in Sept. **$$**

Nantucket Film Festival. *Various venues. Phone 508/ 228-6648. www.nantucketfilmfestival.org.* Like other film festivals worldwide, Nantucket's festival screens new independent films that may not otherwise garner attention. You'll be joined by screenwriters, actors, film connoisseurs and, occasionally, big-name celebrities at the festival's seminars, readings, and discussions. A daily event called Morning Coffee showcases a panel of directors, screenwriters, and actors participating in Q&A with festival-goers, who sip coffee and munch on muffins. Mid-June. **$$$$**

Nantucket Wine Festival. *Phone 508/228-1128. www. nantucketwinefestival.com.* This is a wine festival like no other: take in a wine symposium, a variety of food and wine seminars, a wine auction, and many other events. The Great Wine in Grand Houses event allows you to visit a private mansion, sip fine wines drawn from nearly 100 wineries, and dine on food prepared by some of the world's finest chefs. Reservations are required and should be made as soon as you know you'll be visiting the island. Mid-May. **$$$$**

Sand Castle Contest. *Phone 508/228-1700.* Third Sat in Aug.

Limited-Service Hotels

★ ★ **THE BEACHSIDE AT NANTUCKET.** *30 N Beach St, Nantucket (02554). Phone 508/228-2241; toll-free 800/322-4433; fax 508/228-8901. www.thebeachside.com.* 93 rooms. Closed Nov-Apr. Complimentary continental breakfast. Check-in 3 pm, check-out noon. Restaurant, bar. Outdoor pool. **$**

★ ★ **CLIFFSIDE BEACH CLUB.** *46 Jefferson Ave, Nantucket (02554). Phone 508/228-0618; fax 508/325-4735. www.cliffsidebeach.com.* 27 rooms, all suites. Closed Nov-Apr. Check-in 3 pm, check-out noon. Restaurant, bar. Beach. **$$**

★ ★ **HARBOR HOUSE VILLAGE.** *S Beach St, Nantucket Island (02554). Phone 508/325-1000; toll-free 866/325-9300; fax 508/228-7639. www.nantucketislandre sorts.com.* 104 rooms, 3 story. Check-in 3 pm, check-out 11 am. Restaurant, bar. Outdoor pool. Beach. **$**

★ ★ **NANTUCKET INN.** *27 Macy's Ln, Nantucket (02554). Phone 508/228-6900; toll-free 800/321-8484; fax 508/228-9861. www.nantucketinn.net.* 100 rooms, 2 story. Closed Dec-mid-Apr. Pets accepted; fee. Check-in 3 pm, check-out noon. Restaurant, bar. Fitness room. Indoor pool, outdoor pool, whirlpool. Airport transportation available. **$**

Full-Service Hotel

★ ★ ★ **WHITE ELEPHANT RESORT.** *50 Easton St, Nantucket (02554). Phone 508/228-2500; toll-free 800/475-2637; fax 508/325-1195. www.whiteelephant resort.com.* Step back in time for a game of croquet on a sweeping, manicured lawn at this harborfront resort. 63 rooms, 3 story. Closed Nov-Mar. Check-in 3 pm, check-out 11 am. Restaurant, bar. **$$$**

Full-Service Inns

★ ★ ★ **JARED COFFIN HOUSE.** *29 Broad St, Nantucket (02554). Phone 508/228-2400; fax 508/228-8549. www.jaredcoffinhouse.com.* Historical objets d'art. Restored 1845 mansion. 60 rooms, 3 story. Check-in after 3 pm, check-out 11 am. Restaurant, bar. **$**

★ ★ ★ ★ **THE WAUWINET.** *120 Wauwinet Rd, Nantucket Island (02584). Phone 508/228-0145; toll-free 800/426-8718; fax 508/228-6712. www. wauwinet.com.* Nearly 30 miles out to sea, the idyllic island of Nantucket is a place where crashing waves wash away everyday cares. The Wauwinet embodies the perfect getaway on this magical island. Tucked away on a private stretch of beach, The Wauwinet leads its guests to believe that they have been marooned on a remote island, yet this delightful hotel remains close to the town's charming cobblestone streets, a complimentary jitney ride away. Built in 1876 by ship captains, The Wauwinet's rooms and suites have a sophisticated country style blended with the services of a posh resort. Private beaches fronting the harbor and the Atlantic Ocean are spectacular, and clay tennis courts challenge guests to a match. Whether diners choose to arrive by foot or by sunset cruise on the 26-foot *Wauwinet Lady,* Topper's restaurant (see) promises to be an exceptional event. With a 20,000-bottle wine cellar and an impressive menu, it is an epicurean's delight. 36 rooms, 3 story. Closed Nov-early May. Complimentary full breakfast. Check-in 4 pm, check-out 11 am. Restaurant. Tennis. **$$$$**
🏃

Specialty Lodgings

The following lodging establishments are approved by Mobil Travel Guide, but due to their unique and individualized nature have not been given a traditional Mobil Star rating. Included in this listing you may find bed-and-breakfasts, limited-service inns, guest ranches, and other unique hotel properties.

CARLISLE HOUSE INN. *26 N Water St, Nantucket (02554). Phone 508/228-0720; fax 781/639-1004. www.carlislehouse.com.* Restored whaling captain's house (1765). 17 rooms, 3 story. Closed early Dec-Mar. Children over 10 years only. Complimentary continental breakfast. Check-in 2 pm, check-out 11 am. **$**
🉐

CENTERBOARD GUEST HOUSE. *8 Chester St, Nantucket (02554). Phone 508/228-9696. www. nantucket.net/lodging/centerboard.* Restored Victorian residence (1885). 8 rooms, 3 story. Closed Jan-Feb. Complimentary continental breakfast. Check-in 3 pm, check-out 11 am. **$**
🉐

CENTRE STREET INN. *78 Centre St, Nantucket (02554). Phone 508/228-0199; toll-free 800/298-0199; fax 508/228-8676. www.centrestreetinn.com.* Colonial house built in 1742; some antiques. 14 rooms, 3 story. Closed Jan-Apr. Children over 8 years only. Complimentary continental breakfast. Check-in 3 pm, check-out 11 am. **$**
🉐

COBBLESTONE INN. *5 Ash St, Nantucket (02554). Phone 508/228-1987; fax 508/228-6698.* Built in 1725. 5 rooms, 3 story. Closed Jan-Mar. Complimentary full breakfast. Check-in 2 pm, check-out 11 am. **$**
🉐

MARTIN HOUSE INN. *61 Centre St, Nantucket (02554). Phone 508/228-0678. www.martinhouse inn.net.* Built in 1803. 13 rooms, 3 story. Closed Jan-Feb. Complimentary continental breakfast. Check-in 3 pm, check-out 11 am. Restaurant. **$**
🉐

ROBERTS HOUSE INN. *11 India St, Nantucket (02554). Phone 508/228-0600; toll-free 800/872-6830; fax 508/325-4046. www.robertshouseinn.com.* Built in 1846; established in 1883. 45 rooms, 3 story. Complimentary continental breakfast. Check-in 2 pm, check-out 11 am. **$**

SEVEN SEA STREET INN. *7 Sea St, Nantucket (02554). Phone 508/228-3577; fax 508/228-3578. www.sevenseastreetinn.com.* View of Nantucket Harbor. 11 rooms, 2 story. Children over 5 years only. Complimentary continental breakfast. Check-in 3 pm, check-out 11 am. Whirlpool. **$$**
🉐

SHERBURNE INN. *10 Gay St, Nantucket (02554). Phone 508/228-4425; toll-free 888/577-4425; fax 508/228-8114. www.nantucket.net/lodging/sherburne.* Built in 1835 as a silk factory; period antiques, fireplaced parlors. 8 rooms, 3 story. Children over 6 years only. Complimentary continental breakfast. Check-in 2 pm, check-out 11 am. **$**
🈁

SHIPS INN. *13 Fair St, Nantucket (02554). Phone 508/228-0040; fax 508/228-6254. www.nantucket.net/lodging/shipsinn.net.* Built in 1831 by a sea captain; many original furnishings. 12 rooms, 4 story. Closed Nov-Apr. Complimentary continental breakfast. Check-in 2 pm, check-out 10 am. Restaurant, bar. **$$**
🈁

TUCKERNUCK INN. *60 Union St, Nantucket (02554). Phone 508/228-4886; toll-free 800/228-4886; fax 508/228-4890. www.tuckernuckinn.com.* 20 rooms, 2 story. Check-in 3 pm, check-out 11 am. Restaurant. **$**
🈁

🔍 **VANESSA NOEL HOTEL.** *5 Chestnut St, Nantucket (02554). Phone 508/228-5300. www.vanno.com.* 8 rooms, 3 story. Complimentary continental breakfast. Check-in 1 pm, check-out 11 am. High-speed Internet access. Bar. **$$$**

Restaurants

★ ★ ★ **21 FEDERAL.** *21 Federal St, Nantucket (02554). Phone 508/228-2121; fax 508/228-2962.* Tucked inside a handsome Greek Revival building dating to the mid-1800s, 21 Federal offers diners a rare blend of historic charm and contemporary panache. This stylishly clubby spot is a favorite haunt of the island's beautiful people, both for its delectable New American cuisine and its convivial spirit. The well-rounded menu is sure to please epicureans with its wide selection of meat, poultry, and seafood, while the award-winning wine list and fantastic wines available by the glass delight oenophiles. American menu. Dinner. Closed Jan-Mar. Bar. Outdoor seating. **$$$**

🔍 ★ ★ ★ **AMERICAN SEASONS.** *80 Center St, Nantucket (02554). Phone 508/228-7111; fax 508/325-0779. www.americanseasons.com.* Located on a quiet residential street just a few blocks from the center of town, American Seasons invites guests to embark on a culinary journey across the United States. Patrons dine on sophisticated renditions of regional specialties from New England, Down South, the Wild West, or the Pacific Coast at this unique restaurant where location is the theme. From the charming country décor filled with quaint folk art to the romantic candlelit dining room and patio, the setting is as memorable as the meal. American menu. Dinner. Closed Jan-mid-Apr. Bar. Outdoor seating. **$$$**

★ **ATLANTIC CAFE.** *15 S Water St, Nantucket (02554). Phone 508/228-0570; fax 508/228-8787. www.atlanticcafe.com.* Diners with hearty appetites flock to Atlantic Cafe, where the promise of a rollicking good time and a filling, pub-style meal attracts families and singles alike. Nantucket's nautical history is proudly commemorated here, with ship wheels, harpoons, and boats lining the walls. This popular establishment offers exceptional value with affordable prices, and the large wraparound bar has been the preferred watering hole of locals for decades. American, seafood menu. Lunch, dinner, late-night. Closed late Dec-early Jan. Bar. Children's menu. **$**

🔍 ★ ★ **BLACK EYED SUSAN'S.** *10 India St, Nantucket (02554). Phone 508/325-0308.* Black Eyed Susan's is a funky foodie's dream. This tiny café with just under ten tables lures diners with a penchant for the unusual. Space is tight, but the counter provides front-row seats to the action of the open kitchen. Thai, Mexican, and other international flavors punctuate the fusion menu. Breakfast is especially eye-opening, with traditional dishes taking on exotic bents, and dinner reservations here are truly coveted. Be sure to pick up a bottle of your favorite wine on the way, since this is a BYOB restaurant. International/Fusion menu. Breakfast, dinner. Closed Sun; also Nov-Apr. Casual attire. Reservations recommended. Outdoor seating. No credit cards accepted. **$$**
🈁

★ ★ ★ **BOARDING HOUSE.** *12 Federal St, Nantucket (02554). Phone 508/228-9622; fax 508/325-7109. www.boardinghouse-pearl.com.* Long waits are par for the course at the Boarding House, but this smart restaurant's nouveau cuisine and sexy, youthful scene make it worth the wait. Nestled on a corner in the heart of town, this restaurant enjoys one of the island's most enviable locations. Those in the know book a table outdoors to enjoy people-watching and stargazing, while others seek the excitement of the bustling bar or the intimate setting of the dimly lit downstairs. Seafood and beef serve as the main inspirations behind the creative Asian-influenced menu, and a comprehensive wine list ensures a perfect pairing. American menu. Dinner. Bar. Reservations recommended. Outdoor seating. **$$$** ♿

★ **CAMBRIDGE STREET RESTAURANT.** *12 Cambridge St, Nantucket (02554). Phone 508/228-7109.* For a finger-licking good time, head over to Cambridge Street. This lively restaurant in the center of town features stick-to-your-ribs good food in a cool setting. The barbecue-focused menu is a hit with the young crowd that frequents this place for its all-around fun at a reasonable price. American menu. Lunch, dinner. Closed Jan-Apr. Bar. Casual attire. **$$** ♿

★ ★ ★ **CHANTICLEER.** *9 New St, Nantucket (02564). Phone 508/257-6231; fax 508/257-4154. www.thechanticleerinn.com.* Chef/owner Jean-Charles Berruet delights his guests with expertly prepared food and perfectly professional service. The main dining room is cozy and romantic, with a crackling fireplace, fresh flowers, and a view of the famous rose garden. Make sure to take a stroll through the rose and herb gardens during a visit here and drink in the beauty of the place. French menu. Dinner. Closed Mon; also late Oct-mid-May. Bar. Reservations recommended. Outdoor seating. **$$$$**

★ ★ ★ **CLUB CAR.** *1 Main St, Nantucket (02554). Phone 508/228-1101. www.theclubcar.com.* Lunch and dinner at The Club Car are elegant, but the atmosphere remains casual. The Club Car lounge is housed in a renovated club car from a train that used to run between Steamboat Wharf and Siasconset Village, so the décor is fascinating. The restaurant offers great seats for people-watching along Main Street and the waterfront, and a pianist performs nightly. French menu. Lunch, dinner. Closed Nov-late May. Bar. Reservations recommended. **$$$$** ♿

★ ★ ★ **COMPANY OF THE CAULDRON.** *7 India St, Nantucket (02554). Phone 508/228-4016. www.companyofthecauldron.com.* Romantics adore the Company of the Cauldron. From the charming, ivy-covered exterior to the soft glow of the candlelit dining room to the gentle strains of the harp played in the background, this special restaurant seems crafted straight from a romance novel. While it offers the perfect setting in which to begin or rekindle a love affair, the kitchen's passion for food is yet another reason to visit. The exceptional New American menu changes nightly, surprising and delighting visitors with memo-

rable dishes. American menu. Dinner. Closed Mon; also mid-Dec-May. **$$$**

★ **DOWNYFLAKE.** *18 Sparks Ave, Nantucket (02554). Phone 508/228-4533.* The early bird gets the doughnut at Downyflake. Open at 5 am and serving breakfast until 2 pm, this coffee shop rewards early risers with freshly baked doughnuts still warm from the oven. Traditional breakfast favorites and lunch are also served here, all with a friendly smile. A favorite haunt of islanders, this casual spot is the perfect place to catch up on local gossip while sipping a hot cup of coffee. Breakfast, lunch. Casual attire. **$**

★ **FOG ISLAND CAFE.** *7 S Water St, Nantucket (02554). Phone 508/228-1818. www.fogisland.com.* The line forms early outside the Fog Island Cafe. Best known for its hearty country breakfasts, this casual restaurant is a favorite of visitors and locals alike for its friendly service, relaxed setting, and delicious food. This establishment perfectly conveys the essence of beach living with its breezy ceiling fans and large wood tables and booths. Conveniently located in the heart of town, the Fog Island Cafe's laid-back attitude makes it a perfect choice for the entire family, and its sophisticated comfort food is sure to please diners of all ages. American menu. Breakfast, lunch, dinner, brunch. Casual attire. **$**

★ ★ **LE LANGUEDOC.** *24 Broad St, Nantucket (02554). Phone 508/228-2552; fax 508/228-4682. www.lelanguedoc.com.* For a taste of France off the New England coast, visit Le Languedoc. This charming restaurant, located inside one of Nantucket's historic homes, shares two personalities with diners. Guests may choose the casual, upbeat style of the bistro and accompanying terrace or opt for the intimate, romantic setting of the pricier upstairs dining room. A traditional French menu is served in both settings, and for those who can't venture forth after the superb meal, rooms are available at Le Languedoc's inn. French menu. Dinner. Closed Feb-Mar. Bar. Outdoor seating. **$$$** ♿

★ ★ **NANTUCKET LOBSTER TRAP.** *23 Washington St, Nantucket (02554). Phone 508/228-4200; fax 508/228-6168. www.nantucketlobstertrap .com.* Families and large groups flock to the lively Lobster Trap. Open seasonally and for dinner only, this informal restaurant is known for its friendly service and fun atmosphere. Lobsters are the big draw here, yet the island's famous scallops are a close second. Lines are long, but guests may enjoy drinks and appetizers on the patio while waiting for a table. The Lobster Trap even packages takeout clambakes and other meals to enjoy on the beach or at home. Seafood menu. Dinner. Closed mid-Oct-early May. Bar. Children's menu. Casual attire. Outdoor seating. **$$$**

★ ★ ★ **ORAN MOR.** *2 S Beach St, Nantucket (02554). Phone 508/228-8655.* Climb the stairs to Oran Mor and discover a food lover's heaven. Tucked inside a historic Nantucket house with views across to the harbor, this jewel box treats its visitors to a truly serendipitous setting. The atmospheric fine-dining experience is capped off by a friendly, knowledgeable staff that manages to be attentive without being intrusive. The eclectic menu echoes the restaurant's accessible elegance, with organic ingredients and fresh seafood dominating the subtle yet complex flavors. International menu. Dinner. Closed Dec 25. Bar. Casual attire. **$$$**

★ ★ ★ **THE PEARL.** *12 Federal St, Nantucket (02554). Phone 508/228-9701. www.boardinghouse-pearl.com.* The Pearl brings city chic to Nantucket. This ultra-hip restaurant appeals to a young, fashionable clientele on holiday from the city, yet not wanting to leave sophistication behind. Asian flavors punctuate the mainly seafood dishes here, and the drink menu is decidedly trendy, offering creative takes on the martini, cosmopolitan, and sake, in addition to a complete wine and champagne list. This intimate restaurant has only two seatings per evening, so reservations are a must. International menu. Dinner. Bar. Casual attire. Reservations recommended. Outdoor seating. **$$$$**
D

★ ★ **ROPEWALK.** *1 Straight Wharf, Nantucket (02554). Phone 508/228-8886; fax 508/228-8740. www.theropewalk.com.* With the harbor gently lapping at its doorstep and the island's most luxurious yachts docked just outside, the Ropewalk enjoys one of the best locations on Nantucket. The boating crowd populates this clubby, open-air restaurant where seafood is the specialty. The raw bar here is considered one of the island's best, and the always-hopping bar is tops for drinks with a view. Seafood menu. Dinner. Closed mid-Oct-mid-May. Bar. Children's menu. Outdoor seating. **$$**

★ ★ **SEAGRILLE.** *45 Sparks Ave, Nantucket (02554). Phone 508/325-5700.* Located just a short distance from town, The SeaGrille is a terrific destination for the entire family. This casual restaurant with friendly service specializes in seafood, including New England favorites such as Ipswich clams and Chatham

scrod in addition to raw bar offerings, yet its extensive menu includes many meat, poultry, and game selections to satisfy non-seafood eaters. The quahog chowder is an island favorite and is even shipped via mail order for those who can't get enough of this local dish. Seafood menu. Lunch, dinner. Children's menu. Casual attire. **$$**

★ ★ ★ **SUMMER HOUSE.** *17 Ocean Ave, Nantucket (02554). Phone 508/257-9976.* Nestled in the tiny hamlet of 'Sconset, where rose-covered cottages and wind-swept bluffs are *de rigueur,* the Summer House seduces guests with its spectacular oceanfront setting and superb cuisine. White wicker furnishings and ceiling fans recall the seaside vacations of a former time, while the refined New American menu is firmly rooted in the present. Lunch is available poolside, while the upscale clientele enjoys dinner with an ocean view in the elegant dining room. American menu. Lunch, dinner. Closed mid-Oct-mid-May. Bar. Casual attire. Outdoor seating. **$$$$**

★ ★ ★ **TOPPER'S.** *120 Wauwinet Rd, Nantucket (02554). Phone 508/228-0145; toll-free 800/426-8718; fax 508/325-0657. www.wauwinet.com.* Located in the charming Wauwinet Inn (see), this romantic, sophisticated restaurant is filled with flowers, art, and the island's upper-crust clientele. The food, service, and wine list are all first-rate. At lunch, the menu is tasting style so that diners can sample small portions of several dishes. Nice touches include complimentary sparkling water at dinner, sterling silver pendulum plate carriers, and even gourmet to-go basket lunches if you prefer a picnic. American menu. Lunch, dinner, Sun brunch. Closed late Oct-early May. Bar. Outdoor seating. **$$$$**

★ ★ **WEST CREEK CAFE.** *11 W Creek Rd, Nantucket (02554). Phone 508/228-4943.* Located mid-island, the West Creek Cafe is worth the drive out of town. This sensational restaurant jazzes up the local scene with its refined New American cuisine. Cosmopolitan couples linger over meals in the intimate dining room, where zebra-print banquettes and satin pillows add to the urbane ambience. The menu changes weekly, surprising both loyal visitors and newcomers with its cleverly prepared dishes. American menu. Dinner. Closed Tues; Jan 1, July 4, Dec 25. Bar. Outdoor seating. **$$$**
D

Natick (B-6)

Population 32,170
Elevation 180 ft
Area Code 508
Zip 01760
Information MetroWest Chamber of Commerce, 1671 Worcester Rd, Suite 201, Framingham 01701; phone 508/879-5600
Web Site www.metrowest.org

This town was set aside as a plantation for the "Praying Indians" in 1650 at the request of Reverend John Eliot. A missionary, he believed that he could promote brotherhood between Native Americans and settlers by converting them. After half a century, the Native Americans were crowded out by settlers.

Limited-Service Hotels

★ **HAMPTON INN.** *319 Speen St, Natick (01760). Phone 508/653-5000; toll-free 800/426-7866; fax 508/651-9733. www.hamptoninn.com.* 185 rooms, 7 story. Complimentary continental breakfast. Check-in 3 pm, check-out noon. Fitness room. **$**
🏃

★ ★ **SHERBORN INN.** *33 N Main St, Sherborn (01770). Phone 508/655-9521; fax 508/655-5325. www.sherborninn.com.* 4 rooms, 2 story. Complimentary continental breakfast. Check-in 3 pm, check-out 11 am. Restaurant. **$**

Full-Service Hotel

★ ★ ★ **CROWNE PLAZA.** *1360 Worcester St, Natick (01760). Phone 508/653-8800; toll-free 800/227-6963; fax 508/653-1708. www.crowneplaza.com.* This hotel is located 15 miles west of downtown Boston and has a dramatic, atrium-lobby entrance. Rates include a continental breakfast buffet, evening hors d'oeuvres, and local transportation. Guests will find shops and theaters at the neighboring Natick Mall. 251 rooms, 7 story. Check-out noon. High-speed Internet access. Restaurant, bar. Fitness room. **$**
🏃

Restaurant

★ ★ **SHERBORN INN.** *33 N Main St, Sherborn (01770). Phone 508/655-9521; toll-free 800/552-9742;* *fax 508/655-5325. www.sherborninn.com.* Restored tavern décor. American, Irish menu. Dinner. Bar. **$$**

New Bedford (D-7)

See also Fall River

Settled 1640
Population 93,768
Elevation 50 ft
Area Code 508
Information Bristol County Convention & Visitors Bureau, 70 N Second St, PO Box 976, 02741; phone 508/997-1250 or toll-free 800/288-6263
Web Site www.bristol-county.org

Herman Melville, author of *Moby Dick,* said that the brave houses and flowery gardens of New Bedford were one and all harpooned and dragged up from the bottom of the sea. Whaling did, in fact, build this city. When oil was discovered in Pennsylvania in 1857, the world's greatest whaling port nearly became a ghost town. New Bedford scrapped the great fleet and became a major cotton textile center. More recently, it has thrived on widely diversified industries. New Bedford remains a major Atlantic deep-sea fishing port. The whaling atmosphere is preserved in local museums and monuments, while the Whaling National Historical Park celebrates the town's whaling legacy. In the County Street historic district, many of the mansions built for sea captains and merchants still stand.

What to See and Do

Buttonwood Park & Zoo. *425 Hawthorn St, New Bedford (02740). Phone 508/991-6175. www.bpzoo.org.* Greenhouse; ball fields, tennis courts, playground, picnic area, fitness circuit. Zoo exhibits include elephants, lions, deer, bears, buffalo; seal pool. (Daily; closed Jan 1, Thanksgiving, Dec 25) **$**

Fort Phoenix Beach State Reservation. *Off Hwy 6 and I-95, E via Hwy 6 to Fairhaven, then 1 mile S; follow signs. Phone 508/992-4524.* Swimming; fine view of the harbor. Nearby is Fort Phoenix, a pre-Revolutionary fortification (open to the public). **$**

New Bedford-Cuttyhunk Ferry. *Fisherman's Wharf at Pier 3, New Bedford. Phone 508/992-1432.* (Mid-June-mid-Sept: daily; rest of year: varied schedule) Reservations suggested. **$$$$**

New Bedford Whaling Museum. *18 Johnny Cake Hill, New Bedford (02740). Phone 508/997-0046.* Features an 89-foot half-scale model of whaleship *Lagoda.* Galleries devoted to scrimshaw, local artists; murals of whales and whale skeleton; period rooms and collections of antique toys, dolls, prints, and ship models. Silent movie presentation (July-Aug). (Daily; closed Jan 1, Thanksgiving, Dec 25) **$$$**

Rotch-Jones-Duff House and Garden Museum. *396 County St, New Bedford (02740). Phone 508/997-1401.* Whaling era Greek Revival mansion (1834) and garden, has been maintained to reflect the lives of three families that lived in the house. (Daily) Museum sponsors concerts and programs throughout the year. Tours available, inquire for schedule. Museum shop. **$$**

Seamen's Bethel. *15 Johnny Cake Hill, New Bedford (02740). Phone 508/992-3295.* (1832) "Whaleman's Chapel" referred to by Melville in *Moby Dick.* Prow-shaped pulpit later built to represent Melville's description. Also many cenotaphs dedicated to men lost at sea. Vespers third Sun each month. (Daily)

Steamship Authority. *Phone 508/477-8600.* New Bedford-Martha's Vineyard Ferry. Bus tours, car rentals on Martha's Vineyard. (Mid-May-mid-Oct, daily) Same-day round-trip and one-way trips available. Schedule may vary. **$$$$**

Special Events

Blessing of the Fleet. *Waterfront. Phone 508/999-5231.* July 4 weekend.

Feast of the Blessed Sacrament. *Madeira Ave, Hathaway St, and Tinkham St, New Bedford. Phone 508/992-6911.* North end of town. Largest Portuguese feast in North America; entertainment, parade and amusement rides. Three days usually beginning first weekend in Aug.

First Night New Bedford. *Emerson and Mill sts, New Bedford. Phone toll-free 800/508-5353.* Historic waterfront and downtown. Celebration of arts and culture; fireworks. Dec 31.

Limited-Service Hotel

★ ★ **DAYS INN.** *500 Hathaway Rd, New Bedford (02740). Phone 508/997-1231; toll-free 800/329-7466; fax 508/984-7977.* 151 rooms, 3 story. Check-in 3 pm, check-out 11 am. Restaurant, bar. Indoor pool. Airport transportation available. **$**

Restaurants

★ **ANTONIO'S.** *267 Coggeshall St, New Bedford (02746). Phone 508/990-3636.* Portuguese menu. Lunch, dinner. Bar. Children's menu. Casual attire. No credit cards accepted. **$$**

★ ★ **FREESTONE'S CITY GRILL.** *41 William St, New Bedford (02740). Phone 508/993-7477; fax 508/984-4486. www.freestones.com.* The sumptuous mahogany and marble of Freestone's harks back to the building's heyday as Citizens' Bank in the late 19th century. A popular lunch spot for visitors to the adjacent Whaling National Park, Freestone's also offers contemporary American fare in the evenings. Grilled meatloaf, for example, gets a spicy punch by incorporating andouille sausage into the blend. The chowder here is award-winning, and the drink menu is anything but typical. Desserts are homey and old-fashioned, from the hot fudge brownie to the carrot cake. Seafood menu. Lunch, dinner. Closed Labor Day, Thanksgiving, Dec 25. Bar. Children's menu. Casual attire. **$$**

★ ★ ★ **OCEANNA.** *95 William St, New Bedford (02740). Phone 508/997-8465.* Seafood menu. Lunch, dinner. Closed Sun. Bar. Children's menu. Casual attire. **$$**

Newburyport (A-8)

See also Amesbury

Settled 1635
Population 17,189
Elevation 37 ft
Area Code 978
Zip 01950
Information Greater Newburyport Chamber of Commerce & Industry, 29 State St; phone 978/462-6680
Web Site www.newburyport.chamber.org

Novelist John P. Marquand, who lived in Newburyport, said it "is not a museum piece although it sometimes looks it." High Street is surely a museum of American Federalist architecture. Ship owners and captains built these great houses. The birthplace of the US Coast Guard, Newburyport lies at the mouth of the Merrimack River. The city's early prosperity came from shipping and shipbuilding. It is now a thriving year-round tourist destination.

What to See and Do

Coffin House. *16 High Rd (Hwy 1A), Newburyport (01951). Phone 978/463-2057.* (Circa 1654) Developed in a series of enlargements, features 17th- and 18th-century kitchens, buttery, and parlor with early 19th-century wallpaper; furnishings of eight generations. Tours on the hour. (June-mid-Oct, Wed-Sun) **$$**

Cushing House Museum. *98 High St, Newburyport (01950). Phone 978/462-2681.* (Historical Society of Old Newbury; circa 1810) A Federalist-style mansion, once the home of Caleb Cushing, first envoy to China from US. Museum houses collections of needlework, paperweights, toys, paintings, furniture, silver, clocks, china; library. Also shed, carriage house, and 19th-century garden. (May-Oct, Tues-Sat; closed holidays) **$$**

Custom House Maritime Museum. *25 Water St, Newburyport (01950). Phone 978/462-8681.* Collections of artifacts depicting maritime heritage of area; includes ship models, navigational instruments; decorative arts, library. (Apr-late Dec, Mon-Sat, also Sun afternoons) **$$**

Parker River National Wildlife Refuge. *Newburyport. 3 miles E on Plum Island. Phone 978/465-5753.* Natural barrier beach formed by 6 1/2 miles of beach and sand dunes is the home of many species of birds, mammals, reptiles, amphibians, and plants; saltwater and freshwater marshes provide resting and feeding place for migratory birds on the Atlantic Flyway. Hiking, bicycling, waterfowl hunting, nature trail. (Daily) Closed to public when parking lots are full. Contact Refuge Manager, Northern Blvd, Plum Island (01950).

Special Events

Arts, Flowers, & All that Jazz. *Downtown. Phone 978/462-6680.* Demonstrations, flower and garden show, crafts, exhibits, and jazz concerts. Sun-Mon of Memorial Day weekend.

Fall Harvest Festival. *Downtown. Phone 978/462-6680.* Juried crafts, music, entertainment, food, baking contest. Sun-Mon of Columbus Day weekend.

Yankee Homecoming. *Barthholmes and Market sts, entire city of Newburyport, New Bedford. Phone 978/462-6680.* Celebration includes parades, fireworks, exhibits; river cruises; sailboat and canoe races; craft show; lobster feeds. Last Sat in July-first Sun in Aug.

Limited-Service Hotel

★ ★ **GARRISON INN.** *11 Brown Sq, Newburyport (01950). Phone 978/499-8500; fax 978/499-8555. www.garrisoninn.com.* Restored historic inn (1809). 24 rooms, 4 story. Check-in 3 pm, check-out 11 am. Restaurant, bar. Children's activity center. **$**

Specialty Lodgings

The following lodging establishments are approved by Mobil Travel Guide, but due to their unique and individualized nature have not been given a traditional Mobil Star rating. Included in this listing you may find bed-and-breakfasts, limited-service inns, guest ranches, and other unique hotel properties.

CLARK CURRIER INN. *45 Green St, Newburyport (01950). Phone 978/465-8363. www.clarkcurrierinn .com.* Built 1803 by a shipbuilder. 7 rooms, 3 story. Complimentary full breakfast. Check-in 3 pm, check-out 11 am. **$**

ESSEX STREET INN. *7 Essex St, Newburyport (01950). Phone 978/465-3148; fax 978/462-1907. www.newburyportchamber.org.* Built in 1801; fireplace. 19 rooms, 3 story. Complimentary continental breakfast. Check-in 3-8 pm, check-out 11 am. **$**

MORRILL PLACE. *209 High St, Newburyport (01950). Phone 978/462-2808; toll-free 888/594-4667; fax 978/462-9966.* Built in 1806. 9 rooms, 3 story. Pets accepted, some restrictions. Complimentary continental breakfast. Check-in 4 pm, check-out noon. **$**

WINDSOR HOUSE. *38 Federal St, Newburyport (01950). Phone 978/462-3778; toll-free 888/873-5296; fax 978/465-3443.* Federal mansion (1786) built by lieutenant of the Continental Army for his wedding. 4 rooms, 3 story. Pets accepted, some restrictions. Complimentary full breakfast. Check-in 4 pm, check-out 11 am. **$$**

Restaurants

★ ★ ★ **DAVID'S.** *11 Brown Sq, Newburyport (01950). Phone 978/462-8077; fax 978/462-8085.*

www.davidsrestaurant.com. A favorite of locals and visitors alike, this friendly restaurant serves a wide variety of American fare. Upstairs at The Rim, the theme is Asian. International/Fusion menu. Dinner. Closed Jan 1, Dec 24-25. Bar. Children's menu. **$$$**

★ ★ **GLENN'S GALLEY.** *44 Merrimas St, Newburyport (01950). Phone 978/465-3811; fax 978/465-2013. www.glennsrestaurant.com.* Seafood menu. Lunch, dinner. Closed Mon; holidays. Bar. Children's menu. **$$**

★ **THE GROG.** *13 Middle St, Newburyport (01950). Phone 978/465-8008; fax 978/462-9505. www.thegrog.com.* International/Fusion menu. Lunch, dinner. Closed Dec 25. Bar. **$$**

★ ★ **MICHAEL'S HARBORSIDE.** *1 Tournament Wharf, Newburyport (01950). Phone 978/462-7785; fax 978/465-9981. www.michaelsharborside.com.* Seafood menu. Lunch, dinner. Closed Thanksgiving, Dec 25. Bar. Outdoor seating. **$$**

★ ★ **TEN CENTER STREET.** *10 Center St, Newburyport (01950). Phone 978/462-6652; fax 978/462-6729.* In a restored 1800s Federal-style house. Outdoor seating. American menu. Lunch, dinner. Bar. **$$**

Newton (B-7)

See also Boston

Settled 1630
Population 83,829
Elevation 100 ft
Area Code 617
Information Chamber of Commerce, 199 Wells Ave, Suite 208, PO Box 590268, Newton 02459; phone 617/244-5300
Web Site www.nnchamber.com

Newton, the "Garden City," is actually a city of 13 suburban neighborhoods that have maintained their individual identities. Of the 13, eight have "Newton" in their names: Newton, Newtonville, Newton Centre, Newton Corner, Newton Highlands, West Newton, Newton Upper Falls, and Newton Lower Falls. Five colleges are located here: Boston College, Lasell College, Mount Ida College, Andover-Newton Theological School, and Aquinas Junior College.

What to See and Do

Charles River Canoe & Kayak Center. *2401 Commonwealth Ave, Newton (02466). Phone 617/965-5510. www.ski-paddle.com/cano/canoe.htm.* Whether you're an experienced paddler looking to rent boats by the hour or you're getting geared up to paddle for the first time, Charles River Canoe & Kayak is your starting point. The Charles River offers beautiful views of the Boston skyline and several area universities, as well as diverse waterfowl. Pack a picnic lunch to revive your energy. (Apr-Oct Thurs-Sun; closed Mon-Wed) **$$$**

Jackson Homestead Museum. *527 Washington St, Newton (02458). Phone 617/552-7238. www.newton.ma.us/jackson.* (1809) Once a station on the Underground Railroad. Home of the Newton Historical Society. Changing exhibits; children's gallery; toys; textiles; and tools. (Tues-Sat and Sun afternoon) **$$**

Limited-Service Hotel

★ ★ **HOLIDAY INN.** *399 Grove St, Newton (02462). Phone 617/969-5300; toll-free 800/465-4329; fax 617/965-4280. www.holiday-inn.com.* 191 rooms, 7 story. Check-in 3 pm, check-out noon. Restaurant, bar. Fitness room. Outdoor pool. **$**

Full-Service Hotels

★ ★ ★ **MARRIOTT BOSTON NEWTON.** *2345 Commonwealth Ave, Newton (02466). Phone 617/969-1000; toll-free 800/228-9290; fax 617/527-6914. www.marriott.com.* Perched along the Charles River, this property is just 15 minutes from downtown Boston and 5 minutes from the Waltham Business District. Business travelers will find a convenient 24-hour, self-serve business center and over 16,000 square feet of meeting space. 430 rooms, 7 story. Check-out 1 pm. Restaurant, bar. Fitness room. Indoor pool, outdoor pool, whirlpool. Business center. **$**

★ ★ ★ **SHERATON NEWTON HOTEL.** *320 Washington St, Newton (02158). Phone 617/969-3010; toll-free 800/325-3535; fax 617/630-2976. www.sheraton.com.* All the rooms and suites at this recently renovated property have a creative, contemporary décor with sleek white bedding; a well-designed work area; and warm, mustard-colored walls. Minutes from downtown Boston, an express bus departs for

Faneuil Hall every 20 minutes. 272 rooms, 12 story. Check-in 3 pm, check-out 11 am. High-speed Internet access. Restaurant, bar. Fitness room. Indoor pool. **$**

Restaurant

★ ★ ★ **LUMIERE.** *1293 Washington St, West Newton (02465). Phone 617/244-9199; fax 617/796-9178. www.lumiererestaurant.com.* From the spoon door handle at the entrance, to sheet music, light shades, and Scrabble tiles on the rest room doors, this restaurant's décor is warm and whimsical. The contemporary French cuisine goes beyond bistro without going all the way uptown. French, Mediterranean, Pacific menu. Dinner. Closed Mon; holidays. **$$$**

North Adams (A-2)

See also Williamstown

Settled 1745
Population 14,681
Elevation 707 ft
Area Code 413
Zip 01247
Information Northern Berkshire Chamber of Commerce, 40 Main St; phone 413/663-3735

North Adams is an industrial community set in the beautiful four-season resort country of the northern Berkshires. Its factories make electronic components, textile machinery, wire, machine tools, paper boxes, and other products. Susan B. Anthony was born in nearby Adams in 1820.

What to See and Do

MASS MoCA. *1040 Mass MoCA Way, North Adams (01247). Phone 413/664-4481.* Center for visual, performing, and media arts. Features unconventional exhibits and performances by renowned artists and cultural institutions. Rehearsals and production studios are open to the public. Tours available. (Daily) **$$$** Also here is

> **Kidspace.** *87 Marshall St, North Adams (01247). Phone 413/664-4481.* Children's gallery presents contemporary art in manner that is interesting and accessible. Includes hands-on activity stations where children can create their own works of art. (June-Aug: Mon, Thurs-Sun; rest of year: limited hours) **FREE**

Mohawk Trail State Forest. *E on Hwy 2, near Charlemont. Phone 413/339-5504.* Spectacular scenery. Swimming, fishing; hiking, winter sports, picnicking, camping, log cabins. **$$**

Mount Greylock State Reservation. *1 mile W on Hwy 2, then N on Notch Rd. Phone 413/499-4262.* Mount Greylock, the highest point in the state (3,491 feet), is here. War memorial tower at summit. Fishing; hunting, cross-country skiing, snowmobiles allowed. Picnicking. Lodge, snacks; campsites (mid-May-mid-Oct). Visitor center on Rockwell Road in Lanesborough, off Hwy 7.

Natural Bridge State Park. *1 1/4 miles NE on Hwy 8. Phone 413/663-6392.* A water-eroded marble bridge and rock formations, about 550 million years old, popularized by author Nathaniel Hawthorne. Picnicking. (Mid-May-mid-Oct) **$**

Savoy Mountain State Forest. *E on Hwy 2, near Florida, MA. Phone 413/664-9567.* Brilliant fall foliage. Swimming, fishing, boating (ramp); hiking and riding trails, hunting, winter sports, picnicking, camping, log cabins. Waterfall. **FREE**

Western Gateway Heritage State Park. *115 State St, North Adams (01247). Behind City Hall on Hwy 8. Phone 413/663-8059.* A restored freightyard with six buildings around a cobbled courtyard. Detailed historic exhibits on the construction of the Hoosac Railroad Tunnel. (Daily; closed holidays) **DONATION**

Special Events

Fall Foliage Festival. *57 Main St, North Adams (01247). Phone 413/663-3735.* Parade, entertainment, dancing, children's activities. Late Sept-early Oct.

La Festa. *85 Main St, North Adams (01247). Phone 413/663-3782.* Ethnic festival, ethnic food, entertainment, events. Sixteen days beginning mid-June.

Limited-Service Hotel

★ ★ **HOLIDAY INN BERKSHIRES.** *40 Main St, North Adams, (01247). Phone 413/663-6500; fax 413/663-6380. www.holiday-inn.com.* 86 rooms. Check-in 3 pm, check-out 11 am. Wireless Internet access. Restaurant, bar. Indoor pool, whirlpool. **$**

Northampton (B-3)

Settled 1673
Population 28,978
Elevation 140 ft
Area Code 413
Zip 01060
Information Chamber of Commerce and Visitor Center, 99 Pleasant St; phone 413/584-1900
Web Site www.northamptonuncommon.com

When the famed concert singer Jenny Lind honeymooned in this town on the Connecticut River in 1852, she exclaimed, "Why, this is the paradise of America." But it wasn't always a peaceful town. Northampton was the scene of a frenzied religious revival movement in the first half of the 18th century. The movement stemmed from Jonathan Edwards, a Puritan who came to be regarded as the greatest preacher in New England. Later, the town was the home of President Calvin Coolidge. A granite memorial on the court house lawn honors Coolidge, who once served as mayor.

With its first-class theaters and restaurants, numerous antique shops and art galleries, and charming hotels and inns, Northampton has become a popular tourist destination, particularly among New Yorkers and Bostonians seeking a weekend getaway. The town's thriving arts scene can be credited, at least in part, to its close proximity to five colleges. Mount Holyoke College is in nearby South Hadley, while three schools—Amherst College, Hampshire College, and the University of Massachusetts—are located across the Connecticut River in Amherst. The nation's largest liberal arts college for women, Smith, is located in downtown Northampton. Smith's Museum of Art houses approximately 25,000 objects, including paintings by Picasso and Cézanne, a cast bronze sculpture by Rodin, and more than 5,700 photographic prints.

Just beyond the city limits, the rolling hills and quiet streams of the Pioneer Valley offer splendid recreational opportunities for outdoor enthusiasts. Be it on foot or bike or in a canoe or kayak, the valley's pastoral beauty begs to be explored.

What to See and Do

Arcadia Nature Center and Wildlife Sanctuary, Massachusetts Audubon Society. *127 Combs Rd,* *Easthampton (01027).* 4 miles SW on Hwy 10, follow signs, in Northampton and Easthampton. Phone 413/584-3009. Five hundred fifty acres on migratory flyway; an ancient oxbow of the Connecticut River; self-guiding nature trails; observation tower; courses and programs. Grounds (Tues-Sun). **$$**

Calvin Coolidge Memorial Room. *20 West St,* *Northampton (01060).* Forbes Library, Hwys 9 and 66. Phone 413/587-1011. Displays of the late president's papers and correspondence; also books and articles on Coolidge. Memorabilia includes Native American headdress and beadwork given to him, Mrs. Coolidge's needlework, and photographs. (Mon-Wed; closed holidays; schedule may vary) **FREE**

Historic Northampton Museum Houses. *46-66 Bridge* *St, Northampton (01060).* Phone 413/584-6011. All houses (Tues-Fri, Sat-Sun afternoons). **$$** Nearby are

Damon House. *58 Bridge St, Northampton (01060).* Phone 413/584-6011. (1813) Permanent formal parlor exhibit (circa 1820).

Parsons House. *58 Bridge St, Northampton (01060).* (Circa 1730) Contains exhibits on local architecture.

Shepherd House. (1798) Includes the lifetime collection of one Northampton family and focuses on family lifestyle at the turn of the 19th century.

Look Park. *300 N Main St, Northampton (01062).* NW off Hwy 9. Phone 413/584-5457. Miniature train and Christenson Zoo; boating; tennis; picnicking; playgrounds, ball fields; also here is Pines Theater (musical entertainment, children's theater, and puppet programs, summer). Park (all year). Fees for most facilities. **$**

Smith College. *33 Elm St, Northampton (01063).* Phone 413/584-2700. (1871) (2,700 women) The largest private liberal arts college for women in the United States. On campus are Paradise Pond, named by Jenny Lind; Helen Hills Hills Chapel; William Allan Neilson Library with more than 1 million volumes; Center for the Performing Arts; Plant House and Botanical Gardens; Japanese Garden. Also here is

Museum of Art. *Elm St, Northampton (01063).* A fine collection with emphasis on American and European art of the 19th and 20th centuries. (Sept-May: Tues-Sun; rest of year: Tues-Sat; closed holidays)

Special Events

Eastern National Morgan Horse Show. *Three-County Fairgrounds, Damon Rd and Hwy 9, Northampton (01060).* Phone 413/584-2237. Late July.

Maple Sugaring. *99 Pleasant St, Northampton (01060).* Phone 413/584-1900. Visitors are welcome at many maple camps. Mid-Mar-early Apr.

Springtime in Paradise. *Three-County Fairgrounds, Damon Rd and Hwy 9, Northampton (01060).* Phone 413/584-1900. Major arts festival. Late May.

Three-County Fair. *Three-County Fairgrounds, Damon Rd and Hwy 9, Northampton (01060).* Phone 413/584-2237. www.3countyfair.com. The nation's oldest agricultural fair. Agricultural exhibits, horse racing, parimutuel betting. (Labor Day week)

Limited-Service Hotels

★ ★ **CLARION HOTEL AND CONFERENCE CENTER.** *1 Atwood Dr, Northampton (01060).* Phone 413/586-1211; toll-free 800/582-2929; fax 413/586-0630. www.hampshirehospitality.com. This Clarion is a cross between a conference center and a country inn. With easy access off I-91, seven well-maintained meeting rooms, and a staff that understands the needs of an organization of business travelers, it is well designed for conferences. Yet the wood-paneled lobby and public areas have a rustic feel, with exposed brick, overstuffed furniture, and a large, welcoming gas fireplace. The lobby also opens onto a domed, plant-filled atrium that houses an indoor pool and video arcade. The dome lets light flood the hotel year-round—particularly welcome in the midst of a cold New England winter. 122 rooms, 2 story. Complimentary continental breakfast. Check-in 3 pm, check-out 11 am. Restaurant, bar. Indoor pool, outdoor pool, children's pool. Tennis. **$**
⟂ ⟂

★ ★ **THE HOTEL NORTHAMPTON.** *36 King St, Northampton (01060).* Phone 413/584-3100; fax 413/584-9455. Built in 1927, this elegant brick Colonial Revival-style lodging—the most prominent in Northampton—is listed as a Historic Hotel by the National Trust for Historic Preservation. It's located on a busy street opposite the restored Calvin Theater, within walking distance of historic Northampton's many shops, eclectic restaurants, and cultural attractions. A narrow glass conservatory filled with plants surrounds half the building. The hotel's public areas celebrate its heritage, with framed historical material as well as handsome artwork ranging from Norman Rockwell prints to Japanese woodcuts; the clublike lobby has a large fireplace and lots of reading chairs, complete with a collection of old books on the mantle. Welcoming and spacious guest rooms, which have gracious foyers, feature colonial-inspired floral fabrics and furnishings. Dining options at the hotel include the light and airy Coolidge Park Cafe and the authentic New England Wiggins Tavern, with antiques, pewter and cast-iron implements, exposed beams, dark wood, and an open hearth. 99 rooms, 5 story. Complimentary continental breakfast. Check-in 2:30 pm, check-out 11 am. High-speed Internet access, wireless Internet access. Two restaurants, two bars. Fitness room. **$$**
⟂

Specialty Lodging

The following lodging establishment is approved by Mobil Travel Guide, but due to its unique and individualized nature has not been given a traditional Mobil Star rating. Included in this listing you may find bed-and-breakfasts, limited-service inns, guest ranches, and other unique hotel properties.

AUTUMN INN. *259 Elm St, Northampton (01060).* Phone 413/584-7660; toll-free 800/582-2929; fax 413/586-4808. www.hampshirehospitality.com. About it's a third of a mile from the main gates of Smith College and a mile from the center of Northampton, this hotel sits back from a busy street in an older residential area of town. The property was built in the 1960s to resemble a colonial-era Inn, and well it does. It looks like a two-story colonial brick home on a well-manicured lawn, and it fits in beautifully with the neighborhood's surrounding Victorian- and colonial-style homes. A huge hearth and wood-burning fireplace greet guests in the lobby; patterned after working kitchens of bygone eras, it is replete with copper kettles and cast-iron fixtures. In front of the hearth is a cozy area with tables and chairs where continental breakfast is served each morning. 32 rooms, 2 story. Complimentary continental breakfast. Check-in 3 pm, check-out 11 am. Outdoor pool. **$**
⟂ ⟂

Restaurant

★ ★ **EASTSIDE GRILL.** *19 Strong Ave, Northampton (01060).* Phone 413/586-3347; fax 413/586-2406. American menu. Dinner. Closed Thanksgiving, Dec 24-25. Bar. **$$**

Orleans (Cape Cod) (D-10)

See also Eastham

Settled 1693
Population 6,341
Elevation 60 ft
Area Code 508
Zip 02653
Information Cape Cod Chamber of Commerce, Hwys 6 and 132, PO Box 790, Hyannis 02601-0790; phone 508/362-3225 or toll-free 888/227-3263
Web Site www.capecodchamber.org

Orleans supposedly was named in honor of the Duke of Orleans after the French Revolution. The settlers worked at shipping, fishing, and salt production. Its history includes the dubious distinction of being the only town in America to have been fired upon by the Germans during World War I. The town is now a commercial hub for the summer resort colonies along the great stretch of Nauset Beach and the coves behind it. A cable station, which provided direct communication between Orleans and Brest, France, from 1897 to 1959, was restored to its original appearance and is now open to the public.

What to See and Do

Academy of Performing Arts. *120 Main St, Orleans (02653). Phone 508/255-1963.* Theater presents comedies, drama, musicals, dance. Workshops for all ages.

French Cable Station Museum. *41 S Orleans Rd, Orleans (02653). Hwy 28 and Cove Rd. Phone 508/240-1735.* Built in 1890 as the American end of the transatlantic cable from Brest, France. Original equipment for submarine cable communication on display. (July-Labor Day, Tues-Sat afternoons) **$$**

Nauset Beach. *44 Main St, Orleans (02643). About 3 miles E of Hwy 6 on marked roads. Phone 508/255-1386.* One of the most spectacular ocean beaches on the Atlantic coast is now within the boundaries of Cape Cod National Seashore. Swimming, surfing, fishing; lifeguards. Parking fee.

Limited-Service Hotels

★ **THE COVE.** *13 Hwy 28, Orleans (02653). Phone* 508/255-1203; toll-free 800/343-2233; fax 508/255-7736. www.thecoveorleans.com. 47 rooms, 2 story. Check-out 11 am. Outdoor pool. Business center. **$**
🅿 🖼 🏃

★ **NAUSET KNOLL MOTOR LODGE.** *237 Beach Rd, East Orleans (02643). Phone 508/255-3348; fax 508/247-9184. www.capecodtravel.com.* 12 rooms. Closed late Oct-mid-Apr. Check-out 11 am. **$**

★ **SEASHORE PARK MOTOR INN.** *24 Canal Rd, Orleans (02653). Phone 508/255-2500; toll-free 800/772-6453; fax 508/255-9400. www.seashoreparkinn.com.* 62 rooms, 2 story. Closed Nov-mid-Apr. Complimentary continental breakfast. Check-out 11 am. Indoor, outdoor pool; whirlpool. **$**
🅿 🖼

Specialty Lodgings

The following lodging establishments are approved by Mobil Travel Guide, but due to their unique and individualized nature have not been given a traditional Mobil Star rating. Included in this listing you may find bed-and-breakfasts, limited-service inns, guest ranches, and other unique hotel properties.

THE PARSONAGE INN. *202 Main St, East Orleans (02643). Phone 508/255-8217; toll-free 888/422-8217; fax 508/255-8216. www.parsonageinn.com.* Originally a parsonage (1770) and cobbler's shop. 8 rooms, 2 story. Children over 6 years only. Complimentary full breakfast. Check-in 2 pm, check-out 11 am. **$**
🅿

SHIP'S KNEES INN. *186 Beach Rd, East Orleans (02643). Phone 508/255-1312; fax 508/240-1351. www.shipskneesinn.com.* This inn, a restored sea captain's house (circa 1820), is located near the ocean. The rooms are individually decorated in nautical style and have many antiques and some four-poster beds. 16 rooms, 2 story. Children over 12 years only. Complimentary continental breakfast. Check-in 1 pm, check-out 10:30 am. Outdoor pool. Tennis. **$**
🅿 🖼 🏃

Restaurants

★ ★ **BARLEY NECK INN.** *5 Beach Rd, East Orleans (02653). Phone 508/255-0212; fax 508/255-3626. www.barleyneck.com.* The dining room at the Barley Neck Inn is one of Cape Cod's treasures. Located within a sea captain's home that dates to 1868, this restaurant has one of the nicest settings around. Antique-filled rooms romance diners, who feast primarily on seafood dishes with a French influence. A selection from the well-rounded wine list is the perfect complement to the distinctive cuisine. American menu. Dinner. **$$**

★ **THE BEACON ROOM.** *23 West Rd, Orleans (02653). Phone 508/255-2211.* A covered porch and intimate dining room make for an appealing setting at the delightful Beacon Room, and the eclectic menu covers all the bases with large portions of clever food. American menu. Lunch, dinner. Bar. Casual attire. Outdoor seating. **$$**

★ ★ **CAPTAIN LINNELL HOUSE.** *137 Skaket Beach Rd, Orleans (02653). Phone 508/255-3400; fax 508/255-5377. www.linnell.com.* Chef/owner Bill Conway delivers a delightful dining experience at this charming and romantic restaurant. Take a walk out to the Victorian gazebo and enjoy the smell of lavender and the refreshing ocean breeze, and then settle in for a cozy candlelit dinner. Seafood menu. Dinner. Children's menu. Outdoor seating. **$$$**

★ **DOUBLE DRAGON INN.** *Hwys 6A and 28, Orleans (02653). Phone 508/255-4100.* Chinese, Polynesian menu. Lunch, dinner. Closed Thanksgiving. **$$**

★ **LOBSTER CLAW.** *Hwy 6A, Orleans (02653). Phone 508/255-1800. www.capecod.com/lobclaw.* Nautical décor is all the rage at the delightfully whimsical Lobster Claw restaurant, formerly a cranberry packing factory. This Cape classic is frequented by families who come here for the tongue-in-cheek take on the Massachusetts coast. Lobster is the main event, served broiled, boiled, baked, or stuffed, but the menu does include many other seafood selections. American, seafood menu. Lunch, dinner. Closed mid-Nov-Mar. Bar. Children's menu. **$$**

★ ★ **MAHONEY'S ATLANTIC BAR AND GRILL.** *28 Main St, Orleans (02653). Phone 508/255-5505.* Mahoney's Atlantic Bar and Grill feels like the local watering hole, yet this casual, tavern-style restaurant shows off its culinary talents with an inventive New American menu. Seafood drives the menu, although meat and vegetarian entrées run a close second. Good food and entertainment go hand in hand at Mahoney's, with frequent live music performances. American, seafood menu. Dinner. Bar. Casual attire. Outdoor seating. **$$**

★ ★ ★ **NAUSET BEACH CLUB.** *222 E Main St, East Orleans (02643). Phone 508/255-8547;* fax 508/255-8872. www.nausetbeachclub.com. The Nauset Beach Club shares a taste of Northern Italy with guests. This inviting restaurant features some of the most beloved recipes from northern Italy, and the homemade pastas and desserts are noteworthy. Local seafood is incorporated into many of the enticing entrées. Wine is especially important here, where the list pays tribute to many of the small vineyards in the United States and abroad. Italian menu. Dinner. Bar. Casual attire. Reservations recommended. **$$$**

★ ★ **OLD JAILHOUSE TAVERN.** *28 West Rd, Orleans (02653). Phone 508/255-5245. www.legalseafoods.com.* The Old Jailhouse Tavern, located in part of an old jailhouse, promises a good time. From "jailbirds" chicken wings to "hung jury" sandwiches, this Orleans establishment plays off its former incarnation as an old lockup on its American menu. Perfect for groups, this restaurant even has a special section of the menu devoted to items that are ideal for sharing. Seafood menu. Lunch, dinner. Closed Thanksgiving, Dec 25. Bar. **$$**

★ **SIR CRICKET'S FISH AND CHIPS.** *38 Hwy 6A, Orleans (02653). Phone 508/255-4453.* The English-style fish and chips sold here are the ostensible draw, but fried seafood of all descriptions keeps many loyal fans returning to this take-out window attached to the Nauset Lobster Pool. The fried oyster roll and simple fried fish sandwich are some of the best anywhere on the Cape. If you don't want to eat in the car, there are a couple of tiny tables set up on the asphalt next to the soda machine. Seafood menu. Lunch, dinner. Children's menu. Casual attire. Outdoor seating. No credit cards accepted. **$**

★ ★ **THE YARDARM.** *48 Hwy 28, Orleans (02653). Phone 508/255-4840.* Its location just five minutes from Nauset Beach and Rock Harbor explains the seafood-driven menu at The Yardarm. This well-liked pub is a popular hangout for locals, who come here for the chowder and nightly specials. Yankee pot roast, corned beef and cabbage, and other pub grub round out the menu. American menu. Lunch, dinner. Bar. Children's menu. Casual attire. **$$**

Pittsfield (B-2)

See also Lenox, Stockbridge and West Stockbridge

Settled 1743
Population 48,622
Elevation 1,039 ft
Area Code 413
Zip 01201
Information Berkshire Visitors Bureau, Berkshire Common; phone 413/443-9186 or toll-free 800/237-5747
Web Site www.berkshires.org

Beautifully situated in the Berkshire Hills vacation area, this is also an old and important manufacturing center. It is the home of the Berkshire Life Insurance Company (chartered in 1851) and of industries that make machinery, plastics, gauges, and paper products.

What to See and Do

Arrowhead. *780 Holmes Rd, Pittsfield (01201). Phone 413/442-1793.* (1780) Herman Melville wrote *Moby Dick* while living here from 1850 to 1863; historical exhibits, furniture, costumes; gardens. Video presentation. Gift shop. Headquarters of Berkshire County Historical Society. (Memorial Day weekend-Oct, daily) **$$**

Berkshire Museum. *39 South St (Hwy 7), Pittsfield (01201). Phone 413/443-7171.* Museum of art, natural science, and history, featuring American 19th- and 20th-century paintings; works by British, European masters; artifacts from ancient civilizations; exhibits on Berkshire County history; aquarium; changing exhibits; films, lectures, children's programs. (July-Aug: daily; rest of year: Tues-Sun; closed holidays) **$$$**

Bousquet. *2 miles S on Hwy 7, then 1 mile W, on Dan Fox Dr. Phone 413/442-8316. www.bousquets.com.* Two double chairlifts, three rope tows; snowmaking, patrol, school, rentals; cafeteria, bar, daycare. Longest run 1 mile; vertical drop 750 feet. Night skiing. (Dec-Mar, daily) **$$$$**

Brodie Mountain. *10 miles N on Hwy 7. Phone 413/443-4752. www.skibrodie.com.* Four double chairlifts, two rope tows; patrol, school, rentals, snowmaking; bar, cafeteria, restaurant; nursery. (Nov-Mar, daily) Cross-country trails with rentals and instruction. Half-day rates. Tennis, racquetball, winter camping. **$$$$**

Canoe Meadows Wildlife Sanctuary. *472 W Mountain Rd, Pittsfield (01201). Phone 413/637-0320.* Two hundred sixty-two acres with 3 miles of trails, woods, open fields, ponds; bordering the Housatonic River. (Tues-Sun) **$$**

Hancock Shaker Village. *Hwys 20 and 41, Pittsfield. 5 miles W. Phone 413/443-0188.* An original Shaker site (1790-1960); now a living history museum of Shaker life, crafts, and farming. Large collection of Shaker furniture and artifacts in 20 restored buildings, including the Round Stone Barn, set on 1,200 scenic acres in the Berkshires. Exhibits; seasonal craft demonstrations, Discovery Room activities, café (seasonal); farm animals, heirloom herb and vegetable gardens; museum shop; picnicking. **$$$$**

Jiminy Peak. *37 Corey Rd, Hancock (01237). 9 miles N, then W, between Hwy 7 and Hwy 43. Phone 413/738-5500. www.jiminypeak.com.* One six-passanger, three double chairlifts, J-bar, two quads, three triples; patrol, school, rentals, restaurant, two cafeterias, bar, lodge. Longest run 2 miles; vertical drop 1,140 feet. (Thanksgiving-early Apr, daily) Night skiing. Half-day rates. Also trout fishing; 18-hole miniature golf; Alpine slide and tennis center (Memorial Day-Labor Day); fee for activities. **$$$$**

Special Event

South Mountain Concerts. *South St, Pittsfield (01201). 2 miles S on Hwys 7, 20. Phone 413/442-2106.* Chamber music concerts. Sept-Oct, Sun.

Limited-Service Hotel

★ ★ **CROWNE PLAZA HOTEL.** *1 West St, Pittsfield (01201). Phone 413/499-2000; toll-free 800/227-6963; fax 413/442-0449. www.berkshirecrowne.com.* Just minutes from Tanglewood, the Norman Rockwell Museum, the Hancock Shaker Village, and summer theater, this modern, centrally located hotel offers an alternative to the more prevalent inns and bed-and-breakfasts populating the area. A curved staircase inside a large, welcoming lobby of warm wood and live plants sweeps up to second-floor restaurants and meeting rooms. Guest rooms are large and attractive with one amenity that, for many, is even nicer than the in-room coffee, wireless Internet, or direct-dial phone: Fido and Fluffy are more than welcome. 179 rooms, 12 story. Pets accepted; fee. Check-in 3 pm, check-out noon. High-speed Internet access. Restaurant, bar. Fitness room. Indoor pool, whirlpool. **$**

Full-Service Resort

★ ★ JIMINY PEAK MOUNTAIN RESORT.
Corey Rd, Hancock (01237). Phone 413/738-5500; toll-free 888/454-6469; fax 413/738-5513. www.jiminypeak.com. 96 rooms, 3 story. Check-in 4 pm, check-out 10:30 am. Restaurant. Children's activity center. Fitness room. Two outdoor pools, whirlpool. Tennis. Ski in/ski out. **$**

Restaurant

★ ★ DAKOTA. *1035 South St, Pittsfield (01201). Phone 413/499-7900; fax 413/499-8610. www.dakota restaurant.com.* American menu. Dinner, Sun brunch. Closed Thanksgiving, Dec 25. Bar. Children's menu. Casual attire. Reservations recommended. **$$**

Plymouth (C-8)

Settled 1620
Population 51,701
Elevation 50 ft
Area Code 508
Zip 02360
Information Destination Plymouth, 170 Water St, Suite 10C; phone 508/747-7525 or toll-free 800/872-1620
Web Site www.visit-plymouth.com

On December 21, 1620, 102 men, women, and children arrived on the *Mayflower* to found the first permanent European settlement north of Virginia. Although plagued by exposure, cold, hunger, and disease during the terrible first winter, the colony was firmly established by the next year. Plymouth Rock lies under an imposing granite colonnade, marking the traditional place of landing.

Plymouth now combines a summer resort, beaches, a harbor full of pleasure craft, an active fishing town, and a remarkable series of restorations of the original town.

What to See and Do

Burial Hill. *Just W of Town Square.* Governor Bradford is buried here.

Cole's Hill. *Across the street from Plymouth Rock.* Here Pilgrims who died during the first winter were secretly buried.

Harlow Old Fort House. *119 Sandwich St, Plymouth (02360). Phone 508/746-9497.* (1677) Pilgrim household crafts; spinning, weaving, and candle-dipping demonstrations; herb garden. (July-Oct, Wed-Sat) **$$**

Hedge House. *126 Water St, Plymouth (02360). Opposite Town Wharf. Phone 508/746-0012.* (1809) Period furnishings, special exhibits. (June-Oct, Wed-Sat) **$$**

Howland House. *33 Sandwich St, Plymouth (02360). Phone 508/746-9590.* (1666) Restored Pilgrim house has 17th- and 18th-century furnishings. (Memorial Day-mid-Oct, Mon-Sat, also Sun afternoons and Thanksgiving) **$$**

Mayflower Society House Museum. *4 Winslow St, Plymouth. Off North St. Phone 508/746-2590.* National headquarters of the General Society of Mayflower Descendants. House built in 1754; nine rooms with 17th- and 18th-century furnishings. Formal garden. (July-Labor Day: daily; Memorial Day weekend-June and early Sept-Oct: Fri-Sun) **$$**

Myles Standish State Forest. *194 Cranberry Rd, South Carver (02366). S on Hwy 3, exit 5, Long Pond. Phone 508/866-2526.* Approximately 15,000 acres. Swimming, bathhouse, fishing, boating; hiking and bicycle trails, riding, hunting, winter sports, picnicking (fee), camping (fee; dump station).

National Monument to the Forefathers. *Allerton St and Hwy 44, Plymouth (02360). Phone 508/746-1790.* Built between 1859 and 1889 (at a cost of $155,000) to depict the virtues of the Pilgrims. At 81 feet, it is the tallest solid granite monument in the United States. (May-Oct, daily) **FREE**

Ocean Spray Cranberry World. *158 Water St, Plymouth (02360). Phone 508/866-8190.* Visitor Center with exhibits of the history and cultivation of the cranberry. Half-hour self-guided tours. (May-Nov) **$$$$**

Pilgrim Hall Museum. *75 Court St, Plymouth (02360). On Hwy 3A. Phone 508/746-1620.* (1824) Decorative arts and possessions of first Pilgrims and their descendants; includes furniture, household items, ceramics; only known portrait of a *Mayflower* passenger. (Daily; closed Jan, Dec 25) **$$**

Plimoth Plantation/*Mayflower II*. *137 Warren Ave, Plymouth (02360). Take Hwy 93 S to Hwy 3 S, exit 4*

(Plimoth Plantation Hwy). Continue on Plimoth Plantation Hwy for approximately 1 mile and take the exit for the museum. At the end of the exit ramp, turn right and proceed up the street for 20 yards. Turn right at the sign for the museum into the driveway. Phone 508/746-1622. www.plimoth.org. The Plimoth Plantation, which re-creates a 1627 Pilgrim village, reflects an old-fashioned spelling of the colony that now serves to differentiate the plantation from the modern town. The actors at the plantation play their roles faithfully, pretending no knowledge of the 21st (or even the 18th) century; they wear and use only the clothing, equipment, tools, and cookware that would have been available in the late 17th century. The plantation is large and takes a bit of walking to see. The *Mayflower II* is a full-scale reproduction of the *Mayflower* built by J. W. & A. Upham shipyard in England with oak timbers, hand-forged nails, linen canvas sails, hemp rope, and other historically accurate details. It was sailed from England to Plymouth in 1957 on a 55-day voyage and has remained on display at Plimoth Plantation ever since. Plan to spend a half day to a full day for both exhibits. (Apr-Nov, daily; closed Dec-Mar) **$$$$** On the plantation are

1627 Pilgrim Village. *137 Warren Ave, Plymouth (02362).* Fort-Meetinghouse and 14 houses. Costumed people portray actual residents of Plymouth and re-create life in an early farming community.

Hobbamock's (Wampanoag) Homesite. A large bark-covered house representing Hobbamock's dwelling, as well as specially crafted tools and artifacts, depict the domestic environment of the Wampanoag culture. Staff members explain this rich heritage from a modern-day perspective.

Visitor Center. *137 Warren Ave, Plymouth (02362).* Provides visitors with introduction to this unique museum. Orientation program includes a 12-minute multi-image screen presentation. Exhibits; educational services; museum shop; restaurants, picnic area.

Plymouth Colony Winery. *56 Pinewood Rd, Plymouth (02360). Hwy 44 W, left on Pinewood Rd.* Phone 508/747-3334. Working cranberry bogs. Wine tasting. Watch cranberry harvest activities in fall. Winery (Apr-late Dec: daily; Mar: Fri-Sun; also holidays). **FREE**

Plymouth Harbor Cruises. *10 Town Wharf, Plymouth (02360).* Phone 508/747-2400. One-hour cruises of

historic harbor aboard *Pilgrim Belle,* a Mississippi-style paddlewheeler. (Mid-May-Mid-Oct, daily) Departs from State Pier. **$$$**

Plymouth National Wax Museum. *16 Carver St, Plymouth (02360).* Phone 508/746-6468. Pilgrim story told through narrations and animation; includes 26 life-size scenes and more than 180 figures. (Mar-Nov, daily) **$$$**

Plymouth Rock. *Phone 508/866-2580.* Water St, on the harbor.

Provincetown Ferry. *10 Town Wharf, Plymouth (02360).* Phone 508/747-2400. Round-trip passenger ferry departs State Pier in the morning, returns in the evening. (Mid-June-Labor Day: daily; May-mid-June and after Labor Day-Oct: weekends) **$$$$**

Richard Sparrow House. *42 Summer St, Plymouth (02360).* Phone 508/747-1240. (1640) Plymouth's oldest restored home; craft gallery, pottery made on premises. (Memorial Day weekend-Thanksgiving, Mon-Tues, Thurs-Sun; gallery open through late Dec) **$**

Site of First Houses. *Leyden and Water sts, Plymouth.* Marked by tablets.

Splashdown Amphibious Tours. *58 Seven Hills Rd, Plymouth (02360).* Phone 508/747-7658. One-hour tours of historic Plymouth; half on land, half on water. Hourly departures from Harbor Place and Village Landing. (Mid-Apr-late Oct, daily) **$$$$**

Spooner House. *27 North St, Plymouth (02360).* Phone 508/746-0012. (1747) Occupied by Spooner family for five generations and furnished with their heirlooms. Collections of Asian export wares, period furniture. (June-Oct, Wed-Sat) **$$**

Supersports Family Fun Park. *108 N Main St, Carver (02330). W of Plymoth historical area, junction Hwys 58 and 44.* Phone 508/866-9655. Rides, games, sports, mini-golf, bumper boats. (Daily, call for off-season hours; closed Dec 25) **$$$$**

Swimming. Six public beaches.

Village Landing Marketplace. *170 Water St, Plymouth (02660). Near junction Hwy 44 and Hwy 3A.* Modeled after colonial marketplace; contains a restaurant and specialty shops. Overlooks historic Plymouth Harbor.

Whale-watching. *117 Standish Ave, Plymouth (02360).* Phone 508/746-2643. Four-hour trip to Stellwagen Bank to view world's largest mammals. (Early May-mid-Oct: daily; early Apr-early May and mid-Oct-early Nov: weekends) **$$$$**

Special Events

America's Hometown Thanksgiving Celebration. *Phone 508/747-7525; toll-free 800/872-1620.* Programs for various events may be obtained by contacting Destination Plymouth. Nov (Throughout Thanksgiving weekend).

Autumnal Feasting. *137 Warren Ave, Plymouth (02360). Phone 508/742-1622; toll-free 800/872-1620.* Plimoth Plantation's 1627 Pilgrim Village. A harvest celebration with Dutch colonists from Fort Amsterdam re-creating a 17th-century event. Activities, feasting, games. Columbus Day weekend.

Destination Plymouth Sprint Triathlon. *194 Cranberry Rd, South Carver (02366). Phone 508/866-2526; toll-free 800/872-1620.* Myles Standish State Forest (see). National Championship qualifier includes 1/2-mile swim, 12-mile bike ride, and 4-mile run. July.

Pilgrim's Progress. *Phone toll-free 800/872-1620.* A reenactment of Pilgrims going to church, from Cole's Hill to Burial Hill. Each Fri in Aug; also Thanksgiving.

Limited-Service Hotels

★ **BEST WESTERN COLD SPRING.** *188 Court St, Plymouth (02360). Phone 508/746-2222; toll-free 800/678-8667; fax 508/746-2744. www.coldspringmotel.com.* 60 rooms. Closed Jan-Mar. Complimentary continental breakfast. Check-in 2 pm, check-out 11 am. **$**
🐾

★ ★ **RADISSON HOTEL PLYMOUTH HARBOR.** *180 Water St, Plymouth (02360). Phone 508/747-4900; toll-free 800/333-3333; fax 508/746-2609. www.radisson.com.* Located on scenic Plymouth Harbor midway between Cape Cod and Boston, this inn is near many historic attractions, including Plymouth Rock. 175 rooms, 4 story. Check-out 11 am. High-speed Internet access. Restaurant, bar. Fitness room. Indoor pool. **$**
🧍 🐾

Specialty Lodgings

The following lodging establishments are approved by Mobil Travel Guide, but due to their unique and individualized nature have not been given a traditional Mobil Star rating. Included in this listing you may find bed-and-breakfasts, limited-service inns, guest ranches, and other unique hotel properties.

THE COLONIAL HOUSE INN. *207 Sandwich St (Hwy 3A), Plymouth (02360). Phone 508/747-4274; toll-free 866/747-4274. www.thecolonialhouseinn.com.* 4 rooms. Complimentary continental breakfast. Check-in 4-7 pm, check-out 11 am. Beach. Indoor pool. **$$**
🐾

JOHN CARVER INN. *25 Summer St, Plymouth (02360). Phone 508/746-7100; toll-free 800/274-1620; fax 508/746-8299. www.johncarverinn.com.* 79 rooms, 3 story. Check-out 11 am. Restaurant, bar. Outdoor pool. **$$**
🐾

THE MABBETT HOUSE. *7 Cushman St, Plymouth (02360). Phone 508/830-1911; toll-free 800/572-7829; fax 508/830-9775. www.mabbetthouse.com.* Colonial Revival house; artifacts collected from world travels. 3 rooms, 2 story. Children over 12 years only. Complimentary full breakfast. Check-in 3 pm, check-out 11 am. **$**
🐾

Restaurant

★ **HEARTH AND KETTLE.** *25 Summer St, Plymouth (02360). Phone 508/746-7100; fax 508/746-8299. www.johncarverinn.com.* Servers dressed in colonial attire. Seafood menu. Breakfast, lunch, dinner. Closed Dec 25. Bar. Children's menu. **$$**

Provincetown (Cape Cod) (C-9)

Settled circa 1700
Population 3,431
Elevation 40 ft
Area Code 508
Zip 02657
Information Chamber of Commerce, 307 Commercial St, PO Box 1017; phone 508/487-3424
Web Site www.capecodaccess.com/provincetownchamber

Provincetown is a startling mixture of heroic past and easygoing present; the area may have been explored by Leif Ericson in AD 1004. It is certain that the

Mayflower anchored first in Provincetown Harbor while the Mayflower Compact, setting up the colony's government, was signed aboard the ship. Provincetown was where the first party of Pilgrims came ashore. A bronze tablet at Commercial Street and Beach Highway marks the site of the Pilgrims' first landing. The city attracts many tourists who come each summer to explore the narrow streets and rows of picturesque old houses.

What to See and Do

Commercial Street. To view a shopping district that's steeped in history and still thriving today, visit Provincetown's Commercial Street. Stretching more than 3 miles in length, the narrow street sports art galleries, shops, clubs, restaurants, and hotels. When the street was constructed in 1835, the houses that backed up to it all faced the harbor, which was the principle area of business activity. As you tour the street, note that many of those homes were turned 180 degrees to face the street or had a new "front" door crafted in the back of the house.

Expedition Whydah's Sea Lab & Learning Center. *16 MacMillan Wharf, Provincetown (02657). Phone 508/487-7955.* Archaeological site of sunken pirate ship *Whydah,* struck by storms in 1717. Learn about the recovery of the ship's pirate treasure, the lives and deaths of pirates, and the history of the ship and its passengers. (Apr-mid-Oct: daily; mid-Oct-Dec: weekends and school holidays)

⭐ **Pilgrim Monument & Museum.** *High Pole Hill, Provincetown (02657). Phone 508/487-1310. www.pilgrim-monument.org.* A 252-foot granite tower commemorating the Pilgrims' 1620 landing in the New World; provides an excellent view. (Summer, daily) **$$$** Admission includes

Provincetown Museum. *High Pole Hill, Provincetown (02657). Phone 508/487-1310.* Exhibits include whaling equipment, scrimshaw, ship models, artifacts from shipwrecks; Pilgrim Room with scale model diorama of the merchant ship *Mayflower;* Donald MacMillan's Arctic exhibit; antique fire engine and firefighting equipment; theater history display. (Summer, daily)

Provincetown Art Association & Museum. *460 Commercial St, Provincetown (02657). Phone 508/487-1750.* Changing exhibits; museum store. (Late May-Oct: daily; rest of year: weekends) **DONATION**

Recreation. Swimming at surrounding beaches, including Town Beach, west of the village, Herring Cove and Race Point, on the ocean side. Tennis, cruises, beach buggy tours, and fishing available.

Town Wharf (MacMillan Wharf). *Commercial and Standish sts, Provincetown (02657).* Center of maritime activity. Also here is

Portuguese Princess Whale Watch. *Phone 508/487-2651; toll-free 800/442-3188 (New England).* 100-foot boats offer 3 1/2-hour narrated whale-watching excursions. Naturalist aboard. (Apr-Oct, daily)

Whale-watching. *306 Commercial St, Provincetown (02657). Dolphin Fleet of Provincetown. Phone 508/349-1900; toll-free 800/826-9300.* Offers 3 1/2- to 4-hour trips (mid-Apr-Oct, daily). Research scientists from the Provincetown Center for Coastal Studies are aboard each trip to lecture on the history of the whales being viewed. **$$$$**

Special Event

Provincetown Portuguese Festival. *MacMillian Wharf, Provincetown (02657). Phone 508/487-3424.* Provincetown's fisherman of Portuguese ancestry started this enduring festival over 50 years ago. Each year in late June, the local bishop says Mass at St. Peter's Church and then leads a procession to MacMillan Wharf, where he blesses a parade of fishing boats. The festival that follows features fireworks, concerts, dancing, Portuguese art, and delightful food choices. If you aren't in town for the Provincetown Blessing, check out similar events in Falmouth (July 4) and Hyannis (early July). Last week in June.

Limited-Service Hotels

★ ★ **BEST WESTERN TIDES BEACHFRONT MOTOR INN.** *837 Commercial St, Provincetown (02657). Phone 508/487-1045; toll-free 800/780-7234; fax 508/487-3557. www.bwprovincetown.com.* 64 rooms, 2 story. Closed mid-Oct-mid-May. Check-in 2 pm, check-out 11 am. Restaurant. Outdoor pool. Beach. **$**
🅳 ⛱

★ **WATERMARK INN.** *603 Commercial St, Provincetown (02657). Phone 508/487-0165; fax 508/487-2383. www.watermark-inn.com.* 10 rooms, 2 story, all suites. Check-in 3 pm, check-out 11 am. Beach. **$**
🅳

Full-Service Resorts

★ **THE MASTHEAD RESORT.** *31-41 Commercial St, Provincetown (02657). Phone 508/487-0523; toll-free 800/395-5095; fax 508/481-9251. www.capecodtravel.com/masthead.* 10 rooms, 2 story. Check-out 10 am. Beach. **$**

★ ★ **PROVINCETOWN INN.** *1 Commericial St, Provincetown (02657). Phone 508/487-9500; toll-free 800/942-5388; fax 508/487-2911. www.provincetown inn.com.* 100 rooms, 2 story. Complimentary continental breakfast. Check-out 11 am. Restaurant, bar. Outdoor pool. Beach. **$**

Specialty Lodgings

The following lodging establishments are approved by Mobil Travel Guide, but due to their unique and individualized nature have not been given a traditional Mobil Star rating. Included in this listing you may find bed-and-breakfasts, limited-service inns, guest ranches, and other unique hotel properties.

CROWNE POINTE HISTORIC INN. *82 Bradford St, Provincetown (02657). Phone 508/487-6767; fax 508/487-5554. www.crownepointe.com.* 40 rooms. Complimentary full breakfast. Check-in 4 pm, check-out 11 am. High-speed Internet access. **$$$**

FAIRBANKS INN. *90 Bradford St, Provincetown (02657). Phone 508/487-0386; toll-free 800/324-7265; fax 508/487-3540. www.fairbanksinn.com.* Built in 1776; courtyard. 14 rooms, 2 story. Children over 15 years only. Complimentary continental breakfast. Check-in 2 pm, check-out 11 am. **$**

SNUG COTTAGE. *178 Bradford St, Provincetown (02657). Phone 508/487-1616; fax 508/487-5123. www.snugcottage.com.* Built in 1820. 8 rooms, 2 story. Complimentary full breakfast. Check-in 3 pm, check-out 11 am. **$$**

SOMERSET HOUSE. *378 Commercial St, Provincetown (02657). Phone 508/487-0383; toll-free 800/575-1850; fax 508/487-4746. www.somersethouse inn.com.* Restored 1850s house. 13 rooms, 3 story. Complimentary full breakfast. Check-in 3 pm, check-out 11 am. Beach. **$$**

WATERSHIP INN. *7 Winthrop St, Provincetown (02657). Phone 508/487-0094; toll-free 800/330-9413. www.watershipinn.com.* Built in 1820. 15 rooms, 3 story. Complimentary continental breakfast. Check-in 2 pm, check-out 11:30 am. **$**

WHITE WIND INN. *174 Commercial St, Provincetown (02657). Phone 508/487-1526; toll-free 888/449-9463; fax 508/487-4792. www.whitewindinn .com.* Located opposite the harbor, this inn (1845) was a former shipbuilder's home. 12 rooms, 3 story. Pets accepted, some restrictions; fee. Complimentary continental breakfast. Check-in 2 pm, check-out 11 am. **$**

Restaurants

★ ★ **CAFE EDWIGE.** *333 Commercial St, Provincetown (02657). Phone 508/487-2008.* In a town where many summer folk don't get up until nearly noon, Edwige corners the market in gourmet breakfasts by serving until 1 pm. But chef Stephen Frappolli saves his best New American chops for evening, reveling in New England seafood with dishes like planked local codfish with roasted corn and shiitake mushrooms, and what many consider P'Town's best crab cakes. It's an easy place to miss: Edwige is on the second level. American menu. Breakfast, dinner. Closed Oct 31; also late May. Outdoor seating. **$$**

★ ★ **DANCING LOBSTER CAFE.** *373 Commercial St, Provincetown (02657). Phone 508/487-0900.* With a name like the Dancing Lobster and a waterfront location, it is no wonder that seafood is the backbone of this restaurant's menu. European influences are found throughout the offerings, from the Venetian fish soup to the Basque stew. This place is well liked and the lines are long, even with a reservation. Mediterranean menu. Dinner. Closed Mon; also Dec-May. Bar. Reservations recommended. **$$**

★ ★ **FRONT STREET.** *230 Commercial St, Provincetown (02657). Phone 508/487-9715. www.frontstreetrestaurant.com.* A lovely Victorian building welcomes guests to the well-received Front Street restaurant. This chef-owned restaurant takes great pride in its artful nouveau cuisine. Two menus define the culinary experience here, and whether you choose from the authentic Italian menu or the weekly changing continental one, you are sure to be delighted with the results. Italian menu. Dinner. Closed Jan-Apr. Bar. **$$**

★ **LOBSTER POT.** *321 Commercial St, Provincetown (02657). Phone 508/487-0842; fax 508/ 487-4863.* Perhaps the quintessential Olde Cape Cod restaurant in a town of hip eateries, the Lobster Pot nonetheless thrives by keeping everything as simple as possible, from steamed clams to steamed lobster to the accompanying cole slaw and French fries. There's almost always a line, so snagging a table on the outdoor deck is purely luck of the draw. After your meal, stop by the lobster and chowder market and pick up your favorite items to take home. Seafood menu. Lunch, dinner. Closed Jan. Bar. Casual attire. Outdoor seating. **$$**

★ ★ **LORRAINE'S RESTAURANT.** *133 Commercial St, Provincetown (02657). Phone 508/487-6074. www.lorrainesrestaurant.com.* New American meets Mexican cuisine at the popular Lorraine's Restaurant. From its scenic waterfront location to its easygoing atmosphere, this place practically defines casual dining. Open year-round, this restaurant caters to a laid-back crowd that enjoys a good meal in a cozy environment. Mexican menu. Dinner, late-night. Closed Dec-Mar. Casual attire. **$$**

★ ★ **MARTIN HOUSE.** *157 Commercial St, Provincetown (02657). Phone 508/487-1327; fax 508/487-4514. www.themartinhouse.com.* A warren of tiny, rustic rooms makes up the dining spaces in this utterly charming 18th-century house with five working fireplaces. In summer, you can also dine alfresco by a fountain on the garden terrace. The romantic mood is enhanced by a sleekly contemporary menu that features nightly variants on local oysters, foie gras, and seafood soups (like crab and shrimp with green curry). Vegetarians always have at least one well-considered option, often employing seitan ("wheat meat"). American menu. Dinner. Closed Mon-Wed; also Jan. Bar. Reservations recommended. Outdoor seating. **$$$**

★ ★ **THE MEWS RESTAURANT & CAFE.** *429 Commercial St, Provincetown (02657). Phone 508/487-1500.* Tucked away in the art gallery district, The Mews Restaurant & Café shares two personalities with diners. The first-floor dining room dazzles guests with its beachfront views, stylish setting, and cosmopolitan cuisine, while the upstairs café has an airy feel with a lighter menu. International/Fusion menu. Dinner. Bar. Casual attire. **$$**

★ ★ **NAPI'S.** *7 Freeman St, Provincetown (02657). Phone 508/487-1145; toll-free 800/571-6274; fax 508/ 487-7123.* Napi's takes diners on an art-filled journey around the world. Located on a quiet side street, this restaurant has an art gallery feel, thanks to the many works by local artists displayed on its walls. The menu is a hodgepodge of international specialties, providing diners with a variety of tantalizing choices. International/Fusion menu. Dinner. Bar. Children's menu. **$$**

★ **PUCCI'S HARBORSIDE.** *539 Commercial St, Provincetown (02657). Phone 508/487-1964.* Pucci's Harborside boasts great views and excellent casual American dining. This first-rate restaurant is a perfect stop for both lunch and dinner. Guests feast on gourmet burgers, deliciously messy nachos, and other upscale bar food in a decidedly relaxed setting perched above the harbor. Seafood menu. Lunch, dinner. Closed Nov-mid-Apr. Bar. **$**

★ ★ ★ **RED INN RESTAURANT.** *15 Commercial St, Provincetown (02657). Phone 508/487-0050; fax 508/487-6253.* One of the best places to enjoy fine dining with a view is at the historic Red Inn, a restored colonial building. Views of the harbor, the bay, Long Point lighthouse, and even the shores of the Outer Cape delight sophisticated patrons who dine on imaginative meals. The house special is the porterhouse steak, truly a carnivore's delight. International/Fusion menu. Lunch, dinner, Sun brunch. Closed Dec 25. **$$**

★ ★ **SAL'S PLACE.** *99 Commercial St, Provincetown (02657). Phone 508/487-1279; fax 508/ 487-1279. www.salsplaceprovincetown.com.* Provincetown's quiet West End is home to Sal's Place. This intimate restaurant dishes it up Italian style, earning kudos for its large portions of satisfying food. Seafood is jazzed up with Mediterranean influences, and the pastas are always a great choice. The waterfront location adds to its appeal, and outdoor seating is available seasonally. Italian menu. Dinner. Closed Nov-Apr. Children's menu. Outdoor seating. **$$**

Quincy (B-7)

See also Boston

Settled 1625
Population 88,025
Elevation 20 ft
Area Code 617
Information Tourism and Visitors Bureau, 1250

Hancock St, Suite 802 N, 02169; phone toll-free 888/232-6737

Boston's neighbor to the south, Quincy (QUIN-zee) was the home of the Adamses, a great American family whose fame dates from colonial days. Family members include the second and sixth presidents—John Adams and his son, John Quincy Adams. John Hancock, first signer of the Declaration of Independence, was born here. George Bush, the 41st president, was born in nearby Milton.

Thomas Morton, an early settler, held May Day rites at Merrymount (a section of Quincy) in 1627 and was shipped back to England for selling firearms and "firewater" to the Native Americans.

What to See and Do

★ **Adams National Historic Park.** *1250 Hancock St, Quincy (02169). Phone 617/770-1175.* Administered by the National Park Service. Tickets to sites can be purchased here *only.* (Mid-Apr-mid-Nov: daily; rest of year: Tues-Fri) Golden Eagle Passport accepted (see MAKING THE MOST OF YOUR TRIP). **$$** Includes

The Adams National Historic Site. *135 Adams St, Quincy (02169). Off Furnace Brook Pkwy.* The house (1731), bought in 1787 by John Adams, was given as a national site by the Adams family in 1946. Original furnishings.

John Adams and John Quincy Adams Birthplaces. *133 and 141 Franklin St, Quincy (02169).* Two 17th-century saltbox houses. The elder Adams was born and raised at 133 Franklin Street; his son was born in the other house. While living here, Abigail Adams wrote many of her famous letters to her husband, John Adams, when he was serving in the Continental Congress in Philadelphia and as an arbitrator for peace with Great Britain in Paris. Guided tours.

Josiah Quincy House. *20 Muirhead St, Quincy (02170). Phone 617/227-3956.* (1770) Built on a 1635 land grant, this fine Georgian house originally had a view across Quincy Bay to Boston Harbor; was surrounded by outbuildings and much agricultural land. Long the home of the Quincy family; furnished with family heirlooms and memorabilia. Period wall paneling, fireplaces surrounded by English tiles. Tours on the hour. (July-Aug, Sat-Sun afternoons) **$$**

Quincy Historical Society. *Adams Academy Building, 8 Adams St, Quincy (02169). Phone 617/773-1144.* Museum of regional history; library. (Mon-Sat) **$**

Quincy Homestead. *1010 Hancock St, Quincy (02169). At Butler Rd. Phone 617/472-5117.* Four generations of Quincys lived here, including Dorothy Quincy, wife of John Hancock. Two rooms built in 1686, rest of house dates from the 18th century; period furnishings; herb garden. (May-Oct, Wed-Sun) **$$**

United First Parish Church. *1306 Hancock St, Quincy. At Washington St. Phone 617/773-1290.* (1828) Only church in United States where two presidents—John Adams and John Quincy Adams—and their wives are entombed. Tours (late Apr-mid-Nov, Mon-Sat, Sun afternoons). **$$**

Special Events

Quincy Bay Race Week. *Quincy Yacht Club, Quincy (02169). Phone toll-free 888/232-6737.* Sailing regatta, marine parades, fireworks. July.

South Shore Christmas Festival. *Phone toll-free 888/232-6737.* Includes parade with floats. Sun after Thanksgiving.

Summerfest. *Phone toll-free 888/232-6737.* Concerts on the Green, Ruth Gordon Amphitheatre. Wed, mid-June-Aug.

Full-Service Hotel

★ ★ ★ **MARRIOTT BOSTON QUINCY.** *1000 Marriott Dr, Quincy (02169). Phone 617/472-1000; toll-free 800/228-9290; fax 617/472-7095. www.marriott.com.* 472 rooms, 9 story. Check-in 4 pm, check-out noon. Restaurant, bar. Fitness room. Indoor pool, whirlpool. Business center. **$**
🖥 🏋 ⚓ 🏃

Rockport (A-8)

Settled 1690
Population 7,767
Elevation 77 ft
Area Code 978
Zip 01966
Information Chamber of Commerce, PO Box 67M; phone 978/546-6575 or toll-free 888/726-3922
Web Site www.rockportusa.com

Rockport is a year-round artists' colony. A weather-beaten shanty on one of the wharves has been the subject of so many paintings that it is called "Motif No. 1."

Studios, galleries, summer places, estates, and cottages dot the shore of Cape Ann from Eastern Point southeast of Gloucester all the way to Annisquam.

What to See and Do

Old Castle. *Granite and Curtis sts, Rockport (01966). Pigeon Cove. Phone 978/546-9533.* (1715) A fine example of early 18th-century architecture and exhibits. (July-Aug: daily; rest of year: by appointment) **$$**

The Paper House. *52 Pigeon Hill St, Rockport (01966). Phone 978/546-2629.* Newspapers were used in the construction of the house and furniture. (Apr-Oct) **$**

Rockport Art Association. *12 Main St, Rockport (01966). Phone 978/546-6604.* Changing exhibits of paintings, sculpture, and graphics by 250 artist members. Special events include concerts (see SPECIAL EVENT), lectures, artist demonstrations. (Daily; closed Thanksgiving, Dec 25-Jan 1) **FREE**

Sandy Bay Historical Society & Museums. *40 King St, Rockport (01966). Near railroad station. Phone 978/546-9533.* Early American and 19th-century rooms and objects, exhibits on fishing, granite industry, the Atlantic cable, and a children's room in an 1832 home constructed of granite. (Mid-June-mid-Sept: daily; rest of year: by appointment) **$**

Sightseeing Tours and Boat Cruises. Contact the Chamber of Commerce for a list of companies offering sightseeing, fishing, and boat tours.

Special Event

Rockport Chamber Music Festival. *157 South St, Rockport (01966). Phone 978/546-7391. www.rcmf.org.* Soloists and chamber ensembles of international acclaim have performed at this art colony since 1982. A lecture series and family concert are also featured. Four weekends in June or July.

Limited-Service Hotels

★ ★ **SANDY BAY MOTOR INN.** *173 Main St, Rockport (01966). Phone 978/546-7155; toll-free 800/437-7155; fax 978/546-9131. www.sandybaymotorinn.com.* This inn is conveniently located just a short walk from downtown's quaint shops and galleries and is close to many beaches, theaters, and churches. 80 rooms, 2 story. Pets accepted, some restrictions; fee. Check-out 11 am. Restaurant. Indoor pool, whirlpool. Tennis. **$**

★ ★ **TURK'S HEAD MOTOR INN.** *151 South St, Rockport (01966). Phone 978/546-3436. www.turksheadinn.com.* 28 rooms, 2 story. Closed mid-Oct-Mar. Check-out 11 am. Restaurant. Indoor pool. Two beaches nearby. **$**

Full-Service Inns

★ ★ ★ **EMERSON INN BY THE SEA.** *1 Cathedral Ave, Rockport (Pigeon Cove) (01966). Phone 978/546-6321; toll-free 800/964-5550; fax 978/546-7043. www.emersoninnbythesea.com.* This traditional country inn has hosted guests at its oceanfront Pigeon Cove location since 1846. From March through the end of December visitors can enjoy beautiful ocean views from the pool, porch, restaurant and half the guest rooms. 36 rooms, 4 story. Check-in after 1 pm, check-out noon. Restaurant. Spa. Outdoor pool, whirlpool. **$**

★ ★ ★ **SEACREST MANOR.** *99 Marmion Way, Rockport (01966). Phone 978/546-2211. www.seacrestmanor.com.* Delightful, charming, and intimate, this country inn provides an attentive (but not overbearing) staff. Enjoy afternoon tea or, if in the mood for some fresh air, rent one of the bicycles available for guests. 7 rooms, 2 story. Closed Dec-Mar. Complimentary full breakfast. Check-in after 2 pm, check-out 11 am. Restaurant (inn guests only). **$$**

★ ★ ★ **SEAWARD INN & COTTAGES.** *44 Marmion Way, Rockport (01966). Phone 978/546-3471; toll-free 877/473-2927; fax 978/546-7661. www.seawardinn.com.* Situated on Cape Ann 40 miles northeast of Boston, this inn offers cozy rooms and 9 quaint cottages. Guests can relax in Adirondack chairs along the rocky, Atlantic coast. 39 rooms. Complimentary full breakfast. Check-in 2 pm, check-out 11 am. Restaurant. Airport transportation available. **$**

★ ★ ★ **YANKEE CLIPPER INN.** *127 Granite St, Rockport (01966). Phone 978/546-3407; toll-free 800/545-3699; fax 978/546-9730. www.yankeeclipperinn.com.* Serving guests year-round, this seaside resort offers rolling country gardens, a heated pool and an atmosphere engineered for comfort. Enjoy a splendid meal in the Veranda Restaurant featuring elegant American-Continental cuisine. 16 rooms, 3 story. Closed Jan-Feb. Complimentary full breakfast. Check-out 11 am. Outdoor saltwater pool. Airport transportation available. **$$**

Specialty Lodgings

The following lodging establishments are approved by Mobil Travel Guide, but due to their unique and individualized nature have not been given a traditional Mobil Star rating. Included in this listing you may find bed-and-breakfasts, limited-service inns, guest ranches, and other unique hotel properties.

ADDISON CHOATE INN. *49 Broadway, Rockport (01966). Phone 978/546-7543; toll-free 800/245-7543; fax 978/546-7638. www.addisonchoateinn.com.* This charming bed-and-breakfast is located less than an hour's drive north of Boston at the tip of Cape Ann. Guests can enjoy all the town has to offer including artists' galleries, shops, and, of course, the beaches. 8 rooms, 3 story. Children over 11 years only. Complimentary continental breakfast. Check-in 3 pm, check-out 11 am. **$**

THE INN ON COVE HILL. *37 Mount Pleasant St, Rockport (01966). Phone 978/546-2701; toll-free 888/546-2701; fax 978/576-1095. www.innoncovehill.com.* This inn was built in 1791 from proceeds of pirates' gold found nearby. It is located near the wharf and yacht club. 8 rooms, 3 story. Closed mid-Oct-mid-Apr. Complimentary continental breakfast. Check-in 2 pm, check-out 11 am. **$**

LINDEN TREE INN. *26 King St, Rockport (01966). Phone 978/546-2494; toll-free 800/865-2122; fax 978/546-3297. www.lindentreeinn.com.* 18 rooms, 3 story. Complimentary full breakfast. Check-in 2 pm, check-out 11 am. **$**

PEGLEG RESTAURANT AND INN. *2 King St, Rockport (01966). Phone 978/546-2352; toll-free 800/346-2352. www.pegleginn.com.* 33 rooms. Closed Nov-Mar. Complimentary continental breakfast. Check-in 2 pm, check-out 11 am. Restaurant. **$**

ROCKY SHORES INN & COTTAGES. *65 Eden Rd, Rockport (01966). Phone 978/546-2823; toll-free 800/348-4003.* Mansion built in 1905. 11 rooms, 3 story. Closed mid-Oct-mid-Apr. Complimentary full breakfast. Check-in 3 pm, check-out 11 am. **$**

THE TUCK INN B&B. *17 High St, Rockport (01966). Phone 978/546-7260; toll-free 800/789-7260. www.thetuckinn.com.* Colonial house built in 1790. Within walking distance to downtown and beach. 13 rooms, 2 story. Complimentary continental breakfast. Check-in 2-9 pm, check-out 11 am. Outdoor pool. **$**

Restaurant

★ **BRACKETT'S OCEANIEW.** *25 Main St, Rockport (01966). Phone 978/546-2797. www.bracketts.com.* Seafood menu. Lunch, dinner. Closed Nov-mid-Mar. **$$**

Salem (B-7)

See also Beverly, Danvers, Lynn, Marblehead

Settled 1626
Population 40,407
Elevation 9 ft
Area Code 978
Zip 01970
Information Chamber of Commerce, 63 Wharf St; phone 978/744-0004
Web Site www.salem-chamber.org

In old Salem, the story of early New England life is told with bricks, clapboards, carvings, and gravestones. The town had two native geniuses to immortalize it: Samuel McIntire (1757-1811), master builder, and Nathaniel Hawthorne (1804-1864), author. History is charmingly entangled with the people and events of Hawthorne's novels. Reality, however, could be far from charming. During the witchcraft panic of 1692, 19 persons were hanged on Gallows Hill, another "pressed" to death; at least two others died in jail. Gallows Hill is still here; so is the house of one of the trial judges.

Early in the 18th century, Salem shipbuilding and allied industries were thriving. Salem was a major port. The Revolution turned commerce into privateering.

A Walk through Salem

Salem is a fascinating old port city with a walkable downtown. Begin at the National Park Visitors Center at 2 Liberty Street across from the Museum Place garage. Just around the corner on the pedestrian stretch of Essex Street is the Peabody Essex Museum, New England's ultimate treasure chest of exotica, all of it brought from the farthest points of the globe by Salem sea captains in the decades after the Revolution. The Essex Institute part of the museum houses a collection of portraits and archives, including the actual records of the 1692 witch trials for which Salem is infamous; a short film puts the trials in their historical context. Historic homes on the grounds include the Gardner-Pingree House, showcasing the work of Samuel McIntire. Salem's famous architect, McIntire is known for creating airy Federal-era mansions with elegant carved detailing, arches, and stairways. You might want to detour to see Chestnut Street, famous because it is lined with McIntire mansions (walk west up Essex Street and south on Cambridge Street; return the same route).

West of the museums, turn south off Essex Street to Derby Square, site of Salem's old Town Hall, a graceful brick building dating from 1816 that is now a hospitable visitor center for the Salem Chamber of Commerce. Continue down the square (it's really a mini-park) to Front Street and follow the red line on the sidewalk (the Salem Heritage Trail) down Charter and Liberty streets, past the Old Burying Point Cemetery and the Salem Wax Museum.

Continue down along Derby Street to the Salem Maritime National Historic site on Salem Harbor. The *Friendship*, a fully rigged tall ship, is berthed at Central Wharf. The handsome brick Custom House (1819), where Nathaniel Hawthorne worked, is next door at the head of Derby Wharf. Here, too, is the Elias Hasket Derby House, built by the man who pioneered a new sailing route around the Cape of Good Hope and is said to have been America's first millionaire. The House of Seven Gables, immortalized by Hawthorne, is a few blocks east overlooking the harbor. Retrace your steps (following the red line) up Derby Street and turn up Hawthorne Boulevard to Salem Common. Look for the Salem Witch Museum (Washington Square North), which dramatizes the tale of the witch trials with computerized sound and light. This tour is slightly under 2 miles, but you can hop a trolley—also a good way to gain an overview of sites to begin with—if you tire along the way. Return down Brown Street to your starting point.

Then began the fabulous China trade and Salem's heyday. The captains came home, and Sam McIntire built splendid houses for them that still stand. Shipping declined after 1812. Salem turned to industry, which, together with tourism, is the present-day economic base.

What to See and Do

Chestnut Street. Architecturally, one of the most beautiful streets in America; laid out in 1796.

House of Seven Gables. *54 Turner St, Salem (01970). Off Derby St on Salem Harbor. Phone 978/744-0991. www.7gables.org.* Nathaniel Hawthorne's 1851 novel is said to have been inspired by this home, although he never lived there. You'll enjoy the tour most if you've read the book, because you'll recognize furnishings and areas of the home from Hawthorne's descriptions. Even if you haven't read it, however, you're sure to enjoy the well-preserved estate that dates to 1669, as well as the guide in period clothing. (Daily; closed the first three weeks in Jan) **$$**

Peabody Museum & Essex Institute. *East India Sq, Salem (01970). Phone 978/745-9500; toll-free 866/745-1876.* The Peabody Museum, founded by sea captains in 1799, features five world-famous collections in 30 galleries. Large collections of marine art, Asian export art. Essex Institute features historical interpretations of the area. Peabody Museum (daily; closed Jan 1, Thanksgiving, Dec 25). Essex Institute (daily) **$$$** Admission includes

Crowninshield-Bentley House. *Essex St and Hawthorne Blvd, Salem (01970).* (1727) Reverend William Bentley, minister and diarist, lived here from 1791 to 1819. Period furnishings. (June-Oct: daily; rest of year: Sat-Sun, holidays)

Gardner-Pingree House. *128 Essex St, Salem (01970).* (1804) Designed by McIntire; restored and handsomely furnished. (June-Oct: daily; rest of year: Sat-Sun, holidays)

John Ward House. *161 Essex St, Salem (01970). Behind Essex Institute.* (1684) Seventeenth-century furnishings. (June-Oct: daily; rest of year: Sat-Sun, holidays)

Peirce-Nichols House. *80 Federal St, Salem (01970). Phone 978/745-9500.* (1782) One of the finest examples of McIntire's architectural genius; authentically furnished. (By appointment only)

Pickering Wharf. *174 Derby St, Salem (01970). Adjacent to Salem Maritime National Historic Site.* This 6-acre commercial and residential village by the sea includes shops, restaurants, and a marina.

Pioneer Village: Salem in 1630. *Forest River Park off West St, Salem (01970). Phone 978/744-0991.* Reproduction of early Puritan settlement, includes dugouts, wigwams, and thatched cottages; costumed interpreters. Guided tours. (Late May-Oct, daily) **$$$$**

Ropes Mansion and Garden. *318 Essex St, Salem (01970). Phone 978/745-9500.* (Late 1720s) Gambrel-roofed, Georgian and colonial mansion; restored and furnished with period pieces. The garden (laid out in 1912) is nationally known for its beauty and variety. (June-Oct, daily; limited hours Sun) **$$**

★ **Salem Maritime National Historic Site.** *174 Derby St, Salem (01970). Orientation Center, Central Wharf Warehouse. Phone 978/740-1660. www.nps.gov/sama.* Nine acres of historic waterfront. Self-guided and guided tours. (Daily; Jan 1, Thanksgiving, Dec 25). **$$** Site includes

Custom House. *174 Derby St, Salem (01970). Derby St, opposite wharf. Phone 978/745-0799.* (1819) Restored offices. (Daily; closed Jan 1, Thanksgiving, Dec 25)

Derby House. *174 Derby St, Salem (01970). Phone 978/745-0799.* (1761-1762) Home of maritime merchant Elias Hasket Derby, one of the country's first millionaires. In back are the Derby House Gardens, featuring roses, herbs, and 19th-century flowers. Inquire at Orientation Center for tour information.

Derby Wharf. *174 Derby St, Salem (01970). Off Derby St. Phone 978/740-1660.* Once a center of Salem shipping (1760-1810).

Narbonne House. *Phone 978/745-0799.* A 17th-century house with archaeological exhibits. Inquire at Orientation Center for tour information.

Scale House. *174 Derby St, Salem (01970). Phone 978/745-0799.* (1829) and **Bonded Warehouse** (1819). Site of 19th-century customs operations. (Daily)

Visitor Information. *2 New Liberty St, Salem (01970). Phone 978/744-0004.* In Orientation Center and downtown visitor center at Museum Place, Essex Street.

West India Goods Store. *164 Derby St, Salem (01970).* (1800) Coffee, teas, spices, and goods for sale. (Daily; closed Jan 1, Thanksgiving, Dec 25)

Salem State College. *352 Lafayette St, Salem (01970). Phone 978/542-6200.* (1854) (9,300 students) On campus are

Chronicle of Salem. *Meier Hall.* Mural, 60 feet by 30 feet, depicts Salem history from settlement to present in 50 sequences. (Mon-Fri; closed holidays)

Library Gallery. Art exhibits by local and national artists. (Mon-Sat) **FREE**

Main Stage Auditorium. *352 Lafayette St, Salem (01970). Phone 978/744-3700.* This 750-seat theater presents musical and dramatic productions (Sept-Apr).

Winfisky Art Gallery. Photographs, paintings, graphics, and sculpture by national and local artists. (Sept-May, Mon-Fri) **FREE**

Salem Witch Museum. *19 1/2 Washington Sq, Salem (01970). Follow Hawthorne Blvd to the NW corner of Salem Common. Phone 978/744-1692. www.salem witchmuseum.com.* The Salem Witch Museum recreates the Salem Witch Trials of 1692 with a 30-minute narrated presentation that uses special lighting and life-size figures. The museum may be too frightening for young children. If you're traveling in October, also visit Salem's Haunted Happenings, a Halloween festival that begins in early October and runs through Halloween and features street merchants, plays, witchy games, and haunted houses. (Daily; closed Jan 1, Thanksgiving, Dec 25) **$$**

Stephen Phillips Trust House. *34 Chestnut St, Salem (01970). Phone 978/744-0440.* (1804) Federal-style mansion with McIntire mantels and woodwork. Furnishings, rugs, and porcelains reflect the merchant and seafaring past of the Phillips family. Also here is a carriage barn with carriages and antique automobiles. (Late May-Oct, Mon-Sat) **FREE**

Witch Dungeon Museum. *16 Lynde St, Salem (01970). Phone 978/741-3570.* Reenactment of witch trial of Sarah Good by professional actresses; tour through re-created dungeon where accused witches awaited trial; original artifacts. (May-Nov, daily) **$$**

Witch House. *310 1/2 Essex St, Salem (01970). Phone 978/744-0180.* (1642) Home of witchcraft trial judge Jonathan Corwin. Some of the accused witches may have been examined here. (Mid-Mar-Nov, daily) **$$**

Special Events

Haunted Happenings. *Various sites. Phone 978/744-0004.* Psychic festival, historical exhibits, haunted house, costume parade, contests, dances. Entire month of Oct.

Heritage Days Celebration. *Phone 978-744-0004.* Band concerts, parade, exhibits, and ethnic festivals. Mid-Aug.

Limited-Service Hotel

★ ★ **HAWTHORNE HOTEL.** *18 Washington Sq W, Salem (01970). Phone 978/744-4080; fax 978/745-9842.* 89 rooms, 6 story. Pets accepted, some restrictions; fee. Check-out 11 am. Restaurant. Fitness room. **$**

Specialty Lodging

The following lodging establishment is approved by Mobil Travel Guide, but due to its unique and individualized nature has not been given a traditional Mobil Star rating. Included in this listing you may find bed-and-breakfasts, limited-service inns, guest ranches, and other unique hotel properties.

SALEM INN. *7 Summer St, Salem (01970). Phone 978/741-0680; toll-free 800/446-2995; fax 978/744-8924. www.saleminnma.com.* With individually appointed rooms and suites, many of which feature Jacuzzis, kitchenettes, and fireplaces, this inn provides comfort and luxury without assaulting your wallet. Season packages available. 33 rooms, 4 story. Pets

accepted; fee. Complimentary continental breakfast. Check-in 3 pm, check-out 11 am. **$**

Restaurants

★ ★ **GRAPE VINE.** *26 Congress St, Salem (01970). Phone 978/745-9335; fax 978/744-9335. www.grapevinesalem.com.* American, Italian menu. Dinner. Closed holidays; also Super Bowl Sun. Bar. Outdoor seating. **$$$**

★ ★ **LEGAL SEAFOODS.** *210 Andover St, Peabody (01960). Phone 978/532-4500; fax 978/532-2110.* Seafood menu. Lunch, dinner. Closed Thanksgiving, Dec 25. Bar. Children's menu. **$$**

★ ★ ★ **LYCEUM.** *43 Church St, Salem (01970). Phone 978/745-7665; fax 978/744-7699. www.lyceum salem.com.* One of the area's best restaurants, this comfortable, elegant dining room is located in the building where Alexander Graham Bell made his first phone call in 1877. American menu. Lunch, dinner, Sun brunch. Closed Thanksgiving, Dec 25. Bar. **$$**

★ ★ ★ **RED RAVEN'S LIMP NOODLE.** *75 Congress Ave, Salem (01970). Phone 978/745-8558.* This quirky North Shore restaurant (one of two in town) is known for a menu that blends foods from around the world with a sense of humor and an offbeat setting. The door to the women's room is indicated with a brassiere. Need we say more? International/Fusion menu. Dinner. Closed Sun-Mon; holidays. Bar. **$$**

★ **VICTORIA STATION.** *86 Wharf St, Salem (01970). Phone 978/745-3400; fax 978/745-7460. www.victoriastationinc.com.* Seafood menu. Lunch, dinner. Closed Dec 25. Bar. Children's menu. Outdoor seating. **$**

Sandwich (Cape Cod) (D-8)

See also Bourne

Settled 1637
Population 20,136
Elevation 20 ft
Area Code 508
Zip 02563
Information Cape Cod Canal Region Chamber of

Commerce, 70 Main St, Buzzards Bay 02532; phone 508/759-6000
Web Site www.capecodcanalchamber.org

The first town to be settled on Cape Cod, Sandwich made the glass that bears its name. This pressed glass was America's greatest contribution to the glass industry.

What to See and Do

⭐ **Heritage Plantation.** 67 Grove St, Sandwich (02563). Phone 508/888-3300. www.heritageplantation.org. The Heritage Plantation offers an eclectic mix of beautiful gardens, folk art, antique cars, and military paraphernalia. Visit the Old East Windmill from 1800 and the restored 1912 carousel that's great fun for young and old. Call ahead to find out about unique exhibits, displays, and concerts. Note that the Heritage Plantation is located in the town of Sandwich, the oldest town on the Cape. (Daily, mid-May-mid-Oct) **$$**

Hoxie House & Dexter Gristmill. Water St, Sandwich (02563). Phone 508/888-1173. Restored mid-17th-century buildings. House, operating mill; stone-ground corn meal sold. (Mid-June-mid-Oct, daily)

Sandwich Glass Museum. 129 Main St, Sandwich (02563). Phone 508/888-0251. Internationally renowned collection of exquisite Sandwich Glass (circa 1825-1888). (Apr-Oct, daily) **$$**

Scusset Beach. Hwys 3 and 6, Sandwich (02563). 3 miles NW on Hwy 6A across canal, then 2 miles E at junction Hwy 3 and Hwy 6. Phone 508/362-3225. Swimming beach, fishing pier; camping (fee).

Shawme-Crowell State Forest. 42 Main St, Sandwich (02563). 3 miles W on Hwy 130, off Hwy 6. Phone 508/888-0351. Approximately 2,700 acres. Primitive camping.

Limited-Service Hotels

⭐ **EARL OF SANDWICH MOTEL.** 378 Hwy 6A, East Sandwich (02537). Phone 508/888-1415; toll-free 800/442-3275; fax 508/833-1039. www.earlofsandwich.com. 24 rooms. Pets accepted, some restrictions. Complimentary continental breakfast. Check-out 11 am. **$**
🐾

⭐ **SHADY NOOK INN & MOTEL.** 14 Old Kings Hwy, Sandwich (02563). Phone 508/888-0409; toll-free 800/338-5208; fax 508/888-4039.

www.shadynookinn.com. 30 rooms. Check-out 11 am. Outdoor pool. **$**
🅿 🏊

⭐ **SPRING HILL MOTOR LODGE.** 351 Hwy 6A, East Sandwich (02537). Phone 508/888-1456; toll-free 800/646-2514; fax 508/833-1556. 24 rooms. Check-out 11 am. Outdoor pool. Tennis. **$**
🅿 🏊 🎿

Full-Service Inn

⭐⭐⭐ **DAN'L WEBSTER INN.** 149 Main St, Sandwich (02563). Phone 508/888-3622; toll-free 800/444-3566; fax 508/888-5156. www.danlwebsterinn.com. Modeled on an 18th-century house. 54 rooms, 3 story. Check-in 3 pm, check-out 11 am. Restaurant, bar. Outdoor pool. **$$**
🅿 🏊

Specialty Lodgings

The following lodging establishments are approved by Mobil Travel Guide, but due to their unique and individualized nature have not been given a traditional Mobil Star rating. Included in this listing you may find bed-and-breakfasts, limited-service inns, guest ranches, and other unique hotel properties.

BAY BEACH BED & BREAKFAST. 3 Bay Beach Ln, Sandwich (02563). Phone 508/888-8813; toll-free 800/475-6398; fax 508/888-5416. www.baybeach.com. Overlooking Cape Cod Bay, this private beachfront bed-and-breakfast offers guests a quiet haven from their busy lives. Visitors will enjoy elegant guest room amenities such as fresh flowers, wine and cheese, and fresh fruit in their refrigerator. 6 rooms, 3 story. Closed Nov-mid-May. Children over 16 years only. Complimentary full breakfast. Check-in 2-6 pm, check-out noon. Fitness room. Beach. **$$$**
🅿 🧍

THE BELFRY INN & BISTRO. 8 Jarves St, Sandwich (02563). Phone 800/844-4542; toll-free 800/844-4542; fax 508/888-3922. www.belfryinn.com. Former rectory built in 1882; belfrey access. 14 rooms, 3 story. Children over 10 years only. Complimentary full breakfast. Check-in 3 pm, check-out 11 am. Restaurant. Business center. **$$**
🧍

CAPTAIN EZRA NYE HOUSE BED & BREAKFAST. 152 Main St, Sandwich (02563). Phone 508/888-6142; toll-free 800/388-2278; fax

508/833-2897. www.captainezranyehouse.com. Built in 1829. 6 rooms, 2 story. Children over 10 years only. Complimentary full breakfast. Check-in 2 pm, check-out 11 am. **$**

ISAIAH JONES HOMESTEAD. *165 Main St, Sandwich (02563). Phone 508/888-9115; toll-free 800/526-1625; fax 508/888-9648. www.isaiahjones.com.* An American flag and flower-lined porch beckon guests inside this 1849 Victorian home. The guest rooms, decorated with antiques and country-patterned fabrics, are a great resting stop when visiting this Cape Cod town's many historic sites. 7 rooms, 2 story. Children over 16 years only. Complimentary full breakfast. Check-in 3-6 pm, check-out 11 am. **$**

VILLAGE INN. *4 Jarves St, Sandwich (02563). Phone 508/833-0363; toll-free 800/922-9989; fax 508/833-2063. www.capecodinn.com.* Federal-style house (1837) with wraparound porch, gardens. 8 rooms, 3 story. Children over 8 years only. Complimentary full breakfast. Check-in 3-6 pm, check-out 11 am. **$**

Restaurants

★ ★ **AQUA GRILLE.** *14 Gallo Rd, Sandwich (02563). Phone 508/888-8889.* Located at the Sandwich Marina, the Aqua Grille is a nice spot for catching up with friends over good food. Lunch tantalizes guests with salads, soups, sandwiches, fried seafood, and specials, while the dinner menu intrigues with grilled fish, meats, and pastas. Large windows give the restaurant an airy ambience while showing off great water views. American, seafood menu. Lunch, dinner. Closed Oct-mid-Apr. Bar. Children's menu. Casual attire. Outdoor seating. **$$**

★ ★ **BEEHIVE TAVERN.** *406 Hwy 6A, Sandwich (02563). Phone 508/833-1184.* American, seafood menu. Lunch, dinner. Bar. Children's menu. Casual attire. **$$**

★ ★ **BRIDGE RESTAURANT.** *21 Hwy 6A, Sagamore (02561). Phone 508/888-8144.* The Bridge Restaurant brings an interesting mix to Cape Cod. This family restaurant surprises guests with its menu. From typical regional seafood dishes and Italian meals to Thai specialties and even American comfort food classics, the menu has it all. Warm, friendly service adds to the homey feeling. Italian, seafood menu.

Lunch, dinner. Closed Thanksgiving, Dec 25. Bar. Children's menu. **$**

★ ★ ★ **THE DAN'L WEBSTER INN.** *149 Main St, Sandwich (02563). Phone 508/888-3623; toll-free 800/444-3566; fax 508/888-5156. www.danlwebsterinn.com.* An actual stagecoach inn frequented in the early 1800s by its namesake, Dan'l Webster offers both a colonial-motif tavern with burgers, pizzas, and salads, and a white-tablecloth dining room serving chic contemporary cuisine. Chef and co-owner Robert Catania buys some of his fish and hydroponic vegetables from a local aquafarm, and he has constructed a wine list to match his culinary aspirations. His twin loves entwine in a luscious dish of mixed seafood in white wine sauce. Half portions are available for many dishes. The conservatory dining area overlooks a garden. Seafood menu. Breakfast, lunch, dinner, Sun brunch. Bar. Children's menu. Business casual attire. Valet parking. **$$**

★ **HORIZONS.** *98 Town Neck Rd, Sandwich (02563). Phone 508/888-6166; fax 508/888-9209.* Dining on the Cape is even better when enjoyed tableside at Horizons. This breezily elegant restaurant treats its patrons to unencumbered views of Cape Cod Bay. While the waves gently lap and the sea grass blows in the wind, visitors enjoy fresh seafood for lunch and dinner. Seafood, steak menu. Lunch, dinner. Closed Jan-Apr. Bar. Children's menu. Outdoor seating. **$**

Saugus (B-7)

See also Boston

Settled 1630
Population 26,078
Elevation 21 ft
Area Code 781
Zip 01906

Saugus is the birthplace of the American steel industry. The first ironworks were built here in 1646.

What to See and Do

Saugus Iron Works National Historic Site. *244 Central St, Saugus (01906). Phone 781/233-0050.* Commemorates America's first successful integrated ironworks. Reconstructed furnace, forge, mill on original foundations; furnished 17th-century house; museum; working blacksmith shop; seven working waterwheels; guided tours and demonstrations (Apr-

Oct); film. (Daily; closed Jan 1, Thanksgiving, Dec 25) Contact the National Park Service, Saugus Iron Works National Historic Site, 244 Central Street. **FREE**

Restaurants

★ ★ ★ **DONATELLO.** *44 Broadway, Saugus (01906). Phone 781/233-9975; fax 781/233-8075. www.donatello-restaurant.com.* This northern Italian restaurant is the selection of locals for a special occasion. The pasta is freshly made and if you are a veal fan, this is the place to order the chop. The servers provide the finishing touches to the dining event. Italian menu. Lunch, dinner. Closed July 4, Thanksgiving, Dec 24. Bar. Valet parking. **$$**

★ ★ **HILLTOP STEAK HOUSE.** *855 Broadway, Saugus (01906). Phone 781/233-7700; fax 781/231-3134. www.hilltop-steak-house.com.* Seafood menu. Lunch, dinner. Closed Thanksgiving, Dec 25. Bar. Children's menu. **$$**

★ ★ **ORZO TRATTORIA.** *114 Broadway, Saugus (01906). Phone 781/233-6815. www.orzorestaurant .com.* Italian menu. Lunch, dinner. Bar. Children's menu. Casual attire. **$$**

Somerville

Population 77,478

Sitting to the northwest of Boston, Somerville—just a mile and a half from the city's financial and commercial districts—is a diverse community in which more than 50 different languages are spoken. That diversity is reflected in its restaurant scene, with Union Square and the hip Davis Square serving as prime dining and entertainment destinations. Ample public transportation makes it easy to get to Boston and other suburbs.

South Hadley (B-3)

See also Amherst, Holyoke

Settled circa 1660
Population 17,196
Elevation 257 ft
Area Code 413
Zip 01075
Information Chamber of Commerce, 10 Harwich Place; phone 413/532-6451

Nestled on the banks of the Connecticut River, South Hadley was incorporated as a town in 1775. Twenty years later, the first navigable canal in the United States began operation here. The town remained a busy shipping center until 1847, when the coming of the railroad made shipping by river unprofitable.

What to See and Do

Mount Holyoke College. *50 College St, South Hadley (01075). Phone 413/538-2000.* (1837) (1,950 women) Campus tours (inquire for schedule). On the grounds are

> **Joseph Allen Skinner Museum.** *135 Woodbridge St, South Hadley (01075). Phone 413/538-2085.* Housed in a small Congregational church (1846). Collection of Early American furnishings, decorative arts; one-room schoolhouse. (May-Oct, Wed and Sun, afternoons) **FREE**

> **Mount Holyoke College Art Museum.** *50 College St, South Hadley (01075). Phone 413/538-2245.* Small but choice permanent collection of paintings, drawings, prints, and sculpture; also special exhibitions. (Tues-Fri, also Sat-Sun afternoons; closed college holidays) **FREE**

> **Talcott Arboretum.** *Park St and Lower Lake Rd, South Hadley (01075). Phone 413/538-2199.* Campus features variety of trees and plantings; Japanese meditation, wildflower, and formal perennial gardens; greenhouse complex has collections of exotic plants; flower show (Mar); tours by appointment. (Mon-Fri, also Sat-Sun afternoons; closed holidays) **FREE**

Old Firehouse Museum. *11 N Main St, South Hadley (01075). Phone 413/536-4970.* Served as a firehouse 1888-1974; features firefighting equipment, Native American artifacts, items relating to local history and South Hadley Canal. (June-Sept, Wed and Sun; schedule may vary) **FREE**

Special Event

Women's Regatta. *Phone 413/536-3132.* Brunelle's Marina. Oct.

Springfield (C-3)

See also Holyoke; also see Enfield, CT and Windsor Locks, CT

Settled 1636
Population 152,082
Elevation 70 ft
Area Code 413
Information Greater Springfield Convention & Visitors Bureau, 1441 Main St, 01103; phone 413/787-1548 or toll-free 800/723-1548

Established under the leadership of William Pynchon of Springfield, England, this is now a major unit in the Connecticut River industrial empire. Springfield is also a cultural center with a fine library, museums, and a symphony orchestra, and is the home of Springfield College.

Public Transportation

Buses Pioneer Valley Transit Authority. Phone 413/781-7882

Airport Hartford Bradley International Airport; weather 860/627-3440; cash machines, Terminals A and B

Information Phone 860/292-2000

What to See and Do

Basketball Hall of Fame. *1150 W Columbus Ave, Springfield (01105). Adjacent to I-91.* Phone 413/781-6500. Exhibits on the game and its teams and players; shrine to the sport invented here in 1891 by Dr. James Naismith. Historic items on display; free movies; video highlights of great games; life-size, action blow-ups of Hall of Famers. Major features include: "Hoopla," a 22-minute film; and "The Spalding Shoot-Out," the most popular participatory attraction, which allows visitors to try their skill at scoring a basket of varying heights while on a moving sidewalk. (Daily; closed Jan 1, Thanksgiving, Dec 25) **$$$**

Brimfield State Forest. *24 miles E on Hwy 20, then SE near Brimfield.* Swimming, trout fishing from the shore (stocked); hiking, picnicking. **$**

Forest Park. *200 Trafton Rd, Springfield (01108). Hwy 83 off I-91.* Phone 413/733-2251 *(zoo).* On 735 acres. Nature trails, tennis, swimming pool. Picnicking, playgrounds, ball fields. Zoo (Apr-Nov: daily; rest of year:

Sat-Sun; fee). Duck ponds. Pony rides, train rides (fee for both). Park (all year). **$$**

Granville State Forest. *323 W Hartland Rd, Springfield (01034). 22 miles W off Hwy 57.* Phone 413/357-6611. Scenic gorge, laurel display. Swimming, fishing; hiking, picnicking, camping.

Indian Motocycle Museum. *33 Hendee St, Springfield (01104).* Phone 413/737-2624. Part of the vast complex where Indian motorcycles were made until 1953. On display are historical cycles and other American-made machines; photographs; extensive collection of toy motorcycles; other Native American products, including an early snowmobile and a 1928 roadster. (Daily; closed Jan 1, Thanksgiving, Dec 25) **$$**

Laughing Brook Education Center and Wildlife Sanctuary. *793 Main St, Hampden (01036). 7 miles SE.* Phone 413/566-8034. Woodlands and wetlands, 354 acres. Former house (1782) of children's author and storyteller Thornton W. Burgess. Live animal exhibits of wildlife native to New England. Observation areas of pond, field, and forest habitats. 4 1/2 miles of walking trails; picnic area. (Tues-Sun; also Mon holidays; closed Jan 1, Thanksgiving, Dec 25) **$$**

Municipal Group. *NW side of Court Sq.* Includes renovated Symphony Hall, which, together with the Springfield Civic Center, offers a performing arts complex presenting a variety of concerts, theater, children's productions, dance and sporting events, and industrial shows; 300-foot campanile, modeled after the bell tower in the Piazza San Marco of Venice.

Six Flags New England. *1623 Main St, Agawam (01001). 5 miles W via Hwy 57 and Hwy 159S.* Phone 413/786-9300. www.sixflags.com/parks/newengland. Amusement park, rides, roller coasters; children's area; games and arcades; shows; restaurants. (June-Labor Day: daily; Apr-May, Sept-Oct: weekends only) **$$$$**

Springfield Armory National Historic Site. *1 Armory Sq, Springfield (01105). Old Armory Sq Green, Federal and State sts.* Phone 413/734-8551. US armory (1794-1968) contains one of the largest collections of military small arms in the world. Exhibits include "Organ of Guns," made famous by Longfellow's poem "The Arsenal at Springfield." Film, video presentations. (Tues-Sun; closed Jan 1, Thanksgiving, Dec 25) **FREE**

Springfield Museums at the Quadrangle. *220 State St, Springfield (01103).* Phone 413/263-6800. Includes four museums and a library. **George Walter Vincent Smith Art Museum** houses collection of Asian armor, arms, jade, bronzes, and rugs; 19th-century American paintings, sculpture. **Connecticut River Valley Historical Museum** includes genealogy and local history library; period rooms. **Museum of Fine Arts** has 20 galleries, including an outstanding collection of American and European works. **Science Museum** has an exploration center, early aviation exhibit, aquarium, planetarium, African hall, dinosaur hall. (All buildings Wed-Sun) **$$$**

Storrowton Village. *Eastern States Exposition, 1305 Memorial Ave, West Springfield (01089). On Hwy 147. Phone 413/787-0136.* A group of restored Early American buildings: meeting house, schoolhouse, blacksmith shop, and homes. Old-fashioned herb garden. Dining. Guided tours (June-Labor Day: Mon-Sat; rest of year: by appointment; closed holidays). **$$**

Special Events

Eastern States Exposition (The Big E). *1305 Memorial Ave, West Springfield (01089). Phone 413/737-2443. www.thebige.com. On Hwy 147.* Largest fair in the Northeast; entertainment, exhibits; historic Avenue of States, Storrowton Village; horse show; agricultural events; "Better Living Center" exhibit. Sept.

Glendi Greek Celebration. *Phone 413/787-1548.* Greek folk dances, observance of doctrine and ritual festivities, Greek foods, art exhibits, street dancing. Early Sept.

Hall of Fame Tip-off Classic. *Springfield Civic Center, 1277 Main St, Springfield (01103). Phone 413/781-6500.* Official opening game of the collegiate basketball season with two of the nation's top teams. Mid-Nov.

Indian Day. *Indian Motocycle Museum, 33 Hendee St, Springfield (01104). Phone 413/737-2624.* Gathering of owners and those interested in Indian motorcycles and memorabilia. Third Sun in July.

Peach Festival. *Fountain Park, 833 Tinkham Rd, Wilbraham (01095). Phone 413/599-0010. www.peachfestival.org.* Started in 1985, the Peach Festival has grown into a local tradition in Massachusetts. In recent years, the festival has added amusement park-style rides and a yearly Creature Feature, which screens old horror movies like *The Creature from the Black Lagoon.* Marie Osmond has performed in the past, and citizens and visitors alike draw inspiration from nearby Civil War reenactments. There are also dance competitions and the annual Peach Festival parade and pancake breakfast. Third weekend in Aug.

Peter Pan Slice of Summer. *101 State St, Springfield (01103). Phone 413/733-3800.* A four-day outdoor festival featuring food and music from around the world. Mid-June.

World's Largest Pancake Breakfast. *Phone 413/733-3800.* A battle with Battle Creek, Michigan, to see who can serve the "world's largest breakfast." Features pancake breakfast served at a four-block-long table. Mid-May.

Limited-Service Hotels

★ **HAMPTON INN.** *1011 Riverdale St (Hwy 5), West Springfield (01089). Phone 413/732-1300; toll-free 800/426-7866; fax 413/732-9883. www.hampton-inn.com.* Every member of the family—including the four-legged one—is welcome at this hotel, easily accessible at the intersection of I-90 and I-91. Connecting rooms, cribs, in-room refrigerators, and king rooms with pull-out couches are designed with families in mind, and both kids and adults will enjoy the refreshing outdoor pool. The hotel is located at the entrance to a suburban shopping center with CostCo, Kohl's, and other shops and casual restaurants close by. 126 rooms, 4 story. Pets accepted; fee. Complimentary continental breakfast. Check-in 3 pm, check-out noon. Outdoor pool. **$**
🐾 ➿

★ ★ **HOLIDAY INN DOWNTOWN.** *711 Dwight St, Springfield (01104). Phone 413/781-0900; toll-free 800/465-4329; fax 413/785-1410. www.holiday-inn.com.* Just off I-91 and I-291, this 244-room hotel is slightly north of Springfield's downtown. A welcoming place for families, it has a video arcade, game room, and indoor pool and is close to attractions such as the Basketball Hall of Fame, Dr. Seuss Museum, and Six Flags. Zaffino's, the 12th-floor restaurant, has large windows that take advantage of a beautiful view of the Pioneer Valley and Connecticut River. 244 rooms, 12 story. Pets accepted; fee. Check-in 3 pm, check-out 11 am. High-speed Internet access, wireless Internet access. Restaurant, bar. Fitness room. Indoor pool. Business center. **$**
🐾 🏋 ➿ 🏃

Full-Service Hotels

★ ★ ★ **MARRIOTT SPRINGFIELD.** *1500 Main St, Springfield (01115). Phone 413/781-7111; toll-free 800/228-9290; fax 413/731-8932. www.marriott.com.* The bed—with an extra-thick mattress, duvet with bed skirt, and multiple plush pillows—is the most noticeable aspect of the renovated guest rooms in this contemporary, city-center hotel. It is an elegant focal point in a room that also includes grass-cloth wall coverings, rich maroons and golds, and a bath with polished granite and upgraded fixtures. When you leave your room, you won't have far to go for entertainment: just walk through the hotel (and make sure to look at the artwork in the public areas; much of it was commissioned from local artists on local subjects like the Connecticut River, New England barns, and Dr. Seuss) to the walkway that connects the Marriott to an office tower complex and mall. There you'll find casual restaurants, art galleries, an African American history museum, and even a billiards parlor. 265 rooms, 16 story. Check-in 4 pm, check-out noon. High-speed Internet access. Two restaurants, bar. Fitness room. Indoor pool, whirlpool. Business center. **$$**

★ ★ ★ SHERATON SPRINGFIELD MONARCH PLACE HOTEL

1 Monarch Plz, Springfield (01144). Phone 413/781-1010; fax 413/734-3249. This hotel has one serious health club. The Sheraton Athletic Club is the largest hotel health club west of Boston, is available to private members as well as hotel guests, and has two dozen machines, free weights, a 50-foot swimming pool, a racquetball court, an indoor golf range, and a myriad of fitness classes. Spa services include everything from tanning to massage to manicures. But the health club isn't the only larger-than-life element of this 325-room hotel: rooms surround a 12-story atrium, airy and grand. Public areas are spacious as well and feature local touches such as a folk art mural of Springfield's many historical highlights and points of interest. Throughout the hotel, and in many guest rooms, windows highlight lovely views of the Connecticut River. If you're staying for business, ask for a "smart room," with photocopier and fax machine. And if you're staying for pleasure, the Sheraton's downtown location gives you proximity to the city's museums and shops, and its connection to the Monarch Tower office complex allows you access to additional shopping and dining—sans coat. 325 rooms, 12 story. Check-in 3 pm, check-out noon. High-speed Internet access. Restaurant, bar. Fitness room, fitness classes available. Indoor pool, whirlpool. Business center. **$$**

Restaurants

★ ★ HOFBRAUHAUS.
1105 Main St, West Springfield (01089). Phone 413/737-4905; fax 413/734-7479. www.hofbrauhaus.org. This group-friendly restaurant is a local favorite. With the waitstaff in costume and a world-class array of beer steins, guests are sure to enjoy themselves. American, German menu. Lunch, dinner. Closed Dec 25. Bar. Children's menu. **$$$**

★ IVANHOE.
1422 Elm St, West Springfield (01089). Phone 413/736-4881; fax 413/736-3408. www.theivanhoe.com. American, seafood menu. Lunch, dinner, Sun brunch. Closed Dec 25. Bar. Children's menu. Casual attire. **$$**

★ ★ MONTE CARLO.
1020 Memorial Ave, West Springfield (01089). Phone 413/734-6431; fax 413/788-9119. Italian menu. Lunch, dinner. Closed Mon; Thanksgiving, Dec 25. Bar. Children's menu. **$$**

★ ★ STUDENT PRINCE & FORT.
8 Fort St, Springfield (01103). Phone 413/734-7475; fax 413/739-7303. www.studentprince.com. German, American menu. Lunch, dinner. Bar; imported draft beer. Children's menu. **$$**

Stockbridge and West Stockbridge (B-2)

See also Lenox, Pittsfield

Settled 1734
Population 2,276
Elevation 842 and 901 ft
Area Code 413
Zip Stockbridge, 01262; West Stockbridge, 01266
Information Stockbridge Chamber of Commerce, 6 Elm St, PO Box 224; phone 413/298-5200; or visit Main St Information Booth
Web Site www.stockbridgechamber.org

Established as a mission, Stockbridge was for many years a center for teaching the Mahican. The first preacher was John Sergeant. Jonathan Edwards also taught at Stockbridge. The town is now mainly a summer resort but still has many features and attractions open year round. West Stockbridge is a completely restored market village. Its Main Street is lined with well-kept storefronts, renovated in the style of the

1800s, featuring stained glass, antiques, and hand-crafted articles.

What to See and Do

Berkshire Botanical Garden. *Hwys 102 and 183, Stockbridge (01262). Phone 413/298-3926.* Fifteen-acre botanical garden; perennials, shrubs, trees, antique roses, ponds; wildflower exhibit, herb, vegetable gardens; solar, semitropical, and demonstration greenhouses. Garden shop. Herb products. Special events, lectures. Picnicking. (May-Oct, daily) **$$$**

Chesterwood. *284 Main St, Stockbridge (01262). 2 miles S of junction Hwy 102 and Hwy 183. Phone 413/298-3579.* Early 20th-century summer residence and studio of Daniel Chester French, sculptor of the *Minute Man* statue in Concord and of Lincoln in the Memorial in Washington, DC. Also museum; gardens, woodland walk; guided tours. A property of the National Trust for Historic Preservation. (May-Oct, daily) **$$$**

Children's Chimes Bell Tower. *Main St, Stockbridge (01262).* (1878) Erected by David Dudley Field, a prominent lawyer, as a memorial to his grandchildren. Carillon concerts (June-Aug, daily).

Merwin House "Tranquility". *14 Main St, Stockbridge (01262). Phone 413/298-4703.* (Circa 1825) Brick house in late Federal period; enlarged with a "shingle"-style wing at the end of the 19th century. European and American furniture and decorative arts. (June-mid-Oct, Tues, Thurs, Sat-Sun) **$$**

Mission House. *1 Seargeant St, Stockbridge (01262). Main and Sergeant sts, on Hwy 102. Phone 413/298-3239.* House built in 1739 for the missionary Reverend John Sergeant and his wife, Abigail Williams; now a museum of colonial life. Collection of colonial antiques; Native American museum; gardens and orchard. Guided tours. (Memorial Day weekend-Columbus Day weekend, daily) **$$**

Naumkeag. *1 Seargeant St, Stockbridge (01262). Prospect Hill. Phone 413/298-3239.* Stanford White designed this Norman-style "Berkshire cottage" (1886); the interior has antiques, Oriental rugs, and a collection of Chinese export porcelain. Gardens include terraces of tree peonies, fountains, a Chinese garden and birch walk. Guided tours. (Memorial Day weekend-Columbus weekend, daily) **$$$**

⭐ **Norman Rockwell Museum.** *9 Glendale Rd, Stockbridge (01262). Phone 413/298-4100.* Maintains and exhibits the nation's largest collection of original art by Norman Rockwell. (Daily; closed Jan 1, Thanksgiving, Dec 25) **$$$**

Special Events

Berkshire Theatre Festival. *Berkshire Playhouse, 6 E Main, Stockbridge (01262). Entrance from Hwy 7, Hwy 102. Phone 413/298-5536.* Summer theater (Mon-Sat); Unicorn Theater presents new and experimental plays (Mon-Sat in season); children's theater (July-Aug, Thurs-Sat). Late June-late Aug.

Harvest Festival. *Berkshire Botanical Garden, Hwys 102 and 183, Stockbridge (01262). Phone 413/298-3926.* Celebrates the beginning of the harvest and foliage season in the Berkshire Hills. First weekend in Oct.

Stockbridge Main Street at Christmas. *6 Elm St, Stockbridge and West Stockbridge (01262). Phone 413/298-5200.* Events include a re-creation of Norman Rockwell's painting. Holiday marketplace, concerts, house tour, silent auction, sleigh/hay rides, caroling. First weekend in Dec.

Full-Service Inns

★ ★ ★ **THE RED LION INN.** *30 Main St, Stockbridge (01262). Phone 413/298-5545; fax 413/298-5130. www.redlioninn.com.* Designated a Historic Hotel of America by the National Trust for Historic Preservation, the Red Lion Inn sits on the picturesque and historic Main Street of Stockbridge that has been immortalized by Norman Rockwell. It is one of the few hostelries in New England to operate continuously since pre-1800. Today, the Red Lion offers a combination of guest rooms in the Inn on Main Street and suites among a handful of buildings throughout town, such as the former studio of artist Daniel Chester French and the former home of the Stockbridge Volunteer Fire Department. While there is unmistakable New England charm throughout, there is also an element of surprise: the inn's decorating style definitely bows to noteworthy guests of the past, such as Hawthorne and Longfellow, but it also notes the Red Lion's connections to present-day stars of nearby Tanglewood, such as Bob Dylan. 108 rooms. Pets accepted, some restrictions; fee. Check-in 3 pm, check-out noon. Two restaurants, bar. Fitness room. Outdoor pool. **$$**

⊞ ⤵ 🏋 🛏

★ ★ ★ **WILLIAMSVILLE INN.** *Hwy 41, West Stockbridge (01266). Phone 413/274-6118; fax 413/*

274-3539. *www.williamsvilleinn.com.* A perfect way to escape and get away to the Berkshires. This is an ideal spot to enjoy many of the annual festivals. Breakfast is served daily by the fireplace; for added charm, enjoy afternoon storytelling, held during the summer. 16 rooms, 3 story. Complimentary full breakfast. Check-in 2 pm, check-out 11 am. Restaurant, bar. Outdoor pool. Tennis. **$**

Specialty Lodgings

The following lodging establishments are approved by Mobil Travel Guide, but due to their unique and individualized nature have not been given a traditional Mobil Star rating. Included in this listing you may find bed-and-breakfasts, limited-service inns, guest ranches, and other unique hotel properties.

INN AT STOCKBRIDGE. *Hwy 7 N, Stockbridge (01262). Phone 413/298-3337; toll-free 888/466-7865; fax 413/298-3406. www.stockbridgeinn.com.* A decanter of port in your room. Breakfast at a gleaming, mahogany table in an elegant formal dining room. A large parlor with reading material and chairs by the fire. A stroll through beautifully landscaped gardens on 12 secluded acres. This 1906 Georgian-style inn—the land can be traced back to a missionary family who came to Stockbridge in 1739 to convert the natives to Christianity—contains eight guest rooms. The Cottage House, added in 1997, has four junior suites; The Barn, built in 2001, provides four deluxe suites. Each room is decorated with period antiques and lush fabrics, has traditional furnishings like armoires and four-poster beds, and has a view overlooking the inn's meadows, reflecting pond, or some other calming sight. If you're feeling a bit guilty about all this graceful relaxation, wander into the exercise room for a turn on a cardio machine—although you may want to follow it up with an appointment with the inn's on-call massage therapist. 16 rooms, 2 story. Children over 12 years only. Complimentary full breakfast. Check-in 2 pm, check-out 11 am. Fitness room. Outdoor pool. **$$$**

THE TAGGART HOUSE. *18 W Main St, Stockbridge (01262). Phone 413/298-4303. www.taggarthouse.com.* This lovingly restored and renovated 1800s country house fronts the Housatonic River in the Berkshires. It is elegant, luxurious, sophisticated, intimate, and replete with the finest of antiques and sumptuous furnishings throughout. 4 rooms. Closed Jan-Apr.

Children over 18 years only. Complimentary full breakfast. Check-in 3 pm, check-out noon. **$$$**

Restaurants

★ **MICHAEL'S RESTAURANT & PUB.** *5 Elm St, Stockbridge (01262). Phone 413/298-3530.* Italian menu. Lunch, dinner, late-night. Bar. Children's menu. Casual attire. Reservations recommended. **$$**

★ ★ ★ **THE RED LION.** *30 Main St, Stockbridge (01262). Phone 413/298-5545; fax 413/298-5130. www.redlioninn.com.* The candlelit dining room of this historic inn is filled with antiques, colonial pewter, and crystal. The contemporary New England menu emphasizes local, seasonal produce and offers several vegetarian options. American menu. Breakfast, lunch, dinner, late-night. Bar. Children's menu. Business casual attire. Reservations recommended. Outdoor seating. **$$$**

★ ★ ★ **WILLIAMSVILLE INN.** *Hwy 41, West Stockbridge (01266). Phone 413/274-6118; fax 413/274-3539. www.williamsvilleinn.com.* This cozy dining room has an open fireplace and plenty of candlelight. The walls are lined with book shelves, and you may feel as if you are dining in someone's home—only the food is better. The continental menu includes meat and poultry, salads, seafood, and other standard fare. American, German menu. Dinner. Closed Mon-Wed in Nov-mid-June. Bar. Reservations recommended. **$$**

Sturbridge (C-5)

Settled circa 1730
Population 7,837
Elevation 619 ft
Area Code 508
Zip 01566-1057
Information Tourist Information Center, 380 Main St; phone 508/347-2761 or toll-free 888/788-7274

What to See and Do

⭐ **Old Sturbridge Village.** *1 Old Sturbridge Village, Sturbridge (01566). On Hwy 20 W, 1 mile W of junction I-84 exit 2 and MA Tpke (I-90) exit 9. Phone 508/347-3362; toll-free 800/733-1830. www.osv.org.* A living history museum that re-creates a rural New England town of the 1830s. The museum covers more than 200 acres with more than 40 restored buildings; costumed interpreters demonstrate the life, work, and community celebrations of early 19th-century New Englanders. Working historical farm; many special events; picnic area. (Apr-Nov, daily; closed Dec 25) **$$$$**

Special Event

New England Thanksgiving. *1 Old Sturbridge Village, Sturbridge (01566). Phone 508/347-3362.* Re-creation of early 19th-century Thanksgiving celebration. Includes turkey shoot, hearth cooking and meeting-house service. Thanksgiving Day.

Limited-Service Hotels

★ **COMFORT INN & SUITES COLONIAL.** *215 Charlton Rd (Hwy 20), Sturbridge (01566). Phone 508/347-3306; toll-free 800/228-5151; fax 508/347-3514. www.sturbridgecomfortinn.com.* Located just outside Sturbridge, about a mile northeast of Old Sturbridge Village on Highway 20, this hotel is easily accessible from I-84. It has no restaurant of its own, but it sits in a small commercial center that also includes a Cracker Barrel, a fast-food restaurant, and a convenience store. Pets are allowed only in the older "courtyard units," so make arrangements in advance. 77 rooms, 2 story. Pets accepted, some restrictions; fee. Complimentary continental breakfast. Check-in 2 pm, check-out 11 am. High-speed Internet access. Bar. Fitness room. Indoor pool, outdoor pool, whirlpool. Business center. **$**

★ **ECONO LODGE.** *682 Main St, Sturbridge (01518). Phone 508/347-2324; toll-free 800/446-6900; fax 508/347-7320. www.econolodge.com.* 48 rooms. Complimentary continental breakfast. Check-in 2 pm, check-out 11 am. Outdoor pool. **$**

★ **THE LODGES AT OLD STURBRIDGE VILLAGE.** *Main St, Hwy 20, Sturbridge (01566). Phone 508/347-3327; toll-free 800/733-1830; fax 508/347-3018. www.osv.org.* Right next to the main entrance to Old Sturbridge Village, set back from busy Highway 20, these lodges are part of the Old Sturbridge operation. Families enjoy the residential feel and spaciousness of the six village units, while history buffs appreciate the ambience and details of the ten rooms in the Oliver Wight House, built around 1789 and listed on the National Register of Historic Places. Wight House rooms have an old inn feel, with worn floorboards, nonworking brick fireplaces, four-

poster beds with white chenille bedspreads, and early American furnishings and wallpaper. Village rooms, though more modern, carry on the old-fashioned appeal. Amenities are limited here, but if the history museum is your destination, this hotel is a convenient choice. 57 rooms, 2 story. Closed Dec 25. Check-in 3 pm, check-out 11 am. Outdoor pool. **$**

Full-Service Hotel

★ ★ ★ **STURBRIDGE HOST RESORT.** *366 Main St, Sturbridge (01566). Phone 508/347-7393; toll-free 800/582-3232; fax 508/347-3944. www.fine-hotels.com.* Situated along a scenic country side, this hotel is located across the street from Old Sturbridge Village and allows business travelers to bring the family along for fun. 220 rooms, 3 story. Check-out 11 am. Restaurant, bar. Fitness room. Indoor pool, whirlpool. Tennis. **$**

Full-Service Inn

★ ★ ★ **PUBLICK HOUSE HICTORIC INN.** *295 Main St, Sturbridge (01566). Phone 508/347-3313; toll-free 800/782-5425; fax 508/347-1246. www.publickhouse.com.* Built in 1771, this historic inn has 18th-century ambience with modern conviences. The guest rooms and suites all have private baths, air-conditioning, and are decorated with antiques or reproductions. Many have canopy beds and all are non-smoking rooms. Breakfast, lunch, and dinner is served here seven days a week. 17 rooms, 2 story. Check-in 3 pm, check-out 11 am. Restaurant, bar. Tennis. **$**

Specialty Lodging

The following lodging establishment is approved by Mobil Travel Guide, but due to its unique and individualized nature has not been given a traditional Mobil Star rating. Included in this listing you may find bed-and-breakfasts, limited-service inns, guest ranches, and other unique hotel properties.

COLONEL EBENEZER CRAFTS INN. *Fiske Hill Rd, Sturbridge (01566). Phone 508/347-3141; toll-free 800/782-5425; fax 508/347-5073.* Built in 1786; overlooks woods. 8 rooms, 3 story. Check-in 3 pm, check-out 11 am. Outdoor pool. Tennis. **$**

Restaurants

★ ★ **PUBLICK HOUSE.** *295 Main St, Sturbridge (01566). Phone 508/347-3313; fax 508/347-5073. www.publickhouse.com.* In original colonial structure built in 1771. New England menu. Breakfast, lunch, dinner. Bar. Children's menu. Outdoor seating. **$$$** 🅿

★ ★ **ROM'S RESTAURANT.** *Hwy 131, Sturbridge (01566). Phone 508/347-3349; toll-free 800/766-1952; fax 508/347-1496. www.sturbridge.com.* Italian, American menu. Lunch, dinner. Closed Thanksgiving, Dec 25. Children's menu. **$$**

★ ★ ★ **WHISTLING SWAN.** *502 Main St, Sturbridge (01566). Phone 508/347-2321; fax 508/347-7262. www.thewhistlingswan.com.* There are really two restaurants in one at this local favorite: a quiet, fine dining continental restaurant downstairs and a more casual restaurant upstairs with nightly entertainment. American menu. Lunch, dinner. Closed holidays. Bar. Children's menu. **$$**

Sudbury Center (B-6)

See also Boston, Concord

Settled 1638
Population 16,841
Area Code 978
Zip 01776
Information Board of Selectmen, Loring Parsonage, 288 Old Sudbury Rd, Sudbury; phone 978/443-8891

Sudbury, which has a number of 17th-century buildings, is best known for the Wayside Inn at South Sudbury, which was the scene of Longfellow's *"Tales of a Wayside Inn"* (1863).

What to See and Do

Longfellow's Wayside Inn. *72 Wayside Inn Rd, Sudbury Center (01776). 3 miles SW, just off Hwy 20. Phone 978/443-1776.* (1702) A historical and literary shrine, this is America's oldest operating inn. Originally restored by Henry Ford, it was badly damaged by fire in December 1955, and restored again by the Ford Foundation. Period furniture. (Daily; closed July 4, Dec 25) Also on the property are

Gristmill. *72 Wayside Inn Rd, Sudbury Center (01776).* With waterwheel in operation; stone grinds wheat and corn used by inn's bakery. (Apr-Nov, daily)

Martha Mary Chapel. *72 Wayside Inn Rd, Sudbury Center (01776).* Built and dedicated by Henry Ford in 1940, a nondenominational, nonsectarian chapel. No services; used primarily for weddings. (By appointment)

Redstone School. *72 Wayside Inn Rd, Sudbury Center (01776).* (1798) "The Little Red Schoolhouse" immortalized in "Mary Had a Little Lamb." (May-Oct, daily)

Special Events

Fife & Drum Muster and Colonial Fair. *72 Wayside Inn Rd, Sudbury Center (01776). Phone 978/443-8891.* Muster takes place on field across from Longfellow's Wayside Inn. Fife and drum corps from New England and surrounding areas compete. Colonial crafts demonstrations and sales. Last Sat in Sept.

Reenactment of March of Sudbury Minutemen to Concord on April 19, 1775. *72 Wayside Inn Rd, Sudbury Center (01776). Phone 978/443-1776.* More than 200 costumed men muster on the Common before proceeding to Old North Bridge in Concord. Apr.

Limited-Service Hotels

★ ★ **BEST WESTERN ROYAL PLAZA HOTEL & TRADE CENTER.** *181 W Boston Post Rd, Marlborough (01752). Phone 508/460-0700; toll-free 888/543-9500; fax 508/480-8218. www.bestwestern.com.* 431 rooms, 6 story. Check-out 11 am. Restaurant, bar. Fitness room. Indoor pool. **$$** 🅿 🏃 〰

★ **CLARION HOTEL.** *738 Boston Post Rd, Sudbury (01776). Phone 978/443-2223; toll-free 800/637-0113; fax 978/443-5830. www.choicehotels.com.* 39 rooms, 3 story. Complimentary full breakfast. Check-out 11 am. Fitness room. **$$** 🏃

★ ★ **RADISSON HOTEL MARLBOROUGH.** *75 Felton St, Marlborough (01752). Phone 508/480-0015; toll-free 800/333-3333; fax 508/485-2242. www.radisson.com.* 206 rooms, 5 story. Check-out noon. Restaurant, bar. Fitness room. Indoor pool, whirlpool. **$** 🏃 〰

Specialty Lodgings

The following lodging establishments are approved by Mobil Travel Guide, but due to their unique and individualized nature have not been given a traditional Mobil Star rating. Included in this listing you may find bed-and-breakfasts, limited-service inns, guest ranches, and other unique hotel properties.

THE ARABIAN HORSE INN. *277 Old Sudbury Rd, Sudbury (01776). Phone 978/443-7400; toll-free 800/ 272-2426; fax 978/443-0234. www.arabianhorseinn .com.* Built in 1886. 5 rooms, 3 story. Pets accepted; fee. Complimentary full breakfast. Check-in 3 pm, check-out 11 am. **$$**
🄟 ⬛

LONGFELLOWS WAYSIDE INN. *72 Wayside Inn Rd, Sudbury (01776). Phone 978/443-1776; toll-free 800/339-1776; fax 978/443-8041. www.wayside.org.* Historic inn (1716); self-guided tours through restored public rooms. National historic site; on grounds are Wayside Gristmill and Redstone School, built by former owner Henry Ford. 10 rooms, 2 story. Complimentary full breakfast. Check-in 3 pm, check-out 11 am. Restaurant, bar. **$**

Restaurant

★ ★ **LONGFELLOW'S WAYSIDE INN.** *72 Wayside Inn Rd, Sudbury Center (01776). Phone 978/443-1776; fax 978/443-8041. www.wayside.org.* Seafood, steak menu. Lunch, dinner. Closed July 4, Dec 25. Bar. Children's menu. **$$**

Truro and North Truro (Cape Cod) (C-9)

Settled Truro: circa 1700
Population 2,087
Elevation 20 ft
Area Code 508
Zip Truro 02666; North Truro 02652
Information Cape Cod Chamber of Commerce, Hwys 6 and 132, PO Box 790, Hyannis 02601-0790; phone 508/362-3225 or toll-free 888/227-3263
Web Site www.capecodchamber.org

Truro, named for one of the Channel towns of England, is today perhaps the most sparsely settled part of the Cape—with great stretches of rolling moorland dotted only occasionally with cottages. On the hill above the Pamet River marsh are two early 19th-century churches; one is now the town hall. The countryside is a favorite resort of artists and writers.

What to See and Do

Fishing. Surf casting on Atlantic beaches. Boat ramp at Pamet and Depot roads; fee for use, harbor master on duty.

Highland Light/Cape Cod Light. *Highland Light Rd, North Truro (02652). Phone 508/487-1121. www.lighthouse.cc/highland.* This delightful lighthouse boasts a long and glorious past as the first lighthouse on Cape Cod. Built in 1798 and fueled with whale oil, the lighthouse was rebuilt in 1853 and switched over to an automated facility in 1986. It now shines for 30 miles, the longest visible range of any lighthouse on the Cape. Thoreau stayed in the lighthouse during his wanderings on Cape Cod. Tours are offered 10 am-5 pm daily from May through October. The museum next door, housed in a historic building, is open 10 am-4:30 pm, June through September, and highlights the fishing and whaling heritage of the area. (Daily May-late Oct) **$**

Pilgrim Heights Area. *Off Hwy 6. Phone 508/487-1256.* Interpretive display, self-guided nature trails, picnicking; rest rooms. **FREE**

Swimming. *Head of the Meadow. N on Hwy 6 and W of Chamber of Commerce booth.* **Corn Hill Beach.** *On the bay (fee).* A sticker for all beaches must be purchased from National Park Service Visitor Center or at beach entrances. No lifeguards. Mid-June-Labor Day.

Truro Historical Society Museum. *6 Highland Light Rd, North Truro (02652). Phone 508/487-3397.* Collection of artifacts from the town's historic past, including shipwreck mementos, whaling gear, ship models, 17th-century firearms, pirate chest, and period rooms. (June-Sept, daily) **$$**

Limited-Service Hotel

★ **CROW'S NEST MOTEL.** *49 Shore Rd, North Truro (02652). Phone 508/487-9031; toll-free 800/499-9799. www.capecodtravel.com.* 33 rooms, 2 story. Closed Dec-Mar. Check-out 10 am. Beach. **$**
🄟

Restaurants

★ **ADRIAN'S.** *535 Hwy 6, North Truro (02652). Phone 508/487-4360; fax 508/487-6510. www.adrians restaurant.com.* You won't find red-and-white-checkered tablecloths here. Adrian's, overlooking Cape Cod Bay at the Outer Reach, is light and airy, with a large deck providing optimal views of the water. The menu features Italian classics and a range of creative pizzas, like calamari fra diavolo and melanzane (eggplant). Italian menu. Breakfast, dinner. Closed mid-Oct-mid-May. Bar. Children's menu. Outdoor seating. **$$**

★ ★ **BLACKSMITH SHOP RESTAURANT.** *17 Truro Center Rd, Truro (02666). Phone 508/349-6554.* The Blacksmith Shop Restaurant stands out for its impressive, often daring cuisine. This place caters to slightly adventurous souls who enjoy traveling with their taste buds. From Mexico to Morocco, many of the items on the menu show off an international flair. A historic appearance adds charm, but this restaurant is fully rooted in the present. Seafood menu. Breakfast, dinner, Sun brunch. Closed Dec 25; also Mon-Wed in the off-season. Bar. Children's menu. **$$**

★ **MONTANO'S.** *481 Hwy 6, North Truro (02652). Phone 508/487-2026; fax 508/487-4913. www.montanos.com.* For great Italian cooking on the Cape, visitors snag a table at Montano's. This family-style restaurant offers a full range of classic dishes, and with a large steak menu, the place is paradise for meat lovers as well. From pasta and pizza to fish and meat, Montano's will satisfy the needs of any hungry diner. Italian, seafood menu. Lunch, dinner. Closed Dec 24-25. Bar. Children's menu. Casual attire. **$$**

Waltham (B-7)

See also Boston

Settled 1634
Population 59,226
Elevation 50 ft
Area Code 781
Zip 02154
Information Waltham West Suburban Chamber of Commerce, 84 South St; phone 781/894-4700
Web Site www.walthamchamber.com

The name Waltham, taken from the English town of Waltham Abbey, means "a home in the forest," and is still appropriate today, due to the town's many wooded areas. Originally an agricultural community, Waltham is now an industrial center. It is also the home of Bentley College and Regis College.

What to See and Do

Brandeis University. *415 South St, Waltham (02453). Phone 781/736-4300.* (1948) (3,700 students) The first Jewish-founded nonsectarian university in the United States. Its 250-acre campus includes Three Chapels, Rose Art Museum (Sept-May, Tues-Sun; closed holidays; free); Spingold Theater Arts Center (plays presented Oct-May; fee); and Slosberg Music Center, with classical and jazz performances (Sept-May).

Cardinal Spellman Philatelic Museum. *235 Wellesley St, Weston (02493). 4 miles W on Hwy 20. Phone 781/894-6735.* Exhibition gallery; library. (Tues-Thurs, Sat-Sun; closed holidays) **FREE**

Gore Place. *52 Gore St, Waltham (02453). On Hwy 20 at the Waltham-Watertown line. Phone 781/894-2798.* A living history farm, Gore Place may be New England's finest example of Federal-period residential architecture; changing exhibits; 40 acres of cultivated fields. The mansion, designed in Paris and built in 1805, has 22 rooms filled with examples of Early American, European, and Asian antiques. (Mid-Apr-mid-Nov, daily except Mon) **$$**

Lyman Estate. *185 Lyman St, Waltham (02452). Phone 781/893-7232 (house).* (1793) Designed by Samuel McIntire for Boston merchant Theodore Lyman. Enlarged and remodeled in the 1880s, the ballroom and parlor retain Federal design. Landscaped grounds. Five operating greenhouses contain grape vines, camellias, orchids, and herbs. House open by appointment for groups only. Greenhouses (Mon-Sat, also Sun afternoons). **$$**

Limited-Service Hotels

★ ★ **DOUBLETREE HOTEL.** *550 Winter St, Waltham (02451). Phone 781/890-6767; toll-free 800/222-8733; fax 781/890-8917. www.doubletree.com.* Situated near Lexington and Concord as well as a wealth of historical stops, this hotel has a fitness center, pool, and fully equipped rooms for the business traveler. 275 rooms, 8 story, all suites. Check-in 2 pm, check-out noon. Restaurant, bar. Fitness room. Indoor pool, whirlpool. Business center. **$**

★ ★ **HOME SUITES INN.** *455 Totten Pond Rd, Waltham (02451). Phone 781/890-3000; toll-free 866/335-6175; fax 781/890-0233. www.homesuitesinn.com.* 116 rooms, 3 story, all suites. Complimentary continental breakfast. Check-out 11 am. Restaurant, bar. Outdoor pool. **$**

≋

Full-Service Hotel

★ ★ ★ **THE WESTIN WALTHAM-BOSTON.** *70 3rd Ave, Waltham (02451). Phone 781/290-5600; toll-free 800/228-3000; fax 781/290-5626. www.westin.com.* Just 15 minutes from downtown Boston, this modern hotel has standard rooms providing comfort and service. Many rooms are geared to the business traveler, offering business services such as dataports and faxes. 376 rooms, 8 story. Check-in 3 pm, check-out 1 pm. Restaurant, bar. Fitness room. Indoor pool, whirlpool. Airport transportation available. Business center. **$$**

🕴 ≋ 🏃

Restaurants

★ ★ ★ **GRILL AT HOBBS BROOK.** *550 Winter St, Waltham (02451). Phone 781/487-4263; fax 781/890-9097.* This restaurant is located in the Doubletree Hotel (see). In season, many of the ingredients come from the on-site garden. The plush setting is a quiet, relaxing place to dine. American menu. Breakfast, lunch, dinner. Bar. Children's menu. **$$$**

★ ★ **IL CAPRICCIO.** *888 Main St, Waltham (02451). Phone 781/894-2234; fax 781/891-3227.* Gauzy drapes and glass partitions give this innovative restaurant a chic, urban look. Italian menu. Dinner. Closed Sun; holidays. Bar. **$$$**

★ ★ **NEW GINZA.** *63-65 Galen St, Watertown (02472). Phone 617/923-2100.* Sushi menu. Lunch, dinner. Casual attire. **$$$**

★ ★ **TUSCAN GRILL.** *361 Moody St, Waltham (02453). Phone 781/891-5486; fax 781/647-4204.* Italian menu. Dinner. Closed July 4, Thanksgiving, Dec 24-25. Bar. **$$**

Wellesley *(B-7)*

See also Boston

Settled 1661
Population 26,613
Elevation 141 ft

Area Code 781
Zip 02181
Information Chamber of Commerce, One Hollis St, Suite 111; phone 781/235-2446
Web Site www.wellesleyweb.com/chamber.htm

This Boston suburb was named after an 18th-century landowner, Samuel Welles. It is an educational and cultural center. There are four widely known institutions here: Dana Hall, a girls' preparatory school; Babson College, a business school; Massachusetts Bay Community College; and Wellesley College.

What to See and Do

Wellesley College. *106 Central St, Wellesley (02481). Central and Washington sts, on Hwy 16/135. Phone 781/283-1000.* (1870) (2,200 women) Founded by Henry F. Durant. 500 wooded acres bordering Lake Waban. On campus are Davis Museum and Cultural Center and Margaret C. Ferguson Greenhouses (Daily).

Limited-Service Hotel

★ ★ **WELLESLEY INN ON THE SQUARE.** *576 Washington St, Wellesley (02482). Phone 781/235-0180; toll-free 800/233-4686; fax 781/235-5263. www.wellesleyinn.com.* 70 rooms, 4 story. Check-out 11 am. Restaurant, bar. **$**

🖻

Restaurant

🔍 ★ ★ ★ **BLUE GINGER.** *583 Washington St, Wellesley (02482). Phone 781/283-5790; fax 781/283-5772.* At Blue Ginger, celebrity chef Ming Tsai shows that he is more than just another pretty face on the Food Network. In addition to being able to read from a teleprompter with ease, the man can cook. Fusing East and West, layering sweet with spice, he is a dazzling chef with a colorful palette of culinary talents. This hotspot is packed regularly, so reserve a table early. The menu is filled with drool-worthy dishes like leek-potato pancakes and five-peppercorn grilled sirloin delicately smothered in Roquefort sauce. American menu. Lunch, dinner. Closed Sun. Children's menu. Reservations recommended. Outdoor seating. **$$$**

Wellfleet (Cape Cod) (C-9)

Settled circa 1725
Population 2,749
Elevation 50 ft
Area Code 508
Zip 02667
Information Chamber of Commerce, PO Box 571; phone 508/349-2510
Web Site www.wellfleetchamber.com

Once a fishing town, Wellfleet dominated the New England oyster business in the latter part of the 19th century. It is now a summer resort and an art gallery town, with many tourist homes and cottages. Southeast of town is the Marconi Station Area of Cape Cod National Seashore (see). Fishermen here can try their luck in the Atlantic surf or off deep-sea charter fishing boats.

What to See and Do

Historical Society Museum. *266 Main St, Wellfleet (02667). Phone 508/349-9157.* Marine items, whaling tools, Marconi memorabilia, needlecraft, photograph collection, marine and primitive paintings. (Late June-mid-Sept, Tues-Sat; schedule may vary) **$**

Sailing. Rentals at Wellfleet Marina; accommodates 150 boats; launching ramp, facilities.

Swimming. At numerous bayside and ocean beaches on marked roads off Highway 6. Freshwater ponds with swimming are scattered through woods east of Highway 6. (Parking sticker necessary mid-June to Labor Day.)

Wednesday Night Square Dance. *Town Pier, Holbroook and Commercial sts, Wellfleet (02667). Phone 508/349-0330.* If you want one of the most unique experiences on Cape Cod, visit this old-fashioned square dance, where you can spin your partner round and round based on the instructions of a master caller. If you're not a skilled square dancer, come early, when dance steps are easier to master, and gain confidence as the night progresses. (July-Aug) **FREE**

Wellfleet Bay Wildlife Sanctuary. *291 Hwy 6, South Wellfleet (02663). On W side of Hwy 6. Phone 508/349-2615.* Operated by the Massachusetts Audubon Society. Self-guiding nature trails. Natural history summer day camp for children. Guided nature walks, lectures, classes, Monomoy Island natural history tours. Sanctuary (Memorial Day-Columbus Day: daily; rest of year: Tues-Sun). **$$**

Wellfleet Drive-In Theater. *Hwy 6, Wellfleet (02667). At the Eastham-Wellfleet town line. Phone 508/349-2450. www.wellfleetdrivein.com.* Wellfleet Drive-In Theater, the only outdoor theater on the Cape, projects a family-oriented double feature every evening under the stars. Arrive at 7 pm to get your ideal parking spot; the kids can spend the hour in the play area. Enjoy better concessions than you'll find at any indoor movie theater. (Mid-Oct-mid-Apr) **$$**

Limited-Service Hotel

★ ★ **WELLFLEET MOTEL & LODGE.** *146 Hwy 6, South Wellfleet (02663). Phone 508/349-3535; toll-free 800/852-2900; fax 508/349-1192. www.wellfleetmotel.com.* 65 rooms, 2 story. Check-out 11 am. Restaurant, bar. Indoor pool, outdoor pool, whirlpool. **$**

Specialty Lodging

The following lodging establishment is approved by Mobil Travel Guide, but due to its unique and individualized nature has not been given a traditional Mobil Star rating. Included in this listing you may find bed-and-breakfasts, limited-service inns, guest ranches, and other unique hotel properties.

INN AT DUCK CREEK. *70 Main St, Wellfleet (02667). Phone 508/349-9333; fax 508/349-0234.* Sitting porch overlooks Duck Creek. 25 rooms, 3 story. Closed mid-Oct-mid-May. Complimentary continental breakfast. Check-in 1 pm, check-out 11 am. **$**

Restaurants

★ ★ ★ **AESOP'S TABLES.** *316 Main St, Wellfleet (02667). Phone 508/349-6450.* A perennial favorite, this casual but sophisticated restaurant, located in a restored 1805 house, serves a contemporary menu with New England specialties, such as clam chowder and crab cakes, and more adventurous pastas, salads, and entrées, some of which have a decidedly Asian accent. American menu. Lunch, dinner. Closed mid-Oct-mid-May. Bar. Outdoor seating. **$$**

★ **MOBY DICK'S.** *Hwy 6, Wellfleet (02667). Phone 508/349-9795.* With its red-checkered tablecloths and walls decorated with fishing nets, Moby Dick's is the very definition of a seafood shack. Fish plays a starring role throughout the menu here, from the soups and salads to the sandwiches and entrées. Lobsters and clambakes are popular choices. Plate cleaners take note: the desserts are worth leaving a bit of dinner behind. Seafood menu. Lunch, dinner. Closed mid-Oct-Apr. Children's menu. Casual attire. Outdoor seating. **$$**

★ ★ **SERENA'S.** *545 Hwy 6, Wellfleet (02667). Phone 508/349-9370.* Italian menu. Dinner. Closed Dec-Apr. Casual attire. **$$**

★ ★ **VAN RENSSELAER'S RESTAURANT & RAW BAR.** *1019 Hwy 6, South Wellfleet (02663). Phone 508/349-2127; fax 508/349-1783. www. vanrensselaers.com.* Van Rensselaer's wins kudos for its fantastic cooking and inviting atmosphere. Family-run for more than 30 years, this homey place makes everyone feel like a member of the family. Its comprehensive menu is a real crowd-pleaser, with seafood, meat, vegetarian entrées, and even a children's menu. American menu. Breakfast, dinner. Closed Nov-Mar. Bar. Children's menu. Outdoor seating. **$$**

Westport

Restaurant

★ ★ **THE BACK EDDY.** *1 Bridge Rd, Westport (02790). Phone 508/636-6500. www.backeddy.com.* American menu. Lunch, dinner. Closed Mon-Tues. Casual attire. **$$$**

Williamstown (A-2)

See also North Adams

Settled 1749
Population 8,424
Elevation 638 ft
Area Code 413
Zip 01267

A French and Indian War hero, Colonel Ephraim Williams, Jr., left a bequest in 1755 to establish a "free school" in West Hoosuck, provided the town be renamed after him. In 1765, the town name was changed to Williamstown, and in 1793, the school became Williams College. The life of this charming Berkshire Hills town still centers around the college.

What to See and Do

Sterling and Francine Clark Art Institute. *225 South St, Williamstown (01267). Phone 413/458-9545.* More than 30 paintings by Renoir, other French Impressionists; old-master paintings; English and American silver; American artists Homer, Sargent, Cassatt, Remington. Extensive art library (Mon-Fri). Museum shop. Picnic facilities on grounds. (July-Labor Day: daily; rest of year: Tues-Sun; closed Jan 1, Thanksgiving, Dec 25) **$$$**

Williams College. *54 Sawyer Library Dr, Williamstown (01267). Hwy 7. Phone 413/597-3131.* (1793) (1,950 students) Private liberal arts college; campus has a wide variety of architectural styles, ranging from colonial to Gothic. Chapin Library of rare books is one of nation's finest, housing the four founding documents of the United States. Hopkins Observatory, the nation's oldest (1836), has planetarium shows. Adams Memorial Theatre presents plays. The Paul Whiteman Collection houses Whiteman's recordings and memorabilia. Also here is

Williams College Museum of Art. *15 Lawrence Hall Dr, Williamstown (01267). Main St. Phone 413/597-2429.* Considered one of the finest college art museums in the country. Houses approximately 11,000 pieces. Exhibits emphasize contemporary, modern, American, and non-Western art. Museum shop. (Tues-Sat, also Sun afternoons and Mon holidays; closed Jan 1, Thanksgiving, Dec 25) **FREE**

Limited-Service Hotels

★ **BERKSHIRE HILLS MOTEL.** *1146 Cold Spring Rd, Williamstown (01267). Phone 413/458-3950; toll-free 800/388-9677; fax 413/458-5878. www.berkshire hillsmotel.com.* 21 rooms, 2 story. Complimentary buffet breakfast. Check-out 11 am. Outdoor pool. **$**
🄳 ☕

★ **FOUR ACRES MOTEL.** *213 Main St; Hwy 2, Williamstown (01267). Phone 413/458-8158; fax 413/458-8158. www.fouracresmotel.com.* A beautifully landscaped pool with a mountain view is a highlight of this 31-room motel, situated on Highway 2 just east of the town center. The hotel takes advantage of its location in other ways; in the summer, attractive café tables are set up on a wooden deck so that guests can relax in front of the beautiful scenery. The Four Acres has also made sure that all second-floor rooms have balconies. 31 rooms, 2 story. Complimentary continental breakfast. Check-in 1 pm, check-out 11 am. Outdoor pool. **$**

Full-Service Inns

★ ★ ★ **1896 HOUSE.** *910 Cold Spring Rd, Williamstown (01267). Phone 413/458-1896; toll-free 888/666-1896. www.1896house.com.* As its name suggests, this property offers its guests the choice to stay by the brook or by the pond. The Brookside, hidden from the road by trees, features Cushman rock maple furniture, luxurious amenities, and a beautiful gazebo. The Pondside offers rooms with two queen beds and slightly fewer frills. 29 rooms. Complimentary continental breakfast. Check-out 11 am. Restaurant. Outdoor pool. **$**

★ ★ ★ **THE ORCHARDS.** *222 Adams Rd, Williamstown (01267). Phone 413/458-9611; toll-free 800/225-1517; fax 413/458-3273. www.orchardshotel .com.* Culture seekers adore The Orchards for its tranquil setting and ideal location in the heart of the Berkshires. Grand gates of Vermont granite announce that you've arrived at the European chateau-style property, just east of the village center, off Highway 2 and Adams Road. This delightful hotel is the perfect place to unwind and take in the town's renowned arts festivals, museums, and antiques shops, many of which are within walking distance. Yet its peaceful garden setting makes it feel a million miles away from civilization. Its mood is decidedly relaxed, but sophisticated. The charming guest rooms echo the resort's spirit with a warm décor reminiscent of the English countryside. Luxurious appointments range from Persian rugs and Austrian crystal chandeliers in the public spaces to bay windows and upgraded baths with marble floors in the guest accommodations. All rooms have a refrigerator, cleverly housed in a custom sideboard and stocked with beverages. Yasmin's restaurant (see) serves a mix of continental and American cuisine in an elegant setting, and guests are invited to dine outdoors in the garden during summer months. The experience is sure to transport, with the gentle trickle of the fountain and the heady fragrance of the abundant blooms. 49 rooms, 3 story. Check-in 3 pm, check-out 1 pm. High-speed Internet

access. Restaurant, bar. Fitness room. Outdoor pool, whirlpool. **$$$**

★ ★ ★ **WILLIAMS INN.** *Hwys 7 and 2, Williamstown (01267). Phone 413/458-9371; toll-free 800/828-0133; fax 413/458-2767. www.williamsinn .com.* Owned by Williams College, the Williams Inn is situated on campus just two blocks from the village center. Since Williamstown is dominated by the college, visitors at the inn generally have something in common, and there is a warmth and friendliness among both guests and staff. It also has the feel of a community focal point; the area around the front desk has a wealth of information and local brochures, and staff is ready to answer any and all questions. Another focal point for both guests and locals alike is the inn's entertainment: depending on the season, you can catch anything from jazz to acoustic guitar to cabaret. 125 rooms, 3 story. Check-in 3 pm, check-out 11 am. High-speed Internet access. Restaurant, bar. Indoor pool, whirlpool. **$$**

Restaurants

★ ★ ★ **LE JARDIN.** *777 Cold Spring Rd, Williamstown (01267). Phone 413/458-8032.* Nestled among pines near a trout pond, this lovely restaurant serves traditional French food in a comfortable, homey setting. French menu. Dinner. Closed Tues in Sept-June. Bar. Guest rooms available. **$$**

★ ★ **WATER STREET GRILL.** *123 Water St, Williamstown (01267). Phone 413/458-2175; fax 413/458-4820.* International/Fusion menu. Lunch, dinner. Closed Easter, Thanksgiving, Dec 25. Bar. Children's menu. **$$**

★ ★ ★ **YASMIN'S.** *222 Adams Rd, Williamstown (01267). Phone 413/458-9611; fax 413/458-3273. www. theorchardshotel.com.* The European chefs who rotate through the kitchens of this fine hotel leave their mark on the creative American menu. Among the selections served in the elegant country dining room are Chilean sea bass with thyme flowers and veal loin with wasabi butter. International/Fusion menu. Breakfast, lunch, dinner, Sun brunch. Bar. Children's menu. Outdoor seating. **$$$**

Worcester (B-5)

Settled 1673
Population 172,648
Elevation 480 ft
Area Code 508
Information Worcester County Convention & Visitors Bureau, 30 Worcester Center Blvd, 01608; phone 508/753-2920
Web Site www.worcester.org

The municipal seal of Worcester (WUS-ter) calls it the "Heart of the Commonwealth." One of the largest cities in New England, it is an important industrial center. Also a cultural center, it has some outstanding museums and twelve colleges.

What to See and Do

American Antiquarian Society. *185 Salisbury St, Worcester (01609). Phone 508/755-5221.* Research library is the largest collection of source materials pertaining to the first 250 years of American history. Specializing in the period up to 1877, the library has 2/3 of all pieces known to have been printed in this country between 1640 and 1821. (Mon-Fri; closed holidays. Guided tours Wed afternoons). **FREE**

EcoTarium. *222 Harrington Way, Worcester (01604). 1 1/2 miles E. Phone 508/791-9211.* Contains museum with environmental science exhibits; solar/lunar observatory, multimedia planetarium theater; African Hall. Indoor-outdoor wildlife, aquariums; train ride; picnicking. (Daily; closed holidays) **$$$**

Higgins Armory Museum. *100 Barber Ave, Worcester (01606). Phone 508/853-6015.* Large exhibit of medieval-Renaissance and feudal Japan's arms and armor; paintings, tapestries, stained glass. Armor demonstrations and try-ons. (Tues-Sat, also Sun afternoons; closed holidays) **$$$**

John H. Chaffy Blackstone River Valley National Heritage Corridor. *414 Massasoit Rd, Worcester (01604). Phone 508/755-8899.* This 250,000-acre region extends southward to Providence, Rhode Island (see) and includes myriad points of historical and cultural interest. Visitor center at Massachusetts Audubon Society's Broad Meadow Brook Wildlife Sanctuary; tours and interpretive programs.

Salisbury Mansion. *40 Highland St, Worcester (01609). Phone 508/753-8278.* (1772) House of leading businessman and philanthropist Stephen Salisbury. Restored to 1830s appearance. Guided tours. (Thurs-Sun afternoons; closed holidays) **$$**

Worcester Art Museum. *55 Salisbury St, Worcester (01609). Phone 508/799-4406.* Fifty centuries of paintings, sculpture, decorative arts, prints, drawings, and photography from America to ancient Egypt; changing exhibits; tours, films, lectures. Café, gift shop. (Wed-Sun; closed holidays) **$$$**

Worcester Common Outlets. *100 Front St, Worcester (01608). I-290, exit 16. Phone 508/798-2581.* More than 100 outlet stores can be found at this indoor outlet mall. Food court. (Daily)

Special Event

Worcester Music Festival of the Worcester County Music Association. *Mechanics Hall, 321 Main St, Worcester (01608). Phone 508/752-5608.* The country's oldest music festival; folkdance companies; choral masterworks; symphony orchestras, guest soloists; young people's program. Seven to 12 concerts. Sept-Mar.

Full-Service Hotels

★ ★ ★ **BEECHWOOD HOTEL.** *363 Plantation St, Worcester (01605). Phone 508/754-5789; toll-free 800/344-2589; fax 508/752-2060. www.beechwoodhotel.com.* A 24-hour fitness room, 24-hour business center, free local and long-distance phone calls, free incoming and outgoing faxes, and free high-speed Internet access in all guest rooms—as well as a location just 1.5 miles from downtown Worcester and easy proximity to the Centrium Convention Centre—make this an exceptional business hotel. Yet there is also grace and beauty. A polished foyer with marble floors greets guests, a small seating area around the fireplace beckons you to sit awhile, a restored, antique, stained-glass window draws your glance upward. Stairs lead down to a casual bar, the Harlequin Restaurant, and function rooms such as the Grand Ballroom, which includes the century-old Maria Gill Wilson Room, formerly the chapel at Worcester City Hospital. Whether you're there for business or pleasure, don't forget to keep your eye out for whimsy—such as an antique carousel horse or a jar of gummy bears in your guest room. 73 rooms, 5 story. Pets accepted, some restrictions; fee. Complimentary continental breakfast. Check-in 3 pm, check-out 11 am. High-speed Internet access. Restaurant, bar. Fitness room. Business center. **$$**

★ ★ ★ **CROWNE PLAZA HOTEL.** *10 Lincoln Sq, Worcester (01608). Phone 508/791-1600; toll-free 800/ 628-4240; fax 508/791-1796. www.cpworcester.com.* If fresh-roasted coffee and a location facing Main Street are your idea of hotel perfection, look no further. The Crowne Plaza is modern and amenity-filled, near many cultural venues, close to shopping malls and the booksellers' marketplace, and within ten minutes of most area businesses. Yet the hotel itself is also a place for relaxation, with a large indoor/outdoor pool and a courtyard landscaped with holly and flowering fruit trees. Ask for a room with a balcony, where you can enjoy morning coffee with a view of Lincoln Square. 242 rooms, 9 story. Check-in 3 pm, check-out noon. Wireless Internet access. Restaurant, bar. Fitness room. Indoor pool, outdoor pool, whirlpool. Airport transportation available. Business center. **$$**

Restaurant

★ ★ ★ **CASTLE.** *1230 Main St, Leicester (01524). Phone 508/892-9090; fax 508/892-3620. www.castle restaurant.com.* Owned and operated by the Nicas family since 1950, this "castle", complete with turrets, towers, and a moat, provides a unique dining experience for all the seasons of the year. Choose from one of the two distinctly different dining rooms, the Crusader or the Camelot, each with its own creative menu. French menu. Lunch, dinner. Closed Mon; Jan 1, Thanksgiving, Dec 25. Bar. Children's menu. Outdoor seating. **$$$**

Yarmouth (Cape Cod)

See also Hyannis and Barnstable

Population 11,603
Elevation 20 ft
Area Code 508
Zip 02664
Information Yarmouth Area Chamber of Commerce, PO Box 479; 800/732-1008; or the Cape Cod Chamber of Commerce, Hwy 6 and Hwy 132, PO Box 790, Hyannis 02601-0790; phone 508/362-3225 or toll-free 888/227-3263
Web Site www.capecodchamber.org

Much of the Yarmouth area was developed on the strength of seafaring and fishing in the first half of the 19th century. Well-preserved old houses line Main Street to the north in Yarmouth Port, architecturally among the choicest communities in Massachusetts. Bass River, to the south, also contains many fine estates.

What to See and Do

Cape Symphony Orchestra. *712A Main St, Yarmouth Port (02675). Phone 508/362-1111.* This 90-member professional orchestra performs 15 indoor concerts throughout the year at Barnstable High School's 1,400-seat auditorium. Concerts selections range from classical to pops to special children's events. If you're visiting in summer, catch two outdoor pops concerts—one at the Mashpee Commons in Mashpee at the end of July; the other at Eldredge Park in Orleans in mid-August. (Sept-May; also two concerts in summer) **$$$$**

Captain Bangs Hallet House. *11 Strawberry Ln, Yarmouth Port (02664). Off Hwy 6A, near Yarmouth Port Post Office. Phone 508/362-3021.* Early 19th-century sea captain's home. (June-Oct: Thurs-Sun afternoons; rest of year: by appointment) Botanic trails (all year; donation). Gate house (June-mid-Sept, daily). **$$**

Pewter Crafters of Cape Cod. *933 Hwy 6A, Yarmouthport (02675). Phone 508/362-3407. www. pewtercraftercapecod.com.* The Pewter Crafters studio gives you a chance to view pewter craftspeople plying their trade, and then admire their creations on display. The shop sells both traditional and more contemporary designs of tableware, jewelry, candlesticks, and decanters, so you can take home a unique piece of Cape Cod home with you. (Mon-Sat; hours vary by season)

Swimming. *265 Sisson Rd, South Yarmouth (02645). Phone 508/430-7553.* Nantucket Sound and bayside beaches. Parking fee.

Winslow Crocker House. *250 Hwy 6A, South Yarmouth (02675). On Old King's Hwy, Hwy 6A, in Yarmouth Port. Phone 508/362-4385.* (Circa 1780) Georgian house adorned with 17th-, 18th-, and 19th-century furnishings collected in the early 20th century. Includes furniture made by New England craftsmen in the colonial and Federal periods; hooked rugs, ceramics, pewter. (June-mid-Oct, Tues, Thurs, Sat-Sun) **$$**

Limited-Service Hotels

★ **ALL SEASON MOTOR INN.** *1199 Hwy 28, South Yarmouth (02664). Phone 508/394-7600; toll-free 800/527-0359; fax 508/398-7160. www.allseasons.com.* 114 rooms, 2 story. Check-out 11 am. Restaurant. Fitness room. Outdoor pool, whirlpool. **$**

★ ★ **BEST WESTERN BLUE ROCK RESORT.** *Todd Rd, South Yarmouth (Cape Cod) (02664). Phone 508/398-6962; toll-free 800/780-7234; fax 508/398-1830. www.bestwestern.com.* 44 rooms, 2 story. Closed late-Oct-Mar. Check-out 11 am. Restaurant, bar. Outdoor pool, whirlpool. Golf, 18 holes. Tennis. **$**

★ ★ **BEST WESTERN BLUE WATER ON THE OCEAN.** *2915 Shore Dr, South Yarmouth (02664). Phone 508/398-2288; toll-free 800/367-9393; fax 508/398-1010. www.bestwestern.com.* 106 rooms, 2 story. Check-in 3 pm, check-out 11 am. Restaurant, bar. Children's activity center. Indoor pool, outdoor pool, whirlpool. Tennis. Beach. **$$**

★ **GULL WING SUITES.** *822 Main St (Hwy 28), South Yarmouth (02664). Phone 508/394-9300; fax 508/394-1190. www.ccrh.com.* 136 rooms, 2 story. Check-out 11 am. Indoor pool, outdoor pool, whirlpool. **$**

Full-Service Resorts

★ ★ **RED JACKET BEACH.** *1 S Shore Dr, South Yarmouth (02664). Phone 508/398-6941; toll-free 800/672-0500; fax 508/398-1214. www.redjacketbeach.com.* Found steps away from the coast, this Cape Cod oceanfront resort has private balconies or porches so that guests may enjoy the view. Indoor and outdoor heated pools and complete recreation facilities including spas, sailing, and tennis are available. 150 rooms, 2 story. Closed late Oct-Mar. Check-out 11 am. Restaurant, bar. Children's activity center. Fitness room. Indoor pool, outdoor pool, whirlpool. Tennis. **$$**

★ ★ **RIVIERA BEACH RESORT.** *327 S Shore Dr, Bass River (02664). Phone 508/398-2273; toll-free 800/227-3263; fax 508/398-1202.* 125 rooms, 2 story. Closed Nov-Mar. Check-out 11 am. Restaurant, bar. Children's activity center. Indoor pool, outdoor pool, whirlpool. Beach. **$$**

Full-Service Inn

★ ★ ★ **LIBERTY HILL INN.** *77 Main St, Yarmouth Port (02675). Phone 508/362-3976; toll-free 800/821-3977; fax 508/362-6485. www.libertyhillinn.com.* Built in 1825, this charming bed-and-breakfast features individually appointed rooms, all unique in their décor and feel; many feature fireplaces and canopy beds. 9 rooms, 3 story. Complimentary full breakfast. Check-in 3-9 pm, check-out 11 am. Airport transportation available. **$**

Specialty Lodgings

The following lodging establishments are approved by Mobil Travel Guide, but due to their unique and individualized nature have not been given a traditional Mobil Star rating. Included in this listing you may find bed-and-breakfasts, limited-service inns, guest ranches, and other unique hotel properties.

CAPTAIN FARRIS HOUSE BED & BREAKFAST. *308 Old Main St, Yarmouth (02664). Phone 508/760-2818; toll-free 800/350-9477; fax 508/398-1262. www.captainfarris.com.* With its beautifully landscaped lawns and breathtaking views, this bed-and-breakfast will surely please everyone. Guests can enjoy sailing, canoeing, kayaking, and windsurfing. Antique shopping, bird-watching, and The John F. Kennedy Museum are also nearby. 10 rooms. Children over 10 years only. Complimentary full breakfast. Check-in 3 pm, check-out 11 am. Restaurant. Whirlpool. **$**

COLONIAL HOUSE INN & RESTAURANT. *277 Main St (Hwy 6A), Yarmouth Port (02675). Phone 508/362-4348; toll-free 800/999-3416; fax 508/362-8034. www.colonialhousecapecod.com.* Old mansion (1730s); many antiques, handmade afghans. 21 rooms, 3 story. Pets accepted; fee. Complimentary full breakfast. Check-in 2 pm, check-out noon. Restaurant, bar. Indoor pool, whirlpool. Business center. **$**

INN AT LEWIS BAY. *57 Maine Ave, West Yarmouth (02673). Phone 508/771-3433; toll-free 800/962-6679; fax 508/790-1186. www.innatlewisbay.com.* Located in a quiet seaside neighborhood just one block from Lewis Bay, this Dutch colonial bed-and-breakfast offers guests a relaxing place to vacation. A bountiful breakfast is served each morning, and afternoon refreshments each afternoon. 6 rooms, 2 story. Children over 12 years only. Complimentary full breakfast. Check-in 3-8 pm, check-out 11 am. **$**

🅟

Restaurants

★ ★ **ABBICCI.** *43 Main St, Yarmouth (02675). Phone 508/362-3501; fax 508/362-7802. www.abbicci restaurant.com.* Abbicci's bold interiors prepare diners for the splashy northern Italian cooking available at this restaurant housed within a former sea captain's home. With its clever cuisine, the talented kitchen offers a much-appreciated respite from the seafood shacks and family-style Italian restaurants on the Cape, and its civilized atmosphere is a boon for adults. Italian menu. Dinner. Bar. **$$$**

★ ★ **ARDEO.** *23V Whites Path, South Yarmouth (02664). Phone 508/760-1500.* The bold, contemporary setting of Ardeo is a perfect match for its flavorful Mediterranean cuisine. This sensational spot offers Cape Codders something different, dazzling them with the flavors of Italy, Greece, and the Middle East. From salads, wraps, and panini for lighter dining to homemade pastas and wood-stone pizzas, the menu offers many choices. Mediterranean menu. Lunch, dinner. Bar. Children's menu. Casual attire. **$$**

★ ★ **INAHO.** *157 Main St, Yarmouth Port (02675). Phone 508/362-5522.* Inaho wins praise for its excellent selection of sushi and sashimi. Those who aren't fans of raw fish trumpet the fantastic teriyaki dishes and exceptional tempura. This restaurant has an elegant setting, complete with a traditional Japanese garden with goldfish pond out back. Sushi, Japanese menu. Dinner. Closed Mon; Easter, Thanksgiving, Dec 25. Casual attire. **$$**

🅟

★ ★ **RIVERWAY LOBSTER HOUSE.** *Hwy 28, South Yarmouth (02664). Phone 508/398-2172.* Families and friends enjoy the charm of the Riverway Lobster House. From its traditional white "Cape" building to its seaside menu, this 50-year-old restaurant is the very essence of Cape Cod. Seafood and meat account for most of the menu, although many like to get their hands dirty with this restaurant's well-liked barbecued ribs and chicken. Seafood menu. Dinner. Closed Dec 25. Bar. Children's menu. **$$**

★ ★ **SKIPPER RESTAURANT.** *152 S Shore Dr, South Yarmouth (02664). Phone 508/394-7406; fax 508/394-0627. www.skipper-restaurant.com.* The Skipper is the ultimate beach restaurant and a true Cape landmark. Located across from Yarmouth's Smugglers Beach, this informal restaurant has been entertaining visitors since 1936. Nautical memorabilia decorates the interior, while windows share beach and water views. The all-day dining offers a range of choices, from American fare to local dishes. Seafood menu. Lunch, dinner. Closed Nov-mid-Apr. Bar. Children's menu. Casual attire. Outdoor seating. **$$**

★ ★ **YARMOUTH HOUSE.** *335 Main St, West Yarmouth (02673). Phone 508/771-5154; fax 508/790-2801. www.yarmouthhouse.com.* The Yarmouth House has an inimitable charm. From its amiable staff to its open-air garden complete with wooden water wheel, this restaurant creates a lasting memory. Lunch focuses on sandwiches and burgers, while dinner highlights chicken, veal, seafood, and steaks. Lobster lovers rejoice in the many different recipes served here. Seafood menu. Lunch, dinner. Closed Dec 25. Bar. Children's menu. **$$**

New Hampshire

New Hampshire is a year-round vacation state, offering a variety of landscapes and recreational opportunities within its six unique regions. The lush Lakes Region, dominated by Lake Winnipesaukee, and the Seacoast Region, with its beaches, bays, and historic waterfront towns, are ideal for water sports. The rugged, forested White Mountains offer hiking, camping, dazzling autumn foliage, and excellent skiing. The "little cities" of the Merrimack Valley—Nashua, Manchester, and Concord—are centers of commerce, industry, government, and the arts. Rural 19th-century New England comes alive in the small towns of the Monadnock Region, and many features of these areas come together in the Dartmouth-Lake Sunapee Region, home of Dartmouth College.

The mountains in New Hampshire are known for their rugged "notches" (called "gaps" and "passes" elsewhere), and the old valley towns have a serene beauty. Some of the best skiing in the East can be found at several major resorts here. The state's many parks, antiques shops, art and theater festivals, and county fairs are also popular attractions, and more than half of New England's covered bridges are in New Hampshire.

David Thomson and a small group of colonists settled on the New Hampshire coast near Portsmouth in 1623. These early settlements were part of Massachusetts. In 1679, they became a separate royal province under Charles the Second. In 1776, the Provincial Congress adopted a constitution making New Hampshire the first independent

Population: 1,109,252

Area: 8,992 square miles

Elevation: 0-6,288 feet

Peak: Mount Washington (Coos County)

Entered Union: Ninth of original 13 states (June 21, 1788)

Capital: Concord

Motto: Live Free or Die

Nickname: Granite State

Flower: Purple Lilac

Bird: Purple Finch

Tree: White Birch

Time Zone: Eastern

Web Site: www.visitnh.gov

Fun Facts:

- The first US public library was opened in Peterborough in 1837.
- Open since 1789, the John Hancock Inn in Hancock, NH, is the oldest operating tavern in New England.

colony, seven months before the Declaration of Independence was signed.

Although New Hampshire was the only one of the thirteen original states not invaded by the British during the Revolution, its men fought long and hard on land and sea to bring about the victory. This strong, involved attitude continues in New Hampshire to this day. The New Hampshire presidential primary is the first in the nation, and the town meeting is still a working form of government here.

Manufacturing and tourism are the principal businesses here. Electrical and electronic products, machinery, plastics, fabricated metal products, footwear, other leather goods, and instrumentation

Calendar Highlights

MAY

Lilac Time Festival (*Franconia*). *8 miles W on NH 117, then 4 miles S on US 302, in Lisbon. Phone 603/838-6673.* Celebration of the state flower and observance of Memorial Day. Parade, carnival, vendors, entertainment, special events.

JUNE

Market Square Days (*Portsmouth*). *Phone 603/436-3988.* Summer celebration with 10K road race, street fair, entertainment.

Seacoast Jazz Festival (*Portsmouth*). *For schedule, phone 603/436-3988.* Two stages with continuous performances on the historical Portsmouth waterfront.

JULY

The Old Homestead (*Keene*). *Potash Bowl in Swanzey Center. For schedule, phone 603/352-0697.* Drama of life in Swanzey during 1880s based on the Biblical story of the Prodigal Son; first presented in 1886.

AUGUST

Lakes Region Fine Arts and Crafts Festival (*Meredith*). *Phone Chamber of Commerce 603/279-6121.* Juried show featuring more than 100 New England artists. Music, children's theater, food.

League of New Hampshire Craftsmen's Fair (*Sunapee*). *Mount Sunapee Resort. Phone 603/224-3375. www.nhcrafts.org/annualfair.htm.* More than 200 craftsmen and artists display and sell goods.

Mount Washington Valley Equine Classic (*North Conway*). *Phone Chamber of Commerce, 603/356-3171 or toll-free 800/367-3364.* Horse jumping.

SEPTEMBER

New Hampshire Highland Games (*Lincoln*). *Loon Mountain. Phone toll-free 800/358-7268.* Largest Scottish gathering in the eastern United States. Bands, competitions, concerts, workshops.

Riverfest (*Manchester*). *Phone 603/623-2623.* Outdoor festival with family entertainment, concerts, arts and crafts, food booths, fireworks.

---

are manufactured. Farmers sell poultry and eggs, dairy products, apples, potatoes, garden crops, maple syrup, and sugar. Nicknamed the "Granite State," about 200 types of rocks and minerals, including granite, mica, and feldspar, come from New Hampshire's mountains.

When to Go/Climate

New Hampshire experiences typical New England weather—four distinct seasons with a muddy month or so between winter and spring. Snow in the mountains makes for great skiing in winter; summer temperatures can push up into the 90s.

AVERAGE HIGH/LOW TEMPERATURES (° F)

Concord

Jan 30/7		**May** 69/41		**Sept** 72/46	
Feb 33/10		**June** 77/51		**Oct** 61/35	
Mar 43/22		**July** 80/55		**Nov** 47/27	
Apr 56/32		**Aug** 72/46		**Dec** 34/14	

Mount Washington

Jan 12/-5		**May** 41/39		**Sept** 46/35	
Feb 13/-3		**June** 50/38		**Oct** 36/24	
Mar 20/5		**July** 54/43		**Nov** 27/14	
Apr 29/16		**Aug** 52/42		**Dec** 17/-6	

Parks and Recreation

Water-related activities, hiking, riding, various other sports, picnicking and visitor centers, as well as camping, are available in many state parks. There is an admission charge at most state parks; children under 12 are admitted free. Tent camping $12-$20/night; RV camp sites $24-$30/night. For further information contact the New Hampshire Division of Parks & Recreation, PO Box 1856, Concord 03302. Phone 603/271-3556 or 603/271-3628 (camping reservations).

FISHING AND HUNTING

Nonresident season fishing license: $47; 15-day, $27.50; 7-day, $32; 3-day, $25. Nonresident hunting

THE UPPER CONNECTICUT RIVER VALLEY

The Upper Connecticut River valley forms one of New England's most beautiful and distinctive regions. The river, which now forms the boundary between New Hampshire and Vermont, was northern New England's first highway, and the towns scattered along both its banks were settled long before the interior of either state. Interstate 91 follows the river north for the entire length of this tour, but in numerous places the slower state roads along the river are more rewarding.

Begin in the Vermont village of Putney (I-91, exit 4 in Vermont), known for apples, private schools, crafts shops, and Basketville, the original "world's largest basket store" on Highway 5, just north of the village center. Santa's Land, a Christmas theme park with a petting zoo and miniature railroad, is another mile north on Highway 5. Bellows Falls (I-91, exit 5), the largest natural falls on the entire Connecticut River, is the departure point for the Green Mountain Railroad (Depot St), which offers 26-mile excursion rides aboard the Green Mountain Flyer to Chester Depot and back.

A mile west of Interstate 91, exit 6 on Highway 103, is the Old Rockingham Meeting House, built in 1787, Vermont's oldest unchanged public building. The Vermont Country Store, next door, has an antique cracker-making machine and an extensive stock of old-time products and gadgets. Head back up Interstate 91 to exit 8 and cross the river to New Hampshire. Turn north on this particularly scenic stretch of Highway 12A. In Cornish, North Star Canoes offers access to riverside campsites, as well as a shuttle service upstream so canoeists can paddle downstream through this beautiful landscape. Continue on Highway 12A past the Cornish-Windsor Bridge, said to be the longest covered bridge in the country. Turn at the sign for the St. Gaudens National Historic Site. This one-time home of sculptor Augustus Saint-Gaudens includes models of his most famous statues. The extensive grounds are the site of free Sunday afternoon concerts in July and August.

Backtrack to the covered bridge and cross to Highway 5 in Windsor. Turn left for the American Precision Museum, showcasing early precision tools and changing exhibits. The entrance to Mount Ascutney State Park is 3 miles south of town on Highway 44A, off Highway 5. Within the park, you'll find hiking, camping, and a paved road to the 3,144-foot summit of Mount Ascutney.

In Windsor, follow Highway 5 north to the Old Constitution House, the tavern where delegates gathered in 1777 to draft the state's constitution. Continue north on Highway 5, past Simon Pierce Glass (visitors welcome) to Interstate 91 and follow this scenic highway 14 miles to exit 13 in Norwich.

The Montshire Museum of Science is right there by the river, marked from the exit. Incorporating both states in its name (it began on the New Hampshire side of the river), the Montshire, one of New England's most outstanding museums, is dedicated to demystifying natural phenomena in a way that's fun. Exhibits change but usually include an aquarium, a display on the physics of the bubble, and a hands-on corner geared to preschoolers. There are also extensive nature trails.

Cross the river into Hanover, New Hampshire, and up to the Dartmouth College green. Park (not always easy) and look for the Hood Museum on the green. This modern building houses an outstanding collection, ranging from Assyrian bas reliefs to works by Picasso and Frank Stella. Cross back over the river to Interstate 91, exit 13, and backtrack 3 miles to exit 20, the junction with Interstate 89. **(Approximately 63 miles)**

license: $92; small game, $47; small game 3-day, $23; muzzleloader, $36. Combination hunting and fishing license, nonresident: $127. Fees subject to change. For further information and for the *New Hampshire Freshwater and Saltwater Fishing Digests,* pamphlets that summarize regulations, contact the New Hampshire Fish & Game Department, 2 Hazen Dr, Concord 03301; phone 603/271-3422 or 603/271-3211.

Driving Information

Passengers under 18 years must be in an approved passenger restraint anywhere in vehicle. Children under 4 years must be in an approved safety seat anywhere in vehicle. For further information, phone 603/271-2131.

INTERSTATE HIGHWAY SYSTEM

The following alphabetical listing of New Hampshire towns in this book shows that these cities are within 10 miles of the indicated interstate highways. Check a highway map for the nearest exit.

Highway Number	Cities/Towns within 10 Miles
Interstate 89	Concord, Hanover, New London, Sunapee.
Interstate 91	Hanover.
Interstate 93	Concord, Franconia, Franconia Notch State Park, Franklin, Holderness, Laconia, Lincoln/North Woodstock, Littleton, Manchester, Meredith, Plymouth, Salem.
Interstate 95	Exeter, Hampton Beach, Portsmouth.

Additional Visitor Information

The *New Hampshire Guidebook,* with helpful information on lodging, dining, attractions, and events, is available from the New Hampshire Office of Travel & Tourism, 172 Pembroke Rd, PO Box 1856, Concord 03302. Phone 603/271-2665 or toll-free 800/386-4664. For recorded information about events, foliage, and alpine ski conditions, phone toll-free 800/258-3608.

The League of New Hampshire Craftsmen Foundation offers information on more than 100 galleries, museums, historic sites, craft shops, and craftsmen's studios. Send stamped, self-addressed, business-size envelope to 205 N Main St, Concord 03301; phone 603/224-3375.

There are several welcome centers in New Hampshire; visitors who stop by will find information and brochures most helpful in planning stops at points of interest. Open daily: on I-93 at Hooksett, Canterbury, Salem and Sanborton Boulder; on I-89 at Lebanon, Springfield, and Sutton; on I-95 at Seabrook; and on Hwy 16 at North Conway. Open Memorial Day-Columbus Day: on Hwy 9 at Antrim; on Hwy 3 at Colebrook; on Hwy 4 at Epsom; on Hwy 25 at Rumney; and on Hwy 2 at Shelburne.

Bartlett (C-4)

See also Bretton Woods, Jackson, North Conway

Population 2,290
Elevation 681 ft
Area Code 603
Zip 03812
Information Mount Washington Valley Chamber of Commerce, N Main St, PO Box 2300, North Conway 03860; phone 603/356-5701
Web Site www.mtwashingtonvalley.org

What to See and Do

Attitash Bear Peak Ski Resort. *Hwy 302, Bartlett (03812). Phone 603/374-2368. www.attitash.com.* Two high-speed quad, three quad, three triple, three double chairlifts; three surface lifts; patrol, school, rentals; snowmaking; nursery; cafeteria; bar. Longest run 1 3/4 mile; vertical drop 1,750 feet. (Mid-Nov-late Apr, daily) **Summer recreation:** Alpine Slide, water slides, scenic chairlift, horseback riding, mountain biking, hiking, driving range (mid-June-Labor Day: daily; Memorial Day-mid-June and early Sept-mid-Oct: weekends; fees). **$$$$**

Full-Service Resort

★ ★ **ATTITASH GRAND SUMMIT RESORT AND CONFERENCE CENTER.** *Hwy 302, Bartlett (03812). Phone 603/374-1900; toll-free 800/862-1600; fax 603/340-3040. www.attitashmtvillage.com.* 253 rooms, 3 story. Check-out 11 am. Restaurant, bar. Indoor pool, two outdoor pools, whirlpool. Tennis. Ski in/ski out. **$**
🏊 🎿 🏊

Bretton Woods (C-4)

See also Bartlett, Franconia, Littleton, Mount Washington, Twin Mountain

Settled 1791
Population 10
Elevation 1,600 ft
Area Code 603
Zip 03575

Bretton Woods is located in the heart of the White Mountains on a long glacial plain in the shadow of Mount Washington (see) and the Presidential Range. Mount Washington was first sighted in 1497; however, settlement around it did not begin until 1771 when the Crawford Notch, which opened the way through the mountains, was discovered. In the 1770s, Governor Wentworth named the area Bretton Woods for his ancestral home in England. This historic name was set aside in 1832 when all the tiny settlements in the area were incorporated under the name of Carroll. For a time, a railroad through the notch brought as many as 57 trains a day, and the area grew as a resort spot. A string of hotels sprang up, each more elegant and fashionable than the last. In 1903, the post office, railroad station, and express office reverted to the traditional name—Bretton Woods. Today, Bretton Woods is a resort area at the base of the mountain.

In 1944, the United Nations Monetary and Financial Conference was held here; it established the gold standard at $35 an ounce, organized plans for the International Monetary Fund and World Bank, and chose the American dollar as the unit of international exchange.

What to See and Do

Bretton Woods Ski Area. *5 miles E on Hwy 302. Phone 603/278-3320. www.brettonwoods.com.* Two high-speed quad, quad, triple, two double chairlifts, three surface lifts; patrol, school, rentals, snowmaking; restaurant, cafeteria, bar; child care; lodge. Longest run 2 miles; vertical drop 1,500 feet. (Thanksgiving-Apr, daily) Night skiing (early Dec-Mar, Fri-Sat). 48 miles of cross-country trails. **$$$$**

Crawford Notch State Park. *Bretton Woods. Approximately 8 miles SE on Hwy 302. Phone 603/374-2272.* One of state's most spectacular passes. Mounts Nancy and Willey rise to the west; Mounts Crawford, Webster, and Jackson to the east. Park headquarters is at the former site of the Samuel Willey house. He, his family of six, and two hired men died in a landslide in 1826 when they rushed out of their house, which the landslide left untouched. Fishing, trout-feeding pond. Hiking, walking trails on the Appalachian system. Picnicking, concession. Camping. Interpretive center. (Late May-mid-Oct) In park are

Arethusa Falls. *1 1/2 miles SW of Hwy 302, 6 miles N of Bartlett.* Highest in state; 50-minute walk from parking area.

Flume Cascade. *3 miles N.* A 250-foot fall.

Silver Cascade. *N end of Crawford Notch.* A 1,000-foot cataract.

Full-Service Resort

★ ★ ★ MOUNT WASHINGTON HOTEL.
Hwy 302, Bretton Woods (03575). Phone 603/278-1000; toll-free 800/258-0330; fax 603/278-8838. www.mtwashington.com. This landmark hotel is a true retreat in every way. Enjoy golfing, horseback riding, and bicycle riding during the day and live music, fine dining, and dancing at night with a choice of either live jazz or big band sounds. 200 rooms, 4 story. Check-in 3 pm, check-out 11 am. Restaurants, bar. Children's activity center. Indoor pool, outdoor pool. Golf. Tennis. **$$**
⊠ 🎿 ⛷

Full-Service Inn

★ ★ ★ THE BRETTON ARMS COUNTRY INN.
Hwy 302, Bretton Woods (03575). Phone 603/278-1000; toll-free 800/258-0330; fax 603/278-8838. www.brettonarms.com. Restored in 1896, this inn has a true country atmosphere, offering carriage and sleigh rides as well as a wealth of seasonal recreational facilities. 31 rooms. Check-in 3 pm, check-out 11 am. Restaurant. Children's activity center. Two indoor pools, outdoor pool. Airport transportation available. **$$**
⊠

Restaurant

★ FABYAN'S STATION.
Hwy 302, Bretton Woods (03575). Phone 603/278-2222. www.mtwashington.com. Converted railway station. American menu. Lunch, dinner. Bar. Children's menu. **$$**

Center Ossipee (D-4)

See also Wolfeboro

Population 500
Elevation 529 ft
Area Code 603
Zip 03814
Information Greater Ossipee Area Chamber of Commerce, 127 Hwy 28, Ossipee, 03864-7300; phone 603/539-6201 or toll-free 800/382-2371
Web Site www.ossipeevalley.org

The communities in the Ossipee area are part of a winter and summer sports region centering around Ossipee Lake and the Ossipee Mountains. The mountains also harbor a volcano (extinct for 120 million years) that is considered to be the most perfectly shaped volcanic formation in the world; it is rivaled only by a similar formation in Nigeria. A hike up Mount Whittier offers an excellent view of the formation. In the winter, the area comes alive with snowmobiling, dog sledding, cross-country skiing, and other activities.

What to See and Do

King Pine Ski Area. *Hwy 153, Madison (03849). 11 miles NE via Hwys 25, 153. Phone 603/367-8896. www.kingpine.com.* Triple, double chairlifts; two J-bars; snowmaking; patrol, school, rentals; night skiing; nursery; snack bar; bar. (Early Dec-late Mar, daily) **$$$$**

Sailing. Silver Lake, north and east of village; also **Ossipee Lake**. Marinas with small boat rentals.

Swimming. Ossipee Lake, north and east of village; **Duncan Lake**, south of village.

White Lake State Park. *Hwys 25 and 16, Tamworth (03886). 6 miles N on NH 16. Phone 603/323-7350.* Sandy beach on tree-studded shore. Swimming; trout fishing. Hiking. Picnicking, concessions. Tent camping. (Mid-May-mid-Oct) Snowmobile trails (Dec-Mar). **$$**

Colebrook (B-4)

See also Dixville Notch

Settled 1770
Population 2,444
Elevation 1,033 ft
Area Code 603
Zip 03576
Information North Country Chamber of Commerce, PO Box 1; phone 603/237-8939 or toll-free 800/698-8939
Web Site www.northcountrychamber.org

At the west edge of the White Mountains, Colebrook is the gateway to excellent hunting and fishing in the Connecticut Lakes region. The Mohawk and Connecticut rivers join here. Vermont's Mount Monadnock adds scenic beauty.

What to See and Do

Beaver Brook Falls. *2 miles N on Hwy 145.* A scenic glen.

Coleman State Park. *7 miles E on Hwy 26, then 5 miles N on Diamond Pond Rd. Phone 603/237-4520.* On Little Diamond Pond in the heavily timbered Connecticut Lakes region. Lake and stream fishing; picnicking; primitive camping. (Mid-May-mid-Oct)

Columbia Covered Bridge. *4 miles S on Hwy 3 in Columbia.* Seventy-five feet high.

Shrine of Our Lady of Grace. *2 miles S on Hwy 3. Phone 603/237-5511.* Oblates of Mary Immaculate. More than 50 Carrara marble and granite devotional monuments on 25 acres. Special events throughout the season. Guided tours (Mother's Day-second Sun in Oct, daily). **FREE**

Limited-Service Hotel

★ **NORTHERN COMFORT MOTEL.** *RR 1, Colebrook (03576). Phone 603/237-4440. www.northerncomfortmotel.com.* 19 rooms. Pets accepted; fee. Complimentary continental breakfast. Check-out 11 am. Fitness room. Outdoor pool, whirlpool. **$**

Concord (E-4)

See also Manchester

Settled 1727
Population 36,006
Elevation 288 ft
Area Code 603
Zip 03301
Information Chamber of Commerce, 40 Commercial St; phone 603/224-2508
Web Site www.concordnhchamber.com

New Hampshire, one of the original 13 colonies, entered the Union in 1788—but its capital was in dispute for another 20 years. Concord finally won the honor in 1808. The state house, begun immediately, was finished in 1819. The legislature is the largest (more than 400 seats) of any state. Concord is the financial center of the state and a center of diversified industry as well.

What to See and Do

Canterbury Shaker Village. *288 Shaker Rd, Canterbury (03224). 15 miles N on I-93 to exit 18, then follow signs.* Phone 603/783-9511. www.shakers.org. Pay homage to New Hampshire's Shaker heritage with a visit to this National Historic Landmark museum that offers guided and self-guided tours and a variety of exhibits. (Mid-May-late Oct: daily 10 am-5 pm; Nov-Dec: Sat-Sun 10 am-4 pm; closed Thanksgiving, Dec 25) **$$$**

Capitol Center for the Arts. *44 S Main St, Concord (03301).* Phone 603/225-1111. www.ccanh.com. Renovated historic theater (1920s) is the state's largest. Presents nationally touring Broadway and popular family entertainment all year.

Christa McAuliffe Planetarium. *2 Institute Dr, Concord (03301). I-93, exit 15 E.* Phone 603/271-7831. www.starhop.com. This living memorial to New Hampshire teacher Christa McAuliffe, who died aboard the US space shuttle *Challenger* on January 28, 1986, offers a variety of shows designed for all ages in a 92-seat theater. Some shows are aimed at the very young while others boast 3-D computer graphic effects likely to wow anyone. (Daily; call or visit Web site for show schedule) **$$**

⭐ **Concord Arts & Crafts.** *36 N Main St, Concord (03301).* Phone 603/228-8171. High-quality traditional and contemporary crafts by some of New Hampshire's finest craftsmen; monthly exhibits. (Mon-Sat; closed holidays)

Granite State Candy Shoppe. *13 Warren St, Concord (03301).* Phone 603/225-2591; toll-free 888/225-2531. www.nhchocolates.com. Founded in 1927 by a Greek immigrant, Granite State Candy Shoppe is an old-fashioned candy store that has been delighting sweet tooths ever since with the motto, "We're in the happiness business." Now owned by his grandchildren, many of the founder's original copper kettles are still in use, and each chocolate is dipped one by one. Sure, you can buy these treats on the Internet, but nothing beats a visit to the store where it all began.

League of New Hampshire Craftsmen. *205 N Main St, Concord (03301).* Phone 603/224-1471. www.nhcrafts.org. Six retail galleries throughout the state. Library and resource center for League Foundation members. (Mon-Fri; closed holidays) **FREE**

Museum of New Hampshire History. *6 Eagle Sq, Concord (03301).* Phone 603/226-3189. Historical museum (founded 1823) with permanent and changing exhibits, including excellent examples of the famed Concord Coach; museum store. (Tues-Sat, also Sun afternoons) **$$**

Pat's Peak Ski Area. *8 miles N on I-89 to Hwy 202, then 8 miles W to Hwy 114, then 3 miles S, near Henniker.* Phone 603/428-3245; toll-free 800/728-7732. Triple, two double chairlifts, two T-bars, J-bar, pony lift; patrol, school, rentals, ski shop; snowmaking; cafeteria, lounge; nursery. Night skiing. (Dec-late Mar, daily; closed Dec 25)

Pierce Manse. *14 Penacook St, Concord (03301). 1 mile N of State House.* Phone 603/224-0094. Home of President Franklin Pierce from 1842 to 1848. Reconstructed and moved to the present site; contains many original furnishings and period pieces. (Mid-June-mid-Sept, Mon-Fri; also by appointment; closed July 4, Labor Day) **$**

State House. *107 N Main St, Concord (03301).* Phone 603/271-2154. Hall of Flags; statues, portraits of state notables. (Mon-Fri; closed holidays) **FREE**

Limited-Service Hotels

★ **COMFORT INN.** *71 Hall St, Concord (03301).* Phone 603/226-4100; toll-free 877/424-6423; fax 603/228-2106. www.comfortinn.com. Perfect for budget-conscious families, this hotel provides a number of amenities, including a Nintendo 64 station in each room. 100 rooms, 3 story. Pets accepted, some restrictions; fee. Complimentary continental breakfast. Check-in 3 pm, check-out noon. Indoor pool, whirlpool. **$**

★ **HAMPTON INN.** *515 South St, Bow (03304).* Phone 603/224-5322; toll-free 800/426-7866; fax 603/224-4282. www.hamptoninn.com. 145 rooms, 4 story. Complimentary continental breakfast. Check-out noon. Indoor pool, whirlpool. **$**

Full-Service Inn

★ ★ ★ **COLBY HILL INN.** *The Oaks, Henniker (03242).* Phone 603/428-3281; toll-free 800/531-0330; fax 603/428-9218. www.colbyhillinn.com. This classic New England country inn offers individually decorated rooms and a fine-dining restaurant in a beautiful, wooded setting. 16 rooms, 2 story. Children over 7 years only. Complimentary full breakfast. Check-in

3 pm, check-out 11 am. Restaurant. Outdoor pool. **$$**

Restaurant

★ ★ **COLBY HILL INN.** *The Oaks, Henniker (03242). Phone 603/428-3281; fax 603/428-9218. www.colbyhillinn.com.* A part of the Colby Hill Inn (see) bed-and-breakfast in the New Hampshire countryside, this restaurant features a surprisingly cosmopolitan menu that combines familiar favorites with more contemporary variations. Rustic game meats appear as pepper-crusted duck breast with cranberry-orange syrup and fig-and-sage-glazed venison osso buco. Seafood choices are also featured, such as cedar-plank roasted salmon with a maple-rum glaze, and baked stuffed jumbo shrimp Rockefeller. International/Fusion menu. Dinner. Closed Dec 24-25. **$$$**

Dixville Notch (B-4)

See also Colebrook

Population 30
Elevation 1,990 ft
Area Code 603
Zip 03576

The small village of Dixville Notch shares its name with the most northerly of the White Mountain passes. The Notch cuts through the mountain range between Kidderville and Errol. At its narrowest point, east of Lake Gloriette, is one of the most impressive views in the state. Every four years, Dixville Notch is invaded by the national news media, who report the nation's first presidential vote tally shortly after midnight on election day.

What to See and Do

Balsams/Wilderness Ski Area. *Hwy 26, Dixville Notch (03576). Phone 603/255-3400; toll-free 800/255-0800 (snow conditions, NH only).* Chairlift, two T-bars; patrol, school, rentals, snowmaking; restaurant, cafeteria, bar, nursery, resort. Longest run 1 mile; vertical drop 1,000 feet. (Dec-Mar, daily) Cross-country trails. **$$$$**

Table Rock. *3/4 mile S of Hwy 26, 1/2 mile E of village of Dixville Notch.* Views of New Hampshire, Maine, Vermont, and Québec.

Full-Service Resort

★ ★ ★ **THE BALSAMS.** *Hwy 26, Dixville Notch (03576). Phone 603/255-3400; toll-free 800/255-0600; fax 603/255-4221. www.thebalsams.com.* The Balsams transports guests back to the New England of legend with its impressive architecture and bucolic setting. Built just after the Civil War, this 15,000-acre family-friendly resort is Yankee living at its best. A veritable winter wonderland during snowy months, this destination is a playground year-round with a wide variety of sporting activities and entertainment. Winter is spent downhill skiing, cross-country skiing, snowboarding, and ice skating, while warmer months are enjoyed while playing golf or tennis and enjoying the great outdoors on nature walks. The accommodations have a classic New England country appeal coupled with serene views. Operating on the all-inclusive American plan, The Balsams makes gourmet dining an integral part of the experience here. 204 rooms, 6 story. Closed Apr-mid-May, mid-Oct-mid-Dec. Check-in 4 pm, check-out noon. Restaurant, bar. Children's activity center. Fitness room. Outdoor pool. Golf, 27 holes. Tennis. **$$$**

Dover (E-5)

See also Portsmouth

Settled 1623
Population 25,042
Elevation 57 ft
Area Code 603
Zip 03820
Information Chamber of Commerce, 299 Central Ave; phone 603/742-2218
Web Site www.dovernh.org

With its historic trails and homes, Dover is the oldest permanent settlement in New Hampshire. The town contains the only known existing colonial garrison.

What to See and Do

Woodman Institute. *182-190 Central Ave, Dover (03820). 1/2 mile S on Hwy 108. Phone 603/742-1038.* Garrison House (1675), only garrison in New Hampshire now visible in nearly its original form. Woodman House (1818), residence of the donor, is now a natural history museum with collections of minerals; Native American artifacts; and displays of mammals, fish, amphibians, reptiles, birds, insects;

war memorial rooms. Senator John P. Hale House (1813) contains articles of Dover history and antique furniture. (Apr-Jan, Wed-Sun afternoons; closed holidays) **$$**

Special Event

Cocheco Arts Festival. Mid-July-late Aug.

Limited-Service Hotel

★ **DAYS INN.** *481 Central Ave, Dover (03820). Phone 603/742-0400; toll-free 800/329-7466; fax 603/742-7790. www.dover-durham-daysinn.com.* 50 rooms, 2 story. Pets accepted. Complimentary continental breakfast. Check-out 11 am. Outdoor pool, whirlpool. **$**

Specialty Lodging

The following lodging establishment is approved by Mobil Travel Guide, but due to its unique and individualized nature has not been given a traditional Mobil Star rating. Included in this listing you may find bed-and-breakfasts, limited-service inns, guest ranches, and other unique hotel properties.

SILVER STREET INN. *103 Silver St, Dover (03820). Phone 603/743-3000; fax 603/749-5673. www.silverstreetinn.com.* Victorian house built circa 1880 for a local businessman. 10 rooms, 3 story. Complimentary full breakfast. Check-in 2 pm, check-out 11 am. **$**

Restaurants

★ ★ **FIREHOUSE ONE.** *1 Orchard St, Dover (03820). Phone 603/749-2220; fax 603/740-9846. www.firehouseone.com.* Old restored firehouse (1840), arched doors and windows, tin walls and ceilings, overstuffed chairs. American menu. Lunch, dinner, Sun brunch. Closed July 4, Dec 25. Bar. Children's menu. Reservations recommended. Outdoor seating. **$$**

★ ★ ★ **MAPLES.** *17 Newmarket Rd, Durham (03824). Phone 603/868-7800; toll-free 888/399-9777; fax 603/868-2964. www.threechimneysinn.com.* This restaurant provides wonderful service in an old New England setting that includes beautiful dark wood tables and large, comfortable chairs. The small, intimate dining room allows couples to feel alone. In the summertime, guests will enjoy dining on the patio and

in the winter, the fireplace creates a cozy atmosphere. American menu. Dinner. Outdoor seating. **$$$**

★ **NEWICK'S SEAFOOD.** *431 Dover Point Rd, Dover (03820). Phone 603/742-3205; fax 603/749-6942. www.newicks.com.* Nautical accents. Seafood menu. Lunch, dinner. Closed Thanksgiving, Dec 25. Seafood market. **$$**

Exeter (F-5)

See also Hampton Beach, Portsmouth

Settled 1638
Population 12,481
Elevation 40 ft
Area Code 603
Zip 03833
Information Exeter Area Chamber of Commerce, 120 Water St; phone 603/772-2411
Web Site www.exeterarea.org

A venerable preparatory school and colonial houses belie Exeter's radical history. It had its beginnings in religious nonconformity, led by Reverend John Wheelwright and Anne Hutchinson, both of whom were banished from Massachusetts for heresy. There was an anti-British scuffle in 1734, and by 1774 Exeter was burning Lord North in effigy and talking of liberty. It was made the capital of the state during the Revolution, since there were too many Tories in Portsmouth. Exeter is the birthplace of Daniel Chester French and John Irving.

What to See and Do

American Independence Museum. *1 Governors Ln, Exeter (03833). Phone 603/772-2622.* Site of Revolutionary War-era state treasury building; grounds house Folsom Tavern (1775). (May-Oct, Wed-Sun) **$$**

Exeter Fine Crafts. *61 Water St, Exeter (03833). Phone 603/778-8282.* Work in all media by New Hampshire's finest artisans. (Mon-Sat) **FREE**

Gilman Garrison House. *12 Water St, Exeter (03833). Phone 603/436-3205.* (1676-1690) Built as a fortified garrison with hewn logs; pulley arrangement to raise and lower door still in place. Substantially remodeled in mid-18th century; wing added with 17th- and 18th-century furnishings. (Open by appointment only) **$$**

Phillips Exeter Academy. *20 Main St, Exeter (03833). Phone 603/772-4311.* (1781) (990 students) On 400 acres with more than 100 buildings. Coed school for grades 9-12. Founded by John Phillips, who sought a school for "students from every quarter"; known for its student diversity. On campus are a contemporary library (1971), designed by Louis I. Kahn; the Frederick R. Mayer Art Center; and the Lamont Art Gallery.

Franconia (C-3)

See also Bretton Woods, Franconia Notch State Park, Littleton, Twin Mountain

Population 811
Elevation 971 ft
Area Code 603
Zip 03580
Information Franconia Notch Chamber of Commerce, PO Box 780; phone 603/823-5661 or toll-free 800/237-9007
Web Site www.franconianotch.org

What to See and Do

Frost Place. *Ridge Rd, Franconia (03580). 1 mile S on Hwy 116 to Bickford Hill Rd, right over bridge, left at fork, on to Ridge Rd. Phone 603/823-5510.* Two furnished rooms of Robert Frost's home open to public; memorabilia; poetry trail; 25-minute video. (July-Columbus Day: Wed-Mon afternoons; Memorial Day-June: Sat-Sun afternoons) **$$**

New England Ski Museum. *Franconia Notch Pkwy, Franconia (03580). Hwy 3, exit 34B; near Cannon Mountain Tramway. Phone 603/823-7177; toll-free 800/639-4181. www.nesm.org.* Details history of skiing in the East; exhibits feature skis and bindings, clothing, art, and photographs; vintage films. Gift shop. (Late May-mid-Oct: daily; Dec-late Mar: Mon-Tues, Fri-Sun; closed Dec 25) **FREE**

Special Event

Lilac Time Festival. *8 miles W on NH 117, then 4 miles S on NH 302. Phone 603/838-6673.* Celebration of the state flower and observance of Memorial Day. Parade, carnival, vendors, entertainment, special events. Late May.

Limited-Service Hotels

★ ★ **FRANCONIA VILLAGE HOTEL.** *87 Wallace Hill Rd, Franconia (03580). Phone 603/823-7422; fax 603/823-5638.* In operation since 1923, this inn overlooks the upper rapids of Niagara Falls and is a distinctive historic structure. The inn has an "Olde English" atmosphere and lovely wood-burning fireplaces. 60 rooms, 2 story. Complimentary continental breakfast. Restaurant. Fitness room. Indoor pool, whirlpool. **$**

★ **STONYBROOK MOTEL & LODGE.** *1098 Profile Rd; Hwy 18, Franconia (03580). Phone 603/823-5800; toll-free 800/722-3552. www.stonybrookmotel.com.* 23 rooms. Check-out 11 am. Indoor pool, outdoor pool. **$**

Full-Service Inn

★ ★ ★ **FRANCONIA INN.** *1300 Easton Rd, Franconia (03580). Phone 603/823-5542; toll-free 800/473-5299; fax 603/823-8078. www.franconiainn.com.* Nestled in the White Mountains, this bed-and-breakfast offers spacious and comfortable rooms with breathtaking vistas. 34 rooms, 3 story. Closed Apr-mid-May. Check-in 3 pm, check-out 11 am. Restaurant, bar. Outdoor pool, whirlpool. Tennis. **$**

Specialty Lodgings

The following lodging establishments are approved by Mobil Travel Guide, but due to their unique and individualized nature have not been given a traditional Mobil Star rating. Included in this listing you may find bed-and-breakfasts, limited-service inns, guest ranches, and other unique hotel properties.

HILLTOP INN. *1348 Main St, Sugar Hill (03585). Phone 603/823-5695; toll-free 800/770-5695; fax 603/823-5518. www.hilltopinn.com.* Built in 1895; antiques, quilts. 6 rooms, 2 story. Complimentary full breakfast. Check-in 2-6 pm, check-out 11 am. **$**

LOVETTS INN. *1474 Profile Rd (Hwy 18), Franconia (03580). Phone 603/823-7761; toll-free 800/356-3802; fax 603/823-8802. www.lovettsinn.com.* 22 rooms, 2 story. Closed Apr. Pets accepted, some restrictions; fee. Check-in 2 pm, check-out 11 am. Restaurant, bar. Outdoor pool. **$$**

SUGAR HILL INN. *Hwy 117, Franconia (03580). Phone 603/823-5621; toll-free 800/548-4748; fax 603/823-5639. www.sugarhillinn.com.* Converted farmhouse (circa 1789). 9 rooms. Check-in 3 pm, checkout 11 am. Restaurant (public by reservation), bar. **$$**
🅿

SUNSET HILL HOUSE – A GRAND INN. *231 Sunset Hill Rd, Sugar Hill (03585). Phone 603/823-5522; toll-free 800/786-4455; fax 603/823-5738. www.sunsethillhouse.com.* Built in 1882; beautiful view of mountains, attractive grounds. 28 rooms, 2 story. Complimentary full breakfast. Check-in 3 pm, checkout 11 am. Restaurant. Outdoor pool. Golf. **$$$**
🏊 🏌

Restaurants

★ ★ ★ **THE FRANCONIA INN.** *1300 Easton Rd, Franconia (03580). Phone 603/823-5542; toll-free 800/473-5299; fax 603/823-8078. www.franconiainn.com.* The "Elegant American Cuisine" draws on regional specialties and is influenced by the rich heritage of the cultural mosaic along with unique variations of the classics. Guests will enjoy great views of the White Mountains, the romance of candlelight dining, and the muted strains of Mozart. American menu. Dinner. Closed Apr-mid-May. Bar. Children's menu. **$$**

★ ★ **HORSE & HOUND.** *205 Wells Rd, Franconia (03580). Phone 603/823-5501. www.bestinns.net/usa/hh/horse.html.* International/Fusion menu. Dinner. Closed Sun-Wed. Bar. Children's menu. **$$**
🅿

★ ★ **LOVETTS INN BY LAFAYETTE BROOK.** *1474 Profile Rd (Hwy 18), Franconia (03580). Phone 603/823-7761; fax 603/823-8802. www.lovettsinn.com.* American menu. Dinner. Closed Apr. Bar. Reservations recommended. **$$**
🅿

★ ★ **POLLY'S PANCAKE PARLOR.** *672 Hwy 117, Sugar Hill (03585). Phone 603/823-5575; fax 603/823-5577. www.pollyspancakeparlor.com.* In converted carriage shed (1840). American menu. Breakfast, lunch. Closed Dec-Mar. Children's menu. **$$**

Franconia Notch State Park (C-3)

See also Franconia, Lincoln/North Woodstock

Approximately 7 miles SE of Franconia via Hwy 18 and I-93/Franconia Notch State Pkwy.

This 7-mile pass and state park, a deep valley of 6,440 acres between the Franconia and Kinsman ranges of the White Mountains, has been a top tourist attraction since the mid-19th century. Mounts Liberty (4,460 feet), Lincoln (5,108 feet), and Lafayette (5,249 feet) loom on the east, and Cannon Mountain (4,200 feet) presents a sheer granite face. The Pemigewasset River follows the length of the Notch.

The park offers various recreational activities, including swimming at Sandy Beach; fishing and boating on Echo Lake (junction Hwy 18 and I-93, exit 3); hiking; 8-mile paved bike path through the Notch; skiing; picnicking; camping. Fees for some activities. For further information, contact Franconia Notch State Park, Franconia 03580; phone 603/823-5563.

The Basin. *W of I-93 (Franconia Notch State Pkwy), S of Profile Lake.* Deep glacial pothole, 20 feet in diameter, at the foot of a waterfall, polished smooth by sand, stones, and water.

Cannon Mountain Ski Area. *5 miles S of Franconia via Hwy 18 and I-93 (Franconia Notch State Pkwy), exit 34B or 34C. Phone 603/823-8800. www.cannonmt.com.* Tramway, two quad, three triple, two double chairlifts, pony lift; patrol, school, rentals; snowmaking; cafeterias, bar (beer and wine); nursery. New England Ski Museum. Longest run 2 miles and vertical drop 2,146 feet. (Late Nov-mid-Apr, daily; closed Dec 25) Tramway rising 2,022 feet vertically over a distance of 1 mile in 6 minutes, also operates Memorial Day-mid-Oct: daily; rest of year: weekends (weather permitting).

Flume Gorge & Park Information Center. *15 miles S of Franconia, I-93 (Franconia Notch State Pkwy), exit 34A. Phone 603/745-8391.* Narrow, natural gorge, and waterfall along the flank of Mount Liberty, accessible by stairs and walks; picnicking. Mountain flowers and mosses, Liberty Gorge, the Cascades, covered bridges. Information center offers a 15-minute movie introducing the park every half hour. Interpretive exhibits. Gift shop, cafeteria. (Mid-May-late Oct, daily)

Lafayette Campground. *9 miles S of Franconia Village, off I-93 (Franconia Notch State Pkwy). Phone 603/823-9513.* Fishing. Hiking on Appalachian trail system. Picnicking. Camping. Fees for some activities. (Mid-May-mid-Oct, daily) **$$$$**

Old Man of the Mountain Historic Site. *1,200 ft above Profile Lake, W of I-93 (Franconia Notch State Pkwy), exit 2.* Discovered in 1805, the craggy likeness of a man's face was formed naturally of five layers of granite and was 40 feet high. It tumbled down on May 3, 2003. It was also known as the "Great Stone Face."

Franklin (E-4)

See also Laconia

Settled 1764
Population 8,304
Elevation 335 ft
Area Code 603
Zip 03235
Information Greater Franklin Chamber of Commerce, PO Box 464, phone 603/934-6909
Web Site www.franklin.nh.us/chamber

Franklin was named in 1828 for Benjamin Franklin; until then it was a part of Salisbury. It is the birthplace of Daniel Webster, lawyer, senator, and statesman. The Pemigewasset and Winnipesaukee rivers, joining to form the Merrimack, provide the city with abundant water power.

What to See and Do

Congregational Christian Church. *47 S Main St, Franklin (03235). On US 3. Phone 603/934-4242.* (1820) Church that Daniel Webster attended; tracker action organ. A bust of Webster by Daniel Chester French is outside. (Wed-Thurs mornings, Sun, also by appointment) **FREE**

Tanger Factory Outlet Center. *120 Laconia Rd, Tilton (03276). Approximately 5 miles E on Hwy 3. Phone 603/286-7880. www.tangeroutlet.com.* This large factory outlet center features familiar retailing names like Gap, Wilsons Leather, and Nine West. (May-Dec: Mon-Sat 10 am-9 pm, Sun 10 am-6 pm; Jan-Apr: Sun-Thurs 10 am-6 pm, Fri-Sat 10 am-8 pm)

Limited-Service Hotel

★ **SUPER 8.** *7 Tilton Rd, Tilton (03276). Phone 603/286-8882; toll-free 800/800-8000; fax 603/286-8788. www.super8.com.* Close to all the outdoor activities and entertainment around Lake Winnipesaukee, this budget-friendly hotel puts guests in convenient proximity to swimming, boating, and fishing. 63 rooms, 2 story. Check-in 3 pm, check-out 11 am. **$**

Specialty Lodging

The following lodging establishment is approved by Mobil Travel Guide, but due to its unique and individualized nature has not been given a traditional Mobil Star rating. Included in this listing you may find bed-and-breakfasts, limited-service inns, guest ranches, and other unique hotel properties.

MARIA ATWOOD INN. *71 Hill Rd (Rte 3A), Franklin (03235). Phone 603/934-3666. www.atwood inn.com.* The phrase "stepping back in time" is the perfect way to describe this gorgeous Federal-style bed-and-breakfast, built as a home for its namesake in 1830. Enjoy a traditional country breakfast in the morning, then head out for a day of outdoor ventures such as skiing, hiking, boating, and fishing, or hunt down some quintessential weekend-in-the-country pursuits like antiquing, quilt-making, and outdoor theater. 7 rooms, 3 story. Complimentary full breakfast. Check-in 3 pm, check-out 11 am. **$**

Restaurant

★ **MR D'S.** *428 N Main St, West Franklin (03235). Phone 603/934-3142.* Collection of old-fashioned photographs on walls. American menu. Breakfast, lunch, dinner. Closed holidays. Children's menu. **$$**

Gorham (C-4)

See also Mount Washington, Pinkham Notch, White Mountain National Forest

Settled 1805
Population 3,173
Elevation 801 ft
Area Code 603
Zip 03581
Information Northern White Mountains Chamber of Commerce, 164 Main St, PO Box 298, Berlin 03570; phone 603/752-6060 or toll-free 800/992-7480
Web Site www.northernwhitemountains.com

Commanding the northeast approaches to the Presidential Range of the White Mountains, at the north end of Pinkham Notch (see), Gorham has magnificent views and is the center for summer and winter sports. The Peabody River merges with the Androscoggin in a series of falls. A Ranger District office of the White Mountain National Forest (see) is located here.

What to See and Do

Dolly Copp Campground. *300 Glen Rd, Gorham (03851). 6 miles S on Hwy 16 in White Mountain National Forest.* Phone 603/466-2713. 176 campsites; fishing, hiking, picnicking.

Libby Memorial Pool & Recreation Area. *1/4 mile S on Hwy 16.* Natural pool, bathhouses; picnicking. (Summer, daily, weather permitting)

Moose Brook State Park. *30 Jimtown Rd, Gorham (03581). 2 miles W on Hwy 2.* Phone 603/466-3860. Views of the Presidential Range of the White Mountains; good stream fishing area. Swimming, bathhouse; picnicking; camping. Hiking to Randolph Range. (Late May-early Sept)

Moose Tours. *Hwys 2 and 16, Gorham (03581). Main St.* Phone 603/752-6060. Daily tours leave each evening from the Gorham Informational Booth on a specified route to locate moose for sighting. (Late May-mid-Oct) **$$$**

Mount Washington. *10 miles S on Hwy 16.* (see).

Limited-Service Hotels

★ **MT. MADISON MOTEL.** *365 Main St, Gorham (03581).* Phone 603/466-3622; toll-free 800/851-1136; fax 603/466-3664. www.mtmadisonmotel.com. 33 rooms, 2 story. Check-out 11 am. Outdoor pool. **$**
🛏

★ ★ **ROYALTY INN.** *130 Main St, Gorham (03581).* Phone 603/466-3312; toll-free 800/437-3529; fax 603/466-5802. www.royaltyinn.com. 90 rooms, 2 story. Pets accepted, some restrictions; fee. Check-out 11 am. Restaurant, bar. Fitness room. Indoor pool, outdoor pool. **$**
🐾 🏃 🛏

Full-Service Inn

★ ★ ★ **PHILBROOK FARM INN.** *881 North Rd, Shelburne (03581).* Phone 603/466-3831. www.phil

brookfarminn.com. The fifth generation of Philbrooks now run this historic inn, set on 900 acres of forested property bordered by the Androscoggin River. Built in 1861, the building has been modernized without sacrificing any of the original charm. 18 rooms, 3 story. Closed late Oct-late Dec; also Apr. Pets accepted. Complimentary full breakfast. Check-in noon, check-out 10 am. Restaurant. Outdoor pool. **$**
🐾 🛏

Restaurant

★ ★ **YOKOHAMA.** *288 Main St, Gorham (03581).* Phone 603/466-2501. Japanese menu. Lunch, dinner. Closed Mon; Thanksgiving, Dec 25; also three weeks in Apr. Children's menu. **$$**

Hampton Beach (F-5)

See also Exeter, Portsmouth

Settled 1638
Population 900
Elevation 56 ft
Area Code 603
Zip 03842
Information Chamber of Commerce, 1 Park Ave, PO Box 790; phone 603/926-8717 or toll-free 800/438-2826
Web Site www.hamptonbeaches.com

What to See and Do

Fishing. Charter boats at Hampton Beach piers.

Fuller Gardens. *10 Willow Ave, North Hampton (03862). 4 miles NE via Hwy 1A, just N of Hwy 111.* Phone 603/964-5414. Former estate of the late Governor Alvan T. Fuller featuring extensive rose gardens, annuals, perennials, Japanese garden, and conservatory. (May-Oct, daily) **$$**

Hampton Beach State Park. *3 miles S on Hwy 1A.* Phone 603/926-3784. Sandy beach on Atlantic Ocean. Swimming, bathhouse. Also here is the Sea Shell, a band shell and amphitheater. Camping (hook-ups). (Late May-Labor Day, daily)

Tuck Memorial Museum. *40 Park Ave, Hampton (03842). On Meeting House Green, 4 miles N via Hwy 1A.* Phone 603/929-0781. Home of Hampton Historical Society. Antiques, documents, photographs, early postcards, tools, and toys; trolley exhibit; memorabilia of Hampton history. Restored one-room schoolhouse; fire station. (Mid-June-mid-Sept: Tues-Fri and Sun afternoons; rest of year: by appointment) **FREE**

Special Events

Band concerts. On beach. Evenings. Late June-Labor Day.

Performing Arts Center of Winnacunet High School. *Hwy 101 E, Hampton Beach (03842). Phone 603/926-3073.* Performances in 200-year-old modernized ox barn. Nightly except Mon; matinee Wed, Fri; children's shows Sat. Mid-June-Labor Day.

Limited-Service Hotels

★ ★ **ASHWORTH BY THE SEA.** *295 Ocean Blvd, Hampton Beach (03842). Phone 603/926-6762; toll-free 800/345-6736; fax 603/926-2002. www.ashworthhotel.com.* 105 rooms, 4 story. Check-in 3 pm, check-out noon. Restaurant, bar. Indoor pool. **$**

★ **HAMPSHIRE INN.** *20 Spur Rd (Hwy 107), Seabrook (03874). Phone 603/474-5700; toll-free 800/932-8520; fax 603/474-2886. www.hampshireinn.com.* 35 rooms, 3 story. Complimentary continental breakfast. Check-out 11 am. Fitness room. Indoor pool, whirlpool. Airport transportation available. **$**

★ ★ **HAMPTON FALLS INN.** *11 Lafayette Rd, Hampton Falls (03844). Phone 603/926-9545; toll-free 800/356-1729; fax 603/926-4155. www.hamptonfallsinn.com.* 47 rooms, 3 story. Pets accepted, some restrictions; fee. Check-out 11 am. Restaurant. Indoor pool, whirlpool. **$**

★ ★ **INN OF HAMPTON.** *815 Lafayette Rd, Hampton (03842). Phone 603/926-6771; toll-free 800/423-4561; fax 603/929-2160. www.theinnofhampton.com.* Not to be confused with the chain of a similar name, this inn provides the personalized touches of a bed-and-breakfast but has several rooms providing modern business services. 71 rooms, 2 story. Check-out 11 am. Restaurant. Fitness room. Indoor pool, whirlpool. **$**

Specialty Lodgings

The following lodging establishments are approved by Mobil Travel Guide, but due to their unique and individualized nature have not been given a traditional Mobil Star rating. Included in this listing you may find bed-and-breakfasts, limited-service inns, guest ranches, and other unique hotel properties.

D. W. 'S OCEANSIDE INN. *365 Ocean Blvd, Hampton Beach (03842). Phone 603/926-3542; toll-free 866/623-2674; fax 603/926-3549. www.oceansideinn.com.* This early 1900s beach house overlooking the Atlantic Ocean is an ideal getaway from the grind. Geared toward more mature getaways, the Oceanside is open mid-May through mid-Oct. 10 rooms, 2 story. Complimentary full breakfast. Check-in 2 pm, check-out 11 am. Beach. **$$**

LAMIE'S INN & OLD SALT RESTAURANT. *490 Lafayette Rd, Hampton (03842). Phone 603/926-0330; toll-free 800/805-5050; fax 603/926-0211. www.lamiesinn.com.* 32 rooms, 2 story. Check-in 3 pm, check-out 11 am. Restaurant, bar. Airport transportation available. **$**

Restaurant

★ **NEWICK'S FISHERMAN'S LANDING.** *845 Lafayette Rd, Hampton (03842). Phone 603/926-7646; fax 603/926-7947. www.newicks.com.* Seafood menu. Lunch, dinner. Closed Thanksgiving, Dec 25; Mon-Tues in winter. Children's menu. **$$**

Hanover (D-3)

See also White River Junction, VT

Settled 1765
Population 9,212
Elevation 531 ft
Area Code 603
Zip 03755
Information Chamber of Commerce, PO Box 5105, 216 Nugget Bldg, Main St; phone 603/643-3115
Web Site www.hanoverchamber.org

Established four years after the first settlers came here, Dartmouth College is an integral part of Hanover. Named for the Earl of Dartmouth, one of its original supporters, the school was founded by the Reverend

Eleazar Wheelock "for the instruction of the youth of Indian tribes . . . and others."

What to See and Do

Dartmouth College. *Main and Wheelock sts, Hanover (03755). Phone 603/646-1110.* (1769) (5,400 students) On campus are

Baker Barry Memorial Library. *1 Elm St, Hanover (03755). Wentworth and College sts. Phone 603/646-2560.* (White spire) Two million volumes; notable frescoes by the Mexican artist José Clemente Orozco. (Academic year, daily) Guide service during vacations (Mon-Fri).

Dartmouth Row. *E side of Green.* Early white brick buildings including Wentworth, Dartmouth, Thornton, and Reed halls. Parts of Dartmouth Hall date to 1784.

Hood Museum and Hopkins Center for the Arts. *Opposite S end of Green.* Concert hall, theaters, changing art exhibits. Gallery (daily; free). Performing arts events all year (fees).

Dartmouth Skiway. *Lyme. 15 miles N on Hwy 10 to Lyme, then 3 miles E. Phone 603/795-2143. www.dartmouth.edu/~skiway.* Quad, double chairlift, surface tow; patrol, school; lodge, snack bar. Longest run 1 mile; vertical drop 968 feet. (Mid-Dec-Mar, daily) **$$$$**

Enfield Shaker Museum. *24 Caleb Dyer Ln, Enfield (03748). Phone 603/632-4346.* Museum devoted to Shaker culture on the site where the Shakers established their Chosen Vale in 1793. Includes exhibits, craft demonstrations, workshops, special programs, and extensive gardens. **$$$**

League of New Hampshire Craftsmen. *13 Lebanon St, Hanover (03755). Phone 603/643-5050.* Work by some of New Hampshire's finest craftspeople. (Mon-Sat; closed holidays) **FREE**

⭐ **Saint-Gaudens National Historic Site.** *Rte 12A, Cornish. Approximately 5 miles S on Hwy 10, then 12 miles S off Hwy 12A, across the river from Windsor, VT. Phone 603/675-2175.* Former residence and studio of sculptor Augustus Saint-Gaudens (1848-1907); "Aspet," built circa 1800, was once a tavern. Saint-Gaudens's famous works *The Puritan, Adams Memorial*, and *Shaw Memorial* are among the 100 works on display. Also formal gardens and works by

other artists; sculptor-in-residence; interpretive programs. (Memorial Day-Oct, daily) **$$**

Webster Cottage. *32 N Main St, Hanover (03755). Phone 603/643-6529.* (1780) Residence of Daniel Webster during his last year as a Dartmouth College student; colonial and Shaker furniture, Webster memorabilia. (June-mid-Oct: Wed, Sat-Sun afternoons) **FREE**

Limited-Service Hotel

★ **CHIEFTAIN MOTOR INN.** *84 Lyme Rd, Hanover (03755). Phone 603/643-2550; toll-free 800/845-3557; fax 603/643-5265. www.chieftaininn.com.* View of the Connecticut River. 22 rooms, 2 story. Complimentary continental breakfast. Check-out 11 am. **$$**

Full-Service Inn

★ ★ ★ **HANOVER INN.** *Main and Wheelock sts, Hanover (03755). Phone 603/643-4300; toll-free 800/443-7024; fax 603/646-3744. www.hanoverinn.com.* This inn is located just minutes from Dartmouth College. The guest rooms are decorated with a colonial motif, and guests have access to athletic facilities at the university. 92 rooms, 5 story. Pets accepted, some restrictions; fee. Check-out noon. Restaurant, bar. Fitness room. Airport transportation available. **$$$**

🖼 🏃

Specialty Lodgings

The following lodging establishments are approved by Mobil Travel Guide, but due to their unique and individualized nature have not been given a traditional Mobil Star rating. Included in this listing you may find bed-and-breakfasts, limited-service inns, guest ranches, and other unique hotel properties.

ALDEN COUNTRY INN. *1 Market St, Lyme (03768). Phone 603/795-2222; toll-free 800/794-2296; fax 603/795-9436. www.aldencountryinn.com.* Original inn and tavern built in 1809; antique furnishings. 15 rooms, 4 story. Complimentary full breakfast. Check-in 3 pm, check-out 11 am. Restaurant, bar. **$**

DOWD'S COUNTRY INN. *On the Common, Lyme (03768). Phone 603/795-4712; toll-free 800/482-4712; fax 603/795-4220. www.dowdscountryinn.com.* This charming New England inn is located 10 miles north of Dartmouth College. Close to the Lyme commons, this property is surrounded by trees and provides a wonderful place for guests to relax. 23 rooms, 2 story. Pets accepted, some restrictions; fee. Complimentary full breakfast. Check-in 3 pm, check-out 11 am. **$$**

THE SHAKER INN AT THE GREAT STONE DWELLING. *447 Hwy 4A, Enfield (03748). Phone 603/632-7810; toll-free 888/707-4257. www.the shakerinn.com.* 24 rooms, 4 story. Complimentary full breakfast. Check-in 3 pm, check-out 11 am. Restaurant, bar. Children's activity center. Beach. Golf. **$$**

Restaurants

★ ★ **JESSE'S.** *RR 120, Hanover (03755). Phone 603/643-4111; fax 603/643-3340. www.bluesky restaurants.com.* Victorian décor. American menu. Dinner. Bar. Children's menu. Outdoor seating. **$$**

★ **MOLLY'S.** *43 S Main St, Hanover (03755). Phone 603/643-2570; fax 603/643-6645. www.mollys restaurant.com.* American menu. Lunch, dinner. Closed Thanksgiving, Dec 25. Bar. **$$**

Holderness (D-4)

See also Meredith, Plymouth

Settled 1770
Population 1,694
Elevation 584 ft
Area Code 603
Zip 03245

Holderness is the shopping center and post office for Squam Lake (second-largest lake in the state) and neighboring Little Squam. Fishing, boating, swimming, water sports, and winter sports are popular in this area. The movie *On Golden Pond* was filmed here. A Ranger District office of the White Mountain National Forest is located here.

What to See and Do

League of New Hampshire Craftsmen–Sandwich Home Industries. *32 Main St, Center Sandwich (03227). 12 miles NE via Hwy 113. Phone 603/284-6831.* Work by some of New Hampshire's finest crafts people. (Mid-May-mid-Oct, daily) **FREE**

Squam Lakes Natural Science Center. *23 Science Center Rd, Holderness (03245). Phone 603/968-7194.* www.nhnature.org. If this attraction looks familiar, perhaps you'll recognize it as the site where the 1981 movie *On Golden Pond,* with Henry Fonda and Katharine Hepburn, was filmed. Walking through the woods of this 200-acre wildlife sanctuary, you'll see black bears, deer, bobcats, otters, mountain lions, foxes, and birds of prey in enclosed trailside exhibits. You can also take the Explore Squam boat tour. Picnicking. (May-early Nov, daily 9:30 am-4:30 pm) **$$$**

Squam Lake Tours. *Hwy 113, Holderness (03245). 1/2 mile S on US 3. Phone 603/968-7577.* Two-hour boat tours of the area where *On Golden Pond* was filmed. (May-Oct, three tours daily) **$$$**

Full-Service Inns

★ ★ ★ **GLYNN HOUSE INN.** *59 Highland St, Ashland (03217). Phone 603/968-3775; toll-free 800/637-9599; fax 603/968-9415. www.glynnhouse.com.* This restored 1896 Victorian is located conveniently near Squam Lake in the heart of the White Mountains. 11 rooms, 2 story. Children over 12 years only. Complimentary full breakfast. Check-in 3 pm, check-out 11 am. **$$**

★ ★ ★ **MANOR ON GOLDEN POND.** *Manor Dr (Hwy 3), Holderness (03245). Phone 603/968-3348; toll-free 800/545-2141; fax 603/968-2116. www.manor ongoldenpond.com.* Modeled after an English country estate, this inn is located on the shore of Squam Lake. Activities include tennis, badminton, croquet, and access to a private beach. 37 rooms, 3 story. Children over 12 years only. Complimentary full breakfast. Check-in 3-6 pm, check-out 11 am. Restaurant, bar. Outdoor pool. Tennis. **$$**

Specialty Lodging

The following lodging establishment is approved by Mobil Travel Guide, but due to its unique and individualized nature has not been given a traditional Mobil Star rating. Included in this listing you may find bed-and-breakfasts, limited-service inns, guest ranches, and other unique hotel properties.

INN ON GOLDEN POND. *Hwy 3, Holderness (03245). Phone 603/968-7269; fax 603/968-9226. www.innongoldenpond.com.* Built in 1879; fireplace; rooms individually decorated. 8 rooms, 3 story. Children over 12 years only. Complimentary full breakfast. Check-in 3 pm, check-out 11 am. **$**

Restaurants

★ ★ **COMMON MAN.** *60 Main St, Ashland (03245).* Phone 603/968-7030; fax 603/968-3931. *www.thecman.com.* American menu. Lunch, dinner. Closed Thanksgiving, Dec 24-25. Bar. Children's menu. **$$**

★ ★ **CORNER HOUSE INN.** *22 Main St, Holderness (03227).* Phone 603/284-6219; fax 603/284-6220. This Victorian-style inn (1849) was originally a house and an attached harness shop. Guest rooms are available. American menu. Lunch, dinner. Closed Thanksgiving, Dec 25. **$$**

★ ★ ★ **MANOR ON GOLDEN POND.** *Manor Dr (Hwy 3 and Shepard Hill Rd), Holderness (03245).* Phone 603/968-3348; fax 603/968-2116. *www.manorongoldenpond.com.* Dinner at this cozy inn on Squam Lake is both a delicious and romantic experience. The frequently changing à la carte menu allows you to choose different combinations of New American dishes like duck hash Napolean and sautéed mahi mahi. American menu. Dinner. Bar. Reservations recommended. **$$$**
🅱

Jackson (C-4)

See also Bartlett, Mount Washington, North Conway, Pinkham Notch

Settled 1790
Population 678
Elevation 971 ft
Area Code 603
Zip 03846
Information Chamber of Commerce, PO Box 304; phone 603/383-9356
Web Site www.jacksonnh.com

At the south end of Pinkham Notch (see), Jackson is a center for skiing and a year-round resort. The Wildcat River rushes over rock formations in the village; Wildcat Mountain is to the north. A covered bridge (circa 1870) spans the Ellis River.

What to See and Do

Black Mountain. *2 1/2 miles N on Hwy 16B.* Phone 603/383-4490. *www.blackmt.com.* Triple, double chairlifts, J-bar; patrol, school, rentals; cafeteria; nursery. Longest run 1 mile; vertical drop 1,100 feet.

Heritage-New Hampshire. *2 miles S on Hwy 16 in Glen.* Phone 603/383-9776. Path winds among theatrical sets and takes visitors on a walk through 30 events during 300 years of New Hampshire history. Each set has animation, sounds, and smells to re-create the past, from a stormy voyage to the New World to a train ride through autumn foliage in Crawford Notch. (Late May-early Oct, daily) **$$$**

Jackson Ski Touring Foundation. *Main St and Hwy 16A, Jackson.* Phone toll-free 800/866-3334. *www.jacksonxc.org.* Maintains 95 miles of cross-country trails, connecting inns and ski areas. Instruction, rentals, rescue service. (Dec-mid-Apr, daily; closed Dec 25) **$$$**

Story Land. *2 miles S on Hwy 16 in Glen.* Phone 603/383-4186. Village of storybook settings; Cinderella's castle, Heidi's grandfather's house; themed rides, including raft ride, on 35 acres. (Mid-June-early Sept: daily; early Sept-early Oct: weekends) **$$$$**

Limited-Service Hotels

★ ★ **EAGLE MOUNTAIN HOUSE.** *Carter Notch Rd E, Jackson (03846).* Phone 603/383-9111; toll-free 800/966-5779; fax 603/383-0854. *www.eaglemt.com.* Spectacular view of mountains and forest. 93 rooms, 5 story. Check-out 11 am. Restaurant, bar. Fitness room. Outdoor pool, whirlpool. Golf. Tennis. **$**
🛉 🛏 🕴 🖾

★ **LODGE AT JACKSON VILLAGE.** *Hwy 16, Jackson (03846).* Phone 603/383-9101; toll-free 800/233-5634; fax 603/383-9823. *www.lodgeatjacksonvillage.com.* 32 rooms, 2 story. Check-out 11 am. Outdoor pool. Tennis. **$**
🛏 🖾

★ ★ **STORYBOOK RESORT INN.** *Hwys 302 and 16, Glen (3838).* Phone 603/383-6800; fax 603/383-4678. *www.storybookresort.com.* 78 rooms, 2 story. Check-out 11 am. Restaurant, bar. Fitness room. Indoor pool, two outdoor pools, children's pool. Tennis. **$**
🛉 🛏 🖾

Full-Service Resort

★ ★ ★ **WENTWORTH RESORT HOTEL.** *Hwy 16A and Carter Notch Rd, Jackson (03846).* Phone 603/383-9700; toll-free 800/637-0013; fax 603/383-4265. *www.thewentworth.com.* This elegant country inn, built in 1869, has been in continuous operation for more than a century. Located in the White Mountains, the year-round resort has first-class amenities like a fine-dining restaurant and recreational facilities. 60 rooms, 2 story. Check-out 11 am. Restaurant, bar. Outdoor pool. **$**

Full-Service Inn

★ ★ ★ **INN AT THORN HILL.** *Thorn Hill Rd, Jackson (03846). Phone 603/383-4242; toll-free 800/ 289-8990; fax 603/383-8062. www.innatthornhill.com.* 16 rooms. Children over 8 years only. Check-in 3 pm, check-out 11 am. Restaurant, bar. Fitness room. **$**

Specialty Lodgings

The following lodging establishments are approved by Mobil Travel Guide, but due to their unique and individualized nature have not been given a traditional Mobil Star rating. Included in this listing you may find bed-and-breakfasts, limited-service inns, guest ranches, and other unique hotel properties.

DANA PLACE INN. *Hwy 16, Jackson (03846). Phone 603/383-6822; toll-free 800/537-9276; fax 603/383-6022. www.danaplace.com.* 30 rooms, 2 story. Pets accepted. Complimentary full breakfast. Restaurant, bar. Indoor pool, children's pool, whirlpool. Golf. Tennis. Business center. **$$**

ELLIS RIVER HOUSE. *Hwy 16, Jackson (03846). Phone 603/383-9339; toll-free 800/233-8309; fax 603/383-4142. www.ellisriverhouse.com.* 21 rooms, 3 story. Children over 12 years only. Complimentary full breakfast. Check-in 3 pm, check-out 11 am. Bar. Outdoor pool, whirlpool. **$**

NESTLENOOK FARM RESORT. *Dinsmore Rd, Jackson (03846). Phone 603/383-9443; toll-free 800/ 659-9443; fax 603/383-4515. www.luxurymountaingeta ways.com.* Located on the river, this restored Victorian building is one of the oldest in Jackson (1770). Furnishings include antiques, Tiffany lamps, and 18th-century parlor stoves. 7 rooms, 3 story. Children over 12 years only. Complimentary full breakfast. Check-in 3 pm, check-out 11 am. Outdoor pool. **$$**

Restaurants

★ ★ **CHRISTMAS FARM INN.** *Hwy 16B, Jackson (03846). Phone 603/383-4313; toll-free 800/443-5837; fax 603/383-6495. www.christmasfarminn.com.* In historic building (1786). International/Fusion menu. Breakfast, dinner. Bar. **$$**

★ ★ ★ **INN AT THORN HILL.** *Thorn Hill Rd, Jackson (03846). Phone 603/383-4242; toll-free 800/ 289-8990; fax 603/383-8062. www.innatthornhill.com.* New England fusion menu. Dinner. **$$**

★ **RED PARKA PUB.** *Hwy 302, Glen (03838). Phone 603/383-4344; fax 603/383-9127. www.redparkapub.com.* One room in 1914 railroad car. American menu. Dinner. Closed Thanksgiving, Dec 24. Bar. Children's menu. Outdoor seating. **$**

★ ★ **WILDCAT TAVERN.** *Hwy 16A, Jackson (03846). Phone 603/383-4245; toll-free 800/228-4245; fax 603/383-6456. www.wildcattavern.com.* In historic inn (1896). American menu. Lunch, dinner. Bar. Children's menu. Outdoor seating. **$$**

Jaffrey (F-3)

See also Keene, Peterborough

Settled 1760
Population 5,361
Elevation 1,013 ft
Area Code 603
Zip 03452
Information Chamber of Commerce, PO Box 2; phone 603/532-4549
Web Site www.jaffreycoc.org

Jaffrey, on the eastern slopes of Mount Monadnock, has been a summer resort community since the 1840s.

What to See and Do

Barrett House "Forest Hall." *79 Main St, New Ipswich (03071). 10 miles SE on Hwy 124, then 1/4 mile S on Hwy 123A (Main St). Phone 603/878-2517.* (1800) Federal mansion with third-floor ballroom. Twelve museum rooms contain some of the most important examples of 18th- and 19th-century furniture and antique musical instruments in New England. Extensive grounds with Gothic Revival summer house on terraced hill behind main house. Guided tours. (June-mid-Oct, Thurs-Sun) **$$**

⭐ **Cathedral of the Pines.** *Cathedral Rd, Rindge (03461). 3 miles E on Hwy 124, then 3 miles S. Phone 603/899-3300. www.cathedralpines.com.* International nondenominational shrine. National memorial for all American war dead; Memorial Bell Tower dedicated to women who died in service. Outdoor altar, gardens, museum. (May-Oct, daily)

Monadnock State Park. *116 Poole Memorial Rd, Jaffrey (03452). 2 miles W on Hwy 124, then N. Phone 603/532-8862.* Hikers' mecca; 40-mile network of well-maintained trails on Mount Monadnock (3,165 feet). Summit views of all New England states. Picnicking, camping. Ski touring (Dec-Mar). No pets allowed. **$$**

Jefferson

Settled 1772
Population 965
Elevation 1,384 ft
Area Code 603
Zip 03583
Information Northern White Mountain Chamber of Commerce, 164 Main St, PO Box 298, Berlin 03570; phone 603/752-6060 or toll-free 800/992-7480
Web Site www.northernwhitemountains.com

On the slopes of Mount Starr King in the White Mountains, this resort area is referred to locally as "Jefferson Hill."

What to See and Do

Santa's Village. *1 mile NW on Hwy 2, 1/2 mile W of junction Hwy 116. Phone 603/586-4445.* Santa and tame deer; unique rides; live shows, computerized animation. Playground; picnic area. (Father's Day-Labor Day: daily; after Labor Day-Columbus Day: Sat-Sun) **$$$$**

Six Gun City. *Hwy 2, Jefferson. 4 miles E. Phone 603/586-4592.* Western frontier village; cowboy skits, frontier show, fort, Native American camp, homestead, carriage and sleigh museum, general store, snack bar; miniature horse show; pony and burro rides; bumper boats, water slides, and other rides; miniature golf, games, animals, and antiques. (Mid-June-Labor Day: daily; after Labor Day-Columbus Day: Sat-Sun) **$$$**

Special Event

Lancaster Fair. *6 miles NW in Lancaster. Phone 603/788-2530.* Agricultural exhibits, horse show, entertainment. Labor Day weekend.

Keene (F-3)

See also Jaffrey, Peterborough; see also Brattleboro, VT

Settled 1736
Population 22,430
Elevation 486 ft
Area Code 603
Zip 03431
Information Chamber of Commerce, 48 Central Sq; phone 603/352-1303
Web Site www.keenechamber.com

A modern commercial city, Keene is the chief community of the Monadnock region. Its industries manufacture many products including furniture, machinery, textiles, and toys.

What to See and Do

Colony Mill Marketplace. *222 West St, Keene (03431). Phone 603/357-1240.* Restored 1838 textile mill now transformed into regional marketplace with dozens of specialty shops, an antique center, numerous dining options, and varied entertainment. (Daily)

Horatio Colony House Museum. *199 Main St, Keene (03431). Phone 603/352-0460.* Stately Federalist home (1806) of the son of prominent Keene mill owners. Features treasures collected from Colony's world travels; books, art, antique furniture. (May-mid-Oct: Tues-Sat; rest of year: by appointment) **FREE**

Wyman Tavern. *339 Main St, Keene (03431). Phone 603/352-1895.* (1762) Scene of first meeting of Dartmouth College trustees in 1770; now furnished in 1820s-style. (June-Sept, Thurs-Sat) **$**

Special Events

Cheshire Fair. *Fairgrounds, 319 Monadnock Hwy, North Swanzey (03446). S on Hwy 12. Phone 603/357-4740.* Exhibits; horse and ox pulling contests; entertainment. First week in Aug.

Old Homestead. *At Potash Bowl in Swanzey Center, at Swanzey. 4 miles S on Hwy 32. Phone 603/352-0697.* Drama of life in Swanzey during the 1880s based on the Biblical story of the Prodigal Son; first presented in 1886. Mid-July.

Limited-Service Hotel

★ ★ BEST WESTERN SOVEREIGN HOTEL.

401 Winchester St, Keene (03431). Phone 603/357-3038; toll-free 800/780-7234; fax 603/357-4776. www.bwkeene.com. 131 rooms, 2 story. Pets accepted; fee. Complimentary full breakfast. Check-out noon. Restaurant, bar. Indoor pool. **$**

Restaurants

★ ★ 176 MAIN. *176 Main St, Keene (03457). Phone 603/357-3100; fax 603/357-5500. www.176main.com.* Mexican, Italian, seafood menu. Lunch, dinner. Closed holidays. Bar. Children's menu. Outdoor seating. **$$**

★ THE PUB. *131 Winchester St, Keene (03431). Phone 603/352-3135; fax 603/252-0263.* American menu. Dinner. Closed Dec 25. Bar. Children's menu. **$**

Laconia (D-4)

See also Franklin, Meredith, Wolfeboro

Settled 1777
Population 15,743
Elevation 570 ft
Area Code 603
Zip 03246
Information Chamber of Commerce, 11 Veterans Sq; phone 603/524-5531
Web Site www.laconia-weirs.org

On four lakes (Winnisquam, Opechee, Pauqus Bay, and Winnipesaukee), Laconia is the commercial center of the area known as the "Lakes Region." Besides the resort trade, it has more than a score of factories whose products include knitting machinery, hosiery, knitted fabrics, ball bearings, and electronic components. The headquarters of the White Mountain National Forest (see) is also located here.

What to See and Do

Daytona Fun Park. *Rte 11B, Laconia (03246). Phone 603/366-5461. www.daytonafunpark.com.* Challenge family and friends to miniature Indy Car racing on the go-karts. There's also a climbing wall, batting cages, and miniature golf. (Daily 10 am-11 pm) **$$**

Funspot. *Rte 3 S, Weirs Beach (03246). Phone 603/366-4377. www.funspotnh.com.* Funspot offers more than 500 new and classic games, an indoor golf center, bowling, kiddie rides, minature golf, a driving range, and an on-site tavern and restaurant. Fee ($) for individual attractions. (Mid-June-Labor Day: daily 9 am-midnight; rest of year: Sun-Thurs 10 am-10 pm, Fri-Sat 10 am-11 pm)

Gunstock Recreation Area. *Hwy 11A, Gilford (03249). 7 miles E on Hwy 11A. Phone 603/293-4341; toll-free 800/486-7862. www.gunstock.com.* A 2,400-acre county-operated park.

Summer. Picnic and camp sites (Memorial Day weekend-Columbus Day weekend; fee; hook-ups additional; includes swimming privileges); fireplaces; stocked pond, blazed trails, playground; special events.

Winter. Skiing. Quad, two triple, two double chairlifts, two handle tows; patrol, school, rentals; snowmaking; cafeteria, lounge; nursery. Longest run 2 miles; vertical drop 1,400 feet. Cross-country trails. Night skiing. (Nov-Mar, daily; closed Dec 25) **$$$$**

Half Moon Amusement Arcades. *240-260 Lakeside Ave, Weirs Beach (03246). Phone 603/366-4315. www.weirsbeach.com.* This old-fashioned arcade, just across the street from the scenic Weirs Beach boardwalk, includes a penny arcade, a family fun center and bumper cars. Revisit your teen years with classic games like Pac-Man, Asteroids, Space Invaders, and Pole Position, or let a new generation of game players discover Skeeball and pinball. Fee ($) for individual attractions. (Daily, hours vary)

M/S *Mount Washington*. *Weirs Beach (03246). Phone 603/366-5531; toll-free 888/843-6686. www.cruisenh.com.* Cruise the waters of Lake Winnipesaukee (win-e-puh-SAW-kee), the largest lake in New Hampshire, and enjoy scenic mountain views aboard the M/S *Mount Washington*, which offers daily scenic cruises and dinner dance cruises. Ports of call include Weirs Beach, Wolfeboro, Meredith, Alton Bay, and Center Harbor. (Mid-May-Oct; check Web site or call for schedule) **$$$$**

Queen of Winnipesaukee. *Phone 603/366-5531.* This 46-foot sloop sails from M/S *Mount Washington* dock in Weirs Beach. 1 1/2-hour cruises (July-Labor Day: daily; mid-May-June and early Sept-early Oct: weekends). Two-hour evening, moonlight cruises (July-Aug, Tues-Sat).

Recreation. The Weirs. *306 Union Ave, Laconia (03246). 5 miles N on Hwy 3 at Weirs Beach on Lake Winnipesaukee. Phone 603/524-5046.* Swimming, boating, fishing, sailing, water-skiing, lifeguards, bathhouses; playgrounds, picnic areas, nature trails. Endicott Memorial Stone with initials of 1652 explorers, south end of beach. (Mid-June-Labor Day, daily) **$$**

⭐ **Surf Coaster U.S.A.** *1085 White Oaks Rd, Weirs Beach (03247). 6 miles N on Hwy 3, then E on Hwy 11B. Phone 603/366-5600. www.surfcoasterUSA.com.* Family water park with wave pool, water slides, "Crazy River" inner tube ride, "Boomerang" rides inside translucent glass tubes; raft rentals, sun decks, showers, children's play areas; entertainment, games, prizes. Snack bar. (Mid-June-Labor Day, daily) **$$$$**

Special Event

New Hampshire Music Festival. *88 Alvah Wilson Rd, Laconia (03246). Phone 603/524-1000.* Plymouth State College, in Silver Cultural Arts Center. Symphony/pop concerts. Thurs-Fri; limited Sat performances.

Limited-Service Hotels

★ ★ **B MAE'S RESORT INN & SUITES.** *Rtes 11 and 11B, Gilford (03249). Phone 603/293-7526; toll-free 800/458-3877; fax 603/293-4340. www.bmaesresort.com.* B Mae's Resort Inn and Suites is located at Lake Winnipesaukee and is close to all Weirs Beach attractions. All rooms have a deck or patio. 82 rooms, 2 story. Complimentary continental breakfast. Check-in 3 pm, check-out 11 am. Restaurant, bar. Fitness room. Indoor pool, outdoor pool, whirlpool. **$**
🏃 ⌷

★ **BARTON'S MOTEL.** *1330 Union Ave, Laconia (03246). Phone 603/524-5674. www.bartonsmotel.com.* Located on the shores of Lake Winnipesaukee and minutes from Weirs Beach attractions, Barton's Motel offers scenic water views, as well as swimming and relaxing on its private beach. Amenities include free paddleboats and rowboats, free dockage for boat owners, and an on-site bookstore. 41 rooms. Check-out 11 am. Beach. Outdoor pool. **$**
⌷ ⌷

Lincoln/North Woodstock (C-4)

See also Franconia Notch State Park, Waterville Valley

Population 1,229
Elevation Lincoln, 811 ft; North Woodstock, 738 ft
Area Code 603
Zip Lincoln, 03251; North Woodstock, 03262
Information Chamber of Commerce, NH 112, PO Box 358, Lincoln; phone 603/745-6621 or toll-free 800/227-4191
Web Site www.linwoodcc.org

In a spectacular mountain setting, the villages of Lincoln and Woodstock lie at the junction of the road through Franconia Notch State Park (see) and the Kancamagus Scenic Byway (Hwy 112).

What to See and Do

Clark's Trading Post. *1 mile N of North Woodstock on Hwy 3. Phone 603/745-8913.* Entertainment park has trained New Hampshire black bears, haunted house, replica of 1884 firehouse; 30-minute ride on White Mountain Central railroad. Museum features early Americana, photo parlor, maple cabin, nickelodeons, ice cream parlor. Bumper boats. (July-Labor Day: daily; Memorial Day-June and early Sept-Columbus Day: weekends) **$$$**

Hobo Railroad. *Connector Rd, Lincoln (03251). Railroad St, off Main. Phone 603/745-2135.* Fifteen-mile scenic excursions along the Pemigewasset River. Features restored Pullman Dome dining car. (Daily) **$$$**

Loon Mountain Recreation Area. *3 miles E of Lincoln off Hwy 112 (Kancamagus Hwy). Phone 603/745-8111.* A 7,100-foot gondola, two triple, four double chairlifts, one high-speed quad chairlift, pony lift; patrol, school, rentals, shops, snowmaking; restaurant, cafeterias, bar; nursery; lodge. Longest run 2 1/2 miles; vertical drop 2,100 feet. (Late Nov-mid-Apr, daily) Cross-country trails (Dec-Mar). **Summer activities** include mountain biking (rentals), bike tours, in-line skating, horseback riding, skate park, climbing wall. Gondola also operates Memorial Day-mid-Oct (daily).

Lost River Gorge. *Lost River Rd, North Woodstock. 6 miles W of North Woodstock on Hwy 112, Kinsman*

Notch. *Phone 603/745-8031.* Natural boulder caves, largest known granite pothole in the eastern United States; Paradise Falls; boardwalks with 1,900-foot glacial gorge; nature garden with 300 varieties of native shrubs and flowers; geology exhibits; cafeteria, picnicking. (Mid-May–mid-Oct, daily) Appropriate outdoor clothing recommended. **$$$**

Whale's Tale Water Park. *N on I-93, exit 33, then N on Hwy 3. Phone 603/745-8810.* Wave pool, water slides, "lazy river," children's activity pool; playground; concession, gift shop. (Mid-June–Labor Day: daily; Memorial Day–mid-June: Sat-Sun) **$$$$**

Special Event

New Hampshire Highland Games. *Loon Mountain. Phone toll-free 800/358-7268.* Largest Scottish gathering in the eastern United States. Bands, competitions, concerts, workshops. Three days in Sept.

Limited-Service Hotels

★ **DRUMMER BOY MOTOR INN.** *Hwy 3, Lincoln (03251). Phone 603/745-3661; toll-free 800/762-7275; fax 603/745-9829. www.drummerboymotorinn.com.* 53 rooms. Check-out 11 am. Indoor pool, outdoor pool, whirlpool. **$**
🏊

★ ★ **INDIAN HEAD RESORT.** *RR 1, Box 99, Lincoln (03251). Phone 603/745-8000; toll-free 800/343-8000; fax 603/745-8414. www.indianheadresort.com.* View of mountains. 98 rooms, 2 story. Check-out 11 am. Restaurant, bar. Fitness room. Indoor pool, outdoor pool, whirlpool. Tennis. **$**
🧍 🏊 🎿

★ ★ **INNSEASON RESORTS SOUTH MOUNTAIN.** *Kancamagus Hwy, Lincoln (03251). Phone 603/745-2244; toll-free 800/654-6183; fax 603/745-2317. www.millatloon.com.* 95 rooms, 4 story. Check-out 11 am. Restaurant. Fitness room. Indoor pool, outdoor pool. **$**
🧍 🏊

★ ★ **MOUNTAIN CLUB ON LOON.** *Hwy 112 (Kancamagus Hwy), Lincoln (03251). Phone 603/745-3401; toll-free 800/229-7829; fax 603/745-8224. www.mtnclubonloon.com.* 234 rooms, 6 story. Check-out 11 am. Restaurant, bar. Children's activity center. Fitness room. Indoor pool, outdoor pool, whirlpool. Tennis. **$**
🧍 🏊 🎿

★ ★ **WOODWARDS RESORT.** *Hwy 3, Lincoln (03251). Phone 603/745-8141; toll-free 800/635-8968; fax 603/745-3408. www.woodwardsresort.com.* Located in the heart of the White Mountains, this small motor inn has been family operated since 1956. It is close to skiing, hiking, and other recreational activities. 80 rooms, 2 story. Check-out 11 am. Restaurant, bar. Indoor pool, outdoor pool, whirlpool. Tennis. **$**
🏊 🎿

Specialty Lodging

The following lodging establishment is approved by Mobil Travel Guide, but due to its unique and individualized nature has not been given a traditional Mobil Star rating. Included in this listing you may find bed-and-breakfasts, limited-service inns, guest ranches, and other unique hotel properties.

WOODSTOCK INN. *135 Main St, North Woodstock (03262). Phone 603/745-3951; toll-free 800/321-3985; fax 603/745-3701. www.woodstockinnnh.com.* Victorian house (1890). 24 rooms, 4 story. Complimentary full breakfast. Check-in 3 pm, check-out 11 am. Restaurant, bar. **$**

Restaurants

★ ★ **COMMON MAN.** *Pollard Rd, Lincoln (03217). Phone 603/745-3463; fax 603/745-6868. www.thecman.com.* Converted farmhouse; one of the oldest structures in the city. American menu. Dinner. Closed Dec 24-25. Bar. Children's menu. **$$**

★ ★ **GORDI'S FISH & STEAK HOUSE.** *Kancamagus Hwy, Lincoln (03251). Phone 603/745-6635; fax 603/745-3073.* Contemporary building with Victorian accents. Seafood, steak menu. Dinner. Closed Thanksgiving, Dec 25. Bar. Children's menu. **$$$**

★ ★ **OLD TIMBERMILL PUB & RESTAURANT.** *Main St (Hwy 112), Lincoln (03251). Phone 603/745-3603; fax 603/745-9345.* Converted mill drying shed (1926). Seafood, steak menu. Lunch, dinner. Bar. Outdoor seating. **$$**
🍴

★ **TRUANTS TAVERNE.** *96 Main St, North Woodstock (03262). Phone 603/745-2239. www.truantstaverne.com.* Seafood, steak menu. Lunch, dinner. Closed Thanksgiving, Dec 25. Bar. Children's menu. **$$**

Littleton (C-3)

See also Bretton Woods, Franconia, Twin Mountain

Population 5,827
Elevation 822 ft
Area Code 603
Zip 03561
Information Chamber of Commerce, 120 Main St, PO Box 105; phone 603/444-6561
Web Site www.littletonareachamber.com

Littleton is a resort area a few miles northwest of the White Mountain National Forest (see), which maintains a Ranger District office in nearby Bethlehem. Littleton is also a regional commercial center; its industries produce abrasives and electrical component parts. The Ammonoosuc River falls 235 feet on its way through the community.

What to See and Do

Littleton Historical Museum. *1 Cottage St, Littleton (03561). Phone 603/444-6435.* Photographs, arts and crafts, stereographs, local memorabilia. (Wed afternoons, or by appointment; also Sat in July-Oct) **FREE**

Samuel C. Moore Station. *8 miles W on Hwys 18, 135. Phone 603/653-9232.* Largest conventional hydroelectric plant in New England; a 2,920-foot dam across Connecticut River forms Moore Reservoir, which extends nearly 11 miles and covers an area of 3,490 acres. Visitor center has exhibits (daily). Recreation areas offer hunting, fishing, boat launching, waterskiing, picnicking and nature studies. (Memorial Day-Columbus Day, daily)

Limited-Service Hotel

★ ★ **EASTGATE MOTOR INN.** *335 Cottage St, Littleton (03561). Phone 603/444-3971; toll-free 866/640-3561; fax 603/444-3971. www.eastgatemotorinn.com.* 55 rooms. Pets accepted, some restrictions. Complimentary continental breakfast. Check-out 11 am. Restaurant, bar. Outdoor pool, children's pool. **$**

Full-Service Inn

★ ★ ★ **ADAIR COUNTRY INN.** *80 Guider Ln, Bethlehem (03574). Phone 603/444-2600; toll-free*

888/444-2600; fax 603/444-4823. www.adairinn.com. Built in 1927, this inn is situated on 200 landscaped acres designed by the Olmsted Brothers. The relaxing location is nestled near the 700,000-acre White Mountain National Forest. Guest rooms are furnished with antiques and original artwork and include afternoon tea and homemade desserts. 10 rooms, 3 story. Complimentary full breakfast. Check-in 3 pm, check-out 11 am. Restaurant. Tennis. **$$**

Specialty Lodgings

The following lodging establishments are approved by Mobil Travel Guide, but due to their unique and individualized nature have not been given a traditional Mobil Star rating. Included in this listing you may find bed-and-breakfasts, limited-service inns, guest ranches, and other unique hotel properties.

THAYER'S INN. *111 Main St, Littleton (03561). Phone 603/444-6469; toll-free 800/634-8179. www.thayersinn.com.* Historic inn (1843); antiques, library, sitting room. Cupola open to the public. 39 rooms, 4 story. Check-in 2 pm, check-out 11 am. **$**

WAYSIDE. *3738 Main St, Bethlehem (03574). Phone 603/869-3364; toll-free 800/448-9557; fax 603/869-5765. www.thewaysideinn.com.* This inn was originally a four-room homestead (1825) for the family of President Franklin Pierce. It is located on the Ammonoosuc River with a natural sand beach. 14 rooms. Check-in 3 pm, check-out 11 am. Restaurant, bar. **$**

Restaurants

★ ★ **CLAM SHELL.** *274 Dells Rd, Littleton (03561). Phone 603/444-6445; fax 603/444-5238.* American, seafood menu. Lunch, dinner. Closed Dec 24 (evening)-25. Bar. Children's menu. **$$**

★ **EASTGATE.** *335 Cottage St, Littleton (03561). Phone 603/444-3971. www.eastgatemotorinn.com.* American menu. Dinner. Closed Dec 24. Bar. **$**

★ ★ **ITALIAN OASIS.** *106 Main St, Littleton (03561). Phone 603/444-6995; fax 603/444-4884.* Converted Victorian home (circa 1890). Italian menu. Lunch, dinner. Closed Easter, Thanksgiving, Dec 25. Bar. Outdoor seating. **$$**

★ ★ **ROSA FLAMINGOS.** *Main St, Bethlehem (03574). Phone 603/869-3111.* Italian menu. Lunch, dinner. Closed Easter, Thanksgiving, Dec 25. Bar. Children's menu. Outdoor seating. **$$**

Manchester (F-4)

See also Concord, Nashua

Settled 1722
Population 99,567
Elevation 225 ft
Area Code 603
Information Chamber of Commerce, 889 Elm St, 03101-2000; phone 603/666-6600
Web Site www.manchester-chamber.org

Manchester is a city that has refused to bow to economic adversity. When the Amoskeag Manufacturing Company (cotton textiles), which had dominated Manchester's economy, failed in 1935, it left the city poverty-stricken. With determination worthy of New Englanders, a group of citizens bought the plant for $5 million and revived the city. Now Manchester is northern New England's premier financial center.

What to See and Do

Currier Gallery of Art. *201 Myrtle Way, Manchester (03104). Phone 603/669-6144.* One of New England's leading small museums; 13th- to 20th-century European and American paintings and sculpture; New England decorative art; furniture, glass, silver, and pewter; changing exhibitions, concerts, films, other programs. Tours of Zimmerman House, designed by Frank Lloyd Wright (call for reservations and times, fee). (Mon, Wed-Sun; closed holidays) **$$**

Manchester Historic Association Millyard Museum. *129 Amherst St, Manchester (03104). 2 blocks E of Elm St. Phone 603/622-7531. www.manchesterhistoric.org.* Museum and library with collections illustrating life in Manchester from pre-colonial times to present; permanent and changing exhibits; firefighting equipment; decorative arts, costumes, paintings. (Tues-Sat; closed holidays) **$$**

McIntyre Ski Area. *Kennard Rd, Manchester (03104). Kennard Rd. Phone 603/624-6571.* Two double chairlifts, pony lift; patrol, school, rentals, snowmaking; snack bar. Vertical drop 169 feet. (Dec-Mar, daily)

Palace Theatre. *80 Hanover St, Manchester (03101). Phone 603/668-5588.* Productions in vintage vaudeville/opera house.

Science Enrichment Encounters Museum. *200 Bedford St, Manchester (03101). Phone 603/669-0400.* More than 60 interactive, hands-on exhibits demonstrate basic science principles. (Daily; closed holidays) **$$**

Special Event

Riverfest. *Phone 603/623-2623.* Outdoor festival with family entertainment, concerts, arts and crafts, food booths, fireworks. Labor Day weekend.

Limited-Service Hotels

★ **FAIRFIELD INN.** *860 S Porter St, Manchester (03103). Phone 603/625-2020; toll-free 800/228-2800; fax 603/625-7562. www.fairfieldinn.com.* This hotel is only minutes from the Manchester Airport. 102 rooms, 4 story. Complimentary continental breakfast. Check-in 3 pm, check-out noon. Outdoor pool. Airport transportation available. **$**

★ ★ **FOUR POINTS BY SHERATON.** *55 John Devine Dr, Manchester (03103). Phone 603/668-6110; toll-free 800/368-7764; fax 603/668-0408. www.fourpoints.com/manchester.* This hotel is conveniently located near Manchester Airport, the Mall of New Hampshire, and historic downtown Manchester. 121 rooms, 4 story. Check-in 3 pm, check-out noon. High-speed Internet access. Restaurant, bar. Indoor pool, whirlpool. Airport transportation available. **$**

★ ★ **QUALITY INN BEDFORD.** *121 S River Rd, Bedford (03110). Phone 603/622-3766; fax 603/625-1126.* Located on the site of John Goffe's historic gristmill, this small inn and convention center takes full advantage of its forested setting and proximity to the local business district. 194 rooms, 3 story. Check-out noon. Restaurant, bar. Fitness room. Indoor pool, outdoor pool, whirlpool. Airport transportation available. **$$**

★ ★ **RADISSON HOTEL MANCHESTER.** *700 Elm St, Manchester (03101). Phone 603/625-1000; toll-free 800/333-3333; fax 603/206-4000. www.radisson.com.* With the hotel's location near downtown Manchester, guests can enjoy everything this quaint New England city has to offer, such as shopping, dining, live theater, and museums. 250 rooms, 12 story. Check-in 3 pm, check-out 11 am. Restaurant, bar. Fitness room. Indoor pool, whirlpool. Airport transportation available. Business center. **$**

Full-Service Inn

★ ★ ★ **BEDFORD VILLAGE INN.** *2 Olde Bedford Way, Bedford (03110). Phone 603/472-2001; toll-free 800/852-1166; fax 603/472-2379. www.bedfordvillage inn.com.* This stately New England inn, a converted 1800s barn, is set on beautifully landscaped grounds. The all-suite accommodations feature four-poster beds, Italian marble, and whirlpool bathtubs. A fine restaurant and other top-notch amenities are offered. 14 rooms, 3 story, all suites. Check-in 3 pm, check-out 11 am. Restaurant. **$$**
🅳

Restaurants

★ ★ ★ **BEDFORD VILLAGE INN.** *2 Olde Bedford Way, Bedford (03110). Phone 603/472-2001; toll-free 800/852-1166; fax 603/472-2379. www.bedfordvillage inn.com.* This yellow clapboard structure originally was part of a working farm (1810). Guests can choose from several dining rooms, each with its own distinct character—hand-painted murals, swag drapes, area rugs, or a roaring fireplace. The kitchen turns out updated regional New England cuisine using only the freshest indigenous ingredients. Don't miss the signature dessert, the chocolate bag—white and dark chocolate mousse, fresh berries, and vanilla sponge cake. American menu. Breakfast, lunch, dinner. Closed Dec 25. Bar. **$$$**

★ **PURITAN BACKROOM.** *245 Hooksett Rd, Manchester (03104). Phone 603/669-6890; fax 603/623-3788. www.puritanbackroom.com.* This local favorite serves everything from burgers made from black Angus ground beef to veal parmigiana. There's also a kids' menu (try the smiley-face French fries). Grown-up fans may appreciate the Backroom's extensive beer and wine list and its full bar. Homemade ice cream is also on the menu. The casual atmosphere is welcoming, with its wood-paneled walls, low lighting, and framed folk art. Its easy access from Interstate 93 makes it a convenient stop. American menu. Lunch, dinner. Closed Thanksgiving, Dec 25. Bar. Children's menu. **$$**

Meredith (D-4)

See also Holderness, Laconia, Plymouth

Founded 1768
Population 4,837
Elevation 552 ft

Area Code 603
Zip 03253
Information Chamber of Commerce, 272 Daniel Webster Hwy, PO Box 732; phone 603/279-6121 or toll-free 877/279-6121
Web Site www.meredithcc.org

Between Lakes Winnipesaukee and Waukewan in the Lakes Region, Meredith is a year-round recreation area.

What to See and Do

League of New Hampshire Craftsmen—Meredith/Laconia Arts & Crafts. *279 Daniel Webster Hwy, Meredith (03253). 1 1/2 miles N of Hwys 3 and 104. Phone 603/279-7920.* Work by some of New Hampshire's finest craftspeople. (Daily)

⭐ **Winnipesaukee Scenic Railroad.** *Phone 603/279-5253.* Scenic train rides along the shore of Lake Winnipesaukee. Board in Meredith or Weirs Beach. (Memorial Day-Columbus Day) Fall foliage trains to Plymouth.

Special Events

Altrusa Annual Antique Show and Sale. Third Sat in Sept.

Great Rotary Fishing Derby. Second weekend in Feb.

Lakes Region Fine Arts and Crafts Festival. *Phone 603/279-6121.* Juried show featuring more than 100 New England artists. Music, children's theater, food. Last weekend in Aug.

Full-Service Inn

★ ★ ★ **THE INN AT BAY POINT.** *312 Daniel Webster Hwy, Meredith (03253). Phone 603/279-7006; toll-free 800/622-6455; fax 603/279-6797. www.millfalls.com.* This inn overlooks the shoreline of Egg Harbor. 24 rooms, 4 story. Complimentary continental breakfast. Check-in 3 pm, check-out noon. Restaurant, bar. Fitness room. Beach. Whirlpool. **$$**
🏃

Specialty Lodgings

The following lodging establishments are approved by Mobil Travel Guide, but due to their unique and individualized nature have not been given a traditional Mobil Star rating. Included in this listing you may

Hiking the White Mountains High Huts System

New England's highest mountains are webbed with hiking trails, thanks largely to the Appalachian Mountain Club (AMC), founded in 1876. The club blazed and mapped trails and eventually established an extensive base camp for hikers in Pinkham Notch at the eastern base of Mount Washington; a hostel in Crawford Notch, at the western base; and a chain of eight full-service "high huts" spaced over 56 miles of mountain trails, each a day's hike apart.

The huts are so much a part of the heritage and character of the White Mountains that it would be a shame to hike the Whites without staying at one. Seven offer three full meals in season (mid-June to mid-September) as well as bunks, pillows, and blankets (no sheets). Each hut has its resident naturalist who offers talks and walks. An AMC shuttle van circles trailheads leading to each of the huts so that hikers can begin in one place and emerge at another. It's wise to begin at Pinkham Notch Camp on Highway 16 in the White Mountain National Forest, a source of gear, maps, and weather information. Reservations for all AMC facilities are a must.

One of the most spectacular hikes that utilizes either one or two of the high huts is on Mount Washington itself. Begin with the Crawford Path, dating to 1819, said to be the oldest continually used footpath in America. The trailhead is on Highway 302 across from the AMC Crawford Notch Visitors Center. It follows Gibbs Brook (note the cutoff for Gibbs Falls), then angles off and up. To spend the night at Mizpah Hut Spring Hut (strongly advised), take the Mizpah cut-off. Just 2 miles from Highway 302, this is a good base from which to explore several trails above tree line.

It's also possible, weather permitting, to continue on the Crawford Path, ascending in moderate grades, with spectacular open views alternating with patches of scrub and woods. The trail ascends steadily via Mount Pierce, Mount Eisenhower, and Mount Monroe, reaching the Lake of the Clouds Hut at 7 miles. Spend the night.

Descend back to Highway 302 via the Ammonoosuc Ravine Trail, which begins just south of the Lake of the Clouds and follows the Ammonoosuc River steeply for the first 2 miles of the 3-mile descent. There are numerous cascades and spectacular views, but many people prefer to do this hike in reverse, ascending rather than descending such a steep trail. It's also possible to cheat by taking the White Mountain Cog Railway from its base off Highway 302 (near the trailhead for this trail) to the summit of Mount Washington, hiking down to the Lake of the Clouds, and then either down the Ammonoosuc Ravine or Crawford Path. Check with the AMC before hiking anywhere in the Whites.

find bed-and-breakfasts, limited-service inns, guest ranches, and other unique hotel properties.

THE INN AT MILL FALLS. *312 Daniel Webster Hwy, Meredith (03253). Phone 603/279-7006; toll-free 800/622-6455; fax 603/279-6797. www.millfalls.com.* Actually three stately inns in one, this historic lakeside vacation development offers a charming respite from busy urban life. A covered marketplace of galleries and shops is just one of the many full-service amenities. 54 rooms, 5 story. Check-in 3 pm, check-out 11 am. Indoor pool, whirlpool. **$$**

OLDE ORCHARD INN. *RR Box 256, Moultonborough (03254). Phone 603/476-5004; toll-free 800/598-5845; fax 603/476-5419.*

www.oldeorchardinn.com. This quaint inn was built in 1790 and was converted to a bed-and-breakfast 150 years later. Guests will enjoy the lounge with fireplace, massaging easy chair, and library. 9 rooms. Complimentary full breakfast. Check-in 3 pm, check-out 11 am. **$**

Restaurants

★ ★ **HART'S TURKEY FARM.** *Hwys 3 and 104, Meredith (03253). Phone 603/279-6212; fax 603/279-4433. www.hartsturkeyfarm.com.* If you feel like a little family-style Thanksgiving during your trip, check out Hart's turkey dinners with all the trimmings. You'll also find turkey potpies, turkey croquettes, and even turkey burgers. American menu. Lunch, dinner. Children's menu. **$$**

★ ★ **MAME'S.** *8 Plymouth St, Meredith (03253). Phone 603/279-4631; fax 603/279-8646. www.mamesrestaurant.com.* Converted brick house and barn (1825). American menu. Lunch, dinner. Bar. Children's menu. **$$**

Mount Washington (C-4)

See also Bretton Woods, Gorham, Jackson

10 miles S of Gorham on Hwy 16.

Mount Washington is the central peak of the White Mountains and the highest point in the northeastern United States (6,288 feet). At the summit is a 54-acre state park with an information center, first-aid station, restaurant, and gift shop. The mountain has the world's first cog railway, completed in 1869; a road to the top dates to 1861. P. T. Barnum called the view from the summit "the second-greatest show on earth."

The weather on Mount Washington is so violent that the timberline is at about 4,000 feet; in the Rockies it is nearer 10,000 feet. In the treeless zone are alpine plants and insects, some unique to the region. The weather station here recorded a wind speed of 231 miles per hour in April, 1934—a world record. The lowest temperature recorded was -49° F; the year-round average is below freezing. The peak gets nearly 15 feet of snow each year.

What to See and Do

⭐ **Cog railway.** *Hwy 302, Bretton Woods (03589). Base station road, off Hwy 302, 4 miles E of junction Hwys 3 and 302; on W slope of mountain. Phone 603/846-5404; toll-free 800/922-8825.* Allow at least three hours for round trip. (May-Memorial Day weekend: weekends; after Memorial Day weekend-Nov: daily) **$$$$**

Great Glen Trails. *Hwy 16, Gorham (03581). Phone 603/466-2333.* Located at the base of Mount Washington, this all-season, nonmotorized recreational trails park features biking programs (rentals), hiking programs (guide or unguided), kayak and canoe tours, and workshops in summer; cross-country skiing, snowshoeing, and snow tubing in winter.

(Daily; closed Apr) For a detailed brochure with schedule and fees, contact Hwy 16, Pinkham Notch, Gorham 03581. **$$$**

Hiking trails. *Phone 603/466-2725.* Many crisscross the mountain; some reach the top. Hikers should check weather conditions at Pinkham Notch headquarters before climbing. **FREE**

Mount Washington auto road. *Hwy 16, Gorham. Approaches from the E side, in Pinkham Notch, 8 miles S of Gorham on Hwy 16. Phone 603/466-3988.* Trip to the summit of Mount Washington takes approximately 30 minutes each way. *Note:* make sure your car is in good condition; check brakes before starting. (Mid-May-mid-Oct, daily, weather permitting) Guided tour service available (daily). **$$$$**

Mount Washington Summit Museum. *Hwy 302, Sargent's Purchase. Top of Mount Washington. Phone 603/466-3388.* Displays on life in the extreme climate of the summit; rare flora and fauna; geology, history. (Memorial Day-Columbus Day, daily)

Nashua (E-4)

See also Manchester, Peterborough, Salem

Settled 1656
Population 79,662
Elevation 169 ft
Area Code 603
Information Greater Nashua Chamber of Commerce, 146 Main St, 2nd floor, 03060; phone 603/881-8333
Web Site www.nashuachamber.com

Originally a fur trading post, Nashua's manufacturing began with the development of Merrimack River water power early in the 19th century. The city, second largest in New Hampshire, has more than 100 diversified industries ranging from computers and tools to beer.

What to See and Do

Anheuser-Busch, Inc. *221 Daniel Webster Hwy (Hwy 3), Merrimack (03054). Everett Tpke exit 10. Phone 603/595-1202.* Guided tours of brewery; sampling room; gift shop. Children only with adult; no pets. **FREE** Adjacent is

Clydesdale Hamlet. *221 Daniel Webster Hwy, Merrimack (03054). Phone 603/595-1202.* Buildings modeled after a 19th-century European-style farm are the living quarters for the famous Clydesdales (at least 15 are here at all times); carriage house contains vintage wagons. **FREE**

Silver Lake State Park. *Silver Lake Rd, Hollis (03049). 8 miles W on Hwy 130 to Hollis, then 1 mile N off Hwy 122. Phone 603/465-2342.* One thousand-foot sand beach on a 34-acre lake; swimming, bathhouse; picnicking. (Late June-Labor Day)

Special Event

American Stage Festival. *14 Court St, Milford (03060). 5 miles NW off Hwy 101.Phone 603/886-7000.* Five plays; music events, children's series. June-Sept.

Limited-Service Hotels

★ **FAIRFIELD INN.** *4 Amherst Rd, Merrimack (03054). Phone 603/424-7500; toll-free 800/228-2800. www.fairfieldinn.com.* 116 rooms, 3 story. Complimentary continental breakfast. Check-out noon. Outdoor pool. **$**

★ ★ **HOLIDAY INN.** *9 Northeastern Blvd, Nashua (03062). Phone 603/888-1551; toll-free 888/801-5661; fax 603/888-7193. www.holiday-inn.com.* 208 rooms, 4 story. Pets accepted; fee. Check-out noon. Restaurant, bar. Fitness room. Outdoor pool. **$**

Full-Service Hotels

★ ★ ★ **CROWNE PLAZA.** *2 Somerset Pkwy, Nashua (03063). Phone 603/886-1200; toll-free 800/ 962-7482; fax 603/595-4199. www.crowneplaza.com.* Just 15 miles from Manchester Airport and 40 miles from Boston's Logan Airport, this full-service hotel is in the heart of the high-tech "southern tier." 250 rooms, 8 story. Check-out noon. Restaurant, bar. Fitness room. Indoor pool, whirlpool. Airport transportation available. **$**

★ ★ ★ **SHERATON NASHUA HOTEL.** *11 Tara Blvd, Nashua (03062). Phone 603/888-9970; toll-free 800/325-3535; fax 603/888-4112. www.sheraton.com.* This contemporary hotel offers a comfortable stay for business or leisure travelers. 337 rooms, 7 story. Check-out noon. Restaurant, bar. Children's activity center. Fitness room. Indoor pool, outdoor pool, whirlpool. Business center. **$**

Restaurants

★ **HANNAH JACK TAVERN.** *Greeley St and Daniel Webster Hwy, Merrimack (03054). Phone 603/424-4171; fax 603/424-4172.* This restaurant is located in a 200-year-old colonial building. American menu. Lunch, dinner. Closed July 4, Dec 25. Bar. Children's menu. **$$**

★ **NEWICK'S.** *696 Daniel Webster Hwy, Merrimack (03054). Phone 603/429-0262; toll-free 800/640-0262; fax 603/429-0675. www.newicks.com.* Seafood menu. Lunch, dinner. Closed Thanksgiving, Dec 25. Bar. Children's menu. **$$**

New London (E-3)

See also Sunapee

Population 3,180
Elevation 825 ft
Area Code 603
Zip 03257
Information Chamber of Commerce, Main St, PO Box 532; phone 603/526-6575 or toll-free 877/526-6575
Web Site www.newlondonareanh.com

What to See and Do

Ragged Mountain. *10 miles E on Hwy 11, then 7 miles N on Hwy 4 to Danbury, then 1 1/2 miles E on Hwy 104 to access road. Phone 603/768-3475. www.ragged-mt.com.* Two triple, three double chairlifts, three surface tows; patrol, school, rentals, snowmaking; cafeteria, bar. Longest run 1 3/4 miles; vertical drop 1,250 feet. (Mid-Nov-Mar, daily) Cross-country skiing. **$$$$**

Special Event

Barn Playhouse. *209 Main St, New London (03257). Off Hwy 11. Phone 603/526-4631.* Live theater presentations nightly; Wed matinees. Also Mon children's attractions. Mid-June-Labor Day.

Limited-Service Hotel

★ **FAIRWAY MOTEL.** *Country Club Ln, New London (03257). Phone 603/526-6040; fax 603/526-9622.* 12 rooms. Check-out 11 am. Outdoor pool. **$**

Full-Service Inn

★ ★ ★ **INN AT PLEASANT LAKE.** *125 N Pleasant St, New London (03257). Phone 603/526-6271; toll-free 800/626-4907; fax 603/526-4111. www.innat pleasantlake.com.* Situated between the lake and Mount Kearsarge, this gabled country inn affords a quiet, relaxing vacation. Three common rooms are decorated like a comfortable house, and the inn has access to a private beach. 12 rooms, 3 story. Complimentary full breakfast. Check-in 3 pm, check-out 11 am. Restaurant. Fitness room. **$**

Specialty Lodgings

The following lodging establishments are approved by Mobil Travel Guide, but due to their unique and individualized nature have not been given a traditional Mobil Star rating. Included in this listing you may find bed-and-breakfasts, limited-service inns, guest ranches, and other unique hotel properties.

FOLLANSBEE INN. *Hwy 114, North Sutton (03260). Phone 603/927-4221; toll-free 800/626-4221; fax 603/927-6307. www.follansbeeinn.com.* This homey 1840 country inn, located on the south shore of Keyzar Lake, has a wraparound porch, individually decorated rooms, and a relaxing atmosphere. 18 rooms, 3 story. Closed two weeks in Nov and Apr. Children over 10 years only. Complimentary full breakfast. Check-in 3 pm, check-out 11 am. **$**

NEW LONDON INN. *353 Main St, New London (03257). Phone 603/526-2791; toll-free 800/526-2791; fax 603/526-2749. www.newlondoninn.net.* This inn was built in 1792. 23 rooms, 3 story. Complimentary continental breakfast. Check-in 3 pm, check-out 11 am. Restaurant, bar. **$**

Restaurants

★ ★ **MILLSTONE.** *Newport Rd (Hwy 11 W), New London (03257). Phone 603/526-4201. www.millstone restaurant.com.* American menu. Lunch, dinner, Sun brunch. Closed Dec 25. Children's menu. Casual attire. **$$**

★ ★ **NEW LONDON INN.** *353 Main St, New London (03257). Phone 603/526-2791; fax 603/526-2749. www.newlondoninn.net.* American menu. Dinner. Closed Mon. Children's menu. Reservations recommended. **$$**

★ ★ **POTTER PLACE INN.** *88 Depot St, Andover (03216). Phone 603/735-5141. www.potterplaceinn.com.* House built in the 1790s; country atmosphere. International/Fusion menu. Dinner. Closed Sun-Mon in Nov-Apr. Bar. **$$**

Newport (E-3)

See also Sunapee

Settled 1765
Population 6,110
Elevation 797 ft
Area Code 603
Zip 03773
Information Chamber of Commerce, 2 N Main St; phone 603/863-1510

Newport is the commercial headquarters for the Lake Sunapee area. Its industries include machine tools, woolens, clothing, and firearms. The Town Common Historic District has many churches and Colonial and Victorian houses.

What to See and Do

Fort at No. 4. *267 Springfield Rd, Charlestown (03603). 10 miles W on Hwy 11/103, then 11 miles S on Hwy 11/12. Phone 603/826-5700.* Reconstructed French and Indian War log fort, complete with stockade, Great Hall, cow barns, and living quarters furnished to reflect 18th-century pioneer living. Exhibits include Native American artifacts, demonstrations of colonial crafts and an audiovisual program. (Memorial Day-late Oct, daily) **$$$**

North Conway (C-4)

See also Bartlett, Jackson, Pinkham Notch

Settled 1764
Population 2,100
Elevation 531 ft
Area Code 603
Zip 03860
Information Mount Washington Valley Chamber of Commerce, 1267 Main St, PO Box 2300; phone 603/356-5701 or toll-free 800/367-3364
Web Site www.mtwashingtonvalley.org

The heart of the famous Mount Washington valley region of the White Mountains, this area also includes

Bartlett, Glen, Jackson, Conway, Redstone, Kearsarge, and Intervale. Mount Washington, seen from the middle of Main Street, is one of the great views in the East.

What to See and Do

Conway Scenic Railroad. *38 Norcross Cir, North Conway (03860). Depot on Main St. Phone 603/356-5251.* Steam and diesel trains depart from restored Victorian station (1874) for an 11-mile (55-minute) round trip. The Valley Train explores the Saco River valley (mid-May-Oct: daily; mid-Apr-mid-May, Nov-Dec: weekends); the Notch Train travels through Crawford Notch (mid-Sept-mid-Oct: daily; late June-mid-Sept: Tues-Thurs, Sat). Railroad museum. **$$$**

Covered bridges. In Conway, Jackson, and Bartlett.

Echo Lake State Park. *2 miles W, off Hwy 302. Phone 603/356-2672.* Mountain lake in the shadow of White Horse Ledge. Scenic road to 700-foot Cathedral Ledge, a dramatic rock formation; panoramic views of the White Mountains and the Saco River Valley. Swimming, picnicking. (Late June-Labor Day)

Factory outlet stores. *Hwy 16, North Conway (03860). Phone 603/356-2225.* Many outlet malls and stores can be found along Highway 16. Contact the Chamber of Commerce for more information.

League of New Hampshire Craftsmen. *2526 Main St, North Conway (03860). Phone 603/356-2441.* Work by some of New Hampshire's finest craftspeople. (Daily) **FREE**

Mount Cranmore. *1 mile E off Hwy 302 (Hwy 16). Phone 603/356-7070; toll-free 800/786-6754. www.cranmore.com.* Express quad, triple, double chairlift to summit, three double chairlifts to north, south, and east slopes, four surface lifts; patrol, school, rentals; snowmaking; restaurant, bar, cafeterias; day care. Longest run 1 3/4 miles; vertical drop 1,200 feet. (Nov-Apr, daily)

Sacobound. *Hwy 302, 2 miles E of Center Conway. Phone 603/447-3002.* Specializes in rafting, canoeing, kayak touring, and paddling school. Programs include guided whitewater rafting trips, whitewater canoe and kayak school, and calmwater and whitewater canoe rentals. (May-Oct) **$$$$**

Special Events

Eastern Slope Playhouse. *2760 Main St, North Conway (03860). Phone 603/356-5776.* On grounds of Eastern Slope Inn Resort (see LIMITED-SERVICE HOTELS). Mount Washington Valley Theatre Company presents four Broadway musicals. Tues-Sun. Late June-early Sept.

Mount Washington Valley Equine Classic. *Phone 603/356-3171; toll-free 800/367-3364.* Horse jumping. Mid-Aug.

Mud Bowl. *Hog Coliseum, North Conway (03860).* Sept.

Limited-Service Hotels

★ ★ **BEST WESTERN RED JACKET MOUNTAIN VIEW RESORT & CONFERENCE CENTER.** *Hwy 16, North Conway (03860). Phone 603/356-5411; toll-free 800/752-2538; fax 603/356-3842. www.bestwestern.com.* 152 rooms, 3 story. Check-out 11 am. Restaurant, bar. Children's activity center. Fitness room. Indoor pool, outdoor pool. Tennis. **$**

★ **COMFORT INN.** *Hwys 16 and 302, North Conway (03860). Phone 603/356-8811; toll-free 800/228-5150; fax 603/356-7770. www.choicehotels.com.* 39 rooms, 2 story. Check-out 11 am. Outdoor pool. **$**

★ ★ **EASTERN SLOPE INN RESORT.** *2760 Main St, North Conway (03860). Phone 603/356-6847; toll-free 800/862-1600; fax 603/356-8732. www.easternslopeinn.com.* 146 rooms, 3 story. Check-out 10 am. Restaurant. Indoor pool, whirlpool. Tennis. **$**

★ ★ **THE FOX RIDGE.** *Hwy 16, North Conway (03860). Phone 603/356-3151; toll-free 800/343-1804; fax 603/356-0096. www.foxridgeresort.com.* 136 rooms, 2 story. Closed late Oct-mid-May. Check-out 11 am. Restaurant. Children's activity center. Indoor pool, outdoor pool. Tennis. **$**

★ ★ **GREEN GRANITE INN.** *Hwys 16 and 302, North Conway (03860). Phone 603/356-6901; toll-free 800/468-3666; fax 603/356-6980. www.greengranite.com.* 91 rooms, 2 story. Complimentary continental breakfast. Check-in 3 pm, check-out 11 am. Fitness room. Indoor pool, outdoor pool, whirlpool. **$**

★ **NORTH CONWAY MOUNTAIN INN.** *Main St, North Conway (03860). Phone 603/356-2803; toll-free 800/319-4405. www.northconwaymountaininn.com.* 32 rooms, 2 story. Check-out 10 am. **$**

★ **SWISS CHALETS VILLAGE INN.** *Hwy 16A, Intervale (03845). Phone 603/356-2232; toll-free 800/831-2727; fax 603/356-7331. www.swisschaletsvillage.com.* Rooms in Swiss chalet-style buildings; on 12 acres. 42 rooms, 3 story. Pets accepted; fee. Complimentary continental breakfast. Check-out 11 am. Outdoor pool. **$**

★ ★ ★ **WHITE MOUNTAIN HOTEL & RESORT.** *W Side Rd, North Conway (03860). Phone 603/356-7100; toll-free 800/533-6301. www.whitemountainhotel.com.* This 80-room resort is surrounded by the White Mountain National Forest (see) and is next to Echo Lake State Park. 80 rooms, 3 story. Check-in 3 pm, check-out 11 am. Restaurant, bar. Fitness room. Outdoor pool, whirlpool. Golf. Tennis. **$**

Full-Service Hotel

★ ★ **NORTH CONWAY GRAND HOTEL.** *72 Common Ct, North Conway (03860). Phone 603/356-9300; toll-free 800/648-4397; fax 603/356-6028. www.northconwaygrand.com.* This hotel is located in the White Mountain region and offers its guests a fitness facility, shopping (on premise) at more than 40 outlet stores, and access to many local attractions including skiing, golfing, mountain biking, hiking, and additional shopping. A casual restaurant is also on-site. 200 rooms, 4 story. Check-out 11 am. Restaurant, bar. Fitness room. Indoor pool, whirlpool. **$**

Specialty Lodgings

The following lodging establishments are approved by Mobil Travel Guide, but due to their unique and individualized nature have not been given a traditional Mobil Star rating. Included in this listing you may find bed-and-breakfasts, limited-service inns, guest ranches, and other unique hotel properties.

1785 INN. *3582 N White Mountain Hwy, North Conway (03860). Phone 603/356-9025; toll-free 800/421-1785; fax 603/356-6081. www.the1785inn.com.* This colonial-style building (1785) is located on 6 acres and features original fireplaces and Victorian antiques. Guests will enjoy views of the river and

Mount Washington. 17 rooms, 3 story. Complimentary full breakfast. Check-in 2 pm, check-out noon. Restaurant. Outdoor pool. **$**

BUTTONWOOD INN. *Mt Surprise Rd, North Conway (03860). Phone 603/356-2625; toll-free 800/258-2625; fax 603/356-3140. www.buttonwoodinn.com.* Located on 17 wooded acres on the mountainside, this Cape Cod-style building (1820s) features many antiques and a library. 10 rooms, 2 story. Complimentary full breakfast. Check-in 3 pm, check-out 11 am. Outdoor pool. **$**

CRANMORE MOUNTAIN LODGE. *Kearsarge St, off Hwy 16, North Conway (03860). Phone 603/356-2044; toll-free 800/356-3596; fax 603/356-4498. www.cml1.com.* Located on 12 acres, this historic guest house (1860) was once owned by Babe Ruth's daughter. On the grounds, there are farm animals and a duck pond. 22 rooms, 3 story. Complimentary full breakfast. Check-in 3 pm, check-out 11 am. Restaurant. Outdoor pool, whirlpool. Tennis. **$**

DARBY FIELD COUNTRY INN. *185 Chase Hill Rd, Albany (03818). Phone 603/447-2181; toll-free 800/426-4147; fax 603/447-5726. www.darbyfield.com.* View of Presidential Mountains. 13 rooms, 3 story. Children over 2 years only. Complimentary full breakfast. Check-in 2-6 pm, check-out 9-11 am. Outdoor pool. **$$**

EASTMAN INN. *2331 White Mountain Hwy, North Conway (03846). Phone 603/356-6707; toll-free 800/626-5855; fax 603/356-7708. www.eastmaninn.com.* This inn was built in 1777. 34 rooms, 3 story. Complimentary full breakfast. Check-in 3 pm, check-out 11 am. **$$**

THE FOREST, A COUNTRY INN. *Hwy 16A, Intervale (03845). Phone 603/356-9772; toll-free 877/854-6535; fax 603/356-5652. www.forest-inn.com.* This inn has been in operation since 1890. 11 rooms, 3 story. Complimentary full breakfast. Check-in 3 pm, check-out 11 am. Outdoor pool. **$**

MERRILL FARM RESORT. *428 White Mountain Hwy, North Conway (03860). Phone 603/447-3866; toll-free 800/445-1017. www.merrillfarm.com.*

Converted farmhouse (1885) and cottages on the Saco River. 63 rooms, 2 story. Complimentary full breakfast. Check-in 3 pm, check-out 11 am. Restaurant. Outdoor pool, whirlpool. **$**

SNOWVILLAGE INN. *Stewart Rd, Snowville (03832). Phone 603/447-2818; toll-free 800/447-4345; fax 603/447-5268. www.snowvillageinn.com.* This secluded inn on 10 acres features a panoramic view of the mountains. 18 rooms. Restaurant. **$**

Restaurants

★ ★ ★ **1785 INN.** *3582 White Mountain Hwy, North Conway (03860). Phone 603/356-9025; fax 603/356-6081. www.the1785inn.com.* Dinner in the fine dining room of this lovely inn is casual and cozy. The extensive continental menu includes creative veal preparations, as well as a wide variety of appetizer and entrée selections. American, French menu. Dinner. Closed Dec 25. **$$**

★ **BELLINI'S.** *33 Seavey St, North Conway (03860). Phone 603/356-7000; fax 603/356-6122. www.bellinis.com.* Italian menu. Dinner. Closed Tues. Bar. Children's menu. **$$**

★ **HORSEFEATHERS.** *Main St, North Conway (03860). Phone 603/356-2687; fax 603/356-9368. www.horsefeathers.com.* Neighborhood nostalgia; landmark restaurant. American menu. Lunch, dinner. Closed Thanksgiving, Dec 25. Bar. **$$**

Peterborough (F-3)

See also Jaffrey, Keene, Nashua

Settled 1749
Population 5,239
Elevation 723 ft
Area Code 603
Zip 03458
Information Greater Peterborough Chamber of Commerce, PO Box 401; phone 603/924-7234
Web Site www.peterboroughchamber.com

This was the home of composer Edward MacDowell (1861-1908). Edward Arlington Robinson, Stephen Vincent Benét, Willa Cather, and Thornton Wilder,

among others, worked at the MacDowell Colony, a thriving artists' retreat, which made Peterborough famous.

What to See and Do

Greenfield State Park. *Forest Rd, Greenfield. 9 miles N on Hwy 136, then W on unnumbered road. Phone 603/547-3497.* On 401 acres. Swimming, bathhouse; fishing. Picnicking, concessions. Camping (dump station) with separate beach. (Mid-May-mid-Oct)

Miller State Park. *Rte 101 E, Peterborough. 4 miles E. Phone 603/924-3672.* First of the New Hampshire parks. Atop the 2,288-foot Pack Monadnock Mountain; walking trails on summit; scenic drive; picnicking. (June-Labor Day: daily; May and Labor Day-Nov: Sat-Sun, and holidays)

New England Marionette Opera. *24 Main St, Peterborough (03248). Phone 603/924-4333.* Largest marionette facility in the country devoted to opera. (Mid-May-late Dec, Sat evenings, also Sun matinee; closed July 4, Thanksgiving)

Peterborough Historical Society. *19 Grove St, Peterborough (03458). Phone 603/924-3235.* Exhibits on the history of the area; historical and genealogical library. (Mon-Fri) **$$**

Sharon Arts Center. *457 Hwy 123, Sharon (03458). 5 miles SE on Hwy 123, in Depot Sq. Phone 603/924-7256.* Gallery and crafts center. (Daily) **FREE**

Limited-Service Hotel

★ **JACK DANIELS MOTOR INN.** *80 Concord St, Peterborough (03458). Phone 603/924-7548; fax 603/924-7700. www.jackdanielsmotorinn.com.* 17 rooms, 2 story. Check-out 11 am. **$**

Full-Service Inn

★ ★ ★ **HANCOCK INN.** *33 Main St, Hancock (03449). Phone 603/525-3318; toll-free 800/525-1789; fax 603/525-9301. www.hancockinn.com.* In continuous operation since 1789, the interior of this country inn is reminiscent of 18th-century New England. Sit by the fire in the red-walled dining room and order the famous Shaker cranberry pot roast to finish the day. 11 rooms, 3 story. Children over 12 years only. Complimentary full breakfast. Check-in 2 pm, check-out 11 am. Restaurant. **$$**

Specialty Lodging

The following lodging establishment is approved by Mobil Travel Guide, but due to its unique and individualized nature has not been given a traditional Mobil Star rating. Included in this listing you may find bed-and-breakfasts, limited-service inns, guest ranches, and other unique hotel properties.

GREENFIELD INN. *Hwys 31 N and 136, Greenfield (03047). Phone 603/547-6327; toll-free 800/678-4144; fax 603/547-2418. www.greenfieldinn.com.* 15 rooms, 2 story. Complimentary full breakfast. Check-in 4 pm, check-out 11 am. $
🅿

Restaurant

★ ★ ★ **HANCOCK INN.** *33 Main St, Hancock (03449). Phone 603/525-3318; fax 603/525-9301. www.hancockinn.com.* Delight in the flavors of the past at this historic restaurant, in operation since 1789. American menu. Dinner. Closed Dec 25. Reservations recommended. $$$

Pinkham Notch (C-4)

See also Gorham, Jackson, North Conway

Approximately 7 miles N on Hwy 16.

Named for Joseph Pinkham, a 1790 settler, this easternmost White Mountain pass is closest to Mount Washington. The headquarters for the Appalachian Mountain Club Hut System is here.

What to See and Do

Glen Ellis Falls Scenic Area. *E of Hwy 16, 12 miles N of Glen in White Mountain National Forest (see).*

Wildcat Ski & Recreation Area. *Hwy 16, Pinkham Notch (03846). 10 miles N of Jackson. Phone 603/466-3326; toll-free 800/255-6439. www.skiwildcat.com.* Express quad, three triple chairlifts; patrol, school, rentals; snowmaking; cafeteria, nursery. Longest run 2 miles; vertical drop 2,100 feet. (Mid-Nov-early May, daily; closed Thanksgiving, Dec 25) Skyride gondolas operate Memorial Day-mid-October for mountain and fall foliage viewing (daily). $$$$

Plymouth (D-4)

See also Holderness, Meredith, Waterville Valley

Settled 1764
Population 5,811
Elevation 660 ft
Area Code 603
Zip 03264
Information Chamber of Commerce, PO Box 65; phone 603/536-1001 or toll-free 800/386-3678
Web Site www.plymouthnh.org

Since 1795, Plymouth's varied industries have included lumber, pig iron, mattresses, gloves, and sporting goods. It has been a resort center since the mid-19th century.

What to See and Do

Mary Baker Eddy Historic House. *58 Stinson Lake Rd, Rumney (03266). Approximately 7 miles W via Hwy 25 to Stinson Lake Rd, then approximately 1 mile N to N side of the Village of Rumney. Phone 603/786-9943.* Residence of Mary Baker Eddy from 1860 to 1862, prior to the founding of the Christian Science Church. (May-Oct, Tues-Sun; closed holidays) $

Plymouth State College. *17 High St, Plymouth (03264). 1 block W of business center. Phone 603/535-5000.* (1871) (3,500 students) A member of the University System of New Hampshire. Art exhibits in galleries and Lamson Library. Music, theater, and dance performances in Silver Cultural Arts Center (some fees). Planetarium shows. Tours.

Polar Caves Park. *705 Old Rte 25, Rumney (03266). 5 miles W on Tenney Mountain Hwy (Hwy 25). Phone 603/536-1888.* Glacial caves; animal exhibits; local minerals; scenic rock formations; maple sugar museum; gift shops, picnicking. (Early May-late Oct, daily) $$$

Limited-Service Hotel

★ **BEST INN.** *304 Main St, Plymouth (03264). Phone 603/536-2330; toll-free 800/237-8466; fax 603/536-2686. www.bestinn.com.* 38 rooms, 2 story. Pets accepted. Complimentary continental breakfast. Check-out 11 am. Outdoor pool. $
🅿 🐾 🏊

Restaurant

★ **TREE HOUSE.** *3 S Main St, Plymouth (03264). Phone 603/536-4084; fax 603/536-1916. www.thetree houserestaurant.com.* American menu. Lunch, dinner. Closed Thanksgiving, Dec 25. Bar. Children's menu. **$$**

Portsmouth (E-5)

See also Dover, Exeter, Hampton Beach

Settled 1630
Population 25,925
Elevation 21 ft
Area Code 603
Information Greater Portsmouth Chamber of Commerce, 500 Market St, PO Box 239, 03802-0239; phone 603/436-3988 or 603/436-1118
Web Site www.portsmouthchamber.org

A tour of Portsmouth's famous houses is like a tour through time, with colonial and Federal architecture from 1684 into the 19th century. One-time capital of New Hampshire, Portsmouth was also the home port of a dynasty of merchant seamen who grew rich and built accordingly. The old atmosphere still exists in the narrow streets near Market Square.

The US Navy Yard, located in Kittery, Maine (see), on the Piscataqua River, has long been Portsmouth's major "industry." The peace treaty ending the Russo-Japanese War was signed at the Portsmouth Navy Yard in 1905.

What to See and Do

Children's Museum of Portsmouth. *280 Marcy St, Portsmouth (03801). Phone 603/436-3853.* Arts and science museum featuring mock submarine, space shuttle, lobster boat, exhibits, and gallery. (Summer and school vacations: daily; rest of year: Tues-Sat, also Sun afternoons) **$$**

Fort Constitution. *4 miles E on Hwy 1B in Newcastle.* (1808) The first cannon was placed on this site in 1632; in 1694, it was known as Fort William and Mary. Information about a British order to stop gunpowder from coming into the colonies, brought by Paul Revere on December 13, 1774, caused the Sons of Liberty from Portsmouth, New Castle, and Rye to attack and capture a fort that held five tons of gunpowder the next day. Much of this powder was used at

Bunker Hill by the patriots. This uprising against the King's authority was one of the first overt acts of the Revolution. Little remains of the original fort except the base of its walls. Fort Constitution had been built on the same site by 1808; granite walls were added during the Civil War. (Mid-June-early Sept: daily; late May-mid-June, late Sept-mid-Oct: weekends, holidays only)

⭐ **Fort Stark State Historic Site.** *Wild Rose Ln, New Castle. Approximately 5 miles E off Hwy 1B. Phone 603/436-7406.* A former portion of the coastal defense system dating to 1746, exhibiting many of the changes in military technology from the Revolutionary War through World War II. The fort is situated on Jerry's Point, overlooking the Piscataqua River, Little Harbor, and Atlantic Ocean. (Late May-mid-Oct, Sat-Sun)

Old Harbour Area. *Located on Historic Waterfront; Hwy 95 exit 7.* Features craftspeople, unique shops, bookstores, restaurants.

Portsmouth Harbor Cruises. *64 Ceres St, Portsmouth (03801). Old Harbor District. Phone 603/436-8084; toll-free 800/776-0915.* Narrated historical tours aboard the 49-passenger M/V *Heritage.* 90-minute harbor, 2 1/2-hour Isles of Shoals, 1-hour cocktail, 90-minute sunset cruises, 2 1/2-hour inland river cruise, fall foliage cruise. (Mid-June-Oct)

⭐ **Portsmouth Historic Homes.** *Middle and State sts, Portsmouth (03801). Phone 603/436-1118.* The Historic Associates, part of the Greater Portsmouth Chamber of Commerce, has walking tour maps for six historic houses; maps are available free at the Chamber of Commerce, 500 Market St. The houses include

Governor John Langdon House. *143 Pleasant St, Portsmouth (03801). Phone 603/436-3205.* (1784) John Langdon served three terms as governor of New Hampshire and was the first president *pro tempore* of the US Senate. House's exterior proportions are monumental; interior embellished with excellent woodcarving and fine Portsmouth-area furniture. George Washington was entertained here in 1789. Architect Stanford White was commissioned to add the large wing at the rear with dining room in the Colonial Revival style. Surrounded by landscaped grounds with gazebo, rose and grape arbor, and restored perennial garden beds. Tours (June-mid-Oct, Wed-Sun; closed holidays). **$$**

John Paul Jones House. *43 Middle St, Portsmouth (03801). At State St. Phone 603/436-8420.* (1758) Where the famous naval commander twice boarded; now a museum containing period furniture, collections of costumes, china, glass, documents, weapons. Guided tours (June-mid-Oct, Thurs-Mon; closed Tues-Wed). **$$**

Moffatt-Ladd House. *154 Market St, Portsmouth (03801). Phone 603/436-8221.* (1763) Built by Captain John Moffatt; later the home of General William Whipple, his son-in-law, a signer of the Declaration of Independence. Many original 18th- and 19th-century furnishings. Formal gardens. (Mid-June-mid-Oct, daily) **$$**

Rundlet-May House. *364 Middle St, Portsmouth (03801). Phone 603/436-3205.* (1807) Federalist, three-story mansion. House sits on terraces and retains its original 1812 courtyard and garden layout; landscaped grounds. House contains family furnishings and accessories, including many fine examples of Federalist craftsmanship and the latest technologies of its time. (June-mid-Oct, Wed-Sun afternoons) Guided tours (Mon-Sat; Sun afternoons). Grounds available for rental. **$$**

Warner House. *150 Daniel St, Portsmouth (03801). At Chapel St. Phone 603/436-5909.* (1716) One of New England's finest Georgian houses, with scagliola in the dining room, restored mural paintings on the staircase walls, beautiful paneling, a lightning rod on the west wall said to have been installed by Benjamin Franklin in 1762, five portraits by Joseph Blackburn, appropriate furnishings. (June-mid-Oct, Mon-Sat; Sun afternoons) Guided tours. **$$**

Wentworth-Gardner House. *50 Mechanic St, Portsmouth. Phone 603/436-4406.* (1760) Excellent example of Georgian architecture. Elaborate woodwork, scenic wallpaper, magnificent main staircase. (Mid-June-mid-Oct, Tues-Sun afternoons) **$$**

⭐ **Star Island and Isles of Shoals.** *315 Market St, Portsmouth (03801). Depart from Barker's Wharf. Phone 603/431-5500.* The M/V *Thomas Laighton* makes cruises to historic Isles of Shoals, Star Island walkabouts, lobster clambake river cruises, fall foliage excursion, and others. Party ship. (Mid-June-Labor Day, daily) **$$$$**

⭐ **Strawbery Banke Museum.** *454 Court St, Portsmouth (03801). Hancock and Marcy sts, downtown, follow signs. Phone 603/433-1100.* Restoration of a 10-acre historic waterfront neighborhood; site of the original Portsmouth settlement. 42 buildings dating from 1695 to 1950. Nine houses: Captain Keyran Walsh House (1796), Governor Goodwin Mansion (1811), Chase House (1762), Captain John Wheelwright House (1780), Thomas Bailey Aldrich House (1790), Drisco House (1790s), Rider-Wood House (1840s), Abbott Grocery Store (1943), and the William Pitt Tavern (1766) are restored with period furnishings. Shops, architectural exhibits, pottery shop, and demonstrations; tool, photo, archaeological and house construction exhibits; family programs and activities, special events, tours; picnicking, coffee shop. (May-Oct, Mon-Sat; Sun afternoons) Guided tours (Nov-Dec; Feb-Mar, Thurs-Sun). **$$$**

Special Events

Market Square Days. *Downtown, Portsmouth. Phone 603/436-3988.* Summer celebration with 10K road race, street fair, and entertainment. June.

Seacoast Jazz Festival. *Phone 603/436-2848.* Two stages with continuous performances on the historical Portsmouth waterfront. Last Sun in June.

Limited-Service Hotels

⭐ **COMFORT INN.** *1390 Lafayette Rd, Portsmouth (03801). Phone 603/433-3338; toll-free 800/552-8484; fax 603/431-1639. www.choicehotels.com.* 121 rooms, 6 story. Complimentary continental breakfast. Check-out 11 am. Fitness room. Indoor pool, whirlpool. **$**
🏃 🛏

⭐ **FAIRFIELD INN.** *650 Borthwick Ave, Portsmouth (03801). Phone 603/436-6363; toll-free 800/228-2800; fax 603/436-1621. www.fairfieldinn.com.* 105 rooms, 4 story. Complimentary continental breakfast. Check-out noon. High-speed Internet access. Outdoor pool. **$**
🛏

⭐ ⭐ **HOLIDAY INN.** *300 Woodbury Ave, Portsmouth (03801). Phone 603/431-8000; toll-free 800/465-4329; fax 603/431-2065. www.holiday-inn.com.* 130 rooms, 6 story. Check-out 11 am. Restaurant, bar. Fitness room. Indoor pool. **$**
🏃 🛏

⭐ **THE PORT INN.** *505 Hwy 1 Bypass S, Portsmouth (03801). Phone 603/436-4378; toll-free 800/282-7678; fax 603/436-4378. www.theportinn.com.* 57 rooms, 2 story. Complimentary continental breakfast. Check-out 11 am. Outdoor pool. **$**

Full-Service Hotels

★ ★ ★ **SHERATON HARBORSIDE HOTEL PORTSMOUTH.** *250 Market St, Portsmouth (03801). Phone 603/431-2300; toll-free 800/325-3535; fax 603/431-7805. www.sheraton.com.* This hotel is located in the downtown historic district on the Piscataqua River. 200 rooms, 5 story. Check-out noon. Restaurant, bar. Fitness room. Indoor pool. Airport transportation available. Business center. **$**

★ ★ ★ **SISE INN.** *40 Court St, Portsmouth (03801). Phone 603/433-1200; toll-free 877/747-3466; fax 603/431-0200. www.someplacesdifferent.com.* This Queen Anne-style home was built in 1881 for the prosperous businessman and merchant John E. Sise. The Victorian décor is reflected throughout the guest rooms. 34 rooms, 3 story. Complimentary continental breakfast. Check-in 4 pm, check-out 11 am. **$$**

Restaurants

★ ★ **METRO.** *20 High St, Portsmouth (03801). Phone 603/436-0521; fax 603/433-1894. www.themetro restaurant.com.* This American bistro tempts diners with a nightly veal special; fresh, flavorful seafood; and other contemporary preparations. American menu. Lunch, dinner. Closed Sun; Thanksgiving, Dec 25. Bar. **$$**

★ **PIER II.** *10 State St, Portsmouth (03801). Phone 603/436-8100.* Seafood, steak menu. Lunch, dinner. Closed Thanksgiving, Dec 25; also Jan. Bar. Children's menu. Valet parking. Outdoor seating. **$$**

Salem (F-4)

See also Nashua

Population 25,746
Elevation 131 ft
Area Code 603
Zip 03079
Information Greater Salem Chamber of Commerce, 224 N Broadway, PO Box 304; phone 603/893-3177
Web Site www.salemnhchamber.org

What to See and Do

★ **America's Stonehenge.** *105 Haverhill Rd, North Salem (03079). 5 miles E of I-93, just off Hwy 111. Phone 603/893-8300. www.stonehengeusa.com.* A megalithic calendar site dated to 2000 BC, with 22 stone buildings on more than 30 acres. The main site features a number of stone-constructed chambers and is surrounded by miles of stone walls containing large, shaped monoliths that indicate the rising and setting of the sun at solstice and equinox, as well as other astronomical alignments, including lunar. (Daily; closed Thanksgiving, Dec 25) **$$$**

Canobie Lake Park. *85 N Policy St, Salem (03079). 1 mile E of I-93, exit 2. Phone 603/893-3506. www.canobie.com.* Bring your bravery—and a change of clothes—for rides such as the Boston Tea Party Shoot-the-Chute water ride; the Corkscrew Coaster, which features two upside-down spins; and the Starblaster, which simulates a blast into outer space. You'll also find tamer options like bumper cars and kiddie rides. (Late Apr-late Sept; call for hours) **$$$$**

Robert Frost Farm. *Hwy 28, Derry. 1 mile SW on Hwy 38, then NW on Hwy 28. Phone 603/432-3091.* Home of poet Robert Frost from 1900 to 1911; period furnishings; audiovisual display; poetry-nature trail. (June-Labor Day: daily; after Labor Day-mid-Oct: weekends only) **$$**

Rockingham Park. *Rockingham Park Blvd, Salem. Exit 1 off I-93. Phone 603/898-2311.* Thoroughbred horse racing. Live and simulcast racing (daily).

Limited-Service Hotels

★ **FAIRFIELD INN.** *8 Keewaydin Dr, Salem (03079). Phone 603/893-4722; toll-free 800/228-2800; fax 603/893-2898. www.fairfieldinn.com.* 105 rooms, 4 story. Complimentary continental breakfast. Check-out noon. Outdoor pool. **$**

★ ★ **HOLIDAY INN.** *1 Keewaydin Dr, Salem (03079). Phone 603/893-5511; toll-free 800/465-4329; fax 603/894-6728. www.holiday-inn.com.* 85 rooms, 6 story. Complimentary continental breakfast. Check-out 11 am. Restaurant. Fitness room. Outdoor pool. **$**

Sunapee (E-3)

See also New London, Newport

Population 2,559
Elevation 1,008 ft
Area Code 603
Zip 03782
Information New London — Lake Sunapee Region Chamber of Commerce, PO Box 532; phone 603/526-6575 or toll-free 877/526-6575
Web Site www.lakesunapeenh.org

This is a year-round resort community on beautiful Lake Sunapee.

What to See and Do

M/V Kearsarge Restaurant Ship. *Phone 603/763-4030.* Buffet dinner while cruising around Lake Sunapee.

M/V Mount Sunapee II Excursion Boat. *Sunapee Harbor, Lake Ave, Sunapee. Off Hwy 11. Phone 603/763-4030.* 1 1/2-hour narrated tours of Lake Sunapee. Boat rentals, kayaks, canoes; gift shops, restaurants; concerts. (Mid-June-Labor Day: daily; mid-May-mid-June and after Labor Day-mid-Oct: Sat-Sun)

Mount Sunapee State Park. *1 mile S off Hwy 103. Phone 603/763-2356.* 2,714 acres.

Summer. Swimming beach, bathhouse (fee); trout pool; picnicking, playground, concession; chairlift rides (fee). Displays by artists and craftspeople. (Memorial Day weekend; mid-June-early Sept: daily; early Sept-Columbus Day: weekends)

Winter. Skiing. One high-speed detachable quad, two fix grip quads, three quad, two triple, double chairlift, four surface lifts; patrol, school, rentals; cafeteria; snowmaking; nursery. 60 slopes and trails. Snowboarding. (Dec-Apr, daily) **$$$$**

Snowhill at Eastman Ski Area. *6 Club House Ln, Grantham (03753). 4 miles N on Hwy 11, then 6 miles N on I-89, exit 13. Phone 603/863-4500. www.eastman-lake.com.* Ski Touring Center has 30 kilometers of cross-country trails; patrol, school, rentals; bar, restaurant. Summer facilities include Eastman Lake (swimming, boating, fishing); 18-hole golf, tennis; indoor pool; hiking. (Dec-Mar, daily; closed Dec 25)

Special Event

League of New Hampshire Craftsmen's Fair. *Mount Sunapee Resort, Sunapee. Phone 603/224-3375. www.nhcrafts.org/annualfair.htm.* More than 300 craftspeople and artists display and sell goods. Aug.

Limited-Service Hotel

★ **BURKEHAVEN AT SUNAPEE.** *179 Burkehaven Hill Rd, Sunapee (03782). Phone 603/763-2788; toll-free 800/567-2788; fax 603/763-9065. www.burkehavenatsunapee.com.* 10 rooms. Check-out 11 am. Outdoor pool. Tennis. **$**
🖨 🏊 🎿

Specialty Lodgings

The following lodging establishments are approved by Mobil Travel Guide, but due to their unique and individualized nature have not been given a traditional Mobil Star rating. Included in this listing you may find bed-and-breakfasts, limited-service inns, guest ranches, and other unique hotel properties.

CANDLELITE INN. *5 Greenhouse Ln, Bradford (03221). Phone 603/938-5571; toll-free 888/812-5571; fax 603/938-2564. www.candleliteinn.com.* Built in 1897; gazebo porch. 6 rooms, 3 story. Complimentary full breakfast. Check-in 3 pm, check-out 11 am. **$**
🖨

DEXTERS INN & TENNIS CLUB. *258 Stagecoach Rd, Sunapee (03782). Phone 603/763-5571; toll-free 800/232-5571. www.dextersnh.com.* This inn is located on a 20-acre estate. 2 story. Pets accepted, some restrictions; fee. Complimentary full breakfast. Check-in 3 pm, check-out 11 am. Outdoor pool. Tennis. **$$**
🐾 🏊 🎿

Twin Mountain (C-3)

See also Bretton Woods, Franconia, Littleton

Population 760
Elevation 1,442 ft
Area Code 603
Zip 03595
Information Chamber of Commerce, PO Box 194; phone toll-free 800/245-8946
Web Site www.twinmountain.org

What to See and Do

Mount Washington. *E off US 302.* (see).

Limited-Service Hotels

★ **FOUR SEASONS MOTOR INN.** *Birch Rd and Rte 3, Twin Mountain (03595).* Phone 603/846-5708; toll-free 800/228-5708. www.4seasonsmotorinn.com. 24 rooms, 2 story. Check-out 11 am. Outdoor pool. **$**

★ **SHAKESPEARE'S INN.** *675 Hwy 3, Twin Mountain (03595). Phone 603/846-5562; fax 603/846-5782. www.shakespearesinn.com.* At the base of the White Mountains. 33 rooms, 2 story. Closed Apr-May, Nov-Dec. Check-out 10:30 am. Restaurant. Outdoor pool. Tennis. **$**

Specialty Lodging

The following lodging establishment is approved by Mobil Travel Guide, but due to its unique and individualized nature has not been given a traditional Mobil Star rating. Included in this listing you may find bed-and-breakfasts, limited-service inns, guest ranches, and other unique hotel properties.

NORTHERN ZERMATT INN & MOTEL. *529 Hwy 3 N, Twin Mountain (03595). Phone 603/846-5533; toll-free 800/535-3214; fax 603/846-5664. www.zermattinn.com.* Former boarding house (circa 1900) for loggers and railroad workers. 17 rooms, 3 story. Complimentary continental breakfast. Check-in 3 pm, check-out 11 am. Outdoor pool. **$**

Waterville Valley (D-4)

See also Lincoln/North Woodstock, Plymouth

Founded 1829
Population 151
Elevation 1,519 ft
Area Code 603
Zip 03215
Information Waterville Valley Region Chamber of Commerce, RFD 1, Box 1067, Campton 03223; phone 603/726-3804 or toll-free 800/237-2307
Web Site www.watervillevalleyregion.com

Although the resort village of Waterville Valley was developed in the late 1960s, the surrounding area has been attracting tourists since the mid-19th century, when summer vacationers stayed at the Waterville Inn. Completely encircled by the White Mountain National Forest, the resort, which is approximately 11 miles northeast of Campton, offers a variety of winter and summer activities, as well as spectacular views of the surrounding mountain peaks.

What to See and Do

Waterville Valley Ski Area. *1 Ski Area Rd, Waterville Valley (03215). 11 miles NE of Campton on Hwy 49. Phone toll-free 800/468-2553. www.waterville.com.* Three double, two triple chairlifts, two quad chairlifts, T-bar, J-bar, four platter pulls; patrol, school; retail, rental and repair shops; snowmaking; restaurants, cafeterias, lounge; nursery. 52 ski trails; longest run 3 miles; vertical drop 2,020 feet. Half-day rates. (Mid-Nov-mid-Apr, daily) Ski Touring Center with 46 miles of cross-country trails; rentals, school, restaurants. Summer facilities include nine-hole golf, 18 clay tennis courts, small boating, hiking, fishing, bicycling; entertainment. Indoor sports center (daily). Contact Waterville Valley Resort, Town Square. **$$$$**

Limited-Service Hotels

★ ★ **SNOWY OWL INN.** *4 Village Rd, Waterville Valley (03215). Phone 603/236-8383; toll-free 800/766-9969; fax 603/236-4890. www.snowyowlinn.com.* This inn is situated in the heart of Waterville Valley and the White Moutain National Forest. The lobby atrium has natural wood and a three-story fieldstone fireplace. 83 rooms, 4 story. Complimentary continental breakfast. Check-out 11 am. Fitness room. Indoor pool, outdoor pool, whirlpool. **$**

★ ★ **VALLEY INN & TAVERN.** *1 Tecumseh Rd, Waterville Valley (3215). Phone 603/236-8336; toll-free 800/343-0969; fax 603/236-4294. www.valleyinn.com.* 52 rooms, 5 story. Complimentary continental breakfast. Check-in 4 pm, check-out 11 am. Restaurant, bar. Fitness room. Indoor/outdoor pool, whirlpool. **$**

Restaurant

★ ★ **WILLIAM TELL.** *Rte 49, Thornton (03223). Phone 603/726-3618; fax 603/726-4722.* American menu. Dinner, Sun brunch. Closed Wed. Bar. Children's menu. Outdoor seating. **$$**

White Mountain National Forest

This national forest and major New Hampshire recreation area includes the Presidential Range and a major part of the White Mountains. There are more than 100 miles of roads and 1,128 miles of foot trails. The Appalachian Trail, with eight hostels, winds over some spectacular peaks. Eight peaks tower more than a mile above sea level; the highest is Mount Washington (6,288 feet). Twenty-two mountains rise more than 4,000 feet. There are several well-defined ranges, divided by deep "notches" and broader valleys. Clear streams rush through the notches; mountain lakes and ponds dot the landscape. Deer, bear, moose, and bobcat roam the wilds; trout fishing is good.

The US Forest Service administers 23 campgrounds with more than 700 sites ($12-$16/site/night), also picnicking sites for public use. There is lodging within the forest; for information, reservations contact the Appalachian Mountain Club, Pinkham Notch, Gorham 03581; phone 603/466-2727. There are also many resorts, campsites, picnicking, and recreational spots in private and state-owned areas. A visitor center (daily) is at the Saco Ranger Station, 33 Kancamagus Hwy, Conway 03818; phone 603/447-5448. Information stations are also located at exits 28 and 32, off Interstate 93 and at Franconia Notch State Park Visitor Center. For further information, contact the Supervisor, White Mountain National Forest, 719 N Main St, Laconia 03246; phone 603/528-8721.

The following cities and villages in and near the forest are included in this book: Bartlett, Bretton Woods, Franconia, Franconia Notch State Park, Gorham, Jackson, Lincoln/North Woodstock Area, Mount Washington, North Conway, Pinkham Notch, Twin Mountain, and Waterville Valley. For information on any of them, see the individual alphabetical listing.

Wolfeboro (D-4)

See also Center Ossipee, Laconia

Settled 1760
Population 4,807
Elevation 573 ft

Area Code 603
Zip 03894
Information Chamber of Commerce, 312 Central Ave, PO Box 547; phone 603/569-2200 or toll-free 800/516-5324
Web Site www.wolfeboro.com-chamber

Wolfeboro has been a resort area for more than two centuries; it is the oldest summer resort in America. In the winter it is a ski touring center with 40 miles of groomed trails.

What to See and Do

Clark House. *337 S Main St, Wolfeboro (03894). Phone 603/569-4997.* Wolfeboro Historical Society is housed in Clark family homestead (1778), a one-room schoolhouse (circa 1820) and a firehouse museum. Clark House has period furnishings and memorabilia; the firehouse museum contains restored firefighting equipment dating to 1842. (July-Aug, Mon-Sat) **DONATION**

Lake Winnipesaukee cruises. (See LACONIA)

Wentworth State Park. *6 miles E on Hwy 109. Phone 603/569-3699.* On Lake Wentworth. Swimming; bathhouse. Picnicking. (Late June-Labor Day)

Wright Museum. *77 Center St, Wolfeboro (03894). Phone 603/569-1212. www.wrightmuseum.org.* Showcases American enterprise during World War II. Collection of tanks, Jeeps, and other military vehicles, period memorabilia. (May-Oct, daily; weekends only Apr and Nov; closed Dec-Mar) **$$**

Limited-Service Hotel

★ ★ **LAKEVIEW INN & MOTOR LODGE.** *200 N Main St, Wolfeboro (03894). Phone 603/569-1335; fax 603/569-9426. www.lakeviewinn.net.* This inn was built in 1768 on king's land grant. 17 rooms, 2 story. Complimentary continental breakfast. Check-out 11 am. Restaurant, bar. **$**

Full-Service Inn

★ ★ ★ **THE WOLFEBORO INN.** *90 N Main St, Wolfeboro (03894). Phone 603/569-3016; toll-free 800/451-2389; fax 603/569-5375. www.wolfeboroinn.com.* Built in 1812, this inn has a fabulous location on Lake Winnipesaukee in one of America's oldest summer resort towns. Many rooms offer Wolfeboro Bay views and all include a boat ride and private beach access during summer months. 44 rooms, 3 story. Complimentary continental breakfast. Check-in 3 pm, check-out 11 am. Restaurant. **$**

Rhode Island

Giovanni da Verrazano, a Florentine navigator in the service of France, visited the Narragansett Bay of Rhode Island in 1524; however, it wasn't until 1636 that the first permanent white settlement was founded. Roger Williams, a religious refugee from Massachusetts, bought land at Providence from the Narragansetts. Williams fled what he considered puritanical tyranny and established a policy of religious and political freedom in his new settlement. Soon others began similar communities, and in 1663, King Charles II granted them a royal charter, officially creating the "State of Rhode Island and Providence Plantations."

Although the smallest state in the nation and smaller than many of the counties in the United States, Rhode Island is rich in American tradition. It is a state of firsts. Rhode Islanders were among the first colonists to take action against the British, attacking British vessels in its waters. On May 4, 1776, the state was the first to proclaim independence from Great Britain, two months before the Declaration of Independence was signed. In 1790, Samuel Slater's mill in Pawtucket became America's first successful water-powered cotton mill, and in 1876, polo was played for the first time in the United States in Newport.

Rhode Island has a tradition of manufacturing skill. The state produces machine tools, electronic equipment, plastics, textiles, jewelry, toys, and boats. The famous Rhode Island Red Hen was developed by farmers in Little Compton. Rhode Island is also for those who follow the sea. With more than 400 miles of coastline, visitors can swim, sail, fish, or relax in the many resort areas.

Population: 1,003,464
Area: 1,054 square miles
Elevation: 0-812 feet
Peak: Jerimoth Hill (Providence County)
Entered Union: Thirteenth of original 13 states (May 29, 1790)
Capital: Providence
Motto: Hope
Nickname: Ocean State
Flower: Violet
Bird: Rhode Island Red Hen
Tree: Red Maple
Time Zone: Eastern
Web Site: www.visitrhodeisland.com
Fun Facts:
- The White Horse Tavern, built in 1673, is the oldest operating tavern in the United States.
- Portsmouth is home to the oldest schoolhouse in the United States; it was built in 1716.

When to Go/Climate

The weather in Rhode Island is more moderate than in other parts of New England. Breezes off Narragansett Bay make summer humidity bearable and winter temperatures less bitter than elsewhere in the region.

AVERAGE HIGH/LOW TEMPERATURES (° F)

Providence

Jan 37/19	May 67/47	Sept 74/54
Feb 38/21	June 77/57	Oct 64/43
Mar 46/29	July 82/63	Nov 53/35
Apr 57/38	Aug 81/62	Dec 41/24

Calendar Highlights

FEBRUARY

Mid-winter New England Surfing Championship *(Narragansett). Narragansett Town Beach. Phone the Eastern Surfing Association, 401/789-1954.*

Newport Winter Festival *(Newport). Phone 401/ 849-8048, 401/847-7666, or toll-free 800/326-6030.* Ten days of food, festivities, and music. More than 200 cultural and recreational events and activities.

MAY

Gaspee Days *(Warwick). Phone Gaspee Days Committee, 401/781-1772 or toll-free 800/492-7942.* Celebration of the capture and burning of British revenue schooner *Gaspee* by Rhode Island patriots; arts and crafts, concert, foot races, battle reenactment, muster of fife and drum corps, parade, and contests.

JUNE

Spring Festival of Historic Houses *(Providence). Phone 401/831-7440.* Sponsored by the Providence Preservation Society. Tours of selected private houses and gardens.

JULY

Hot Air Balloon Festival *(Kingston). University of Rhode Island. Phone 401/783-1770.* Two-day event features hot air balloon rides, parachute demonstrations, arts and crafts, and music.

Newport Music Festival *(Newport). Phone 401/847-7090.* Chamber music, held in Newport's fabled mansions.

Parks and Recreation

Water-related activities, hiking, riding, various other sports, picnicking, and visitor centers, as well as camping, are available in many state parks. Most are open sunrise to sunset. Parking fee at beaches: weekdays, $6-$12/car; weekends, holidays, $7-$14/car. Camping $14-$20/night; with electric and water $18-$25; sewer $20-$35. No pets allowed. A map is available at the Division of Parks & Recreation, Department of Environmental Management, 2321 Hartford Ave, Johnston 02919. Phone 401/222-2632.

FISHING AND HUNTING

No license is necessary for recreational saltwater game fishing. Freshwater fishing license: nonresident, $31; three-day tourists' fee, $16. Both large-mouth bass and northern pike can be found in Worden Pond; trout can be found in Wood River.

Hunting license: nonresident, $41. Resident licenses and regulations may be obtained at city and town clerks' offices and at most sporting goods shops. Nonresident licenses may be obtained by contacting DEM-Licensing, 235 Promenade St,

Providence 02908; phone 401/222-3576. For further information write Division of Fish & Wildlife, Department of Environment Management, Government Center, Wakefield 02879. Phone 401/789-3094.

Driving Information

Children ages 4-12 must be in approved passenger restraints anywhere in a vehicle; ages 3 and under must use approved safety seats. Phone Governor's Office of Highway Safety at 401/222-3024.

INTERSTATE HIGHWAY SYSTEM

The following alphabetical listing of Rhode Island towns in this book shows that these cities are within 10 miles of the indicated interstate highway. Check a highway map for the nearest exit.

Highway Number	Cities/Towns within 10 Miles
Interstate 95	East Greenwich, Pawtucket, Providence, Warwick, Westerly.

Additional Visitor Information

Contact the Rhode Island Economic Development Corporation Division of Marketing & Commu

THE ROAD LESS TRAVELED

Newport and South County are the shoreline destinations that most people head for when they visit Rhode Island. As a result, both areas become clogged with traffic and tourists during the summer. But Rhode Island has a quiet eastern coast along its border with Massachusetts that is an ideal area for a day trip. The drive to the coastal towns of Tiverton and Little Compton takes about 50 minutes from Providence and passes through the attractive harbor town of Bristol, which is on Narragansett Bay. From downtown Providence, take Highway 195 east to exit 7, Highway 114 South. Stay on this highway through Barrington, Warren, and Bristol. (In Warren, you may want to stop for the dozens of antiques and second-hand shops that line Main and Water sts.) Highway 114 (Main St in Warren) becomes Hope Street in Bristol, and here you'll be charmed by the many elegant Federal-era houses (some of them bed-and-breakfast inns) that show how wealthy this town was in the period before the Civil War. South of the town, a turn-of-the-century mansion and estate called Blithewold is open to the public for tours.

Drive over the Mount Hope Bridge into the Aquidneck Island town of Portsmouth. You won't see much of this town, however, as you turn left onto Highway 24 to cross the Sakonnet River Bridge into Tiverton. Turn right onto Highway 77 South, and stay on this road through Tiverton and Little Compton. (Highway 77 ends rather ignominiously in a parking lot with a view of the ocean at Sakonnet Point in Little Compton.) There's only one traffic light along the length of Highway 77, and that's at the intersection with Highway 179, an area known as Tiverton Four Corners. In this vicinity, you'll find some delightful shops, including a gourmet take-out place where you can pick up food for a picnic and Gray's Ice Cream, which has been making dozens of homemade flavors at this spot since the 1920s. Continuing south on Highway 77, you'll pass open farmland with lovely vistas of Narragansett Bay. Little Compton is a wealthy summer community, so there's very little commerce in town, and you'll see old farmhouses that are now used as summer homes.

You can return by the same route, or turn right onto Highway 24 North in Tiverton to drive into Fall River, Massachusetts, then head west back to Providence on Highway 195. **(Approximately 40 miles)**

---

nications, 1 W Exchange St, Providence 02903. Phone 401/222-2601 or toll-free 800/556-2484. The *Providence Journal-Bulletin Almanac* is an excellent state reference book and may be obtained from the Providence *Journal*, 75 Fountain St, Providence 02902.

There are several information centers in Rhode Island; visitors will find information and brochures most helpful in planning stops at points of interest. Two of the information centers are located: off Interstate 95 in Richmond (daily); and 7 miles south of Providence in Warwick, at T. F. Green Airport.

Block Island (F-6)

(By ferry from Providence, Newport, and Point Judith; by air from Westerly. Also by ferry from New London, CT, and Montauk, Long Island)

Settled 1661

Population 620
Elevation 9 ft
Area Code 401
Zip 02807
Information Chamber of Commerce, Water St, PO Drawer D; phone 401/466-2982 or toll-free 800/383-2474
Web Site www.blockislandchamber.com

Block Island, Rhode Island's "air-conditioned" summer resort, covers 21 square miles. Lying 12 miles out to sea from Point Judith, it received its nickname because it is 10 to15 degrees cooler than the mainland in summer and consistently milder in winter. Although Verrazano saw the island in 1524, it was named for the Dutch explorer Adriaen Block, who landed here in 1614. Until the resort trade developed, this island community was devoted to fishing and farming. Settler's Rock on Corn Neck Road displays plaques on the boulder listing the first settlers.

In recent years, Block Island has become a favorite "nature retreat" for people seeking to escape fast-paced city living. More than 40 rare and endangered species of plants and animals can be found on the island, of which 1/4 is in public trust. The Nature Conservancy has designated Block Island as "one of the 12 last great places in the Western Hemisphere."

What to See and Do

Ferry service. *304 Great Island Rd, Point Judith (02882). Phone 401/783-4613.*

Block Island/Montauk, Long Island. *Phone 516/668-5009.* (Mid-June-Labor Day, one trip daily)

Block Island/New London, CT. Two-hour trip. (Mid-June-Labor Day, one trip daily, extra trips Fri)

Block Island/Point Judith. Advance reservations for vehicles; all vehicles must be on pier 45 minutes before sailing. (Mid-June-mid-Sept: eight round trips daily; early May-mid-June, mid-Sept-Oct: four round trips daily; rest of year: one round trip daily)

Block Island/Providence/Newport. Departs from either Providence or Newport. (Late June-Labor Day, one trip daily) Nonvehicular ferry.

Fishing. Surf casting from most beaches; freshwater ponds for bass, pickerel, perch; deep-sea boat trips for tuna, swordfish from Old Harbor.

Fred Benson Town Beach. *1/2 mile N to Crescent Beach.* Swimming, bathhouse, lifeguards; picnicking, concession. Parking.

Natural formations. Mohegan Bluffs. West of Southeast Light lighthouse off Mohegan Trail, are 185-foot clay cliffs that offer a fine sea view. **New Harbor,** 1 mile west on Ocean Avenue, is a huge harbor made by cutting through sand bar into Great Salt Pond.

New England Airlines. *Phone 401/466-5881; toll-free 800/243-2460.* Twelve-minute scheduled flights between Westerly State Airport and Block Island State Airport; also air taxi and charter service to all points. (Daily) Phone 401/466-5881, 401/596-2460, or toll-free 800/243-2460.

North Light. Lighthouse built in 1867 at the tip of the island near Settler's Rock, now houses a maritime museum. Bordering the dunes are a seagull rookery and wildlife sanctuary.

Limited-Service Hotel

★ ★ **SPRING HOUSE.** *52 Spring St, Block Island (02807). Phone 401/466-5844; toll-free 800/234-9263; fax 401/466-2633. www.springhousehotel.com.* 49 rooms, 3 story. Closed in winter. Complimentary continental breakfast. Check-out 11 am. Restaurant, bar. Airport transportation available. **$$**
🅟

Specialty Lodging

The following lodging establishment is approved by Mobil Travel Guide, but due to its unique and individualized nature has not been given a traditional Mobil Star rating. Included in this listing you may find bed-and-breakfasts, limited-service inns, guest ranches, and other unique hotel properties.

THE 1661 INN & GUEST HOUSE. *1 Spring St, Block Island (02807). Phone 401/466-2421; toll-free 800/626-4773; fax 401/466-3162. www.blockisland resorts.com.* Located on a secluded island, this inn benefits from the unspoiled beaches, grassy cliffs, and rolling hills speckled with wildflowers. 21 rooms, 2 story. Complimentary full breakfast. Check-in 2 pm, check-out 11 am. Tennis. Airport transportation available. **$$$**
🛋

Restaurants

★ ★ **FINN'S SEAFOOD.** *Water St, Block Island (02807). Phone 401/466-2473; fax 401/466-2769.* Seafood menu. Lunch, dinner. Closed Nov-Apr. Bar. Outdoor seating. **$$$**

★ ★ ★ **HOTEL MANISSES DINING ROOM.** *1 Spring St, Block Island (02807). Phone 401/466-2836; fax 401/466-3162. www.blockislandresorts.com.* Stone-walled dining room and glass-enclosed garden room. International/Fusion menu. Dinner. Closed Mon-Fri in mid-Feb-Apr; Dec-mid-Feb. Bar. Children's menu. Outdoor seating. **$$$**

★ ★ **MOHEGAN CAFE.** *Water St, Block Island (02807). Phone 401/466-5911; fax 401/466-2664.* Seafood menu. Lunch, dinner. Closed Thanksgiving, Dec 25. Bar. Children's menu. **$$**
🅟

Bristol (D-7)

See also Portsmouth, Providence

Settled 1669
Population 21,625
Elevation 50 ft
Area Code 401
Zip 02809
Information East Bay County Chamber of Commerce, 654 Metacom Ave, PO Box 250, Warren 02885-0250; phone 401/245-0750
Web Site www.eastbaychamber.org

King Philip's War (1675-1676) began and ended on the Bristol peninsula between Mount Hope and Narragansett bays; King Philip, the Native American rebel leader, headquartered the Wampanoag tribe in the area. After the war ended, Bristol grew into an important port, and by the turn of the 18th century, the town was the fourth-busiest port in the United States. Bristol was the home of General Ambrose Burnside, Civil War officer and sometime governor and senator. The town was the site of the famous Herreshoff Boatyard, where many America's Cup winners were built. Roger Williams University (1948) is located in Bristol.

What to See and Do

Blithewold Mansion and Gardens. *101 Ferry Rd, Bristol (02809). 2 miles S on Hwy 114 (Ferry Rd); on Bristol Harbor overlooking Naragansett Bay. Phone 401/253-2707. www.blithewold.org.* Blithewold Mansion, Gardens and Arboretum is a beautifully landscaped historic public garden situated on Bristol Harbor with sweeping views overlooking Narragansett Bay. A 45-room mansion, trees, lawns, flowers, gardens, and the sea combine to produce an aesthetic experience that is exciting and refreshing. Concerts are held on the grounds in the summer. (Daily) **$$$**

Colt State Park. *2 1/2 miles NW off Hwy 114.* Three-mile scenic drive around shoreline of former Colt family estate on east side of Narragansett Bay. Fishing, boating; hiking and bridle trails, picnicking. Concerts in Stone Barn. **$** In park is

Coggeshall Farm Museum. *Colt State Park, Poppasquash Rd, Bristol. Off Hwy 114. Phone 401/253-9062.* Working farm from 18th and 19th centuries; vegetables, herbs, animals; colonial craft demonstrations. (Tues-Sun; closed Jan) (See SPECIAL EVENTS) **$$**

Haffenreffer Museum of Anthropology. *300 Tower St, Bristol (02809). 1 mile E of Metacom Ave, Hwy 136, follow signs; overlooks Mount Hope Bay. Phone 401/253-8388.* Brown University museum features Native American objects from North, Central, and South America; Eskimo collections; African and Pacific tribal arts. (June-Aug: Tues-Sun; rest of year: Sat-Sun) **$**

Herreshoff Marine Museum. *1 Burnside St, Bristol (02809). Phone 401/253-5000. www.herreshoff.org.* Herreshoff Manufacturing Company produced some of America's greatest yachts, including eight winners of the America's Cup. Exhibits include yachts manufactured by Herreshoff, steam engines, fittings; photographs and memorabilia from "golden age of yachting." (May-Oct, Mon-Fri afternoons; also Sat-Sun, limited hours) **$$**

Hope Street. *Hope St, Bristol. On Hwy 114.* Famous row of colonial houses.

Prudence Island. Ferry from Church Street dock.

Special Event

Harvest Fair. *Coggeshall Farm Museum, Colt State Park, Poppasquash Rd, Bristol (02809). Phone 401/253-9062.* During the day, workers mill around dressed in colonial garb, and craftspeople demonstrate weaving, pottery and blacksmith techniques at Coggeshall Farm Museum. Pony rides, a silent auction, music, magic and live farm animals are also found at the fair. Weekend in mid-Sept.

Specialty Lodgings

The following lodging establishments are approved by Mobil Travel Guide, but due to their unique and individualized nature have not been given a traditional Mobil Star rating. Included in this listing you may find bed-and-breakfasts, limited-service inns, guest ranches, and other unique hotel properties.

ROCKWELL HOUSE INN. *610 Hope St, Bristol (02809). Phone 401/253-0040; toll-free 800/815-0040; fax 401/253-1811. www.rockwellhouseinn.com.* Set on a half-acre of land, this 1809 inn has the state's largest tulip tree on its property and is conveniently located within walking distance to Narragansett Bay, many antiques shops, and restaurants. Guest rooms feature ceiling fans and stenciled borders. 4 rooms, 2 story.

Children over 12 years only. Complimentary full breakfast. Check-in 4 pm, check-out 11 am. **$$**

WILLIAMS GRANT INN. *154 High St, Bristol (02809). Phone 401/253-4222; toll-free 800/596-4222; fax 401/254-0986. www.wmgrantinn.com.* House built in 1808; original fireplaces, artwork, many antiques. 5 rooms, 2 story. Children over 12 years only. Complimentary full breakfast. Check-in noon-10 pm, check-out 11 am. **$**

Restaurants

★ ★ **LOBSTER POT.** *119-121 Hope St, Bristol (02809). Phone 401/253-9100; fax 401/253-7225.* Seafood menu. Lunch, dinner. Closed Mon. Bar. Children's menu. **$$$**

★ ★ **NATHANIEL PORTER INN.** *125 Water St, Warren (02885). Phone 401/245-6622; fax 401/247-2277. www.nathanielporterinn.com.* This house built in 1795 features colonial décor and antiques. American menu. Dinner, Sun brunch. Closed Mon. Bar. Children's menu. **$$**

Charlestown (E-6)

See also Narragansett, Westerly

Population 6,478
Elevation 20 ft
Area Code 401
Zip 02813
Information Chamber of Commerce, 4945 Old Post Rd; phone 401/364-3878
Web Site www.cshell.com/ccc

Charlestown, named for King Charles II of England, was originally called Cross Mills for two gristmills that once stood here. Charlestown was first settled along the coast by summer residents and by permanent residents after World War II. The town's past can be seen in Fort Ninigret, the historic Native American church, and the Royal Indian Burial Ground.

What to See and Do

Burlingame State Park. *Kings Factory Rd, Charlestown (02813). 2 miles SW via Hwy 1. Phone 401/322-7337.* More than 2,000 acres with wooded area. Swimming, lifeguard, fishing, boating; picnicking, concession. Tent and trailer camping (mid-Apr-Oct).

Kimball Wildlife Refuge. *Montauk Rd, Charlestown (02813). 2 1/2 miles SW on US 1, Windswept Farm exit, left onto Montauk Rd.* Thirty-acre refuge on the south shore of Watchaug Pond has nature trails and programs.

Swimming, fishing. At several Block Island Sound beaches; S of Hwy 1 on Charlestown Beach Rd; Green Hill Rd; Moonstone Rd.

Special Events

August Meeting of the Narragansett Indian Tribe. *Narragansett Indian church grounds, Charlestown (02813). Phone 401/364-1101.* Dancing, music, storytelling. Said to be the oldest continuous meeting in the country. Second week in Aug.

Seafood Festival. *4945 Old Post Rd, Charlestown (02813). Phone 401/364-3878.* Seafood vendors, amateur seafood cook-off, helicopter rides, antique car show. First Sat-Sun in Aug.

Theatre-by-the-Sea. *364 Cards Pond Rd, Matunuck (02879). 7 miles NE via Hwy 1, then S off Matunuck Beach Rd exit to Cards Pond Rd. Phone 401/782-8587.* Historic barn theater (1933) presents professionally staged musicals. Restaurant, bar, cabaret. Tues-Sun evenings; matinees Thurs; children's shows July-Aug, Fri only. June-Sept.

East Greenwich (D-6)

See also Warwick

Population 11,865
Elevation 64 ft
Area Code 401
Zip 02818
Information Chamber of Commerce, 591 Main St; phone 401/885-0020
Web Site www.eastgreenwichchamber.com

Sometimes referred to as "the town on four hills," East Greenwich, on Narragansett Bay, is a sports and yachting center. Nathanael Greene and James M. Varnum organized the Kentish Guards, who protected the town during the Revolution, here in 1774. The Guards are still active today.

What to See and Do

Kentish Guards Armory. *92 Pierce St, East Greenwich (02818). Phone 401/821-1628.* (1843) Headquarters of the Kentish Guards, local militia chartered in 1774 and still active; General Nathanael Greene was a charter member. (By appointment only) **$**

Old Kent County Court House. *125 Main St, East Greenwich (02818). Phone 401/886-8606.* (1750) Remodeled in 1909 and 1995.

Varnum House Museum. *57 Pierce St, East Greenwich (02818). Phone 401/884-4110.* (1773) Mansion of a Revolutionary War officer and lawyer; period furnishings, colonial items, gardens. (June-Sept, by appointment) **$**

Varnum Memorial Armory and Military Museum. *6 Main St, East Greenwich. Phone 401/884-4110.* (1913) Museum displays uniforms and armaments from the Revolutionary through the Vietnam wars. (By appointment) **DONATION**

Glocester

Population 5,011
Elevation 422 ft
Area Code 401
Zip 02859
Information Blackstone Valley Tourism Council, 171 Main St, Pawtucket 02860; phone 401/724-2200 or toll-free 800/454-2882 (outside RI)

What to See and Do

Brown & Hopkins Country Store. *1179 Putnam Pike, Chepachet (02814). 3 miles SE on Hwy 100 to Hwy 44 (Main St). Phone 401/568-4830.* (1799) Nation's oldest continuously operating country store; inside are antiques, gourmet food, penny candy, and a café. (Wed-Sun; closed holidays)

Casimir Pulaski State Park. *3 miles SE on Hwy 100, 6 miles W on Hwy 44. Phone 401/568-2085.* Park has 100 acres with lake. Swimming beach; cross-country skiing, picnicking. Pavilion (reservation required). (Late May-early Sept)

George Washington State Campground. *1826 Putnam Pike, Glocester (02859). 3 miles SE on Hwy 100, 4 miles W on Hwy 44. Phone 401/568-2013.* Swimming beach, fishing, boating; hiking trail, picnicking, camping (no fires). (Mid-Apr-mid-Oct) **$**

Jamestown (E-6)

See also Newport

Settled circa 1670
Population 4,999
Elevation 8 ft
Area Code 401
Zip 02835
Information Jamestown Chamber of Commerce, PO Box 35; phone 401/423-3650
Web Site www.jamestownri.com/chamber

Jamestown is centered around the Jamestown Ferry landing, but technically the town also includes all of Conanicut—one of three main islands in Narragansett Bay. The island is connected by bridges to Newport on the east (toll) and to the mainland on the west (free). While much of Jamestown was burned by the British in 1775, some old houses do remain.

The restored Conanicut Battery, a Revolutionary redoubt 2 miles south on Beavertail Road, is open to the public and is the second-highest point on the island.

What to See and Do

Fishing. Striped bass, tuna, flounder, bluefish. For boat charter inquire at East Ferry slip.

Jamestown Museum. *92 Narragansett Ave, Jamestown (02835). Phone 401/423-3771.* Photos and displays pertain to town and old Jamestown ferries. (Late June-Labor Day, Tues-Sat afternoons) **DONATION** The Jamestown Historical Society also maintains the

> **Old Windmill.** *1 1/2 miles N on North Rd. Phone 401/423-1798.* (1787) Restored to working order. (Mid-June-mid-Sept, Sat-Sun afternoons) **DONATION**

Sydney L. Wright Museum. *26 North Rd, Jamestown (02835). Located in the library. Phone 401/423-7280.* Exhibits of Native American and early colonial artifacts from Conanicut Island. (Mon-Sat)

Watson Farm. *North Rd, Jamestown. S of Hwy 138. Phone 401/423-0005.* (1796) This 280-acre farm on Conanicut Island is being worked as a typical New England farm. Self-guided tour of farm and pastures with focus on land-use history. (June-mid-Oct: Tues, Thurs, and Sun afternoons) **$$**

Kingston (E-6)

See also Narragansett, Newport, North Kingstown

Population 6,504
Elevation 242 ft
Area Code 401
Zip 02881
Information Chamber of Commerce, 328 Main St, PO Box 289, Wakefield 02880; phone 401/783-2801; or the South County Tourism Council, Stedman Government Center, 4808 Tower Hill Rd, Wakefield 02879; phone 401/789-4422 or toll-free 800/548-4662
Web Site www.southcountyri.com

Known as Little Rest until 1825, Kingston was once forestland bought from the Narragansett. Early settlers were farmers who built a water-powered mill in an area still known as Biscuit City. Here, the state constitution was ratified, and a law was passed abolishing slavery in the state. Kingston overlooks a fertile flood plain, which geologists believe was an ancient river. Kingston is also the home of the University of Rhode Island.

What to See and Do

Helme House. *2587 Kingstown Rd, Kingston (02881). Phone 401/783-2195.* (1802) Gallery of the South County Art Association. (Wed-Sun) **FREE**

Kingston Library. *2605 Kingstown Rd, Kingston (02881). Phone 401/783-8254.* (1776) Visited by George Washington and Benjamin Franklin, this building housed the Rhode Island General Assembly at the time the British occupied Newport. (Mon-Sat)

Museum of Primitive Art and Culture. *1058 Kingstown Rd, Peace Dale (02879). 2 miles S via Hwy 108. Phone 401/783-5711.* 1850s post office building; prehistoric artifacts from New England, North America, South Seas, Africa, Europe, and Asia. (Tues-Thurs; limited hours; also by appointment) **DONATION**

Night Heron Nature Cruises. *Phone 401/783-9977; toll-free 888/644-8476.* Offers snorkeling, nature, sunrise, sunset, and undersea nightlife cruises. Each cruise offers two or more departures daily.

Special Event

Hot Air Balloon Festival. *University of Rhode Island, 404 Wordens Pond Rd C, Kingston (02881). Phone*

401/783-1770. Two-day event features hot air balloon rides, parachute demonstrations, arts and crafts, and music. Late July or early Aug.

Specialty Lodging

The following lodging establishment is approved by Mobil Travel Guide, but due to its unique and individualized nature has not been given a traditional Mobil Star rating. Included in this listing you may find bed-and-breakfasts, limited-service inns, guest ranches, and other unique hotel properties.

LARCHWOOD INN. *521 Main St, Wakefield (02879). Phone 401/783-5454; toll-free 800/275-5450; fax 401/783-1800. www.larchwoodinn.com.* This inn was built in 1831. 18 rooms, 3 story. Pets accepted, some restrictions; fee. Check-in 1 pm, check-out 11 am. Restaurant, bar. **$**
🅳 🏹

Restaurant

★ ★ **LARCHWOOD INN.** *521 Main St, Wakefield (02879). Phone 401/783-5454; fax 401/783-1800. www.larchwoodinn.com.* American menu. Breakfast, lunch, dinner. Bar. **$**

Little Compton (E-7)

See also Portsmouth

Population 3,339
Area Code 401
Zip 02837
Information Town Hall, PO Box 523; phone 401/635-4400; or the Newport County Convention and Visitors Bureau, 23 America's Cup Ave, Newport 02840; phone 401/849-8048 or toll-free 800/976-5122
Web Site www.gonewport.com

In Little Compton's old burial ground lie the remains of the first white woman born in New England, Elizabeth Alden Pabodie, the daughter of John and Priscilla Alden.

What to See and Do

Gray's Store (1788). *4 Main St, Adamsville (02837). 7 miles NE on local road. Phone 401/635-4566.* First post office in the area (1804) features antique soda fountain, wheeled cheese, candy, and tobacco cases. (Daily; closed Sun and holidays in winter)

Sakonnet Point. *5 Bluff Head Ave, Little Compton (02837).* Swimming beaches, fishing. Harbor with lighthouse.

Sakonnet Vineyards. *162 W Main, Little Compton (02837). Phone 401/635-8486.* Tour of winery and vineyard. Wine tasting (daily). **FREE**

Wilbor House. *1 mile S on Hwy 77 at West Rd. Phone 401/635-4035.* (1690) Seventeenth-century house with 18th- and 19th-century additions was restored in 1956 by local historical society; period furnishings, antique farm, and household implements. Display of carriages and sleighs in 1860 barn. Also one-room schoolhouse, artist's studio. (Mid-June-mid-Sept: Wed-Sun, also by appointment) **$$**

Narragansett (E-6)

See also Block Island, Charlestown, Kingston, Newport

Settled 1675
Population 14,985
Elevation 20 ft
Area Code 401
Zip 02882
Information Narragansett Chamber of Commerce, The Towers Narragansett Visitors Center Ocean Rd; phone 401/783-7121
Web Site www.narragansettri.com/chamber

Part of the township of South Kingstown until 1901, Narragansett was named after the indigenous people who sold their land to the first area settlers. Once a center for shipbuilding, the town's center is still referred to as Narragansett Pier. Between 1878 and 1920, Narragansett was a well-known, elegant summer resort with many fine "cottages" and hotels. The most prominent landmark of that time was the Narragansett Casino. The casino's main entrance and covered promenade, "the Towers" on Ocean Road, is the only surviving element of that complex; the rest was lost in a devastating fire in 1900. Today, Narragansett's most important industries are commercial fishing and tourism. It is also the home of the University of Rhode Island's renowned Graduate School of Oceanography, located at the Bay Campus on South Ferry Road.

What to See and Do

Block Island Ferry. *304 Great Island Rd, Point Judith (02882). 5 miles S on Ocean Rd, 1 mile W on Sand Hill*

Cove Rd. Phone 401/783-4613. Automobile ferries to Block Island from Point Judith and New London, Connecticut. (Summer, daily)

Fishing. Wide variety of liveries at Narragansett Pier and the surrounding waterfront villages. Fishing tournaments are held throughout summer.

Point Judith. *1460 Ocean Rd, Narragansett (02882). 6 miles S of center on Ocean Ave, to Coast Guard Station and Lighthouse. Phone 401/789-0444.* Fine sea view.

South County Museum. *Strathmore St, Narragansett (02882). Phone 401/783-5400. www.southcounty museum.org.* Antiques representing rural life in 19th-century Rhode Island; costumes, vehicles, and nautical equipment. Farm and blacksmithing displays; toys. Country kitchen, general store, cobbler's shop. Also complete turn-of-the-century letterpress print shop. (May-Oct, Wed-Sun) **$$**

Swimming. Public beaches at **Narragansett Pier,** pavilion, fees; **Scarborough State Beach,** 1 1/2 miles S on Ocean Ave. **Salty Brine Beach,** Ocean Ave, protected by seawall, fishing; **Roger Wheeler State Beach,** west of Point Judith, playground, picnic tables, concession; parking (fee). Similar facilities at other beaches.

⭐ **The Towers.** *1/4 mile S on Hwy 1.* This Romanesque entrance arch flanked by rounded, conical-topped towers is a grandiose and sad reminder of McKim, Mead, and White's 19th-century casino, destroyed by fire in 1900, and Narragansett's own past as summer mecca for the rich and fashionable. Today, the Tourist and Information Center is located here.

Special Event

Mid-winter New England Surfing Championship. *Narragansett Town Beach, Narragansett. Phone 401/789-1954.* For information, contact the Eastern Surfing Association, 126 Sayles Ave, Pawtucket, 02860. Third Sat in Feb.

Restaurant

★ ★ **COAST GUARD HOUSE.** *40 Ocean Rd, Narragansett (02882). Phone 401/789-0700; fax 401/789-4399. www.thecoastguardhouse.com.* Former Coast Guard station (1888); ocean view. Seafood menu. Lunch, dinner, Sun brunch. Closed Dec 24-25. Bar. Children's menu. Outdoor seating. **$$**

Newport (E-7)

See also Block Island, Jamestown, Kingston, Narragansett, Portsmouth

Founded 1639
Population 28,227
Elevation 96 ft
Area Code 401
Zip 02840
Information Newport County Convention & Visitors Bureau, 23 America's Cup Ave; phone 401/849-8048 or toll-free 800/976-5122
Web Site www.gonewport.com

Few cities in the country have a history as rich and colorful as that of Newport, and fewer still retain as much evidence of their great past. The town was founded by a group of men and women who fled the religious intolerance of Massachusetts. They established the first school in Rhode Island the following year. Shipbuilding, for which Newport is still famous, began in 1646. The first Quakers to come to the New World settled in Newport in 1657. They were followed in 1658 by 15 Jewish families who came here from Holland. Newport produced the state's first newspaper, the *Rhode Island Gazette.*

Newport took an active part in the Revolution; local residents set fire to one British ship and continued to fire on others until the British landed 9,000 men and took possession. The city was occupied for two years; it was not until the French fleet entered the harbor that the British withdrew their forces.

Newport's fame as a summer resort began after the Civil War when many wealthy families, including the August Belmonts, Ward McAllister, Harry Lehr, Mrs. William Astor, and Mrs. Stuyvesant Fish, made the town a center for lavish and sometimes outrageous social events. Parties for dogs and one for a monkey were among the more bizarre occasions. Hostesses spent as much as $300,000 a season entertaining their guests. Although less flamboyant than it was before World War I, the summer colony is still socially prominent.

Today, Newport is famous for its boating and yachting, with boats for hire at many wharves. A bridge (toll) connects the city with Jamestown to the west.

Additional Visitor Information

The Newport County Convention and Visitor's Bureau maintains an information center at 23 America's Cup Avenue (daily). Tickets to most tourist attractions are offered for sale. An eight-minute video, maps, general tourist information, and group tours and convention information are available. For further information, phone 401/849-8048 or toll-free 800/976-5122.

The Preservation Society of Newport County publishes material on all Society properties. It sells combination tickets at all buildings under its administration and provides sightseeing information. Phone 401/847-1000.

What to See and Do

Artillery Company of Newport Military Museum. *23 Clarke St, Newport (02840). Phone 401/846-8488.* Military dress of many nations and periods. (June-Sept: Wed-Sat, also Sun afternoons; rest of year: by appointment) **$$**

Brick Market. *127 Thames St, Newport (02840). Long Wharf and Thames St. Phone 401/846-0813.* Home of the Newport Historical Society. Built by Peter Harrison, architect of Touro Synagogue, in 1762 as a market and granary. The restored building and surrounding area house boutiques and restaurants. (Daily)

CCInc Auto Tape Tours. *Phone 201/236-1666.* This 90-minute cassette offers a mile-by-mile self-guided tour of Newport. Available at Paper Lion, Long Wharf Mall, and Gateway Visitor Information Center. Includes tape and recorder rental. Tape also may be purchased directly from CCInc, PO Box 227, 2 Elbrook Dr, Allendale, NJ 07401. **$$$$**

⭐ **Cliff Walk.** *Begins at Memorial Blvd.* Scenic walk overlooking Atlantic Ocean adjoins many Newport "cottages." Designated a National Recreational Trail in 1975. **FREE**

Easton's Beach. *Memorial Blvd (Hwy 138), Newport.* Well-developed public beach has bathhouse, snack bar, antique carousel, picnic area, and designated surfing area. (Mid-June-Labor Day: daily; early June: weekends). **$$$**

Fort Adams State Park. *Harrison Ave and Ocean Dr, Newport (02840). Phone 401/847-2400.* Park surrounds Fort Adams, the second-largest bastioned fort in the United States between 1799 and 1945. The rambling 21-acre fort (guided tours only) was constructed of stone over a 33-year period. Beach swimming, fishing, boating (launch, ramps, hoist); soccer and rugby fields, picnicking. (Memorial Day-Labor Day, daily)

Friends Meeting House. *Farewell and Marlborough sts, Newport (02840). Phone 401/846-0813.* (1699) Site of New England Yearly Meeting of the Society of Friends until 1905; meeting house, expanded in 1729 and 1807, spans three centuries of architecture and construction. Guided tours through Newport Historical Society. (By appointment) **FREE**

⭐ **Historic Mansions and Houses.** Combination tickets to the Elms, the Breakers, Rosecliff, Marble House, Hunter House, Chateau-sur-Mer, Kingscote, and Green Animals topiary gardens (see PORTSMOUTH) are available at any of these houses.

Astors' Beechwood. *580 Bellevue Ave, Newport (02840). Phone 401/846-3772.* Italianate summer residence of Mrs. Caroline Astor, *the* Mrs. Astor. Theatrical tour of house includes actors portraying Mrs. Astor's servants and society guests. (Mid-May-mid-Dec: daily; rest of year: weekends only) **$$$**

Belcourt Castle. *657 Bellevue Ave, Newport (02840). 2 miles S on Hwy 138A. Phone 401/846-0669.* (1891) Designed by Richard Morris Hunt in French château style, this 62-room house was the residence of Oliver Hazard Perry Belmont and his wife, Alva Vanderbilt Belmont, who built Marble House when married to William K. Vanderbilt. Belcourt is unique for the inclusion of stables within its main structure; Belmont loved horses. Contains the largest collection of antiques and objets d'art in Newport; gold coronation coach; large collection of stained-glass windows. Tea served. Special events scheduled throughout year. (Daily; closed Jan, Thanksgiving, Dec 25) **$$$**

Breakers. *44 Ochre Point Ave, Newport (02840). Phone 401/847-1000.* (1895) Seventy-room, northern Italian palazzo designed by Richard Morris Hunt is the largest of all Newport cottages and is impressive by its sheer size; contains original furnishings. Children's playhouse cottage has scale-size kitchen, fireplace, playroom. Built for Mr. and Mrs. Cornelius Vanderbilt. (Apr-Oct, daily) **$$$$**

Chateau-sur-Mer. *474 Bellevue Ave, Newport (02840). Phone 401/847-1000.* (1852) Victorian mansion remodeled in 1872 by Richard Morris

Hunt has landscaped grounds with Chinese moon gate. Built for William S. Wetmore, who made his fortune in the China trade. (May-Oct: daily; rest of year: weekends) **$$$**

Edward King House. *Aquidneck Park, 35 King St, Newport (02840). Phone 401/846-7426.* (1846) Villa by Richard Upjohn is considered one of the finest Italianate houses in the country. Used as senior citizens' center. Tours. (Mon-Fri)

Elms. *367 Bellevue Ave, Newport (02840). Phone 401/847-1000.* (1901) Modeled after 18th-century Chateau d'Asnieres near Paris, this restored "cottage" from Newport's gilded age boasts elaborate interiors and formal, sunken gardens that are among the city's most beautiful. Built for Edward J. Berwind, Philadelphia coal magnate. (May-Oct: daily; Nov-Mar: Sat-Sun) **$$$**

Hammersmith Farm. *Ocean Dr, Newport. Phone 401/846-0420.* The unofficial summer White House during the Kennedy Administration. The farm dates to 1640; 28-room, shingle-style summer house was added in 1887 by John Auchincloss; descendant Hugh D. Auchincloss married Janet Lee Bouvier, mother of Jacqueline Bouvier Kennedy; rambling cottage was site of wedding reception of John and Jacqueline Kennedy. Gardens designed by Frederick Law Olmsted. Not open to the public; private residence.

Hunter House. *54 Washington St, Newport (02840). Phone 401/847-6543.* (1748) Outstanding example of colonial architecture features gambrel roof, 12-on-12 panel windows, broken pediment doorway. Furnished with pieces by Townsend and Goddard, famous 18th-century cabinet makers. (May-Oct: daily; Apr: weekends) **$$$**

Kingscote. *253 Bellevue Ave, Newport (02840). Phone 401/847-1000.* (1839) Gothic Revival cottage designed by Richard Upjohn; in 1881, McKim, Mead, and White added the "aesthetic" dining room, which features Tiffany-glass wall and fixtures. Outstanding Chinese export paintings and porcelains. Built for George Noble Jones of Savannah, Georgia, Kingscote is considered the nation's first true summer "cottage." (May-Sept: daily; Apr and Oct: weekends) **$$$**

Marble House. *596 Bellevue Ave, Newport (02840). Phone 401/847-1000.* (1892) French-style palace designed by Richard Morris Hunt is the most sumptuous of Newport cottages. Front gates, entrance, and central hall are modeled after Versailles. House is named for the many kinds of marble used on interior, which also features lavish use of gold and bronze. Original furnishings include dining room chairs made of gilded bronze. Built for Mrs. William K. Vanderbilt. On display are yachting memorabilia and restored Chinese teahouse where Mrs. Vanderbilt held suffragette meetings. (Apr-Oct: daily; rest of year: weekends) **$$$**

Rosecliff. *548 Bellevue Ave, Newport (02840). Phone 401/847-6543.* (1902) Designed by Stanford White after the Grand Trianon at Versailles, Rosecliff boasts the largest private ballroom in Newport and famous heart-shaped staircase. Built for socialite Mrs. Hermann Oelrichs. (Apr-Oct, daily) **$$$**

Samuel Whitehorne House. *416 Thames St, Newport (02840). Phone 401/849-7300.* (1811) Features exquisite furniture, silver, and pewter made by 18th-century artisans; Chinese porcelain, Irish crystal, and Pilgrim-era furniture; garden. (May-Oct: Mon, Fri-Sun and holidays; or by appointment, 24-hour advance notice is necessary) **$$**

Wanton-Lyman-Hazard House. *17 Broadway, Newport (02840). Phone 401/846-0813.* (Circa 1675) Oldest house in Newport, one of the finest Jacobean houses in New England, the site of the 1765 Stamp Act riot; restored; 18th-century garden; guided tours. (Mid-June-late Aug, Tues-Sat; closed holidays) **$**

Whitehall Museum House. *311 Berkeley Ave, Middletown (02842). 3 miles NE. Phone 401/846-3116.* (1729) Restored, hip-roofed country house built by Bishop George Berkeley, British philosopher and educator; garden. (July-Aug: daily; June: by appointment only) **$$**

⭐ **International Tennis Hall of Fame & Museum.** *194 Bellevue Ave, Newport (02840). Easton's Beach. Phone 401/849-3990.* World's largest tennis museum features interactive and dynamic exhibits detailing the history of the sport. Tennis equipment, fashions, trophies, and memorabilia on display in the famous Newport Casino, built in 1880 and designed by McKim, Mead, and White. (Daily; closed Thanksgiving, Dec 25) Grass courts available (May-Oct). **$$$**

Newport Art Museum and Art Association. *76 Bellevue Ave, Newport (02840). Opposite Touro Park. Phone 401/848-8200.* Changing exhibitions of contemporary and historical art are housed in 1864 mansion designed by Richard Morris Hunt in the "stick-style" and in 1920 Beaux Arts building. Lectures, performing arts events, evening musical picnics; tours. (Tues-Sun, afternoons; closed holidays) **$$**

Newport Historical Society Museum. *82 Touro St, Newport (02840). Adjacent to Seventh Day Baptist Meeting House. Phone 401/846-0813.* Colonial art; Newport silver and pewter, china, Early American glass, furniture. (Tues-Sat; closed holidays) Walking tours of colonial Newport (Mid-June-Sept, Fri-Sat; fee). **FREE**

Newport Jai alai. *150 Admiral Kalbfus Rd, Newport (02840). At base of Newport Bridge. Phone 401/849-5000; fax 401/846-0290. www.newportgrand.com.* Pari-mutuel betting. (Daily)

Newport Navigation. *Newport Harbor Hotel and Marina, 49 America's Cup Ave, Newport (02840). Phone 401/849-3575.* One-hour narrated cruise of Narragansett Bay and Newport Harbor aboard the *Spirit of Newport.* (May-Oct, daily) **$$$**

Old Colony and Newport Railroad. *Terminal, America's Cup Ave, Newport. Phone 401/624-6951.* Vintage one-hour train ride along a scenic route to Narragansett Bay. (July-early Sept: Sat-Sun; May-June and mid-Sept-Nov: Sun; also Christmas season) **$$$**

Oldport Marine Harbor Tours. *1 Sayers Wharf, Newport (02840). Phone 401/847-9109.* One-hour cruise of Newport Harbor aboard the *Amazing Grace.* (May-mid-Oct, daily) **$$$**

Old Stone Mill. *Touro Park, Mill St and Bellevue Ave, Newport.* Origin of circular stone tower supported by arches is unknown. Although excavations (1948-1949) have disproved it, some people still believe structure was built by Norsemen. **FREE**

Redwood Library and Athenaeum. *50 Bellevue Ave, Newport (02840). Phone 401/847-0292.* Designed by master colonial architect Peter Harrison; thought to be oldest library building (1750) in continuous use in United States; used by English officers as a club during Revolution. Collections include part of original selection of books and early portraits. (Mon-Sat; closed holidays) **FREE**

Seventh Day Baptist Meeting House. *82 Touro St, Newport (02840). Adjacent to Newport Historical Society. Phone 401/846-0813.* (1729) Historical church built by master builder Richard Munday.

Touro Synagogue National Historic Site. *72 Touro St, Newport (02840). Phone 401/847-4794. www.tourosynagogue.org.* The oldest synagogue (1763) in America, a Georgian masterpiece by the country's first architect, Peter Harrison, contains the oldest Torah in North America, examples of 18th-century crafts, and a letter from George Washington; worship services follow the Sephardic Orthodox ritual of the founders.

Trinity Church. *Queen Anne Sq, Newport (02840). Phone 401/846-0660.* (1726) First Anglican parish in state (1698), Trinity has been in continuous use since it was built. George Washington and philosopher George Berkeley were communicants. Interior features Tiffany windows and an organ tested by Handel before being shipped from London. Tours. **FREE**

Viking Boat Tour. *23 Americas Cup Ave, Newport (02840). The Viking Queen leaves Goat Island Marina off Washington St. Phone 401/847-6921.* One-hour narrated trip includes historic Newport, yachts, waterfront mansions; also available is extended trip with tour of Hammersmith Farm (see). (May-Oct)

Viking Bus Tour. *Gateway Tourist Center, 23 America's Cup Ave, Newport (02840). Phone 401/847-6921.* Two-, three-, and four-hour narrated trips cover 150 points of interest, including mansions and restored areas. (Schedules vary) Three-hour trips include admission to one mansion; four-hour trips include admission to two mansions. **$$$$**

White Horse Tavern. *42 Marlborough St, Newport (02840). Phone 401/849-3600.* (1673) Oldest operating tavern in the nation. (Daily)

Special Events

Christmas in Newport. *23 America's Cup Ave, Newport (02840). Phone 401/849-6454.* A month-long series of activities including concerts, tree lighting, and craft fairs. Dec.

JVC Jazz Festival. *Fort Adams State Park, Newport (02840). Phone 401/847-3700.* Mid-Aug.

Newport Irish Heritage Month. *Throughout town. Phone 401/845-9123.* A variety of Irish heritage and theme events; films, concerts, plays, arts and crafts, exhibits; food and drink; parade and road race. Mar.

Newport Music Festival. *163 Glen Farm Rd, Newport (02840). Phone 401/847-7090.* Chamber music held in Newport's fabled mansions. Three concerts daily. Mid-July.

Newport Winter Festival. *23 America's Cup Ave, Newport (02840). Phone 401/849-8048; toll-free 800/ 326-6030.* Ten days of food, festivities, music. More than 200 cultural and recreational events and activities. Late Jan-early Feb.

Limited-Service Hotels

★ ★ **COURTYARD BY MARRIOTT.** *9 Commerce Dr, Middletown (02842). Phone 401/849-8000; toll-free 888/686-5067; fax 401/849-8313. www.courtyard.com.* 148 rooms, 3 story. Check-out noon. Restaurant. Fitness room. Indoor pool, outdoor pool, whirlpool. Business center. **$**

★ ★ **MILL STREET INN.** *75 Mill St, Newport (02840). Phone 401/849-9500; toll-free 800/392-1316; fax 401/848-5131. www.millstreetinn.com.* The Mill Street Inn is a blend of Newport's past and present. Its location in a restored 19th-century mill (1890) evokes images of Newport's industrial history, but the exposed brick walls and wood beams in the hotel's interior are contemporary. 23 rooms, 3 story, all suites. Complimentary full breakfast. Check-in 3 pm, check-out 11 am. **$$**

Full-Service Hotels

★ ★ ★ **HOTEL VIKING.** *1 Bellevue Ave, Newport (02840). Phone 401/847-3300; fax 401/848-4864. www.hotelviking.com.* Situated on Bellevue Avenue within Newport's Historic Hill, Hotel Viking exudes New England elegance. The hotel sits atop the highest point in the city, offering guests an impressive vista of the town below. The lavish lodging spot is removed from the throngs of tourists, and guests can unwind, away from crowds, in the luxurious accommodations. 222 rooms, 5 story. Pets accepted. Check-in 3 pm, check-out 11 am. High-speed Internet access. Two restaurants, bar. Fitness room, spa. Indoor pool, whirlpool. Business center. **$$**

★ ★ ★ **HYATT REGENCY NEWPORT.** *1 Goat Island, Newport (02840). Phone 401/851-1234; toll-free 800/633-7313; fax 401/846-7210. www.newport.hyatt.com.* Located on private Goat Island, this hotel is less than a mile from downtown and offers spectacular views of Newport Harbor and Narragansett Bay. 267 rooms, 9 story. Check-in 4 pm, check-out 11 am. Restaurant, bar. Fitness room, spa. Indoor pool, outdoor pool. Tennis. Airport transportation available. Business center. **$$**

★ ★ ★ **MARRIOTT NEWPORT.** *25 America's Cup Ave, Newport (02840). Phone 401/849-1000; toll-free 800/458-3066; fax 401/849-3422. www.newportmarriott.com.* Located in the heart of the historic district, overlooking Newport Harbor, this comfortable hotel is close to recreational facilities. 319 rooms, 7 story. Check-in 4 pm, check-out 11 am. High-speed Internet access. Restaurant, bar. Fitness room. Indoor pool. Tennis. Business center. **$$$**

★ ★ ★ **NEWPORT HARBOR HOTEL AND MARINA.** *49 America's Cup Ave, Newport (02840). Phone 401/847-9000; toll-free 800/955-2558; fax 401/849-6380. www.nhhm.com.* This hotel is located in the beautiful harbor of Newport and is surrounded by yachts, restaurants, and shops. Activities abound, whether guests choose to read a book and listen to the waves, visit 19th-century mansions, charter a boat, or play tennis or squash. 133 rooms, 4 story. Check-in 4 pm, check-out 11 am. High-speed Internet access. Restaurant, bar. Indoor pool. **$$**

Full-Service Resort

★ ★ ★ **THE INN AT CASTLE HILL.** *590 Ocean Dr, Newport (02840). Phone 401/849-3800; toll-free 888/466-1355; fax 401/849-3838. www.castlehillinn.com.* This inn and lighthouse, perched at the tip of the peninsula, is an area landmark. 25 rooms, 3 story. Children over 12 years only. Complimentary full breakfast. Check-in 3 pm, check-out 11 am. Restaurant, bar. Beach. **$$**

Specialty Lodgings

The following lodging establishments are approved by Mobil Travel Guide, but due to their unique and individualized nature have not been given a traditional Mobil Star rating. Included in this listing you may find bed-and-breakfasts, limited-service inns, guest ranches, and other unique hotel properties.

1760 FRANCIS MALBONE HOUSE. *392 Thames St, Newport (02840). Phone 401/846-0392; toll-free 800/846-0392; fax 401/848-5956. www.malbone.com.* Located in the historic harborfront neighborhood, this beautifully restored colonial home was built in

1760. Wake to a gourmet breakfast, recharge with afternoon tea after a day of exploring, and then retreat to a Queen Anne-style room. 20 rooms, 3 story. Complimentary full breakfast. Check-in 2 pm, check-out 11 am. **$$$**

IVY LODGE. *12 Clay St, Newport (02840). Phone 401/849-6865; toll-free 800/834-6865; fax 401/849-2919. www.ivylodge.com.* This lodge is located in the heart of Newport's Mansion District. Activities include walking and touring local mansions, swimming at the nearby beach, and shopping. 8 rooms, 3 story. No children allowed. Complimentary full breakfast. Check-in 3 pm, check-out 11 am. **$$**

MELVILLE HOUSE. *39 Clarke St, Newport (02840). Phone 401/847-0640; fax 401/847-0956. www.melvillehouse.com.* Built around 1750, this historic colonial-style bed-and-breakfast is located in the center of the historic district on a street lit by gas. It is within walking distance to sailboats, antiques shops, and galleries, as well as the Tennis Hall of Fame and many famous mansions. 7 rooms, 2 story. Children over 12 years only. Complimentary full breakfast. Check-in 3 pm, check-out 11 am. **$$**

PILGRIM HOUSE. *123 Spring St, Newport (02840). Phone 401/846-0040; toll-free 800/525-8373; fax 401/848-0357. www.pilgrimhouseinn.com.* The Pilgrim House (circa 1810) features tastefully furnished rooms—complete with sleigh beds, comfy quilts, and period armoires and end tables—which allow guests to relax after a day of sightseeing in Newport's Historic Hill District. Guests can nibble on breakfast treats from the third-story deck, which looks out onto the harbor and the mouth of Narragansett Bay. 11 rooms, 3 story. Children over 12 years only. Check-in 3 pm, check-out 11 am. **$**

THE WILLOWS OF NEWPORT ROMANTIC INN AND GARDEN. *8 Willow St, Historic Point, Newport (02840). Phone 401/846-5486; fax 401/849-8215. www.thewillowsofnewport.com.* Located just three blocks from downtown and the waterfront, this bed-and-breakfast features a "secret garden" with birds, flowers, and a waterfall flowing into a heart-shaped fish pond. Room amenities include robes, fresh flowers, and breakfast in bed. Other room features are antique furnishings and canopy beds. 7 rooms, 3 story. Closed Feb-Mar. No children allowed.

Complimentary continental breakfast. Check-in 3 pm, check-out 11 am. **$$**
🅳

Restaurants

★ ★ ★ **CANFIELD HOUSE.** *5 Memorial Blvd, Newport (02840). Phone 401/847-0416; fax 401/847-5754. www.marshallslocuminn.com/canfield.htm.* Chef Sam Williamson adds a creative twist to continental cooking at this elegant restaurant in a former casino. High ceilings, dark wood paneling, crystal chandeliers, and other refined touches give an air of celebration to any meal here. American menu. Dinner. Closed Mon; Thanksgiving, Dec 25. Bar. **$$**

★ ★ **CHRISTIE'S OF NEWPORT.** *351 Thames St, Newport (02840). Phone 401/847-5400; fax 401/847-4970. www.christiesofnewport.com.* Seafood menu. Lunch, dinner. Closed Dec 25. Bar. Children's menu. Outdoor seating. **$$$**

★ ★ **LA FORGE CASINO.** *186 Bellevue Ave, Newport (02840). Phone 401/847-0418; fax 401/846-9170. www.laforgerestaurant.com.* Built in 1880. French, American menu. Lunch, dinner, Sun brunch. Closed Thanksgiving, Dec 25. Bar. Children's menu. Outdoor seating. **$$**

★ ★ ★ **LA PETITE AUBERGE.** *19 Charles St, Newport (02840). Phone 401/849-6669; fax 401/849-2519.* Located in the historic 1714 Stephen Decatur house, this classic restaurant has lace tablecloths, antique furnishings, and tableside service. French menu. Dinner. Closed Jan 1, Thanksgiving, Dec 25. Bar. Outdoor seating. **$$$**
🅳

★ ★ ★ **LE BISTRO.** *41 Bowen's Wharf, Newport (02840). Phone 401/849-7778. www.lebistronewport .com.* This casually elegant bistro on Bowmen's Wharf has been serving fresh, flavorful New England specialties and classic French food for decades. French menu. Lunch, dinner. Bar to 1 am. **$$$**
🅳

★ ★ **THE MOORING.** *Sayer's Wharf, Newport (02840). Phone 401/846-2260; fax 401/846-8950. www.mooringrestaurant.com.* Seafood menu. Lunch, dinner. Closed Thanksgiving, Dec 25. Bar. Children's menu. Outdoor seating. **$$**

★ **RHODE ISLAND QUAHOG COMPANY.** *250 Thames St, Newport (02840). Phone 401/848-2330.* Mexican décor in 1894 music hall. Barbecue, Southwestern menu. Lunch, dinner. Closed Dec 25. Bar. Children's menu. Outdoor seating. **$**
🅳

★ ★ ★ **WHITE HORSE TAVERN.** *26 Marlborough St, Newport (02840). Phone 401/849-3600; fax 401/849-7317. www.whitehorsetavern.com.* Located in a building that dates to 1687, this cozy restaurant has exposed hand-hewn beams, open fireplaces, and a romantic atmosphere. The menu is a blend of regional New England dishes. New England menu. Lunch, dinner, Sun brunch. Closed Jan 1, Dec 25. Bar. Jacket required (dinner). **$$$**
🅳

North Kingstown (D-6)

See also Kingston, Providence, Warwick

Settled 1641
Population 23,786
Elevation 51 ft
Area Code 401
Zip 02852
Information North Kingstown Chamber of Commerce, 8045 Post Rd; phone 401/295-5566
Web Site www.northkingstown.com

North Kingstown was originally part of a much larger area named for King Charles II. The settlement was divided in 1722, creating North Kingstown and South Kingstown, as well as other townships.

What to See and Do

Casey Farm. *Boston Neck Rd, Saunderstown. 3 1/2 miles S on Hwy 1A (past Jamestown Bridge approach). Phone 401/295-1030.* (Circa 1750) Once the site of Revolutionary War activities, this farm was built and continuously occupied by the Casey family for 200 years. Views of Narrangansett Bay and Conanicut Island. Restored and operating farm with animals, organic gardens; 18th-century farmhouse with family paintings, furnishings; outbuildings. (June-Oct: Tues, Thurs, and Sat afternoons) **$$**

Gilbert Stuart Birthplace. *815 Gilbert Stuart Rd, North Kingstown (02874). 5 miles S off Hwy 1A, NW of Saunderstown. Phone 401/294-3001.* Birthplace of portraitist Gilbert Stuart (1755-1828). Antique furnishings; snuffmill powered by wooden waterwheel; partially restored gristmill. Guided tours (half hour). (Apr-Oct: Mon-Thurs, Sat-Sun) **$$**

Main Street, Wickford Village. *North Kingstown. E from center.* There are 20 houses built before 1804; on side streets are 40 more.

Old Narragansett Church. *Church Ln, North Kingstown (02874). Phone 401/294-4357.* (1707) Episcopal. Tours. (Mid-June-Labor Day, Fri-Sun)

Smith's Castle. *55 Richard Smith Dr, North Kingstown (02852). 1 1/2 miles N on Hwy 1. Phone 401/294-3521.* (1678) Blockhouse (circa 1638), destroyed by fire in 1676 and rebuilt in 1678, is one of the oldest plantation houses in the country and the only known existing house where Roger Williams preached; 17th- and 18th-century furnishings; 18th-century garden. (June-Aug: Mon, Thurs-Sun, afternoons; May and Sept: Fri-Sun, afternoons; also by appointment) **$$**

Special Events

Festival of Lights. House tours, hayrides. First weekend in Dec.

Wickford Art Festival. *Wickford Village, 36 Beach St, North Kingstown (02852). Phone 401/294-6840.* Approximately 250 artists and artisans from around the country. Second weekend in July.

Pawtucket (D-6)

See also Providence

Settled 1671
Population 72,644
Elevation 73 ft
Area Code 401
Information Blackstone Valley Tourism Council, 175 Main St, 02860; phone 401/724-2200 or toll-free 800/454-2882 (outside RI)
Web Site www.tourblackstone.com

This highly concentrated industrial center, first settled by an ironworker who set up a forge at the falls on the Blackstone River, is recognized by historians as the birthplace of the Industrial Revolution in America. It was here in Pawtucket, named for the Native American phrase "falls of the water," that Samuel Slater founded the nation's first water-powered cotton mill. The town has since become one of the largest cities in the state and a major producer of textiles, machinery, wire, glass, and plastics.

What to See and Do

Slater Memorial Park. *Newport Ave and Hwy 1A, Pawtucket (02862). Phone 401/728-0500.* Within 200-acre park are sunken gardens; Rhode Island Watercolor Association Gallery (Tues-Sun); historical Daggett House (fee); carousel (July-Aug: daily; May-June and Sept-Oct: weekends only; fee). Tennis, playing fields, picnicking. **FREE**

Slater Mill National Historic Site. *67 Roosevelt Ave, Pawtucket (02862). Phone 401/725-8638.* Nation's first water-powered cotton mill (1793) was built by Samuel Slater; on-site are also Wilkinson Mill (1810) and Sylvanus Brown House (1758). Mill features restored water-power system, including raceways and 8-ton wheel; operating machines; spinning and weaving demonstrations; slide show. (June-Labor Day: Tues-Sun; Mar-May and after Labor Day-mid-Dec: weekends; closed holidays) **$$**

Special Events

Arts in the Park Performance Series. *Slater Memorial Park, Newport Ave and Hwy 1A, Pawtucket (02862).* Tues-Thurs and Sun, July-Aug.

Octoberfest Parade and Craft Fair. First weekend in Oct.

Pawtucket Red Sox. *McCoy Stadium, 1 Ben Mondor Way, Pawtucket (02860). Phone 401/724-7300. www.pawsox.com.* AAA farm team of the Boston Red Sox.

St. Patrick's Day Parade. First weekend in Mar.

Portsmouth (D-7)

See also Bristol, Little Compton, Newport

Founded 1638
Population 16,857
Elevation 122 ft
Area Code 401
Zip 02871
Information Newport County Convention and Visitor's Bureau, 23 America's Cup Ave, Newport 02840; phone 401/849-8048 or toll-free 800/976-5122
Web Site www.gonewport.com

Originally called Pocasset, Portsmouth was settled by a group led by John Clarke and William Coddington, who were sympathizers of Anne Hutchinson of Massachusetts. Soon after the town was first begun,

Anne Hutchinson herself, with a number of fellow religious exiles, settled here and forced Clarke and Coddington to relinquish control. Coddington then went south and founded Newport, with which Portsmouth temporarily united in 1640. Fishing, shipbuilding, and coal mining were the earliest sources of revenue. Today, Portsmouth is a summer resort area.

Portsmouth Fun Fact

Portsmouth is home to the oldest schoolhouse in the United States. It was built in 1716.

What to See and Do

Butterfly Zoo. *594 Aquidneck Ave, Middletown (02842). Phone 401/849-9519.* The only New England operation that breeds, raises, releases, and sells butterflies. View a wide variety of butterflies, including a preserved specimen of one believed to be the world's largest. (Tues-Sun) **$$**

⭐ **Green Animals.** *Portsmouth (02871). Off Hwy 114. Phone 401/847-6543.* Topiary gardens planted in 1880 with California privet, golden boxwood, and American boxwood sculpted into animal forms, geometric figures, and ornamental designs; also rose garden, formal flower beds. Children's toy collection in main house. (May-Oct, daily) **$$$**

Prescott Farm and Windmill. *2009 W Main Rd (Hwy 114), Middletown (02842). Phone 401/847-6230.* Restored buildings include an operating windmill (circa 1810), General Prescott's guard house, and a country store stocked with items grown on the farm. (Apr-Nov, daily) Tours (Mon-Fri). **$**

Restaurant

⭐ ⭐ **SEAFARE INN.** *3352 E Main Rd, Portsmouth (02871). Phone 401/683-0577; fax 401/683-2910. www.seafareinn.com.* Dine on chef George Karousos's creative cuisine in one of the seven dining rooms of this 1887 Victorian inn. White linen tablecloths, fine silver, and friendly service make for a most enjoyable evening. American menu. Dinner. Closed Sun-Mon; Jan 1, Dec 24-25. Jacket required. **$$**

Providence (D-6)

See also Bristol, Fall River, North Kingstown, Pawtucket, Warwick

Settled 1636
Population 160,728
Elevation 24 ft
Area Code 401
Information Providence Warwick Convention & Visitors Bureau, One W Exchange St, 02903; phone 401/274-1636 or toll-free 800/233-1636
Web Site www.pwcvb.com

Grateful that God's providence had led him to this spot, Roger Williams founded a town and named it accordingly. More than three-and-a-half centuries later, Providence is the capital and largest city of the State of Rhode Island and Providence Plantations, the state's official title.

In its early years, Providence was a farm center. Through the great maritime epoch of the late 18th century and first half of the 19th century, clipper ships sailed from Providence to China and the West Indies. During the 19th century, the city became a great industrial center, which today still produces widely known Providence jewelry and silverware. Providence is also an important port of entry.

Providence's long history has created a blend of old and new: modern hotels and office buildings share the streets with historic houses. Benefit Street, overlooking Providence's modern financial district, has one of the largest concentrations of colonial houses in America. The city's location along the upper Narragansett Bay and numerous cultural opportunities each provide many varied attractions for the visitor. In addition, Providence is the southern point of the Blackstone River Valley National Heritage Corridor, a 250,000-acre region that extends to Worcester, Massachusetts (see).

What to See and Do

Arcade. *Westminster St, Providence (02903). Phone 401/598-1049.* (1828) First indoor shopping mall with national landmark status. More than 35 specialty shops; restaurants.

Brown University. *45 Prospect St, Providence (02912). Phone 401/863-1000.* (1764) (7,500 students) Founded as Rhode Island College; school was renamed for Nicholas Brown, a major benefactor and son of a founder, in 1804. Brown is the seventh-oldest college in the United States and a member of the Ivy League. Pembroke College for Women (1891), named for the Cambridge, England *alma mater* of Roger Williams, merged with the men's college in 1971. Here are

Annmary Brown Memorial. *21 Brown St, Providence (02904). N of Charlesfield St. Phone 401/863-1994.* (1907) Paintings; Brown family memorabilia. (Mon-Fri afternoons, by appointment)

David Winton Bell Gallery. *List Art Center, 64 College St, Providence (02908). Phone 401/863-2932.* (1971) Historical and contemporary exhibitions. (Late Aug-May, Tues-Sun; closed holidays)

John Carter Brown Library. *George and Brown sts, Providence (02912). S side of campus green. Phone 401/863-2725.* (1904) Library houses exhibits, books, and maps relating to the exploration and settlement of America. (Mon-Sat; closed school vacations) **FREE**

John Hay Library. *20 Prospect St, Providence (02906). Across from Van Wickle gates. Phone 401/863-3723.* (1910) Named for Lincoln's secretary John Hay (Brown, 1858), library houses extensive special collections including Lincoln manuscripts, the Harris collection of American poetry and plays, and university archives. (Mon-Fri) **FREE**

Rockefeller Library. *10 Prospect St, Providence (02912). Phone 401/863-2167.* (1964) Named for John D. Rockefeller Jr. (Brown, 1897), library houses collections in the social sciences, humanities, and fine arts. (Daily; closed school vacations) **FREE**

University Hall. (1770) The original "college edifice" serves as the main administration building.

Wriston Quadrangle. *On Brown St near John Carter Brown Library.* (1952) Square named for president-emeritus Henry M. Wriston.

Cathedral of St. John. *271 N Main St, Providence (02903). At Church St. Phone 401/331-4622.* (1810) This Georgian structure with Gothic detail was built on the site of King's Church (1722). (Daily) **FREE**

First Baptist Church in America. *75 N Main St, Providence (02903). At Waterman St. Phone 401/454-3418.* Oldest Baptist congregation in America, established in 1638; the present building was erected

by Joseph Brown in 1775. Sun morning service. (Mon-Fri; closed holidays)

First Unitarian Church. *1 Benevolent St, Providence (02906). Phone 401/421-7970.* (1816) Organized as First Congregational Church in 1720, the church was designed by John Holden Greene and has the largest bell ever cast by Paul Revere. **FREE**

Governor Stephen Hopkins House. *15 Hopkins St, Providence (02903). Opposite courthouse. Phone 401/421-0694.* (1707) House of signer of Declaration of Independence and ten-time governor of Rhode Island; 18th-century garden; period furnishings. (Apr-Dec, Wed and Sat afternoons, also by appointment) Children only with adult. **DONATION**

John Brown House. *52 Power St, Providence (02906). At Benefit St. Phone 401/331-8575.* (1786) Georgian masterpiece by Joseph Brown, brother of John. George Washington was among the guests entertained in this house. Museum of 18th-century china, glass, Rhode Island antiques, and paintings; John Brown's chariot (1782), perhaps the oldest American-made vehicle extant. Guided tours. (Jan-Feb: Fri-Sun; rest of year: Tues-Sun; closed holidays) **$$$** The historical society also maintains a

Library. *121 Hope St, Providence (02906). At Power St.* One of the largest genealogical collections in New England; Rhode Island imprints dating to 1727; newspapers, manuscripts, photographs, films. (Tues-Sat) **FREE**

Johnson & Wales University. *8 Abbott Park Pl, Providence (02903). Phone 401/598-1000; toll-free 800/342-5598.* (1914) (8,000 students) Two- and four-year degree programs are offered in business, hospitality, food service, and technology. Tours available by appointment (free). On campus is the

Culinary Archives & Museum. *315 Harborside Blvd, Providence (02905). Trade Center at Harborside Campus. Phone 491/598-2805.* Dubbed the "Smithsonian of the food service industry," this museum contains more than 200,000 items related to the fields of culinary arts and hospitality collected and donated by Chicago's chef Louis Szathmary. Includes rare US presidential culinary autographs; tools of the trade from the third millennium BC; Egyptian, Roman, and Asian spoons more than 1,000 years old; gallery of chefs; original artwork; hotel and restaurant silver; and periodicals related to the field. Guided tours. (Tues-Sat by appointment; closed holidays) **$$**

Lincoln Woods State Park. *2 Manchester Print Works Rd, Providence (02865). 5 miles N via Hwy 146, S of Breakneck Hill Rd. Phone 401/723-7892.* More than 600 acres. Swimming, bathhouse, freshwater ponds, fishing, boating; hiking and bridle trails, ice skating, picnicking, concession. Fees for some activities.

Museum of Rhode Island History at Aldrich House. *110 Benevolent St, Providence (02906). Phone 401/331-8575.* Exhibits on Rhode Island's history. Headquarters for Rhode Island Historical Society. (Tues-Fri; closed Jan 1, Thanksgiving, Dec 25) **$$$**

North Burial Ground. *N Main St (Hwy1), Providence. 1 mile N of Market Sq.* Graves of Roger Williams and other settlers.

Old State House. *150 Benefit St, Providence (02903). Phone 401/222-2678.* Where the General Assembly of Rhode Island met between 1762 and 1900. Independence was proclaimed in the Old State House two months before the Declaration was signed in Philadelphia. (Mon-Fri; closed holidays) **FREE**

Providence Athenaeum Library. *251 Benefit St, Providence (02903). Phone 401/421-6970.* (1753) One of the oldest subscription libraries in the United States; housed in a Greek Revival building designed by William Strickland in 1836. Rare book room includes original Audubon elephant folios; small art collection. (Daily; summer, Mon-Fri; closed holidays, also two weeks in early Aug) Tours. **FREE**

Providence Children's Museum. *100 South St, Providence (02903). Phone 401/273-5437.* Many hands-on exhibits, including a time-travel adventure through Rhode Island's multicultural history, wet-and-wild exploration of water, and hands-on geometry lab. Traveling exhibits. Weekly programs. Gift shop. (Sept-June: Tues-Sun; rest of year: daily) **$$**

Providence Preservation Society. *21 Meeting St, Providence (02903). Phone 401/831-7440.* The Providence Preservation Society offers brochures and tour booklets for several historic Providence neighborhoods. (Mon-Fri) **$$**

Rhode Island School of Design. *2 College St, Providence (02903). Phone 401/454-6100.* (1877) (1,960 students) One of the country's leading art and design schools. Tours. On campus are

RISD Museum. *224 Benefit St, Providence (02903). Phone 401/454-6500.* Collections range from ancient to contemporary. (Tues-Sun; closed holidays) **$$**

Woods-Gerry Gallery. *62 Prospect St, Providence (02906). Phone 401/454-6141.* Mansion built 1860-1863 has special exhibits by students, faculty, and alumni. Call for schedule.

Rhode Island State House. *82 Smith St, Providence (02903). Phone 401/222-2357.* Capitol by McKim, Mead, and White was completed in 1901. Building contains a Gilbert Stuart full-length portrait of George Washington and the original parchment charter granted to Rhode Island by Charles II in 1663. *Independent Man* statue on dome. Guided tours. Building (Mon-Fri; closed holidays and second Mon in Aug). **FREE**

Roger Williams National Memorial. *282 N Main St, Providence (02903). Phone 401/521-7266.* This 4 1/2-acre park, at the site of the old town spring, commemorates founding of Providence and contributions made by Roger Williams to civil and religious liberty; slide presentation, exhibit. (Daily; closed Jan 1, Dec 25) **FREE**

Roger Williams Park. *1000 Elmwood Ave, Providence (02905). 3 miles S on Elmwood Ave. Phone 401/785-9450.* The park has 430 acres of woodlands, waterways, and winding drives. Japanese garden, Betsy Williams's cottage, and greenhouses. (Daily; closed Jan 1, Thanksgiving, Dec 25) **FREE** Also in the park are

Museum of Natural History and Cormack Planetarium. *1000 Elmwood Ave, Providence (02905). Phone 401/785-9450.* Anthropology, geology, astronomy, and biology displays; educational and performing arts programs. (Daily; closed Jan 1, Thanksgiving, Dec 25) **$**

Zoo. *1000 Elmwood Ave, Providence (02907). Phone 401/785-3510.* Children's nature center, tropical building, African plains exhibit; Marco Polo exhibits; over 600 animals. Educational programs; tours. (Daily; closed Dec 25) **$$$**

Special Events

Spring Festival of Historic Houses. *21 Meeting St, Providence (02903). Phone 401/831-7440.* Sponsored by the Providence Preservation Society. Tours of selected private houses and gardens. Second weekend in June.

WaterFire. *Waterplace Park, 101 Regent Ave, Providence (02908). Phone 401/272-3111.* Floating bonfires in the Providence River accompanied by music. Call for schedule.

Limited-Service Hotels

★ ★ **COURTYARD BY MARRIOTT PROVIDENCE DOWNTOWN.** *32 Exchange Terr, Providence (02903). Phone 401/272-1191; toll-free 800/ 321-2211; fax 401/272-1416. www.courtyard.com.* 216 rooms. Check-in 3 pm, check-out noon. Fitness room. Indoor pool, whirlpool. **$**

★ ★ **JOHNSON & WALES INN.** *213 Taunton Ave, Seekonk (02771). Phone 508/336-8700; toll-free 800/232-1772; fax 508/336-3414. www.jwu.edu/jwinn.* 86 rooms, 5 story. Check-out 11 am. Restaurant, bar. Business center. **$**

★ ★ **RADISSON HOTEL PROVIDENCE HARBOR.** *220 India St, Providence (02903). Phone 401/272-5577; toll-free 800/333-3333; fax 401/272-0251. www.radisson.com.* 136 rooms, 6 story. Check-in 3 pm, check-out 11 am. Restaurant, bar. Fitness room. Whirlpool. Airport transportation available. Business center. Overlooks the harbor. **$$**

Full-Service Hotels

★ ★ ★ **MARRIOTT PROVIDENCE.** *1 Orms St, Providence (02904). Phone 401/272-2400; toll-free 800/937-7768; fax 401/273-2686. www.marriott.com.* This Marriott's downtown location allows guests to be just steps from Newport shopping, entertainment, and a charming neighborhood of Colonial homes. The rooms' rich fabrics and the pool area's sleek design give the hotel a cosmopolitan vibe. 346 rooms, 6 story. Check-in 3 pm, check-out noon. High-speed Internet access. Restaurant, bar. Fitness room. Indoor pool, outdoor pool. Airport transportation available. Business center. **$$**

★ ★ ★ **THE WESTIN PROVIDENCE.** *1 W Exchange St, Providence (02903). Phone 401/598-8000; toll-free 800/301-1111; fax 401/598-8200. www.starwood.com.* At the convention center and adjacent to the Providence Place Mall, this hotel has business-friendly guest rooms and an indoor rooftop pool. 364 rooms, 25 story. Pets accepted, some restrictions; fee. Check-in 3 pm, check-out noon. High-speed Internet access. Restaurant, bar. Fitness room. Indoor pool, whirlpool. Business center. **$$**

Specialty Lodgings

The following lodging establishments are approved by Mobil Travel Guide, but due to their unique and individualized nature have not been given a traditional Mobil Star rating. Included in this listing you may find bed-and-breakfasts, limited-service inns, guest ranches, and other unique hotel properties.

CHRISTOPHER DODGE HOUSE. *11 W Park St, Providence (02908). Phone 401/351-6111; fax 401/351-4261. www.providence-hotel.com.* 5 rooms. Complimentary full breakfast. Check-in 3 pm, check-out 11 am. **$$**

HISTORIC JACOB INN. *120 Jacob St, Providence (02940). Phone 508/336-9165; toll-free 888/336-9165; fax 508/336-0951.* 10 rooms, all suites. Complimentary full breakfast. Check-in 3 pm, check-out 11 am. Outdoor pool. Tennis. **$$$**

OLD COURT BED & BREAKFAST. *144 Benefit St, Providence (02903). Phone 401/751-2002; fax 401/272-4830. www.oldcourt.com.* Built in 1863 as a rectory, this bed-and-breakfast overlooks the Old State House and features antique furnishings, chandeliers, and memorabilia from the 19th century. 10 rooms, 3 story. Children over 12 years only. Complimentary full breakfast. Check-in 4 pm, check-out 11 am. **$**

Restaurants

★ ★ **ADESSO.** *161 Cushing St, Providence (02906). Phone 401/521-0770; fax 401/521-1777.* Italian menu. Dinner. Closed July 4, Thanksgiving, Dec 25. Bar. **$$**

★ **THE CACTUS GRILLE.** *800 Allens Ave, Providence (02905). Phone 401/941-0004; fax 401/941-0175.* Mexican menu. Lunch, dinner. Closed Dec 25. Bar. Children's menu. Casual attire. **$$**

★ ★ **HEMENWAY'S SEAFOOD GRILL.** *1 Providence-Washington Plz, Providence (02903). Phone 401/351-8570; fax 401/351-8594.* Seafood menu. Lunch, dinner. Closed Thanksgiving, Dec 25. Bar. Children's menu. Valet parking. Outdoor seating. **$$$**

★ ★ **INDIA.** *123 Dorrance St, Providence (02903). Phone 401/278-2000; fax 401/778-7001.* Indian menu. Lunch, dinner. Bar. Casual attire. **$$**

★ ★ ★ **MILL'S TAVERN.** *101 N Main St, Providence (02903). Phone 401/272-3331.* Mill's Tavern has a knack for improving on the classics. From its smart design and young, energetic vibe to its appealing menu, this winning restaurant housed in a former mill turns tradition on its head. The hurricane-lamp chandeliers, exposed beams, and wharf mosaic are a nod to the taverns of the past, while the marble-topped bar and open kitchen are decidedly modern. The menu echoes the classic-contemporary sentiment with a wide variety of creatively prepared seasonal dishes, many utilizing the dream kitchen's wood-burning oven, wood grill, and rotisserie. Part comfort food, part nouveau cuisine, this menu dazzles the palate with its whimsical pairings and simple yet sophisticated preparations. A raw bar rounds out the offerings, while those in the know save room for dessert. The warm, knowledgeable staff is the perfect complement to this casually elegant restaurant, providing professional and thorough service without being stuffy or intrusive. American menu. Dinner. Business casual attire. Reservations recommended. Valet parking. **$$$**

★ ★ **PANE E VINO.** *365 Atwells Ave, Providence (02903). Phone 401/223-2230; fax 401/223-4322.* Italian menu. Dinner. Closed Sat; holidays. Bar. Casual attire. Outdoor seating. **$$**

★ ★ ★ **POT AU FEU.** *44 Custom House St, Providence (02903). Phone 401/273-8953; fax 401/273-8963.* This restaurant features a casual, bistro-style dining downstairs and a more formal upstairs. French menu. Lunch, dinner. Closed Sun; holidays. Bar. **$$$**

Warwick (D-6)

See also East Greenwich, North Kingstown, Providence

Population 85,427
Elevation 64 ft
Area Code 401
Information Department of Economic Development, City Hall, 3275 Post Rd, 02886; phone 401/738-2000 or toll-free 800/492-7942
Web Site www.warwickri.com

Warwick, the second-largest city in Rhode Island, is the location of T. F. Green Airport, the state's largest commercial airport. With 39 miles of coastline on Narragansett Bay, the city has more than 15 marinas. Warwick is a major retail and industrial center. The geographic diversity of Warwick promoted a decentralized pattern of settlement, which gave rise to a number of small villages including Pawtuxet, Cowesett, and Conanicut.

What to See and Do

Cadillac Shopping Outlet. *1689 Post Rd, Warwick (02888). Phone 401/738-5145.* Discounted brand-name clothing for men, women, and children. (Daily)

Goddard Memorial State Park. *345 Ives Rd, Warwick (02818). E side of Greenwich Cove, E of town via Forge and Ives rds. Phone 401/884-2010.* Approximately 490 acres with swimming at Greenwich Bay Beach (bathhouse), fishing, boating; bridle trails, nine-hole golf (fee), ice skating, picnicking, concessions, playing fields, and fireplaces (fee). **$**

Historic Pontiac Mills. *334 Knight St, Warwick (02886). Phone 401/737-2700.* Portions of an 1863 mill complex have been restored and now house approximately 80 small businesses, artisans, and shops. (Daily). Also open-air market (Sat-Sun).

Walking Tour of Historic Apponaug Village. *Post Rd and Greenwich Ave, Warwick (02886). Phone toll-free 800/492-7942.* More than 30 structures of historic and/or architectural interest are noted on walking tour brochure available through the Department of Economic Development, Warwick City Hall, 3275 Post Rd, Apponaug 02886. **FREE**

Warwick Mall. *400 Bald Hill Rd, Warwick (02886). Phone 401/739-7500.* Renovated and expanded; largest mall in the state. More than 90 specialty shops and four department stores. Outdoor patio, video wall, topiary gardens. Weekly special events. (Daily)

Special Events

Gaspee Days. *Phone 401/781-1772; toll-free 800/492-7942.* Celebration of the capture and burning of British revenue schooner *Gaspee* by Rhode Island patriots; arts and crafts, concert, footraces, battle reenactment, fife and drum corps muster, parade, contests. May-June.

Warwick Heritage Festival. *Warwick City Park, Warwick. Phone toll-free 800/492-7942.* Revisit history with this weekend reenactment. Nov, Veterans Day weekend.

Limited-Service Hotel

★ ★ **RADISSON AIRPORT HOTEL WARWICK / PROVIDENCE.** *2081 Post Rd,*

Warwick (02886). Phone 401/739-3000; fax 401/732-9309. www.radisson.com. 111 rooms. Complimentary continental breakfast. Check-in 3 pm, check-out noon. Restaurant, bar. Airport transportation available. **$**

✈

Full-Service Hotel

★ ★ ★ **CROWNE PLAZA.** 801 Greenwich Ave, Warwick (02886). Phone 401/732-6000; toll-free 800/227-6963; fax 401/732-4839. www.crowneplazari.com. Located just 8 miles from downtown and 3 miles from the airport, this is a suburban hotel with contemporary décor. 266 rooms, 6 story. Pets accepted, some restrictions. Check-in 3 pm, check-out 11 am. High-speed Internet access. Restaurant, bar. Fitness room. Indoor pool, whirlpool. Airport transportation available. Business center. **$$**

🛎 ✈ 🛏 🏃

Westerly (E-5)

See also Block Island, Charlestown

Founded 1669
Population 21,605
Elevation 50 ft
Area Code 401
Zip 02891
Information Westerly-Pawcatuck Area Chamber of Commerce, 1 Chamber Way; phone 401/596-7761 or toll-free 800/732-7636; or the South County Tourism Council, Stedman Government Center, 4808 Tower Hill Rd, Wakefield 02879; phone 401/789-4422 or toll-free 800/548-4662
Web Site www.westerlychamber.org

Westerly, one of the oldest towns in the state, was at one time known for its nearby granite quarries. Today, local industries include textiles, the manufacture of fishing line, and tourism.

What to See and Do

Babcock-Smith House. 124 Granite St, Westerly (02891). Phone 401/596-4424. (Circa 1732) This two-story, gambrel-roofed Georgian mansion was residence of Dr. Joshua Babcock, Westerly's first physician and friend of Benjamin Franklin. Later it was home to Orlando Smith, who discovered granite on the grounds. Furniture collection covers 200 years; toys date to 1890s; colonial garden and culinary herb garden. (July-mid-Sept: Wed, Sun; May-June and mid-Sept-mid-Oct: Sun only) **$**

Misquamicut State Beach. 257 Atlantic Ave, Westerly (02891). 5 miles S off Hwy 1A. Phone 401/596-9097. Swimming, bathhouse (fee), fishing nearby; picnicking, concession. (Mid-June-early Sept, daily) Parking fee. **$$$**

Watch Hill. 6 miles S on Beach St, via Avondale. Historical community of handsome summer houses, many dating from the 1870s; picturesque sea views. Located here are

Flying Horse Carousel. Original amusement ride built in 1867.

Lighthouse. (1856) Granite lighthouse built to replace wooden one built in 1807; lit by oil lamp until 1933, when replaced by electric. Museum exhibit (Tues and Thurs, afternoons).

Limited-Service Hotels

★ **BREEZEWAY RESORT.** 70 Winnapaug Rd, Misquamicut Beach (02891). Phone 401/348-8953; toll-free 800/462-8872; fax 401/596-3207. www.breezewayresort.com. 50 rooms, 2 story. Complimentary continental breakfast. Check-out 11 am. Bar. Outdoor pool. **$**

🅿 🛏

★ ★ **SHELTER HARBOR INN.** 10 Wagner Rd, Westerly (02891). Phone 401/322-8883; toll-free 800/468-8883; fax 401/322-7907. www.shelterharborinn.com. This relaxing country inn is off the beaten path—but well worth the detour! The main house—a sprawling, early 1800s farmhouse—manages to be cozy and inviting. Guests can curl up in front of the fireplace with a book from the inn's library or explore Shelter Harbor's grounds. 24 rooms, 2 story. Complimentary full breakfast. Check-in 3 pm, check-out 11 am. Restaurant, bar. Tennis. **$**

🎾

★ **WINNAPAUG INN.** 169 Shore Rd, Westerly (02891). Phone 401/348-8350; toll-free 800/288-9906; fax 401/596-8654. www.winnapauginn.com. Winnapaug Pond is adjacent. 49 rooms. Complimentary continental breakfast. Check-out 11 am. **$**

🛏

Specialty Lodging

The following lodging establishment is approved
by Mobil Travel Guide, but due to its unique and
individualized nature has not been given a traditional
Mobil Star rating. Included in this listing you may
find bed-and-breakfasts, limited-service inns, guest
ranches, and other unique hotel properties.

VILLA BED & BREAKFAST. *190 Shore Rd,
Westerly (02891). Phone 401/596-1054; toll-free 800/
722-9240; fax 401/596-6268. www.thevillaatwesterly.
com.* This bed-and-breakfast is a romantic hideaway
with flower gardens, Italian porticos, and verandas.
The complimentary breakfast can be enjoyed in the
dining area or by the pool. Close by is Misquamicut
Beach, the Foxwoods Casino, the Mystic Aquarium
and the ferry to Block Island. 6 rooms, 3 story.
Complimentary continental breakfast. Check-in 3-6
pm, check-out 11 am. Outdoor pool, whirlpool. **$**
🏊

Restaurant

★ ★ **VILLA TROMBINO.** *112 Ashway Rd, Westerly
(02891). Phone 401/596-3444.* Italian, American menu.
Dinner. Closed Mon; Thanksgiving, Dec 24-25. Bar.
Children's menu. **$$**

Vermont

Vermont was the last New England state to be settled. The earliest permanent settlement date is believed to be 1724. Ethan Allen and his Green Mountain Boys made Vermont famous when they took Fort Ticonderoga from the British in 1775. Claimed by both New York and New Hampshire, Vermont framed a constitution in 1777. It was the first state to prohibit slavery and the first to provide universal male suffrage, regardless of property or income. For 14 years, Vermont was an independent republic, running its own postal service, coining its own money, naturalizing citizens of other states and countries, and negotiating with other states and nations. Vermont became the 14th state in 1791.

Although Vermont is usually thought of as a farm state, more than 17 percent of the labor force is in manufacturing. Machinery, food, wood, plastic, rubber, paper, electrical, and electronic products are made here. Dairy products lead the farm list, with sheep, maple sugar and syrup, and apples and potatoes following. Vermont leads the nation in its yield of marble and granite; limestone, slate, and talc are also quarried and mined.

Tall steeples dominate the towns, forests, mountains, and countryside where one can walk the 260-mile Long Trail along the Green Mountain crests. Vermont has one of the highest concentrations of alpine ski areas and cross-country ski touring centers in the nation. Fishing and hunting are excellent; resorts range from rustic to elegant.

When to Go/Climate

Vermont enjoys four distinct seasons. Comfortable summers are followed by brilliantly colored falls and typically cold New England winters. Heavy

Population: 562,758
Area: 9,273 square miles
Elevation: 95-4,393 feet
Peak: Mount Mansfield (Lamoille County)
Entered Union: March 4, 1791 (14th state)
Capital: Montpelier
Motto: Freedom and Unity
Nickname: Green Mountain State
Flower: Red Clover
Bird: Hermit Thrush
Tree: Sugar Maple
Fair: Early September in Rutland
Time Zone: Eastern
Web Site: www.travel-vermont.com
Fun Facts:
- Vermont produces the largest amount of maple syrup in the United States.
- The first Ben & Jerry's Ice Cream store opened in Burlington in 1978.

snowfall makes for good skiing in winter, while spring thaws bring on the inevitable muddy months. Summer and fall are popular times to visit.

AVERAGE HIGH/LOW TEMPERATURES (° F)

Burlington

Jan 25/8	**May** 67/45	**Sept** 69/49
Feb 28/9	**June** 76/55	**Oct** 57/39
Mar 39/22	**July** 81/60	**Nov** 44/30
Apr 54/34	**Aug** 78/58	**Dec** 30/16

Parks and Recreation

Water-related activities, hiking, riding, various other sports, picnicking, camping, and visitor centers are available in many of Vermont's state parks. Day use areas (Memorial Day weekend-Labor Day, daily): over age 14, $2.50/person; ages 4-13, $2; under 4 free. Boat rentals, $5/hour. Paddleboats, $5/half hour. Canoe rentals, $5/hour.

Calendar Highlights

FEBRUARY

Winter Carnival *(Brattleboro)*. Week-long festival includes ski races, parade, ice show, sleigh rides, road races.

APRIL

Maple Sugar Festival *(St. Albans)*. Phone 802/524-5800 or 802/524-2444. A number of producers welcome visitors who join sugarhouse parties for sugar-on-snow, sour pickles, and raised doughnuts. Continuing events; arts and crafts; antiques; wood-chopping contests.

JUNE

Mountain Bike World Cup Race Mt. Snow. *(West Dover)*. Phone toll-free 800/245-7669. More than 1,500 cyclists from throughout the world compete in downhill, dual slalom, and circuit racing events.

JULY

Festival on the Green *(Middlebury)*. Phone 802/388-0216. Classical, modern, and traditional dance; chamber and folk music; theater and comedy presentations.

SEPTEMBER

Vermont State Fair *(Rutland)*. Phone 802/775-5200. Exhibits of arts and crafts, flowers, produce, home arts, pets, animals, maple sugaring. Entertainment, agricultural displays, hot air ballooning. Daily special events.

Camping: $15/night, lean-to $22 at areas with swimming beaches; $13/night, lean-to $20 at areas without swimming beaches. Reservations of at least 2 days (3 days mid-May-Oct) and maximum of 21 days may be made by contacting park or Department of Forests, Parks, and Recreation, 103 S Main St, Waterbury 05671-0603, with full payment. Pets are allowed on leash only. Phone 802/241-3655.

FISHING AND HUNTING

Nonresident fishing license: season $41; 7-day $30; 3-day $20; 1-day $15. Nonresident hunting license: $85; $25 for those under 18 years. Nonresident small game license: $40. In order for a nonresident to obtain a hunting license, he/she must prove that he/she holds a license in his/her home state. Bow and arrow license (hunting or combination license also required): nonresident $25. Combination hunting and fishing license: nonresident $110. For *Vermont Guide to Fishing*, contact the Fish and Wildlife Department, 103 S Main St, Waterbury 05671-0501. Phone 802/241-3700.

Driving Information

All vehicle occupants must be secured in federally approved safety belts. Children ages 1-4 must be secured in approved child safety devices. When the number of occupants exceeds the number of safety belts, children take priority and must be secured. Children under age 1 must use approved safety seats. Phone 802/828-2665.

INTERSTATE HIGHWAY SYSTEM

The following alphabetical listing of Vermont towns in this book shows that these cities are within 10 miles of the indicated Interstate highways. Check a highway map for the nearest exit.

Highway Number	Cities/Towns within 10 Miles
Interstate 89	Barre, Burlington, Montpelier, St. Albans, Swanton, Waterbury, White River Junction.
Interstate 91	Bellows Falls, Brattleboro, Fairlee, Grafton, Lyndonville, Newfane, Newport, St. Johnsbury, Springfield, White River Junction, Windsor, Woodstock.

Additional Visitor Information

Vermont is very well documented. The Vermont Official Transportation Map, as well as numerous descriptive folders, are distributed free by the Vermont Department of Tourism and Marketing,

THE BEST OF VERMONT

From Montpelier, take Interstate 89 to exit 10, then head up Highway 100 to the Ben & Jerry's ice cream factory. This is the state's top tourist attraction—and for good reason. The 30-minute factory tour begins with a short movie about the company's founders, Ben Cohen and Jerry Greenfield. From there, tour groups head to the production facilities, where the ice cream production process is explained. The last stop on the tour—and the most popular—is the FlavoRoom, where visitors can enjoy delicious samples of Ben & Jerry's most popular flavors. Don't forget to stop in at the gift shop for the perfect Vermont souvenirs!

Continue on Highway 100 to the village of Stowe. Depending on the season, you can spend your time here biking, hiking, or cross-country skiing. Take the gondola to the top of Mount Mansfield (Vermont's highest peak at 4,393 feet) for dramatic views of the area. Enjoy a walk along the riverside Stowe Recreation Path, or simply relax at one of the many inns, shops, and restaurants. From Stowe, continue on to Smugglers Notch (Hwy 108), a high, scenic pass that runs from Stowe (open summer only), through the scenic Mount Mansfield State Forest, and on to the village of Jeffersonville. Most tourists return by the same route, but there is an interesting loop return through Johnson and Morristown. Once back at Interstate 89, continue on to Burlington, Vermont's largest city and a departure point for ferries. Visitors will enjoy biking or in-line skating along Lake Champlain, shopping, or stopping at the restaurants along the Church Street Marketplace. Be sure to take time for a guided tour of Ethan Allen Homestead, one of the top attractions in Vermont. South of Burlington on Highway 7 is the town of Shelburne, also a departure point for ferries. The big draw here is the Shelburne Museum, which is located on 45 acres and includes such items as a working carousel; a 5,000-piece hand-carved miniature traveling circus; a lighthouse; an authentic country store; farm equipment; and *Ticonderoga*, a 200-foot sidewheel steamboat. From the eclectic and bizarre to the historic and educational, the Shelburne Museum is bound to have something of interest for everyone in your group—don't miss it! You'll also want to make time for trips to Shelburne Farms and the Vermont Teddy Bear Company. **(Approximately 436 miles round-trip from Boston)**

6 Baldwin St, Drawer 33, Montpelier 05633-1301; phone 802/828-3237 or toll-free 800/837-6668. Visitor centers are located off Interstate 89 in Guilford (daily); off Interstate 89 in Highgate Springs (daily); off Highway 4 in Fair Haven (daily); and off Interstate 93 in Waterford (daily).

The Vermont Chamber of Commerce, PO Box 37, Montpelier 05601, distributes *Vermont Traveler's Guidebook* of accommodations, restaurants, and attractions; phone 802/223-3443. *Vermont Life*, one of the nation's best known and respected regional quarterlies, presents photo essays on various aspects of life in the state; available by writing *Vermont Life*, 6 Baldwin St, Montpelier 05602. Another excellent source of information on the state is *Vermont: An Explorer's Guide* (The Countryman Press, Woodstock, VT, 1994) by Christina Tree and Peter Jennison; a comprehensive book covering attractions, events, recreational facilities, accommodations, restaurants, and places to shop. It is available in bookstores.

Various books on Vermont are also available from the Vermont Historical Society, Vermont Museum, Pavilion Building, 109 State St, Montpelier 05609.

For information regarding Vermont's Long Trail, along with other hiking trails in the state, contact the Green Mountain Club, 4711 Waterbury Stowe Rd, Waterbury Center 05677; phone 802/244-7037. The Department of Agriculture, 116 State St, Drawer 20, Montpelier 05602-2901, has information on farms offering vacations and maple sugarhouses open to visitors.

Several Vermont-based companies offer inn-to-inn bicycle tours from May through October (months vary). Tours range in length from two days to several weeks; most are designed to accommodate all levels of cyclists. Bicycling enthusiasts can obtain a brochure entitled *Bicycle Touring in Vermont* from the Vermont Department of Tourism and Marketing, 6 Baldwin St, Drawer 33, Montpelier 05633-1301; phone 802/828-3237.

Arlington (E-1)

See also Bennington, Dorset, Manchester and Manchester Center

Settled 1763
Population 2,299
Elevation 690 ft
Area Code 802
Zip 05250

What to See and Do

Battenkill River. *103 S Main St, Arlington (05250). Phone 802/241-3700.* Trout and fly fishing on the Battenkill River.

Candle Mill Village. *316 Old Mill Rd, East Arlington (05252). 1 1/2 miles E on Old Mill Rd. Phone 802/375-6068.* Three buildings, including a gristmill built in 1764 by Remember Baker of the Green Mountain Boys; many music boxes, candles, cookbook and teddy bear displays. (Daily; closed holidays) **FREE**

Norman Rockwell Exhibition. *3772 Hwy 7A, Arlington (05250). Phone 802/375-6423.* Hundreds of magazine covers, illustrations, advertisements, calendars, and other printed works are displayed in an historic 1875 church in the illustrator's hometown. Hosts are Rockwell's former models. Twenty-minute film. (Daily; closed Easter, Thanksgiving, Dec 25) **$**

Limited-Service Hotel

★ **CANDLELIGHT MOTEL.** *4893 Hwy 7A, Arlington (05200). Phone 802/375-6647; toll-free 800/348-5294; fax 802/375-2566. www.candlelightmotel .com.* 17 rooms. Complimentary continental breakfast. Check-in 1 pm, check-out 11 am. Outdoor pool. **$**
🅟 ⛱

Full-Service Inns

★ ★ ★ **ARLINGTON INN.** *3904 Hwy 7A, Arlington (05250). Phone 802/375-6532; toll-free 800/443-9442; fax 802/375-6534. www.arlingtoninn.com.* This dramatic Greek Revival-style mansion, with columns lining the front porch and entrance, was built in 1848 and has been operating as an inn since 1888. It's listed on the National Register of Historic Places. Spread throughout the main house and several converted outbuildings, the varied guest rooms feature impressive antiques; some have double-sided

fireplaces and Jacuzzi tubs. If you'd like a more historical room, opt for the main house; the carriage house and parsonage have been renovated with modern architectural details, such as cathedral ceilings and skylights. The 3-acre grounds include a walking path, gazebo, and small stone fountain with waterfall. 18 rooms, 2 story. Complimentary full breakfast. Check-in 3 pm, check-out 11 am. Restaurant, bar. **$$**

★ ★ ★ **ARLINGTON'S WEST MOUNTAIN INN.** *River Rd and Hwy 313, Arlington (05250). Phone 802/375-6516; fax 802/375-6553. www.westmountaininn.com.* This century-old, seven-gabled inn, located on a mountainside, is furnished with a mix of antiques and country classics. Surrounded by woodland acres with wildflowers, a bird sanctuary and llamas, this hideaway provides guests with many activities. 18 rooms, 3 story. Check-in 2 pm, check-out noon. Restaurant (public by reservation), bar. **$$**

Specialty Lodging

The following lodging establishment is approved by Mobil Travel Guide, but due to its unique and individualized nature has not been given a traditional Mobil Star rating. Included in this listing you may find bed-and-breakfasts, limited-service inns, guest ranches, and other unique hotel properties.

HILL FARM INN. *458 Hill Farm Rd, Arlington (05250). Phone 802/375-2269; toll-free 800/882-2545; fax 802/375-9918. www.hillfarminn.com.* North of Arlington's town center, Hill Farm Road takes visitors to a rural spot that feels very much like the farm it once was. On 50 acres fronting the Battenkill River, the inn consists of a historic guest house (1790) and a classic white farmhouse (1830), along with several outlying cottages housing family suites and efficiencies. Sheep, goats, and chickens wander about outside to amuse kids and adults alike. Inside, the guest rooms have simple country charm; no phones are there to distract from the peaceful feeling, although some rooms do have televisions. 15 rooms, 2 story. Complimentary full breakfast. Check-in 3 pm, check-out 11 am. **$**
🅟

Restaurant

★ ★ ★ **ARLINGTON INN.** *3904 Hwy 7A, Arlington (05250). Phone 802/375-6532; toll-free 800/443-9442; fax 802/375-6534. www.arlingtoninn.com.* This landmark historic inn was built in 1848 as a private home and has been in operation since 1888. Guests enjoy the romance and elegance of the Victorian atmosphere and can dine fireside with a candlelight dinner for two. Seafood menu. Dinner. Closed Mon; Dec 24-25. Bar. Children's menu. **$$$**

Barre (C-2)

See also Montpelier, Waitsfield, Warren, Waterbury

Settled 1788
Population 9,482
Elevation 609 ft
Area Code 802
Zip 05641
Information Central Vermont Chamber of Commerce, PO Box 336; phone 802/229-4619
Web Site www.central-vt.com

Barre (BA-rie) has a busy, industrial air. It is home to the world's largest granite quarries and a granite finishing plant. Many highly skilled European stonecutters have settled here. A popular summer area, Barre serves as an overflow area for nearby ski resorts in winter.

What to See and Do

Goddard College. *123 Pitkin Rd, Plainfield (05667). 5 miles N on Hwy 14, then 4 miles NE on Hwy 2. Phone 802/454-8311.* (400 students) Several buildings designed by students; formal gardens. Theater, concerts.

Groton State Forest. *126 Boulder Beach Rd, Groton (05046). 19 miles E on Hwy 302, then N on Hwy 232, near Groton. Phone 802/584-3822.* This 25,625-acre area includes 3-mile-long Lake Groton (elevation 1,078 feet) and six other ponds. Miles of trails have been established to more remote sections of the forest. Nine developed recreation areas. Swimming, bathhouse, fishing, boating (rentals); nature trail, snowmobiling, picnicking, concession. Four campgrounds (dump station), lean-tos. (Memorial Day-Columbus Day)

Hope Cemetery. *On Hwy 14 at N edge of town. Phone 802/229-5711.* "Museum" of granite sculpture. Headstones rival finest granite carvings anywhere. Carved by craftsmen as final tribute to themselves and their families.

Robert Burns. *Phone 802/229-4619.* This granite statue of the poet stands near the city park in downtown. Erected in 1899 by admirers of the poet; regarded as one of the world's finest granite sculptures.

Rock of Ages Quarry and Manufacturing Division. *773 Graniteville Rd, Graniteville (05654). Exit 6 from I-89 or 2 miles S on Hwy 14, then 3 1/2 miles SE on Main St. Phone 802/476-3119.* Skilled artisans creating monuments; picnic area. Visitor center (May-Oct, daily). Manufacturing Divison (all year, Mon-Fri). 30-minute quarry shuttle tour (June-Oct, Mon-Fri; fee). **FREE**

Youth Triumphant. *City park.* Erected Armistice Day, 1924. Benches around the memorial create a whisper gallery; whispers on one side of oval can be easily heard on other side.

Special Event

Old Time Fiddlers' Contest. *Barre Auditorium, 61 Seminary Hill, Barre (05641). Phone 802/476-0256.* This event is dedicated to preserving and promoting Old-Time Fiddling and its related arts and skills. Usually last weekend in Sept.

Limited-Service Hotel

★ **HOLLOW INN AND HOTEL.** *278 S Main St, Barre (05641). Phone 802/479-9313; toll-free 800/998-9444; fax 802/476-5242. www.hollowinn.com.* 41 rooms, 2 story. Pets accepted; fee. Complimentary continental breakfast. Check-out 11 am. Fitness room. Outdoor pool, whirlpool. **$**

Specialty Lodgings

The following lodging establishments are approved by Mobil Travel Guide, but due to their unique and individualized nature have not been given a traditional Mobil Star rating. Included in this listing you may find bed-and-breakfasts, limited-service inns, guest ranches, and other unique hotel properties.

GREEN TRAILS INN. *24 Stone Rd, Brookfield (05036). Phone 802/276-3412; toll-free 800/243-3412. www.greentrailsinn.com.* Buildings date to 1790 and 1830. On site of famed Floating Bridge. 13 rooms, 3 story. Children over 10 years only. Complimentary full breakfast. Check-in 3 pm, check-out 11 am. Restaurant. Airport transportation available. **$**

SHIRE INN. *Main St, Chelsea (05038). Phone 802/685-3031; toll-free 800/441-6908; fax 802/685-3871. www.shireinn.com.* This Federal-style house was built in 1832. 6 rooms, 2 story. Children over 7 years only. Complimentary full breakfast. Check-in 3 pm, check-out 11 am. **$$**

Bellows Falls (E-2)

See also Brattleboro, Grafton, Springfield

Settled 1753
Population 3,313
Elevation 299 ft
Area Code 802
Zip 05101
Information Great Falls Regional Chamber of Commerce, 55 Village Square, PO Box 554; phone 802/463-4280
Web Site www.gfrcc.org

The first construction work on a US canal was started here in 1792. Later, nine locks raised barges, rafts, and small steamers over the falls. In 1983, a series of fish ladders extending 1,024 feet was constructed to restore Atlantic salmon and American shad to their migratory route up the Connecticut River. Power from the river helps make this an industrial town; wood products, paper, and wire cord are among the chief products. Ben & Jerry's ice cream has a nationwide distribution center here.

What to See and Do

Adams Gristmill. *End of Mill Hill St, Bellows Falls. Phone 802/463-3734.* (1831) Former mill; museum contains early electrical equipment, implements used in paper manufacturing and farming. (By appointment)

Green Mountain Railroad. *54 Depot Sq, Bellows Falls (05101). 1/4 mile N. Phone 802/463-3069.* Green Mountain Flyer offers scenic train rides through three river valleys. (Late June-Labor Day: Tues-Sun; mid-Sept-Columbus Day: daily) **$$$**

Native American Petroglyphs. *On riverbanks near Vilas Bridge. Phone 802/463-4280.* Carvings on rocks, unique among Native American works, by members of an early American people; as early as AD 1000.

Rockingham Meetinghouse. *7 Village Sq, Rockingham. 5 miles N on Hwy 103; 1 mile W of I-91 exit 6 on Old Rockingham Rd. Phone 802/463-3964.* (1787) Restored in 1907; colonial architecture, antique glass windows; old burying ground with quaint epitaphs. (Mid-June-Labor Day, daily) **$**

Special Event

Rockingham Old Home Days. *Rockingham Meetinghouse, 7 Village Sq, Rockingham.* Celebrates the founding of the meetinghouse. Dancing, outdoor cafés, sidewalk sales, entertainment, fireworks; pilgrimage to meetinghouse last day. First weekend in Aug.

Bennington (F-1)

See also Arlington, Green Mountain National Forest, Manchester and Manchester Center, Wilmington

Settled 1761
Population 16,451
Elevation 681 ft
Area Code 802
Zip 05201
Information Information Booth, 100 Veterans Memorial Dr; phone 802/447-3311 or toll-free 800/229-0252
Web Site www.bennington.com

Bennington was headquarters for Ethan Allen's Green Mountain Boys, known to New Yorkers as the "Bennington Mob," in Vermont's long struggle with New York. On August 16, 1777, this same "mob" won a decisive battle of the Revolutionary War. Bennington has three separate areas of historic significance: the Victorian and turn-of-the-century buildings downtown; the colonial houses, church, and commons in Old Bennington (1 mile W); and the three covered bridges in North Bennington.

What to See and Do

Bennington Battle Monument. *15 Monument Cir, Old Bennington (05201). Phone 802/447-0550.* A 306-foot monolith commemorates a Revolutionary War victory. Elevator to observation platform (mid-Apr-Oct, daily). Gift shop. **$**

Bennington College. *Hwy 67A and College Dr, Bennington (05201). Phone 802/442-5401.* (1932) (787 students) Introduced progressive methods of education; became coeducational in 1969. The Visual and Performing Arts Center has special exhibits. Summer programs and performances.

Bennington Museum. *Main St, Bennington (05201).* *Phone 802/447-1571.* Early Vermont and New England historical artifacts, including American glass, paintings, sculpture, silver, furniture; Bennington pottery, Grandma Moses paintings, 1925 "Wasp" luxury touring car. Schoolhouse Museum contains Moses family memorabilia; Bennington flag; other Revolutionary War collections. (Daily; closed Thanksgiving, Dec 25) Genealogical library (by appointment). **$$**

Long Trail. *Phone 802/447-3311.* A path for hikers leading over the Green Mountains to the Canadian border, crosses Highway 9 approximately 5 miles east of Bennington. A section of the trail is part of the Appalachian Trail.

Old First Church. *Monument Ave, Old Bennington (05201). Phone 802/447-1223.* (1805) Example of early colonial architecture; original box pews; Asher Benjamin steeple. Guided tours. (Memorial Day-mid-Oct, daily) Adjacent is

Old Burying Ground. *Phone 802/447-3311.* Buried here are poet Robert Frost and those who died in the Battle of Bennington.

Park-McCullough House Museum. *Park and West St, North Bennington. N via Hwy 67A. Phone 802/442-5441.* (1865) A 35-room Victorian mansion with period furnishings; stable with carriages; costume collection; Victorian gardens; child's playhouse. (Early May-Oct, daily) Special events are held throughout the year. **$$**

Shaftsbury State Park. *22 Shaftsbury State Park Rd, Shaftsbury (05262). 10 1/2 miles N on Hwy 7A. Phone 802/375-9978.* The 26-acre Lake Shaftsbury, a former millpond, is surrounded by 101 acres of forests and wetlands. Swimming, fishing, boating (rentals); nature and hiking trails, picnicking. (Memorial Day-Labor Day) **$**

Valley View Horses & Tack Shop, Inc. *Northwest Hill Rd, Pownal. 9 miles S on Hwy 7. Phone 802/823-4649 (for fees).* Full-service equestrian facility offers guided trail rides and horse rentals (by the hour). Also "Pony Express" pony rides at the stables for young riders. Western tack shop. (Daily)

Woodford State Park. *142 State Park Rd, Woodford (05201). Approximately 10 miles E on Hwy 9. Phone 802/447-7169.* At 2,400 feet, this 400-acre park has the highest elevation of any park in the state. Swimming, fishing, boating (no motors; rentals); nature and hiking trails, picnicking, tent and trailer sites (dump station), lean-tos. (Memorial Day-Columbus Day) **$**

Special Events

Antique and Classic Car Show. Car show, swap meet, craft festival, car corral, tractor pull events, food and, entertainment are some of the activities at this annual show. Second weekend after Labor Day.

Mayfest. *www.bennington.com/bbc/mayfest.* Mayfest is a day for shopping for handmade crafts, eating tasty food and watching street entertainment. Sat of Memorial Day weekend.

Limited-Service Hotels

★ **BENNINGTON MOTOR INN.** *143 W Main St, Bennington (05201). Phone 802/442-5479; toll-free 800/359-9900. www.coolcruisers.net/ benningtonmotorinn.htm.* 16 rooms, 2 story. Check-out 11 am. **$**
🐕

★ **BEST WESTERN NEW ENGLANDER MOTOR INN.** *220 Northside Dr, Bennington (05201). Phone 802/442-6311; toll-free 800/780-7234; fax 802/442-5885. www.bestwestern.com.* 58 rooms, 2 story. Complimentary continental breakfast. Check-out 11 am. Outdoor pool. **$**
🏊

★ **KNOTTY PINE.** *130 Northside Dr, Bennington (05201). Phone 802/442-5487; fax 802/442-2231. www.bennington.com/knottypine.* 21 rooms. Check-out 11 am. Outdoor pool. **$**
🐕 🏊

★ ★ **VERMONTER MOTOR LODGE.** *2964 West Rd, Bennington (05201). Phone 802/442-2529; fax 802/442-0879. www.sugarmapleinne.com.* 31 rooms. Pets accepted, some restrictions; fee. Check-out 11 am. Restaurant. **$**
🍽

Full-Service Inn

★ ★ ★ **FOUR CHIMNEYS INN.** *21 West Rd, Bennington (05201). Phone 802/447-3500; toll-free 800/649-3503; fax 802/447-3692. www.fourchimneys.com.* This elegant 1783 inn is set on 11 acres of trees and rolling grass fields. Guest rooms blend modern amenities with an old-world feel. 11 rooms, 3 story.

Complimentary continental breakfast. Check-in 2 pm, check-out 11 am. Restaurant. **$$**
🖪

Specialty Lodging

The following lodging establishment is approved by Mobil Travel Guide, but due to its unique and individualized nature has not been given a traditional Mobil Star rating. Included in this listing you may find bed-and-breakfasts, limited-service inns, guest ranches, and other unique hotel properties.

SOUTH SHIRE INN. *124 Elm St, Bennington (05201). Phone 802/447-3839; fax 802/442-3547. www.southshire.com.* Inside and out, this inn is reminiscent of the Victorian era from its shingled façade to the mahogany paneling, leaded glass doors, and ornate moldings of its common rooms. All units have period furnishings. 9 rooms, 2 story. Children over 12 years only. Complimentary full breakfast. Check-in 3 pm, check-out 11 am. **$**
🖪

Brandon (D-1)

See also Middlebury, Rutland

Settled 1761
Population 4,223
Elevation 431 ft
Area Code 802
Zip 05733
Information Brandon Area Chamber of Commerce, PO Box 267; phone 802/247-6401
Web Site www.brandon.org

Brandon is a resort and residential town located at the western edge of the Green Mountains. The first US electric motor was made in nearby Forestdale by Thomas Davenport.

What to See and Do

Branbury State Park. *Hwy 53, Salisbury. 3 miles NE on Hwy 73, then N on Hwy 53, E shore of Lake Dunmore. Phone 802/247-5925.* This 76-acre park has swimming, 1,000-foot sand beach, fishing, boating, sailing; nature and hiking trails, picnicking, concession, camping (dump station), lean-tos. (Memorial Day-Columbus Day)

Mount Independence. *Hwys 22A and 73 W, Orwell (05760). 16 miles W via Hwys 73 and 22A. Phone 802/ 759-2412.* Wooded bluff on shore of Lake Champlain, part of Revolutionary War defense complex. Fort built in 1776 across from Fort Ticonderoga to house 12,000 troops and to protect colonies from northern invasion; evacuated in 1777. Least disturbed major Revolutionary War site in the country; four marked trails show ruins of fort complex. (Late May-early Oct, daily) **$$**

Stephen A. Douglas Birthplace. *2 Grove St (Hwy 7), Brandon (05733). Phone 802/247-6401.* Cottage where the "Little Giant" was born in 1813. Douglas attended Brandon Academy before moving to Illinois in 1833. (By appointment) **FREE**

Full-Service Inn

★ ★ ★ **LILAC INN.** *53 Park St, Brandon (05733). Phone 802/247-5463; toll-free 800/221-0720; fax 802/ 247-5499. www.lilacinn.com.* This colonial home, built in 1909, is on the National Register of Historic Places and is a peaceful, romantic getaway. Enjoy a book in the library, practice on the putting green, or take a drive to nearby historic Fort Ticonderoga. 9 rooms, 2 story. Complimentary full breakfast. Check-in 3 pm, check-out 11 am. Restaurant. **$$**

Specialty Lodging

The following lodging establishment is approved by Mobil Travel Guide, but due to its unique and individualized nature has not been given a traditional Mobil Star rating. Included in this listing you may find bed-and-breakfasts, limited-service inns, guest ranches, and other unique hotel properties.

THE BRANDON INN. *20 Park St, Brandon (05733). Phone 802/247-5766; toll-free 800/639-8685; fax 802/247-5768. www.historicbrandoninn.com.* This inn was built in 1786. 37 rooms, 3 story. Check-in 3 pm, check-out 11 am. Restaurant, bar. Outdoor pool. **$**
🏊

Restaurant

★ ★ **LILAC INN.** *53 Park St, Brandon (05733). Phone 802/247-5463; toll-free 800/221-0720; fax 802/247-5499. www.lilacinn.com.* International/Fusion menu. Dinner, brunch. Closed Mon-Tues. Bar. Outdoor seating. **$$$**

Brattleboro (F-2)

See also Bellows Falls, Greenfield, Keene, Marlboro, Newfane, Wilmington

Settled 1724
Population 12,241
Elevation 240 ft
Area Code 802
Zip 05301
Information Brattleboro Area Chamber of Commerce, 180 Main St; phone 802/254-4565
Web Site www.brattleboro.com

The first settlement in Vermont was at Fort Dummer (2 miles S) in 1724. Rudyard Kipling married a Brattleboro woman and lived here in the 1890s. Brattleboro is a resort area and an industrial town.

What to See and Do

Brattleboro Museum & Art Center. *10 Vernon St, Brattleboro (05301). Union Railroad Station. Phone 802/257-0124.* Exhibits change periodically and feature works by New England artists; history exhibits; permanent display of Estey organ collection; frequent performances and lecture programs. (Mid-May-Nov, Tues-Sun; closed holidays) **$**

Creamery Bridge. *Approximately 2 miles W on Hwy 9. Phone 802/254-4565.* (1879) One of Vermont's best-preserved covered bridges.

Harlow's Sugar House. *Bellows Falls Rd, Putney. 3 miles N via I-91, exit 4; on Hwy 5. Phone 802/387-5852.* Observe working sugarhouse (Mar-mid-Apr). Maple exhibit and products. Pick your own fruit in season: strawberries, blueberries, raspberries, apples; also cider in fall. (Daily; closed Dec 25, also Jan-mid-Feb) **FREE**

Living Memorial Park. *Guilford St, Brattleboro (05301). 2 miles W, just off Hwy 9. Phone 802/254-5808.* Swimming pool (mid-June-Labor Day). Ball fields, lawn games, tennis courts, skiing (T-bar; Dec-early Mar), ice skating (mid-Nov-early Mar). Picnicking, playground. Special events during summer. Fee for some activities.

Santa's Land. *655 Bellows Falls Rd, Putney (05346). 12 miles N on Hwy 5 or I-91, exits 4 or 5. Phone 802/387-5550.* Christmas theme village; visit with Santa, railroad ride, carousel. Petting zoo; gardens.

Concessions. (Memorial Day weekend-Dec 24, daily; closed Thanksgiving) **$$$**

Special Events

Winter Carnival. Week-long festival includes ski races, parade, ice show, sleigh rides, road races. Feb.

Yellow Barn Music Festival. *10 miles N via I-91 or Hwy 5 in Putney, behind the Public Library. Phone 802/387-6637; toll-free 800/639-3819.* Five-week chamber music festival. Students and well-known guest artists perform concerts. Also Special Performance Series, children's concerts. Tues, Fri, Sat evenings, some Thurs, Sun, July-Aug.

Limited-Service Hotel

★ **LATCHIS HOTEL.** *50 Main St, Brattleboro (05301). Phone 802/254-6300; fax 802/254-6304. www.latchis.com.* This hotel is located in Brattleboro's eclectic downtown historic district. Built in Art Deco-style in 1938, the Latchis Building is on the National Register of Historic Places—it's one of the few Art Deco buildings in Vermont. The building also houses the Latchis Theatre, which shows first-run art films, and the Lucca Bistro and its downtown brewpub. Inside, the hotel's public areas are pure Art Deco: terrazzo floors, mirrors, chrome fixtures, and neoclassical friezes (the designer was the son of Greek immigrants). Guest rooms have a more traditional New England look, although they retain a 1930s charm. For breakfast, muffins are delivered to the room, and in-room refrigerators are stocked with bottles of juice. 30 rooms, 4 story. Complimentary continental breakfast. Check-in 2 pm, check-out 11 am. **$**

Full-Service Hotel

★ ★ **QUALITY INN.** *1380 Putney Rd, Brattleboro (05301). Phone 802/254-8701; toll-free 866/254-8701; fax 802/257-4727. www.qualityinnbrattleboro.com.* North of the town center on busy Route 5, the river road along the Connecticut, this hotel is one of the few full-service, technologically up-to-date lodgings in the area. It's convenient to Interstate 91 and just north of the Route 9 bridge to New Hampshire. Families enjoy the recreation area, with a small pool (better for kids than lap swimmers), whirlpool, game room, sauna, and small fitness room. A surprising touch is that the hotel's restaurant serves Indian food, which is available through room service as well; a variety of dining alternatives are nearby. 104 rooms, 2 story. Pets accepted; fee. Complimentary continental breakfast. Check-in 3 pm, check-out 11 am. Wireless Internet access. Restaurant, bar. Fitness room. Indoor pool, outdoor pool, whirlpool. **$**

Burlington (B-1)

See also Shelburne

Settled 1773
Population 39,127
Elevation 113 ft
Area Code 802
Zip 05401
Information Lake Champlain Regional Chamber of Commerce, 60 Main St, Suite 100; phone 802/863-3489 or toll-free 877/686-5253
Web Site www.vermont.org

Burlington, on Lake Champlain, is the largest city in Vermont. It is the site of the oldest university and the oldest daily newspaper (1848) in the state, the burial place of Ethan Allen, and the birthplace of philosopher John Dewey. It has a diversity of industries. The lakefront area offers a park, dock, and restaurants.

Burlington Fun Fact

The first Ben and Jerry's Ice Cream store opened in Burlington in 1978.

What to See and Do

Battery Park. *Hwy 127 and Pearl St, Burlington (05401). Phone 802/863-3489.* View of Lake Champlain and Adirondacks. Guns here drove back British warships in War of 1812.

Bolton Valley Ski/Summer Resort. *4302 Bolton Access Rd, Bolton Valley (05477). 20 miles E at 4302 Bolton Valley Access Rd, off Hwy 2 in Bolton; I-89 exits 10, 11. Phone toll-free 877/926-5866. www.boltonvalleyvt.com.* Resort has quad, four double chairlifts; one surface lift; school, patrol, rentals; snowmaking; cafeteria, restaurants, bar; nursery. Forty-three runs, longest run over 3 miles; vertical drop 1,600 feet. (Nov-Apr, daily) Sixty-two miles of cross-country trails. Also summer activities.

Burlington Ferry. *Leaves King St Dock. Phone 802/864-9804 (for schedule, other trips).* Makes one-hour trips across Lake Champlain to Port Kent, NY (mid-May-mid-Oct, daily). Refreshments. **$$$$**

Church Street Marketplace. *135 Church St, Burlington (05401). Phone 802/863-1648.* Four traffic-free blocks, from the Unitarian Church, designed in 1815 by Peter Banner, to City Hall at the corner of Main Street. Buildings are a mix of Art Deco and 19th-century architectural styles and house more than 100 shops, restaurants, galleries, and cafés. The bricked promenade is spotted with vendors and street entertainers.

Discovery Museum. *51 Park St, Essex Junction (05452). On Hwy 2A. Phone 802/878-8687.* "Hands-on" children's museum offers participatory exhibits in the physical and natural sciences, history, art. (Tues-Sun; closed holidays)

⭐ **Ethan Allen Homestead and Museum.** *1 Ethan Allen Homestead, Burlington (05401). 2 miles N off Hwy 127. Phone 802/865-4556. www.ethanallenhomestead.org.* Ethan Allen had a colorful history as a frontiersman, military leader, land speculator, suspected traitor, and prisoner of war. This preserved pioneer homestead, set amid rolling fields with views of the nearby river, was his last home. Here you'll find a re-created hayfield and kitchen gardens, plus the 1787 farmhouse. One-hour guided tours are available. (May-Oct: daily; Nov-Apr: call for schedule) **$**

Ethan Allen Park. *North Ave and Ethan Allen Pkwy, Burlington (05401). Phone 802/863-3489.* Part of Ethan Allen's farm. Ethan Allen Tower (Memorial Day-Labor Day, Wed-Sun afternoons and evenings) with view of Adirondacks and Lake Champlain to the west, Green Mountains to the east. Picnicking. **FREE**

Excursion Cruises. *Burlington Boathouse, 266 Pine St, Burlington (05401). Phone 802/862-8300. Spirit of Ethan Allen III,* replica of a vintage sternwheeler and Lake Champlain's largest excursion vessel, offers sightseeing sunset, moonlight, brunch, and dinner cruises on Lake Champlain; both decks enclosed and heated. Reservations required for dinner cruises. (June-Oct) **$$$$**

Green Mountain Audubon Center. *20 miles SE via I-89, Richmond exit, in Huntington near the Huntington-Richmond line. Phone 802/434-3068.* Center has 230 acres with trails through many Vermont habitats, including beaver ponds, hemlock swamp, brook, river, marsh, old farm fields, woodland, and sugar orchard. Educational nature center with classes, interpretive programs, and special projects. Open all year for hiking, snowshoeing, and cross-country skiing. Grounds, office (hours vary). Fee for some activities. Adjacent is

Birds of Vermont Museum. *900 Sherman Hollow Rd, Huntington (05462). Phone 802/434-2167. www.birdsofvermont.org.* This museum displays wood carvings of 450 species of local birds, all done by a single artist. It also offers nature trails and recorded bird songs. (May-Oct, daily 10 am-4 pm) **$**

Lake Champlain Chocolates. *750 Pine St, Burlington (05401). Phone 802/864-1807. www.lakechamplain chocolates.com.* Large glass windows afford visitors a view of the chocolate-making process at this small-scale factory. The gift shop on-site usually features in-store chocolate-making demonstrations on Saturdays, when the factory itself is closed. (Tours: Mon-Fri 9 am-2 pm on the hour; factory store: Mon-Sat 9 am-6 pm, Sun noon-5 pm; closed holidays) **FREE**

Sherman Hollow Cross-Country Skiing Center. *10 miles SE on I-89 to exit 11, then E on Hwy 2, then S on Huntington Rd to Sherman Hollow Rd, then W. Phone 802/434-4553.* The area has 25 miles of groomed, one-way, double-tracked cross-country ski trails; more than 3 miles of lighted trails for night skiing; a warming hut; and a restaurant. Rentals are available. (Dec-Apr) **$$$**

St. Michael's College. *1 Winooski Park, Colchester (05439). N via I-89 to exit 15, then 1/4 mile NE on Hwy 15, in Winooski-Colchester. Phone 802/654-2000.* (1904) (1,700 students) Chapel of St. Michael the Archangel (daily). Also professional summer theater at St. Michael's Playhouse.

University of Vermont. *Waterman Bldg, 85 S Prospect St, Burlington (05405). Phone 802/656-3480.* (1791) (10,000 students) Fifth-oldest university in New England. Graduate and undergraduate programs. On campus are the **Billings Center,** of architectural significance; **Bailey-Howe Library,** largest in the state; Georgian-designed **Ira Allen Chapel,** named for the founder; and the **Old Mill,** classroom building with cornerstone laid by General Lafayette in 1825. Also here is

Robert Hull Fleming Museum. *61 Colchester Ave, Burlington (05405). Phone 802/656-0750.* American, European, African, pre-Columbian, and Oriental art; changing exhibits. (Limited hours) **DONATION**

Special Events

Discover Jazz Festival. *230 College St, Burlington (05401). Phone 802/863-7992.* A jazz extravaganza with more than 150 live performances taking place in city parks, clubs, and restaurants. Ten days in early June.

St. Michael's Playhouse. *McCarthy Arts Center, St. Michael's College, Colchester (05439). Phone 802/654-2535.* Summer theater. Professional actors perform four plays (two weeks each). Tues-Sat, late June-late Aug.

Vermont Mozart Festival. *110 Main St, Burlington (05401). Phone 802/862-7352.* Features 26 chamber concerts in picturesque Vermont settings including the Trapp Family Meadow, Basin Harbor Club in Vergennes, and Shelburne Farms on Lake Champlain. Mid-July-early Aug.

Limited-Service Hotels

★ ★ **BEST WESTERN WINDJAMMER INN & CONFERENCE CENTER.** *1076 Williston Rd, South Burlington (05403). Phone 802/863-1125; toll-free 800/371-1125; fax 802/658-1296. www.bestwestern.com/windjammerinn.* 177 rooms, 2 story. Pets accepted, some restrictions; fee. Complimentary continental breakfast. Check-out 11 am. Restaurant. Fitness room. Indoor pool, outdoor pool, whirlpool. Airport transportation available. **$**

★ ★ **CLARION HOTEL.** *1117 Williston Rd, South Burlington (05403). Phone 802/658-0250; toll-free 800/252-7466; fax 802/660-7516. www.clarionvermont.com.* 130 rooms, 2 story. Pets accepted, some restrictions; fee. Check-out noon. Restaurant, bar. Fitness room. Indoor pool, children's pool. Airport transportation available. **$**

★ **COMFORT INN.** *1285 Williston Rd, South Burlington (05403). Phone 802/865-3400; toll-free 800/228-5150; fax 802/846-3411. www.choicehotels.com.* 105 rooms, 3 story. Pets accepted, some restrictions; fee. Complimentary continental breakfast. Check-out noon. Fitness room. Outdoor pool. **$**

★ **HOLIDAY INN EXPRESS.** *1712 Shelburne Rd, South Burlington (05403). Phone 802/860-1112; toll-free 800/874-1554; fax 802/846-1926. www.innvermont.com.* 78 rooms, 3 story, all suites.

Complimentary continental breakfast. Check-out noon. Airport transportation available. **$**

★ **WILSON INN.** *10 Kellogg Rd, Essex Junction (05452). Phone 802/879-1515; toll-free 800/521-2334; fax 802/764-5149. www.wilsoninn.com.* 32 rooms, 3 story, all suites. Pets accepted, some restrictions; fee. Complimentary continental breakfast. Check-out 11 am. Outdoor pool. **$**

Full-Service Hotels

★ ★ ★ **THE INN AT ESSEX–A SUMMIT HOTEL.** *70 Essex Way, Essex (05452). Phone 802/878-1100; toll-free 800/727-4295; fax 802/878-0063. www.innatessex.com.* Each room at this inn is individually decorated with 18th-century period-style furniture. The meals are prepared by the New England Culinary Institute. 97 rooms, 3 story. Check-out 11 am. Restaurant. Airport transportation available. **$$**

★ ★ ★ **SHERATON BURLINGTON HOTEL AND CONFERENCE CENTER.** *870 Williston Rd, South Burlington (05403). Phone 802/865-6600; toll-free 800/677-6576; fax 802/865-6670. www. sheraton.com.* 309 rooms, 4 story. Pets accepted; fee. Check-out noon. Restaurant, bar. Fitness room. Indoor pool, whirlpool. Airport transportation available. Business center. **$**

Restaurants

★ **DAILY PLANET.** *15 Center St, Burlington (05401). Phone 802/862-9647; fax 802/862-6693.* European-style café. American menu. Lunch, dinner, brunch. Closed holidays. Bar. **$$**

★ ★ **ICE HOUSE.** *171 Battery St, Burlington (05401). Phone 802/864-1800; fax 802/864-1801.* Converted icehouse. Seafood, steak menu. Lunch, dinner, Sun brunch. Children's menu. Outdoor seating. **$$**

★ ★ ★ **PAULINE'S.** *1834 Shelburne Rd, South Burlington (05401). Phone 802/862-1081; fax 802/862-6842. www.paulinescafe.com.* This friendly, casual restaurant has a strong local following. American menu. Lunch, dinner. Closed Dec 24 (evening)-25. Bar. Children's menu. Outdoor seating. **$$**

★ ★ **PERRY'S FISH HOUSE.** *1080 Shelburne Rd, South Burlington (05403). Phone 802/862-1300. www.perrysfishhouse.com.* Dinner. Closed Thanksgiving, Dec 25. Bar. Children's menu. **$$**

Dorset (E-1)

See also Arlington, Manchester and Manchester Center, Peru

Settled 1768
Population 1,918
Elevation 962 ft
Area Code 802
Zip 05251
Information Dorset Chamber of Commerce, PO Box 121; phone 802/867-2450
Web Site www.dorsetvt.com

This charming village is surrounded by hills 3,000 feet high. In 1776, the Green Mountain Boys voted for Vermont's independence here. The first marble quarry in the country was opened in 1785 on nearby Mount Aeolus.

Special Event

Dorset Theatre Festival. *Cheney Rd, Dorset. Phone 802/867-5777.* Professional theater company presents five productions. May-Labor Day.

Full-Service Inns

★ ★ ★ **DORSET INN.** *Church and Main sts, Dorset (05251). Phone 802/867-5500; toll-free 877/367-7389; fax 802/867-5542. www.dorsetinn.com.* This 1796 inn, located where the Green Mountain Boys plotted their fight against the British, strives to blend colonial elements with modern amenities. Individually decorated guest rooms feature private baths, antique furnishings, and wall-to-wall carpets. Established in 1796, this is the oldest continuously operating inn in Vermont. 31 rooms, 3 story. Check-in 2 pm, check-out 11 am. Restaurant, bar. **$**

★ ★ ★ **INN AT WEST VIEW FARM.** *2928 Hwy 30, Dorset (05251). Phone 802/867-5715; toll-free 800/769-4903; fax 802/867-0468. www.innatwestview farm.com.* This restored farmhouse, which overlooks the Vermont countryside, is the perfect setting for a quiet, relaxing country vacation. Guest rooms feature private baths with large, soft towels and comfortable sitting areas. 10 rooms, 2 story. Complimentary full breakfast. Check-in 3 pm, check-out 11 am. Restaurant, bar. **$**

Specialty Lodging

The following lodging establishment is approved by Mobil Travel Guide, but due to its unique and individualized nature has not been given a traditional Mobil Star rating. Included in this listing you may find bed-and-breakfasts, limited-service inns, guest ranches, and other unique hotel properties.

BARROWS HOUSE INN. *3156 Hwy 30, Dorset (05251). Phone 802/867-4455; toll-free 800/639-1620; fax 802/867-0132. www.barrowshouse.com.* 28 rooms. Pets accepted, some restrictions; fee. Check-in early afternoon, check-out 11 am. Restaurant, bar. Outdoor pool. Tennis. **$$**

Restaurants

★ ★ ★ **BARROWS HOUSE INN.** *3156 Hwy 30, Dorset (05251). Phone 802/867-4455; toll-free 800/639-1620; fax 802/867-0132. www.barrowshouse.com.* Choose between the clubby tavern, the bright greenhouse, or the more formal dining room to enjoy the eclectic regional cuisine served in this charming inn. American menu. Breakfast, dinner. Bar. Children's menu. **$$$**

★ ★ **INN AT WEST VIEW FARM.** *2929 Hwy 30, Dorset (05251). Phone 802/867-5715; toll-free 800/769-4903; fax 802/867-0468. www.innatwestviewfarm.com.* This restaurant is located in a converted 1850 farmhouse. American menu. Dinner. Closed Tues-Wed; also Apr; first two weeks in Nov. Bar. **$$**

Fairlee (D-3)

See also White River Junction

Population 883
Elevation 436 ft
Area Code 802
Zip 05045
Information Town Offices, Main St, PO Box 95; phone 802/333-4363

Special Events

Chicken Barbecue. *On the Common, Main St, Fairlee.* Phone 802/333-4363. July 4.

Vermont State Open Golf Tournament. *Lake Morey Inn Country Club, Fairlee. Phone 802/333-4311.* Mid-June.

Full-Service Resort

★ ★ **LAKE MOREY RESORT.** *Club House Rd, Fairlee (05045). Phone 802/333-4311; toll-free 800/423-1211; fax 802/333-4553. www.lakemoreyresort.com.* 144 rooms, 3 story. Check-in 2 pm, check-out 11 am. Restaurant, bar. Children's activity center. Fitness room. Indoor pool, outdoor pool, whirlpool. Golf. Tennis. **$**

Grafton (E-2)

See also Bellows Falls, Londonderry, Newfane, Springfield

Population 602
Elevation 841 ft
Area Code 802
Zip 05146
Information Great Falls Regional Chamber of Commerce, 55 Village Square, PO Box 554, Bellows Falls 05101; phone 802/463-4280
Web Site www.gfrcc.org

This picturesque New England village is a blend of houses, churches, galleries, antiques shops, and other small shops—all circa 1800. Founded in pre-Revolutionary times under the patronage of George III, Grafton became a thriving mill town and modest industrial center after the damming of the nearby Saxton River. When water power gave way to steam, the town began to decline. Rescued, revived, and restored by the Windham Foundation, it has been returned to its former attractiveness. A creek curling through town and the peaceful air of a gentler era contribute to the charm of this village, considered a paradise for photographers.

What to See and Do

Grafton Ponds Cross-Country Ski Center. *Townshend Rd, Grafton. Phone 802/843-2400.* Featuring more than 16 miles of groomed trails; school, rentals; concession, warming hut. (Dec-Mar, daily; closed Dec 25) In summer, walking and fitness trails (no fee). **$$$$**

The Old Tavern at Grafton. *92 Main St, Grafton (05146). Main St and Townshend Rd. Phone 802/843-2231. www.old-tavern.com.* (1801) Centerpiece of village. Visited by many famous guests over the years, including several presidents and authors; names inscribed over the desk. Furnished with antiques, colonial décor. Former barn converted to lounge; annex is restored from two houses; dining by reservations. (May-Mar, daily)

Full-Service Inn

★ ★ ★ **OLD TAVERN AT GRAFTON.** *92 Main St, Grafton (05146). Phone 802/843-2231; toll-free 800/843-1801; fax 802/843-2245. www.old-tavern.com.* This picturesque New England inn offers its guests a haven from their busy lives. Guests will enjoy the stone walls, colorful flowers, afternoon tea, tennis, bicycles, and pond. The individually decorated guest rooms and houses feature antique Chippendale and Windsor furnishings. 46 rooms, 3 story. Closed Apr. Children over 7 years only. Complimentary full breakfast. Check-in 4 pm, check-out 11 am. Restaurant, bar. Tennis. **$**
🖼

Specialty Lodging

The following lodging establishment is approved by Mobil Travel Guide, but due to its unique and individualized nature has not been given a traditional Mobil Star rating. Included in this listing you may find bed-and-breakfasts, limited-service inns, guest ranches, and other unique hotel properties.

INN AT WOODCHUCK HILL FARM. *Woodchuck Hill Rd, Grafton (05146). Phone 802/843-2398. www. woodchuckhill.com.* First farmhouse in town (1790). On 200 acres; pond. 10 rooms, 3 story. Complimentary full breakfast. Check-in 1 pm, check-out 11 am. **$**
🖼

Green Mountain National Forest

See also Bennington, Manchester and Manchester Center, Rutland, Warren

This 360,000-acre tract lies along the backbone of the Green Mountains, beginning at the Massachusetts line. Its high point is Mount Ellen (4,083 feet). The 260-mile Long Trail, a celebrated hiking route, extends the length of the state; about 80 miles of it are within the forest.

Well-maintained gravel roads wind through the forests of white pine, hemlock, spruce, yellow birch, and sugar maple; there are many recreation areas and privately owned resorts. Hunting and fishing are permitted in the forest under Vermont regulations. There are whitetailed deer, black bear, ruffed grouse, and other game, plus brook, rainbow, and brown trout.

Developed and primitive camping, swimming, and picnicking are found throughout the forest, as are privately operated alpine ski areas and ski touring centers. Fees charged at some recreation sites and at developed campsites.

What to See and Do

Moosalamoo Recreation Area. *99 Ranger Rd, Rochester (05767). Within Green Mountain National Forest. Phone 802/747-6700.* This 20,000-acre area features trails from which all the forest's diverse natural beauty can be viewed. Winter activities include cross-country skiing on groomed, specially marked trails; also alpine skiing. The nation's oldest long-distance hiking trail, the Long Trail, runs the Moosalamoo border for nearly 15 miles. Biking allowed on roads and some trails. Camping facilities abound in the area. (Daily)

Jeffersonville (B-2)

See also Stowe, Swanton

Population 462
Elevation 459 ft
Area Code 802
Zip 05464
Information Smugglers' Notch Area Chamber of Commerce, PO Box 364
Web Site www.smugnotch.com

What to See and Do

Smugglers' Notch. *4323 Hwy 108 S, Jeffersonville (05464). 5 miles S on Hwy 108. Phone 802/644-8851; toll-free 800/451-8752.* Resort has five double chairlifts, three surface lifts; school, rentals; snowmaking; concession area, cafeteria, restaurants; nursery, lodge. 60 runs, longest run over 3 miles; vertical drop 2,610 feet. (Thanksgiving-mid-Apr, daily) More than 25 miles of cross-country trails (Dec-Apr, daily; rentals), ice skating. Summer activities include ten swimming pools, three water slides; tennis, miniature golf, driving range. **$$$$**

Full-Service Resort

★ ★ **SMUGGLERS' NOTCH RESORT.** *4323 Hwy 108 S, Jeffersonville (05464). Phone 802/644-8851; toll-free 800/451-8752; fax 802/644-1230. www.smuggs.com.* Located in rural Vermont, this resort caters to family vacationers and has activities tailored to the four seasons of the year. 525 rooms, 3 story. Check-in 5 pm, check-out 10 am. Restaurant, bar. Children's activity center. Fitness room. Eight outdoor pools, whirlpool. Tennis. Ski in/ski out. Airport transportation available. **$**

Specialty Lodging

The following lodging establishment is approved by Mobil Travel Guide, but due to its unique and individualized nature has not been given a traditional Mobil Star rating. Included in this listing you may find bed-and-breakfasts, limited-service inns, guest ranches, and other unique hotel properties.

SINCLAIR INN BED & BREAKFAST. *389 Hwy 15, Jericho (05465). Phone 802/899-2234; toll-free 800/433-4658; fax 802/899-2007. www.sinclairinnbb.com.* This restored Queen Anne Victorian inn was built in 1890. 6 rooms, 3 story. Children over 12 years only. Complimentary full breakfast. Check-in 3 pm, check-out 11 am. **$**

Killington (D-2)

See also Plymouth, Rutland, Woodstock

Population 50
Elevation 1,229 ft
Area Code 802
Zip 05751
Information Killington Chamber of Commerce, PO Box 114; phone 802/773-4181 or toll-free 800/337-1928
Web Site www.killingtonchamber.com

What to See and Do

Gifford Woods State Park. *34 Gifford Woods, Killington (05737). On Hwy 100, 1 mile N of Jct Hwy 4. Phone 802/775-5354.* This 114-acre park has fishing at nearby pond, boat access to Kent Pond. Foot trails (Appalachian Trail passes through park). Virgin forest with picnic facilities. Tent and trailer sites (dump station), lean-tos. (Memorial Day-Columbus Day)

Killington Resort. *4763 Killington Rd, Killington (05751). 5 miles SW of Jct Hwy 4 and Hwy 100, N. Phone 802/422-3261 (ski reports); toll-free 800/621-6867. www.killington.com.* Comprises 1,200 acres with seven mountains (highest elevation 4,241 feet). Two gondolas, six high-speed quad, six quad, six triple, four double chairlifts, eight surface lifts; patrol, school, rentals; snowmaking; mountaintop restaurant (with observation decks), six cafeterias, bars; children's center, nursery; lodging. More than 200 runs; longest run 10 miles, vertical drop 3,150 feet. Snowboarding; snow tubing. (Oct-June, daily) The resort offers

Pico Alpine Slide and Scenic Chairlift. *Phone 802/621-6867.* Chairlift to top of mountain slope; control speed of own sled on the way down. Sports center and restaurant below. (Late May-mid-Oct)

Summer activities. Resort activities include a tennis school (Memorial Day-Sept), 18-hole golf, mountain biking (rentals), in-line skating/skateboarding park; gondola rides to view foliage; two water slides. (July 4-Sept)

Limited-Service Hotels

★ ★ **CASCADES LODGE.** *58 Old Mill Rd, Killington Village (05751). Phone 802/422-3731; toll-free 800/345-0113; fax 802/422-3351. www.cascadeslodge.com.* 46 rooms, 3 story. Complimentary full breakfast. Check-out 11 am. Restaurant, bar. Fitness room. Indoor pool, whirlpool. Ski in/ski out. **$**

★ ★ **GREY BONNET INN.** *831 Hwy 100, Killington (05751). Phone 802/775-2537; toll-free 800/342-2086; fax 802/775-3371. www.greybonnetinn.com.* 40 rooms, 3 story. Closed Apr-May, late Oct-late Nov. Check-out 11 am. Restaurant, bar. Fitness room. Indoor pool, outdoor pool, whirlpool. Tennis. **$**

★ ★ **KILLINGTON PICO MOTOR INN.** *64 Hwy 4, Killington (05751). Phone 802/773-4088; toll-free 800/ 548-4713; fax 802/775-9705. www.killingtonpico.com.* 29 rooms. Complimentary full breakfast. Check-out 11 am. Restaurant, bar. Outdoor pool, whirlpool. **$**

★ **SHERBURNE-KILLINGTON MOTEL.** *1946 Hwy 4, Killington (05751). Phone 802/773-9535; toll-free 800/366-0493; fax 802/773-0011. www.lodging killington.com.* View of mountains. 20 rooms. Complimentary continental breakfast. Check-out 11 am. Outdoor pool. **$**

★ ★ **SUMMIT LODGE.** *Killington Mountain Rd, Killington (05751). Phone 802/422-3535; toll-free 800/635-6343; fax 802/422-3536. www.summitlodge vermont.com.* 45 rooms, 3 story. Check-out 11 am. Restaurant, bar. Two outdoor pools, whirlpool. Tennis. Airport transportation available. **$**

Full-Service Resorts

★ ★ ★ **CORTINA INN AND RESORT.** *103 Hwy 4, Killington (05751). Phone 802/773-3333; toll-free 800/451-6108; fax 802/775-6948. www.cortinainn.com.* This cozy inn and resort is a perfect choice for a country getaway weekend. Guests can enjoy activities year-round. 91 rooms. Complimentary full breakfast. Check-out 11 am. Restaurant, bar. Fitness room. Indoor pool, whirlpool. Tennis. Airport transportation available. **$**

★ ★ ★ **INN OF THE SIX MOUNTAINS.** *2617 Killington Rd, Killington (05751). Phone 802/422-4302; toll-free 800/228-4676; fax 802/422-4321. www.sixmountains.com.* Tucked away in the mountains of Killington, this resort is a family pleaser year-round. 13 rooms, 3 story. Complimentary full breakfast. Check-in 4 pm, check-out noon. Restaurant, bar. Fitness room. Indoor pool, outdoor pool, whirlpool. Tennis. **$**

Full-Service Inn

★ ★ ★ **RED CLOVER INN.** *7 Woodward Rd, Mendon (05701). Phone 802/775-2290; toll-free 800/752-0571; fax 802/773-0594. www.redcloverinn.com.* This 1840s country inn is situated on 13 acres and boasts wonderful views of the Green Mountains. The guest rooms are individually appointed with antiques and country woodwork. 14 rooms, 2 story. Pets accepted, some restrictions; fee. Children over 12 years only. Complimentary full breakfast. Check-in 2 pm, check-out 11 am. Restaurant. Outdoor pool. **$$$**

Specialty Lodging

The following lodging establishment is approved by Mobil Travel Guide, but due to its unique and individualized nature has not been given a traditional Mobil Star rating. Included in this listing you may find bed-and-breakfasts, limited-service inns, guest ranches, and other unique hotel properties.

VERMONT INN. *Hwy 4, Killington (05751). Phone 802/775-0708; toll-free 800/541-7795; fax 802/773-2440. www.vermontinn.com.* 18 rooms, 2 story. Closed mid-Apr-late May. Children over 6 years only. Check-in 2 pm, check-out 11 am. Restaurant, bar. Fitness room. Outdoor pool, whirlpool. Tennis. **$$**

Restaurants

★ ★ ★ **HEMINGWAY'S.** *4988 Hwy 4, Killington (05751). Phone 802/422-3886. www.hemingways restaurant.com.* Housed in a charming 19th-century house and warmed by a glowing fireplace, elaborate fresh country flower arrangements, glass-enclosed gardens, and a stone-walled wine cellar, Hemingway's is an enchanting restaurant for romance, where fine dining feels comfortable and warm. The chef offers several choices (a nightly changing wine-tasting menu in addition to a six-course feasting menu, a four-course vegetable menu, and a three-course prix fixe menu), each prepared with seasonal ingredients, regional seafood, and farm-raised poultry and game. Hemingway's is known for its robust, American-style fare—notably the pecan-crusted Vermont lamb with crispy potatoes and green beans, and the wood-grilled quail with cheddar corn cakes and black-eyed pea vinaigrette. Handmade breads and a diverse wine list are other delicious perks. International menu. Dinner. Closed Mon-Tues; also mid-Apr-mid-May, late Oct-mid-Nov. Bar. Casual attire. **$$$$**

★ ★ ★ **RED CLOVER.** *7 Woodward Rd, Mendon (05702). Phone 802/775-2290; toll-free 800/752-0571.* Sophisticated inn dining in three candlelit dining rooms (two have fireplaces) distinguish this charming country inn. Friendly service completes the experience. Dinner. Closed Sun; also day after Easter-day after Memorial Day. Bar. **$$**

★ ★ **VERMONT INN.** *Hwy 4, Killington (05751). Phone 802/775-0708; toll-free 800/541-7795; fax 802/773-2440. www.vermontinn.com.* Fireside dining.

Seafood menu. Dinner. Closed mid-Apr-Memorial Day. Bar. Children's menu. **$$**

Londonderry (E-2)

See also Grafton, Manchester and Manchester Center, Peru, Stratton Mountain, Weston

Founded 1770
Population 1,506
Elevation 1,151 ft
Area Code 802
Zip 05148
Information Londonderry Area Chamber of Commerce Mountain Marketplace, PO Box 58; phone 802/824-8178
Web Site www.londonderryvt.com

Limited-Service Hotel

★ ★ **DOSTAL'S RESORT LODGE.** *441 Magic Mountain Access Rd, Londonderry (05148). Phone 802/ 824-6700; toll-free 800/255-5373; fax 802/824-6701. www.dostals.com.* 50 rooms, 2 story. Closed Nov-mid-Dec. Check-out 11 am. Restaurant, bar. Indoor pool, outdoor pool, whirlpool. Tennis. **$**
🄳 🌊 🎿

Specialty Lodgings

The following lodging establishments are approved by Mobil Travel Guide, but due to their unique and individualized nature have not been given a traditional Mobil Star rating. Included in this listing you may find bed-and-breakfasts, limited-service inns, guest ranches, and other unique hotel properties.

FROG'S LEAP INN. *7455 Hwy 100, Londonderry (05148). Phone 802/824-3019; toll-free 877/376-4753; fax 802/824-3657. www.frogsleapinn.com.* This historic building (1842) is situated on 32 wooded acres. 17 rooms, 2 story. Closed three weeks in Apr and one week in Nov. Check-in 2 pm, check-out 11 am. Restaurant. Outdoor pool. Tennis. **$**
🌊 🎿

LONDONDERRY INN. *Hwy 100, Londonderry (05155). Phone 802/824-5226; fax 802/824-3146. www.londonderryinn.com.* This inn is a former farmhouse (1826). 25 rooms, 3 story. Complimentary continental breakfast. Check-in 2 pm, check-out 11 am. Restaurant. Outdoor pool. **$**
🄳 🌊

SWISS INN. *249 Hwy 11, Londonderry (05148). Phone 802/824-3442; toll-free 800/847-9477; fax 802/824-6313. www.swissinn.com.* 19 rooms, 2 story. Complimentary full breakfast. Check-out 11 am. Restaurant, bar. Outdoor pool. Tennis. **$**
🄳 🌊 🎿

Ludlow (E-2)

See also Okemo State Forest, Plymouth, Springfield, Weston

Population 2,302
Area Code 802
Zip 05149
Information Ludlow Area Chamber of Commerce, Okemo Market Pl, PO Box 333; phone 802/228-5830

What to See and Do

Crowley Cheese Factory. *103 Healdville Rd, Healdville (05758). Phone 802/259-2340.* (1882) Oldest cheese factory in the United States; still makes cheese by hand as in the 19th century. Display of tools used in early cheese factories and in home cheesemaking. Watch the process and sample the product. (Mon-Fri) **FREE**

Green Mountain Sugar House. *820 Hwy 100 N, Ludlow (05149). 4 miles N on Hwy 100 N. Phone 802/228-7151.* Working maple sugar producer on shore of Lake Pauline. Shop offers syrup, candies, crafts, and gifts. (Daily) **FREE**

Okemo Mountain Ski Area. (See OKEMO STATE FOREST)

Full-Service Inn

🔍 ★ ★ ★ **THE GOVERNOR'S INN.** *86 Main St, Ludlow (05149). Phone 802/228-8830; toll-free 800/468-3766; fax 802/228-2961. www.thegovernorsinn.com.* Skiers with a penchant for history are smitten by The Governor's Inn. The challenging slopes of Okemo Mountain are just a short distance away, and the inn provides convenient shuttle service from its doorstep to the base of the mountain. Non-skiers are instantly enchanted by Vermont's country charms while perusing the antiques shops and country stores of the village. The inn itself, dating to 1890, is a Victorian masterpiece in every detail. Floral patterns, period furniture, and antiques reflect a bygone era, and gas-lit stoves and fireplaces in many rooms add a romantic ambience. Breakfast is a truly

elegant affair, where tables are gracefully set with silver, crystal, and china. The talented chef's gourmet picnic baskets are heartwarming and delicious, and dinner is an equally inspired event. Diners taken with the cuisine may participate in one of the fantastic Culinary Magic Cooking Seminars, where the kitchen's secrets are happily shared. 9 rooms, 3 story. Closed late Dec; also two weeks in Apr and two weeks in Nov. Children over 12 years only. Complimentary full breakfast. Check-in 2 pm, check-out 11 am. Restaurant. **$$**
🅱

Specialty Lodgings

The following lodging establishments are approved by Mobil Travel Guide, but due to their unique and individualized nature have not been given a traditional Mobil Star rating. Included in this listing you may find bed-and-breakfasts, limited-service inns, guest ranches, and other unique hotel properties.

ANDRIE ROSE INN. *13 Pleasant St, Ludlow (05149). Phone 802/228-4846; toll-free 800/223-4846; fax 802/228-7910. www.andrieroseinn.com.* This cozy inn was built in 1829 and is nestled at the base of Okemo Mountain. The guest rooms are appointed with antiques, skylights, and whirlpool tubs. 23 rooms, 2 story. Complimentary full breakfast. Check-in 3 pm, check-out 11 am. **$**
🅱

COMBES FAMILY INN. *953 E Lake Rd, Ludlow (05149). Phone 802/228-8799; toll-free 800/822-8799; fax 802/228-8704. www.combesfamilyinn.com.* This restored farmhouse (1891) is on 50 acres and near Lake Rescue. 11 rooms, 2 story. Closed mid-Apr–mid-May. Pets accepted. Check-in 2 pm, check-out 11 am. Restaurant. **$**
🅱 🐾

GOLDEN STAGE INN. *399 Depot St, Proctorsville (05153). Phone 802/226-7744; toll-free 800/253-8226; fax 802/226-7882. www.goldenstageinn.com.* 9 rooms. Check-in 3-9 pm, check-out 11 am. Restaurant (public by reservation), bar. Outdoor pool. **$$**
🏊

INN AT WATER'S EDGE. *45 Kingdom Rd, Ludlow (05149). Phone 802/228-8143; toll-free 888/706-9736. www.innatwatersedge.com.* 11 rooms. Complimentary full breakfast. Check-in 4 pm, check-out 11 am. **$$**

Lyndonville (B-3)

See also St. Johnsbury

Settled 1781
Population 1,255
Elevation 720 ft
Area Code 802
Zip 05851
Information Lyndon Area Chamber of Commerce, PO Box 886; phone 802/626-9696
Web Site www.lyndonvermont.com

Home of small industries and trading center for the surrounding dairy and stock raising farms, Lyndonville lies in the valley of the Passumpsic River. Five covered bridges, the earliest dating to 1795, are located within the town limits.

What to See and Do

Burke Mountain Ski Area. *1 mile N on Hwy 5, then 6 miles NE on Hwy 114, in Darling State Park. Phone 802/626-3322. www.skiburke.com.* Area has two chairlifts, one Pomalift, J-bar; school, rentals; snowmaking. Two cafeterias, two bars; nursery. Forty-three runs, longest run approximately 2 1/2 miles; vertical drop 2,000 feet. More than 57 miles of cross-country trails. (Thanksgiving-early Apr, daily)

Lake Willoughby. *18 miles N on Hwy 5A.* Beaches, water sports, fishing; hiking trails to the summit of Mount Pisgah, at 2,741 feet.

Limited-Service Hotel

★ **COLONNADE INN.** *28 Back Center Rd, Lyndonville (05851). Phone 802/626-9316; toll-free 877/435-3688; fax 802/626-1023.* 40 rooms, 2 story. Complimentary continental breakfast. Check-out 11 am. **$**
🅱

Specialty Lodging

The following lodging establishment is approved by Mobil Travel Guide, but due to its unique and individualized nature has not been given a traditional Mobil Star rating. Included in this listing you may find bed-and-breakfasts, limited-service inns, guest ranches, and other unique hotel properties.

THE WILDFLOWER INN. *Darling Hill Rd, Lyndonville (05851). Phone 802/626-8310; toll-free 800/627-8310; fax 802/626-3039. www.wildflowerinn.com.* Family-oriented inn on 500 acres; barns, farm animals; sledding slopes. Art gallery. 25 rooms, 2 story. Closed two weeks in Apr and Nov. Complimentary full breakfast. Check-in 3 pm, check-out 11 am. Restaurant. Children's activity center. Outdoor pool, children's pool, whirlpool. Tennis. **$**

Manchester and Manchester Center (E-1)

See also Arlington, Bennington, Dorset, Green Mountain National Forest, Londonderry, Peru, Stratton Mountain

Settled 1764
Population 3,622
Elevation 899 and 753 ft
Area Code 802
Zip Manchester 05254; Manchester Center 05255
Information Manchester and the Mountains Regional Chamber of Commerce, 5046 Main St, Suite 1; phone 802/362-2100 or toll-free 800/362-4144
Web Site www.manchestervermont.net

These towns have been among Vermont's best-loved year-round resorts for 100 years. The surrounding mountains make them serenely attractive, and the ski business has added to their following. Bromley Mountain, Stratton Mountain, and other areas lure thousands each year. A Ranger District office of the Green Mountain National Forest is located here.

What to See and Do

American Museum of Fly Fishing. *3657 Main St, Manchester (05254). VT Historic Hwy 7A and Seminary Ave. Phone 802/362-3300. www.amff.com.* This museum, founded in 1968 by fishermen who wanted to ensure that the history of their sport would not be lost, is a mecca for anglers of all ages. Collection of fly-fishing memorabilia; tackle of many famous persons, including Dwight D. Eisenhower, Ernest Hemingway, Andrew Carnegie, Winslow Homer, Bing Crosby, and others. (Mon-Fri 10 am-4 pm; closed holidays) **$**

Emerald Lake State Park. *65 Emerald Lake Ln, North Dorset (05253). 6 miles N on Hwy 7. Phone 802/362-1655.* This 430-acre park has rich flora in a limestone-based bedrock. Swimming beach, bathhouse, fishing (also in nearby streams), boating (rentals); nature and hiking trails, picnicking, concession. Tent and trailer sites (dump station), lean-tos. (Memorial Day-Columbus Day)

✪ Equinox Sky Line Drive. *1A St and Bruno Dr, Manchester and Manchester Center (05250). 5 miles S on VT Historic Hwy 7A. Phone 802/362-1114.* A spectacular 5-mile paved road that rises from 600 to 3,835 feet; parking and picnic areas along road; view from top of Mount Equinox. Fog or rain may make mountain road dangerous and travel inadvisable. (May-Oct, daily) No large camper vehicles. **$$$**

Factory outlet stores. *Hwy 11/30, Manchester Center (05255). Phone 802/362-2100.* Many outlet stores can be found in this area, mainly along Highway 11/30 and at the intersection of Highway 11/30 and Highway 7A. Contact the Chamber of Commerce for a complete listing of stores.

Historic Hildene. *1005 Hildene Rd, Manchester Village. 2 miles S via VT Historic Hwy 7A. Phone 802/362-1788.* (1904) The 412-acre estate of Robert Todd Lincoln (Abraham Lincoln's son) includes a 24-room Georgian manor house, held in the family until 1975; original furnishings; carriage barn; formal gardens; nature trails. Tours. (Mid-May-Oct, daily) **$$$**

Merck Forest & Farmland Center. *8 miles NW on Hwy 30 to East Rupert, then 2 1/2 miles W on Hwy 315. Phone 802/394-7836.* Includes 3,100 acres of unspoiled upland forest, meadows, mountains, and ponds; 28 miles of roads and trails for hiking and cross-country skiing. Fishing; picnicking, camping (reservations required). Educational programs. Fees for some activities.

Southern Vermont Arts Center. *West Rd, Manchester. 1 mile N off West Rd. Phone 802/362-1405; toll-free 800/639-3819.* Painting, sculpture, prints; concerts, music festivals; botany trail; café. Gift shop. (Late May-mid-Oct, Tues-Sun) **$$$**

Limited-Service Hotels

★ ASPEN MOTEL. *Hwy 7A N, Manchester Center (05255). Phone 802/362-2450; fax 802/362-1348. www.thisisvermont.com/aspen.* 24 rooms. Check-out 11 am. Outdoor pool. **$**

★ **MANCHESTER VIEW.** *Hwy 7A and High Meadow Way, Manchester Center (05255). Phone 802/362-2739; toll-free 800/548-4141; fax 802/362-2199. www.manchesterview.com.* 35 rooms, 2 story. Check-out 11 am. Fitness room. Outdoor pool. **$**

★ **OLYMPIA MOTOR LODGE.** *7259 Main St, Manchester Center (05255). Phone 802/362-1700; fax 802/362-1705. www.olympia-vt.com.* 24 rooms, 2 story. Check-out 11 am. Bar. Outdoor pool. Tennis. **$**

★ **WEATHERVANE MOTEL.** *2212 Main St, Hwy 7A, Manchester (05254). Phone 802/362-2444; toll-free 800/687-8382; fax 802/362-4616. www.weathervane motel.com.* 22 rooms. Complimentary continental breakfast. Check-in 3 pm, check-out 11 am. Outdoor pool, whirlpool. **$**

Full-Service Resort

★ ★ ★ **THE EQUINOX.** *3567 Main St, Manchester Village (05254). Phone 802/362-4700; toll-free 800/362-4747; fax 802/362-4861. www.equinoxresort.com.* Since 1769, The Equinox has welcomed visitors with open arms. This premier resort set on 1,100 acres has long been a favorite of notables, including Abraham Lincoln's family, who vacationed here in the 1800s. Located on historic Route 7A in the shadow of Mount Equinox, this classic New England getaway offers guests a truly well-rounded adventure. From world-class golf at the Gleneagles golf course and skiing at nearby Stratton and Bromley mountains to falconry, Orvis fly fishing and shooting schools, and even off-road driving with Hummers and Land Rovers, this place is a paradise for sports enthusiasts. The Avanyu Spa and nearby shopping in Manchester Village appeal to others, and three restaurants combine historic charm and classic fare for enjoyable dining experiences. 183 rooms, 4 story. Check-in 4 pm, check-out 11 am. Three restaurants, bar. Fitness room, fitness classes available, spa. Indoor pool, whirlpool. Golf, 18 holes. Tennis. Airport transportation available. Business center. **$$$$**

Full-Service Inns

★ ★ ★ **RELUCTANT PANTHER INN AND RESTAURANT.** *39 West Rd, Manchester (05254). Phone 802/362-2568; toll-free 800/822-2331. www.*

reluctantpanther.com. This lovely inn was built in 1850 by a local wealthy blacksmith. The owners have refurbished the property and were able to retain two of the original fireplaces. 13 rooms. No children allowed. Complimentary full breakfast. Check-in 3 pm, check-out 11 am. Restaurant. **$$**

★ ★ ★ **VILLAGE COUNTRY INN.** *3835 Main St, Historic Hwy 7A, Manchester (05254). Phone 802/362-1792; toll-free 800/370-0300; fax 802/362-7238. www.villagecountryinn.com.* Located in the charming village of Manchester, this small bed-and-breakfast is perfect for a romantic getaway. Guest rooms are adorned with lace, chintz, and canopied beds. Relax in the formal living room that has a fieldstone fireplace and an old working sleigh as the coffee table. 32 rooms, 3 story. Pets accepted, some restrictions; fee, Children over 12 years only. Complimentary full breakfast. Check-in 2 pm, check-out 11 am. Restaurant, bar. Outdoor pool. **$**

Specialty Lodgings

The following lodging establishments are approved by Mobil Travel Guide, but due to their unique and individualized nature have not been given a traditional Mobil Star rating. Included in this listing you may find bed-and-breakfasts, limited-service inns, guest ranches, and other unique hotel properties.

1811 HOUSE. *Hwy 7A, Manchester (05254). Phone 802/362-1811; toll-free 800/432-1811; fax 802/362-2443. www.1811house.com.* Each guest room at the inn is named for individuals that were prominent in the history of the Manchester. Gardens grace 7 1/2 acres around the inn. 13 rooms, 2 story. Children over 16 years only. Complimentary full breakfast. Check-in 2 pm, check-out 11 am. Bar. Tennis. **$$**

INN AT MANCHESTER. *Hwy 7A, Manchester (05254). Phone 802/362-1793; toll-free 800/273-1793; fax 802/362-3218. www.innatmanchester.com.* A lovely inn where guests find "peace, pancakes, and pampering," this 19th-century Victorian structure has been beautifully restored to its original grandeur. 18 rooms, 3 story. Children over 8 years only. Complimentary full breakfast. Check-in 2 pm, check-out 11 am. Outdoor pool. **$$**

MANCHESTER HIGHLANDS INN. *216 Highland Ave, Manchester Center (05255). Phone 802/362-4565; toll-free 800/743-4565; fax 802/362-4028. www. highlandsinn.com.* 15 rooms, 3 story. Complimentary full breakfast. Check-in 2 pm, check-out 11 am. Outdoor pool. **$**

PALMER HOUSE. *Hwy 7A, Manchester Center (05255). Phone 802/362-3600; toll-free 800/917-6245; fax 802/362-3600. www.palmerhouse.com.* This 20-acre resort is located in the heart of Manchester, nestled in the surrounding mountains. 50 rooms. Children over 12 only. Check-in 3 pm, check-out 11 am. Fitness room. Indoor pool, outdoor pool, whirlpool. Golf, 9 holes. Tennis. **$$**

WILBURTON INN. *River Rd, Manchester Village (05254). Phone 802/362-2500; toll-free 800/648-4944; fax 802/362-1107. www.wilburton.com.* Set on a hill that overlooks the Battenkill Valley, this 20-acre Victorian estate is a terrific choice for a weekend in New England. Guests can enjoy many activities on the property or enjoy the shopping nearby. The spacious grounds feature sculptured displays, and the inn offers mountain views. 30 rooms, 3 story. Complimentary full breakfast. Check-in 1 pm, check-out 11 am. Restaurant, bar. Outdoor pool. Tennis. **$$**

Restaurant

★ ★ ★ **BLACK SWAN.** *Hwy 7A, Manchester (05254). Phone 802/362-3807. www.blackswanrestaurant.com.* This restaurant is a converted farmhouse built in the 1800s. International/Fusion menu. Dinner. Closed Thanksgiving. Bar. **$$**

Marlboro (F-2)

See also Brattleboro, Wilmington

Settled 1763
Population 924
Elevation 1,736 ft
Area Code 802
Zip 05344

What to See and Do

Marlboro College. *South Rd, Marlboro. 2 1/2 miles S of Hwy 9. Phone 802/257-4333.* (1946) (300 students)

Arts and sciences, international studies. On campus is Drury Art Gallery (Mon-Fri; closed holidays).

Special Event

Marlboro Music Festival. *Phone 802/254-2394.* Marlboro College campus. Chamber music concerts. Mid-July-mid-Aug.

Middlebury (C-1)

See also Brandon, Vergennes

Settled 1761
Population 8,034
Elevation 366 ft
Area Code 802
Zip 05753
Information Addison County Chamber of Commerce Information Center, 2 Court St; phone 802/388-7951 or toll-free 800/733-8376
Web Site www.midvermont.com

Benjamin Smalley built the first log house here just before the Revolution. In 1800, the town had a full-fledged college. By 1803, there was a flourishing marble quarry and a women's academy run by Emma Hart Willard, a pioneer in education for women; today, it is known as Middlebury College. A Ranger District office of the Green Mountain National Forest is located here; map and guides for day hikes on Long Trail are available.

What to See and Do

Congregational Church. *27 N Pleasant St, Middlebury (05753). On the Common. Phone 802/388-7634.* (1806-1809) Built after a plan in the *Country Builder's Assistant* and designed by architect Lavius Fillmore. Architecturally, one of finest in Vermont. (Mid-June-Aug, Fri-Sat)

Henry Sheldon Museum. *1 Park St, Middlebury (05753). Phone 802/388-2117.* Comprehensive collection of 19th-century "Vermontiana" in brick house (1829) with black marble fireplaces. Authentic furnishings range from hand-forged kitchen utensils to country and high-style furniture. Museum also features oil portraits, pewter, Staffordshire, clocks, pianos, toys, dolls, and local relics. Guided and self-guided tours. (Daily; closed holidays) **$$**

Historic Middlebury Village Walking Tour. *2 Court St, Middlebury (05753). Phone 802/388-7951.* Contact the Addison County Chamber of Commerce Information Center for map and information.

Middlebury College. *W of town on Hwy 125. Phone 802/443-5000.* (1800) (1,950 students) Famous for the teaching of arts and sciences; summer language schools; Bread Loaf School of English and Writers' Conference. College includes

Bread Loaf. *10 miles E on Hwy 125. Phone 802/388-7951.* Site of nationally known Bread Loaf School of English in July and annual Writers' Conference in August. Also site of Robert Frost's cabin. In winter, it is the Carroll and Jane Rikert Ski Touring Center.

Emma Willard House. *Phone 802/388-7951.* Location of first women's seminary (1814), now admissions and financial aid offices.

Middlebury College Museum of Art. *Hwy 30, Middlebury (05753). Phone 802/443-5007.* (Tues-Sun; closed Jan 1, Thanksgiving, Dec 25) **FREE**

Middlebury College Snow Bowl. *13 miles E on Hwy 125, just E of Bread Loaf. Phone 802/388-4356.* Area has triple, two double chairlifts; patrol, school, rentals; snowmaking; cafeteria. Fourteen runs. (Early Dec-early Apr, daily; closed Dec 25) **$$$$**

Old Stone Row. *Phone 802/388-7951.* Includes Painter Hall (1815), the oldest college building in the state.

⭐ **Starr Library.** *Phone 802/388-7951.* Has a collection of works by Robert Frost and other American writers. (Daily; closed holidays)

UVM Morgan Horse Farm. *74 Battell Dr, Weybridge (05753). 2 1/2 miles NW off Hwy 23. Phone 802/388-2011.* Breeding and training farm for internationally acclaimed Morgan horses; owned by the University of Vermont. Daily workouts and training can be viewed. Guided tours, slide presentations. (May-Oct, daily) **$$**

Vermont State Craft Center at Frog Hollow. *1 Mill St, Middlebury (05753). Phone 802/388-3177.* Restored mill overlooking Otter Creek Falls houses an exhibition and sales gallery with works of more than 300 Vermont craftspeople. Special exhibitions, classes and workshops. (Spring-fall: daily; rest of year: Mon-Sat; closed holidays) **FREE**

Special Events

Addison County Home and Garden Show. Exhibits, demonstrations. Usually last weekend in Mar.

Festival on the Green. *Main St and Hwy 7, Middlebury (05753).* Village green. Classical, modern, and traditional dance; chamber and folk music; theater and comedy presentations. Early July.

Winter Carnival. The oldest and largest student-run carnival in the country includes fireworks, an ice show and ski competitions; held on the campus of Middlebury College. Late Feb.

Limited-Service Hotel

★ ★ **MIDDLEBURY INN.** *14 Court House Sq, Middlebury (05753). Phone 802/388-4961; toll-free 800/842-4666; fax 802/388-4563. www.middleburyinn.com.* This inn was established in 1827. 45 rooms, 3 story. Pets accepted, some restrictions. Complimentary continental breakfast. Check-in 3 pm, check-out 11 am. Restaurant, bar. **$$**
🐾

Full-Service Inn

★ ★ ★ **SWIFT HOUSE INN.** *25 Stewart Ln, Middlebury (05753). Phone 802/388-9925; fax 802/388-9927. www.swifthouseinn.com.* This inn is composed of three separate buildings, each with its own character and charm. Rooms are individually decorated and feature four-poster beds and handmade quilts. 2 story. Complimentary continental breakfast. Check-in 3 pm, check-out 11 am. Restaurant. **$$**

Specialty Lodging

The following lodging establishment is approved by Mobil Travel Guide, but due to its unique and individualized nature has not been given a traditional Mobil Star rating. Included in this listing you may find bed-and-breakfasts, limited-service inns, guest ranches, and other unique hotel properties.

WAYBURY INN. *457 E Main (Hwy 125), East Middlebury (05743). Phone 802/388-4015; toll-free 800/348-1810; fax 802/388-1248. www.wayburyinn.com.* Constructed as a stagecoach stop; an inn since 1810. Near Middlebury College. 14 rooms. Complimentary full breakfast. Check-in 3 pm, check-out 11 am. Restaurant, bar. **$**
🗓

Montpelier (C-2)

See also Barre, Waitsfield, Waterbury

Settled 1787
Population 8,247
Elevation 525 ft
Area Code 802
Information Central Vermont Chamber of Commerce, PO Box 336, Barre 05641; phone 802/229-5711
Web Site www.central-vt.com

The state capital, on the banks of the Winooski River, is also a life insurance center. Admiral Dewey, victor at Manila Bay, was born here. A popular summer vacation area, Montpelier absorbs the overflow from the nearby ski areas in winter.

What to See and Do

Hubbard Park. *22 Corse St, Montpelier (05602). 1 mile NW, on Hubbard Park Dr. Phone 802/223-5141.* A 110-acre wooded area with picnic area (shelter, fireplaces, water). Stone observation tower (1932). **FREE**

Morse Farm. *1168 County Rd, Montpelier (05602). 3 miles N via County Rd (follow signs on Main St). Phone 802/223-2740; toll-free 800/242-2740.* Maple sugar and vegetable farm in rustic, wooded setting. Tour of sugar house; view sugarmaking process in season (Mar-Apr); slide show explains process off-season. Gift shop. (Daily; closed Easter, Dec 25) **FREE**

State House. *115 State St, Montpelier (05633). Phone 802/828-2228.* (1859) Made of Vermont granite; dome covered with gold leaf. (Mon-Fri, also Sat late morning-early afternoon July-mid-Oct) **FREE**

Thomas Waterman Wood Art Gallery. *36 College St, Montpelier (05602). In Vermont College Arts Center. Phone 802/828-8743.* Oils, watercolors, and etchings by Wood and other 19th-century American artists. Also American artists of the 1920s and '30s; changing monthly exhibits of works of contemporary local and regional artists. (Tues-Sun afternoons; closed holidays) **$**

Vermont Department of Libraries. *109 State St, Montpelier (05602). Pavilion Office Bldg. Phone 802/828-3261.* Local and state history collections. (Mon-Fri; closed holidays) **FREE**

Vermont Historical Society Museum, Library. *109 State St, Montpelier (05602). Pavilion Office Bldg, adjacent to State House. Phone 802/479-8500.* Historical exhibits. (Tues-Sun; closed holidays) **$$**

Limited-Service Hotel

★ **COMFORT INN.** *213 Paine Turnpike N, Montpelier (05602). Phone 802/229-2222; toll-free 800/228-5150; fax 802/229-2222. www.choicehotels.com.* 89 rooms, 3 story. Complimentary continental breakfast. Check-out 11 am. Bar. Airport transportation available. **$**

Full-Service Hotel

★ ★ ★ **CAPITOL PLAZA HOTEL AND CONFERENCE CENTER.** *100 State St, Montpelier (05602). Phone 802/223-5252; toll-free 800/274-5252; fax 802/229-5427. www.capitolplaza.com.* Located in the heart of Montpelier and across the street from the historic State House, this hotel has been serving Vermont's lawmakers and tourists since the 1930s. 56 rooms, 4 story. Check-out 11 am. Restaurant, bar. **$**

Full-Service Inns

★ ★ ★ **INN AT MONTPELIER.** *147 Main St, Montpelier (05602). Phone 802/223-2727; fax 802/223-0722. www.innatmontpelier.com.* Take a trip back to the early 1800s with a visit to this historic inn. The two stately buildings that make up this inn showcase Greek and Colonial Revival woodwork, numerous fireplaces, and a magnificent front staircase. 19 rooms, 2 story. Complimentary continental breakfast. Check-in 3-9 pm, check-out 11 am. **$**
🄳

★ ★ ★ **THE INN ON THE COMMON.** *1162 N Craftsbury Rd, Craftsbury Common (05827). Phone 802/586-9619; toll-free 800/521-2233; fax 802/586-2249. www.innonthecommon.com.* Nestled under a large maple tree, this inn, which consists of three restored Federal-style houses, offers colorful gardens and wooded hillsides. Individually decorated guest rooms feature antiques, artwork, and sitting areas. 16 rooms, 2 story. Pets accepted, some restrictions; fee. Check-in 1 pm, check-out 11 am. Restaurant, bar. Outdoor pool. Tennis. **$$**
🄳 🐾 🏊 ⛷

Specialty Lodging

The following lodging establishment is approved by Mobil Travel Guide, but due to its unique and individualized nature has not been given a traditional Mobil Star rating. Included in this listing you may find bed-and-breakfasts, limited-service inns, guest ranches, and other unique hotel properties.

NORTHFIELD INN. *228 Highland Ave, Northfield (05663). Phone 802/485-8558. www.thenorthfieldinn .com.* This inn was built in 1901 and is furnished with period pieces. 28 rooms, 3 story. Children over 15 years only. Complimentary full breakfast. Check-in 3-6 pm, check-out 11 am. **$**
⬛ 🖼️

Restaurant

★ ★ **CHEF'S TABLE.** *118 Main St, Montpelier (05602). Phone 802/229-9202; fax 802/223-9285. www.necidining.com/chefmain.htm.* International/ Fusion menu. Dinner. Closed Sun; holidays. Bar. **$$$**

Newfane (F-2)

See also Brattleboro, Grafton

Settled 1774
Population 1,555
Elevation 536 ft
Area Code 802
Zip 05345
Information Town Clerk, PO Box 36; phone 802/365-7772
Web Site www.newfanevt.com

Originally settled high on Newfane Hill, this is a charming, sleepy town. American poet Eugene Field spent many summer holidays here.

What to See and Do

Jamaica State Park. *48 Salmon Hole Ln, Jamaica. 13 miles W on Hwy 30. Phone 802/874-4600.* On 758 acres. Old train bed along West River serves as trail to Ball Mountain Dam. Fishing; hiking trails, picnicking, tent and trailer sites (dump station), lean-tos. Whitewater canoeing on river. (May-Columbus Day) **$$**

Scott Covered Bridge. *Over the West River in Townshend, 5 miles N via Hwy 30.* (1870) Longest single span in state (166 feet), built with lattice-type trusses. Together, the three spans total 276 feet. Other two spans are of king post-type trusses.

Townshend State Forest. *2755 State Forest Rd, Townshend (05353). 6 miles N, off Hwy 30. Phone* 802/365-7500. A 1,690-acre area with foot trail to Bald Mountain (1,580 feet). Swimming at nearby Reservoir Recreation Area; hiking trails, picnic sites, tent and trailer sites. (May-Columbus Day)

Windham County Courthouse. *On the green.* (1825)

Windham County Historical Society Museum. *Main St, Newfane (05345). On Hwy 30, across from the Village Green. Phone 802/365-4148.* Contains artifacts from the 21 towns of Windham County; exhibits on the Civil War and the Vermont Regiment. (Memorial Day-Columbus Day, Wed-Sun) **DONATION**

Full-Service Inn

★ ★ ★ **WINDHAM HILL INN.** *311 Lawrence Dr, West Townshend (05359). Phone 802/874-4080; toll-free 800/944-4080; fax 802/874-4702. www.windhamhill.com.* Capture the peacefulness and serenity that can be found at this charming and elegant 1825 country estate perched amidst 160 well-maintained acres. Relax, surrounded by lush trees, fields, and an impressive rock wall border. Guests will find the views to be extraordinary, the rooms handsomely furnished, and the service warm and extremely friendly. 21 rooms, 3 story. Children over 12 years only. Check-in 2 pm, check-out 11 am. Restaurant. Outdoor pool. Tennis. **$$**
⬛ 🖼️ 🎿

Specialty Lodging

The following lodging establishment is approved by Mobil Travel Guide, but due to its unique and individualized nature has not been given a traditional Mobil Star rating. Included in this listing you may find bed-and-breakfasts, limited-service inns, guest ranches, and other unique hotel properties.

FOUR COLUMNS INN. *21 West St, Newfane (05345). Phone 802/365-7713; toll-free 800/787-6633; fax 802/365-0022. www.fourcolumnsinn.com.* Located in the center of the country village of Newfane, yet nestled at the foot of a 150-acre private mountain, this 16-room inn combines historic charm with modern convenience. While some rooms are without TVs, they do have wireless Internet access. The décor is charmingly old-fashioned, yet all comfort: king beds, queens, sleigh beds, iron four-poster beds. Many suites have two-sided fireplaces, most rooms have whirlpools or soaking tubs, and everywhere there are fine art prints and antiques that provide interest without being fussy. The popular front suite has a whirlpool under large windows that overlook the village center and a huge, walk-in shower with 12 jets. Local lore says the four columns of this 1833 inn were initiated by the original owner's wife, who was Southern and missed her native architecture. 16 rooms. Pets accepted, some restrictions; fee. Complimentary continental breakfast. Check-in 2 pm, check-out 11 am. Restaurant, bar. Outdoor pool. **$$$**

Restaurants

★ ★ ★ **FOUR COLUMNS.** *21 West St, Newfane (05345). Phone 802/365-7713; toll-free 800/787-6633; fax 802/365-0022. www.fourcolumnsinn.com.* Chef Greg Parks has been cooking at this charming inn for many years, but his cuisine is as contemporary as you can find. American menu. Breakfast, dinner. Closed Tues. Bar. Casual attire. Reservations recommended. Outdoor seating. **$$$**

★ ★ ★ **OLD NEWFANE INN.** *Hwy 30, Newfane (05345). Phone 802/365-4427; toll-free 800/784-4427. www.oldnewfaneinn.com.* Timbered ceilings, brick fireplaces, and pewter cover plates add to the colonial charm of this historic 1787 landmark. French, Swiss menu. Breakfast, dinner. Closed Mon; Apr-mid-May, Nov-mid-Dec. Bar. Casual attire. Reservations recommended. **$$**

Newport (A-3)

Settled 1793
Population 4,434
Elevation 723 ft
Area Code 802
Zip 05855
Information Chamber of Commerce, The Causeway; phone 802/334-7782

Just a few miles from the Canadian border, Newport lies at the southern end of Lake Memphremagog. Rugged Owl's Head (3,360 feet) guards the western shore of the lake. Recreational activities in the area include swimming, fishing, boating, camping, skiing, and snowmobiling.

What to See and Do

Goodrich Memorial Library. *70 Main St, Newport (05855). Phone 802/334-7902.* Artifacts of old

Vermont in historic building; animal display. (Mon-Sat; closed holidays) **FREE**

Haskell Opera House & Library. *1 Caswell Ave, Derby Line (05830). 8 miles N via Hwy 5, on Caswell Ave, also in Stanstead, QC, Canada. Phone 802/873-3022. www.haskellopera.org.* Historic turn-of-the-century building owned jointly by local Canadian and US residents. First floor houses library with reading room in United States, book stacks in Canada. Second floor is historic turn-of-the-century opera house that preserves much of its antiquity (seats 400) with audience in United States, stage in Canada. Summer concert series (fee). Tours (Tues-Sat, fee)

Newport's *Princess*. *City Dock. Phone 802/334-6617.* Cruise Lake Memphremagog in both United States and Canadian waters aboard sternwheeler with turn-of-the-century décor. Cruises include Sightseeing (90 minutes), Pizza (90 minutes, reservations required), Buffet Dinner (two hours, reservations required), Moonlight (90 minutes), and Weekend Brunch (90 minutes, reservations required). (May-Oct, daily; departures vary)

Northeast Kingdom Tours. *3 Clough St, Newport (05855). Phone 802/334-8687.* Escorted bus tours depart from Newport Municipal Building and local motels. Narrated trips (two and four hours) explore international border region (Vermont/Canada); includes stops at dairy farm and Old Stone House museum. Cruises on Lake Memphremagog and trips to Montréal also available.

Old Stone House. *28 Old Stone House Rd, Orleans (05860). 11 miles SE via Hwy 5S or I-91 S to Orleans, then 2 miles NE on unnumbered road to Brownington Village. Phone 802/754-2022.* (1836) Museum housed in four-story granite building with antique furniture; early farm, household, and military items; 19th-century schoolbooks. (July-Aug: daily; mid-May-June, Sept-mid-Oct: Mon-Tues, Fri-Sun) **$$**

Limited-Service Hotel

★ **SUPER 8.** *974 E Main St, Derby (05829). Phone 802/334-1775; toll-free 800/800-8000; fax 802/334-1994. www.super8.com.* 52 rooms, 2 story. Complimentary continental breakfast. Check-out 11 am. **$**

Champlain Islands Bicycle Tour

A land chain composed of the Alburg peninsula and three islands—Isle La Motte, North Hero, and South Hero—straggles down the middle of Lake Champlain. The islands are connected by bridges to one another and by causeways to the mainland. Together they comprise Grand Isle Country (population 4,000).

This is old farm and resort country. In the 19th century, visitors arrived by lake steamer to stay at farms. Roads are flat and little trafficked once you are off Highway 2 (the main road down the spine of the islands). Views are splendid: east across the lake to Vermont's Green Mountains and west to New York's Adirondacks. Isle La Motte, the smallest and quietest of the islands, is beloved by bicyclists.

The obvious place to begin a loop here is in the parking lot at St. Anne's Shrine on Highway 129 in the northwestern corner of the island. Here an open-sided Victorian chapel on the shore marks the site of Vermont' first French settlement in 1666. There is a public beach, a picnic area in a large pine grove, and a large statue of Samuel de Champlain, who is credited with discovering New England's largest lake.

Pedal south from the shrine along the West Shore Road. Mountain bike rentals are available from Bike Shed Rentals, located a mile below the shrine. At 2.4 miles note the magnificent views west to the Adirondacks from the public boat access. At 3.7 miles the road turns to hard-packed dirt for 1.3 miles. Look for Fisk Farm (44 West Shore Rd), a complex of buildings that includes an attractive bed-and-breakfast and gallery, also the ruins of a large old stone house that Vice President Theodore Roosevelt was visiting when he received the news that President McKinley had been shot. Beside the farm is the Fisk Quarry, the oldest in Vermont and part of a 480-million-year-old coral reef that underlies the southern third of the island. Open to the public, the quarry is studded with fossils that represent some of the most primitive life earth has known.

Keep to the main road as it curves to the east (pavement resumes), past Hall's Apple Orchards, which has been in the same family since the early 1800s. Its farmhouse is built of the island's distinctive "marble" (dark limestone). The road continues north past the Isle La Motte Historical Society, housed in an old schoolhouse; look for another reef (said to be 450 million years old) in a nearby field. At 7.4 miles you are at the four corners that mark the middle of Isle La Motte village with its country store and picnic benches by the pond. Another fine old stone building houses the public library. At 9 miles turn onto Shrine Road and bear left at the "Y". Follow the paved road back to the shrine. The total loop is 10 miles.

North Hero

See also Swanton

Population 502
Elevation 111 ft
Area Code 802
Zip 05474
Information Champlain Islands Chamber of Commerce, PO Box 213; phone 802/372-8400
Web Site www.champlainislands.com

What to See and Do

North Hero State Park. *3803 Lakeview Dr, North Hero (05474). 6 miles N, off Hwy 2 near South Alburg. Phone 802/372-8727.* A 399-acre park located in the north part of the Champlain Islands; extensive shoreline on Lake Champlain. Swimming, fishing, boating (ramps); hiking trails, playground, tent and trailer sites (dump station), lean-tos. (Memorial Day-Labor Day)

Special Event

Royal Lippizan Stallions of Austria. *6231 Arbor Blvd West, North Hero (34119).* Summer residence of the stallions. Performances Thurs and Fri evenings, Sat and Sun afternoons. For ticket prices, contact Chamber of Commerce. July-Aug.

Limited-Service Hotel

★ ★ **SHORE ACRES INN.** *237 Shore Acres*

Dr, North Hero (05474). Phone 802/372-8722. www.shoreacres.com. 23 rooms. Pets accepted, some restrictions; fee. Check-out 10:30 am. Restaurant, bar. Tennis. **$**

Full-Service Inn

★ ★ ★ **NORTH HERO HOUSE INN.** *Hwy 2, North Hero (05474). Phone 802/372-4732; toll-free 888/ 525-3644; fax 802/372-3218. www.northherohouse.com.* This inn, built in 1800, is surrounded by spectacular views of the Green Mountains and Mount Mansfield. Activities are available year-round. 26 rooms, 3 story. Complimentary continental breakfast. Check-in 2 pm, check-out 11 am. Restaurant, bar. Tennis. **$$**

Specialty Lodging

The following lodging establishment is approved by Mobil Travel Guide, but due to its unique and individualized nature has not been given a traditional Mobil Star rating. Included in this listing you may find bed-and-breakfasts, limited-service inns, guest ranches, and other unique hotel properties.

THOMAS MOTT ALBURG HOMESTEAD B&B. *63 Blue Rock Rd, Alburg (05440). Phone 802/796-4402; toll-free 800/348-0843. www.thomas-mott-bb.com.* This restored farmhouse (1838) overlooks the lake. 4 rooms, 2 story. Children over 6 years only. Complimentary full breakfast. Check-in 3 pm, check-out 11 am. **$**

Restaurant

★ ★ **NORTH HERO HOUSE.** *Hwy 2, North Hero (05474). Phone 802/372-4732; fax 802/372-3218. www.northherohouse.com.* Breakfast, dinner, Sun brunch. Bar. Outdoor seating. **$$**

Okemo
State Forest (E-2)

See also Ludlow, Weston

Mount Okemo (3,372 feet), almost a lone peak in south central Vermont near Ludlow, commands splen-did views of the Adirondacks, the White Mountains, the Connecticut Valley, and Vermont's own Green Mountains. A road goes to within 1/2 mile of the mountain top (summer, fall; free); from there, it's an easy hike to the fire tower at the top. Surrounding Mount Okemo is the 4,527-acre state forest, which is primarily a skiing area.

Area has seven quad, three triple chairlifts, two Pomalifts, J-bar; patrol, school, rentals; snowmaking; cafeteria, restaurants, bar; nursery; 83 runs, longest run 4 1/2 miles; vertical drop 2,150 feet. (Early Nov-mid-Apr, daily) For information about area lodging, phone toll-free 800/786-5366.

Peru (E-2)

See also Dorset, Londonderry, Manchester and Manchester Center, Stratton Mountain, Weston

Settled 1773
Population 324
Elevation 1,700 ft
Area Code 802
Zip 05152

This small mountain village has many fine examples of classic New England architecture, such as the Congregational Church (1846). Spectacular views of the Green Mountains surround this skiing center; it is also a popular area for fishing, hunting, and hiking.

What to See and Do

Bromley Mountain Ski Area. *2 miles SW on Hwy 11. Phone 802/824-5522. www.bromley.com.* Area has two quad, five double chairlifts, two mitey-mites, J-bar; patrol, school, rentals; snowmaking; two cafeterias, restaurant, two lounges; nursery. Forty-two runs, longest run over 2 miles; vertical drop 1,334 feet. (Mid-Nov-mid-Apr, daily)

Bromley Alpine Slide. *Rte 11, Peru. Phone 802/ 824-5522.* Speed-controlled sled ride and scenic chairlift; café, picnic area. Outdoor deck. Multistate view. (Late May-mid-Oct, daily, weather permitting) **$$$**

Summer activities. Includes miniature golf, thrill sleds, children's theater. (Mid-June-mid-Oct)

Hapgood Pond Recreation Area. *2 miles NE on Hapgood Pond Rd, in Green Mountain National Forest.*

Phone 802/824-6456. Swimming, fishing, boating; picnicking, camping. Fee for various activities. **$$**

J.J. Hapgood Store. *Main St, Peru. Phone 802/824-5911.* (1827). General store featuring interesting old items; also penny candy, maple syrup, cheese. (Daily)

Wild Wings Ski Touring Center. *North Rd, Peru. 2 1/2 miles N on North Rd. Phone 802/824-6793.* Ski school, rentals; warming room; concession. Twelve miles of groomed cross-country trails. **$$$**

Plymouth (D-2)

See also Killington, Ludlow, Woodstock

Population 440
Elevation 1,406 ft
Area Code 802
Zip 05056
Information Town of Plymouth, HC 70, Box 39A; phone 802/672-3655

Seemingly unaware of the 21st century, this town hasn't changed much since July 4, 1872, when Calvin Coolidge was born in the back of the village store, still in business today. A country road leads to the cemetery where the former president and six generations of his family are buried. Nearby is the Coolidge Visitor Center and Museum, which displays historical and presidential memorabilia.

What to See and Do

Calvin Coolidge State Forest. *855 Coolidge St Park Rd, Plymouth (05056). 1 mile N off Hwy 100A, Calvin Coolidge Memorial Hwy. Phone 802/672-3612.* A 16,165-acre area. Hiking, snowmobile trails. Picnic facilities. Tent and trailer sites (dump station), primitive camping, lean-tos. (Memorial Day-Columbus Day)

Plymouth Cheese Corporation. *Town Hwy 4, Plymouth. Phone 802/672-3650.* Cheese, canned products, maple syrup, and honey. Cheese processed Mon-Wed. (Facility open late May-Nov: daily; rest of year: Mon-Fri; closed Jan 1, Thanksgiving, Dec 25) **FREE**

President Calvin Coolidge Homestead. *Coolidge Memorial Dr, Plymouth Notch. 1 mile NE on Hwy 100A. Phone 802/672-3773.* Restored to its early 20th-century appearance. Calvin Coolidge was sworn in by his father in the sitting room in 1923. The Plymouth Historic District also includes the General Store that was operated by the president's father, the house

where the president was born, the village dance hall that served as the 1924 summer White House office, the Union Church with its Carpenter Gothic interior, the Wilder House (birthplace of Coolidge's mother), the Wilder Barn with 19th-century farming equipment, a restaurant, and a visitor center with museum. (Late May-mid-Oct, daily) **$$**

Limited-Service Hotel

★ **FARMBROOK MOTEL.** *706 Hwy 100A, Plymouth (05056). Phone 802/672-3621.* 12 rooms. Check-out 11 am. **$**
🐾

Full-Service Resort

★ ★ ★ **HAWK INN AND MOUNTAIN RESORT.** *HCR 70 Box 64, Plymouth (05056). Phone 802/672-3811; toll-free 800/685-4295; fax 802/672-5585. www.hawkresort.com.* From rooms at the inn to luxurious mountainside villas on the 1,200 acres of this resort, guests can enjoy privacy and peace, as well as a variety of activities. 200 rooms. Check-in 4 pm, check-out 11 am. Restaurant, bar. Children's activity center. Fitness room. Indoor pool, outdoor pool, whirlpool. Tennis. Airport transportation available. **$$$**
🏋️ 🛏️ 🎿

Rutland (D-1)

See also Brandon, Green Mountain National Forest, Killington

Settled 1761
Population 18,230
Elevation 648 ft
Area Code 802
Information Chamber of Commerce, 256 N Main St; phone 802/773-2747
Web Site www.rutlandvermont.com

This is Vermont's second-largest city. Its oldest newspaper, the *Rutland Herald,* has been published continuously since 1794. The world's deepest marble quarry is in West Rutland. The office of the supervisor of the Green Mountain National Forest is located here.

What to See and Do

Chaffee Center for the Visual Arts. *16 S Main St, Rutland (05701). On Hwy 7, opposite Main St Park.*

Phone 802/775-0356. Continuous exhibits of paintings, graphics, photography, crafts, sculpture. Print room; gallery shop; annual art festivals (mid-Aug, Columbus Day weekend); other special events. (Mon, Wed-Sun; closed holidays) **FREE**

Hubbardton Battlefield and Museum. *654 Hwy 4 E, Rutland (05701). 7 miles W via Hwy 4, exit 5.* Phone 802/759-2412. On July 7, 1777, the Green Mountain Boys and colonial troops from Massachusetts and New Hampshire stopped British forces pursuing the American Army from Fort Ticonderoga. This was the only battle of the Revolution fought on Vermont soil and the first in a series of engagements that led to the capitulation of Burgoyne at Saratoga. Visitor Center with exhibits. Battle monument; trails; picnicking. (Memorial Day-Columbus Day, Wed-Sun) **$**

Mountain Top Cross-Country Ski Resort. *N via Hwy 7, then 10 miles NE on unnumbered road, follow signs.* Phone 802/483-2311; toll-free 800/445-2100. Patrol, school, rentals; snowmaking; concession area, restaurant at the inn. Sixty-eight miles of cross-country trails. Ice skating, horse-drawn sleigh rides. (Nov-Mar, daily)

New England Maple Museum. *Hwy 7, Pittsford. 7 miles N on Hwy 7.* Phone 802/483-9414. One of the largest collections of antique maple sugaring artifacts in the world; two large dioramas featuring more than 100 hand-carved figures; narrated slide show; demonstrations, samples of Vermont foodstuffs; craft and maple product gift shop. (Mid-Mar-Dec 24, daily; closed Thanksgiving) **$$**

Norman Rockwell Museum. *654 Hwy 4 E, Rutland (05701).* Phone 802/773-6095. More than 2,000 pictures and Rockwell memorabilia spanning 60 years of artist's career. Includes the *Four Freedoms,* Boy Scout series, many magazine covers, including all 323 from the *Saturday Evening Post,* and nearly every illustration and advertisement. (Daily; closed holidays) Gift shop. **$$**

⭐ **Vermont Marble Exhibit.** *61 Main St, Proctor (05765). 2 miles W on Hwy 4, then 4 miles N on Hwy 3, adjacent to Vermont Marble Company factory.* Phone 802/459-3311; toll-free 800/451-4468. Exhibit explains how marble is formed and the process by which it is manufactured. Displays; sculptor at work; balcony view of factory; "Gallery of the Presidents"; movie on the marble industry; marble market, gift shop. (June-Oct: daily; rest of year: Mon-Sat) **$$**

Wilson Castle. *W Proctor Rd, Center Rutland. 2 1/2 miles W on Hwy 4, then 1 mile N on West Proctor Rd.* Phone 802/773-3284. This 32-room 19th-century mansion on a 115-acre estate features 19 open proscenium arches, 84 stained-glass windows, 13 imported tile fireplaces, a towering turret and parapet; European and Asian furnishings; art gallery; sculpture; 15 other buildings. Picnic area. Guided tours. (Late May-mid-Oct, daily) **$$$**

Special Events

Green Mountain International Rodeo. *Phone 802/773-2747.* PRCA rodeo. Free pony rides, petting zoo. Bands, dancing. Mid-June.

Vermont State Fair. Exhibits of arts and crafts, flowers, produce, home arts, pets, animals, maple sugaring. Daily special events. Late Aug-early Sept.

Limited-Service Hotels

★ **BEST WESTERN INN & SUITES RUTLAND/KILLINGTON.** *Hwy 4 E, Rutland (05701).* Phone 802/773-3200; toll-free 800/720-7234; fax 802/773-6615. www.bestwestern.com. 56 rooms, 2 story. Complimentary continental breakfast. Check-out 11 am. Fitness room. Outdoor pool. Tennis. **$**
🅳 🏃 🏊 🎿

★ **COMFORT INN.** *19 Allen St, Rutland (05701).* Phone 802/775-2200; toll-free 800/432-6788; fax 802/775-2694. www.choicehotels.com. 104 rooms, 3 story. Complimentary continental breakfast. Check-out 11 am. Indoor pool, whirlpool. **$**
🏊

★ ★ **HOLIDAY INN.** *476 Hwy 7 S, Rutland (05701).* Phone 802/775-1911; toll-free 800/462-4810; fax 802/775-0113. www.holidayinn-vermont.com. 151 rooms. Check-out noon. Restaurant, bar. Fitness room. Indoor pool, whirlpool. Airport transportation available. Business center. **$**
🏃 🏊 🏃

Full-Service Resort

★ ★ ★ **MOUNTAIN TOP INN.** *195 Mountain Top Rd, Chittenden (05737).* Phone 800/445-2100; toll-free 800/445-2100; fax 802/483-6373. www.mountaintopinn.com. Nestled in the Green Mountains of Vermont, right by the lake, the guest rooms offer the finest in New England tradition. The candlelit dining room has magnificent views. 60 rooms. Closed

Apr and first three weeks in Nov. Pets accepted; fee. Restaurant, bar. Outdoor pool. Golf. Tennis. **$$**
🅿 ☎ ⛱ 📶 ⛷

Specialty Lodgings

The following lodging establishments are approved by Mobil Travel Guide, but due to their unique and individualized nature have not been given a traditional Mobil Star rating. Included in this listing you may find bed-and-breakfasts, limited-service inns, guest ranches, and other unique hotel properties.

INN AT RUTLAND. *70 N Main St, Rutland (05701). Phone 802/773-0575; toll-free 800/808-0575; fax 802/775-3506. www.innatrutland.com.* This Victorian mansion was built in 1893 and has been lovingly restored to its former elegance. Rooms are furnished with thoughtful attention to detail that beckons guests to experience the charm of a time long since forgotten. 11 rooms, 3 story. Complimentary full breakfast. Check-in 3 pm, check-out 11 am. **$**
🅿

MAPLEWOOD INN. *VT 22A S, Fair Haven (05743). Phone 802/265-8039; toll-free 800/253-7729; fax 802/265-8210. www.maplewoodinn.net.* Listed on the National Register of Historic Places, this Greek Revival inn offers guest rooms with period décor, perfect for a romantic getaway. Guests are close to sightseeing and can enjoy hot beverages and cordials in the sitting room. 5 rooms, 2 story. Complimentary full breakfast. Check-in 3-9 pm, check-out 11 am. **$**
🅿

Restaurant

★ ★ **COUNTRYMAN'S PLEASURE.** *Townline Rd, Mendon (05701). Phone 802/773-7141; fax 802/747-4959. www.countrymanspleasure.com.* Austrian-born chef/owner Hans Entinger has been serving Middle European specialties for more than 20 years in this personable, country inn environment. Candlelight and open fireplaces add to the ambience. German, Austrian menu. Dinner. Closed Mon; Dec 24-25. Bar. Children's menu. **$**

Shelburne (C-1)

See also Burlington, Vergennes

Settled 1763
Population 5,871

Elevation 148 ft
Area Code 802
Zip 05482
Information Town Hall, 5420 Shelburne Rd, PO Box 88; phone 802/985-5110
Web Site www.shelburnevt.org

Shelburne is a small, friendly town bordering Lake Champlain. West of town are the Adirondack Mountains; to the east are the Green Mountains. The Shelburne Museum has one of the most comprehensive exhibits of early American life.

What to See and Do

Charlotte-Essex Ferry. *King St Dock, Burlington (05401). 5 miles S on Hwy 7 to Charlotte, then 2 miles W to dock. Phone 802/864-9804 (for schedule).* Makes 20-minute trips across Lake Champlain to Essex, NY (Apr-Jan, daily). (See BURLINGTON). **$$$**

Mount Philo State Park. *5 miles S on Hwy 7, then 1 mile E on local road. Phone 802/425-2390.* A 648-acre mountaintop park offering beautiful views of the Lake Champlain Valley. Picnicking, camping, lean-tos. Entrance and camp roads are steep; not recommended for trailers. (Memorial Day-Columbus Day)

Shelburne Farms. *1611 Harbor Rd, Shelburne (05482). Phone 802/985-8686.* Former estate of Dr. Seward Webb and his wife, Lila Vanderbilt, built at the turn of the 20th century; beautifully situated on the shores of Lake Champlain. The grounds, landscaped by Frederick Law Olmstead and forested by Gifford Pinchot, once totaled 3,800 acres. Structures include the Webbs' mansion, Shelburne House, a 110-room summer "cottage" built in the late 1800s on a bluff overlooking the lake; a five-story farm barn with a courtyard of more than 2 acres; and the coach barn, once the home of prize horses. Tours (Memorial Day-mid-Oct, daily; closed holidays). Also hayrides; walking trail. Visitor center, phone 802/985-8442. Cheese shop (all year, daily). Overnight stays available. **$$$**

⭐ **Shelburne Museum.** *5555 Shelburne Rd, Shelburne (05482). On Hwy 7, in center of town. Phone 802/985-3346. www.shelburnemuseum.org.* Founded by Electra Webb, daughter of Sugar King H. O. Havemeyer, this stupendous collection of Americana is located on 45 acres of parklike setting with 37 historic buildings containing items such as historic circus posters, toys, weather vanes, trade signs, and an extensive collection of wildfowl decoys and dolls. American and European paintings and prints (including works by Monet and

Grandma Moses) are on display as well. Also here is the 220-foot sidewheel steamboat *Ticonderoga,* which carried passengers across Lake Champlain in the early part of the century and is now the last vertical beam passenger and freight sidewheel steamer intact in the United States; a working carousel and a 5,000-piece hand-carved miniature traveling circus; a fully intact lighthouse; one-room schoolhouse; authentic country store; the only two-lane covered bridge with footpath in Vermont; blacksmith shop; printing and weaving demonstrations; farm equipment and more than 200 horse-drawn vehicles on display. Visitor orientation film; free jitney; cafeteria; museum stores; free parking. (Late May-late Oct: daily; rest of year: limited hours) **$$$$**

Vermont Teddy Bear Company. *(Hwy 7), 6655 Shelburne Rd, Shelburne (05482). 1 mile S. Phone 802/ 985-3001. www.vermontteddybear.com.* The guided tour of this factory shows the process of handcrafting these famous stuffed animals. The on-site gift shop ensures that you won't go home empty handed. The Bear Shop opens at 9 am daily; call for a tour schedule. **$**

Vermont Wildflower Farm. *4750 Shelburne Ave, Shelburne (05482). 5 miles S via Hwy 7. Phone 802/ 425-3500.* Acres of wildflower gardens, flower fields, and woodlands; pond and brook. Changing slide/ sound show (every half hour). Gift shop. (May-late Oct, daily) **$$**

Limited-Service Hotel

★ **DAYS INN.** *3229 Shelburne Rd, Shelburne (05482). Phone 802/985-3334; toll-free 800/329-7466; fax 802/985-3419. www.daysinn.com.* 58 rooms, 2 story. Complimentary continental breakfast. Check-out 11 am. Outdoor pool. **$**

Springfield (E-2)

See also Bellows Falls, Grafton, Ludlow

Settled 1761
Population 9,579
Elevation 410 ft
Area Code 802
Zip 05156
Information Chamber of Commerce, 14 Clinton St, Suite 6; phone 802/885-2779
Web Site www.springfieldvt.com

The cascades of the Black River once provided power for the machine tool plants that stretch along Springfield's banks. Lord Jeffrey Amherst started the Crown Point Military Road to Lake Champlain from here in 1759. Springfield has been the home of many New England inventors. It is also the headquarters of the Amateur Telescope Makers who meet at Stellafane, an observatory site west of Highway 11.

What to See and Do

Eureka Schoolhouse. *Charlestown Rd, Springfield (05156). Phone 802/885-2779.* Oldest schoolhouse in the state; built in 1790. Nearby is a 100-year-old lattice-truss covered bridge. (Memorial Day-Columbus Day, daily) **$$**

Reverend Dan Foster House & Old Forge. *6 miles N on Valley St to Weathersfield Center Rd. Phone 802/885-2779.* Historic parsonage (1785) contains antique furniture, textiles, utensils, farm tools; old forge has working machinery and bellows. Guided tours. For further information contact the Chamber of Commerce. (Late June-Sept, Thurs-Mon or by appointment)

Springfield Art and Historical Society. *9 Elm Hill, Springfield (05156). Phone 802/885-2415.* American art and artifacts. Collections include Richard Lee pewter, Bennington pottery, 19th-century American paintings, costumes, dolls, toys; Springfield historical items. Changing exhibits. (May-Nov, Tues-Fri; closed holidays) **FREE**

Special Event

Vermont Apple Festival and Craft Show. *Phone 802/885-2779.* Family activities, cider pressing, apple pie bake-off, entertainment, crafts. Columbus Day weekend.

Limited-Service Hotel

★ ★ **HOLIDAY INN EXPRESS.** *818 Charlestown Rd, Springfield (05156). Phone 802/885-4516; toll-free 800/465-4329; fax 802/885-4595. www.holiday-inn.com.* Just off Interstate 91, exit 7, this family-friendly hotel back onto a wooded hill. Some rooms have refrigerators and microwaves, and the connected Howard Johnson's restaurant provides meal service. 88 rooms, 2 story. Complimentary continental breakfast. Check-in 3 pm, check-out noon. Restaurant, bar. Fitness room. Indoor pool. Business center. **$**

Full-Service Inn

★ ★ ★ **THE INN AT WEATHERSFIELD.** *Hwy 106, Perkinsville (05151). Phone 802/263-9217; toll-free 800/477-4828; fax 802/263-9219. www.weathersfield inn.com.* The rooms at this inn transport guests to a colonial countryside atmosphere full of charm and tranquility. Shopping, state parks, hiking, skiing, and sleigh and carriage rides are just minutes away. A gourmet, candlelit dinner can be enjoyed on the premises. 12 rooms, 2 story. Children over 8 years only. Complimentary full breakfast. Check-in 1 pm, check-out 11 am. Restaurant. **$**

🄳

Specialty Lodgings

The following lodging establishments are approved by Mobil Travel Guide, but due to their unique and individualized nature have not been given a traditional Mobil Star rating. Included in this listing you may find bed-and-breakfasts, limited-service inns, guest ranches, and other unique hotel properties.

HARTNESS HOUSE. *30 Orchard St, Springfield (05156). Phone 802/885-2115; toll-free 800/732-4789; fax 802/885-2207. www.hartnesshouse.com.* Part historic inn, part aviation museum and working observatory, the Hartness House is tied up in aviation, astronomy, and invention. A former Vermont governor, James Hartness was an inventor who built a series of underground tunnels in which he could work in undisturbed peace and quiet. He was also an aviation pioneer with a fascination for amateur astronomy and telescope making. After his death, his heirs combined his passions, and today three of the workrooms in Hartness's underground tunnels have been turned into a museum containing hundreds of exhibits related to amateur astronomy, telescope making, and astronomical lens and mirror making, as well as early-1900s photographs of Springfield and the Hartness House. But those more interested in resting than questing can take heart: the underground tunnels also lead to the original 1903 Hartness House, all polished wood and winding staircases, with a cozy, plant-filled living room on the ground floor and 14 guest rooms above. Two added wings wrap around the pool, one with eight rooms, the other with 24. The Hartness House is surrounded by 32 acres of woods and winding nature trails; the proprietors will be happy to make you a sack lunch to take along as you follow a path along a mountain stream. 43 rooms, 3 story. Pets accepted, some restrictions; fee. Compli-

mentary full breakfast. Check-in 3 pm, check-out 11 am. Wireless Internet access. Restaurant, bar. Outdoor pool. **$**

🐾 🏊

STONE HEARTH INN. *698 Hwy 11 W, Chester (05143). Phone 802/875-2525; toll-free 888/617-3656; fax 802/875-4688. www.thestonehearthinn.com.* Restored farm house (1810); antiques. 10 rooms, 3 story. Complimentary full breakfast. Check-in 4 pm, check-out 11 am. Bar. **$$**

🄳

St. Albans (B-1)

See also Swanton

Settled 1785
Population 7,339
Elevation 429 ft
Area Code 802
Zip 05478
Information Chamber of Commerce, 2 N Main St; phone 802/524-2444
Web Site www.stalbanschamber.com

This small city is a railroad town (Central Vermont Railway) and a center of maple syrup and dairy interests. It was a stop on the Underground Railroad and has had a surprisingly violent history. Smugglers used the city as a base of operations during the War of 1812. On October 19, 1864, the northernmost engagement of the Civil War was fought here when a small group of Confederates raided the three banks in town and fled to Canada with $200,000. In 1866, the Fenians, an Irish organization pledged to capture Canada, had its headquarters here.

What to See and Do

Brainerd Monument. *Greenwood Cemetery, S Main St, St. Albans. Phone 802/524-2444.* A father's revengeful commemoration of his son's death in Andersonville Prison.

Burton Island State Park. *St. Albans Bay. On island in Lake Champlain; 5 miles W on Hwy 36, then 3 miles SW on unnumbered road to Kamp Kill Kare State Park access area, where passenger ferry service (fee) is available to island; visitors may use their own boats to reach the island. Phone 802/879-5674.* This 253-acre park offers swimming beach, fishing, canoeing (rentals), boating (rentals, marina with electrical hook-ups);

nature and hiking trails, picnicking, concession, tent sites, lean-tos. (Memorial Day-Labor Day)

Chester A. Arthur Historic Site. *Fairfield. 10 miles W via Hwy 36 to Fairfield, then follow an unpaved road to the site. Phone 802/828-3226.* Replica of the second house of the 21st president (Arthur was vice president and became president in 1881 when James Garfield died); nearby is the brick church (1830) where Arthur's father was a preacher. Exhibit of Chester A. Arthur's life and career. Rural setting; picnic area. (Late May-mid-Oct, Wed-Sun 11 am-5 pm) **DONATION**

Lake Carmi State Park. *Hwy 236 and Marshfarm Rd, Enosburg Falls (05450). 15 miles NE on Hwy 105 to North Sheldon, then 3 miles N on Hwy 236. Phone 802/879-5674.* This 482-acre park features rolling farmland; 2-mile lakefront, swimming beach, bathhouse, fishing, boating (ramps, rentals); nature trails, picnicking, concession, tent and trailer sites (dump station), lean-tos. (Memorial Day-Labor Day)

St. Albans Historical Museum. *Church St, St. Albans. Phone 802/527-7933.* Toys, dolls, clothing, train memorabilia; farm implements; St. Albans Confederate Raid material, photographs; library and reference room; re-created doctor's office with medical and X-ray collections; items and documents of local historical interest. (June-Sept, Tues-Sat, also by appointment)

Special Events

Bay Day. Family activity day. Great Race, one-legged running, family games; volleyball, canoeing, and bicycling. Concessions. Fireworks. July 4 weekend.

Civil War Days. *Taylor Park, St. Albans.* A three-day event depicting scenes of the Civil War in St. Albans, the northernmost point where the war was fought. Reenactment of major battle, entertainment, antiques. Mid-Oct.

Maple Sugar Festival. A number of producers welcome visitors who join sugarhouse parties for sugar-on-snow, sour pickles, and raised doughnuts. Continuing events, arts and crafts, antiques, woodchopping contests. Usually last weekend in Apr.

Limited-Service Hotel

★ **COMFORT INN.** *813 Fairfax Rd, St. Albans (05478). Phone 802/524-3300; toll-free 800/228-5150; fax 802/524-3300. www.vtcomfortinn.com.* 63 rooms, 3

story. Complimentary continental breakfast. Checkout noon. Fitness room. Indoor pool. **$**

St. Johnsbury (C-3)

See also Lyndonville

Settled 1787
Population 7,608
Elevation 588 ft
Area Code 802
Zip 05819
Information Northeast Kingdom Chamber of Commerce, 357 Western Ave, Suite 2; phone 802/748-3678 or toll-free 800/639-6379
Web Site www.vermontnekchamber.org

This town was named for Ethan Allen's French friend, St. John de Crève Coeur, author of *Letters from an American Farmer.* The town gained fame and fortune when Thaddeus Fairbanks invented the platform scale in 1830. Fairbanks scales, maple syrup, and manufacturing are among its major industries.

What to See and Do

Fairbanks Museum and Planetarium. *1302 Main St, St. Johnsbury (05819). Phone 802/748-2372.* Exhibits and programs on natural science, regional history, archaeology, anthropology, astronomy, and the arts. More than 4,500 mounted birds and mammals; antique toys; farm, village, and craft tools; Northern New England Weather Broadcasting Center; planetarium; Hall of Science; special exhibitions in Gallery Wing. (Mon-Sat, also Sun afternoons; closed Jan 1, Dec 25) Planetarium (July-Aug: daily; rest of year: Sat-Sun only). Museum and planetarium closed holidays. **$$**

Maple Grove Farms of Vermont Factory Tours & Maple Museum. *1052 Portland St, St. Johnsbury (05819). Phone 802/748-5141. www.maplegrove.com.* Learn all about "Vermont's first industry" on this factory tour, which offers glimpses into the process of making pure maple syrup and maple candy. Top it off by tasting the various grades of syrup available in the Cabin Shop, and you're sure to leave with your sweet tooth sated. (Mon-Fri 8 am-2 pm; closed holidays) **$**

St. Johnsbury Athenaeum and Art Gallery. *1171 Main St, St. Johnsbury (05819). Phone 802/748-8291.* Works by Albert Bierstadt and artists of the Hudson River School. (Mon-Sat; closed holidays) **DONATION**

Special Event

St. Johnsbury Town Band. *Courthouse Park, St. Johnsbury.* One of the oldest continuously performing bands (since 1830) in the country plays weekly outdoor evening concerts. Contact the Chamber of Commerce for further information. Mon, mid-June-late Aug.

Limited-Service Hotels

★ **FAIRBANKS MOTOR INN.** *32 Western Ave, St. Johnsbury (05819). Phone 802/748-5666; fax 802/748-1242.* 46 rooms, 3 story. Pets accepted; fee. Complimentary continental breakfast. Check-out 11 am. Outdoor pool. **$**

★ **HOLIDAY MOTEL.** *222 Hastings St, St. Johnsbury (05819). Phone 802/748-8192; fax 802/748-1244.* 34 rooms. Check-out 11 am. Outdoor pool. **$**

Full-Service Inn

★ ★ ★ **RABBIT HILL INN.** *48 Lower Waterford Rd, Lower Waterford (05848). Phone 802/748-5168; toll-free 800/762-8669; fax 802/748-8342. www.rabbithillinn.com.* Nestled between the river and mountains of picturesque northern Vermont, the Rabbit Hill Inn is quintessential New England at its best. Meandering pathways and covered bridges take guests back in time to the 18th century in this postcard-perfect village. Romantics flock to this old-fashioned inn, which dates to 1795, to rediscover simple pleasures and enjoy country pursuits. Souls are soothed after a walk in the meadow, while the spring-fed pool cools and relaxes. Many guests meet in the public rooms to play classic board games, often making new friends as they piece together puzzles. Befitting a bed-and-breakfast, the mornings are met with freshly baked temptations and lavish buffets; afternoon tea lures visitors from their repose; and evenings bring sensational five-course dinners. Undeniably lovely, the guest rooms are a valentine to visitors with canopy beds and soft colors. 19 rooms, 3 story. Closed first two weeks of Apr and first two weeks of Nov. Children over 13 years only. Complimentary continental breakfast. Check-in 2 pm, check-out 11 am. Restaurant, bar. **$$$**

Restaurant

★ ★ ★ **RABBIT HILL.** *48 Lower Waterford Rd, Lower Waterford (05848). Phone 802/748-5168; fax 802/748-8542. www.rabbithillinn.com.* Chef Russell Stannard's five-course dinner menu highlights his creative style of cooking. The hardwood floors, wainscoting, area rugs, and other decorative accents afford an elegant setting in which to enjoy it. American menu. Dinner. Bar. Reservations recommended. **$$$**

Stowe (B-2)

See also Highgate Springs, Jeffersonville, Waterbury

Settled 1794
Population 3,433
Elevation 723 ft
Area Code 802
Zip 05672
Information Stowe Area Association, Main St, PO Box 1320; phone 802/253-7321 or toll-free 877/467-8693
Web Site www.gostowe.com

Stowe is a year-round resort area, with more than half of its visitors coming during the summer. Mount Mansfield, Vermont's highest peak (4,393 feet), offers skiing, snowboarding, snowshoeing, and skating in the winter. Summer visitors enjoy outdoor concerts, hiking, biking, golf, tennis, and many events and attractions, including a Ben & Jerry's ice cream tour.

What to See and Do

Alpine Slide. *Hwy 108, N of Stowe Village. Phone 802/253-7321.* Chairlift takes riders to a 2,300-foot slide that runs through the woods and open field. Speed controlled by rider. (Memorial Day-mid-June: weekends and holidays; mid-June-Labor Day: daily; after Labor Day-mid-Oct: weekends and holidays) **$$$**

Elmore State Park. *Hwy 12, Lake Elmore. N on Hwy 100, then S on Hwy 12, at Lake Elmore. Phone 802/888-2982.* This 709-acre park offers swimming beach, bathhouse, fishing, boating (rentals); hiking trails (one trail to Elmore Mountain fire tower), picnicking, concession, tent and trailer sites (dump station), lean-tos. Excellent views of Green Mountain Range; fire tower. (Memorial Day-Columbus Day)

Mount Mansfield State Forest. This 38,000-acre forest can be reached from Underhill Flats, off Highway 15, or from Stowe, north on Highway 108, through Smugglers' Notch, a magnificent scenic drive. The Long Trail leads to the summit of Mount Mansfield from the north and south. There are three state recreation areas in the forest. **Smugglers' Notch** (phone 802/253-4014 or 802/479-4280) and **Underhill** (phone 802/899-3022 or 802/879-5674) areas offer hiking, skiing, snowmobiling, picnicking, camping (dump station). **Little River Camping Area** (phone 802/244-7103 or 802/479-4280), northwest of Waterbury, offers swimming, fishing, boating (rentals for campers only); hiking, camping. (Memorial Day-Columbus Day)

Stowe Mountain Auto Road. *Approximately 6 miles NW of Stowe off Hwy 108.* A 4 1/2-mile drive to the summit. (Mid-May-mid-Oct, daily)

Stowe Mountain Resort. *5781 Mountain Rd, Stowe (05672). NW via Hwy 108.* Phone 802/253-3000; toll-free 800/253-4754. www.stowe.com. Resort has quad, triple, six double chairlifts; Mighty-mite handle tow; patrol, school, rentals; snowmaking; cafeterias, restaurants, bar, entertainment; nursery. Forty-seven runs, longest run more than 3 1/2 miles; vertical drop 2,360 feet. Night skiing. (Mid-Nov-mid-Apr, daily) Summer activities include three outdoor swimming pools; alpine slide (mid-June-early Sept, daily), mountain biking (rentals), gondola rides, in-line skate park, fitness center, spa, recreation trail, tennis, golf. Nearby is

Mount Mansfield Gondola. *Hwy 108, N of Stowe Village.* An eight-passenger enclosed gondola ride to the summit of Vermont's highest peak. Spectacular view of the area. Restaurant and gift shop. (Late May-mid-June: weekends; mid-June-mid-Oct: daily)

Stowe Recreation Path. *Stowe Village.* An approximately 5-mile riverside path designed for nature walks, bicycling, jogging, and in-line skating. **FREE**

Special Events

Stoweflake Balloon Festival. *1746 Mountain Rd, Stowe (05672). Stoweflake Resort Field, Hwy 108.* Phone 802/253-7321. More than 20 balloons launched continuously. Second weekend in July.

Trapp Family Meadow Concerts. *700 Trapp Hill Rd, Stowe (05672).* Phone 802/253-7321. Classical concerts in the Trapp Family Lodge Meadow. Sun evenings, late June-mid-Aug.

Limited-Service Hotel

★ ★ **GREEN MOUNTAIN INN.** *18 S Main St, Stowe (05672).* Phone 802/253-7301; fax 802/253-5096. Modern comforts are not lacking at this historic prop-

erty close to many attractions of Stowe. 100 rooms, 3 story. Pets accepted, some restrictions; fee. Check-in 3 pm, check-out 11 am. Two restaurants, bar. Fitness room. Outdoor pool. **$$**

Full-Service Resorts

★ ★ **GOLDEN EAGLE RESORT.** *511 Mountain Rd, Stowe (05672).* Phone 802/253-4811; toll-free 800/626-1010; fax 802/253-2561. www.goldeneagleresort.com. Families will feel welcome year-round at this resort close to Stowe. 94 rooms. Check-in 3 pm, check-out 11 am. Restaurant, bar. Fitness room. Indoor pool, outdoor pool, whirlpool. Tennis. **$**

★ ★ **GREY FOX INN AND RESORT.** *990 Mountain Rd, Stowe (05672).* Phone 800/544-8454; toll-free 800/544-8454; fax 802/253-8344. www.stowegreyfoxinn.com. Late-19th-century farmhouse; library. 42 rooms, 3 story. Check-in 2 pm, check-out 11 am. Restaurant. Fitness room. Indoor pool, outdoor pool, whirlpool. **$**

★ ★ ★ **STOWEFLAKE MOUNTAIN RESORT & SPA.** *1746 Mountain Rd, Stowe (05672).* Phone 802/253-7355; toll-free 800/253-2232; fax 802/253-6858. www.stoweflake.com/home.php. Stoweflake Mountain Resort is the ultimate New England getaway. This comprehensive resort treats guests to a well-rounded experience filled with golf and other sports, fine dining, and an exceptional spa. The accommodations cover all the bases, from standard guest rooms to townhouses, and all feature a warm New England spirit. The 50,000-square-foot spa is a veritable temple of relaxation, and the treatment menu goes beyond the ordinary to surprise and delight guests. The chef pays special attention to spa guests with separate calorie-conscious selections on the menus, although his regular menu's masterful creations from organic and locally grown ingredients are sure to tempt those watching their waistlines. 164 rooms, 2 story. Check-in 3 pm, check-out 11 am. Two restaurants, bar. Fitness room, spa. Indoor pool, outdoor pool, whirlpool. Business center. **$$**

★ ★ ★ **TOPNOTCH RESORT & SPA.** *4000 Mountain Rd, Stowe (05672).* Phone 802/253-8585; toll-free 800/451-8686; fax 802/253-9263. www.topnotch-resort.com. Topnotch Resort & Spa, tucked away on 120 acres in the Green Mountains, is a year-round resort. The first sign of snowfall attracts avid skiers who appreciate the proximity to some of Vermont's best skiing, while warmer months draw tennis players to the comprehensive facility with nine indoor and four outdoor courts and a renowned academy. Sybarites visit throughout the year to reap the physical and spiritual rewards of the 23,000-square-foot spa, where innovative therapies increase personal well-being. Guests watching their waistlines revel in the resort's spa cuisine: Maxwell's delights with steaks and seafood, and Buttertub Bistro & Lounge is the very definition of après-ski, with fireside cocktails and live entertainment. English manor house meets Vermont countryside in the guest accommodations. 126 rooms, 3 story. Pets accepted. Check-in 3:30 pm, check-out 11:30 am. High-speed Internet access, wireless Internet access. Restaurant, bar. Children's activity center. Fitness room, fitness classes available, spa. Indoor pool, outdoor pool, whirlpool. Tennis. Airport transportation available. Business center. **$$$**

★ ★ **TRAPP FAMILY LODGE.** *700 Trapp Hill Rd, Stowe (05672). Phone 802/253-8511; toll-free 800/826-7000; fax 802/253-5740. www.trappfamily.com.* "The hills are alive" at this resort run by the inspiration for the famous movie and play. Take advantage of all Vermont has to offer, or join in a guest sing-a-long. 73 rooms, 4 story. Check-in 3 pm, check-out 11 am. Restaurant, bar. Fitness room. Indoor pool, two outdoor pools. Tennis. **$$**

Full-Service Inns

★ ★ ★ **EDSON HILL MANOR.** *1500 Edson Hill Rd, Stowe (05672). Phone 802/253-7371; toll-free 800/621-0284; fax 802/253-4036.* This inn is located on 225 acres of a rolling hillside with a view of the Green Mountains. 25 rooms. Check-in 2 pm, check-out 11 am. Restaurant, bar. **$$**

★ ★ ★ **YE OLDE ENGLAND INNE.** *433 Mountain Rd, Stowe (05672). Phone 802/253-7558; toll-free 800/643-1553; fax 802/253-8944. www.englandinn.com.* This elegant 1893 English inn offers guests a truly delightful stay. From the charmingly appointed rooms furnished in Laura Ashley-style to the Mr. Pickwicks Polo Pub where strangers are strangers no more, this warm and inviting inn is a welcome respite. 30 rooms, 5 story. Check-in 3

pm, check-out 11 am. Restaurant, bar. Outdoor pool, whirlpool. **$$**

Specialty Lodging

The following lodging establishment is approved by Mobil Travel Guide, but due to its unique and individualized nature has not been given a traditional Mobil Star rating. Included in this listing you may find bed-and-breakfasts, limited-service inns, guest ranches, and other unique hotel properties.

THREE BEARS AT THE FOUNTAIN. *1049 Pucker St, Stowe (05672). Phone 802/253-7671; toll-free 800/898-9634; fax 802/253-8804. www.threebearsbandb.com.* Built in 1826; one of the oldest guesthouses in Stowe. 6 rooms, 2 story. Complimentary full breakfast. Check-in 3 pm, check-out 10:30 am. Outdoor pool. **$**

Stratton Mountain (E-2)

See also Londonderry, Manchester and Manchester Center, Peru

Area Code 802
Zip 05155

What to See and Do

Stratton Mountain. *Stratton Mountain Rd, Londonderry. Off Hwy 30. Phone 802/297-2200. www.stratton.com.* A high-speed gondola, two high-speed six-passenger, three quad, one triple, two double chairlifts, two surface lifts; patrol, school, rentals; snowmaking; cafeterias, restaurants, bars; nursery, sports center. Ninety runs, longest run 3 miles; vertical drop 2,003 feet. (Mid-Nov-mid-Apr, daily) More than 17 miles of cross-country trails (Dec-Mar, daily), rentals; snowboarding. Summer activities include gondola ride; horseback riding, tennis, golf (school), festivals, concert series. **$$$$**

Special Events

Labor Day Street Festival. *Phone 802/297-2200.* Festival with continuous entertainment, specialty foods, imported beer, activities for children. Labor Day weekend.

Stratton Arts Festival. *Stratton Mountain Base Lodge. Phone 802/297-2200.* Paintings, photography, sculpture, and crafts; special performing arts events, craft demonstrations. Mid-Sept-mid-Oct.

Limited-Service Hotel

★ ★ THE INN AT STRATTON MOUNTAIN.

RR 1 Box 145, Stratton (05155). Phone 802/297-2200; toll-free 800/787-2886; fax 802/297-4084. www.stratton.com. This conveniently located mountain resort includes a ski-in/ski-out lodge. In winter there are ski trails spanning 500 acres to keep guests busy, while golf and tennis are the attraction during warmer months. 110 rooms, 4 story. Check-in 5 pm, check-out 10 am. Children's activity center. Fitness room. Indoor pool, three outdoor pools, whirlpool. Golf. Tennis. Ski in/ski out. **$**

Swanton (A-1)

See also Jeffersonville, North Hero, St. Albans

Population 2,360
Elevation 119 ft
Area Code 802
Zip 05488
Information Chamber of Commerce, PO Box 210; phone 802/868-7200

The location of this town, just 2 miles east of Lake Champlain, makes it an attractive resort spot.

What to See and Do

Missisquoi National Wildlife Refuge. *371 N River St, Swanton (05488). 2 1/2 miles W via Hwy 78. Phone 802/868-4781.* More than 6,400 acres, including much of the Missisquoi River delta on Lake Champlain; primarily a waterfowl refuge (best in Apr, Sept, and Oct), but other wildlife and birds may be seen. Fishing; hunting, hiking and canoe trails. (Daily) **FREE**

Special Event

Swanton Summer Festival. *On Village Green.* Band concerts, square dancing, rides, children's events, parades, arts and crafts. Last weekend in July.

Full-Service Resort

★ ★ TYLER PLACE FAMILY RESORT. *Old*

Dock Rd, Highgate Springs (05460). Phone 802/868-3301; toll-free 802/868-4000; fax 802/868-5621. www.tylerplace.com. This resort is designed for vacationing families. Accommodations have a country flavor and are designed with kids in mind. The resort is set on a mile of lakeshore and 165 acres of land. Guests will enjoy the paddleboats, kayaks, fishing, pools, and many other activities. 39 rooms, 2 story. Closed Labor Day-late May. Check-in 3 pm, check-out 10 am. Restaurant, bar. Children's activity center. Fitness room. Indoor pool, outdoor pool, children's pool. Tennis. **$**

Vergennes (C-1)

See also Middlebury, Shelburne

Settled 1766
Population 2,578
Elevation 205 ft
Area Code 802
Zip 05491
Information Vergennes Chamber of Commerce, PO Box 335; phone 802/877-0080

Vergennes is one of the smallest incorporated cities in the nation (one square mile). It is also the oldest city in Vermont and the third oldest in New England.

What to See and Do

Button Bay State Park. *5 Button Bay State Park Rd, Vergennes (05491). 6 miles W on Button Bay Rd, just S of Basin Harbor. Phone 802/475-2377.* This 236-acre park on a bluff overlooking Lake Champlain was named for the buttonlike formations in the clay banks; spectacular views of Adirondack Mountains. Swimming pool, fishing, boating (rentals); nature and hiking trails, picnicking, tent and trailer sites (dump station). Museum, naturalist. (Memorial Day-Columbus Day)

Chimney Point State Historic Site. *Hwys 17 and 125, Addison (05491). 6 miles S via Hwy 22A, then 8 miles SW via Hwy 17, at the terminus of the Crown Point Military Rd on shoreline of Lake Champlain. Phone 802/759-2412.* This 18th-century tavern was built on the site of a 17th-century French fort. Exhibits on the Native American and French settlement of Champlain Valley and Vermont. (Memorial Day-Columbus Day, Wed-Sun) **$**

John Strong Mansion. *6656 Hwy 17 W, West Addison (05491). 6 miles SW via Hwy 22A, on Hwy 17. Phone 802/759-2309.* (1795) Federalist house; restored and furnished in the period. (Mid-May-mid-Oct, Fri-Sun) **$$**

Kennedy Brothers Factory Marketplace. *11 Main St, Vergennes (05491). Phone 802/877-2975.* Renovated 1920s brick creamery building features gift, crafts, and antiques shops. Deli, ice cream shop, picnic area. (Daily; closed Jan 1, Thanksgiving, Dec 25) **FREE**

Rokeby Museum. *4334 Hwy 7, Ferrisburgh (05456). 2 miles N on Hwy 7, 6 miles S of ferry route on Hwy 7. Phone 802/877-3406.* (Circa 1785) Ancestral home of abolitionist Rowland T. Robinson was a station for the Underground Railroad. Artifacts and archives of four generations of the Robinson family. Set on 85 acres, farmstead includes an ice house, a creamery, and a stone smokehouse. Special events year-round. Tours. (Mid-May-mid-Oct, Thurs-Sun) **$$**

Full-Service Resort

★ ★ ★ **BASIN HARBOR CLUB.** *Basin Harbor Rd, Vergennes (05491). Phone 802/475-2311; toll-free 800/622-4000; fax 802/475-6545. www.basinharbor.com.* Located on Lake Champlain, this 700-acre property offers guest rooms in the lodge or cottages spread out over the acreage. Fresh local ingredients are used to prepare the breakfast and dinner meals served in the main dining room. 117 rooms. Closed Nov-mid-May. Pets accepted, some restrictions; fee. Check-in 4 pm, check-out 11 am. Restaurant, bar. Children's activity center. Fitness room. Beach. Outdoor pool. Golf. Tennis. Airport transportation available. **$$**

Specialty Lodging

The following lodging establishment is approved by Mobil Travel Guide, but due to its unique and individualized nature has not been given a traditional Mobil Star rating. Included in this listing you may find bed-and-breakfasts, limited-service inns, guest ranches, and other unique hotel properties.

STRONG HOUSE INN. *94 W Main St, Vergennes (05491). Phone 802/877-3337; fax 802/877-2599. www.stronghouseinn.com.* This historic Federal-style inn is furnished in period furniture and antiques and is set on 6 acres of walking trails, gardens, and ponds. Nearby are many activities, including hiking, golfing, cycling, and fishing. 14 rooms, 2 story. Children over 8 years only. Complimentary full breakfast. Check-in 3 pm, check-out 11 am. **$$**

Waitsfield (C-2)

See also Barre, Montpelier, Warren, Waterbury

Population 1,422
Elevation 698 ft
Area Code 802
Zip 05673
Information Sugarbush Chamber of Commerce, General Wait House - Hwy 100, PO Box 173; phone 802/496-3409 or toll-free 800/828-4748
Web Site www.sugarbushchamber.org

This region, known as "the Valley," is a popular area in summer as well as in the winter ski season.

What to See and Do

Mad River Glen Ski Area. *Hwy 17, Waitsfield. 5 miles W of Hwy 100. Phone 802/496-3551. www.madriverglen.com.* Area has three double, two single chairlifts; patrol, school, rentals; snowmaking; cafeterias, restaurant, bar; nursery. Forty-four runs, longest run 3 miles; vertical drop 2,000 feet. (Dec-Apr, daily) **$$$$**

Full-Service Inn

★ ★ **TUCKER HILL INN.** *Hwy 17, Waitsfield (05673). Phone 802/496-3983; toll-free 800/543-7841. www.tuckerhill.com.* 22 rooms. Check-in 2 pm, check-out 11 am. Restaurant, bar. Outdoor pool. Tennis. **$$**

Specialty Lodgings

The following lodging establishments are approved by Mobil Travel Guide, but due to their unique and individualized nature have not been given a traditional Mobil Star rating. Included in this listing you may find bed-and-breakfasts, limited-service inns, guest ranches, and other unique hotel properties.

1824 HOUSE INN BED AND BREAKFAST. *2150 Main St, Waitsfield (05673). Phone 802/496-7555; toll-free 800/426-3986; fax 802/496-7559. www.1824house.com.* This restored 1824 farmhouse features feather beds, Oriental rugs, and down quilts. 8

rooms, 2 story. Complimentary full breakfast. Check-in 4 pm, check-out 11 am. Whirlpool. **$**

THE INN AT THE ROUND BARN. *1661 E Warren Rd, Waitsfield (05673). Phone 802/496-2276; fax 802/496-8832. www.theroundbarn.com.* Located on more than 200 acres of mountains, ponds, and meadows, this unique inn has, as the name implies, a round barn that is fully restored and is the setting for weddings, meetings, and other functions. Activities for guests abound in this year-round destination. 12 rooms, 2 story. Complimentary full breakfast. Check-in 3 pm, check-out 11 am. Indoor pool. **$$**

LAREAU FARM COUNTRY INN. *Hwy 100, Waitsfield (05673). Phone 802/496-4949; toll-free 800/833-0766; fax 802/496-7979. www.lareaufarminn.com.* Farmhouse and barn built by the area's first physician. 13 rooms, 2 story. Complimentary full breakfast. Check-in 3 pm, check-out 10:30 am. **$**

THE WAITSFIELD INN. *5267 Main, Waitsfield (05673). Phone 802/496-3979; toll-free 800/758-3801; fax 802/496-3970. www.waitsfieldinn.com.* 14 rooms, 2 story. Closed Apr, Nov. Check-in 3 pm, check-out 11 am. **$**

Restaurants

★ **RESTAURANT DEN.** *Hwy 100, Waitsfield (05673). Phone 802/496-8880.* Lunch, dinner. Closed Thanksgiving, Dec 25. Bar. Outdoor seating. **$$**

★ ★ **THE STEAK PLACE AT TUCKER HILL.** *Hwy 17, Waitsfield (05673). Phone 802/496-3983. www.tuckerhill.com.* Dinner. Bar. Children's menu. Outdoor seating. **$$**

Warren (C-2)

See also Barre, Green Mountain National Forest, Waitsfield, Waterbury

Population 1,172
Elevation 893 ft
Area Code 802
Zip 05674
Information Sugarbush Chamber of Commerce, PO

Box 173, Waitsfield 05673; phone 802/496-3409 or toll-free 800/828-4748
Web Site www.sugarbushchamber.org

What to See and Do

Sugarbush Golf Course. *Golf Course Rd, Warren. 3 miles NW via Hwy 100. Phone 802/583-2722.* An 18-hole championship course designed by Robert Trent Jones Sr.; driving range; nine-hole putting green; championship tees (6,524 yards). Restaurant. (May-Oct, daily) Reservations recommended. **$$$$**

Sugarbush Resort. *Sugarbush Access Rd, Warren. 3 miles NW, off Hwy 100. Phone 802/583-2381; toll-free 800/537-8427. www.sugarbush.com.* Area has seven quad, three triple, six double chairlifts; four surface lifts; patrol, school, rentals; concession area, cafeteria, restaurant, bar; nursery. One hundred seven runs, longest run more than 2 miles; vertical drop 2,650 feet. (Early Nov-early May, daily) **$$$$**

Sugarbush Soaring Association. *2 miles NE via Hwy 100, at Sugarbush Airport. Phone 802/496-2290.* Soaring instruction, scenic glider rides. Picnicking, restaurant. (May-Oct, daily) Reservations preferred.

Full-Service Resort

★ ★ ★ **SUGARBUSH INN.** *2405 Sugarbush Access Rd, Warren (05674). Phone 802/583-6114; toll-free 800/537-8427; fax 802/583-6132. www.sugarbush.com.* Snowshoeing, snow tubing, ice skating and horse-drawn sleigh rides are available on property. 238 rooms. Check-in 6 pm, check-out 11 am. Restaurant, bar. Fitness room. Indoor pool, outdoor pool, whirlpool. Golf. Tennis. **$**

Full-Service Inn

★ ★ ★ **THE PITCHER INN.** *275 Main St, Warren (05674). Phone 802/496-6350; toll-free 888/867-4824; fax 802/496-6354. www.pitcherinn.com.* This romantic inn on the Mad River was constructed on the site of an inn of the same name originally built in the 1700s. Skiers are drawn here, and the inn thoughtfully accommodates them with a locker room for ski storage and a boot and glove warmer. Rustic yet rich and elegant guest accommodations in the main house draw upon Vermont's colonial history and are individually decorated in themes like the Mallard Room and the School Room, while two suites in the adjacent barn are perfect for families. The inn's intimate restaurant,

which serves breakfast and dinner, boasts a 6,500-bottle wine cellar. 9 rooms, 3 story. Check-in 3 pm, check-out 11 am. Restaurant, bar. **$$$$**
🅓

Specialty Lodging

The following lodging establishment is approved by Mobil Travel Guide, but due to its unique and individualized nature has not been given a traditional Mobil Star rating. Included in this listing you may find bed-and-breakfasts, limited-service inns, guest ranches, and other unique hotel properties.

SUGARTREE INN. *2440 Sugarbush Access Rd, Warren (05674). Phone 802/583-3211; toll-free 800/666-8907; fax 802/583-3203. www.sugartree.com.* 9 rooms, 3 story. Closed three weeks in Apr. Children over 7 years only. Complimentary full breakfast. Check-in 3 pm, check-out 11 am. Restaurant. **$**
🅓

Restaurant

★ ★ ★ **THE COMMON MAN.** *3209 German Flats Rd, Warren (05674). Phone 802/583-2800; fax 802/583-2826. www.commonmanrestaurant.com.* Located in Vermont's Mad River Valley, this restaurant offers superb dining. The 1880s restored barn is a perfect setting for this casual dining spot. American menu. Dinner. Closed Thanksgiving, Dec 25. Children's menu. **$$**

Waterbury (C-2)

See also Barre, Montpelier, Stowe, Waitsfield, Warren

Population 4,589
Elevation 428 ft
Area Code 802
Zip 05676
Information Central Vermont Chamber of Commerce, PO Box 336, Barre 05641; phone 802/229-5711

Centrally located near many outstanding ski resorts, including Stowe, Mad River Valley, and Bolton Valley, this area is also popular in summer for hiking, backpacking, and bicycling.

What to See and Do

Ben & Jerry's Ice Cream Factory Tour. *I-89, exit 10, then N on Hwy 100. Phone 802/244-8687; toll-free* 866/258-6877. www.benjerry.com. This half-hour guided tour, offered every 30 minutes (and even more frequently in summer and fall), takes visitors through the ice cream factory that cranks out such beloved flavors as Cherry Garcia and Chunky Monkey. The tour includes a seven-minute "moovie," views of the production line (except on weekends), and free samples in the FlavoRoom. There's also a gift shop, where you can pick up one of those famous tie-dyed cow T-shirts and a few pints to take home. (Daily; closed Jan 1, Thanksgiving, Dec 25) **$**

Camel's Hump Mountain. *8 miles SW of town on dirt road, then 3 1/2-mile hike to summit.* State's third-highest mountain. Trail is challenging. Weather permitting, Canada can be seen from the top.

Cold Hollow Cider Mill. *3600 Waterbury-Stowe Rd, Waterbury Center (05677). 3 1/2 miles N on Hwy 100. Phone 802/244-8771; toll-free 800/327-7537. www.coldhollow.com.* One of the largest cider mills in New England features a 43-inch rack-and-cloth press capable of producing 500 gallons of cider an hour; also jelly-making operations (fall). Samples are served. **FREE**

Little River State Park. *3444 Little River Rd, Waterbury (05676). 2 miles W off Hwy 2. Phone 802/244-7103.* This 12,000-acre park offers swimming, fishing; nature and hiking trails, tent and trailer sites (dump station), lean-tos. (Memorial Day-Columbus Day)

Long Trail. *Phone 802/229-5711.* A 22-mile segment of backpacking trail connects Camel's Hump with Mount Mansfield, the state's highest peak. Primitive camping is allowed on both mountains. Recommended for the experienced hiker.

Winter recreation. Area abounds in downhill, cross-country, and ski touring facilities; also many snowmobile trails.

Limited-Service Hotel

★ ★ **BEST WESTERN WATERBURY-STOWE.** *45 Blush Hill Rd, Waterbury (05676). Phone 802/244-7822; toll-free 800/621-7822; fax 802/244-6395. www.bestwestern.com.* 79 rooms, 2 story. Check-out noon. Restaurant, bar. Fitness room. Indoor pool. Tennis. **$**
🏃 🏊 🎿

Specialty Lodgings

The following lodging establishments are approved by Mobil Travel Guide, but due to their unique and individualized nature have not been given a traditional Mobil Star rating. Included in this listing you may find bed-and-breakfasts, limited-service inns, guest ranches, and other unique hotel properties.

BLACK LOCUST INN. *5088 Waterbury-Stowe Rd, Waterbury Center (05677). Phone 802/244-7490; toll-free 800/366-5592; fax 802/244-8473. www.blacklocustinn.com.* Surrounded by black locust trees, this restored 1832 farmhouse offers guest rooms with private baths and down comforters. A three-course hearty breakfast is served using local produce. In the evening, wines and hot and cold hors d'oeuvres are complimentary. The inn is close to all major ski areas. 6 rooms, 2 story. Children over 12 years only. Complimentary full breakfast. Check-in 2 pm, check-out 11 am. **$**

THATCHER BROOK INN. *Hwy 100, Waterbury (05676). Phone 802/244-5911; toll-free 800/292-5911; fax 802/244-1294. www.thatcherbrook.com.* Built in 1899; twin gazebos with front porch. 22 rooms, 2 story. Complimentary full breakfast. Check-in 3 pm, check-out 10:30 am. Restaurant. **$**

Restaurant

★ ★ ★ **THATCHER BROOK.** *Hwy 100 N, Waterbury (05676). Phone 802/244-5911; fax 802/244-1294. www.thatcherbrook.com.* This candlelit and cozy restaurant has four dining rooms that are appointed with antiques and oil paintings. The "romantic room" is perfect for couples seeking privacy. French menu. Dinner. Bar. Children's menu. Outdoor seating. **$$**

West Dover (F-2)

See also Wilmington

Population 250
Elevation 1,674 ft
Area Code 802
Zip 05356
Information Mount Snow Valley Region Chamber of Commerce, Hwy 9, W Main St, PO Box 3, Wilmington 05363; phone 802/464-8092 or toll-free 877/887-6884
Web Site www.visitvermont.com

What to See and Do

Mount Snow Ski Area. *9 miles N on Hwy 100, in Green Mountain National Forest. Phone 802/464-8501; toll-free 800/245-7669 (lodging).* Area has two quad, six triple, nine double chairlifts; patrol, school, rentals; snowmaking; cafeterias, restaurant, bars, entertainment; nursery. More than 100 trails spread over five interconnected mountain areas (also see WILMINGTON); shuttle bus. Longest run 2 1/2 miles; vertical drop 1,700 feet. Half-day rates. (Nov-early May, daily)

Special Events

Mountain Bike World Cup Race. *Mount Snow Ski Area, West Dover. Phone toll-free 800/245-7669.* More than 1,500 cyclists from throughout the world compete in downhill, dual slalom, and circuit racing events. Mid-June.

Mount Snow Foliage Craft Fair. *Mount Snow Ski Area, West Dover.* New England area artisans exhibit pottery, jewelry, glass, graphics, weaving, and other crafts; entertainment. Columbus Day weekend.

Full-Service Inn

★ ★ ★ **THE INN AT SAWMILL FARM.** *Hwy 100 and Crosstown Rd, West Dover (05356). Phone 802/464-8131; toll-free 800/493-1133; fax 802/464-1130. www.theinnatsawmillfarm.com.* While its location in southern Vermont makes it an easy jaunt from New York or Boston, the Inn at Sawmill Farm's sophisticated yet low-key attitude is what draws city slickers to its bucolic setting. This converted barn is perfectly situated for skiers to hit the slopes of nearby Mount Snow, while others enjoy trawling for antiques or casting a rod in the region's trout ponds. Lazy afternoons are spent picnicking on the lovely grounds filled with ponds and luscious blooms. Weathered floors and hand-hewn posts and beams hint at the original construction, yet this inn has a decidedly polished flair. Moods are instantly elevated in the lovely guest rooms, where rich colors and floral prints delight visitors. Despite its sleepy address, the inn's restaurant is anything but country. Its haute cuisine rivals that of many of its city competitors, and dessert is simply not to be missed. 21 rooms, 2 story. Closed late Mar-Memorial Day. Complimentary full breakfast. Check-in 3 pm, check-out noon. Restaurant. Fitness room. Outdoor pool. Tennis. **$$$$**

Specialty Lodgings

The following lodging establishments are approved by Mobil Travel Guide, but due to their unique and individualized nature have not been given a traditional Mobil Star rating. Included in this listing you may find bed-and-breakfasts, limited-service inns, guest ranches, and other unique hotel properties.

THE FOUR SEASONS INN. *145 Rte 100, West Dover (05356). Phone 802/464-8303; fax 802/531-4500 or 802/463-3373. www.fourseasonsinn.com.* 18 rooms. No children allowed. Complimentary full breakfast. Check-in 3 pm, check-out 11 am. Wireless Internet access. Bar. Outdoor pool.**$$**
🖾 🖾

WEST DOVER INN. *108 Hwy 100, West Dover (05356). Phone 802/464-5207; fax 802/464-2173. www.westdoverinn.com.* This inn, built in 1846, was a stagecoach stop and a general store. 12 rooms, 2 story. Closed mid-Apr-Memorial Day. Children over 12 years only. Complimentary full breakfast. Check-in 2 pm, check-out 11 am. Restaurant. **$**
🖾

Restaurant

★ ★ ★ THE INN AT SAWMILL FARM. *Hwy 100 and Crosstown Rd, West Dover (05356). Phone 802/464-8131; toll-free 800/493-1133; fax 802/464-1130. www.theinnatsawmillfarm.com.* Only in a town that wears charm and hospitality like a comfortable old jacket—West Dover—can an old sawmill and barn be transformed into a sophisticated but unpretentious haven for weary urban food lovers. The Sawmill Inn was purchased by the Williams family in 1967 and has weathered the years with grace, maintaining its commitment to quality ingredients and family-style warmth. Decorated like a New England fairy tale, with exposed beams and hanging chandeliers, the restaurant oozes serenity and calm and is the perfect place to relax for an evening of pampering and delicious home-style cooking. The restaurant features a seasonal American menu specializing in locally farmed game such as quail, pheasant, rabbit, and venison. The impressive wine list heaves at the seams, with a selection of 1,285 wines in the 30,000-bottle cellar. All this from a little old barn. American menu. Breakfast, dinner. Closed late Mar-Memorial Day. Bar. Casual attire. Reservations recommended. **$$$**

Weston (E-2)

See also Londonderry, Ludlow, Okemo State Forest, Peru

Population 620
Elevation 1,295 ft
Area Code 802
Zip 05161

Once nearly a ghost town, Weston is now a serene village secluded in the beautiful hills of Vermont. Charming old houses are situated around a small common, and shops are scattered along Main Street. Weston is listed on the National Register of Historic Places.

What to See and Do

Farrar-Mansur House Museum. *N side of Common.* (1797) Restored house/tavern with nine rooms. Period furnishings; paintings. Guided tours. (July-Aug: Mon-Fri; Memorial Day-Columbus Day: weekends) **$$**

Greendale Camping Area. *2 miles N on Hwy 100, 2 miles W on Greendale Rd in Green Mountain National Forest.* Picnicking, camping (fee).

Old Mill Museum. *Hwy 100, Weston. In center of village.* Museum of old-time tools and industries; tinsmith in residence. Guided tours (July-Aug). (Memorial Day-Columbus Day, daily) **DONATION**

Vermont Country Store. *Hwy 100, Weston. S of Village Green. Phone 802/824-3184.* Just like those Granddad used to patronize—rock candy and other old-fashioned foodstuffs. (Mon-Sat; closed Thanksgiving, Dec 25)

Weston Bowl Mill. *Just N of Common on Hwy 100. Phone 802/824-6219.* Wooden bowls, other wooden household products made on premises. Seconds available. (Daily; closed Easter, Thanksgiving, Dec 25) **FREE**

Weston Playhouse. *Hwy 100, Weston. Village Green. Phone 802/824-5288; fax 802/717-1032. www.westonplayhouse.org.* One of the oldest professional theater companies in the state. Restaurant; cabaret.

Specialty Lodgings

The following lodging establishments are approved by Mobil Travel Guide, but due to their unique and individualized nature have not been given a traditional Mobil Star rating. Included in this listing you may find bed-and-breakfasts, limited-service inns, guest ranches, and other unique hotel properties.

THE COLONIAL HOUSE. *287 Hwy 100, Weston (05161). Phone 802/824-6286; toll-free 800/639-5033; fax 802/824-3934. www.cohoinn.com.* 2 story. Complimentary full breakfast. Check-in 1 pm, check-out 11 am. Restaurant. **$**

WILDER HOMESTEAD INN. *25 Lawrence Hill Rd, Weston (05161). Phone 802/824-8172; toll-free 877/838-9979; fax 802/824-5054. www.wilderhomestead.com.* This Federal-style country inn was built in 1827 and overlooks the river. 7 rooms, 3 story. Closed two weeks in Apr. Children over 12 years only. Complimentary full breakfast. Check-in 2 pm, check-out 11 am. **$**

White River Junction (D-2)

See also Fairlee, Hanover, Windsor, Woodstock

Settled 1764
Population 2,521
Elevation 368 ft
Area Code 802
Zip 05001

Appropriately named, this town is the meeting place of the Boston & Maine and Central Vermont railroads, the White and Connecticut rivers, and two interstate highways.

What to See and Do

Quechee Gorge. *About 8 miles W on Hwy 4.* Often referred to as Vermont's "Little Grand Canyon," the Ottauquechee River has carved out a mile-long chasm that offers dramatic views of the landscape and neighboring towns.

Limited-Service Hotel

★ **COMFORT INN.** *8 Sykes Mountain Ave, White River Jct (05001). Phone 802/295-3051; toll-free 800/ 628-7727; fax 802/295-5990. www.choicehotels.com.* In a commercial area near the junction of Interstate 91 and Interstate 89 and near several restaurants, this hotel appeals to budget-minded travelers. It lacks its own fitness facilities, but guests have full privileges at a health club about 1/2 mile away. 94 rooms, 4 story. Pets accepted. Complimentary continental breakfast. Check-in 2 pm, check-out 11 am. High-speed Internet access, wireless Internet access. Outdoor pool. **$**

Wilmington (F-2)

See also Bennington, Brattleboro, Marlboro, West Dover

Population 1,968
Elevation 1,533 ft
Area Code 802
Zip 05363
Information Mount Snow Valley Region Chamber of Commerce, Hwy 9, W Main St, PO Box 3; phone 802/464-8092 or toll-free 877/887-6884
Web Site www.visitvermont.com

What to See and Do

Haystack Ski Area. *3 miles NW, off Hwy 100. Phone 802/464-8501; toll-free 800/245-7669 (lodging).* Resort has double, three triple chairlifts; patrol, school, rentals, snowmaking; concession, cafeteria, bar, nursery, lodges. More than 100 trails spread over five interconnecting mountain areas (see WEST DOVER); shuttle bus. Longest run 1 1/2 miles; vertical drop 1,400 feet. (Dec-Mar, daily) Golf, pro shop; restaurant, bar (early May-mid-Oct). **$$$$**

★ **Molly Stark State Park.** *705 Hwy 9 E, Wilmington (05363). Approximately 4 miles E on Hwy 9. Phone 802/464-5460.* A 158-acre park named for wife of General John Stark, hero of Battle of Bennington (1777); on west slope of Mount Olga (2,438 feet). Fishing in nearby lake; hiking trails, tent and trailer sites (dump station), lean-tos. Fire tower with excellent views. (Memorial Day-Columbus Day)

Mount Snow Resort. *3 miles NW, off Hwy 100. Phone 802/464-8501; toll-free 800/245-7669 (lodging). www.mountsnow.com.* Resort has three high-speed quads, quad, ten triple, four double chairlifts, two surface lifts; patrol, school, rentals; snowmaking; concession, cafeteria, bar; nursery, lodges. More than 100 trails spread over five interconnecting mountain areas (see WEST DOVER); shuttle bus. Longest run 1 1/2 miles; vertical drop 1,700 feet. (Dec-Mar, daily) Golf, pro shop; restaurant, bar (early May-mid-Oct). **$$$$**

Special Events

Deerfield Valley Farmers Day Exhibition. Pony pull, midway rides; horse show, livestock judging, entertainment. Late Aug.

The Nights Before Christmas. *Throughout Wilmington and West Dover. Phone 802/464-8092.* Celebrates holiday season with caroling, torchlight parade, fireworks, tree lighting. Festival of Light, living nativity, and children's hayrides. Late Nov-late Dec.

Limited-Service Hotel

★ **HORIZON INN.** *Hwy 9 E, Wilmington (05363). Phone 802/464-2131; toll-free 800/336-5513; fax 802/464-8302. www.horizoninn.com.* This family-friendly lodge is just east of the ski town of Wilmington and sits off Route 9, the area's major east/west route. It's close to the resort mountain locations of Mount Snow, Haystack, and Stratton and is in the heart of southern Vermont "fall foliage country." Family-owned and -run, it has a homey feel, particularly in its large, informal basement lounge with 60-inch TV. The second-floor dining room, serving American food, is filled with Norman Rockwell art and Hummel figurines. 29 rooms, 2 story. Check-in 2 pm, check-out 11 am. Restaurant, bar. Fitness room. Indoor pool, whirlpool. **$**

🏋 🏊

Full-Service Inns

★ ★ ★ **HERMITAGE INN.** *Coldbrook Rd, Wilmington (05363). Phone 802/464-3511; fax 802/464-2688. www.hermitageinn.com.* Bring your cross-country skis and ski in/ski out of this picturesque inn, sitting on the crest of a hill just down the road from Haystack and close to Mount Snow. In the fall, shoot clay pigeons or go pheasant hunting on the private, 200-acre hunting preserve. In the summer, enjoy croquet or other lawn games. And at any time of the year, visit the inn's fine-dining restaurant, if only to sample the extensive wine list; *Wine Spectator* magazine has pronounced it "one of the greatest wine lists in the world" (be sure to visit the inn's wine shop and buy a bottle of your favorite to take home). The guest rooms are equally sumptuous. There are four in the main house, seven in the adjoining wine house, and four in the carriage house, each with a wood-burning fireplace and a collection of New England antiques. If the inn looks familiar, it's undoubtedly because you have seen it in a painting by the artist Michel

Delacroix. The original, "Winter in New England," now hangs in the Hermitage Inn. 15 rooms, 2 story. Complimentary full breakfast. Check-in 2 pm, check-out 11 am. Restaurant, bar. Ski in/ski out. **$**

🅳 🏊

★ ★ ★ **WHITE HOUSE OF WILMINGTON.** *178 Hwy 9 E, Wilmington (05363). Phone 802/464-2135; toll-free 800/541-2135; fax 802/464-5222. www.whitehouseinn.com.* A historic old inn with an indoor/outdoor pool, steam room, sauna, and tanning room? Lawn games in the summer...tubing, cross-country skiing, and snowshoeing in the winter...trails for hiking year-round.... There is much to do at this country mansion, built in 1915 as a summer home for a wealthy lumber baron. Restorations began in 1978, but today the inn retains many of its original, elegant details, such as the front hallway's wallpaper, made in France at the turn of the century; and the secret staircase, a guest favorite. The original house has nine guest rooms, some with fireplaces and some with both fireplaces and whirlpool tubs; an adjoining guest house has eight additional rooms that have been designed for families. Downstairs, it's easy to picture a lumber baron entertaining his wealthy friends in from the city for a weekend of skiing or croquet: there they are after a game of croquet, sipping lemonade in front of the huge fireplace in the lounge (where today there are jigsaw puzzles in progress) or dining elegantly in the main dining room, where guests sup in equal elegance today. 25 rooms. Closed Apr. Children over 8 years only. Complimentary full breakfast. Check-in 2 pm, check-out 11 am. Restaurant, bar. Fitness room. Indoor pool, outdoor pool. Ski in/ski out. **$$**

🅳 🏋 🏊 🏊

Specialty Lodging

The following lodging establishment is approved by Mobil Travel Guide, but due to its unique and individualized nature has not been given a traditional Mobil Star rating. Included in this listing you may find bed-and-breakfasts, limited-service inns, guest ranches, and other unique hotel properties.

TRAIL'S END - A COUNTRY INN. *5 Trail's End Ln, Wilmington (05363). Phone 802/464-2727; toll-free 800/859-2585; fax 802/464-5532. www.trailsendvt.com.* 5 rooms, 2 story. Complimentary full breakfast. Check-in 2 pm, check-out 11 am. Outdoor pool. Tennis. **$**

🅳 🏊 🎾

Restaurants

★ ★ ★ **HERMITAGE.** *Coldbrook Rd, Wilmington (05363). Phone 802/464-3511; fax 802/464-2688. www.hermitageinn.com.* Nestled at the foot of southern Vermont's Green Mountains, this restaurant is part of the inn bearing the same name. There is a 40,000-bottle wine cellar and many of the labels are available in the gift shop along with the homemade preserves and other delicacies. American menu. Dinner, Sun brunch. Bar. **$$$**
🅿

★ ★ **WHITE HOUSE.** *178 Hwy 9 E, Wilmington (05363). Phone 802/464-2135; toll-free 800/541-2135; fax 802/464-5222. www.whitehouseinn.com.* American menu. Dinner. Bar. Casual attire. **$$**

Windsor (E-2)

See also White River Junction

Settled 1764
Population 3,714
Elevation 354 ft
Area Code 802
Zip 05089
Information White River Area Chamber of Commerce, PO Box 697, White River Junction 05001; phone 802/295-6200

Situated on the Connecticut River in the shadow of Mount Ascutney, Windsor once was the political center of the Connecticut Valley towns. The name "Vermont" was adopted, and its constitution was drawn up here. Inventors and inventions flourished here in the 19th century; the hydraulic pump, a sewing machine, coffee percolator, and various refinements in firearms originated in Windsor.

What to See and Do

American Precision Museum. *196 Main St, Windsor (05089). Phone 802/674-5781.* Exhibits include hand and machine tools; illustrations of their uses and development. Housed in former Robbins and Lawrence Armory (1846). (Late May-Oct: daily; rest of year: by appointment) **$$**

Constitution House. *16 N Main St, Windsor (05089). Phone 802/672-3773.* An 18th-century tavern where the constitution of the Republic of Vermont was signed on July 8, 1777. Museum. (Mid-May-mid-Oct, Wed-Sun) **$**

Covered bridge. Crossing the Connecticut River; longest in the United States.

Mount Ascutney State Park. *3 miles S off Hwy 5 on Hwy 44A; I-91 exit 8. Phone 802/674-2060.* This 1,984-acre park has a paved road to summit of Mount Ascutney (3,144 feet). Hiking trails, picnicking, tent and trailer sites (dump station), lean-tos. (Memorial Day-Columbus Day)

Vermont State Craft Center at Windsor House. *54 Main St, Windsor (05089). Phone 802/674-6729.* Restored building features works of more than 250 Vermont craftspeople. (June-Dec: daily; rest of year: Mon-Sat) **FREE**

Wilgus State Park. *6 miles S on Hwy 5. Phone 802/674-5422.* This 100-acre park overlooks the Connecticut River. Canoe launching. Hiking trails. Wooded picnic area. Tent and trailer sites (dump station), lean-tos. (Memorial Day-Columbus Day)

Full-Service Inn

★ ★ ★ **JUNIPER HILL INN.** *153 Pembroke Rd, Windsor (05089). Phone 802/674-5273; toll-free 800/359-2541; fax 802/674-2041. www.juniperhillinn.com.* Teddy Roosevelt slept here. No wonder: the exterior of this magnificent 1902 Classical Revival mansion, perched atop 14 acres of hillside, is just a prelude to the elegance that lies within. A 30-x-40-foot Great Hall features a floor-to-ceiling fireplace. A 5-x-15-foot table sits within a massive Gathering Room. The library, tucked within the west wing, is a perfect place to sit by the fire and play a board game or two. In the Gentleman's Sitting Parlor, one can have a brandy and a quiet chat. It's all designed to make you feel as though you are a guest at the country home of your (very wealthy) aunt, who invited you to the outskirts of historic Windsor to forget your cares and enjoy life. Sleep in a four-poster bed, sniff the fragrance of fresh flowers, soak in a claw-foot tub—while sipping a sherry—and awaken to a deluxe breakfast. 16 rooms, 3 story. Closed two weeks in Nov; three weeks in late Mar-early Apr, Children over 12 years only. Complimentary full breakfast. Check-in 3 pm, check-out 11 am. Restaurant. Outdoor pool. **$$**
🅿 🏊

Woodstock (D-2)

See also Killington, Plymouth, White River Junction

Settled 1768
Population 3,212
Elevation 705 ft
Area Code 802
Zip 05091
Information Chamber of Commerce, 18 Central St, PO Box 486; phone 802/457-3555
Web Site www.woodstockvt.com

The antique charm of Woodstock has been preserved, at least in part, by determination. Properties held for generations by descendants of original owners provided built-in zoning long before Historic District status was achieved. When the iron bridge that crosses the Ottauquechee River at Union Street was condemned in 1968, it was replaced by a covered wooden bridge.

What to See and Do

Billings Farm & Museum. *Hwy 12, Woodstock. Phone 802/457-2355.* Exhibits include operating dairy farm and an 1890s farmhouse. (May-late Oct, daily)

Covered bridge. *Center of village.* (1968) First one built in Vermont since 1895. Two others cross the Ottauquechee River: one 3 miles W (1877), another 4 miles E, at Taftsville (1836).

Kedron Valley Stables. *Hwy 106 S, South Woodstock. 5 miles S on Hwy 106. Phone 802/457-1480.* Hayrides, sleigh rides, picnic trail rides; indoor ring; riding lessons by appointment.

Marsh-Billings-Rockefeller National Historic Park. *54 Elm St, Woodstock (05091). On Hwy 12, 1/2 mile N of Woodstock Village Green. Phone 802/457-3368.* Includes Marsh-Billings-Rockefeller mansion, which contains extensive collection of American landscape paintings. Mansion is surrounded by 550-acre Mount Tom forest. Interpretive tours of the mansion, its grounds and gardens, and the Mount Tom forest are available. Reservations recommended. Park also offers hiking, nature study, and cross-country skiing. (June-Oct, daily)

Silver Lake State Park. *10 miles NW via Hwy 12 to Barnard, on Silver Lake. Phone 802/234-9451.* This 34-acre park offers a swimming beach, bathhouse, fishing, boating (rentals); picnicking, concession, tent and trailer camping (dump station), lean-tos. Within walking distance of Barnard Village. (Memorial Day-Labor Day, daily)

Suicide Six Ski Area. *14 The Green, Woodstock (05091). 3 miles N on Hwy 12 (S Pomfret Rd). Phone 802/457-1666.* Area has two double chairlifts, J-Bar; patrol, PSIA school, rentals, snowmaking; cafeteria, wine and beer bar, lodge. Twenty-two runs, longest run 1 mile; vertical drop 650 feet. Site of the first ski tow in the United States (1934). (Early Dec-late Mar, daily) **$$$$**

Vermont Institute of Natural Science. *Church Hill Rd, Woodstock. 1 1/2 miles SW. Phone 802/457-2779.* Property includes a 75-acre preserve with trails (daily). Raptor Center, an outdoor museum, has 26 species of hawks, owls, and eagles (summer, daily; winter, Mon-Sat). Gift shop. **$$**

Walking Tours Around Woodstock. *Phone 802/457-2450.* There are one- and two-hour tours of Historic District, covering more than 1 mile; departing from Chamber of Commerce information booth on the green. (Mid-June-mid-Oct: Mon, Wed, and Sat) **$$**

Woodstock Country Club. *14 The Green, Woodstock (05091). Phone 802/457-2112.* An 18-hole championship golf course, ten tennis courts, paddle tennis, cross-country skiing center with more than 35 miles of trails; rentals, instruction, tours. Restaurant, lounge. (Daily; closed Apr and Nov) Fee for activities.

Woodstock Historical Society. *26 Elm St, Woodstock (05091). Phone 802/457-1822.* Dana House (1807) has 11 rooms spanning 1750-1900, including a children's room; also silver, glass, paintings, costumes, furniture; research library; Woodstock-related artifacts, photographs. Farm and textile equipment. Gift shop. (Mid-May-late Oct, daily)

Limited-Service Hotels

★ **POND RIDGE MOTEL.** *506 Hwy 4 W, Woodstock (05091). Phone 802/457-1667. www.vtliving.com/pond ridgemotel.* Kids will enjoy playing on the huge lawn of this older-style, family-friendly motel, located on 6 1/2 acres of private frontage along the Ottauquechee River, 1.8 miles west of historic Woodstock Green. In front are a gazebo and big shade trees; in the back are a pond and the Ottauquechee, both great places for splashers and waders. Benches and picnic tables have been set up along the river. Rooms have lovely views of the water. 20 rooms. Check-in 1 pm, check-out 11 am. **$**
🄳

★ **THE SHIRE RIVERVIEW.** *46 Pleasant St, Woodstock (05091). Phone 802/457-2211; fax 802/457-5836. www.shiremotel.com.* A wraparound porch with rocking chairs is undoubtedly the first thing that will catch your eye as you approach this soft gray and white retreat. Well situated just east of Woodstock's historic village center, the Shire Riverview has a prime spot overlooking the Ottauquechee River, the Marsh-Billings-Rockefeller National Park, and the natural beauty of Vermont's rolling hills. The Shire takes full advantage of its views, with large windows and French doors and a veranda where guests can take morning coffee and tea. Rooms are spacious; there are value rooms without views but with full amenities, and other rooms and suites with plush four-poster beds and mahogany furniture, well-coordinated fabrics and colors, and large baths with upgraded amenities. There's no restaurant, but with the heart of Woodstock within walking distance, no worries. 43 rooms. Check-in 2 pm, check-out 11 am. **$**

Full-Service Resort

★ ★ ★ **WOODSTOCK INN & RESORT.** *14 The Green, Woodstock (05091). Phone 802/457-1100; toll-free 800/448-7900; fax 802/457-6699. www.woodstockinn.com.* The Woodstock Inn & Resort, on the south side of the Woodstock green, is the Vermont getaway of dreams. From its classic New England architecture to its gracious charm, this resort makes its way into travelers' hearts. An inn has stood on this spot since the 18th century, lending a deep sense of history. An enormous fireplace welcomes guests. The rooms and suites are sweet renditions of traditional Vermont style, with handmade quilts, built-in alcoves, and original prints. While the accommodations are exceedingly inviting and plush, the plethora of outdoor activities encourages guests to leave the confines of their cocoonlike rooms. Downhill and cross-country skiing are two of the resort's most popular winter activities, while the Woodstock Country Club's prestigious course draws golfers. Biking, canoeing, fishing, horseback riding, and nature walks are among the many ways to enjoy the picturesque countryside, and the town's shops and other attractions are within walking distance. After a long day, three restaurants satisfy diners with fine dining, casual fare, and traditional tavern-style food. In season, children's programs are organized around sports, area attractions, and even a special "Kids' Day in the Kitchen." The inn offers many packages combining all sorts of activities and meal plans.

142 rooms, 3 story. Check-in 3 pm, check-out 11 am. Three restaurants, bar. Children's activity center. Fitness room, fitness classes available. Indoor pool, outdoor pool, whirlpool. Golf, 18 holes. Tennis. Business center. **$$**

Full-Service Inns

★ ★ ★ **KEDRON VALLEY INN.** *Hwy 106, South Woodstock (05091). Phone 802/457-1473; toll-free 800/836-1193; fax 802/457-4469. www.kedronvalleyinn.com.* Just 5 miles outside Woodstock, this small historic inn makes a good base while enjoying the local activities. Guests can partake in antique shopping or browsing in local shops. 26 rooms, 3 story. Closed Apr. Pets accepted. Check-in 3:30 pm, check-out 11:30 am. Restaurant, bar. **$$**

★ ★ ★ **QUECHEE INN AT MARSHLAND FARM.** *1619 Quechee Main St, Quechee (05059). Phone 802/295-3133; toll-free 800/235-3133; fax 802/295-6587. www.quecheeinn.com.* This inn was built in 1793 and has been restored to its 19th-century beginnings with many modern conveniences. 24 rooms, 2 story. Complimentary full breakfast. Check-in 3 pm, check-out 11 am. Restaurant, bar. **$$**

★ ★ ★ ★ ★ **TWIN FARMS.** *Stage Rd, Barnard (05031). Phone 802/234-9999; toll-free 800/894-6327; fax 802/234-9990. www.twinfarms.com.* Travelers searching for the ultimate Vermont farmhouse, where rocking chairs line the porch, deer gambol on the lawn, and fireplaces warm hearts and souls on chilly evenings, need look no further than Twin Farms. This remarkable inn appeals to the naturalist in all guests with its magnificent 300 acres of ponds, wooded valleys, and rolling lawns carpeted in brilliant wildflowers or blanketed in pure ivory snow. The accommodations weave together quintessential New England charm with a cosmopolitan twist. From the clean lines and simple furnishings of the Orchard Cottage and the seductive Moroccan style of the Meadow Cottage to the vaulted ceilings of twig artistry in the Treehouse, the designs spark the imaginations of their residents. Vermont's lush landscape serves as the inspiration for the kitchen's gourmet meals, with organic ingredients from local farms determining the menus, while its ever-changing seasons never cease to amaze. 15 rooms, 2 story. Closed Apr. No children allowed. Complimentary continental breakfast.

Check-in 4 pm, check-out noon. Restaurant (guests only). Fitness room; Japanese furo tubs. Spa. Tennis. Ski in/ski out. **$$$$**

Specialty Lodgings

The following lodging establishments are approved by Mobil Travel Guide, but due to their unique and individualized nature have not been given a traditional Mobil Star rating. Included in this listing you may find bed-and-breakfasts, limited-service inns, guest ranches, and other unique hotel properties.

APPLEBUTTER INN. *Happy Valley Rd, Woodstock (05091). Phone 802/457-4158. www.applebutterinn.com.* This restored Federal-style house (1850) features period furnishings. 6 rooms, 2 story. Complimentary full breakfast. Check-in 3 pm, check-out 10:30 am. **$**

CANTERBURY HOUSE BED AND BREAKFAST. *43 Pleasant St, Woodstock (05091). Phone 802/ 457-3077; toll-free 800/390-3077; fax 802/457-4630. www.thecanterburyhouse.com.* Victorian home built in 1880; antiques. 7 rooms, 3 story. No children allowed. Complimentary full breakfast. Check-in 2 pm, check-out 10:30 am. Restaurant. **$**

CHARLESTON HOUSE. *21 Pleasant St, Woodstock (05091). Phone 802/457-3843; fax 802/457-2512. www.charlestonhouse.com.* Greek Revival house built in 1835; many antiques. 9 rooms, 2 story. Complimentary full breakfast. Check-in 3 pm, check-out 11 am. **$$**

THE LINCOLN INN AT THE COVERED BRIDGE. *530 Woodstock Rd, Woodstock (05091). Phone 802/457-3312; fax 802/457-5808. www.lincolninn.com.* This renovated farmhouse's (circa 1869) property is bordered by the Ottauquechee River and a covered bridge. 6 rooms, 2 story. Complimentary full breakfast. Check-in 3 pm, check-out 11 am. Restaurant. **$**

MAPLE LEAF INN. *Hwy 12, Barnard (5031). Phone 802/234-5342; toll-free 800/516-2753. www.mapleleafinn.com.* Just gazing at this white, porch-wrapped farmhouse will relax arriving guests. The property is nestled on 16 acres of maple and birch trees near the quaint town of Woodstock, where antiques stores, unique shops and outdoor recreations abound. 7 rooms, 3 story. Complimentary full breakfast. Check-in 3-6 pm, check-out 11 am. **$$**

PARKER HOUSE INN. *1792 Quechee Main St, Quechee (05059). Phone 802/295-6077; fax 802/296-6696. www.theparkerhouseinn.com.* Victorian home (1857); former senator's residence. 7 rooms, 3 story. Complimentary full breakfast. Check-in 3 pm, check-out 11 am. Restaurant. **$**

WINSLOW HOUSE. *492 Woodstock Rd, Woodstock (05091). Phone 802/457-1820; toll-free 866/457-1820; fax 802/457-1820. www.thewinslowhousevt.com.* Farmhouse built in 1872; period furnishings. 4 rooms, 2 story. Closed two weeks in Apr. Pets accepted, some restrictions; fee. Children over 10 years only. Complimentary full breakfast. Check-in 3 pm, check-out 11 am. Wireless Internet access. **$**

WOODSTOCKER BED AND BREAKFAST. *61 River St, Woodstock (05091). Phone 802/457-3896; fax 802/457-3897. www.woodstockervt.com.* Built in 1830; individually decorated rooms. 9 rooms, 2 story. Complimentary full breakfast. Check-in 3 pm, check-out 11 am. Whirlpool. **$**

Restaurants

★ ★ ★ **BARNARD INN.** *5518 Hwy 12, Barnard (05031). Phone 802/234-9961; fax 802/234-5590.* The original brick structure of this house, built in 1796, is a perfect host for this charming restaurant. French menu. Dinner. Closed Sun-Mon. Bar. Children's menu. **$$**

★ ★ ★ **KEDRON VALLEY.** *Hwy 106, South Woodstock (05091). Phone 802/457-1473. www.kedronvalleyinn.com.* The dining room of this elegant inn offers an updated menu. Vermont-raised produce and meat are featured, and the friendly service has a certain Vermont charm. Breakfast, dinner. Closed Wed except fall foliage season and week of Dec 25; also Apr. Bar. Children's menu. **$$**

★ ★ ★ **PRINCE AND THE PAUPER.** *24 Elm St, Woodstock (05091). Phone 802/457-1818. www.princeandpauper.com.* Chef/owner Chris Balce welcomes you to his country restaurant with candlelit

tables and hand-hewn beams. International/Fusion menu. Dinner. Closed Thanksgiving, Dec 25. Bar. Outdoor seating. **$$$**
🅓

★ ★ ★ **QUECHEE INN AT MARSH-LAND FARM.** *1119 Quechee Main St, Quechee (05059). Phone 802/295-3133; fax 802/295-6587. www.quecheeinn.com.* The restaurant is in the main house of this inn, which dates to 1793 and overlooks the Ottauquechee River. The cuisine is served in a casual but sophisticated setting, with a wine list to match. International/Fusion menu. Dinner. Bar. Children's menu. **$$$**
🅓

★ ★ ★ **SIMON PEARCE.** *Main St, Quechee (05059). Phone 802/295-1470; fax 802/295-2853. www.simonpearce.com.* Part of the glassblowing and pottery complex that has become an emblem of Vermont, this spacious, contemporary restaurant has beautiful, forested views of the Ottauquechee River. International/Fusion menu. Lunch, dinner. Closed Thanksgiving, Dec 25. Outdoor seating. **$$$**

★ ★ ★ **WOODSTOCK INN.** *14 The Green, Woodstock (05091). Phone 802/457-1100; fax 802/457-6699. www.woodstockinn.com.* This quaint restaurant has an understated elegance and is a perfect choice for a romantic meal with softly candlelit tables. A short drive from Hanover's Dartmouth College. Changing menu. Dinner, Sun brunch. Bar. Children's menu. Jacket suggested (Memorial Day-Labor Day). Outdoor seating. **$$$**

A Parisian-flavored side trip is only two hours from Burlington. Montréal has the largest French population outside of Europe; nearly two-thirds of its people speak French. While in Montréal, take time to wander the narrow, winding streets in the Old City section. But don't think that Montréal is all history; the city also has a very modern, elegant feel.

Montréal, QC

2 hours, 155 miles from Burlington, VT

Settled 1642
Population 1,800,000
Elevation 117 ft (36 m)
Area Code 514
Information Tourisme-Québec, CP 979, H3C 2W3; phone 514/873-2015 or toll-free 800/363-7777
Web Site www.tourisme-montreal.org

Blessed by its location on an island at the junction of the St. Lawrence and Ottawa rivers, Montréal has served for more than three centuries as a gigantic trading post; its harbor can accommodate more than 100 oceangoing vessels. While it is a commercial, financial, and industrial center, Montréal is also an internationally recognized patron of the fine arts, hosting several acclaimed festivals attended by international enthusiasts.

A stockaded, indigenous settlement called Hochelaga when it was discovered in 1535 by Jacques Cartier, the area contained a trading post by the early 1600s; but it was not settled as a missionary outpost until 1642 when the Frenchman Paul de Chomedey, Sieur de Maisonneuve, and a group of settlers, priests, and nuns founded Ville-Morie. This later grew as an important fur trading center, and from here men such as Jolliet, Marquette, Duluth, and Father Hennepin set out on their western expeditions.

Montréal remained under French rule until 1763 when Canada was surrendered as a possession to the British under the Treaty of Paris. For seven months during the American Revolution, Montréal was occupied by Americans, but it was later regained by the British.

Today, Montréal is an elegantly sophisticated city. Two-thirds of its people are French-speaking, and its French population is the largest outside of Europe. The city is also extremely international, with more than 80 ethnic groups represented in the metropolitan region. The largest of these include Italian, Jewish, Muslim, Greek, and Chinese. City neighborhoods, attractions, and markets reflect this diversity.

Montréal is made up of two parts: the Old City, in the same area as the original Ville-Morie, which is a maze of narrow streets, restored buildings, and old houses, best seen on foot; and the modern Montréal, with its many skyscrapers, museums, theaters, restaurants, and glittering nightlife. Sainte-Catherine Street's boutiques and department stores are a shopper's paradise, while Crescent Street's café-terrasses encourage people-watching while sipping coffee in the sunshine.

When there is inclement weather, head for Montréal's underground city, an impressive pedestrian network more than 19 miles (30 kilometers) long, providing access to hundreds of shops and restaurants, several area attractions, and businesses. The underground also provides access to one of the most unique subway systems in the world. Each station has been decorated by a different architect in a different style, and visitors have called it "the largest underground art gallery in the world." Mont-Royal rises from the center of the island-city to a height of 764 feet (233 meters), affording a panoramic view. Calèches (horse-drawn carriages) provide tourists with a charming means of viewing the city and are, with the exception of bicycles, the only vehicles permitted in some areas of Mount Royal Park. Adjacent to the park is the Westmount area, a section of meandering roads and charming older homes of the early 1900s with delightful English-style gardens.

In 1967, Montréal hosted Expo '67, celebrating Canada's centennial. The summer Olympic games were held here in 1976.

Additional Visitor Information

Québec Tourism, PO Box 979, Montréal, H3C 2W3; phone toll-free 800/363-7777 or in person at Infotouriste, 1001 rue du Square-Dorchester (between Peel and Metcalfe sts); also office at Old Montréal, Place Jacques-Cartier, 174 Notre-Dame St E; all have helpful information for tourists. The Consulate General of the United States is located on 1155 rue St. Alexandre, at Placé Felip-Martin, at the corner of René Levesque Blvd; phone 514/398-9695. Public transportation is provided by the Societé de Transport de la Communauté Urbaine de Montréal (STCUM), phone 514/288-6287.

Public Transportation

Airport Montréal Dorval International Airport.

Information Phone 514/394-7377 or toll-free 800/465-1213

Lost and Found Phone 514/636-0499

Airlines Air Canada, Air Canada Jazz, Air Canada Tango, Air Creebec, Air France, Air Inuit, Air Saint-Pierre, Air Transat, Allegheny Airlines, American Airlines, American Express, Atlantic Coast Airlines, Atlantic Southeast Airlines, Austrian Airlines, British Airways, CanJet, Chautauqua Airlines, Comair, Continental Airlines, Continental Express, Corsair, CSA Czech Airlines, Cubana, Delta Air Lines, Egypt Air, First Air, Hydro-Quebec, Japan Air Lines, Jetsgo, KLM Royal Dutch, Lufthansa, Mesaba Airlines, Mesa Airlines, Mexicana, Northwest Airlines, Olympic Airways, PSA Airlines, Quebecair Express, Royal Air Maroc, Swiss, United Airlines, WestJet, Zip

What to See and Do

Angrignon Park. *3400 des Trinitaires Blvd, Montréal (H4E 4J3). Phone 514/872-3816.* On 262 acres (106 hectares) with more than 21,600 trees; lagoons, river; playground, picnicking, bicycling, iceskating, cross-country skiing. (Daily) **$$**

Caleche tours. Horse-drawn carriages depart from Place d' Armes, Mount Royal Park, or Old Port of Montréal. **$$$$**

Casino Montréal. *1 Ave du Caino, Montréal (H3C 4W7). Housed in Expo 67's famous French Pavilion. Phone 514/392-2746; toll-free 800/665-2274. www. casinos-quebec.com.* The Casino de Montréal offers

guests a variety of games, with more than 120 gaming tables as well as 3,060 slot machines. (Open 24 hours)

Dorchester Square. *1555 Peel St, Montréal.* In the center of Montréal, this park is a popular meeting place. Also here is Mary Queen of the World Cathedral, a 1/3-scale replica of St. Peter's in Rome, as well as the information center of Montréal and Tourisme Québec. **FREE**

Fort Lennox. *Saint-Paul-de-l'ile-aux-Noix, 1 61st Ave, Montréal (J0J 1G0). Off Rte 223. www.parcscanada.gc.ca.* Located on Île-aux-Noix, Fort Lennox was designed to protect against an American invasion. Costumed guides provide visitors with insight into the history of these fortifications. On-site are picnic tables, outdoor game equipment, a snack bar, and a souvenier stand. (Daily 10 am-6 pm; mid-May-mid-June: Mon-Fri 10 am-5 pm; Sept-mid-Oct: Mon-Fri by appointment only) **$$**

Gray Line bus tours. *1140 Wellington St, Montréal (H3C 1V8). Phone 514/934-1222. www.grayline.com.* The well-known Gray Line offers various sightseeing and package tours of Montréal, with stops at the Biodome, Notre-Dame Basilica, and Chinatown. Buses depart from Dorchester Square. (May-Oct) **$$$$**

La Fontaine Park. *Sherbrooke and Ave du Parc Lafontaine, Montréal. Phone 514/872-2644.* Outdoor enthusiasts delight in this park for its many recreational oportunities. Along with paddleboating on two manmade lakes, visitors may enjoy foot paths and bicycle trails, and, in the winter, cross-country skiing, ice skating, and snowshoeing. **FREE**

Maison St.-Gabriel. *Pointe-Saint-Charles, 2146 place Dublin, Montréal (H3K 2A2). Phone 514/935-8136. www.maisonsaint-gabriel.qc.ca.* Built in the late 17th century as a farm; also served as school for Marguerite Bourgeoys, founder of the Sisters of the Congrégatun de Notre-Dame, who looked after young French girls who were to marry the early colonists. The site includes vegetable, herb, and flower gardens; a stone barn; and the house itself, complete with period furnishings and tools, and items of French-Canadian heritage, including woodcuts from ancient churches and chapels. (Apr-late June, Sept-mid-Dec: Tues-Sun guided tours at 1 pm, 2 pm, 3 pm, and 4 pm; late June-early Sept: Tues-Sun 11 am-5 pm) **$$$**

McCord Museum of Canadian History. *690 Sherbrooke St W, Montréal. Phone 514/398-7100. www.mccord-museum.qc.ca.* Extensive and diverse collections including the most important First Nations collection in Quebec, Canadian costumes and textiles, and the Notman photographic archives. (Tues-Fri 10 am-6 pm; Sat-Sun 10 am-5 pm; closed Mon except for holidays and during summer)

McGill University. *805 Sherbrooke St Ouest, Montréal (H3A 2K6). Phone 514/398-6555. www.mcgill.ca.* (30,580 students) McGill's 80-acre (32-hectares) main campus is set between the lower slopes of Mount Royal and the downtown commercial district. Originally established as the Royal Institution for the Advancement of Learning from land and money left by Scottish immigrant James McGill, it was later renamed McGill University and chartered in 1821. Walking tours are given by students who offer insight into student life and the history of the university. **FREE**

⭐ **Montréal Botanical Garden.** *4101 rue Sherbrooke Est, Montréal (H1X 2B2). Phone 514/872-1400. www.ville.montreal.qc.ca/jardin.* Within 180 acres (73 hectares) grow more than 26,000 species and varieties of plants; 30 specialized sections include roses, perennial plants, heath gardens, flowery brooks, bonsai, carnivorous plants, and an arboretum; one of the world's largest orchid collections; seasonal flower shows. The bonsai and penjing collections are two of the most diversified in North America. Chinese and Japanese gardens; restaurant, tea room. Parking (fee). (Daily 9 am-4 pm, summer to 6 pm) **$$$** Also here (and included in admission) is

> **Insectarium de Montréal.** *4581 Sherbrooke St E, Montréal. Phone 514/872-1400. www.ville.montreal.qc.ca/insectarium.* The Insectarium features a collection of more than 350,000 insects in a building designed to resemble a stylized insect. Interactive and participatory exhibits take visitors through aviaries and living displays in six geographically-themed areas. Includes a butterfly aviary (summer), and a children's amusement center. (Daily 9 am-5 pm, summer to 7 pm)

Montréal Canadiens (NHL). *1260 de La Gauchetiere SW, Montréal. Phone 514/790-1245. www.canadiens.com.* Formed in 1910, the Canadiens played their first game on the Jubilee rink, beating the Cobalt Silver Kings in overtime. The team is a 24-time Stanley Cup winner, most recently winning the coveted trophy during the 1992-1993 season. Games are played at the Bell Center, which also hosts various concerts and special events.

Montréal Harbour Cruises. *Depart from Quai de L'Horloge in Old Montréal, at the foot of Berri St and from Quai Jacque Cartier. Phone 514/842-9300; toll-free 800/667-3131.* Various guided cruises and dinner excursions (1-4 hours); bar service. Reservations are advised. Contact Croisières Vieure-Port de Montréal, Quai de l'Horlage, C.P. 1085, Succ. Place d'Armes, H2Y 3J6. (May-mid-Oct, daily) **$$$$**

Montréal Museum of Fine Arts. *1379-80 Sherbrooke St Ouest, Montréal. Phone 514/285-2000; toll-free 800/899-6873. www.mmfa.qc.ca.* (Musée des beaux-arts de Montréal) Canada's oldest art museum (founded in 1860) has a wide variety of displays, ranging from Egyptian statues to 20th-century abstracts. Canadian section features old Québec furniture, silver, and paintings. (Tues-Sun 11 am-6 pm; Wed to 9 pm) **DONATION**

Montréal Planetarium. *1000 rue Saint-Jacques Ouest, Montréal (H3C 1G7). Phone 514/872-4530. www.planetarium.montreal.qc.ca.* See the stars at the Montréal Planetarium, where its 385-seat theater holds multimedia astronomy shows, with projectors creating all features of the night sky. Just outside the theater are temporary and permanent exhibits on the solar system, meteorites, fossils, and other astronomy-related topics. (Daily; hours vary by season, call for information) **$$**

Musée d'art contemporain de Montréal. *185 Sainte-Catherine St W, Montréal. Phone 514/847-6226. www.macm.org.* The only museum in Canada that is devoted exclusively to modern art. Gift shop, bookstore, garden, restaurant. (Tues-Sun 11 am-6 pm, Wed 11 am-9 pm)

Museum of Decorative Arts. *2200 rue Crescent, Montréal (H3G 2B8). Phone 514/284-1252.* Historic mansion Chateau Dufresne (1918), partially restored and refurnished, now houses international exhibitions of glass, textiles, and ceramic art; changing exhibits. (Wed-Sun; closed Jan 1, Dec 25) **$$**

⭐ **Old (Vieux) Montréal.** *Bounded by McGill, Berri, Notre-Dame sts, and the St. Lawrence River. www.old.montreal.qc.ca.* The city of Montréal evolved from the small settlement of Ville-Marie founded by de Maisonneuve in 1642. The largest concentration of 19th-century buildings in North America is found here; several original dwellings remain, while many other locations are marked by bronze plaques throughout the area. The expansion of this settlement led to what is now known as Old Montréal. The area roughly forms a 100-acre (40-hectare) quadrangle which corresponds approximately to the area enclosed within the original fortifications. Some major points of interest are

Chateau Ramezay. *280 Notre-Dame St E, Montréal (H2Y 1C5). In front of City Hall. Phone 514/861-3708. www.chateauramezay.qc.ca.* This historic building was constructed in the 18th century, and was once the home of the governors of Montréal, the West Indies Company of France, and the Governors-General of British North America. It opened as a museum in 1895, and today is the oldest private museum in Québec. Collections include furniture, paintings, costumes, porcelain, manuscripts, and art objects of the 17th-19th centuries. (June-Sept: daily 10 am-6 pm; Oct-May: Tues-Sun 10 am-4:30 pm) **$$$**

Notre-Dame Basilica. *110 rue Notre-Dame Ouest, Montréal. Phone 514/842-2925; toll-free 866/842-2925.* In 1672, a church described as "one of the most beautiful churches in North America" was erected on the present Notre-Dame street. When this became inadequate for the growing parish, a new church designed by New Yorker James O'Donnell was built. It was completed in 1829 and two towers and interior decorations were added later. *Le Gros Bourdon,* a bell cast in 1847 and weighing 24,780 pounds (11,240 kilograms), is in Perseverance Tower; there is a ten-bell chime in Temperance Tower. Built of Montréal limestone, the basilica is neo-Gothic in design with a beautiful main altar, pulpit, and numerous statues, paintings, and stained-glass windows. (Late June-Labor Day: daily 7 am-8 pm; rest of year: to 6 pm) **$**

Notre-Dame-de-Bonsecours Church. *400 rue St.-Paul, Montréal (H2Y 1H4). Phone 514/282-8670. www.marguerite-bourgeoys.com.* Founded in 1657 by teacher Marguerite Bourgeoys, and rebuilt 115 years later, this is one of the oldest churches still standing in the city. With its location near the Port of Montréal, parishioners often prayed here for the safety of the community's sailors. In recognition of this, many fishermen and other mariners presented the church with miniature wooden ships, which hang from the vaulted ceiling today. The tower offers views of the river and city. Housed here is the Marguerite Bourgeois museum (fee), which features objects pertaining to early settlers. (May-Oct: Tues-Sun 10 am-5 pm; Nov-mid-Jan, mid-Mar-Apr: 11 am-3:30 pm) **FREE**

Place d'Armes. *St. Sulpice and Notre-Dame sts, Montréal. Phone 514/877-6810.* A square of great historical importance and center of Old Montréal. The founders of Ville-Marie encountered the Iroquois here in 1644 and rebuffed them. In the square's center is a statue of de Maisonneuve, first governor of Montréal, and at one end is the St. Sulpice seminary (1685) with an old wooden clock (1710), oldest building in Montréal. At 119 St. Jacques St is the **Bank of Montréal.** This magnificent building contains a museum with collection of currency, mechanical savings banks, photographs, reproduction of old-fashioned teller's cage. (Mon-Fri; closed holidays) Some of the most important financial houses of the city are grouped around the square. **FREE**

Place Jacques-Cartier. *Between rue Notre-Dame and rue de la Commune.* Named for the discoverer of Canada, this was once a busy marketplace. Today, restaurants, cafés, bars, cyclists, in-line skaters, and street performers are found around the plaza, which is closed off to traffic. The oldest monument in the city, the Nelson Column, is in the square's upper section.

Ste. Paul St. *Montréal.* The oldest street in Montréal. The mansions of Ville-Marie once stood here, but they have been replaced by commercial houses and office buildings.

Old Port of Montréal. *De la Commune St, Montréal. Between the St. Lawrence River and Old Montréal. Phone 514/496-7678; toll-free 800/971-7678. www.oldportofmontreal.com.* A departure point for boat cruises and a recreation and tourist park hosting exhibitions, special events, and entertainment. Also here is

The Montréal Science Centre. *King-Edward Pier, 333 de la Commune St W, Montréal (H2Y 2E2). Phone 514/496-4724; toll-free 877/496-4724. www.montrealsciencecentre.com.* Uncover the mysteries of science and technology through multimedia and hands-on exhibits, an IMAX theater, and more. (Late Apr-mid-June: daily 10 am-5 pm; mid-June-early Sept: Sun-Thurs 10 am-5 pm, Fri-Sat 10 am-9 pm; winter: Tues-Sun 10 am-5 pm, closed Mon except on legal holidays) **$$$$**

Olympic Park. *4141 Pierre de Coubertin Ave, Montréal (H1V 3N7). Phone 514/252-4737; toll-free 877/997-0919. www.rio.gouv.qc.ca.* The stadium was the site of the 1976 Summer Olympic Games and is now home of the Montréal Expos baseball team and les

Alouettes de Montréal football team. The world's tallest inclined tower (626 feet or 191 meters, leaning, and at a 45-degree angle), once used to open and close the retractable roof, features an observation deck. (Due to problems with the roof, it was replaced in 1988 with one that does not open.) On-site are a cafeteria and souvenir shop. Tours of the stadium are given daily. **$$$** Adjacent stadium is

Biodome de Montréal. *4777 Pierre-De Coubertin Ave, Montréal (H1V 1B3). Phone 514/868-3000. www.biodome.qc.ca.* The former Olympic Velodrome has been transformed into an environmental museum that combines elements of a botanical garden, aquarium, zoo, and nature center. Four ecosystems—Laurentian Forest, Tropical Forest, Polar World, and St.-Laurent Marine—sustain thousands of plants and small animals. The Biodome also features a 1,640 feet (500-meter) Nature Path with text panels and maps, and Naturalia, a discovery room. (Daily 9 am-4 pm, summer to 6 pm; closed Jan 1, Dec 25) **$$$$**

Parc du Mont-Royal. *Cote des Neiges and Remembrance rds, Montréal. Phone 514/843-8240. www.lemontroyal.qc.ca.* Designed by the creator of Central Park in New York City, Parc du Mont-Royal is also a park located in the heart of a city. Popular with visitors to Montréal, there is something for everyone here: cycling, hiking, picnicking, paddleboating, cross-country skiing, and snowshoeing. (Bikes, paddleboats, skis, and showshoes may be rented at the park). (Daily 6 am-midnight) **FREE**

Parc Jean-Drapeau. *1 Circuit Gilles-Villeneuve, Montréal (H3C 1A9). Phone 514/872-6120. www.parcjeandrapeau.com.* Two islands in the middle of the St. Lawrence River; access via Jacques-Cartier Bridge or Metro subway. Île Ste.-Hélène (St. Helen's Island) was the main anchor site for Expo '67; now a 342-acre (138-hectare) multipurpose park with three swimming pools; picnicking; cross-country skiing, snowshoeing. Île Notre-Dame (Notre Dame Island), to the south, was partly built up from the river bed and was an important activity site for Expo '67. Here is Gilles-Villeneuve Formula 1 racetrack (see SPECIAL EVENTS); also beach, paddleboats, windsurfing, and sailing. Some fees. (Daily) Also located here are

David M. Stewart Museum. *20 Chemin Tour L'Île, St. Helen Island (H3C 4G6). Phone 514/861-6701. www.stewart-museum.org.* The Stewart Museum houses artifacts such as maps, firearms, kitchen utensils, engravings, and navigational and scientific instruments that trace Canadian history from the 16th to 19th centuries. (May-Oct: daily 10 am-6 pm; rest of year: Wed-Mon 10 am-5 pm; closed Jan 1, Dec 25) **$$$**

Floral Park. *Île Notre-Dame.* Site of Les Floralies Internationales 1980; now permanent, it displays a collection of worldwide flowers and plants. Walking trails; pedal boats, canoeing; picnic area; snack bar and restaurant. Some fees. (Third week in June-mid-Sept, daily)

La Ronde. *Île Sainte-Hélène, 22 Chemin Macdonald, Montréal (H3C 6A3). Phone 514/397-2000. www.laronde.com.* A 135-acre amusement park with 35 rides, including a 132-foot (40-meter) high wooden roller coaster; arcades, entertainment on a floating stage; water-skiing; live cartoon characters, children's village; circus, boutiques, and restaurants. (Mid-May-late Oct: days, hours vary, call for information) **$$$$**

The Old Fort. (1820-1824) Oldest remaining fortification of Montréal; only the arsenal, powder magazine, and barracks building still stand. Two military companies dating to the 18th century, La Compagnie Franche de la Marine and the 78th Fraser Highlanders, perform colorful military drills and parades (late June-Aug, Wed-Sun).

Parc Safari. *850 Rte 202, Hemmingford (J0L 1H0). 33 miles (56 kilometers) S on Hwy 15 to exit 6, then follow zoo signs. Phone toll-free 800/465-8724. www.parcsafari.com.* Features 750 animals, rides, and shows, children's theater and play area, swimming beach; drive-through wild animal reserve; picnicking, restaurants, boutiques. (Mid-May-mid-Sept, daily) **$$$$**

Place des Arts. *175 rue Ste.-Catherine St Ouest, Montréal. Phone 514/842-2112 (tickets). www.pdarts.com.* This four-theater complex is the heart of Montréal's artistic life. L'Opéra de Montréal, the Montréal Symphony Orchestra, les Grands Ballets Canadiens, and La Compagnie Jean-Duceppe theatrical troupe have their permanent home here. Other entertainment includes chamber music, recitals, jazz, folk singers, variety shows, music hall, theater, musicals, and modern and classical dance.

⭐ **Pointe-a-Calliere, the Montréal Museum of Archaeology and History.** *350 Place Royale, Montréal (H2Y 3Y5). Corner of Place Youville in Old Montréal. Phone 514/872-9150. www.pac.museum.qc.ca.* Built in 1992 over the actual site of the founding of Montréal, the main museum building, the **Eperon,** actually rests on pillars built around ruins dating from the town's first cemetery and its earliest fortifications, which are now in its basement. Two balconies overlook this archaeological site, and a 16-minute multimedia show is presented using the actual remnants as a backdrop. From here, visitors continue underground, amid still more remnants, to the **Archaeological Crypt,** a structure that allows access to many more artifacts and remains; architectural models beneath a transparent floor illustrate five different periods in the history of Place Royale. The **Old Customs House (Ancienne-Douane)** houses thematic exhibits on Montréal in the 19th and 20th centuries. Permanent and changing exhibits. Café; gift shop. (July-Aug: Mon-Fri 10 am-6 pm, Sat-Sun 11 am-6 pm; rest of year: Tues-Fri 10 am-5 pm, Sat-Sun 11 am-6 pm) **$$$**

Rafting Montréal. *8912 La Salle Blvd, La Salle (H8P 1Z9). Phone 514/767-2230.* Rafting and hydro-jet trips on the Lachine Rapids of the St. Lawrence River. (May-Sept, daily; reservations required) **$$$$**

St. Joseph's Oratory of Mont Royal. *3800 Chemin Queen Mary, Montréal (H3V 1H6). On N slope of Mt Royal. Phone 514/733-8211. www.saint-joseph.org.* The chapel was built in 1904 as a tribute to St. Joseph by Brother Andre, a member of the Congregation of Holy Cross. A larger crypt church was completed in 1917, when crowds coming to see Brother Andre and pray to St. Joseph were getting too large for the chapel. Today, the main church is a famous shrine attracting more than 2 million pilgrims yearly. A basilica with a seating capacity of 2,200 was founded in 1924; the dome towers over the city, and a 56-bell carillon made in France is outstanding. The Oratory's museum features 200 nativity scenes from 100 different countries. (Daily 10 am-5 pm) **DONATION**

Universite de Montréal. *2900 boul Édouord-Montpetit, Montréal. Phone 514/343-6111. www.umontreal.ca/ang.* (1920) (58,000 students) On the north slope of Mount Royal.

Special Events

Antiques Bonaventure. *900 de la Gauchetiere St Ouest, Montréal (H5A 1G1). Phone 514/933-6375. www.place bonaventure.com.* Held in Place Bonaventure's East Exhibition Hall, this antiques show features exhibits of private and public collections for sale, where more than 100 dealers participate. Mid-June.

Canadian Grand Prix. *Parc Jean-Drapeau, Montréal. Phone 514/350-0000. www.grandprix.ca.* Held annually since 1967, this Formula 1 race took place on the Mont-Tremblant Circuit until 1977. At that time, the track was considered too dangerous, and the then-named Île-Notre-Dame Track was built. The first race at the new track was held in 1978, and was won by Gilles Villeneuve, Canada's first F1 driver. In 1982, when Villeneuve was tragically killed during practice laps at the Belgian Grand Prix, the track was re-named in his honor. If you wish to attend this event, make sure to purchase tickets well in advance; they can be extremely hard to come by, as this event is quite popular. Mid-June.

Fete Nationale. *82 rue Sherbrooke Ouest, Montréal (H2X 1X3). Phone 514/849-2560.* St.-Jean-Baptiste, patron saint of the French Canadians, is honored with three days of festivities surrounding the provincial holiday. The celebration includes street festivals, a bonfire, fireworks, musical events, and parades. Mid-June.

International Fireworks Competition. *Île Sainte-Hélène, 22 Chemin Macdonald, Montréal (H3C 6A3). Phone 418/523-3389. www.montrealfireworks.com.* Held in Montmorency Falls Park, this musical fireworks competition attracts master fireworks handlers from around the world, who each present a 30-minute display. Fireworks start at 10 pm, rain or shine. Late June-late July.

Just for Laughs Festival. *1594 St. Denis, Montréal. Phone 514/845-2322. www.hahaha.com.* This comedy festival features comic talent from all over the world. Shows are performed in more than 25 venues along St. Denis Street and are broadcast to millions of viewers worldwide. Artists who have performed at past festivals include Jerry Seinfeld, Jay Leno, Rowan Atkinson, Jon Stewart, Lily Tomlin, and the cast of "The Simpsons." Mid-July.

Montréal Bike Fest. *1251 Rachel St E, Montréal (H2J 2J9). Phone 514/521-8687.* An entire week of events celebrating the bicycle, ending with Le Tour de ile when 40,000 cyclists ride through the streets of Montréal. Includes a 16-mile (26-kilometers) outing for up to 10,000 children. Late May-early June.

Montréal Highlights Festival. *822 Sherbrooke St Est, Montréal (H2L 1K4). Phone toll-free 800/363-7777.* Spotlights the city's cultural and artistic diversity. Mid-Feb-early Mar.

Montréal International Jazz Festival. *822 Sherbrooke St Est, Montréal (H2L 1K4). Phone 514/871-1881; toll-free 888/515-0515. www.montrealjazzfest.com.* More than 1,200 musicians and a million music lovers from around the world gather to celebrate jazz and other types of music. The ten-day fest includes more than 350 indoor and outdoor concerts. Late June-early July.

World Film Festival. *1432 de Bleury St, Montréal (H3A 2J1). Phone 514/848-3883. www.ffm-montreal.org.* Montréal's World Film Festival was organized to celebrate all types of cinema, from documentaries and drama to comedy and science fiction. Amateur and well-known filmmakers alike participate in the event, which screens films from nearly 70 countries. Late Aug-early Sept. **$$$$**

Limited-Service Hotels

★ ★ **COURTYARD BY MARRIOTT MONTRÉAL DOWNTOWN.** *410 Sherbrooke St Ouest, Montréal (H3A 1B3). Phone 514/844-8855; toll-free 800/321-2211; fax 514/844-0912. www.marriott.com.* This budget-friendly hotel is close to the convention center and McGill University, as well as the site of the Montréal Jazz Festival. Nearby access to the subway makes exploring farther-reaching areas of the city easy. 157 rooms, 26 story. Complimentary continental breakfast. Check-in 3 pm, check-out noon. High-speed Internet access. Restaurant, bar. Fitness room. Indoor pool, whirlpool. **$**

★ ★ **HOLIDAY INN SELECT MONTRÉAL.** *99 Viger Ave Ouest, Montréal (H2Z 1E9). Phone 514/878-9888; toll-free 888/878-9888; fax 514/878-6341. www.yul-downtown.hiselect.com.* Pagoda-topped building in Chinatown area. 235 rooms, 8 story. Check-in 3 pm, check-out noon. One restaurant, two bars. Fitness room. Indoor pool, whirlpool. Business center. **$$**

★ ★ **HOSTELLERIE LES TROIS TILLEULS.** *290 Richelieu St, St-Marc-Sur-Richelieu (G0L 2E0). Phone 514/856-7787; fax 514/584-3146. www.lestroistilleuls.com.* This 1880s farmhouse is tucked away to give visitors a quiet and relaxing stay. Located an hour's drive from town, this hotel offers rooms with a view of the Richelieu River. 59 rooms, 3 story. Check-out noon. Restaurant, bar. Indoor pool. Tennis. Business center. **$**

★ ★ ★ **HOSTELLERIE RIVE GAUCHE.** *1810 Richelieu Blvd, Beloeil (J3G 4S4). Phone 450/467-4477; fax 450/467-0525. www.hostellerierivegauche.com.* Just 20 minutes from downtown Montréal, this hotel offers year-round recreation. All rooms have views of the Richelieu River or Mont St.-Hilaire. 22 rooms, 3 story. Check-out noon. Restaurant, bar. Indoor pool. Tennis. **$**

★ ★ **HOTEL CHERIBOURG.** *2603 Chemin du Parc, Orford (J1X 8C8). Phone 819/843-3308; toll-free 800/567-6132; fax 819/843-2639. www.cheribourg.com.* 97 rooms, 3 story. Check-out noon. Restaurant, bar. Fitness room. Indoor pool, outdoor pool, whirlpool. Tennis. **$**

★ ★ **HOTEL LE CANTLIE SUITES.** *1110 Sherbrooke St Ouest, Montréal (H3A 1G9). Phone 514/842-2000; toll-free 800/567-1110; fax 514/844-7808. www.hotelcantlie.com.* From this elegantly furnished hotel, guests can enjoy views of the Montréal skyline, the St. Lawrence River, and Mount Royal. The extra-spacious guest rooms feature limited kitchens, separate work areas, and fax machines. A heated rooftop pool entertains in warmer weather, while the Mezzanine Bar offers opportunities for mingling year-round. 250 rooms, all suites. Check-in 3 pm, check-out noon. Wireless Internet access. Restaurant, bar. Fitness room. Outdoor pool. Business center. **$$**

★ ★ ★ **HOTEL NELLIGAN.** *106 rue St. Paul Ouest, Montréal (H2Y 1Z3). Phone 514/788-2040; toll-free 877/788-2040; fax 514/788-2041. www.hotelnelligan.com.* This boutique hotel consists of two connected buildings, both thought to be built between 1830 and 1840. Don't think that means that the Nelligan is old and musty, however. The hotel's exposed-brick and stone walls hint at its lengthy history, but it provides all the modern touches that guests expect in an urban hotel, including wireless high-speed Internet access in common areas, multiline phones, and a minibar in every room. Down comforters, terrycloth bathrobes, evening turndown service, daily ice delivery, and windows that open onto the streets of Old Montréal ensure guests' comfort. A wine and cheese reception is offered daily, and the on-site restaurant, Verses, serves French fare in a hip and trendy setting. 63 rooms. Complimentary continental breakfast. Check-in 3 pm, check-out noon. High-speed Internet access. Restaurant, bar. Fitness room, fitness classes available. Business center. **$$**

★ ★ **NOVOTEL.** *1180 rue de la Montagne, Montréal (H3G 1Z1). Phone 514/861-6000; toll-free 800/668-6835; fax 514/861-0992. www.novotelmontreal.com.* One block north of the Molson Centre, a venue for sporting events and concerts, this hotel is located in the heart of Montréal and its downtown shopping district. 228 rooms, 9 story. Pets accepted; fee. Check-in 3 pm, check-out 1 pm. High-speed Internet access. Restaurant, bar. Fitness room. Business center. **$**

★ ★ **QUALITY INN.** *6680 Taschereau Blvd, Brossard (J4W 1M8). Phone 450/671-7213; toll-free 800/267-3837; fax 450/671-7041. www.qualityinn.com.* 91 rooms, 3 story. Complimentary continental breakfast. Check-out noon. Restaurant, bar. Outdoor pool. **$**

Full-Service Hotels

★ ★ ★ **CHATEAU VERSAILLES HOTEL.** *1659 Sherbrooke St Ouest, Montréal (H3H 1E3). Phone 888/933-8111; toll-free 888/933-8111; fax 514/933-6867. www.versailleshotels.com.* Located at the start of Montréal's famous Miracle Mile shopping district, this hotel has rooms in either renovated Victorian houses or the modern 14-story tower. Minutes by metro to the Molson Centre, home of the Montréal Canadiens, and the Place des Arts. 65 rooms, 15 story. Pets accepted, some restrictions; fee. Complimentary continental breakfast. Check-in 3 pm, check-out noon. Wireless Internet access. Restaurant, bar. Fitness room. Business center. **$$**

★ ★ ★ **DELTA MONTRÉAL.** *475 President Kennedy Ave, Montréal (H3A 1J7). Phone 877/814-7706; toll-free 800/268-1133; fax 506/443-3499. www.deltamontreal.com.* In the middle of everything—that's Delta Montréal! It's located in the heart of downtown, near the Convention Centre and the Place des Arts. Shoppers, art lovers, and history buffs choose this modern, inviting hotel with oversized rooms, most with balconies. Fitness buffs can work out at Delta's elaborate spa and sports center complete with squash courts, while those who prefer more leisurely pursuits can enjoy French cuisine at Le Bouquet or relax at Le Cordial, the hotel's full-service bar. 456 rooms, 23 story. Pets accepted; fee. Check-in

3 pm, check-out noon. High-speed Internet access. Restaurant, bar. Children's activity center. Fitness room, fitness classes available. Indoor pool, whirlpool. Business center. **$**

★ ★ ★ **FAIRMONT THE QUEEN ELIZABETH.** *900 Rene Levesque Blvd Ouest, Montréal (H3B 4A5). Phone 514/861-3511; toll-free 800/441-1414; fax 514/954-2256. www.fairmont.com.* All of Montréal is at your disposal while staying at The Fairmont The Queen Elizabeth. This masterpiece of contemporary sophistication is in the city center, located above the train station and linked to the massive underground system of shops and restaurants. Situated near the city's many businesses, this hotel is a popular choice among corporate travelers who appreciate the full-service business center and health club amenities. This historic hotel's modern flair surprises and delights guests. Eye-popping colors are juxtaposed with dazzling designs, creating a sensual ambience in the public and private rooms. Dining is an event savored by hotel guests and locals alike, who frequent the renowned Beaver Club for its gourmet meals and hunting lodge atmosphere and the convivial, Mediterranean-inspired Le Montréalais Bistrot-Bar-Restaurant. 1,039 rooms, 21 story. Pets accepted; fee. Check-in 4 pm, check-out noon. High-speed Internet access. Two restaurants, bar. Fitness room. Indoor pool, children's pool, whirlpool. Business center. **$$**

★ ★ ★ **HILTON MONTRÉAL BONAVENTURE.** *1 Place Bonaventure, Montréal (H5A 1E4). Phone 514/878-2332; toll-free 800/267-2575; fax 514/878-3881. www.hiltonmontreal.com.* Penthouse life is glorious inside this hotel perched on top of the Place Bonaventure Exhibition Hall. There are acres of rooftop gardens to explore and a year-round outdoor pool. The central city location is perfect for sight-seeing in Old Montréal, gambling at the casino, or shopping the underground boutiques. 395 rooms, 2 story. Pets accepted, some restrictions. Check-in 3 pm, check-out noon. High-speed Internet access. Restaurant, bar. Fitness room. Indoor pool, outdoor pool. Business center. **$$**

★ ★ ★ **HILTON MONTRÉAL DORVAL AIRPORT.** *12505 Cote de Liesse, Montréal (H9P 1B7). Phone 514/631-2411; fax 514/631-0192. www.dorval.hilton.com.* 494 rooms, 10 story. Check-in

4 pm, check-out noon. Restaurant, bar. Fitness room. Indoor pool, whirlpool. Business center. **$**

★ ★ ★ **HILTON MONTRÉAL/LAVAL.** *2225, autoroute des Laurentides, Montréal (H7S 1Z6). Phone 450/682-2225; fax 450/682-8492. www.hilton.com.* 170 rooms, 5 story. Check-in 4 pm, check-out noon. Restaurant, bar. Fitness room. Indoor pool, whirlpool. Business center. **$$**

★ ★ ★ **HOTEL DU FORT.** *1390 rue du Fort, Montréal (H3H 2R7). Phone 514/938-8333; toll-free 800/565-6333; fax 514/938-2078. www.hoteldufort.com.* This traditional-style hotel puts its emphasis on providing upscale service and the comforts of home. Understated guest rooms include kitchenettes and windows that open out onto city views. The on-site restaurant offers a nice continental breakfast buffet, and room service options include menus from area restaurants. 124 rooms. Check-in 3 pm, check-out noon. High-speed Internet access. Restaurant, bar. Fitness room. Business center. **$$$**

★ ★ ★ **HOTEL GAULT.** *449 rue Ste. Hélène, Montréal (H2Y 2K9). Phone 514/904-1616; toll-free 800/250-1625; fax 514/904-1717. www.hotelgault.com.* You might not expect to find an ultramodern hotel in a historic neighborhood, but the Hotel Gault is exactly that. Opened in 2002, it's set in a restored stone-façaded building. Inside, you'll find interiors of glass, concrete, and steel, with warm woods to keep the place from feeling overly cold or unfriendly. Soundproofed guest rooms feature flat-screen TVs, CD and DVD players, and comfortable workstations, as well as heated bathroom floors; some have private terraces. A variety of living spaces are available, so you can choose the setup that best fits your needs during your stay. 30 rooms. Check-in 3 pm, check-out noon. High-speed Internet access. Restaurant, bar. Fitness room. Business center. **$$**

★ ★ ★ **HOTEL INTERCONTINENTAL MONTRÉAL.** *360 Rue Ste. Antoine Ouest, Montréal (H2Y 3X4). Phone 514/987-9900; toll-free 800/361-3600; fax 514/847-8730. www.montreal.intercontinental.com.* Located in downtown Montréal, a short walk from the popular Old Town, which has cobblestone roads, art galleries, shops, and restaurants. 357 rooms, 17 story. Pets accepted, some restrictions; fee. Check-

in 3 pm, check-out noon. High-speed Internet access. Two restaurants, one bar. Fitness room, spa. Indoor pool. Business center. **$$**

★ ★ ★ **HOTEL L'EAU A LA BOUCHE.** *3003 Bd Ste.-Adele, Sainte Adele (J8B 2N6). Phone 450/229-2991; fax 450/229-7573.* 25 rooms, 3 story. Check-in 4 pm, check-out noon. Restaurant, bar. Fitness room, spa. **$$**

★ ★ ★ **HOTEL LE GERMAIN.** *2050 Mansfield, Montréal (H3A 1Y9). Phone 514/849-2050; toll-free 877/333-2050; fax 514/849-1437. www.hotelboutique.com.* This distinctive boutique hotel offers hospitality, comfort, and relaxation in an elegant setting, while providing state-of-the-art work equipment. The convenient downtown location makes it close to shopping, museums, concert halls, and movie theaters. Guest rooms feature original photos by Louis Ducharme, natural lighting, duvets, and dual-line phones. 101 rooms, 13 story. Pets accepted; fee. Complimentary full breakfast. Check-in 3 pm, check-out noon. High-speed Internet access. Restaurant, bar. Fitness room. **$$**

★ ★ ★ ★ **HOTEL LE ST. JAMES.** *355 Saint Jacques St, Montréal (H2Y-1N9). Phone 866/841-3111; toll-free 866/841-3111; fax 514/841-1232. www.hotellestjames.com.* When guests check into the majestic Hotel Le St. James, it's customary for the staff to provide their canine or feline companions with an individual bed and a selection of gourmet snacks. Yes, pets are pampered here—but so are the humans. And then some. Each room and suite is individually decorated with antiques and art, and each is appointed with much-appreciated luxuries like goose-down comforters, Frette linens, and scented toiletries by Penhaligon's of London. Business travelers also will appreciate the in-room high-speed Internet access, not to mention the complimentary shoeshines and a morning paper. Even the architecture makes you feel important. A former bank, the building's imposing façade features ornate moldings and details fully restored to their 1870s grandeur. Inside, the lobby boasts crystal chandeliers, Grecian columns, high tea service, and an impressive center staircase that simply begs for grand entrances—with your pet or alone. 61 rooms. Pets accepted, some restrictions; fee. Check-in 3 pm, check-out 1 pm. High-speed Internet access. Restaurant, bar. Fitness room. Business center. **$$$$**

★ ★ ★ **HOTEL OMNI MONT-ROYAL.** *1050 Sherbrooke St Ouest, Montréal (H2A 2R6). Phone 514/284-1110; toll-free 800/843-6664; fax 514/845-3025. www.omnihotels.com.* This property is centrally located in downtown Montréal and at the foot of Mount Royal. 299 rooms, 31 story. Pets accepted; fee. Check-in 3 pm, check-out 1 pm. High-speed Internet access, wireless Internet access. Two restaurants, two bars. Fitness room, fitness classes available. Indoor pool, outdoor pool, whirlpool. Business center. **$$**

★ ★ ★ **HOTEL PLACE D'ARMES.** *701 Cote de la Place d'Armes, Montréal (H2Y 2Y6). Phone 514/842-1887; toll-free 888/450-1887; fax 514/842-6469. www.hotelplacedarmes.com.* Step from Old Montréal's centuries-old charm into new millennium modishness at Hotel Place d'Armes. The boutique hotel's ultra-modern black-and-white décor will delight the most sophisticated traveler's expectations. Best of all, you may purchase and take home any guest room item that strikes your fancy. 48 rooms, 6 story. Complimentary continental breakfast. Check-in 3 pm, check-out noon. High-speed Internet access. One restaurant, two bars. Fitness room. **$$**

★ ★ ★ **HOTEL ST. PAUL.** *355 rue McGill, Montréal (H2Y 2E8). Phone 514/380-2200; toll-free 866/380-2202; fax 493/031-5155. www.hotelstpaul.com.* Set in a restored Beaux Arts building—a historic landmark—the Hotel St. Paul is all about contemporary cool. Upon checking in, make sure to stop and admire the striking alabaster fireplace in the lobby. Guest room floors revolve around two themes: earth (lit in red) and sky (lit in blue). The spare accommodations feature large windows, modern furnishings, and animal-skin accents; suites add two-person tubs and custom-made stone sinks. The on-site restaurant, Cube, serves fresh seasonal cuisine. 120 rooms. Check-in 3 pm, check-out noon. High-speed Internet access. Restaurant, bar. Fitness room. Business center. **$$$**

★ ★ ★ **HYATT REGENCY MONTRÉAL.** *1255 Jeanne Mance, Montréal (H5B 1E5). Phone 514/982-1234; toll-free 800/361-8234; fax 514/285-1243. www.montreal.hyatt.com.* Enjoy a lively urban retreat at Wyndham Montréal. A part of the elaborate shopping, dining, and entertainment center Complexe des Jardins and adjacent to Place des Arts, the hotel also has underground access to Montréal's Convention Center. Its indoor pool opens onto a terrace garden with a cascading waterfall. Fine French cuisine awaits guests at Café Fleuri. 605 rooms, 12 story. Check-in 3 pm, check-out noon. Restaurant, bar. Fitness room. Indoor pool, whirlpool. Business center. **$$**

★ ★ ★ **LA PINSONNIERE.** *124 rue St.-Raphael, Cap a l'Aigle (G0T 1B0). Phone 418/665-4431; toll-free 800/387-4431; fax 418/665-7156. www.lapinsonniere .com.* 25 rooms, 3 story. Check-in 4 pm, check-out noon. Restaurant, bar. Fitness room, spa. **$$**

★ ★ ★ **LE SAINT SULPICE.** *414 rue Saint Sulpice, Montréal (H2Y 2V5). Phone 514/288-1000; toll-free 800/297-0144; fax 514/288-0077.* Step back in time at this new luxury hotel, located in the historic part of Montréal, behind the Notre-Dame Basilica and a block from the Old Port. Accommodations are loft-style or one-bedroom suites, half of which boast fireplaces, with some suites overlooking the sun-filled courtyard. Sample steaks and seafood as well as regional specialties in S Le Restaurant. The Essence Health Center features beautifying treatments in addition to modern exercise equipment. 108 rooms, all suites. Check-in 3 pm, check-out noon. Restaurant, bar. Fitness room. **$$**

★ ★ ★ **LOEWS HOTEL VOGUE.** *1425 rue de la Montagne, Montréal (H3G 1Z3). Phone 514/285-5555; toll-free 800/465-6654; fax 514/849-8903. www.loewshotels.com.* The fresh spirit and chic modernity of the Loews Hotel Vogue breathes new life into old-world Montréal. Located in the business district of the "Paris of Canada," this hip hotel's vivid colors, plush amenities, and superb service make it a favorite of the jet set. The accommodations provide sleek shelter with silk upholstered furnishings, while creature comforts like oversized bathrooms appeal to the sybarite in every guest. Visitors are well cared for here, with a gracious concierge who attends to all needs, and efficient business and fitness centers. From bistros to brasseries, Montréal is known for its food, and this hotel is no exception. Don't miss L'Opéra Bar, the place to see and be seen in this charming city. 142 rooms, 9 story. Pets accepted. Check-in 3 pm, check-out 1 pm. High-speed Internet access. Restaurant, bar. Fitness room. Business center. **$$**

★ ★ ★ **MARRIOTT MONTRÉAL CHATEAU CHAMPLAIN.** *1050 de la Gauchetiere, Montréal (H3B 4C9). Phone 514/878-9000; toll-free 800/200-5909; fax 514/878-6761. www.marriotthotels.com/yulcc.* Both veteran travelers and first-time visitors to Marriott Chateau Champlain are met with comfort and convenience in the heart of downtown Montréal. Charming Art Nouveau décor adorns the guest rooms, while blooming azaleas accent the cozy lobby seating. Hospitality rules at the Mediterranean-flavored Le Samuel de Champlain restaurant, while Le Senateur Bar satisfies discriminating tastes. 611 rooms, 36 story. Check-in 3 pm, check-out noon. High-speed Internet access. Restaurant, bar. Fitness room, spa. Indoor pool, whirlpool. **$$**

★ ★ ★ **THE RITZ-CARLTON, MONTRÉAL.** *1228 Sherbrooke St Ouest, Montréal (H3G 1H6). Phone 514/842-4212; toll-free 800/363-0366; fax 514/842-3383. www.ritzcarlton.com.* Old-world refinement is the calling card of The Ritz-Carlton, Montréal. This classic hotel is perfectly situated to take in the inimitable charm of this slice of France in North America. It is a leisure traveler's dream, with the quaint Old Town, Olympic Center, and renowned museums located just a short distance from the hotel. From the genteel public spaces to the sumptuously appointed rooms and suites, the mood here is resolutely distinguished. The Ritz-Carlton standards of service are legendary, and guests are treated with kid gloves from the moment of arrival. Gastronomic pleasures abound here at the elegant Le Café de Paris and the romantic Le Jardin du Ritz, noted for its lush garden setting with trickling fountain and endearing duck pond. 229 rooms, 9 story. Pets accepted; fee. Check-in 3 pm, check-out noon. High-speed Internet access. Restaurant, bar. Fitness room. Business center. **$$**

★ ★ ★ **SOFITEL MONTRÉAL.** *1155 Rue Sherbrooke Ouest, Montréal (H3A 2N3). Phone 514/285-9000; fax 514/289-1155.* Modern and elegant, this hotel is set at the foot of Parc Mont Royal on Sherbrooke Street, close to galleries, boutiques, and the historic center of the city. Enjoy morning croissants and evening cocktails in Le Bar; dine on Provençal-inspired cuisine in Renoir; and work off your indulgences in the hotel's fitness center and sauna. 258 rooms. Pets accepted, some restrictions. Check-in 3 pm, check-out noon. Restaurant, bar. Fitness room. Business center. **$$**

★ ★ ★ **SUPER 8 MONTRÉAL - WEST/ VAUDREUIL.** *21700 Trans-Canada Hwy, Vaudreuil (J7V 8P3). Phone 450/424-8898; fax 450/424-8898.* This European-inspired property sits along the shore of Lac des Deux Montagnes. 117 rooms, 6 story. Check-out noon. Restaurant, bar. Fitness room. Indoor pool, whirlpool. Tennis. **$$**

Full-Service Inns

★ ★ ★ **AUBERGE DU VIEUX-PORT.** *97 de la Commune Ouest, Montréal (H2Y 1J1). Phone 514/876-0081; toll-free 888/660-7678; fax 514/876-8923. www.aubergeduvieuxport.com.* Once a depot, then a warehouse, general store, and grocery store, this historic landmark building served several functions before becoming a hotel. Built in 1882 along the St. Lawrence River, it was transformed into a hotel in 1995, with Les Ramparts restaurant serving up fine, French cuisine, and a rooftop terrace affording a panoramic view of the St. Lawrence River. Guests are pampered with a full breakfast, afternoon wine and cheese, daily newspaper, a CD library, free e-mail access, and more. 27 rooms. Complimentary full breakfast. Check-in 3 pm, check-out noon. Restaurant. **$$**

★ ★ ★ **AUBERGE HANDFIELD.** *555 Richelieu Blvd, St-Marc-Sur-Richelieu (J0L 2E0). Phone 450/584-2226; fax 450/584-3650. www.aubergehandfield.com.* Guests can chose between a room with a view of the garden or river. Small shops and boutiques are nearby with a larger shopping mall only a ten-minute drive away. 56 rooms, 2 story. Check-in 3 pm, check-out noon. Restaurant, bar. Fitness room. Outdoor pool, whirlpool. **$**

★ ★ ★ **AUBERGE HATLEY.** *325 rue Virgin, CP330, North Hatley (J0B 2C0). Phone 819/842-2451; toll-free 800/336-2451; fax 819/842-2907. www.aubergehatley.com.* This charming inn, in a 1903 Victorian-style mansion, overlooks Lake Massawippi and has with a rustic décor of leather chairs, carved wood, and brick hearths. Enjoy hiking and antiquing in spring and fall and skiing in winter. 25 rooms, 3 story. Complimentary full breakfast. Check-in 4 pm, check-out noon. Restaurant. Outdoor pool. **$$$**

Specialty Lodgings

The following lodging establishments are approved by Mobil Travel Guide, but due to their unique and individualized nature have not been given a traditional Mobil Star rating. Included in this listing you may find bed-and-breakfasts, limited-service inns, guest ranches, and other unique hotel properties.

ANGELICA BLUE B&B. *1213 Ste. Elizabeth, Montréal (H2X 3C3). Phone 514/844-5048; toll-free 800/878-5048; fax 514/844-2114. www.angelicablue .com.* This Victorian row house bed-and-breakfast dates to the late 1800s, featuring warm, sunny accommodations in the heart of downtown Montréal. A full breakfast with different hot entrées is served daily. Guests have access to a TV room, a fully equipped kitchen, and washing and ironing facilities. 6 rooms. Complimentary full breakfast. Check-in 4 pm, check-out 11 am. **$**

AUBERGE DE LA FONTAINE. *1301 rue Rachel Est, Montréal (H2J 2K1). Phone 514/597-0166; toll-free 800/597-0597; fax 514/597-0496. www.auber gedelafontaine.com.* Don't look for calico or buttons and bows at Auberge de la Fontaine. Its individually decorated guest rooms feature the bold colors and sleek designs expected in a sophisticated city inn. Say "bon jour" with a complimentary continental buffet in the lobby's attractive breakfast area. Then, after a busy day of meetings or sightseeing, stroll the inviting paths in the park across the street where you'll find the fountain that gives the inn its name. Auberge's well-informed staff delights in matching guests' dining preferences with the perfect choice of restaurants, perhaps on nearby lively St. Denis Street. Afterward, comfortable beds offer blissful slumber. 21 rooms, 3 story. Complimentary full breakfast. Check-in 3 pm, check-out noon. **$$**

LE PETIT PRINCE B&B. *1384 Overdale Ave, Montréal (H3G 1V3). Phone 514/938-2277; toll-free 877/938-9750; fax 514/935-9750. www.montreal bandb.com.* This bed-and-breakfast is well suited to its urban location. Rather than frills and lace, you'll find artsy and contemporary style in this stone-façaded townhouse. All areas of the home feature exposed-brick walls, while guest room furnishings include modern four-poster and sleigh beds and funky artwork by local artists. Each room has a mini-fridge and a two-person whirlpool tub; two rooms have functional fireplaces, while the other two have large private balconies. 4 rooms. Complimentary full breakfast.

Check-in 4 pm, check-out 11 am. Wireless Internet access. **$$**

LE TRAVERSIN B&B. *4124 rue Ste. Hubert, Montréal (H2L 4A8). Phone 514/597-1546. www. homeniscience.com.* The four rooms in this restored home, built in 1912, afford guests comfortable accommodations with private or shared bathrooms and amenities such as feather duvets, slippers, bathrobes, and TVs. Guests enjoy an extensive breakfast in the large dining room or mingle in the living room. After a day spent exploring St.-Denis Street, and nearby downtown Montréal, retire to Le Traversin's private garden and hot tub, open from the end of April to December, or to the terrace. 4 rooms. Complimentary continental breakfast. Check-in 3 pm, check-out noon. **$$**

LES BONS MATINS. *1393 Argyle Ave, Montréal (H3G 1V5). Phone 514/931-9167; toll-free 800/588-5280; fax 514/931-1621. www.bonsmatins.com.* Guests stay in rooms in adjoining restored century-old townhomes in the heart of Montréal, close to main thoroughfares Sainte-Catherine Street and Crescent Street, and area attractions. Antiques and paintings by a family artist decorate rooms, all with private baths with accoutrements such as bathrobes and natural bath products. In addition to the business communications system in guest rooms, there is also a Windows XP workstation made available to guests. A full gourmet breakfast is served daily in the dining room. Other amenities include a private parking lot, living room with fireplace, garden, and a terrace. 7 rooms. Complimentary full breakfast. Check-in 3 pm, check-out noon. **$$**

MANOIR HARVARD. *4805 Harvard Ave, Montréal (H3X 3P1). Phone 514/488-3570; toll-free 888/373-3570; fax 514/590-0797. www.manoirharvard.com.* This stone-and-wood Victorian oozes country charm. The landscaped grounds feature old-fashioned gardens, easily viewed from the terrace. Guest rooms have queen- or king-size beds and are furnished with lovely antiques. Should you wish to escape the tranquility, Manoir Harvard is close to the Villa Maria metro station and is just steps from Monkland Village's cafés and shops. 5 rooms. Complimentary full breakfast. Check-in 3 pm, check-out noon. **$$**

Restaurants

★ ★ ★ **AU PIED DE COCHON.** *536 Rue Duluth Est, Montréal (H2L1A9). Phone 514/281-1114; fax 514/ 281-1116.* French menu. Dinner, late-night. Closed

Mon. Bar. Business casual attire. Reservations recommended. **$$$**

★ **AU TOURNANT DE LA RIVIERE.** *5070 Salaberry, Carignan (J3L 3P9). Phone 450/658-7372; fax 450/658-7372.* French menu. Lunch, dinner, Sun brunch. **$$$**

★ ★ **AUBERGE HANDFIELD.** *555 Richelieu Blvd, St.-Marc-Sur-Richelieu (J0L 2E0). Phone 450/584-2226; fax 450/584-3650. www.aubergehandfield.com.* French menu. Breakfast, lunch, dinner, Sun brunch. Closed Mon; also mid-Jan-early May. Bar. Children's menu. Casual attire. Reservations recommended. Outdoor seating. **$$$**

★ **BEN'S DELICATESSEN.** *990 de Maisonneuve Blvd, Montréal (H3A 1M5). Phone 514/844-1001; fax 514/844-1002.* Deli menu. Lunch, dinner, late-night. Casual attire. **$**

★ ★ ★ **BICE RISTORANTE.** *1504 Rue Sherbrooke Ouest, Montréal (H3G 1L3). Phone 514/937-6009; fax 514/937-6023. www.bicemontreal.com.* Located in the western section of Sherbrooke Street, the Montréal location of this upscale Italian restaurant chain offers good food with careful service in an elegant, modern setting. Italian menu. Lunch, dinner. Closed Dec 24-26; also early-mid-Jan. Bar. Casual attire. Reservations recommended. Valet parking. Outdoor seating. **$$$**

★ ★ **BIDDLE'S JAZZ AND RIBS.** *2060 rue Aylmer, Montréal (H3A 2E3). Phone 514/842-8656; fax 514/842-2665.* American menu. Lunch, dinner. Bar. Casual attire. Reservations recommended. Outdoor seating. **$$**

★ ★ ★ **BISTRO A CHAMPLAIN.** *75 Chemin Masson, Ste. Marguerite (J0T 1L0). Phone 450/228-4988; fax 450/228-4893. www.bistroachamplain.com.* Located on the edge of Lake Masson in the Laurentian Mountains, this elegant, rustic restaurant draws an international clientele. French menu. Dinner. Closed Mon-Tues. **$$$**

★ ★ ★ **CAFE DE PARIS.** *1228 Sherbrooke St W, Montréal (H3G 1H6). Phone 514/842-4212; fax 514/842-4907. www.ritzcarlton.com.* This premier dining room is located in the Ritz Carlton Hotel. Elegant presentations and smooth service are the hallmarks of this sophisticated room. French menu. Breakfast, lunch, dinner, brunch. Bar. Children's menu. Casual attire. Valet parking. Outdoor seating. **$$$**

★ **CAFE STE. ALEXANDRE.** *518 Duluth St E, Montréal (H2L 1A7). Phone 514/849-4251; fax 514/908-1518.* Greek menu. Lunch, dinner. Children's menu. Casual attire. Reservations recommended. Outdoor seating. **$$**

★ ★ ★ **CAFI FERREIRA.** *1446 rue Peel, Montréal (H3A 1S8). Phone 514/848-0988; fax 514/848-9375.* This restaurant is one of the most stylish dining rooms in Montréal. The friendly staff serves up wonderful Portuguese cuisine. The menu emphasizes fresh fish and is accompanied by a comprehensive selection of Portuguese wines and ports. Portuguese menu. Lunch, dinner. Closed Sun. Bar. Casual attire. Reservations recommended. **$$$**

⚲ ★ ★ ★ **CHEZ LA MERE MICHEL.** *1209 Guy St, Montréal (H3H 2K5). Phone 514/934-0473; fax 514/939-0709.* In a city with volumes of competition, this fine French restaurant has succeeded in its downtown historic-home location since 1965. Guests will feel like they've stepped into a painting, from the quaint flower-lined walkway to the small, slightly cluttered rooms filled with eclectic collectibles. The menu is classic and well prepared, including a fantastic strawberry Napoleon for dessert. French menu. Dinner. Closed Sun. Casual attire. **$$$**

★ ★ ★ **CUBE.** *355 McGill St, Montréal (H2Y2E8). Phone 514/876-2823; fax 514/380-2200.* French menu. Lunch, dinner. Bar. Casual attire. Reservations recommended. **$$$**

⚲ ★ ★ **GLOBE.** *3455 Blvd St.-laurent, Montréal. Phone 514/284-3823; fax 514/284-3531. www.restaurantglobe.com.* French menu. Dinner, late-night. Bar. Casual attire. Reservations recommended. **$$$**

★ ★ **IL CORTILE.** *1442 Sherbrooke Ouest, Montréal (H3G 1K3). Phone 514/843-8230.* This classic Italian trattoria set in the middle of an urban section of town is a quiet oasis from the hustle and bustle of the city. Perfect pastas and risottos are just the beginning—the traditional menu offers an authentic taste of seasonal cooking. Italian menu. Lunch, dinner. Closed Dec 24-25. Bar. Casual attire. Reservations recommended. Outdoor seating. **$$$**

★ ★ **JARDIN NELSON.** *407 Place Jacques-Cortier, Montréal (H2Y3B1). Phone 514/861-5731. www.jardin nelson.com.* American, French menu. Lunch, dinner, brunch. Closed Nov-Mar. Bar. Casual attire. Reservations recommended. Outdoor seating. **$$**
🅳

★ ★ ★ **KATSURA MONTRÉAL.** *2170 rue de la Montagne, Montréal (H3G 1Z7). Phone 514/849-1172; fax 514/849-1775. www.restaurantkatsura.com.* Japanese menu. Lunch, dinner. Closed holidays. Bar. Casual attire. **$$**

★ ★ ★ **L'EAU A LA BOUCHE.** *3003 Ste. Adèle Blvd, Ste. Adèle (J8B 2N6). Phone 450/229-2991; toll-free 888/828-2991; fax 450/229-7573. www.leau alabouche.com.* Tucked into the maple, birch, and pine forests surrounding the Laurentian Mountains, near the village of Sainte-Adèle, you will find L'eau a la Bouche, a charming little restaurant located on the property of the even more enchanted Hotel L'eau a la Bouche. The restaurant is set in a Bavarian-style wooden house that feels like it just popped out of a Hans Christian Andersen fairy tale. The gourmet menu is built around local produce, fish, meat, and homegrown herbs and vegetables, woven together and dressed up with a perfect dose of French technique and modern flair. Attentive, thoughtful service and a vast wine list make this luxurious dining experience unforgettable. French menu. Breakfast, dinner. Closed holidays. Bar. **$$$**

★ ★ **L'EXPRESS.** *3927 Ste. Denis, Montréal (H2W 2M4). Phone 514/845-5333; fax 514/843-7576.* It is not easy to be the "in" place for more than 20 years, but somehow this classic French bistro has managed to pull it off. The food is consistently good, and the scene remains forever first rate. French menu. Lunch, dinner. Closed Dec 25. Bar. Casual attire. Reservations recommended. **$$**

★ ★ **LA GAUDRIOLE.** *825 Laurier Est, Montréal (H2O 1G7). Phone 514/276-1580; fax 514/276-8842. www.lagaudriole.com.* French menu. Lunch, dinner. Closed Jan 1-8 and July 18-Aug 4. Reservations recommended. **$$$**

★ **LA LOUISIANE.** *5850 rue Sherbrooke Ouest, Montréal (H4A 1X5). Phone 514/369-3073; fax 514/369-3702.* Dinner. Closed Mon. **$$**

★ ★ ★ **LA MAREE.** *404 Place Jacques Cartier, Montréal (H2Y 3B2). Phone 514/861-8126; fax 514/861-3954.* Situated in Old Montréal, this romantic dining room offers classic French cuisine in an ornate, Louis XIII atmosphere. The historic 1808 building is just the place to enjoy old-fashioned, formal service and a great bottle of wine from the cellar. French menu. Lunch, dinner. Closed Jan 1, Dec 25. Bar. Casual attire. Reservations recommended. Outdoor seating. **$$$**

★ ★ ★ **LA RAPIERE.** *1155 rue Metcalfe, Montréal (H3B 2V6). Phone 514/871-8920; fax 514/871-1923.* Southwestern French cooking with a personal touch is the draw at this casual, sophisticated restaurant in downtown Montréal. Cassoulet, foie gras, and other specialties from southwestern France are served in a typical country-French setting. French menu. Lunch, dinner. Closed Sun; holidays; also mid-July-mid-Aug, 15 days in Dec. Bar. Jacket required. Reservations recommended. **$$$**

★ **LA SAUVAGINE.** *1592 Rte 329 Nord, Ste.-Agathe (J8C 2Z8). Phone 819/326-7673; fax 819/326-9351. www.lasauvagine.com.* French menu. Dinner. Closed Mon-Tues off-season. **$**

★ ★ ★ **LALOUX.** *250 Ave Des Pins Est, Montréal (H2W 1P3). Phone 514/287-9127; fax 514/281-0682. www.laloux.com.* One of the few "bistro parisiens" in Montréal, this local favorite features excellent cuisine du marche served in a sober but refined environment. The waitstaff is very professional and knowledgeable about food, wines, and their pairing. French menu. Lunch, dinner. Closed Jan 1, Dec 25. Bar. Casual attire. Reservations recommended. Outdoor seating. **$$$**

★ ★ **LE CAFE FLEURI.** *1255 rue Jeanne Mance, Montréal (H5B 1E5). Phone 514/285-1450; toll-free 800/996-3426; fax 514/285-1243. www.wyndham.com.* French menu. Breakfast, lunch. Bar. Children's menu. Outdoor seating. **$$**

★ ★ **LE CHRYSANTHEME.** *1208 Crescent, Montréal (H3G 2A9). Phone 514/397-1408.* Chinese menu. Lunch, dinner. Closed Mon; last week in July, Dec 23-Jan 3. Bar. Casual attire. **$$**
🅳

★ **LE JARDIN DE PANOS.** *521 Duluth St Est, Montréal (H2L 1A8). Phone 514/521-4206; fax 514/521-8766. www.lejardindepanos.com.* Greek menu. Lunch, dinner. Closed Dec 25. Children's menu. Casual attire. Outdoor seating. **$$**

★ ★ **LE KEG/BRANDY'S.** *25 rue St. Paul Est, Montréal (H2Y 1G2). Phone 514/871-9093; fax 514/871-9818. www.kegsteakhouse.com.* Steak menu.

Dinner. Closed Dec 25. Bar. Children's menu. Casual attire. **$$$**

★ ★ ★ **LE LUTETIA.** *1430 rue de la Montagne, Montréal (H3G 1Z5). Phone 514/288-5656; fax 514/288-9658. www.hoteldelamontagne.com.* Located in the popular l'Hotel de la Montagne, along with a piano bar and discotheque, this restaurant serves cuisine in a comfortable rococo setting. The service is gracious and accommodating, the décor pleasant and interesting. French menu. Breakfast, lunch, dinner. Bar. Children's menu. Casual attire. Reservations recommended. **$$$**

★ ★ **LE MAISTRE.** *5700 Monkland, Montréal (H4A 1E6). Phone 514/481-2109; fax 514/481-2109. www.clic1.com.* French menu. Lunch, dinner. Closed Mon. Reservations recommended. Outdoor seating. **$$**
🅳

★ ★ ★ **LE MAS DES OLIVIERS.** *1216 rue Bishop, Montréal (H3X 2R2). Phone 514/861-6733; fax 514/861-7838.* This small, traditional French restaurant has been offering rich cuisine in a Provençal setting for more than 30 years. French menu. Lunch, dinner. Closed Dec 24-Jan 3. Bar. Casual attire. Reservations recommended. **$$$**
🅳

★ ★ ★ **LE MITOYEN.** *652 Place Publique, Ste. Dorothee Laval, Montréal (H7X 1G1). Phone 450/689-2977; fax 450/689-0385.* Envision a quaint village green surrounding a picturesque fountain. On the east side nestles a charming country 1870 cottage featuring the best of French cuisine: Le Mitoyen. Chef/proprietor Richard Bastien plans his menus around the freshest the market can offer, taking as much pride in his sparkling kitchen as he does in his quietly elegant dining rooms, cozily sized for intimate dining for individuals, couples, or groups. Gracious servers in time-honored country tradition welcome guests as honored friends. Both native Montréalers and out-of-towners enjoy the exquisite fare and homey atmosphere. French menu. Lunch, dinner. Closed Mon. Outdoor seating. **$$$**

★ ★ **LE MUSCADIN.** *639 Notre Dame Ouest, Montréal (H3C 1H8). Phone 514/842-0588. www.lemuscadin.ca.* Italian menu. Lunch, dinner. Closed Sun; Dec 24-Jan 3. Casual attire. Reservations recommended. Outdoor seating. **$$$**

★ ★ **LE PARCHEMIN.** *1333 rue University, Montréal (H3A 2A4). Phone 514/844-1619; fax 514/844-7873. www.leparchemin.com.* French menu. Lunch, dinner. Closed Sun; Jan 1, Dec 25. Bar. Casual attire. **$$$**

★ ★ **LE PARIS.** *1812 Ste Catherine Ouest, Montréal (H3H 1M1). Phone 514/937-4898; fax 514/937-1726.* French menu. Lunch, dinner. Closed Dec 24-25. Casual attire. Reservations recommended. **$$**
🅳

★ ★ ★ **LE PIEMONTAIS.** *1145-A Rue de Bullion, Montréal. Phone 514/861-8122; fax 514/861-6041.* Experience authentic, Piedmont-region cuisine at this comfortable Italian restaurant where the proprietor makes everyone feel like a regular. Simple but artfully prepared dishes are presented with professional and attentive service. Italian menu. Lunch, dinner. Closed Sun; third week in July-Aug 15. Casual attire. Reservations recommended. **$$$**

★ ★ ★ **LE PIMENT ROUGE.** *1170 Peel, Montréal (H3B 4P2). Phone 514/866-7816; fax 514/866-1575. www.lepimentrouge.com.* The bold cuisine of China's Szechwan province is gloriously prepared at Le Piment Rouge, an open, airy, contemporary restaurant located in the former Windsor Hotel. Set in a historic turn-of-the-century building, the restaurant has an up-to-the-minute design and features towering arched windows and an enormous wine rack on display in the center of the dining area. Signature dishes include spicy peanut butter dumplings (a recipe the restaurant is credited with inventing in Montréal) and General Tao chicken served with a special (read: secret) homemade sauce. Le Piment Rouge is a hotspot, drawing local politicians, financiers, and the token celebrity on occasion. Beer is always a good choice with Chinese food, but Le Piment Rouge also stocks more than 3,000 wines if you're craving something with a cork, not a bottle cap. Chinese menu. Lunch, dinner. Bar. Business casual attire. Valet parking. **$$**

★ ★ **LE STE. AMABLE.** *410 Place Jacques Cartier, Montréal (H2Y 2E2). Phone 514/866-3471; fax 514/393-8958. www.st-amable.com.* French menu. Lunch, dinner. Bar. Casual attire. Reservations recommended. Outdoor seating. **$$**
🅳

★ ★ ★ **LES CAPRICES DE NICOLAS.** *2072 rue Drummond, Montréal (H3G 1W9). Phone 514/282-9790; fax 514/288-0249. www.lescaprices.com.* The intimate candlelight and romantic indoor/outdoor garden combine to make this restaurant a true special-occasion destination. Given the classic, very formal service, it is a pleasant surprise to find the French dishes on the menu refreshingly updated with light, vibrant flavors and seasonal market produce. A wine list of 500 labels adds to the excitement. French menu. Dinner. Closed Dec 24-Jan 10. Bar. Jacket required. Reservations recommended. **$$$**

★ ★ **LES CONTINENTS.** *360 rue St.-Antoine Ouest, Montréal (H2Y 3X4). Phone 514/987-9900; toll-free 800/361-3600; fax 514/987-0004. www.inter continental.com.* French menu. Breakfast, lunch, dinner. Closed Easter weekend. Bar. Children's menu. Casual attire. **$$$**

★ ★ ★ **LES HALLES.** *1450 rue Crescent, Montréal (H3G 2B6). Phone 514/844-2328; fax 514/849-1294. www.restaurantleshalles.com.* A traditional French menu awaits guests at this Montréal restaurant. It also offers an "owners surprise," for which guests are treated to a tasting menu put together just for them. French menu. Dinner. Closed Sun; holidays; Dec 23-Jan 21. Bar. Casual attire. **$$$**

★ ★ ★ **LES REMPARTS.** *93 rue de la Commune Est, Montréal (H2Y 1G1). Phone 514/392-1649; toll-free 888/660-7678; fax 514/876-8923. www.rest aurantlesremparts.com.* Located in the basement of the Auberge du Vieux-Port, on the site of Montréal's original fortress, this restaurant offers a comfortable, cozy atmosphere with professional, attentive service. French menu. Lunch, dinner. Closed Dec 24-25. Bar. Children's menu. Casual attire. Reservations recommended. Outdoor seating. **$$$**

★ ★ ★ **LES TROIS TILLEULS.** *290 rue Richelieu, Montréal (J0L 2E0). Phone 514/856-7787; toll-free 800/263-2230; fax 450/584-3146. www.lestroistilleuls .com.* Modern interpretations of classic French cuisine, complemented by home baking, are served in this 1880s farmhouse. Gardens and terrace offer views of the St. Lawrence River. Located on the South Shore, 35 minutes from downtown Montréal. French menu. Breakfast, lunch, dinner, brunch. Bar. Children's menu. Casual attire. Reservations recommended. Outdoor seating. **$$$$**

★ ★ ★ **MED BAR AND GRILL.** *3500 Blvd St. Laurent, Montréal (H2X 2V1). Phone 514/844-0027; fax 514/844-6848. www.medgrill.com.* If you're seeking a spot to see and be seen, or a chic place to linger over luscious cocktails while perched amidst Montréal's most stylish set, Med Bar and Grill is an excellent option. But the restaurant is not only a hot venue for drinking and lounging, it also happens to be a great place to sit down and eat. The food is upscale but remains fun and inviting. Reading the menu will make your stomach growl. Classic dishes of the Mediterranean are given a modern spin here, reflecting the seasons and incorporating the region's bountiful produce. Grilled veal chops with celery and potato puree, topped with pistachios and porcini mushrooms, and crunchy ravioli stuffed with slowly simmered braised rabbit, spinach, shitake mushrooms, and raisins are signature dishes. Med Bar and Grill is that rare dining spot where style and substance come together winningly. Mediterranean menu. Dinner. Closed Sun; Jan 1, Dec 25. Bar. Casual attire. Reservations recommended. Valet parking. **$$$**

★ ★ **MIKADO.** *368 Rue Laurier Ouest, Montréal (H2V 2B7). Phone 514/279-4809; fax 514/274-4006.* Japanese menu. Lunch, dinner. Closed Jan 1, Dec 25. Bar. Reservations recommended. **$$**

★ ★ **MOISHE'S.** *3961 St. Laurent Blvd, Montréal (H2W 1Y4). Phone 514/845-3509.* Steak menu. Lunch, dinner. Bar. Casual attire. Reservations recommended. **$$$**

★ ★ ★ **NUANCES.** *1 Ave de Casino, Montréal (H3C 4W7). Phone 514/392-2708; toll-free 800/665-2274; fax 514/864-4951. www.casinos-quebec.com.* Montréal has a certain Parisian flair to it. Many of its restaurants embrace this sophisticated, elegant French ambience, offering guests a dining experience on par with those found in the Rive Gauche. Nuances is one such restaurant. This stylish, modern bistro, located within the Montréal Casino, is swathed in soothing earth tones and decorated with original works by local artists custom-designed for the space. The upscale menu stars exquisitely updated French cuisine assembled from a cast of nature's best seasonal products. Signature plates include salmon fume with potato galette and herbed cream, earthenware-baked loin of lamb, and a steamy hot chocolate cake served with vanilla sauce. Both the chef and the sommelier developed the wine list, so the selections match up nicely with the très Français menu. French menu. Dinner. Bar. Jacket required. Reservations recommended. Valet parking. **$$$**

★ ★ **PRIMADONNA.** *3479 boul St. Laurent, Montréal (H2S 3C7). Phone 514/282-6644; fax 514/*

282-9260. Italian menu. Lunch, dinner. Bar. Casual attire. Reservations recommended. **$$$$**
🅿

★ ★ **QUELLI DELLA NOTTE.** *6834 Blvd St. Laurent, Montréal. Phone 514/271-3929; fax 514/271-3429. www.quelli.ca.* Italian menu. Lunch, dinner. Closed Sun. Bar. Children's menu. **$$$**
🅿

★ ★ ★ **QUEUE DE CHEVAL.** *1221 boul René-Lévesque Ouest, Montréal (H3G 1T1). Phone 514/390-0090; fax 514/390-1390. www.queuedecheval.com.* Prime, dry-aged meats are the showstoppers at Queue de Cheval, a rustic, chateau-styled steakhouse accented with deep, rich maple wood and tall, vaulted ceilings in the heart of downtown Montréal. Set in a renovated historic property, with a giant open grill and an arching staircase at its center, Queue de Cheval buzzes nightly with a lively, stylish, carnivorous crowd. The classic steakhouse menu offers USDA Prime beef that is dry-aged for five weeks, butchered in house, and then spiced up with bold, robust flavors before being grilled to juicy perfection. As you'd expect from a steakhouse, the wine list complements the cuisine with a great selection of rich, meaty reds. Those in search of less meat won't have to order in from another restaurant, however. The menu has a generous raw bar, a terrific selection of salads and vegetarian appetizers, and a shimmering Fresh Fish Market that features a selection of about six fish nightly, which the kitchen will prepare grilled, whole-roasted, or seared with a choice of toppings and crusts. Steak menu. Lunch, dinner. Closed Dec 25, 31. Bar. Business casual attire. Reservations recommended. Valet parking. Outdoor seating. **$$$**

★ ★ **RESTAURANT CHANG THAI.** *2100 Crescent St, Montréal. Phone 514/286-9994.* Thai menu. Lunch, dinner. Bar. Casual attire. **$$**
🅿

★ ★ **RESTAURANT CHEZ LEVEQUE.** *1030 rue Laurier Ouest, Montréal (H2V 2K8). Phone 514/279-7355; fax 514/279-1737.* French menu. Breakfast, lunch, dinner. Bar. Children's menu. Reservations recommended. **$$**

★ **RESTAURANT DAOU.** *519 Faillon Est, Montréal (H2R 1L6). Phone 514/276-8310; fax 514/334-6720.* Lebanese menu. Lunch, dinner. Closed Mon. **$$**

★ ★ **RESTAURANT SHO-DAN.** *2020 Metcalfe, Montréal (H3A 1X8). Phone 514/987-9987; fax 514/*
987-9967. *www.sho-dan.com.* Japanese menu. Lunch, dinner. Closed Jan 1, Dec 25. Bar. Casual attire. **$$**

★ ★ ★ **RISTORANTE DA VINCI.** *1180 Bishop, Montréal (H3G 2E3). Phone 514/874-2001; fax 514/874-9499. www.davinci.qc.ca.* This charming restaurant offers an authentic atmosphere, warm, attentive service, and well-prepared traditional dishes made with fresh ingredients. Italian menu. Lunch, dinner. Closed Sun; Dec 24-25, Dec 31-Jan 2. Bar. Casual attire. Reservations recommended. Outdoor seating. **$$$**
🅿

★ ★ **ROSALIE RESTAURANT.** *1232 Rue de la Montagne, Montréal. Phone 514/392-1970; fax 514/392-1772. www.rosalierestaurant.com.* French bistro menu. Lunch, dinner. Bar. Casual attire. Reservations recommended. Outdoor seating. **$$**

★ ★ **SOUVENIRS D'INDOCHINE.** *243 Mont-Royal Ouest, Montréal. Phone 514/848-0336.* Lunch, dinner. **$$$**

★ ★ **SZECHUAN.** *400 rue Notre Dame St Ouest, Montréal (H2Y 1V3). Phone 514/844-4456; fax 514/844-7235.* Chinese menu. Lunch, dinner. Closed Sun; Jan 1, Dec 25. Bar. Casual attire. Reservations recommended. **$$$**

★ ★ **TOKYO SUKIYAKI.** *7355 Mountain Sights Ave, Montréal (H4P 2A7). Phone 514/737-7245.* Japanese menu. Dinner. Closed Mon; Dec 23-Jan 8. Bar. Casual attire. Reservations recommended. **$$$**
🅿

★ ★ ★ ★ **TOQUE!** *900 place Jean-Paul Riopelle, Montréal (H2Z 2B2). Phone 514/499-2084; fax 514/499-0292. www.restaurant-toque.com.* The presentations at Toque!, a graceful, luxurious, contemporary French restaurant, are breathtaking. Plates are garnished with such impeccable attention to detail that you may spend several minutes debating whether or not to take out your digital camera before devouring it. But look at it this way: since you are probably at Toque! to eat, and not to simply stare, mouth agape, at the magnificent culinary artwork on the plate, don't feel bad about ruining it with your fork. Just dig in. The talented and hospitable chef, Norman Laprise, would be quite hurt if you didn't, not to mention that tasting food with your eyes is nothing compared to tasting it with your mouth. Laprise wields magic with a whisk and uses locally farmed ingredients to create a miraculous menu of sophisticated, avant-garde French fare. If you've got one meal in Montréal, Toque! is one place that you should not overlook. French menu. Lunch, dinner. Closed Sun-Mon; also two weeks in late Dec-early Jan. Bar. Business casual attire. Reservations recommended. **$$$**

★ ★ **ZEN.** *1050 rue Sherbrooke Ouest, Montréal (H3A 2R6). Phone 514/499-0801; fax 514/284-1162. www.omnihotels.com.* Chinese menu. Lunch, dinner. Closed Easter, Thanksgiving, Dec 25. Bar. Children's menu. Casual attire. Reservations recommended. **$$$**

Index

Notes

Notes

Notes

Notes

Notes

Notes

Notes

Notes

Notes

Notes

Notes

Notes

Notes

Notes

Notes